Ellicott's Commentary on the Whole Bible

A Verse by Verse Explanation

EDITED BY
CHARLES JOHN ELLICOTT

VOLUME IV

Job —— Isaiah

WIPF & STOCK · Eugene, Oregon

Wipf and Stock Publishers
199 W 8th Ave, Suite 3
Eugene, OR 97401

Ellicott's Commentary on the Whole Bible Volume IV
Job - Isaiah
By Ellicott, Charles J.
ISBN 13: 978-1-4982-0139-1
Publication date 7/28/2016
Previously published by Cassell, 1897

This is a reprint of the 1959 Zondervan edition. Originally published in 1897 by Cassell as A Bible Commentary for English Readers.

Job
BY
THE REV. STANLEY LEATHES, D.D.
Late Professor of Hebrew, King's College, London.

The Psalms
BY
THE REV. ARCHDEACON AGLEN, M.A.

Proverbs
BY
THE REV. J. W. NUTT, M.A.
Late Fellow of All Souls' College, Oxford.

Ecclesiastes
BY
THE REV. G. SALMON, D.D.
Provost of Trinity College, Dublin.

The Song of Solomon
BY
THE REV. ARCHDEACON AGLEN, M.A.

Isaiah
BY
THE VERY REV. E. H. PLUMPTRE, D.D.
Late Dean of Wells.

CONTENTS

	PAGE
INTRODUCTION TO JOB	1
JOB	7
INTRODUCTION TO THE PSALMS	79
THE PSALMS	85
INTRODUCTION TO THE PROVERBS	303
THE PROVERBS	305
INTRODUCTION TO ECCLESIASTES	359
ECCLESIASTES	366
INTRODUCTION TO THE SONG OF SOLOMON	385
THE SONG OF SOLOMON	387
EXCURSUS ON NOTES TO THE SONG OF SOLOMON	404
INTRODUCTION TO ISAIAH	409
ISAIAH	416

THE BOOK OF JOB

INTRODUCTION
TO
THE BOOK OF JOB

I. Plan of the Book.—Great as are the difficulties connected with, and many as are the differences of opinion concerning, the Book of Job, there is and can be neither difficulty nor difference of opinion as to the plan on which the work is constructed. This is at once simple and obvious. There is, *first*, an historical prologue, just sufficient to make the reader acquainted with and interested in the hero of the book; relating who he was and what was the occasion of the following controversy, but nothing more. *Secondly*, a dialogue or argument carried on between Job and three of his friends who came to him in his great calamity. Each of the friends is answered by Job three times; but as the book is now found, the third friend only replies twice, unless, as some suppose, Zophar's third speech is to be discovered at chap. xxvii. 13, and Job's reply at chap. xxix. 1. This great discussion or controversy which constitutes the main substance of the book is introduced by the solemn curse pronounced by Job upon the day of his birth in chap. iii. *Thirdly*, after the three friends have ceased to accuse Job, another speaker comes forward in the person of Elihu, who is specially introduced to us at chap. xxxii. 2. He is distressed both at the tone assumed by Job and at the way in which the friends have conducted the argument, and proceeds to take a somewhat different and intermediate position; his share in the discussion is continued through the next six chapters. *Fourthly*, the reply of the Lord as the hitherto unseen witness but now manifested judge and umpire in the great argument, which extends from chap. xxxviii. to the end of chap. xli. or the beginning of chap. xlii. And, *fifthly*, there is an historical conclusion or epilogue, which gives us the sequel of Job's history till his death.

II. Object.—This can only be gathered from a survey of the facts and incidents recorded, which are briefly these:—Job was a man famous in his age and country for his piety and integrity. Up to a certain period also he was notoriously happy and prosperous, till a succession of ruthless calamities fell upon him with tremendous and unexampled severity; and in one day he was deprived of his ten children and of all his substance. We are further told that this was by the express permission of the Almighty, who had given him over to the power of Satan because that evil spirit had alleged that the piety of Job was not disinterested, but only for selfish ends. It may be presumed, therefore, that Satan challenged the Almighty in the case of Job, and that the Almighty accepted his challenge. It must, however, be carefully noted that the reader only, and not the several characters in this discussion, is supposed to be acquainted with this fact, for had it appeared openly at any point of the argument there would at once have been an end to the discussion. The several speakers were shooting arrows in the dark; the reader only occupies a vantage-ground in the light afforded by a knowledge of the secret. Satan, however, is not mentioned again after his disappearance in the second chapter. The result, therefore, of his challenge of the Almighty is only to be discovered in the sequel of the history. We are especially told that Job sinned not, nor charged God foolishly, up to the point when Satan put forth his hand and touched his person. Nor are we told that he did so afterwards; on the contrary, from the words of God in chap. xlii. 7, we are rather led to imply the contrary. We may infer, therefore, that the outspokenness of Job, seeing it was accompanied with faith in God, profound and unswerving, was not displeasing to the Almighty, and was not reckoned as sin; albeit Job was fain to repent himself in dust and ashes at the actual manifestation of the Lord. It was not, however, on his repentance, but on his intercession on behalf of his friends, that the Lord turned the captivity of Job (chap. xlii. 10); and then his prosperity once more returned to him. Seven sons and three daughters were again born to him, and his cattle and substance became twice as much as they had been at the first. Such is the summary of the narrative of Job, from which alone we can gather the *object* of the book, and this, it would seem, must be capable of being expressed in the several truths which are obviously to be deduced from it; and these are:—

(1) Severity of affliction is not a proof of special iniquity—it does not vary as sin varies. The sinner may escape—the innocent may suffer. Because a man is exceptionally stricken, he is not, therefore, exceptionally guilty—because a man is especially prosperous, he is not, therefore, especially holy. This is a truth which is confirmed to us by the repeated experience of life; but notwithstanding this continued experience of it, the reminder thereof is oftentimes most needful and salutary in affliction, while it is always valuable as a corrective in our judgment of others. To inculcate this truth must assuredly have been part of the object of the Book of Job, if not the main and sole object; but we may learn that—

(2) Righteousness is its own reward, independently of all the inequalities of fortune. The position and the arguments of Job would have been altogether different if he had not had the testimony of a good conscience. It makes all the difference to the *impetus* of adversity whether it overtakes the innocent or the guilty. This is clearly one of the inferences that the Book of Job suggests, whether or not it was part of the object contemplated by the writer. The powerlessness of accumulated adversity to overthrow the truly righteous man is taught us by the history of Job. He is proof against all the slings and arrows of outrageous

fortune. He can still trust God, and God will justify him. This is verily a priceless lesson, and it is unquestionably taught by the history of Job.

(3) Hope is not only brighter, but truer also than despair; the dark days of Job were not destined to be his last. He had in himself a principle of vitality which could and would survive them. The Lord, after he had tried him, gave him not only what he had before, but twice as much also as he had had before. To be sure, the children he had lost could not be restored to him; but his tears for them were wiped away by the smiles of others, and the closed page of their history was replaced by the open page of the history of others as yet unsullied and full of hope—the sweeter and brighter because of the dark background. To enforce this truth, and to remind men of it, must surely have been part of the object of him who wrote the Book of Job; and when the storm is raging it is no small consolation to remember that the sun will shine brightly after it, and perhaps the more brightly because of it. If Job had not suffered exceptionally, no one would have recorded his history or remembered his name. He would not have been known for his patience had he not been known for his sufferings. The one, therefore, is not only the condition of the other, but contains also in itself the promise of the other, even though in certain cases that promise may not visibly be fulfilled, as, for a time and while the anguish lasted, it certainly was not in the case of Job.

(4) Satan is not to be permitted to triumph over man. He shamelessly challenged the Most High to produce an instance, even where the conditions were most promising, of one who served Him for anything more than could be gained therefrom. The challenge was accepted, and Satan was foiled. He proposes the challenge, but when the issue of it is to be declared, by the course of circumstances, he is not forthcoming. His judgment goes by his default; his defeat is proclaimed by his non-appearance, although by that alone. At the same time, while man is so far justified against his ghostly adversary, the Almighty also is vindicated; for He will be no man's debtor, and, therefore, all that Job had in his prosperity is restored to him, and in respect of worldly substance twice as much. This also is one of the lessons of Job, whether or not it was the designed object of the writer to inculcate it, upon which we are hardly competent to pronounce. It may be observed incidentally that this is virtually the teaching also of the third chapter of Genesis; while the word "enmity," verse 15 (אֵיבָה, 'êybhah), and the name Job (אִיּוֹב, 'yyobh), *the assaulted one,* and therefore the hated one, present an unquestionable although significant point of contact, inasmuch as the two words are derived from the same root (אָיַב), *hated,* or *was an enemy.*

(5) Job is a typical character; for it is hardly possible to suppose that his history is not intended to be typical of the condition of man in life, and, therefore, in its degree typical of the Son of Man in His cross and passion, and in the eventual glory of His resurrection. What is true of the type must be true of the race; and what is true of the race must be true of the Head of the race. I am far from saying that this was all foreseen by the writer of Job; but so far as the history of Job is capable of teaching the essential truth of human life to man, it must also foreshadow and reflect the history of Him who was the truth itself, and this not because of any power of arbitrary and mechanical prediction in the writing or the writer, but because the writing was inherently, essentially, and intensely true to human nature, which was the nature that Christ took.

So far, then, without reference to the authorship of Job, or to its place in the Canon, we are perfectly warranted in regarding it as pointing to Him, because it points to and expresses the deepest and most essential truth of that human life and nature of which He was the deepest and the most essential truth.

(6) The object of Job was unquestionably didactic: it was intended to teach and inculcate all the lessons that we can derive from it. The writer cannot be suspected of writing without a purpose, but must fairly be credited with all the wisdom and doctrine with which his work is fraught, whether or not it was consciously present to his mind, even as Shakespeare must fairly be credited with all the wisdom and truth that Coleridge or Schlegel or Goethe could detect in "Hamlet." Job also, from its inherent characteristics, is a cosmopolitan book. It inculcates truth without reference to any religious systems. It aims at justifying the ways of God to man as man, whether under the Law or the Gospel, or independently of the light of either, seeing that it not improbably preceded both. It takes the broadest possible view both of the character of God and of the position of man, and deals with the mighty problem of the moral government of God, towards which it offers the only solution possible under the circumstances.

III. **Character.**—The Book of Job is a Divine book, and marked with the distinctive features that characterise the other books of revelation. For instance, it assumes the possibility and the fact of God's revelation of Himself, and is in no way staggered at the thought of God's holding direct intercourse with man. Those who demur to this position can so far have nothing in common with the writer of Job. It is a foregone conclusion with him that this intercourse and the manifestation or revelation it implies was not only a possibility, but an historic fact. However true it may be that the Lord speaks out of other whirlwinds than that of Job, it is no subjective or ordinary voice which said, *Ye have not spoken of me the thing that is right as my servant Job hath.* Here, then, we discover the first characteristic feature of the book, and one that binds it closely to the collection of which it forms a part; the verdict, therefore, that we pass on this matter will inevitably influence all our judgment of the book. It will have no other authority than we consent to allow it unless we accept its testimony in this respect, while if we do, it will at once speak to us with the very highest authority. But, *secondly,* the book is essentially non-Jewish and non-Israelite in character. The hero Job was not of the chosen race; and, what is more, there is no trace of a consciousness of the existence of any such race; while it is included among the sacred books of the Hebrews, it is distinctly non-Hebrew in character. There seem to be but two ways in which we can reasonably account for this circumstance—either the book must have been derived from some foreign source and adopted into and appropriated by the literature of Israel, in which case it furnished a solitary, and an improbable, instance; or it must be the record and monument of a time when the nationality of Israel was as yet undefined and indistinct, before Israel had become conscious of its own existence as a nation; in other words, before the Exodus. My own opinion inclines very strongly to this belief, for to suppose, which is the only other alternative, that in the palmy days of the literature of Israel any Israelite would have entirely divested himself of his nationality, and his national recollections and prejudices, and have set himself the task of bringing back and reconstructing the life and manner of a bygone age, and have thrown himself so successfully into the surroundings of the past as to betray no token of his own condition and circumstances, is absolutely impossible. The Book of Job knows nothing of Moses, or the Exodus, the Temple, the kingdom, or the Law (once only in chap. xxii. 22 is the word *law* used in a merely general sense—*receive the law at his mouth*), or of any of the later incidents in the history of Israel. It would have been strange if, being conversant with them, no allusion to them had anywhere escaped the writer; but so it is, and this makes the book essentially non-Hebrew in character; but, nevertheless, *thirdly*, it is in no sense alien from or antagonistic to the faith of Israel; on the contrary, it takes that view of Divine things which, as a matter of fact, the unaided speculations of man have never risen to, and displays that knowledge of God which is not found outside the compass of revelation. This is a feature which must on no account be overlooked in dealing with the Book of Job. *Fourthly*, the book is unquestionably historical—first, because it clearly professes to be so; secondly, because, although parables and allegories are to be found in Scripture, it does not appear that any one book is purely allegorical, or is intended to be so. If the Book of Ruth, for example, or the Book of Job, is mere allegory—that is, romance—then a death-blow is struck at the root of all history, and like the gods in the story of Nala, we stand upon air when we seem to touch the ground. A tradition is found in the Talmud to the effect that "Job did not exist, and was not a created man, but the work is a parable;" but this is shown to be worthless by the reasons above given, and from the way in which the persons in Job are linked to names and places otherwise known to us, and from the general circumstantiality of the narrative. It is, of course, possible to throw doubt on the reality of anything, but there is no *reason* to doubt the reality of Job.

IV. Integrity.—The most superficial observer can see that there is a great difference in style (if only the difference of prose and poetry) between the narrative portions of the book and the argumentative; the important feature is the frequency of the name Jehovah in the former, and its occurrence but once in the latter (chap. xii. 9); still it is to be observed that Job himself, who uses it here, has already used it thrice in chap. i. 21, and precisely in the same way, which is that, namely, of ascribing all things both good and evil to God (comp. ii. 10 and xii. 6, 9). It may be questioned, however, whether this obvious difference of style is anything more than is needful from the exigency of the case in passing from narrative to elevated discussion; certainly we cannot allow that this difference shows the book to be other than a consistent whole, and warrants us in assigning the narrative parts to a different hand. In short, these narrative parts are indispensable to the understanding of the others, which, except as fragments preserving the sentiments of the several speakers, can have had no existence independent of them. He, therefore, who is responsible for the book in its present form is so far responsible for both alike; though, of course, no further responsible for the several speeches than responsible for their general accuracy in rightly representing the several speakers. Some, indeed, have supposed that the speech of Elihu is an interpolation, though, of course, without the slightest ground. Artistically his speech holds its proper place as leading up gradually from the un-qualified condemnation of the friends, and Job's longing for vindication, to the ultimate appearance and justification of the Lord as judge and umpire in the controversy. It would, therefore, be as reasonable to excise Job's curse as to omit the speech of Elihu. In short, the book as we have it is unquestionably a consistent whole, nor is there any reason to suppose that it ever existed in any other form.

V. Date.—Opinions as to the date of Job have varied from the age of the patriarchs to that of the Captivity, or even later, that is to say, 800 or 1,000 years. As the supporters of the several theories have uniformly appealed to the critical and linguistic reasons, this may serve to show the vagueness and uncertainty of much that arrogates to itself the name of criticism. He who could not tell the difference between a work of the time of the Conquest and one of our own day could hardly claim to be a critic; and though it is true that the language of the Old Testament was far less liable to change than our own, yet this may be taken as an instance not altogether inappropriate or unfair. Of course, if the Book of Job is in any sense authentic—*i.e*, a record of actual fact—its date as a composition cannot be put very much later than the occurrence of its facts—that is, than the age of Job. Now, it so happens that the age of Job is, within certain limits, ascertainable—*e.g*., we are told that he lived a hundred and forty years after his recovery from his great trials. As he had ten children, who appear to have been all grown up when his calamities overtook him, we can hardly suppose him to have been less than sixty or seventy at this time. It has, indeed, been suggested that, as Job's substance was doubled, so also the years of his life may have been, and this would correspond with some such number. At all events, he must have been 200 or 210 years old at the time of his death. If, then, we may trust these numbers, which must depend upon the authentic character of the narrative, we may find in them at least some guide to the age of Job. It cannot have been, with all due deference to those who think otherwise, within 100 years of the Captivity (Renan, *Livre de Job*, p. xxxvi.), because at that time there is no evidence that the life of man was prolonged to such an extent. Neither, again, can it have been (assuming for the moment the authenticity of Genesis) in the age of the earlier patriarchs of Gen. v., because then the period of human life was yet longer; but in the case of Abraham, Isaac, and Jacob, we meet with the ages of 175. 180, and 147 years respectively. These would furnish us with some approximation to the supposed age of Job, which, however, we may regard as having been exceptionally prolonged. It would seem, therefore, antecedently probable that the age at which Job lived was approximately that of the Hebrew patriarchs. Now it so happens that most of the names occurring in connection with Job are found also in what we may roughly call the age of these patriarchs, when, as it appears, human life was not uncommonly at least twice as long as it is now. For instance, in Gen. xxv. 3 we find Sheba and Dedan among the sons of Abraham by Keturah. It was apparently a band of Sheba's retainers or descendants who fell upon Job's cattle (chap. i. 15). Sheba and Dedan are also mentioned among the sons of Cush and Ham (Gen. x. 7), and it has been supposed that Keturah was of Canaanite, and therefore of Hamite origin, and that Sheba was reckoned to Ham through her; at all events, Sheba, and Dedan, and Shuah, from whom we seem to have Bildad the Shuhite, were among those of his descendants whom Abraham during his lifetime

JOB.

sent away "eastward to the land of the East," to which Job himself belonged. Here, then, we seem to have some sort of clue to the time and place of Job. Uz, again, is mentioned as a descendant of Shem in Gen. x. 23; and in xxii. 21, he is said to have been the son of Nahor, and brother of Chesed, possibly the father of the Chasdim or Chaldeans of Job i. 17. Job thus may be traced perhaps through Uz to Nahor the brother of Abraham; at all events, there is a similarity in the names found in both cases. Once more, Eliphaz was the son of Esau and father of Amalek (Gen. xxxvi. 10, 12), and Teman was the son of Eliphaz, so that Eliphaz the Temanite, the friend of Job, may probably either have been this man or a descendant of his. Tema, again (Job vi. 19), was a descendant of Ishmael (Gen. xxv. 15), so that these lines, however faint, all point to what we may call the age of the patriarchs between Abraham and Moses for the time at which Job flourished. It is plain also that a generation or two was enough to establish a tribe or family, for when Israel came out of Egypt, Amalek the grandson of Esau had become a powerful people, who were even regarded as ancient (Num. xxiv. 20). The only nearer guide we have to the precise age of Job is on the supposition that Eliphaz the Temanite was the son of Esau of that name (though it is strange he should be called after the name of his own son), in which case the children of Jacob would be contemporary with Job. Following out this supposition, the late Dr. Lee of Cambridge calculated that Job died forty-seven years before the Exodus (*Book of Job*, p. 34). Whether or not this is correct, there at least seems to be very good reason to believe that the age of Job fell between the entry of the Israelites into Egypt and the Exodus. If so, we then are able to arrive at some idea as to the—

VI. Author of the Book of Job.—There is nothing whatever to guide us on this point except the evidence of the book itself, coupled with any such considerations as have already been noticed. There is but one solitary fragment of tradition, which is that Job, like the Pentateuch, was the work of Moses. This may be worth nothing critically, but as a tradition it is simply the only one that exists. If, however, the age of Job was that of the patriarchs between Abraham and Moses, as there is every reason to believe, and if the book is authentic, as its place in the Canon would seem to imply, then there is no one so likely as Moses to whom it can be referred. If it was written before the Exodus, that would account for the silence of the book with reference to that and to all subsequent events of Jewish history; and while the influence of the Book of Job is traceable in the Psalms and prophets, it manifests various points of contact with the Book of Genesis, which alone of the books of Moses can have been in existence at that time. It is not improbable, but, on the contrary, highly probable, that Job himself may have thrown together the various speeches of himself and his friends—and manifestly no one would have been so fit to do this as himself; but we can hardly account for the acceptance of the book by the people of Israel, unless it had been specially commended to them by some one in the position of the great Law-giver; and who so likely as he to have supplied the historical framework of the book, and reduced it to its ultimate form? I venture to think that the Mosaic origin of the book is really more probable than the Solomonic or the Exile origin of it. Certain phrases in Job are peculiar to, or characteristic of, Moses: for instance, עֲבֻדָּה רַבָּה —*ăbhuddah rabbah* (Job i. 3 and Gen. xxvi. 14); "the sons of God" (Job i. 6 and Gen. vi. 2); "the fire of God" (Job i. 16 and Gen. xix. 24); "his bone and his flesh" (Job ii. 4 and Gen. ii. 23); "they lifted up their voice, and wept" (Job ii. 12 and Gen. xxi. 16, xxvii. 38, xxix. 11); "they scattered dust toward heaven" (Job ii. 12 and Exod. ix. 10); the "seven oxen and seven rams" of Job xlii. 8 and Num. xxiii. 1; the strange word קְשִׂיטָה (*qĕsitah*), found only in Job xlii. 11, Gen. xxxiii. 19, and Josh. xxiv. 32; the "earring of gold" (Job xlii. 11 and Gen. xxiv. 22), used afterwards by Solomon (Prov. xi. 22, xxv. 12); "their father gave them inheritance among their brethren" (Job xlii. 15; comp. Num. xxvii. 7). Bearing in mind that there are but three chapters in which to trace these similarities, they are even more numerous than we could expect to find them. Besides this we may mention, in the book generally the name of God, Shaddai, the Almighty, which is so frequent in Job, but, with the exception of the Pentateuch, is not found above twice in any other book, and only eight times in all the other books together; the notion of Divine communications conveyed in sleep, as in the case of Abraham, Jacob, &c.; wealth consisting in flocks and herds, and the like. There is no mention in Job of Tarshish, Hermon, or Lebanon; but, on the other hand, Jordan is mentioned. There is a possible allusion to the Fall (Job xxxi. 33) and to the Deluge (Job xxii. 16), though this is not certain in either case. The grosser forms of idolatry of a later age are not mentioned in Job, but only sun and moon worship (chap. xxxi. 26—28). The Rephaim of Gen. xiv. 5, Deut. ii. 11, 20, iii. 11, 13 are mentioned (Job xxvi. 5). The character given to Job (chap. i. 1) is like that ascribed to the patriarchs Jacob (Gen. xxv. 27) and Joseph (Gen. xlii. 18; comp. Gen. vi. 9 and xvii. 1). The feasting of Job's sons every one in his day is like the feast on Pharaoh's birthday in the history of Joseph. "Naked came I out of my mother's womb, and naked shall I return thither" (chap. i. 21) is an echo of "Dust thou art, and unto dust shalt thou return" (Gen. iii. 19). The "deep sleep falling on men" (Job iv. 13; xxxiii. 15) is like the "deep sleep" that fell on Adam and Abram (Gen. ii. 21, xv. 12); but the word here used occurs only three times elsewhere. There is a probable allusion to the destruction of Sodom and Gomorrha in Job xviii. 15; and the "side" in Job xviii. 12 may possibly mean the "wife," in allusion to Gen. ii. 22. The "harp" and the "organ" of Job xxi. 12 and xxx. 31 are identical with Gen. iv. 21, but not found in juxtaposition elsewhere, nor at all except in Ps. cl. 3, 4. In Job xxxi. 32 there seems to be a reference to Gen. xix. 2. In Job xxxii. 8, xxxiii. 4, 6; comp. Gen. ii. 7 (נְשָׁמָה —*nĕshāmah*—is used in all). In Job xxxiv. 12; comp. Gen. xviii. 25. In Job xxxiv. 20, 25 one might almost imagine an allusion to the death of the firstborn. In Job iii. 18 we, at all events, find the נֹגֵשׂ —*noghēs*— of the bondage; while in Job xxii. 30 there may possibly be an allusion to the intercession of Abraham for Sodom. At all events, these points of contact between Job and the Book of Genesis, which under the supposition of the Mosaic origin of the book could have been the only part of the Bible in existence when Job was written, and the early history of which must, at any rate, have been familiar to Moses, are at least strong enough and many enough to give support to the theory, if they do not establish it conclusively. It must be borne in mind that we have every reason to believe that the several books of the Bible were the work of well-known actors in the Bible history, and not of casual and insignificant authors. In the New

Testament it is so with the Acts of the Apostles and the Epistle to the Hebrews, and it is probably so in every case in the Old Testament. It is not likely that there is in the Old Testament the work of any man who is not known to us from the history, whether in the case of Chronicles, Judges, Ruth, or Job. But if this is so, as seems most probable on every ground, and if we are right in maintaining the antiquity of Job, then there is no one so likely to have written it as Moses. Indeed, with the exception of Job himself (whose virtual authority for the book must be presupposed in any case, if it is a true history), there is no one else who can have written it. We find here that acquaintance with desert life, and with Egypt, for example, which were combined in Moses, but scarcely in any one else. The pyramids may perhaps be spoken of in Job iii. 14; while the familiarity with the crocodile and the ostrich, not to mention other points, sufficiently shows this.

VII. Doctrine of the Book of Job.—There is distinct knowledge of God as the Creator of man, and the Author of nature (chaps. ix., xxviii. 8, 9). "Thine hands have made me and fashioned me." "Remember, I beseech thee, that thou hast made me as the clay; and wilt thou bring me into dust again?" (chap. xiv. 15). "Thou wilt have a desire to the work of thy hands" (chap. xxvi. 8, 10). The speeches of Elihu and of the Lord abundantly show that they identify the Author of nature with the moral Governor. In Elihu's words, "the spirit of God hath made me, and the breath of the Almighty hath given me life" (chap. xxxiii. 4.), he not only recognises God as his Creator, but even does so in words which almost involve the knowledge of Gen. ii. 7, when they are compared together; while in declaring the righteousness of God as the ultimate Judge (chap. xxxiv. 12), he almost repeats the words of Abraham. It is hardly possible to read Job without reading into it a variety of allusions to other books, and discovering points which will largely tend to confirm our preconceived notions, whatever they may be; but these considerations must be borne in mind:—(1) Is the date of Job likely to be early or late? Formerly it was always regarded as one of the oldest books in existence; but though some have put it as low down as the Captivity, and of course thought they discovered reasons in the book itself for doing so, it seems to me beyond all question that, as the book undeniably describes a very early state of society, so it must belong to that early period. (2) If the traditional and apparent succession of the books of Scripture is in the main correct, then there can have been only one book of the whole which was in existence when Job was written, namely, the Book of Genesis; now, on the supposition that the records of this book were known, then it is not a little remarkable that the points of contact between the two are numerous and striking. And therefore, (3) so far as this is the case, the fact must be allowed to go some way in confirmation of this hypothesis as the right one. The theocratic tone of Job is exactly that of Genesis. The history of Joseph (e.g.) in that book presents in its view of human life a marked resemblance to the teaching of the Book of Job, and to the development of the history of Job. God is regarded in Job as Supreme and Independent, Holy and Incorruptible (chaps. xv. 15, xxii. 2—4), Immortal and Eternal (chap. x. 5), Spiritual and Invisible (chaps. ix. 11, xxvi. 13), the Hearer and Answerer of prayer (chap. xxxiii. 26), the King of kings (chap. xxxiv. 19), the Preserver of men (chaps. xxxiii. 28, xii. 10), the Giver of wisdom (chap. xxxv. 11, &c.), the Ruler of nations (chap. xii. 23, &c.). In the words of Job x. 9, he almost declares his knowledge of what God had said to Adam (Gen. iii. 18), and so far as this is the case he accepts that record as a true revelation of God.

There is evidence in Job of acquaintance with, and the study of, astronomy, in which considerable advancement must have been made (chaps. ix. 9, xxxviii. 31, 32, &c.). The description of the war-horse in chap. xxxix. is one of the most famous in Job, and this points to a knowledge of Egypt, in which horses were abundant (Gen. xlvii. 17, xlix. 17; Exod. ix. 3, xiv. 9, 23, xv. 1, 21). Mining operations and the achievements of early engineering were familiar to the writer of Job (chap. xxviii.), as were the riches and the solitudes of the desert. In fact, the range of observation, experience, and reflection is probably larger in Job not only than that of any other book of the Bible, but also of any other book whatever of the same extent. While, however, there is no trace in Job of a knowledge of any other composition than that of Genesis, it is significant to observe the manifest—

VIII. Effect of this Book on other Books of Scripture.—The evidences of this are so numerous that they can only be touched upon here. Foremost comes the famous instance of Jeremiah's complaint unto God (chap. xx.), in which he curses the day of his birth, like Job. It is plain that one of these pre-supposes the other, and no one of any critical discernment can doubt which is the original. (See Renan xxxiv.) Next, there is Ps. viii. 4, which almost repeats Job vii. 17— at least, in its idea. Comp. Ps. xi. 6, Job xv. 34, xxii. 20; Lam. iii. 7, Job i. 10; Eccles. v. 15, Job i. 21; Ps. lviii. 8, Job iii. 16; Prov. ii. 4, Job iii. 21; Isa. xxxv. 3, "Strengthen ye the weak hands, and confirm the feeble knees;" Job iv. 4, "Thy words have upholden him that was falling, and thou hast strengthened the feeble knees;" comp. Heb. xii. 12; comp. also Ezek. vii. 17, and xxi. 7, and Isa. xiii. 7. With Ps. xxxvii. 25, "I have been young, and now am old," &c., comp. Job iv. 8. With Ps. xc. 7, "In the morning it is green," &c., comp. Job iv. 20 and viii. 12. Indeed, the language of Psalms, Proverbs, and the prophets abounds with traces of the influence of Job; in fact, so manifest is this that it has been made the basis of a theory that Job was written in the age of David and Solomon. But, as before said, its ancient existence and authority, which will equally account for this knowledge, is inherently more probable. It is in the substantial teaching of the book, no less than in the reproduction of its language, that we can discern traces of its influence. For instance, in the teaching of Job xiii. 16 ("He also shall be my salvation: for an hypocrite shall not come before him") there is the germ not only of all the stern morality of the prophets, but also that of the grace and sweetness of the Gospel itself. And so completely was it felt that *faith* was *the* lesson of Job, that his *patience*, which was manifested in the deep undercurrent of resignation and confidence (chap. xiii. 15) rather than in the outward repression of complaint, has passed into a proverb (James v. 11). He was patient, however, because of his intense faith; and to the exhibition of this character of faith as seen in Job how much may we not ascribe of the trust, resignation, and confidence of the Psalms? With the exception, however, of Job and the Psalms, no book of the Bible so honours and inculcates faith as the Book

JOB.

of Genesis (*e.g.*, in chap. xv. 6), which, we have seen, the writer of Job must have known.

IX. **Canonicity.**—Job belongs to the *third* section of the Hebrew writings, being classed with the Psalms, Proverbs, &c. And this for obvious reasons, because it was not a book of the Law, and it could not be classed with the prophets. But its canonicity has never been doubted. Its very place, however, in the Canon must be owing to its connection with some great writer of authority; and this is the more obvious because of its being in no sense an Israelitish book. When, however, we bear in mind the fact of its position among the sacred writings of Israel, the sublimity, purity, and simplicity of its teaching and aim, we must not only confess that it is in many respects the most marvellous book in existence, but that it towers far above all other books in the grandeur of its poetry, the nobility of its sentiments, and the splendour of its diction. And in the contemplation of these features, we are led by a species of induction to the acknowledgment of its true—

X. **Inspiration,** for no judgment of the Book of Job can be adequate or just which does not recognise in the facts about it sufficiently clear indications of an origin not of the unaided speculations of man, but the product, if we will only accept it, of an authorised and inspired communication on the part of God. If things happened as the Book of Job says they did, then we must have in that record of them a veritable revelation of the Most High.

THE BOOK OF JOB

CHAPTER I.—⁽¹⁾ There was a man in the land of Uz, whose name *was* Job; and that man was ^aperfect and upright, and one that feared God, and eschewed evil. ⁽²⁾ And there were born unto him seven sons and three daughters. ⁽³⁾ His ¹substance also was seven thousand sheep, and three thousand camels, and five hundred yoke of oxen, and five hundred she asses, and a very great ²household; so that this man was the greatest of all the ³men of the east.

⁽⁴⁾ And his sons went and feasted in their houses, every one his day; and sent and called for their three sisters to eat and to drink with them. ⁽⁵⁾ And it was so, when the days of *their* feasting were gone about, that Job sent and sanctified them, and rose up early in the morning, and offered burnt offerings *according* to the number of them all: for Job said, It may be that my sons have sinned, and ^bcursed God in their hearts. Thus did Job ⁴continually.

⁽⁶⁾ Now there was a day when the sons of God came to present themselves be-

---

B.C. cir. 1520.

a ch. 2. 3.
1 Or, *cattle.*
2 Or, *husbandry.*
3 Heb., *sons of the east.*
b 1 Kin. 21. 10, 13.
4 Heb., *all the days.*

⁽¹⁾ **There was a man in the land of Uz.**—The first mention of this name is in Gen. x. 23, where Uz is said to have been one of the sons of Aram, who was one of the sons of Shem. (Comp. 1 Chron. i. 17.) Another Uz (in the Authorised Version spelt Huz) is mentioned in Gen xxii. 21 as the firstborn of Nahor, the brother of Abraham. A third form of this name is mentioned in Gen. xxxvi. 28 among "the sons of Seir the Horite, who inhabited the land " of Edom. (Comp. 1 Chron. i. 42.) It is probable that each of these is to be associated with a different district: the first perhaps with that of the Lebanon—a district near Damascus is still called El-Ghutha; the second with that of Mesopotamia or Chaldea; and the third with the Edomite district south of Palestine. From the mention of "the land of Uz" (Lam. iv. 21) and "the kings of the land of Uz" (Jer. xxv. 20), where in each case the association seems to be with Edom, it is probable that the land of Job is to be identified rather with the district south and south-east of Palestine.

Whose name was Job.—The name is really *Iyyov*, and is carefully to be distinguished from the Job (*Yov*) who was the son of Issachar (Gen. xlvi. 13), and from the Jobab (*Yovav*) who was one of the kings of Edom (Gen. xxxvi. 33), with both of which it has been confounded. The form of the name may suggest the signification of "the assaulted one," as the root from which it appears to be derived means "was an enemy."

Perfect and upright . . .—Noah in like manner is said to have been "perfect" (Gen. vi. 9). Abram was required to be so (Gen. xvii. 1), and Israel generally (Deut. xviii. 13), though the adjective in these places is not quite the same as that used here; and our Lord required the same high standard of His disciples (Matt. v. 48), while He also, through the gift of the Spirit, made it possible. The character here given to Job is that in which wisdom is declared to consist. (Comp. xxviii. 28.) It has the twofold aspect of refusing the evil and choosing the good, of aiming at a lofty ideal of excellence and of shunning that which is fatal or opposed to it.

⁽²⁾ **Seven sons and three daughters.**—The like number was restored to him after his probation (chap. xlii. 13).

⁽³⁾ **The men of the east.**—This term is indefinite with regard to the three districts above mentioned, and might include them all. The Arabs still call the Hauran, or the district east of Jordan, the land of Job. It is said to be a lovely and fertile region, fulfilling the conditions of the poem.

⁽⁴⁾ **Every one his day.**—*i.e.*, probably his birthday. (Comp. Gen. xl. 20, xxi. 8; and in the New Testament Matt. xiv. 6, Mark vi. 21.)

⁽⁵⁾ **Job sent and sanctified them . . .**—The earliest records of society exhibit the father of the family acting as the priest. This is one of the passages that show Job was outside the pale and influence of the Mosaic law, whether this was owing to his age or his country. His life in this respect corresponds with that of the patriarchs in Genesis more nearly than any other in Scripture.

Cursed God.—The word used here and in verse 11 and chap. ii. 5, 9, and also in 1 Kings xxi. 10, 13, of Naboth, is literally *blessed;* that in chap. iii. 1, *e.g.*, &c., being quite different. The contrast in chaps. i. 22 and ii. 10 shows the Authorised Version to be substantially right, however this contradictory sense is obtained. Many languages have words which are used in opposite senses. (Comp. *e.g.*, our "cleave to" and "cleave.") The use of *bless* in the sense of *curse* may be a euphemism, or it may arise from giving to it the meaning of *saluting* or *bidding farewell to*, and so *dismissing*. This use is not elsewhere found than in the passages cited above.

⁽⁶⁾ **Sons of God.**—Comp. chap. xxxviii. 7, Gen. vi. 2, 4; and for the sense comp. 1 Kings xxii. 19. The phrase probably means *the angels;* or at all events an incident in the unseen spiritual world is referred to simultaneous with a corresponding one on earth. (Comp. 1 Cor. xi. 10.) In the latter sense, a solemn thought is suggested by it to those who join in the public worship of God.

Satan.—The word appears in the Old Testament as the name of a specific person only here and in Zech.

Satan is Permitted   JOB, I.   *to Tempt Job.*

fore the LORD, and ¹Satan came also ²among them. ⁽⁷⁾ And the LORD said unto Satan, Whence comest thou? Then Satan answered the LORD, and said, From *ᵃgoing to and fro in the earth, and from walking up and down in it.* ⁽⁸⁾ And the LORD said unto Satan, ³Hast thou considered my servant Job, that *there is* none like him in the earth, a perfect and an upright man, one that feareth God, and escheweth evil? ⁽⁹⁾ Then Satan answered the LORD, and said, Doth Job fear God for nought? ⁽¹⁰⁾ Hast not thou made an hedge about him, and about his house, and about all that he hath on every side? thou hast blessed the work of his hands, and his ⁴substance is increased in the land. ⁽¹¹⁾ But put forth thine hand now, and touch all that he hath, ⁵and he will curse thee to thy face. ⁽¹²⁾ And the LORD said unto Satan, Behold, all that he hath *is* in thy ⁶power; only upon himself put not forth thine hand. So Satan went forth from the presence of the LORD.

⁽¹³⁾ And there was a day when his sons and his daughters *were* eating and drinking wine in their eldest brother's house:

1 Heb., *the adversary.*

2 Heb., *in the midst of them.*

a 1 Pet. 5. 8.

3 Heb., *Hast thou set thy heart on.*

4 Or, *cattle.*

5 Heb., *if he curse thee not to thy face.*

6 Heb., *hand.*

7 Or, *A great fire.*

8 Heb., *rushed.*

9 Heb., *from aside,* &c.

⁽¹⁴⁾ and there came a messenger unto Job, and said, The oxen were plowing, and the asses feeding beside them: ⁽¹⁵⁾ and the Sabeans fell *upon them,* and took them away; yea, they have slain the servants with the edge of the sword; and I only am escaped alone to tell thee. ⁽¹⁶⁾ While he *was* yet speaking, there came also another, and said, ⁷The fire of God is fallen from heaven, and hath burned up the sheep, and the servants, and consumed them; and I only am escaped alone to tell thee. ⁽¹⁷⁾ While he *was* yet speaking, there came also another, and said, The Chaldeans made out three bands, and ⁸fell upon the camels, and have carried them away, yea, and slain the servants with the edge of the sword; and I only am escaped alone to tell thee. ⁽¹⁸⁾ While he *was* yet speaking, there came also another, and said, Thy sons and thy daughters *were* eating and drinking wine in their eldest brother's house: ⁽¹⁹⁾ and, behold, there came a great wind ⁹from the wilderness, and smote the four corners of the house, and it fell upon the young men, and they are dead; and I only am escaped alone to tell thee.

---

iii. 12, and possibly in 1 Chron. xxi. 1 and Ps. cix. 6. If this psalm is David's, according to the inscription, no reliance can be placed on speculations as to the late introduction of a belief in Satan among the Jews, nor, therefore, on any as to the lateness of these early chapters of Job. Precisely the same word is used, apparently as a common name, in the history of Balaam (Num. xxii. 22, 32), also in 1 Sam. xxix. 4, and 1 Kings v. 4, xi. 14, 23, 25, where it can hardly be otherwise. Here only and in Zechariah it is found with the definite article "the adversary." The theory of the personality of the evil one must largely depend upon the view we take of these and other passages of Scripture as containing an authoritative revelation.

⁽⁷⁾ **From going to and fro . . .**—Compare our Lord's words in Matt. xiii. 25: "and went his way." St. Peter evidently had this passage in mind (1 Pet. v. 8, "walketh about").

⁽⁹⁾ **Doth Job fear God for nought?**—Manifesting the worst kind of scepticism, a disbelief in human goodness. Satan knows that the *motive* of an action is its only value, and by incrimination calumniates the motives of Job. The object of the book is thus introduced, which is to exhibit the integrity of human conduct under the worst possible trial, and to show man a victor over Satan.

⁽¹²⁾ **All that he hath is in thy power . . .**—Mighty as the principle of evil is in the world, it is nevertheless held in check by One who directs it to His own ends. Such is the uniform teaching of Scripture. We are not under the uncontrolled dominion of evil, strong as the temptation may be at times to think so. (See 2 Cor. xii. 7, 9; 1 Thess. ii. 18, &c.)

⁽¹⁵⁾ **The Sabeans.**—Literally, *Sheba.* Three persons named Sheba are found in Genesis: (1) The son of Raamah and grandson of Cush (Gen. x. 7); (2) the son of Jokshan and grandson of Abraham (Gen. xxv. 3); (3) The son of Joktan and grandson of Eber (Gen. x. 28). It is probably the second who is referred to here, whose descendants led a predatory and marauding kind of life in the country bordering on that of Job. (Comp. Ezek. xxxviii. 13.)

⁽¹⁶⁾ **The fire of God.**—Whether or not we understand this phrase as in the margin, it can hardly mean anything else than lightning. (Comp. Gen. xix. 24, and 2 Kings. i. 10—14.) It is characteristic of the Old Testament poetry to see in the convulsions of nature the immediate action of the Most High; but perhaps it is intended throughout Job that we should see more than this, as the book undoubtedly assumes to be the record of a Divine revelation.

⁽¹⁷⁾ **The Chaldeans.**—Literally, *Chasdim,* or descendants of Chesed (Gen. xxii. 22; see Note on verse 1). This name reappears in the classic Carduchia and in the modern Kurdistan, as well as in the more familiar Chaldæa; it being a well-known philological law that *r* and *l* and *r* and *s* are interchangeable. It is to be noted that this calamity arose from the opposite quarter to the last, illustrating the well-known fact that troubles never come alone, and that causes of a widely different nature seem to combine to overthrow the falling man.

⁽¹⁸⁾ **Thy sons and thy daughters.**—See verse 13. The marvellous accumulation of disasters points us to the conclusion that it was the distinct work of Satan, according to the permission given him (verse 12), and consequently supernatural.

(20) Then Job arose, and rent his ¹mantle, and shaved his head, and fell down upon the ground, and worshipped, (21) and said,

*ᵃNaked came I out of my mother's womb,
And naked shall I return thither:
The LORD gave, and the LORD hath taken away;
Blessed be the name of the LORD.*

(22) In all this Job sinned not, nor ²charged God foolishly.

CHAPTER II.—(1) Again there was a day when the sons of God came to present themselves before the LORD, and Satan came also among them to present himself before the LORD. (2) And the LORD said unto Satan, From whence comest thou? And ᵇSatan answered the LORD, and said, From going to and fro in the earth, and from walking up and down in it. (3) And the LORD said unto Satan, Hast thou considered my servant Job, that *there is* none like him in the earth, ᶜa perfect and an upright man, one that feareth God, and escheweth evil? and still he holdeth fast his integrity, although thou movedst me against him, ³to destroy him without cause. (4) And Satan answered the LORD, and said, Skin for skin, yea, all that a man hath will he give for his life. (5) But put forth thine hand now, and touch his bone and his flesh, and he will curse thee to thy face. (6) And the LORD said unto Satan, Behold, he *is* in thine hand; ⁴but save his life.

(7) So went Satan forth from the presence of the LORD, and smote Job with sore boils from the sole of his foot unto his crown. (8) And he took him a potsherd to scrape himself withal; and he sat down among the ashes.

(9) Then said his wife unto him, Dost thou still retain thine integrity? curse God, and die. (10) But he said unto her, Thou speakest as one of the foolish women speaketh. What? shall we receive good at the hand of God, and shall we not receive evil? In all this did not Job sin with his lips.

(11) Now when Job's three friends heard of all this evil that was come upon him, they came every one from his own place; Eliphaz the Temanite, and Bildad the Shuhite, and Zophar the Naamathite: for they had made an appointment to-

---

1 Or, *robe*.
ᵃ Eccles. 5. 15; 1 Tim. 6. 7.
2 Or, *attributed folly to God*.
ᵇ ch. 1. 7.
ᶜ ch. 1. 1, 8.
3 Heb., *to swallow him up*.
4 Or, *only*.

---

(20) **And worshipped.**—Compare the conduct of David (2 Sam. xii. 20) and of Hezekiah (2 Kings xix. 1). Moments of intense sorrow or trial, like moments of intense joy, force us into the immediate presence of God.

(21) **Thither.**—If taken literally, can only refer to the *womb*, which in that case must here mean the earth, with a probable allusion to Gen. iii. 19. (Comp. Job xvii. 14.)

Blessed be the name of the Lord.—The very word used in a contrary sense (verse 11). Thus was Satan foiled for the *first* time.

(22) **Foolishly.**—The same word as at chap. xxiv. 12, signifying reproach or guilt. It is a noun derived from the adjective rendered "unsavoury" in chap. vi. 6.

II.

(1) **And Satan came also.**—See chap. i. 7. St. Peter applies to Satan the verb from which we have *peripatetic*.

(4) **Skin for skin.**—This is a more extreme form of the insinuation of chap. i. 9. He means Job takes care to have his *quid pro quo;* and if the worst come to the worst, a man will give up everything to save his life. If, therefore, Job can save his life at the price of subservience to God, he will willingly pay that price rather than die; but his service is worth no more than that selfish object implies.

(6) **But save his life.**—God's faithfulness cannot fail even if, as Satan hints, Job's should do so (2 Tim. ii. 13). There was one who cared for Job's life more than he cared for it himself.

(7) **Sore boils.**—Supposed to be Elephantiasis, an extreme form of leprosy, in which the skin becomes clotted and hard like an elephant's, with painful cracks and sores underneath.

(9) **Then said his wife.**—Thus it is that a man's foes are they of his own household (Micah vii. 6; Matt. x. 36, &c.). The worst trial of all is when those nearest to us, instead of strengthening our hand in God and confirming our faith, conspire to destroy it.

(10) **Shall we receive good . . . ?**—The words were fuller than even Job thought; for merely to receive evil as from *God's* hands is to transmute its character altogether, for then even calamities become blessings in disguise. What Job meant was that we are *bound* to expect evil as well as good from God's hands by a sort of compensation and even-handed justice, but what his words *may* mean is a far more blessed truth than this. There is a sublime contrast between the temptation of Job and the temptation of Christ (Matt. xxvi. 39—42, &c.). (Comp. Heb. v. 8.) *This* was the lesson Job was learning.

(11) **Eliphaz the Temanite.**—Teman was the son of Eliphaz, the son of Esau, to whose family this Eliphaz is probably to be referred (Gen. xxxvi. 4, 10, 11). If so, this may roughly indicate the date of the book. The inhabitants of Teman, which lay north-east of Edom, were famed for their wisdom (Jer. xlvii. 7).

Bildad the Shuhite probably derived his origin from Shuah, the son of Abraham by Keturah (Gen. xxv. 2). Of the district from which Zophar the Naamathite came nothing is known. It probably derived its name from a Naamah or Naaman, of which there were several (*e.g.*, Gen. iv. 22; 1 Kings xiv. 21; Gen. xlvi. 21; Num. xxvi. 40; 2 Kings v. 1), as names of persons or places called after them.

gether to come to mourn with him and to comfort him. (12) And when they lifted up their eyes afar off, and knew him not, they lifted up their voice, and wept; and they rent every one his mantle, and sprinkled dust upon their heads toward heaven. (13) So they sat down with him upon the ground seven days and seven nights, and none spake a word unto him: for they saw that *his* grief was very great.

CHAPTER III.—(1) After this opened Job his mouth, and cursed his day. (2) And Job ¹spake, and said,
(3) *a* "Let the day perish wherein I was born,
And the night *in which* it was said,
There is a man child conceived.
(4) Let that day be darkness; let not God regard it from above,
Neither let the light shine upon it.
(5) Let darkness and the shadow of death ²stain it;
Let a cloud dwell upon it;
³Let the blackness of the day terrify it.
(6) *As for* that night, let darkness seize upon it;
⁴Let it not be joined unto the days of the year,
Let it not come into the number of the months.
(7) Lo, let that night be solitary,
Let no joyful voice come therein.
(8) Let them curse it that curse the day,
Who are ready to raise up ⁵their mourning.
(9) Let the stars of the twilight thereof be dark;
Let it look for light, but *have* none;
Neither let it see ⁶the dawning of the day:
(10) Because it shut not up the doors of my *mother's* womb,
Nor hid sorrow from mine eyes.
(11) Why died I not from the womb?
Why did I *not* give up the ghost when I came out of the belly?
(12) Why did the knees prevent me?
Or why the breasts that I should suck?
(13) For now should I have lain still and been quiet,
I should have slept: then had I been at rest,
(14) With kings and counsellors of the earth,
Which built desolate places for themselves;
(15) Or with princes that had gold,
Who filled their houses with silver:
(16) Or as an hidden untimely birth I had not been;
As infants *which* never saw light.

1 Heb., *answered.*
a ch. 10. 18, 19; Jer. 20. 14.
2 Or, *challenge it.*
3 Or, *let them terrify it, as those who have a bitter day.*
4 Or, *let it not rejoice among the days.*
5 Or, *a leviathan.*
6 Heb., *the eyelids of the morning.*

---

(12) **And knew him not.**—Compare the converse statement descriptive of the love of him who could recognise his lost son under a disguise as great as that of Job, or even greater (Luke xv. 20).

(13) **So they sat down with him upon the ground seven days.**—Compare the conduct of David (2 Sam. xii. 16), and see also Gen. l. 10; 1 Sam. xxxi. 13; Ezek. iii. 15. There is a colossal grandeur about this description which is in keeping with the majesty and hoary antiquity of the poem.

III.

(1) **After this opened Job his mouth.**—There is a striking similarity between this chapter and Jer. xx. 14—18, so much so that one must be borrowed from the other; the question is, which is the original? Is Jeremiah the germ of this? or is this the tree from which a branch has been hewn by Jeremiah? Our own conviction is that Job is the original, inasmuch as this chapter is indispensable to the development of the poem; but in Jeremiah the passage occurs casually as the record of a passing mood of despair. It is, moreover, apparently clear that Jeremiah is quoting Job as he might quote one of the Psalms or any other writing with which he was familiar. He was applying to daily life the well-known expression of a patriarchal experience, whereas in the other case the words of Job would be the ideal magnifying of a commonplace and realistic experience.

(4) **Regard.**—Literally, *require, ask for, and so manifest care about.* (Comp. Deut. xi. 12.)

(5) **Stain.**—Literally, *redeem*—*i.e.*, claim as their rightful inheritance. The other meaning enters into this word, as in Isa. lxiii. 3; Mal. i. 7.

Blackness of the day—*i.e.*, preternatural darkness, inopportune and unexpected darkness, like that of eclipses, &c.

(6) **Let it not be joined.**—Rather, *let it not rejoice among*, as one of the glorious procession of nights.

(8) **That curse the day**—*i.e.*, Let those who proclaim days unlucky or accursed curse that day as pre-eminently so; or let them recollect that day as a standard or sample of cursing. "Let it be as cursed as Job's birthday."

These people are further described as being ready to arouse leviathan (Authorised Version, "raise up their mourning"), or the crocodile—persons as mad and desperate as *that*. Let the most hopeless and reckless of mankind select that day as the one which they would choose to curse. This seems to be Job's meaning.

(9) **The dawning . . .**—Literally, *the eyelids of the dawn.*

(12) **Prevent**—*i.e.*, "Why was I nursed with care, instead of being allowed to fall to the ground and be killed?"

(14) **Desolate places**—*i.e.*, gorgeous tombs and splendid sepulchres, which, being tenanted only by the dead, are desolate; or it may mean that the places so built of old are now ruined and desolate. In the former sense it is possible that the Pyramids may here be hinted at.

(16) **Untimely birth.**—Another condition which would have relieved him from the experience of suffering.

The Ease of Death.   JOB, IV.   *Eliphaz Reproveth him.*

(17) There the wicked cease *from* troubling;
And there the ¹weary be at rest.
(18) *There* the prisoners rest together;
They hear not the voice of the oppressor.
(19) The small and great are there;
And the servant *is* free from his master.
(20) Wherefore is light given to him that is in misery,
And life unto the bitter *in* soul;
(21) Which ²long for death, but it *cometh* not;
And dig for it more than for hid treasures;
(22) Which rejoice exceedingly,
And are glad, when they can find the grave?
(23) *Why is light given* to a man whose way is hid,
ᵃAnd whom God hath hedged in?
(24) For my sighing cometh ³before I eat,
And my roarings are poured out like the waters.
(25) For ⁴the thing which I greatly feared is come upon me,
And that which I was afraid of is come unto me.
(26) I was not in safety, neither had I rest,
Neither was I quiet; yet trouble came.

1 Heb., *wearied in strength.*

2 Heb., *wait.*

ᵃ ch. 19. 8.

3 Heb., *before my meat.*

4 Heb., *I feared a fear, and it came upon me.*

5 Heb., *a word.*

6 Heb., *who can refrain from words?*

7 Heb., *the bowing knees.*

ᵇ Pro. 22. 8; Hos. 10. 13.

8 That is, *by his anger,* as Isa. 30. 33.

CHAPTER IV.—(1) Then Eliphaz the Temanite answered and said,
(2) *If* we assay ⁵to commune with thee, wilt thou be grieved?
But ⁶who can withhold himself from speaking?
(3) Behold, thou hast instructed many,
And thou hast strengthened the weak hands.
(4) Thy words have upholden him that was falling,
And thou hast strengthened ⁷the feeble knees.
(5) But now it is come upon thee, and thou faintest;
It toucheth thee, and thou art troubled.
(6) *Is* not *this* thy fear, thy confidence,
Thy hope, and the uprightness of thy ways?
(7) Remember, I pray thee, who *ever* perished, being innocent?
Or where were the righteous cut off?
(8) Even as I have seen, ᵇthey that plow iniquity,
And sow wickedness, reap the same.
(9) By the blast of God they perish,
And ⁸by the breath of his nostrils are they consumed.

---

(17) **There**—*i.e.*, in the grave, the place indicated, but not distinctly expressed.

(18) **The oppressor.**—As this is the word rendered *taskmaster* in Exodus, some have thought there may be an allusion to that history here.

(20) **Wherefore is light given.**—Comp. the connection between life and light in Ps. xxxvi. 9 and John i. 4.

(23) **Hedged in.**—The same expression was used in an opposite sense in chap. i. 10.

(25) **For the thing which I greatly feared** . . . —Comp. Prov. xxviii. 14. It means that he had always had in remembrance the uncertainty and instability of earthly things, and yet he had been overtaken by a calamity that mocked his carefulness and exceeded his apprehensions.

IV.

(2) **If we assay.**—Rather, perhaps, *Has one ever assayed?* or, *Has a word ever been tried?* It appears from chap. xxix. 9, 10, that Job was held in great honour and reverence by all, and Eliphaz regarded him with awe such as would have constrained him to be silent, but he is so convinced that Job is wrong and deserves reproof, that he cannot refrain from speaking. He strikes a note, however, which the friends all sound, namely, that it is the wicked who suffer, and that all who suffer must be wicked. This, in a variety of forms, is the sum and substance of what they have to say.

(3) **Behold, thou hast instructed many.**—There is a conspicuous want of feeling in Eliphaz. Without any true sympathy, however, he may have given the outward signs of it (chap. ii. 12, 13). He charges Job with inability to derive from his own principles that support which he had expected them to afford to others, and seems almost to rejoice malevolently that one who had been so great a help to others was now in need of help himself. "Calamity touches thee, and thou art overwhelmed by it."

(6) **Is not this thy fear, thy confidence . . . ?**—The meaning seems to be, "Should not thy fear or piety be thy confidence, and the uprightness of thy ways thy hope? Should not the piety thou wast so ready to commend to others supply a sufficient ground of hope for thyself?" Or we may understand, "Is not thy reverence, thy confidence, thy hope, and thy integrity shown to be worthless if thou faintest as soon as adversity toucheth thee?" The drift of the speaker is virtually the same in either case.

(7) **Remember, I pray thee, who ever perished, being innocent?**—He challenges Job's experience, and quotes his own in proof of the universal connection between sin and suffering. In so doing, his object may be to insinuate that Job is sinful; or, as seems perhaps more probable, and certainly more gracious, to prove to him that if he is what he was supposed to be, that itself is a ground of hope, inasmuch as no innocent person is allowed to perish. He utters here a half-truth, which, however, is after all true, inasmuch as God will never *fail*, though He may *try*, those who trust in Him.

(8) **They that plow iniquity.**—Comp. Gal. vi. 7, 8; and comp. also the strange expression of Isa. v. 18,

11

His Vision and   JOB, V.   *its Teaching.*

(10) The roaring of the lion, and the voice of the fierce lion,
And the teeth of the young lions, are broken.
(11) The old lion perisheth for lack of prey,
And the stout lion's whelps are scattered abroad.
(12) Now a thing was secretly brought to me,
And mine ear received a little thereof.
(13) In thoughts from the visions of the night,
When deep sleep falleth on men,
(14) Fear ² came upon me, and trembling,
Which made ³ all my bones to shake.
(15) Then a spirit passed before my face;
The hair of my flesh stood up:
(16) It stood still, but I could not discern the form thereof:
An image *was* before mine eyes,
⁴ *There was* silence, and I heard a voice, *saying*,
(17) Shall mortal man be more just than God?
Shall a man be more pure than his maker?
(18) Behold, he ᵃ put no trust in his servants;
⁵ And his angels he charged with folly:
(19) How much less *in* them that dwell in ᵇ houses of clay,
Whose foundation *is* in the dust,
Which are crushed before the moth?
(20) They are ⁶ destroyed from morning to evening:
They perish for ever without any regarding *it*.
(21) Doth not their excellency *which is* in them go away?
They die, even without wisdom.

CHAPTER V.—(1) Call now, if there be any that will answer thee;
And to which of the saints wilt thou ⁷ turn?
(2) For wrath killeth the foolish man,
And ⁸ envy slayeth the silly one.
(3) I have seen the foolish taking root:

Margin notes:
1 Heb., *by stealth.*
2 Heb., *met me.*
3 Heb., *the multitude of my bones.*
4 Or, *I heard a still voice.*
a ch. 15. 15; 2 Pet 2. 4.
5 Or, *nor in his angels, in whom he put light.*
b 2 Cor. 5. 1.
6 Heb., *beaten in pieces.*
7 Or, *look?*
8 Or, *indignation.*

---

(11) **The old lion perisheth . . .**—This means that even though wickedness is joined with strength, it is equally unable to prosper. It is to be observed that no less than five different words are here used for *lion*, showing that these animals must have been common and of various kinds in Job's country.

(12) **Now a thing.**—He now proceeds to enforce and illustrate what he has said in highly poetical language, which has been versified in one of Byron's Hebrew Melodies.

Secretly brought to me.—Literally, *was stolen for me.* Joseph uses the same expression of himself in Gen. xl. 15.

Mine ear received a little, compared with the inexhaustible resources remaining unrevealed. The word used for *little* is only found once again, and in the mouth of Job (chap. xxvi. 14).

(13) **In thoughts from the visions of the night.**—The Book of Genesis exhibits the same idea of revelation through visions of the night, *e.g.,* chaps. xv. 1, xx. 3, xxx. 11, xl. 5, xli. 1, xlvi. 2; afterwards it is not common, except in the Book of Daniel. The word rendered "thoughts" only occurs once again, in Job xx. 2. The "deep sleep" of this place is like a reminiscence of Gen. ii. 21 and xv. 12. It is used again in Job xxxiii. 15, otherwise only once in 1 Sam. xxvi. 12, once in Prov. xix. 15, and once in Isa. xxix. 10.

(15) **A spirit passed before my face.**—It is vain to argue from this passage that spiritual essences are capable of being seen by the bodily eye, because, first of all, the language is highly figurative and poetical, and because, secondly, every one understands that a spiritual manifestation can be made only to the spirit. The notion, therefore, of *seeing* a spirit is absurd in itself, because it involves the idea of seeing the invisible; but it is conceivable that the perceptions of the inner spirit may be so vivid as to assume the character of outward manifestations.

(17) **Shall mortal man be more just than God?**—This is the burden, or refrain, upon which the friends of Job are for ever harping. It is perfectly orthodox, but at the same time perfectly inadequate to deal with the necessities of Job's case. He is willing to admit that it is impossible for any man to be just with God; but then arises Job's dilemma, Where is God's justice if He punishes the innocent as the guilty? The word rendered "mortal" man is really *weak, frail* man, involving, it may be, the idea of *mortality,* but not immediately suggesting it. As far as mortality implies sin, the notion of being *just* is absurd; and even a *strong* man—such is the antithesis—cannot be more pure than He that made him, who, it is assumed, must be both strong and righteous.

(18) **Behold, he put no trust in his servants.**—The statement is a general one; it does not refer to any one act in the past. We should read *putteth* and *chargeth.* Eliphaz repeats himself in chap. xv. 15.

(19) **Houses of clay.**—This may perhaps contain an allusion to Gen. xi. 3.

Are crushed before the moth?—That is to say, are so frail that even the moth destroys them.

(20) **From morning to evening.**—The process is continual and unceasing, and when we consider the ravages of time on history, we may well say, as in verse 20, that "none regardeth it."

The next verse, however, may seem to imply that they themselves are unmindful of their decay, it is so insidious and so complete.

V.

(1) **Call now.**—The speaker now becomes more personal and direct in his tone and bearing. He insinuates that Job is "unwise" and "silly," and promises swift destruction for all such.

(3) **I cursed.**—The word means, "I was able to declare distinctly, and I did declare without hesitation, that his

Man Born to Trouble.   JOB, V.   *The End of God's Correction.*

But suddenly I cursed his habitation.
(4) His children are far from safety,
    And they are crushed in the gate,
      neither *is there* any to deliver *them*.
(5) Whose harvest the hungry eateth up,
    And taketh it even out of the thorns,
    And the robber swalloweth up their substance.
(6) Although ¹affliction cometh not forth of the dust,
    Neither doth trouble spring out of the ground;
(7) Yet man is born unto ²trouble, as ³the sparks fly upward.
(8) I would seek unto God, and unto God would I commit my cause:
(9) *a* Which doeth great things ⁴and unsearchable;
    Marvellous things ⁵without number:
(10) Who giveth rain upon the earth,
    And sendeth waters upon the ⁶fields:
(11) *b* To set up on high those that be low;
    That those which mourn may be exalted to safety.
(12) *c* He disappointeth the devices of the crafty,
    So that their hands ⁷cannot perform *their* enterprise.
(13) *d* He taketh the wise in their own craftiness:
    And the counsel of the froward is carried headlong.
(14) *e* They ⁸meet with darkness in the daytime,
    And grope in the noonday as in the night.
(15) But he saveth the poor from the sword,
    From their mouth, and from the hand of the mighty.
(16) *f* So the poor hath hope, and iniquity stoppeth her mouth.
(17) *g* Behold, happy *is* the man whom God correcteth:

---

1 Or, *iniquity*.
2 Or, *labour*.
3 Heb., *the sons of the burning coal lift up to fly.*
a ch. 9. 10; Ps. 72. 18; Rom. 11. 33.
4 Heb., *and there is no search*.
5 Heb., *till there be no number*.
6 Heb., *out-places*.
b 1 Sam. 2. 7; Ps. 113. 7.
c Neh. 4. 15; Ps. 33. 10; Isa. 8. 10.
7 Or, *cannot perform any thing*.
d 1 Cor. 3. 19.
e Deut. 28. 29.
8 Or, *run into*.
f Ps. 107. 42.
g Prov. 3. 12; Heb. 12. 5; James 1. 12; Rev. 3. 19.

---

lot would be as follows." All these general results of experience have the sting of insinuation in them that they contain the key to Job's unfortunate condition. There is secret unsoundness there which is the cause of the manifest and open misery. It is impossible that a man so stricken should be otherwise than, for some unknown reason, the guilty victim of the righteous wrath of a just judge.

(4) **They are crushed.**—Rather, perhaps, *they crush one another*. Their internal rivalries and dissensions bring them to ruin. They exemplify the house divided against itself.

(5) **Whose harvest the hungry eateth up.**—The meaning becomes more pointed if we understand the wicked man himself as the subject whose harvest he shall eat famishing and have to take from among the thorns—there shall be so little, and that little choked with thorns. The word "robber" is perhaps a *trap*, or *snare*. Some of the old versions use other vowels, and read, "the thirsty swallow up," making the parallelism complete.

(6, 7) **Although affliction. . . .**—These two verses are confessedly very difficult. It is hard to see also the connection between sparks flying upwards and man's being born to trouble. It seems to give better sense if we understand Eliphaz comparing man's lot as prepared for him by God with his own pride and presumptuous ambition. Man is born to labour, but, like sparks of fire, he makes high his flight. Trouble and toil is no accidental growth, but a lot appointed by God, which would be beneficial if man did not thwart it by his own pride. They lift themselves up and soar on high like sparks of fire with daring and presumptuous conduct, and so bring on themselves condign punishment. The same word means *trouble* and *toil*, and it may be understood in the two consecutive verses in these cognate, but slightly different, senses. It would be no consolation to Job to tell him that man was born to trouble; besides, it is a sentiment more likely to proceed from the patient himself than from the spectator.

(11) **To set up on high those that be low.**—Thus his doctrine is that man's exaltation must come from God, and not from his own vain strivings. (Comp. Ps. lxxv. 4—10, and the prayer of Hannah, 1 Sam. ii. 6—8; also Ps. cxiii. 7, &c.)

(12) **So that their hands cannot perform their enterprise.**—Or, *so that their hands can do nothing that is sound or of worth, can accomplish nothing effectual*.

(13) **He taketh the wise.**—St. Paul quotes the former half of this verse in his warning to the Corinthians (1 Cor. iii. 19): "The wisdom of this world is foolishness with God. For it is written, He taketh the wise in their own craftiness." The word rendered "froward" means *crooked, perverse*, or *tortuous*. The name Naphtali is derived from the same root (Gen. xxx. 8).

(14) **Darkness in the daytime.**—This is possibly an allusion to the Egyptian plague of darkness "that may be felt" (Ex. x. 21), as the words used are similar. This may be a note of probable date. (Compare Isa. lix. 10, where the thoughts correspond, but the words differ.) This is one of the many passages of Job in which there seems to be an indication of some acquaintance with the events related in the Pentateuch, though the points of contact are too slight for us to be quite sure of it.

(15) **From the sword, from their mouth.**—It is merely a matter of grammatical nicety whether we regard the sword as coming forth from their mouth, or as identical with what comes forth from it, or as the first of three things from which the poor are delivered. It is worthy of special note that the Lord is thus conceived of and represented as the *Saviour*, and the Saviour of them who have no saviour. Is not this an idea confined to the circle of the sacred writings? At all events, it so abounds and predominates in them as to be pre-eminently, if not exclusively, characteristic of them.

(16) **Iniquity stoppeth her mouth.**—See Ps. cvii. 42, where the same phrase occurs.

(17) This is probably the original of Prov. iii. 12, which is itself quoted by the writer of the Epistle to

The Happiness of those   JOB, VI.   *who Endure God's Chastening*

Therefore despise not thou the chastening of the Almighty:
(18) ᵃ For he maketh sore, and bindeth up:
He woundeth, and his hands make whole.
(19) ᵇ He shall deliver thee in six troubles:
Yea, in seven there shall no evil touch thee.
(20) In famine he shall redeem thee from death:
And in war ¹from the power of the sword.
(21) Thou shalt be hid ²from the scourge of the tongue:
Neither shalt thou be afraid of destruction when it cometh.
(22) At destruction and famine thou shalt laugh:
Neither shalt thou be afraid of the beasts of the earth.
(23) ᶜ For thou shalt be in league with the stones of the field:
And the beasts of the field shall be at peace with thee.
(24) And thou shalt know ³that thy tabernacle *shall be* in peace;
And thou shalt visit thy habitation, and shalt not ⁴sin.
(25) Thou shalt know also that thy seed *shall be* ⁵great,
And thine offspring as the grass of the earth.
(26) Thou shalt come to *thy* grave in a full age,
Like as a shock of corn ⁶cometh in in his season.
(27) Lo this, we have searched it, so it *is*;
Hear it, and know thou *it* ⁷for thy good.

CHAPTER VI.—(1) But Job answered and said,
(2) Oh that my grief were throughly weighed,
And my calamity ⁸laid in the balances together!
(3) For now it would be heavier than the sand of the sea:
Therefore ⁹my words are swallowed up.
(4) ᵈ For the arrows of the Almighty *are* within me,

Marginal notes:
a Deut. 32. 39; 1 Sam. 2. 6; Isa. 30. 26; Hos. 6. 1.
b Ps. 91. 3.
1 Heb., *from the hands*.
2 Or, *when the tongue scourgeth*.
c Hos. 2. 18.
3 Or, *that peace is thy tabernacle*.
4 Or, *err*.
5 Or, *much*.
6 Heb., *ascendeth*.
7 Heb., *for thyself*.
8 Heb., *lifted up*.
9 That is, *I want words to express my grief*.
d Ps. 38. 2.

---

the Hebrews (chap. xii. 5), while the spirit of it is expressed by St. James and St. John in the Revelation. (See the margin.) This is the only place in Job in which the word here used for *happy*—which is the very first word of the Psalms, and is used five-and-twenty times in them alone—is found.

(18) **He maketh sore, and bindeth up.**—The sentiment here expressed is one of those obvious ones which lose all their force from familiarity with them, but which come home sometimes in sorrow with a power that is boundless, because Divine.

(19) **In six troubles.**—The special form of speech here used is characteristic mainly of the Proverbs (see chaps. vi. 16, xxx. 15, 18, 21). Since evil was emphatically *touching* Job, the actual irony of these words must have been bitter indeed.

(20) **He shall redeem thee.**—It is rather, *he hath redeemed thee*, as though the speaker could appeal to Job's own experience in the matter which itself became a ground of confident hope for the future.

(21) **Shalt thou be afraid.**—Comp. the expression in verse 15.

(22) **Neither shalt thou be afraid of the beasts of the earth.**—Literally, *and of the beasts of the earth be not thou afraid*.

(23) **For thou shalt be in league.**—Literally, *for with the stones of the field shall thy covenant be, and the beasts of the field shall be made to be at peace with thee*.

(24) **Sin.**—The word rendered "sin" literally means also *to miss the mark*, as in Judges xx. 16, and that is probably its meaning here: *Thou shalt visit thy dwelling-place, and miss nothing*, since one does not see very clearly why the promise of not sinning is connected with visiting the habitation or fold.

(25) **Great.**—The word means also *numerous*, which seems to suit the parallelism better here. The whole description is a very beautiful and poetical one of the perfect security of faith, though it is to a certain extent vitiated by its want of strict correspondence with facts, of which the very case of Job was a crucial instance. This was the special problem with which his friends had to deal, and which proved too hard for them. May we not learn that the problem is one that can only be solved in practice and not in theory?

(26) **Thou shalt come to thy grave.**—There is not improbably a contrast implied here between *going into* the grave and *going up* (see the margin) to the barn. The grave in such a case is not the melancholy end of life, but rather the passage to a higher life for which one is already ripe. "Henceforth there is laid up for me a crown of righteousness," &c. (2 Tim. iv. 8).

(27) **So it is.**—It is the boastful confidence of Eliphaz which is so hard to bear. He speaks as though Job's experience were as nothing to his. "This is mine: take it to thyself, and make it thine."

VI.

(1) **But Job answered and said.**—Job replies to Eliphaz with the despair of a man who has been baulked of sympathy when he hoped to find it. We cannot trace, nor must we expect to find, the formal reply of a logical argument. Eliphaz, he feels, has so misjudged his case that he is neither worthy of a direct reply nor susceptible of one. It is enough for him to reiterate his complaint, and long for one who can enter into it.

(3) **Swallowed up.**—That is, *words are useless and powerless to express it*. (See the margin.)

(4) **The poison whereof drinketh up my spirit.**—Rather, *the poison whereof my spirit imbibeth*, the rendering of the Authorised Version being ambiguous.

The poison whereof drinketh up my spirit:
The terrors of God do set themselves in array against me.
(5) Doth the wild ass bray ¹when he hath grass?
Or loweth the ox over his fodder?
(6) Can that which is unsavoury be eaten without salt?
Or is there *any* taste in the white of an egg?
(7) The things *that* my soul refused to touch *are* as my sorrowful meat.
(8) Oh that I might have my request;
And that God would grant *me* ²the thing that I long for!
(9) Even that it would please God to destroy me;
That he would let loose his hand, and cut me off!
(10) Then should I yet have comfort;
Yea, I would harden myself in sorrow: let him not spare;
For I have not concealed the words of the Holy One.

(11) What *is* my strength, that I should hope?
And what *is* mine end, that I should prolong my life?
(12) *Is* my strength the strength of stones? or *is* my flesh ³of brass?
(13) *Is* not my help in me? and is wisdom driven quite from me?
(14) ⁴To him that is afflicted pity *should be shewed* from his friend;
But he forsaketh the fear of the Almighty.
(15) My brethren have dealt deceitfully as a brook,
And as the stream of brooks they pass away;
(16) Which are blackish by reason of the ice,
And wherein the snow is hid:
(17) What time they wax warm, ⁵they vanish:
⁶When it is hot, they are ⁷consumed out of their place.
(18) The paths of their way are turned aside;

¹ Heb., *at grass.*
² Heb., *my expectation.*
³ Heb., *brasen.*
⁴ Heb., *To him that melteth.*
⁵ Heb., *they are cut off.*
⁶ Heb., *in the heat thereof.*
⁷ Heb., *extinguished.*

Do set themselves in array against me.—Like hosts marshalling themselves for battle. "If the ox or the ass will not low or bray so long as he is satisfied, so neither should I complain if I had no valid cause. My groaning is the evidence of a great burden, and consequently the disdainful way in which you treat it is insipid and distasteful to me—my soul refuseth to touch your proffered remedies; they are as loathsome meat to me." According to some, the words rendered "the white of an egg" mean *the juice of purslain.*

(8) **Oh that I might have my request.**—Baffled in the direction of his fellow-creatures, he turns, like many others, to God as his only hope, although it is rather from God than in God that his hope lies. However exceptional Job's trials, yet his language is the common language of all sufferers who think that relief, if it comes, must come through change of circumstances rather than in themselves in relation to circumstances. Thus Job looks forward to death as his only hope; whereas with God and in God there were many years of life and prosperity in store for him. So strong is this feeling in him, that he calls death the thing that he longs for, his hope or expectation. (Comp. chap. xvii., where even the hope that he had in death seems to have passed away and to have issued in blank hopelessness.)

(9) **Even that it would please God . . .**—The sequence of thought in these verses is obscure and uncertain. The speaker may mean that, notwithstanding all that might befall him, his consolation would still be that he had never denied the words of the Holy One. The words "I would harden myself in sorrow" are the most doubtful, not occurring elsewhere in Scripture. Some render the two clauses, "I would exult, or rejoice, in pain that spareth not;" but "Let him not spare," or "Though he spare not," seems preferable. Others render, "Though I burn in sorrow."

(10) **Concealed**—*i.e.*, denied. The same was the confidence of the Psalmist (Ps. xl. 9, 10). (Comp. Acts xx. 20.)

(11) **Prolong my life.**—This is the literal rendering; but some understand *be patient*, as in our phrase, long-suffering.

(13) **Is not my help in me?**—It is in passages such as these that the actual meaning of Job is so obscure and his words so difficult. The sense may be, "Is it not that I have no help in me, and wisdom is driven quite from me?" or yet again, "Is it because there is no help in me that therefore wisdom is driven far from me?" as is the case by your reproaches and insinuations. (See especially chap. v. 2, 27.)

(14) **But he forsaketh the fear of the Almighty.**—It is difficult to determine the precise relation of dependent clauses in an archaic language like the Hebrew; but the Authorised Version is, at all events, not correct here, the sense rather being, "Even to one that forsaketh the fear of the Almighty;" or, perhaps, better still, "lest he should forsake;" or, "he may even forsake," &c.

(15) **Have dealt deceitfully as a brook.**—This is one of the most celebrated poetical similes in the book, and carries us to life in the desert, where the wadys, so mighty and torrent-like in the winter, are insignificant streams or fail altogether in summer. So when the writer saw the Guadalquiver (or mighty wady) at Cordova, in August, it was a third-rate stream, running in many divided currents in its stony bed.

(18) **They go to nothing.**—It is doubtful whether this applies to the streams or to the caravans. Thus, "The paths of their way are turned aside and come to nought;" or, "The caravans that travel by the way of them turn aside, and go into the waste and perish." The nineteenth verse seems to suggest the latter as the more probable.

They go to nothing, and perish.
(19) The troops of Tema looked,
The companies of Sheba waited for them.
(20) They were confounded because they had hoped;
They came thither, and were ashamed.
(21) ¹For now ye are ²nothing;
Ye see *my* casting down, and are afraid.
(22) Did I say, Bring unto me?
Or, Give a reward for me of your substance?
(23) Or, Deliver me from the enemy's hand?
Or, Redeem me from the hand of the mighty?
(24) Teach me, and I will hold my tongue:
And cause me to understand wherein I have erred.
(25) How forcible are right words!
But what doth your arguing reprove?
(26) Do ye imagine to reprove words,
And the speeches of one that is desperate, *which are* as wind?
(27) Yea, ³ye overwhelm the fatherless,
And ye dig *a pit* for your friend.
(28) Now therefore be content, look upon me;
For *it is* ⁴evident unto you if I lie.
(29) Return, I pray you, let it not be iniquity;
Yea, return again, my righteousness *is* ⁵in it.
(30) Is there iniquity in my tongue?
Cannot ⁶my taste discern perverse things?

CHAPTER VII.—(1) *Is there* not ⁷an appointed time to man upon earth?
Are not his days also like the days of an hireling?
(2) As a servant ⁸earnestly desireth the shadow,
And as an hireling looketh for *the reward of* his work:

1 Or, *For now ye are like to them.* Heb., *to it.*
2 Heb., *not.*
3 Heb., *ye cause to fall upon.*
4 Heb., *before your face.*
5 That is, *in this matter.*
6 Heb., *my palate.*
7 Or, *a warfare.*
8 Heb., *gapeth after.*

---

(19) **The troops of Tema.**—Fürst says of Tema that it was a tract in the north of the Arabian Desert, on the borders of the Syrian one, where traffic was carried on from the Persian Gulf to the Mediterranean by caravans (Isa. xxi. 14; Jer. xxv. 23; chap. vi. 19). Sheba, as understood here, was probably a district on the Arabian Gulf (see chap. i. 15), where merchants trafficked with the distant cities of the East, as well as enriched themselves with the plunder of their neighbours, as in chap. i. 15.

(20) **They were confounded.**—Comp. Jeremiah's description of the famine (Jer. xiv. 3). (See margin.)

(21) **For now ye are nothing.**—"Surely now ye are become like *it*," *i.e.*, that wady; or, according to another reading followed in the text of the Authorised Version, "Ye have become nothing: ye have seen an object of terror, and are terrified: ye have seen my broken-down condition, and are dismayed at it."

(22) **Did I say, Bring unto me?**—"It is not as though I had abused your former kindness. I never laid myself under obligations to you; I never asked for your help before. Had I done so, I might have wearied out your patience, and brought upon myself your present conduct justly; but you cannot convict me of this."

(25) **How forcible are right words!**—"How forcible are words of uprightness! But what doth your reproof reprove? Open rebuke is better than secret love; better to be honestly and openly rebuked by you than be subject to the secret insinuations which are intended to pass for friendship."

(26) **Do ye imagine to reprove words . . . ?**—"It cannot be your intent to reprove mere words, as mine confessedly are (verse 3), and as you seem to count them (verse 13). If so, they are hardly worthy the trouble bestowed upon them, but might be left to answer themselves."

(27) **Yea, ye overwhelm the fatherless.**—Rather, probably, *Ye would cast lots upon the fatherless, and make merchandise of your friend.* This is more in accordance with the language, and preserves the parallelism.

(28) **Now therefore be content** to look upon me; for it will be evident unto you if I lie; or, *for surely I shall not lie to your face.*

(29) **Return, I pray you.**—"Do not regard the case as settled, but come again and examine it; try once more before you decide there is no unrighteousness in my case;" or, as some understand it, in my *tongue*, which is expressed immediately afterwards, and is here anticipated in the pronoun *her.* This rendering is certainly confirmed by verse 30.

(30) **Is there iniquity?**—Or, *injustice in my tongue? Is my taste so perverted that it cannot perceive what is perverse?* "Ye appear to think that I am wholly incapable of judging my own cause because it is my own; but if ye will only condescend to return in due course, ye shall find that I know what is right as well as you, and that there is no more vicious reasoning in me than there is with you, and probably less." It is difficult to draw out the argument of Job in the logical form of our Western thought, and to trace the line of connection running through it. If we look at it in detail—as we must in order to explain it—then we are apt to look at it piecemeal, and miss the thread; but in point of fact it is just this very thread which it is so difficult to detect and retain from one chapter to another.

VII.

In this chapter Job turns away from his friends to God, to whom he appeals for compassion (verses 1—11). He asks whether man hath not a campaign to serve upon earth. The English Version suggests a limited period; but it is apparently not so much that as what is required to be done in the period. "Hath not man a time of service upon earth? Is he not appointed to sorrow (verses 5—7), because his life is one of toil? Is not his life a life of servitude? and is he not like a very slave?" Job does not regret that man's time is short upon earth, for he says that he longs eagerly

Job is Weary of Life, JOB, VII. *and Hopeth for Death.*

(3) So am I made to possess months of vanity,
And wearisome nights are appointed to me.
(4) When I lie down, I say,
When shall I arise, and ¹the night be gone?
And I am full of tossings to and fro
Unto the dawning of the day.
(5) My flesh is clothed with worms and clods of dust;
My skin is broken, and become loathsome.
(6) ᵃ My days are swifter than a weaver's shuttle,
And are spent without hope.
(7) O remember that my life *is* wind:
Mine eye ²shall no more ³see good.
(8) The eye of him that hath seen me shall see me no *more*:
Thine eyes *are* upon me, and ⁴I *am* not.
(9) *As* the cloud is consumed and vanisheth away:
So he that goeth down to the grave shall come up no *more*.
(10) He shall return no more to his house,
Neither shall his place know him any more.
(11) Therefore I will not refrain my mouth;
I will speak in the anguish of my spirit;
I will complain in the bitterness of my soul.
(12) *Am* I a sea, or a whale, that thou settest a watch over me?
(13) When I say, My bed shall comfort me,
My couch shall ease my complaint;
(14) Then thou scarest me with dreams,
And terrifiest me through visions:
(15) So that my soul chooseth strangling,
And death rather ⁵than my life.
(16) I loathe *it*; I would not live alway:
Let me alone; for my days *are* vanity.
(17) ᵇ What *is* man, that thou shouldest magnify him?
And that thou shouldest set thine heart upon him?
(18) And *that* thou shouldest visit him every morning,
And try him every moment?
(19) How long wilt thou not depart from me,

1 Heb., *the evening be measured?*
a ch. 16. 22.; Ps. 90. 6; & 102. 11; & 103. 15; & 144. 4; Isa. 40. 6; Jam. 4. 14.
2 Heb., *shall not return.*
3 *to see,* that is, *to enjoy.*
4 That is, *I can live no longer.*
5 Heb., *than my bones.*
b Ps. 8. 4; & 144. 3; Heb. 2. 6.

---

for his end, but he regrets that it is so full of misery. The context, therefore, shows that it is the character of the appointed time, and not the shortness of it, that he laments.

(4) **When I lie down, I say.**—Or, *When I lie down, then I say, When shall I arise? But the night is long, and I am filled with tossings to and fro till the morning twilight.*

(5) **With worms and clods of dust.**—It is characteristic of Elephantiasis that the skin becomes hard and rugous, and then cracks and becomes ulcerated.

(8) **Shall see me no more.**—That is, *thine own eyes shall look for me, but I shall be no more.* So LXX. and Vulg.

(9) **As the cloud is consumed.**—It is a fine simile that man is as evanescent as a cloud; and very apt is the figure, because, whether it vanishes on the surface of the sky or is distributed in rain, nothing more completely passes away than the summer cloud. It is an appearance only, which comes to nought.

(10) **Neither shall his place . . .**—This language is imitated in Ps. ciii. 16. We need not force these words too much, as though they forbad our ascribing to Job any belief in a future life or in the resurrection, because, under any circumstances, they are evidently and accurately true of man as we know him here. Even though he may live again in another way, it is not in this world that he lives again, and it is of this world and of man in this world that Job is speaking. And man, in the aspect of his mortality, is truly a pitiable object, demanding our compassion and sympathy. Happily, the appeal to man's Maker is not in vain, and He who has made him what he is has looked upon his misery.

Consequently Job can say, therefore, "I will not refrain my mouth; I will speak in the anguish of my spirit; I will complain in the bitterness of my soul."

(12) **Am I a sea, or a whale . . . ?**—This very hard verse it seems most reasonable to explain, if we can, from Scripture itself: *e.g.,* in Jer. v. 22 we read, "Fear ye not me? saith the Lord: will ye not tremble at my presence, which have placed the sand for the bound of the sea?" The writer was probably familiar with Egypt when the Nile, which is still called the sea, was carefully watched and guarded by dykes that its overflow might not destroy the land. So Job exclaims, "Am I like the sea, or one of its monsters—like that Leviathan which Thou hast made to take his pastime therein, that Thou keepest guard over me and makest me thy prisoner continually, shutting me up on every side so fast in prison that I cannot get free?"

(15) **So that my soul** maketh choice of strangling and death rather than a life like this. Literally, *than these my bones,* or, as some take it, *a death by these my members:* a death inflicted by myself, suicide.

(16) **I loathe it**—*i.e.,* the thought of self-destruction; or, *I loathe my life;* or, according to others (see the margin), *I waste away:* this, however, is perhaps less probable. Then the thought comes with a ray of comfort, "I shall not live for ever;" for this seems more in accordance with the context than the Authorised Version: "I would not live always."

(17, 18) **What is man . . . ?**—Here is another point of contact with Ps. viii. 5; but the spirit of the Psalmist was one of devout adoration, whereas that of Job is one of agony and desperation.

(19) **Till I swallow down my spittle.**—This is doubtless a proverbial expression, like "the twinkling of an eye," or "while I fetch a breath."

Nor let me alone till I swallow down my spittle?

(20) I have sinned; what shall I do unto thee, O thou preserver of men?
Why hast thou set me as a mark against thee,
So that I am a burden to myself?

(21) And why dost thou not pardon my transgression,
And take away mine iniquity?
For now shall I sleep in the dust;
And thou shalt seek me in the morning, but I *shall* not *be*.

CHAPTER VIII.

(1) Then answered Bildad the Shuhite, and said,

(2) How long wilt thou speak these *things?*
And *how long shall* the words of thy mouth *be like* a strong wind?

(3) *ª*Doth God pervert judgment?
Or doth the Almighty pervert justice?

(4) If thy children have sinned against him,
And he have cast them away ¹for their transgression;

(5) *ᵇ*If thou wouldest seek unto God betimes,
And make thy supplication to the Almighty;

(6) If thou *wert* pure and upright;
Surely now he would awake for thee,
And make the habitation of thy righteousness prosperous.

(7) Though thy beginning was small,
Yet thy latter end should greatly increase.

(8) *ᶜ*For enquire, I pray thee, of the former age,
And prepare thyself to the search of their fathers :

(9) (For *ᵈ*we *are but of* yesterday, and know ²nothing,
Because our days upon earth *are* a shadow :)

(10) Shall not they teach thee, *and* tell thee,
And utter words out of their heart?

(11) Can the rush grow up without mire?
Can the flag grow without water?

a Deut. 32. 4; 2 Chr. 19. 7; Dan. 9. 11.

¹ Heb., *in the hand of their transgression.*

b ch. 22. 23.

c Deut. 4. 32.

d Gen. 47. 9 ; 1 Chr. 29. 15 ; ch. 7. 6; Ps. 39. 5 ; & 144. 4.

² Heb., *not.*

---

(20) **I have sinned**—*i.e.,* "Putting the case that I have sinned, yet what then can I do unto Thee, O thou keeper of men?" with a possible allusion to verse 12, though the verb is not the same.

O thou preserver of men.—"Why hast Thou set me as a mark for Thee to expend all Thine arrows upon?" or, "Why hast Thou made me to be Thy stumbling-block, so that Thou ever comest into collision against me, so that I am become a burden to myself?"

(21) **And why dost thou not pardon my transgression?**—In Job's belief, sin was the origin of all disaster, and so he thinks that if he were but pardoned his sorrows would pass away. Our Lord has not discouraged the belief when He has taught us that His miracle of healing the paralytic was accompanied with the assurance of forgiveness (*e.g.,* Matt. ix. 2; Mark ii. 5; Luke v. 20).

VIII.

The burden of Bildad's speech is very much what that of Eliphaz was: the justice of God, and the impossibility of one who is not a wicked man being forsaken of God and punished. This, which is emphatically the problem of the Book of Job, was the great practical problem of the Old World, as we see from Ps. xxxvii. and the like. It is a problem which not seldom weighs heavily on our own hearts even in the light of the Gospel, though, of course, since the redemption of the Cross of Christ this problem has once for all been practically solved. What is so conspicuous in the speeches of Job's friends is their total want of refinement and delicacy of feeling. They blurt out without the slightest compunction the most unscrupulous charges, and they cast the most reckless insinuations against him. Here, for instance, Bildad does not hesitate to say that Job's sons died for their transgressions *because* God is a righteous God, and He would not have been righteous had they, being innocent, perished. Thus, in order to save the credit of the righteous God facts must be distorted or misrepresented to any extent, as though God were not a God of truth as well as of righteousness.

(4) **And he have cast them away.**—Literally, *then he sent them away.* By means of their transgression; it became their destruction.

(6) **If thou wert pure and upright.**—Of course, then, there is but one inference : thou art not pure and upright. These are verily the wounds of a friend which are not faithful. Bildad brings to the maintenance of his point the experience of former generations. He wishes to be very orthodox in his assertions, and to base his statements upon authority, and he appeals to the experience of former ages long gone by, and calls them to attest the truth of what he says. He also, like Eliphaz, uses figures, and has recourse to metaphor, only his figures are highly obscure and admit of various explanations. We give that which seems to commend itself most to us. It appears, then, that Bildad contemplates two representative characters, the two which are so prominent throughout this book—namely, the righteous and the wicked. He depicts the latter first, and describes him under the likeness of the paper-reed, or rush that grows in the mire of Egyptian swamps, which, though surrounded with moisture, yet as a matter of fact is liable soon to wither: so is the wicked man, according to this moralist and philosopher. He is surrounded by mercies and blessings, but they avail him nought; he withereth in the midst of abundance.

(11) **The flag** is the plant of Gen. xli. 2, which the cattle feed upon. This figure is enforced by a second, that, namely, of the spider's web, the most fragile and transient of tenements.

The Hypocrite's Judgment. JOB, IX. *Job's Answer to Bildad.*

⁽¹²⁾ ^aWhilst it *is* yet in his greenness, and not cut down,
It withereth before any *other* herb.
⁽¹³⁾ So *are* the paths of all that forget God;
And the ^bhypocrite's hope shall perish:
⁽¹⁴⁾ Whose hope shall be cut off,
And whose trust *shall be* ¹a spider's web.
⁽¹⁵⁾ He shall lean upon his house, but it shall not stand:
He shall hold it fast, but it shall not endure.
⁽¹⁶⁾ He *is* green before the sun,
And his branch shooteth forth in his garden.
⁽¹⁷⁾ His roots are wrapped about the heap,
And seeth the place of stones.
⁽¹⁸⁾ If he destroy him from his place,
Then *it* shall deny him, *saying,* I have not seen thee.
⁽¹⁹⁾ Behold, this *is* the joy of his way,
And out of the earth shall others grow.
⁽²⁰⁾ Behold, God will not cast away a perfect *man,*
Neither will he ²help the evil doers:
⁽²¹⁾ Till he fill thy mouth with laughing, and thy lips with ³rejoicing.
⁽²²⁾ They that hate thee shall be clothed with shame;
And the dwelling place of the wicked ⁴shall come to nought.

CHAPTER IX.—⁽¹⁾ Then Job answered and said,
⁽²⁾ I know *it is* so of a truth:
But how should ^cman be just ⁵with God?
⁽³⁾ If he will contend with him,
He cannot answer him one of a thousand.
⁽⁴⁾ *He is* wise in heart, and mighty in strength:
Who hath hardened *himself* against him, and hath prospered?
⁽⁵⁾ Which removeth the mountains, and they know not:
Which overturneth them in his anger.
⁽⁶⁾ Which shaketh the earth out of her place,
And the pillars thereof tremble.
⁽⁷⁾ Which commandeth the sun, and it riseth not;
And sealeth up the stars.
⁽⁸⁾ ^dWhich alone spreadeth out the heavens,
And treadeth upon the ⁶waves of the sea.

a Ps. 129. 6; Jer. 17. 6.
b ch. 11. 20; & 18. 14; Ps. 112. 10; Prov. 10. 28.
1 Heb., *a spider's house.*
2 Heb., *take the ungodly by the hand.*
3 Heb., *shouting for joy.*
4 Heb., *shall not be.*
c Ps. 143. 2.
5 Or, *before God?*
d Gen. 1. 6.
6 Heb., *heights.*

⁽¹⁵⁾ **It shall not endure.**—The description of the wicked man ends here.

⁽¹⁶⁾ **He is green.**—Here begins, as we understand it, another and an opposite picture, which fact is marked in the Hebrew by an emphatic pronoun. "Green is *he* (see verse 6) before the sun, &c., quite unlike the watery paper-plant. This man is verdant and luxuriant, not in the midst of moisture, but even before the sun." There is not the same promise of verdure, but a greater realisation of it.

⁽¹⁷⁾ **His roots are wrapped about.**—This is the cause of his continual luxuriance, that his roots receive moisture from below, where they are wrapped about the spring which fertilises them underneath; they are planted near to a perennial fountain, and therefore (see verse 6) "he is green before the sun."

And seeth the place of stones.—Rather, *the house of stones*—*i.e.,* the stone house. He seeth the permanent and durable edifice of stone which is the habitation of civilisation and culture, and here his holding is so firm that, even if plucked up, his roots and suckers are so numerous that they leave behind them descendants and offshoots, so that out of his earth others grow; or, more correctly, out of another dust they grow. Even if transplanted, this luxuriant tree will flourish equally well in another soil.

⁽²¹⁾ **Till he fill thy mouth with laughing.**—Rather, *he will yet fill thy mouth with laughter—afflicted though thou hast been, thou shalt again rejoice.* The attitude of Bildad is one of unsympathetic selfishness. He wishes to think well of his friend because he is *his* friend, but he cannot reconcile his afflicted condition with any theory of righteous government, and therefore is driven to *suspect* that all is not right with him, though he feels warranted in promising him that if he casts away that secret sin all shall yet be well with him. We may say that if the contrast here indicated is not intended by the speaker, then we must consider the "he" of verse 16 the person before spoken of, and must understand his luxuriance of a merely apparent luxuriance; but then in that case one is at a loss to see why the "he" of verse 16 should be emphasised as it is in the Hebrew.

IX.

Then Job answered . . .—Job's reply to Bildad differs from that to Eliphaz, inasmuch as he exposes the hollowness of Bildad's position by sapping his foundation. Admitting the general propriety of all he has said, he confronts him with the anterior question, "How can weak man be just with God?" and this is the question, if fairly dealt with, which must always confound shallow generalisers like Bildad.

⁽³⁾ **If he will contend with him.**—If man choose to contend with God, he cannot answer Him one question of a thousand, once in a thousand times.

⁽⁷⁾ **And sealeth up the stars.**—Comp. chap. xli. 15. The idea of shutting up, taking away the power of, &c., is contained in the expression "sealing."

⁽⁸⁾ **Waves of the sea.**—Literally, *high place of the sea:* the sea, when and where it runs *mountains high.* The various physical phenomena of earthquake, eclipse, and hurricane are here described as the field of Divine action and the operations of His hands.

God's Great Works.   JOB, IX.   Man's Feebleness.

⁽⁹⁾ ^aWhich maketh ¹Arcturus, Orion, and Pleiades,
And the chambers of the south.
⁽¹⁰⁾ ^bWhich doeth great things past finding out;
Yea, and wonders without number.
⁽¹¹⁾ Lo, he goeth by me, and I see *him* not:
He passeth on also, but I perceive him not.
⁽¹²⁾ ^cBehold, he taketh away, ²who can hinder him?
Who will say unto him, What doest thou?
⁽¹³⁾ *If* God will not withdraw his anger,
The ³proud helpers do stoop under him.
⁽¹⁴⁾ How much less shall I answer him,
And choose out my words *to reason* with him?
⁽¹⁵⁾ Whom, though I were righteous, *yet* would I not answer,
But I would make supplication to my judge.
⁽¹⁶⁾ If I had called, and he had answered me;
Yet would I not believe that he had hearkened unto my voice.
⁽¹⁷⁾ For he breaketh me with a tempest,
And multiplieth my wounds without cause.
⁽¹⁸⁾ He will not suffer me to take my breath,
But filleth me with bitterness.
⁽¹⁹⁾ If *I speak* of strength, lo, *he is* strong:
And if of judgment, who shall set me a time *to plead?*
⁽²⁰⁾ If I justify myself, mine own mouth shall condemn me:
If I say, I *am* perfect, it shall also prove me perverse.
⁽²¹⁾ *Though* I *were* perfect, *yet* would I not know my soul:
I would despise my life.
⁽²²⁾ This *is* one *thing,* therefore I said *it,*
He destroyeth the perfect and the wicked.
⁽²³⁾ If the scourge slay suddenly,

a ch. 38. 31, &c.; Amos 5. 8.

¹ Heb., *Ash, Cesil, and Cimah.*

b ch. 5. 9.

c Isa. 45. 9; Jer. 18. 6; Rom. 9. 20.

² Heb., *who can turn him away?*

³ Heb., *helpers of pride,* or, *strength.*

⁽⁹⁾ **Which maketh Arcturus . . .**—This shows us that in the time of this writer, whoever he was, his fellow-countrymen had attained to such knowledge of astronomy as is here implied in the specific names of definite constellations. The Great Bear is the glory of the northern hemisphere, Orion of the southern sky, and the Pleiades of the east; the chambers of the north are the unknown and unexplored regions, of which the speaker has no personal experience.

⁽¹⁰⁾ **Which doeth great things.**—He adopts the very words his former antagonist, Eliphaz, had used in chap. v. 9.

⁽¹¹⁾ **He passeth on also.**—This, again, is an expression Eliphaz had used in chap. iv. 15. Here in words of great sublimity Job depicts the unapproachable majesty of God omnipotent, but invisible, and shows the utter hopelessness of entering into judgment with Him. Unfortunately, though this is a proposition to which all must assent, yet none is virtually so much repudiated or practically so often contravened. Men still cast about to justify themselves before God, and will do so till the end of time; but it is in teaching such as this that the Book of Job has laid the foundation of the Gospel by preparing for its acceptance by overthrowing man's natural and habitual standing-ground in himself.

⁽¹²⁾ **What doest thou?**—Putting the case even that God were, so to say, in the wrong, and the assailant, yet even then He would maintain His cause from sheer might, and crush His adversary.

⁽¹³⁾ **Proud helpers.**—Literally, *helpers of Rahab.* (See Isa. xxx. 7; Ps. lxxxvii. 4.) But whether Rahab was Egypt, or a poetical name for the lost archangel, it is impossible to say. If the former, then there is a probable allusion here to the overthrow of Pharaoh and his hosts; but we lack evidence to make it plain. The phrase is evidently used as expressing the very ideal of strength—the race of the giants.

⁽¹⁵⁾ **Though I were righteous.**—He now puts the alternative case: that he were actually righteous; yet even then supplication, and not assertion, would best become him.

⁽¹⁷⁾ **He breaketh me . . .**—This is one of the three passages in which this word is found, the other two being Gen. iii. 15, "It shall *bruise,*" &c., and Ps. cxxxix. 11, "If I say the darkness shall *cover* me."

⁽¹⁸⁾ **Take my breath.**—The action being that of breathing again after complete exhaustion—recovering breath and the power to breathe, &c. "If I say I am perfect, it also shall prove me perverse by the very act of saying so; because for man to maintain his righteousness before God is at once to proclaim his iniquity. The finite cannot come into competition with the Infinite, nor measure itself therewith."

⁽¹⁹⁾ **If I speak of strength.**—All this is the most uncompromising acknowledgment of the absolute inability of man to stand in judgment before God. The whole of this is so very abrupt and enigmatical that it is extremely difficult to be sure of the argument, though naturally the general drift of it is obvious enough. "If it were a trial of strength—Who is Almighty?—and if it was a matter of judgment, is He not judge and court together? and what authority that He would acknowledge could give me the opportunity of pleading my cause before Him? Were I righteous, my own mouth would show me wicked; were I perfect, then would it or He prove me perverse. Were I perfect, I should not know myself, or know it myself. I despise my life under such conditions; therefore, said I, it is all one: He destroyeth the perfect and the wicked alike."

⁽²³⁾ **The scourge slay suddenly.** — Probably meaning that in the case of hidden calamity overtaking an innocent man, He, God, will laugh at it: that is to say, take no more notice of it than if it furnished Him

Man's Innocency not to be   JOB, IX.   *Condemned by his Afflictions.*

He will laugh at the trial of the innocent.
(24) The earth is given into the hand of the wicked :
He covereth the faces of the judges thereof ;
If not, where, and who *is* he ?
(25) Now my days are swifter than a post :
They flee away, they see no good.
(26) They are passed away as the ¹ ² swift ships :
As the eagle *that* hasteth to the prey.
(27) If I say, I will forget my complaint,
I will leave off my heaviness, and comfort *myself:*
(28) I am afraid of all my sorrows,
I know that thou wilt not hold me innocent.

(29) *If* I be wicked, why then labour I in vain ?
(30) If I wash myself with snow water,
And make my hands never so clean ;
(31) Yet shalt thou plunge me in the ditch,
And mine own clothes shall ³ abhor me.
(32) For *he is* not a man, as I *am, that* I should answer him,
And we should come together in judgment.
(33) Neither is there ⁴ any ⁵ daysman betwixt us,
That might lay his hand upon us both.
(34) Let him take his rod away from me,
And let not his fear terrify me :
(35) *Then* would I speak, and not fear him;
⁶ but *it is* not so with me.

---

1 Heb., *ships of desire.*
2 Or, *ships of Ebeh.*
3 Or, *make me to be abhorred.*
4 Heb., *one that should argue.*
5 Or, *umpire.*
6 Heb., *but I am not so with myself.*

---

with sport. The very fact of such calamity befalling, as it often does, the innocent is at all events, in one view, a proof of His indifference to it who, by the exercise of His providence, could easily interpose to prevent it, and so looks as if He verily winked at it. Job's argument is the argument of a man who wilfully shuts out faith in his estimate of God's dealings; not that Job is devoid of faith, but in the course of arguing with his friends, who maintain the strict, rigid justice of God, he confronts them with the severe logic of facts, which they can neither contradict nor explain. Of course, for the very requirements of argument, he takes the pessimist view of the Divine providence, and declares even that the earth is given over into the hands of the wicked man. "He covereth the face of the judges thereof; and if it is not He that doeth this, who is it ? there can be none other. He either doeth the evil Himself, or He permits it to be done ; and what is the difference, supposing Him able to prevent it ?" When we review the disorders of the earth—and how much more in Job's days was it so—all must admit that faith is sorely tried ; and even faith can render but a very partial explanation of them, so that such a line as this is fully justified, when the adversary is determined to maintain that all is rose-coloured, happy, and equal as Job's friends did. They had before them an instance of inequality in the Divine conduct, and they must either make it square with the Divine justice or give up the contest. They could not do the one, and were unwilling to do the other; it only remained, therefore, for Job to assert the inequality of the Divine dealings, and he puts the case as strongly as he can, all the time, it must never be forgotten, *holding fast his faith in God*, so that at the last he is even justified by God, who says to his friends, "Ye have not spoken of me that which is right, like my servant" (Job xlii. 8).

(25) **Swifter than a post.**—The runner, with his messages and dispatches. He now turns away from the contemplation of God and His dealings to that of his own misery.

(26) **Swift ships.**—What is meant by the swift ships, or ships of Desire, no one knows. Literally, *ships of Eveh*, probably a proper name, and perhaps referring to a particular kind of boat in use on the Nile; if so, this is one instance out of many of Job's acquaintance with Egypt. The Vulgate has, *naves poma portantes.* Job is a problem to himself; he is confident of his innocence, and yet he is confident that that very innocence will avail him nothing before God, he is sure that he must be condemned. Now, it is impossible to deny that this is the very attitude of the Gospel; it is, therefore, if we bear in mind the vast antiquity of the confession, both a witness to the truth of the Gospel and an anticipation of it that God alone could give. Indeed, it is hopelessly impossible to enter into the position of Job unless we are ourselves enlightened with the teaching of the Gospel, and able to look at it from the Gospel standpoint. While, therefore, admitting this fact, we are the better able to appreciate the wonderful confession Job is about to make in verses 32, 33.

(32, 33) **For he is not a man, as I am** . . .—Is not that confession, if we believe that such a daysman as Job longed for has been given, itself a witness that it came from God, and was given by God ? The light that has shined upon us was shining then in the heart of Job, and shines for ever in the pages of his book. Job felt, as he had been taught to feel, that in himself there not only was no hope, but no possibility of justification with God, unless there should be an umpire and impartial mediator, who could make the cause of both his own, and reconcile and unite the two in himself. It is useless to inquire what other particular form the aspiration of Job may have taken, or how far he understood and meant what he said ; but here are his words, and this is what they must mean, and it is for us to adore the wisdom by which they were taught accurately to correspond with what we know has been given to us by God. We know that a daysman has laid his hand upon us both; and while we see that this is what Job wanted, we cannot but see more plainly that this is what we want. It is to be observed that this word daysman, or judge, is immediately connected with the Scripture phrase, "the *day* of the Lord," and St. Paul's words, "the *day* shall declare it" (1 Cor. iii. 13).

(35) **It is not so with me.**—Literally, *I am not so with me.* The words are variously understood : "It is not so with me," *i.e.*, "I am not thus without fear," as the former part of the verse supposes; or, "I am not so as ye suppose," *i.e.*, guilty, but innocent; or, "Am I not right with myself ?" *i.e.*, inwardly conscious of my integrity and innocence (chap. x. 1).

CHAPTER X.—(1) My soul is ¹weary of my life;
I will leave my complaint upon myself;
I will speak in the bitterness of my soul.
(2) I will say unto God, Do not condemn me;
Shew me wherefore thou contendest with me.
(3) *Is it* good unto thee that thou shouldest oppress,
That thou shouldest despise ²the work of thine hands,
And shine upon the counsel of the wicked?
(4) Hast thou eyes of flesh? or seest thou as man seeth?
(5) *Are* thy days as the days of man? *are* thy years as man's days,
(6) That thou enquirest after mine iniquity,
And searchest after my sin?
(7) ³Thou knowest that I am not wicked;
And *there is* none that can deliver out of thine hand.
(8) Thine hands ⁴have made me
And fashioned me together round about;
Yet thou dost destroy me.
(9) Remember, I beseech thee, that thou hast made me as the clay;
And wilt thou bring me into dust again?
(10) ᵃHast thou not poured me out as milk,
And curdled me like cheese?
(11) Thou hast clothed me with skin and flesh,
And hast ⁵fenced me with bones and sinews.
(12) Thou hast granted me life and favour,
And thy visitation hath preserved my spirit.
(13) And these *things* hast thou hid in thine heart:
I know that this *is* with thee.
(14) If I sin, then thou markest me,
And thou wilt not acquit me from mine iniquity.
(15) If I be wicked, woe unto me;
And *if* I be righteous, *yet* will I not lift up my head.
I am full of confusion; therefore see thou mine affliction;
(16) For it increaseth. Thou huntest me as a fierce lion:
And again thou shewest thyself marvellous upon me.
(17) Thou renewest ⁶thy witnesses against me,
And increaseth thine indignation upon me;
Changes and war *are* against me.

1 Or, *cut off while I live.*
2 Heb., *the labour of thine hands.*
3 Heb., *It is upon thy knowledge.*
4 Heb., *took pains about me.*
a Ps. 139. 14, 15, 16.
5 Heb., *hedged.*
6 *That is, thy plagues.*

X.

In this chapter Job reaches the climax of his complaint, which leaves him in the land of thick darkness, where the light is as darkness.

(1) **I will leave.**—Or, according to some, *I will give free vent to the complaint that is upon me.* (Comp. verse 27 of the last chap.)

(2) **I will say unto God . . .**—This is a model of prayer for all, combining the prayer of the publican (Luke xviii. 13), and a prayer for that light for which we long so earnestly in times of affliction and darkness.

(7) **That I am not wicked.**—The meaning is rather, *that I shall not be found guilty.* It is not like the appeal of Peter (John xxi. 17). See the language borrowed by the Psalmist (Ps. cxix. 73).

(9) **Into dust.**—Comp. Ps. xxii. 15.

(10) **Poured me out as milk.**—An allusion to the embryo. (See Ps. cxxxix. 13—16.)

(13) **These things hast thou hid in thine heart.**—Job implies that his sense of God's goodness is embittered by the thought that while showing him such kindness, He had in reserve for him the trials and sorrows under which he was then labouring: while showering good upon him, He intended eventually to overwhelm him with affliction. This was the purpose He had hidden in His heart.

(14) **If I sin . . .** —"If I had sinned Thou wouldst have marked me for punishment, and from mine iniquity Thou wouldst not acquit me. If I had been guilty, woe unto me! and if righteous, I must not lift up my head like an innocent person. I am full of shame, therefore behold Thou mine affliction, for only by Thy taking note of it can I find relief."

(16) **For it increaseth.**—This verse is very obscure. Some understand it thus: "But is it so glorious a thing that Thou shouldst hunt me like a fierce lion, and then again show Thyself mysterious and wonderful towards me? hunting me like a lion, and yet hiding alike Thy person and Thy motive from me?" Or the subject is the *head* of the former verse, "And if it exalt itself, Thou huntest me," &c. Or again, as in the Authorised Version, the subject is the affliction, "For it increaseth: Thou huntest me," &c.

(17) **Thou renewest thy witnesses against me.**—Some understand this of the sores on Job's person, which his friends regarded as witnesses—proofs of his guilt; but it seems more probable that the figure is forensic: "Thou still bringest fresh witnesses against me, and multipliest thine anger against me, so that relays of them, even a host, are against me; for they come upon me host after host—these witnesses of Thine anger, the ministers of Thy vengeance." The sublimity of this indictment against God is only equalled by the sense of terrific awe with which one reads it. The language is Job's, and so far has the sanction of Holy Writ; but we may surely learn therefrom the condescension as well as the loving-kindness of the Most High.

(18) *Wherefore then hast thou brought me forth out of the womb?
Oh that I had given up the ghost, and no eye had seen me!
(19) I should have been as though I had not been;
I should have been carried from the womb to the grave.
(20) *Are not my days few? cease *then*,
And let me alone, that I may take comfort a little,
(21) Before I go *whence* I shall not return,
Even to the land of darkness and the shadow of death;
(22) A land of darkness, as darkness *itself*;
And of the shadow of death, without any order,
And *where* the light *is* as darkness.

CHAPTER XI.—(1) Then answered Zophar the Naamathite, and said,
(2) Should not the multitude of words be answered?
And should [1] a man full of talk be justified?
(3) Should thy [2] lies make men hold their peace?
And when thou mockest, shall no man make thee ashamed?
(4) For thou hast said, My doctrine *is* pure,
And I am clean in thine eyes.
(5) But oh that God would speak, and open his lips against thee;
(6) And that he would shew thee the secrets of wisdom,
That *they are* double to that which is!
Know therefore that God exacteth of thee *less* than thine iniquity *deserveth*.
(7) Canst thou by searching find out God?
Canst thou find out the Almighty unto perfection?
(8) *It is* [3] as high as heaven; what canst thou do?
Deeper than hell; what canst thou know?
(9) The measure thereof *is* longer than the earth,
And broader than the sea.
(10) If he [4] cut off, and shut up, or gather together,
Then [5] who can hinder him?

a ch. 3. 11.
b See ch. 7. 6 & 8. 9.
[1] Heb., *a man of lips*.
[2] Or, *devices*.
[3] Heb., *the heights of heaven*.
[4] Or, *make a change*.
[5] Heb., *who can turn him away?*

---

(19) **Wherefore then hast thou brought me forth?**—Here Job reverts to the strain of his original curse (chap. iii. 11, &c.).

(20) **Cease then, and let me alone.**—According to another reading, "Let him cease, and let me alone." In reading this reply of Job's, one cannot but feel that it moves upon the very verge of blasphemy, and is only redeemed therefrom by its pervading reverence and deep undertone of faith. Job never gives up his faith in God, though, like Jacob, he wrestles with Him in the dark, and the issue shows that God is not displeased with such an unburdening of the soul that keeps close to the straight line of truth, which is, after all, one of the many manifestations of God.

XI.

(1) **Zophar**, the third of Job's friends, has a clearly defined character, distinct from that of the others; he is the ordinary and common-place moral man, who expresses the thoughts and instincts of the many. Eliphaz was the poet and spiritual man, who sees visions and dreams dreams; Bildad was the man who rested on authority and appealed to tradition; Zophar is the man of worldly wisdom and common sense. In some respects he is the most offensive of the three. He is astonished that Job has not been silenced by the replies of the other two, and thinks he can do no less than help to silence him. Thus he at once begins with "a multitude of words," and "full of talk," and "lies," and "mockery." Zophar stands on a lower level, and drags Job down to it. He refracts his protestations of innocence against himself, and charges him with iniquity in making them. His longing also to come into judgment with God (chap. ix. 32) he turns back upon himself, being confident that it could not fail to convict him were he to do so.

(4) **Clean in thine eyes** is variously referred to God, to mortal men (verse 3), and to Job himself (chap. xxxii. 1). The first seems most to be preferred, for at all events Job had hypothetically spoken of himself as righteous before God (chap. x. 15). (Comp. chap. ix. 30, &c.) Zophar, therefore, who professes superior wisdom, desires that God would show Job how far short he falls of it: that He would show him the hidden things, the secrets of wisdom; for sound wisdom is manifold: it has many aspects, and lies as it were fold over fold in unexpected complexities, defying the shallow and unscrutinising gaze; and were He to do this, Job would find out to his dismay that God still credited him part of the penalty due to him.

(6) **They are double to that which is!**—This translation conveys no sense, and is not a translation; see the last Note.

(7) **Canst thou by searching find out God?**—Literally, *Canst thou attain to the searching out of God?*

(8) **It is as high as heaven.**—Literally, *The heights of heaven; what canst thou do? it is deeper than the grave; what canst thou know?*

(10) **If he cut off.**—It is the same word as "a spirit passed before me" (chap. iv. 15); and as Job himself used (chap. ix. 11): "he passeth on, but I perceive him not." "If, then," says Zophar, "God acteth thus, or if He delivers up a man into the hands of his enemies, or if He calls together a multitude against him—alluding apparently to chaps. ix. 11, 12, and x. 17, where the word rendered *changes* is a derivative of the word here rendered "cut off"—then who can turn Him back from His intent?" adopting Job's own question at chap. ix. 12: "Who can hinder Him?" Some understand the three terms forensically: "if He arrest, and im-

(11) For he knoweth vain men:
 He seeth wickedness also; will he not then consider it?
(12) For ¹vain man would be wise,
 Though man be born like a wild ass's colt.
(13) If thou prepare thine heart,
 And stretch out thine hands toward him;
(14) If iniquity be in thine hand, put it far away,
 And let not wickedness dwell in thy tabernacles.
(15) For then shalt thou lift up thy face without spot;
 Yea, thou shalt be stedfast, and shalt not fear:
(16) Because thou shalt forget thy misery,
 And remember it as waters that pass away:
(17) And thine age ²shall be clearer than the noonday;
 Thou shalt shine forth, thou shalt be as the morning.
(18) And thou shalt be secure, because there is hope;
 Yea, thou shalt dig about thee, and thou shalt take thy rest in safety.
(19) ᵃAlso thou shalt lie down, and none shall make thee afraid;
 Yea, many shall ³make suit unto thee.
(20) But the eyes of the wicked shall fail,
 And ⁴they shall not escape,
 And ᵇtheir hope shall be as ⁵the giving up of the ghost.

CHAPTER XII.—(1) And Job answered and said,
(2) No doubt but ye are the people,
 And wisdom shall die with you.
(3) But I have ⁶understanding as well as you;
 ⁷I am not inferior to you:
 Yea, ⁸who knoweth not such things as these?
(4) I am as one mocked of his neighbour,
 Who calleth upon God, and he answereth him:
 The just upright man is laughed to scorn.
(5) He that is ready to slip with his feet

1 Heb., empty.
2 Heb., shall arise above the noon-day.
a Lev. 26. 6.
3 Heb., intreat thy face.
4 Heb., flight shall perish from them.
b ch. 8. 14 & 18. 14.
5 Or, a puff of breath.
6 Heb., an heart.
7 Heb., I fall not lower than you.
8 Heb., with whom are not such as these?

---

prison, and hold assize;" but it is probable that Job's own statements are alluded to.

(11) **He knoweth vain men.**—Though he regardeth it not: that is, seemeth not to see it.

(12) **For vain man would be wise**, &c., is extremely difficult, because it is hard to distinguish subject and predicate. Literally, it runs, *And hollow man is instructed, and the wild ass's colt is born a man.* Whether it means that if God did not thus conceal His observation of human actions, the very fool and the most obstinate would become instructed and disciplined, whereas now they are allowed to go on in their folly and obstinacy; or whether it is meant that, notwithstanding the dealings of Providence, hollow-hearted man is still devoid of heart, and every son of Adam at his birth is a very wild ass colt; or whether, again, it is meant that by reason of the Divine discipline the hollow-hearted man is disciplined, and the very wild ass colt is born a man and humanised, it is hard to decide. The uncertainty in part arises from our not knowing the exact meaning of the first verb: whether it is to get understanding or to be deprived of it—for either is possible. Another way of taking the context is to refer the last clause of verse 11, not to God, but to man. Man sees not that God sees him, for an empty man will get understanding when a wild ass's colt is born a man—that is, the latter is as likely as the former. One point is pretty clear, that by the wild ass's colt Zophar means Job. However, he suggests that if he will become something better and wiser, and will put away his secret sin, which he is convinced must cling to him, then he shall again know prosperity and be established in it.

(17) **Thine age shall be clearer than the noonday.**—Rather, *there shall arise for thee a lifetime brighter than the noonday; thou shalt soar on high; thou shalt be like the morning*, which is conceived of as having wings (Ps. cxxxix. 9). (Comp. Mal. iv. 2, of the Sun of Righteousness.) This is how we understand the word rendered *thou shalt shine forth.* Many take it as a substantive, meaning *darkness*, in which case we must render, *though there be darkness, thou shalt be as the morning.*

(18) **Thou shalt dig about thee.**—Rather, *thou shalt look around or search about thee, and see that thou canst lie down in safety.* (Comp. Josh. ii. 2, and Job. xxxix. 29.) The same word means, indeed, to *dig* and to *blush;* but both meanings are incongruous and inadmissible here.

(20) **As the giving up of the ghost.**—Omit the *as* of comparison; or do so, and take the margin. Thus ends the first part of this mighty argument, the first fytte of this grand poem.

XII.

(1) **And Job answered and said.**—Each of the friends has now supplied his quota, and Job proceeds to reply to the third, showing that he is far more conversant with the wisdom and majesty of God than they are themselves, though in their own esteem they alone are wise.

(4) **I am as one mocked of his neighbour.**—The laughing-stock of his companion—he who called on God, and He answered him. This is either the character Job claims for himself, or it is the supposed taunt of his friends—the righteous and the perfect a laughing-stock, or, the righteous and the perfect might be a laughing-stock. Ridicule is no test of truth or of merit.

(5) **Is as a lamp despised in the thought of him that is at ease.**—This rendering conveys no sense. The meaning is either that the lamp or torch

Job Maintaineth himself   JOB, XII.   *against his Friends.*

Is as a lamp despised in the thought of him that is at ease.

(6) The tabernacles of robbers prosper, And they that provoke God are secure; Into whose hand God bringeth *abundantly*.

(7) But ask now the beasts, and they shall teach thee; And the fowls of the air, and they shall tell thee:

(8) Or speak to the earth, and it shall teach thee: And the fishes of the sea shall declare unto thee.

(9) Who knoweth not in all these That the hand of the LORD hath wrought this?

(10) In whose hand *is* the ¹soul of every living thing, And the breath of ²all mankind.

(11) *ᵃ*Doth not the ear try words? and the ³mouth taste his meat?

(12) With the ancient *is* wisdom; And in length of days understanding.

(13) ᵇWith him *is* wisdom and strength, He hath counsel and understanding.

(14) Behold, he breaketh down, and it cannot be built again:

He ᵇshutteth ⁵up a man, and there can be no opening.

(15) Behold, he withholdeth the waters, and they dry up: Also he sendeth them out, and they overturn the earth.

(16) With him *is* strength and wisdom: The deceived and the deceiver *are* his.

(17) He leadeth counsellors away spoiled, And maketh the judges fools.

(18) He looseth the bond of kings, And girdeth their loins with a girdle.

(19) He leadeth princes away spoiled, and overthroweth the mighty.

(20) ᶜHe removeth away ⁶the speech of the trusty, And taketh away the understanding of the aged.

(21) He poureth contempt upon princes, And ⁷weakeneth the strength of the mighty.

(22) He discovereth deep things out of darkness, And bringeth out to light the shadow of death.

(23) He increaseth the nations, and destroyeth them: He enlargeth the nations, and ⁸straiteneth them *again*.

---

1 Or, *life.*
2 Heb., *all flesh of man.*
a ch. 34. 3.
3 Heb., *palate.*
4 That is, *With God.*
b Is. 22. 22; Rev. 3. 7.
5 Heb., *upon.*
c ch. 32. 9.
6 Heb., *the lip of the faithful.*
7 Or, *looseth the girdle of the strong.*
8 Heb., *leadeth in.*

---

prepared for feet tottering and uncertain in the darkness is disregarded and rejected by those who are at ease, and need no such aid; in which case one does not see very clearly why Job compares himself to such a torch: or, more probably, there is contempt for calamity in the thoughts of him that is at ease, it is ready at hand for them who are tottering with their feet.

(6) **Into whose hand God bringeth abundantly.**—Some understand these words, *to him that bringeth his god in his hand* (comp. Hab. i. 11, 16); but the other seems more in accordance with the usage. (Comp., *e.g.*, Prov. iii. 27, &c.)

(9) **Who knoweth not in all these that the hand of the Lord hath wrought this?**—This is the only place in the dialogue parts of Job in which the sacred name of Jehovah is found, and Job's very use of the word in such a context is the clearest evidence of the superior knowledge that he claims. No one of his friends makes use of the name; but Job uses it here, and shows thereby his knowledge of the covenant name.

(11) **Doth not the ear try words?**—Bildad had appealed to the wisdom of authority and tradition, but Job reminds him that it is given to the wise man not to accept everything he has received, but to discriminate. He allows that wisdom is the prerogative of age, but reminds him that the Ancient of Days must needs be wise indeed.

(14) **Behold, he breaketh down . . .**—God has equal power over the moral and physical world.

(18) **He looseth the bond of kings.**—He looseth the confederacy of kings, by which they bind themselves together, and girdeth them to fight against each other. Some understand it of the girdle of servitude in contrast to the girdle of state.

(19) **He leadeth princes.** — Some understand *priests* rather than *princes*. The word appears to be used in both senses; here the parallelism seems to suit *princes* better. The latter part of this chapter seems to re-echo the sentiments of Eliphaz in chap. v. 11—16; but, instead of giving them the optimist direction he had sketched, he confesses that his own position is rather one of blank despair. Eliphaz is quite sure he possesses the key to the interpretation of the ways of Providence. Job ever fears that his ignorance is so profound as to amount almost to sheer hopelessness. Job is thus the type of a man who has felt the hollowness and unreality of traditional orthodoxy, and is feeling his way in thick darkness, sustained, nevertheless, by an unquenchable faith that there is light, and that the light will eventually dawn. That this character is the more acceptable to the God of truth is made abundantly clear in the sequel. It is to be observed, however, that Job's breadth of view far exceeds that of Eliphaz, inasmuch as the latter generalises vaguely, while Job declares that not men, but *nations*, are the subjects of God's guiding providence.

(23) **He increaseth the nations, and destroyeth them.**—The latter part of this chapter teaches us a truth that is apt to be forgotten in the present day, which is, nevertheless, the key to much of the history of the world. Why is it that nations are marked with such characteristic differences? as, for instance, the Greeks, the Romans, and the Jews in ancient times; the French, the English, and the Germans in our own. Why is it that the counsel of the wisest sometimes faileth, as with

Job Reproveth his Friends   JOB, XIII.   *of Partiality*

(24) He taketh away the heart of the chief of the people of the earth,
And causeth them to wander in a wilderness *where there is* no way.
(25) They grope in the dark without light,
And he maketh them to ¹stagger like a drunken *man*.

CHAPTER XIII.—(1) Lo, mine eye hath seen all *this*,
Mine ear hath heard and understood it.
(2) What ye know, *the same* do I know also :
I *am* not inferior unto you.
(3) Surely I would speak to the Almighty,
And I desire to reason with God.
(4) But ye *are* forgers of lies, ye *are* all physicians of no value.
(5) O that ye would altogether hold your peace !
And it should be your wisdom.
(6) Hear now my reasoning,
And hearken to the pleadings of my lips.

(7) Will ye speak wickedly for God ?
And talk deceitfully for him ?
(8) Will ye accept his person ? will ye contend for God ?
(9) Is it good that he should search you out ?
Or as one man mocketh another, do ye *so* mock him ?
(10) He will surely reprove you, if ye do secretly accept persons.
(11) Shall not his excellency make you afraid ?
And his dread fall upon you ?
(12) Your remembrances *are* like unto ashes,
Your bodies to bodies of clay.
(13) ²Hold your peace, let me alone,
That I may speak, and let come on me what *will*.
(14) Wherefore do I take my flesh in my teeth,
And put my life in mine hand ?
(15) Though he slay me, yet will I trust in him :

1 Heb., *wander*.

2 Heb., *be silent from me*.

Ahitophel—the bravery of the boldest sometimes forsaketh them? but because there is One working underneath it all for His own ends and to His own glory, as seemeth Him good. Zophar, with all his common sense, had scarcely risen to the perception of this truth, for while Job maintained that there was always a deeper depth, he was prepared, at all events, to imply that the dealings of God were intelligible, and approved themselves to the conceptions of human equity. Job, on the other hand, declared that they were inscrutable, and, consequently, from their very darkness, suggested the necessity for faith. His teaching here may seem to savour of fatalism, but that is simply because he deals only with one side of the problem. Had he found occasion, he would have stated with equal force the correlative truth of the absolute responsibility of man, even though but as clay in the hands of the potter; for, in fact, were it not so, how then should God judge the world? Into the mazes of this problem Job enters not, being concerned with other questions and mysteries. Job's conception, therefore, of the righteous government of God as far transcended that of his friends as their estimate of his righteousness fell short of the truth. Justly, therefore, he exclaims, "I am not inferior unto you."

XIII.

(2) **I am not inferior unto you.**—*I fall not short of you.* But it is this very sense of the inscrutableness of God's dealings that makes him long to come face to face with God, and to reason with Him on the first principles of His action. As it is manifestly the traditionally orthodox position that his friends assume, it is refreshing to find that there may be some truth spoken for God by what is not so reckoned, and that more ultimate truth may exist in honest doubt than is sometimes found in the profession of a loosely-held creed. So the Laureate :

    "There lives more truth in honest doubt,
    Believe me, than in half the creeds."

(4) **Ye are forgers of lies.**—He now retorts upon his friends in terms not more deferential than their own, and calls them scrapers together, or patchers up, of falsehood, and physicians who are powerless to heal, or even to understand the case. He feels that they have failed miserably and utterly to understand *him*.

(5) **O that ye would altogether hold your peace !** is singularly like the sentiment of Prov. xvii. 28. Their wisdom will consist in listening to his wisdom rather than displaying their own folly.

(7) **Will ye speak wickedly for God ?**—And now, in these verses, he gives utterance to a sublime truth, which shows how truly he had risen to the true conception of God, for he declares that He, who is no respecter of persons, desires to have no favour shown to Himself, and that in seeking to show favour they will greatly damage their own cause, for He is a God of truth, and by Him words as well as actions are weighed, and therefore nothing that is not true can stand any one in stead with Him.

(9) **As one man mocketh another.**—As one man, with mingled flattery and deception, seeks to impose upon another.

(12) **Remembrances**—*i.e.,* "Wise and memorable saws of garnered wisdom are proverbs of ashes, worthless as the dust, and fit for bodies of clay like your bodies." Or, as some understand it, "Your high fabrics, or defences, are fabrics of clay," as an independent parallelism.

(13) **Hold your peace.**—He now prepares to make a declaration like the memorable one in chap. xix. He resolves at all hazards to face God in judgment.

(14) **Wherefore do I take my flesh in my teeth.**—This is probably the meaning of this verse, which, however, should not be read interrogatively: "At all risks, come what come may, I will take my flesh in my teeth, and put my life in my hand."

(15) **Though he slay me, yet will I trust in him.**—This rendering is almost proverbial; but, to say

26

But I will ¹maintain mine own ways before him.
⁽¹⁶⁾ He also *shall be* my salvation:
For an hypocrite shall not come before him.
⁽¹⁷⁾ Hear diligently my speech, and my declaration with your ears.
⁽¹⁸⁾ Behold now, I have ordered *my* cause;
I know that I shall be justified.
⁽¹⁹⁾ Who *is* he *that* will plead with me?
For now, if I hold my tongue, I shall give up the ghost.
⁽²⁰⁾ Only do not two *things* unto me:
Then will I not hide myself from thee.
⁽²¹⁾ Withdraw thine hand far from me:
And let not thy dread make me afraid.
⁽²²⁾ Then call thou, and I will answer:
Or let me speak, and answer thou me.
⁽²³⁾ How many *are* mine iniquities and sins?
Make me to know my transgression and my sin.
⁽²⁴⁾ Wherefore hidest thou thy face,
And holdest me for thine enemy?
⁽²⁵⁾ Wilt thou break a leaf driven to and fro?
And wilt thou pursue the dry stubble?
⁽²⁶⁾ For thou writest bitter things against me,
And ᵃmakest me to possess the iniquities of my youth.
⁽²⁷⁾ Thou puttest my feet also in the stocks,
And ²lookest narrowly unto all my paths;
Thou settest a print upon the ³heels of my feet.
⁽²⁸⁾ And he, as a rotten thing, consumeth,
As a garment that is moth eaten.

CHAPTER XIV.—⁽¹⁾ Man *that is* born of a woman *is* ⁴of few days,
And full of trouble.
⁽²⁾ ᵇHe cometh forth like a flower, and is cut down:

1 Heb., *prove, or, argue.*
a Ps. 25. 7.
2 Heb., *observest.*
3 Heb., *roots.*
4 Heb., *short of days.*
b ch. 8. 9: Ps. 102. 11, & 103. 15, & 144. 4.

---

the least, its accuracy is very doubtful, for the better reading does not warrant it, but runs thus: *Behold He will slay me. I have no hope; yet will I maintain my ways before Him.* It is true we thus lose a very beautiful and familiar resolve; but the expression of living trust is not less vivid. For though there is, as there can be, no gleam of hope for victory in this conflict, yet, notwithstanding, Job will not forego his conviction of integrity; for the voice of conscience is the voice of God, and if he knows himself to be innocent, he would belie and dishonour God as well as himself in renouncing his innocence.

⁽¹⁶⁾ **He also shall be my salvation.**—Comp. Ps. xxvii. 1, &c. It is characteristic of Job that, living, as he probably did, outside the pale of Israel, he nevertheless shared the faith and knowledge of God's chosen people; and this cannot be said of any other nation, nor does any literature give evidence of it. Indeed, it is this which most markedly distinguishes Job from his friends, in that he can and does trust God unreservedly, in spite of all adverse circumstances, overwhelming as they were; while his friends are ignorant of the great central fact that He is Himself the sinner's hope, and are content to rest only upon vague and bald generalities. It is because, therefore, he has said, and can say, "He is and will be my salvation," that he can also say, "I know that I shall be justified, that I am righteous, because I trust in Him" (Gen. xv. 6). We do not, in thus speaking, import the Gospel into Job, but exhibit that in Job which had already been manifest in Abraham, and probably recorded of him.

⁽¹⁹⁾ **If I hold my tongue, I shall give up the ghost.**—A marvellous confession, equivalent to, "If I give up my faith in Him who is my salvation, and my personal innocence, which goes hand-in-hand therewith, I shall perish. To give up my innocence is to give up Him in whom I hold my innocence, and in whom I live."

⁽²⁰⁾ **Will I not hide myself from thee**—*i.e.*, "I shall not be hidden"—quite a different word from that in Gen. iii. 10, though the comparison of the two places is not without interest.

⁽²¹⁾ **Withdraw thine hand far from me.**—That is, "Cease to torture me bodily, and to terrify me mentally; let me at least have freedom from physical pain and the undue apprehension of Thy terrors."

⁽²³⁾ **How many are mine iniquities?**—We must be careful to note that alongside with Job's claim to be righteous there is ever as deep a confession of personal sin, thus showing that the only way in which we can understand his declarations is in the light of His teaching who convicts of sin before He convinces of righteousness.

⁽²⁵⁾ **Wilt thou break a leaf.**—His confession of sin here approaches even to what the Psalmist describes as the condition of the ungodly (Ps. i. 4).

⁽²⁶⁾ **For thou writest bitter things against me.**—Exquisitely plaintive and affecting is this confession.

⁽²⁷⁾ **Thou puttest my feet also in the stocks.**—This is illustrated by the language of the Psalms (Ps. lxxxviii. 8, cxlii. 7, &c.). There is a difficulty in these two verses, arising from the pronouns. Some understand the subject to be the fetter: "Thou puttest my feet in the fetter that watcheth over all my paths, and imprinteth itself upon the roots of my feet, and it (the foot) consumeth like a rotten thing, and like a garment that is moth-eaten." Others refer the "he" to Job himself; and others to man, the subject of the following chapter. In the Hebrew future tense the third person feminine and the second person masculine are alike, and the word for fetter, which is only found here and at chap. xxxiii. 11, where Elihu quotes these words, may possibly be feminine in this place, though it is clear that Elihu understood Job to be speaking of God. Probably by the "he" introduced so abruptly is meant the object of all this watching and persecution.

XIV.

⁽¹⁾ **Man that is born of a woman is of few days.**—He now takes occasion to dilate on the miserable estate of man generally, rising from the particular instance in himself to the common lot of the

The Shortness of Life   JOB, XIV.   *and Certainty of Death.*

He fleeth also as a shadow, and continueth not.

(3) And dost thou open thine eyes upon such an one,
And bringest me into judgment with thee?[1]

(4)[1] Who *a*can bring a clean *thing* out of an unclean? not one.

(5) *b*Seeing his days *are* determined,
The number of his months *are* with thee,
Thou hast appointed his bounds that he cannot pass;

(6) Turn from him, that he may [2]rest,
Till he shall accomplish, as an hireling, his day.

(7) For there is hope of a tree, if it be cut down, that it will sprout again,
And that the tender branch thereof will not cease.

(8) Though the root thereof wax old in the earth,
And the stock thereof die in the ground;

(9) *Yet* through the scent of water it will bud,
And bring forth boughs like a plant.

(10) But man dieth, and [3]wasteth away:

Yea, man giveth up the ghost, and where *is* he?

(11) *As* the waters fail from the sea,
And the flood decayeth and drieth up:

(12) So man lieth down, and riseth not:
Till the heavens *be* no more, they shall not awake,
Nor be raised out of their sleep.

(13) O that thou wouldest hide me in the grave,
That thou wouldest keep me secret, until thy wrath be past,
That thou wouldest appoint me a set time, and remember me!

(14) If a man die, shall he live *again*?
All the days of my appointed time will I wait, till my change come.

(15) Thou shalt call, and I will answer thee:
Thou wilt have a desire to the work of thine hands.

(16) *c*For now thou numberest my steps:
Dost thou not watch over my sin?

(17) My transgression *is* sealed up in a bag,
And thou sewest up mine iniquity.

(18) And surely the mountain falling [4]cometh to nought,

---

1 Heb., *Who will give.*
a Ps. 51. 5.
b ch. 7. 1.
2 Heb., *cease.*
3 Heb., *is weakened,* or, *cut off.*
c Ps. 139. 2.
4 Heb., *fadeth.*

---

race. It is not improbable that these words should be connected with the last of the former chapter. *He, as a rotten thing, consumeth—a man born of woman, short of days and full of trouble, who came forth as a flower and was (began to be) cut off (at once); who fled as the shadow that abideth not.* After having resolved to come into judgment with God, he pictures to himself the miserable creature with whom God will have to contend if He contends with *him*.

(4) **Who can bring a clean thing . . .**—How can man be clean that is born of woman, who is unclean? This question is reiterated by Bildad (chap. xxv. 4). We ought perhaps, however, rather to render "Oh, that the clean could come forth from the unclean! but none can."

(6) **Accomplish.**—Rather, *have pleasure in; rejoice at the day when his wages are paid him.* Job had used the same image before (chap. vii. 2). Job now proceeds to enlarge on the mortality of man, comparing him, as is so often done in all literature, to the vegetable produce of the earth (Isa. xl. 7, lxv. 22); with this difference, however—that a tree will sprout again when it is cut down, but even a strong man succumbs to death. "Yea, man giveth up the ghost, and where is he?"

(11) **As the waters fail from the sea** seems commonly to have been misunderstood from its having been taken as a comparison; but there is no particle denoting comparison in the Hebrew. Moreover, the water never fails from the sea, nor do great rivers like the Nile or the Euphrates ever dry up. The comparison that is implied, but not expressed, is one of contrariety. *The waters will have failed from the sea, and the rivers will have wasted and become dry, and yet the man who hath lain down (in death) will not arise:* i.e., sooner than that shall happen, the sea will fail and the great rivers become dry. This appears to give a sense far better and more appropriate to the context. The Authorised Version obscures the obvious meaning of the passage by the introduction of the "as," which is not wanted. There is no hope of any future life, still less of any resurrection here; but neither can we regard the language as involving an absolute denial of it. What Job says is equally true even in full view of the life to come and of the resurrection; indeed, there seems to glimmer the hope of an ardent though unexpressed longing, through the very language that is used. At all events, the statement uttered so confidently is not proof against the inevitable doubt involved in verse 14.

(14) **If a man die, shall he live again?**—Why ask the question if it were absolutely certain that he would not? "All the days of my warfare—*i.e.*, as long as I live—I will hope, till my change or transition from life to death comes, that Thou shalt call and I shall answer Thee, that Thou wilt long for the work of Thine hands."

(16) **For now thou numberest my steps: dost thou not watch over my sin?**—"It is sealed up in a bag, and Thou fastenest up mine iniquity. But persecution so persistent would wear out the strongest, even as the mountain and the rock are gradually worn away. How much more then must I be the subject of decay? for Thou destroyest the hope of man when he dieth, so that he no longer has any interest in the welfare or any concern in the adversity of his children after him; only in his own person he has pain, and his own soul within him mourneth."

And the rock is removed out of his place.
(19) The waters wear the stones :
Thou ¹washest away the things which grow *out* of the dust of the earth ;
And thou destroyest the hope of man.
(20) Thou prevailest for ever against him, and he passeth :
Thou changest his countenance, and sendest him away.
(21) His sons come to honour, and he knoweth *it* not ;
And they are brought low, but he perceiveth *it* not of them.
(22) But his flesh upon him shall have pain,
And his soul within him shall mourn.

CHAPTER XV.—(1) Then answered Eliphaz the Temanite, and said,
(2) Should a wise man utter ²vain knowledge,
And fill his belly with the east wind ?
(3) Should he reason with unprofitable talk ?
Or with speeches wherewith he can do no good ?
(4) Yea, ³thou castest off fear, and restrainest ⁴prayer before God.
(5) For thy mouth ⁵uttereth thine iniquity,
And thou choosest the tongue of the crafty.
(6) Thine own mouth condemneth thee, and not I :
Yea, thine own lips testify against thee.
(7) *Art* thou the first man *that* was born ?
Or wast thou made before the hills ?
(8) ᵃHast thou heard the secret of God ?
And dost thou restrain wisdom to thyself ?
(9) What knowest thou, that we know not ?
What understandest thou, which *is* not in us ?
(10) With us *are* both the grayheaded and very aged men,
Much elder than thy father.
(11) *Are* the consolations of God small with thee ?
Is there any secret thing with thee ?
(12) Why doth thine heart carry thee away ?
And what do thy eyes wink at,
(13) That thou turnest thy spirit against God,
And lettest *such* words go out of thy mouth ?
(14) ᵇWhat *is* man, that he should be clean ?
And *he which is* born of a woman, that he should be righteous ?

¹ Heb., *overflowest.*
² Heb., *knowledge of wind.*
³ Heb., *thou makest void.*
⁴ Or, *speech.*
⁵ Heb., *teacheth.*
a Rom. 11. 34.
b 1 Kin. 8. 46 ; 2 Chr. 6. 36 ; ch. 14. 4 ; Ps. 14.3 ; Prov. 20. 9 ; 1 John 1. 8.

XV.

Eliphaz returns to the argument with the repetition of what he and his friends have said before. He reproaches Job, professes a high idea of the majesty and righteousness of God, and reiterates the assertion that the wicked man, by the sure retribution of the Divine Providence, receives the reward of his iniquity in this world. In verse 16 he uses strong general language, which is probably meant to reflect on Job, and the inference is suggested that Job himself, because so sorely chastened, must be wicked.

(2) **Should a wise man utter vain knowledge . . .**—Job therefore is not wise, and his words have been vain and windy.

(3) **Should he reason with unprofitable talk ?**—Nay, his arguments, though pretentious and apparently recondite, are unprofitable, and can do no good.

(4) **Yea, thou castest off fear.**—The tendency also of Job has been to encourage a kind of fatalism (*e.g.*, chap. xii. 16—25), and therefore to check the offering of prayer to God, besides setting an example which, if followed, as from Job's position it was likely to be, would lead to murmuring and blasphemy.

(5) **Thy mouth uttereth thine iniquity.**—These words may mean either " Thy mouth teacheth thine iniquity," or " Thine iniquity teacheth thy mouth," and the second clause must be taken adversatively or otherwise according as we understand the meaning, " Thy mouth proclaimeth thine iniquity, though thou choosest the tongue of the crafty, and so contrivest in some degree to conceal it ; " or, " Thine iniquity teacheth thy mouth its eloquence, and by consequence thou choosest the tongue of the crafty." We incline to the latter, though it is fair to say that the next verse seems rather to favour the other meaning.

(7) **Art thou the first man that was born ?**—This is a retort upon chap. xii. 2, 7, and 9, where Job had claimed equal knowledge for the inanimate creation.

(11) **Are the consolations of God small with thee ?**—This is one of the obscure phrases of Job upon which it is very difficult to decide. The Authorised Version gives very good sense, which seems to suit the context in the following verse ; but it is susceptible of other phases of meaning : *e.g.*, " or a word that dealeth gently with thee (2 Sam. iv. 5), such as ours have been (?) " ; or " the word that he hath spoken softly with thee " (but see verse 8) ; or, again, " the consolations of God may mean strong consolations (Ps. lxxx. 11), such as ours have been, spoken in strong language," in which case the second clause would mean, " Was thine own speech gentle ? " " Small with thee " means, of course, *too small for thee.*

(12) **What do thy eyes wink at ?**—Or, Why do they wink ? as though it was only thou who perceivedst it.

(14) **What is man ?**—This is the ceaseless burden. (See chaps. iv. 17, ix. 2, xxv. 4, &c.)

(15) "Behold, he putteth no trust in his saints;
Yea, the heavens are not clean in his sight.
(16) How much more abominable and filthy *is* man,
Which drinketh iniquity like water?
(17) I will shew thee, hear me;
And that *which* I have seen I will declare;
(18) Which wise men have told
From their fathers, and have not hid *it*:
(19) Unto whom alone the earth was given,
And no stranger passed among them.
(20) The wicked man travaileth with pain all *his* days,
And the number of years is hidden to the oppressor.
(21) ¹A dreadful sound *is* in his ears:
In prosperity the destroyer shall come upon him.
(22) He believeth not that he shall return out of darkness,
And he is waited for of the sword.
(23) He wandereth abroad for bread, saying, Where *is it*?
He knoweth that the day of darkness is ready at his hand.
(24) Trouble and anguish shall make him afraid;
They shall prevail against him, as a king ready to the battle.
(25) For he stretcheth out his hand against God,
And strengtheneth himself against the Almighty.
(26) He runneth upon him, *even* on *his* neck,
Upon the thick bosses of his bucklers:
(27) Because he covereth his face with his fatness,
And maketh collops of fat on *his* flanks.
(28) And he dwelleth in desolate cities,
And in houses which no man inhabiteth,
Which are ready to become heaps.
(29) He shall not be rich, neither shall his substance continue,
Neither shall he prolong the perfection thereof upon the earth.
(30) He shall not depart out of darkness;
The flame shall dry up his branches,

a ch. 4. 18.

¹ Heb., *A sound of fears.*

---

(15) **Behold.**—Comp. chaps. iv. 18, v. 5.

(16) **How much more abominable and filthy is man . . .**—This strong language, thus couched in general terms, is doubtless intended to reflect on Job, otherwise it would not need to have been so strong.

(18) **Which wise men have told from their fathers.**—Here he adopts the language of Bildad (chap. viii. 8), appealing both to his own experience and that of universal tradition in an age prior to civil commotion and foreign disturbance.

(20) **Travaileth with pain.**—This and the following verses contain the result of this experience. Here, again, we have a highly-coloured and poetical description of the oppressor, true to the character of the speaker in chap. iv. 12, &c. We should read verse 20: *The wicked man travaileth with pain all his days, even the number of years that are laid up for the oppressor.* It is not an independent statement, as in the Authorised Version. A sound of terror is for ever in his ears lest the spoiler should come upon him in his prosperity—he always seems to dread his war-swoop. And this condition of darkness within, which contrasts so painfully with his outward prosperity, he sees no escape from; he is ever in fear of a sword hanging over him, like Damocles.

(23) **He wandereth abroad for bread.**—This is one of the points in which the picture seems inconsistent, because overdrawn, except that forage as well as plunder may be the object of marauding raids.

(24) **As a king ready to the battle.**—Or, They prevail against him like a king: he is destined to be like a ball (comp. Isa. xxii. 18), the tennis-ball of calamity.

(25) **For he stretcheth out his hand.**—It is instructive to note the difference in time indicated here. "Because he *hath stretched* out his hand against God, and *behaveth* himself proudly against the Almighty. He runneth upon Him with haughty neck, with the thick bosses of his bucklers;" fully protected as he supposes against the vengeance of the Most High. (Comp. Ps. x. 6, 11, &c.) The English version, with less probability, represents the armour as being God's; on the contrary, it is the wicked man's prosperity which hath thus blinded and hardened him. (See Deut. xxxii. 15; Ps. xvii. 10.)

(28) **Which are ready to become heaps.**—This completes the description of the haughty tyrant. He dwelt in cities that are to be desolate, or that are desolate, which are ready to become heaps. This may point either to what they were in his intention, or to what he had made them, or to what, in the opinion of the speaker, they were likely to become, notwithstanding his having fortified and dwelt in them.

(29) **He shall not be rich.**—Now comes the destiny which awaits him in the judgment of the speaker. "Neither shall he prolong the perfection thereof upon the earth." The word rendered "perfection thereof" occurs nowhere else, so that it is very doubtful what it means. Some render, "Neither shall their produce (that of the wicked) bend (luxuriantly) to the earth;" or, "their possessions or achievements extend on the earth."

(30) **He shall not depart out of darkness.**—See verse 22. "By the breath of his mouth shall he go away." What this means is not very clear: probably as in chap. xi. 20; or, "When he expires it shall be the end of him; he shall leave nothing permanent that is destined to last;" or, "He shall pass away suddenly and completely, like his own breath."

Job Complaineth of   JOB, XVI.   *his Friend's Unmercifulness.*

And by the breath of his mouth shall he go away.
(31) Let not him that is deceived trust in vanity:
For vanity shall be his recompence.
(32) It shall be ¹accomplished before his time,
And his branch shall not be green.
(33) He shall shake off his unripe grape as the vine,
And shall cast off his flower as the olive.
(34) For the congregation of hypocrites *shall be* desolate,
And fire shall consume the tabernacles of bribery.
(35) ᵃThey conceive mischief, and bring forth ²vanity,
And their belly prepareth deceit.

CHAPTER XVI.—(1) Then Job answered and said,
(2) I have heard many such things:
³ᵇ Miserable comforters *are* ye all.
(3) Shall ⁴vain words have an end?
Or what emboldeneth thee that thou answerest?
(4) I also could speak as ye *do*:
If your soul were in my soul's stead,
I could heap up words against you,
And shake mine head at you.
(5) *But* I would strengthen you with my mouth,
And the moving of my lips should asswage *your grief*.
(6) Though I speak, my grief is not asswaged:
And *though* I forbear, ⁵what am I eased?
(7) But now he hath made me weary:
Thou hast made desolate all my company.
(8) And thou hast filled me with wrinkles, *which* is a witness *against me*:
And my leanness rising up in me beareth witness to my face.
(9) He teareth *me* in his wrath, who hateth me:
He gnasheth upon me with his teeth;
Mine enemy sharpeneth his eyes upon me.
(10) They have gaped upon me with their mouth;
They have smitten me upon the cheek reproachfully;
They have gathered themselves together against me.

1 Or, *cut off.*

a Ps. 7. 14; Is. 59. 4.

2 Or, *iniquity.*

3 Or, *troublesome.*

b ch. 13. 4.

4 Heb., *words of wind.*

5 Heb., *what goeth from me.*

---

(31) **Let not him that is deceived trust in vanity.**—Or, *Let him not trust in vanity deceiving himself.* (Comp. James i. 26; 1 Sam. xii. 21.)

(32) **It shall be accomplished.**—That is, paid in full before its time.

The remainder of this chapter calls for little explanation. In it the speaker only repeats the orthodox and familiar saw that the wicked are punished in life, and therefore, by implication, the good rewarded: a maxim which fails utterly in the face of afflictions like those of Job, unless, as his friends insinuated, he was one of the wicked. After stating the doom of the ungodly, Eliphaz, in the last verse, sums up the character of those he has been denouncing. Not only are they evil in themselves, but they hatch evil; but it is evil that recoils on themselves.

(34) **Desolate.**—This was Job's own word (chap. iii. 7), and as it is an uncommon word, there may be some intentional reference to his use of it.

XVI.

(1) **Then Job answered.**—Job, in replying, ceases to continue the argument, which he finds useless; but, after complaining of the way his friends have conducted it, and contrasting the way in which they have treated him with that in which he would treat them were they in his case, he proceeds again to enlarge upon his condition, and makes a touching appeal to Heaven, which prepares us for the more complete confession in chap. xix. He ends by declaring that his case is desperate.

(2) **I have heard many such things.**—Trite rather than true, or at least the whole truth.

"Common is the common-place,
And vacant chaff well meant for grain."

(3) **Shall vain words have an end?**—The English idiom rather requires, "Shall *not* vain words have an end? for if not, what emboldeneth or provoketh thee that thou answerest?" Eliphaz had contributed nothing to the discussion in his last reply; he had simply reiterated what had been said before.

(4) **If your soul.**—*i.e., person*="If you were in my place, I could heap up words," &c. It is doubtful whether this is in contrast to what comes afterwards in the fifth verse, as in the Authorised Version, or whether it may not be in parallelism with it; thus: "I would make myself a companion to you—condole and sympathise with you in words, and shake my head at you as a mark of sympathy." The phrase differs somewhat from that in Ps. xxii. 7; Isa. xxxvii. 22, where to shake the head expresses contempt and derision.

(6) **Though I speak . . .**—"I cannot but reply, though to reply gives me no relief."

(7) **But now he hath made me weary.**—He turns again, in his passionate plaint, to God, whom he alternately speaks of in the third person and addresses in the second. "Thou hast made desolate all my company," by destroying all his children and alienating the hearts of his friends.

(8) **Witness against me.**—As in chap. x. 17. The wrinkles in his body, caused by the disease, were a witness against him; and certainly, in the eyes of his friends, they furnished unquestionable proof of his guilt.

(9) **He teareth me in his wrath.**—Terrible as the language is that Job has used against God, he seems here almost to exceed it, for he calls Him his adversary. It is hardly possible not to understand the expression of

| Job's Afflictions. | JOB, XVII. | He Maintaineth his Innocence. |

⁽¹¹⁾ God ¹hath delivered me to the ungodly,
And turned me over into the hands of the wicked.
⁽¹²⁾ I was at ease, but he hath broken me asunder:
He hath also taken *me* by my neck, and shaken me to pieces,
And set me up for his mark.
⁽¹³⁾ His archers compass me round about,
He cleaveth my reins asunder, and doth not spare;
He poureth out my gall upon the ground.
⁽¹⁴⁾ He breaketh me with breach upon breach,
He runneth upon me like a giant.
⁽¹⁵⁾ I have sewed sackcloth upon my skin,
And defiled my horn in the dust.
⁽¹⁶⁾ My face is foul with weeping,
And on my eyelids *is* the shadow of death;
⁽¹⁷⁾ Not for *any* injustice in mine hands:
Also my prayer *is* pure.
⁽¹⁸⁾ O earth, cover not thou my blood,
And let my cry have no place.
⁽¹⁹⁾ Also now, behold, my witness *is* in heaven,
And my record *is* ²on high.
⁽²⁰⁾ My friends ³scorn me:
But mine eye poureth out *tears* unto God.
⁽²¹⁾ O that one might plead for a man with God,
As a man *pleadeth* for his ⁴neighbour!
⁽²²⁾ When ⁵a few years are come,
Then I shall go the way *whence* I shall not return.

CHAPTER XVII.—⁽¹⁾ My ⁶breath is corrupt, my days are extinct,
The graves *are ready* for me.
⁽²⁾ *Are there* not mockers with me?
And doth not mine eye ⁷continue in their provocation?
⁽³⁾ Lay down now, put me in a surety with thee;

Marginal notes:
1 Heb., *hath shut me up.*
2 Heb., *in the high places.*
3 Heb., *are my scorners.*
4 Or, *friend.*
5 Heb., *years of number.*
6 Or, *spirit is spent.*
7 Heb., *lodge.*

God, for though he immediately speaks of his friends, yet just afterwards he openly mentions God.

⁽¹¹⁾ **The ungodly and the wicked** are the terms he retorts upon his friends, and they have certainly earned them. Now follows—

⁽¹²⁾ **I was at ease.**—A highly poetical passage, in which Job becomes, as it were, a St. Sebastian for the arrows of God. It is hardly possible to conceive a more vivid picture of his desolate condition under the persecuting hand of the Almighty.

⁽¹⁵⁾ **I have sewed sackcloth upon my skin.** —Referring, probably, to the state of his skin, which had become hard and rugged as sackcloth. As the second half of the verse must be figurative, there seems to be no reason to understand the first half otherwise.

⁽¹⁶⁾ **Foul.**—Rather, perhaps, *red*, as with wine.

⁽¹⁷⁾ **Not for any injustice.**—Literally, *for no injustice*, just as in Isa. liii. 9: "because he had done no violence," should be "not because he had done any violence, or because deceit was in his mouth."

⁽¹⁸⁾ **Let my cry have no place.**—That is, "Let there be no place in the wide earth where my cry shall not reach: let it have no resting place: let it fill the whole wide earth."

⁽¹⁹⁾ **My witness is in heaven.**—It is very important to note passages such as these, because they help us to understand, and serve to illustrate, the famous confession in chap. xix. This is surely a wonderful declaration for a man in the position of Job. What can the believer, in the full light of the Gospel revelation, say more, with the knowledge of One in heaven ever making intercession for him? And yet Job's faith had risen to such a height as this, and had grasped such a hope as this. In no other book of the Bible is there such a picture of faith clinging to the all-just God for justification as in the Book of Job.

⁽²⁰⁾ **My friends scorn me.**—Or, as an apostrophe, "Ye my scorners who profess and ought to be my friends: mine eye poureth out tears unto God that He would maintain the right of man with God, and of the son of man with his neighbour;" or, "that one might plead for man with God as the son of man pleadeth for his neighbour"—this is what he has already longed for in chap. ix. 33.

⁽²²⁾ **When a few years are come.**—Literally, *years of number*, which means either "years than can be easily numbered," as *men of number* (Gen. xxxiv. 20) is used to express *few men*; or "years that are numbered," that is, allotted, determined. It is strange to find Job speaking, in his condition, of *years*, but so, for that matter, is it to find a man so sorely tormented as he was indulging in so long an argument. Perhaps this shows us that the narrative of Job is intended to be an ideal only, setting forth the low estate of sin-stricken humanity: this is only thrown out as a suggestion, no weight is assigned to it more than it may chance to claim. Perhaps, however, these words are spoken by Job in contemplation of his condition as a *dying* man, even had he not been so afflicted.

XVII.

⁽¹⁾ **My breath is corrupt.**—As it is said to be in Elephantiasis. Some understand it, "My spirit is consumed." (See margin.)

The graves.—*i.e., the grave is mine—my portion.* The plural is frequently used for the singular in Hebrew, as, *e.g.*, in the case of the word *blood*, which is commonly plural, though with us it is never so used.

⁽²⁾ **Mine eye continue in their provocation?**— "It sees, and can see nothing else; has nothing else to look upon": a bitter reproach against his friends.

⁽³⁾ **Lay down now . . .**—*i.e., Give now a pledge; be surety for me with Thyself.* He has declared that he has a witness in the heavens, but he desires some *present* token of the vindication to come of which he is confident, and so he asks God to give him such a pledge. This is virtually the same prayer that we find Hezekiah using (Isa. xxxviii. 14): "O Lord, I am oppressed: under-

The Hope of the Righteous,   JOB, XVII.   *though Afflicted by the Wicked.*

Who *is* he *that* will strike hands with me?

(4) For thou hast hid their heart from understanding:
Therefore shalt thou not exalt *them*.

(5) He that speaketh flattery to *his* friends,
Even the eyes of his children shall fail.

(6) He hath made me also a byword of the people;
And ¹aforetime I was as a tabret.

(7) Mine eye also is dim by reason of sorrow,
And all ²my members *are* as a shadow.

(8) Upright *men* shall be astonied at this,
And the innocent shall stir up himself against the hypocrite.

(9) The righteous also shall hold on his way,
And he that hath clean hands ³shall be stronger and stronger.

(10) But as for you all, do ye return, and come now:
For I cannot find *one* wise *man* among you.

(11) My days are past, my purposes are broken off,
Even ⁴the thoughts of my heart.

(12) They change the night into day:
The light *is* ⁵short because of darkness.

(13) If I wait, the grave *is* mine house:
I have made my bed in the darkness.

(14) I have ⁶said to corruption, Thou *art* my father:
To the worm, *Thou art* my mother, and my sister.

(15) And where *is* now my hope? as for my hope, who shall see it?

(16) They shall go down to the bars of the pit,
When *our* rest together *is* in the dust.

¹ Or, *before them.*
² Or, *my thoughts.*
³ Heb., *shall add strength.*
⁴ Heb., *the possessions.*
⁵ Heb., *near.*
⁶ Heb., *cried, or, called.*

---

take for me," that is, "Be surety for me." (See also Ps. cxix. 122: "Be surety for thy servant for good.") There is that in man which demands exact and rigorous fulfilment or expiation of non-fulfilment. Job felt that his only hope of this fulfilment or expiation of non-fulfilment lay with God Himself: that same God who had put this sense of obligation within him; therefore he says, "Be surety for me with Thyself." He longed for the daysman who should lay his hand upon both him and God; he now longs for that surety with God that God alone can give. The surety must be Divine if his witness is in the heavens; it must be the witness of God to God himself. In this wonderful way does the language of Job fit in with all that we have since and elsewhere learnt of the persons in the Godhead.

Who is he that will strike hands with me?—This was the method of becoming surety; but he knows that there is no one among his friends who will do this, or that could do it if he would. (Comp. Ps. xlix. 7.)

(4) **Their heart.**—*i.e.*, the heart of his friends.

(5) **He that speaketh flattery to his friends.**—The three words thus rendered are, from their very brevity, most obscure. Literally, they run: *for a portion he will tell friends.* But what is the meaning of this? Some render, "He denounceth his friends for a prey," *i.e.*, such is the conduct of Job's friends towards Job. Others understand it, "He would say, friends should take their part," *i.e.*, any one who would undertake to be surety for me would naturally expect my friends to share the responsibility; but so far from this, the eyes of his sons would fail in looking for it; they would never see it.

(6) **He** (*i.e.*, God) **hath made me also a byword of the people; and aforetime I was as a tabret.**—Or, *I am become as a tabret, or drum openly, i.e.*, a signal of warning. "My case will be fraught with warning for others." But some render it, "I am become an open abhorrence, or one in whose face they spit." The general meaning is perfectly clear, though the way it may be expressed varies.

(8) **Upright men shall be astonied.**—"As a result of the warning my case would give, upright men would be astonished at it, innocent men would be encouraged, and the righteous would persevere and wax bold."

(10) **But as for you all, do ye return.**—This is probably said with irony. "Come again and renew the argument between us; but I shall not be able to find a wise man among you. I am willing to listen to your argument, but I am confident as to the result of it."

For I cannot find.—Rather, *and I shall not find: i.e.*, if ye renew the argument.

(12) **They change the night into day.**—Comp. chap. xi. 17. So little did his friends enter into his case that they wanted him to believe that his night of trial was the reverse of darkness, and that there was light at hand. This was to him only the more painful mockery, because of its contrast to his felt condition. He, on the contrary, says that his only hope is in the grave. "The light," say they, "is near unto the darkness; that it is near before the darkness cometh; they try to persuade me that prosperity is close at hand."

(16) **They shall go down to the bars of the pit.**—The last verse of this chapter, which is itself one of the most difficult, is the most difficult of all. The difficulty consists in this: *the bars of the grave* are masculine, and the verb, *they shall go down,* is feminine plural; it seems improbable that *the bars of the grave* should be the subject of the verb (though perhaps not absolutely impossible); but if *the bars of the grave* are the place to which the going down is, as in the Authorised Version, then what is the subject to the verb, go down, seeing that *hope,* the apparent subject, is a feminine singular? Some render "it shall go down," but this is in defiance of the grammar, though, probably, the meaning it conveys is not far from the truth. The words clearly express a condition of utter despair, and that Job's only hope of rest is in the grave. It is a rule in Hebrew grammar that when the verb precedes its subject it need not agree with it in gender or number; but here the verb must, at all events, come after its subject, and consequently, it is very difficult to determine what that subject is. The only apparent subject is to be found in the *corruption* of the *worm* of verse 14; but they, instead of going down to the grave, are already there.

CHAPTER XVIII.—⁽¹⁾ Then answered Bildad the Shuhite, and said,
⁽²⁾ How long *will it be ere* ye make an end of words?
Mark, and afterwards we will speak.
⁽³⁾ Wherefore are we counted as beasts,
And reputed vile in your sight?
⁽⁴⁾ He teareth ¹himself in his anger:
Shall the earth be forsaken for thee?
And shall the rock be removed out of his place?
⁽⁵⁾ Yea, the light of the wicked shall be put out,
And the spark of his fire shall not shine.
⁽⁶⁾ The light shall be dark in his tabernacle,
And his ²candle shall be put out with him.
⁽⁷⁾ The steps of his strength shall be straitened,
And his own counsel shall cast him down.
⁽⁸⁾ For he is cast into a net by his own feet,
And he walketh upon a snare.
⁽⁹⁾ The gin shall take *him* by the heel,
And the robber shall prevail against him.
⁽¹⁰⁾ The snare *is* ³laid for him in the ground,
And a trap for him in the way.
⁽¹¹⁾ Terrors shall make him afraid on every side,
And shall ⁴drive him to his feet.
⁽¹²⁾ His strength shall be hungerbitten,
And destruction *shall be* ready at his side.
⁽¹³⁾ It shall devour the ⁵strength of his skin:
Even the firstborn of death shall devour his strength.
⁽¹⁴⁾ ᵃHis confidence shall be rooted out of his tabernacle,
And it shall bring him to the king of terrors.
⁽¹⁵⁾ It shall dwell in his tabernacle, because *it is* none of his:
Brimstone shall be scattered upon his habitation.

1 Heb., *his soul.*
2 Or, *lamp.*
3 Heb., *hidden.*
4 Heb., *scatter him.*
5 Heb., *bars.*
a ch. 8. 14 & 11. 20; Ps. 112. 10; Prov. 10. 28.

XVIII.

⁽¹⁾ **How long?**—Bildad begins very much as Job himself had done (chap. xvi.).

⁽³⁾ **Wherefore are we counted as beasts.**—Referring to Job's words (chaps. xiii. 4, &c., xvi. 2, &c.). In this chapter there is a marked increase in his harshness and violence. It has, however, a certain resemblance to chap. viii., inasmuch as Bildad works out a simile here, as he did there; and in verse 16 the two similes touch. In verse 2, which resembles chap. viii. 2, we must supply, as the Authorised Version does, *Will it be ere?* or the negative, *Will ye not make?* &c., or else we must render, "How long [will ye speak thus]? Make an end of words," &c. The plural is used because Job is regarded as the representative of a class, or else as we use the plural instead of the singular in addressing a person.

⁽⁴⁾ **He teareth himself in his anger.**—As Eliphaz had charged Job (chap. xv. 4) with the evil tendencies of his speeches, so Bildad here compares him to a maniac, and assumes that the effect of his teaching will be to banish God from the earth, and remove the strength and hope of man. The last clause is a direct quotation from Job in chap. xiv. 18; it looks, therefore, very much like a wilful perversion of Job's words, for it is clear that he used them very differently. Even if there were no intentional misrepresentation Bildad applies Job's words to his own purposes. The drift of his question is, "Can you expect the course of God's providence to be altered for you? On the contrary, the retribution that awaits the wicked is sure and swift; for verily (verse 5) the light of the wicked shall be put out."

⁽⁷⁾ **The steps of his strength.**—*i.e.,* his giant strides. He shall be the victim of his own devices, and when they seem to hold out the hope of prosperity shall lead him to destruction. (Comp. Ps. cxli. 11.)

⁽⁸⁾ **He is cast into a net.**—Job had compared himself to one hunted by the Almighty (chap. x. 16), and Bildad here describes the evil man as snared in a net, but it is one for which he has no one to thank but himself. It is his own pit he falls into; the insinuation being that Job is likewise responsible for his calamities, which are the punishment of his sin. It is to be observed that in this and the following verses the speaker heaps together every word he can find descriptive of the art of snaring.

⁽¹¹⁾ **Shall drive him to his feet.**—Comp. chap. xv. 21. One feels very much tempted to understand this, as the English undoubtedly suggests, *shall startle him to his feet,* but the true meaning is, more probably, *shall chase him at his heels.*

⁽¹²⁾ **His strength.**—By "strength" some understand his firstborn son, as Gen. xlix. 3, but it is not necessary to take it otherwise than literally.

Destruction shall be ready at his side.—Or, according to some, *for his halting:* shall lie in wait for his tripping in order to overthrow him.

⁽¹³⁾ **The strength of his skin.**—This verse should probably be rendered, "It shall devour the members of his body, even the firstborn of death shall devour his members;" and by the "firstborn of death" is probably to be understood some wasting disease such as Job's, the phrase being so used as a euphemism.

⁽¹⁴⁾ **His confidence shall be rooted out.**—Rather, *he shall be rooted out of his tent which he trusted was his own.*

The king of terrors.—Perhaps the most remarkable personification of unseen forces to be found in the Bible.

⁽¹⁵⁾ **It shall dwell in his tabernacle.**—Or, "There shall dwell in his tent they that are none of his," or "which is no longer his": *i.e.,* terrors shall dwell, or, "which is none of his" may hint that it had been violently taken from some one else. "Brimstone

(16) His roots shall be dried up beneath,
And above shall his branch be cut off.
(17)ᵃ His remembrance shall perish from the earth,
And he shall have no name in the street.
(18)¹ He shall be driven from light into darkness,
And chased out of the world.
(19) He shall neither have son nor nephew among his people,
Nor any remaining in his dwellings.
(20) They that come after *him* shall be astonied at his day,
As they that ²went before ³were affrighted.
(21) Surely such *are* the dwellings of the wicked,
And this *is* the place of *him that* knoweth not God.

CHAPTER XIX.—(1) Then Job answered and said,
(2) How long will ye vex my soul,
And break me in pieces with words?
(3) These ten times have ye reproached me:
Ye are not ashamed *that* ye ⁴make yourselves strange to me.
(4) And be it indeed *that* I have erred,
Mine error remaineth with myself.

(5) If indeed ye will magnify *yourselves* against me,
And plead against me my reproach:
(6) Know now that God hath overthrown me,
And hath compassed me with his net.
(7) Behold, I cry out of ⁵wrong, but I am not heard:
I cry aloud, but *there is* no judgment.
(8) He hath fenced up my way that I cannot pass,
And he hath set darkness in my paths.
(9) He hath stripped me of my glory,
And taken the crown *from* my head.
(10) He hath destroyed me on every side, and I am gone:
And mine hope hath he removed like a tree.
(11) He hath also kindled his wrath against me,
And he counteth me unto him as *one of* his enemies.
(12) His troops come together, and raise up their way against me,
And encamp round about my tabernacle.
(13) He hath put my brethren far from me,
And mine acquaintance are verily estranged from me.

ᵃ Prov. 2. 22.

¹ Heb., *They shall drive him.*

² Or, *lived with him.*

³ Heb., *laid hold on horror.*

⁴ Or, *harden yourselves against me.*

⁵ Or, *violence.*

---

shall be scattered on his dwelling" is probably an allusion to the cities of the plain (Gen. xix.).

(16) **His roots shall be dried up.**—With tacit allusion to what he had said in chap. viii. 12, and also to the destruction of Job's own offspring, which had already been accomplished.

(17) **His remembrance shall perish.**—This is the doom which above all others is dreaded by the modern roamers of the desert. (Comp. also Jer. xxxv. 19.)

(19) **He shall have neither son nor nephew.**—"He shall have neither his own son's son among his people, nor any remaining, where he sojourned."

(20) **Shall be astonied at his day.**—That is, his doom, or destiny. He shall stand forth as a warning and monument to all.

(21) **Dwellings of the wicked.**—That is to say, of the wicked man. As Bildad designedly uses the singular here, there can be little doubt that he as designedly intended this terrible and cruel picture to represent Job himself.

XIX.

(2) **How long?**—Job begins as Bildad himself had begun in both cases. His last speech had been so offensive and unfeeling that Job may well ask "How long will ye *vex my soul*, and break me in pieces with *words?*" Moreover, Bildad had infused a kind of personal malice into his charges, which Job felt most keenly, so that he is constrained to ask, "If indeed I have erred, doth not my error remain with myself? I alone suffer for it, and ye do not even sympathise or suffer with me."

(6) **Know now that God hath overthrown me.**—Bildad had spoken a great deal about the wicked being snared by his own sin, and now Job, without actually quoting his words—for he uses a word for *net* that Bildad had not used—speaks to their substance. It is *God* who has taken him in His net and compassed him about therewith. This is the assertion he has made before (chaps. xvi. 7, xiii. 27, &c.).

(7) **Behold I cry out of wrong.**—The description he now gives of himself as persecuted and forsaken by God is necessary to enhance the value of the confession he is about to make. Severely has God dealt with him, but that severity of dealing has only drawn him nearer to God and made him trust the more. He groups together a rich variety of figures to express his desolate condition. He is suffering assault, and can get no protection or redress; he is imprisoned on every side, his hope is torn up like the tree of which he had before spoken (chap. xiv. 7).

(11) **He hath also kindled . . .**—Comp. chap. xvi. 9, 12, &c.

(13) **He hath put my brethren far from me.**—The Psalmist has apparently copied this in Ps. lxxxviii. 8. The sense of human desertion is hardly less terrible than that of being forsaken by God, and this has been added to him. It is not easy to read these sad complaints of Job without seeing how fitly they apply to the sorrows of the Man of sorrows. Those who, with the present writer,

(14) My kinsfolk have failed,
And my familiar friends have forgotten me.
(15) They that dwell in mine house, and my maids,
Count me for a stranger: I am an alien in their sight.
(16) I called my servant, and he gave *me* no answer;
I intreated him with my mouth.
(17) My breath is strange to my wife,
Though I intreated for the children's sake of ¹mine own body.
(18) Yea, ²young children despised me;
I arose, and they spake against me.
(19) ᵃAll ³my inward friends abhorred me:
And they whom I loved are turned against me.
(20) My bone cleaveth to my skin ⁴and to my flesh,
And I am escaped with the skin of my teeth.
(21) Have pity upon me, have pity upon me, O ye my friends;
For the hand of God hath touched me.
(22) Why do ye persecute me as God,
And are not satisfied with my flesh?
(23) ⁵Oh that my words were now written!
Oh that they were printed in a book!
(24) That they were graven with an iron pen
And lead in the rock for ever!
(25) For I know *that* my redeemer liveth,

1 Heb., *my belly.*
2 Or, *the wicked.*
a Ps. 41. 9. & 55. 20.
3 Heb., *the men of my secret.*
4 Or, *as.*
5 Heb., *Who will give,* &c.

---

believe in the overruling presence of the Holy Ghost will adore His wisdom in this fitness; but at all events it shows how completely Christ entered into the very heart of human suffering, in that the deepest expressions of suffering inevitably remind us of Him, whether those expressions are met with in the Book of Job, in the Psalms of David, or in the Lamentations of Jeremiah.

(17) **Though I intreated for the children's sake of mine own body.**—Rather, *and so is my affection or kindness* (see Ps. lxxvii. 10, where the same word occurs) *to the children of my mother's womb, i.e., my brethren.* Others render, *I am become offensive to,* &c.

(19) **My inward friends.**—That is, *my intimate friends: the men of my counsel who are familiar with my secret affairs.*

(20) **My bone cleaveth to my skin and to my flesh** in one indistinguishable mass, and I have escaped with the skin of my teeth, because the teeth have no skin, or, as others explain, because the teeth have fallen out. This expression, which is by no means clear in the context, has passed into a proverb expressive of a very narrow escape—a meaning which can only by inference be obtained from this place in Job.

(21) **Have pity upon me.**—Now comes once more an exceeding great and bitter cry. (Comp. chap. xvi. 20.)

(22) **Why do ye persecute me as God?**—Comp. chap. xvi. 9.

(23) **Oh that my words were now written!**—Some understand this to refer to the words he is about to utter; by others they are interpreted generally. The former view is probably owing to the Christian acceptation given to them, and the consequently great importance attaching to them. Since, however, the three verses, 25—27, are manifestly more emphatic than any he has yet spoken, though they do not stand quite alone, there is no reason why it should not be especially these very words which he desires more than any others to have recorded. Perhaps the "now"=*here* shows this.

Oh that they were printed.—This points us to primitive time, when writing materials and the use of writing involved more or less of *engraving,* as, for instance, in later times was the case with tablets of wax.

(25) **For I know that my redeemer liveth.**—We must carefully note all the passages which lead up to this one. First, we must bear in mind that Bildad (chap. xviii. 17—20) had threatened Job with the extinction of his *name and memory,* so he now appeals to the verdict of futurity, and with what success we ourselves who read and repeat and discuss his words are witnesses. Then in Job's own speeches we have, as early as chap. ix. 32—35. his longing for *a daysman* to come between himself and God. Then in chaps. x. 7, xiii. 15—19, he emphatically declares his innocence, and appeals to God as conscious of it. In chap. xvi. 19, he affirms that his *witness is in the high heavens;* in verse 21 of the same chapter he longs for an *advocate* to plead his cause. In chap. xvii. 3 he calls upon God to *be surety for him.* Therefore he has already recognised God as his *judge,* his *umpire,* his *advocate,* his *witness,* and *surety,* and in some cases by formal confession of the fact, in others by earnest longing after and aspirations for some one to act in that capacity. Here, then, he goes a step further in expression, if not by implication, and declares his knowledge that he has a *Goel* or Redeemer. This *goel* was the name given to the next of kin whose duty it was to redeem, ransom, or avenge one who had fallen into debt or bondage, or had been slain in a family feud. In Ruth, for instance, the goel is he who has to marry the widow of his relative, and to continue his name. The various and conditional functions, then, of this *Goel,* Job is assured, God will take upon Himself for him; He will avenge his quarrel (comp. Ps. xxxv. 1, 23), He will be surety for him. He will vindicate him before men and before God Himself; He will do for him what none of his professed friends would undertake to do. And as to this matter, he has not the slightest doubt: he states most emphatically that he himself *knows* that this *Goel* liveth. "And I, even I know; as for me, I know that my Vindicator is living, that He liveth, is a reality existing now, and not one to come into existence hereafter, though His manifestation may be a thing of the future, for He shall stand at the last upon the earth," or, "He shall stand last upon earth" (comp. Isa. xl. 8), that is, after all others have passed away and gone down to the bars of the tomb. Now, this alone is assuredly a marvellous confession. It states the reality and eternity of God. It is faith in the *I am.* This same epithet of Redeemer is applied to God in Ps. xix. 15; Isa. lix. 20; in the former passage it is coupled with rock, which was the term Bildad had applied to God (chap. xviii. 4).

Faith in the Resurrection.   JOB, XX.   *Reply of Zophar.*

And *that* he shall stand at the latter day upon the earth:
(26) ¹And *though* after my skin *worms* destroy this *body*,
Yet in my flesh shall I see God:
(27) Whom I shall see for myself,
And mine eyes shall behold, and not ²another;
Though my reins be consumed ³within me.
(28) But ye should say, Why persecute we him,
⁴Seeing the root of the matter is found in me?
(29) Be ye afraid of the sword:
For wrath *bringeth* the punishments of the sword,
That ye may know *there is* a judgment.

CHAPTER XX.—(1) Then answered Zophar the Naamathite, and said,
(2) Therefore do my thoughts cause me to answer,
And for *this* ⁵I make haste.
(3) I have heard the check of my reproach,
And the spirit of my understanding causeth me to answer.
(4) Knowest thou *not* this of old, since man was placed upon earth,
(5) ªThat the triumphing of the wicked *is* ⁶short,
And the joy of the hypocrite *but* for a moment?
(6) Though his excellency mount up to the heavens,
And his head reach unto the ⁷clouds;
(7) Yet he shall perish for ever like his own dung:

¹ Or, *After I shall awake, though this body be destroyed, yet out of my flesh shall I see God.*
² Heb., *a stranger.*
³ Heb. *in my bosom.*
⁴ Or, *and what root of matter is found in me?*
⁵ Heb., *my haste is in me.*
ª Ps. 37. 35, 36.
⁶ Heb., *from near.*
⁷ Heb., *cloud.*

Upon the earth is literally, *upon dust*; the word is thus used in Job xli. 33. This usage of the same words in the same book, where the meaning is not ambiguous, is strongly against the rendering some have preferred: *over the dust*, or *over my dust*.

(26) **And though after my skin.**—The word *skin* is probably put by the common metonymy of a part for the whole for *body*. "After they have thus destroyed my skin," or "after my skin hath been thus destroyed"—or, "and after my skin hath been destroyed—this shall be: that even from my flesh I shall see God"—referring, probably, in the first instance, to his present personal faith, notwithstanding the corruption produced by his disease. "I can and do still *see* God, whom I know as my Redeemer;" but perhaps more probably put in contrast to this present knowledge as implying something yet to come, when the Redeemer stands at the last upon the earth, which also seems to be yet further expressed in the following verse.

(27) **My reins be consumed within me.**—*i.e.*, with longing to see Him; literally, *my reins are consumed in my bosom.* The words "in my flesh" may mean *from my flesh*, or, *without my flesh*. Taken in the former sense and applied to the future, it is hard not to recognise in them, at the least, some dim conception of a resurrection.

(27) **Whom I shall see for myself.**—The words "see for myself" may mean *see on my side, i.e.*, as my Judge and Avenger; or they may be the personal intensifying of the conviction which seems confirmed by the words, "and not a stranger." Do Job's words then teach the doctrine of the resurrection? Possibly not directly, but they express the firm conviction of that faith of which the resurrection is the only natural justification; they express a living trust in a living personal God, who, if He is to come into contact with man, cannot suffer His Holy One to see corruption nor leave His soul in hell. How far Job believed in the resurrection of the flesh hereafter, he certainly believed there was life out of death and through death here; and no man can believe in a living God and not believe that He must and will triumph over death. It is possible for us to believe in some dogma about the resurrection, and yet not believe in God. In this respect we shall be unlike Job. It is impossible for us to believe as he did and not be ready and thankful to believe in the resurrection of Christ, and of those who belong to Christ, as soon as the fact is proclaimed to us on sufficient authority. In this way, and for this reason, the confession of Job rightly stands at the head of the Christian Office for the Burial of the Dead, which looks forward to the resurrection, and lays fast hold thereon. Those who decline to see in Job's confession any knowledge or hope of a resurrection, must not forget that they have also to explain and account for Isaiah xxvi. 19.

(28) **Seeing the root of the matter.**—This verse is variously understood, according as "the root of the matter" is interpreted of the cause of suffering or the essence of piety. "For ye say, How we will persecute him, and that the root of the matter is found in me." The Authorised Version takes the other view. It seems preferable to render, "For ye say, What is a persecuted man to Him (why should He persecute any man without cause?), and therefore the root of the matter (*i.e.*, the cause of the afflictions) is, *i.e.*, must be found in me."

(29) **Be ye afraid . . .**—Job threatens his friends with that condign punishment of which they regarded him as a conspicuous example.

XX.

(1) **Then answered Zophar.**—Zophar retorts with yet greater vehemence than before, and assumes a more ornate and elaborate style, still reiterating the former burden of the speedy doom of the wicked man.

(2) **Therefore.**—That is, because of the eagerness that is in him. His spirit is stirred in him, and impels him to reply.

(3) **I have heard the check of my reproach.**—Rather, *I have heard*, or, *I hear the reproof of my shame*: that is, a reproof that puts me to shame, or is intended to do so.

The spirit of my understanding causeth me to answer.—Or, more literally, *Out of my understanding my spirit answereth me*, or *causeth me to answer.* He professes to be moved by an impulse within, which he cannot but obey.

(5) **The triumphing of the wicked is short.**—He affirms that the destruction of the wicked is not only certain, but speedy. (Comp. Ps. ciii. 16 and chap. vii. 8, 10.)

The State and Portion   JOB, XX.   *of the Wicked.*

They which have seen him shall say, Where *is* he?

(8) He shall fly away as a dream, and shall not be found:
Yea, he shall be chased away as a vision of the night.

(9) The eye also *which* saw him shall *see him* no more;
Neither shall his place any more behold him.

(10) ¹His children shall seek to please the poor,
And his hands shall restore their goods.

(11) His bones are full *of the sin* of his youth,
Which shall lie down with him in the dust.

(12) Though wickedness be sweet in his mouth,
Though he hide it under his tongue;

(13) *Though* he spare it, and forsake it not;
But keep it still ²within his mouth:

(14) *Yet* his meat in his bowels is turned,
It is the gall of asps within him.

(15) He hath swallowed down riches,
And he shall vomit them up again:
God shall cast them out of his belly.

(16) He shall suck the poison of asps:
The viper's tongue shall slay him.

(17) He shall not see the rivers,
³The floods, the brooks of honey and butter.

(18) That which he laboured for shall he restore,
And shall not swallow *it* down:
⁴According to *his* substance *shall* the restitution *be,*
And he shall not rejoice *therein.*

(19) Because he hath ⁵oppressed *and* hath forsaken the poor;
Because he hath violently taken away an house which he builded not;

(20) ᵃSurely he shall not ⁶feel quietness in his belly,
He shall not save of that which he desired.

(21) ⁷There shall none of his meat be left;
Therefore shall no man look for his goods.

(22) In the fulness of his sufficiency he shall be in straits:
Every hand of the ⁸wicked shall come upon him.

(23) When he is about to fill his belly,
God shall cast the fury of his wrath upon him,
And shall rain *it* upon him while he is eating.

(24) He shall flee from the iron weapon,
And the bow of steel shall strike him through.

(25) It is drawn, and cometh out of the body;
Yea, the glittering sword cometh out of his gall:

---

1 Or, *The poor shall oppress his children.*
2 Heb., *in the midst of his palate.*
3 Or, *streaming brooks.*
4 Heb., *according to the substance of his exchange.*
5 Heb., *crushed.*
a Eccles. 5. 13, 14.
6 Heb., *know.*
7 Or, *there shall be none left for his meat.*
8 Or, *troublesome.*

---

(10) **His children shall seek to please the poor.**—That is, shall seek their favour by making good what had been taken from them, or otherwise; or it may be rendered, *the poor shall oppress his children.*

(11) **His bones are full of the sin of his youth.**—Rather, *of his youth,* or *youthful vigour,* as in chap. xxxiii. 25: "He shall return to the days of his youth," and Ps. lxxxix. 46: "The days of his youth hast thou shortened." "Though he is in the full vigour of life, yet it shall lie down with him in the dust."

(12) **Though wickedness be sweet in his mouth.**—He draws a picture of the wicked man after the pattern of a gourmand or glutton, which, if it were intended to apply to Job, was a fresh instance of heartless cruelty, as well as of an entire want of discernment of character, and of unfitness for the office of judge he was so ready to assume. It is possible that the reproach here aimed at Job was that of inordinate love of riches, which Zophar extracts from the bare fact of his having been a wealthy man.

(17) **The brooks of honey and butter.**—He uses language which might lead one to suppose he was familiar with the promise of Canaan, except that, as the phrase is not precisely identical, it may perhaps rather show a community of proverbial language, and that the *land flowing with milk and honey* may have been an expression in use, and not one original with the Pentateuch.

(18) **That which he laboured for shall he restore** . . .—The latter part of this verse is probably right; but it may be, "According to the substance that he hath gotten he shall not rejoice."

(19) **Because he hath oppressed and forsaken** . . .—For these insinuations there was not a vestige of ground, but Job formally rebuts them in chap. xxxi.

(20) **Quietness in his belly.**—"Because he knew no quietness within him, (Comp. Isa. lvii. 20, 21.) he shall not save ought of that which he desireth."

(21) **There shall none of his meat be left.**—Rather, *There was nothing left that he devoured not, therefore his prosperity shall not endure.*

(22) **The hand of** every one that is in misery shall come upon him: *i.e.,* in retaliation, or possibly, but less probably, every blow of a miserable man, which can render a man miserable, shall come upon him.

(24) **He shall flee from the iron weapon, and.**—That is, if he escaped one mischance, another should overtake him.

(25) **Yea, terrors overtake him.**—Even when he has escaped a second and a third calamity, terrors shall still be upon him. This was all perfectly true in a sense, yea, even a truism, but it was utterly false in its application to Job himself.

The Portion of the Wicked.   JOB, XXI.   *Sometimes the Wicked Prosper.*

Terrors *are* upon him.
(26) All darkness *shall be* hid in his secret places:
A fire not blown shall consume him;
It shall go ill with him that is left in his tabernacle.
(27) The heaven shall reveal his iniquity;
And the earth shall rise up against him.
(28) The increase of his house shall depart,
And *his goods* shall flow away in the day of his wrath.
(29) This *is* the portion of a wicked man from God,
And the heritage ¹appointed unto him by God.

CHAPTER XXI.—(1) But Job answered and said,
(2) Hear diligently my speech,
And let this be your consolations.
(3) Suffer me that I may speak;
And after that I have spoken, mock on.
(4) As for me, *is* my complaint to man?
And if *it were so*, why should not my spirit be ²troubled?
(5) ³Mark me, and be astonished,
And lay *your* hand upon *your* mouth.
(6) Even when I remember I am afraid,
And trembling taketh hold on my flesh.
(7) ᵃWherefore do the wicked live,
Become old, yea, are mighty in power?
(8) Their seed is established in their sight with them,
And their offspring before their eyes.
(9) Their houses ⁴*are* safe from fear,
Neither *is* the rod of God upon them.
(10) Their bull gendereth, and faileth not;
Their cow calveth, and casteth not her calf.
(11) They send forth their little ones like a flock,
And their children dance.
(12) They take the timbrel and harp,
And rejoice at the sound of the organ.
(13) They spend their days ⁵in wealth,
And in a moment go down to the grave.
(14) ᵇTherefore they say unto God, Depart from us;
For we desire not the knowledge of thy ways.
(15) What *is* the Almighty, that we should serve him?
And what profit should we have, if we pray unto him?
(16) Lo, their good *is* not in their hand:
The counsel of the wicked is far from me.

¹ Heb., *of his decree from God.*
² Heb., *shortened?*
³ Heb., *Look unto me.*
ᵃ Ps. 17. 10 & 73. 12; Jer. 12. 1; Hab. 1. 16.
⁴ Heb., *are peace from fear.*
⁵ Or, *in mirth.*
ᵇ ch. 22. 17.

---

(26) **All darkness shall be hid in his secret places.**—Rather, *All darkness, every kind of disaster, is laid up for his secret treasures.*
A fire not blown.—By human hands, &c.
(27) **The heaven shall reveal his iniquity.**—All nature shall combine to bring about his ruin, which is, in fact, decreed by God. We here take leave of Zophar, who does not reply again; he has exhausted himself, notwithstanding verse 2.

XXI.

(1) **But Job answered.**—Having, in chap. xix., declared his belief in a retribution to come, Job now proceeds to traverse more directly Zophar's last contention, and to show that even in this life there is not the retribution which he maintained there was.

(2) **Hear diligently my speech.**—"Listen to my words, and let *that* be the consolation you give me."

(4) **Is my complaint to man?**—"It is not to man that I complain. I do not ask for your sympathy, and, therefore, why should ye resent an offence that is not given? If, however, I did ask it, might not my spirit with good reason be impatient? But, on the contrary, my complaint is to God; and, concerning the ways of God, I venture to ask why it is that His justice is so tardy; and this is a problem which when I remember it I am troubled, and horror taketh hold on my flesh, so difficult and arduous is it."

(8) **Their seed is established in their sight.**—Not only are they mighty in power themselves, but they leave their power to their children after them (comp. Ps. xvii. 14). This contradicts what Eliphaz had said (chap. xv. 34), what Bildad had said (chap. xviii. 19), and what Zophar had said (chap. xx. 10).

(9) **Their houses are safe from fear.**—On the contrary, Zophar had just said that "a fire not blown should consume him" (chap. xx. 26), and Bildad (in chap. xviii. 15) that "destruction should dwell in his tabernacle, and brimstone be scattered on his habitation."

(11, 12) **They send forth their little ones . . .**—In striking contrast to the fate of Job's own children, and in contradiction to what Eliphaz had said (chap. xv. 29—33).

(13) **In a moment.**—They go down to death without being made to feel the lingering tortures that Job had to undergo.

(14) **Therefore they say unto God.**—Should be, *Yet they said unto God, Depart from us,* &c.

(16) **Lo, their good** (*i.e.*, their prosperity) **is not in their own hand.**—And that constitutes the mystery of it; for it is God who gives it to them; or the words may be a hypothetical answer to his statement, thus, "Lo, thou repliest, their prosperity is not," &c.; and then the words, "the counsel of the wicked is far from me," are Job's indignant repudiation of all knowledge of their reasoning.

(17) How oft is the ¹candle of the wicked put out!
And *how oft* cometh their destruction upon them!
God distributeth sorrows in his anger.
(18) They are as stubble before the wind,
And as chaff that the storm ²carrieth away.
(19) God layeth up ³his iniquity for his children:
He rewardeth him, and he shall know *it*.
(20) His eyes shall see his destruction,
And he shall drink of the wrath of the Almighty.
(21) For what pleasure *hath* he in his house after him,
When the number of his months is cut off in the midst?
(22) Shall *any* teach God knowledge?
Seeing he judgeth those that are high.
(23) One dieth ⁴in his full strength,—being wholly at ease and quiet.
(24) His ⁵breasts are full of milk,
And his bones are moistened with marrow.
(25) And another dieth in the bitterness of his soul,
And never eateth with pleasure.
(26) They shall lie down alike in the dust,
And the worms shall cover them.
(27) Behold, I know your thoughts,
And the devices *which* ye wrongfully imagine against me.
(28) For ye say, Where *is* the house of the prince?
And where *are* ⁶the dwelling places of the wicked?
(29) Have ye not asked them that go by the way?
And do ye not know their tokens,
(30) ᵃThat the wicked is reserved to the day of destruction?
They shall be brought forth to ⁷the day of wrath.
(31) Who shall declare his way to his face?
And who shall repay him *what* he hath done?
(32) Yet shall he be brought to the ⁸grave,
And shall ⁹remain in the tomb.
(33) The clods of the valley shall be sweet unto him,
And every man shall draw after him,
As *there are* innumerable before him.
(34) How then comfort ye me in vain,
Seeing in your answers there remaineth ¹⁰falsehood?

1 Or, *lamp*.
2 Heb., *stealeth away*.
3 That is, *the punishment of his iniquity*.
4 Heb., *in his very perfection, or, in the strength of his perfection*.
5 Or, *milk pails*.
6 Heb., *the tent of the tabernacles of the wicked?*
a Prov. 16. 4.
7 Heb., *the day of wraths*.
8 Heb., *graves*.
9 Heb., *watch in the heap*.
10 Heb., *transgression?*

(17) **How oft is the candle of the wicked put out?**—This and the following verse are either a concession on the part of Job, as much as to say, "I admit that it is as you say with the wicked;" or else they should be read interrogatively, "How often is it that we do see this?"

(19) **God layeth up his iniquity** (*i.e.,* the punishment of it) **for his children,** may be the hypothetical reply of the antagonists in the mouth of Job, and the second clause his own retort: "Let him repay it to himself that he may know it."

(20) **His eyes shall see his destruction.**—This may be understood as the continuation of Job's suggested amendment of the Divine government. "His own eyes should see his destruction, and he should drink of the wrath, &c. For what concern or interest hath he in his house after him when the number of his months is cut off, &c."

(22) **Shall any teach God knowledge?** may be regarded as the hypothetical reply of the antagonist. If the reader prefers to understand these latter verses in any other way, it is open to him to do so, but in our judgment it seems better to understand them thus. The supposed alternative hypothetical argument seems to throw much light upon them.

(23) **One dieth.**—Job enlarges on the inequality of human fate, showing that death is the only equaliser.

(24) **His breasts.**—This is an uncertain word, occurring only here. Some understand it literally of *milk-pails,* others of the lacteals of the human body, which certainly suits the parallelism better.

(26) **They shall lie down alike in the dust.**—Not only, therefore, is the inequality of their life a stumbling-block, but so also is the equality which obliterates all distinction between them in death.

(28) **Of the prince**—*i.e., of the generous, virtuous, princely man?*—the antithesis to the wicked man. "Behold I know your thoughts, for ye say, How can we tell who is virtuous and who is wicked? and consequently we know not to which catalogue you belong." They had all along been insinuating that, though he seemed to be righteous, he was really wicked.

(29) **Their tokens**—*i.e., the marks and evidences of their experience, and the conclusions at which they had arrived.*

(30—33) **That the wicked. . . .**—These verses contain the result of their experience.

(32) **And shall remain in the tomb.**—The word rendered tomb is rendered *shock of corn* in chap. v. 26, and is not found in the sense of tomb elsewhere. It is doubtful, therefore, whether this is its meaning here. The verse may mean: "He shall be borne to the grave, and men shall watch over his sheaves," *i.e.,* his possessions; or "He shall be borne to the grave with as much deference as when he used to watch over his sheaves" (to protect them from robbery).

(33) **The clods of the valley shall be sweet unto him.**—Death is robbed of its repulsiveness and horror, seeing that all will be glad to join in his funeral procession, and after him all men will draw (in endless procession), and before him they will be without number.

(34) **There remaineth falsehood.**—Or, *all that is left of them is transgression,* that is to say, it is not only worthless, but yet more, it is even harmful and wrong.

The Answer of Eliphaz.   JOB, XXII.   *His Accusation of Job.*

CHAPTER XXII.—⁽¹⁾ Then Eliphaz the Temanite answered and said,
⁽²⁾ Can a man be profitable unto God,
   ¹ As he that is wise may be profitable unto himself?
⁽³⁾ *Is it* any pleasure to the Almighty, that thou art righteous?
   Or *is it* gain *to him*, that thou makest thy ways perfect?
⁽⁴⁾ Will he reprove thee for fear of thee?
   Will he enter with thee into judgment?
⁽⁵⁾ *Is* not thy wickedness great?—and thine iniquities infinite?
⁽⁶⁾ For thou hast taken a pledge from thy brother for nought,
   And ² stripped the naked of their clothing.
⁽⁷⁾ Thou hast not given water to the weary to drink,
   And thou hast withholden bread from the hungry.
⁽⁸⁾ But *as for* ³ the mighty man, he had the earth;
   And the ⁴ honourable man dwelt in it.
⁽⁹⁾ Thou hast sent widows away empty,
   And the arms of the fatherless have been broken.
⁽¹⁰⁾ Therefore snares *are* round about thee,
   And sudden fear troubleth thee;
⁽¹¹⁾ Or, darkness, *that* thou canst not see;
   And abundance of waters cover thee.
⁽¹²⁾ *Is* not God in the height of heaven?
   And behold ⁵ the height of the stars, how high they are!
⁽¹³⁾ And thou sayest, ⁶ How doth God know?
   Can he judge through the dark cloud?
⁽¹⁴⁾ Thick clouds *are* a covering to him, that he seeth not;
   And he walketh in the circuit of heaven.
⁽¹⁵⁾ Hast thou marked the old way— which wicked men have trodden?
⁽¹⁶⁾ Which were cut down out of time,
   ⁷ Whose foundation was overflown with a flood:
⁽¹⁷⁾ ^a Which said unto God, Depart from us:
   And what can the Almighty do ⁸ for them?
⁽¹⁸⁾ Yet he filled their houses with good *things*:
   But ^b the counsel of the wicked is far from me,
⁽¹⁹⁾ ^c The righteous see *it*, and are glad:
   And the innocent laugh them to scorn.

Marginal notes:
1 Or, *if he may be profitable*, doth his *good success* depend *thereon?*
2 Heb., *stripped the clothes of the naked.*
3 Heb., *the man of arm.*
4 Heb., *eminent, or, accepted for countenance.*
5 Heb., *the head of the stars.*
6 Or, *what.*
7 Heb., *a flood was poured upon their foundation.*
a ch. 21. 14.
8 Or, *to them?*
b ch. 21. 16.
c Ps. 107. 42.

XXII.

⁽¹⁾ **Then answered Eliphaz.**—Eliphaz proceeds to reply in a far more exaggerated and offensive tone than he has yet adopted, accusing Job of definite and specific crimes. He begins by asserting that the judgment of God cannot be other than disinterested, that if, therefore, He rewards or punishes, there cannot be anything personal in it.

⁽²⁾ **As he that is wise.**—It is probably an independent statement: "Surely he that is wise is profitable, &c."

⁽⁴⁾ **Will he reprove thee.**—That is, *Because He standeth in awe of thee. Will He justify his dealings with thee?*

⁽⁵⁾ **Is not thy wickedness great?**—This was mere conjecture and surmise, arising simply from a false assumption: namely, that a just God can only punish the wicked, and that therefore those must be wicked whom He punishes.

⁽⁶⁾ **Thou hast taken a pledge from thy brother.**—These specific charges, false as they were, show the depth to which Eliphaz had sunk.

⁽⁸⁾ **But as for the mighty man.**—By the "mighty and the honourable" man is probably meant Job. Some understand the words from verses 5—10 inclusive, as the words spoken by God on entering into judgment with Job (verse 4); but this hardly seems probable.

^(10, 11) **Snares . . . about thee.**—That is, *Fear troubleth thee, or darkness, &c.* "If darkness and abundance of waters cover thee so that thou canst not see, is not God in the high heavens, though thou canst not see Him. God is too great to take note of the affairs of men, their sin or their good deeds. He is so far off that He cannot see what goes on in the earth, for His dwelling-place is in heaven." Eliphaz attributes to Job the kind of sentiments that he had himself attributed to the wicked man in the last chapter, verse 14, &c.

⁽¹⁵⁾ **Hast thou marked the old way. . . ?**—Rather, *Dost thou keep the old way which the wicked men trod? Dost thou hold their tenets?*

⁽¹⁶⁾ **Which were cut down out of time.**—Or, *which were snatched away before their time.* It is generally supposed that there is an allusion here to the history of the Flood; if so, the reference is of course very important in its bearing on the age of that record, since the Book of Job can hardly fail to be very old itself.

Whose foundation was overflown with a flood.—Or, *upon whose foundation a stream was poured out;* or, *whose foundation became as a flowing stream;* or, *whose foundation is like a flowing stream:* that is, their principles are infectious, and bear all before them.

⁽¹⁷⁾ **Which said unto God, Depart from us.**—Here again he attributes to Job the very thoughts he had ascribed to the wicked (chap. xx. 14, 15).

⁽¹⁸⁾ **Yet he filled their houses.**—The bitterness of his irony now reaches its climax in that he adopts the very formula of repudiation Job had himself used (chap. xiv. 16).

⁽¹⁹⁾ **The righteous see it.**—That is, *the destruction of the wicked, as in the days of Noah.*

(20) Whereas ¹our substance is not cut down,
But ²the remnant of them the fire consumeth.
(21) Acquaint now thyself ³with him, and be at peace:
Thereby good shall come unto thee.
(22) Receive, I pray thee, the law from his mouth,
And lay up his words in thine heart.
(23) ᵃIf thou return to the Almighty, thou shalt be built up,
Thou shalt put away iniquity far from thy tabernacles.
(24) Then shalt thou lay up gold ⁴as dust,
And the *gold* of Ophir as the stones of the brooks.
(25) Yea, the Almighty shall be thy ⁵defence,
And thou shalt have ⁶plenty of silver.
(26) For then shalt thou have thy delight in the Almighty,
And shalt lift up thy face unto God.
(27) Thou shalt make thy prayer unto him,
And he shall hear thee, and thou shalt pay thy vows.
(28) Thou shalt also decree a thing, and it shall be established unto thee:
And the light shall shine upon thy ways.
(29) When *men* are cast down, then thou shalt say, There *is* lifting up;
And he shall save ⁷the humble person.
(30) ⁸He shall deliver the island of the innocent:
And it is delivered by the pureness of thine hands.

CHAPTER XXIII.— (1) Then Job answered and said,

Marginal notes:
1 Or, *estate.*
2 Or, *their excellency.*
3 That is, *with God.*
a ch. 8. 5.
4 Or, *on the dust.*
5 Or, *gold.*
6 Heb., *silver of strength.*
7 Heb., *him that hath low eyes.*
8 Or, *the innocent shall deliver the island.*

---

(20) **Whereas our substance . . .**—These are probably the words of the righteous and the innocent: "Surely they that did rise up against us are cut off, and the remnant of them the fire hath consumed." The rendering in the Authorised Version is probably less correct, though in that also these words seem to be those of the innocent in verse 19.

(21) **Acquaint now thyself with him.**—As he himself had done in chap. v., and as Zophar had done in chap. xi., Eliphaz proceeds to give Job some good advice. "Thereby good shall come unto thee," or "Thereby shall thine increase be good;" or perhaps he means that peace and rest from the obstinate questionings he was disturbed with would come to him thereby.

(22) **The law from his mouth.**—It would be highly interesting to know whether by this *law* (Torah), the Law, the Torah, was in any way alluded to. One is naturally disposed to think that since Job seems to be the one Gentile book of the Old Testament, the one book in which the literature of Israel touches the world at large, it must, therefore, be prior to the Law, or else have been written in independence and ignorance of it. The former seems by far the more reasonable supposition, and certainly the life depicted appears to be that of the patriarchal times before the giving of the Law. And yet, on the other hand, it is hard to know what could be meant by "His words" prior to the Mosaic Revelation, unless, indeed, the expression is a witness to the consciousness of that inner revelation of the voice of God in the conscience which the holy in all ages have never wanted.

(23) **Thou shalt put away iniquity.**—All this implies the imputation of apostasy and iniquity to Job.

(24) **The gold of Ophir.**—And, moreover, that the wealth for which he was so famous among the children of the East was the accumulation of iniquity and wrong-doing. The sense probably is, "Put thy treasure on a level with the dust, and the gold of Ophir among the stones of the brooks": that is, reckon it of no more value than such stones; do not set thine heart upon it. The situation of Ophir has always been a matter of dispute. Josephus placed it in India (*Antt.* viii. 6, § 4), as do some moderns; others suppose it to have been an Indian colony in Southern Arabia, and others have placed it on the east coast of Africa.

(25) **The Almighty shall be thy defence.**—Rather, And the Almighty shall be thy treasure, and precious silver unto thee. The word thus qualifying silver occurs only three other times in the Bible: Ps. xcv. 4, "The *strength* of the hills"; Num. xxii. 23 and 24, "the *strength* of a unicorn." Its original idea is probably brightness or splendour.

(26) **Then shalt thou have thy delight in the Almighty.**—Zophar had told him the same thing, that he should lift up his face *without spot* (chap. xi. 15).

(28) **Thou shalt also decree a thing.**—As, for instance, in the memorable case of Abraham's intercession for Sodom, to which there is not improbably an allusion here.

(29) **There is lifting up.**—This may be its meaning, but some understand it in a bad sense: "When men are cast down, then thou shalt say, It was pride that caused their fall."

(30) **He shall deliver the island of the innocent** is undoubtedly an error for *He shall deliver him that is not innocent*: that is, either God shall deliver, or the humble person, if that is the subject of the former clause; the humble-minded man would have saved them. "He would have delivered him that is not innocent; yea, even so shall he be delivered by the cleanness of thy hands," as the ten righteous would have saved Sodom. It is remarkable that this, which is the last word of Eliphaz, has in it the significance of a prophecy, for it is exactly thus that the history of Job closes; and Eliphaz himself exemplified his own promise in being indebted to Job for the act of intercession by which he was pardoned, together with his friends; chap. xlii. 8, 9.

XXIII.

(1) **Then Job answered.**—Job replies to the insinuations of Eliphaz with the earnest longing after God and the assertion of his own innocence; while in the twenty-fourth chapter he laments that his own case is but one of many, and that multitudes suffer from the oppression of man unavenged, as he suffers from the stroke of God.

Job's Longing to Appear before God. JOB, XXIII. *He declares his Innocence.*

(2) Even' to day *is* my complaint bitter:
¹My stroke is heavier than my groaning.
(3) Oh that I knew where I might find him!
That I might come *even* to his seat!
(4) I would order *my* cause before him,
And fill my mouth with arguments.
(5) I would know the words *which* he would answer me,
And understand what he would say unto me.
(6) Will he plead against me with *his* great power?
No; but he would put *strength* in me.
(7) There the righteous might dispute with him;
So should I be delivered for ever from my judge.
(8) Behold, I go forward, but he *is* not there;
And backward, but I cannot perceive him:
(9) On the left hand, where he doth work, but I cannot behold *him:*
He hideth himself on the right hand, that I cannot see *him*:
(10) But he knoweth ²the way that I take:
When he hath tried me, I shall come forth as gold.
(11) My foot hath held his steps,
His way have I kept, and not declined.
(12) Neither have I gone back from the commandment of his lips;
³I have esteemed the words of his mouth more than ⁴my necessary *food*.
(13) But he *is* in one *mind,* and who can turn him?
And *what* ᵃhis soul desireth, even *that* he doeth.
(14) For he performeth *the thing that is* appointed for me:
And many such *things are* with him.
(15) Therefore am I troubled at his presence:
When I consider, I am afraid of him.
(16) For God maketh my heart soft,—and the Almighty troubleth me:
(17) Because I was not cut off before the darkness,
Neither hath he covered' the darkness from my face.

1 Heb., *my hand.*

2 Heb., *the way that is with me.*

3 Heb., *I have hid, or, laid up.*

4 Or, *my appointed portion.*

ᵃ Ps 115. 3.

---

(2) **Even to day.**—Or, *Still is my complaint bitter or accounted rebellion; yet is my stroke heavier than my groaning: my complaint is no just measure of my suffering.*

(3) **Oh that I knew where I might find him.**—The piteous complaint of a man who feels that God is with him for chastisement, but not for healing.

(6) **Plead against me.**—Rather, *Would he plead with me,* or *contend with me in the greatness of his power? Nay; but he would have regard unto me; he would consider my case.* Eliphaz had bidden Job to acquaint himself with God, and return unto Him (chap. xxii. 23); Job says there is nothing he longs for more than to come into His presence.

(7) **There the righteous might dispute.**—He has learnt this marvellous truth, which the Gospel has so effectually brought to light, that it is God the Saviour who is Himself the refuge from God the Judge (John xii. 47); and then, in the solemn conviction of His presence, he makes use of the most sublime language expressive of it, being assured, though He may hide Himself with the express purpose of not interfering in his cause, yet that all things work together for good to them that love Him (Rom. viii. 28), and that when his time of trial is over, he himself will come forth like gold. Job's case teaches us that if an innocent man is falsely accused, God's honour is vindicated and maintained by his holding fast his conviction of innocence rather than by his yielding to the pressure of adversity and owning to sins he has not committed, or relaxing his hold on innocence by yielding to irritability.

(12) **I have esteemed the words of his mouth more than my necessary food.**—Comp. John iv. 32—34. Or, *I have treasured up the words, &c., according to the statute prescribed to me,* or *from my own law:* i.e., "I made it a principle with myself to treasure up the words of His mouth." The LXX. and the Vulg. have a differing reading, and render *in my bosom.*

(13) **He is one, or in one.**—Job either declares His unique sovereignty or His unchangeable purpose. The context seems to support the latter, in which case the sense given by the Authorised Version is correct.

(14) **He performeth the thing that is appointed for me.**—"He will accomplish my appointed lot; He will complete that which He has decreed for me; and like these things there are many (more) with Him" (chap. x. 13). Job is disposed to take the full measure of the worst, like a pessimist, that being steeled against it, he may be prepared; and so steeled, he still trusts God. (Comp. chap. xiii. 15, Authorised Version.)

(15) **Therefore am I troubled at his presence.**—i.e., invisible though it be, and undiscoverable as He is on every hand (verses 8, 9), Job is in a strait betwixt two (Phil. i. 23). The victim of an ever present paradox and dilemma; afraid of God, yet longing to see Him; conscious of His presence, yet unable to find Him; assured of His absolute justice, and yet convinced of his own suffering innocence. His history, in fact, to the Old World was what the Gospel is to the New: the exhibition of a perfectly righteous man, yet made perfect through suffering. It was therefore an effort at the solution of the problem of the reconciliation of the inequality of life with the justice of God.

(16) **For God maketh my heart soft.**—That is, "He has made it full of apprehension and fear, and the Almighty hath troubled me in these two respects: that He did not cut me off before the darkness, so that I had never been born, or that He did not hide darkness from mine eyes after giving me life." (Comp. chap. iii.

CHAPTER XXIV.—⁽¹⁾ Why, seeing times are not hidden from the Almighty,
Do they that know him not see his days?
⁽²⁾ *Some* remove the ᵃlandmarks;
They violently take away flocks, and ¹feed *thereof*.
⁽³⁾ They drive away the ass of the fatherless,
They take the widow's ox for a pledge.
⁽⁴⁾ They turn the needy out of the way:
The poor of the earth hide themselves together.
⁽⁵⁾ Behold, *as* wild asses in the desert,
Go they forth to their work; rising betimes for a prey:
The wilderness *yieldeth* food for them and for *their* children.
⁽⁶⁾ They reap *every one* his ²corn in the field:
And ³they gather the vintage of the wicked.
⁽⁷⁾ They cause the naked to lodge without clothing,
That *they have* no covering in the cold.

ᵃ Deu. 19. 14 & 27. 17.

1 Or, *feed them*.

2 Heb., *mingled corn*, or, *dredge*.

3 Heb., *the wicked gather the vintage*.

⁽⁸⁾ They are wet with the showers of the mountains,
And embrace the rock for want of a shelter.
⁽⁹⁾ They pluck the fatherless from the breast,
And take a pledge of the poor.
⁽¹⁰⁾ They cause *him* to go naked without clothing,
And they take away the sheaf *from* the hungry:
⁽¹¹⁾ *Which* make oil within their walls,
And tread *their* winepresses, and suffer thirst.
⁽¹²⁾ Men groan from out of the city,
And the soul of the wounded crieth out:
Yet God layeth not folly *to them*.
⁽¹³⁾ They are of those that rebel against the light;
They know not the ways thereof,
Nor abide in the paths thereof.
⁽¹⁴⁾ The murderer rising with the light—killeth the poor and needy,
And in the night is as a thief.
⁽¹⁵⁾ The eye also of the adulterer waiteth for the twilight,

11, 20, &c.) We may understand this of the physical suffering to which he was subjected, or of the mental distress and perplexity under which he laboured.

XXIV.

⁽¹⁾ **Why, seeing times are not hidden.**—Job, in this chapter, gives utterance to this perplexity, as it arises, not from his own case only, but from a survey of God's dealings with the world generally. "Why is it," he asks, "since times and events are not hidden from the Almighty, that they who know Him—that is, believe in and love Him—do not see His days?"—that is, His days of retribution and judgment. Even those who love and serve God are as perplexed about His principles of government as those who know Him not. It is to be observed that the position of the second negative in the Authorised Version of this verse renders it highly ambiguous to the majority of readers. This ambiguity would entirely disappear if we read *see not* instead of "not see."

⁽²⁾ **Some remove the landmarks.**—Now follows a description of the wrong-doings of various classes of men. The removal of landmarks was expressly provided against by the Mosaic Law (Deut. xix. 14, xxvii. 17).

And feed thereof.—Rather, probably, *feed them*: *i.e.,* pasture them, the more easy to do when the landmarks are so removed.

⁽³⁾ **They drive away the ass.**—The ass and the ox, the fatherless and the widow presumably having no more than one. He first describes the oppression of the country, and then that of the city (verse 12). We seem here to catch a glimpse of the sufferings of some oppressed and subject aboriginal race, such as the Canaanites may have been to the Jews, though there is probably no allusion to them. But, at all events, the writer and the speaker seem to have been familiar with some abject and servile race, who haunted the desert and suffered at the hands of the more powerful tribes. Man's inhumanity to man is, unhappily, a crime of very long standing.

⁽⁶⁾ **They reap every one his corn.**—Or, probably, *the corn*, that is, *of the wicked tyrant*. While they reap his corn and cut his provender, they have to go without themselves.

⁽¹⁰⁾ **They cause him to go naked without clothing.**—Rather, *they go about*, or, *so that they go about, naked without clothing* (the tautology is expressive in Hebrew, though meaningless in English), *and an hungered they carry the sheaves*.

⁽¹²⁾ **Men groan from out of the city.**—Here a survey of the oppressions wrought within the city walls is taken.

Yet God layeth not folly to them.—That is, to those who are the cause of their wrongs, their oppressors.

⁽¹³⁾ **They are of those that rebel against the light.**—A very remarkable expression, which seems to anticipate the teaching of St. John (chap. i. 9, &c.).

⁽¹⁴⁾ **With the light.**—The mention of light as a moral essence suggests its physical analogue, so that by the contrast of the one with the violence done to the other, the moral turpitude of the wrong-doing is heightened. It seems impossible to interpret the light in the former case (verse 13) otherwise than morally, and if so, the mention of the "ways thereof" and the "paths thereof" is very remarkable. The order in which these crimes of murder, adultery, and theft are mentioned according, as it does, with that in the *Decalogue*, is, at all events, suggestive of acquaintance with it.

There is a Secret Judgment   JOB, XXV.   *for the Wicked.*

Saying, No eye shall see me: and ¹disguiseth *his* face.

⁽¹⁶⁾ In the dark they dig through houses, *Which* they had marked for themselves in the daytime:
They know not the light.

⁽¹⁷⁾ For the morning *is* to them even as the shadow of death:
If *one* know *them, they are* in the terrors of the shadow of death.

⁽¹⁸⁾ He *is* swift as the waters;—their portion is cursed in the earth:
He beholdeth not the way of the vineyards.

⁽¹⁹⁾ Drought and heat ²consume the snow waters:
So doth the grave *those which* have sinned.

⁽²⁰⁾ The womb shall forget him;
The worm shall feed sweetly on him;
He shall be no more remembered;
And wickedness shall be broken as a tree.

⁽²¹⁾ He evil entreateth the barren *that* beareth not:
And doeth not good to the widow.

⁽²²⁾ He draweth also the mighty with his power:
He riseth up, ³and no *man* is sure of life.

⁽²³⁾ *Though* it be given him *to be* in safety, whereon he resteth;
Yet his eyes *are* upon their ways.

⁽²⁴⁾ They are exalted for a little while,
But ⁴are gone and brought low;
They are ⁵taken out of the way as all *other,*
And cut off as the tops of the ears of corn.

⁽²⁵⁾ And if *it be* not *so* now, who will make me a liar,
And make my speech nothing worth?

CHAPTER XXV.—⁽¹⁾ Then answered Bildad the Shuhite, and said,
⁽²⁾ Dominion and fear *are* with him,

---

1 Heb., *setteth his face in secret.*
2 Heb., *violently take.*
3 Or, *he trusteth not his own life.*
4 Heb., *are not.*
5 Heb., *closed up.*

⁽¹⁶⁾ **Which they had marked for themselves in the daytime.**—Or, as some understand, *they seal* (*i.e.*, *shut*) *themselves up in the daytime*. It is said that it is still the custom in Eastern cities for such persons to endeavour to obtain access to the harem in female attire.

They know not the light.—Compared with verse 13, shows strongly the different usage of the expression in the two cases.

⁽¹⁸⁾ **He is swift.**—That is—each of these rebels against the light *is swift to make his escape over the face of the waters.* So we ought to read it, and not, with Authorised Version, as a comparison.

Their portion is cursed in the earth.—That is, *men so regard it;* it has an evil name, and is of bad repute.

He beholdeth not.—Rather, *he*—that is, each of them—*turneth not the way of the vineyards,* which is frequented and cultivated, but chooseth rather lone, desolate, solitary, and rugged paths.

⁽¹⁹⁾ **So doth the grave those which have sinned.**—Job had already spoken of the sudden death of the wicked as a blessing (chaps. ix. 23, xxi. 13), as compared with the lingering torture he himself was called upon to undergo.

⁽²⁰⁾ **The womb shall forget him.**—Some understand this verse as expressing what *ought* rather to be the doom of the wicked. "His own mother *should* forget him; the worm should feed sweetly on him; he should be no more remembered; and *then* unrighteousness would be broken as a tree."

⁽²²⁾ **He draweth also the mighty.**—He now appears to revert to his former line, and describes another case—that, namely, of a great tyrant who draws others by his influence and example to the same courses.

He riseth up, and no man is sure of his life.—Being so completely under his sway.

⁽²³⁾ **Though it be given.**—"Yea, he, that is each of them, giveth him tribute, &c., that he may be secure and stable."

Yet his eyes—that is, the great tyrant's eyes—**are upon their ways.**—They are exalted for a little while, but are soon gone, and are taken out of the way like all others. Some understand the subject of the first verb, "he giveth him to be in security," to be God, and that also makes very good sense, for while God so allows him to be secure, His eyes are on their ways, the ways of all of them. In this case, however, verse 24 does not correspond so well with what Job has already said of the impunity with which the wicked are wicked, unless indeed the *suddenness* of their fate is the main point of his remarks, as in verse 19.

⁽²⁵⁾ **And if it be not so now.**—Job also has his facts, as ready and as incontrovertible as those of his friends, and yet irreconcilable with theirs.

XXV.

⁽¹⁾ **Then answered Bildad.**—Bildad attempts no formal reply to Job's statements, he merely falls back upon the position twice assumed by Eliphaz before (chaps. iv. 17—21 and xv. 14—16), and twice allowed also by Job (chap. xiv. 4)—the impossibility of man being just with God—and therefore implies the impiety of Job in maintaining his righteousness before God. God, he says, is almighty, infinite, and absolute. How can any man contend with Him, or claim to be pure in His sight? This is the final speech of the friends. Bildad no longer accuses Job; he practically owns himself and his companions worsted in argument, seeing that he attempts no reply, but reiterates truisms that are independent of the special matter in hand. Job, in chap. xxiii. 3—12, had spoken of his longing for the Divine judgment; so Bildad labours to deprive him of that confidence, as though he would say, "I have nothing to do with your facts, nor can I explain them; but be that as it may, I am certain that you, or any mortal man, cannot be pure in the sight of God."

⁽²⁾ **Dominion and fear are with him.**—He is absolute in sovereignty and terrible in power, so that

45

Bildad's Objection. JOB, XXVI. *Job's Answer to him.*

He maketh peace in his high places.
(3) Is there any number of his armies?
And upon whom doth not his light arise?
(4) *a* How then can man be justified with God?
Or how can he be clean *that is* born of a woman?
(5) Behold even to the moon, and it shineth not;
Yea, the stars are not pure in his sight.
(6) How much less man, *that is* *b* a worm?
And the son of man, *which is* a worm?

CHAPTER XXVI.—(1) But Job answered and said,
(2) How hast thou helped *him that is* without power?
How savest thou the arm *that hath* no strength?
(3) How hast thou counselled *him that* hath no wisdom?
And how hast thou plentifully declared the thing as it is?
(4) To whom hast thou uttered words?
And whose spirit came from thee?
(5) Dead *things* are formed
From under the waters, ¹ and the inhabitants thereof.
(6) *c* Hell *is* naked before him,—and destruction hath no covering.
(7) He stretcheth out the north over the empty place,
And hangeth the earth upon nothing.
(8) He bindeth up the waters in his thick clouds;
And the cloud is not rent under them.
(9) He holdeth back the face of his throne,
And spreadeth his cloud upon it.
(10) He hath compassed the waters with bounds,
² Until the day and night come to an end.
(11) The pillars of heaven tremble—and are astonished at his reproof.
(12) He divideth the sea with his power,
And by his understanding he smiteth through ³ the proud.

a ch. 4. 17, &c., & 15. 14, &c.
b Ps. 22. 6.
1 Or, *with the inhabitants.*
c Pro. 15. 11.
2 Heb., *until the end of light with darkness.*
3 Heb., *pride.*

even in His high places, and among His celestial hosts, He maintaineth peace and harmony.

(3) **Is there any number of his armies?**—He is also so glorious that He dispenses of His glory to His innumerable hosts of angels. Glorious as they are, they but reflect His glory; and what then must not that be? but if so, how utterly hopeless for man to think he can have any purity to compete with His, or that He will acknowledge to be such. Man also is by nature and birth unclean. (Comp. Ps. li. 5.)

(5) **Even to the moon and stars**, pure and chaste as their light is, they are not clean before Him (comp. chap. iv. 18), for the stars rise and set, and once in every month the moon hides her face.

(6) **How much less man** . . .—Comp. Pss. viii. 4, xxii. 6; Isa. xli. 14, &c.

XXVI.

(1) **Then answered Job.**—Job himself has virtually said much the same as Bildad (chaps. ix. 2, xiv. 4), so he makes no further comment on his remarks here, but merely asks how he has helped him thereby, or others like him in a weak and helpless condition.

(3) **The thing as it is?**—Rather, *How hast thou plentifully declared sound knowledge?*

(4) **To whom.**—That is, "Is it not to one who had said the same thing himself? Was it not my own breath, my own teaching, that came forth from you?" He then proceeds to show that it is not only the starry heavens that declare the glory of God, but the under world likewise, and the universe generally.

(5) **Dead things are formed.**—The Hebrew word is *the Rephaim,* who were among the aboriginal inhabitants of the south of Palestine and the neighbourhood of the Dead Sea, and it is used to express the dead and the inhabitants of the nether world generally. The word rendered *are formed* probably means either *are pierced* or *tremble*: that is, they are pierced through with terror, or they tremble, with a possible reference to the state of the dead as the prey of corruption, though spoken of them where they are beyond the reach of it. All the secrets of this mysterious, invisible, and undiscoverable world are naked and open before Him—the grave lies naked and destruction is uncovered.

(7) **He stretcheth out the north over the empty place, and hangeth the earth upon nothing.**—If these words mean what they seem to do—and it is hard to see how they can mean anything else—then they furnish a very remarkable instance of anticipation of the discoveries of science. Here we find Job, more than three thousand years ago, describing in language of scientific accuracy the condition of our globe, and holding it forth as a proof of Divine power. Some have attempted to explain the latter clause of the destitution caused by famine; but that is precluded by the terms of the first clause.

(8) **He bindeth up the waters.**—The idea of the waters being bound up in the clouds, so that the clouds are not rent thereby, is similar to that in Gen. i. 7. The conception is that of a vast treasury of water above the visible sky, which is kept there in apparent defiance of what we know as the laws of gravitation, and which all experience would show was liable to fall of itself.

(9) **He holdeth back the face.**—Or, *covereth the face of his throne in the heavens, spreading his rack of cloud upon it.*

(10) **He hath compassed the waters with bounds.**—Rather, *He hath described a circle upon the face of the waters, unto the confines of light and darkness.* The phenomenon described is that of the horizon at sea, which is a perfect circle, and which is the limit apparently of light, and beyond which is darkness, for all is invisible.

(11) **The pillars of heaven tremble.**—The phenomenon of storm and tempest is alluded to.

(12) **He divideth the sea.**—The word is taken in the two opposite senses of *stirring up* and *calming*;

(13) By his spirit he hath garnished the heavens;
His hand hath formed the crooked serpent.
(14) Lo, these *are* parts of his ways:
But how little a portion is heard of him?
But the thunder of his power who can understand?

CHAPTER XXVII.—(1) Moreover Job ¹continued his parable, and said,
(2) *As* God liveth, *who* hath taken away my judgment;
And the Almighty, *who* hath ²vexed my soul;
(3) All the while my breath *is* in me,
And ³the spirit of God *is* in my nostrils;
(4) My lips shall not speak wickedness,
Nor my tongue utter deceit.
(5) God forbid that I should justify you:
Till I die I will not remove mine integrity from me.
(6) My righteousness I hold fast, and will not let it go:
My heart shall not reproach *me* ⁴so long as I live.
(7) Let mine enemy be as the wicked,
And he that riseth up against me as the unrighteous.
(8) ᵃFor what *is* the hope of the hypocrite, though he hath gained,
When God taketh away his soul?
(9) ᵇWill God hear his cry—when trouble cometh upon him?
(10) Will he delight himself in the Almighty?
Will he always call upon God?
(11) I will teach you ⁵by the hand of God:
That which *is* with the Almighty will I not conceal.
(12) Behold, all ye yourselves have seen *it*;
Why then are ye thus altogether vain?
(13) This *is* the portion of a wicked man with God,

1 Heb., *added to take up.*
2 Heb., *made my soul bitter.*
3 That is, the breath which God gave him.
4 Heb., *from my days.*
a Mat. 16. 26.
b Prov. 1. 28; Ezek. 8. 18; John 9. 31; James 4. 3.
5 Or, *being in the hand, &c.*

---

perhaps the latter is more appropriate to the context, which seems to speak of God's *mastery* over nature.

By his understanding he smiteth through the proud.—Literally, *Rahab*, which certainly is at times a name for Egypt (see Isa. li. 9, *e. g.*), and which, if used in that sense here, can only refer to the signal judgments on Egypt at the Exodus. According to our view of this matter will be the indication derived therefrom of the date of Job.

(13) **The crooked serpent.**—By this expression is doubtless meant the forked lightning-flash, though it is difficult to determine whether any, or what mythological ideas may underlie the expression, or whether it is anything more than a figure derived from the natural world, which suggested the similitude of the flying serpent. Others understand by it the constellation of the Northern Dragon, to whose influence storms were ascribed.

(14) **These are parts.**—Literally, *ends*—just the merest outskirts. For "is heard" we may render *do we hear;* and for "the thunder of His power," *the thunder of His mighty deeds.* We can only hear the faintest whisper of His glory, and cannot understand or endure the full-toned thunder of His majesty. Here, then, is Job's final reply to the arguments of his friends. He shows himself even more conscious than they of the grandeur and holiness of God; but that has in no way rendered his position as a sufferer more intelligible—rather the reverse—nor theirs as defenders of the theory of exact retribution. He cannot understand and they cannot explain; but while he rejects their explanations, he rests secure in his own faith.

XXVII.

(1) **Job continued his parable.**—The remainder of Job's speech—now, for the first time, called his *parable*—consists of his determination not to renounce his righteousness (verses 2—6); his own estimate of the fate of the wicked (verses 7—23); his magnificent estimate of the nature of wisdom (chap. xxviii.); his comparison of his former life (chap. xxix.) with that of his present experience (chap. xxx.); his final declaration of his innocent and irreproachable conduct (chap. xxxi.).

(2) **As God liveth, who hath taken away my judgment.**—Job's faith leads him to see that, though there may be no explanation for his sufferings, yet they are laid upon him by God for purposes of His own, which are veiled from him.

(5) **God forbid that I should justify you.**—To admit the wickedness with which his friends charged him would have been to justify them—to say that they were right and he was wrong. This he resolves not to do.

(6) **My heart shall not reproach me.**—Or, *doth not reproach me for any of my days.*

(7) **Let mine enemy be as the wicked.**—While, however, he admits that the wicked is often a prosperous man, he declares that he has no envy for him, but would have only his adversaries to be like him.

(8) **What is the hope?**—Better, *What is the hope of the godless, though he get him gain, when God taketh away his soul?*

(10) **Will he delight himself?**—It is only the godly who can say, "Whom have I in heaven but Thee, and there is none upon earth that I desire in comparison with Thee;" and again, "I will praise Thy name, because it is so *comfortable;*" but this man hath no promise that he can plead, and therefore no assurance of access at all times to the presence of God.

(11) **I will teach you.**—Better, *I will teach you of the hand of God;* or, *what is in the power of God.*

(12) **Behold, all ye yourselves have seen it.**—That is, "You have seen me so proclaim the great power of God."

(13) **This is the portion of a wicked man.**—Some have thought that the remainder of this chapter, if not chap. xxviii. also, constitutes the missing third speech of Zophar, and that the usual words, "Then answered Zophar the Naamathite, and said," have dropped

The Blessings of the Wicked JOB, XXVIII. *turned into Curses.*

And the heritage of oppressors, *which* they shall receive of the Almighty.
⁽¹⁴⁾ If his children be multiplied, *it is* for the sword:
And his offspring shall not be satisfied with bread.
⁽¹⁵⁾ Those that remain of him shall be buried in death:
And *a* his widows shall not weep.
⁽¹⁶⁾ Though he heap up silver as the dust,
And prepare raiment as the clay;
⁽¹⁷⁾ He may prepare *it*, but the just shall put *it* on,
And the innocent shall divide the silver.
⁽¹⁸⁾ He buildeth his house as a moth,
And as a booth *that* the keeper maketh.
⁽¹⁹⁾ The rich man shall lie down, but he shall not be gathered:
He openeth his eyes, and he *is* not.
⁽²⁰⁾ *b* Terrors take hold on him as waters,
A tempest stealeth him away in the night.
⁽²¹⁾ The east wind carrieth him away, and he departeth:
And as a storm hurleth him out of his place.
⁽²²⁾ For *God* shall cast upon him, and not spare:
¹ He would fain flee out of his hand.
⁽²³⁾ *Men* shall clap their hands at him,
And shall hiss him out of his place.

CHAPTER XXVIII.—⁽¹⁾ Surely there is ² a vein for the silver,
And a place for gold *where* they fine *it*.
⁽²⁾ Iron is taken out of the ³ earth,
And brass *is* molten *out of* the stone.
⁽³⁾ He setteth an end to darkness,
And searcheth out all perfection:
The stones of darkness, and the shadow of death.
⁽⁴⁾ The flood breaketh out from the inhabitant;
Even the waters forgotten of the foot:
They are dried up, they are gone away from men.
⁽⁵⁾ *As for* the earth, out of it cometh bread:
And under it is turned up as it were fire.

a Ps. 78. 64.
b ch. 18. 11.
1 Heb., *in fleeing he would flee.*
2 Or, *a mine.*
3 Or, *dust.*

---

out; but whatever may so be gained in symmetry seems to be lost in dramatic effect. We have seen that Bildad had but little to say, and that was only a few truisms; it is not surprising, therefore, that when it came to the turn of Zophar he had nothing more to say, and Job was left virtually master of the field. It is, however, a little remarkable that, supposing these words to be rightly ascribed to Job, he should precisely adopt those with which Zophar had concluded (chap. xx. 29). Perhaps Job is willing to show how completely he is prepared to accept the facts of his friends, although he will not admit their inferences. He, like them, is quite ready to allow that the prosperity of the wicked must be seeming rather than real, and that it must eventually come to nought.

⁽¹⁵⁾ **Those that remain of him shall be buried in death.**—That is, as the context shows, it shall be obscure, and excite no sympathy; their very death shall be as it were a burial, and shall consign them to oblivion.

His widows.—That is, those commonly hired for the purpose of making lamentation for the dead, or the widows of those that remain of him.

⁽¹⁹⁾ **But he shall not be gathered.**—Some ancient versions read, "but he shall do so no more;" but the "gathering" may refer to his wealth. "He openeth his eyes, and it (*i.e.*, his wealth) is not;" or it may mean that as soon as he openeth his eyes, hoping to enjoy his riches, he shall be no more, but be suddenly cut off. This sense appears to accord with the following verses.

⁽²²⁾ **For God shall cast upon him.**—The Authorised Version supplies *God* as the subject; but we obtain very good sense by understanding it of the man who constantly fled from his power now being only too glad of the opportunity of avenging himself on him, while he or others clap their hands at him, and hiss him from his place.

XXVIII.

⁽¹⁾ **Surely there is a vein for the silver.**—In this chapter Job draws out a magnificent contrast between human skill and ingenuity and Divine wisdom. The difficulty to the ordinary reader is in not perceiving that the person spoken of in verse 3 is *man*, and not God. Man possesses and exercises this mastery over nature, but yet is ignorant of wisdom unless God bestows it on him. That Job should say this is but natural, after his painful experience of the want of wisdom in his friends.

⁽³⁾ **He setteth an end to darkness.**—May be read thus, *Man setteth an end to darkness, and searcheth out to the furthest bound the stones of darkness and the shadow of death.*

⁽⁴⁾ **The flood breaketh out . . .** is very uncertain. We may render, *Man breaketh open a shaft where none sojourneth; they are forgotten where none passeth by*: *i.e.*, the labourers in these deserted places, they hang afar from the haunts of men, they flit to and fro. Or it may be, *The flood breaketh out from the inhabitants, even the waters forgotten of the foot: they are dried up, they are gone away from man:* that is, the very course of rivers is subject to the will and power of man. Those who walk over the place forget that it was once a river, so completely has man obliterated the marks of it.

⁽⁵⁾ **As for the earth . . .**—While the ploughman and the reaper till and gather the fruits of the earth on its surface, the miner far below maintains perpetual fires, as also does the volcanic mountain, with its fields and vineyards luxuriant and fertile on its sides.

(6) The stones of it *are* the place of sapphires:
And it hath ¹dust of gold.
(7) *There is* a path which no fowl knoweth,
And which the vulture's eye hath not seen:
(8) The lion's whelps have not trodden it,
Nor the fierce lion passed by it.
(9) He putteth forth his hand upon the ²rock;
He overturneth the mountains by the roots.
(10) He cutteth out rivers among the rocks;
And his eye seeth every precious thing.
(11) He bindeth the floods ³from overflowing;
And *the thing that is* hid bringeth he forth to light.
(12) But where shall wisdom be found?
And where *is* the place of understanding?
(13) Man knoweth not the price thereof;
Neither is it found in the land of the living.
(14) *ª*The depth saith, It *is* not in me:
And the sea saith, *It is* not with me.
(15) ⁴It *ᵇ*cannot be gotten for gold,
Neither shall silver be weighed *for* the price thereof.
(16) It cannot be valued with the gold of Ophir,
With the precious onyx, or the sapphire.
(17) The gold and the crystal cannot equal it:
And the exchange of it *shall not be for* ⁵jewels of fine gold.
(18) No mention shall be made of ⁶coral, or of pearls:
For the price of wisdom *is* above rubies.
(19) The topaz of Ethiopia shall not equal it,
Neither shall it be valued with pure gold.
(20) *ᶜ*Whence then cometh wisdom?
And where *is* the place of understanding?
(21) Seeing it is hid from the eyes of all living,
And kept close from the fowls of the ⁷air.
(22) Destruction and death say,
We have heard the fame thereof with our ears.
(23) God understandeth the way thereof,
And he knoweth the place thereof.
(24) For he looketh to the ends of the earth,
And seeth under the whole heaven;
(25) To make the weight for the winds;

1 Or, *gold ore.*
2 Or, *flint.*
3 Heb., *from weeping.*
a Rom. 11. 33. 34.
4 Heb., *Fine gold shall not be given for it.*
b Prov. 3. 14 & 8. 11, 19 & 16. 16.
5 Or, *vessels of fine gold.*
6 Or, *Ramoth.*
c ver. 12.
7 Or, *heaven.*

---

(6) **The stones of it are the place of sapphires.**—So ingenious is man that he discovereth a place of which the stones are sapphires and the very dust gold, and a path that no bird of prey knoweth, and which the falcon's eye hath not seen.

(9) **He putteth forth his hand upon the rock.**—The process described is that of tunnelling and excavating, and that of making canals and lining them with stone; and in the course of such works many precious things would be discovered. The canals and cisterns were made so accurately that they retained the water, and did not even weep or trickle.

(12) **But where shall wisdom be found?**—With magnificent effect comes in this question, after the gigantic achievements of man just recounted; notwithstanding his industry, science, and skill, he is altogether ignorant of true wisdom. Neither his knowledge nor his wealth can make him master of that; nor can he find it where he discovers so many other secret and precious things.

(17) **The exchange of it.**—Or, according to some, *the attraction of it.* The remainder of this chapter calls for little remark: its unrivalled sublimity is patent, and comment is superfluous. There is a general resemblance between this chapter and Prov. viii., and both seem to imply a knowledge of the Mosaic narrative of creation.

(22) **Destruction and death say.**—That destruction and death should have heard the fame of wisdom is natural, as it consists in departing from the evil which leads to their abode.

(23) **God understandeth the way thereof.**—God is the author of wisdom, and His fear is the beginning thereof; so with His infinite knowledge of the universe He cannot but be cognisant of the place and way thereof. It is to be observed that while the foundation of wisdom is said to be coeval with that of the world, the very existence of wisdom in relation to man implied the existence of evil, because except by departing from evil there could for man be no wisdom, though evil itself may undoubtedly involve and imply the deflection from a previously existing right. *Wrong,* for example, is what is *wrung* aside from the right. The two ideas which Job starts with are man's ignorance of the *price* and the *place* of wisdom. Neither he nor nature knows the place of it: neither all living, nor the deep, nor the sea; and as for its price, though man is prepared to give any high price for the costly stones and jewels of the earth, yet all that he has to give is not to be mentioned in comparison with the value of wisdom. Wisdom, however, is to be purchased by the poor, as we may infer from the language of the prophet Isaiah (chap. lv. 1), or, at all events, that which ranks with wisdom; and in like manner Christ represented the kingdom of heaven as a pearl of great price, which would demand all that a man had to buy it, and yet he represented the poor as those especially to whom it was preached. It is true that the wisdom of which

And he weigheth the waters by measure.
(26) When he made a decree for the rain,
And a way for the lightning of the thunder:
(27) Then did he see it, and ¹declare it;
He prepared it, yea, and searched it out.
(28) And unto man he said,
Behold, ᵃthe fear of the Lord, that *is* wisdom;
And to depart from evil *is* understanding.

CHAPTER XXIX.—(1) Moreover Job ²continued his parable, and said,
(2) Oh that I were as *in* months past,
As *in* the days *when* God preserved me;
(3) When his ³candle shined upon my head,
And *when* by his light I walked *through* darkness;
(4) As I was in the days of my youth,
When the secret of God *was* upon my tabernacle;
(5) When the Almighty *was* yet with me,
When my children *were* about me;
(6) When I washed my steps with butter,
And the rock poured ⁴me out rivers of oil;
(7) When I went out to the gate through the city,
When I prepared my seat in the street!
(8) The young men saw me, and hid themselves:
And the aged arose, *and* stood up.
(9) The princes refrained talking,
And laid *their* hand on their mouth.
(10) ⁵The nobles held their peace,
And their tongue cleaved to the roof of their mouth.
(11) When the ear heard *me*, then it blessed me;
And when the eye saw *me*, it gave witness to me:
(12) Because I delivered the poor that cried,
And the fatherless, and *him that had* none to help him.
(13) The blessing of him that was ready to perish came upon me:
And I caused the widow's heart to sing for joy.

¹ Or, *number it.*
a Ps. 111. 10; Prov. 1. 7 & 9. 10.
² Heb., *added to take up.*
³ Or, *lamp.*
⁴ Heb., *with me.*
⁵ Heb., *the voice of the nobles was hid.*

Job speaks (verse 28) is in no way connected with the Gospel of the kingdom; but yet, if the words of the wise are indeed given from one Shepherd, it is impossible not to recognise a central thought underlying all such words, if not in the separate minds of the wise at heart, in the original mind of the one Shepherd. So we can see that that which is true of wisdom as described by Job receives its illustration from that which is true of the Gospel of the kingdom and of the evangelical promises of Isaiah.

(27) The terms employed with reference to the Lord's knowledge of wisdom are remarkable. They are: (1) seeing, or intuition; (2) declaring or numbering, ratiocination; (3) preparing or establishing, determination; (4) searching out, or investigation. Each of these actions implies the operation of mind, and is so far opposed to the fatality of an impersonal law or the fixed necessity of an inevitable nature.

(28) **And unto man he said.**—No one can for a moment suppose that this is an historical statement, or is to be treated as being one; but it is nevertheless profoundly and universally true. It is the wisdom of man as man to fear the Lord and to depart from evil; and this is God's primary revelation to man, which virtually underlies and is involved in all others. When we are told, as we are elsewhere, that the fear of the Lord is the *beginning* of wisdom, this implies that the fear of the Lord does not supersede, though it may be essential to, any other revelation, or any other development of wisdom, or any other manifestation of it. It is to be observed that the word rendered "the Lord" here is not the four-lettered name Jehovah which was used by Job in chap. xii. 9, but the other name for the Divine Being (Adonai), which was in later times universally substituted for the name Jehovah by the Jews in reading.

XXIX.

(1) **Job continued his parable.**—In this chapter he recounts wistfully his past happiness. In his case it was indeed not without cause, though in point of fact he was *then* passing through a time of trial which was itself bringing fast on his time of deliverance, and which was to make his name famous throughout the world and in all time. And in most similar cases we have need to bear in mind the words of Solomon (Eccles. vii. 10): "Say not thou, What is the cause that the former days were better than these? for thou dost not enquire wisely concerning this."

(2) **Preserved.**—Or, *watched over me.* When does God not watch over us, if we only knew it?

(3) **When his candle shined.**—See Isa. 1. 10.

(4) **In the days of my youth.**—Literally, *my autumn:* i.e., in the ripeness, maturity of my days. He was then in the depth of winter. (Comp. the words "in which it seemed always afternoon.") Some suppose, however, that as with the ancient and modern Jews the year began with the autumn, it is used much in the same way as we use spring.

The secret of God.—Or, *the counsel of God.*

(7) **To the gate.**—There business was transacted. (Comp. the expression, which is still used with reference to the Turkish Empire, of "the Sublime Porte," or the supreme Place of government; Ps. cxxvii. 5; Jer. xxxv. 20, &c.)

(9) **The princes retrained talking.**—Comp. Isa. lii. 15.

(11) **When the ear heard me, then it blessed me.**—This is a direct negative to the charges of Eliphaz in chap. xxii. 6, &c. He has felt them too deeply to pass them by in total silence.

(14) I put on righteousness, and it clothed me:
My judgment *was* as a robe and a diadem.
(15) I was eyes to the blind,—and feet *was* I to the lame.
(16) I *was* a father to the poor:
And the cause *which* I knew not I searched out.
(17) And I brake [1] the jaws of the wicked,
And [2] plucked the spoil out of his teeth.
(18) Then I said, I shall die in my nest,
And I shall multiply *my* days as the sand.
(19) My root *was* [3] spread out by the waters,
And the dew lay all night upon my branch.
(20) My glory *was* [4] fresh in me,
And my bow was [5] renewed in my hand.
(21) Unto me *men* gave ear,
And waited, and kept silence at my counsel.
(22) After my words they spake not again;
And my speech dropped upon them.
(23) And they waited for me as for the rain;
And they opened their mouth wide *as* for the latter rain.
(24) *If* I laughed on them, they believed *it* not;
And the light of my countenance they cast not down.
(25) I chose out their way, and sat chief,
And dwelt as a king in the army,
As one *that* comforteth the mourners.

CHAPTER XXX.—(1) But now *they that are* [6] younger than I have me in derision,
Whose fathers I would have disdained
To have set with the dogs of my flock.
(2) Yea, whereto *might* the strength of their hands *profit* me,
In whom old age was perished?
(3) For want and famine *they were* [7] solitary;
Fleeing into the wilderness
[8] In former time desolate and waste.
(4) Who cut up mallows by the bushes,
And juniper roots *for* their meat.
(5) They were driven forth from among men,

[1] Heb., *the jaw-teeth, or, the grinders.*
[2] Heb., *cast.*
[3] Heb., *opened.*
[4] Heb., *new.*
[5] Heb., *changed.*
[6] Heb., *of fewer days than I.*
[7] Or, *dark as the night.*
[8] Heb., *yesternight.*

---

(14) **I put on righteousness.**—Comp. Isa. lxi. 10, xxviii. 5, lxii. 3; 2 Tim. iv. 8; James i. 12; 1 Peter v. 4; 1 Thess. ii. 19. His judgment, the result of his personal righteousness, was as a robe of honour and a crown of glory to him.

It clothed me.—Literally, *it clothed itself with me.* First, righteousness is the garment, and then he is the garment to righteousness. (Compare the expressions "Put ye on the Lord Jesus Christ," Rom. xiii. 14, and 2 Cor. v. 2, 3, 4, and the Hebrew of Ps. cxliii. 9, where "I flee unto thee to hide me" is, *I have covered myself with thee,* or, *have hidden me with thee.*) This is the Gospel truth of the interchange of sin and righteousness between Christ and the believer. He bears our sins; we are clothed with the robe of His righteousness.

(18) **I shall die in my nest.**—Very touching is this spontaneous expression of his almost unconscious hope when in prosperity. Some have suggested the transposition of these three verses to the end of the chapter. Though this is obviously their natural position in one sense, yet in another it is less natural. The same thing is to be seen in the last four verses of chapter xxxi. They carry on the previous vindication from verse 34, which had been broken by the parenthesis in verses 35—37.

(19) **My root was spread.**—It is perhaps better to read this and the next verse in the present: "My root is spread out . . . and the dew lieth. My glory is fresh in me, and my bow is renewed." (Comp. Gen. xlix. 24.)

(24) **If I laughed on them.**—That is, "They would not believe that I could be so affable to them, could so condescend to them—they looked up to me with the greatest deference."

(25) **I sat.**—It is still the custom among the Jews for mourners to sit upon the ground and for one who wishes to console them to occupy a seat above them. Such is Job's pathetic lamentation over the days that were gone. He appears before us as a conspicuous example of one who had worn the poet's crown of sorrow in the remembrance of happier things in time of sorrow. He is the type and representative of suffering humanity, of man waiting for redemption, but as yet unredeemed. It is in this way that he points us on to Christ, who, Himself the Redeemer, went through all the sorrows of sinful and unredeemed humanity. He is able to describe his former state and all its glory and bliss, while his friends are constrained to listen in silence. They have said their worst, they have aspersed and maligned his character, but they have not silenced him; he is able to make the most complete vindication of all his past life, to contrast its happiness with the present contempt and contumely of it, so much owing to them and their heartless, unsympathetic treatment of him, while they can make no reply.

XXX.

(1) **Whose fathers I would have disdained.**—Rather, *whose fathers I disdained to set.* The complaint is that the children of those who were so inferior to him should treat him thus.

(2) **Whereto might the strength of their hands profit me,** is the description of the fathers; verse 3 *seqq.* describes their children. The people here spoken of seem to have been somewhat similar to those known to the ancients as Troglodytes (Herod. iv. 183, &c.), the inhabitants of caves, who lived an outcast life and had manners and customs of their own.

(They cried after them as *after a* thief;)
⁽⁶⁾ To dwell in the cliffs of the valleys,
In ¹caves of the earth, and *in* the rocks.
⁽⁷⁾ Among the bushes they brayed;
Under the nettles they were gathered together.
⁽⁸⁾ *They were* children of fools, yea, children of ²base men:
They were viler than the earth.
⁽⁹⁾ ᵃAnd now am I their song, yea, I am their byword.
⁽¹⁰⁾ They abhor me, they flee far from me, ³And spare not to spit in my face.
⁽¹¹⁾ Because he hath loosed my cord, and afflicted me,
They have also let loose the bridle before me.
⁽¹²⁾ Upon *my* right *hand* rise the youth;
They push away my feet,
And they raise up against me the ways of their destruction.
⁽¹³⁾ They mar my path,—they set forward my calamity,
They have no helper.
⁽¹⁴⁾ They came *upon me* as a wide breaking in *of waters*:
In the desolation they rolled themselves *upon me*.
⁽¹⁵⁾ Terrors are turned upon me:
They pursue ⁴my soul as the wind:
And my welfare passeth away as a cloud.
⁽¹⁶⁾ And now my soul is poured out upon me;
The days of affliction have taken hold upon me.
⁽¹⁷⁾ My bones are pierced in me in the night season:
And my sinews take no rest.
⁽¹⁸⁾ By the great force *of my disease* is my garment changed:
It bindeth me about as the collar of my coat.
⁽¹⁹⁾ He hath cast me into the mire,
And I am become like dust and ashes.
⁽²⁰⁾ I cry unto thee, and thou dost not hear me:
I stand up, and thou regardest me *not*.
⁽²¹⁾ Thou art ⁵become cruel to me:
With ⁶thy strong hand thou opposest thyself against me.
⁽²²⁾ Thou liftest me up to the wind;
Thou causest me to ride *upon it*,
And dissolvest my ⁷substance.
⁽²³⁾ For I know *that* thou wilt bring me *to* death,
And *to* the house appointed for all living.

¹ Heb., *holes.*
² Heb., *men of no name.*
ᵃ Ps. 35.15. & 69.12.
³ Heb., *and withhold not spittle from my face.*
⁴ Heb., *my principal one.*
⁵ Heb., *turned to be cruel.*
⁶ Heb., *the strength of thy hand.*
⁷ Or, *wisdom.*

They are desolate with want and famine. They flee into the wilderness on the eve of wasteness and desolation, or when all is dark (yesternight), waste, and desolate. It is evident that Job must have been familiar with a people of this kind, an alien and proscribed race living in the way he mentions.

⁽⁷⁾ **Among the bushes they brayed.**—Herodotus says their language was like the screeching of bats, others say it was like the whistling of birds. This whole description is of the mockers of Job, and therefore should be in the present tense in verses 5, 7, and 8, as it may be in the Authorised Version of verse 4.

⁽⁸⁾ **They were viler than the earth.**—Rather, *They are scourged out of the land,* or *are outcasts from the land.*

⁽⁹⁾ **And now am I their song.**—See the references in the margin, which show that it is quite appropriate to give to the complaints of Job a Messianic interpretation.

⁽¹¹⁾ **Because he hath loosed my cord.**—Better, *his:* i.e., "God hath loosed the cord of his bow and they have cast off all restraint before me."

⁽¹²⁾ **The youth**—i.e., the young brood, rabble.

⁽¹³⁾ **They have no helper**—i.e., probably without deriving therefrom any help or advantage themselves.

⁽¹⁴⁾ **As a wide breaking in of waters.**—Or, *as through a wide breach they come.* "In the midst of the crash they roll themselves upon me;" or, "instead of a tempest" (*i.e.,* like a tempest) "they roll themselves upon me."

⁽¹⁵⁾ **They pursue**—i.e., "the terrors chase or pursue my honour:" i.e., *my soul;* or it may be, "Thou (i.e., God) chasest."

⁽¹⁸⁾ **My garment changed.**—Some render "By His (i.e., God's) great power the garment (of my skin) is disfigured;" and others, "With great effort must my garment be changed because of the sores to which it clings? It bindeth me about as closely as the collar of my coat."

⁽¹⁹⁾ **He hath cast me into the mire.**—He now turns more directly to God, having in verse 16 turned from man to his own condition—*dust and ashes.* This latter phrase is used but three times in Scripture: twice by Job (here and chap. xlii. 6), and once by Abraham (Gen. xviii. 27).

⁽²⁰⁾ **Thou regardest me not.**—The Authorised Version understands that the negative of the first clause must be supplied in the second, as is the case in Ps. ix. 18: "The needy shall not alway be forgotten; the expectation of the poor shall *not* perish for ever." Others understand it, "I stand up (*i.e.,* to pray) in the attitude of prayer, and Thou lookest at me," *i.e.,* and doest no more with mute indifference.

⁽²²⁾ **Thou liftest me up to the wind.**—Some render this verse, "Thou liftest me up to the wind, and causest me to ride upon it; Thou dissolvest me in thy blast;" others understand him to express the contrast between his former prosperous state and his present low condition: "Thou usedst to raise me up and make me ride upon the wind, and now Thou dissolvest my substance, my very being." (Comp. Ps. cii. 10: "Thou hast lifted me up and cast me down.")

⁽²⁴⁾ **Though they cry in his destruction.**—

(24) Howbeit he will not stretch out *his* hand to the ¹grave,
Though they cry in his destruction.
(25) ᵃDid not I weep ²for him that was in trouble?
Was *not* my soul grieved for the poor?
(26) When I looked for good, then evil came *unto* me:
And when I waited for light, there came darkness.
(27) My bowels boiled, and rested not:
The days of affliction prevented me.
(28) I went mourning without the sun:
I stood up, *and* I cried in the congregation.
(29) ᵇI am a brother to dragons, and a companion to ³owls.
(30) My skin is black upon me,
And my bones are burned with heat.
(31) My harp also is *turned* to mourning,
And my organ into the voice of them that weep.

¹ Heb., *heap.*
ᵃ Ps. 35. 13; Rom. 12. 15.
² Heb., *for him that was hard of day?*
ᵇ Ps. 102. 6.
³ Or, *ostriches.*
c 2 Chron. 16. 9; ch. 34. 21; Prov. 5. 21 & 15. 3.
⁴ Heb., *Let him weigh me in balances of justice.*

CHAPTER XXXI. — ⁽¹⁾ I made a covenant with mine eyes;
Why then should I think upon a maid?
⁽²⁾ For what portion of God *is there* from above?
And *what* inheritance of the Almighty from on high?
⁽³⁾ *Is* not destruction to the wicked?
And a strange *punishment* to the workers of iniquity?
⁽⁴⁾ ᶜDoth not he see my ways,—and count all my steps?
⁽⁵⁾ If I have walked with vanity,
Or if my foot hath hasted to deceit;
⁽⁶⁾ ⁴Let me be weighed in an even balance,
That God may know mine integrity.
⁽⁷⁾ If my step hath turned out of the way,
And mine heart walked after mine eyes,
And if any blot hath cleaved to mine hands;

This is a very obscure verse. Some render it, "Surely against a ruinous heap he will not put forth his hand; though it be in his destruction *one may utter* a cry because of these things." Others, understanding the word rendered "ruinous heap" otherwise, render "Howbeit, God will not put forth His hand to bring man to death and the grave when there is earnest prayer for them, nor even when in calamity proceeding from Him there is a loud cry for them:" that is to say, "I know that Thou wilt dissolve and destroy me, and bring me to the grave, though Thou wilt not do so when I pray unto Thee to release me by death from my sufferings. Thou wilt surely do so, but not in my time or according to my will, but only in Thine own appointed time, and as Thou seest fit." This is one of those passages that may be regarded as hopelessly uncertain. Each reader will make the best sense he can of it, according to his judgment. That Job should speak of himself as a *ruinous heap* seems very strange; neither is it at all clear what "these things" are because of which a cry is uttered. Certainly the *significance* given by the other rendering is much greater. "His destruction" must mean, at all events, *the destruction that cometh from Him*; and if this is so, the sense given is virtually that of the Authorised Version.

(25) **Did not I weep for him?**—Job declares that he has not withheld that sympathy with sorrow and suffering for which he himself has asked in vain.

(26) **When I looked for good.**—Before, in chap. iii. 25, 26, he had spoken as one who did not wish to be the *fool* of prosperity, and so overtaken unawares by calamity, and who therefore looked at things on the darker side; now he speaks as one who hoped for the best, and yet, notwithstanding that hope, was disappointed and deceived.

(27) **My bowels boiled.**—The sense is better expressed by the present, "My bowels boil, and rest not. Days of affliction have overtaken me unawares." (See last verse.)

(28) **I went mourning without the sun.**—Rather, *I go mourning without the sun*; or, according to some, "blackened, but not by the sun." We give the preference to the other.

I stood up, and I cried in the congregation —*i.e.*, not merely in secret, but in the face of all men.

(29) **Dragons and owls** are, according to some moderns, *jackals* and *ostriches*.

(31) **My harp also is turned to mourning.**— Or, *Therefore is my harp turned to mourning, and my pipe into the voice of them that weep.* The musical instruments here named, like those of Gen. iv. 21, are respectively the stringed and wind instruments.

XXXI.

⁽¹⁾ **I made a covenant with mine eyes.**—Job makes one grand profession of innocence, rehearsing his manner of life from the first; and here he does not content himself with traversing the accusations of his friends, but professes his innocence also of sins less manifest to the observance of others, and affecting the secret conduct and the heart—namely, sensual transgression and idolatry. His object, therefore, is to show his friends that he has really been more upright than their standard demanded or than they supposed him to be, till his affliction made them suspect him; and this uprightness was the consequence of rigid and inflexible adherence to principle, for he made a covenant with his eyes, as the avenues of sinful desires. (Comp. Matt. v. 28.)

⁽²⁾ **What portion of God is there from above?** —Comp. the remonstrance of Joseph (Gen. xxxix. 9).

⁽³⁾ **Is not**—*i.e.*, Is not this the *portion* of verse 2?

⁽⁴⁾ **Doth not he.**—The "He" is emphatic, obviously meaning God. His appeal is to the All-seeing knowledge of God, whom nothing escapes, and who is judge of the hearts and reins (Pss. vii. 9, xliv. 21; Jer. xvii. 10, xx. 12). (Comp. Acts xxv. 11.)

⁽⁷⁾ **If my step hath turned out of the way** —The form of the expression is very emphatic: the narrow way of strict integrity and righteousness. (Compare the expression applied to the first believers, Acts ix. 2—*men of the way*.)

(8) Then let me sow, and let another eat;
 Yea, let my offspring be rooted out.
(9) If mine heart have been deceived by a woman,
 Or *if* I have laid wait at my neighbour's door;
(10) *Then* let my wife grind unto another,
 And let others bow down upon her.
(11) For this *is* an heinous crime;
 Yea, it *is* an iniquity *to be punished by* the judges.
(12) For it *is* a fire *that* consumeth to destruction,
 And would root out all mine increase.
(13) If I did despise the cause of my manservant
 Or of my maidservant, when they contended with me;
(14) What then shall I do when God riseth up?
 And when he visiteth, what shall I answer him?
(15) Did not he that made me in the womb make him?
 And ¹did not one fashion us in the womb?
(16) If I have withheld the poor from *their* desire,
 Or have caused the eyes of the widow to fail;
(17) Or have eaten my morsel myself alone,
 And the fatherless hath not eaten thereof;
(18) (For from my youth he was brought up with me, as *with* a father,
 And I have guided ²her from my mother's womb;)
(19) If I have seen any perish for want of clothing,
 Or any poor without covering;
(20) If his loins have not blessed me,
 And *if* he were *not* warmed with the fleece of my sheep;
(21) If I have lifted up my hand against the fatherless,
 When I saw my help in the gate:
(22) *Then* let mine arm fall from my shoulder blade,
 And mine arm be broken from ³the bone.
(23) For destruction *from* God *was* a terror to me,
 And by reason of his highness I could not endure.
(24) If I have made gold my hope,
 Or have said to the fine gold, *Thou art* my confidence;
(25) If I rejoiced because my wealth *was* great,
 And because mine hand had ⁴gotten much;
(26) If I beheld ⁵ the sun when it shined,
 Or the moon walking ⁶ *in* brightness;
(27) And my heart hath been secretly enticed,
 Or ⁷my mouth hath kissed my hand:
(28) This also *were* an iniquity *to be punished by* the judge:
 For I should have denied the God *that is* above.
(29) If I rejoiced at the destruction of him that hated me,
 Or lifted up myself when evil found him:
(30) Neither have I suffered ⁸ my mouth to sin
 By wishing a curse to his soul.
(31) If the men of my tabernacle said not,
 Oh that we had of his flesh! we cannot be satisfied.

1 Or, *did he not fashion us in one womb?*
2 That is, *the widow.*
3 Or, *the chanel-bone.*
4 Heb., *found much.*
5 Heb., *the light.*
6 Heb., *bright.*
7 Heb., *my hand hath kissed my mouth.*
8 Heb., *my palate.*

---

(10) **Then let my wife grind**—*i.e.*, perform all menial offices, like a slave.

(13) **If I did despise.**—In chap. xxii. 8, Eliphaz had insinuated that Job had favoured the rich and powerful, but had oppressed and ground down the weak. He now meets this accusation, and affirms that he had regarded his own servants even as brethren, because partakers of a common humanity.

(15) **Did not he that made me in the womb make him?**—He here meets the charges of Eliphaz (chap. xxii. 6, 7, 9).

(18) **For from my youth he.**—The pronouns refer to the fatherless of verse 17 and to the widow of verse 16.

(19) **If I have seen any perish for want of.**—Or, *any wanderer without.*

(23) **I could not endure.**—Rather, *I was unable to act thus.*

(24) **If I have made gold my hope.**—He here refers to the admonition of Eliphaz (chap. xxii. 23, 24), and declares that such had not been his practice.

(26) **If I beheld the sun.**—It is remarkable that the kind of idolatry repudiated by Job is that only of sun and moon worship. He seems to have been ignorant of the more material and degraded kinds.

(28) **By the judge.**—Rather, perhaps, *by my judge*, *i.e.*, God; unless, indeed, there be any reference to the Mosaic law (Deut. xvii. 2—7), which does not seem likely.

(29) **If I rejoiced at the destruction.**—He now proceeds to the realm of the wishes and thoughts, and is, therefore, far more thorough and searching with his own case than his friends had been.

(31) **Oh that we had of his flesh!**—We should never be satisfied therewith. (Comp. the similar expression, chap. xix. 22.)

Job's Last Words   JOB, XXXII.   *to his Friends.*

(32) The stranger did not lodge in the street:
But I opened my doors ¹to the traveller.
(33) If I covered my transgressions ²as Adam,
By hiding mine iniquity in my bosom:
(34) Did I fear a great multitude,
Or did the contempt of families terrify me,
That I kept silence, *and* went not out of the door?
(35) Oh that one would hear me!
³Behold, my desire *is, that* the Almighty would answer me,
And *that* mine adversary had written a book.
(36) Surely I would take it upon my shoulder,
And bind it *as* a crown to me.
(37) I would declare unto him the number of my steps;
As a prince would I go near unto him.
(38) If my land cry against me,
Or that the furrows likewise thereof ⁴complain;
(39) If I have eaten ⁵the fruits thereof without money,
Or have ⁶caused the owners thereof to lose their life:
(40) Let thistles grow instead of wheat,
And ⁷cockle instead of barley.
The words of Job are ended.

CHAPTER XXXII. — (1) So these three men ceased ⁸to answer Job, because he *was* righteous in his own eyes.

Marginal notes:
1 Or, *to the way.*
2 Or, *after the manner of men.*
3 Or, *behold, my sign is that the Almighty will answer me.*
4 Heb., *weep.*
5 Heb., *the strength thereof.*
6 Heb., *caused the soul of the owners thereof to expire, or, breathe out.*
7 Or, *noisome weeds.*
8 Heb., *from answering.*

---

(32) **I opened my doors to the traveller.**—The manners of Gen. xix. 2, 3, Judg. xix. 20, 21, if not the incidents there recorded, are here implied. "The traveller" is literally *the road* or *way*: *i.e.*, the wayfarer.

(33) **As Adam.**—Or, *as man*, *i.e.*, commonly does. There may or may not be here some indication of acquaintance with the narrative of Genesis. (See the margin.)

(35) **Oh that one would hear me!**—The rendering noticed in the margin is probably the right one—*Oh that I had one to hear me! Lo, here is my mark! i.e.*, my signature, my declaration, which I am ready to subscribe; and oh that mine adversary had written a book! More correctly, perhaps, "That I had the book or indictment that my adversary hath written; would that I had it in black and white before me, that I might deal with it accordingly, and answer it point to point." Here, then, is the same deviation from strict sequence of order that we observed in chap. xxix. 18. Verses 35—37 ought to come after verses 38—40; but the writer's ideas of symmetry and order were not as ours, and this, in some respects, may be more natural, though, strictly speaking, less correct.

(37) **I would declare**—*i.e.*, "I would readily give an account of all my actions, and meet him with alacrity and perfect confidence." Others suppose the meaning to be, "I would meet him as I would meet a prince, with the utmost deference and respect, not at all as an enemy, but as one worthy of all honour and regard." The actual meaning is uncertain. On the other hand, he has been spoken of by his friends: as a fool (chap. v. 2), by Eliphaz; as a man full of words, a liar, and a mocker (chap. xi. 2, 3), by Zophar; as perverse, wicked, and iniquitous (chap. xi. 12, 14); a blasphemer and a hypocrite, by Eliphaz (chap. xv. 4, 5, 13, 16, 34, &c.); as wicked, a robber, and ignorant of God, by Bildad (chap. xviii. 5, 14); as wicked and a hypocrite, by Zophar (chap. xx. 5); as extortionate and oppressive (verses 15, 19, &c.); as a tyrant and an impious man, by Eliphaz (chap. xxii. 5, 9, 13, 17, &c.).

(38) **Or that the furrows likewise thereof complain.**—Rather, *Or if the furrows thereof weep together*—a strong impersonation to express the consequence of oppression and wrong-doing. It is to be observed that throughout this defence Job has far more than traversed the indictment of his friends. He has shown that he has not only not broken the moral law, as they insinuated, but, much more, has shown himself exemplary in all the relations of life, so that, according to the narrator of the history, he was not only one that *feared God and eschewed evil* (chap. i. 1), but also was *perfect, i.e.,* of sincere and consistent conduct and *upright.*

XXXII.

(1) **So these three men ceased.**—The next six chapters are taken up with the reply of a fourth person not before mentioned, but who appears to have been present during the discussion, and who is described as Elihu, the son of Barachel the Buzite, of the kindred of Ram. The name appears to mean, *He is my God*. The person from whom he was descended seems to have been the son of Nahor, Abraham's brother (Gen. xxii. 21); and a city of the like name is mentioned in Jer. xxv. 23. There is a Ram mentioned in Ruth iv. 19, who was the great grandson of Judah; but we can hardly suppose this was the Ram of whose kindred Elihu was. On the other hand, we have no clue to the identification; for even if, with some, we suppose him to have been the same as Aram, the son of Kemuel, and great nephew of Abraham, it is not easy to see how a descendant of Buz, his uncle, should have been described as of the kindred of Ram. One tradition identifies Ram with Abraham, but this is mere conjecture, and in this case highly improbable; the only inference we can draw is that this specification of Elihu serves to show that he was a real, and not an imaginary, personage. The Targum speaks of Elihu as a relative of Abraham. If we are right in putting the life of Elihu so far back, the whole position and surroundings of Job's history become the more probable, because what is told us of Abraham and the patriarchs corresponds with the description and character of Job; and then, also, the traditional Mosaic origin of the Book of Job becomes the more probable.

Because he was righteous in his own eyes.—This appears from chaps. iii. 26, vi. 10, 29, x. 7, xiii. 15, xix. 6, &c., xxiii. 7, 10, 11, 12, xxvii. 6, xxix. 12, &c.

Elihu's Anger against Job   JOB, XXXII.   *and his Three Friends.*

(2) Then was kindled the wrath of Elihu the son of Barachel the Buzite, of the kindred of Ram: against Job was his wrath kindled, because he justified [1] himself rather than God. (3) Also against his three friends was his wrath kindled, because they had found no answer, and *yet* had condemned Job. (4) Now Elihu had [2] waited till Job had spoken, because they *were* [3] elder than he. (5) When Elihu saw that *there was* no answer in the mouth of *these* three men, then his wrath was kindled. (6) And Elihu the son of Barachel the Buzite answered and said,

I *am* [4] young, and ye *are* very old;
Wherefore I was afraid, and [5] durst not shew you mine opinion.
(7) I said, Days should speak,
And multitude of years should teach wisdom.
(8) But *there is* a spirit in man:
And *a* the inspiration of the Almighty giveth them understanding.
(9) Great men are not *always* wise:
Neither do the aged understand judgment.

(10) Therefore I said, Hearken to me;—I also will shew mine opinion.
(11) Behold, I waited for your words;—I gave ear to your [6] reasons,
Whilst ye searched out [7] what to say.
(12) Yea, I attended unto you,
And, behold, *there was* none of you that convinced Job,
Or that answered his words:
(13) Lest ye should say, We have found out wisdom:
God thrusteth him down, not man.
(14) Now he hath not [8] directed *his* words against me:
Neither will I answer him with your speeches.
(15) They were amazed, they answered no more:
[9] They left off speaking.
(16) When I had waited, (for they spake not,
But stood still, *and* answered no more;)
(17) *I said,* I will answer also my part,—
I also will shew mine opinion.
(18) For I am full of [10] matter,
[11] The spirit within me constraineth me.

1 Heb., *his soul.*
2 Heb., *expected Job in words.*
3 Heb., *elder for days.*
4 Heb., *few of days.*
5 Heb., *I feared.*
a ch. 38. 36; Prov. 2. 6; Eccles. 2. 26; Dan. 1. 17 & 2. 21.
6 Heb., *understandings.*
7 Heb., *words.*
8 Or, *ordered his words.*
9 Heb., *they removed speeches from themselves.*
10 Heb., *words.*
11 Heb., *the spirit of my belly.*

---

(2) **Because he justified himself rather than God.**—See chap. xix. 6. Job maintained his innocence, and could not understand how his affliction could be reconciled with the justice of God. Yet, at the same time, he declared that God was his salvation (chap. xiii. 16), and that it was impossible for man to be absolutely just with God (chap. ix. 2, 28), though at the same time he might hope in His righteousness (chap. xxiii. 3 *seqq.*).

(3) **They had found no answer.**—They could not reply unto Job, nor deny that he had been in conduct such as he said he had been, and yet they concluded that he must be wicked because God had smitten him.

(4) **Now Elihu had waited till Job had spoken.**—Literally, *Had waited in words for or regarding Job*; that is, as some understand it, had waited to speak unto Job, or, more probably, had waited till the argument was closed to declare his opinion with reference to Job. The line taken by Elihu is an intermediate one, and is neither that of Job nor his friends. He admits the integrity of Job—or, at least, he does not deny it—although he uses very strong expressions as to the course which Job has adopted (chap. xxxiv. 7—9, 35—37); but he considers that the Divine afflictions have a disciplinary object, and that they may be sent because God has discerned the seeds of unfaithfulness and defection in the sufferer; and this may serve to explain their purpose in the case of Job. He has very lofty ideas of the righteousness of God (chap. xxxiv. 10, &c.), and of His power and majesty (chap. xxxvii. 28). He holds that with regard to the Almighty we cannot find Him out, but that we may safely trust His mercy and His justice. This is the position to which he leads Job when the Lord answers him out of the whirlwind.

(6) **I am young.**—The way in which Elihu comes forward is very interesting, and full of character. It gives us also a picture of the times and habits.

(8) **But there is a spirit in man.**—Rather, *But it is the spirit in man.*

And the inspiration of the Almighty.—Rather, *And the breath of the Almighty that giveth them understanding.* It is the expression used in the Mosaic narrative of the origin of man, and may perhaps show acquaintance on the part of the writer with that narrative (Gen. ii. 7). Elihu means to say that it is not years so much as the spirit and illumination of the Almighty that maketh a man pre-eminent in wisdom.

(9) **Great men are not always wise.**—That is, *old men.* He had just before said that he was "little in days" (verse 6); or it may be used in the sense of number, many, or multitudes. (Comp. what Job himself said, chap. xii. 2: "No doubt because ye are a *people* wisdom will die with you.")

(10) **Therefore I said.**—Equivalent to, *Therefore I say.* It is what he says now, as the result of former convictions.

(12) **There was none of you.**—In Elihu's judgment there was no one who touched the main point of the argument with Job.

(13) **Lest ye should say.**—That is, "I resolved to speak, lest ye should think yourselves wise, and that God was afflicting him on account of his sins." God is declaring his guilt in such a way that man's opinion matters little.

(15) **They were amazed.**—The force is given better by substituting the present tense, "They are amazed, they answer no more: they have not a word to say."

(16) **When I had waited.**—Or, as some render it, "And shall I wait because they speak not?" But they stand still and make no further reply.

His eagerness to Speak.   JOB, XXXIII.   *He Reasons with Job.*

(19) Behold, my belly *is* as wine *which* ¹hath no vent;
It is ready to burst like new bottles.
(20) I will speak, ²that I may be refreshed:
I will open my lips and answer.
(21) Let me not, I pray you, accept any man's person,
Neither let me give flattering titles unto man.
(22) For I know not to give flattering titles;
In so doing my maker would soon take me away.

CHAPTER XXXIII.—(1) Wherefore, Job, I pray thee, hear my speeches,
And hearken to all my words.
(2) Behold, now I have opened my mouth,
My tongue hath spoken ³in my mouth.
(3) My words *shall be of* the uprightness of my heart:
And my lips shall utter knowledge clearly.
(4) The Spirit of God hath made me,
And the breath of the Almighty hath given me life.
(5) If thou canst answer me,
Set *thy words* in order before me, stand up.

(6) *a* Behold, I am ⁴according to thy wish in God's stead:
I also am ⁵formed out of the clay.
(7) Behold, my terror shall not make thee afraid,
Neither shall my hand be heavy upon thee.
(8) Surely thou hast spoken ⁶in mine hearing,
And I have heard the voice of *thy* words, *saying,*
(9) I am clean without transgression, I *am* innocent;
Neither *is there* iniquity in me.
(10) Behold, he findeth occasions against me,
He counteth me for his enemy,
(11) He putteth my feet in the stocks,—
he marketh all my paths.
(12) Behold, *in* this thou art not just:
I will answer thee, that God is greater than man.
(13) Why dost thou strive against him?
For ⁷he giveth not account of any of his matters.
(14) For God speaketh once,—yea twice,
yet man perceiveth it not.
(15) In a dream, in a vision of the night,

Margin: 1 Heb., *is not opened.*   2 Heb., *that I may breathe.*   3 Heb., *in my palate.*   *a* ch. 9. 35 & 13. 20.   4 Heb., *according to thy mouth.*   5 Heb., *cut out of the clay.*   6 Heb., *in mine ears.*   7 Heb., *he answereth not.*

---

(19) **New bottles.**—Or *wine-skins.* (Comp. Matt. ix. 17.)

(22) **In so doing my maker would soon take me away.**—Or perhaps the meaning may be, "My Maker will almost have to forgive me:" that is, for being too candid, frank, and straightforward; for speaking too plainly. Some commentators regard Elihu's character with great disfavour, and consider him to be an empty and arrogant talker, mainly, perhaps, from verses 18, 19; others accept him as a wise and pious friend of Job, who not only gave him good advice, but perhaps more nearly than any other of the disputants hit the truth about Job's afflictions. We are probably more right in this latter view, because at the climax of the poem we do not read that Elihu had any share in the condemnation which was passed by God on the three friends of Job. He is not noticed for either praise or blame.

It is to be observed that the last eight verses of this chapter are a kind of soliloquy, unlike the former part of it, which was addressed to the friends, or the next chapter, which is addressed to Job.

XXXIII.

(1) **Wherefore, Job, I pray thee.**—He begins by professing his sincerity and integrity; and with reference to Job's expressed desire to find an umpire (chap. ix. 33), and one who would maintain his right with God (chap. xvi. 21), he declares that he is ready to do so, and that he is, like Job, made out of the clay, and consequently disposed to deal favourably with him.

(7) **Neither shall my hand be heavy upon thee**—*i.e.*, I will deal gently with thee, and not be harsh.

(9) **I am clean without transgression.**—Job has nowhere used this language; but many of his statements were capable of being so perverted and misrepresented (chaps. ix. 20, 21, xvi. 17, xxiii. 10—12, xxvii. 5, 6). This shows that Elihu even was incapable of entering fully into Job's position. He did not understand that a man could alone be righteous in proportion as he trusted God, but that, trusting God, he was righteous with His righteousness. This was the truth that Job dimly perceived and was faintly, though surely, striving after; and to his friends it was unintelligible, and not wholly apprehended by Elihu.

(10) **Behold, he findeth occasions against me.**—See chaps. xiii. 24, 26, 27, xix. 11.

(11) **He putteth my feet in the stocks.**—Referring, probably, to chap. xiii. 27.

(12) **Behold, in this thou art not just.**—But had not Job said the same thing? (chap. ix. 2, &c., 14, &c.); and is it possible to conceive that any one could think otherwise, more especially as Elihu used the word which specially means man in his frailty?

(13) **Why dost thou strive against him?**—Job had not striven against God, he had only expressed his longing to come into judgment with Him (chap. xxiii. 3, &c.). Job was striving with and against the darkness that was round about His throne, not with the justice of God, which he entirely trusted. Some render the last clause of the verse, "For none can answer any of His words," but the Authorised Version seems preferable.

(14) **For God speaketh once, yea twice.**—The two ways are dilated upon (verses 15—18 and 19—26). Abimelech (Gen. xx. 3) and Daniel (Dan. iv. 5) were

57

When deep sleep falleth upon men, in slumberings upon the bed;
(16) Then ¹he openeth the ears of men,—and sealeth their instruction,
(17) That he may withdraw man *from his* ²*purpose,*
And hide pride from man.
(18) He keepeth back his soul from the pit,
And his life ³from perishing by the sword.
(19) He is chastened also with pain upon his bed,
And the multitude of his bones with strong *pain:*
(20) ᵃSo that his life abhorreth bread,—and his soul ⁴dainty meat.
(21) His flesh is consumed away, that it cannot be seen;
And his bones *that* were not seen stick out.
(22) Yea, his soul draweth near unto the grave,
And his life to the destroyers.
(23) If there be a messenger with him, An interpreter, one among a thousand,
To shew unto man his uprightness:
(24) Then he is gracious unto him, and saith,
Deliver him from going down to the pit:
I have found ⁵ a ransom.
(25) His flesh shall be fresher ⁶than a child's:
He shall return to the days of his youth:
(26) He shall pray unto God, and he will be favourable unto him:
And he shall see his face with joy:
For he will render unto man his righteousness.
(27) ⁷He looketh upon men, and *if any* say,
I have sinned, and perverted *that which was* right,
And it profited me not;
(28) ⁸He will deliver his soul from going into the pit,
And his life shall see the light.

1 Heb., *he revealeth,* or *uncovereth.*
2 Heb., *work.*
3 Heb., *from passing by the sword.*
a Ps. 107.
4 Heb., *meat of desire.*
5 Or, *an atonement.*
6 Heb., *than childhood.*
7 Or, *He shall look upon men, and say, I have sinned,* &c.
8 Or, *He hath delivered my soul,* &c., *and my life.*

---

instances of this first method. (Comp. also Gen. xv. 12. &c., xxviii. 12, &c.)

(16) **Then he openeth the ears of men and sealeth.**—Comp. chap. xiv. 17: "My transgression is sealed in a bag." "He openeth their ear," that is, He showeth them that He will decree, confirm, and seal up their chastisement, the sentence that is to be executed upon them, if they will not repent. If taken in the sense of instruction, it must mean that He will complete and confirm it.

(17) **From his purpose.**—Rather, *That He may withdraw man from carrying out his evil actions, and may remove that pride from man which he secretly cherishes.* This is the main point of Elihu's teaching: that the purposes of God are disciplinary, to keep man from the sin which otherwise he would be prone to commit. In this way Job might have been a righteous man, and yet be justly chastened lest he should prove unrighteous.

(19) **He is chastened.**—This is the second manner in which God speaks—first by dreams, &c., then by afflictions.

And the multitude of his bones with strong pain.—Or, reading it otherwise, we may render, *And with continual strife in his bones*—*e.g.,* rheumatism and gout.

(23) **To show unto man his uprightness.**—Some render, "to show unto man what is right for him," but it seems rather to mean, *to declare concerning that man his uprightness,* to plead his cause before God and be his advocate. (Comp. 1 Kings xiv. 13; 2 Chron. xix. 3, &c.)

This angel, who is one among a thousand, and discharges the function of an interpreter, is a remarkable anticipation of the existence of that function with God which is discharged by the Advocate with the Father (1 John ii. 1; Rom. viii. 34; Heb. vii. 25). It is impossible for us who believe that all Scripture is given by inspiration of God not to see in this an indication of what God intended afterwards to teach us concerning the intercession and mediation of the Son and the intercession of the Holy Spirit on behalf of man (Rom. viii. 26). (Comp. John xiv. 16.)

(24) **Then he is gracious unto him**—*i.e.,* God is gracious; He accepts the mediation of the mediating angel. These words of Elihu's must have fallen on Job's ear with a grateful and refreshing sound, confirming to him his longing for the daysman (chap. ix. 33).

And saith—*i.e.,* to the destroying angels of verse 22. It is remarkable that it is *God* who finds the ransom, as it was by God's grace that the interpreting angel was forthcoming. It is not man's righteousness that has saved him, but the ransom that God has found, even though God, who judgeth the actions, may have justly recognised what of righteousness there was in man.

(26) **He will be favourable unto him.**—Very beautiful is this description of the restoration of the penitent sinner and his recovery from sickness. He shall thankfully resort unto the house of God with joy, for that He has rewarded him according to his righteousness, which was the fruit of faith (Gen. xv. 6; Ps. xxxii. 1, 2).

(27) **He looketh upon men, and if any say.**—Rather, *He looketh upon men, and saith, I have sinned,* &c.: that is the confession of the restored sinner. Some render it, *He shall sing before men,* but hardly so probably or appropriately.

(28) **He will deliver his soul.**—There are two readings in the Hebrew here, of which one is represented by the Authorised Version; but the better one is, "He hath redeemed my soul from going into the pit, and my life shall see the light"—this is part of the restored man's confession, which appears to be continued till the speaker resumes in verse 29.

Elihu accuses Job of   JOB, XXXIV.   *charging God with Injustice.*

(29) Lo, all these *things* worketh God—
    ¹oftentimes with man,
(30) To bring back his soul from the pit,
    To be enlightened with the lights of the living.
(31) Mark well, O Job, hearken unto me:
    Hold thy peace, and I will speak.
(32) If thou hast any thing to say, answer me:
    Speak, for I desire to justify thee.
(33) If not, hearken unto me:
    Hold thy peace, and I shall teach thee wisdom.

CHAPTER XXXIV.—(1) Furthermore Elihu answered and said,
(2) Hear my words, O ye wise *men*;
    And give ear unto me, ye that have knowledge.
(3) *ᵃ*For the ear trieth words,—as the ²mouth tasteth meat.
(4) Let us choose to us judgment:
    Let us know among ourselves what *is* good.
(5) For Job hath said, I am righteous:
    And God hath taken away my judgment.
(6) Should I lie against my right?
    ³My wound *is* incurable without transgression.
(7) What man *is* like Job, *who* drinketh up scorning like water?
(8) Which goeth in company with the workers of iniquity,
    And walketh with wicked men.
(9) For he hath said, It profiteth a man nothing
    That he should delight himself with God.
(10) Therefore hearken unto me, ye ⁴men of understanding:
    *ᵇ*Far be it from God, *that he should do* wickedness;
    And *from* the Almighty, *that he should commit* iniquity.
(11) *ᶜ*For the work of a man shall he render unto him,
    And cause every man to find according to *his* ways.
(12) Yea, surely God will not do wickedly,

Marginal notes:
1 Heb., *twice and thrice.*
a ch. 12. 11.
2 Heb., *palate.*
3 Heb., *mine arrow.*
4 Heb., *men of heart.*
b Deut. 32. 4; ch. 8. 3 & 36. 23; Ps. 92. 15; Rom. 9. 14.
c Ps. 62. 12; Prov. 24. 12; Jer. 32. 19; Ezek. 33. 20; Matt. 16. 27; Rom. 2. 6; 2 Cor. 5. 10; 1 Pet. 1. 17; Rev. 22. 12.

---

(30) **To bring back his soul.**—Here, again, is the very key-note of Elihu's doctrine. God's dealings are for the purpose of education and discipline, and this is what he wishes to impress upon Job.

(32) **I desire to justify thee.**—He wishes to justify Job before his friends, that is, to maintain that his afflictions are not on account of past sin, but as a preservative against possible future defection. This being so, he considers that Job's case may justly be defended, and Job himself vindicated against his friends.

XXXIV.

(1) **Furthermore Elihu.**—Elihu here hardly makes good the profession with which he starts, for he begins immediately to accuse Job in no measured language. Elihu makes, indeed, a great profession of wisdom, and expressly addresses himself to the wise (verse 2), and insists upon the necessity of discrimination (verses 3, 4). It is to be observed that Job himself had given utterance to much the same sentiment in chap. xii. 11.

(5) **For Job hath said.**—See chaps. xiii. 18, 19, and xxvii. 2, especially.

(6) **Should I lie against my right?**—Comp. chap. xxvii. 2—6.

My wound is incurable.—Literally, *my arrow*, i.e., the arrow which hath wounded me. (See chaps. xvi. 11, xvii. 1, &c.)

Without transgression.—That is to say, *on my part*. (See chap. xvi. 17.) Some understand the former clause, "Notwithstanding my right, I am accounted a liar," but the Authorised Version is more probably right.

(7) **Who drinketh up scorning?**—The same word had been applied to Job by Zophar (chap. xi. 3), "And when thou *mockest*, shall no man make thee ashamed?" and the same reproach by Eliphaz (chap. xv. 16).

(8) **And walketh with wicked men.**—This was the charge that was brought against Job by Eliphaz (chaps. xv. 4, 5, xxii. 15).

(9) **It profiteth a man nothing.**—Comp. what Job had said (chaps. ix. 20—22, 30, 31, x. 6, 7, 14, 15). Eliphaz had virtually said the same thing, though the form in which he cast it was the converse of this (see chap. xxii. 3), for he had represented it as a matter of indifference to *God* whether man was righteous or not, which was, of course, to sap the foundations of all morality; for if God cares not whether man is righteous or not, it certainly cannot *profit* man to be righteous. On the other hand, Eliphaz had in form uttered the opposite doctrine (chap. xxii. 21).

(10) **Ye men of understanding.**—Elihu now appeals to the men of understanding, by whom he can hardly mean the three friends of whom he has already spoken disparagingly, but seems rather to appeal to an audience, real or imagined, who are to decide on the merits of what he says. This is an incidental indication that we are scarcely intended to understand the long-continued argument as the record of an actual discussion. Elihu begins to take broader ground than the friends of Job, inasmuch as he concerns himself, not with the problems of God's government, but with the impossibility of His acting unjustly (Gen. xviii. 25), and the reason he gives is somewhat strange—it is the fact that God is irresponsible, He has not been put in charge over the earth; but His authority is ultimate and original, and being so, He can have no personal interests to secure at all risks; He can only have in view the ultimate good of all His creatures, for, on the other hand, if He really desired to slay them, their breath is in His hands, and He would only have to recall it. The earth and all that is in it belongs to God: it is His own, and not another's entrusted to Him; His self-interest, therefore, cannot come into collision with the welfare of His creatures, because their welfare

God who is Almighty   JOB, XXXIV.   *Cannot be Unjust.*

Neither will the Almighty pervert judgment.
(13) Who hath given him a charge over the earth?
Or who hath disposed ¹the whole world?
(14) *ᵃIf he set his heart ²upon man,
If he gather unto himself his spirit and his breath;*
(15) ᵇAll flesh shall perish together,
And man shall turn again unto dust.
(16) If now *thou hast* understanding, hear this:
Hearken to the voice of my words.
(17) Shall even he that hateth right ³govern?
And wilt thou condemn him that is most just?
(18) *Is it fit* to say to a king, *Thou art* wicked?
And to princes, *Ye are* ungodly?
(19) *How much less to him* that ᶜaccepteth not the persons of princes,
Nor regardeth the rich more than the poor?
For they all *are* the work of his hands.
(20) In a moment shall they die,
And the people shall be troubled at midnight, and pass away:
And ⁴the mighty shall be taken away without hand.
(21) ᵈFor his eyes *are* upon the ways of man,
And he seeth all his goings.
(22) *There is* no darkness, nor shadow of death,
Where the workers of iniquity may hide themselves.
(23) For he will not lay upon man more *than right;*
That he should ⁵enter into judgment with God.
(24) He shall break in pieces mighty men ⁶without number,
And set others in their stead.

¹ Heb., *all of it?*
ᵃ Ps. 104. 29.
² Heb., *upon him.*
ᵇ Gen. 3.19; Eccles. 12. 7.
³ Heb., *bind?*
ᶜ Deut. 10. 17; 2 Chr. 19. 7; Acts 10. 34; Rom. 2. 11; Gal. 2. 6; Eph. 6. 9; Col. 3. 25; 1 Pet. 1. 17.
⁴ Heb., *they shall take away the mighty.*
ᵈ 2 Chron. 16, 9; ch. 31. 4; Prov. 5, 21 & 15. 3; Jer. 16. 17.
⁵ Heb., *go.*
⁶ Heb., *without searching out.*

---

is the welfare of that which is His—of that, therefore, in which He Himself has the largest interest. The argument is a somewhat strange one to us, but it is sound at bottom, for it recognises God as the prime origin and final hope of all His creatures, and assumes that His will can only be good, and that it must be the best because it is His. (Comp. St. John x. 12, 13.)

(13) **Who hath disposed the whole world?**—Or, *Who hath set the whole world upon Him?* i.e., entrusted it to His care; in the other sense it means, "Who but He hath made the whole world, and who, therefore, can have the interest in it which He must have?"

(14) **If he set his heart upon man.**—Or, *upon himself.* It is ambiguous: and so, likewise, the next clause is. We must either regard it as the consequence of the former one—"If He set His heart upon Himself, had regard to His own interest, then He would gather unto Himself His own spirit and His own breath"—or we must do as some do: supply the "if" at the beginning of it, and read it as in the Authorised Version. In this sense, the setting His heart upon man would mean in a bad sense—to do him injury. In doing him injury He would, in fact, injure His own. The effect of His setting His heart on man would be that all flesh would perish together, and man would turn again to his dust; but then God would have injured His own, and not another's, in so doing. It is hardly possible that the writer of this last clause should have been ignorant of Gen. iii. 19. The speech of Elihu is marked with entire self-confidence.

(17) **Shall even he. . . .**—The argument is that one who holds such a position of absolute rule cannot be other than most just. He who is fit to rule must be just, and He who is the ultimate ruler must be fit to rule, and must, therefore, be just; but if He is absolutely just, how shall we condemn His government or Him on account of it, even though we cannot explain it all or reconcile it with our view of what is right?

Him that is most just, is rather *him that is just* and *mighty,* i.e., not only just, but able also to execute justice because mighty.

(18) **Is it fit to say to a king?**—The argument is from the less to the greater. "Who could challenge a king or princes? and if not a king, how much less the King of kings?" There is a strong ellipse in the Hebrew, but yet one that is naturally supplied. (Comp. Ps. cxxxvii. 5.)

(20) **In a moment shall they die**—i.e., "they all alike die, rich and poor together; the hour of death is not hastened for the poor nor delayed for the rich. They all alike die."

Even at midnight the people are troubled. . . .—It is hard to think that the writer did not know of Exodus xii. 29. It is better to read these statements as habitual presents and not as futures: "In a moment they die, even at midnight—the people are shaken and pass away," &c.

(21) **His eyes are upon the ways of man.**—He is not only just and mighty, but He is also all-wise; He cannot therefore err.

(22) **There is no darkness.**—As Job had perhaps seemed to imply in chap. xxiv. 13—16.

(23) **For he will not lay upon man more than right**—i.e., so much that he should enter into judgment with God. This is probably the meaning, as the Authorised Version; but some render, "He needeth not yet again to consider a man that he should go before God in judgment." He hath no need to consider any man's case twice or to rectify His first decision. He is infallible, and cannot do otherwise than right, whatever He does.

(24) **Without number.**—Rather, *in an unsearchable manner,* as before, verse 20, "without hand," i.e., without human means.

(25) **Therefore.**—We should expect *because* rather; but the writer, believing in God's justice, infers that since God acts thus He knoweth the works of man, and has grounds for acting as He acts.

(25) Therefore he knoweth their works,
And he overturneth *them* in the night,
so that they are ¹destroyed.
(26) He striketh them as wicked men—
²in the open sight of others;
(27) Because they turned back ³from him,
And would not consider any of his ways:
(28) So that they cause the cry of the poor to come unto him,
And he heareth the cry of the afflicted.
(29) When he giveth quietness, who then can make trouble?
And when he hideth *his* face, who then can behold him?
Whether *it be done* against a nation, or against a man only:
(30) That the hypocrite reign not,—lest the people be ensnared.
(31) Surely it is meet to be said unto God,
I have borne *chastisement*, I will not offend *any more*:
(32) *That which* I see not teach thou me:
If I have done iniquity, I will do no more.
(33) ⁴*Should it be* according to thy mind? he will recompense it.
Whether thou refuse, or whether thou choose; and not I:
Therefore speak what thou knowest.
(34) Let men ⁵of understanding tell me,
And let a wise man hearken unto me.
(35) Job hath spoken without knowledge,
And his words *were* without wisdom.
(36) ⁶My desire *is that* Job may be tried unto the end
Because of *his* answers for wicked men.
(37) For he addeth rebellion unto his sin,
He clappeth *his hands* among us,
And multiplieth his words against God.

CHAPTER XXXV.—⁽¹⁾ Elihu spake moreover, and said,
(2) Thinkest thou this to be right,
That thou saidst, My righteousness *is* more than God's?
(3) For thou saidst, What advantage will it be unto thee?
And, What profit shall I have, ⁷*if I be cleansed* from my sin?
(4) ⁸I will answer thee,—and thy companions with thee.

---

1 Heb., *crushed.*
2 Heb., *in the place of beholders.*
3 Heb., *from after him.*
4 Heb., *Should it be from with thee?*
5 Heb., *of heart.*
6 Or, *My father, let Job be tried.*
7 Or, *by it more than by my sin?*
8 Heb., *I will return to thee words.*

---

(26) **He striketh them as wicked men.**—Rather, *in the place of wicked men he striketh them*: *i.e.*, the wicked—that is, "He executeth His judgments in the sight of all beholders, striking down wicked men in their very place, so that there can be no doubt as to who are stricken or why they are stricken."

(27) **Because they turned back from him.**—Elihu, therefore, as well as Job's other friends, believed in the direct execution of God's judgments.

(29) **When he giveth quietness, who then can make trouble?**—This is probably the meaning, but literally it is, *Who can condemn?*

Or against a man only.—Rather, *against a man alike*: *i.e.*, it is all one in either case. He judges nations as He judges individuals, and individuals as He does nations.

(30) **That the hypocrite reign not.**—Rather, (whether God is provoked), *on account of an ungodly man reigning, or by the snares of a whole people*: *i.e.*, the corruption of a nation, *e.g.*, Sodom, &c.

(31, 32) **I have borne chastisement . . .**—These verses express the attitude that should be assumed towards God: one of submission and penitence.

(33) **Should it be according to thy mind?** is obscure from its abruptness. We understand it thus: "Should he recompense it (*i.e.*, a man's conduct) according to thy mind, with thy concurrence, whether thou refusest or whether thou choosest?"

And not I—*i.e.*, "Then why not according as I refuse or choose? If thou art to influence and direct His dealing and government, why may not I? why may not any one? And if so, He is no longer supreme or absolute. What knowest thou, then? Speak, if thou hast anything to say to this reasoning."

(34) **Let men of understanding tell me.**—Rather, *Men of understanding will say to me*, or, *agree with me; and every wise man that heareth me will say*, &c.

(36) **My desire is that Job may be tried.**—There seems to be reason to prefer the marginal rendering, and consider the words as addressed to God: "Oh my Father, let Job be tried, &c." "*Pater mi probetur Job*," Vulg. Elihu's words cannot have fallen upon Job with more acceptance or with lighter weight than those of his other friends. He must have felt, however, that his cause was safe with God, whatever the misunderstanding of men.

Because of his answers for wicked men.—Rather, *his answering like wicked men*.

(37) **He clappeth his hands among us.**—As though he were confident of victory in argument.

XXXV.

(2) **My righteousness is more than God's.**—See chap. xix. 6, &c. Job had not in so many words said this, but what he had said was capable of being so represented, and perhaps seemed to involve it. (Comp. chaps. ix. 22, x. 15.) Here, again, there was a misrepresentation of what Job had said. He certainly did not mean that he was none the better for being righteous; on the contrary, he had distinctly said, "Let mine enemy be as the wicked," &c. (chap. xxvii. 7, &c.), because *he* could not delight himself in God; but it was perfectly true that he had said that his righteousness had not delivered him from suffering.

(4) **And thy companions.**—Elihu professes to answer Job's friends as well as himself, but what he says (verse 5, &c.) is very much what Eliphaz had said before (chaps. xv. 14, &c., xxii. 3, &c., and Bildad

Comparison is not   JOB, XXXVI.   *to be Made with God.*

(5) Look unto the heavens, and see;
And behold the clouds *which* are higher than thou.
(6) If thou sinnest, what dost thou against him?
Or *if* thy transgressions be multiplied, what doest thou unto him?
(7) *a* If thou be righteous, what givest thou him?
Or what receiveth he of thine hand?
(8) Thy wickedness *may hurt* a man as thou *art*;
And thy righteousness *may profit* the son of man.
(9) By reason of the multitude of oppressions they make *the oppressed* to cry:
They cry out by reason of the arm of the mighty.
(10) But none saith, Where *is* God my maker,
Who giveth songs in the night;
(11) Who teacheth us more than the beasts of the earth,
And maketh us wiser than the fowls of heaven?
(12) There they cry, but none giveth answer,
Because of the pride of evil men.
(13) *b* Surely God will not hear vanity,
Neither will the Almighty regard it.
(14) Although thou sayest thou shalt not see him,
Yet judgment *is* before him; therefore trust thou in him.
(15) But now, because *it is* not so, ¹ he hath visited in his anger;
Yet ² he knoweth *it* not in great extremity:
(16) Therefore doth Job open his mouth in vain;
He multiplieth words without knowledge.

CHAPTER XXXVI.—(1) Elihu also proceeded, and said,
(2) Suffer me a little, and I will shew thee

a ch. 22 3; Ps. 16. 2; Rom. 11. 35.
b ch. 27. 9; Prov. 1. 28; Isa. 1. 15; Jer. 11. 11.
1 That is, *God.*
2 That is, *Job.*

---

in chap. xxv.). It is indeed true that God is too high to be affected by man's righteousness or unrighteousness, but it does not follow therefore that He is indifferent, for then He would not be a righteous judge. (See Note on chap. xxxiv. 9.)

(9) **By reason of the multitude of oppressions.**—The argument seems to be that among men there may be oppression, but not with an almighty and just Judge. The right course, therefore, is to wait. "Men may, indeed, complain because of the oppression of an earthly tyrant; but how canst *thou* say thou beholdest Him not?" (See chap. ix. 9.)

(10) **But none saith.**—Some render this, "But he who giveth songs in the night saith not, Where is God my Maker," *i.e.*, the selfish and luxurious oppressor, who spendeth the night in feasting and revelry. This is an intelligible meaning. On the other hand, though the phrase, "who giveth songs in the night," has become proverbial, and, with the meaning assigned to it, is very beautiful, it may be doubted whether it is so obvious or natural in this place. This is a matter for individual taste and judgment to decide. If it is understood of God, it ascribes to Him the turning of sorrow into gladness, and the night of affliction into joy—an office which is, indeed, frequently assigned to God, but of which the appropriateness is not so manifest here. The decision of this question will perhaps partly depend upon the view we take of the words which follow—"Where is God my Maker?"—whether they are part of the cry of the oppressed or whether they are the words of Elihu. If the latter, then they become more intelligible; if otherwise, it is difficult to see their special appropriateness in this particular place. Perhaps it is better to regard them as the words of Elihu.

(11) **Who teacheth us.**—Or it may be, *Who teacheth us by, and maketh us wise by*, &c. Then the sense will be that the oppression is so severe that the victims of it forget that God can give songs in the night, and that He has favoured men more than the beasts of the field, and that, as not one sparrow can fall to the ground without Him, so He has even numbered the hairs of those who are of more value to Him than many sparrows.

(13) **God will not hear vanity.**—Some understand this as part of the cry in verse 12: "Seeing it is all in vain, God doth not hear, neither doth the Almighty regard it."

(14) **Although thou sayest thou shalt not see him.**—Rather, *Dost not behold Him.*

(15) **But now, because it is not so,** is very obscure. The Authorised Version refers the first clause to God and the second to Job. Perhaps we may render, *But now, what His anger has visited upon thee is as nothing* (compared with thy deserts); *yea, He hath not regarded the great abundance* (of thy sin), *i.e.*, hath not visited it with anger. *Therefore doth Job*, &c. Others render it, "But now, because it is not so (*i.e.*, there is no judgment), He hath visited in His anger, *saith Job*, and He regardeth it not, *saith He*, in His exceeding arrogance;" or, "But now, because He hath not visited in His anger, neither doth He much regard arrogance, therefore Job," &c. The word thus rendered *arrogance* is not found elsewhere; it appears to mean abundance or superfluity. Of these renderings, the first seems to give the better sense. The general bearing of the verse is perhaps apparent however rendered, namely, that Job is encouraged in his murmurings, because God hath dealt too leniently with him. Elihu's reproaches must have been some of the heaviest that Job had to bear. Happily the judgment was not to be long deferred. (See chap. xxxviii. 1.)

XXXVI.

(1) **Elihu also proceeded.**—It is not easy to acquit Elihu of some of the "arrogance" he was so ready to ascribe to Job. He professes very great zeal for God, but it is hard to see that some of his great professions are warranted. For instance, he says—

Elihu shows that God   JOB, XXXVI.   *is Just in all His Ways.*

(1) That *I have* yet to speak on God's behalf.

(3) I will fetch my knowledge from afar, And will ascribe righteousness to my Maker.

(4) For truly my words *shall* not *be* false: He that is perfect in knowledge *is* with thee.

(5) Behold, God *is* mighty, and despiseth not *any*: He *is* mighty in strength *and* ²wisdom.

(6) He preserveth not the life of the wicked: But giveth right to the ³poor.

(7) ᵃ He withdraweth not his eyes from the righteous: But with kings *are they* on the throne; Yea, he doth establish them for ever, and they are exalted.

(8) And if *they be* bound in fetters, *And* be holden in cords of affliction;

(9) Then he sheweth them their work, And their transgressions that they have exceeded.

(10) He openeth also their ear to discipline, And commandeth that they return from iniquity.

(11) If they obey and serve *him*, They shall ᵇspend their days in prosperity, And their years in pleasures.

(12) But if they obey not,—⁴they shall perish by the sword, And they shall die without knowledge.

(13) But the hypocrites in heart heap up wrath: They cry not when he bindeth them.

(14) ⁵They die in youth,—and their life *is* among the ⁶unclean.

(15) He delivereth the ⁷poor in his affliction, And openeth their ears in oppression.

(16) Even so would he have removed thee out of the strait Into a broad place, where *there is* no straitness; And ⁸that which should be set on thy table *should be* full of fatness.

(17) But thou hast fulfilled the judgment of the wicked: ⁹Judgment and justice take hold *on* thee.

(18) Because *there is* wrath, *beware* lest he take thee away with *his* stroke: Then a great ransom cannot ¹⁰deliver thee.

(19) Will he esteem thy riches? *No*, not gold, nor all the forces of strength.

(20) Desire not the night,—when people are cut off in their place.

---

1 Heb., *that there are yet words for God.*
2 Heb., *heart.*
3 Or, *afflicted.*
a Ps. 34. 15.
b ch. 21. 13.
4 Heb., *they shall pass away by the sword.*
5 Heb., *Their soul dieth.*
6 Or, *sodomites.*
7 Or, *afflicted.*
8 Heb., *the rest of thy table.*
9 Or, *judgment and justice should uphold thee.*
10 Heb., *turn thee aside.*

---

(3) **I will fetch my knowledge from afar.**—But is not this what Bildad had said before him? (chap. viii. 8, &c.); and yet the teaching of verse 6 is not very different from his.

(4) **He that is perfect in knowledge.**—We may presume that he meant God; but in the Authorised Version it looks very much as though he meant himself. (Comp. chap. xxxvii. 16.) So apparently Vulg., "*perfecta scientia probabitur tibi.*"

(7) **From the righteous**—*i.e.*, the righteous man. (Comp. Ps. cxiii. 5—8.)

(9) **Then he sheweth them their work.**—The true nature of their conduct and their transgressions, that they have behaved themselves proudly. This is Elihu's special doctrine, that God's chastisements are by way of discipline, to reform the future rather than to chastise the past.

(11) **They shall spend their days in prosperity.**—It is, perhaps, not more easy to reconcile this teaching of Elihu's with the realities of actual fact than it is the notions of Job's friends as to direct retribution in life.

(13) **The hypocrites in heart.**—The words rather mean *the godless or profane in heart*.

They cry not.—That is, cry not for help.

When he bindeth them.—That is, as in verse 8, he has been speaking especially of one kind of affliction, like that, namely, of Joseph.

(15) **He delivereth the poor in his affliction.**—The point of Elihu's discourse is rather that He delivereth the afflicted by his affliction; He makes use of the very affliction to deliver him by it as a means, "and openeth their ears by oppression."

(16) **Even so would he have removed thee.** It is possible to understand this verse somewhat otherwise, and the sense may perhaps be improved. Elihu may be speaking, not of what God would have done, but of what He has actually done: "Yea, also He hath removed thee from the mouth of an adversary, even ease and abundance in the place of which there was no straitness, and that which came down upon thy table full of fatness; but thou art full of the judgment of the wicked, therefore justice and judgment take hold on thee." "God, in His mercy, saw that thou wast in danger, and He removed the cause of temptation, and thy chastisement would have been of short duration hadst thou been submissive and resigned; but thou hast been bold and daring, like the wicked, and hast reaped the judgment of the wicked."

(18) **Because there is wrath.**—"For there is wrath: now, therefore, beware lest He take thee away with one stroke, so that great ransom cannot deliver thee." Literally it is, *let not a great ransom deliver thee*, but the sense is probably like the Authorised Version.

(19) **No, not gold, nor all the forces of strength.**—The words here are doubtful. Some render, "Will He esteem thy riches, that thou be not in distress?" or, "all the forces of thy strength;" others, "Will thy cry avail, that thou be not in distress?" &c.; but there is authority for the Authorised Version.

(20) **Desire not the night**—*i.e.*, of death, as Job had done (chaps. xvi. 22, xvii. 13, &c., xix. 27), or, as

(21) Take heed, regard not iniquity:
For this hast thou chosen rather than affliction.
(22) Behold, God exalteth by his power:—who teacheth like him?
(23) Who hath enjoined him his way?
Or who can say, Thou hast wrought iniquity? ¹
(24) Remember that thou magnify his work,—which men behold.
(25) Every man may see it;—man may behold *it* afar off.
(26) Behold, God *is* great, and we know *him* not,
Neither can the number of his years be searched out.
(27) For he maketh small the drops of water:
They pour down rain according to the vapour thereof:

¹ Heb., *the roots.*

² Heb., *that which goeth up.*

(28) Which the clouds do drop
And distil upon man abundantly.
(29) Also can *any* understand the spreadings of the clouds,
Or the noise of his tabernacle?
(30) Behold, he spreadeth his light upon it,
And covereth ¹the bottom of the sea.
(31) For by them judgeth he the people;
He giveth meat in abundance.
(32) With clouds he covereth the light;
And commandeth it *not to shine* by *the cloud* that cometh betwixt.
(33) The noise thereof sheweth concerning it,
The cattle also concerning ²the vapour.

CHAPTER XXXVII.—(1) At this also my heart trembleth,

all events, his words might be understood. For "people," read *peoples: i.e.,* nations.

(21) **Regard not iniquity.**—Or, perhaps, the special sin of longing for death, for thou hast desired to die rather than bear thine affliction. Alas! Job's case is not a solitary one, for who that has been tried as he was has not longed for the end?

(22) **Behold, God exalteth by his power.**—The rest of Elihu's speech is splendidly eloquent. He dilates on the power and majesty of God, and appears to be speaking in contemplation of some magnificent natural phenomenon—as the tempest, or hurricane, or whirlwind—out of which the Lord ultimately spake (chap. xxxviii. 1). It is probable that this storm was beginning to gather, and that it suggested the glorious imagery of Elihu's speech. The points are that (1) God is the source of greatness; (2) that there is no teacher like Him (verse 22); (3) that He is absolute as well as almighty (verse 23); (4) that He is unsearchable and eternal (verse 26).

(24) **Which men behold.**—Some render it, "Whereof men sing," but the other seems to suit the context best.

(27) **The drops of water.**—The origin and first beginnings of the tempest are described. "He maketh small," or draweth up by exhalation. "They pour down rain," or "they distil in rain from His vapour," or "belonging to the vapour thereof." The rain is first absorbed, and then distilled and poured down.

(29) **The spreading of the clouds**—*i.e.,* how the clouds are spread over the heavens, and heaped up one upon the other like mountains in the skies when the storm gathers.

Or the noise of His tabernacle?—Or the thunderings of His pavilion (Ps. xviii. 12).

(30) **His light** appears to mean here the lightning which flashes forth from the cloud.

And covereth the bottom of the sea.—Literally, *it hath covered the roots of the sea: i.e.,* it, the lightning, or He, God, hath covered those clouds which are composed of the roots of the sea, that is, the drops of water which are exhaled from the sea.

(31) **For by them**—*i.e.,* these roots of the sea, these drops of water, these rain-clouds. "He judgeth peoples" by withholding them, or "giveth meat in abundance" by sending rain on the earth; or He may use them in excess, to chastise nations by inundations and the like. The change from *roots of the sea* to *bottom of the sea* in the Authorised Version has obscured the meaning of "them" in the next verse, unless, indeed, we understand it generally, *by these things.*

(32) **With clouds.**—The word here rendered "clouds" really means *hands,* and there seems to be no good reason why it should be otherwise understood. The verse will then read, "He covereth the lightning with His hands, and giveth it a charge that it strike the mark;" or, according to some, "giveth it a charge against the assailant." The figure is that of a man hurling a stone or bolt, and taking aim; and a very fine one the image is. The Authorised Version cannot be right with its five inserted words.

(33) **The noise thereof sheweth concerning it.**—This verse is extremely difficult, and the sense very uncertain. We may translate the first clause, "The noise thereof (*i.e.,* the crash of the thunder) declareth concerning Him:" it is His voice, and speaks of Him; but the last clause is almost unintelligible. The words as they stand mean, or may mean, *cattle even concerning a goer up;* but what this means who shall say? Possibly, *the thunder-crash telleth the cattle even concerning Him who goeth up: i.e.,* even the cattle show, by their terror, that the thunder speaketh to them of God, who goeth up on high. (See Pss. xxix. 9, lxviii. 4, 18, xlvii. 5.) Some render the last clause, "The cattle also concerning Him as He riseth up;" or, "The cattle also concerning the rising storm." There can be no doubt but that the general meaning is that all nature participateth in the terror caused by the thunder, which is regarded as the audible voice of God; but what the exact expression of this general thought may be it is very hard to say.

There should be no break between this chapter and the next.

XXXVII.

(1) **At this also my heart trembleth.**—Elihu is discoursing of the same matter. He says, "Not only are the cattle terrified, but at this also *my* heart trembleth and is moved out of its place. Hark! listen to the sound of His voice."

God is to be Feared   JOB, XXXVII.   *because of His great Works.*

And is moved out of his place.
(2) ¹Hear attentively the noise of his voice,
And the sound *that* goeth out of his mouth.
(3) He directeth it under the whole heaven,
And his ²lightning unto the ³ends of the earth.
(4) After it a voice roareth :
He thundereth with the voice of his excellency ;
And he will not stay them when his voice is heard.
(5) God thundereth marvellously with his voice ;
Great things doeth he, which we cannot comprehend.
(6) For ᵃhe saith to the snow, Be thou *on* the earth ;
⁴Likewise to the small rain,
And to the great rain of his strength.
(7) He sealeth up the hand of every man ;
That all men may know his work.
(8) Then the beasts go into dens,—and remain in their places.
(9) ⁵Out of the south cometh the whirlwind :
And cold out of the ⁶north.
(10) By the breath of God frost is given :
And the breadth of the waters is straitened.
(11) Also by watering he wearieth the thick cloud :
He scattereth ⁷his bright cloud :
(12) And it is turned round about by his counsels :
That they may do whatsoever he commandeth them
Upon the face of the world in the earth.
(13) He causeth it to come, whether for ⁸correction,
Or for his land, or for mercy.
(14) Hearken unto this, O Job :
Stand still, and consider the wondrous works of God.
(15) Dost thou know when God disposed them,
And caused the light of his cloud to shine ?
(16) Dost thou know the balancings of the clouds,
The wondrous works of him which is perfect in knowledge ?
(17) How thy garments *are* warm,
When he quieteth the earth by the south *wind* ?
(18) Hast thou with him spread out the sky,

1 Heb., *Hear in hearing.*
2 Heb., *light.*
3 Heb., *wings of the earth.*
a Ps. 147. 16, 17.
4 Heb., *and to the shower of rain, and to the showers of rain of his strength.*
5 Heb., *Out of the chamber.*
6 Heb., *scattering winds.*
7 Heb., *the cloud of his light.*
8 Heb., *a rod.*

---

(3) **He directeth it.**—Or, *sendeth it forth:* *i.e.*, the noise and rumbling which fills all heaven.

(4) **After it a voice roareth**—*i.e.*, the thunderclap which follows the lightning-flash.

And he stayeth them not (or will not stay them) **when his voice is heard.**—What does this mean? We understand it, "Yet none can track them (*i.e.*, the thunder and the lightning) when His voice is heard. They travel in paths which none can explore. Vivid as the lightning is, who shall pursue its course?"

(6) **For he saith to the snow.**—All the operations of nature obey the behest of God—the snow, the gentle showers, the drenching downpour. By means of these He sealeth up the hand of every man, obstructing and impeding their works and movements, so that all the men whom He has made may know it or know Him. This is the plain meaning, which the Authorised Version gives somewhat less clearly. Men may learn from these things that they and their works are under the control of God. They are not the entirely free agents they suppose.

(8) **Then the beasts go into dens.**—And not man only, but the beasts likewise, have to take refuge in their dens and coverts.

(9) **Out of the south.**—Rather, *out of its chamber* (see chap. ix. 9) cometh the whirlwind, or typhoon : and cold from the northern constellations, from the quarter of the heavens where they shine.

(10) **The breadth of the waters is straitened.**—Firm, like a molten mass.

(11) **He wearieth the thick cloud.**—Also He ladeth the thick cloud with moisture, maketh it to be charged with rain. "He scattereth the cloud of His lightning," that is, which containeth His lightning. Others render, "Yea, the bright sun weareth out (disperseth) the thick cloud; it scattereth the cloud that holds His lightning. And it (the cloud) is turned round about by His counsels, that they may do His purpose, even all which He commandeth them, upon the face of the habitable world." Whether for correction, or for His land generally, or whether He causeth the rain to come as a special mercy :—these are the various purposes for which God reserves His showers.

(15) **Light of His cloud**—*i.e.*, lightning, as before. "Dost thou know all the secrets of God's thunderbolts, at whom and how He will use them?" Some understand this otherwise : "Dost thou know when God setteth the sun over them (the clouds), and causeth the light (*i.e.*, the sun) to shine upon His cloud?" *i.e.*, "Dost thou know how God useth the sun to disperse the clouds?"

(16) **The balancings of the clouds.**—How they are poised and suspended in the sky. "Ye clouds, that far above me *float* and pause."—Coleridge.

(17) **When he quieteth the earth.**—Or, *When the earth is still.*

(18) **Spread out the sky.**—Some understand this of the action of the sun in dispersing the clouds; but it seems more probable that it refers to God. "Hast thou spread out with Him the magnificent dome of heaven?" The words used, however, imply *the clouds* rather than the cloudless sky which resembles a burnished mirror; so that it is not improbable that the sun may be the subject here and in the following verses.

God's Wisdom Unsearchable.   JOB, XXXVIII.   *God's Answer to Job.*

Which is strong, *and as* a molten looking glass?
(19) Teach us what we shall say unto him;
For we cannot order *our speech* by reason of darkness.
(20) Shall it be told him that I speak?
If a man speak, surely he shall be swallowed up.
(21) And now *men* see not the bright light which *is* in the clouds:
But the wind passeth, and cleanseth them.
(22) ¹Fair weather cometh out of the north:
With God *is* terrible majesty.
(23) *Touching* the Almighty, we cannot find him out: *he is* excellent in power,
And in judgment, and in plenty of justice: he will not afflict.
(24) Men do therefore fear him:
He respecteth not any *that are* wise of heart.

1 Heb., *Gold.*

2 Heb., *make me know.*

a Ps. 104. 5; Prov. 30. 4.

3 Heb., *if thou knowest understanding.*

4 Heb., *sockets.*

5 Heb., *made to sink.*

b Ps. 104. 9.

CHAPTER XXXVIII.—(1) Then the Lord answered Job out of the whirlwind, and said,
(2) Who *is* this that darkeneth counsel By words without knowledge?
(3) Gird up now thy loins like a man;
For I will demand of thee, and ²answer thou me.
(4) *a*Where wast thou when I laid the foundations of the earth?
Declare, ³if thou hast understanding.
(5) Who hath laid the measures thereof, if thou knowest?
Or who hath stretched the line upon it?
(6) Whereupon are the ⁴foundations thereof ⁵fastened?
Or who laid the corner stone thereof;
(7) When the morning stars sang together,
And all the sons of God shouted for joy?
(8) *b*Or *who* shut up the sea with doors,

---

(19) **Teach us what we shall say unto** (or, *concerning*) **him**—*i.e.*, the sun. "He is altogether hidden by the clouds; but is he gone? is he not still there behind them?"

(20) **Be swallowed up.**—The sense will vary, according as we understand this of God or of the sun. In the first case, it is a simple expression of awe at God's majesty: "Shall it be told Him that I would speak? If a man speak, surely he shall be swallowed up;" but unquestionably the sense is clearer if we understand it of the sun: "Shall it be told of him? Shall I, indeed, speak it? or hath any man ever ventured to say, in such a case, that the sun is swallowed up, extinguished?"

(21) **And now men see not the bright light**—*i.e.*, the sun. "But he is bright behind the clouds, and when the wind has passed over them and cleared them away, even the north wind, he will come forth like gold; but upon God there is terrible majesty. Though the sun is hidden, we shall see him again, but who shall ever find out God?" It is manifest that this rendering adds great sublimity, and points to the opening of the next chapter.

(23) **Touching the Almighty, we cannot find him out.**—He is excellent, or mighty, in power and justice, &c.

(24) **Men do therefore fear him.**—Or, "Therefore men may fear Him; but as for the wise in heart, no one even of them shall see Him." This may be, and probably is, the meaning, though the literal rendering is that of the Authorised Version, which, however, involves a somewhat doubtful sentiment in itself, for God, we may believe, does regard or respect those who are truly wise. In the original there is a very manifest play on the words, which it is impossible to preserve, between yĕre'u and yireh—*men shall fear, but none shall see.*

XXXVIII.

(1) **Then the Lord answered Job.**—This chapter brings the grand climax and catastrophe of the poem. Unless all was to remain hopelessly uncertain and dark, there could be no solution of the questions so fiercely and obstinately debated but by the intervention of Him whose government was the matter in dispute. And so the Lord answered Job out of *the* whirlwind, or tempest: that is to say, the tempest which had been long gathering, and which had been the subject of Elihu's remarks. The one argument which is developed in the remaining chapters is drawn from man's ignorance. There is so much in nature that man knows not and cannot understand, that it is absurd for him to suppose that he can judge aright in matters touching God's moral government of the world. Though Job is afterwards (chap. xlii. 8) justified by God, yet the tone of all that God says to him is more or less mingled with reproach.

(2) **Who is this?**—The question may be answered by Job's own words (chap. xiv. 1). It is a man as so described, a dying and enfeebled man, like Job himself, not even a man in his best estate, but one so persecuted and exhausted as Job: one, therefore, altogether unequal to the task he has undertaken.

That darkeneth counsel.—That is, probably, *my counsel*, which was the matter under debate. The words, however, are often used proverbially in a general sense. Such discussions, carried on, as they cannot but be, in entire ignorance by blind mortals, must to God's omniscience seem thus, and cannot be otherwise than the darkening of counsel by words without knowledge.

(4) **Where wast thou?**—The comparison of the creation of the world to the building of an edifice is such a concession to the feebleness of man as serves of itself to heighten the effect of the inevitable answer to the question preferred.

(7) **The morning stars.**—The context seems to suggest that by the stars are meant the angels entrusted with their guardianship, from whence Milton has borrowed his conceptions. The magnificent sublimity of the expression and the thought needs no comment.

When it brake forth, *as if* it had issued out of the womb?
(9) When I made the cloud the garment thereof,
And thick darkness a swaddling-band for it,
(10) And ¹brake up for it my decreed *place*,
And set bars and doors,
(11) And said, Hitherto shalt thou come, but no further:
And here shall ²thy proud waves be stayed?
(12) Hast thou commanded the morning since thy days;
And caused the dayspring to know his place;
(13) That it might take hold of the ³ends of the earth,
That the wicked might be shaken out of it?
(14) It is turned as clay *to* the seal; and they stand as a garment.
(15) And from the wicked their light is withholden,
And the high arm shall be broken.
(16) Hast thou entered into the springs of the sea?
Or hast thou walked in the search of the depth?
(17) Have the gates of death been opened unto thee?
Or hast thou seen the doors of the shadow of death?
(18) Hast thou perceived the breadth of the earth?

Declare if thou knowest it all.
(19) Where *is* the way *where* light dwelleth?
And *as for* darkness, where *is* the place thereof,
(20) That thou shouldest take ⁴it to the bound thereof,
And that thou shouldest know the paths *to* the house thereof?
(21) Knowest thou *it*, because thou wast then born?
Or *because* the number of thy days *is* great?
(22) Hast thou entered into the treasures of the snow?
Or hast thou seen the treasures of the hail,
(23) Which I have reserved against the time of trouble,
Against the day of battle and war?
(24) By what way is the light parted,
Which scattereth the east wind upon the earth?
(25) Who hath divided a watercourse for the overflowing of waters,
Or a way for the lightning of thunder;
(26) To cause it to rain on the earth, *where* no man *is*;
On the wilderness, wherein *there is* no man;
(27) To satisfy the desolate and waste *ground*;
And to cause the bud of the tender herb to spring forth?
(28) Hath the rain a father?

1 Or, *established my decree upon it.*
2 Heb., *the pride of thy waves.*
3 Heb., *wings.*
4 Or, *at.*

(10) **And brake up for it my decreed place.**—Rather, *And prescribed for it my decree*: that is to say, determined the boundaries of its abode. When we bear in mind the vast forces and unstable nature of the sea, it seems a marvel that it acknowledges any limits, and is held in restraint by them.

(12) **And caused the dayspring to know his place.**—Changing, as it does, from day to day with the changing seasons.

(13) **Shaken out of it.**—The figure is that of a man shaking a cloth (chap. xxiv. 15—17).

(14) **As clay to the seal.**—In the darkness every object is without form and void, just as clay or wax, which has no distinctness of shape till the seal is applied, and then the impression is clear and manifest. So with the coming of the daylight after darkness. We should rather render, *It is changed as clay under the seal, and all things stand forth as in their proper raiment.*

(16) **The search of the depth**—*i.e.*, the secret recesses of it. The "springs of the sea" are rather, perhaps, the *mazes, intricacies, &c. of the trackless, pathless deep.* This leads to the cognate thought of the bottomless pit of death (verse 17).

(18) **Perceived.**—Or rather, perhaps, *comprehended*. **The breadth of the earth.**—The earth being conceived of as a vast plain (comp. verse 13). Unscientific as all this language is, it is not a little remarkable that the majestic sublimity of it is not one whit affected thereby.

(20) **That thou shouldest take it**—*i.e.*, go with or track it.

(21) **Knowest thou it?**—It is better to read this verse without an interrogation, as sublime irony. "Doubtless thou knowest all this, for thou wast born then, and the number of thy days is so great!"

(23) **The time of trouble.**—As was the case with the Canaanites, in Josh. x. 11. (Comp. Ps. xviii. 13.)

(24) **By what way is the light parted?**—*i.e.*, distributed in turn to all the inhabitants of the earth.
The east wind.—As naturally suggested by the origin of light and the mention of it.

(25) **Who hath divided a watercourse.**—Rather, *cleft a channel for the water-flood.*

(26) **To cause it to rain on the earth.**—Because God is mindful of His creation, independently of the wants of man.

Or who hath begotten the drops of dew?
(29) Out of whose womb came the ice?
And the hoary frost of heaven, who hath gendered it?
(30) The waters are hid as *with* a stone,
And the face of the deep ¹is frozen.
(31) Canst thou bind the sweet influences of ²³Pleiades,
Or loose the bands of ⁴Orion?
(32) Canst thou bring forth ⁵Mazzaroth in his season?
Or canst thou ⁶guide Arcturus with his sons?
(33) Knowest thou the ordinances of heaven?
Canst thou set the dominion thereof in the earth?
(34) Canst thou lift up thy voice to the clouds,
That abundance of waters may cover thee?
(35) Canst thou send lightnings, that they may go,
And say unto thee, ⁷Here we *are*?
(36) ᵃWho hath put wisdom in the inward parts?
Or who hath given understanding to the heart?
(37) Who can number the clouds in wisdom?
Or ⁸who can stay the bottles of heaven,
(38) ⁹When the dust ¹⁰groweth into hardness,
And the clods cleave fast together?
(39) ᵇWilt thou hunt the prey for the lion?
Or fill ¹¹the appetite of the young lions,
(40) When they couch in *their* dens,
And abide in the covert to lie in wait?
(41) ᶜWho provideth for the raven his food?
When his young ones cry unto God,
They wander for lack of meat.

CHAPTER XXXIX. — (1) Knowest thou the time when the wild goats of the rock bring forth?
Or canst thou mark when ᵈthe hinds do calve?
(2) Canst thou number the months *that* they fulfil?
Or knowest thou the time when they bring forth?
(3) They bow themselves, they bring forth their young ones,
They cast out their sorrows.
(4) Their young ones are in good liking, they grow up with corn;
They go forth, and return not unto them.
(5) Who hath sent out the wild ass free?
Or who hath loosed the bands of the wild ass?
(6) Whose house I have made the wilderness,
And the ¹²barren land his dwellings.
(7) He scorneth the multitude of the city,
Neither regardeth he the crying ¹³of the driver.

---

1 Heb., *is taken.*
2 Or, *the seven stars.*
3 Heb., *Cimah.*
4 Heb., *Cesil.*
5 Or, *the twelve signs.*
6 Heb., *guide them.*
7 Heb., *behold us.*
a ch. 32. 8; Eccles. 2. 26.
8 Heb., *who can cause to lie down.*
9 Or, *When the dust is turned into mire.*
10 Heb., *is poured.*
b Ps. 104. 21.
11 Heb., *the life.*
c Ps. 147. 9; Matt. 6. 26.
d Ps. 29. 9.
12 Heb., *salt places.*
13 Heb., *of the exactor.*

---

(30) **The waters are hid.**—Or, *The waters hide themselves and become like stone.* Water loses its familiar quality, and is turned into stone.

(31) **The sweet influences.**—With reference to their supposed effect on weather and the like, or perhaps the word means *chain* or *band*, with allusion to their group—"Glitter like a swarm of fire-flies tangled in a silver braid." The context, however, of "the bands of Orion" seems rather to favour the other view. "Canst thou regulate the influences exerted by these several constellations in either direction of increase or diminution?"

(32) **Mazzaroth** is commonly understood to mean the signs of the Zodiac, and by the children of Arcturus the three stars in the tail of Ursa Major.

(33) **The ordinances of heaven.**—Comp. chap. xxviii. 26. That is, the recurring seasons and their power of influencing the earth.

(36) **Wisdom in the inward parts.**—The mention of the inward parts and the heart here, in the midst of natural phenomena, perplexes every one; but it is a natural solution to refer them to the lightnings personified: "Who hath put such understanding in their inward parts?"

(37) **Who can stay the bottles of heaven?**—This is understood in two opposite senses—of pouring out the bottles or of laying them up in store. It is not easy to decide which is most in accordance with the context, for the context also is somewhat uncertain, according as we interpret the solid mass of thick mud or of hard, dry soil. The survey of physical phenomena ends with this verse.

(39) **Wilt thou hunt the prey?**—The new chapter ought to begin here with this verse, inasmuch as the animal creation now passes under review.

(41) **They wander for lack of meat.**—The second clause is not a direct statement, but is dependent on the previous one; thus: "When his young ones cry unto God, when they wander for lack of meat."

XXXIX.

(4) **They grow up with corn.**—Or more probably, perhaps, *in the open field*, as the word means according to some.

(7) **The crying of the driver.**—Or, *the shoutings of the taskmaster.* The word is the same as is applied to the taskmasters of Egypt, and this suggests the question whether or not there may be a reminiscence of that bondage here.

God's Governance   JOB, XXXIX.   *of all Created Things.*

⁽⁸⁾ The range of the mountains *is* his pasture,
And he searcheth after every green thing.
⁽⁹⁾ Will the unicorn be willing to serve thee,—or abide by thy crib?
⁽¹⁰⁾ Canst thou bind the unicorn with his band in the furrow?
Or will he harrow the valleys after thee?
⁽¹¹⁾ Wilt thou trust him, because his strength *is* great?
Or wilt thou leave thy labour to him?
⁽¹²⁾ Wilt thou believe him, that he will bring home thy seed,
And gather *it into* thy barn?
⁽¹³⁾ *Gavest thou* the goodly wings unto the peacocks?
Or ¹wings and feathers unto the ostrich?
⁽¹⁴⁾ Which leaveth her eggs in the earth,
And warmeth them in dust,
⁽¹⁵⁾ And forgetteth that the foot may crush them,
Or that the wild beast may break them.
⁽¹⁶⁾ She is hardened against her young ones, as though *they were* not her's:
Her labour is in vain without fear;
⁽¹⁷⁾ Because God hath deprived her of wisdom,
Neither hath he imparted to her understanding.
⁽¹⁸⁾ What time she lifteth up herself on high,
She scorneth the horse and his rider.
⁽¹⁹⁾ Hast thou given the horse strength?
Hast thou clothed his neck with thunder?
⁽²⁰⁾ Canst thou make him afraid as a grasshopper?
The glory of his nostrils *is* ²terrible.
⁽²¹⁾ ³He paweth in the valley, and rejoiceth in *his* strength:
He goeth on to meet ⁴the armed men.
⁽²²⁾ He mocketh at fear, and is not affrighted;
Neither turneth he back from the sword.
⁽²³⁾ The quiver rattleth against him,
The glittering spear and the shield.
⁽²⁴⁾ He swalloweth the ground with fierceness and rage:
Neither believeth he that *it is* the sound of the trumpet.
⁽²⁵⁾ He saith among the trumpets, Ha, ha;
And he smelleth the battle afar off,
The thunder of the captains, and the shouting.
⁽²⁶⁾ Doth the hawk fly by thy wisdom,
And stretch her wings toward the south?

Marginal notes: 1 Or, *the feathers of the stork and ostrich.*   2 Heb., *terror.*   3 Or, *His feet dig.*   4 Heb., *the armour.*

⁽⁹⁾ **The unicorn.**—It is a mistake to identify this animal with the rhinoceros, as was formerly done; it is more probably the same with the buffalo, or wild ox. The most glaring form of the mistake is in Ps. xxii. 22: "Thou hast heard me also from among the *horns* of the *unicorns*." The way in which the animal is here spoken of, as in analogous contrast to the domestic ox, suggests that it is not wholly dissimilar. It is familiar and homely toil that the wild ox is contemplated as being put to, in the place of tame cattle, whose work it is.

⁽¹²⁾ **Wilt thou believe him?**—*i.e.*, *trust him*, as in the former verse "Wilt thou [trust" was, rather, *Wilt thou feel confidence in him?*

⁽¹³⁾ **Gavest thou the goodly wings unto the peacocks?**—Rather, *The wing of the ostrich is superb, but are her pinions and her feathers like the stork's?* Ostrich feathers are said to be worth from £8 to £15 a pound; but, beautiful and valuable as they are, they are hardly like the plumage of a bird, and are not so used for flight; on the contrary, the ostrich runs like a quadruped, it is stated at the rate sometimes of fifty or sixty miles an hour.

⁽¹⁴⁾ **Which leaveth her eggs.**—The ostrich only sits upon her eggs at night, when the cold would chill and destroy them; by day the heat of the sand continues the process of hatching.

⁽¹⁸⁾ **She lifteth up herself.**—That is, either from the nest when she comes to maturity, or when she sets out to run. The ostrich has a habit of running in a curve, which alone enables horsemen to overtake and kill or capture her. As in verse 13 a comparison seems to be drawn between the ostrich and the stork, so here, probably, the subject spoken of is the stork. Swift and powerful as the ostrich is, yet no sooner does the stork, on the contrary, rise on high into the air than she—as, indeed, any bird—can baffle the pursuit of horsemen.

⁽¹⁹⁾ **Thunder**—*i.e.*, with *terror*, such as thunder causes. Some refer it to the moving or shaking of the mane.

⁽²⁰⁾ **Canst thou make him afraid as a grasshopper?**—Rather, *Hast thou made him to leap as a locust?*

⁽²¹⁾ **He paweth . . . he rejoiceth.**—The first verb is plural, and the second singular. "They paw" (literally, *dig*), and "he rejoiceth."

⁽²⁴⁾ **Neither believeth he**—*i.e.*, he disregardeth the summons of the trumpet, as though he did not believe that it gave the call to war.

⁽²⁵⁾ **He saith among the trumpets**—Literally, *when there are plenty of trumpets*: *i.e.*, as often as the trumpet soundeth.

⁽²⁶⁾ **Doth the hawk fly?**—The more symmetrical order of these descriptions would be for the ostrich to have come *after* the war-horse and before the hawk; in that case there would have been a gradual transition from the fleetest of quadrupeds to the fleetest of birds

Job Humbles himself. JOB, XL. *God's Demand of him.*

(27) Doth the eagle mount up ¹at thy command,
And make her nest on high?
(28) She dwelleth and abideth on the rock,
Upon the crag of the rock, and the strong place.
(29) From thence she seeketh the prey,—
and her eyes behold afar off.
(30) Her young ones also suck up blood:
And *ᵃ*where the slain *are*, there *is* she.

CHAPTER XL.—(1) Moreover the LORD answered Job, and said,
(2) Shall he that contendeth with the Almighty instruct *him*?
He that reproveth God, let him answer it.
(3) Then Job answered the LORD, and said,
(4) Behold, I am vile; what shall I answer thee?
I will lay mine hand upon my mouth.
(5) Once have I spoken; but I will not answer:
Yea, twice; but I will proceed no further.
(6) Then answered the LORD unto Job out of the whirlwind, and said,

(7) ᵇGird up thy loins now like a man:
I will demand of thee, and declare thou unto me.
(8) ᶜWilt thou also disannul my judgment?
Wilt thou condemn me, that thou mayest be righteous?
(9) Hast thou an arm like God?
Or canst thou thunder with a voice like him?
(10) ᵈDeck thyself now *with* majesty and excellency;
And array thyself with glory and beauty.
(11) Cast abroad the rage of thy wrath:
And behold every one *that is* proud, and abase him.
(12) Look on every one *that is* proud, *and* bring him low;
And tread down the wicked in their place.
(13) Hide them in the dust together;—
and bind their faces in secret.
(14) Then will I also confess unto thee
That thine own right hand can save thee.
(15) Behold now ²behemoth, which I made with thee;
He eateth grass as an ox.

---

¹ Heb., *by thy mouth.*
a Matt. 24. 28; Luke 17. 37.
b ch. 38. 3.
c Ps. 50. 21; Rom. 3. 4.
d Ps. 104. 1.
² Or, *the elephant,* as some think.

---

by means of the ostrich, which, though winged like a bird, cannot use its wings as birds do, but only run on the ground like a quadruped.

(30) **Where the slain are, there is she.**—Comp. Matt. xxiv. 28, and Luke xvii. 37.

XL.

(2) **Shall he that contendeth with the Almighty instruct him?**—Rather, *Can he that reproveth (e.g.,* Job) *contend with the Almighty?* or, *Can the contending with the Almighty instruct Him?* "Art thou prepared still to dispute and contend with God? or, if thou dost, is there any hope that thou wilt instruct (*i.e.*, convince) Him in argument? Let him that argueth with God (*i.e.*, Job) answer this question." It might, perhaps, tend to make these verses (verses 4, 5) more effective if we transposed them after chap. xlii. 6, and regarded them as the very climax of the poem, as some have done. But this is not necessary, and is an arrangement that has no support from external evidence. If, however, it were adopted, Job's resolution, "Once have I spoken; but I will speak no more: yea, twice; but I will not again" (verse 5), would not be literally inconsistent, as it now is, with what he says in chap. xlii. 1—6.

(8) **Wilt thou also disannul my judgment?**—Comp. what Job said in chaps. xix. 6, 7, xxvii. 2. God is about to show Job his inability to govern the world and administer judgment among men, so as to rule them morally, from his acknowledged inability to govern the more formidable animals of the brute creation. If he cannot restrain them, how is it likely that he will be able to tread down the wicked in their place? And if he cannot hold the wicked in check and compel them to submission, how, any more, can he protect himself from their violence? how can he save himself from the outbursts of their fury? or, if not save himself from them, how much less can he deliver himself from the hand of God? If he cannot hide them in the dust together, and bind them (*i.e.*, restrain the threatenings of their rage in the hidden world) in the secret prison-house, how much less can he save himself, and be independent of the help of a saviour?

(15) **Behoth.**—The identification of behemoth has always been a great difficulty with commentators. The word in Hebrew is really the natural plural of behēmāh, which means *domestic cattle;* and this fact would suggest the idea that more than one animal may be meant in the description (verses 15—24), which scarcely seems to answer to one and the same. In this way the verses 15—20 would describe very well the elephant, and verses 21—24 the hippopotamus. The objection to this is, that behēmāh is commonly used of domestic cattle in contrast to wild beasts, whereas neither the elephant nor the hippopotamus can come under the category of domestic animals. There is a word in Coptic (p-ehe-emmou, meaning water-ox), used for the hippopotamus, which may, perhaps, lie concealed in behemoth. Then the difficulty is to make the description answer throughout to the hippopotamus (*e.g.*, verse 20), since the hippopotamus does not frequent mountains, neither does it exactly eat grass like an ox (verse 15).

Which I made with thee.—Fellow-creatures of thine, to inhabit the world with thee: thus skilfully reminding him that he had a common origin with the beasts.

(16) Lo now, his strength *is* in his loins,
And his force *is* in the navel of his belly.
(17) ¹He moveth his tail like a cedar:
The sinews of his stones are wrapped together.
(18) His bones *are as* strong pieces of brass;
His bones *are* like bars of iron.
(19) He *is* the chief of the ways of God:
He that made him can make his sword to approach *unto him*.
(20) Surely the mountains bring him forth food,
Where all the beasts of the field play.
(21) He lieth under the shady trees,
In the covert of the reed, and fens.
(22) The shady trees cover him *with* their shadow;
The willows of the brook compass him about.
(23) Behold, ²he drinketh up a river, *and* hasteth not:
He trusteth that he can draw up Jordan into his mouth.
(24) ³He taketh it with his eyes: *his* nose pierceth through snares.

CHAPTER XLI.—(1) Canst thou draw out ⁴leviathan with an hook?
Or his tongue with a cord ⁵*which* thou lettest down?
(2) Canst thou put an hook into his nose?
Or bore his jaw through with a thorn?
(3) Will he make many supplications unto thee?
Will he speak soft *words* unto thee?
(4) Will he make a covenant with thee?
Wilt thou take him for a servant for ever?
(5) Wilt thou play with him as *with* a bird?
Or wilt thou bind him for thy maidens?
(6) Shall the companions make a banquet of him?
Shall they part him among the merchants?
(7) Canst thou fill his skin with barbed irons?
Or his head with fish spears?
(8) Lay thine hand upon him,—remember the battle, do no more.
(9) Behold, the hope of him is in vain:
Shall not *one* be cast down even at the sight of him?
(10) None *is so* fierce that dare stir him up:
Who then is able to stand before me?

1 Or, *He setteth up.*
2 Heb., *he oppresseth.*
3 Or, *Will any take him in his sight, or, bore his nose with a gin?*
4 That is, *a whale*, or, *a whirlpool.*
5 Heb., *which thou drownest?*

---

(16) **In the navel.**—Rather, *in the sinews, or muscles.*
(17) **The sinews of his stones.**—Rather, *of his thighs.*
(18) **Strong pieces.**—Or, perhaps, *tubes.* His limbs are like bars of iron.
(19) **He is the chief of the ways of God.**—This is surely more applicable to the elephant than the hippopotamus, considering the great intelligence and usefulness of the elephant. The last clause is very obscure. Some render, "He only that made him can bring his sword near unto him;" or, "He that made him hath furnished him with his sword." Others, "He that would dress him (as meat) let him come near him with his sword!" indicating the inequality of the contest. Perhaps a combination of the first and last is best—"Let his Maker (but no one else venture to) approach him with His sword."
(21) **He lieth under the shady trees.**—If this description applies to any *one* animal, it seems on the whole more appropriate to the elephant than the hippopotamus. No doubt the judgment of critics has been biassed by their pre-conceived notions about the circumstances under which they suppose the Book of Job to have been written; and the author was more likely, it is thought, to have been acquainted with the river-horse of Egypt than with the elephant of India, though, to be sure, elephants abound also in Africa, and may very well have been known to the writer of Job from that quarter, if the other is less likely.
(23) **Behold, he drinketh up a river.**—This verse is better rendered, *Behold, if a river overflow* (or, *is violent*), *he trembleth not* (or, *hasteneth not*); he is confident, though Jordan swell up to his mouth.
(24) **His nose pierceth through snares.**—Some render, "Shall any take him with snares? while he is looking, shall any pierce through his nose?" The sense seems to be rather, *Let one take him by his eyes:* i.e., by allurements placed before him, as elephants are taken. *By means of snares one may pierce his nose.* The Authorised Version seems to be less probably right.

XLI.

(1) **Leviathan.**—There can be little doubt that by this is meant the crocodile or alligator, whatever may be the true meaning of behemoth.
Or his tongue . . .—Some render, "or press down his tongue with a cord"; but the Authorised Version seems preferable.
(2) **Hook.**—Or, *cord of rush.*
A thorn.—Or, *spike* or *hook.*
(4) **A servant for ever.**—The crocodile being probably quite untameable.
(6) **Shall the companions make a banquet of him?**—Or, *Shall the bands of fishermen make traffic of him?* or, *dig a pit for him?*—the former suiting the parallelism better.
(8) **Remember the battle.**—"Bear in mind what thou dost attempt, and thou wilt not do it again."
(9) **Behold the hope of him is in vain**—*i.e.,* the hope of the rash man who would venture to attack him: **at the sight of him,** *i.e.,* the infuriated crocodile.
(10) **None is so fierce that dare stir him up.**—"If, therefore, the creatures of My hand strike so much terror, how far more terrible must I be? If thou canst

God's Great Power   JOB, XLI.   *in the Leviathan.*

(11) Who hath prevented me, that I should repay him?
ᵃWhatsoever is under the whole heaven is mine.
(12) I will not conceal his parts,
Nor his power, nor his comely proportion.
(13) Who can discover the face of his garment?
Or who can come to him ¹with his double bridle?
(14) Who can open the doors of his face? His teeth *are* terrible round about.
(15) His ²scales *are his* pride,
Shut up together *as with* a close seal.
(16) One is so near to another,—that no air can come between them.
(17) They are joined one to another,
They stick together, that they cannot be sundered.
(18) By his neesings a light doth shine,
And his eyes *are* like the eyelids of the morning.
(19) Out of his mouth go burning lamps, —*and* sparks of fire leap out.
(20) Out of his nostrils goeth smoke,
As *out* of a seething pot or caldron.
(21) His breath kindleth coals,—and a flame goeth out of his mouth.
(22) In his neck remaineth strength,
And ³sorrow is turned into joy before him.
(23) ⁴The flakes of his flesh are joined together:
They are firm in themselves; they cannot be moved.
(24) His heart is as firm as a stone;
Yea, as hard as a piece of the nether *millstone.*
(25) When he raiseth up himself, the mighty are afraid:
By reason of breakings they purify themselves.
(26) The sword of him that layeth at him cannot hold:
The spear, the dart, nor the ⁵habergeon.
(27) He esteemeth iron as straw, *and* brass as rotten wood.
(28) The arrow cannot make him flee:
Sling-stones are turned with him into stubble.
(29) Darts are counted as stubble:
He laugheth at the shaking of a spear.
(30) ⁶Sharp stones *are* under him:
He spreadeth sharp pointed things upon the mire.
(31) He maketh the deep to boil like a pot:
He maketh the sea like a pot of ointment.

ᵃ Ps. 24. 1. & 50. 12; 1 Cor. 10. 26.
¹ Or, *within.*
² Heb., *strong pieces of shields.*
³ Heb., *sorrow rejoiceth.*
⁴ Heb., *The fallings.*
⁵ Or, *breastplate.*
⁶ Heb., *sharp pieces of the potsherd.*

---

not save thyself from them, how much less canst thou be saved without Me?" (See chap. xl. 14.) The first clause may be understood thus: "He is not so cruel (the common meaning of the word rendered *fierce*)—*i.e.*, to himself—that he should venture to rouse him up."

(11) **Who hath prevented me?**—It is manifest that this appeal would come more appropriately at the end of the following detailed description than, as it does here, just before it. "Who hath prevented me," &c., of course means, *Who hath first given to me, that I should repay him?*

(13) **Who can discover . . . ?**—Rather, *Who can strip off his outer garment? i.e.*, his scales, which are the covering of his skin. *Who shall come within his double bridle, i.e.*, the doubling of his jaw? Who would venture a limb within his jaws? This seems to be the meaning, rather than "Who shall come to him with his double bridle," forsooth to take him therewith?

(14) **Who can open the doors of his face?**—*i.e.*, his mouth. Round about his teeth is terror.

(18) **By his neesings a light doth shine, and his eyes are like the eyelids of the morning** —*i.e.*, fiery red and glowing.

(20) **Out of his nostrils goeth smoke, as out of a seething pot or caldron.**—The last word is uncertain: it is the same as was rendered in the Authorised Version "hook" at verse 2; and taking the same sense here, we may render, *as of a seething pot and rushes: i.e.*, a pot made hot with rushes.

(22) **Sorrow is turned into joy before him.**— Literally, *and before him danceth fear,* or *pining sorrow exulteth before him.* A marvellous personification of the terror which goes with him wherever he goes.

(23) **The flakes of his flesh**—*i.e.*, the parts that in other animals hang down: *e.g.*, dewlaps, &c., are not flabby, as with them.

(24) **His heart**—*i.e.*, his nature, his disposition. This seems to be the meaning, rather than the physical organ of life.

(25) **By reason of breakings**—*i.e.*, the waves he makes in the water, or the breakings he makes among the plants and trees in the water.

They purify themselves—*i.e.*, they are beside themselves; they are so overwhelmed with terror, that they take themselves off, as those who have to dwell apart for uncleanness.

(26) **The sword of him that layeth at him.**— Literally, *As to one approaching him* (to slay him), *his sword cannot stand; it will snap in his hand.*

(29) **Darts.**—Rather, *clubs.*

(30) **He spreadeth sharp pointed things upon the mire.**—Some render, "He spreadeth, as it were, a threshing-wain upon the mire." The statement is, that he not only can lie without inconvenience upon sharp-pointed things, but his own body presents a sharp surface to the mud he lies on.

(31) **The sea**—*i.e.*, not necessarily the salt water, for the Nile is still called the sea by the Arabs, and so with many other large rivers. Example, the "sea-wall" of the Thames below Gravesend.

Job submits himself   JOB, XLII.   *to God.*

(32) He maketh a path to shine after him;
One would think the deep *to be* hoary.
(33) Upon earth there is not his like,—
¹who is made without fear.
(34) He beholdeth all high *things*:
He *is* a king over all the children of pride.

CHAPTER XLII. — (1) Then Job answered the LORD, and said,
(2) I know that thou canst do every *thing*,
And *that* ²no thought can be withholden from thee.
(3) *ᵃ* Who *is* he that hideth counsel without knowledge?
Therefore have I uttered that I understood not;

Things too wonderful for me, which I knew not.
(4) Hear, I beseech thee, and I will speak:
I will demand of thee, and declare thou unto me.
(5) I have heard of thee by the hearing of the ear:
But now mine eye seeth thee.
(6) Wherefore I abhor *myself*,—and repent in dust and ashes.
(7) And it was so, that after the LORD had spoken these words unto Job, the LORD said to Eliphaz the Temanite, My wrath is kindled against thee, and against thy two friends: for ye have not spoken of me the thing that is right, as my servant Job hath. (8) Therefore take

¹ Or, *who behave themselves without fear.*

² Or, *no thought of thine can be hindered.*

a ch. 38. 2.

(33, 34) **Upon earth there is not his like.**—Some have proposed to take away the last two verses of chap. xli. from their connection with the crocodile, and to transpose them, referring them to man, so as to come before verse 8, understanding them thus: "There is one whose like is not upon earth, who is made without dread. He seeth every high thing, and is king over all the proud beasts. To Him then I say (verse 8), Lay thine hand upon him; remember the battle, and do so no more. Lo! his hope is deceived. Is he indeed cast down at the very sight of him? He is not so cruel to himself that he should rouse him up. Who then can stand before me? Who hath first given to me, that I should have to repay him? That which is under the whole heavens is mine." It cannot be denied that this makes very good sense, but it seems to be too great a liberty to take with the text as we find it to adopt this as the true order of the verses; for in that case, what is there that we might not deal with in a like manner? Those who advocate this transposition in the order of the verses would also place chap. xl. 1—5 so as to follow chap. xl. 6, in this manner: "Then Job answered the Lord and said, I know that thou canst do everything, and that no purpose can be withholden from thee, or that no purpose of thine can be restrained." Then the next words come in as the implied answer of God: "Who is this that hideth my counsel for want of knowledge?" To which Job replies: "Therefore (I confess that) I have uttered without understanding things too wonderful for me, which I knew not." Again God replies, as in chaps. xxxviii. 3 and xl. 7: "Hear, I beseech thee and I will speak, I will demand of thee, and declare thou unto me;" to which Job answers: "I have heard of thee by the hearing of the ear, but now mine eye seeth thee. Wherefore I abhor what I have said, and repent it in dust and ashes." Then the Lord answered Job and said, "Is he that contended with the Almighty reproved? Does he acknowledge his discomfiture? He that argueth with God, let him answer this question." Then Job answered the Lord and said, "Behold I am vile. What shall I answer thee? I lay my hand before my mouth; once I have spoken, but I will not answer; yea twice, but I will not do so again." There is a certain amount of sharpness and point obtained in thus making this confession the climax of the poem, and a kind of formal consistency is secured in regarding this resolution as Job's last utterance instead of making him speak again, as he does, according to the present order, in chap xlii. 2. But this consistency is formal rather than real, inasmuch as there is no inconsistency in the *tone* of chap. xlii. 2 *seqq.*, and the promise of chap. xl. 5. Whatever advantage may be derived from the re-arrangement will be a matter for individual taste rather to decide, which will vary with the individual; and at all events, the climax of chap. xlii. 6 as it stands is a very noble one, and we may question whether we can heighten its grandeur.

XLII.

(3) **Who is he that hideth counsel?**—It is quite obvious that the right way of understanding these verses is, as in Isa. lxiii. 1—6, after the manner of a dialogue, in which Job and the Lord alternately reply. "Who is this that hideth counsel without knowledge?" were the words with which God Himself joined the debate in chap. xxxviii. 2; and therefore, unless we assign them to Him here also, we must regard them as quoted by Job, and applied reflectively to himself; but it is far better to consider them as part of a dialogue.

(4) **Hear, I beseech thee.**—This cannot in like manner be appropriately assigned to Job, but, as in chaps. xxxviii. 3 and xl. 7, must be referred to God; then the confession of verses 5 and 6 comes in very grandly. How much of our knowledge of God is merely hearsay? and it is not till the experimental teaching of the Holy Ghost has revealed God to our consciences that we really see Him with the inward eye. The confession of Job, therefore, is the confession of every converted man. Compare in a much later and very different, and yet analogous sphere, the confession of St. Paul (Gal. i. 16).

(7) **And it was so.**—The verdict that is spoken against the friends of Job is based rather on the tone and spirit of what they have said than on any of their actual words, for many of these are conspicuous for their wisdom, truth, and beauty. But throughout they had been on the wrong side, and seemed to think that the cause of God had need to be upheld at all risks, and that it might even be required to tell lies for God (chap. xiii. 7); and it was this that provoked the Divine indignation.

(8) **Therefore take unto you now seven bullocks and seven rams.**—It is remarkable that

unto you now seven bullocks and seven rams, and go to my servant Job, and offer up for yourselves a burnt offering; and my servant Job shall pray for you: for ¹him will I accept: lest I deal with you *after your* folly, in that ye have not spoken of me *the thing which is* right, like my servant Job. ⁽⁹⁾ So Eliphaz the Temanite and Bildad the Shuhite *and* Zophar the Naamathite went, and did according as the LORD commanded them: the LORD also accepted ²Job.

⁽¹⁰⁾ And the LORD turned the captivity of Job, when he prayed for his friends: also the LORD ³gave Job twice as much as he had before. ⁽¹¹⁾ Then came there unto him all his brethren, and all his sisters, and all they that had been of his acquaintance before, and did eat bread with him in his house: and they be-

1 Heb., *his face,* or, *person.*

2 Heb., *the face of Job.*

3 Heb., *added all that had been to Job unto the double.*

moaned him, and comforted him over all the evil that the LORD had brought upon him: every man also gave him a piece of money, and every one an earring of gold.

⁽¹²⁾ So the LORD blessed the latter end of Job more than his beginning: for he had fourteen thousand sheep, and six thousand camels, and a thousand yoke of oxen, and a thousand she asses. ⁽¹³⁾ He had also seven sons and three daughters. ⁽¹⁴⁾ And he called the name of the first, Jemima; and the name of the second, Kezia; and the name of the third, Kerenhappuch. ⁽¹⁵⁾ And in all the land were no women found *so* fair as the daughters of Job: and their father gave them inheritance among their brethren.

⁽¹⁶⁾ After this lived Job an hundred

---

the sacrifices prescribed for Job's friends were similar to those which Balaam prescribed for Balak (Num. xxiii. 2—29). This is probably one indication out of many that the age of Job was that of Moses, or before it. "My servant Job shall pray for you." This, strange to say, was the very promise with which Eliphaz himself had closed his third and last speech. His words therefore received a striking fulfilment in the case of himself and his friends. The intercession of Job seems to show us that his character is a typical one, representing to us the character of Christ as the sufferer and the mediator on behalf of man; and as in Job there is no trace of acquaintance with the Divine covenant, the book shows us a sort of anticipation of the Gospel to the Gentile world, that the mercies of God are not limited, as some have thought, to the chosen race, but that the principles of God's action are the same universally. He deals with men upon a principle of mediation: whether the mediator be Moses, as the mediator of the first covenant; or Job, who was the accepted mediator for his friends beyond the pale of the covenant; or whether the mediator be Jesus Christ, as the one Mediator between God and man.

⁽¹⁰⁾ **When he prayed for his friends.**—Job's personal discipline was not complete till he passed from the sphere of his own sorrows to the work of intercession for his friends, and it was through the very act of this self-oblivion and self-sacrifice that his own deliverance was brought about. When he prayed for his friends, we are told, the Lord turned his own captivity: that is, restored and re-instated him in prosperity even greater than before.

This is the true moral of all human history, which is to be accomplished in the world of the regeneration, if not here. All sorrow is fraught with the promise and the hope of future blessedness, and to know that is to rob sorrow of its pain. It is impossible to reap the full gain of it when the burden presses, but, as far as it can be done, sorrow is mitigated. Had Job been able to look forward with confidence to his actual deliverance, he would have been able to bear his affliction; it was because he could not that all was dark. And after all there are sorrows and afflictions for which there is no deliverance like Job's; there is a captivity which can never be turned in this life, and for this the only hope is the sure hope of the Gospel, and the promise which in its degree is afforded by the history of Job: for if Job's is a representative history, as we are bound to believe it must be, then the lesson of it must be that what is not explained or mended here will be explained and mended hereafter. It is God alone who can enlighten the darkness which surrounds His counsels; but at the same time we must remember that with Him is the well of life, and in His light we shall see light.

⁽¹¹⁾ **Every man also gave him a piece of money.**—The Hebrew word is *kesîtâh,* which is found also in the narrative of Jacob's purchase of the field of the children of Hamor (Gen. xxxiii. 19). Some have supposed, from a comparison of this passage with Gen. xxiii. 16, which relates the corresponding transaction between Abraham and the sons of Heth, that the value of the *kesîtâh* was four shekels, but this is, of course, not certain from these narratives. Tradition says that the *kesîtâh* was a coin with the figure of a lamb stamped upon it.

⁽¹²⁾ **Fourteen thousand sheep.**—The number of Job's cattle here is exactly the double of those in chap. i. 3. That Job's latter end should be blessed had been the promise of all his friends (chaps. v. 24, &c., viii. 7—20, &c., xi. 16, &c., xxii. 27, &c.), but then it was hampered with a condition which involved the falsehood of all Job's previous life, and it was the unjust imputation of this falsehood to Job which was an offence against the truth of God, and was so regarded by Him. Truth had to be violated in order that God's justice might stand, which was the greatest possible offence and indignity to the Divine justice.

⁽¹⁴⁾ **Jemima.**—This name perhaps means *as fair as the day.*

Kezia—*i.e.,* cassia, an aromatic bark, much prized by the ancients. (See Ps. xlv. 9.)

Kerenhappuch—*i.e.,* the horn for containing kohl for the eyes. The Eastern women are in the habit of painting the upper part of the eyelids with stibium, so that a black edge is formed about them and they seem larger. (See 2 Kings ix. 30; Jer. iv. 30.) The meaning of this name is the paint-box for this purpose.

⁽¹⁶⁾ **An hundred and forty years.**—The particularity of this detail forbids us to suppose that the

| *Job's Children.* | JOB, XLII. | *His Age and Death.* |

and forty years, and saw his sons, and his sons' sons, *even* four generations.

⁽¹⁷⁾ So Job died, *being* old and full of days.

---

character of Job was other than real; his great age also shows that he must be referred to the very early patriarchal times, probably anterior to Moses.

⁽¹⁷⁾ **So Job died, being old and full of days.**—Such is the close of this mysterious book, which deals with the greatest problems that can engage the human mind, and shows us the way in which the ancients solved them, and the help which God vouchsafed them, apart from His covenant revelation and before the dawning of the Gospel light. And the great lesson of the history is the way in which the malice of Satan is foiled. He had insinuated that all service of God was interested and done for advantage. Job had clearly shown that he was capable of loving God even under the most severe afflictions; and the issue which was eventually brought about was no contradiction of this fact, inasmuch as it was entirely hidden from Job till long after his probation was ended, and therefore could have no influence upon his patience and faith. It is remarkable that Job is only twice mentioned in Scripture, once in the Old Testament and once in the New. Ezekiel was acquainted with Job's history (chap. xiv. 14, 20), and St. James (chap. v. 11) refers to him as a familiar standard of patience. It is evident, however, that the Book of Job was well known, from the many instances in the Psalms and elsewhere in which we find traces of the influence produced by familiarity with the language of the book.

THE BOOK OF PSALMS

INTRODUCTION TO THE BOOK OF PSALMS

I. Preliminary.—The Psalms appear in the earliest classification we have of the Hebrew Scriptures, viz., that of the New Testament, as one of the three great divisions of sacred literature, side by side with the Law and the Prophets. In the more elaborate arrangement of the Talmudic Canon, they lose their distinctive title in the more general one of *Hagiographa* or sacred writings (in Hebrew, *Kethubim*),[*] at the head of which they stand, in the order adopted in the Hebrew Bibles.[†] In the Septuagint this threefold division, not having been settled at the time of that translation, does not of course appear, and the Psalms there are classed with the poetical and didactic books, as in our English Bibles. It is often assumed that the title *Psalms* in Luke xxiv. 44 means the whole of the *Hagiographa*, the whole being named after its most important part. It is, however, more probable that the pre-eminence there given to the Psalms is due to another reason. The threefold division into Law, Prophets, and Psalms, was not a popular mode of designating the Scriptures as a whole, but an arrangement arising out of the use of the synagogue, where the Psalms supplied the lesson for the afternoon, as the Prophets did for the morning, of the Sabbath. The collection in its present form bears evidence of adaptation to the exigencies of the synagogue services.[‡] It was, however, originally made for the (Second) Temple service, and for musical purposes. It was the Jewish hymnal. This appears in the names by which it was known. In Hebrew the book is that of the *Tehillim*, or shortly, *Tillim*,[§] that is, *praises*. The Greek name is in one Codex ψαλμοί, in another ψαλτήριον (the *Lyre*), from which comes *Psalter*.[||] The Hebrew word for *psalm* (*mizmôr*), whatever be the root idea of the term, apparently denotes a composition, not merely lyric, like *shir*, and so capable of being sung, but one actually set to music and accompanied by music.

Another indication that the choral service of the Temple or the Synagogue was the object of the compilation of the Psalms, and indeed of the composition of many of them, is found in the titles prefixed to a great number of the hymns. The meaning of these titles, and their bearing upon the difficult questions of date and authorship, will be discussed in the individual psalms. Here it is only necessary to call the reader's attention to the musical character of many of them. Some, for instance, convey directions to the choir or choir-master: in the Authorised Version, "To the chief musician" (Pss. xi., xiii., &c.). To this is sometimes added the kind of instruments to be employed (Pss. v., vi., liv., &c.), or the name of a musician or designation of a body of musicians (Pss. lxii., lxxvii.). Others apparently indicate the tune to which the psalm is to be sung, or the compass of the voices for which it is suitable (Pss. ix., xxii., lvi., vi., xii.). Others, again, bring the Psalter into close connection with the Levitical guilds or families, the Asaphites and the Korahites (Pss. l., lxxiii.—lxxxiii., xlii.—xlix.), whose connection with the Temple worship is elaborately described in the Book of Chronicles.

But there is, besides, ample historical testimony which corroborates what the nature of many of the Psalms, as well as the titles of others, would lead us to conclude—that the whole collection was intended for public worship. That the use of the Psalter in the various branches of the Christian Church is a continuation of its original purpose and use in the Jewish Church, is proved by Talmudic directions,[*] and that the use had begun at an early time and continued unbroken through all the fortunes of Israel is shown by notices in the historical books, in the apocryphal books, and in the New Testament.

Its character as the Jewish hymnal once recognised, the Psalter will be found to answer, so to speak, frankly and openly the many questions that can and must be asked of its composition, arrangement, &c., even if on all points the answer cannot be so complete as we could wish. For instance we see at once from the analogy of hymn-books of modern churches that the collection is likely to turn out to be a compilation of works of different authors and different times, composed with various purposes, and on a vast variety of subjects, and only so far connected as being capable of use in the public worship of the Church; and this the most cursory glance at the Book of Psalms is sufficient to establish.

There is, however, this important difference between the Jewish and other hymn-books; it is rare that into one of the latter a poem not having a distinct religious

---

[*] This term, which simply means "writings," no doubt came gradually into use after the Canon, as far as the Law and Prophets were concerned, was formed, and seems to indicate that the books included in it were at first held in less esteem.

[†] This arrangement is not universal in Hebrew MSS. The Spanish MSS. and the Masorah place the *Chronicles* at the head of this division. *Ruth* took the place of honour according to one Jewish Canon, and according to another *Job* preceded the Psalter, as in the LXX., Vulgate, and our Bible.

[‡] Grätz has pointed out that the number of Psalms in the collection was not invariably a hundred and fifty, but sometimes only a hundred and forty-seven. This variation was due to the fact that, like the Pentateuch, the Psalter was read through in three years, and the number of Sabbaths that do not clash with a festival varies from a hundred and forty-seven to a hundred and fifty in different periods of three years.

[§] The full form was *sepher tehillim*, which was gradually abbreviated to *tehillim, tillim, tillin, tilli*.

[||] Comp. the frequent use of the words *harp, lyre*, to denote books of poetry.

[*] Tradition, as embodied in the Talmud, has preserved the liturgical form in use in the Herodian Temple, and it is confirmed by notices in Josephus, who was an eye-witness. Psalms were sung by Levites to a musical accompaniment after the presentation of wine on the altar, when all the congregation were on their bended knees.

end is introduced. We do not in Christian hymn-books light upon old battle pieces, or patriotic ballads, or village songs of harvest and vintage, and it is rare that among the authors of church hymns we find a name of one recognised as great in poetry. In our own literature, though there is hardly one of our really great poets who has not written some poetry which we may call sacred, not one has contributed to the many collections of hymns. Even Milton left nothing, save translations of Psalms, that is sung in church; Wordsworth's ecclesiastical sonnets have not found their way into hymn-books; nor are Coleridge's hymns "To the Earth" or "In the Vale of Chamouni," embodied in any church hymnal. The case was wholly otherwise in the hymnal of Israel. There, not to depart from the traditions embodied in the titles, we find historic pieces, records of personal adventure, songs of travel and tempest, of fight and festival, and at least one song of love; and these, or many of them, are, according to tradition, from the pens of some of the greatest bards the country produced. The reason of this difference is of course the acknowledged fact that poetical and religious inspiration were in Israel one and the same. With the one exception of the Song of Solomon, nothing has been preserved which was not religious either in tone or intention. Rarely could the muse of Hebrew song find a voice till moved by religious feeling and fervour: rarely was the religious purpose absent. There are many pieces of poetry actually preserved in the Canon which were not made use of by the collectors of hymns, and yet the same sacred character marks them. Such, for instance, is David's elegy over Saul (2 Sam. i. 17—27), and such his last words (2 Sam. xxiii. 1—7). Deborah's magnificent ode (Judges v.) is another example, and the many hymns scattered up and down the prophetical books. To form the hymnal of the Jewish Church, then, it was not necessary to bespeak hymns for this or that occasion, for a temple dedication, a thanksgiving for victory, for the marriage of a king, for harvest or vintage festival. Enough were there ready to the collector's hand, sung at the village gathering, chanted by exulting soldiers, carolled forth at high festival with accompaniment of harp or horn. Some, no doubt, had a distinctive liturgical origin, but more were adapted for liturgic use. Many were put together entirely from older songs, to serve better than the originals for the Temple service; but more were taken just as they were, or, as hymn collectors have always allowed themselves a license in this respect, with slight alterations and additions. Having thus the whole poetic wealth of the nation from which to draw, the psalm collectors eagerly ransacked it. Indeed, the Psalter has sometimes been described as an *anthology* of Hebrew poetry. This it is not, for there is certainly as much of poetical matter in the rest of Scriptures as in the Psalms, but there is, it may be said with equal certainty, as truly great and noble poetry within the collections as we find in any of the other books. We cannot say that Isaiah contributed any of the Psalms, or the author of the Book of Job. Moses only by a suspicious title and Jeremiah only by the conjectures of critics, have a place in these collections. But there are psalms worthy of the pen of the greatest of these. And so truly is the Psalter representative of Hebrew poetry, that there is not one of the styles in which the bards of Israel made either successful or tentative efforts of which specimens are not to be found in it. Not only does it supply the greatest examples of lyric song, but of the best that Israel else produced. That which was almost its peculiar creation—*Didactic* or *Gnomic* poetry—that species of poetry which its distinguishing genius, prophecy, made its own, the nearest approach it ever made to the *Epos*, and even what steps it took in dramatic art, are all worthily represented in the books arranged for public worship. It can hardly be doubted that some at least of the power which the Psalter has exercised, and still exercises, is due to this poetic character.* And if poetically the psalms compare so favourably with modern hymns in that which forms their chief and most important characteristic, they not only compare to advantage with ancient literature, but present themselves as unique at the time of their origin. Even among other nations of a Semitic origin there was nothing like them. Hymns to the gods of Greece have been preserved, but how vast is their difference from the Psalms. Let the reader compare one of those translated by Shelley, with any song out of the Psalter. Pretty compliments, and well turned flatteries intended to propitiate, he will find, set, indeed, in melodious verse that celebrates the birth of gods and demi-gods; but no wrestling in prayer with tearful eyes and downcast head, and the full assurance of faith, such as has made the Psalms for all time the expression of the devotional feelings of men.

II. **Contents and formation of the Psalter.—**
BOOK I., Psalms i.—xli., all ascribed to David, except Pss. i., ii., x., xxxiii., where the omission of an inscription is easily accounted for. The name *Jehovah* is principally, but not exclusively, used throughout this book.

BOOK II., Pss. xlii.—lxxii., comprising the following groups: Pss. xlii.—xlix., Korahite; xliii., which is anonymous, is properly part of xlii.; Ps. l., Asaphic; Pss. li.—lxv., Davidic; Pss. lxvi., lxvii., anonymous; Pss. lxviii.—lxx., Davidic; Ps. lxxi., anonymous; Ps. lxxii., Solomonic. The use of the name *Elohim* is characteristic of this book.

BOOK III., Pss. lxxiii.—lxxxix., comprising: Pss. lxxiii.—lxxxiii., Asaphic; Pss. lxxxiv., lxxxv., Korahite; Pss. lxxxvi., Davidic; Pss. lxxxvii., lxxxviii., Korahite, the latter having a supplementary inscription "to Heman the Ezrahite," Ps. lxxxix. ascribed to Ethan. Though used an almost equal number of times, the name Jehovah is plainly not so congenial to this book as *Elohim*.

BOOK IV., Pss. xc.—cvi., comprising: Ps. xc., ascribed to Moses; Pss. xci.—c., anonymous; Ps. ci., Davidic; Ps. cii., "A prayer of the afflicted;" Ps. ciii., Davidic; Pss. civ.—cvi., anonymous. The divine names are used here and in the next book indifferently.

BOOK V., Pss. cvii.—cl., comprising: Ps. cvii., anonymous; Pss. cviii.—cx., Davidic; Pss. cxi.—cxix., anonymous; Pss. cxi., cxii., cxiii., have *Hallejuhah* in the place of an inscription; Pss. cxx.—cxxxiv. "Songs of degrees" (of these Pss. cxxii., cxxiv., cxxxi., cxxxiii. are in the Hebrew Bible, but not in the LXX., ascribed to David, and Ps. cxxvii. to Solomon); Pss. cxxxv.—cxxxvii., anonymous; Ps. cxxxv. being inscribed "Hallejuhah, a psalm of praise;" Pss. cxxxviii.—cxlv., Davidic;

---

* The distinguished commentator on the Psalms, Grätz (Kritischer Commentar zu den Psalmen nebst Text und Uebersetzung Von Dr. H. Grätz, Breslau, 1882), says that, taken as a whole, the Psalms *lack* the qualifications of poetry of the highest order, viz., unity, depth of imagination, loftiness of speech, and an elegant rhythm. He probably stands alone in his opinion. For the poetical form see below, § 5. The only unity possible in a collection of separate lyric pieces is one of purpose and spirit, and the religious history of the Psalter, the hold it has taken on the heart of the world, is sufficient evidence of the existence of such unity, as the influence it has had on the poetry of Christendom is sufficient proof of the depth of its imagination and the power of its speech.

Pss. cxlvi.—cl., anonymous, each beginning with "Hallejuhah."

This arrangement does not correspond with that of the LXX. and Vulg., which put together Pss. ix. and x., cxiv., cxv., and separate Pss. cxvi. and cxlvii. into two. There are also considerable variations in the titles. The LXX. ascribe seventeen to David, which have no author named in the Hebrew, one to Jeremiah (Ps. cxxxvii.), four to Haggai and Zechariah (Pss. cxxxviii., cxlvi.—cxlviii.) making at the same time the omissions noticed above, while other less important variations show themselves.

The complete absence of any perspicuous method in this table is the first point that strikes us. It is told that in the first century of our era an ambitious scribe wished to classify the Psalms and arrange them on some more intelligible plan, but was met by the objection that it would be impiety to meddle with what David had left in such confusion. Modern scholars have not been so scrupulous, and many attempts at classification have been made, none, perhaps, with complete success, but even the worst with this result—to show how entirely without plan the last compiler of the Psalter worked, or rather to suggest that he made no attempt at classification, but found certain collections or groups already formed, and merely attached others to them so as to serve for the purpose of public worship, without either endeavouring to improve on a previous system or invent one of his own. That such collections previously existed there can hardly be a doubt. Just so much plan appears in the arrangement of the whole as to show it, for surely no collector would have taken the trouble to bring all the Davidic psalms which occur in the first and second books together, unless he were intending to make, as far as he could, a complete collection of such psalms. Indeed, the compiler of Books I. and II. himself declares he has effected this object by the statement, "The prayers of David the son of Jesse are ended," which can mean nothing else than that there were, in the writer's knowledge, no more to be found. We may even perhaps assume that before the bulk of the others bearing the inscription "of David" were discovered, not only Books I. and II., but also III. and IV., had taken their present shape, or surely the last redactor would have placed those occurring in Book V. nearer the others of the same reputed authorship.

The position of groups called from their titles Asaphic and Korahite psalms in Books III. and IV., points to the same conclusion. Unless the last compiler had found them already spread over two books, he surely would have grouped them together. Another distinct group, which seems to owe its arrangement to some previous hand, appears under the title "songs of degrees."

The groups, too, known as the *Hallel* psalms, were evidently formed for purposes of public singing, and not on any system affecting the whole collection of psalms.

The general conclusion is, that the Psalter owes its shape chiefly to what we may call the accidents of growth. Whenever the last redaction was made, individual psalms, nay, whole groups of psalms, may have been inserted, or added; but the addition was made without regard to any definite system, either chronological or artistic. The previous grouping may even have been interfered with, and to some extent disordered, by the latest hand that touched the Psalter.

On the other hand, so much of chronological sequence as naturally must show itself in a collection of compositions which has grown with time, may have been so far recognised and continued as that most of the very late psalms occur towards the end, while the earlier Books I. and II. were—except in one particular—but very slightly, perhaps from the same motive, interfered with.

This one particular relates to Psalms i. and ii. That these were by the Rabbis regarded as one composition, and were placed at the head of the collection with a purpose (see Introduction, Pss. i. and ii.) can hardly now be questioned. It is also probable that they owe their position to the latest, or, at all events, a very late hand. The collector of the Davidic psalms of Book I. would hardly have begun his collection with an orphan psalm, as the Rabbis call those wanting inscriptions; whereas a late compiler, who had already under his hand many such, would not pay any regard to a point of the kind. Wishing to strike at once the key-note of the whole collection, and to place at the opening of the Psalms a composition presenting the covenant relation in both its aspects, as affecting the individual towards ungodly individuals and the nation towards uncovenanted nations, and at the same time to bring into prominence the dignity of the written law, and the glory of the Messianic hope, he would select the two hymns most strikingly suiting his purpose, and weld them into one inaugurating psalm.

III. **The titles of the Psalms.**—Preliminary to any attempt at discussion of the authorship of the Psalms or the date of the composition and collection, the titles or inscriptions found at the head of so large a number of them claim notice, as being apparently the only guide followed in the arrangement of the Psalter as it has come down to us.

In the Hebrew Bible 116 psalms have inscriptions of some kind. The rest, 34 in number, are called by the Rabbis "orphan" psalms. In the Greek Bible no psalm has been left without a heading, except the first and second. An indication of the difference of opinion as to the value of these headings is supplied by the numbering of the verses. When the text of the Hebrew Bible received its present shape they were evidently regarded as an integral part of the Psalms, forming in many cases the first verse, to the great inconvenience in reference, since in all versions they have been treated as prefatory and not as part of the composition. That this opinion was not as old as the ancient versions is shown by the liberties the translators took with the inscriptions. They evidently did not, like the Fathers and later Jews, regard them as of equal importance with the text of the Psalms; and this very fact prepares the way for that criticism to which they have been in modern times subjected.

On the other hand, the fact that the LXX. found the inscriptions in their copies, proves that they were not the invention of those who incorporated them with the Psalms. Nay, it is often argued that because the translators were so perplexed by some of the musical directions as to have made hopeless nonsense of them, these at least, and by implication the titles generally, must be of an antiquity considerably greater than the version of the LXX., lapse of time having rendered these musical terms obscure. They may, however, have been obscure not from antiquity but from novelty. Newly-invented technical terms offer as much difficulty to a translator as obsolete words, and the musical system of Palestine was not improbably quite unknown at Alexandria long after it had come into use. On the other side it must be noticed that the translators allowed themselves considerable license with the titles even when they understood them, both changing and supplementing them, and generally treating them not as authoritative, but merely as convenient, finding them in many points defective, and often capable of improvement. This mode of treatment is not confined to the LXX. The Syriac allows itself the same freedom, and in one case prefixes a most interesting, but at the same time most tantalising heading, "from an ancient document."

Since such was the point of view of the old versions, it may justly be claimed by modern scholarship, that the inscriptions are open ground, coming to us with no kind of external authority, and to be judged in each separate case on their merits. They may here embody a tradition, here merely represent a clever guess, but whether due to popular tradition or Rabbinical adventure, the value of each inscription depends on the support it receives from the contents of the Psalm to which it has been affixed, and not to any authority from its age or position.

The meaning of the many obscure and perplexing musical inscriptions will be discussed as they present themselves. But one inscription, since it designates a whole group of psalms calls for notice here. It is that prefixed to the fifteen psalms, cxx.—cxxxiv., "a song of degrees." This translation comes through the Vulgate, *canticum graduum*; but song of *steps* or *ascents* would more nearly represent the Hebrew. The inscription was plainly intended to describe either the purpose for which the Psalms were composed, or some use to which they were adapted, for we may dismiss the theory that it describes a peculiarity of rhythm, a step-like progression, which is indeed audible in some of them, but only very faintly or not at all in most.*

Three accounts have been given of these psalms.

(1). They were composed to celebrate the return from the Captivity, and the title means "songs of going up." This view, however, must be abandoned. Some of the poems may very probably have been composed in honour of this event, but others of them (Pss. cxx., cxxii., cxxxiv.) have nothing to do with the march homewards from exile. Nor does the inscription really refer to that event. It is true that the verb from which the noun is formed is the usual word for journeying from the Babylonian low country to Palestine, and in Ezra vii. 9 the very noun in the singular is used of the return, but the *plural* cannot well refer to it.

(2). They are pilgrim songs which were chanted by the caravans as they journeyed to Jerusalem to the yearly feasts. This view is more natural, but against it is the fact that some of the hymns seem in no way suitable for such a use, and there is no historical authority (though strong probability) that any such custom prevailed. The form of the noun is also, in the opinion of many scholars, against this theory.

(3). They were psalms chanted by the Levites at the feast of Tabernacles as they stood during the water-drawing on the steps leading from the court of the men to that of the women. They are in fact literally "step songs." In favour of this view there is the fact that the number of the steps so occupied was *fifteen*, corresponding with the number of the Psalms. It is gathered also from the Talmud that these very Psalms were actually sung in this position. The inscription "songs of steps" not only exactly suits this explanation, but is what we should expect a rubrical title to be. (Comp. the *Graduale* of the Romish Church). This is also the explanation given by the Rabbinical authorities, on which we have to rely for our knowledge of Jewish ritual.

IV. **Authorship and Date of the Psalms.**—The discovery that little historical value was to be attached to the titles, at once opened up the difficult question as to the authorship and date of every part of the collection, and, unfortunately, without knowing the principle on which the collectors worked in prefixing the titles, we are without the benefit of profiting by their errors. That they thought they were working on materials extending through the whole possible period of the nation's literature, is shown by the ascription of one Psalm (xc.) to Moses. That, however, they did not work with the intention of making their collection representative of all the different ages of greatest literary vigour in that long period, is evident from the exclusion of the Song of Deborah, and the Psalm of Hannah, which would have served as examples of the times of the Judges. Nor are more than two Psalms allotted to the prolific age of Solomon (Pss. xxxii. and cxxvii.), and none at all to the revivals under Hezekiah and Josiah.

Apparently the first purpose was to collect and edit only Davidic psalms. Others, of Levitical origin, were soon added. But the tendency to attribute more and more of the hymns to David becomes evident as the collection goes on, and shows itself more decidedly still in the LXX.* By the time of Christ the whole Psalter had acquired the name of the royal poet, and in the phraseology of the Eastern and Western churches alike, it is simply called "David," while the Æthiopic version closes with the words "David is ended." Modern criticism has gone as far or even farther in the opposite direction. Ewald refers to David and *his time* only *seventeen* psalms; Grätz, a more recent commentator on the Psalms, grudgingly allows him part of *one*, the xviiith. The question of authorship, in so far as data exist for it, must be discussed with every individual psalm. Doubtless a very large part of the collection is due to the Levites. The inscriptions point that way, as well as the musical associations of the psalter. Within this body not only were the rites of the national religion preserved and continued, but its best spirit, as we know from the histories, was kept alive by them. In times when even the priests were carried away by the idolatrous influences of the court, Levites were found more "upright in heart," to struggle against the corrupt tendencies of the times, or throw themselves into any movement for reform (2 Chron. xxix. 34, xxxiv. 8—13). Professionally a religious body, they were certain to be the first victims of religious persecution, and we cannot doubt that they were generally among that better part of the community whose voice is so constantly lifted up in the psalms, now in plaintive prayer, now in fierce denunciation against the prevailing idolatries and apostacies. Add to this that they often

---

* The peculiarity is really nothing more than a variety of Hebrew verse, not confined to these Psalms (Comp. Pss. xciii., xcvi.; Is. xvii. 12, seq.. xxvi. 5, seq.; and especially Jud. v. 3, 5, 6, &c.) in accordance with which the sense is carried to a climax by the repetition of some prominent word, *e.g.*, in Ps. cxxi. 3, 4.

He will not suffer thy foot to move,
Thy keeper will not slumber,
Behold *slumbereth* not and *sleepeth* not
The *keeper* of Israel.

This device is hardly apparent in Pss. cxx., cxxvii., cxxix., cxxxi., and not at all in Pss. cxxviii., cxxxii.

* The LXX. allot to David Pss. x., xxxiii., xliii., lxvii., lxxi., xci., xciii.—xcix., civ., cxxxvii. On the other side it omits the Davidic inscription in cxxii., cxxiv., cxxxi., cxxxiii. (The numbers refer to the Hebrew Bible.)

suffered from negligence in paying the tithes, and were therefore literally among those poor afflicted ones, whose constancy to the Theocratic ideal is to be rewarded as in Pss. xxii. and xxxvii., which console the true seekers of God with the hope of temporal as well as spiritual blessings.*

The task of discovering individual authors for the Psalms must be given up; that of ascertaining the date of composition is hardly less difficult since so many have no strongly-marked individuality, and greatly resemble one another. Critics have, however, placed the largest number of the Psalms in four periods of history.

(1). Before the Captivity.
(2). During the Captivity.
(3). From the Captivity to the Maccabees.
(4). In the Maccabean (or subsequent) age.

Still, within limits so large it is often next to impossible to decide on the precise date of a psalm. Certain general features, however, present themselves as tests, and these have been followed here, and will be found noticed in the particular introductions.

The most important question with regard to these periods relates to the Maccabean age. In the controversy as to the existence of psalms of this period, critics of the greatest eminence are found on each side. If (see below) it can be proved that the Canon, as far as regards the Psalter, was not closed till after the reign of the Asmonean Queen Alexandra (Salome) then there is no external argument against Maccabean Psalms, while there is in many cases strong internal evidence in their favour. Nay, there is the strongest *a priori* probability that times so stirring, and marked by such a striking revival of patriotic and religious sentiment, should have given birth to poetry.

The question of the close of the Psalter has received a new light from the discovery of Grätz, that, according to tradition embodied in the Talmud, the night service, alluded to in Ps. cxxxiv., did not become part of Jewish ritual before the re-inauguration of the *Water Libation* during the Feast of Tabernacles by Queen Alexandra. This, if certain, brings the composition of that psalm, and, by implication, others of the "songs of degrees," down to the middle of the first century before Christ, and gives for the whole range over which the Psalter extends, counting from David, a period of eight hundred years.

V. **Nature of the verse.**—Of quantity and metre, in the sense a Greek would have used the words, Hebrew poetry knows nothing.

It is even doubtful whether any regard was paid to the number of *syllables* in a line, as distinguished from words. Nor did rhyme lend its charm to Hebrew verse.† Its music is heard rather in the succession of sentences than the succession of words. Single lines show no certain indication of a rule of quantity or accent, guiding and regulating the flow of thought, but when two or more are taken together, there is found to be a rhythmical proportion or symmetry between them, which has received various names, but is most usually, after Bishop Lowth's terminology, called *Parallelism*.* This term, though mathematical rather than poetic, serves well to express the essential peculiarity of Hebrew verse, in which the lines are so balanced one against the other, that thought corresponds to thought, in repetition, amplification, contrast or response. We might make a rough analogy by comparing the rhythmic movement of verse to the time-beats of a clock or watch. Other languages divide the verses into measured feet, as a watch ticks off the seconds; but Hebrew offers line to line with the longer, more solemn, and more majestic beat of the pendulum of a large clock. If one sentence balances another, so that voice and sense stop together, the natural cadence thus produced satisfies the Hebrew ear, though, very generally, the effect is improved by an actual equality in the number of words in the two clauses.

It is convenient to speak of parallelism as *simple* or *complex* according as the verse formed by it consists of two members or more than two.

The perfect form exhibits a symmetry both in form and expression; there is a balance not only in the sense, but in the order and arrangement of the words, the lines being of equal length and identical in structure, verb answering to verb, and noun to noun, as in Ps. xix. 2.

"Day to day uttereth speech,
And night to night sheweth knowledge."

This form is variously called the *synonymous* or *cognate* parallelism. The second line may be an exact echo or repetition of the first, as in verse 1 of the same psalm.

"The heavens declare the glory of God,
And the sky sheweth his handy-work."

But generally it either explains and illustrates the first line, as in Ps. xviii. 14.

"Yea, he sent out his arrows and scattered them,
And he shot out his lightnings and discomfited them."

Or it gives a new turn to the thought, and carries it on, as Ps. lxxvii. 1.

"My voice is unto God, and I cry aloud,
My voice is unto God, and he will hearken unto me."

The Psalms offer endless modifications of this perfect form. Sometimes the similarity of sense is dropped, while that of form remains. Often a graceful diversity is introduced by inverting the order of the words, as in the example above given, from Ps. cxix. 1, where in the Hebrew the clauses run

"The heavens declare the glory of God,
And the works of his hands shews the sky."

a figure which the Greeks called *chiasmus*, and which in Hebrew poetry is often called *introverted parallelism*. Comp. Ps. cvii. 9, 16, where the English partially repeats the figure.

Often again the principal element is not one of resemblance, but of progression, as in Ps. cxxix. 3.

"The ploughers ploughed upon my back,
And made long furrows."

Here the echo is not so much in the sense as in the construction of the clauses. The balance is maintained in the number and order of the words employed, though an entirely new thought is introduced. Indeed, sometimes, the rhythm almost disappears. There is still a manifest intention of parallelism, but the charm of the echo is gone. We are very near prose in such verses as Ps. cvii. 38, &c.

"He blesseth them so that they multiply exceedingly,
And suffereth not their cattle to decrease."

---

* Grätz has worked out this theory fully, and even goes so far as to adopt from the Hebrew (*anavim*) a name for this class of Psalm-writing Levites. He justly observes that while poor in material things, they were intellectually and morally far above the rest of the nation.

† Instances of assonance indeed are common, and the appearance of the same suffix, sometimes in five or six words together, shows that the Hebrew ear was pleased with a frequent repetition of identical sounds. Some of the Liturgical Psalms, *e.g.*, cvi., show a special tendency to this device.

* Other names are "rhyme of sentiment;" "thought rhythm;" "sentence rhythm."

PSALMS.

For this kind of parallelism the name *synthetic* was adopted by Lowth, but *epithetic* has been suggested as an improvement.

The alphabetical poems, presently to be noticed, show how the Hebrew poets of the later ages tried to supply to this kind of verse something of the definiteness wanting from the lax nature of their parallelism.

If *contrast* between the two clauses takes the place of resemblance, we get the second of the two principal forms of parallelism, the *antithetic* or, as it has been called from its prevalence in the Book of Proverbs, the *gnomic* or *sententious* rhythm. Here, as in the former case, the degrees of the antithesis are various. Sometimes the opposition extends to all the terms, as

"They are bowed down and fallen,
But we are risen and stand."—Ps. xx. 8.

Sometimes it is confined to one, and sometimes it discovers itself only as a contrast of sentiment without extending to the several terms. The Psalms do not afford many examples for this kind of verse, but the following fall more or less distinctly under it, Pss. i. 6, xv. 4.

The poetic mood, however, does not at all times submit to the constraint of fixed metre, and even the simple style of Hebrew has to allow of many a licence to be elastic enough for the passion of lyric song.

In the development from the simple rhythm, the *complex* forms of verse followed the analogy of rhymed stanzas in English and other modern poetry. Just as the original rhyming couplets have developed into verses of every possible variety, so the simple Hebrew rhythm has undergone countless variations and numerous combinations. The *rhyme* of *thought* has been treated like the *rhyme* of *sound*. In this way grew up what is generally called the strophe system of the Psalms.

That a division of Psalms into stanzas, or strophes, is not an arbitrary arrangement, is proved by the occurrence of two marked features. The first of these is the Refrain, which itself in many of the hymns serves to mark the verse structure. This feature may, perhaps, be traced to the liturgical use of the Psalms, the chorus alone being sung by the full choir, while the priest or Levite chanted the rest. The most perfect examples are offered by Pss. xlii., xliii., xlvi., xlviii., lvii., lxxx.

The other, which still more convincingly points to the fact that psalms were composed in stanzas is afforded by the alphabetical or acrostic psalms.* In these compositions, which are (counting Pss. ix. and x. as one) eight in number, the letters of the Hebrew alphabet are used as the letters of names and words are used in modern acrostics. There are as many as five variations in the mode and its use in the Psalter.

In the Psalms cxi., cxii., each *line* has its own initial letter, and in the original each line consists generally of three words.

In Pss. xxv., xxxiv., cxlv., which are arranged in couplets, only the first line of the couplet shows the initial letter.

Ps. xxxvii. is arranged in stanzas of four lines, the first line only of each having the initial letter.

The author of Psalms ix., x., apparently intended to begin every line of his quatrains with the same letter, but abandoned it for a simpler plan after the first stanza (comp. Lam. iii.)

In the cxixth. Psalm the alphabetic system has been carried out most completely and elaborately. It consists of twenty-two long stanzas, composed each of eight couplets, each of the eight beginning with the same letter. This laboured result first suggested to Bishop Lowth his examination into the principle of Hebrew poetry. It certainly furnishes a proof of the existence of a verse structure and a guide for dividing other poems into their constituent stanzas.

VI. **The purpose and scope of the Psalms.**—The covenant ideal in its bearing on individuals and on the nation at large in its relation to other nations (prominently put forward in the first two Psalms) may be said to furnish its purpose to the Psalter. This theocratic ideal was not born into the heart of the people at once, but was developed by a long and painful discipline after many failures and much suffering; and all this finds its reflection in the Psalms.

According to the two aspects under which it is viewed, this covenant ideal appears in the portrait of the perfectly just and upright individual, or in the picture of a prosperous and happy nation. The latter, however, is often represented in the person of its anointed king, or Messiah, to whom, even in the darkest and saddest days, the eyes of the race can hopefully turn. This identification of the ideal people with the ideal sovereign must always be borne in mind in reading the Psalms. It follows of necessity from the *locus standi* so commonly assumed by the writers, who, under their own personality, really present the fortunes of the community, its sufferings and trials, its hopes and fears. Thus the changeful destinies of the race are represented as involved in the fortunes of one individual, and this individual is very often the perfect King. It is in consequence of this that we can find in the Psalms, not only the Jews' Messiah, but the Christians' Christ, not only the victorious and triumphant monarch, but the despised and suffering Son of Man.

Another point in regard to the covenant ideal as presented in the Psalter must be noticed. The *character* of the upright individual is described from a *religious* rather than a *moral* point of view. The highest moral standard is touched in the Psalms, but it is, so to speak, touched from above, not from below; it is conceived of by reference to God and the requirements for one who would tread His courts, not by reference to the moral excellence of the qualities themselves that go to make up the perfect character. Hence proceeds a far stricter ethical sentiment than that which attends a merely moral code, a sentiment which regards a breach of the law not only as a lapse from the right, but as treason against God. Where, therefore, a moral standard would demand accusation and condemnation, the standard of the Psalmist cries for denunciation as of a recreant and apostate to a great cause. What are called the *imprecatory* psalms may possibly, sometimes, combine with their religious and patriotic vehemence some elements less pardonable. Party and even personal bitterness may sometimes lend the words a sting. They are certainly not so suited for Christian worship as the prayers and praises which form the greater part of the Psalter. But their difficulty, as component part of a Jewish book of devotion, vanishes when we reflect that the wicked, on whose head the curses fell, were at once foes to their nation and apostates from their religion, and in many cases actually represented public enemies such as churches and states even of Christian times have thought it right to denounce with anathemas.

---

* This species of poem is not confined to the Psalter. Four out of the five chapters of the Lamentations and part of the last chapter of the Book of Proverbs are alphabetical.

THE BOOK OF PSALMS

PSALM I.

(1) Blessed ᵃ *is* the man that walketh not in the counsel of the ¹ungodly, nor standeth in the way of sinners, nor sitteth in the seat of the scornful.

(2) But his delight *is* in the law of the LORD; ᵇ and in his law doth he meditate day and night. (3) And he shall be like a tree ᶜ planted by the rivers of water, that bringeth forth his fruit in his

a Prov. 4. 14.
1 Or, *wicked.*
b Josh. 1. 8; Ps. 119. 1.
c Jer. 17. 8.

Book I.

Psalm i. has generally been regarded as a kind of preface or introduction to the rest of the Psalter. The absence of an inscription favours this view, since this absence is rare in the first book. (See *General Introduction*.) It is still further favoured by the traditional arrangement which left the psalm without a number, combining it with Psalm ii.—a tradition supported by the reading of some MSS. in Acts xiii. 33 (see *New Test. Com.*). There are also some slight similarities of phraseology between the first two psalms, but no resemblance of style or matter, such as would be found if they had been originally one composition. At the same time, the two psalms seem to have been placed side by side by the compilers of the collection in order to form together such a general introduction. In the one we see the blessing attending the loyal fulfilment of the covenant of Jehovah in the case of the individual; in the other in the case of the nation at large, under its ideal prince. Just as the righteous man in Ps. i. is contrasted with the wicked *individuals*, so in Ps. ii. the chosen Israel is contrasted with the surrounding nations who do not submit voluntarily to Jehovah; and, combined, the two strike the key-note of the whole Psalter, the faithfulness of God's dealings with men, whether in their individual or national relation to Him, and the indissoluble connection between righteousness and blessing. It is true that in Ps. ii. the word "wicked" in connection with the heathen does not occur, but throughout the Psalter the two ideas are inseparable, and are undoubtedly implied there. It must be noticed too that Ps. i. presents the contrast of the *just* and the *wicked* in the same view which meets us in almost every psalm : not so much a moral as a religious view; the covenant relation is always presupposed. The *just* or *righteous* is the Israelite faithful to Jehovah and His Law; the *ungodly* or *wicked* is the Jew who makes light of his legal duties, whether in thought, act, or talk. (See Note 1.)

For determining the date, there is not only the indication of a comparatively late composition afforded by the growing reverence for the written Law (*tôrah*), but also the extreme probability that Jeremiah xvii. 8 is founded on this psalm, which approximately fixes the furthest limit to which it may be brought down. The use of the word "scorners," a word of frequent use in the Book of Proverbs (and actually defined in Prov. xxi. 24), but not found anywhere else in the Psalter, connects this psalm with the period which produced that book. It harmonises also with the dominant feeling of the later period of the monarchy. The conjecture that Solomon wrote it is interesting, but rests on insufficient ground.

In character, the psalm is simple and didactic, with an easy flowing style, not rising to any great height of poetry, either in its thought or diction. The parallelism is regular but varied.

(1) **Blessed.**—The Hebrew word is a plural noun, from the root meaning to be "straight," or "right." Literally, *Blessings to the man who*, &c.

Walketh . . . standeth . . . sitteth.—Better, *went, stood, sat.* The good man is first described on the negative side. In the short summary of evil from which he has been saved, it is the custom of commentators to see an epitome of the whole history of sin. But the apparent gradation was a necessity of the rhythm. The three terms employed, however, for evil have distinctive significations. (1) *The ungodly.* Properly, restless, wanting in self-control, victims of ungoverned passion, as defined in Isa. lvii. 20. (2) *Sinners.* General term for wrong-doers. (3) *Scornful.* A proverbial word, defined in Prov. xxi. 24: Aquila has "mockers;" Symmachus "impostors;" the LXX. "pests;" Vulgate "pest." The words expressing the *conduct* and the *career*, "counsel," "way," are aptly chosen, and correspond with "went," "stood." Possibly "seat" should be "assembly." (Comp. Ps. cvii. 32.) It has an official sound, and without unduly pressing the language, we think of the graduation in vice which sometimes ends in deliberate preference for those who despise virtue. (Comp. Ps. xxvi. 4, 5.)

(2) **But.**—The Hebrew is an elliptical expression implying a strong contrast, "nay but," "on the contrary."

The positive side of a good man's character is now described according to the standard which prevailed when the written law first came truly into force.

In the law of Jehovah is his delight.—Or, *to the law of Jehovah is his inclination.* The Hebrew word means primarily "to bend."

Meditate.—Literally, *murmur* (of a dove, Isa. xxxviii. 14; of men lamenting, Isa. xvi. 7; of a lion growling, Isa. xxxi. 4; of muttered charms, viii. 19). (Comp. Josh. i. 8, which might have suggested this).

(3) **And he.**—Better, *So is he.* For the image so forcible in an Eastern clime, where vegetation depends on proximity to a stream, comp. Pss. lii. 8, xcii. 12; Isa. xliv. 4; and its development in Jer. xvii. 7, 8. The full moral bearing of the image appears in our Lord's parabolic saying, "a good tree cannot bring forth corrupt fruit, nor an evil tree good fruit." The physical growth of a tree has in all poetry served as a ready emblem of success, as its decay has of failure. (Recall Wolsey's

The Unhappiness   PSALMS, II.   *of the Ungodly.*

season; his leaf also shall not ¹ wither; and whatsoever he doeth shall prosper.

(4) The ungodly *are* not so but *are* ᵃlike the chaff which the wind driveth away. (5) Therefore the ungodly shall not stand in the judgment, nor sinners in the congregation of the righteous.

(6) For the LORD knoweth the way of the righteous: but the way of the ungodly shall perish.

PSALM II.

(1) Why ᵇ do the heathen ² rage, and the people ³ imagine a vain thing?

1 Heb., *fade*.
ᵃ Ps. 35. 5; Isa. 17. 13.
ᵇ Acts 4. 25.
2 Or, *tumultuously assemble*.
3 Heb., *meditate*.

---

comment on his fall in Shakespeare's *Henry VIII*.) Nor has the moral significance of vegetable life been ignored. "If," says a German poet, "thou wouldest attain to thy highest, go look upon a flower, and what that does unconsciously do thou consciously." In Hebrew poetry a moral purpose is given to the grass on the mountain side and the flower in the field, and we are taught that "there is not a virtue within the widest range of human conduct, not a grace set on high for man's aspiration, which has not its fitting emblem in vegetable life."—*Bible Educator*, ii., p. 179.

For the general comparison of a righteous man to a tree, comp. Pss. lii. 8 (the olive), cxxviii. 3 (vine); Hos. xiv. 6 (olive and cedar). Naturally the actual kind of tree in the poet's thought interests us. The oleander suggested by Dean Stanley (*Sinai and Palestine*, 146), though answering the description in many ways, fails from its want of fruit to satisfy the principal condition. For, as Bishop Hall says, "Look where you will in God's Book, you shall never find any lively member of God's house, any true Christian, compared to any but a *fruitful* tree." Probably the *palm* meets all the conditions best. (Comp. Ps. xcii. 12.)

The last clause, "Whatsoever he doeth, it shall," &c., is obscure in construction. The best rendering is, *all that he doeth he maketh to prosper*, which may mean either "the righteous man carries out to a *successful end* all his enterprises," or "all that he begins he brings to a maturity."

(4) **The ungodly.**—Better, *Not so the ungodly*.

But are like.—They shall be winnowed out of the society of the true Israel by the fan of God's judgment. The image is a striking one, although so frequent as almost to have become a poetical commonplace (Hab. iii. 12; Joel iii. 14; Jer. li. 33; Isa. xxi. 10). (See *Bible Educator*, iv. 4.)

(5) **Therefore.**—Notice contrast with verse 1. Those who had deliberately chosen the assembly of the scornful will have no place in that of the good.

Shall not stand.—Properly, *shall not rise*. Probably like our phrase, "shall not hold up his head." Will be self-convicted, and shrink away before God's unerring scrutiny, like the man without a wedding garment in our Lord's parable (Matt. xxii. 12). The LXX. and Vulg. have "rise again," as if with thought of an after state.

The congregation of the righteous.—A phrase repeating itself in different forms in the Psalms. It implies either *Israel* as opposed to the heathen, or *faithful* Israel as opposed to those who had proved disloyal to the covenant. In theory all the congregation was holy (Num. xvi. 3), but we meet in the Psalms with the feeling expressed in the Apostle's words, "They are not all Israel that are of Israel."

(6) **Knoweth**—*i.e., recogniseth with discriminative discernment and appreciation*. (Comp. Pss. xxxi. 7 and cxliv. 3; Exod. ii. 25; also John x. 14. So Shakespeare, *As You Like It*: "I know you are my eldest brother, and in the gentle condition of blood you should so know me.")

The way of the ungodly shall perish.—This is explained by Ps. cxii. 10, "the *desire* of the wicked shall perish;" all his plans and ambitions shall come to nought. The metaphor is illustrated by Job vi. 18, where an unjust course is compared to a stream that suddenly dries up and disappears.

II.

As Psalm i. describes the results of fulfilling the covenant for the individual by contrasting the condition of those who fail in their allegiance, so Psalm ii. shows how the covenant relation exalts Israel over the heathen; but some particular political situation seems to be indicated. Jerusalem appears to be threatened by a confederacy of hostile and rebellious powers—a confederacy that took advantage of the succession of a young and inexperienced monarch to throw off the bonds of subjection and tribute. David, Solomon, Ahaz, and Uzziah, have each of them been regarded as the hero and theme of the poem, but in each case there is some lack of correspondence between the history and the psalm. The psalm must therefore be regarded as expressing an ideal view of the future—an ideal which the poet felt, from his historic knowledge of the past, would not shape itself except under difficulties and opposition. Doubtless there were in his mind the prophetic words spoken of David's son, "I will be his father, and he shall be my son"—words embodying the vital principle of the Hebrew monarchy, the essential idea of the Israelitish polity, that the king was only a regent in God's name, the deputy of Jehovah, and the chosen instrument of His will. Starting from these words, the poet shapes an ideal monarchy and an ideal king—one who, though encountered by the worst forms of opposition, would prove himself a true son of David, and by his fidelity to his God and nation, a true son of God. Undismayed by the threatening aspect of things, and with prophetic words ringing in his ears, the youthful monarch aims at re-asserting God's supremacy over the heathen, and imposing once more that restraint of His law and religion from which they longed to be free. A view of the psalm alone explains its want of exact historic coincidence, and vindicates the claims universally made for it of Messianic prevision; for there is but a step between the ideal king and the Messianic king—a step which, though perhaps unconsciously, the poets and prophets of Israel were for ever taking.

The psalm is lyric, with intense dramatic feeling. The poet begins and ends in his own person; but we hear the heathen muttering their threats, Jehovah answering them in thunder from heaven, and holding animated dialogue with His anointed, who, in turn, takes up the address, and declares His Divine mission and asserts His power. The strophical arrangement is fairly marked.

(1) **Why do the heathen rage?**—Better, *Why did nations band together, or muster?* The Hebrew occurs only here as a verb, but derivatives occur in

The Kingdom	PSALMS, II. *of Christ.*

(2) The kings of the earth set themselves, and the rulers take counsel together, against the LORD, and against his anointed, *saying,* (3) Let us break their bands asunder, and cast away their cords from us.

(4) *a* He that sitteth in the heavens shall laugh: the LORD shall have them in derision. (5) Then shall he speak unto them in his wrath, and [1] vex them in his sore displeasure.

(6) Yet have I [2] set my king [3] upon my holy hill of Zion.

(7) I will declare [4] the decree: the LORD hath said unto me, *b* Thou *art* my Son; this day have I begotten thee. (8) *c* Ask of me, and I shall give *thee* the heathen *for* thine inheritance, and the uttermost parts of the earth *for* thy possession. (9) *d* Thou shalt break them with a rod of iron; thou shalt dash them in pieces like a potter's vessel.

a Prov. 1. 23.
[1] Or, *trouble.*
[2] Heb., *anointed.*
[3] Heb., *upon Zion, the hill of my holiness.*
[4] Or, *for a decree.*
b Acts 13. 33; Heb. 1. 5.
c Ps. 72. 8.
d Rev. 2. 27, & 19. 15.

Pss. lv. 14, lxiv. 2: in the first, of a *festive crowd;* in the second, of a *conspiracy allied with some evil intent.* This fixes the meaning here, *band together,* possibly as in Aquila's translation, with added sense of *tumult.* The LXX. have "grown restive," like horses; Vulg., "have raged."

Imagine.—Better, *meditate,* or *plan.* Literally, as in Ps. i. 2, only here in bad sense, *mutter,* referring to the whispered treasons passing to and fro among the nations, "a maze of mutter'd threats and mysteries." In old English "imagine" was used in a bad sense; thus Chaucer, "nothing list him to be *imaginatif,*" *i.e., suspicious.* The verb in this clause, as in the next, is in the present, the change being expressive: Why *did* they plot? what *do* they hope to gain by it?

(2) **Set themselves**—*i.e., with hostile intent,* as in Jer. xlvi. 4, where the same word is used of warriors: "Stand forth with your helmets."

Rulers.—Properly, *grave dignitaries.*

Take counsel.—Better, *have taken their plans,* and are now mustering to carry them into effect. Notice the change of tense: in the first clause, the poet *sees,* as it were, the array; in the second, he goes back to its origin.

Against the Lord.—Notice the majestic simplicity of this line. The word Messiah is applicable in its first sense to any one anointed for a holy office or with holy oil (Lev. iv. 3, 5, 16). Its distinctive reference to an expected prince of the chosen people, who was to redeem them from their enemies, and fulfil completely all the Divine promises for them, probably dates from this psalm, or more distinctly from this psalm than from any one passage. At least, that the traditional Jewish interpretation had fastened upon it as of this importance is shown by the frequent and emphatic quotation of this psalm in the New Testament. (See New Testament use of these verses in Acts iv. 25, and Note in *New Testament Commentary.*)

(3) **Let us break.**—The whispered purpose now breaks out into loud menace, and we hear their defiance pass along the ranks of the rebels.

Cords.—The LXX. and Vulg. have "yoke," which is in keeping with the metaphor of a restive animal. (Comp. Isa. lviii. 6 and x. 27.)

(4) **He that sitteth.**—Here the psalm, with a sublimity truly Hebrew, turns from the wild confusion on earth to the spectacle of God looking down with mingled scorn and wrath on the fruitless attempts of the heathen against His chosen people.

Laugh.—We speak of the "irony of events"; the Hebrew ascribes irony to God, who controls events.

(5) **Then.**—An emphatic particle, marking the climax; possibly equal to "Lo! behold." The grand roll of the words in the original is like the roll of the thunder, and is rendered more effective by its contrast with the quiet manner of verse 4.

And vex them.—Literally, *and greatly* (the verb is in the intensive conjugation) *terrify them in his nostrils and in his heat.*

(6) **Yet have I.**—The pronoun is very emphatic: "You *dare* to revolt, it is *I* who have given this office to the king."

Set.—Literally, *poured out,* as of melted metal; used of the Divine Spirit (Isa. xxix. 10), of a libation (Exod. xxx. 9), and of pouring melted metal into a mould (Isa. xl. 19); from the latter use, to *establish,* or *set up,* is a natural transition. Gesenius and Ewald give a different sense to the word *pour,* and follow Symmachus in translating *anointed,* which agrees well with the mention of the Messiah (verse 4). The LXX. and Vulg. have "but I was appointed king by him," making the Anointed begin his speech here, instead of at the next verse.

(7) **I will declare.**—The anointed king now speaks himself, recalling the covenant made with him by Jehovah at his coronation.

I will tell.—Better, *Let me speak concerning the appointment.* The word rendered *decree* in our version is derived from a root meaning to engrave, and so stands for any formal agreement, but it is usually an ordinance clearly announced by a prophet or some other commissioned interpreter of the Divine will, and consecrated and legalised by mutual adoption by king and people.

The Lord hath.—Better, *Jehovah said unto me:* that is, at that particular time, the day which the great event made the new birthday, as it were, of the monarch, or perhaps of the monarchy. From the particular prince, of whose career, if we could identify him with certainty, this would be the noblest historical memorial, the Psalmist—if, indeed, any one historic personage was in his thought at all—let his thoughts and hopes range, as we certainly may, on to a larger and higher fulfilment. The figure of an *ideal prince* who was always about to appear, but was never realised in any actual successor on the throne, may possibly, by the time of this psalm, have assumed its great place in the nation's prophetic hopes. Certainly the whole line of tradition claims the passage in a Messianic sense. (See Note, verse 2; and in *New Testament Commentary,* Note to Acts xiii. 33; Heb. i. 5, v. 5. For the king, spoken of as *God's son,* see Ps. lxxxix. 26, 27, and comp. 2 Sam. vii. 14.)

(9) **Thou shalt break.**—The LXX. translated, "thou shalt pasture them," understanding by the rod (Heb., *shevet*), as in Lev. xxvii. 32, a shepherd's crook. (Comp. Ezek. xx. 37; Micah vii. 14.) Elsewhere the rod is a sceptre (Ps. cxxv. 3); in Prov. xxii. 15 it is a rod of correction. The use to be made of it—*to dash*

Kings called on to   PSALMS, III.   *accept Christ's Kingdom.*

(10) Be wise now therefore, O ye kings: be instructed, ye judges of the earth. (11) Serve the LORD with fear, and rejoice with trembling. (12) Kiss the Son, lest he be angry, and ye perish *from* the way, when his wrath is kindled but a little.

a Prov. 16. 20; Isa. 30. 18; Jer. 17. 7; Rom. 9. 33, & 10. 11; 1 Pet. 2. 6.

b 2 Sam. 15. 15.

a Blessed *are* all they that put their trust in him.

PSALM III.

A Psalm of David, *b* when he fled from Absalom his son.

(1) LORD, how are they increased that

---

the nations in pieces, as one breaks a potter's vessel—points to the latter of these significations here.

"Then shalt thou bring full low
With iron sceptre bruised, and them disperse
Like to a potter's vessel shivered so." (*Milton's trans.*)

Verse 10 begins the fourth section of the poem. Subject princes are warned to be wise in time, and, as a religious duty as well as a political necessity, to submit to Jehovah.

Rejoice with trembling.—Literally, *quake*, referring to the motion of the body produced by strong emotion, and therefore used both of joy and terror. Our version follows the LXX.; most of the old versions paraphrase the word: Chaldean, "pray"; Syriac, "cleave to him"; Arabic, "praise him." It is historically interesting to remember that the words of this verse—*et nunc reges intelligite*—formed the legend of the medal struck in England after the execution of Charles I.

(12) **Kiss the Son.**—This familiar translation must be surrendered. It has against it the weight of all the ancient versions except the Syriac. Thus the Chaldaic has, "receive instruction"; LXX., followed by Vulg., "lay hold of discipline." Symmachus and Jerome render "pay pure adoration." Aquila has "kiss with discernment." *Bar*, in the sense of "son," is common in Chaldee, and is familiar to us from the Aramaic patronymics of the New Testament: *e.g.*, *Bar-Jonas*, *Bar-nabas*, &c. The only place where it occurs in Heb., is Prov. xxxi. 2, where it is repeated three times; but the Book of Proverbs has a great deal of Aramaic colouring. Our psalmist uses *ben* for "son" in verse 7, and it is unlikely that he would change to so unusual a term, unless *nashshekû-bar* were a proverbial saying, and of this there is no proof. Surely, too, the article or a suffix would have been employed. "Kiss son" seems altogether too abrupt and bald even for Hebrew poetry. The change of subject also in the co-ordinate clause, "lest he (*i.e.*, Jehovah, as the context shows) be angry," is very awkward. As to the translation of the verb, the remark of Delitzsch, that it means "to kiss, and nothing else," is wide of the mark, since it must in any case be taken *figuratively*, with sense of *doing homage*, as in Gen. xli. 40 (margin), or *worshipping* (1 Kings xix. 18; Hosea xiii. 2). The most consistent rendering is, therefore, *proffer pure homage* (to Jehovah), *lest he be angry*. It may be added that the current of Rabbinical authority is against our Authorised version. Thus R. Solomon: "Arm yourselves with discipline;" (so, with a slight variation, one of the latest commentarists, E. Reuss: "Arm yourselves with loyalty";) another Rabbi: "Kiss the covenant"; another, "Adore the corn." Among the best of modern scholars, Hupfeld renders "yield sincerely"; Ewald, "receive wholesome warning"; Hitzig, "submit to duty"; Grätz (by emendation), "give good heed to the warning."

From the way.—The LXX. and Vulg. amplify and explain "from the righteous way" It is the way in following which, whether for individuals or nations,

alone there is peace and happiness. (See Note Ps. cxix. 1.)

When his wrath.—Better, *for his wrath is soon kindled*, or *easily kindled*.

Put their trust.—Better, *find their refuge*.

Notice in the close of the psalm the settled and memorable belief that good must ultimately triumph over evil. The rebels against God's kingdom must be conquered in the noblest way, by being drawn into it.

III.

With this psalm the hymn-book of Israel properly begins. The title indicates it as the first psalm of a Davidic collection formed at some time previous to the arrangement of the rest of the Psalter—a date, however, which we cannot recover. We also find ourselves on probable historical ground. The only reason to suspect the tradition embodied in the title which refers Ps. iii. to the time of the flight from Absalom, is in the mention of "the holy mountain"; and this is explained as in Note to verse 4. There is a beautiful conjecture which connects the two psalms with the actual day of the flight from Jerusalem—the day of whose events we have a more detailed account than of any other in Jewish history. The close connection of the two psalms is seen by a comparison of Ps. iv. 7 with Ps. iii. 3, and Ps. iii. 5 with Ps. iv. 8, and of both with the narrative in 2 Sam. xv., xvi., and xvii.

The absence of any allusion to Absalom by name may be accounted for by the tender feeling of the fond father for the rebellious son. Ewald calls attention to the evidence in the tone of Ps. iii., not only of a tried religious sense, but also of the elasticity and strength supplied by a peaceful sleep. "The calmer mood of a cheerful morning" comes to crown the constancy of a faith which is not of yesterday, but has been built up by a lifetime. The same eminent critic declares that here "the elevation, the stamp, the style of David are unmistakable." The rhythmical arrangement is so artistic that we must suppose the poem composed at leisure, after the excitement of the rout was over.

Title.—A Psalm of David. Heb., *Mizmôr ledavid*, the usual form of announcing authorship. *Mizmôr*, which occurs only in the inscriptions to psalms, must be regarded as the technical term for a particular kind of lyric composition, and possibly originated with David. It corresponds to ψαλμὸς in the Greek version; and whether the root from which it is derived primarily means "to prune," or is, as some think, a word formed to express the sound of a harp-string when struck, it means *a song composed for musical accompaniment*, as is shown by its being sometimes united with *shir*, the generic name for song. (See titles to Pss. xlviii., lxvi.)

(1) **How ... many.**—"And Absalom and *all the people*, the men of Israel, came to Jerusalem" (2 Sam. xvi. 15). Ahithophel counsels Absalom to take 12,000 men, and go in instant pursuit of the fugitive. Hushai's advice shows, of course, the exaggeration of flattery: "Therefore I counsel that all Israel be generally

trouble me! many *are* they that rise up against me. (2) Many *there be* which say of my soul, *There is* no help for him in God. Selah.

(3) But thou, O Lord, *art* a shield ¹for me; my glory, and the lifter up of mine head.

(4) I cried unto the Lord with my voice, and he heard me out of his holy hill. Selah. (5) *ᵃ*I laid me down and slept; I awaked; for the Lord sustained me. (6) *ᵇ*I will not be afraid of ten thousands of people, that have set *themselves* against me round about.

(7) Arise, O Lord; save me, O my God: for thou hast smitten all mine enemies *upon* the cheek bone; thou hast broken the teeth of the ungodly. (8) *ᶜ*Salvation *belongeth* unto the Lord: thy blessing *is* upon thy people. Selah.

1 Or, *about.*
a Ps. 4. 8.
b Ps. 27. 3.
c Isa. 43. 11; Hos. 13. 4.
2 Or, *overseer.*

PSALM IV.

To the ²chief Musician on Neginoth, A Psalm of David.

(1) Hear me when I call, O God of my

---

gathered unto thee, from Dan even to Beersheba, as the sand which is by the sea for multitude."

(2) **There is no help.**—According to the current creed, misfortune implied wickedness, and the wicked were God-forsaken. David, too, had sent back Zadok with the Ark, which in the popular view meant sending away the power and the presence of God. Even Zadok seemed to share this feeling; and David's words to him, "thou a seer" (2 Sam. xv. 27), seem to contain something of a rebuke.

Selah.—This curious word must apparently remain for ever what it has been ever since the first translation of the Bible was made—the puzzle of ordinary readers, and the despair of scholars. One certain fact about it has been reached, and this the very obscurity of the term confirms. It has no ethical significance, as the Targum, followed by some other of the old versions and by St. Jerome, implies, for in that case it would long ago have yielded a satisfactory meaning. There are many obscure words in Hebrew, but their obscurity arises from the infrequency of their use; but *selah* occurs no less than seventy-one times in the compass of thirty-nine psalms, and three times in the ode of Habakkuk (Hab. iii. 3, 9, 13). It is pretty certain that the sense "for ever," which is the traditional interpretation of the Rabbinical schools, does not suit the majority of these places, and no other moral or spiritual rendering has ever been suggested; nor is it a poetical word, marking the end of a verse or the division into strophes, for it occurs sometimes in the very middle of a stanza, as in Pss. xx. 3, 4, xxxii. 4, 5, and lii. 3, 4, and often at the end of a psalm (Ps. xlvi.). There is only one conclusion, now universally admitted, that *selah* is a musical term, but in the hopeless perplexity and darkness that besets the whole subject of Hebrew music, its precise intention must be left unexplained. The conjecture that has the most probability on its side makes it a direction to *play loud.* The derivation from *sâlah,* "to raise," is in favour of this view. The fact that in one place (Ps. ix. 16) it is joined to *higgaion,* which is explained as a term having reference to the sound of stringed instruments, lends support to it, as also does the translation uniformly adopted in the Psalms by the LXX.: διάψαλμα—if, indeed, that word means interlude. It is curious that the interpretation next in favour to Ewald's makes the meaning of *selah* exactly the opposite to his—*piano* instead of *forte*—deriving it from a word meaning "to be silent," "to suspend."

(3) **For me.**—Better, *behind me.* A protection from the emissaries of Absalom, now on his track.

My glory, and the lifter up of mine head.—Comp.—
"O et praesidium et dulce decus meum."
Horace, *Ode* I., i. 2.

The significance of this sublime trust comes out as we read in 2 Sam. xv. 30 how the humiliated monarch went barefoot over Olivet, with head bent down and muffled in his mantle; no glory or dignity left; mute and humiliated under the insults and curses of Shimei.

(4) **With my voice.**—That is, *aloud.* The verbs are present, expressing the habit of the royal psalmist.

(6) **That have set themselves**—*i.e., have arrayed themselves as for battle.* (See 1 Kings xx. 12.)

(7) **Thou hast smitten . . . broken.**—Better, *thou smitest . . . breakest.* The enemies are conceived of as wild beasts, like the lion and bear of the adventures of David's own youth, whom God would render harmless to him.

(8) **Thy blessing . . .**—Rather, *let thy blessing be upon thy people.* It is not the statement of a fact, but an intercessory prayer. The true Shepherd of His people was a noble and generous man. This close, as Ewald says, "throws a bright light on the depth of his noble soul."

IV.

This psalm most probably belongs to the same occasion as that which produced Psalm iii. (see Introduction to that psalm), but was sung in an hour of still greater trial. Standing by itself, indeed, it might have been written by any prophet struggling against the dislike and opposition of his fellow-citizens. The rhythm is irregular. Psalm iv. was one of those repeated by Augustine at his conversion.

Title.—**To the chief musician.**—(Margin, *overseer.*) The rendering of a word occurring fifty-five times in the inscriptions, and in Hab. iii. 19. Whatever be the primary meaning of the root-word, whether *to be bright* or *strong,* the form here employed must imply "one who has obtained the mastery," or "holds a superior post." Hence "master," "director," or "overseer" (2 Chron. ii. 18, xxxiv. 12). But from the description in 1 Chron. xv. 16, *et seq.,* we see that the musical directors, as they are considered to be (Asaph, Heman, and Ethan), had themselves cymbals, and took part in the performance, and hence the word would answer to a leader of the band; but as in the case of the Psalms there is vocal music as well, perhaps "precentor" is the best equivalent. The LXX., followed by the Vulg., render "to the end"—a phrase difficult to explain, but which possibly had an eschatological reference rather than a musical.

On Neginoth.—Another musical term occurring, with a slight variation in the preposition, in the titles of six psalms. Its derivation from a root, meaning

righteousness: thou hast enlarged me *when I was* in distress; ¹have mercy upon me, and hear my prayer.

⁽²⁾ O ye sons of men, how long *will ye turn* my glory into shame? *how long will* ye love vanity, *and* seek after leasing? Selah. ⁽³⁾ But know that the LORD hath set apart him that is godly for himself: the LORD will hear when I call unto him.

⁽⁴⁾ Stand in awe, and sin not: commune with your own heart upon your bed, and be still. Selah. ⁽⁵⁾ Offer *ᵃ* the sacrifices of righteousness, and put your trust in the LORD.

⁽⁶⁾ *There be* many that say, Who will

1 Or, *be gracious unto me.*

a Ps. 50. 14, & 51. 19.

"to touch the strings," as well as the connection in which it is found, point to the explanation (almost universally given), "upon stringed instruments," or, "with harp accompaniment." It seems natural to join the two directions — "to the conductor of those playing on stringed instruments," or, "to the leader of the harps."

⁽¹⁾ **Hear me.**—Better, *In my crying hear me, God of my righteousness.*

The conception of God as supremely just, and the assertor of justice, is one of the noblest legacies from the Hebrew faith to the world. It is summed up in the question, "Shall not the judge of all the earth do right?" The strength of the innocent in the face of calumny or oppression lies in the appeal to the eternal source of righteousness.

Thou hast enlarged.—Better, *in my straitness Thou* (or, *Thou who*) *hast made room for me.* This is a thought very common in the Psalter, and apparently was a favourite phrase of David's, occurring in Ps. xviii. 19 (comp. verse 36), and in other psalms attributed to him.

⁽²⁾ **Sons of men.**—A literal rendering of a Hebrew phrase generally interpreted as "men of high degree." Luther translates "gentlemen" (see Ps. xlix. 2), where it is "high," as contrasted with "low." (Comp. Ps. lxii. 9, "men of high degree.")

How long?—Literally, *how long to shame my glory?* which, after the analogy of Ps. xxxvii. 26, "his seed is for a blessing," must mean *How long shall my glory be for shame* (*opprobrio*)*?* The LXX. and Vulg. follow a different and probably correct reading: "How long will ye be heavy (or slow) of heart?" They also indicate that an interrogative has dropped out before the second clause, so that it is rightly supplied by the Authorised Version.

Seek after.—In Hebrew the intensive conjugation, *to seek earnestly*, or *again and again.*

Leasing—*i.e., lying.* (Comp. verse 6.) So in Wycliffe's New Testament: "Whanne he speketh leesing, he speketh of his own; for he is a leere, and is fader of it" (John viii. 44). "Lesyngmongers" (1 Tim. i. 10). Chaucer uses the word; and it is common in *Piers Ploughman.* Shakespeare also knows the word:—

"Now Mercury indue thee with leasing,
For thou speakest well of fools."—*Twelfth Night.*

(See *Bible Educator*, iv. 3.) Milton's translation is—

"To love, to seek, to prize
Things false and vain, and nothing else but lies."

For "Selah," see Note, Ps. iii. 2.

From this verse we gather that the report of the calumny uttered against him in Jerusalem had reached the king's ears.

⁽³⁾ **But know.**—It is the privilege of true and heroic natures to rise to a consciousness of their strength and dignity in the hour of peril, and when the victims of unjust persecution. Besides his innate greatness, David has a grandeur and dignity, derived from his deep sense of the covenant between God and His anointed, and his own imperfect but sincere endeavour to act worthily the part of God's vice-regent on earth. His selection by Jehovah is an unanswerable reply to his calumniators, and the surest proof of his own uprightness.

Hath set apart.—That is, *has distinguished* or *honoured.* So rightly the LXX. and Vulg. The Hebrew word occurs in Exod. viii. 22, ix. 4, xi. 7, of severance between Israel and Egypt. (Comp. Ps. xvii. 7.)

Godly.—Heb. *chasid*, properly, *graced* or *gracious*, according as it is used of Israel or of the God of Israel. The *covenant* relationship is more prominent in the word than a moral excellence, though this is presupposed. See Ps. l. 5, where the word appears to be defined. There is a difficulty in the construction: *lô* (*to him*) may go either with the verb or the object. By comparison with Ps. xvii. 7, we take it with the latter. LXX., "his holy one."

⁽⁴⁾ **Stand in awe.**—Literally, *tremble,* whether with *fear* or *anger.* But the rendering of the LXX., "be angry," quoted in Eph. iv. 26, though etymologically correct, is plainly inadmissible here. (See *New Testament Commentary.*)

Commune—*i.e.*, reflect on your conduct, let the still hours of the night bring calmer and wiser thoughts with them. The LXX. and Vulg. translate "repent" instead of "be still." This supposes the words to be addressed to the *enemies.* But the next verse makes this doubtful. Probably the clause is a general reflection on the proper conduct of Israelites when in trouble.

⁽⁵⁾ **Sacrifices of righteousness.**—Comp. Ps. li. 18, 19; Deut. xxxiii. 19. The context in both places directs to the translation "right" or "due" sacrifices, *i.e.*, sacrifices duly and religiously performed.

⁽⁶⁾ **There be many.**—Around the fugitive king were many whose courage was not so high, nor their faith so firm, as his. He hears their expressions of despair—

"Talking like this world's brood."—MILTON.

It is better to translate the words of these faint-hearted ones by the future, as in Authorised Version; not by the optative, as Ewald and others.

Lift thou up . . .—This is an echo of the priestly benediction (Num. vi. 24, *et seq.*), which must so often have inspired the children of Israel with hope and cheerfulness during their desert wanderings—which has breathed peace over so many death-beds in Christian times.

The Hebrew for "lift" is doubly anomalous, and is apparently formed from the usual word "to lift," with a play upon another word meaning "a banner," suggesting to the fearful followers of the king that Jehovah's power was ready to protect him. The Vulg. follows the LXX. in rendering, "The light of thy countenance

The Happiness of God's Favour. PSALMS, V. *David's Prayer to God.*

shew us *any* good? Lord, lift thou up the light of thy countenance upon us. ⁽⁷⁾ Thou hast put gladness in my heart, more than in the time *that* their corn and their wine increased.

⁽⁸⁾ ^a I will both lay me down in peace, and sleep: for thou, Lord, only makest me dwell in safety.

PSALM V.
To the chief Musician upon Nehiloth, A Psalm of David.

⁽¹⁾ Give ear to my words, O Lord, consider my meditation. ⁽²⁾ Hearken unto the voice of my cry, my King, and my God: for unto thee will I pray. ⁽³⁾ ^b My voice shalt thou hear in the morning, O Lord; in the morning will I direct *my prayer* unto thee, and will look up.

⁽⁴⁾ For thou *art* not a God that hath pleasure in wickedness: neither shall evil dwell with thee. ⁽⁵⁾ The foolish shall not stand ¹ in thy sight: thou hatest all workers of iniquity. ⁽⁶⁾ Thou shalt destroy them that speak leasing: the Lord will abhor ² the bloody and deceitful man.

a Ps. 3. 5.
b Ps. 130. 6.
¹ Heb., *before thine eyes.*
² Heb., *the man of bloods and deceit.*

---

was made known by a sign over us:" *i.e.*, shone so that we recognised it.

⁽⁷⁾ **Thou hast.**—Either "Thou hast put a gladness in my heart more than when their corn and new wine are much," or, "More than when one has much corn," &c. The expression is one of pregnant brevity for, "A gladness greater than that when corn and wine are plentiful."

⁽⁸⁾ **Both.**—Better, *and at once*. So the LXX. and Vulg.: "At the very moment." (Comp. Isa. xlii. 14.) This, too, is the meaning of "withal," used to render the same Hebrew word in Ps. cxli. 10.

Thou, Lord, only.—The authority of all the ancient Versions, including the LXX. and Vulg., is for taking the adverb with the predicate, not with the subject as in the Authorised Version: "Thou, Jehovah, makest me to dwell alone in safety." We see from Jer. xlix. 31, Micah vii. 14, that isolation from other nations was, in the Hebrew view, a guarantee against danger. This certainly favours the view that the poem is national rather than individual.

For the concluding verses of the psalm Luther had a great affection, and desired Ludvig Teuffel to set them as the words of a requiem for him.

V.

Verse 7 makes the inscription to this psalm suspicious. (See Note.) The address, "my king," also denoting the theocratic relation of Jehovah to His people, seems more natural in an invocation supposed to come from the entire faithful Israel—an invocation for help against the idolatrous part of the nation now in power, and preparing, if not actually beginning, persecution. The psalm is therefore rightly assigned to the troublous times of the later monarchy, possibly the reign of Manasseh. The bitterness of possible estrangement from the Temple and its services makes itself visible enough here, in feelings natural to this period. It is plain that when Psalm v. was composed the adherents of Jehovah's religion were the objects of dislike and calumny.

The parallelism is marked and well sustained.

Title.—Properly, *to the leader on the flutes* or *to the precentor, with flute accompaniments*. (See Note to inscription, Ps. iv.)

Nehiloth.—Properly, *nechîlôth*: that is, *bored instruments*. The LXX., followed by the Vulg., translate, "on behalf of the heiress," *i.e.*, according to Augustine, "the Church;" but this is founded on a wrong etymology. Some Rabbins, deriving from a Chaldee word meaning "a swarm of bees," make it refer to the multitudes reciting the psalm; others to the humming or hoarse sound of the musical accompaniment; others to a particular tune, "the drones." Of the use of flutes in the religious services of the Hebrews we have proof in 1 Sam. x. 5, 1 Kings i. 40, Isa. xxx. 29. Possibly the plural form may indicate the double flute. (See *Bible Educator*, ii. 89.)

⁽¹⁾ **Meditation.**—From a root cognate with the word translated meditate in Ps. i. 2, with primary sense of *mutter* or *murmur*. Here "whispered prayer," in contrast to "words" in first clause, and to "voice of my cry" in the next. It echoes clause 1: "while unto thee will I pray" corresponds to "meditation."

⁽³⁾ The daily morning sacrifice sees the Psalmist in the Temple. The word "direct," or, better, *prepare*, is the same employed in Lev. i. 8, 12, vi. 12, of the priest laying out the wood for the sacrifice, or the parts of the offering itself, and suggest that the author may himself have been a priest. The word "offering" should be supplied, instead of "prayer." Henry Vaughan's fine hymn—

"When first thine eyes unveil, give thy soul leave
  To do the like "—

was probably suggested by this verse.

Look up.—The Hebrew is from the root which forms "Mizpeh," or "watch-tower." The psalmist looks up for the answer to his prayer as the seer on his tower (Hab. ii. 1) looked up for his inspiration. The usual attitude of prayer in the East was then, as now, either standing or prostrate, the hands lifted up or spread out (Exod. ix. 33; Pss. xxviii. 2, cxxxiv. 2, cxli. 2). To raise the eyes was not so usual. Virgil, describing the capture of Cassandra by the Greeks, makes her look up, but only because her hands were bound.

"Ad coelum tendens ardentia lumina frustra,
  Lumina—nam teneras arcebant vincula palmas."

⁽⁴⁾ **Neither shall evil.**—Better, *the wicked man is not thy guest.* For the same thought, see Ps. xv.; and for the opposite, of God coming to dwell with the godly, Isa. lvii. 15.

⁽⁵⁾ **Foolish.**—Literally, *shiners*—*i.e.*, displayers of self; or, perhaps, *self-praisers, boasters.*

Shall not stand.—As distinguished men before kings (Prov. xxii. 29); as angels in the court of the heavenly King (Job i. 6).

⁽⁶⁾ **Leasing.**—See Ps. iv. 2.

Bloody.—Margin, literally, *of bloods and deceit.* So LXX. and Vulg.

(7) But as for me, I will come into thy house in the multitude of thy mercy: and in thy fear will I worship toward [1] thy holy temple.

(8) Lead me, O LORD, in thy righteousness because of [2] mine enemies; make thy way straight before my face. (9) For there is no [3] faithfulness [4] in their mouth; their inward part is [5] very wickedness; [6] their throat is an open sepulchre; they flatter with their tongue. (10) [a] Destroy thou them, O God; let them fall [7] by their own counsels; cast them out in the multitude of their transgressions; for they have rebelled against thee.

[1] Heb., the temple of thy holiness.
[2] Heb., those which observe me.
[3] Or, stedfastness.
[4] Heb., in his mouth, that is, in the mouth of any of them.
[5] Heb., wickedness.
[a] Rom. 3. 13.
[6] Or, make them guilty.
[7] Or, from their counsels.
[8] Heb., thou coverest over, or, protectest them.
[9] Heb., crown him.
[10] Or, upon the eighth.
[b] Ps. 38. 1.

(11) But let all those that put their trust in thee rejoice: let them ever shout for joy, because [8] thou defendest them: let them also that love thy name be joyful in thee. (12) For thou, LORD, wilt bless the righteous; with favour wilt thou [9] compass him as with a shield.

PSALM VI.

To the chief Musician on Neginoth [10] upon Sheminith, A Psalm of David.

(1) O [b] LORD, rebuke me not in thine anger, neither chasten me in thy hot displeasure. (2) Have mercy upon me, O LORD; for I am weak: O LORD, heal

---

(7) **House . . . temple.**—These words must certainly be taken literally, and not, as Hupfeld suggests, metaphorically, or in a spiritual sense with reference to verse 4. The reference to worship hardly allows the rendering *palace*, though the derivation of the Hebrew word permits it. No doubt either explanation is possible; but neither would have been suggested but for the title to the psalm; and it is clear (see *General Introduction*) that historical exactness was not regarded in affixing the psalm-titles.

Worship.—Literally, *prostrate myself towards*, as in 1 Kings viii. 29; Ps. xxviii. 2. (Comp. Daniel's attitude of prayer towards Jerusalem, and that of the Moslems now towards Mecca.)

(8) **Enemies.**—Literally, *those watching for, or lying in wait*. Aquila and Jerome both give "those lying in ambush." God's guidance and protection would enable the good man to avoid their snares, and to walk straight in the way of righteousness. To walk in God's way is to walk in safety.

(9) **In their mouth.**—See margin.

Wickedness.—Properly, *an abyss*, from root "to fall," hence in parallelism with "open sepulchre" in next clause. This is an instance of introverted parallelism, "mouth" answering to "tongue." (See *Bible Educator*, iii. 50.)

An open sepulchre.—At once *dangerous* and *noisome*.

Flatter.—Literally, *make smooth the tongue*. (Comp. Ps. xii. 2.) Shakespeare uses "smooth tongue." Comp. also—

"The subtle fiend,
Though only strong with anger and disdain,
Dissembled, and this answer *smooth* returned."
MILTON, *Par. Lost.*

(10) **Destroy.**—Literally, *make or count guilty*.

Transgressions.—Literally, *revolts*, thus being in close synonymous parallelism with the next clause. Or else, as in margin and in ancient versions, LXX., Vulg., and Syriac, "Let them fall from their counsels:" *i.e.*, "let their plots fail."

On the imprecations in the Psalms see *General Introduction*, vi.

(11) **Rejoice.**—From root meaning primarily *bright*. Prov. xiii. 9: "The light of the righteous rejoiceth."

Shield.—Heb., *tsinnah*. The long large shield fit for a giant (1 Sam. xvii. 7, 41), which could protect the whole body.

Luther, when asked at Augsburg where he should find shelter if his patron, the Elector of Saxony, should desert him, replied, "under the shield of heaven." The image is finely elaborated in Browning's *Instans Tyrannus*:—

"When sudden—How think ye the end?
Did I say 'without friend?'
Say, rather, from marge to blue marge,
The whole sky grew his targe
With the sun's self for visible boss;
While an arm ran across
Which the earth heaved beneath like a breast
Where the wretch was safe pressed.
Do you see? Just my vengeance complete.
The man sprang to his feet,
Stood erect, caught at God's skirts, and prayed—
So I was afraid."

VI.

The end of this plaintive poem seems to belong to a different situation from the beginning. At first it sounds like a voice from a bed of sickness, of sickness likely to terminate fatally. But at verse 8 the tone changes. We hear no longer of sickness; but of enemies and wicked men, and prayer gives place to defiance and triumph. Can then the sufferings described in the former part be of the soul instead of the body? In any other than Hebrew literature we should answer in the negative. But with such passages as Isa. i. 5, 6 before us we feel that no picture of physical pain and disease is too vivid or too personal to express moral evil. Rightly, therefore, has the Church made this the first of the penitential psalms. As the personality of the writer is thus merged we need not attempt to recover it. Perhaps he intended it not only to be merged, but lost in the collective application to the suffering faithful in Israel. The Exile period best suits this confession of national sin. The rhythm is fine and well sustained.

Title. For *chief musician* and *Neginoth*, see introduction to Ps. iv. "Upon Sheminith," Heb., *upon the Sheminith*, comp. title to Ps. xii. Margin, *on the eighth*, which has been very variously understood, and still waits for a satisfactory explanation.

(1) **O Lord, rebuke me not.**—Repeated with change of one word in Ps. xxxviii. 1. The sublime thought that pain and sorrow are a discipline of love might be found in these words (as in Ps. xciv. 12; Prov. iii. 11, 12; Jer. x. 24; Heb. xii. 3, 11; Rev. iii. 19), did not the context show that the sufferer in this case is praying for the chastisement to be altogether removed.

(2) **I am weak.**—Properly, *wither*, or *waste with disease*, or *languish*, as in Hosea iv. 3; Isa. xvi. 8.

me; for my bones are vexed. (3) My soul is also sore vexed: but thou, O LORD, how long?

(4) Return, O LORD, deliver my soul: oh save me for thy mercies' sake. (5) *a* For in death *there is* no remembrance of thee: in the grave who shall give thee thanks? (6) I am weary with my groaning; [1] all the night make I my bed to swim; I water my couch with my tears. (7) Mine eye is consumed because of grief; it waxeth old because of all mine enemies.

(8) *b* Depart from me, all ye workers of iniquity; for the LORD hath heard the voice of my weeping. (9) The LORD hath heard my supplication; the LORD will receive my prayer.

(10) Let all mine enemies be ashamed and sore vexed: let them return *and* be ashamed suddenly.

PSALM VII.

Shiggaion of David, which he sang unto the LORD, concerning the [2] words of Cush the Benjamite.

(1) O LORD my God, in thee do I put

a Ps. 30. 9 & 88. 11, & 115. 17, & 118. 17; Isa. 38. 18.

1 Or, *every night.*

b Matt. 7. 23, & 25. 41; Luke 13. 27.

2 Or, *business.*

Vexed.—So LXX. and Vulg. Literally, *affrighted.* (Comp. Virgil's *gelidusque per ima cucurrit Ossa tremor.*)

(3) **But thou, O Lord, how long?**—Comp. Ps. xc. 13. This is "belief in unbelief." *Domine quousque* was Calvin's motto. The most intense grief, it was said, could never extract from him another word. In its national form this faith amid despair is shown in Zech. i. 12. (Comp Rev. vi. 10.)

(5) **For in death.**—As in Ps. xxx. 9, the sufferer urges as a further reason for Divine aid the loss Jehovah would suffer by the cessation of his praise. The Israelite's natural dread of death was intensified by the thought that the grave separated him from all the privileges of the covenant with God. (Comp. Isa. xxxviii. 18.) There can be neither remembrance of His past mercies there, nor confession of His greatness. The word translated *grave,* in exact parallelism with *death,* is *sheôl,* or *underworld,* in the early conception merely a vast sepulchral cave, closed as rock-tombs usually were by gates of stone or iron (Isa. xxxviii. 10; Job xvii. 16). The derivation of the word is disputed, but the primary meaning appears to have been *hollowness.* It occurs sixty-five times in the Bible, and is rendered in the Authorised version three times "pit," and then with curious impartiality thirty-one times "grave," and as many "hell." When it ceased to be merely a synonym for "grave," and began to gather a new set of ideas we cannot ascertain. It was before the time of which we have any contemporary records. But it acquired these new ideas very slowly. *Sheol* was for a very long time only a magnified grave, into which all the dead, bad and good alike, prince and peasant, went; where they lay side by side in their niches, as the dead do in the loculi of eastern tombs now, without sense of light or sound, or any influence from the upper world (1 Kings ii. 2; Job xxx. 23; Ps. lxxxix. 48). It is something more than death, but it is not life. The "sleep of death" expresses it. As in Homer's Hades, the dead are men without the minds or energies of men—"soulless" men; so the dead in the Hebrew conception are *rephaim,* that is, weak, shadowy existences. Indeed, the Biblical representation is even less tolerable than the Greek. Homer's heroes retain many of their interests in the living world; they rejoice in the prosperity of their friends—their own approval or disapproval makes a difference to those still on earth—and, apart from this continued connection with the upper air, they had gone to a realm of their own, with its sovereign lord, its laws and customs, its sanctions, and penalties. Not so in the Jewish belief—"the dead know not anything"; "there is no wisdom in sheol." It would be of no use for God to show any wonders among those incapable of perceiving them (Eccles ix. 5—10; Ps. lxxxviii. 10). They have passed altogether from all the interests and relations of life, even from the covenant relation with Jehovah. (Comp. Isa. xxxviii. 18; Ps. cxv. 17.) How the Hebrew conscience, helped, possibly, by the influence of foreign ideas, gradually struggled into a higher light on these subjects, belongs to the history of eschatology. The fact that Ps. vi. reflects the earlier undeveloped doctrine, is an argument against any very late date for it.

(6) **I water my couch with tears.**—Comp. *Odyssey,* xvii. 102:

"Say, to my mournful couch shall I ascend?
The couch deserted now a length of years,
The couch for ever watered with my tears."—
Pope's *trans.*

Orientals indulge in weeping and other outward signs of emotion, which Western nations, or, at all events, the Teutonic races, try to suppress or hide.

(7) **Consumed**—*i.e., sunken;* literally, *fallen away.* The LXX. use the same word employed to render *vexed* in verse 2. Grief has brought the signs of premature age (Job xvii. 7; Ps. xxxi. 9, and Note there). (See Homer's *Odyssey,* xix. 360, "Quickly do mortals grow old from trouble.")

(8) **Depart from me.**—After the night of sorrow comes the morning of revived faith and confidence, if not of joy. The poet can turn to address his maligners with the assurance that God has heard his prayer, which in his agony he poured out, as he feared at the time, into deaf and unsympathising ears.

(10) **Let all mine enemies.**—Better rendered either by the present or future. The Psalmist with the eye of faith sees the answer to his prayer.

Return—*i.e.,* retire discomfited and in failure.

"My enemies shall all be blank, and dasht
With much confusion : then grow red with shame;
They shall return in haste the way they came,
And in a moment shall be quite abashed."—
Milton's *trans.*

VII.

In this psalm we seem to be once more on sure historical ground. It not only breathes the feeling when David and his outlawed band were daily evading the snares laid for them by the emissaries of Saul, but seems to refer pointedly to the two most romantic incidents in all that romantic period—the chance encounter of pursuer and pursued—(1) In the cave of En-gedi, and (2) (if the two are not the same under different versions) in the wilderness of Ziph (1 Sam. xxiv. and xxvi.); at least, no other recorded incidents

my trust: save me from all them that persecute me, and deliver me: ⁽²⁾ lest he tear my soul like a lion, rending *it* in pieces, while *there is* [1] none to deliver.

⁽³⁾ O LORD my God, if I have done this; if there be iniquity in my hands; ⁽⁴⁾ if I have rewarded evil unto him that was at peace with me; (yea, I have delivered him that without cause is mine enemy:) ⁽⁵⁾ let the enemy persecute my soul, and take *it;* yea, let him tread down my life upon the earth, and lay mine honour in the dust. Selah.

⁽⁶⁾ Arise, O LORD, in thine anger; lift up thyself because of the rage of mine enemies: and awake for me *to* the judgment *that* thou hast commanded. ⁽⁷⁾ So shall the congregation of the people compass thee about: for their sakes therefore return thou on high.

[1] Heb., *not a deliverer.*

---

in the Bible fall in so well, either as occasions for its composition or as illustrations of its spirit. We can readily imagine that there would be men (for Cush, see Note to Title) who would turn even these instances of David's generosity into occasions of slander against him, and that he would pour out his feelings under such unjust provocation in song.

Against this must be noticed the occurrence of an Aramaic word in verse 9, which suggests a late date for the poem.

The poetical form is uncertain.

Title.—Shiggaion is either a variation of *Higgaion* (Ps. ix. 16), and means generally, as the LXX. render it, "poem or psalm;" or it is derived from *shâgah, to wander,* and denotes a wild passionate ode—*cantio erratica,* as some of the old expositors describe it. The Greeks called such a composition *Dithyrambic.* Gesenius makes it simply "a song of praise." "Cush," or *Kush,* cannot be identified. The mistake of the LXX. in writing it *Chus* has led some to connect it with the Hebrew name for an Ethiopian, and to regard it as a nickname, "the blackamoor." The fact of the tribal relation with Saul is quite enough to allow us to conjecture that Cush was some person high in favour with that monarch, servilely eager to injure David. **Concerning the words.**—This is better than the margin, "business," since verse 4 shows that the author's indignation arose from some calumny of him.

⁽¹⁾ **In thee do I put my trust.**—Or, *in thee have I taken refuge.*

⁽²⁾ **Lest he tear.**—The poet turns from the thought of his enemies generally to the one who has just made himself conspicuous. Such a change from plural to singular often occurs in the Psalms. (Comp. Ps. xli. 5, 6.)

Rending it in pieces.—The LXX., followed by the Vulg. (so too the Syriac), take the verb in its primitive sense of "snatch away," and translate, "there being none to redeem or deliver." So Milton: "Tearing, and no rescue nigh." Notice the comparison of human enemies to beasts of prey—a reminiscence of the lion and the bear of his youth, so constantly present to David. (Comp. Ps. iii. 7; 1 Sam. xvii. 37.)

⁽³⁾ **This**—*i.e., this with which I am charged*—the Benjamite's slander.

If there be iniquity.—A comparison with 1 Sam. xxiv. 12, 13, and still more 1 Sam. xxvi. 18, shows how closely this psalm is connected with the two notorious instances of David's magnanimous and generous conduct towards Saul.

⁽⁴⁾ **Yea, I have**—*i.e., on the contrary, so far from returning evil for good, I have returned good for evil.* With allusion, there can be little doubt, to the incidents referred to in the last Note. From metrical reasons, and also to avoid the abruptness of the change of construction, Ewald conjectures that two clauses have dropped out of the text, and restores as follows—

"If I have rewarded evil unto him that dealt friendly with me
(And cunning unto him that was at peace with me,
Yea, if I have not rewarded his soul with good),
And delivered him that without cause is my enemy."

Milton's translation gives yet another colour to the passage—

"If I have wrought
Ill to him that meant me peace,
Or to him have rendered less,
And not freed my foe for nought."

The conjecture of a corruption of the text is supported by the rendering of the LXX. and Vulg., and a very slight change gives the probable rendering: "If I have returned evil to him that dealt friendly with me, and injured my enemy without cause."

⁽⁵⁾ **Let the enemy.**—Better, *let an enemy.*

Persecute.—Literally, *burn.* (See Note on Ps. x. 2.)

Tread.—Used of a potter treading the clay (Isa. xli. 25); of the trampling of horses (Ezek. xxvi. 11); of a herd trampling down their pasture (Ezek. xxxiv. 28).

Dust.—Either as Ps. xxii. 15, "the dust of death," and if so, then *khabôd'.*

Honour must be the soul or life, as plainly in Pss. xvi. 9, lvii. 8, where the Authorised Version has "glory." The parallelism is in favour of this. On the other hand, to lay one's honour in the dust is a common figurative phrase. Shakespeare, *K. Hen. VI.,* i. 5, "Now, France, thy glory droopeth to the dust"; and *Coriol.* iii. 1, "And throw their power in the dust."

Selah.—See Note on Ps. iii. 2. This is one of the places which suggest its interpretation as a direction to the music, to strike up with passion and force.

⁽⁶⁾ In the rapid succession of abrupt utterance of feeling in ejaculations, we see the excitement of the poet's mind.

Of the rage.—Better, *against the rage,* unless we may correct to "in *thy* rage." The LXX. and Vulg. read, "in the ends of," which Jerome explains as meaning, "exalt thyself by making an end of my enemies." Syriac, "Be thou lifted up upon the necks of my enemies."

And awake for me.—Better, arranged in two petitions: *yea, awake for me; prepare the judgment.* There is some difficulty about the syntax of the last clause, but the imperatives suit the parallelism of the context better than the past tenses.

⁽⁷⁾ **So shall.**—This clause is also in the optative: "let the communities of peoples be gathered round thee."

For their sakes.—Rather, *over or above it,* as in LXX. The poet has a vision of judgment. Je-

David sees his Defence   PSALMS, VIII.   *and his Enemies' Destruction.*

(8) The LORD shall judge the people: judge me, O LORD, *a*"according to my righteousness, and according to mine integrity *that is* in me. (9) Oh let the wickedness of the wicked come to an end; but establish the just: *b* for the righteous God trieth the hearts and reins. (10) ¹My defence *is* of God, which saveth the upright in heart. (11) ²God judgeth the righteous, and God is angry *with the wicked* every day. (12) If he turn not, he will whet his sword; he hath bent his bow, and made it ready. (13) He hath also prepared for him the instruments of death; he ordaineth his arrows against the persecutors.

(14)*c* Behold, he travaileth with iniquity, and hath conceived mischief, and brought forth falsehood. (15) ³ He made a pit, and digged it, *d* and is fallen into the ditch *which* he made. (16) His mischief shall return upon his own head, and his violent dealing shall come down upon his own pate.

(17) I will praise the LORD according to his righteousness: and will sing praise to the name of the LORD most high.

PSALM VIII.

To the chief Musician upon Gittith,
A Psalm of David.

(1) O LORD our God, how excellent *is*

---

a Ps. 18. 20.

b 1 Sam. 16. 7; 1 Chron. 28. 9; Ps. 139. 1; Jer. 11. 20 & 17. 10, & 20. 12.

1 Heb., *My buckler is upon God.*

2 Or, *God is a righteous judge.*

c Job 15. 35; Isa. 59. 4; Jam. 1. 15.

3 Heb., *He hath digged a pit.*

d Ps. 9. 15, & 10. 2; Prov. 5. 22.

---

hovah summons the nations, arranges them at His tribunal, and then returns to His high throne to preside. This explanation is more consonant with the context (see next verse) than to suppose the judgment to have taken place between the two clauses of the verse, and the departure of God into the height "as a victor after battle" (Delitzsch), or "in proof of His supremacy as judge" (Ewald). This picture of arraigned nations is certainly in favour of the view which makes the psalm the expression of the feelings of the community rather than of an individual.

(8) **The Lord shall.**—Better, *Jehovah judgeth the nations.* Everything is complete, and the work of judgment begins. The poet prays that his sentence may be according to his own consciousness of righteousness and integrity. Of this plea of innocence Jerome says, "David could not say this; this properly belongs to the Saviour, who was sinless." Others think it is the ideal Israel, which stands before Jehovah's tribunal. But we may compare Job's protestations of innocence, and his persistent demand for a trial. David (if he is the author) refers naturally to his innocence of the charge calumniously brought against him. As between Saul and himself, his conduct had been blameless.

(9) **Establish.**—Literally, *let him stand erect.*

For the righteous God trieth.—Better, *thou trier of hearts and reins, thou just God.* The Hebrew word translated *try* is used, like it, for testing metals (Ps. xii. 6; Prov. xvii. 3).

(10) **My defence.**—Literally, as in margin, *my shield is upon God.* (Comp. Ps. lxii. 7, "In God is my salvation," where the Hebrew is as here, "God is my shield-bearer.") Another explanation appears in Milton's translation—

"On God is cast
My defence, and in Him lies,
In Him who both just and wise,
Saves the upright at heart at last."

(11) **God judgeth.**—The two clauses answer to each other; so the margin, "God is a righteous judge, and God avengeth every day." LXX., "God is a just judge, and strong and longsuffering, not letting loose his anger every day." Vulg., "Still is he not angry with the wicked?" Syriac, "God is the judge of righteousness. He is not angry every day." It has been proposed to read *veál*—"and not"—instead of *veél*—"and God"—conformably to these versions, but unnecessarily.

(12) **If he turn not.**—The Hebrew is doubly idiomatic. Translate *surely* (see Heb. iii. 11, with Note in *New Testament Commentary*), *He will again whet His sword.* It is true that the verb *to turn* in the sense of *repetition* usually precedes the other verb immediately, without, as here, any other words intervening.

Bent.—Literally, *trodden,* showing that the foot was used by the Israelites to bend the bow, as by archers now. (Smith's *Bible Dictionary,* "Arms.")

(13) **Instruments of death.**—That is, *deadly weapons.*

Against the persecutors.—Literally, *for those burning;* so LXX. and Vulg. The meaning appears to be, "His arrows he makes into fiery arrows"—*i.e.,* tips them with fire, by wrapping them in burning tow. Latin, *malleoli.* (Comp. Eph. vi. 16, with Note, in *New Testament Commentary.*) Milton's "rattling storm of arrows barb'd with fire," refers to the same custom.

(14) **Behold, he travaileth.**—The poet's thought recurs to the calumniator, whose sin has deserved all this Divine wrath, and he sees the truth that God's judgments are not arbitrary, but follow naturally on sin as its consequence. The verb "travaileth" gives the general figure, which is elaborated in the two clauses which describe the stages of conception and pregnancy. (For the image, comp. Job xv. 35.)

(15) **He hath made.**—Better, *he digged a pit, and hollowed it out.* Milton: "He digged a pit, and delved it deep."

(15) **Pate.**—A word retained from Coverdale's translation, and common in the Elizabethan age. In Shakespeare it is frequent—

"My invention
Comes from my pate,
As bird-lime does from frieze."

For the moral, comp. 1 Sam. xxv. 29.

Verses 15 and 16 are quoted by Eusebius of the overthrow of Maxentius by Constantine, with special reference to the fact that in preparing a bridge of boats he had prepared the means for his own destruction.

VIII.

This psalm has been aptly called a lyric echo of the first chapter of Genesis. There is no reason to doubt the traditional ascription to David. This exquisite little poem is a record of his shepherd's days, when, under the midnight sky of Palestine, brilliant with stars, he mused on things deep and high, on

thy name in all the earth! who hast set thy glory above the heavens.

(2) ᵃ Out of the mouth of babes and sucklings hast thou ¹ordained strength because of thine enemies, that thou mightest still the enemy and the avenger.

(3) When I consider thy heavens, the

ᵃ Matt. 21. 16.

¹ Heb., *founded*.

---

the mystery of the universe and man's place in it, his relation to the Creator on the one hand, to the rest of creation on the other.

The form of the poem is perfect and yet simple. A spontaneous burst of praise to the Creator of the glorious world is followed by the inevitable feeling of the insignificance and weakness of man, compared with the majestic march of the shining worlds above him. But like a flash of light comes the claim of kinship with the Author of them all, and a twofold proof of this heavenly origin: the lisping tongues of infants, which can impose silence on those who impiously question it; and the sovereignty man asserts by his superior endowments over the rest of living creation.

Title.—Upon Gittith. (Comp. Pss. lxxxi. and lxxxiv.) The LXX. and Vulg. render, "for the wine-presses," as if the word were *gittôth*; and this has been explained to refer either to the festivities of the vintage time, or to the prophecies which describe how the nations would be trodden down as in a wine-press. Another derivation makes it a kind of *flute*, from a word meaning "to hollow out." But the most probable and now generally accepted explanation connects it with *Gath*, the Philistine town. A Talmudic paraphrase for "upon Gittith" is "on the *kinnor* which was brought from Gath." According to this, it was a Philistine lute, just as there was an Egyptian flute and a Doric lyre. Others think it refers to a particular tune, perhaps the march of the Gittite guard (2 Sam. xv. 18).

From a comparison of the three psalms so inscribed, it cannot be a title having any reference to the subject.

(1) **O Lord our Lord.**—*Jehovah our Lord*. For the first time in the Book of Psalms the personal feeling is consciously lost sight of in a larger, a national, or possibly human feeling. The poet recognises God's relation to the whole of mankind as to the whole material creation. Thus the hymn appropriately lent itself to the use of the congregation in public worship, though it does not follow that this was the object of its composition.

Excellent.—The LXX. and Vulg., "wonderful." Better, *great or exalted*.

Who hast set . . .—The translation of this clause is uncertain. It must be determined by the parallelism, and by the fact that the poet, in verse 4, merely expands the thought he had before expressed. There is plainly some error in the text since it is ungrammatical. The proposed emendations vary considerably. The ancient versions also disagree. The Authorised Version may be retained, since it meets all the requirements of the context, and is etymologically correct; though, grammatically, Ewald's correction, which also agrees with the Vulg., is preferable, "Thou whose splendour is raised above the heavens." The precise thought in the poet's mind has also been the subject of contention. Some take the clause to refer to the praises raised in Jehovah's honour higher than the heavens, a thought parallel to the preceding clause; others, to the visible glory spread over the sky. Others see an antithesis. God's glory is displayed on earth in His *name*, His *real* glory is above the heavens. Probably only a general sense of the majesty of Him "that is higher than the highest" (Eccl. v. 8), and "whom the heaven of heavens cannot contain" (1 Kings viii. 27), occupied the poet's mind.

(2) **Babes and sucklings.**—Better, *young children and sucklings*. A regular phrase to describe children from one to three years old (1 Sam. xv. 3, xxii. 19). The *yonek*, or suckling, denotes an earlier stage of the nursing period (which, with Hebrew mothers, sometimes extended over three years, 2 Macc. vii. 27, and on Talmudic authority could not be less than two years) than the *ôlel*, which is applied to children able to play about on the streets (Jer. ix. 21; Lam. iv. 4). (See Dr. Ginsburg on *Eastern Manners and Customs*: *Bible Educator*, i. 29.)

Ordained strength . . .—At the first glance, the LXX. translation, as quoted in Matt. xxi. 16 (see Note, *New Testament Commentary*), "Thou hast perfected praise," seems to be correct, from a comparison with Ps. xxix. 1, where *strength* translates the same Hebrew word, and plainly means *homage*. This expresses, doubtless, part of the thought of the poet, that in a child's simple and innocent wonder lies the truest worship; that God accomplishes the greatest things and reveals His glory by means of the weakest instruments—a thought which was seized upon by our Lord to condemn the want of spirituality in the scribes and Pharisees. But the context, speaking the language of war, seems to demand the primitive meaning, *stronghold* or *defence*. The truth which the Bible proclaims of the innate divinity of man, his essential likeness to God, is the principal subject of the poet; and in the princely heart of innocence of an unspoilt child he sees, as Wordsworth saw, its confirmation. "Trailing clouds of glory do we come, From God who is our home." Such a proof is strong even against the noisy clamour of apostate men, who rebel against the Divine government, and lay upon God the blame of their aberration from His order. "His merry babbling mouth provides a defence of the Creator against all the calumnies of the foe" (Ewald). Others think rather of the faculty of speech, and the wonder and glory of it.

The avenger.—Properly, *him who avenges himself*.

(3) **When I consider.**—Literally, *see, scan*.

Ordained.—Or, as in margin, *founded—i.e., created, formed*; but the English word aptly introduces the idea of *order* in the *kosmos*. Comp.:—

"Know the cause why music was ordained?
—SHAKESPEARE.

In our humid climate we can hardly imagine the brilliance of an Eastern night. "There," writes one of a night in Palestine, "it seems so, bearing down upon our heads with power are the steadfast splendours of that midnight sky;" but, on the other hand, the fuller revelations of astronomy do more than supply the place of this splendour, in filling us with amazement and admiration at the vast spaces the stars fill, and their mighty movements in their measured orbits.

work of thy fingers, the moon and the stars, which thou hast ordained; (4) *a* what is man, that thou art mindful of him? and the son of man, that thou visitest him? (5) For thou hast made him a little lower than the angels, and hast crowned him with glory and honour. (6) Thou madest him to have dominion over the works of thy hands; *b* thou hast put all *things* under his feet: (7) ¹ all sheep and oxen, yea, and the beasts of the field; (8) the fowl of the air, and the fish of the sea, *and whatsoever* passeth through the paths of the seas.

(9) O Lord our Lord, how excellent *is* thy name in all the earth!

a Job 7. 17; Ps. 144. 3; Heb. 2. 6.

b 1 Cor. 15. 27.

1 Heb., *Flocks and oxen all of them.*

PSALM IX.

To the chief Musician upon Muth-labben, A Psalm of David.

(1) I will praise *thee*, O Lord, with my whole heart; I will shew forth all thy

---

(4) **Man ... son of man ...**—The first, possibly, with suggestion of frailty; the second to his life derived from human ancestry. The answer to this question must always touch the two poles, of human frailty on the one hand, and the glory of human destiny on the other. " O the grandeur and the littleness, the excellence and the corruption, the majesty and the meanness, of man."—*Pascal.*

The insignificance of man compared to the stars is a common theme of poetry; but how different the feeling of the Hebrew from that of the modern poet, who regrets the culture by which he had been

" Brought to understand
A sad astrology, the boundless plan
That makes you tyrants in your iron skies,
Innumerable, pitiless, passionless eyes,
Cold fires, yet with power to burn and brand
His nothingness into man."—TENNYSON: *Maud.*

And yet, again, how far removed from the other pole of modern feeling, which draws inanimate nature into close sympathy with human joy or sorrow, expressed in the following words:—" When I have gazed into these stars, have they not looked down upon me as if with pity from their serene spaces, like eyes glistening with heavenly tears over the little lot of man?"—*Carlyle.*

(5) The Hebrew poet dwells on neither of these aspects, but at once passes on to the essential greatness of man and his superiority in creation, by reason of his moral sense and his spiritual likeness to God. Another English poet sings to the stars:—

" 'Tis to be forgiven
That, in our aspirations to be great,
Our destinies o'erleap their mortal state,
And claim a kindred with you."
—BYRON: *Childe Harold.*

But the psalmist looks beyond the bright worlds to a higher kinship with God Himself.

For thou hast made him a little lower than the angels.—Literally, *thou makest him want but a little from God: i.e.,* hast made him little less than Divine. We should read, however, instead of " for thou," " and thou hast made," &c. The Authorised Version follows the LXX. in a translation suggested doubtlessly by the desire to tone down an expression about the Deity that seemed too bold. That version was adopted in his quotation by the author of the Epistle to the Hebrews (Heb. ii. 6, 7). (See Note in *New Testament Commentary*.) Undoubtedly the word Elohim, being used to express a class of supernatural beings, includes angels as well as the Divine being (1 Sam. xxviii. 13; Zech. xii. 8). But here there is nothing in the context to suggest limitation to one part of that class.

Crowned.—Or, *compassed.*

(6) The poet continues, in a rapturous strain, to complete the cycle of animated nature, and to describe man's kingship over all other created beings. For St. Paul's expansion of the thought, and elevation of it into yet a higher sphere, see 1 Cor. xv. 27.

(8) **And whatsoever passeth.**—This is more poetical than to render " the fish of the sea who pass," &c.

Paths of the seas.—Comp. Homer's ὑγρὰ κέλευθα. The repetition of the first thought of the poem, binding the contents together as in a wreath, is the one touch of art it displays.

IX.

In the LXX. and Vulg., Psalms ix. and x. are combined into one. This arrangement appears the more ancient of the two, and possibly is original; for (1) Psalms x. and xxxiii. are the only compositions of the original Davidic collection (Pss. iii.—xli.) without a title. The absence in each case is accounted for in the same way—Psalm xxxiii. had apparently, by a mistake, been joined to Psalm xxxii. before the collection was made; Psalms ix. and x. had not been then separated. (2) The whole piece was originally alphabetical. This acrostic arrangement was either in the beginning very imperfect, or has been deranged by some later hand. The latter is most probable, as it is not by any means likely that two pieces, each with an imperfect attempt at a structure as easy in accomplishment as fanciful in design, should have been first composed, then brought side by side in a collection, and finally combined; whereas a later writer, anxious to adopt to his purpose some earlier work, might either have disregarded the alphabetical arrangement, or possibly have overlooked it. For the details of the arrangement, see below; and for the alphabetical psalms generally, see *General Introduction.* (3) These two psalms have in common certain characteristic turns of expression, which occur rarely elsewhere.

The Hebrew division, no doubt, is based on the fact, that while at first sight Psalm ix. seems to be a thanksgiving for victory, breathing only triumph and hope, Ps. x. is a prayer against violence and blood. But Psalm ix. 13 is quite in the tone of Psalm x. And again, Psalm x. 12, 13 gives an exact echo of Psalm ix. 19, 20. From verse 12, indeed, Psalm x. is as triumphant and hopeful in its tone as Psalm ix. Probably, when used by the later writer, the clouds had darkened round Israel, or round himself personally; for it is difficult to decide whether the psalms are expressions of individual or national feeling. But he still found that he could adopt the victorious ending as well as the confident beginning. The acrostic proceeds regularly from *aleph* to *gimmel* (Ps. ix. 1—6); *daleth* is wanting. Four verses (8—11) begin with *vaw*, and the arrangement proceeds regularly to *yod* (verse 18). For *caph*, which should succeed, *koph* is substituted (verse 20);

marvellous works. (2) I will be glad and rejoice in thee: I will sing praise to thy name, O thou most High.

(3) When mine enemies are turned back, they shall fall and perish at thy presence. (4) For ¹thou hast maintained my right and my cause; thou satest in the throne judging ²right. (5) Thou hast rebuked the heathen, thou hast destroyed the wicked, thou hast put out their name for ever and ever.

(6) ³O thou enemy, destructions are come to a perpetual end: and thou hast destroyed cities; their memorial is perished with them. (7) But the LORD shall endure for ever: he hath prepared his throne for judgment. (8) And ᵃhe shall judge the world in righteousness, he shall minister judgment to the people in uprightness.

(9) ᵇThe LORD also will be ⁴a refuge for the oppressed, a refuge in times of trouble. (10) And they that know thy name will put their trust in thee: for thou, LORD, hast not forsaken them that seek thee.

(11) Sing praises to the LORD, which dwelleth in Zion: declare among the

---

1 Heb., *thou hast made my judgment*.
2 Heb., *in righteousness*.
3 Or, *The destructions of the enemy are come to a perpetual end; and their cities hast thou destroyed*, &c.
a Ps. 96. 13, & 98. 9.
b Ps. 37. 39 & 46. 1, & 91. 2.
4 Heb., *an high place*.

---

and the arrangement is taken up correctly with *lamed*, in Psalm x. 1. Here it suddenly ceases. *Mem, nun, samech, ayin, pe,* and *tsaddi* are wanting; but *koph* appears again in verse 12, and the other letters duly succeed to the end of the psalm. The authorship and date of the combined psalms cannot be ascertained. Their redaction for congregational use must be referred to post-exile times.

Title.—For the "chief musician," see *Introduction* to Psalm iv.

Upon Muth-labben.—*Al muth-labben*. Of the perplexing titles, this is one of the most perplexing. No conjecture of the meaning of the Hebrew as it stands is satisfactory. The text must be emended. It is evident from the LXX. rendering, "on account of the mysteries of the son," that they had before them a different text from ours. Our text has, therefore, probably become corrupted. Now Psalm xlvi. has as part of its title *libeney Kôrah al-alamôth*; and if these words were to be transposed, and *al* omitted from the beginning, and *y* from the end, we should have the same Hebrew letters as in *Almuth-labben*. Neither assumption is difficult to suppose; and though the emendation does not remove us from the region of conjecture, it narrows it. For the meaning of *al-alamôth*, see *Introduction* to Psalm xlvi.

(1) The alphabetic arrangement is begun in its completest form. Every clause of the first stanza begins with *Aleph*.

(3) **When.**—Literally, *in the turning of mine enemies back*, which may be either *when* they turned, or *because* they turned, or possibly with both ideas combined. The older versions have *when*. Verses 2 and 3 form one sentence, "I will be glad and rejoice in thee . . . when mine enemies are turned back, (when) they fall and perish at thy presence."

Fall.—Better, *stumble through weakness.* So the LXX., "are weak."

(4) **Thou hast maintained my right.**—Literally, *thou hast made my judgment,* as the LXX. and Vulg. For this confidence in the supreme arbiter of events compare Shakspeare :—

"Is this your Christian counsel? Out upon you!
Heaven is above all yet. There sits a Judge
That no king can corrupt."—*Henry VIII.*

(5) **Put out.**—Better, *blotted out.* The family is extinct and its name erased from the civil register. (See Pss. lxix. 28, cix. 13.) The *Daleth* stanza is wanting.

(6) **O thou enemy . . .**—This vocative gives no intelligible meaning. Translate, *As for the enemy, they are made an utter wreck and perpetual ruin.*

Destructions.—Properly, *desolations, ruins,* from a word meaning "to be dried up."

Come to a perpetual end.—Properly, *are completed for ever.*

Thou hast destroyed.—Some understand the relative: "the cities which thou hast destroyed."

Their memorial.—Better, *their very memory is perished;* literally, *their memory, theirs.* (Comp. "He cannot flatter, he"—Shakespeare, *King Lear*). The LXX. and Vulg. read, "with a sound," referring to the crash of falling cities. Some would substitute *enemies* for cities, but they lose the emphasis of the passage, which points to the utter evanishment from history of great cities as a consequence and sign of Divine judgment. Probably the poet thinks of Sodom and Gomorrha, whose overthrow left such a signal mark on the thought of Israel. We think of the mounds of earth which alone represent Nineveh and Babylon.

"'Mid far sands,
The palm-tree cinctured city stands,
Bright white beneath, as heaven, bright blue,
Leans over it, while the years pursue
Their course, unable to abate
Its paradisal laugh at fate.
One morn the Arab staggers blind
O'er a new tract of earth calcined
To ashes, silence, nothingness,
And strives, with dizzy wits, to guess
Whence fell the blow."—R. BROWNING: *Easter Day.*

(7) **But the Lord shall endure.**—Better, *but Jehovah sits enthroned for ever,* being in close parallelism with the next clause, "For judgment has erected his throne."

(8) **And he . . . .**—Better, *and he it is who.* The pronoun is emphatic.

(9) **The Lord also.**—Better, *but let Jehovah.*

Refuge.—Properly, *a stronghold:* a citadel into which the persecuted would retreat.

Oppressed.—Properly, *crushed.*

Trouble.—From root meaning "to cut off from." Sc., "provisions," "water," and the like. Its cognate in Jer. xiv. 1, xvii. 8, means "drought." The phrase "in times of trouble" recurs in Ps. x. 1.

(10) **They that know.**—They who know the name of Jehovah will trust Him, because they know it to be a watchword of strength and protection.

Seek.—From root meaning "to tread" or "frequent a place," possibly with allusion to frequenting the courts of the Temple.

He Prays that he may PSALMS, X. *have Cause to Praise Him.*

people his doings. ⁽¹²⁾ ^aWhen he maketh inquisition for blood, he remembereth them: he forgetteth not the cry of the ¹humble.

⁽¹³⁾ Have mercy upon me, O LORD; consider my trouble *which I suffer* of them that hate me, thou that liftest me up from the gates of death: ⁽¹⁴⁾ that I may shew forth all thy praise in the gates of the daughter of Zion: I will rejoice in thy salvation.

⁽¹⁵⁾ ^bThe heathen are sunk down in the pit *that* they made: in the net which they hid is their own foot taken.

⁽¹⁶⁾ The LORD is known *by* the judgment *which* he executeth: the wicked is snared in the work of his own hands. Higgaion. Selah. ⁽¹⁷⁾ The wicked shall

a Gen. 9. 5.

¹ Or, *afflicted.*

b Ps. 7. 16.

² Heb., *In the pride of the wicked he doth persecute.*

c Ps. 7. 16, & 9. 16; Prov. 5. 22.

be turned into hell, *and* all the nations that forget God. ⁽¹⁸⁾ For the needy shall not alway be forgotten: the expectation of the poor shall *not* perish for ever.

⁽¹⁹⁾ Arise, O LORD; let not man prevail: let the heathen be judged in thy sight. ⁽²⁰⁾ Put them in fear, O LORD: *that* the nations may know themselves *to be but* men. Selah.

PSALM X.

⁽¹⁾ Why standest thou afar off, O LORD? *why* hidest thou *thyself* in times of trouble?

⁽²⁾ ²The wicked in *his* pride doth persecute the poor: ^clet them be taken in the devices that they have imagined.

---

(12) **When.**—Better, *for he maketh inquisition*; literally, *the seeker of bloods*: *i.e.*, "the avenger of blood." The allusion is to the *goel*, the nearest relative of the murdered man, who must, according to Oriental custom, avenge him. The verbs are better in the past, "remembered," "forgot not."

Them—*i.e.*, the sufferers to be mentioned now.

Humble.—This follows the Hebrew margin. Better here, *the afflicted*. In the Hebrew the two readings give two forms from the same root, generally taken to have, one of them, an ethical, the other, a physical sense; but the distinction is not borne out by Biblical use.

(13, 14) It is natural to take these verses as the cry for help just mentioned.

Consider.—Literally, *see my suffering from my haters*.

My lifter up from the gates of death.—For the gates of *sheol*, see Note to Ps. vi. 5. (Comp. Ps. cvii. 18, and the Homeric phrase "the gates of Hades.") We might perhaps paraphrase "from the verge of the grave," if it were not for the evident antithesis to "gates of the daughter of Zion" in the next verse. We understand, therefore, "gates" in sense of "power," "rule," the gate being the seat of the judge or king, and so, like our "court," synonymous for his power. (Comp. Sublime Porte.)

Daughter of Zion—*i.e.*, Zion itself (see Isa. xxxvii. 22): a common personification of cities and their inhabitants. So of Edom (Lam. iv. 21); of Babylon (Ps. cxxxvii. 8, &c.).

(15) Comp. Ps. vii. 16.

(16) **The Lord.**—Better, *Jehovah hath made himself known. He hath executed judgment, snaring the wicked in the work of his own hands.*

Higgaion. Selah.—*Higgaion* occurs three times in the Psalms—here, Ps. xix. 14, and Ps. xcii. 4 (Heb.). In the two latter places it is translated; in Ps. xix. 14, "meditation;" in Ps. xcii. 4, "solemn sound." Both meanings are etymologically possible, but the word apparently indicates some change in the music, or possibly, as joined with *selah*, a direction to some particular part of the orchestra.

(17) **The wicked.**—This is a most unfortunate rendering. The true translation is, *the wicked shall return*, as in LXX. and Vulg. (not "be turned") *to the grave*, i.e., *to dust*, according to the doom in Gen. iii. 19,

or *to the unseen world*, as in Job xxx. 23; Ps. xc. 1—3; or the verbs may be imperative, as in LXX. and Vulg., *let them return*. The verse is closely connected with the previous one. The wicked are bringing about their own destruction, and so witnessing to the righteous judgment of Jehovah. There is an intensity about the original word, *lisheôlah*, with its double sign of direction, "right down to the world of death."

And all.—Better, *the heathen all, forgetters of God.*

(18) **Not alway.**—In the original the negative comes emphatically at the commencement, ruling both clauses, as in Ps. xxxv. 19.

The expectation of the poor.—The sufferer's hope will at some time be realised: the hope of being righted. In this confidence the psalmist goes on to call on Jehovah to appear as judge.

(19) **Let not man prevail.**—Better, *let not mere man be defiant.*

(20) **Put them in fear.**—There is a difficulty about the reading. The LXX., Vulg., and Syriac read "place a lawgiver or master over them." So Syriac, "law." Hitzig conjectures, "set a guard upon them." With the present reading apparently the rendering should be, *put a terror upon them*: *i.e.*, "give such a proof of power as to trouble and subdue them."

X.

See *Introduction* to Ps. ix.

(3) **Afar off.**—Comp. Pss. xxii. 1, 2, 19, xxxv. 22, &c.

Hidest.—Isa. i. 15 supplies the ellipsis, "thine eyes," used of a judge bribed to wink at offence. 1 Sam. xii. 3; comp. Lev. xx. 4), of indifference to suffering (Prov. xxviii. 27); LXX. and Vulg., "to overlook."

(2) **The wicked.**—Better, *in the pride of the wicked, the sufferer burns.* (So LXX., Aquila, Symmachus, and Vulg.) Not to be taken of indignation felt by the sufferers, but literally of the afflictions they endure. The Authorised Version rendering of the next clause takes the wicked as the subject of the verb; but it preserves the parallelism better, and is more in accordance with the rest of the psalm (verses 8, 9, 10), to understand it of the "humble," the singular changing to the plural in the subject when supplied: "they (the sufferers) are taken (the verb is in the pre-

A Complaint of   PSALMS, X.   *the Outrages of the Wicked.*

(3) For the wicked boasteth of his ¹heart's desire, and ²blesseth the covetous, *whom* the LORD abhorreth. (4) The wicked, through the pride of his countenance, will not seek *after God:* ³God *is* not in all his ª thoughts. (5) His ways are always grievous; thy judgments *are* far above out of his sight: *as for* all his enemies, he puffeth at them. (6) He hath said in his heart, I shall not be moved: for *I shall* ⁴never *be* in adversity. (7) ᵇ His mouth is full of cursing and ⁵deceit and fraud: under his tongue *is* mischief and ⁶vanity. (8) He sitteth in the lurking places of the villages: in the secret places doth he murder the innocent: his eyes ⁷are privily set against the poor. (9) He lieth in wait ⁸secretly as a lion in his den: he lieth in wait to catch the poor: he doth catch the poor, when he draweth him into his net. (10) ⁹ He croucheth, *and* humbleth himself, that the poor may fall ¹⁰by his strong ones. (11) He hath said in his heart, God hath forgotten: ᶜhe hideth his face; he will never see *it*.

1 Heb., *soul's.*
2 Or, *the covetous blesseth himself, he abhorreth the Lord.*
3 Or, *all his thoughts are, There is no God.*
ª Ps. 14. 1, & 53. 1.
4 Heb., *unto generation and generation.*
ᵇ Rom. 3. 14.
5 Heb., *deceits.*
6 Or, *iniquity.*
7 Heb., *hide themselves.*
8 Heb., *in the secret places.*
9 Heb., *he breaketh himself.*
10 Or, *into his strong parts.*
ᶜ Ps. 94. 7.

---

sent) in the plot which they (the wicked) have devised."

(3) **For the wicked boasteth.**—Literally, *for the wicked speaketh praise to the lust of his soul*, which has been understood either as in the Authorised Version, "prides himself upon his evil desires," or "prides himself in or according to his sinful wish," as LXX., Vulg., Syriac, and Chaldee. The former of these follows most naturally on verse 2. His wiles, so successful in snaring his victim, are a cause of self-gratulation. The representation of the villain addressing his own evil passions in laudatory terms is highly poetic. So the rich fool in the parable congratulates his soul on his greed.

And blesseth.—Rather, *curseth* by a common *euphemism.* (Comp. 1 Kings xxi. 23; Job i. 5.)

The covetous—properly, *robber*—may either be subject or object, as also may "Jehovah;" or being a participle, may be adverbial (as Ewald). Hence we get, besides the Authorised Version and the margin, either, "the robber curses (and) despises Jehovah," or, "he greedily (literally, *robbing*) curses, despises Jehovah;" the last makes a better echo to the first clause. The LXX. and Vulg. read, "The wicked is praised; the sinner has irritated the Lord," getting the second subject from the next verse.

(4) **The wicked.**—The Authorised Version has quite missed the meaning of this verse. Translate, *the wicked in his haughtiness* (literally, *height of his nostril.* Comp. the common expression, 'to turn up one's nose at a person') *saith He will not requite it* (*i.e.*, punish; comp. verse 13). *There is no God in all his thought.* (Comp. Pss. xiv. 1, liii. 1.)

(5) **His ways are always grievous.**— Better, *his enterprises always succeed.* This meaning is obtained from Job xx. 21, "nothing escaped his covetousness, therefore his prospering shall not last," and from the cognate of the verb "strength." Perhaps, however, "his ways are always strong" implies only the bold and reckless course with which a tyrant pursues his end. (Comp. Ps. lxxiii. 12.)

Thy judgments . . .—Literally, *a height thy judgments far above him.* (Comp. Ps. xxxvi. 6.)

Puffeth—*i.e.*, *in scorn.* (Comp. Ps. xii. 5.) South uses the word in this sense, "It is really to defy heaven to *puff* at damnation, and bid omnipotence do its work." It is especially forcible after the description of the haughty attitude of the wicked, with his nose high in the air, snorting out contempt against his foes, disdaining God and man alike.

(6) **I shall not.**—The meaning of the verse is clear, but the construction is involved. Literally, *I shall not be moved to generation and generation, which not in evil.* The LXX. and Vulg. omit the relative altogether. The best rendering is, "I shall never be moved at any time: I who am without ill."

(7) **Cursing and deceit.**—From the connection of cursing with deceit (comp. Hosea iv. 2, "swearing and lying"), we must understand perjury.

(8) **In lurking places . . .**—*i.e.*, in ambush.

Villages.—Properly, enclosed spaces, but then, like our "town" (*ton*, an enclosure), for any collection of dwellings; and in Lev. xxv. 31, "an unwalled place"; applied also to a nomadic encampment (Gen. xxv. 16).

Privily set.—Literally, *hid*: *i.e.*, watched secretly.

The poor.—The Hebrew word, occurring three times in this psalm (verses 10, 14), is peculiar to it. The root idea is *darkness*; hence here, by an easy transition, *obscure, humble.* Symmachus has "feeble." But Mr. Burgess suggests that we may in all three places keep the root idea, *darkness.* Translate, *his eyes hide* (*i.e.*, *wait) for the darkness*; and comp. Job xxiv. 15. "The eye of the adulterer waiteth for the twilight."

"The Arab robber lurks like a wolf among these sand-heaps, and often springs out suddenly upon the solitary traveller, robs him in a trice, and then plunges again into the wilderness of sandhills and reedy downs, where pursuit is fruitless. Our friends are careful not to allow us to straggle about or linger behind, and yet it seems absurd to fear a surprise here—Khaifa before our eyes, Acre in our rear, and travellers in sight on both sides. Robberies, however, do often occur just where we now are. Strange country; and it has always been so."—Thomson, *The Land and Book.*

(9) **Lieth in wait.**—A confusion of metaphor. The wicked is first, the lion watching for his prey, and then the hunter snaring animals. "Poor," here—better, *afflicted* (see Ps. ix. 12). Translate, *in his hiding-place he lurks, as a lion in his lair, lurks to seize a sufferer, seizes a sufferer, drawing him into his net.*

(10) **By his strong ones.**—Possibly, *by his strong claws*, recurring to the metaphor of the lion. Some (Jerome, Perowne, and apparently Syriac), instead of "croucheth," render "is crushed," making the sufferer its subject. There is a various reading to the text, but in either case the image of the beast gathering himself together for a spring is admissible. Or, keeping the primary sense of darkness, render, *he crouches and skulks, and lies darkly down in his strong places.* This avoids the anomaly of taking the plural noun with a singular verb. For the adverbial use of the plural noun, see Isa. 1. 10; Ps. cxxxix. 14.

(11) **Hideth.**—Better, *hath hidden.*

A Prayer for Remedy.   PSALMS, XI.   *David's Trust in God.*

(12) Arise, O Lord; O God, lift up thine hand: forget not the ¹humble.

(13) Wherefore doth the wicked contemn God? he hath said in his heart, Thou wilt not require *it*.

(14) Thou hast seen *it*; for thou beholdest mischief and spite, to requite *it* with thy hand: the poor ²committeth himself unto thee; thou art the helper of the fatherless.

(15) Break thou the arm of the wicked and the evil *man*: seek out his wickedness *till* thou find none.

(16) ᵃ The Lord *is* King for ever and ever: the heathen are perished out of his land.

(17) Lord, thou hast heard the desire of the humble: thou wilt ³prepare their heart, thou wilt cause thine ear to hear:

(18) To judge the fatherless and the oppressed, that the man of the earth may no more ⁴oppress.

1 Or, *afflicted*.

2 Heb., *cleaveth*.

a Ps. 29. 10 & 145. 13, & 146. 10; Jer. 10. 10; Lam. 5. 19.

3 Or, *establish*.

4 Or, *terrify*.

5 Heb., *in darkness*.

b Hab. 2. 20.

PSALM XI.

To the chief Musician, A Psalm of David.

(1) In the Lord put I my trust: how say ye to my soul, Flee *as* a bird to your mountain? (2) For, lo, the wicked bend *their* bow, they make ready their arrow upon the string, that they may ⁵privily shoot at the upright in heart.

(3) If the foundations be destroyed, what can the righteous do?

(4) ᵇ The Lord *is* in his holy temple, the Lord's throne *is* in heaven: his eyes behold, his eyelids try, the children of men. (5) The Lord trieth the righteous: but the wicked, and him that loveth violence, his soul hateth.

---

(12) Here the acrostic arrangement is resumed with *koph*.

(14) **The poor committeth himself.**—Better, *the helpless leaveth it to Thee*. By a slight alteration in the division of the Hebrew letters, and of the pointing, we should get, *It is against thee that he is strong in darkness*. (See Notes above, verses 8, 10.)

(15) **Seek out.**—The meaning of the verse is clear, from Ps. xxxvii. 36, and Isa. xli. 12, where we see that *to seek and not find* was a proverb expressing "riddance of evil;" but the construction is difficult. The first clause should end at "wicked," the words "and the evil" being absolute; and the verbs, which are in form either second or third person, should be taken in the second. Translate, *and as for the evil man, thou shalt look for his wickedness, and not find it* (*thou*=anybody), which preserves the proverbial tone. So the LXX., "his sin shall be sought, and not be found").

(16) **The Lord is King.**—If the psalm has hitherto been personal, it here swells out into a larger strain of national hope and faith.

(18) **Oppressed.**—See Ps. ix. 9. "God's choice acquaintances are humble men."—*Leighton*.

That the man.—Literally, *that may not continue to terrify* (or *defy*) *mere man from the earth*, which may mean that mere mortals may have to confess their weakness in comparison with God. But Ps. ix. 20, where the same word is used, indicates that it is here used in a contemptuous sense of the "heathen." "That the nations from the earth (*i.e.*, spread over the earth) may know themselves to be but men, and no longer defy Israel and Israel's God."

XI.

The tradition assigning this psalm to David is accepted by some of the greatest of modern scholars, but it is difficult to assign it to any known period of his history. Both in his troubles under Saul and in the rebellion of Absalom, he adopted the flight which this poet scorns as unworthy of one whose conscience is clear, and whose faith in Jehovah is sure; and yet the tone of the psalm is too personal to allow it to be taken as merely representative of a type of character, though it certainly stands as a rebuke for ever to those pusillanimous friends who are always ready to counsel flight or compromise, even when the very principles of right and wrong are at stake.

The poetical form is irregular.

(1) **Put I my trust.**—Better, as in Ps. vii. 1, *I find my refuge*.

Flee as a bird.—Literally, *flee ye a bird*. The plural verb, with the singular noun, offers a difficulty which is not obviated by the reading which changes the verb to the singular, since *your mountain* has the plural suffix. We may supply the sign of comparison, as elsewhere sometimes omitted (Ps. xxii. 14); "flee ye *like* a bird;" or we may, with Ewald, take the noun as collective—*a flock of birds*. The idea of trepidation is conveyed in the original by the verb, which suggests the hurried flap of wings. Dr. Thomson, in *The Land and the Book*, finds in the habits of the dove an illustration of the passage; and compares Ps. lv. 6, "Oh that I had wings as a dove!"

(2) **Privily.**—See margin, which preserves the image of the archer lurking in a dark corner.

(3) **The foundations.**—By this word must be understood the principles of morality, which are the foundation of society. Symmachus and Jerome render "laws." But the rendering "What could the righteous do?" is doubtful. The image is of a house shattered by an earthquake (comp. Ps. lxxxii. 5); in such a case how find safety? The LXX. and Vulg. have "Since they have destroyed what thou hast established, what has the righteous done?" The order of the Hebrew words seems to support this rendering, "While morality has been overthrown, the righteous what has *he* done?" A suggested emendation, involving but a slight change in the Hebrew letters, would produce, however, a far better sense: "If the foundations be destroyed, what will become of the *tower*, or *superstructure?*"

(4) **Temple.**—Here, plainly from the parallelism, not any earthly building, but *the heavenly palace of the Divine King*. One thought of God's supreme righteousness, high above earth's anarchy and sin, is enough to reassure the psalmist and make him strong. "God's in His heaven; all's right with the world."—Browning, *Pippa Passes*.

The Justice of God.   PSALMS, XII.   *A Prayer for Help.*

(6) Upon the wicked he shall rain snares, fire and brimstone, and ¹an horrible tempest: *this shall be* the portion of their cup.

(7) For the righteous LORD loveth righteousness; his countenance doth behold the upright.

PSALM XII.

To the chief Musician ² upon Sheminith, A Psalm of David.

(1) ³ Help, LORD; for the godly man ceaseth; for the faithful fail from among the children of men. (2) They speak vanity every one with his neighbour: *with* flattering lips *and* with ⁴ a double heart do they speak.

(3) The LORD shall cut off all flattering lips, *and* the tongue that speaketh ⁵ proud things: (4) who have said, With our tongue will we prevail; our lips ⁶ *are* our own: who *is* lord over us?

(5) For the oppression of the poor, for the sighing of the needy, now will I arise, saith the LORD; I will set *him* in safety *from him that* ⁷ puffeth at him.

1 Or, *a burning tempest.*
2 Or, *upon the eighth.*
3 Or, *save.*
4 Heb., *an heart and an heart.*
5 Heb., *great things.*
6 Heb., *are with us.*
7 Or, *would ensnare him.*

---

(6) **Rain snares.**—Or *nooses.* (Comp. 1 Cor. vii. 35.) This is certainly an extraordinary figure, and various emendations have been suggested. Ewald's "coals of fire" (*pecham* for *pachim*) is the best (comp. Ps. xviii. 13, where the Hebrew word, however, is *gechalim*, "live, or red coals"; while *pecham* is used in Prov. xxvi. 21 as *fuel* for fire, in contrast with *live coals*; but in Isa. xliv. 12 and liv. 16 it is itself plainly *burning coal.*) He arranges the clauses thus: "Causeth to rain upon wicked men coals of fire with brimstone; a glowing blast is the portion of their cup."

"Put we our quarrel to the will of Heaven,
Who, when he sees the hours ripe on earth,
Will rain hot vengeance on offenders' heads."
—SHAKESPEARE: *Rich. II.*, i. 2.

Horrible tempest.—Literally, *wind of heats;* Vulg., *spiritus procellarum;* Targum, *storm and whirlwind;* as in Latin, *aestus* combines the ideas of heat and violent motion; so the Hebrew word here. Probably, therefore, we must think of a hot, poisonous wind—the *simoom.*

Or may we see one more reminiscence of the fate of Sodom and Gomorrha stamped indelibly on the Hebrew mind?

(7) **His countenance.**—Better, *the upright shall behold His countenance.* This beautiful religious hope finds its highest expression in the beatitude on the pure in heart. The beatific vision in Dante is its most glorious poetical development. By the vision of God the Hebrew poet means triumph of right and the acknowledgment of his innocence—light and peace after darkness and trouble, as in Job xxxiii. 26. (Comp. Pss. xvii. 15, xli. 12.)

XII.

The tradition of the Davidic authorship must be discarded here. The psalm is an elegy, but not for personal suffering. It is a lament over the demoralisation of men and the corruption of social life. Neither faith nor law are left; falsehood, duplicity, and hypocrisy succeed everywhere, and the honest men are so lost in the mass of wickedness that they seem to have disappeared altogether. We find similar complaints in Micah vii. 2, Isa. lvii. 1, and Jer. v. 1. But God has not left Himself without a witness. Prophetic voices have been raised—perhaps Isaiah's—in noble assertion of truth and justice, and the poet recalls one such voice, proclaiming the coming and the establishment of a righteous kingdom upon earth, the hope of which had already become the consolation and stay of the faithful.

The insertion of this oracle in verse 5 interferes with the rhythm, which else is even and regular.

For *Title,* see *Introduction* to Ps. vi.

(1) **Ceaseth.**—Intransitive, as in Ps. vii. 9.

The faithful.—The Vulg. and Syriac treat this word as abstract: "truth," "faithfulness." So Ewald; but the parallelism here, as in Ps. xxxi. 23, requires it in the concrete. (Comp. 2 Sam. xx. 19.) The Hebrew is cognate with "amen," and Luther has "amen's leute," *people as good as their word.*

(2) **Vanity.**—So in Ps. xli. 6 and Job xxxv. 13. Literally, *evil.* "Falsehood" would be better. This verse may have been in St Paul's mind (Ephes. iv. 25).

Flattering lips.—Literally, *lips of smoothness.* (Comp. Note, Ps. v. 9.)

With a double heart.—Literally, *with a heart and a heart.* (Comp. 1 Chron. xii. 33.) "One for the Church, another for the Change; one for Sundays, another for working-days; one for the king, another for the Pope. A man without a heart is a wonder, but a man with two hearts is a monster."—Thos. Adams, A.D. 1614.

(3) **The Lord shall.**—Translate, *May Jehovah cut off.*

Proud things.—Literally, *great things.* Vulg., *linguam magniloquam.*

(4) **With our tongue.**—This is the proud saying just mentioned, and is plainly a boast of the power possessed by those who have the ear of persons in authority, and can adroitly "make the worse appear the better cause"; or being themselves in high places, can, like Angelo in *Measure for Measure,* defy the accusations of their victims:—

"Who will believe thee, Isabel?
My place in the State
Will so your accusation overweigh
That you shall stifle in your own report,
And smell of calumny."

But there is great difference of opinion as to the proper rendering, "with our tongues will we prevail." Some render, "we are masters of our tongues"; others, "with our tongues we confederate": *i.e.,* "our tongues are our allies." The last rendering agrees best with the next clause.

Our lips are our own.—Literally, *are with us: i.e.,* on our side. (Comp. 2 Kings ix. 32.)

(5) **For the oppression**—*i.e.,* on account of the oppression. Here, as in so many psalms and prophecies, we have an ancient oracle of God introduced. The poet first quotes it, and then in verse 6 contrasts its truth and genuineness with the false speeches of hypocrites.

I will set.—Literally, *I will set in safety; he blows at it:* which may mean either, "I will ensure him of the

(15) As for me, I will behold thy face in righteousness: I shall be satisfied, when I awake, with thy likeness.

PSALM XVIII.

To the chief Musician, *A Psalm* of David, the servant of the LORD, who spake unto the LORD the words of *a* this song in the day *that* the LORD delivered him from the hand of all his enemies, and from the hand of Saul: And he said,

(1) I will love thee, O LORD, my strength. (2) The Lord *is* my rock, and my fortress, and my deliverer; my God, ¹my strength, in whom I will trust; my buckler, and the horn of my salvation, *and* my high tower. (3) I will call upon the LORD, *who is worthy* to be praised: so shall I be saved from mine enemies. (4) *b* The sorrows of death compassed me, and the floods of ²ungodly men made me afraid. (5) The ³sorrows of hell compassed me about:

a 2 Sam. 22.

1 Heb., *my rock.*

b Ps. 116. 3.

2 Heb., *Belial.*

3 Or, *cords.*

---

(15) **I**—is emphatic. The satisfaction of worldly men is in their wealth and family honours, that of the poet in the sun of God's presence and the vision of His righteousness. (Comp. Note, Ps. xi. 7.)

Instead of "likeness," render *image*, or *appearance*. But what does the poet mean by the hope of seeking God when he wakes? Some think of rising to peace after a perplexing trouble; others of health after suffering; others of the sunlight of the Divine grace breaking on the soul. But the literal reference to night in verse 3 seems to ask for the same reference here. Instead of waking to a worldling's hope of a day of feasting and pleasure, the psalmist wakes to the higher and nobler thought that God—who in sleep (so like death, when nothing is visible), has been, as it were, absent—is now again, when he sees once more (LXX.), found at his right hand (comp. end of Ps. xvi.), a conscious presence to him, assuring him of justice and protection. But as in Ps. xvi., so here, we feel that in spite of his subjection to the common notions about death the psalmist may have felt the stirrings of a better hope. Such "cries from the dark," even if they do not prove the possession of a belief in immortality, show how the human heart was already groping its way, however blindly, towards it.

XVIII.

This magnificent ode is David's, if anything at all of David's has come down to us. Its recurrence in 2 Sam. xxii., the mention of the monarch by name in the last verse (see, however, Note), and the general contents, in the eyes of all but one or two critics*, bear out the tradition of the title.

If no other literary legacy had been left by the Hebrew race, we should have from this psalm a clear conception of the character of its poetic genius. Its wealth of metaphor, its power of vivid word-painting, its accurate observation of nature, its grandeur and force of imagination, all meet us here; but above all, the fact that the bard of Israel wrote under the mighty conviction of the power and presence of Jehovah. The phenomena of the natural world appealed to his imagination as to that of poets generally, but with this addition, that they were all manifestations of a supreme glory and goodness behind them.

In rhythm the poem is as fine as in matter.

Title.—See 2 Sam. xxii. 1. The differences are such as might be expected between a piece in a collection of hymns and the same introduced into an historical book.

(1) **I will love thee.**—Better, *Dearly do I love thee*. The line is wanting in Samuel.

My strength.—This strikes the keynote of the whole poem. The strong, mighty God is the object in David's thought throughout. It is a warrior's song, and his conception of Jehovah is a warrior's conception.

(2) **Rock.**—Better here, *cliff*, keeping "rock" for the next clause. In the first figure the ideas of height and shelter, in the second of broad-based and enduring strength, are predominant.

Fortress.—Properly, *mountain castle*. We have the joint figure of the lofty and precipitous cliff with the castle on its crest, a reminiscence—as, in fact, is every one in this "towering of epithets"—of scenes and events in David's early life.

My God . . .—Better, *my God, my rock, I trust in Him*. God is here *El*, "the strong one." In Samuel, "God of my rock."

Horn of my salvation.—The allusion seems to be not to a means of attack, like the horn of an animal, but to a mountain peak (called "horn" in all languages—so κέρας, Xen. *Anab.* v. 6; "Cornua Parnassi," Statius, *Theb.* v. 532; and so in Hebrew, Isa. v. 1, see margin), such as often afforded David a safe retreat. Render "my peak of safety."

High tower.—The LXX. and Vulgate have "helper." (Comp. Ps. ix. 9.) The word comes in so abruptly, that doubtless the addition in Samuel, "and my refuge, my Saviour, thou savest me from violence," was part of the original hymn, completing the rhythm.

(3) Presents a trifling verbal variation from Samuel.

(4) **The sorrows of death.**—The Hebrew word may mean either *birth pangs* (LXX. and Acts ii. 24, where see Note, *New Testament Commentary*), or *cords*. The figure of the hunter in the next verse, "the snares of death," determines its meaning there to be *cords* (see margin). It is best, therefore, to keep the same rendering here: but there can be little doubt that the version in Samuel, *breakers*, or *waves*, is the true one, from the parallelism—

"Waves of death compassed me,
And billows of Belial terrified me."

For *Belial*, see Deut. xiii. 13. Here the parallelism fixes its meaning, "ruin." For the ideas of peril and destruction, connected by the Hebrews with waves and floods, comp. verse 16, also Pss. xxxii. 6, xlii. 7, lxix. 1. Doubtless the tradition of the Flood and of the Red Sea helped to strengthen the apprehensions natural in a country where the river annually overflowed its banks, and where a dry ravine might at any moment become a dangerous flood. The hatred of the sea arose from quite another cause—viz., the dread of it as a highway for invasion.

(5) **Hell.**—Heb., *sheôl*. (See Note on Ps. vi. 5.)

Prevented—*i.e.*, suddenly seized upon. The poet seems to feel the cords already tightening on his limbs.

---

* Grätz, the latest commentator, allows part of this psalm to be David's.

The Corruption of Man.   PSALMS, XV.   *The Hope of the Exiles.*

There is no God. They are corrupt, they have done abominable works, *there is* none that doeth good.

(2) The LORD looked down from heaven upon the children of men, ^ato see if there were any that did understand, *and* seek God. (3) They are all gone aside, they are *all* together become ¹ filthy: *there is* none that doeth good, no, not one.

(4) Have all the workers of iniquity no knowledge? who eat up my people *as* they eat bread, and call not upon the LORD. (5) There ² were they in great fear: for God *is* in the generation of the righteous. (6) Ye have shamed the counsel of the poor, because the LORD *is* his refuge.

(7) ³Oh that the salvation of Israel *were* come out of Zion! when the LORD bringeth back the captivity of his people, Jacob shall rejoice, *and* Israel shall be glad.

a Rom. 3. 10.
1 Heb., *stinking.*
2 Heb., *they feared a fear.*
3 Heb., *Who will give,* &c.
b Ps. 24. 3, &c.
4 Heb., *sojourn.*

PSALM XV.

A Psalm of David.

(1) LORD, ^bwho shall ⁴abide in thy tabernacle? who shall dwell in thy holy hill?

---

therefore speculative atheism, but practical—a denial of the moral government of God—so that fool and wicked become almost synonymous.

They have done abominable works.—Literally, *they have made to be abhorred their works.* The LXX. and Vulg. have caught the sense, "They have become abominable in their practices." Instead of works, Ps. liii. has "iniquity."

(2) **Looked down.**—Literally, *bent forward to look as from a window.* (Comp. Cant. vi. 10.)

Did understand.—Better, *any man of understanding,* in contrast with "fool," in verse 1, and certainly meaning one who regulates his conduct on the conviction of the existence of a holy and just God.

(3) **Filthy.**—Better, *corrupt* or *putrid.* Comp. the Roman satirist's description of his age:—

"Nothing is left, nothing for future times
To add to the full catalogue of crimes.
The baffled sons must feel the same desires
And act the same mad follies as their sires.
Vice has attained its zenith."—JUVENAL: *Sat.* i.

Between verses 3 and 4 the Alexandrian MS. of the LXX., followed by the Vulg. and the Arabic, insert from Rom. iii. 13—18, the passage beginning, "Their throat is an open sepulchre." The fact of these verses, which are really a *cento* from various psalms and Isaiah, following immediately on the quotation of verses 2 and 3, led the copyist to this insertion. (See Note in *New Testament Commentary* to Rom. iii. 13.)

(4) **Have all the workers of iniquity no knowledge?**—*i.e.,* are they so senseless as not to perceive the consequences of their wrong-doing? or if we point the verb as the LXX. and Vulg., "shall they not know?" *i.e.,* they are sure to find out to what their wickedness is leading them.

Who eat up.—Literally, *eating my people, they have eaten bread; on Jehovah they have not called,* which is usually explained, as in Authorised Version, "to devour God's people has been as usual and as regular as the daily meal." Another rendering is "whilst eating my people they have eaten bread, regardless of Jehovah," *i.e.,* they have gone on in their security eating and drinking, with no thought of the vengeance preparing for them by the God of the oppressed race. Some, however, prefer to divide the two clauses, "Ah, they shall see—all the workers of iniquity who eat my people—they eat bread (*i.e.,* live) regardless of Jehovah." This makes a better parallelism. A comparison with Micah iii. 3, 4, suggests that this verse of the psalm was a proverbial saying. (For the image, comp. Jer. x. 25; and Homer's "people-devouring kings.")

(5) **There were they.**—Literally, *there they feared a fear, i.e.,* terror overtook them. Ps. liii. adds, "which was no fear." The local "there" brings the scene before us as in a picture. We see them *there* before us, these wicked men; *there* in the midst of their intrigues, or their exactions, or their pleasures, the hand of God seizes them, and lo! they are struck with fear. We evidently have not here any indication by which to fasten on a particular event. Whether the addition in Ps. liii. gives any is discussed there.

For God is.—For the singular variation in Ps. liii. consult Note on verse 5 of that psalm. The uneasy sense that, after all, the good have God on their side—this general truth is implied in the phrase "generations of the righteous," even if first employed of faithful Israel—is always a cause of fear to the wicked.

(6) **Counsel.**—This confidence, this piety, this appeal addressed to the supreme Protector, is in this verse called the "counsel," the "plan" of the sufferer, and the poet asks, "Would ye then make the sufferer blush for such a thought?" "No, for Jehovah is his refuge." The Authorised Version has here missed the sense by rendering in the past tense.

(7) **Oh that.**—The thoughts of the exiles turn to the Holy City as the one source of deliverance, as if Jehovah's power would only manifest itself from His hallowed abode. So Daniel looked towards Jerusalem in his prayer. (Comp. the same feeling in Isa. xl. 9, 10.) For the expression "turn the captivity," or, to keep the Heb. idiom, "turn the turning," comp. Pss. lxxxv. 1, cxxvi. 1; Hosea vi. 2; Joel iii. 1. It appears, however, besides its literal reference to the exile, to have been applied proverbially to the removal of any misfortune (Job xlii. 10).

XV.

This is the portrait of a perfect character after the ideal of Israel. We naturally compare with it, on the one hand, the heathen types of perfection as we see them in the ethical philosophy of Greece and Rome, and, on the other, the Christian standard as we see it in the New Testament and in modern literature, and the result is to leave us in wonder and admiration before this figure of stainless honour drawn by an ancient Jewish poet. "Christian chivalry," it has been said, "has not drawn a brighter." In heart and tongue, in deed and word, as a member of society and as an individual, the character of Ps. xv. is without reproach.

| The Psalmist Describes | PSALMS, XVI. | the Perfect Man. |

(2) ᵃ He that walketh uprightly, and worketh righteousness, and speaketh the truth in his heart. (3) *He that* backbiteth not with his tongue, nor doeth evil to his neighbour, nor ¹ taketh up a reproach against his neighbour. (4) In whose eyes a vile person is contemned; but he honoureth them that fear the LORD. *He that* sweareth to *his own* hurt, and changeth not. (5) ᵇ *He that* putteth not out his money to usury, nor taketh reward against the innocent. He that doeth these *things* shall never be moved.

a Isa. 33. 15.
1 Or, *receiveth*, or, *endureth*.
b Ex. 22. 25; Lev. 25. 36; Deut. 23. 19; Ezek. 18. 8, & 22. 12.
2 Or, *A golden Psalm of David*.

PSALM XVI.

² Michtam of David.

(1) Preserve me, O God: for in thee

The psalm makes no pretence to art either in form or style.

(1) **Abide . . . dwell.**—Properly, as in margin, *sojourn* like a passing guest, and *dwell* like a resident. But here the two terms are apparently used as synonyms. It was the natural form in which to put the question at Jerusalem, where God had His abode in the Temple, and we may paraphrase it thus: "What constitutes a true and genuine citizen of the kingdom of God?" The form of Wordsworth's poem, "Who is the happy warrior? who is he," &c., was possibly suggested by the Psalm, and it may be read with advantage by the side of it.

(2) **Uprightly.**—Literally, *he whose walking is perfect rectitude*. In Prov. xxviii. 18 the same phrase occurs. Comp. Isa. xxxiii. 15.

Speaketh the truth in his heart—*i.e.*, both *thinks and speaks the truth*.

> "This above all: to thine own self be true,
> And it must follow as the night the day,
> Thou canst not then be false to any man."
> SHAKSPEARE: *Hamlet*.

(3) **He that backbiteth not.**—Literally, *he has not footed it on his tongue*. Very expressive of those who go about from house to house carrying tittle-tattle. (Comp. 1 Tim. v. 13.)

Reproach.—The Hebrew word has a striking derivation. Properly, *the stripping of the trees of autumn fruit*; so, *stripping honour and reputation from a person*. Two different words are in the Hebrew for "neighbour." Translate, "Who does no ill to his friend, nor carries a reproach against his neighbour." The marginal *receiveth*, or *endureth*, is quite against the context.

(4) **In whose eyes.**—The first clause is obscure. The subject and predicate are not clearly marked; but the Authorised Version gives the right sense. It is quite out of keeping with the context to make both verbs predicates, and to translate, "He is despised and rejected in his own eyes," *i.e.*, thinks humbly of himself. The meaning is, "Those deserving contempt are contemned; but the good who fear Jehovah are honoured."

To his own hurt.—Literally, *to do evil, i.e.*, to himself (see Lev. v. 4). The LXX., by transposing the letters, read, "to his neighbour;" and the English Prayer Book version has apparently combined the two thoughts: "Who sweareth to his neighbour, and disappointeth him not, even though it were to his own hindrance."

> "His words are bonds, his oaths are oracles,
> His love sincere, his thoughts immaculate;
> His tears pure messengers sent from his heart,
> His heart is far from fraud as heaven from earth."
> SHAKSPEARE: *Two Gentlemen of Verona*.

(5) Usury was not forbidden in the legitimate commercial dealings with foreigners (Deut. xxiii. 20); and the laws against it seem to have had exclusive reference to dealings among Israelites themselves, and were evidently enacted more with a view to the protection of the poor than because the idea of usury in itself was considered wrong (Exod. xxii. 25; Lev. xxv. 36). So here the context plainly seems to limit the sin of usury to unjust application of the principle, being connected with bribery. Against "biting" usury (the Hebrew word primarily means "bite") all governments find it necessary to legislate, as we see in the case of the money-lenders of our own time; but with the employment of capital put out on interest for legitimate purposes of trade, neither Hebrew feeling generally, as the whole career of the race shows, nor the higher minds among them, as we see by our Lord's parable of the talents, were averse. The best illustrations of invectives of prophets and psalmists against extortionate usurers are supplied by Shakspeare's play, *The Merchant of Venice*.

XVI.

Ewald's arguments for grouping this psalm with Psalms xvii. and xlix., as those of one time, and even one author, are almost irresistible; and this not merely from the general similarity of language and sentiment, but especially from the feelings expressed about death. The vision of immortality wanting to the early Jews, to Moses, even to David, has at length, however faintly and dimly, dawned. It will be long before it becomes a world-belief, or even a definite individual hope. But the germ of a truth so great must grow, as we see it growing in the Book of Job, till the time is ripe for apostles to quote the words of the ancient poets, as if they had not only felt for themselves the necessity of an immortal existence, but had seen prophetically how in Christ it would be assured to men.

Psalm xvi. is decidedly individual in its experience, and the inscription to David as author receives a certain amount of probability from a comparison of verse 5 with 1 Sam. xxvi. 19. But such slight indications give way before the reference to the bloody sacrifices in verse 4, which brings the date down to a time subsequent at least to Solomon.

The parallelism in this psalm is scarcely traceable.

Title.—Michtam (*Mikhtam*) occurs in five other psalms (lvi.—lx.)—all, like Psalm xvi., ascribed to David. The greatest uncertainty attaches to the word. The marginal explanation rests on the derivation from *kethem* (gold, Job xxviii. 16—19), and may be illustrated by the "golden sayings" of Pythagoras (comp. *Golden Legend*), an obvious expression for something rare and precious. Others compare the *Moallakat* of Mecca, poems written in "golden" letters. The LXX., "a pillar inscription" (Vulg., *tituli inscriptio*), follows another possible derivation, but does not suit the contents of those psalms so inscribed. Some take Mikhtam as a variety of *Mikhtab* (a writing). Most probably

do I put my trust. (2) O my soul, thou hast said unto the LORD, Thou art my Lord: "my goodness *extendeth* not to thee; (3) *but* to the saints that *are* in the earth, and *to* the excellent, in whom *is* all my delight.

(4) Their sorrows shall be multiplied that ¹hasten *after* another *god*: their drink-offerings of blood will I not offer, nor take up their names into my lips.

(5) ᵇ The LORD *is* the portion ²of mine inheritance and of my cup: thou maintainest my lot. (6) The lines are fallen unto me in pleasant *places*; yea, I have a goodly heritage. (7) I will bless the LORD, who hath given me counsel: my reins also instruct me in the night seasons.

(8) ᶜ I have set the LORD always before me: because *he is* at my right hand, I shall not be moved. (9) Therefore my heart is glad, and my glory rejoiceth:

a Job 22. 2, & 35. 7; Ps. 50. 9.

1 Or, *give gifts to another.*

b Deut. 32. 9; Lam. 3. 24.

2 Heb., *of my part.*

c Acts 2. 25.

---

some musical direction, the key to which is lost, is conveyed by the word.

(1) **For in thee.**—Better, *for I have found refuge in thee* (as in Pss. vii. 1, xi. 1). The verb is in the preterite.

(2) **Thou hast said.**—The text of this passage is exceedingly corrupt. This appears (1) from the actual existence of various readings, (2) by the variations in the ancient versions, both from the Hebrew and each other. It will be best to take verses 2 and 3 together first. The consensus of the ancient versions in favour of the first person, "I said," instead of "thou hast said" (the italicised words *O my soul*, are a mere gloss from the Chaldee), gives for verse 2 the plain and intelligible rendering

I said to Jehovah, Thou art my Lord,
I have no good besides thee.

Verse 3 also requires emendation, being quite unintelligible as it stands. The simplest device is to omit the conjunction and recognise one of those changes of person so agreeable to Hebrew, when the verse will run—

"And of the saints who are in the earth,
They are the excellent in whom is all my delight."

The Authorised Version, in inserting "extendeth," introduces the fine thought that

"Merit lives from man to man,
And not from man, O God, to Thee;"

but it could not have been the thought of the original, since "my good," as verses 5 and 6 show, equals "happiness," not "conduct."

(4) **Their sorrows.**—This verse offers also great variation in the ancient versions. The literal text runs *Their sorrows* [or, *idols*] (*fem.*) *are multiplied* (*masc.*); *another they hasten* [or, *change*]. *I will not pour out their libations from blood, and will not take their names upon my lips*, which, with one or two slight changes in the punctuation, becomes—

"They shall multiply their sorrows
Who change to another god:
I will not pour out their bloody libations,
Nor take their names on my lips."

At the same time, from the evident allusion to the curse on Eve in Gen. iii. 16, and the fact that the verb rendered "hasten" (comp. margin) means to buy a wife, it seems that the psalmist had the common prophetical figure for idolatry, viz., adultery, in his mind; but as he is not speaking of the Church as a whole, he does not work it out as the prophets do, by representing the idolaters as adulteresses.

The "libations of blood" seem to refer to the ghastly rites of Moloch and Chemosh. For the last clause comp. Exod. xxiii. 13. To the Hebrews the very name of a god included a predication of his power. Hence the avoidance of even mentioning *baal*, but substituting *bosheth*, *i.e.*, shameful thing, for it, even in proper names.

(5) **The portion.**—There is allusion here to the Levitical portion (Num. xviii. 20): "I am thy portion and thine inheritance." The poet, whom we must imagine exiled from his actual inheritance in Canaan, consoles, and more than consoles himself, with the sublime thought that this "better part" could not be taken away from him. Perowne quotes Savonarola's fine saying, "What must not he possess who possesses the possessor of all!" and St. Paul's, "All things are yours; for ye are Christ's, and Christ is God's;" which rather recalls Deut. xxxii. 9, where the correlative truth to Num. xviii. 20 occurs.

For the figure of the cup, see Ps. xi. 6. It had already become a synonym for "condition in life."

Thou maintainest.—The Hebrew word is peculiar, and causes grammatical difficulties; but the sense is clear. God does not only dispose (cast) the lot of the man in covenant relation to Him—He does that even for unbelievers—but holds it fast in His hand. (See this use of the verb, Amos i. 5, 8; Prov. v. 5.) At the same time Hitzig's conjecture (*tômid* for *tômikh*), is very plausible, "Thou art ever my lot."

(6) **The lines are fallen unto me.**—The allusion is to the "measuring cords" by which allotments of land were measured, and they are said to "fall" possibly because after the measurement the portions were distributed by "lot" (Josh. xvii. 5; Micah ii. 5).

(7) **Given me counsel . . .**—*i.e.*, led me to a right and happy choice of the way of life.

My reins—*i.e.*, my heart.

Instruct me.—Better, *warn me*. Conscience echoes the voice of God. The Hebrew word, from a root meaning *bind*, includes the sense of obligation. Once heard, the Divine monition becomes a law to the good man, and his own heart warns him of the slightest danger of deviation from it.

(8) **At my right hand.**—Comp. Pss. cix. 31, cx. 5, cxxi. 5. The image seems to be a military one: the shield of the right-hand comrade is a protection to the man beside him.

(9) **Glory.**—Heb., *khabôd*; but probably the poet wrote *khabed*, *i.e.*, *liver*, or (comp. "reins" above, and the common use of the word "bowels") *heart*. The LXX. paraphrase *tongue*. The passage was so quoted in Acts ii. 25. (Comp. Pss. lvii. 8, cviii. 1.) "With the best member that I have" (Prayer Book).

Shall rest in hope.—This follows the Vulg. The LXX. also have "shall tabernacle in hope." The true rendering, however, is *shall rest in security*. In "heart, soul, flesh," the poet comprises the whole

The Life Everlasting. PSALMS, XVII. *David's Confidence in his Integrity.*

my flesh also shall ¹rest in hope. ⁽¹⁰⁾ ᵃFor thou wilt not leave my soul in hell; neither wilt thou suffer thine Holy One to see corruption. ⁽¹¹⁾Thou wilt shew me the path of life: in thy presence *is* fulness of joy; at thy right hand *there are* pleasures for evermore.

¹ Heb., *dwell confidently.*

ᵃ Acts 2. 31, & 13. 35.

PSALM XVII.

A Prayer of David.

⁽¹⁾ Hear ²the right, O LORD, attend

² Heb., *justice.*

³ Heb., *without lips of deceit.*

unto my cry, give ear unto my prayer, *that goeth* ³not out of feigned lips. ⁽²⁾ Let my sentence come forth from thy presence; let thine eyes behold the things that are equal. ⁽³⁾ Thou hast proved mine heart; thou hast visited *me* in the night; thou hast tried me, *and* shalt find nothing; I am purposed *that* my mouth shall not transgress. ⁽⁴⁾ Concerning the works of men, by the word of thy lips I have kept *me*

---

living man. (Comp. 1 Thess. v. 23.) The psalmist feels that the body must share with the soul the immunity from evil which is insured by fellowship with God. Carried out to its full issue, the logical conclusion of this is the doctrine of immortality; but we must not see a *conscious* reference to it here.

⁽¹⁰⁾ **Leave.**—Rather, *commit,* or *give up.*

In hell.—Better, *to the unseen world* (Sheôl), as in Ps. vi. 5, where see Note.

Holy One.—Better, *thy chosen,* or *favoured,* or *beloved One.* Heb., *chasîd,* which, starting from the idea of one standing in a state of covenant favour with Jehovah, gathers naturally, to this passive sense, an active one of living conformably to such a state; "gracious" as well as "graced," "blessing" as well as "blessed;" and so generally as in Authorised Version, "saint," "holy" (see Pss. iv. 3, cxlv. 17, and especially Ps. l. 5, "My saints, those who have made a covenant with me by sacrifice.") The received Heb. text has the word in the plural, but with the marginal note that the sign of the plural is superfluous. The weight of MS. authority of all the ancient versions, and of the quotations Acts ii. 27, xiii. 35, is for the singular.

Corruption.—Heb., *shachath,* a pit (from root, meaning *to sink in*), as in Ps. vii. 15, where LXX. rightly "abyss," though here and generally "destruction" (not "corruption"), as if from *shakhath,* "to destroy." Even in Job xvii. 14 "the pit" would give as good a parallelism to "worm" as "corruption." The meaning of the passage is clearly that Jehovah will not abandon His beloved to death. "To be left to Sheôl" and "to see the pit" are synonyms for "to die," just as "to see life" (Eccles. ix. 9, Authorised Version, "live joyfully") is "to be alive;" or, as in next clause, "to make to see the path of life." At the same time we discern here the first faint scintillation of that light of immortality which we see struggling to break through the darkness in all the later literature of Israel; the veil over the future of the individual, if not lifted, is stirred by the morning breath of a larger faith, and so the use is justified which is made of this passage in the New Testament (Acts ii. 25). (See *New Testament Commentary.*)

⁽¹¹⁾ **There are.**—The italics in the Authorised Version spoil the triplet:—

"Thou wilt show me the path of life,
In thy presence fulness and joy,
At thy right hand pleasures for evermore."

It is another image for the same thought which dominates the psalm—the thought of the happiness of being with God. The fair heritage, the serene happiness, the enduring pleasure always to be found at God's right hand, are all different modes of expressing the same sense of complete satisfaction and peace given by a deep religious trust touched, ever so faintly, by a ray of a larger hope beginning to triumph over death itself.

XVII.

For the general scope of this psalm, compare Introduction to Ps. xvi.; for particular points of resemblance, compare Ps. xvii. 8 with Ps. xvi. 1; Ps. xvii. 3 with Ps. xvi. 7; Ps. xvii. 7, 14 with Ps. xvi. 8, &c.; and many linguistic analogies only seen in the Hebrew. It would be satisfactory if we could actually identify the author—doubtless the same man—of the two; but if we lose sight of him in thinking of the righteous part of Israel generally, suffering under the attacks of the ungodly or the heathen, and with only its faith to sustain it, the question of authorship loses its importance.

The psalm is entirely without rhythmic art.

Title.—A prayer. From Ps. lxxii. 20, "the prayers of David the son of Jesse are ended," we naturally regard *tephillah,* i.e., prayer, as a name applicable to all the pieces of the collection, though it only actually occurs as an inscription five times, and only one—the present—belongs to the first two books.

⁽¹⁾ **Hear the right.**—Or (see margin), *justice.* Some ancient versions read, "Hear, Lord of righteousness." Others make it concrete: "Hear me, the righteous;" but the Authorised Version has the true sense.

⁽²⁾ **Let my sentence**—*i.e.,* let my cause be tried before Thy tribunal, where it is sure of success, since I am innocent and Thou art just. The second clause is better in the present, "Thine eyes behold," &c.

The things that are equal.—Heb., *meysharim,* which may be either abstract, *rectitude,* or concrete, *the just* (Cant. i. 4, Note), or adverbial, *justly.*

⁽³⁾ **In the night** (as Ps. xvi. 7).—The time of calm reflection and self-examination. Some, however, taking this verse in connection with verse 15, think the poem was composed at night.

I am purposed.—The Hebrew word presents a difficulty. It is better to take it as a noun—*counsels,* and here, as generally, *evil* counsels—and join it to the preceding, not (as in the Authorised Version) the following words.

"Thou hast proved my heart,
Thou hast visited me in the night,
Thou hast found no malice in me,
My mouth doth not transgress. *or*
It (malice) doth not pass my mouth."

"I offend"—that is, "neither in thought nor word." The LXX., Vulg., Syr., Chald., and Arab. versions support this arrangement.

⁽⁴⁾ **Concerning the works of men**—*i.e., as regards the actions of men,* or *in ordinary human actions;*

David shows the Pride   PSALMS, XVII.   *and Craft of His Enemies.*

from the paths of the destroyer. (5) Hold up my goings in thy paths, *that* my footsteps ¹slip not.

(6) I have called upon thee, for thou wilt hear me, O God: incline thine ear unto me, *and hear* my speech. (7) Shew thy marvellous lovingkindness, O thou ²that savest by thy right hand them which put their trust *in thee* from those that rise up *against them*. (8) Keep me as the apple of the eye, hide me under the shadow of thy wings, (9) from the wicked ³that oppress me, *from* ⁴my deadly enemies, *who* compass me about. (10) They are inclosed in their own fat:

with their mouth they speak proudly. (11) They have now compassed us in our steps: they have set their eyes bowing down to the earth; (12) ⁵like as a lion *that* is greedy of his prey, and as it were a young lion ⁶lurking in secret places.

(13) Arise, O LORD, ⁷disappoint him, cast him down: deliver my soul from the wicked, ⁸which is thy sword: (14) ⁹from men *which are* thy hand, O LORD, from men of the world, *which have* their portion in *this* life, and whose belly thou fillest with thy hid *treasure*: ¹⁰ they are full of children, and leave the rest of their *substance* to their babes.

1 Heb., *be not moved.*
2 Or, *that savest them which trust in thee from those that rise up against thy right hand.*
3 Heb., *that waste me.*
4 Heb., *my enemies against the soul.*
5 Heb., *The likeness of him (that is, of every one of them) is as a lion that desireth to ravin.*
6 Heb., *sitting.*
7 Heb., *prevent his face.*
8 Or, *by thy sword.*
9 Or, *From men, by thine hand.*
10 Or, *their children are full.*

---

for the expression comp. Job xxxi. 33; and Hos. vi. 7, where the margin has *Adam*.

By the word of thy lips.—Some take this clause closely with the foregoing, and render, "against the word," &c.; but the Authorised Version is better. The Divine standard for action, not the human or worldly, influences the writer.

I have kept me.—Literally, *I for my part have observed ways of violence*. But usage (Prov. ii. 20) almost compels us to understand by this, "I have kept ways of violence," which is impossible here. Hence we have either to give the verb the unusual sense "guard against," or suppose an error in the text.

(5) **Hold up.**—Not, as in the Authorised Version, imperative, which is directly opposed to the context. The psalmist still asserts his innocence. Render:—

    My course kept close in thy tracks,
    My footsteps have not wavered.

(Comp. Job xxiii. 11; Ps. xli. 12.)

Paths.—Literally, *wheel-tracks*.

(6) **I**—is emphatic, "As for me, *I*," &c.

(7) **Shew.**—Literally, *Separate*; but (comp. Ps. iv. 3), from its use to express God's providential care of Israel in distinction to other nations, acquires in addition the idea of wonder and miracle (Exod. viii. 22, ix. 4, xi. 7, &c.). The LXX. and Vulgate, "make thy mercies appear wonderful."

(8) **Apple of the eye.**—Literally, *little man, daughter of the eye*. The *mannikin* is, of course, the reflection seen in the pupil. *Daughter* is either a contraction of a word meaning cavity, or is the common Hebrew idiom which by *son* or *daughter of* expresses relation, as *sons of the bow* = *arrows*. In fact, the curious Hebrew phrase is substantially like the Greek κόρη and Latin *pupa*, or *pupilla*, even to the gender.

Hide me under the shadow of thy wings.—The figure of the sheltering wings of the parent bird, so common in Hebrew literature, generally refers to the eagle or vulture, as in Deut. xxxii. 10, 11, the source of both the beautiful images of the text. Our Lord's use of the figure is made more tender by the English rendering, "hen" (Matt. xxiii. 37). (See Note *New Testament Commentary*.)

(9) **Deadly.**—Literally, *with the soul*, or *life*, or better, as in the Syriac, "against the life," and so *deadly*. Others take it adverbially with the verb, "eagerly compass."

(10) **They are inclosed . . .**—Literally, *Their fat have they shut up*. So LXX. and Vulgate, without indicating the meaning. But the "proudly" of the next clause suggests that "fat" is only a figure for the conceit of prosperity, and as that verb is active, the word *mouth* should be joined with it as object from the next clause, "In their conceit they shut their mouth; (when they do speak) they speak proudly."

(11) **They have now . . .**—Evidently the meaning is, *Wherever we go they surround us like curs*, i.e., they dog our footsteps. But the text is confused.

They have set.—Literally, *they fix their eyes to cast on the earth*, which may mean, "they fix their eyes on me, ready to strike me to the ground." Ewald, "they direct their eyes through the land to strike." But Mr. Burgess suggests a translation at once simple and convincing. He brings the first word back from the next verse, and points it *our blood*, instead of the awkward *his likeness*. He thus gets, "They have set their eyes to shed our blood on the earth." For the Hebrew verb in similar sense, comp. Isa. lxvi. 12.

(12) **Young lion.**—Heb., *kephir*. The Hebrew has seven different names for the lion. Milton's description of Satan naturally recurs to the reader—

    "About them round
    A lion now he stalks with fiery glare."

(13) **Disappoint.**—Rather, *go to meet*, as a champion defending some one.

Which is thy sword.—This thought, making the wicked God's weapons of wrath (Isa. x. 5), is arbitrarily introduced by the Authorised Version, and is quite out of keeping with the context. Translate "*with* thy sword," either understanding a preposition, or treating the accusative as an adverb of manner; as an adverb of time and place it is common. Similarly in the next verse, "*with* thy hand from men of the world."

(14) **Of the world.**—Literally, *of time*. Heb., *cheled*, "that which creeps on," an expression anticipating the New Testament use of *world*. (Comp. Job xxi. 7—14.)

Their portion in this life—contrasts with Ps. xvi. 5.

Thy hid treasure.—*That which thou hast stored up*, which is sometimes in a good sense (Ps. xxxi. 19; Prov. xiii. 22), sometimes in a bad (Job xxi. 19). But ought we not to translate—

    "With thy treasure thou fillest their womb:
    They are full of children."

These two lines are thus in close parallelism, while the last clause of the verse, "and leave," &c., answers to "which have their portion in this life."

A Psalm of PSALMS, XVIII. *Praise to God.*

(15) As for me, I will behold thy face in righteousness: I shall be satisfied, when I awake, with thy likeness.

PSALM XVIII.

To the chief Musician, *A Psalm* of David, the servant of the LORD, who spake unto the LORD the words of *a* this song in the day *that* the LORD delivered him from the hand of all his enemies, and from the hand of Saul: And he said,

(1) I will love thee, O LORD, my strength. (2) The Lord *is* my rock, and my fortress, and my deliverer; my God, ¹my strength, in whom I will trust; my buckler, and the horn of my salvation, *and* my high tower.

(3) I will call upon the LORD, *who is worthy* to be praised: so shall I be saved from mine enemies. (4) *b* The sorrows of death compassed me, and the floods of ²ungodly men made me afraid. (5) The ³sorrows of hell compassed me about:

a 2 Sam. 22.
1 Heb., *my rock.*
b Ps. 116. 3.
2 Heb., *Belial.*
3 Or, *cords.*

---

(15) **I**—is emphatic. The satisfaction of worldly men is in their wealth and family honours, that of the poet in the sun of God's presence and the vision of His righteousness. (Comp. Note, Ps. xi. 7.)

Instead of "likeness," render *image,* or *appearance.* But what does the poet mean by the hope of seeking God when he wakes? Some think of rising to peace after a perplexing trouble; others of health after suffering; others of the sunlight of the Divine grace breaking on the soul. But the literal reference to night in verse 3 seems to ask for the same reference here. Instead of waking to a worldling's hope of a day of feasting and pleasure, the psalmist wakes to the higher and nobler thought that God—who in sleep (so like death, when nothing is visible), has been, as it were, absent—is now again, when he sees once more (LXX.), found at his right hand (comp. end of Ps. xvi.), a conscious presence to him, assuring him of justice and protection. But as in Ps. xvi., so here, we feel that in spite of his subjection to the common notions about death the psalmist may have felt the stirrings of a better hope. Such "cries from the dark," even if they do not prove the possession of a belief in immortality, show how the human heart was already groping its way, however blindly, towards it.

XVIII.

This magnificent ode is David's, if anything at all of David's has come down to us. Its recurrence in 2 Sam. xxii., the mention of the monarch by name in the last verse (see, however, Note), and the general contents, in the eyes of all but one or two critics*, bear out the tradition of the title.

If no other literary legacy had been left by the Hebrew race, we should have from this psalm a clear conception of the character of its poetic genius. Its wealth of metaphor, its power of vivid word-painting, its accurate observation of nature, its grandeur and force of imagination, all meet us here; but above all, the fact that the bard of Israel wrote under the mighty conviction of the power and presence of Jehovah. The phenomena of the natural world appealed to his imagination as to that of poets generally, but with this addition, that they were all manifestations of a supreme glory and goodness behind them.

In rhythm the poem is as fine as in matter.

Title.—See 2 Sam. xxii. 1. The differences are such as might be expected between a piece in a collection of hymns and the same introduced into an historical book.

(1) **I will love thee.**—Better, *Dearly do I love thee.* The line is wanting in Samuel.

---

* Grätz, the latest commentator, allows part of this psalm to be David's.

My strength.—This strikes the keynote of the whole poem. The strong, mighty God is the object in David's thought throughout. It is a warrior's song, and his conception of Jehovah is a warrior's conception.

(2) **Rock.**—Better here, *cliff,* keeping "rock" for the next clause. In the first figure the ideas of height and shelter, in the second of broad-based and enduring strength, are predominant.

Fortress.—Properly, *mountain castle.* We have the joint figure of the lofty and precipitous cliff with the castle on its crest, a reminiscence—as, in fact, is every one in this "towering of epithets"—of scenes and events in David's early life.

My God . . .—Better, *my God, my rock, I trust in Him.* God is here *El,* "the strong one." In Samuel, "God of my rock."

Horn of my salvation.—The allusion seems to be not to a means of attack, like the horn of an animal, but to a mountain peak (called "horn" in all languages—so κέρας, Xen. *Anab.* v. 6; "Cornua Parnassi," Statius, *Theb.* v. 532; and so in Hebrew, Isa. v. 1, see margin), such as often afforded David a safe retreat. Render "my peak of safety."

High tower.—The LXX. and Vulgate have "helper." (Comp. Ps. ix. 9.) The word comes in so abruptly, that doubtless the addition in Samuel, "and my refuge, my Saviour, thou savest me from violence," was part of the original hymn, completing the rhythm.

(3) Presents a trifling verbal variation from Samuel.

(4) **The sorrows of death.**—The Hebrew word may mean either *birth pangs* (LXX. and Acts ii. 24, where see Note, *New Testament Commentary*), or *cords.* The figure of the hunter in the next verse, "the snares of death," determines its meaning there to be *cords* (see margin). It is best, therefore, to keep the same rendering here: but there can be little doubt that the version in Samuel, *breakers,* or *waves,* is the true one, from the parallelism—

"Waves of death compassed me,
And billows of Belial terrified me."

For *Belial,* see Deut. xiii. 13. Here the parallelism fixes its meaning, "ruin." For the ideas of peril and destruction, connected by the Hebrews with waves and floods, comp. verse 16, also Pss. xxxii. 6, xlii. 7, lxix. 1. Doubtless the tradition of the Flood and of the Red Sea helped to strengthen the apprehensions natural in a country where the river annually overflowed its banks, and where a dry ravine might at any moment become a dangerous flood. The hatred of the sea arose from quite another cause—viz., the dread of it as a highway for invasion.

(5) **Hell.**—Heb., *sheôl.* (See Note on Ps. vi. 5.)

Prevented—*i.e.,* suddenly seized upon. The poet seems to feel the cords already tightening on his limbs.

the snares of death prevented me. (6) In my distress I called upon the LORD, and cried unto my God: he heard my voice out of his temple, and my cry came before him, *even* into his ears. (7) Then the earth shook and trembled;¹ the foundations also of the hills moved and were shaken, because he was wroth. (8) There went up a smoke ¹ out of his nostrils, and fire out of his mouth devoured: coals were kindled by it. (9) He bowed the heavens also, and came down: and darkness *was* under his feet. (10) And he rode upon a cherub, and did fly: yea, he did fly upon the wings of the wind. (11) He made darkness his secret place; his pavilion round about him *were* dark waters *and* thick clouds of the skies. (12) At the brightness *that was* before him his thick clouds passed, hail *stones* and coals of fire. (13) The LORD also thundered in the heavens, and the

¹ Heb., *by his.*

He is not dead yet, but like to them who go down to *sheôl*. This verse has one verbal difference from Samuel.

(6) **Out of his temple.**—Rather, *palace*—plainly, as in Pss. xi. 4, xxix. 9, the heavenly abode of Jehovah.

My cry.—In Samuel only, " my cry in his ears."

(7) **The earth shook.**—The sudden burst of the storm is the Divine answer to the sufferer's prayer. For similar manifestations comp. Ps. lxviii. 7, 8, lxxvii. 14–20; Amos ix. 5; Micah i. 3; Hab. iii. 4; but here the colours are more vivid, and the language more intense. In fact, the whole realm of poetry cannot show a finer feeling for nature in her wrath. We first hear the rumbling of the earth, probably earthquake preceding the storm (for volcanic phenomena of Palestine see Stanley's *Sinai and Palestine*, 124), or possibly only its distant threatening. Comp.

"Earth groans as if beneath a heavy load."
BYRON.

Foundations also of the hills.—In Sam., " of the heavens"—*i.e.*, the hills, called also "the pillars of heaven" (Job. xxvi. 11).

(8) **A smoke.**—Now the thunder-cloud forms—smoke, as it were, from the nostrils of God (comp. Ps. lxxiv. 1; Deut. xxix. 20: the literal rendering is, " there ascended smoke in his nostrils ")—and intermittent flashes of lightning dart forth and play about the distant summits, seeming to devour everything in its path. (Comp. the expression " lambent flame.")

Coals were kindled by it.—Rather, *flaming coals blazed from it*.

(9) **Darkness.**—Better, *black cloud*. The dark masses of rain-cloud are now gathered, and bend to the earth under the majestic tread of God. (Comp. Nahum i. 3, " and the clouds are the dust of his feet." (Comp. Ps. cxliv. 5.)

(10) **Cherub.**—See Exod. xxv. 19. This passage alone would show how naturally the idea of winged attendants on the Divine Being grew out of the phenomena of cloud and storm. No doubt many features of the developed conception were derived from contact with Assyrian art, but for the poetry of this passage we have only to think of those giant pinions into which cloud so often shapes itself, this clause being in close parallelism with " wings of the wind." The variation in Samuel, "appeared" for "did fly," is, no doubt, a transcriber's error. For the picture we may compare Oceanus' approach in *Prometheus Vinctus* :—

"On the back of the quick-winged bird I glode,
And I bridled him in
With the will of a God."
MRS. BROWNING'S *translation*.

It has been, however, conjectured that for *kherûb* we should read *rekhûb*, " chariot," as in Ps. civ. 3. Comp.

"And rushed forth on my chariot of wings manifold."—*Ibid.*

(11) **Secret place.**—Better, *veil*. Comp. Job xxii. 14; Lam. iii. 44. A better arrangement of the members of this verse is, *He made darkness His veil round about Him; His tent He made of dark waters and black clouds*. Literally, *darkness of waters and blacknesses of clouds*. (Comp. Ps. xcvii. 2; Job xxxvi. 29.) In Samuel, instead of " blacknesses" of clouds, the expression used is " bendings," or " collectings," and the parallelism is marred by the omission of " his veil."

Always present to the Hebrew imagination, God is still invisible, veiled by thick clouds, and far withdrawn in His own ineffable brightness.

This verse gives suggestion of that momentary lull so common before the final fury of a storm bursts. In the Hebrew imagery Jehovah stays His winged car, and draws round Him, as if to take up His abode within them, thick curtains of cloud.

"We often see, against some storm,
A silence in the heavens, the rack stand still,
The bold winds speechless, and the orb below
As hush as death."—SHAKSPEARE: *Hamlet*.

(12) **At the brightness.**—This is obscure. Literally, *From the brightness before him his clouds passed through* (Heb., *avar*—LXX., διῆλθον; Vulg., *transierunt*) *hail and fiery coals*. In Samuel it is " From the brightness before him flamed fiery coals," which is the description we should expect, and, doubtless, gives the sense we are to attach to our text. Through the dark curtain of clouds the lightnings dart like emanations from the Divine brightness which they hide. The difficulty arises from the position of *avaiv*, " his clouds," which looks like a subject rather than an object to *avrû*. It has been conjectured, from comparison with Samuel, that the word has been inserted through error, from its likeness to the verb. If retained it must be rendered as object, " Out of the brightness of his presence there passed through his clouds hail and fiery coals." And some obscurity of language is pardonable in a description of phenomena so overpowering and bewildering as " a tempest dropping fire." A modern poet touches this feeling :—

"Then fire was sky, and sky fire,
And both one brief ecstasy,
Then ashes."—R. BROWNING, *Easter Day*.

In the Authorised Version the thought is of a sudden clearing of the heavens, which is not true to nature, and the clause " hailstones and coals of fire " comes in as an exclamation, as in the next verse. But there it is probably an erroneous repetition, being wanting in Sam. and in the LXX. version of the psalm. Notice how the feeling of the terrible fury of the storm is heightened by the mention of " hail," so rare in Palestine.

(13) **In the heavens.**—The version in Samuel is "from the heavens," which is better. For the thunder as God's voice see Ps. xxix. 3, and Note.

for His Manifold   PSALMS, XVIII.   *and Marvellous Blessings.*

Highest gave his voice; hail *stones* and coals of fire. (14) Yea, he sent out his arrows, and scattered them; and he shot out lightnings, and discomfited them. (15) Then the channels of waters were seen, and the foundations of the world were discovered at thy rebuke, O LORD, at the blast of the breath of thy nostrils. (16) He sent from above, he took me, he drew me out of ¹many waters. (17) He delivered me from my strong enemy, and from them which hated me: for they were too strong for me.

(18) They prevented me in the day of my calamity: but the LORD was my stay. (19) He brought me forth also into a large place; he delivered me, because he delighted in me.

(20) The LORD rewarded me according to my righteousness; according to the cleanness of my hands hath he recompensed me. (21) For I have kept the ways of the LORD, and have not wickedly departed from my God. (22) For all his judgments *were* before me, and I did not put away his statutes from me. (23) I was also upright ²before him, and I kept myself from mine iniquity. (24) Therefore hath the LORD recompensed me according to my righteousness, according to the cleanness of my hands ³in his eyesight.

(25) With the merciful thou wilt shew thyself merciful; with an upright man thou wilt shew thyself upright; (26) with the pure thou wilt shew thyself pure; and with the froward thou wilt ⁴shew

1 Or, *great waters.*
2 Heb., *with.*
3 Heb., *before his eyes.*
4 Or, *wrestle.*

---

(14) **He sent out.**—In the majesty of the storm we have almost forgotten its cause, the Divine wrath against the enemies of the poet. They are abruptly recalled to our remembrance in the suffix ("them") of the verbs in this verse. So the LXX. and Vulg. Many ancient interpreters, however, understood by *them* "the lightnings," while Ewald would carry the pronoun on to the "waters" in the next verse. Instead of "shot" (*rab*) many render as if it were the adjective "many," "his numerous lightnings." But comp. Ps. cxliv. 6 and the verse in Samuel.

(15) **The channels.**—The description of the storm ends with the fury of the wind and the effects of the tempest on the earth's surface. Comp. Ps. xxix., and Milton:—

> "Either tropic now
> 'Gan thunder and both ends of heaven the clouds,
> From many a horrid rift abortive pour'd
> Fierce rain with lightning mix'd, water with fire,
> In ruin reconciled; nor slept the winds
> Within their stony caves, but rush'd abroad
> From the four hinges of the world and fell
> On the vex'd wilderness."
> —Par. Reg. iv. 409-416.

Here, to suit the poet's purpose (see next verse), the rage of the tempest is made to spend itself on the water-floods. The "channels" are either torrent beds (Isa. viii. 7; Ps. xlii. 1; Job vi. 15), or as in Samuel (where for "waters" the text has "sea") the depths of ocean. (Comp. Jonah ii. 5.)

(16) **He drew me.**—By an exquisite transition from the real to the figurative the poet conceives of these parted waters as the "floods of affliction" (verse 5), from which Jehovah has rescued him by means of the very storm which was sent, in answer to his prayer, to overwhelm his enemies. Render at once more literally and forcibly, "He laid hold of me and drew me out of great waters." The conception undoubtedly is that the "gates of death" are under these floods, and those being now parted, the sufferer can be reached and rescued.

Verses 17, 18, 19 show trifling variations between the two copies of the psalm.

(18) **Prevented.**—Better, *fell upon me unawares*. See this use of the verb, generally however used in a good sense, in verse 5.

(19) **A large place.**—Comp. Ps. iv. 1. But there is direct historical allusion to the settlement of Israel in Canaan, as will be seen by a comparison of the Hebrew with Exod. iii. 8, and Num. xiv. 8.

(20—23) For this protestation of innocence comp. Pss. vii., xvii. and Job, *passim*. Self-righteous pride and vindication of one's character under calumny are very different things. If taken of the nation at large, comp. Num. xxiii. 21. Here, also, the text in Samuel offers one or two trifling variations from ours.

(25—27) It is better to change all the futures into our present. We cannot explain this description of God's attitude to man, as if the poet were merely dealing with the conception of the Divine formed in the breast. No doubt his words are amply true in this sense. The human heart makes its God like itself, and to the pure and just He will be a pure and just God, to the cruel and unjust, cruel and unjust. But the definite mention of recompense in verse 24, and the reference to active interposition in behalf of the just in verse 27, leave us no option but to understand by "shew thyself" in verses 25 and 26, not an inward conception, but an external manifestation. It is, in fact, nothing more than a re-statement of the truth of which the history of Pharaoh is the most signal historic declaration, and which we maintain whenever we speak of the natural consequences of sin as retributive justice, the truth which is summed up in the text, "whatsoever a man soweth that shall he also reap." We must at the same time remember that the form of the statement in the psalm is due to the view current in Israel before the development of the conception of Satanic agency, that all suggestions, evil as well as good, came from the mind of the Supreme Disposer of events.

(25) **Man.**—The text of Samuel has "hero" (*gebôr* instead of *gebar*).

(26) **Froward . . . froward.**—The use of this one word to render two different Hebrew terms is so far correct, as they both come from roots meaning primarily *to twist*. Both are combined in Prov. viii. 8, "froward (margin, *twisted*) or perverse," and both are contrasted with "righteousness." Plainly the metaphor might apply either to the character itself, "twisted round," "awry," "perverse," or to the line of conduct pursued, "bent," "crooked," or "wrong," the opposite of "straight," or

thyself froward. ⁽²⁷⁾ For thou wilt save the afflicted people; but wilt bring down high looks. ⁽²⁸⁾ For thou wilt light my ¹candle: the LORD my God will enlighten my darkness. ⁽²⁹⁾ For by thee I have ²run through a troop; and by my God have I leaped over a wall.

⁽³⁰⁾ *As for* God, his way *is* perfect: *ᵃthe word of the LORD is ³tried: he is a buckler to all those that trust in him.

⁽³¹⁾ ᵇ For who *is* God save the LORD? or who *is* a rock save our God? ⁽³²⁾ *It is* God that girdeth me with strength, and maketh my way perfect. ⁽³³⁾ He maketh my feet like hinds' *feet*, and setteth me upon my high places. ⁽³⁴⁾ He teacheth my hands to war, so that a bow of steel is broken by mine arms.

⁽³⁵⁾ Thou hast also given me the shield of thy salvation: and thy right hand hath holden me up, and ⁴thy gentleness hath made me great. ⁽³⁶⁾ Thou hast enlarged my steps under me, that ⁵my feet did not slip. ⁽³⁷⁾ I have pursued mine enemies, and overtaken them: neither did I turn again till they were consumed. ⁽³⁸⁾ I have wounded them that they were not able to rise: they are fallen under my feet.

⁽³⁹⁾ For thou hast girded me with strength unto the battle: thou hast ⁶subdued under me those that rose up against me. ⁽⁴⁰⁾ Thou hast also given me the necks of mine enemies; that I might destroy them that hate me. ⁽⁴¹⁾ They cried, but *there was* none to save *them: even* unto the LORD, but he answered them not. ⁽⁴²⁾ Then did I beat them small as the dust before the wind: I did cast them out as the dirt in the

---

1 Or, *lamp.*
2 Or, *broken.*
a Ps. 12. 6, & 119. 140; Prov. 30. 5.
3 Or, *refined.*
b Deut. 32. 31, 39; 1 Sam. 2. 2; Ps. 86. 8; Isa. 45. 5.
4 Or, *with thy meekness thou hast multiplied me.*
5 Heb., *mine ancles.*
6 Heb., *caused to bow.*

"right." "Froward" = *from ward* (opposite to "toward"), seems to have more of the latter idea, but may combine both—*a disposition turned away from good.* The poet therefore says, "God will turn away from those who turn away from him," a thought which even with the Christian revelation we must admit true, for still it is true that—

"He that shuts love out, in turn shall be
Shut out from love."—TENNYSON.

⁽²⁷⁾ **High looks.**—See variation in Samuel.
The afflicted people.—Better, *afflicted folk*, with no distinctive reference to Israel, except, of course, when the poem became adapted for congregational use.

⁽²⁸⁾ **For thou wilt.**—Better, *Thou makest bright my lamp.* In Samuel, "It is thou Jehovah who art my lamp." This obvious metaphor is common in Hebrew, as in all literature. Light is an emblem of prosperity, happiness, or life itself. (Comp. Job xviii. 6, xxi. 17; Prov. xiii. 9, &c.). It happens to be used very frequently of David and his family (1 Kings xi. 36, xv. 4; 2 Kings viii. 19). Comp. Ps. cxxxii. 17.

⁽²⁹⁾ Better with the verbs in the present—

"For by thee I scatter a troop,
By thee I scale walls."

A graphic reminiscence of warlike exploits. Some, however, read from Samuel "break down," instead of "leap over."

⁽³⁰⁾ **Tried.**—"Sterling gold," not dross. (Comp. Ps. xii. 6; and for "shield," Ps. v. 12.) Prov. xxx. 5 seems to be taken from this verse.

⁽³¹⁾ Comp. Deut. xxxii. 31, where we see that "rock" was a common term among the tribes of Canaan for their divinities. Notice some trifling variations in Samuel.

⁽³²⁾ The verse should run on closely from the last. The italics spoil it.
Girdeth.—The importance of the girdle in a country where the dress was loose and flowing is shown by many passages of Scripture. It is essential to the warrior as here (comp. Ephes. vi. 14, and the Greek expression, "to be girt" = *to be armed*), but also for all active exertion.
Way.—Here, not of conduct, but the *military path*, the march. Notice the variation in Samuel.

⁽³³⁾ This verse is borrowed in Hab. iii. 19. For *swiftness* as an essential of a warrior in Oriental esteem comp. 2 Sam. i. 23, and the invariable epithet in Homer's *Iliad*, "swift-footed Achilles." For "hind" comp. Gen. xlix. 21. Observe "his feet" in Samuel.
My high places.—With allusion to the mountain fortresses the poet had scaled and won.

⁽³⁴⁾ **So that a bow.**—Better, *and mine arms bend a bow of copper.* For the *copper bow* comp. Job xx. 24. *Nechushah*, χαλκὸς, is certainly not *steel*, whether the custom of hardening iron was known to the Jews or not (see Jer. xv. 12, and art. "Steel," in Smith's *Biblical Dict.*). The LXX. and Vulgate have, "thou hast made mine arms a bow of copper." For this test of strength we naturally compare the famous bow of Ulysses—

"So the great master drew the mighty bow,
And drew with ease."—*Odyssey*, POPE'S *trans.*

⁽³⁵⁾ **Thy gentleness.**—Or, *meekness*, as in margin. We cannot afford to sacrifice this striking foreshadowing of His saying of Himself, "I am meek and lowly," to the scare of a word like *anthropomorphism.* Why be afraid to speak of the Divine Being as *meek* any more than as *jealous.* The LXX. and Vulgate have "discipline," probably through this timidity.

⁽³⁶⁾ **Thou hast enlarged my steps.**— Comp. Ps. xxxi. 8, which explains the phrase; also verse 19 above.

^(37–40) Another retrospective glance of the poet over his past wars. Notice slight variations in Samuel.

⁽⁴⁰⁾ **Thou hast also given.**—Literally, *and as to mine enemies, thou gavest to me the back*, which either means "turned to flight so that only their backs were visible" (Jer. xviii. 17 and Ps. xxi. 12), or alludes to the common symbolism of defeat—trampling on an enemy's neck.

⁽⁴¹⁾ **Cried.**—Sam. xxii. has "looked."
⁽⁴²⁾ **Before the wind.**—In Samuel, the weaker "of the earth."
Cast them out—*i.e.*, sweep them before me. In Samuel "stamp and tread them out." So LXX. here "grind," or "pound."

streets. (43)Thou hast delivered me from the strivings of the people; *and* thou hast made me the head of the heathen: a people *whom* I have not known shall serve me. (44)¹As soon as they hear of me, they shall obey me: ²the strangers shall ³ ⁴submit themselves unto me. (45)The strangers shall fade away, and be afraid out of their close places.

(46) The LORD liveth; and blessed *be* my rock; and let the God of my salvation be exalted. (47)*It is* God that ⁵avengeth me, and ⁶subdueth the people under me. (48)He delivereth me from mine enemies: yea, thou liftest me up above those that rise up against me: thou hast delivered me from the ⁷violent man.

(49)ᵃTherefore will I ⁸give thanks unto thee, O LORD, among the heathen, and sing praises unto thy name.

(50)Great deliverance giveth he to his king; and sheweth mercy to his anointed, to David, and to his seed for evermore.

PSALM XIX.

To the chief Musician, A Psalm of David.

(1) The ᵇ heavens declare the glory of

---

1 Heb., *At the hearing of the ear.*
2 Heb., *the sons of the stranger.*
3 Or, *yield feigned obedience.*
4 Heb., *lie.*
5 Heb., *giveth avengements for me.*
6 Or, *destroyeth.*
7 Heb., *man of violence.*
a Rom. 15. 9.
8 Or, *confess.*
b Gen. 1. 6.

---

(43) **People.**—The parallelism favours the interpretation which takes "people" as equivalent to *peoples*—the Gentiles. But as in Samuel it is "my people," explain it of the early political troubles of David. Notice also in Samuel "preserved," instead of "made."

(44) **As soon as**—*i.e.*, at the bare mention of my victories. An actual instance is recorded (2 Sam. viii. 9, *seq.*). For the expression, comp. Job xlii. 5.

The strangers shall.—See margin. More literally, *come with flattery*. In Samuel the two clauses are transposed and slightly varied.

(45) **Fade away**—*i.e.*, wither like vegetation before a scorching blast.

Be afraid out of their close places.—Better, *come trembling out of their castles*. LXX. and Vulgate have "grew old and came limping from their paths."

(46—50) The psalm concludes with a burst of joyous praise, in which the previous figures are recalled in brief touches.

(49) In Rom. xv. 9, St. Paul quotes this verse, together with Deut. xxxii. 43 and Ps. cxvii. 1, as proof that salvation was not in God's purpose confined to the Jews. It seems almost too magnificent a thought in David, that he could draw the surrounding nations within the circle of the religion as he had drawn them within the dominion of Israel. Nor is it likely that an individual would use such an expression. Israel as a nation might praise God "among the nations." Therefore this verse is adduced as an argument by those who assign a later date to the psalm. But perhaps we are only to think of the nations as brought (see verse 44) an *unwilling* audience of the praises which the conqueror raises to his God for the strength that had subdued them.

(50) This verse is by many treated as a late liturgical addition to the hymn. The change to the third person is certainly somewhat suggestive of this, but by no means conclusive.

The question of the relation of the two copies of this hymn to each other is far too complicated and difficult for discussion here. Each has been again and again claimed as the original. The best explanation of the variations is that the compositions were independent copies of some original, and that the psalm, like many others, was altered in preparation for the choir use.

XIX.

The abrupt change in rhythm, and apparently in thought, at verse 7 of this poem suggests a compilation from two originally distinct pieces. This view, it is true, is not supported by any ancient texts or versions, and, among modern scholars, there are some of eminence who still maintain the original unity. They urge that the psalm merely repeats what is the fundamental principle of the Theocracy, which is expressly testified by the Old Testament from the earliest times—the identity of the God of Revelation with the Creator of the universe. But this gives a very imperfect, and hardly a correct, explanation of the psalm. For the second part does not treat the moral law as a revelation of God to man, but as a revelation to man of his duties, and implies that man continually needs forgiveness for lapsing from the road of right. It would be truer to the spirit of the Old Testament to urge that a poet, thrown by the contemplation of the glory of the heavens into a state of religious emotion, naturally passes on to the Law where he has had prepared for him a guide and help in his religion. But for the original separation of the two pieces, the versification, the tone, the poetic feeling all plead. It was, however, an inspired moment when they were united, and thus made to suggest the deep truth that man's obedience to the Divine will, though it cannot be so unswerving as that of the heavens, but is inconstant, and often fails, yet is of a higher order, and is fruitful of yet higher and nobler praise than all the evidence of power and majesty in the outward works of God. The glory of conscious above that of unconscious obedience did not definitely present itself, perhaps, to the mind of him who completed the poem, but it is latent there. The sun leaping forth from his eastern tent to flame through his glorious day, knows nothing of the self-questionings and fears felt by God's human servant trying to do His will. It is only by a bold metaphor that Wordsworth can connect the idea of duty with the law which "preserves the stars from wrong." More in harmony with the feeling suggested by the psalm is the answer put by another poet into the mouth of nature to console the human soul ashamed of its "struggling task'd morality" in view of the serene service of earth and sky—

> "'Ah! child,' she cried, 'that strife Divine,
> Whence was it, for it is not mine?
> There is no effort on my brow;
> I do not strive, I do not weep;
> I rush with the swift spheres, and glow
> In joy, and when I will, I sleep.'"
> MATTHEW ARNOLD.

The Davidic authorship of the first part of the psalm is hardly to be questioned.

(1) **The heavens declare.**—Better, *the heavens are telling*. The poet is even now gazing at the sky, not philosophising on a familiar natural phenomenon,

God's Glory   PSALMS, XIX.   *Shown in Creation,*

God; and the firmament sheweth his handywork. ⁽²⁾ Day unto day uttereth speech, and night unto night sheweth knowledge. ⁽³⁾ *There is* no speech nor language, ^{1 2} *where* their voice is not heard. ⁽⁴⁾ *^a* ³ Their line is gone out through all the earth, and their words to the end of the world. In them hath he set a tabernacle for the sun, ⁽⁵⁾ which *is* as a bridegroom coming out of his chamber, *and* rejoiceth as a strong man to run a race. ⁽⁶⁾ His going forth *is* from the end of the heaven, and his circuit unto the ends of it: and there is nothing hid from the heat thereof.

¹ Or, *without these their voice is heard.*

² Heb., *without their voice heard.*

a Rom. 10. 18.

³ Or, *Their rule,* or, *direction.*

---

nor is he merely enjoying beauty. Not only is his æsthetic faculty satisfied, but his spirit, his religious nature is moved. He has an immediate apprehension, an intuition of God. He is looking on the freshness of the morning, and all he sees is telling of God, bringing God before him. This constitutes the essence of the greater part of Hebrew poetry. This is the inspiration of the bard of Israel—a *religious* inspiration. The lower, the æsthetic perception of beauty, is ready at every moment to pass into the higher, the religious emotion. All truly great poetry partakes of this elevation—Hebrew poetry in its highest degree. Some lines from Coleridge's "Hymn before Sunrise in the Vale of Chamouni" not only supplies a modern example, but explains the moral, or rather spiritual process, involved—

> "O dread and silent mount! I gazed upon thee
> Till thou, still present to the bodily sense,
> Did'st vanish from my thought; entranced in prayer,
> *I worshipped the Invisible alone.*"

(See an article on "God in Nature and in History," in the *Expositor* for March, 1881.)

⁽²⁾ **Uttereth.**—Literally, *pours out,* or *makes to well up,* like a fountain, undoubtedly in reference to the light streaming forth.

Sheweth.—Literally, *breathes out;* perhaps with reference to the cool evening breeze, so welcome in the East. (See Cant. ii. 17, Note.) Notice that it is not here the heavens that are telling (as in verse 1) the tale of God's glory to man, or "to the listening earth," as in Addison's well-known hymn, but day tells its successor day, and night whispers to night, so handing on, as if from parent to son, the great news.

⁽³⁾ **There is no speech.**—The literal rendering is *Not speech, not words, their voice is not heard.* Explaining this is (1) the English version (Bible and Prayer Book) and (if intelligible at all) the LXX. and Vulg.: "There is no speech nor language without their (the heavens') speech being heard (*i.e.*, understood)." But this gives an inadmissible sense to *davar,* which does not mean language, but a spoken word. Besides, it was not a likely thought for the psalmist, that the Divine tradition of the heavens, while it travels over the whole earth, would be everywhere intelligible. (2) "It is not speech, it is not words *whose* voice is inaudible," *i.e.*, unintelligible, but, on the contrary, it is a manifestation to all the world. But the parallelism is against this. The line "their voice is not heard" is but the rhythmic echo of "there is no speech nor word." (3) We therefore keep close to the literal rendering, *There is no speech, there are no* (uttered) *words, their voice is inaudible;* understanding the poet to say, that the manifestation of the Creator's glory, which he has just imagined the heavens proclaiming, and of which each succeeding day hands on the tale, is not made in audible words. The communication of the sky is *eloquent,* but mute; its voice is for the heart and emotion, not the ear. So Addison—

> "What though in solemn silence all
> Move round this dark terrestrial ball,
> What though no real voice or sound
> Amidst their radiant orbs be found?
> In reason's ear they all rejoice
> And utter forth a glorious voice,
> For ever singing as they shine
> The hand that made us is Divine."

⁽⁴⁾ **Their line.**—Heb., *kav,* a cord, used of a plummet line (Zech. i. 16); a measuring cord (Jer. xxxi. 39, where also same verb, *gone forth*). In Isa. xxviii. 10, the word is used ethically for a definition or law. But neither of these seems very appropriate here. The verse wants *sound* or *voice,* and words of this intention actually appear in the LXX., Vulg., Symmachus, Jerome, and the Syriac.

The use which St. Paul makes of these words (Rom. x. 18) is as natural as striking. The march of truth has always been compared to the spread of light. But the allegorical interpretation based on the quotation, making the heavens a figure of the Church and the sun of the Gospel, loses the force and beauty of the Apostle's application.

In them hath . . .—This clause is not only rightly joined to verse 4, but concludes a stanza: the relative in the next verse of the Authorised Version mars the true construction.

A tabernacle.—The tent-chamber into which the sun retired after his day's journey, and from which he started in the morn, Aurora, or dawn (according to Grecian mythology) drawing back the curtains for his departure, was naturally a conception common to all nations. That the phenomena of sunset should engage the poet's attention before those of sunrise was inevitable in a race who reckoned "the evening and the morning were the first day." The LXX. and Vulg. completely spoil the picture by rendering "he hath pitched his tent in the sun."

⁽⁵⁾ **Which is.**—Better, *and he is.* The suddenness of the Oriental sunrise is finely caught in the image of the uplifted tent-curtain and appearance of the radiant hero ("strong man;" Heb., *gibbor.* Comp. Judges v. 31). This want of twilight, this absence of silent preparation for the supreme moment, distinguishes Eastern songs of sunrise from the poetry of the West. There are no musterings of "mute companies of changeful clouds," no "avant couriers of the light," no "grey lines fretting the clouds as messengers of day." Unheralded, unannounced, the sun leaps forth in all his splendour—a young bridegroom with the joy of the wedding-day still on his countenance, a hero leaping forth on his path of conquest and glory. How different the suggested feeling of this from the wistful tenderness of Milton's dawn coming forth "with pilgrim steps in amice grey;" or Shakspeare's "morn in russet clad," that "walks o'er the dew" of the high eastern hill.

Chamber.—Heb., *chuphah,* a marriage chamber or bed (Joel ii. 16). In later Hebrew the canopy

And in   PSALMS, XX.   *His Law.*

(7) The ¹law of the LORD *is* perfect, ²converting the soul: the testimony of the LORD *is* sure, making wise the simple. (8) The statutes of the LORD *are* right, rejoicing the heart: the commandment of the LORD *is* pure, enlightening the eyes. (9) The fear of the LORD *is* clean, enduring for ever: the judgments of the LORD *are* ³true *and* righteous altogether. (10) More to be desired *are they* than gold,ª yea, than much fine gold: ᵇsweeter also than honey and ⁴the honeycomb. (11) Moreover by them is thy servant warned: *and* in keeping of them *there is* great reward.

(12) Who can understand *his* errors? cleanse thou me from secret *faults*. (13) Keep back thy servant also from presumptuous *sins*; let them not have dominion over me: then shall I be upright, and I shall be innocent from ⁵the great transgression. (14) Let the words of my mouth, and the meditation of my heart, be acceptable in thy sight, O LORD, ⁶my strength, and my redeemer.

PSALM XX.

To the chief Musician, A Psalm of David.

(1) The LORD hear thee in the day of

1 Or, *doctrine*.
2 Or, *restoring*.
3 Heb. *truth*.
ª Ps. 119. 72, 127; Prov. 8, 19.
ᵇ Ps. 119. 103.
4 Heb., *the dropping of honeycombs*.
5 Or, *much*.
6 Heb., *my rock*.

---

carried over the wedded pair, or even the marriage itself.

Rejoiceth.—Literally, *leaps for joy*.

A race.—Better, *his race*, i.e., his daily course or journey.

(7) **The law.**—The ear catches even in the English the change of rhythm, which is as marked as the change of subject. Instead of the free lyric movement of the preceding verse, we come suddenly upon the most finished specimen of didactic poetry in regular metre, exhibiting a perfect balance of expression as well as of thought, so perfect in the original, that in verses 7—9 the number of words is the same in each clause. In each clause, too, the Law, under one or another of its many names and aspects, is praised, first for its essential character, then for its results.

The law . . . . the testimony.—These are collective terms embracing, under different regards, the whole body of statutes and precepts in the Jewish code. The law, *tôrah*, means in its primary use "instruction," and therefore is used of prophecy (Isa. i. 10, viii. 16), but here undoubtedly bears its common and more limited sense. Testimony, from a root meaning "to repeat," suggests the solemn earnestness and insistance of the Divine commands.

The description "perfect" and "sure" suggests the lofty ideal prescribed by the Law, and the reliance which the Hebrew might place upon it as a rule of conduct. The word "simple" is generally used in a bad sense, but here has its primary meaning, "open," "ingenuous," "impressible," easily led either towards folly or wisdom.

(8) **Right.**—Here in its original sense of "straight," or direct. A fine moral insight suggested this touch. The road of duty, when plain and unmistakable, inspires a sense of gladness, even if it be difficult and dangerous.

> "Stern Lawgiver, yet thou dost wear
> The Godhead's most benignant grace;
> Nor know we anything so fair
> As is the smile upon thy face.
> Flowers laugh before thee on their beds,
> And fragrance in thy footing treads."
>   WORDSWORTH'S *Ode to Duty*.

Enlightening the eyes.—Not here as in Ps. xiii. 3 (see Note) physically, but morally (comp. Ps. cxix. 105); the whole nature of one who lives in the light of truth is illuminated.

(9) **The fear of the Lord.**—Here plainly not a moral quality of the individual, but, as in Prov. xv. 33 (comp. Deut. xvii. 19), religion, the service demanded by the Law, which, being "pure and undefiled," endures, while the false systems of idolatrous nations perish. Based on the eternal principle of right, the judgments of God, it is eternal as they are.

(10) **Honeycomb.**—(See margin.) The honey that drops from the comb is the finest and purest.

(11) **Warned.**—Better, *illuminated, instructed*.

(12) His eulogium on the Law was not Pharisaic or formal, for the poet instantly gives expression to his sense of his own inability to keep it. If before we were reminded of St. Paul's, "The law is holy, and the commandment holy, and just, and good," (Rom. vii. 12), his own spiritual experience, contained in the same chapter, is here recalled: "For the good that I would I do not: but the evil that I would not, that I do."

Who can understand.—In the original the abruptness of the question is very marked and significant. *Errors who marks? From unconscious ones clear me*, i.e., pronounce me innocent, not cleanse, as in Authorised Version.

(13) **Presumptuous sin.**—The Heb., from root meaning to "boil up" or "over," is properly masculine, and always elsewhere means proud or arrogant men. (So Symmachus and Aquila.) Hence here explain, "Keep thy servant from the companionship of arrogant men, so that they may not get dominion over me, and lead me away from thy Law."

The great transgression.—Rather, *a great transgression*, though even without the article it is possible the particular sin of *idolatry* is intended.

(14) **Meditation.**—Heb., *higgaion*. (See Pss. ix. 16, xcii. 3.)

XX.

This psalm is addressed to a king going to battle, and was plainly arranged for part-singing in the Temple. The congregation lead off with a prayer for the monarch's success (1—5). The priest, or the king himself, as priest, after watching the successful performance of the sacrificial rites, pronounces his confidence of the victory (6—8), upon which the shout, "God save the king!" is raised by the whole host, which acclaim again sinks down into the calmer prayer, "May he hear us when we cry."

The transparent language of the poem and its simple arrangement, the smooth symmetry of the rhythm, and the quiet advance in thought, are all in favour of its being a hymn carefully composed for a public occasion and not a poetical effusion of the feelings of the moment. It is not therefore necessary to discuss the authorship or the question of what particular king it was intended

A Psalm of Prayer PSALMS, XXI. *for Blessing on the King.*

trouble; the name of the God of Jacob ¹defend thee. (2) Send ²thee help from the sanctuary, and ³strengthen thee out of Zion; (3) Remember all thy offerings, and ⁴accept thy burnt sacrifice: Selah. (4) Grant thee according to thine own heart, and fulfil all thy counsel.

(5) We will rejoice in thy salvation, and in the name of our God we will set up *our* banners: the LORD fulfil all thy petitions.

(6) Now know I that the LORD saveth his anointed; he will hear him ⁵from his holy heaven ⁶with the saving strength of his right hand. (7) Some *trust* in chariots, and some in horses: but we will remember the name of the LORD our God. (8) They are brought down and fallen: but we are risen, and stand upright.

(9) Save, LORD: let the king hear us when we call.

1 Heb., *set thee on an high place.*
2 Heb., *thy help.*
3 Heb., *support thee.*
4 Heb., *turn to ashes: or, make fat.*
5 Heb., *from the heaven of his holiness.*
6 Heb., *by the strength of the salvation of his right hand.*

PSALM XXI.

To the chief Musician, A Psalm of David.

(1) The king shall joy in thy strength, O LORD; and in thy salvation how greatly shall he rejoice! (2) Thou hast given him

---

for. It may be taken as a type of the sacrificial hymn. There is, however, a strong Jewish tradition which connects its use, if not its composition, with Hezekiah (Stanley, *Jewish Church*, ii. 461).

(1) **Day of trouble . . . God of Jacob.**—This certainly recalls the patriarch's words (Gen. xxxv. 3), "I will make there an altar unto God, who answered me in the day of my distress." The "name" alone of the God of Jacob was a safeguard to the people, called after their great forefather "Israel." So even under the shadow of the greatness of human monarchs and heroes whole peoples have often felt secure and strong, using no other weapon but his name.

Defend thee.—Better, *set thee up on high* (comp. lxix. 29, xci. 14) *as in a fortress, out of the reach of foes.*

(3) **All thy offerings.**—The king is sacrificing, according to custom, before battle (1 Sam. xiii. 9), the burnt offering (*ôlah*, from root to "go up," *i.e.*, of the smoke) and the bloodless offering (*minchah*, from root "to portion out") of fine flour. (See Lev. ii. 1.) Since the word rendered in our version *memorial* (Lev. xxiv. 7), which is a derivative of the verb here rendered "remember," has been proved by eminent scholars to signify "incense," we may believe the psalmist meant—

"Accept the incense of all thy *minchah*,
And the fat of thy *ôlah*."

Indeed Mr. Burgess would render "smell" and "relish."

Accept.—Literally, *make fat* (Ps. xxiii. 5, "anointest") *i.e.*, regard or receive as a fat or a worthy offering. The objection to the alternative rendering, "turn to ashes," *i.e.*, "consume," (Lev. ix. 24; 1 Kings xviii. 38), is that the Hebrew word never elsewhere has that sense, but only that of "cleansing from ashes."

(5) **We will set up our banners.**—Rather, *we will wave our banners.* (Comp. *Cant.* vi. 10.) The whole army, or their representatives, assembled in the Temple courts, raise the encouraging shout.

(6) **Now know I.**—Better, *now know I that Jehovah hath saved his anointed, i.e.*, the king who is the subject of the poem, it being out of keeping with the rest of the poem to understand "Israel" or the "ideal" king here. The *now* is emphatic. After seeing the sacrifice performed, and feeling sure of its acceptance, this confidence is expressed.

From his holy heaven.—The prayer in verse 2 had mentioned the sanctuary as the residence of the Divine power, and its symbol, the ark, being deposited there (1 Sam. iv. 4). The inspiration now expresses a yet higher conviction. The manifestation of succour will not be through any earthly symbol of God's might, but *immediately* from His dwelling-place on high.

With the saving.—Better, *with the might of the help of.*

(7) **Trust.**—The poetry is weakened by the insertion of this word. Render, *These in chariots and these on horses; but we in the name of Jehovah our God make boast.* The mention of horses and chariots suggests a Syrian war, since the armies of Syria were peculiarly strong in this arm. For an interesting historical reference to this verse, see Macaulay's *Hist. of England*, chap. ix.

(8) **Stand upright.**—We seem to see a whole battle fought before our eyes, in which those formerly struck down rise, and returning to the fight, beat off their foes, and in their turn lay them low. "We were fallen, but have risen, and stand upright."

(9) **Save Lord . . .**—The Authorised Version follows the accentuation of the Masoretic text, but spoils the rhythm, and interrupts the sense. The LXX. and Vulg., followed by all modern commentators, dividing the verse differently render, "Jehovah, save the king," whence our National Anthem. Jehovah thus becomes the subject of the verb *hear* in the last clause. "May He hear us in the day of our calling." The change from second to third person is characteristic of the Hebrew manner of conquering emotion, and allowing the close of a poem to die away in calm and subdued language. (Comp. Ps. cx. 7.)

XXI.

The preceding psalm was a prayer for success; this is a thanksgiving after victory. Possibly, as many think, the two refer to the same event, and are by the same author. The composition is also similar, since here also the arrangement is for a part song. The people—probably a chorus of maidens (see Note to verse 3), or of Levites—meet the returning hero, with their shouts of praise to Jehovah (verses 1—7). The monarch himself is then addressed, perhaps by the leader of the procession (verses 8—12), and the whole concourse again unite in a burst of praise to God at the end. The rhythm is weak and ill-sustained.

(1) **The king shall.**—Rather, *the king is exulting in thy might* (which has secured the victory he prayed for), *and in thy help how greatly glad is he.*

(2) **Request.**—The Hebrew word occurs nowhere else, but is connected with a root, *to be poor*, and, therefore, *in want*. The "not" is emphatic: "And the re-

A Thanksgiving for PSALMS, XXII. *the King's Victory.*

his heart's desire, and hast not withholden the request of his lips. Selah. (3) For thou preventest him with the blessings of goodness: thou settest a crown of pure gold on his head. (4) He asked life of thee, *and thou gavest it him, even* length of days for ever and ever. (5) His glory *is* great in thy salvation: honour and majesty hast thou laid upon him. (6) For thou hast ¹made him most blessed for ever: thou hast ²made him exceeding glad with thy countenance.

(7) For the king trusteth in the LORD, and through the mercy of the most High he shall not be moved.

(8) Thine hand shall find out all thine enemies: thy right hand shall find out those that hate thee. (9) Thou shalt make them as a fiery oven in the time of thine anger: the LORD shall swallow them up in his wrath, and the fire shall devour them. (10) Their fruit shalt thou destroy from the earth, and their seed from among the children of men. (11) For they intended evil against thee: they imagined a mischievous device, *which* they are not able *to perform*. (12) Therefore ³shalt thou make them turn their ⁴back, *when* thou shalt make ready *thine arrows* upon thy strings against the face of them.

(13) Be thou exalted, LORD, in thine own strength: *so* will we sing and praise thy power.

PSALM XXII.

To the chief Musician upon ⁵Aijeleth Shahar, A Psalm of David.

(1) My *ᵃ* God, my God, why hast thou forsaken me? *why art thou so* far ⁶from

Marginal notes:
1 Heb., *set him to be blessings.*
2 Heb., *gladded him with joy.*
3 Or, *thou shalt set them as a butt.*
4 Heb., *shoulder.*
5 Or, *the hind of the morning.*
ᵃ Matt. 27. 46; Mark 15. 34.
6 Heb., *from my salvation.*

---

quest of his lips thou hast by no means withheld." The mention in verse 4 of a prayer for long life, or perhaps, rather, continuance of life, suggests that this "request" was uttered in sickness. On the other hand the general tone of the psalm connects it with a victory.

(3) **Thou preventest**—*i.e.,* comest to meet him. The word "prevent" is familiar in this sense in the English collect: "Prevent us, O Lord, in all our doings." (Comp. Ps. lxxix. 8; 1 Thess. iv. 15.) The "crown" is by some identified with that won by David at Rabbah Moab. Others make it refer to a coronation. Ewald thinks of a birthday celebration. Probably no more is intended than a symbol of victory and rejoicing. Maidens were accustomed to meet a monarch returning in victory, and to offer a *crown,* or *garland,* which was a symbol of extraordinary rejoicing. (Comp. 1 Sam. xviii. 6; Ps. lxviii. 11; Cant. iii. 11; Wisd. ii. 8; Judith xv. 13; 3 Macc. vii. 16.)

(4) **For ever and ever.**—This is merely a term for indefinite length. (Comp. the common salutation of a king: 1 Kings i. 31; Neh. ii. 3; Dan. iii. 9.) An allusion to the eternal kingdom of the Messiah is not to be forced on the passage.

(6) **Most blessed.**—Literally, *blessings.* The idiom is similar to that in Ps. i. 1.

With thy countenance.—Rather, *In thy presence.* (Comp. Ps. xvi. 11.)

(8) **Thine.**—The psalm has hitherto been addressed to Jehovah. It now turns in prophetic strain to the king.

(9) **Thou shalt make . . .**—As it stands the figure is most obscure. Lam. v. 10 is not analogous. Here the fire and not the blackness of the smoky oven is the object of comparison. A very slight literal change gives the sense obviously required: *Thou shalt put them into a fiery oven.* The figure is not drawn from Sodom and Gomorrah, but from a smelter's furnace. (Comp. Isa. xxxi. 9; Mal. iii. 3. For the custom in its literal horror, see Jer. xlviii. 45, xlix. 2; Amos ii. 1, where the reference is to the Transjordanic tribes.) The Philistines subjected their enemies to a similar treatment (Judges xv. 6).

In the time of thine anger.—Literally, *of thy face, i.e.,* by thy very appearance. The dread majesty of God's face is often thus spoken of (Ps. xxxiv. 16; Lev. xx. 6). Here the same awful power of withering the wicked with a glance is ascribed to the representative of Jehovah. (Comp. Prov. xvi. 14, 15, xix. 12.) But, as if startled by the boldness of his own figure, the poet instantly refers to Jehovah.

In his wrath.—Literally, *in his nostril,* in direct parallelism with "face" in last clause.

(10) **Their fruit.**—More fully, "fruit of the womb" (Pss. cxxvii. 3, cxxxii. 11).

(11) **For they.**—Better, *though they have intended evil against thee, have plotted mischief, they have no power at all.*

(12) **Therefore.**—Literally, *for thou shalt put them shoulder* (*pones eos dorsum,* Vulg.). *Upon thy strings thou shalt aim against the face of them:* Ewald renders: "Shalt strike them back·" but the English version seems to explain rightly To "give the neck of an enemy" (Ps. xviii. 4) is a similar form of expression.

(13) **Thou.**—Again the song turns to address Jehovah.

So will we sing and praise.—Better, *We will both with song and lyre celebrate Thy power.*

XXII.

The fact that Jesus uttered from His cross the words of bitter woe that begin this poem, have given and must ever give it a special interest and importance. It was natural that Christian sentiment should fasten lovingly on it, and almost claim it, not only as a record of suffering typical of our Lord's suffering, but as actually in every detail prophetic of Him. But the signs of a true Messianic character of prophecy are to be looked for in moral likeness, not in accidental resemblances of situation, or coincidences of language, and in this sense Ps. xxii. must ever be considered Messianic.

Nothing in David's recorded life bears out the title. The identification of the sufferer with Jeremiah, though much more probable, is excluded by the joyous and hopeful tone of the conclusion of the poem. But is it an individual sufferer at all, and not rather suffering Israel whose profound misery in the first part, and whose happy restoration in the second, the poet depicts?

If such an interpretation suits the description of the suffering servant of Jehovah in Isa. lii., liii., as many

David Complains   PSALMS, XXII.   *in Great Distress.*

helping me, *and from* the words of my roaring?

(2) O my God, I cry in the daytime, but thou hearest not; and in the nightseason, and ¹am not silent.

(3) But thou *art* holy, O thou that inhabitest the praises of Israel.

(4) Our fathers trusted in thee: they trusted, and thou didst deliver them.

(5) They cried unto thee, and were delivered: they trusted in thee, and were not confounded.

(6) But I *am* a worm, and no man; a reproach of men, and despised of the people. (7) ᵃ All they that see me laugh me to scorn: they ²shoot out the lip, they shake the head, *saying*, (8) ᵇ³ He trusted on the LORD *that* he would deliver him: let him deliver him, ⁴ seeing he delighted in him.

(9) But thou *art* he that took me out of the womb: thou ⁵ didst make me hope *when I was* upon my mother's breasts.

(10) I was cast upon thee from the womb: thou *art* my God from my mother's belly.

(11) Be not far from me; for trouble *is* near; for *there is* ⁶none to help. (12) Many bulls have compassed me: strong *bulls*

1 Heb., *there is no silence to me.*
ᵃ Matt. 27. 39.
2 Heb., *open.*
ᵇ Matt. 27. 43.
3 Heb., *He rolled himself on the Lord.*
4 Or, *if he delight in him.*
5 Or, *keptest me in safety.*
6 Heb., *not a helper.*

---

critics think (comp. Isa. xlix. 3), it suggests itself for this psalm which has so many points of analogy with that passage (see Notes). The herds of wild beasts that surround the sufferer are more appropriate as a figure of hostile tribes than of personal enemies, and the vivid picture of suffering in verses 14 and 15 are not less applicable to the material condition of an oppressed nation than the description in Isa. i. 5, 6 is to the moral condition. (Comp. Isa. lii. 14.) Such a view certainly suits the conclusion of the psalm better than any other. The individual sufferer at all events there disappears, and his fortunes merge in those of the nation (notice the change to the plural in verses 26 and 29), and the brilliant prospect of a time when the tale of God's righteousness shall be handed down from generation to generation is that of the prophet who has mourned his country's woes rather than his own, and has seen in faith the prayers of Israel heard, and the promises made to her amply performed.

Still, the strong personal tone in the opening of the poem suggests that this prophet was himself closely identified with the sufferings he depicts, and shared them not only in sympathy but in reality, and the great consensus of opinion looks for the author among the sufferers in the exile, and probably among the Levites. (See Note, verse 26.) The rhythm is irregular, suited to such a dirge.

Upon Aijeleth Shahar.—More correctly, *upon Ayyeleth ha-shachar, i.e.,* upon the hind of the morning, a phrase which at once suggests either an instrument so named, or a particular tune to which the psalm was to be sung, as we might say, "to the tune of 'As pants the hart.'" The latter is the view to which all the best commentators have now unanimously come. It is not worth while even to notice other conjectures.

(1) **My God, my God.** — Heb., *Eli, Eli, lama azavtani,* where the Targum paraphrases *sabbacthani,* the form used by our Saviour on the cross. (See Notes, *N. T. Comm.,* Matt. xxvii. 46; Mark xv. 34.) The LXX. and Vulgate insert "look upon me." (Comp. English Prayer Book version.) For the despairing tone comp. Ps. lxxx. 14. It suits the whole of pious Israel in her times of trouble even better than any individual.

The second part of the verse is obscure from its lyric conciseness, but the Authorised Version has given the meaning, though sacrificing the rhythm—

  "My God, my God, why hast thou forsaken me,
    Far from my aid, from the words of my groaning?"

i.e., far from listening *to* the words that escape me only in groans.

Roaring.—A word used generally of a lion (Isa. v. 29; comp. Judges xiv. 5); but also of a man (Ps. xxxviii. 9). Hitzig's conjecture, "from my cry," instead of "from my help," is very plausible, since it makes the parallelism complete and involves a very slight change. The LXX. and Vulg. have "the words of my offences."

(2) **And am not silent.**—This misses the parallelism, which evidently requires "O my God, I cry in the daytime, and thou answerest not; in the night, and find no repose."

(3) **But.**—In spite of his seeming desertion the poet still believes Jehovah is the God of the covenant—still the Holy One in whom His people could trust.

The phrase "inhabiting the praises of Israel," recalls the more usual "thou that dwellest between the cherubims" (1 Sam. iv. 4; 2 Sam. vi. 2; Pss. lxxx. 1, xcix. 1, where see Note). But the idea here is more spiritual. The ever-ascending praises of His people become a throne for the Divine King, and take the place of the outstretched wings of the cherubim. Perhaps there is a reminiscence of Exod. xv. 11, 12. This explanation is at once more literal and better than the Rabbinical, "enthroned *as* the praises." (Comp. Aquila: "as the hymns.")

(5) **Confounded**—*i.e.,* ashamed.

(6) **Worm.**—An indication of extreme degradation and helplessness. (Comp. Isa. xli. 14.)

(7) **Laugh me to scorn.**—LXX., ἐξεμυκτήρισαν, the verb used by St. Luke in his description of the crucifixion (Luke xxiii. 35).

Shoot out the lip.—Literally, *open with the lip* (Ps. xxxv. 21; Job xvi. 10). We use the expression, "curl the lip."

(8) **He trusted.** — So the LXX. (Comp. Matt. xxvii. 43.) So, too, Ewald among moderns. But generally the form *gol* (short for *gōl*) is taken as an imperative. Literally, *roll thyself on God.* (Comp. Ps. xxxvii. 5; Prov. xvi. 3, margin.)

(9) **But.**—Better, *For.* Faith that turns to God in spite of derision is the best answer to derision.

Thou didst make me hope.— Better, *thou didst make me repose on my mother's breast.*

(12) **Bulls of Bashan.**—For "Bashan" see Num. xxi. 33; for its pastures and cattle, comp. Deut. xxxii. 14, and for the figures, Amos iv. 1. Instead of "fat bulls," the LXX. and Vulgate paraphrase "strong ones of Bashan." The point of the comparison lies in the wantonness and insolence of pampered pride, displayed by the minions of fortune.

of Bashan have beset me round. ⁽¹³⁾ They ¹ gaped upon me *with* their mouths, *as* a ravening and a roaring lion.

⁽¹⁴⁾ I am poured out like water, and all my bones are ² out of joint: my heart is like wax; it is melted in the midst of my bowels. ⁽¹⁵⁾ My strength is dried up like a potsherd; and my tongue cleaveth to my jaws; and thou hast brought me into the dust of death. ⁽¹⁶⁾ For dogs have compassed me: the assembly of the wicked have inclosed me: *^a* they pierced my hands and my feet. ⁽¹⁷⁾ I may tell all my bones: they look *and* stare upon me.

⁽¹⁸⁾ *^b* They part my garments among them, and cast lots upon my vesture.

⁽¹⁹⁾ But be not thou far from me, O LORD: O my strength, haste thee to help me. ⁽²⁰⁾ Deliver my soul from the sword; ³ my darling ⁴ from the power of the dog. ⁽²¹⁾ Save me from the lion's mouth: for thou hast heard me from the horns of the unicorns.

⁽²²⁾ *^c* I will declare thy name unto my brethren: in the midst of the congregation will I praise thee.

⁽²³⁾ Ye that fear the LORD, praise him; all ye the seed of Jacob, glorify him; and fear him, all ye the seed of Israel. ⁽²⁴⁾ For he hath not despised nor abhorred the affliction of the afflicted; neither hath he hid his face from him; but when he cried unto him, he heard.

⁽²⁵⁾ My praise *shall be* of thee in the great congregation: I will pay my vows before them that fear him.

⁽²⁶⁾ The meek shall eat and be satisfied: they shall praise the LORD that

---

Marginal notes: 1 Heb., *opened their mouths against me.* 2 Or, *sundered.* *^a* Matt. 27. 35; Mark 15. 24; Luke 23. 33; John 19. 23, 37. *^b* Luke 23. 34; John 19. 23, 24. 3 Heb., *my only one.* 4 Heb., *from the hand.* *^c* Heb. 2. 12.

⁽¹³⁾ **Ravening.**—Literally, *tearing in pieces.* (Comp. Lam. ii. 15, 16, iii. 10.)

Roaring.—Comp. Amos iii. 4.

⁽¹⁴⁾ The state of hopeless prostration into which the victim of these terrible foes is brought could not be more powerfully described. It is a state of entire dissolution. Again Lam. ii. 2 offers a close parallel.

Out of joint.—Perhaps, better, *stand out as in a state of emaciation.* (Comp. verse 17.) Literally, *separate themselves.* In other places, however, "bones" is used in the sense in which we use "fibres," in such a phrase as "all the fibres of his frame."

⁽¹⁵⁾ **My strength.**—The conjecture, "my palate," instead of "my strength," improves the parallelism. Others, but not so happily, "my moisture."

The dust of death.—Comp. Shakspeare's "Macbeth:"

"The way to dusty death."

⁽¹⁶⁾ **Dogs.**—Literally, *barkers.* (For the wild scavenger dogs of the East, comp. 1 Kings xii. 19, &c.) Symmachus and Theodotion render, "hunting dogs."

The assembly of the wicked denotes the factious nature of the attacks on the sufferer. His enemies have combined, as savage animals, to hunt in packs. Comp. Virgil, Æn. ii. 351:—

"lupi ceu
Raptores atra in nebula."

They pierced.—The word thus rendered has formed a battle-ground for controversy. As the Hebrew text at present stands the word reads *kâari* (like a lion). (Comp. Isa. xxxviii. 13.) But no intelligible meaning can be got out of "like a lion my hands and my feet." Nor does the plan commend itself of dividing the verses differently, and reading, "The congregation of wicked men have gathered round me like a lion. On my hands and my feet I can tell all my bones." The punctuation of the text must therefore be given up, and a meaning sought by changing the reading. The necessity of a change is supported both by the ancient versions and by some MSS., and also by the Masora; though considerable difference exists as to what the word should be read. If the authority of the ancient versions alone were to decide, some verb in the past tense must be read, but the most reasonable course is to accept the present text, but with a different vowel, treating it as a participle, with suffix, of *kûr*, whose root-idea, according to Ewald, is "to bind;" but, according to most other scholars is "to dig." It is, however, so doubtful whether it can mean *to dig through*—i.e., to pierce—that it is better to understand here a binding of the limbs so tightly as to *dig into* them, and wound them. Render: "The band of villains [literally, *breakers*] surrounded me, binding my hands and feet so as to cut them."

⁽¹⁸⁾ **They part my garments . . .**—i.e., as of one already dead. The word "garment" (*beged*) and "vesture" (*lebûsh*) are synonymous terms for the same article of dress—the modern *abba*, or *plaid*, the usual outer garment of the Bedouin. The latter is a more poetic term. (See *Bib. Dict.*, art. "Dress.") The application of the verse in John xix. 24, &c., adds a refinement not present in the psalm.

⁽¹⁹⁾ **Darling.**—See margin. The Hebrew word is used of an only child, Gen. xxii. 2, 12, Judges xi. 34; of a person left desolate, Pss. xxv. 16, lxviii. 6; here as a synonym for "soul" or "life." We may compare the common Homeric expression, φίλον κῆρ.

⁽²¹⁾ **Unicorns.**—See Num. xxiii. 22; either "buffaloes" or "antelopes." There is some uncertainty about the translation of the second clause of this verse. It may be (1) "And from the horns of buffaloes hear me," i.e., hear me calling for help from the horns, &c.; or (2) "Save me from the lion's mouth, and from the horns of buffaloes Thou hast heard me"—a sudden transition from plaintive prayer to exultant faith; or (3), following the LXX. and Vulg., "And from the horns of buffaloes save me, poor and humble as I am." The first is, on the whole, preferable, as preserving the parallelism better.

⁽²²⁾ **I will declare.**—For the application of this verse in Heb. ii. 12, see *New Testament Commentary.*

^(23, 24) These verses contain the substance of the poet's joyful announcement.

⁽²⁶⁾ **The meek.**—Better, *The afflicted.* This term, combined here with so many expressions for the worship of Jehovah, points to the Levites.

Your heart.—LXX. and Vulg., "their," which carries on the construction better. But such sudden changes of person are common in Hebrew; see even

The Glorious Future. PSALMS, XXIII. *The Good Shepherd.*

seek him: your heart shall live for ever. ⁽²⁷⁾ ^a All the ends of the world shall remember and turn unto the LORD: and all the kindreds of the nations shall worship before thee. ⁽²⁸⁾ For the kingdom *is* the LORD's: and he *is* the governor among the nations. ⁽²⁹⁾ All *they that be* fat upon earth shall eat and worship: all they that go down to the dust shall bow before him: and none can keep alive his own soul.

⁽³⁰⁾ A seed shall serve him; it shall be accounted to the Lord for a generation. ⁽³¹⁾ They shall come, and shall declare his righteousness unto a people that shall be born, that he hath done *this*.

a Ps. 2. 8, & 72. 11, & 86. 9.

b Isa. 40. 11; Jer. 23. 4; Ezek. 34. 11, 12, 23; John 10. 11; 1 Pet. 2. 25.

1 Heb., *pastures of tender grass.*

2 Heb., *waters of quietness.*

c Ps. 3. 6, & 118. 6.

PSALM XXIII.

A Psalm of David.

⁽¹⁾ The LORD *is* ^bmy shepherd; I shall not want. ⁽²⁾ He maketh me to lie down in ¹green pastures: he leadeth me beside the ²still waters. ⁽³⁾ He restoreth my soul: he leadeth me in the paths of righteousness for his name's sake.

⁽⁴⁾ Yea, though I walk through the valley of the shadow of death, ^cI will

---

next verse. The feast that was made after a great sacrifice, such as 2 Chron. vii. 5, not improbably suggested the figure of the banquet at which all the restored of Israel should meet; afterwards elaborated in the prophets (comp. Isa. xxv. 6), and adopted in its refined spiritual sense by our Lord (Luke xiv. 16).

The prophetic glance reaches further than the immediate occasion, and in the sufferer's triumphant sense of vindication and restoration he embraces the whole world. (Comp. Jer. xvi. 19.) The interposition of Divine judgment in favour of Israel will warn the nations into sudden recollection of Him, and bring them submissive to His throne.

⁽²⁹⁾ **Shall eat.**—The figure of the banquet is resumed from verse 26, and extended. The mention of the "fat upon earth," as included in this feast, seems certainly out of place, and injures the parallelism. We must change the text to either (1) "Shall eat and do homage all earth's mourners," or (2) "Ah! to him shall be bowed all the fat ones of earth."

They that go down to the dust—*i.e.*, those on the point to die through their sufferings.

And none can keep.—Better, *And he who cannot keep his soul alive.* Literally, *has not kept.* But the parallelism shows that this is not spoken of those actually dead, but of those not able from poverty to keep body and soul together.

⁽³⁰⁾ **A seed . . .**—Better, *Posterity shall serve Him. About Jehovah it shall be told to the* (coming) *generation.* The article makes for this interpretation. Others, as in Ps. lxxxvii. 6, understand a reference to the census; but the parallelism is against this reference. The next verse repeats the same thought in another form.

⁽³¹⁾ **They shall come**—*i.e.*, the generation just foretold: it shall announce His righteousness to a still younger generation (literally, *to a people born*) that He wrought. The tale of Jehovah's goodness to Israel would be handed on from age to age,

"His triumphs would be sung
By some yet unmoulded tongue."

XXIII.

Under two images equally familiar in Hebrew poetry —that of the shepherd watching over his flock, and of the banquet where Jehovah presides over the just —this psalm expresses the tranquillity and happiness of those who are conscious of the Divine protection. But, after the Hebrew lyric manner, direct allusions to circumstances mingle with the images. We think therefore of some real person and some actual experience, and not of an allegorical reference to the return of the people of Israel from exile, or of the guidance of the rescued nation from Egypt through the wilderness, which were favourite modes of explanation among the Rabbis. The mention of the house of Jehovah seems decisive against the Davidic authorship, which else it would be fascinating to accept, breathing, as the exquisite verse does, the freshness and beauty of the "sweet singer's" early shepherd days. The feast, too, under the enemies' eyes, might have been a reminiscence of Mahanaim; but if David's fortunes have thus coloured the psalm, it must have been through the mind of some later writer. The rhythm of the poem is as tender as the thought.

⁽¹⁾ **Shepherd.**—This image, as applied to God, appears in Hebrew literature first (Gen. xlviii. 15, xlix. 24) of his relation to the individual (comp. Ps. cxix. 176); as the shepherd of His people the image is much more frequent (Pss. lxxviii. 52, lxxx. 1; Isa. xl. 11, lxiii. 11; Ezek. xxxiv.; Micah vii. 14).

⁽²⁾ The verbs in these verses are not to be understood as futures, but as presents, describing the customary condition of the poet. "The psalmist describes himself as one of Jehovah's flock, safe under His care, absolved from all anxieties by the sense of this protection, and gaining from this confidence of safety the leisure to enjoy, without satiety, all the simple pleasures which make up life—the freshness of the meadow, the coolness of the stream. It is the most complete picture of happiness that ever was or can be drawn. It represents that state of mind for which all alike sigh, and the want of which makes life a failure to most; it represents that heaven which is everywhere if we could but enter it, and yet almost nowhere because so few of us can" (*Ecce Homo*, 5, 6).

⁽³⁾ **Restoreth my soul**—*i.e.*, refresheth, recreateth, quickeneth.

For his name's sake.—God's providential dealings are recognised as in accordance with His character for great graciousness.

⁽⁴⁾ **The valley of the shadow of death . . .**—This striking expression, to which the genius of Bunyan has given such reality, was probably on Hebrew lips nothing more than a forcible synonym for a dark, gloomy place. Indeed, the probability is that instead of *tsal-mâveth* (shadow of death), should be read, *tsalmúth* (shadow, darkness), the general signification being all that is required in any one of the fifteen places where it occurs. It is true it is used of the "grave" or "underworld" (Job x. 21, 22). But it is

Confidence in God. PSALMS, XXIV. *God's Lordship in the Earth.*

fear no evil: for thou *art* with me; thy rod and thy staff they comfort me. (5) Thou preparest a table before me in the presence of mine enemies: thou ¹ anointest my head with oil; my cup runneth over.

(6) Surely goodness and mercy shall follow me all the days of my life: and I will dwell in the house of the LORD ² for ever.

1 Heb., *makest fat.*
2 Heb., *to length of days.*
a Deut. 10. 14; Job 41. 11; Ps. 50. 12; 1 Cor. 10. 26, 28.
b Job 38. 6; Ps. 104. 5, & 136. 6.
c Ps. 15. 1.
d Isa. 33. 15, 16.
3 Heb., *The clean of hands.*

PSALM XXIV.
A Psalm of David.

(1) The *a* earth *is* the LORD'S, and the fulness thereof; the world, and they that dwell therein. (2) *b* For he hath founded it upon the seas, and established it upon the floods. (3) *c* Who shall ascend into the hill of the LORD? or who shall stand in his holy place? (4) *d* ³ He that hath clean

---

also used of the "darkness of a dungeon" (Ps. cvii. 10), of "the pathless desert" (Jer. ii. 6); or, possibly, since it is there parallel with *drought*, of "the blinding darkness of a sandstorm," and metaphorically of "affliction" (Isa. ix. 2), and of the "dull heavy look" that grief wears (Job xvi. 16).

By *valley* we must understand a deep ravine. Palestine abounds in wild and gloomy valleys, and shepherd life experiences the actual peril of them. Addison's paraphrase catches the true feeling of the original—

"Though in the path of death I tread,
With gloomy horrors overhead."

Thy rod and thy staff.—Used both for *guiding* and *defending* the flock.

(5) Such a sudden transition from the figure of the flock to that of a banquet is characteristic of Hebrew poetry.

Preparest—*i.e.*, *spreadest* or *furnishest*, the usual phrase (Prov. ix. 2; Isa. xxi. 5). (For the same figure of the hospitable host applied to God, see Job xxxvi. 16; Isa. xxv. 6; and the well-known parables in the New Testament.)

In the presence of mine enemies.—We must imagine the banquet spread on some secure mountain height, in sight of the baffled foe, who look on in harmless spite.

My cup runneth over.—Literally, *My cup is abundant drink*. Cup, in the sense of portion, has already occurred (Pss. xi. 6, xvi. 5). The LXX. has, "Thine intoxicating cup, how excellent it is;" Vulg. the same, but with "my" instead of "thy."

(6) **I will dwell.**—As the text stands it must be translated *I will return (and abide) in the house of Jehovah*.

The house of the Lord can hardly be anything but the Temple; though some commentators treat this even as figurative of membership in the Divine family.

XXIV.

Here, as in Ps. xix., we come upon a poem made up of two separate pieces, united without due regard to the difference both of tone and rhythm, which strikes even an English reader. The piece from verses 1 to 6 inclusive falls into three stanzas, of four, five, and four lines respectively. The second piece, though evidently intended to be sung in parts, falls into triplets. Notice also that the didactic character of the first ode does not harmonise with the warlike march of the second. In the first, moreover, it is the pious Israelite who is, by virtue of the correspondence of his character to the godlike, to ascend the Holy Mountain; in the second, it is Jehovah Himself who comes to claim admission into the fortress by virtue of His prowess in battle, or, more exactly, it is the ark which represents Him, and which was understood by its presence to secure victory, which is brought in triumph to that hill where it was henceforth to have its home. The fact that in the early part of the psalm Jehovah appears in full possession of His mountain, which is already a centre for pious worshippers, seems to bring its composition down to a time posterior to the removal of the ark to Zion. Apart from the rhythmical difficulty, the unity of the poem might possibly be vindicated by the supposition that it was composed not for this first removal, but for some subsequent return of the ark.

This hymn was naturally adopted by Christians as figurative of the Resurrection and Ascension.

(1) **The Lord's.**—The majesty of Jehovah as Lord of the universe is a reason to the psalmist for insisting on rectitude and sincerity in those who become His worshippers. St. Paul uses the same truth, referring to this place (1 Cor. x. 26), to show that all things are innocent and pure to the pure; so that a Christian (apart from a charitable regard for the weak) may eat whatever is sold in the shambles, without troubling himself to inquire whether it has been offered to idols or not.

(2) **Upon the seas.**—For the idea of the earth resting on water, comp. Ps. cxxxvi. 6; Prov. viii. 25—29. In Genesis the dry land emerges from the water, but is not said to be founded on it. In Job xxvi. 7 the earth is said to be hung upon nothing. The idea of a water foundation for the earth naturally grew out of the phenomenon of springs, before it was scientifically explained.

(3, 4) For the elaboration of this answer, see Ps. xv. and Isa. xxxiii. 15, 18. "The answer is remarkable, as expressing in language so clear that a child may understand it, the great doctrine that the only service, the only character which can be thought worthy of such a habitation, is that which conforms itself to the laws of truth, honesty, humility, justice, love. Three thousand years have passed, Jerusalem has fallen, the Jewish monarchy and priesthood and ritual and religion have perished; but the words of David still remain, with hardly an exception, the rule by which all wise and good men would measure the worth and value of men, the greatness and strength of nations" (Stanley, *Canterbury Sermons*).

(4) **His soul.**—The Hebrew margin is "my soul," a reading confirmed by the Alexandrian Codex of the LXX. The Rabbis defend it by saying *soul* here = *name* (comp. Amos vi. 8; Jer. li. 14), and *to lift up to vanity* = *to take in vain*.

Vanity.—Evidently, from the parallelism, in the sense of *falsehood*, as in Job xxxi. 5.

Deceitfully.—Literally, *to fraud*, from a root meaning *to trip up*. The LXX. and Vulg. add (from Ps. xv.) "to his neighbour."

hands, and a pure heart; who hath not lifted up his soul unto vanity, nor sworn deceitfully. (5) He shall receive the blessing from the LORD, and righteousness from the God of his salvation. (6) This *is* the generation of them that seek him, that seek thy face, ¹O Jacob. Selah.

(7) Lift up your heads, O ye gates; and be ye lift up, ye everlasting doors; and the King of glory shall come in. (8) Who *is* this King of glory? The LORD strong and mighty, the LORD mighty in battle.

(9) Lift up your heads, O ye gates; even lift *them* up, ye everlasting doors; and the King of glory shall come in. (10) Who *is* this King of glory? The LORD of hosts, he *is* the King of glory. Selah.

PSALM XXV.

A Psalm of David.

(1) Unto thee, O LORD, do I lift up my soul. (2) O my God, I ᵃtrust in thee: let me not be ashamed, let not mine enemies triumph over me. (3) Yea, let none that wait on thee be ashamed: let them be ashamed which transgress without cause.

(4) ᵇShew me thy ways, O LORD; teach me thy paths. (5) Lead me in thy truth, and teach me: for thou *art* the God of my salvation; on thee do I wait all the day. (6) Remember, O LORD, ᶜ²thy tender mercies and thy lovingkindnesses; for they *have been* ever of old. (7) Remember not the sins of my youth, nor my transgressions: according to thy mercy remember thou me for thy goodness' sake, O LORD.

(8) Good and upright *is* the LORD: therefore will he teach sinners in the way. (9) The meek will he guide in judgment: and the meek will he teach his way. (10) All the paths of the LORD *are* mercy and truth unto such as keep his covenant and his testimonies.

---

1 Or, *O God of Jacob.*

a Ps. 22. 5, & 31. 1, & 34. 8; Isa. 28. 16; Rom. 10. 11.

b Ps. 27. 11, & 83. 11, & 119.

c Ps. 103. 17, & 106. 1, & 107. 1; Jer. 33. 11.

2 Heb., *thy bowels.*

---

(5) **Righteousness.**—This is the real blessing that comes from God. That virtue is her own reward, is the moral statement of the truth. The highest religious statement must be looked for in Christ's "Beatitudes."

(6) **O Jacob.**—The address to Jacob is certainly wrong, and therefore many critics, following the LXX. and Syriac, rightly insert, as in our margin, the words "O God of."

(7) **Gates.**—The LXX. and Vulgate miss this fine personification, by rendering "princes" instead of "heads."

"Lift up your gates, O princes."

The sacrifice of the poetry to antiquarianism, by introducing the idea of a "portcullis," is little less excusable. The poet deems the ancient gateways of the conquered castle far too low for the dignity of the approaching Monarch, and calls on them to open wide and high to give room for His passage.

Everlasting doors.—Better, *ancient doors,* "gates of eld;" an appropriate description of the gates of the grim old Jebusite fortress, "so venerable with unconquered age." For *ôlam* in this sense comp. the giants "of old" (Gen. vi. 4), the "everlasting hills" (Gen. xlix. 26, &c.), and see Note to Ps. lxxxix. 1.

The King of glory shall come in.—This name, in which the claim for admission is made, connects the psalm immediately with the ark; that glory, which had fled with the sad cry *Ichabod,* has returned; the symbol of the Divine presence and of victory comes to seek a lasting resting-place.

(8) **Who . . .**—But the claim is not unchallenged. The old heathen gates will not at once recognise the new-comer's right of admission.

The Lord strong and mighty.—But it is the right of conquest—

"Jehovah, the strong, the mighty, Jehovah, mighty in battle."

(10) **The Lord of hosts.**—A second challenge from the reluctant gates serves as the inauguration of the great name by which the Divine nature was especially known under the monarchy. (For its origin and force, see Note on 1 Sam. i. 3.)

XXV.

This acrostic psalm offers nothing definite for ascertaining its date, but is usually referred to the exile times, when the faithful among the captive Israelites were "waiting" (verses 3, 5, 21) for the redemption of their race. It is full of plaintive appeal to God for help, and reflects that disposition to trust entirely to the Divine pity, which is characteristic of the better minds of Israel under affliction. Indeed we may hear here the voice of the community acknowledging the sins of its younger days (verse 7) before trouble had come to teach the Divine lesson of penitence and hope of forgiveness.

(3) **Wait on thee.**—More literally, as in LXX., *wait for thee,* with idea of strong endurance. The root means to *make strong by twisting.* (Comp. verses 5 and 21, where the same word occurs, though in a different conjugation.) The Vulgate has *qui sustinent te,* "who maintain thee," *i.e.,* as their God. The Authorised Version is in error in following the imperative of the LXX. in this verse. It should run, *none that wait for thee shall be ashamed.*

Transgress without cause. — Better, *practise treachery in vain.* The Hebrew word is translated *dealt treacherously,* Judges ix. 23.

Without cause.—Literally, *empty.*

(5) **Lead me in thy truth.**—Better, *make me walk in*—i.e., make me to have an actual experience of the Divine faithfulness in my passage through life.

(6) **Ever of old.**—Better, *from ancient times*

(8) "With recollections clear, august, sublime,
Of God's great Truth and Right immutable,
She queened it o'er her weakness."—A. H. CLOUGH.

(10) **Mercy and truth.**—Or, *grace and truth;* recalling John i. 4—17, and showing how the conception

(11) For thy name's sake, O LORD, pardon mine iniquity; for it is great. (12) What man is he that feareth the LORD? him shall he teach in the way that he shall choose. (13) His soul ¹shall dwell at ease; and his seed shall inherit the earth. (14) ᵃThe secret of the LORD is with them that fear him; ²and he will shew them his covenant. (15) Mine eyes are ever toward the LORD; for he shall ³pluck my feet out of the net. (16) Turn thee unto me, and have mercy upon me; for I am desolate and afflicted. (17) The troubles of my heart are enlarged: O bring thou me out of my distresses. (18) Look upon mine affliction and my pain; and forgive all my sins. (19) Consider mine enemies; for they are many; and they hate me with ⁴cruel hatred. (20) O keep my soul, and deliver me: let me not be ashamed; for I put my trust in thee. (21) Let integrity and uprightness preserve me; for I wait on thee.

(22) Redeem Israel, O God, out of all his troubles.

PSALM XXVI.
A Psalm of David.

(1) Judge me, O LORD; for I have walked in mine integrity: I have trusted also in the LORD; therefore I shall not slide. (2) ᵇExamine me, O LORD, and prove me; try my reins and my heart. (3) For thy lovingkindness is before mine eyes: and I have walked in thy truth. (4) ᶜI have not sat with vain persons, neither will I go in with dissemblers. (5) I have hated the congregation of evil doers; and will not sit with the wicked. (6) I will wash mine hands in innocency: so will I compass thine altar, O LORD: (7) that I may publish with the voice of thanksgiving, and tell of all thy wondrous works.

(8) LORD, I have loved the habitation of thy house, and the place ⁵where thine honour dwelleth.

(9) ⁶Gather not my soul with sinners,

Marginal notes:
1 Heb., *shall lodge in goodness.*
a Prov. 3. 32.
2 Or, *and his covenant to make them know it.*
3 Heb., *bring forth.*
4 Heb., *hatred of violence.*
b Ps. 7. 9.
c Ps. 1. 1.
5 Heb., *of the tabernacle of thy honour.*
6 Or, *Take not away.*

---

of God and His ways was gradually passing over from the domain of the Law to that of the Gospel.

(12) **What man is he . . . ?**—For the emphatic question compare Ps. xxxiv. 12.

The way that he shall choose.—Rather, *the way that he should choose—i.e.,* the way of right choice. The LXX. and Vulg., however, refer it to God—"the way in which He took delight."

(13) **Shall dwell.**—Literally, *shall lodge the night* (comp. margin); but here, as in Ps. xlix. 12, with added sense of permanency.

(14) **Secret.**—Rather, *familiar intercourse* (so Symmachus). The Hebrew word primarily means *couch,* and then the confidential talk of those sitting on it. In Jer. vi. 11, xv. 17, the word is rendered "assembly." The English word *board* offers a direct analogy. The word *divan* seems to have had a history exactly the reverse. (Comp. Ps. lv. 14, "sweet counsel.")

And he will shew them his covenant.—Literally, *and his covenant to make them know.* This is closely parallel with the preceding clause. The communion enjoyed by the pious is the highest covenant privilege.

(17) **The troubles.**—The consensus of commentators is for a different division of the Hebrew words.

. . . "Relieve my sore heart,
And release me from my distress."

(22) This verse, beginning with *Pe,* was apparently a later addition. Not only is it an isolated line, interfering with the alphabetical arrangement, but it also differs from the rest of the psalm by employing *Elohim* in the place of *Jehovah.* (Comp. Ps. xxxiv. 22.)

XXVI.

A priestly or Levitical psalm (see verses 6—8), calm and regular, composed of twelve verses, each verse a distich. The writer has nothing to reproach himself with; he can appeal to the strict tribunal of God without fear. The protest against apostasy is evidently made not for himself alone, but for the pious part of the community.

(1) **Judge me**—*i.e.,* do me justice, "vindicate me."

I shall not slide.—Rather, *I have trusted in Jehovah without wavering.*

(2) **Try.**—Rather, *purify,* according to the right reading. LXX., *try by fire.*

(3) **For thy lovingkindness . . .**—God's favour was before him as an encouragement, and God's truth formed the rule of his life.

(4) **Dissemblers**—*i.e.,* hypocrites.

(5) **Evil doers.**—With idea of violence; from a root meaning to *break in pieces.*

(6) **I will wash.**—First a symbolical action (Deut. xxi. 6 *seq.*; Matt. xxvii. 24), then a figure of speech (Job ix. 30; Ezek. xxxvi. 25). The Levitical authorship or, at all events, the Levitical character of the psalm appears from comparison of this with Exod. xxx. 17 *seq.*

So will I.—Better, *that I may,* &c. There is no other reference in Jewish literature to the custom of pacing round the altar, but it was a very natural and obvious addition to a gorgeous ceremonial—like the processions in churches where a high ceremonial is adopted. It is, however, implied from the Talmud that it was part of the ceremonial of the Feast of Tabernacles for people to march round the altar with palms.

(7) **That I may . . .**—Literally, *to make to hear the voice of praise.*

(9) **Gather not.**—Better as in margin. The psalmist prays that he may be spared to worship in the sanctuary, when doom falls on evildoers and carries them off. The LXX. and Vulg. have "destroy not."

The Psalmist Sustains his Faith PSALMS, XXVII. *by the Power of God,*

nor my life with ¹bloody men: ⁽¹⁰⁾in whose hands *is* mischief, and their right hand is ²full of bribes. ⁽¹¹⁾But as for me, I will walk in mine integrity: redeem me, and be merciful unto me. ⁽¹²⁾My foot standeth in an even place: in the congregations will I bless the LORD.

PSALM XXVII.
A Psalm of David.

⁽¹⁾ The LORD *is* ᵃmy light and my salvation; whom shall I fear? ᵇthe LORD *is* the strength of my life; of whom shall I be afraid? ⁽²⁾ When the wicked, *even* mine enemies and my foes, ³came upon me to eat up my flesh, they stumbled and fell. ⁽³⁾ ᶜThough an host should encamp against me, my heart shall not fear: though war should rise against me, in this *will* I *be* confident. ⁽⁴⁾ One *thing* have I desired of the LORD, that will I seek after; that I may dwell in the house of the LORD all the days of my life, to behold ⁴the beauty of the LORD, and to enquire in his temple. ⁽⁵⁾ For in the time of trouble he shall hide me in his pavilion: in the secret of his tabernacle shall he hide me; he shall set me up upon a rock.

¹ Heb., *men of blood.*
² Heb., *filled with.*
ᵃ Mic. 7. 8.
ᵇ Ps. 118. 6.
³ Heb., *approached against me.*
ᶜ Ps. 3. 6.
⁴ Or, *the delight.*

---

(12) My foot standeth.—It seems more in accordance with the general drift of the poem to take this verse, *When I stand in an even or level place* [*i.e.*, when I am rescued from the difficulties which now beset me] *I will praise Jehovah in the congregation.*

XXVII.

The opening of this ode reads like the expression of a warrior's faith. On the other hand, verses 4 and 6 point to a Levitical origin. Probably a priest or Levite speaks here for the nation at large, deprived for the present, by foreign persecution, of the regular Temple services. The tone is confident and even triumphant till we come to verse 7, when an abrupt change occurs both in feeling and rhythm. The situation which inspired these latter verses was plainly sad—quite changed from the confidence of the earlier part. Nor is it only that the attitude of praise is changed for that of prayer, but the religious experience of this writer is plainly of a different kind from that of the author of the earlier part. He has had "fears within" as well as "fightings without." He shrinks from the anger of God, and dreads that the Divine favour may be withdrawn (verse 9). Many therefore regard the psalm as composite, the work of two different minds. The opening rhythm resembles that of Ps. xi. 7–9, and this part of the psalm may be arranged in six verses of four lines each, resembling English common metre verse (see General Introduction, V.). The latter part is irregular. The Codex Vat. of the LXX. and the Vulg. add to the title the words "before he was anointed," which only serve to make the question of date of composition still more perplexing.

(1) The Lord is my light.—This noble thought appears nowhere else so grandly, though we may compare Isa. lx. 1. The Latin of the Vulgate, "Dominus illuminatio mea," is the motto of the University of Oxford, and expands in a new but true direction the thought of the ancient bard. To him, Jehovah was the guiding and cheering beacon-fire, proclaiming his victory and pointing him the happy homeward way. From this to the belief in God as the source both of moral and intellectual light, is a long but glorious stage, along which the world has been guided by such words as Isa. lx. 1, still more by the recognition of the incarnate Son as the Light of men (John i. 5, iii. 19, xii. 46, &c.).

Strength.—Better, *defence* or *bulwark*; Heb., *maôz*, rendered "rock," Judg. vi. 26 (margin, *strong place*); used in Isa. xvii. 9 of fortified cities; as here, Ps. xxxvii. 39, xliii. 2; LXX., "shields;" Vulg., "protector."

(2) When . . .—Literally, *In the coming against me (of) the wicked to devour my flesh—my enemies and my foes to me—themselves stumbled and fell.* Job xix. 22 would allow us to understand those who eat up flesh, as a figure for calumniators and detractors; but the context marks out the situation so clearly as that of a warrior, that we rather take it as a general metaphor for savage and violent attacks. *To me,* is an emphatic repetition—*my enemies, mine.*

(3) Though an host.—Literally, *Though a camp should encamp.*

In this.—Either *in this circumstance* or *in spite of this.* (Comp. Ps. lxxviii. 32.) The LXX. ἐν ταύτῃ, followed by μίαν in the next clause, seems to refer it to the hope about to be expressed. The Rabbinical commentators (*e.g.*, Aben Ezra and Rashi) refer back to the beginning of the psalm. "In this"—viz., that Jehovah is my light—"do I trust." Rosenmüller refers it to "the battle" just mentioned, *in ipsa pugna.*

(4) To behold the beauty.—Literally, *to see into the favour*—*i.e.,* to meditate on the graciousness of God.

To enquire . . .—Literally, *to look into*, either judicially or critically; here, "to *ponder* or *meditate.*" Ewald, however, and others add with notion of pleasure, "refresh myself," but on doubtful authority. Some Rabbis, connecting *bākar* with *boker*, the morning, render, "to attend in the morning," while some commentators would entirely spiritualise the wish, as if the actual attendance on the House of God were not in the poet's thoughts. But the words breathe—only in even a higher key—the feeling of Milton's well-known

"But let my due feet never fail
To walk the studious cloister's pale," &c.

A mere transposition of letters would give an easy sense, "to *offer* in thy Temple."

(5) Pavilion.—A *booth* or *hut*; also of the lair of wild beasts (Ps. x. 9; Jer. xxv. 38). (Comp. Job xxxviii. 40.)

Secret of his tabernacle.—Better, *hiding place of his tent* (*ôhel*), the regular word for the tent of the congregation, but also used generally of a habitation of any kind—not necessarily of the tent set up for the ark by David at Zion (2 Sam. vi. 17). The clause, "He shall set me up upon a rock"—*i.e.,* for safety—shows that the tent is also used figuratively for shelter; but there may also be a thought of the

(6) And now shall mine head be lifted up above mine enemies round about me: therefore will I offer in his tabernacle sacrifices ¹of joy; I will sing, yea, I will sing praises unto the LORD. (7) Hear, O LORD, *when* I cry with my voice: have mercy also upon me, and answer me. (8) ² *When thou saidst,* Seek ye my face; my heart said unto thee, Thy face, LORD, will I seek. (9) Hide not thy face *far* from me; put not thy servant away in anger: thou hast been my help; leave me not, neither forsake me, O God of my salvation. (10) When my father and my mother forsake me, then the LORD ³will take me up. (11) ᵃTeach me thy way, O LORD, and lead me in ⁴a plain path, because of ⁵mine enemies. (12) Deliver me not over unto the will of mine enemies: for false witnesses are risen up against me, and such as breathe out cruelty. (13) *I had fainted*, unless I had believed to see the goodness of the LORD in the land of the living. (14) ᵇWait on the LORD: be of good courage, and he shall strengthen thine heart: wait, I say, on the LORD.

PSALM XXVIII.
A Psalm of David.

(1) Unto thee will I cry, O LORD my rock; be not silent ⁶to me: ᶜlest, *if* thou be silent to me, I become like them that go down into the pit. (2) Hear the voice of my supplications, when I cry unto thee, when I lift up my hands ⁷toward thy holy oracle.

1 Heb., *of shouting.*
2 Or, *My heart said unto thee, Let my face seek thy face,* &c.
3 Heb., *will gather me.*
a Ps. 25. 4, & 86. 11, & 119.
4 Heb., *a way of plainness.*
5 Heb., *those which observe me.*
b Ps. 31. 24; Isa. 25. 9; Hab. 2. 3.
6 Heb., *from me.*
c Ps. 143. 7.
7 Or, *towards the oracle of thy sanctuary.*

---

sure asylum to be found in the tabernacle of the congregation.

(6) **Sacrifices of joy.**—Literally, *of shouting;* so LXX. and Vulg., *hostiam vociferationis.* The custom of blowing trumpets (Num. x. 10; comp. Ecclus. l. 16—18) at the time of the burnt offering illustrates this expression even if there is no direct allusion to it.

I will sing, yea.—Better, *I will sing and play.*

(7) The change of tone so marked here, from the warlike to the plaintive, leads to the supposition that verses 7—12 are interpolated from another song of quite another kind in contents, art, and period.

I cry with my voice—*i.e.*, aloud.

(8) **When thou saidst.**—The margin rightly rejects these words, and restores the order of the Hebrew; but the text of the Authorised Version really gives its meaning.

The thought seems borrowed from seeking admission to a royal personage to ask a favour.

(9) **Far.**—This is unnecessary and misleading.

(11) **Enemies.**—Comp. Pss. lvi. 2, liv. 7, lix. 10, 11. Ewald, "malignant liers in wait"; so Aquila.

(12) By slightly changing a letter, we avoid the awkward ellipse in verse 13, and get

"Such as breathe out cruelty *against me,*
So that I did not believe to see," &c.

(14) **He shall strengthen.**—Better, *let thy heart be strong.*

Wait . . .—Heb., *wait for Jehovah, and wait for Jehovah.*

XXVIII.

This psalm gives no distinct indication of its authorship or date of composition. The writer appears to be in a critical condition of health (verse 1), and fears death as a mark of Divine punishment, involving him, though innocent, with the wicked. If the psalm is the product of one pen and time, and is really the expression of individual feeling, the writer was a king (verse 8). But the last two verses seem, both in rhythm and tone, to be from another hand, and to be the expression of national, not individual, confidence and hope. In the first seven verses the parallelism is hardly marked at all.

(1) **My rock.**—Heb., *tsûr*, from a root implying "bind together" (Deut. xiv. 25), not necessarily therefore with sense of height, but with that of strength and solidity. Thus Tyre (or Tsûr) is built on a broad shelf of rock. We see from Deut. xxxii. 30, 31; 1 Sam. ii. 2, that "rock" was a common metaphor for a tutelary deity, and it is adopted frequently for Jehovah in the Psalms and poetical books. Sometimes in the Authorised Version it is rendered "strong" (Pss. lx. 9, lxxi. 3; see margin). The LXX. (followed by Vulg.) here, as generally, apparently through timidity, suppresses the metaphor, and renders "my God." In the song of Moses in Deuteronomy, the metaphor occurs nine times, and Stanley thinks it was derived from the granite peaks of Sinai (*Jewish Church*, p. 195).

Be not silent to me.—Vulg. and margin, rightly, "from me." The word rendered "silent" appears, like κωφὸs in Greek, to have the double meaning of deaf and dumb, and is apparently from an analogous derivation. (See Gesenius, *Lex., sub voce.*) Hence we might render, "turn not a deaf ear to me," or "turn not from me in silence."

Them that go down into the pit—*i.e., the dead*, or *those just about to die* (Ps. xxx. 3). In Ps. lxxxviii. 4, the expression is parallel to "My life draweth nigh unto the grave;" pit (*bôr*) is either the sepulchre (as Isa. xiv. 19), or the world of the dead (Ps. lxxxviii. 4). The two significations pass one into the other. This expression suggests that the psalmist was on a bed of sickness.

(2) **Lift up my hands.**—For interesting illustrations of this Oriental custom see Ex. ix. 29; 1 Kings viii. 22, &c. Compare the well-known line:—

"If, knowing God, they lift not hands of prayer."
TENNYSON: *Morte d'Arthur.*

Holy oracle.—Better, *the shrine of thy sanctuary* (see margin)—*i.e.*, the holy of holies, the adytum, or inner recess of the Temple in which the ark was placed, as we see from 1 King vi. 19—22. The Hebrew word, which is of doubtful derivation, is, with the exception of this place, only found in Kings and Chronicles. The margin, "the oracle of thy sanctuary," is a better rendering than the text.

(3) Draw me not away with the wicked, and with the workers of iniquity, ᵃwhich speak peace to their neighbours, but mischief *is* in their hearts. (4) Give them according to their deeds, and according to the wickedness of their endeavours: give them after the work of their hands; render to them their desert. (5) Because they regard not the works of the LORD, nor the operation of his hands, he shall destroy them, and not build them up.

(6) Blessed *be* the LORD, because he hath heard the voice of my supplications.

(7) The LORD *is* my strength and my shield; my heart trusted in him, and I am helped: therefore my heart greatly rejoiceth; and with my song will I praise him. (8) The LORD *is* ¹their strength, and he *is* the ²saving strength of his anointed.

(9) Save thy people, and bless thine inheritance: ³feed them also, and lift them up for ever.

ᵃ Ps. 12. 2; Jer. v. 8.
¹ Or, *his strength.*
² Heb., *strength of salvations.*
³ Or, *rule.*
⁴ Heb., *ye sons of the mighty.*

PSALM XXIX.
A Psalm of David.

(1) Give unto the LORD, O ⁴ye mighty, give unto the LORD glory and strength.

---

(3) **Draw me not.**—Better, *Drag me not.* In Ezek. xxxii. 18 *seq.*, we have a magnificent vision of judgment, in which the wicked nations are represented as being dragged to death and destruction. In the person of the poet, Israel prays not to be involved in such a punishment. The words "which speak peace" may refer to some overture of alliance from such, or it may be generally those who "hide hatred with lying lips" (Prov. x. 18).

(4) **Give them according to their deeds.**—The justice of the *lex talionis* was deeply impressed on the mind of Israel, and we need not wonder to find its enforcement made the subject of prayer. A general notice of the imprecations of the Psalms will be found in the General Introduction (VI.). Here it is enough to remark that there is no indication of personal animosity or vindictiveness. The poet, even if expressing his own feelings, was identified with devout Israel, to whom it was natural not only to expect from Jehovah the manifestation of judgment which could alone remove the conditions that were so unfavourable to the true religion, but also to pray He would at the same time vindicate Himself and justify those faithful to Him. (Comp. for the general thought Isa. iii. 8—11.) In the actual course of God's providence, the retribution is often very accurately apportioned to the evil deed, and the Bible contains many strong instances—*e.g.*, that of Adonibezek (Judges i. 5, 7).

(5) **The works of the Lord, nor the operation of his hands**—*i.e.*, His strict and even-handed justice, which the wicked forget or, deceived by appearances (Isa. v. 19), ignore. For the contrast between "build up" and "pull down," compare Jer. xlii. 10. This verse is in that prophet's style (Jer. i. 10, xviii. 9).

(6) This burst of thanksgiving, breaking in on the poet's prayer, has led to the supposition that an interval elapsed between the composition of the former part of the psalm and this verse, and that the writer takes up his pen to record the answer his supplications have received. Others regard the psalm as composed by the union of two distinct pieces. Others again treat verse 6 as an interpolation. It certainly seems discordant with the rhythm as well as with the sense of the rest.

(7) **Therefore my heart greatly rejoiceth.**—Better, *danceth for joy,* as in the Prayer Book. Another possible translation is, "And when I have been helped my heart will dance for joy."

With my song.—Literally, *from my song,* but the reading is doubtful. The LXX. have "my flesh has flourished," which is probably correct.

(8) **Their strength**—*i.e.*, the strength of His people, who are throughout in the poet's thought, even if it is the individual and not the community that speaks. The LXX. and Vulg. read (comp. Ps. xxix. 11) "to his people."

Saving strength.—Better, *stronghold of salvation.* (See margin.)

(9) **Feed . . . lift them up.**—These words suggest comparison with Isa. xl. 11, lxiii. 9. The incorporation of this petition in the *Te Deum* is one of those interesting facts that link the Christian worship with the Jewish.

XXIX.

This is a piece of storm-music which the poetry of no country or age has surpassed, so vividly, or rather audibly, is the tempest—and an Oriental tempest—presented to us. To the Hebrew a storm, at once terrible and magnificent, was the direct manifestation of the grandeur of God, and here the poet gives the liveliest expression to that feeling by representing all the phenomena as the immediate result of the Divine utterance—consequent on, if not produced by, the thunder, the Divine voice. The very form—in the monotone of its short, incisive, strictly parallel clauses—has been rightly supposed to be intended as an echo of successive peals of thunder, always equal, and always terrible. Some commentator has suggested that this hymn was composed by David to be sung during a thunderstorm. But it wants no such inept conjecture to discern the fitness of the psalm to take its place in a religious service. The poet himself has prepared for such an adaptation by his conception. Two scenes are presented—one on earth, where we see the storm sweeping majestically along from the north to the south over the length of Palestine; the other in heaven, where the "sons of God"—*i.e.*, all the angelic intelligences and powers—stand as spectators of the grand drama below, and at the invocation of the poet raise the cry, "Glory," in praise of the Divine greatness and power. The versification is perfectly regular, but presents instances of that step-like progression which characterises Deborah's song, and the psalms of Degrees. The two concluding lines are evidently a liturgic addition, and did not form part of the original ode. (See Note.)

(1) **Ye mighty.**—Heb., *benê-elim.* Literally, *sons of gods* (not *sons of God,* since *elim* is never used by itself like *Elohim* for God). If, however, which is possible, it is used in a general sense for beings of supernatural power, but inferior to God, the expression *benê-elim* for angels would be intelligible, *i.e.*, for angels (comp.

(2) Give unto the LORD ¹the glory due unto his name; worship the LORD ²in the beauty of holiness.

(3) The voice of the LORD *is* upon the waters: the God of glory thundereth: the LORD *is* upon ³many waters. (4) The voice of the LORD *is* ⁴powerful; the voice of the LORD *is* ⁵full of majesty. (5) The voice of the LORD breaketh the cedars; yea, the LORD breaketh the cedars of Lebanon. (6) He maketh them also to skip like a calf; Lebanon and *ᵃ* Sirion like a young unicorn. (7) The voice of the LORD ⁶divideth the flames of fire. (8) The voice of the LORD shaketh the wilderness; the LORD shaketh the wilder-

1 Heb., *the honour of his name*.
2 Or, *in his glorious sanctuary*.
3 Or, *great waters*.
4 Heb., *in power*.
5 Heb., *in majesty*.
a Deut. 3. 9.
6 Heb., *cutteth out*.

Job i. 6; Isa. vi. 3) in the widest sense as ministers of God, and so including the lightning and storm. (Comp. Ps. civ. 4.) The poet calls on the grand forces of nature themselves to offer praise to their Divine Master, for the glory which they have been commissioned to reveal. It is they who at the beginning and end alike of the psalm sing the praises of Him, who summoned them to speak to men in His name, and make His voice to be heard. The Prayer Book version, "bring young rams," comes from the LXX. and Vulg. The reading probably arose from a marginal gloss. It is the reading of five MSS. of Kennicott and five of De Rossi.

(2) **In the beauty of holiness.**—Better, *in holy attire*; an image borrowed from the splendid vestments of the priests and Levites (2 Chron. xx. 21; Ps. cx. 3). So the presences that attend the courts of heaven are bidden to be robed in their most magnificent attire, as for a high and sacred ceremony.

(3) **The voice.**—The invocation to the angels over, the storm bursts, and seven successive peals of thunder mark its course of fury and destruction. It is first heard rolling over the waters from the west (comp. 1 Kings xviii. 44), unless the "waters" and "many waters," as in Ps. xviii. 11, 12, refer to the gathered masses of rain-cloud, when we might compare

> "Then broke the thunder
> Like a whole sea overhead."
> BROWNING: *Pippa Passes*.

The Hebrew *kôl* ("voice"), used also of any loud sound (2 Sam. xv. 10, of the trumpet; Ezek. i. 24, of water), is sometimes used (Gen. iv. 10; Isa. lii. 8) to call attention, like our "Hark!" So Ewald here. Others refer it to the thunder, as in Ps. lxxvii. 18; but it seems better to take it for the combined noise of the storm, thunder, wind, and rain, as in Shakespeare—

> "The gods who keep this *pudder* o'er our heads."

(4) **Powerful; full of majesty.**—Better literally, as in LXX. and Vulg., *in might, in majesty*.

(5) **The voice of the Lord breaketh.**—Better more literally, *The voice of Jehovah breaking the cedars, and Jehovah hath shivered the cedars of Lebanon*. (The verb in the second clause is an intensive of that used in the first.) The range of Lebanon receives the first fury of the storm. Its cedars, mightiest and longest-lived of Eastern trees, crash down, broken by the violence of the wind. (For cedar, see 2 Sam. vii. 2.) It has been objected that the thunder should not be made the agent in the destruction; but comp. Shakespeare—

> "And thou, all-shaking thunder,
> Smite flat the thick rotundity o' the world!
> Crack Nature's moulds, all germens spill at once,
> That make ingrateful man!"—*King Lear*, Act iii., sc. 2.

(6) Those trees that are not snapped off, bending to the storm, and swaying in the wind, seem to bound like wild buffaloes. (Comp. Ps. cxiv. 4.)

Sirion, according to Deut. iii. 9 (which see), was the Sidonian name of Hermon. Here the whole of the range of Anti-Libanus.

Unicorn.—See Ps. xxii. 21, Note.
There is some ambiguity about the suffix, *them*. It may relate to the mountains instead of the cedars, and some commentators divide the clauses thus: "He maketh them skip; like a calf Lebanon, and Sirion like a young buffalo." It is not, however, necessary to suppose, with some, that an earthquake accompanies the storm; the apparent movement of the hills being introduced to heighten the effect of the violence of the tempest.

(7) **The voice . . .**—Literally, *the voice of Jehovah cleaving flames of fire*. The word is used of hewing stone and wood (Isa. x. 15). The reference to lightning in this verse is universally admitted, some even seeing an allusion to the brief and sudden flash in the single clause of which the sentence is composed. But the most various explanations are given of the image employed. One of these—that of beating out as from an anvil—may be set aside as clumsy and unworthy of the poet. But the comparison with Isa. li. 9, and Hosea vi. 5, where the same verb is used of God's "judgments," makes it possible that the lightnings here are regarded as "thought-executing fires," and if language would allow, we might translate "hewing with flames of fire," and illustrate by

> "And ever and anon some bright white shaft
> Burnt through the pine-tree roof, here burnt and there,
> As if God's messenger through the close wood screen
> Plunged and replunged his weapon at a venture,
> Feeling for guilty thee and me."
> BROWNING: *Pippa Passes*.

But this, though the usual ancient translation, is now generally rejected in favour of the allusion to "forked lightning," as we call it, the *ignes trisulci* of Ovid, a natural metaphor by which to try to represent the "nimble stroke of quick cross-lightnings." For the apparent physical mistake in making thunder the agent in producing the lightning, see Note on verse 5.

(8) **The voice of the Lord shaketh.**—Literally, *maketh to tremble*. The allusion is, doubtless, to the effect of the storm on the sands of the desert. The tempest has moved southward over Palestine, and spends its last fury on the southern wilderness, and the poet seizes on what is one of the most striking phenomena of a storm in such a district—the whirlwind of sand. "But soon Red Sea and all were lost in a sandstorm, which lasted the whole day. Imagine all distant objects entirely lost to view, *the sheets of sand fleeting along the surface of the desert like streams of water*, the whole air filled, though invisibly, with a tempest of sand, driving in your face like sleet" (Stanley, *Sinai and Palestine*, p. 67). For Kadesh, see Num. xiii. 26. Here the term appears to be used in a large and general sense for the whole southern desert.

The Power of God.   PSALMS, XXX.   *Thanks for Deliverance.*

ness of Kadesh. (9) The voice of the LORD maketh the hinds [1] to calve, and discovereth the forests: and in his temple [2] doth every one speak of *his* glory. (10) The LORD sitteth upon the flood; yea, the LORD sitteth King for ever.

(11) The LORD will give strength unto his people; the LORD will bless his people with peace.

PSALM XXX.

A Psalm *and* Song *at* the dedication of the house of David.

(1) I will extol thee, O LORD; for thou hast lifted me up, and hast not made my foes to rejoice over me. (2) O LORD my God, I cried unto thee, and thou hast healed me. (3) O LORD, thou hast brought up my soul from the grave: thou hast kept me alive, that I should not go down to the pit.

(4) Sing unto the LORD, O ye saints of his, and give thanks [3] at the remembrance of his holiness. (5) For [4] his anger *endureth but* a moment; in his favour *is* life: weeping may endure [5] for a night, but [6] joy *cometh* in the morning.

Marginal notes:
1 Or, *to be in pain.*
2 Or, *every whit of it uttereth, &c.*
3 Or, *to the memorial.*
4 Heb., *there is but a moment in his anger.*
5 Heb., *in the evening.*
6 Heb., *singing.*

---

(9) **Maketh the hinds to calve.**—Literally, *maketh the hinds writhe (with pain).* (See margin. Comp. Job xxxix. 1, where the hind's habit of hiding its young for safety is alluded to, a habit which the violence of the storm makes it forget.) Both Plutarch and Pliny notice the custom of shepherds to collect their flocks during a thunderstorm, for such as are left alone and are separated, are apt, through terror, to cast their young.

Discovereth the forests.—The word "discovereth" comes from the LXX. and Vulgate. Literally, *peels* or *strips*—the effects both of wind and lightning. Passing over the sands of the Arabah, the storm has reached the "acacias and palms and vegetation which clothe the rocks of granite and porphyry in the neighbourhood of Petra." *Forests* may seem rather a large word for such vegetation, but Stanley remarks of the Arabah that "the shrubs at times give it almost the appearance of a jungle." Similar effects of a storm upon a forest are described by Tennyson in *Vivien*:

> "Scarce had she ceased when out of heaven a bolt
> (For now the storm was close above them) struck,
> Furrowing a giant oak, and javelining
> With darted spikes and splinters of the wood
> The dark earth round. He raised his eyes and saw
> The tree that shone white-listed thro' the gloom."

In his temple.—Better, *in his palace*—i.e., the heavenly palace, as in Pss. xi. 4, xviii. 6. (See verse 1.) The angelic spectators of the magnificent drama enacted below them cry (not merely speak *of*, as Authorised Version, but *utter* the word) each one, "Glory," obeying the poet's invocation in the prelude. Notice that the effect of the storm on *men* is supposed to be all summed up in the poet's own attitude of listening awe. There is no actual mention of this part of creation; but one feels from the poem that while inanimate nature trembles and suffers, and the godlike intelligences of heaven are engaged in praise, *man* listens and is mute.

(10) **The Lord sitteth.**—Better, *Jehovah was throned upon the flood, and Jehovah will be throned a king for ever.* The word translated "flood" is exclusively, except in this place, applied to the Deluge (Gen. vi., vii.). Hence we must suppose that the poet was recalled to the thought of the great Flood by the torrents of rain now falling. Jehovah sat then upon the waters as their King, and so He will for ever be throned on high above the storms of earth. Or, perhaps, the Deluge may have passed into a proverbial term for any great rain.

(11) **The Lord will give.**—This verse appears to have been a liturgic addition, to give the poem a religious tone. (See Introduction.)

XXX.

This psalm, which is plainly an expression of thankfulness for recovery from a dangerous, and nearly fatal, sickness, does not in a single line or word bear out the title, which suggests either the dedication of the site of the future temple (2 Sam. xxiv.; 1 Chron. xxi.) or of the citadel on Zion (2 Sam. v. 11), or of the re-dedication of the palace profaned by Absalom. On the other hand, the fact that the psalm is, in the Jewish ritual, used at the Feast of Dedication, the origin of which is to be found in 1 Macc. iv. 52 *seq.*, suggests that the title may have been appended after the institution of that feast, in order to give an historical basis for the use of the psalm. The reason of its choice we must look for in the feelings produced by the first successes in the war of independence. After the sad period of humiliation and persecution, the nation felt as the writer of this psalm felt—as if saved from the brink of the grave. Thus the psalm is in application national, though in origin and form individual. Who the author was, it is vain to conjecture; the tone and even the language suggest Hezekiah or Jeremiah. (See Notes.) The parallelism is not strongly marked.

(1) **Thou hast lifted me up.**—The Hebrew word seems to mean to *dangle*, and therefore may be used either of *letting down* or *drawing up*. The cognate noun means *bucket*. It is used in Exod. ii. 19, literally of drawing water from a well; in Prov. xx. 5, metaphorically of counsel. Here it is clearly metaphorical of *restoration from sickness*, and does not refer to the incident in Jeremiah's life (Jer. xxxviii. 13), where quite a different word is used.

(3) **Grave.**—*Sheôl.* (See Note to chap. vi. 5.)

That I should not go down to the pit.—This follows a reading which is considered by modern scholars ungrammatical. The ordinary reading, rightly kept by the LXX. and Vulg., means *from these going down to the pit,* i.e., from the dead. (Comp. Ps. xxviii. 1.)

(4) **Sing unto . . .**—Better, *Play to Jehovah, ye saints of his.* (See Note, Ps. xvi. 10.)

And give thanks.—Better, *and sing praises to his holy name.* (See margin.) Possibly Ex. iii. 15 was in the poet's mind. (Comp. Ps. xcvii. 12.)

(5) **For his anger.**—Literally,

> "For a moment (is) in his anger,
> Life in his favour;
> In the evening comes to lodge weeping,
> But at morning a shout of joy."

Some supply *comes to lodge* with the last clause, but the image is complete and finer without. It is tho-

(6) And in my prosperity I said, I shall never be moved. (7) LORD, by thy favour thou hast ¹made my mountain to stand strong: thou didst hide thy face, *and* I was troubled. (8) I cried to thee, O LORD; and unto the LORD I made supplication. (9) What profit *is there* in my blood, when I go down to the pit? *ª* Shall the dust praise thee? shall it declare thy truth? (10) Hear, O LORD, and have mercy upon me: LORD, be thou my helper. (11) Thou hast turned for me my mourning into dancing: thou hast put off my sackcloth, and girded me with gladness; (12) to the end that ² *my* glory may sing praise to thee, and not be silent. O LORD my God, I will give thanks unto thee for ever.

1 Heb., *settled strength for my mountain.*

a Ps. 6. 5, & 88. 11, & 115. 17.

2 That is, my tongue, or, my soul.

b Ps. 22. 5; Isa. 49. 23.

PSALM XXXI.

To the chief Musician, A Psalm of David.

(1) In *ᵇ*thee, O LORD, do I put my trust; let me never be ashamed: deliver me in thy righteousness. (2) Bow

---

roughly Oriental. Sorrow is the wayfarer who comes to the tent for a night's lodging, but the metaphor of his taking his leave in the morning is not carried on, and we have instead the sudden waking with a cry of joy, sudden as the Eastern dawn, without twilight or preparation. Never was faith in the Divine love more beautifully expressed. (Comp. Isa. liv. 7, 8.)

(6) **And in.**—Better, *But as for me, in,* &c. The pronoun is emphatic. The mental struggle through which the psalmist had won his way to this sublime faith is now told in the most vivid manner, the very soliloquy being recalled.

Prosperity.—Better, *security.*

I shall never be moved.—Better, *I shall never waver.*

(7) **Lord, by thy favour**—*i.e., and all the while thou* (not my own strength) *hadst made me secure.* The margin gives the literal rendering, but the reading varies between the text "to my mountain," "to my honour" (LXX., Vulg., and Syriac), and "on mountains," the last involving the supply of the pronoun "me." The sense, however, is the same, and is obvious. The mountain of strength, perhaps mountain fortress, is an image of secure retreat. Doubtless Mount Zion was in the poet's thought.

Thou didst . . .—The fluctuation of feeling is well shown by the rapid succession of clauses without any connecting conjunctions.

(8) **I cried to thee.**—The very words of "this utter agony of prayer" are given. But it is better to keep the futures in verse 8, instead of translating them as *preterites,* and make the quotation begin here. So Symmachus, "Then I said, *I will cry to thee, O Lord,*" &c.

(9) **What profit . . .**—*i.e.,* to God. For the conception of death as breaking the covenant relation between Israel and Jehovah, and so causing loss to Him as well as to them (for Sheôl had its own king or shepherd, *Death*) by putting an end to all religious service, comp. Hezekiah's song; Isa. xxxviii. 18. Comp. also Ps. vi. 5, and note Ps. lxxxviii. 11.) Plainly as yet no hope, not even a dim one, had arisen of praising God beyond the grave. The vision of the New Jerusalem, with the countless throngs of redeemed with harps and palms, was yet for the future.

(11) **Thou hast turned for me.**—This verse gives the answer to the prayer. *Mourning* is literally *beating the breast,* and therefore *dancing* forms a proper parallelism; or else, according to one derivation of the word, *machôl* would suggest *piping.* (See margin, Pss. cxlix. 3, cl. 4; see Smith's *Bible Dictionary,* under "Dance;" and *Bible Educator,* vol. ii., p. 70; and comp. Note to Song of Solomon vi. 13.)

(12) **My glory.**—The suffix is wanting in the Hebrew, and in all the older versions except LXX. and Vulg. The Chaldee versions make the word concrete and render "the nobles." The Syriac, reading the verb in a different person, makes *glory* the object—"then will I sing to thee, Glory." *My* glory would, as in Ps. cviii. 1, mean *my heart.* (See Note, Ps. xvi. 9.) Without the pronoun, we must (with Jerome) understand by "glory" renown or praise, which, as it were, itself raises songs; or it must be concrete, "everything glorious."

XXXI.

This psalm is full of tantalising expressions, which raise the expectation of a satisfactory historical basis for its composition, only to disappoint by the obscurity of their allusion. On the one hand, the figures of the stronghold and rock (verses 2, 3) not only suggest David as the author, but, from the mode of their introduction, at first seem to point to some definite locality, as *Keilah* or *Ziklag* (verse 7). But we are instantly transported into another circle of images and situations which recall Jeremiah and his fortunes. Moreover, the psalm oscillates between plaintive prayer and assured trust in a way to indicate that we cannot here have the experience of one single event, but the gathered sentiments of a whole lifetime; or, perhaps, which is more likely, the expression of a universal sentiment, the picture of a national situation where power was on one side and right on the other, in which the interests of religion and the discharge of religious duties were opposed by the contemptuous hostility of an idolatrous society. The enemies, at all events, who appear here are those who hate the pious Israelite because they themselves adore other gods (verse 6)—they are the wicked—their arms are recrimination, calumny, contempt, the insolence of the powerful against the humble and weak. The psalm seems, therefore, to reflect the later times of the monarchy, when the pure religion of Jehovah had to struggle against idolatrous tendencies favoured in high places. The recurrence of phrases very common in his writings show that if Jeremiah was not the author of the psalm, he was very familiar with it, or the writer of the psalm was imbued with his style. The versification is irregular.

(1) The words of this verse are interesting as being the last words of Xavier, and as concluding the *Te Deum.*

Verses 1—3 occur again with slight variations in Ps. lxxi. 1—3.

Let me never.—Literally, *let me not for ever be ashamed.*

(2) **My strong rock.**—Literally,

"Thou art to me for a rock of a stronghold,
For a house of fortresses to save me."

down thine ear to me; deliver me speedily: be thou ¹my strong rock, for an house of defence to save me. ⁽³⁾ For thou *art* my rock and my fortress; therefore for thy name's sake lead me, and guide me. ⁽⁴⁾ Pull me out of the net that they have laid privily for me: for thou *art* my strength.

⁽⁵⁾ ᵃ Into thine hand I commit my spirit: thou hast redeemed me, O LORD God of truth.

⁽⁶⁾ I have hated them that regard lying vanities: but I trust in the LORD. ⁽⁷⁾ I will be glad and rejoice in thy mercy: for thou hast considered my trouble; thou hast known my soul in adversities; ⁽⁸⁾ and hast not shut me up into the hand of the enemy: thou hast set my feet in a large room.

⁽⁹⁾ Have mercy upon me, O LORD, for I am in trouble: mine eye is consumed with grief, *yea*, my soul and my belly. ⁽¹⁰⁾ For my life is spent with grief, and my years with sighing: my strength faileth because of mine iniquity, and my bones are consumed. ⁽¹¹⁾ I was a reproach among all mine enemies, but especially among my neighbours, and a fear to mine acquaintance: they that did see me without fled from me. ⁽¹²⁾ I am forgotten as a dead man out of mind: I am like ²a broken vessel. ⁽¹³⁾ For I have heard the slander of many: fear *was* on every side: while they took counsel together against me, they devised to take away my life.

⁽¹⁴⁾ But I trusted in thee, O LORD: I said, Thou *art* my God.

⁽¹⁵⁾ My times *are* in thy hand: deliver me from the hand of mine enemies, and

¹ Heb., *to me for a rock of strength.*
ᵃ Luke 23. 46.
² Heb., *a vessel that perisheth.*

⁽³⁾ **Rock.**—As rock in this verse is *selâ* (LXX. and Vulg., "strength") instead of *tsûr*, as in verse 2, it is better to render "for thou art my cliff fortress;" literally, *cliff and fortress.*

For thy name's sake—*i.e.*, because Thou hast this name of rock and fortress.

Lead me, and guide me.—The future is better,

"Thou wilt lead and guide me."

To pray for protection and then stoutly affirm belief, as in verse 3, has been called illogical; but it is the logic of the heart if not of the intellect; the logic, it may be added, of every prayer of faith.

⁽⁴⁾ **The net.**—This image is a common one in the Psalms. (Comp. Ps. x. 9, &c.)

Laid privily.—Literally, *hidden.* Translate still by the future, *thou wilt pull me out.*

⁽⁵⁾ **I commit.**—Most memorable, even among expressions of the Psalms, as the dying words of our Lord Himself (Luke xxiii. 46), and a long line of Christian worthies. Polycarp, Bernard, Huss, Henry V., Jerome of Prague, Luther, Melancthon, are some of the many who have passed away comforted and upheld by the psalmist's expression of trust. But death was not in his thought, it was in life, amid its troubles and dangers, that he trusted (Hebrew, *deposited as a trust*) his spirit (*rûach*, comp. Isa. xxxviii. 16) to God. But the gift brought to the altar by the seer of old, has been consecrated anew and yet anew.

Lord God of truth.—Comp. 2 Chron. xv. 3, where, as here, there is a contrast between Jehovah and idols; but also, as in Deut. xxxii. 4, the "faithful God."

⁽⁶⁾ **Lying vanities.**—Literally, *breath of lies* (Jonah ii. 8), undoubtedly *idols*, as the parallelism in Jer. viii. 19 shows. It was the term adopted by the Deuteronomist (chap. xxxii. 21) and apparently brought into use by him.

⁽⁸⁾ **Shut me up into the hand.**—This is the exact phrase used by David (1 Sam. xxiii. 11, 12) in consulting the Divine oracle by the ephod. But this does not prove the authorship, for it was evidently a common phrase. (See 1 Sam. xxiv. 18, xxvi. 8; 2 Kings xvii. 4.)

Large room.—Comp. Pss. iv. 1 and xviii. 19.

⁽⁹⁾ **Mine eye is consumed . . .**—Comp. Ps. vi. 7. It was an old idea that the eye could weep itself away. It is an actual fact that the disease *glaucoma* is very much influenced by mental emotions.

Belly.—Better, *body*—both mind and body were suffering.

⁽¹⁰⁾ **Iniquity.**—Gesenius and Ewald understand, the *suffering* that follows on sin rather than the *iniquity* itself, a meaning that certainly seems to suit the context better. The LXX. and Vulg. have "poverty."

⁽¹¹⁾ The adverb rendered *especially* seems out of place. It is therefore better to take it as a noun, in the sense of burden, a sense etymologically probable.

"Because of all mine oppressors I have become a reproach,
And to my neighbours a burden,
And a fear to my acquaintance."

Fled.—Literally, *fluttered away like frightened birds.*

⁽¹²⁾ **Broken vessel.**—A favourite image with Jeremiah (chaps. xix. 11, xxii. 28, xxv. 34, xlviii. 38), but not peculiar to him among the prophets. (Comp. Hos. viii. 8, and see Introduction to this psalm.)

⁽¹³⁾ Again comp. Jer. xx. 10, which reproduces word for word the first two clauses. The expression rendered "fear on every side" was actually a motto of the prophet (Jer. vi. 25; xx. 3, margin; xlvi. 5, xlix. 29. Comp. Lam. ii. 22). But the most probable derivation makes the noun mean not *terror* but *conspiracy*, while for *slander* here we must render *whisper*.

"For I heard the whispering of the many,
'Conspiracy all around.'"

Under cover of a pretended general panic they were really, as the psalmist saw, plotting evil against him.

⁽¹⁴⁾ **But I.**—Emphatic, in contrast to the pretended panic and in spite of the real dangers around him.

⁽¹⁵⁾ **My times are in thy hand**—*i.e.*, the vicissitudes of human life (LXX. and Vulg. have "my destinies") are under Divine control, so that the machinations of the foe cannot prevail against one whom God intends to deliver. For the expression comp. 1 Chron. xxix. 30, "the times that went over him," Isa. xxxiii. 6.

The Great Goodness of God. PSALMS, XXXII. *Exhortation to Love God.*

from them that persecute me. ⁽¹⁶⁾ Make thy face to shine upon thy servant: save me for thy mercies' sake. ⁽¹⁷⁾ Let me not be ashamed, O LORD; for I have called upon thee: let the wicked be ashamed, *and* ¹let them be silent in the grave. ⁽¹⁸⁾ Let the lying lips be put to silence; which speak ²grievous things proudly and contemptuously against the righteous.

⁽¹⁹⁾ *ª Oh* how great *is* thy goodness, which thou hast laid up for them that fear thee; *which* thou hast wrought for them that trust in thee before the sons of men! ⁽²⁰⁾ Thou shalt hide them in the secret of thy presence from the pride of man: thou shalt keep them secretly in a pavilion from the strife of tongues.

⁽²¹⁾ Blessed *be* the LORD: for he hath shewed me his marvellous kindness in a ³strong city. ⁽²²⁾ For I said in my haste, I am cut off from before thine eyes: nevertheless thou heardest the voice of my supplications when I cried unto thee.

⁽²³⁾ O love the LORD, all ye his saints: *for* the LORD preserveth the faithful, and plentifully rewardeth the proud doer. ⁽²⁴⁾ *ᵇ* Be of good courage, and he shall strengthen your heart, all ye that hope in the LORD.

PSALM XXXII.

⁴*A Psalm* of David, Maschil.

⁽¹⁾ Blessed *is he whose* ᶜtrangression *is*

---

1 Or, *let them be cut off for the grave.*
2 Heb., *a hard thing.*
a Isa. 64. 4; 1 Cor. 2. 9.
3 Or, *fenced city.*
b Ps. 27. 14.
4 Or, *A Psalm of David giving instruction.*
c Rom. 4. 7.

The sense of security in this trusting phrase may be contrasted with the feeling of danger in another Hebrew phrase, "my soul is continually in my hand," Ps. cxix. 109.

⁽¹⁶⁾ **Make thy face to shine.**—As in chap. iv. 6, an echo of the priestly blessing. (Num. vi. 24—26.)

⁽¹⁸⁾ **Silence.**—As a different word is used from that rendered *silent* in verse 17, translate *let the lying lips be made dumb.*

Grievous.—Better, *arrogant*, as in 1 Sam. ii. 3. (Comp. Ps. xciv. 4.) So in Ps. lxxv. 5, "a stiff neck" is *a neck thrown impudently back.*

Proudly and contemptuously.—Literally, *in pride and contempt.*

⁽¹⁹⁾ **Laid up.**—Better, *hidden*, (Heb. *tsâphan;* comp. Ps. xvii. 14; Obad. 6), as a treasure for the faithful, and now brought out and displayed in the presence "of the sons of men."

⁽²⁰⁾ **The secret of thy presence.**—Better, *in the hiding-place of thy countenance*, a beautiful thought and common in the Psalms, although expressed by different images. In Ps. xxvii. 5, "the hiding-place of his tabernacle;" lxi. 4, "of his wings;" xci. 1, "of his shadow."

The form the same image takes in the Christian's hope is beautifully expressed by Tennyson:

"To lie within the light of God as I lie upon your breast,
And the wicked cease from troubling and the weary are at rest."

Pride.—Better, *rough* or *wrangling talk*, as the parallelism shows and the LXX. confirm; and, referring back to verse 18, Gesenius renders the word "conspiracies."

⁽²¹⁾ **Shewed me his marvellous kindness . . .**—Better, *made his kindness distinguished* or *manifest*, referring to verse 19.

In a strong city.—Some see a reference to David's adventures at Ziklag or Keilah; others to Jeremiah's in Jerusalem (Jer. xxxviii.). It is, however, better to regard it merely as a general image of the Divine protection.

⁽²²⁾ **In my haste . . .**—Literally, *in my fleeing away in fear.* Jerome, Aquila, and Symmachus, "in my confusion."

⁽²³⁾ **Preserveth the faithful.**—Or, perhaps, by rendering by the abstract instead of the concrete, *keeps faith.* The LXX. and Vulg. have "requireth truths."

⁽²⁴⁾ **Be of good courage.**—Cf. Ps. xxvii. 14.

XXXII.

No other Old Testament saint that we know of could have written this psalm except David. And yet at the outset we are met by the fact that the history makes David's repentance after each of his great sins turn on the reproof of a prophet. Before this voice from without reached him he appears, as far as the historical narrative can tell us, to have been quite unconscious of having done wrong. Moreover, the last half of the psalm (verses 7—12) represents quite a different situation from the first, not that of a penitent mourning his sin, but of a just and godly man rejoicing in the guidance of a good Providence, and contrasting the state of peace and security enjoyed under that guidance with the condition of the ungodly. But even a prophetic glance from the outside cannot read the whole history of a soul, while one who can feel profoundly is not unlikely, when reviewing the past, to dwell exclusively on the intense sense of guiltiness before God, without referring to the outward circumstance which may have suddenly brought it home to him. "The song is plainly ancient, original throughout, the token of a powerful mind." This is Ewald's judgment, not lightly to be set aside. And if we are not led away by the interest of a particular situation, but consider how David, wishing to express in song the happiness of penitence, might colour his half-didactic purpose with the recollection of his own personal experience of sin and forgiveness, a recollection still vivid with him, we shall not wonder at the apparent contradiction between the beginning and end of the psalm, and may readily allow the correctness of the inscription. The versification is fine.

"Augustine used often to read this psalm with weeping heart and eyes, and had it before his death written on the wall over his sick-bed, that he might exercise himself therein, and find comfort therein in his sickness." (Quoted by Perowne from Selnecker.)

Title.—Maschil (*maskhîl*), a title prefixed to thirteen psalms, and in several cases joined to musical directions. By derivation it might indicate a *didactic* poem. So the LXX., "a psalm of understanding" or "for under-

forgiven, *whose* sin *is* covered. (2) Blessed *is* the man unto whom the LORD imputeth not iniquity, and in whose spirit *there is* no guile.

(3) When I kept silence, my bones waxed old through my roaring all the day long. (4) For day and night thy hand was heavy upon me: my moisture is turned into the drought of summer. Selah.

(5) I acknowledged my sin unto thee, and mine iniquity have I not hid. *a* I said, I will confess my transgressions unto the LORD; and thou forgavest the iniquity of my sin. Selah.

(6) For this shall every one that is godly pray unto thee [1] in a time when thou mayest be found: surely in the floods of great waters they shall not come nigh unto him. (7) *b* Thou *art* my hiding place; thou shalt preserve me from trouble; thou shalt compass me about with songs of deliverance. Selah.

(8) I will instruct thee and teach thee in the way which thou shalt go: [2] I will guide thee with mine eye. (9) *c* Be ye not as the horse, *or* as the mule, *which* have no understanding: whose mouth must be held in with bit and bridle, lest they come near unto thee.

a Prov. 28. 13; Isa. 65. 24; 1 John 1. 9.
[1] Heb., *in a time of finding.*
b Ps. 9. 9.
[2] Heb., *I will counsel thee, mine eye shall be upon thee.*
c Prov. 26. 3.

---

standing;" the Vulg., *intellectus*; and Jerome, *intellectus* or *eruditio*. (Comp. the margin.) Against this, however, must be set the fact that only two out of the thirteen hymns with this title can possibly be considered *didactic*. But in Ps. xlvii. 7, the word is joined to a term meaning to play or sing (Authorised Version, "sing ye praises with understanding") in such a way as to indicate a musical reference, a reference fully borne out by some of the titles, and also by the description of the Levitical musicians, 2 Chron. xxx. 22, by the participle of this verb, as "those who play skilfully with good taste." Hence render "a skilful song."

(1, 2) **Transgression—sin—iniquity.**—The same terms used here to express the compass and heinousness of sin are found, though in different order, in Exod. xxxiv. 7. For St. Paul's reading of this passage, see Rom. iv. 6, 7.

(3) **When I kept.**—He describes his state of mind before he could bring himself to confess his sin (the rendering of the particle *ki* by *when*, comp. Hosea xi. 1, is quite correct). Like that knight of story, in whom

"His mood was often like a fiend, and rose
And drove him into wastes and solitudes
For agony, who was yet a living soul,"

this man could not live sleek and smiling in his sin, but was so tortured by "remorseful pain" that his body bore the marks of his mental anguish, which, no doubt, "had marr'd his face, and marked it ere his time."

My bones waxed old.—For this expression comp. Ps. vi. 2.

(4) **Thy hand was heavy.**—The verb, as in "kept silence" in verse 3, is properly present—the agony is still vividly present.

My moisture.—The Hebrew word is found only once besides (Num. xi. 8), where the Authorised Version has "fresh oil;" the LXX. and Vulg., "an oily cake." Aquila has "of the breast of oil," reading the word erroneously. Here both LXX. and Vulg. seem to have had a different reading, "I was turned to sorrow while the thorn was fixed in." Symmachus translates somewhat similarly, but by "to destruction" instead of "to sorrow." Aquila, "to my spoiling in summer desolation." These readings, however, mistake the *lamed*, which is part of the word, for a preposition. Gesenius connects with an Arabic root, *to suck*, and so gets the meaning *juice* or *moisture*.

Into the drought of summer.—This is the best rendering of the Hebrew, though it might be either "as in summer dryness" or "with summer heat." Some understand literally a *fever*, but it is better to take it figuratively of the *soul-fever* which the whole passage describes.

(5) **I acknowledged.**—The fact that this verb is future, as also "I will confess" in the next clause, as well as the requirements of the passage, uphold Hupfeld's suggestion that "I said" has changed its place, and should be replaced at the beginning of the verse. (Comp. Ps. lxxiii. 15, and Note.) The sense is,

"I said, 'I will acknowledge my sin unto thee,
And I did not hide mine iniquity.
(I said) 'I will confess my transgression unto Jehovah,
And thou forgavest the guilt of my sin."

(6) **For this**—*i.e.*, for this cause.
Shall every one.—Better, *let every one.*
In a time . . .—See margin. The expression, "time of finding," is, of course, elliptical. The Authorised Version explains by Isa. lv. 6; but Isa. xlv. 8 would suggest that "forgiveness" or "acceptance" is the word to be supplied. More probably still some general word, as "goal" or "object," is required, the phrase being rendered by the LXX., "in the appointed time;" by the Vulg., "opportune."

Surely.—This adds emphasis to the statement, whether we render after Prov. xiii. 10, "only unto him," or as in Authorised Version. "He—the godly—is the man whom, when the floods rise, they shall not harm." The floods may either be an image of Divine judgment, as in Nah. i. 8, or of temptation and trial, as in Matt. vii. 24—27.

(8) **I will guide thee with mine eye.**—The Hebrew may be rendered either "I will advise—with mine eye upon thee," or "I will fix mine eye upon thee," which is the translation by the LXX., and to be preferred. This verse changes so abruptly to the first person that it is better, with most of the old interpreters and, among moderns, with Ewald, Hitzig, and Reuss, to suppose them the words of deliverance that sound so sweet in the psalmist's ears.

(9) **Whose mouth.**—Here the text has evidently suffered, and the exact meaning is lost. There are also verbal difficulties. The word translated "mouth" elsewhere (except Ps. ciii. 5, where see Note) means "ornament," and the literal rendering of the text as it stands is, *with bit and bridle his ornament to hold, not approaching to thee*. This may mean that the animal is harnessed, either "that it may not approach," or "because without harness it will not approach."

God is to be Praised PSALMS, XXXIII. *for His Goodness and Power.*

⁽¹⁰⁾ Many sorrows *shall be* to the wicked: but he that trusteth in the LORD, mercy shall compass him about. ⁽¹¹⁾ Be glad in the LORD, and rejoice, ye righteous: and shout for joy, all *ye that are* upright in heart.

PSALM XXXIII.

⁽¹⁾ Rejoice in the LORD, O ye righteous; *for* praise is comely for the upright. ⁽²⁾ Praise the LORD with harp: sing unto him with the psaltery *and* an instrument of ten strings. ⁽³⁾ Sing unto him a new song; play skilfully with a loud noise.

⁽⁴⁾ For the word of the LORD *is* right; and all his works *are done* in truth. ⁽⁵⁾ He loveth righteousness and judgment: ^a the earth is full of the ¹ goodness of the LORD. ⁽⁶⁾ ^b By the word of the LORD were the heavens made; and all the host of them by the breath of his mouth. ⁽⁷⁾ He gathereth the waters of the sea together as an heap: he layeth up the depth in storehouses. ⁽⁸⁾ Let all the earth fear the LORD: let all the inhabitants of the world stand in awe of him. ⁽⁹⁾ For he spake, and it was *done*; he commanded, and it stood fast.

⁽¹⁰⁾ ^c The LORD ² bringeth the counsel of the heathen to nought: he maketh the devices of the people of none effect. ⁽¹¹⁾ ^d The counsel of the LORD standeth for ever, the thoughts of his heart ³ to all generations.

⁽¹²⁾ ^e Blessed *is* the nation whose God *is* the LORD; *and* the people *whom* he hath chosen for his own inheritance. ⁽¹³⁾ The LORD looketh from heaven; he beholdeth all the sons of men. ⁽¹⁴⁾ From

---

a Ps. 119. 64.

1 Or, *mercy*.

b Gen. 1. 6, 7.

c Isa. 19. 3.

2 Heb., *maketh frustrate*.

d Prov. 19. 21; Isa. 46. 10.

3 Heb., *to generation and generation*.

e Ps. 65. 4, & 144. 15.

In either case the general application is the same. Horses and mules can only be rendered obedient by restraints that are unworthy of a rational creature. The LXX. and Vulg. have "jaws" instead of "mouth," and Ewald follows them, and renders the last clause, "of those who approach thee unfriendly."

XXXIII.

This is a hymn of praise to Jehovah, as at once Almighty Creator and Ruler of the universe, and the Protector of His chosen people. It was plainly for liturgical use, and beyond this, as even the compilers of the collection left it anonymous, it is useless to inquire into its authorship or date. All that we see clearly is that faith in the protection of Jehovah and not in material force, that which we regard as the traditional faith of Israel, had by this time been firmly implanted. Both in rhythm, which is fine and well sustained, and subject this psalm bears a close relation to Ps. cxlvii.

⁽¹⁾ **Rejoice.** — A common hymnic word, meaning properly to "shout," or "sing for joy."

⁽²⁾ **Harp.** — Heb., *khinnôr* (LXX. and Vulg., "cithara"), most probably a trigon or three-cornered harp, such as may be seen sculptured in Egyptian bas-reliefs. The number of strings probably varied, as different accounts are given. (See *Bible Educator*, i. 19.)

With the psaltery and an instrument of ten strings.—Properly, as LXX. and Vulg., "with the ten-stringed psaltery." (See 1 Sam. x. 5.) Evidently a more elaborate instrument than the *khinnôr*, and with greater capacities. (See *Bible Educator*, i. 70, and art. "Psaltery" in Smith's *Biblical Dictionary*.) From the Greek *psalterion* comes the title "psalter" for the Book of Psalms. By its derivation it meant an instrument played with the fingers. The word was in use in old English:—

"And before hem went minstrels many one,
As harpes, pipes, lutes, and sautry."
CHAUCER: *The Flower and the Leaf*, 237.

⁽³⁾ **A new song.**—This expression occurs in Pss. xcvi. 1, xcviii. 1, cxlix. 1; Isa. xlii. 10; Judith xvi. 13, and was adopted in Rev. v. 9, xiv. 3. The term apparently marked the revival of national psalmody after the Captivity. "Behold, the former things are come to pass, and *new* things do I declare . . . Sing unto the Lord a new song" (Isa. xlii. 9, 10).

Play skilfully with a loud noise.—The latter words represent a Hebrew expression of common hymnic use, describing the full choral effect when instruments and voices were joined in the service of the sanctuary (Pss. xcv. 1, c. 1, &c.). Some, however, limit it (after Lev. xxv. 9) to the trumpet accompaniment, and render—

"Strike the harp deftly for him,
Amid the blare of trumpets."

⁽⁴⁾ **Right.**—The first inspiring cause of praise for a faithful Israelite is the righteousness of the God of the Covenant. But the pregnant expression, "word of Jehovah," naturally leads him on from the thought of its *truth* to the thought of its *power*, and in verses 6 and 7 we have praise of the creative act of the Almighty.

⁽⁶⁾ **The breath of his mouth.**—This is plainly only a synonym for *word*. (Comp. Isa. xi. 4, where "breath of his lips" is used for the Divine sentence of judgment upon the heathen.)

⁽⁷⁾ **As an heap.**—The image explains itself (so we speak of waves "mountains high") without reference to the passage either of the Red Sea or the Jordan. Still less is there a comparison to *heaps of corn*, some think, since *storehouses* in the next clause are not necessarily *barns*, but *reservoirs*. But the LXX., Vulg., and all ancient interpreters read *nôd* ("a skin"), instead of *nêd* ("a heap"), and make the reference to the *rain*, the clouds being considered as *bottles*. With this comp. Job xxxviii. 37.

⁽¹⁰⁾ **The Lord bringeth.**—The thought now passes on to the irresistible rule of Jehovah. His counsel stands for all generations, and being *righteous* as well as *eternal*, frustrates the counsel and thoughts of the heathen, while His chosen people (verse 12) rest in stable peace under the Theocracy. (Comp. Acts v. 38.) The word *devices* in verse 10 should be *thoughts*, as in verse 11, or, better in both, *purposes*.

Verse 12 is the pivot, as it were, on which the whole psalm turns, and was doubtless sung in full chorus.

133

Confidence in God.   PSALMS, XXXIV.   *God's Answer to Prayer.*

the place of his habitation he looketh upon all the inhabitants of the earth. (15) He fashioneth their hearts alike; he considereth all their works. (16) There is no king saved by the multitude of an host: a mighty man is not delivered by much strength. (17) An horse *is* a vain thing for safety: neither shall he deliver *any* by his great strength.

(18) *a* Behold, the eye of the LORD *is* upon them that fear him, upon them that hope in his mercy; (19) to deliver their soul from death, and to keep them alive in famine.

(20) Our soul waiteth for the LORD; he *is* our help and our shield. (21) For our heart shall rejoice in him, because we have trusted in his holy name. (22) Let thy mercy, O LORD, be upon us, according as we hope in thee.

a Job 36. 7; Ps. 34. 15; 1 Pet. 3. 12.

PSALM XXXIV.

A Psalm of David, when he changed his behaviour before ¹Abimelech; who drove him away, and he departed.

(1) I will bless the LORD at all times: his praise *shall* continually *be* in my mouth. (2) My soul shall make her boast in the LORD: the humble shall hear *thereof,* and be glad.

(3) O magnify the LORD with me, and let us exalt his name together. (4) I sought the LORD, and he heard me, and delivered me from all my fears. (5) ²They looked unto him, and were lightened: and their faces were not ashamed. (6) This poor man cried, and the LORD heard *him,* and saved him out of all his troubles.

(7) The angel of the LORD encampeth round about them that fear him, and delivereth them.

¹ Or, *Achish,* 1 Sam. 21. 13.

² Or, *They flowed unto him.*

---

(15) **He fashioneth.**—Better,

"Moulding their hearts for all,
Observing all their deeds."

The Hebrew word rendered "fashion" is that used of a potter moulding clay.

(16) **There is no king.**—Better, *The king doth not triumph by the greatness of his force.*

(17) **Safety.**—Better, *victory.* (Comp. Hab. iii. 8.) The allusion is to the war-horse.

(20—22) **Hope—wait—trust.**—The Hebrew language was naturally rich in words expressive of that attitude of expectancy which was characteristic of a nation whose golden age was not in the past, but in the future —a nation for which its great ancestor left in his dying words so suitable a motto—

"I have waited for thy salvation, O Lord,"

and which, while itself held back outside the promised land of the hope of immortality, was to be the birth-race of the great and consoling doctrine that alone could satisfy the natural craving expressed by the moralist in the well-known line—

"Man never is, but always to be, blest;"

and by the Christian apostle—

"For here we have no continuing city, but we seek one to come."

XXXIV.

This psalm consists of a string of pious sayings of a proverbial kind, all beautiful in themselves, but combined with no art beyond the alphabetical arrangement, and even this, as in Ps. xxv., not strictly carried out. A common authorship with that psalm is marked by the same omission of the *Vau* stanza, and by the completion of the number 22 by an extra *Pe* stanza at the end. Certainly the composition is of a time far later than David, and the inscription (see Note) is of no historic value. A late, even an Aramaic origin, is indicated by the meaning of *nahar* in verse 5, and possibly by the fact that the *Pe* stanza must have originally preceded that beginning with *Ayin*—an error due to the common Aramaic tendency to interchange *Ayin* and *Tsadde.* But beyond this there is nothing by which to appropriate the psalm to any particular period, still less to any particular event or individual, and it reads more like a gnomic composition expressive of the faith of the pious community than as the outpouring of individual feeling.

Title.—There seems little doubt that this title was suggested by the form of the word rendered "taste" in verse 8, *taamû,* reminding the compiler of *taamô* ("his behaviour," 1 Sam. xxi. 13), combined with that of *tithhalêl* ("shall boast," verse 2), with *yithholêl* ("he is mad," 1 Sam. xxi. 14). At least no other conjecture can account for an inscription so entirely foreign to the contents of the psalm, and containing besides an historical blunder in the king's name (the margin corrects it).

(2) **Humble.**—See Note on Ps. ix. 12. The LXX. and Vulg., "the meek." It means here those who have learnt patience in the school of suffering.

(5) **Were lightened.**—The Hebrew verb means properly "to flow," but by a natural process, as in the common phrases "streams of light," "floods of light," acquired in Aramaic the sense of "shining." Such must be its meaning in Isa. lx. 5, almost the echo of the thought in the psalm, the thought of a reflex of the Divine glory lighting up the face of those who in trouble seek God. (Theodoret has "He who approaches God, receives the rays of intellectual light.") We naturally think of the dying Stephen.

As to the construction, the subject must either be supplied from verse 2, or it must be general. The LXX. and Vulg. avoid the difficulty by changing to the second person.

(6) **This poor man.**—Better, *this sufferer*—i.e., either the writer, or Israel personified.

(7) **The angel of the Lord** is an expression which has given rise to much discussion. From comparison with other passages it may be (1) any commissioned agent of God, as a prophet (Haggai i. 13). (2) One of the celestial court (Gen. xxii. 11). (3) Any manifestation of the Divine presence, as the flame in the bush (Exod. iii. 2), the winds (Pss. xxxv. 5, 6, civ. 4). (4) Jehovah Himself, as in the phrase "the angel of

(8) O taste and see that the LORD *is* good: blessed *is* the man *that* trusteth in him.
(9) O fear the LORD, ye his saints: for *there is* no want to them that fear him.
(10) The young lions do lack, and suffer hunger: but they that seek the LORD shall not want any good *thing*.
(11) Come, ye children, hearken unto me: I will teach you the fear of the LORD. (12) *a* What man *is he that* desireth life, *and* loveth *many* days, that he may see good? (13) Keep thy tongue from evil, and thy lips from speaking guile. (14) Depart from evil, and do good; seek peace, and pursue it.
(15) *b* The eyes of the LORD *are* upon the righteous, and his ears *are open* unto their cry. (16) The face of the LORD *is* against them that do evil, to cut off the remembrance of them from the earth.

(17) *The righteous* cry, and the LORD heareth, and delivereth them out of all their troubles.
(18) The LORD *is* nigh ¹unto them that are of a broken heart; and saveth ²such as be of a contrite spirit. (19) Many *are* the afflictions of the righteous: but the LORD delivereth him out of them all. (20) He keepeth all his bones: not one of them is broken. (21) Evil shall slay the wicked: and they that hate the righteous ³shall be desolate. (22) The LORD redeemeth the soul of his servants: and none of them that trust in him shall be desolate.

a 1 Pet. 3. 10.
b Job 36. 7; Ps. 33. 18; 1 Pet. 3. 12.
1 Heb., *to the broken of heart*.
2 Heb., *contrite of spirit*.
3 Or, *shall be guilty*.

PSALM XXXV.
A Psalm of David.

(1) Plead *my cause*, O LORD, with them that strive with me: fight against them that fight against me. (2) Take hold of

---

his presence" (Isa. lxiii. 9). It may very well be, therefore, that the psalmist uses it here in a general sense for the Divine manifestation of protection. We thus avoid the difficulty in the image of *one* angel encamping round the sufferer, which other commentators try to avoid by supposing *angel* to mean either a *troop* of angels, or *captain* or *chief* of an angelic army. But for this difficulty, we should connect the psalmist's words immediately with the well-known incident in Jacob's life at Mahanaim, or with the story of Elisha and "the horses and chariots of fire" round about him. We certainly must not let go the beautiful thought that round God's elect—

"The spangled hosts keep watch in squadrons bright."

(8) **Taste.**—Comp. Heb. vi. 4; 1 Peter ii. 3.

(10) **Young lions.**—See Note, Ps. xvii. 12. The young lion is the emblem of power and self-resource. Yet these sometimes lack, but the earnest seekers after Divine truth and righteousness never. Instead of "lions," the LXX. and Vulgate have "the rich."

(11) **Come, ye children . . .**—A common proverbial style. See Prov. i. 8, and *passim*. (Comp. also 1 John ii. 1, &c.)

(12) **Desireth life.**—Better, *the man delighting in life*. These gnomic sayings are echoes from the book of Proverbs. (See especially Prov. iv. 23.)

(14) **And do good.**—Negative goodness is not sufficient. Practical good must be added.

(15) **The eyes.**—A verse quoted in 1 Pet. iii. 12. (See *New Testament Commentary*). This psalm had a deep hold on the national mind. With the expression, "his ears to their cry," we may compare the phrase, "to have a person's ear."

(16) **To cut off.**—Notice the fear, so intense and recurring to the Semitic mind, of the extinction of race. (Comp. Ps. xxi. 10; Job xviii. 17, &c.)

This verse, according to the sense, should certainly change places with verse 15. This would disarrange the acrostic, bringing *pe* before *ayin*; but, as in Lam. ii., iii., and iv. the same sequence of letters occurs, we are led to the conclusion that the order of the alphabet was not definitely or invariably fixed in respect of

these two letters, a licence intelligible enough when we remember that *tsadde*, which follows *pe*, was often interchanged with *ayin*, which precedes it.

(20) **Broken.**—See John xix. 36, *N. Test. Commentary*.

(21) **Desolate.**—Better (as in margin), *shall be found guilty*, or *condemned*.

(22) **Redeemeth.**—Comp. Ps. xxv. 22, which begins with the same letter, out of its place, and the same word.

XXXV.

This psalm opens in a warlike tone, so as to suggest a soldier for its author, and for its occasion the eve of some battle. But we soon (verses 7, 8, 11, 12) perceive that these warlike expressions are only metaphors, and that the foes of the poet are malicious slanderers and scoffers of the pious Israelites—it may be the court party in the time of one of the later kings, or, more probably, the anti-national party (see Note, verse 16) at a later time, the innovators affected by Persian or Grecian influence. Few good critics, at all events, consider the psalm Davidic. Some ascribe it to Jeremiah. But whoever was its author, it expresses, not an individual feeling alone, but that of a community despised and maligned for its piety, and appealing to Jehovah against its oppressors, with that longing for retributive justice which in an individual becomes, in a Christian view, wickedly vindictive, but to the Old Testament Church was the vindication of the Divine honour which was pledged to do justice to the chosen but afflicted people. The parallelism is fine and well sustained.

(1) **Plead my cause.**—Better, *Strive, O Jehovah, with them that strive with me*. The construction requires this, and the parallelism suggests recourse to arms rather than to the law.

Fight.—Literally, *devour*. (Comp. Num. xxiv 8. "He shall eat up the nations." So a Latin author—

"Qua medius pugnæ vorat agmina vortex."
SILIUS: *Punic.* iv. 230.

Comp. Shakespeare—

"If the wars eat us not up."—*Coriolanus*, Act i., sc. 1.)

(2) **Shield and buckler.**—Better, *buckler and shield*, as the first (Heb., *magen*) suggests a small, the

shield and buckler, and stand up for mine help. (3) Draw out also the spear, and stop *the way* against them that persecute me: say unto my soul, I *am* thy salvation. (4) ᵃLet them be confounded and put to shame that seek after my soul: let them be turned back and brought to confusion that devise my hurt. (5) ᵇLet them be as chaff before the wind, and let the angel of the LORD chase *them*. (6) Let their way be ¹dark and slippery: and let the angel of the LORD persecute them.

(7) For without cause have they hid for me their net *in* a pit, *which* without cause they have digged for my soul. (8) Let destruction come upon him ²at unawares; and let his net that he hath hid catch himself: into that very destruction let him fall.

(9) And my soul shall be joyful in the LORD: it shall rejoice in his salvation. (10) All my bones shall say, LORD, who *is* like unto thee, which deliverest the poor from him that is too strong for him, yea, the poor and the needy from him that spoileth him? (11)³False witnesses did rise up; ⁴they laid to my charge *things* that I knew not. (12) They rewarded me evil for good to the ⁵spoiling of my soul. (13) But as for me, when they were sick, my clothing *was* sackcloth: I ⁶humbled my soul with fasting; and my prayer

a Ps. 40. 14, & 70. 3.
b Job 21. 18; Ps. 1. 4; Isa. 29. 5; Hos. 13. 3.
1 Heb., *darkness and slipperiness.*
2 Heb., *which he knoweth not of.*
3 Heb., *Witnesses of wrong.*
4 Heb., *they asked me.*
5 Heb., *depriving.*
6 Or, *afflicted.*

---

latter (*tsinnah*) a large shield covering the whole body. Greek, θυρεός (see Note, Ps. v. 12.) Notice that the poet, in the intensity of his purpose, overlooks the anomaly of arming a warrior with two shields at once. The bold flight of imagination that could picture the Divine Being as a warrior, a picture common in Hebrew poetry, but here more vividly realised than anywhere else except Isa. lxiii. 1, may well excuse such a lapse.

(3) **Draw out also the spear**—*i.e.*, from the sheath, that seems to have been used to guard its point. So δουροδόκη (Homer, *Odyssey,* i. 128).

Stop the way.—So LXX., Vulg., and all ancient versions. Many modern scholars, however, are disposed to treat the word *segor* not as the imperative of a verb, but as a noun, equivalent to the Greek σάγαρις, Latin, *securis,* a Persian and Scythian weapon mentioned by Herodotus (i. 215, iv. 70) and Xenophon (*Anab.,* iv. 4, 16), and generally taken for a *battle-axe,* but by some as a *short curved sword* or a *scimitar.* It is identified by Sir Henry Rawlinson with the *khanjar* of modern Persia, "a short curved double-edged dagger, almost universally worn." The Bedouins of modern Egypt use a *schagur.*

The adoption of this rendering makes an excellent parallelism, and suits the word rendered "against," which really means "to meet," and suggests an onset instead of a mere passive attitude of defence.

(4) **Confounded.**—Comp. verse 26.

(5) **As chaff.**—Comp. Ps. i. 4, and see Note. There can be little doubt that the "angel of Jehovah" in this and the following verse is (comp. Ps. civ. 4) a personification of the "hurricane" itself, which drives before it all obstacles, and overwhelms even whole armies in dangerous places.

(6) **Dark and slippery.**—See margin. Delitzsch supposes an allusion to the passage of the Red Sea, but the picture suggests rather the passage of some dangerous mountain pass in a raging storm. "The tracks in the limestone hills of Palestine are often worn as smooth as marble; comp. Ps. lxxiii. 18" (quoted from Kay, in the *Speaker's Commentary*).

(7) **Have they hid . . .**—Literally, *they have hid for me the pit of their net,* which, as it stands, can mean nothing but a "pit with a net in it," such as was used to entrap lions and other wild beasts. But it is better to remove the word "pit" to the second clause, thus doing away with the necessity of supplying a relative, and improving the rhythm.

"For unprovoked they hid a net for me,
Unprovoked they digged a pit for my soul."

(8) **Let destruction.**—There is considerable difficulty here, and the ancient versions, by their variations, seem to point to some confusion in the text. The LXX., no doubt, are right in reading the pronouns as plurals, instead of singular. The word translated "destruction" means, primarily, a *storm,* or the *crash* that accompanies a storm (Prov. i. 27), and if with the Syriac we might supply a clause, both parallelism and sense would be complete.

"Let men come upon him (them) unexpectedly.
Let the net which he had catch himself,
The pit which he (they) digged, let him (them) fall into it,
In ruin let him (them) fall into it."

For "unawares," see margin and Note, Song of Sol. vi. 12.

(10) **All my bones.**—As we say, "all the fibres of my body." (Comp. Pss. vi. 2, xxxiv. 20.)

The poor . . . the poor.—Better, *the sufferer . . . the sufferer.*

(12) **To the spoiling of my soul.**—Literally, *desolation to my soul.* We may paraphrase,

"They rewarded me evil for good,
Which to me was desolation."

(13) **And my prayer returned into mine own bosom.**—This has been most variously explained. The context evidently implies something done for the benefit of the whilome friends for whom, in their sickness, the poet had worn sackcloth, and had fasted and adopted all the other signs of mourning. We must therefore set aside (1) the idea of *fruitless* prayer, in spite of the analogy of Matt. x. 13, Luke x. 6. (2) The notion that the answer to the prayer came back to the psalmist himself, instead of to those for whom it was offered, must also be set aside. And (3) we must reject the notion of secret, *i.e.,* silent prayer, in spite of Prov. xvii. 23, xxi. 14, since all the "outward and visible" signs of mourning are indicated, and the very object was to show sympathy and interest.

There remains (1) the literal, *and my prayer turned upon my bosom,* referring to the posture described in verse 14. (Comp. 1 Kings xviii. 42, where, however, there is no express mention of prayer.) The words

The Psalmist Prays for Help, PSALMS, XXXVI. *and for his Enemies' Confusion.*

returned into mine own bosom. (14) I ¹behaved myself ²as though *he had been* my friend *or* brother: I bowed down heavily, as one that mourneth *for his* mother. (15) But in mine ³adversity they rejoiced, and gathered themselves together: *yea,* the abjects gathered themselves together against me, and I knew *it* not; they did tear *me,* and ceased not: (16) with hypocritical mockers in feasts, they gnashed upon me with their teeth.

(17) Lord, how long wilt thou look on? rescue my soul from their destructions, ⁴my darling from the lions.

(18) ᵃ I will give thee thanks in the great congregation: I will praise thee among ⁵ much people. (19) Let not them that are mine enemies ⁶wrongfully rejoice over me: *neither* let them wink with the eye that hate me without a cause. (20) For they speak not peace: but they devise deceitful matters against *them that are* quiet in the land. (21) Yea, they opened their mouth wide against me, *and* said, Aha, aha, our eye hath seen *it.* (22) *This* thou hast seen, O Lord: keep not silence: O Lord, be not far from

| 1 Heb., *walked.* |
| 2 Heb., *as a friend, as a brother to me.* |
| 3 Heb., *halting.* |
| 4 Heb., *my only one.* |
| a Ps. 40. 9, 10, & 111. 1. |
| 5 Heb., *strong.* |
| 6 Heb., *falsely.* |
| 7 Heb., *Ah, ah, our soul.* |
| 8 Heb., *my righteousness.* |

me. (23) Stir up thyself, and awake to my judgment, *even* unto my cause, my God and my Lord.

(24) Judge me, O Lord my God, according to thy righteousness; and let them not rejoice over me. (25) Let them not say in their hearts, ⁷Ah, so would we have it: let them not say, We have swallowed him up. (26) Let them be ashamed and brought to confusion together that rejoice at mine hurt: let them be clothed with shame and dishonour that magnify *themselves* against me. (27) Let them shout for joy, and be glad, that favour ⁸my righteous cause: yea, let them say continually, Let the Lord be magnified, which hath pleasure in the prosperity of his servant.

(28) And my tongue shall speak of thy righteousness *and* of thy praise all the day long.

PSALM XXXVI.

To the chief Musician, *A Psalm* of David the servant of the Lord.

(1) The transgression of the wicked saith within my heart, *that there is* no

---

were, as it were, muttered into his bosom. This is the view of Ewald and Delitzsch, but seems prosaic. (2) The far more probable meaning, *my prayer came back again and again to my bosom, i.e.,* was repeated over and over again; just as we say, "the thought recurred to my mind." (Comp. the common phrase for thoughts coming upon the heart, Jer. iii. 16, vii. 31, etc.) The Hebrew verb has this frequentative sense in one of its conjugations.

(14) **I bowed down heavily.**—Better, *I went squalid, and bowed down,* alluding to the neglected beard and person, and to the dust and ashes of Oriental mourning.

(15) **In mine adversity.**—Better, *at my fall.*

The abjects . . .—The Hebrew word occurs only here. It is derived from a root meaning *to smite,* but its form is perplexing. The ancient versions all give it an active sense. LXX. and Vulg. "whips"; Symmachus, "smiters"; Chaldee, "the wicked who smite me with their words," probably a correct paraphrase. The passive, "these smitten," or "abjects," is due to R. Kimchi.

And I knew it not—*i.e.,* either (1) "unawares," as in verse 8; (2) "for what reason I knew not"; (3) "whom I knew not"; (4) "and I was innocent." Of these possible explanations (2) is to be preferred.

(16) **With hypocritical mockers in feasts.**—This clause is full of difficulty. The LXX. and Vulg. have, "they tempted me, they mocked me with a mocking"; Symmachus, "in hypocrisy, with feigned words"; Chaldee, "with derisive words of flattery." All these take the word rendered in the Authorised Version, "feasts," as a cognate of a word in Isa. xxviii. 11, translated "stammering," but which means rather, "barbarisms." (Comp. Isa. xxxiii. 19.) The word

rendered "hypocritical" more properly means "profane" or "impious." With these meanings we get a very good sense (with evident reference to the malicious attacks of foreigners, or of the anti-national party that affected foreign ways) *in the manner of profane barbaric barbarisms,* or *with profanity and barbarism.*

As to the rendering "feasts," it comes from treating the word as the same used (1 Kings xvii. 13) for a "cake." "Cake-mockers" are explained to be parasites who hang about the tables of the rich, getting their dinner in return for their buffooneries. (Comp. the Greek ψωμοκόλακες; Latin, *bucellarii.*)

(17) **Darling . . .** see margin and Note to Psalm xxii. 20.

The lions is another suitable epithet for the hostile foreign party, so bitter against the genuine Israelite.

(19) **Wink.**—Prov. vi. 13, x. 10; a common gesture of agreement among confederates.

(20) **Quiet in the land.**—For the construction, comp. Isa. xxiii. 8: "The honourable of the earth." They are evidently the pious Jews who wished to preserve their national life and religion against foreign influence and intervention, and certainly among them were Levites.

(23) **Stir up thyself.**—Comp. Ps. vii. 6.

XXXVI.

This psalm consists of three distinctly defined stanzas of nearly equal length. The first portrays the wicked man who has reached the lowest grade of impiety. The second exalts the goodness and justice of God. The third, which is, in a sort, a practical application of the others, expresses, under the form of a prayer, the right choice to make between the two tendencies, the pious and the impious. The sudden transition at the end of

fear of God before his eyes. (2) For he flattereth himself in his own eyes, ¹until his iniquity be found to be hateful. (3) The words of his mouth *are* iniquity and deceit: he hath left off to be wise, *and* to do good. (4) He deviseth ²mischief upon his bed; he setteth himself in a way *that is* not good; he abhorreth not evil.

1 Heb., *to find his iniquity to hate.*
2 Or, *vanity.*
a Ps. 57. 10, & 108. 4.
3 Heb., *the mountains of God.*
4 Heb., *precious.*

(5) ᵃThy mercy, O LORD, *is* in the heavens; *and* thy faithfulness *reacheth* unto the clouds. (6) Thy righteousness *is* like ³the great mountains; thy judgments *are* a great deep: O LORD, thou preservest man and beast. (7) How ⁴excellent *is* thy lovingkindness, O God! therefore the children of men

---

the first stanza has led some critics to pronounce the psalm composite. But what else can the heart, which would not sink beneath the oppressive sense of the accumulated sin and misery of earth, do, but turn suddenly and confidently to the thought of an infinite and abiding goodness and truth. The only resource of faith that would not fail is to appeal from earth to heaven, and see, high over all the fickleness and falsehood of men, the faithfulness of God: strong above all the insolence and tyranny of the wicked His eternal justice: large, deep, and sure, when all other supports seem to fail, His vast and unchanging love.

Those who understand by "God's house," in verse 8, the Temple, reject the Davidic authorship. But understood of the world generally, or, better, of the heavenly abode of the Divine, it does not serve as an indication of date, and there is nothing else in the poem to decide when it was written. The parallelism is varied.

Title.—For "servant of the Lord," as applied to David, see Ps. xviii. (title).

(1) **The transgression of the wicked saith within my heart . . .**—The literal rendering of the present Hebrew text is, *An utterance of sin to the wicked within my heart.* The common phrase rendered in our version, "Thus saith Jehovah," is here imitated, "Thus saith sin." "To the wicked" cannot, as some explain, mean "concerning the wicked." The only possible meaning of the text as it stands is therefore, "Thus saith sin to (me) the wicked man in my heart." But there can be no question that the psalmist wrote "in *his* heart," since all the ancient versions, with the exception of the Chaldee Paraphrase, followed this reading, and some MSS. still show it. This gives us a very fine sense. Sin is personified as the evil counsellor or prompter sitting in the heart of the wicked to suggest evil thoughts: *Sin in the wicked man's heart is his oracle.* Conscience is on the wrong side.

There is no fear . . .—This is not the suggestion of sin just mentioned, but an explanation of the condition into which the wicked man has sunk. Impiety and irreverence have so corrupted his nature, that sin has become his oracle.

(2) **For he flattereth . . .**—Literally, *For he* (or, *it*) *makes smooth to him in his eyes to find out his evil to hate.* (See margin.) A sentence of great difficulty. We must seek for the key to the interpretation of these words in the balance of the two phrases, "before his eyes," "in his own eyes," and must take the two verses together. They form, in fact, an example of introverted parallelism. (See Gen. Introduction.)

Sin is the wicked man's oracle in his heart;
No fear of God is before his eyes;
He makes all smooth to himself in his eyes.
As to the discovery of his guilt that is his hate;

Or,

The discovery of his guilt is the only thing he hates.

This reading takes the two infinitives as subject and complement with the copula understood. It would be strange if Hebrew, which, above all languages, makes the infinitive do duty in various ways, offered no instance of such a use. (For *matsa aven* in the sense of the *discovery of guilt*, comp. Gen. xliv. 16; Hos. xii. 8, etc.)

(3, 4) From the secret promptings of sin, the description of the ungodly passes on to its issues in words and deeds. It is an awful picture of wickedness of a man abandoning himself without check or remorse to the inspiration of his own evil heart. He goes from bad to worse. In a great English tragedy, the murderer, though he has determined to wade farther in blood, yet prays against the horror of nightly temptations:

"Merciful powers,
Restrain in me the cursed thoughts that nature
Gives way to in repose.

But this man "deviseth mischief upon his bed." When even the worst criminals shudder at their own deeds, whispering to their "deaf pillows" the agonies that creep over them with darkness and silence, this ungodly man of the Hebrew poet's picture is occupied rather in scheming fresh villainies; even then *he abhorreth not evil*, or better, *rejecteth not*, catches rather at every fresh suggestion, and shapes it to his end.

(5) **Thy mercy, O Lord, is in . . .**—Better,

Jehovah, to the heavens (reacheth) thy grace,
Thy faithfulness to the sky.

i.e., there are no narrower bounds of divine mercy and truth.

(6) **Great mountains.**—See margin, and compare Ps. lxxx. 10, "cedars of God." So too the rain is called "God's brook." The epithet not only implies greatness and dignity, but also has reference to God as Creator.

A great deep.—The reference, as usual, with the words *deep, depth,* is to the great abyss of waters, of which the seas were regarded as the surface.

The twofold comparison in this verse recalls Wordsworth's lines—

"Two voices are there: one is of the sea,
One of the mountains—each a mighty voice."

but while to the modern poet the voice is *Liberty*, to the ancient Hebrew it is *Righteousness*. The majesty of the hills has often suggested the supremacy of right over wrong—

"Thou hast a voice, great mountain, to repeal
Large codes of fraud and woe."

The calm of the infinite sea has often soothed agitated souls. Hebrew poetry connected both immediately with God, the uplifted strength of the hills became an emblem of His eternal truth; the depth and expanse of the infinite sea of His outspread goodness and inexhaustible justice.

(7) **How excellent.**—Better, *how precious.*

Therefore . . .—Better, the simple conjunction, *and sons of men, they find shelter,* &c.

Prayer for God's Favour. PSALMS, XXXVII. *The Short Career of the Wicked.*

put their trust under the shadow of thy wings. ⁽⁸⁾ They shall be ¹abundantly satisfied with the fatness of thy house; and thou shalt make them drink of the river of thy pleasures. ⁽⁹⁾ For with thee *is* the fountain of life: in thy light shall we see light.

⁽¹⁰⁾ O ²continue thy lovingkindness unto them that know thee; and thy righteousness to the upright in heart. ⁽¹¹⁾ Let not the foot of pride come against me, and let not the hand of the wicked remove me. ⁽¹²⁾ There are the workers of iniquity fallen: they are cast down, and shall not be able to rise.

1 Heb., *watered.*

2 Heb., *draw out at length.*

a Prov. 28.17, & 24.1.

3 Heb., *in truth,* or, *stableness.*

PSALM XXXVII.

A Psalm of David.

⁽¹⁾ Fret ^anot thyself because of evildoers, neither be thou envious against the workers of iniquity. ⁽²⁾ For they shall soon be cut down like the grass, and wither as the green herb.

⁽³⁾ Trust in the LORD, and do good; *so* shalt thou dwell in the land, and ³verily thou shalt be fed. ⁽⁴⁾ Delight thyself

---

Shadow of thy wings.—See Ps. xvii. 8, Note.

⁽⁸⁾ **They shall be abundantly satisfied.**—Better, in order to preserve the parallelism, literally, *They shall drink to the full.* LXX. and Vulg., "They shall be intoxicated with," &c.

Fatness, therefore, is not here the fat of the sacrificial offerings, but the stream of grace flowing from above, to enrich men as the rain enriches the earth. (Comp. Ps. lxv. 11, where "fatness" means "fertilising showers.")

The **house** of God may either be the whole earth (Gesenius), or, more probably, *heaven,* just as the temple is used (Pss. xi. 4, xviii. 6, xxix. 9). God's lovingkindness is regarded as

"An endless fountain of immortal drink,
Pouring unto us from the heaven's brink."
KEATS: *Endymion.*

⁽⁹⁾ **In thy light.**—Better, *by thy light.* This wonderful verse inspired Milton's sublime invocation:

"The author of all being,
Fountain of light, thyself invisible
Amidst the glorious brightness where thou sitt'st."

It contains the germ of that moral and spiritual teaching which had its highest development in the Epistles of St. John. But the original intention of the words seems to be that the favour and bounty of God commend themselves as divine in origin, especially to those in the covenant relation.

⁽¹¹⁾ **The foot of pride . . . the hand of the wicked.**—The one tramples on the lowly; the other is full of violence.

Remove.—Better, *expel,* but we have no indication from where. Perhaps from the Temple.

⁽¹²⁾ **There . . .**—*Of place.* The poet has some definite incident in his mind, but has not told enough for us to identify it.

XXXVII.

This psalm is mainly composed of quotations and adaptations from older writings, especially the Book of Proverbs (see notes *passim*), which are strung together with no other art than that suggested by the alphabetical arrangement, all having one end, to comfort the pious Israelite under the spectacle of successful wickedness, confirming him in his trust in Jehovah, and warning him neither to envy the prospects of the impious, nor to despair of his own state. It is by no means a speculative poem. It does not treat the perplexing problems of life philosophically. The poet has one answer, and only one, for the questions handled so pathetically and profoundly in the Book of Job. The happiness of the wicked cannot endure, and the justice of Jehovah will assuredly re-establish the right, punishing the godless and recompensing the patience and fidelity of the godly. This one conviction—sincere expression of the religious faith of Israel at any period before the captivity—is repeated many times, but never departs from the form of simple assertion. No argument is used, for none is felt to be required. Such conviction as the poet's only needs affirmation. The time of the exile when the hope of regaining the Promised Land was the consolation of the pious, probably produced the psalm.

⁽¹⁾ **Fret . . .**—This verb, repeated in verses 7, 8, is found besides only in Prov. xxiv. 19. Its meaning is *to heat or inflame oneself.*

Neither be thou envious . . .—This has a similar root-meaning (comp. our "burn with jealousy"), and so is in close parallelism with "fret." This verse occurs almost word for word in Prov. iii. 31, xxiii. 16, xxiv. 1, and Ps. lxxiii. 3.

⁽²⁾ **For they . . .**—This inevitable metaphor for the brevity of human life, made still more forcible in an Eastern clime where vegetation is so rapid both in growth and decay, and generally in the Bible applied, without distinction of good or bad, with a mournful sigh over human weakness, becomes here a source of comfort to the godly man.

Green herb.—Literally, *greenness of herbage.*

⁽³⁾ The alphabetic structure helps the poet to make an emphatic threefold exhortation to piety. *Trust in Jehovah; commit thy way to Jehovah; rest in Jehovah.*

So shalt thou dwell . . .—The Authorised Version is quite right in taking the verbs in this clause as futures. (Comp. verses 11, 18, 22.) Emigration, when referred to by the prophets (Jer. xxv. 5, xxxv. 15), is always represented as compulsory, and it was a promise of preservation from it, not a warning against it, that the pious Israelite needed.

And verily thou shalt be fed.—Taken literally this promise may be addressed to the Levites, and may contain allusion to their precarious condition, dependent as they were on offerings and tithes, but the Hebrew may also have the meanings: (1) *Thou shalt feed on* (or *enjoy*) *stability* (or *security*). (Comp. Isa. xxxiii. 6: "and wisdom and knowledge shall be the stability of thy times.") (2) *Thou shalt pasture on faithfulness, i.e.,* be supported by God's truth and righteousness as by a rich pasture. (Comp. Ps. xxiii. 1, and, for the expression, Prov. xv. 14, "feedeth on foolishness.") Possibly both were combined in the

The Different State of   PSALMS, XXXVII.   *the Godly and the Wicked.*

also in the LORD; and he shall give thee the desires of thine heart. ⁽⁵⁾ ^{1 a}Commit thy way unto the LORD; trust also in him; and he shall bring *it* to pass. ⁽⁶⁾ And he shall bring forth thy righteousness as the light, and thy judgment as the noonday. ⁽⁷⁾ ²Rest in the LORD, and wait patiently for him: fret not thyself because of him who prospereth in his way, because of the man who bringeth wicked devices to pass. ⁽⁸⁾ Cease from anger, and forsake wrath: fret not thyself in any wise to do evil. ⁽⁹⁾ For evildoers shall be cut off: but those that wait upon the LORD, they shall inherit the earth. ⁽¹⁰⁾ For yet a little while, and the wicked *shall not be:* yea, thou shalt diligently consider his place, and it *shall* not *be*. ⁽¹¹⁾ ^bBut the meek shall inherit the earth; and shall delight themselves in the abundance of peace. ⁽¹²⁾ The wicked ³plotteth against the just, and gnasheth upon him with his teeth. ⁽¹³⁾ ^cThe LORD shall laugh at him: for he seeth that his day is coming. ⁽¹⁴⁾ The wicked have drawn out the sword, and have bent their bow, to cast down the poor and needy, *and* to slay ⁴such as be of upright conversation. ⁽¹⁵⁾ Their sword shall enter into their own heart, and their bows shall be broken. ⁽¹⁶⁾ A little that a righteous man hath *is* better than the riches of many wicked. ⁽¹⁷⁾ For the arms of the wicked shall be broken: but the LORD upholdeth the righteous. ⁽¹⁸⁾ The LORD knoweth the days of the upright: and their inheritance shall be for ever. ⁽¹⁹⁾ They shall not be ashamed in the evil time: and in the days of famine they shall be satisfied. ⁽²⁰⁾ But the wicked shall perish, and the enemies of the LORD *shall be* as ⁵the fat of lambs: they shall consume; into smoke shall they consume away. ⁽²¹⁾ The wicked borroweth, and payeth not again: but the righteous sheweth mercy, and giveth. ⁽²²⁾ For *such as be* blessed of him shall inherit the earth; and *they that be* cursed of him shall be cut off. ⁽²³⁾ The steps of a *good* man are ⁶ordered by the LORD: and he delighteth in his way. ⁽²⁴⁾ Though he fall, he shall not be utterly cast down: for the LORD upholdeth *him with* his hand. ⁽²⁵⁾ I have been young, and *now* am old; yet have I not seen the righteous forsaken, nor his seed begging bread. ⁽²⁶⁾ *He is* ⁷ ever merciful, and lendeth; and his seed *is* blessed. ⁽²⁷⁾ Depart from evil, and do good; and dwell for evermore. ⁽²⁸⁾ For

Marginal notes: 1 Heb., *Roll thy way upon the LORD*.   *a* Prov. 16. 3; Matt. 6. 25; 1 Pet. 5. 7.   2 Heb., *Be silent to the LORD*.   *b* Matt. 5. 5.   3 Or, *practiseth*.   *c* Ps. 2. 4.   4 Heb., *the upright of way*.   5 Heb., *the preciousness of lambs*.   6 Or, *established*.   7 Heb., *all the day*.

---

psalmist's thought, for the faithfulness of God is the security of man.

⁽⁵⁾ **Commit . . .**—See margin, and Ps. xxii. 8. (Comp. Prov. xvi. 3.) In Ps. lv. 22 the word is different.

⁽⁶⁾ **The light.**—The image is from an Eastern dawn and the progress of the sun to its meridian glory. (Comp. Job xi. 17; Isa. lviii. 10.)

⁽⁷⁾ **Rest . . .**—Better, *Hush! Be still!* See margin. The good man, seeing merit unrewarded and wickedness, on the other hand, constantly successful, is tempted to repine. For a later echo of the poet's thought, irradiated by Christian hope, we may recur to Coleridge's well-known "Complaint" and its "reproof."

⁽⁸⁾ **In any wise to do evil . . .**—Better, *only to do evil*, i.e., only evil can come of it. Comp. Prov. xiv. 23, "tendeth only to penury."

⁽¹⁰⁾ **For yet a little . . .**—Better,

For yet a little while, and the wicked is not;
Thou lookest at his place, and he is not;

i.e., he has dropped out of his place in society, his tribe knows him no more.

⁽¹¹⁾ **Shall inherit.**—A repetition of verse 3.—Better, *are heirs of the land*, i.e., Canaan. Christ's Beatitude (see Matt. v. 3, *N. Test. Commentary*) widens the promise and lifts it to a higher level. The quiet, unpretending, contented servant of God gets more true blessedness out of the earth, and so more truly possesses it, than the ungodly, though they be lords of broad acres.

⁽¹³⁾ **Shall laugh.**—Comp. Ps. ii. 4, Note; his day, i.e., the day of trouble or retribution for the wicked, as we see from Ps. cxxxvii. 7; Job xviii. 20, etc.

⁽¹⁵⁾ **Their sword.**—The *lex talionis*. (Comp. Ps. vii. 15, 16.)

⁽¹⁶⁾ **A little.**—A natural reflection, when it is remembered that great riches bring corresponding cares (Prov. xv. 16), and often lead to ruinous indulgence and luxury (Prov. xiii. 25; Job xx. 12.) Besides, the contentment which is often enjoyed in virtuous poverty seldom dwells with the mammon of unrighteousness.

⁽¹⁷⁾ **The arms** —i.e., of the body, not the sword and bow mentioned above. In contrast, the arms of Jehovah are under the righteous, and uphold him.

⁽¹⁸⁾ **Knoweth.**—See Ps. i. 6, Note.

⁽²⁰⁾ **As the fat of lambs.**—It is now generally allowed that this should be rendered *as the glory of the meadows*, recurring to the image of verse 2. The next clause may then be either, *they are consumed, with smoke they are consumed*; or, *they pass away, like smoke they pass away*.

⁽²³⁾ **The steps.**—Comp. Prov. xx. 24, xvi. 9, passages which are in favour of a general interpretation here, not confined to the good man. Render, *man's steps are established by Jehovah*, i.e., all the stability in human conduct comes from His guidance.

⁽²⁸⁾ **For the Lord.**—In the Hebrew the stanza that should begin with the letter *ayin* is wanting, but may be restored by a very slight change, to agree with the

140

the LORD loveth judgment, and forsaketh not his saints; they are preserved for ever: but the seed of the wicked shall be cut off.

(29) The righteous shall inherit the land, and dwell therein for ever. (30) The mouth of the righteous speaketh wisdom, and his tongue talketh of judgment. (31) The law of his God *is* in his heart; none of his ¹ steps shall slide. (32) The wicked watcheth the righteous, and seeketh to slay him. (33) The LORD will not leave him in his hand, nor condemn him when he is judged.

(34) Wait on the LORD, and keep his way, and he shall exalt thee to inherit the land: when the wicked are cut off, thou shalt see *it*. (35) I have seen the wicked in great power, and spreading himself like ² a green bay tree. (36) Yet he passed away, and, lo, he *was* not: yea, I sought him, but he could not be found. (37) Mark the perfect *man*, and behold the upright, for the end of *that* man *is* peace. (38) But the transgressors shall be destroyed together: the end of the wicked shall be cut off.

(39) But the salvation of the righteous *is* of the LORD: *he is* their strength in the time of trouble. (40) And the LORD shall help them, and deliver them: he shall deliver them from the wicked, and save them, because they trust in him.

¹ Or, *goings.*

² Or, *a green tree that groweth in his own soil.*

PSALM XXXVIII.

A Psalm of David, to bring to remembrance.

(1) O LORD, rebuke me not in thy wrath: neither chasten me in thy hot displeasure. (2) For thine arrows stick fast in me, and thy hand presseth me sore. (3) *There is* no soundness in my flesh because of thine anger; neither *is there any* ³ rest in my bones because of

³ Heb., *peace, or, health.*

Codex Alex., of the LXX., the Vulg. and Symmachus. "The unjust shall be punished."

Probably the transcriber was misled by the *tsaddê* of the next verse, since that letter and *ayin* were often interchanged. (See Note, Ps. xxxiv. 14.)

(35) **In great power.**—Terrible, like a tyrant.

Green bay tree.—The Hebrew word elsewhere implies a "native" as opposed to "a foreigner." So here *an indigenous tree.* "It may be questioned whether any particular tree is intended by the psalmist; but if so, it must have been an evergreen, and may possibly be the Sweet Bay (*Laurus nobilis*), which is a native of Palestine. We met with it near Hebron; on Mount Carmel in great plenty; on Tabor, and in various glades of Galilee and Gilead" (Tristram, *Natural History of Bible,* 338).

The LXX. and Vulg., by slightly altering the text, have, "as cedars of Lebanon."

(36) **Yet he passed away.**—This should be, *And there went one by,* &c. LXX. and Vulg. have, "And I passed by." (Comp. Prayer Book version.)

(37) **For the end of that man is peace.**—This is quite wrongly translated, since *acharith* must here mean, as in Ps. cix. 13; Amos. iv. 2, ix. 1, "posterity." The parallelism decides in favour of this.

> Mark the honest man, and behold the upright;
> For a posterity (shall be) to the man of peace:
> But transgressors are altogether destroyed.
> The posterity of the wicked is destroyed.

So the LXX. and Vulg.

XXXVIII.

Reading only the first part of this psalm (verses 1—11), we should positively assign it to some individual sufferer who had learnt the lesson which St. Jerome says is here taught: "if any sickness happens to the body, we are to seek for the medicine of the soul." But, reading on, we find that the complaint of bodily suffering gives way to a description of active and deadly enemies, who, in the figure so common in the Psalms, beset the pious with snares. It is better, therefore, to think rather of the sufferings of the community of the faithful, who have learnt to attribute their troubles to their own sins, here described, after the manner of the prophets (Isa. i. 6) but even more forcibly, under the figure of distressing forms of sickness.

Title.—Comp. title Ps. lxx. In 1 Chron. xvi. 4 we read, "And he appointed certain Levites to minister before the ark of the Lord, and to *record,* and to *thank* and praise the Lord God of Israel." In the words *thank* and *praise* it is natural to see allusion to the *Hodu* and *Hallelujah* psalms, so called because beginning with those words, and as "to record" is in Hebrew the word used in this title and that to Psalm lxx., it brings these two psalms also in connection with the Levitical duties. "The memorial" was a regular name for one part of the meat offering, and possibly the title is a direction to use these psalms at the moment it was made. The LXX. and Vulg. add, "about the Sabbath," which is possibly a mistake for "for the Sabbath."

(1) **O Lord, rebuke.**—See Note, Ps. vi. 1, of which verse this is almost a repetition.

(2) **For thine arrows . . . .**—The same figure is used of the disease from which Job suffered (elephantiasis? Job vi. 4); of famine (Ezek. v. 16); and generally of divine judgments (Deut. xxxii. 23). By itself it therefore decides nothing as to the particular cause of the Psalmist's grief.

Stick fast.—Better, *have sunk into,* from a root meaning *to descend. Presseth,* in the next clause, is from the same verb. Translate, therefore,

> For thine arrows have fallen deep into me,
> And fallen upon me has thine hand.

(3) **Rest . . .**—Better, *health.* The Hebrew is from a root meaning *to be whole. Peace* (see margin), the reading of the LXX. and Vulg. is a derived meaning.

The Psalmist in Affliction PSALMS, XXXIX. *Declares his Sorrow and Penitence.*

my sin. (4) For mine iniquities are gone over mine head: as an heavy burden they are too heavy for me. (5) My wounds stink *and* are corrupt because of my foolishness.
(6) I am ¹troubled; I am bowed down greatly; I go mourning all the day long. (7) For my loins are filled with a loathsome *disease:* and *there is* no soundness in my flesh. (8) I am feeble and sore broken: I have roared by reason of the disquietness of my heart.
(9) Lord, all my desire *is* before thee; and my groaning is not hid from thee. (10) My heart panteth, my strength faileth me: as for the light of mine eyes, it also ²is gone from me. (11) My lovers and my friends stand aloof from my ³sore; and ⁴my kinsmen stand afar off. (12) They also that seek after my life lay snares *for me:* and they that seek my hurt speak mischievous things, and imagine deceits all the day long.
(13) But I, as a deaf *man,* heard not; and *I was* as a dumb man *that* openeth not his mouth. (14) Thus I was as a man that heareth not, and in whose mouth *are* no reproofs.
(15) For ⁵in thee, O LORD, do I hope: thou wilt ⁶hear, O Lord my God.
(16) For I said, *Hear me,* lest *otherwise* they should rejoice over me: when my foot slippeth, they magnify *themselves* against me. (17) For I *am* ready ⁷to halt, and my sorrow *is* continually before me. (18) For I will declare mine iniquity; I will be sorry for my sin. (19) But mine enemies ⁸*are* lively, *and* they are strong: and they that hate me wrongfully are multiplied. (20) They also that render evil for good are mine adversaries; because I follow *the thing that* good *is.*
(21) Forsake me not, O LORD: O my God, be not far from me. (22) Make haste ⁹to help me, O Lord my salvation.

PSALM XXXIX.
To the chief Musician, *even* to *a* Jeduthun, A Psalm of David.

(1) I said, I will take heed to my

---

1 Heb., *wried.*
2 Heb., *is not with me.*
3 Heb., *stroke.*
4 Or, *my neighbours.*
5 Or, *thee do I wait for.*
6 Or, *answer.*
7 Heb., *for halting.*
8 Heb., *being living, are strong.*
9 Heb., *for my help.*

a 1 Chron. 25. 1.

---

(4) **Are gone over mine head.**—Like waves or a flood. (Comp. Pss. xviii. 15, lxix. 2, 15. Comp. "A sea of troubles."—*Hamlet,* Act iii., scene i.)

(5) **Wounds.**—Better, *stripes,* as in LXX.
Stink and are corrupt.—Both words denote suppuration; the first in reference to the offensive smell, the second of the discharge of matter; the whole passage recalls Isa. i. 6, *seq.*
Foolishness.—Men are generally even more loth to confess their folly than their sins.
(6) **I am troubled**,—Better,

I am made to writhe (see margin),
I am bowed down exceedingly,
All day long I go about squalid.

(See Ps. xxxv. 14, and comp. Isa. xxi. 3.) The usual Oriental signs of mourning are alluded to in the last clause.

(7) **Loathsome disease.**—The Hebrew word is a passive participle of a verb meaning to *scorch,* and here means *inflamed* or *inflammation.* Ewald renders "ulcers." The LXX. and Vulg., deriving from another root meaning *to be light,* or *made light of,* render "mockings."

(8) **I am feeble and sore broken.** — Better, *I am become deadly cold, and am quite worn out.*
Disquietness.—Properly, *roaring.* Thus, *of the sea* (Isa. v. 30), *of lions* (Prov. xix. 12, xx. 2). A very slight alteration once suggested by Hitzig, but since abandoned, would give here, "I roared more than the roaring of a lion."

(9) **All my desire.**—Notice the clutch at the thought of divine justice, as the clutch of a drowning man amid that sea of trouble.

(10) **Panteth.**—Better, *palpitates.* The Hebrew word, like *palpitate,* expresses the beating of the heart, by its sound, *secharchar.*

(11) **Sore** is rather *stroke,* as in margin, or *plague.* His friends, looking on him as "one smitten of God," and thinking "he must be wicked to deserve such pain," abandon him as too vile for their society.
Kinsmen.—Render rather, as in margin, *neighbours,* or *near ones.*

Those who should have been near me stand aloof.

(14) **Reproofs.** — Better, *replies* or *justifications.* (For the whole passage comp. Isa. liii. 7.)
(15) **Thou wilt hear.**—*Thou* is emphatic.
(16) **Lest.**—It is better to carry on the force of the particle of condition:

For I said, Lest they should rejoice over me:
Lest, when my foot slipped, they should vaunt themselves against me.

(18) **Sorry.**—The note of true penitence is here. The sorrow is for the *sin* itself, not for its miserable results.
(19) **But mine enemies are lively.**—See margin. But the parallelism and a comparison with Ps. xxxv. 19 lead to the suspicion that the true reading is "without cause."

XXXIX.

"Undoubtedly," says Ewald, "the finest elegy in the Psalter;" and the same scholar pronounces it original, so that the many points of similarity with the book of Job (see Notes, *passim*) must be taken to indicate the acquaintance of its author with this Psalm. Perhaps it is from this elegy that he takes up the problem offered by the contradictions of life which he carries so much farther. A short refrain (verses 5 and 11) enriches the varied versification.

Title.—The inserted "even" assumes that Jeduthun was the choir-master or leader to whom the musical direction of the Psalm was assigned. But it is possible

ways, that I sin not with my tongue: I will keep ¹my mouth with a bridle, while the wicked is before me. ⁽²⁾ I was dumb with silence, I held my peace, *even* from good; and my sorrow was ²stirred. ⁽³⁾ My heart was hot within me, while I was musing the fire burned: *then* spake I with my tongue, ⁽⁴⁾ LORD, make me to know mine end, and the measure of my days, what it *is*; *that* I may know ³how frail I *am*.

⁽⁵⁾ Behold, thou hast made my days *as* an handbreadth; and mine age *is* as nothing before thee: verily every man ⁴at his best state *is* altogether ᵃ vanity. Selah. ⁽⁶⁾ Surely every man walketh in ⁵a vain shew: surely they are disquieted in vain: he heapeth up *riches*,

1 Heb., *a bridle, or, muzzle for my mouth.*
2 Heb., *troubled.*
3 Or, *what time I have here.*
4 Heb., *settled.*
a Ps. 62. 9, & 144. 4.
5 Heb., *an image.*

---

that the choir itself may have continued to be known by the name of the old master long after he had passed away. Jeduthun (variously written, as in the Hebrew here *Jedithin*) is identified with Ethan (1 Chron. xv. 17) the Merarite, who with Heman the Korahite and Asaph the Gershonite were appointed musical directors (1 Chron. xv. 19) of the Temple service. (Comp. titles of Ps. lxi. and lxxvii.)

⁽¹⁾ **My tongue.**—To enter into the feeling of the poet we must remember the unrestrained way in which Orientals give way to grief. It was natural and becoming for him to "roar" (Ps. xxxviii. 8, &c.) out his indignation or his grief, to mutter (Ps. i. 2, &c.) aloud his prayers, to speak out on every impulse. Now he determines to endure in silence and mutely bear the worst, rather than speak what may in the eyes of the impious be construed into a murmur against Divine Providence, into impatience under the Divine decree. (Comp. Ps. xxxviii. 13, 14.)

With a bridle.—See margin, and comp. Deut. xxv. 4, where the cognate verb occurs. The root-meaning is "stop." For the metaphor comp. James i. 26, and Plato, *Laws*, iii. 701, "the argument, like a horse, ought to be pulled up from time to time, and not be allowed to run away, but held with bit and bridle." (Comp. also Virgil, *Æneid*, vi. 79.)

⁽²⁾ **Even from good.**—This interpretation, while following the LXX., Vulg., and most ancient versions, is suspicious, since the particle, rendered *from*, is not generally used in this sense after a verb expressing silence. Indeed there is only one instance which at all supports this rendering (1 Kings xxii. 3, margin). Nor does the context require or even admit it. If the bright side of things had been so evident that he could speak of it the Psalmist would not have feared reproach for doing so, nor was there cause for his silence "as to the law," the rabbinical mode of explaining the passage. The obvious translation makes the clause parallel with that which follows: "I held my peace *without profit*. My sorrow was increased," *i.e.*, instead of lessening my grief by silence, I only increased it.

Stirred.—The LXX. and Vulg. "renewed," which is nearer the meaning than either the Authorised Version or margin.

⁽³⁾ **The fire burned.**—The attempt at repression only makes the inward flame of feeling burn the more fiercely, till at last it is too much for the resolution that has been formed, and the passion of the heart breaks out in words. Like the modern poet, the Hebrew bard had felt

"'Twere better not to breathe or speak
Than cry for strength, remaining weak,
And seem to find, but still to seek."

But thought is too much for him, and he breaks into speech, not, however, fretfully, still less with bitter invective against others. It is a dialogue with the ruler of destiny, in which frail man wants to face his condition, and know the worst.

⁽⁴⁾ Rhythmically and from every other reason the psalm onward from this verse must be treated as the utterance to which the poet's feelings have at length driven him.

How frail I am.—This is to be preferred to the margin, which follows the LXX. and Vulg. The Hebrew word, from a root meaning to "leave off," though in Isa liii. 3 it means "forsaken," here, as in Ezek. iii. 27, is active, and implies "ceasing to live."

⁽⁵⁾ **Handbreadth.**—Better, *some spans long*. The plural without the article having this indefinite sense.

Mine age.—Literally, *duration*. (See Ps. xvii. 14.) The LXX. and Vulg. have "substance."

Before thee.—Since in God's sight "one day is as a thousand years, and a thousand years as one day." "If nature is below any perception of time, God, at the other extremity of being, is above it. God includes time without being affected by it, and time includes nature, which is unaware of it. He too completely transcends it, his works are too profoundly subject to it, to be otherwise than indifferent to its lapse. But we stand at an intermediate point, and bear affinity with both extremes" (J. Martineau, *Hours of Thought*).

Verily every man . . . .—Better, *nothing but breath is every man at his best*. (Literally, *though standing firm*.) Comp,

"Reason thus with life—
If I do lose thee, I do lose a thing
That none but fools would keep; a breath thou art.
SHAKESPEARE: *Measure for Measure*.

⁽⁶⁾ **Surely every man . . . .**—Better, *only as a shadow walks a man*. A very commonplace of poetry, from the σκιᾶς ὄναρ ἄνθρωποι of Pindar downwards. Thus Sophocles, "I see that we who live are nothing else but images and vain shadows;" Horace, "*Pulvis et umbra sumus*; Burke, "What shadows we are, and what shadows we pursue." The above rendering treats the preposition as the *beth essentiæ*. If, however, we keep the Authorised Version, the thought is of man's life, not as a reality, but as a show, a picture, a phantasma (see margin), and himself only an imaginary actor. But this seems modern for the psalms. Shakespeare, no doubt with this passage in his mind, has combined it with the more obvious image:—

"Out, out, brief candle,
Life's but a walking shadow; a poor player
That struts and frets his hour upon the stage,
And then is heard no more."

Surely they . . .—Better, *Only for a breath they make a stir*.

He heapeth up.—The substantive is left by the Hebrew to be supplied. So we talk of the desire of "accumulating." (For the whole passage, comp. James iv. 13, 14; Luke xii. 16—21.)

and knoweth not who shall gather them.

(7) And now, Lord, what wait I for? my hope *is* in thee. (8) Deliver me from all my transgressions: make me not the reproach of the foolish.

(9) I was dumb, I opened not my mouth; because thou didst *it*. (10) Remove thy stroke away from me: I am consumed by the ¹blow of thine hand. (11) When thou with rebukes dost correct man for iniquity, thou makest ²his beauty to consume away like a moth: surely every man *is* vanity. Selah.

(12) Hear my prayer, O Lord, and give ear unto my cry; hold not thy peace at my tears: *ᵃ*for I *am* a stranger with thee, *and* a sojourner, as all my fathers were. (13) O spare me, that I may recover strength, before I go hence, and be no more.

1 Heb., *conflict.*
2 Heb., *that which is to be desired in him, to melt away.*
ᵃ Lev. 25. 23; 1 Chron. 29. 15; Ps. 119. 19; Heb. 11. 13; 1 Pet. 2. 11.
3 Heb., *In waiting I waited.*
4 Heb., *a pit of noise.*

PSALM XL.

To the chief Musician, A Psalm of David.

(1) ³I waited patiently for the Lord; and he inclined unto me, and heard my cry. (2) He brought me up also out of ⁴an horrible pit, out of the miry clay,

---

. (7) **And now, Lord . . .**—"If such is man's condition, what," says the psalmist, "is my expectation?" We seem to hear the deep sigh with which the words are uttered; and we must remember that the poet can turn for comfort to no hope of immortality. That had not yet dawned. The thought of God's mercy, and the hope of his own moral deliverance, these form the ground of his noble elevation above the oppressive sense of human frailty. The LXX. and Vulg. give it very expressively:—

"And now what is my expectation? Is it not the Lord?
And my substance is with thee."

(8) Here the psalmist recurs to his initial thought, but lets us see deeper down into his heart. It was no mere fancy that if he gave vent to his feelings the wicked might find cause for reproach; the cause was there in his own consciousness of transgression.

The reproach of the foolish.—Better, *The scorn of the fool.* (Comp. Ps. xxii. 6.)

(9) **Thou** is emphatic. Kimchi well explains: "I could not complain of *man*, for it was *God's* doing; I could not complain of *God*, for I was conscious of *my own sin.*"

(10) **Stroke.**—See Note to Ps. xxxviii. 11.

Blow.—Margin, "conflict." A word only found here; from a root meaning *rough*. LXX. and Vulg. have "strength."

Calvin's last words are said to have been a reminiscence of this verse.

(11) **When.**—This is unnecessary. *With judgments for sin Thou chastenest a man.*

Rebukes.—The word rendered "reproofs" in Ps. xxxviii. 14, where see Note.

Beauty.—Literally, *Something desirable.* (See margin.) *Thou, like a moth* (consuming a garment: see Pr. Bk. Version), *causest his desirable things to melt.* (For the image, singularly apt and natural in a country where "changes of raiment" were so prized, and hoarded up as wealth, comp. Job xiii. 28; Matt. vi. 19; James v. 2.)

(12) **For I am a stranger.**—A reminiscence of Gen. xxiii. 4, and adopted 1 Peter ii. 11 from the LXX. (See *New Testament Commentary*, and comp. Heb. xi. 13.) The psalmist, like the Apostle, applies Abraham's words metaphorically to this earthly pilgrimage (comp. 1 Chron. xxix. 15), and pathetically asks why, when the tenure of life is so uncertain, God looks angrily on him? (For the passionate appeal for a respite, comp. Job x. 20, 21, and for the Hebrew conception of the under world, Ps. vi. 5, Note.)

(13) **Recover strength.**—Better, *Let me become cheerful*, i.e., look up with a glad look once more on my face, as the angry look fades from the Divine countenance.

Before.—Literally, *before I go, and am not.* All the words and phrases of this last verse occur in the Book of Job. (See Job vii. 8, 19, 21, xiv. 6, x. 20, 21.)

XL.

The phenomenon presented in this psalm of a burst of praise (verses 1—10), followed by plaintive prayer (verse 11 onwards), is so peculiar, and so contrary to the usual method of psalm composition, as to lead of itself to the conjecture of a composite poem. The fact that verses 13–17 appear again in Psalm lxx., adds some force to this conjecture which is also supported by a marked difference in rhythm, which is finer and better sustained in the second part. We must in any case notice the prophetic power of the singer. In the true spirit of the Hebrew prophets, he exalts spiritual above merely formal religion.

The Davidic authorship is rejected, even by such critics as Delitzsch; and if we must fix on an author, the Deuteronomist suggests himself, or Jeremiah. That the psalm was written after the discovery of the Book of the Law, in Josiah's reign, there can be little doubt.

Title.—See Ps. iii. (title).

(1) **I waited patiently.**—As the margin shows, this is expressed by the common Hebrew idiom the infinitive absolute with the preterite. We may nearly express it by repetition: *I waited and waited.*

Inclined . . .—Either intransitive (comp. Judges xvi. 30), or with ellipse of the word "ear," which usually is found with the verb in this conjugation. (See Pss. xvii. 6, xxxi. 2.)

(2) **Horrible pit.**—The rendering of the margin, "pit of noise," takes *shaôn* in its primary sense, as in Isa. xvii. 12, Ps. lxv. 7, and the idea of a noise of rushing water suits this passage. Most commentators, however, take it here in the sense the cognate bears in Ps. xxxv. 8, "destruction." The LXX. and Vulg. have "misery."

Miry clay.—The word translated "clay" (comp. Ps. lxix. 2) is from a root meaning *to boil up*, or *ferment.* (One of its derivatives means "wine.") Hence "froth," or "slime." LXX., *ilus*; Vulg., *fœx.* A verse of R. Browning's perhaps expresses the poet's image:—

"It frothed by.
A black eddy, bespate with flakes and fumes."

and set my foot upon a rock, *and* established my goings. ⁽³⁾ And he hath put a new song in my mouth, *even* praise unto our God: many shall see *it*, and fear, and shall trust in the LORD.

⁽⁴⁾ Blessed *is* that man that maketh the LORD his trust, and respecteth not the proud, nor such as turn aside to lies. ⁽⁵⁾ Many, O LORD my God, *are* thy wonderful works *which* thou hast done, and thy thoughts *which are* to us-ward: [1] they cannot be reckoned up in order unto thee: *if* I would declare and speak *of them*, they are more than can be numbered.

⁽⁶⁾ *a* Sacrifice and offering thou didst not desire; mine ears hast thou [2] opened: burnt offering and sin offering hast thou not required. ⁽⁷⁾ Then said I, Lo, I come: in the volume of the book *it is* written of me, ⁽⁸⁾ I delight to do thy will, O my God: yea, thy law *is* [3] within my heart.

⁽⁹⁾ I have preached righteousness in the great congregation: lo, I have not refrained my lips, O LORD, thou knowest. ⁽¹⁰⁾ I have not hid thy righteousness within my heart; I have declared thy faithfulness and thy salvation: I have not concealed thy lovingkindness and thy truth from the great congregation.

⁽¹¹⁾ Withhold not thou thy tender mercies from me, O LORD: let thy lovingkindness and thy truth continually preserve me. ⁽¹²⁾ For innumerable evils have compassed me about: mine iniquities have taken hold upon me, so that I am not able to look up; they are more than the hairs of mine head: therefore my heart [4] faileth me.

⁽¹³⁾ Be pleased, O LORD, to deliver me: O LORD, make haste to help me. ⁽¹⁴⁾ *b* Let them be ashamed and confounded together that seek after my soul to destroy it; let them be driven backward and put to shame that wish me evil. ⁽¹⁵⁾ Let them be desolate for a reward of their shame that say unto me, Aha, aha. ⁽¹⁶⁾ Let all those that

[1] Or, *none can order them unto thee.*

a Ps. 51. 16; Isa. 1. 11, & 66. 3; Hos. 6. 6; Matt. 12. 7; Heb. 10. 5.

[2] Heb., *digged.*

[3] Heb., *in the midst of my bowels.*

[4] Heb., *forsaketh.*

b Ps. 35. 4, & 70. 3.

Rock.—The common image of security (Pss. xviii. 2, xxvii. 5), the occurrence of which makes it probable that the "pit" and "clay" are also not realities, but emblems of confusion and danger.

⁽³⁾ **New song.**—See Ps. xxxiii. 3. It seems natural to suppose that this new song is incorporated here; that we have at least the substance of it, if not the words. Possibly the very words are taken up in verse 4. And we are to find the "newness" in the magnificent vindication of spiritual above formal worship.

Shall see it and fear.—Comp. Ps. lii. 6, where there is plainly a reminiscence of this passage.

⁽⁴⁾ **Respecteth not.**—Better, *turneth not towards proud men and false apostates.* The words are, however, somewhat obscure. The LXX. and Vulg. have "vanities and false madnesses." The words we have rendered *false apostates* are by some translated "turners after idols." Idolatry is doubtless implied, but not expressed.

⁽⁵⁾ **Many, O Lord.**—Better,

"In numbers hast Thou made, Thou Jehovah my God,
Wonderful deeds and purposes for us.
There is nothing comparable to Thee. . . .
Would I declare, would I speak,
They are too many to number."

For the third clause, "There is nothing comparable with Thee," which is the rendering of the LXX., Vulg. and Syriac, comp. Isa. xl. 17.

⁽⁶⁾ **Mine ears hast thou opened.**—Literally, *Ears hast thou dug for me*, which can hardly mean anything but "Thou hast given me the sense of hearing." The words are an echo of 1 Sam. xv. 22. The attentive ear and obedient heart, not formal rites, constitute true worship. Comp. the words so frequent on the lips of Christ, "He that hath ears to hear let him hear." The fact that the plural *ears* is used instead of the singular, sets aside the idea of *a revelation*, which is expressed in Isa. xlviii. 8 by "open the ear," and 1 Sam. ix. 15 "uncover the *ear*." Not that the idea is altogether excluded, since the outward ears may be typical of the inward. The same fact excludes allusion to the symbolic act by which a slave was devoted to perpetual servitude (Ex. xxi. 6), because then also only *one ear* was bored. For the well-known variation in the LXX. see *New Testament Commentary*, Heb. x. 5: The latest commentator, Grätz, is of opinion that the text is corrupt, and emends (comp. Ps. li. 16) to, "Shouldest thou desire sacrifice and offering I would select the fattest," a most desirable result if his arguments, which are too minute for insertion, were accepted.

⁽⁷⁾ **Then said I.**—This rendering, which follows the LXX. and Vulg., and is adopted in the Epistle to the Hebrews, must be abandoned. The Hebrew means, *Lo! I come, bringing the book written for me*, which no doubt refers to the Law, which in the person of the poet, Israel here produces as warrant for its conduct. Some see a particular allusion to the discovery of the Book of Deuteronomy in Josiah's reign. But if the conjecture of Grätz be accepted (see preceding Note), the reference will be rather to the Levitical regulation of sacrifice. "Shouldest thou require burnt-offering and sin-offering, then I say, Lo! I bring the book in which all is prescribed me," *i.e.*, I have duly performed all the rites ordained in the book.

The rendering "written *on* me," *i.e.*, "on my heart and mind," might suit the *contents* of the book, but not the *roll* itself.

⁽⁹⁾ **I have preached.**—Literally, *I have made countenances glad.*

Notice the rapid succession of clauses, like successive wave-beats of praise, better than any elaborate description to represent the feelings of one whose life was a thanksgiving.

⁽¹³⁾ **Be pleased.**—From this verse onwards, with some trifling variations which will be noticed under that psalm, this passage occurs as Ps. lxx., where see Notes.

seek thee rejoice and be glad in thee: let such as love thy salvation say continually, The LORD be magnified.

(17) But I *am* poor and needy; yet the Lord thinketh upon me: thou *art* my help and my deliverer; make no tarrying, O my God.

PSALM XLI.

To the chief Musician, A Psalm of David.

(1) Blessed *is* he that considereth [1] the poor: the LORD will deliver him [2] in the time of trouble. (2) The LORD will preserve him, and keep him alive; *and* he shall be blessed upon the earth: and [3] thou wilt not deliver him unto the will of his enemies. (3) The LORD will strengthen him upon the bed of languishing: thou wilt [4] make all his bed in his sickness.

(4) I said, LORD, be merciful unto me: heal my soul; for I have sinned against thee. (5) Mine enemies speak evil of me, When shall he die, and his name perish? (6) And if he come to see *me*, he speaketh vanity: his heart gathereth iniquity to itself; *when* he goeth abroad, he telleth *it*. (7) All that hate me whisper together against me: against me do they devise [5] my hurt. (8) [6] An evil disease, *say they*, cleaveth fast unto

[1] Or, *the weak, or, sick.*
[2] Heb., *in the day of evil.*
[3] Or, *do not thou deliver.*
[4] Heb., *turn.*
[5] Heb., *evil to me.*
[6] Heb., *A thing of Belial.*

XLI.

Recalling the treachery of some pretended friends, the writer in this psalm pronounces, in contrast, a eulogy on those who know how to feel for and show compassion to the suffering. There is nothing, however, to indicate who the author was, or what particular incidents induced him to write. Possibly the sickness is entirely figurative, and the psalm is the expression of the feelings of the community of pious Israelites.

The doxology in verse 13 does not belong to the psalm, but closes the first book of the collection. (See *General Introduction.*) The parallelism is very imperfect.

(1) **Blessed is he.**—This general statement of the great law of sympathy and benevolence—fine and noble however we take it—may be explained in different ways, according as we take the Hebrew word *dal* as *poor*, with the LXX. and Vulg. (comp. Exod. xxx. 15), or with the margin, as *sick, weak in body* (comp. Gen. xli. 19), or give it an ethical sense, *sick at heart.* (Comp. 2 Sam. xiii. 4.) The context favours one of the two latter, and the choice between them depends on whether we take the author's sickness to be *real* or *figurative.* Verse 3 strongly favours the view that the sickness is physical.

Considereth.—The Hebrew word implies wise as well as kindly consideration. So LXX. and Vulg., "he that understands."

(2) **And he shall be blessed.**—Not as in margin Isa. ix. 16, and in Symmachus "called happy," but with deeper meaning, as in Prov. iii. 18. Another derivation is possible, giving the meaning, "he shall be led aright," *i.e.*, shall have right moral guidance. The context, however, does not favour this.

Upon the earth.—Rather, *in the land, i.e.,* of Canaan.

(3) **Will strengthen.**—Literally, *will prop him up, support him.*

Wilt make.—Literally, *hast turned.* Some think with literal allusion to the fact that the Oriental bed was merely a mat, which could be turned while the sick man was propped up. But such literalness is not necessary. To *turn* here is to *change*, as in Pss. lxvi. 6, cv. 29, and what the poet says is that, as in past times, Divine help has come to change his sickness into health, so he confidently expects it will be now, "in his sickness" being equivalent to "in the time of his sickness."

(4) **I said.**—After the general statement, the poet applies it to his own case, which showed such sadly different conduct on the part of friends from whom more than sympathy might have been expected. The pronoun is emphatic: *In my case, I said*, etc.

But it is a singular mark of the psalmist's sincerity and genuineness that he first looks into his own heart for its evil before exposing that of his friends.

(5) **Shall he die . . . perish.**—Better, *When will he die, and his name have perished.*

(6) **And if he come.**—Some one particular individual is here singled out from the body of enemies.

To see.—The usual word for visiting a sick person. (Comp. 2 Sam. xiii. 5; 2 Kings viii. 29.)

Vanity.—Better, *lies.* No more vivid picture of an insincere friend could be given. Pretended sympathy lies at the very bedside, while eye and ear are open to catch up anything that can be retailed abroad or turned into mischief, when the necessity of concealment is over.

The scene of the visit of the king to the death-bed of Gaunt in Shakespeare's *King Richard II.* illustrates the psalmist's position, and the poet may even have had this verse in his mind when he wrote,

"Should dying men flatter with those that live
No, no; *men living flatter those that die.*"

(8) **An evil disease.**—Margin, *thing of Belial.* (For "Belial," see Deut. xiii. 13.) The expression may mean, as in LXX. and Vulg., "a lawless speech," so the Chaldee, "a perverse word." Syriac, "a word of iniquity," or "a physical evil," as in Authorised Version, or "a moral evil." The verse is difficult, not only from this ambiguity, but also from that of the verb, which, according to the derivation we take, may mean "cleave" or "pour forth." Modern scholars prefer the latter, understanding the image as taken from the process of casting metal. *An incurable wound is poured out (welded) upon him.* (Comp. "molten," 1 Kings vii. 24, 30.) This does not, however, suit the context nearly so well as the reading,

"A wicked saying have they directed against me:
Let the sick man never rise again,"

which has the support of the LXX. and Vulg., though they make of the last clause a question, "Shall not the sleeper rise again?"

The Ungratefulness of Friends. PSALMS, XLII. *The Psalmist's Thirst for God.*

him: and *now* that he lieth he shall rise up no more. (9) ᵃYea, ¹mine own familiar friend, in whom I trusted, which did eat of my bread, hath ²lifted up *his* heel against me.

(10) But thou, O LORD, be merciful unto me, and raise me up, that I may requite them.

(11) By this I know that thou favourest me, because mine enemy doth not triumph over me. (12) And as for me, thou upholdest me in mine integrity, and settest me before thy face for ever. (13) Blessed be the LORD God of Israel from ever-lasting, and to everlasting. Amen, and Amen.

ᵃ John 13. 18.

1 Heb., *the man of my peace.*

2 Heb., *magnified.*

3 Or, *A Psalm giving instruction of the sons,* &c.

4 Heb., *brayeth.*

ᵇ Ps. 80. 5.

Book II.

PSALM XLII.

To the chief Musician, ³Maschil, for the sons of Korah.

(1) As the hart ⁴panteth after the water brooks, so panteth my soul after thee, O God. (2) My soul thirsteth for God, for the living God: when shall I come and appear before God? (3) ᵇMy tears have been my meat day

---

(9) **Hath lifted up his heel.**—See margin. The meaning is, possibly, *kicked violently at me.* But Böttcher's conjecture is valuable, "has magnified his fraud against me," which is supported by the LXX. and Vulg., "has magnified his supplanting of me." (For the quotation of this verse in John xiii. 18, see *New Testament Commentary.*) The rights of Oriental hospitality must be remembered, to bring out all the blackness of the treachery here described. The expressive Hebrew idiom, "man of my peace," is retained in the margin. Possibly (see Note, Obad. 7) the second clause recalls another idiom, "man of my bread."

(11) **By this I know.**—Better, *shall know.* His restoration would be a sign of the Divine favour, and a pledge of his victory over his enemies.

Triumph.—Literally, *shout;* "sing a pæan."

(12) **Thou upholdest.**—Here we seem to have the acknowledgment that the prayer just uttered is answered.

(13) **Blessed.**—This doxology is no part of the psalm, but a formal close to the first book of the collection. (See *General Introduction.*)

Book II.

XLII.

It is needless to waste argument on what is seen by every reader at a glance, that Pss. xlii. and xliii. form in reality one poem. In style, in subject, in tone, they might have been recognised as from one time and pen, even if they had been separated in the collection instead of following one on the other, and even if the refrain had not marked them as parts of one composition. (For expressions and feelings interlacing, as it were, the text together, comp. Pss. xlii. 9, 2, 4, with xliii. 2, 4, 4, respectively.) The poems thus united into one are seen to have three equal stanzas. All three stanzas express the complaint of a sufferer sinking under the weight of his misfortunes; the refrain in contrast expresses a sentiment of religious resignation, of unalterable confidence in Divine protection and favour. We can even realise the very situation of the sufferer. We find him not only far from Jerusalem, and longing anxiously for return thither, but actually on the frontier, near the banks of the Jordan, not far from the sources of the river, on the great caravan route between Syria and the far east, on the slopes of Hermon. We seem to see him strain his eyes from these stranger heights to catch the last look of his own native hills, and from the tone of his regrets—regrets inspired not by worldly or even patriotic considerations, but by the forcible separation from the choral service of the Temple, we conjecture him to have been a priest or a Levite.

Title. (See title, Pss. iv., xxxii.) "For the sons of Korah." This is a title of Pss. xlii., xliv.—xlix., lxxxiv., lxxxv., lxxxvii., lxxxviii.

We see from 1 Chron. vi. 16—33, that the Korahites were, when that history was written, professional musicians. Kuenen, in *History of Religion,* p. 204, has pointed out that in the older documents the singers and porters are mentioned separately from the Levites (Ezra vii. 7, 24, x. 23, 24; Neh. vii. 1), and it is only in those of a later date that we find them included in that tribe, when "the conviction had become established, that it was necessary that every one who was admitted in any capacity whatever into the service of the Temple should be a descendant of Levi;" the pedigrees which trace this descent cannot be relied on, and therefore we regard these "sons of Korah" (in one passage a still vaguer appellation, "children of the Korahites," 2 Chron. xx. 19), not as lineally descendants from the Korah of Num. xvi. 1, but as one of the then divisions of the body of musicians who were, according to the idea above noticed, treated as Levitical.

(1) **As the hart panteth.**—"I have seen large flocks of these panting harts gather round the waterbrooks in the great deserts of central Syria, so subdued by thirst that you could approach quite near them before they fled" (Thomson, *Land and Book,* p. 172).

(2) **Thirsteth.**—The metaphor occurs exactly in the same form (Ps. lxiii. 1), and only calls for notice since "God" Himself is here made the subject of the thirst, instead of righteousness, or knowledge, or power, as in the familiar and frequent use of the metaphor in other parts of the Bible, and in other literature.

The living God.—Evidently, from the metaphor, regarded as the fountain or source of life. (Comp. Pss. lxxxiv. 2, xxxvi. 9.)

Appear before God.—Exod. xxiii. 17 shows that this was the usual phrase for frequenting the sanctuary (comp. Ps. lxxxiv. 7), though poetic brevity here slightly altered its form and construction.

(3) **My tears.**—Comp. Pss. lxxx. 5, cii. 9; and Ovid Metam. x. 75, "*Cura dolorque animi lacrimæque alimenta fuere.*"

Where is thy God?—For this bitter taunt comp. Pss. lxxix. 10, cxv. 2; Joel ii. 17, etc.

and night, while they continually say unto me, Where *is* thy God? ⁽⁴⁾ When I remember these *things*, I pour out my soul in me: for I had gone with the multitude, I went with them to the house of God, with the voice of joy and praise, with a multitude that kept holyday. ⁽⁵⁾ Why art thou ¹cast down, O my soul? and *why* art thou disquieted in me? hope thou in God: for I shall yet ²praise him ³*for* the help of his countenance. ⁽⁶⁾ O my God, my soul is cast down within me: therefore will I remember thee from the land of Jordan, and of the Hermonites, from ⁴the hill Mizar. ⁽⁷⁾ Deep calleth unto deep at the noise of thy waterspouts: all thy waves and thy billows are gone over me. ⁽⁸⁾ *Yet* the LORD will command his lovingkindness in the daytime, and in the night his

1 Heb., *bowed down*.
2 Or, *give thanks*.
3 Or, *his presence is salvation*.
4 Or, *the little hill*.

⁽⁴⁾ **When I.**—The conjunction "when" is not expressed, but may be implied from the next clause. Others render, "let me recall these days (*i.e.*, what follows), let me pour out my soul within me" (literally, *upon me*. Comp. Ps. cxlii. 3). But the Authorised Version is better, "when I think of it, my heart must overflow." The expression, "I pour out my soul upon me," may, however, mean, "I weep floods of tears over myself," *i.e.*, "over my lot."

For I had gone with the multitude.—The LXX. and Vulg., as well as the strangeness of the words rendered "multitude" and "went with them," indicate a corruption of the text. Fortunately the general sense and reference of the verse are independent of the doubtful expressions. The poet indulges in a grateful recollection of some great festival, probably the Feast of Tabernacles. (See LXX.)

That kept holyday.—Literally, *dancing* or *reeling*. But the word is used absolutely (Exod. v. 1; Lev. xxiii. 41) for keeping a festival, and especially the Feast of Tabernacles. Dancing appears to have been a recognised part of the ceremonial. (Comp. 2 Sam. vi. 16.)

⁽⁵⁾ **Why art thou.**—The refrain here breaks in on the song like a sigh, the spirit of dejection struggling against the spirit of faith.

Cast down.—Better, as in margin, *bowed down*, and in the original with a middle sense, "why bowest thou down thyself?"

Disquieted.—From root kindred to and with the meaning of our word "hum." The idea of "internal emotion" is easily derivable from its use. We see the process in such expressions as Isa. xvi. 11, "My bowels shall sound like a harp for Moab."

For the help of his countenance.—There is no question but that we must read the refrain here as it is in verse 12, and in Ps. xliii. 5. The LXX. and Vulg. already have done so, and one Hebrew MS. notices the wrong accentuation of the text here. The rhythm without this change is defective, and the refrain unnecessarily altered. Such alteration, however, from comparison of Pss. xxiv. 8, 10, xlix. 12, 20, lvi. 4, 10, lix. 9, 17, is not unusual.

⁽⁶⁾ **Cast down.**—The poet, though faith condemns his dejection, still feels it, and cannot help expressing it. The heart will not be tranquil all at once, and the utterance of its trouble, so natural, so pathetic, long after served, in the very words of the LXX., to express a deeper grief, and mark a more tremendous crisis (John xii. 27; Matt. xxvi. 38).

Therefore will I.—Better, *therefore do I remember thee.* (Comp. Jonah ii. 7.)

From the land of Jordan—*i.e.*, the uplands of the north-east, where the river rises. The poet has not yet passed quite into the land of exile, the country beyond Jordan, but already he is on its borders, and as his sad eyes turn again and again towards the loved country he is leaving, its sacred summits begin to disappear, while ever nearer and higher rise the snow-clad peaks of Hermon.

Hermonites.—Rather, *of the Hermons*, *i.e.*, either collectively for the whole range (as generally of mountains, the Balkans, etc.) or with reference to the appearance of the mountain as a ridge with a conspicuous peak at either end. (See Thomson, *Land and Book*, p. 177.) In reality, however, the group known especially as Hermon has three summits, situated, like the angles of a triangle, a quarter of a mile from each other, and of almost equal elevation. (See Smith's *Bible Dict.*, "Hermon." Comp. *Our Work in Palestine*, p. 246.)

The hill Mizar.—Marg., *the little hill.* So LXX. and Vulg., *a monte modico.* (Comp. the play on the name Zoar in Gen. xix. 20.) Hence some think the poet is contrasting Hermon with Zion. In such a case, however, the custom of Hebrew poetry was to exalt Zion, and not depreciate the higher mountains, and it is very natural to suppose that some lower ridge or pass, over which the exile may be supposed wending his sad way, was actually called "the little," or "the less."

⁽⁷⁾ **Deep calleth unto deep at the noise of thy waterspouts.**—Better, *Flood calleth unto flood at the noise of thy cataracts.* The exile is describing what was before his eyes, and in his ears. There can, therefore, be little doubt that, as Dean Stanley observed, this image was furnished by the windings and rapids of the Jordan, each hurrying to dash itself with yet fiercer vehemence of sounding water over some opposing ledge of rocks "in cataract after cataract to the sea." Thus every step taken on that sorrowful journey offered an emblem of the griefs accumulating on the exile's heart. The word rendered **waterspout** only occurs besides in 2 Sam. v. 8, where the Authorised Version has "gutter," but might translate "watercourse."

All thy waves and thy billows.—From derivation, *breakers and rollers.* The poet forgets the source of his image in its intensity, and from the thought of the cataract of woes passes on to the more general one of "a sea of troubles," the waves of which break upon him or roll over his head. The image is common in all poetry. (Comp. "And as a sea of ills urges on its waves; one falling, another, with huge (literally, *third*) crest, rising."—Æsch., *Seven against Thebes*, 759.)

⁽⁸⁾ **Yet the Lord.**—Better, *By day Jehovah shall command* (or, literally, *Jehovah command*) *his grace.*

And in the night his song—*i.e.*, a song to Him; but the emendation *shirah*, "song," for *shirôh*, "his song," commends itself. The parallelism of this verse seems to confirm the conclusion drawn from the sentence at end of Book II., that the title "prayer,"

song *shall be* with me, *and* my prayer unto the God of my life. (9) I will say unto God my rock, Why hast thou forgotten me? why go I mourning because of the oppression of the enemy? (10) *As* with a ¹sword in my bones, mine enemies reproach me; while they say daily unto me, Where *is* thy God? (11) Why art thou cast down, O my soul? and why art thou disquieted within me? hope thou in God: for I shall yet praise him, *who is* the health of my countenance, and my God.

PSALM XLIII.

(1) Judge me, O God, and plead my cause against an ²ungodly nation: O deliver me ³from the deceitful and unjust man. (2) For thou *art* the God of my strength: why dost thou cast me off? why go I mourning because of the oppression of the enemy? (3) O

1 Or, *killing*.

2 Or, *unmerciful*.

3 Heb., *from a man of deceit and iniquity*.

4 Heb., *the gladness of my joy*.

a Ps. 42. 5, 11.

send out thy light and thy truth: let them lead me; let them bring me unto thy holy hill, and to thy tabernacles. (4) Then will I go unto the altar of God, unto God ⁴my exceeding joy: yea, upon the harp will I praise thee, O God my God. (5) ᵃWhy art thou cast down, O my soul? and why art thou disquieted within me? hope in God: for I shall yet praise him, *who is* the health of my countenance, and my God.

PSALM XLIV.

To the chief Musician for the sons of Korah, Maschil.

(1) We have heard with our ears, O God, our fathers have told us, *what work* thou didst in their days, in the times of old. (2) *How* thou didst drive out the heathen with thy hand, and plantedst them; *how* thou didst afflict the people,

---

and "song" were used indiscriminately for any of the hymns in religious use.

(9) Apparently we have now the very words of the prayer just mentioned.

(10) **As with a sword.**—Margin, *killing*; better, *crushing*. The insertion of the conjunction is erroneous. Render, *with a shattering of my bones*. This, no doubt, refers to actual ill-treatment of the exile by his conductors, who heaped blows, as well as insults, on their captives. We may even suppose this violence especially directed at this particular sufferer, who could not refrain from lingering and looking back, and so irritating his convoy, who would naturally be in a hurry to push forwards. How vividly, too, does the picture of the insulting taunt, "Where is thy God?" rise before us, if we think of the soldiers overhearing the exile's ejaculations of prayer.

XLIII.

(1) **An ungodly nation.**—In the Hebrew simply a negative term, a nation not *khasid*, *i.e.*, not in the covenant. But naturally a positive idea of ungodliness and wickedness would attach to such a term.

(3) **O send out thy light and thy truth: let them lead me.**—Instead of the violent and contemptuous escort of Assyrian soldiers, leading the exile away from the "holy hill," the poet prays for God's light and truth to lead him, like two angel guides, back to it. Light and truth! What a guidance in this world of falsehood and shadow! The *Urim* and *Thummim* of the saints (Deut. xxxiii. 8), the promised attendants of Israel, have been, and are, the escort of all faithful souls in all ages.

(4) **God my God.**—An expression used in this collection instead of the more usual "Jehovah my God." (Comp. xlv. 7, and for its import see *General Introduction*, and Ps. l. 7, Note.)

XLIV.

In spite of the singular used in verses 6, 15, we recognise, in this psalm, a hymn expressive not of individual but of national feeling; a feeling, too, which certainly could not have received such an expression before the exile, before the spell of the fascination of the Canaanitish idolatries had passed away. Nor can the psalm be assigned to the exile period itself, for it does not reflect the profound spiritual insight that characterises the literature which undoubtedly belongs to that time. Ewald places it during the months that disturbed the early years of the return from captivity. The majority of critics, however, prefer the time of Antiochus Epiphanes. It might well have been inspired by one of those reverses, which so often came upon the struggling community of Israel, in consequence of their scrupulous concern for the Sabbath day, which did not even allow them to defend themselves. (See Note, verses 13, 14.) The parallelism is fine and well sustained.

Title.—See title, Pss. xlii., xxxii.

(1) **We have heard.**—The glorious traditions of ancient deliverances wrought by Jehovah for His people were a sacred heritage of every Hebrew. (See Exod. x. 2, xii. 26, seq.; Deut. vi. 20, etc.) This, and all the historical psalms, show how closely interwoven for the Jew were patriotism and religion.

(2) **Thou . . . with thy hand.**—Literally, *Thou, Thy hand*, which may be, as in the Authorised Version, taken as accusative of instrument, or as a repeated subject.

And cast them out.—This entirely misses the meaning and destroys the parallelism. The Hebrew word is that used for a tree spreading its branches out; comp. Jer. xvii. 8; Ezek. xvii. 6, xxxi. 5, and especially Ps. lxxx. 11, a passage which is simply an amplification of the figure in this verse, viz., of a vine or other exotic, planted in a soil cleared for its reception, and there caused to grow and flourish. The pronoun *them* in each clause plainly refers to Israel.

Thou, with thine hand, didst dispossess the heathen,
And planted *them* (Israel) in.
Thou didst afflict the peoples,
But didst make *them* to spread.

Past Deliverances. PSALMS, XLIV. *Present Tribulations.*

and cast them out. ⁽³⁾ For they got not the land in possession by their own sword, neither did their own arm save them: but thy right hand, and thine arm, and the light of thy countenance, because thou hadst a favour unto them.

⁽⁴⁾ Thou art my King, O God: command deliverances for Jacob. ⁽⁵⁾ Through thee will we push down our enemies: through thy name will we tread them under that rise up against us. ⁽⁶⁾ For I will not trust in my bow, neither shall my sword save me. ⁽⁷⁾ But thou hast saved us from our enemies, and hast put them to shame that hated us. ⁽⁸⁾ In God we boast all the day long, and praise thy name for ever. Selah.

⁽⁹⁾ But thou hast cast off, and put us to shame; and goest not forth with our armies. ⁽¹⁰⁾ Thou makest us to turn back from the enemy: and they which hate us spoil for themselves. ⁽¹¹⁾ Thou hast given us [1]like sheep *appointed* for meat; and hast scattered us among the heathen. ⁽¹²⁾ Thou sellest thy people [2]for nought, and dost not increase *thy wealth* by their price. ⁽¹³⁾ *a*Thou makest us a reproach to our neighbours, a scorn and a derision to them that are round about us. ⁽¹⁴⁾ *b*Thou makest us a byword among the heathen, a shaking of the head among the people. ⁽¹⁵⁾ My confusion *is* continually before me, and the shame of my face hath covered me, ⁽¹⁶⁾ for the voice of him that reproacheth and blasphemeth; by reason of the enemy and avenger.

⁽¹⁷⁾ All this is come upon us; yet have we not forgotten thee, neither have we dealt falsely in thy covenant. ⁽¹⁸⁾ Our heart is not turned back, neither have our [3]steps declined from thy way; ⁽¹⁹⁾ though thou hast sore broken us in the place of dragons, and covered us with the shadow of death.

⁽²⁰⁾ If we have forgotten the name of our God, or stretched out our hands to a strange god; ⁽²¹⁾ shall not God search this out? for he knoweth the secrets of the heart. ⁽²²⁾ *c* Yea, for thy sake are we killed all the day long; we are counted as sheep for the slaughter. ⁽²³⁾ Awake, why sleepest thou, O Lord? arise, cast *us* not off for ever. ⁽²⁴⁾ Where-

---

1 Heb., *as sheep of meat.*
2 Heb., *without riches.*
a Ps. 79. 4.
b Jer. 24. 9.
3 Or, *goings.*
c Rom. 8. 36.

⁽³⁾ **The light of thy countenance.**—Notice the contrast to this in verse 24; in times of distress God's face seemed hidden or averted.

⁽⁴⁾ **Thou art my King.**—Literally, *Thou, He, my king,* an idiomatic way of making a strong assertion, *Thou, even thou, art my king, O God.* (Comp. Isa. xliii. 25.) What God has done in the past may be expected again, and for a moment the poet forgets the weight of actual trouble in the faith that has sprung from the grateful retrospect over the past.

⁽⁵⁾ **Push down.**—The image of the original is lost here, the LXX. have retained it. It is that of a buffalo or other horned animal driving back and goring its enemies. Deut. xxxiii. 17 applies it as a special description of the tribe of Joseph. The figure is continued in the next clause; the infuriated animal tramples its victim under foot.

⁽¹⁰⁾ **For themselves**—*i.e.,* at their own will, an expression denoting the completeness of the overthrow of the Jews; they lie absolutely at their enemies' pleasure.

⁽¹¹⁾ **Like sheep.**—The image of the sheep appointed for the slaughter; and unable to resist, recalls Isa. liii. 6, 7, but does not necessarily connect the Psalm with the exile period, since it was a figure likely to suggest itself in every time of helpless peril.

⁽¹²⁾ **For nought.**—Literally, *for not riches* (comp. Jer. xv. 13); notice the contrast to Ps. lxxii. 14.

And dost not increase thy wealth by their price.—This rendering takes the verb as in Prov. xxii. 16; but to make the two places exactly parallel, we should have "dost not increase *for thee.*" It is better, therefore, to make the clause synonymous with the last, and render *thou didst not increase in* (the matter *of*) *their price, i.e.,* thou didst not set a high price on them.

^(13, 14) These verses become very suggestive, if we refer them to one of those periods under the Seleucidæ, when the Jews were so frequently attacked on the Sabbath, and from their scrupulous regard to it would make no resistance.

⁽¹⁴⁾ **Shaking of the head.**—Comp. Ps. xxii. 7.

⁽¹⁵⁾ **The shame.**—Better take *the face* as a second object—*shame hath covered me as to my face, i.e., covered my face.* Though the record of the facts of a sad reality, these verses have also the value of a prophecy sadder still. Twenty centuries of misery are summed up in these few lines, which have been most literally repeated,

"By the torture, prolonged from age to age,
By the infamy, Israel's heritage;
By the Ghetto's plague, by the garb's disgrace,
By the badge of shame, by the felon's place."
R. BROWNING: *Holy Cross Day.*

⁽¹⁹⁾ **In the place of dragons.**—This expression evidently means *a wild desert place,* from comparison with Jer. ix. 11, x. 22, xlix. 33. So Aquila has "an uninhabitable place." The rendering *dragons* for *tannim* arose from its resemblance to *tannin* (sea monster). The *tan* must be a wild beast, since it is connected with *ostriches* (Isa. xxxiv. 13) and *wild asses,* whom it resembles in *snuffing up the wind* (Jer. xiv. 6), and is described as uttering a mournful howl (Isa. xliii. 20; Micah i. 8; Job xxx. 29). The jackal is the animal that best answers these requirements. The LXX. and Vulg., which give various different renderings for the word, have here, "in the place of affliction."

Shadow of death.—See Note, Ps. xxiii. 4.

⁽²²⁾ **For thy sake.**—For St. Paul's quotation of this verse (Rom. viii. 36), see Note, *N. Test. Commentary.*

⁽²³⁾ **Why sleepest.**—Comp. Ps. vii. 6, and see **refs.**

fore hidest thou thy face, *and* forgettest our affliction and our oppression? ⁽²⁵⁾ For our soul is bowed down to the dust: our belly cleaveth unto the earth.

⁽²⁶⁾ Arise ¹ for our help, and redeem us for thy mercies' sake.

PSALM XLV.

To the chief Musician upon Shoshannim, for the sons of Korah, ² Maschil, A Song of loves.

⁽¹⁾ My heart ³ is inditing a good matter: I speak of the things which I have made touching the king: my tongue *is* the pen of a ready writer.

⁽²⁾ Thou art fairer than the children of men: grace is poured into thy lips: therefore God hath blessed thee for ever.

⁽³⁾ Gird thy sword upon *thy* thigh, O *most* mighty, with thy glory and thy majesty. ⁽⁴⁾ And in thy majesty ⁴ ride prosperously because of truth and meekness *and* righteousness; and thy right hand shall teach thee terrible things.

---

¹ Heb., *a help for us.*
² Or, *of instruction.*
³ Heb., *boileth, or, bubbleth up.*
⁴ Heb., *prosper thou, ride thou.*

XLV.

From Calvin downwards this psalm has been recognised as an ode celebrating the nuptials of some king. Indeed, the retention, as part of its title, of "song of loves," when the poem was incorporated into the Temple hymn-book, seems to show that this secular character was admitted even then. There is just enough of historical allusion in the psalm to invite conjecture as to the monarch who is its theme, and too little to permit of his identification. (See Notes to verses 8, 9, 12.) But, as in the case of the longer and more pronounced epithalamium, the Song of Solomon, religious scruples soon rejected this secular interpretation, and sought by allegorical and mystical explanations to bring the poem more within the circle of recognised sacred literature. With the glowing prophetic visions of a conquering Messiah floating before the imagination, it was most natural for the Jews to give the psalm a distinctive Messianic character. Equally natural was it for Christians to adopt the psalm as allegorical of the marriage of the Church with the Divine Head—a mode of interpretation which, once started, found in every turn and expression of the psalm some fruitful type or symbol. The rhythm is flowing and varied.

Title.—Upon Shoshannim, i.e., upon lilies. The same inscription occurs again in Ps. lxix. and in an altered form in Pss. lx. and lxxx., where see Notes. The most probable explanation makes it refer to the *tune* to which the hymn was to be sung. (Comp. the title of Ps. xxii. &c.) As to the actual flower intended by *shoshannim*, see Note, Song of Sol. ii. 1. The expression, *a song of loves*, means either a love song (so Aquila), or a *song of the beloved*. Symm., LXX., and Vulg., *for the beloved*, or a *song of charms, i.e.*, a pleasant song. The first is more in keeping with the evident origin and intention of the poem. (See besides titles Pss. iv., xlii., xxxii.)

⁽¹⁾ **Inditing.**—A most unhappy rendering of a word, which, though only used here, must, from the meaning of its derivative (a "pot," or "cauldron"), have something to do with a *liquid*, and means either to "boil over" or to "bubble up." The LXX. and Vulg. have apparently thought of the bursting out of a fountain: *eructavit*. Symmachus has, "been set in motion." The "spring," or "fountain," is a common emblem of inspired fancy:—

"Ancient *founts* of inspiration *well* through all my fancy yet."
TENNYSON: *Locksley Hall.*

A good matter.—That is, a theme worthy a poet's song. Luther: "A fine song."

I speak of the things which I have made touching the king.—This rendering follows the LXX., Vulg., and most of the older translations. Perhaps, however, we are to understand Aquila and Symmachus as rendering "my poems;" and undoubtedly the true rendering is, *I am speaking: my poem is of a king* (not *the* king, as in Authorised Version).

My tongue . . .—So lofty a theme, so august a subject, inspires him with thoughts that flow freely. The *ready* or *expeditious scribe* (LXX. and Vulg., "A scribe writing quickly") was, as we learn from Ezra vii. 6, a recognised form of praise for a distinguished member of that body, one of whose functions was to make copies of the Law.

⁽²⁾ **Thou art fairer.**—Better, *Fair art thou; aye, fairer than*, &c. We may thus reproduce the Hebrew expression, which, however, grammatically explained, must convey this emphasis. The old versions render: "Thou art fair with beauty;" or, "Thou hast been made beautiful with beauty."

Grace is poured into thy lips.—Better, *A flowing grace is on thy lips*, which may refer either to the beauty of the mouth, or to the charm of its speech. Cicero, himself the grandest example of his own expression, says of another that "Persuasion had her seat upon his lips;" while Christian commentators have all naturally thought of Him at whose "words of grace" all men wondered.

Therefore.—This word is apparently out of place. But there is nothing harsh in rendering: *Therefore, we say, God hath blessed thee for ever.* And we are struck by the emphasis of its occurrence in verses 7 and 17, as well as here. Ewald seems to be right in printing the clause so begun as a kind of refrain. The poet enumerates in detail the beauties of the monarch and his bride, and is interrupted by the acclaim of his hearers, who cannot withhold their approving voices.

⁽³⁾ **Gird thy sword . . . O most mighty.**— Or, perhaps, *Gird on thy sword in hero guise*; or, *Gird on thy hero's sword*. The object of the poet's praise is as heroic in war as he is beautiful in person.

With thy glory and thy majesty.—This adverbial use of the accusatives may be right, but it seems better to take them in apposition with sword. His weapon was the monarch's glory and pride. Some commentators see here a reference to the custom of girding on the sword said to be still observed at the elevation to the throne of a Persian or Ottoman prince. But the next verse shows that we have rather an ideal picture of the royal bridegroom's prowess in war.

⁽⁴⁾ **And in thy majesty.**—The repetition of this word from the last verse (conjunction included) is suspicious, especially as the LXX., followed by the Vulg., render, "Direct (thine arrows or thine aim")."

Ride prosperously . . .—Literally, *proceed, ride;* expressing, according to a common Hebrew

(5) Thine arrows *are* sharp in the heart of the king's enemies; *whereby* the people fall under thee.

(6) ᵃThy throne, O God, *is* for ever and ever: the sceptre of thy kingdom *is* a right sceptre. (7) Thou lovest righteousness, and hatest wickedness: therefore God, thy God, hath anointed thee with the oil of gladness above thy fellows.

(8) All thy garments *smell* of myrrh, and aloes, *and* cassia, out of the ivory palaces, whereby they have made thee glad. (9) Kings' daughters *were* among thy honourable women: upon thy right hand did stand the queen in gold of Ophir.

ᵃ Heb. 1. 8.

---

usage, by two verbs what we express by adverb and verb.

Because of . . .—Better, *In behalf of.* So LXX. and Vulg. There is a difficulty from the absence of the conjunction in the Hebrew before the last of the triad of virtues. The LXX. have it, but may have supplied it, as the Authorised Version does. Some render, "meek righteousness," or, slightly changing the pointing, "the afflicted righteous."

And thy right hand shall teach . . .—If we keep this rendering, we must picture the warrior with his right hand extended, pointing to the foe whom he is about to strike with his deadly arrows. But even this seems somewhat tame; and as the verb rendered "teach" is in 1 Sam. xx. 20 used for "shooting arrows," and "arrows" are mentioned immediately in the next verse, it seems obvious to render: *And thy right hand shall shoot terrors,* or, *terribly.* (Comp. Ps. lxv. 5.)

(5) **Thine arrows.**—Our version has transposed the clauses of this verse. The original is more vivid.

"Thine arrows are sharpened—
The people under Thee fall—
Against the heart of the king's enemies."

The poet actually sees the battle raging before him.

(6) **Thy throne, O God, is for ever and ever.**—This is the rendering of the LXX., Vulg., and of the versions generally. But whether they supposed the words to be addressed to the Divine Being, or that the theocratic king is thus styled, is uncertain. The Christian use of the verse as applied to the Messiah (Heb. i. 8, Note, *New Testament Commentary*) does not help us to explain how the monarch, who is the poet's theme here, could be addressed as God. The use of *Elohim* in Ps. lxxxii. 6, xcvii. 7, Exod. xxii. 28, hardly offers a satisfactory parallel, and even 1 Sam. xxviii. 13 (where we should render, "I saw a *god,* &c.) hardly prepares us to find such an emphatic ascription to an earthly king, especially in an *Elohistic* psalm. Two alternative renderings present themselves—(1) Thy throne of God is for ever . . . *i.e.,* thy divine throne. (Comp. Ps. xxxi. 2, "thy refuge of strength.") (2) Thy throne is of God for ever, which is grammatically preferable, and with which may be compared 1 Chron. xxix. 23, "the throne of the Lord."

(7) **The oil of gladness.**—Comp. "oil of joy," Isa. lxi. 3. Here too it may be merely employed as a figure of happiness, but the bath and, no doubt, subsequent anointing, formed part of the Oriental marriage proceedings. (See *Arabian Nights, passim.*)

Fellows—*i.e.,* the *paranymphs,* or attendants on the bridegroom.

(8) **All thy garments smell of** . . .—Or, perhaps, from the last verse (and comparing Ps. cxxxiii. 2, and the customs there referred to), *are anointed with.* The spices mentioned may have been ingredients of "the oil of gladness."

Myrrh . . . **cassia.**—These spices formed part of the sacred oil described Exod. xxx. 23, 24. On the other hand, for the custom of perfuming clothes, beds, &c., comp. Song of Sol. v. 5; Prov. vii. 17.

For myrrh see Gen. xxxvii. 25.

Aloes.—Heb. *ahălôth* (sometimes *ahălim*), a word formed from the native name *aghil* (Cochin China and Siam are its homes), which also appears in *eaglewood* (*Aquilaria agallochum*). The *lign aloes* of Num. xxiv. 6, was most probably a different tree from that whose *resin* forms the precious perfume here mentioned. (See *Bib. Ed.* i. 243.)

Cassia.—See Note Exod. xxx. 24.

The Oriental's love for these mixtures of many fragrant spices has been finely caught in some modern lines.

"Heap cassia, sandal-buds, and stripes
Of labdanum, and aloe-balls,
Smeared with dull nard an Indian wipes
From out her hair, such balsam falls
From seaside mountain pedestals,
From tree-tops where tired winds are fain—
Spent with the vast and howling main—
To treasure half their island gain."
R. BROWNING: *Paracelsus.*

Out of the ivory palaces, whereby they have made thee glad.—Rather, *out of the ivory palaces music* (literally, *strings*) *has made thee glad.*

Of the many conjectured explanations this, though somewhat grammatically doubtful, is in all other respects preferable. Indeed, it would have been strange if a nuptial ode, giving a picture of the splendour and pomp accompanying the marriage, had missed the mention of music, and at this verse we may imagine the doors of the palace thrown open for the issue of the bridal train (comp. the procession immediately after the bath in the weddings in the *Arabian Nights*), not only allowing the strains of music to float out, but also giving a glimpse into the interior, where, surrounded by her train of ladies, the queen-bride stands.

The word rendered "palace" (generally "temple,") may from its derivation be only a spacious place, and so a receptacle. On the other hand, Amos iii. 15 shows that ivory was frequently used as an ornament of the houses of the rich, and Ahab's "ivory house" (1 Kings xxii. 39) is familiar.

(9) **Honourable women.**—Literally, *precious ones, i.e.,* possibly the favourites of the harem. See Prov. vi. 26, where this word *precious* is used (comp. Jer. xxxi. 20), or there may be an allusion to the costliness and magnificence of the harem rather than to affection for its inmates. Perhaps both senses are combined in the word, and we may compare Shakspere's

"The *jewels* of our father, with washed eyes
Cordelia leaves you."

Upon thy right hand.—Comp. 1 Kings ii. 19.

Did stand.—Better, *was stationed,* referring to the position assigned to the bride when the marriage procession was formed.

In gold of Ophir.—Or, possibly, *as* (*i.e.,* precious as) *gold of Ophir,* a common use of this particle. For

(10) Hearken, O daughter, and consider, and incline thine ear; forget also thine own people, and thy father's house; (11) so shall the king greatly desire thy beauty: for he *is* thy Lord; and worship thou him.

(12) And the daughter of Tyre *shall be there* with a gift; *even* the rich among the people shall intreat ¹thy favour.

(13) The king's daughter *is* all glorious within: her clothing *is* of wrought gold. (14) She shall be brought unto the king in raiment of needlework: the virgins her companions that follow her shall be brought unto thee. (15) With gladness and rejoicing shall they be brought: they shall enter into the king's palace.

(16) Instead of thy fathers shall be thy children, whom thou mayest make princes in all the earth. (17) I will make thy name to be remembered in all generations: therefore shall the people praise thee for ever and ever.

PSALM XLVI.

To the chief Musician ²for the sons of Korah, A Song upon Alamoth.

(1) God *is* our refuge and strength, a very present help in trouble. (2) Therefore will not we fear, though the earth be removed, and though the mountains be carried into ³the midst of the sea; (3) *though* the waters thereof roar *and* be troubled, *though* the mountains shake with the swelling thereof. Selah.

1 Heb., *thy face.*
2 Or, *of.*
3 Heb., *the heart of the seas.*

Ophir and its gold see 1 Kings ix. 28. The LXX. and Vulg. miss the proper name, and read, "clothed in golden vesture and many-coloured."

(10) **Hearken.**—The address now turns to the bride.

(11) **Worship thou him.**—Literally, *Bow down or prostrate thyself.*

(12) **And the daughter of Tyre**—*i.e.,* Tyre itself and the Tyrians. (See Note Ps. ix. 14.) Render,

The Tyrians with a gift entreat thy favour,
The rich ones of the people.

The objection that Tyre was never subject to Israel is not conclusive, since the gifts may be complimentary presents, such as Hiram sent to Solomon, not tribute. (See next Note.)

Entreat thy favour.—Literally, *stroke thy face* (comp. Job xi. 19, Prov. xix. 6); or since the root-idea is one of *polishing* or *making bright,* we may render "makes thy face bright or joyful," *i.e.,* with pleasure at the splendid gifts.

(13) **The king's daughter is all glorious within**—*i.e.,* in the interior, in the inner room of the palace. The next clause would alone dismiss the reference to moral qualities from which has sprung such a wealth of mystic interpretation. But what palace is intended? Certainly not that of the royal bridegroom, since the procession (see verse 14) has not yet reached its destination. We must therefore think of her waiting, in all the splendour of her bridal array, in her own apartments, or in some temporary abode.

Wrought gold—*i.e., textures woven with gold.* The Hebrew word is used also of gems set in gold. The Eastern tales just referred to speak of the custom of repeatedly changing the bride's dress during the marriage ceremonies, every time presenting her in greater magnificence than before.

(14) **In raiment of needlework.**—This is now more generally understood of rich tapestry carpets spread for the procession. (Comp. Æsch. *Agam.* 908—910.)

(16) **Whom thou mayest make princes.**—Historical illustrations have been found in 1 Kings xxii. 26, where Joash, David's son, appears as a governor or a prince of a city (comp. Zeph. i. 8), and in the division of his realm into principalities by Solomon. (1 Kings iv. 7.)

XLVI.

This psalm reflects the feelings with which a people, secure in the sense of Divine protection, looks on while surrounding nations are convulsed, and calmly awaits the issue. Such a situation was that of Israel in the seventh century B.C., while the giant powers of Egypt and Assyria were rending the East by their rivalries, and also during the wars of the Ptolemies and Seleucidæ. The former period suggests itself as the more probable date of the psalm, from its resemblance to much of the language of Isaiah when dealing with events that culminated in the destruction of Sennacherib's army. Compare especially the recurrence of the expression, "God is with us," *Elohim immānû,* with the prophet's use of the name *Immanuel.* The refrain, though missing after the first stanza, marks the regular poetical form.

Title.—For the first part see titles Pss. iv., xlii., *A song upon 'alămôth.* This plainly is a musical direction, but the precise meaning must still remain matter of conjecture. Since *'alămôth* means maidens, the most natural and now generally received interpretation is "a song for sopranos." (Comp. title Ps. vi.)

(1) **Refuge and strength.**—Better, *a refuge and stronghold,* or *a sure stronghold,* as in Luther's hymn,

Ein feste Burg ist unser Gott.

A very present help.—Better, *often found a help.*

(2) **Though the earth be removed.**—Literally, *at the changing of the earth.* Possibly with the same figure implied, which is expressed, Ps. cii. 26, of the worn-out or soiled vesture. The psalmist was thinking of the sudden convulsion of earthquake, and figures Israel fearless amid the tottering kingdoms and falling dynasties. Travellers all remark on the signs of tremendous volcanic agency in Palestine.

It is interesting to compare the heathen poet's conception of the fearlessness supplied by virtue (Hor. *Ode* iii. 3).

(3) **Though the waters . . .**—The original is very expressive in its conciseness:

"They roar, they foam, its waters."

Comp. Homer's equally concise description, including

The Psalmist's Confidence in God. PSALMS, XLVII. *A Song of Praise.*

⁽⁴⁾ There *is* a river, the streams whereof shall make glad the city of God, the holy *place* of the tabernacles of the most High. ⁽⁵⁾ God *is* in the midst of her; she shall not be moved: God shall help her, ¹*and that* right early. ⁽⁶⁾ The heathen raged, the kingdoms were moved: he uttered his voice, the earth melted. ⁽⁷⁾ The LORD of hosts *is* with us; the God of Jacob *is* ²our refuge. Selah.

⁽⁸⁾ Come, behold the works of the LORD, what desolations he hath made in the earth. ⁽⁹⁾ He maketh wars to cease unto the end of the earth; he breaketh the bow, and cutteth the spear in sunder; he burneth the chariot in the fire.

¹ Heb., *when the morning appeareth.*

² Heb., *an high place for us.*

³ Or. *of.*

⁽¹⁰⁾ Be still, and know that I *am* God: I will be exalted among the heathen, I will be exalted in the earth. ⁽¹¹⁾ The LORD of hosts *is* with us, the God of Jacob *is* our refuge. Selah.

PSALM XLVII.

To the chief Musician, A Psalm ³ for the sons of Korah.

⁽¹⁾ O clap your hands, all ye people; shout unto God with the voice of triumph. ⁽²⁾ For the LORD most high *is* terrible; *he is* a great King over all the earth. ⁽³⁾ He shall subdue the people under us, and the nations under our feet. ⁽⁴⁾ He shall choose our inheritance for us, the excellency of Jacob whom he loved. Selah.

---

in three words the "rush," the "swell," and the "roar" of ocean (*Iliad*, xxiii. 230).

Swelling.—Or, *pride*. (Comp. Job xxxviii. 11.) The change in construction in this verse seems to confirm the suspicion that the refrain has dropped away.

⁽⁴⁾ **A river . . .**—Heb., *nāhar, i.e.*, a perennial stream, as distinguished from *nāchal*, a torrent bed dry except in the rainy season. Plainly, then, the "Cedron" is not here alluded to. But many commentators think "Siloam" is intended. (See Stanley, *Sinai and Palestine*, p. 180, and comp. Isa. xii. 3; Ezek. xlvii. 1—5; John vii. 37.)

There may not, however, be any such local allusion. The river, flowing calmly and smoothly along, may be only a symbol of the peace and blessing of the Divine presence, as the tumult and tempest of the sea in the last verse are of the world's noisy troubles. Indeed, the LXX. (comp. Prayer Book version) seems to connect the river of this verse with the waters of the preceding.

Streams.—See Note on Ps. i. 3, where the same word occurs.

⁽⁵⁾ **Right early.**—Literally, *at the turning of the morning*. Evidently metaphorical of the dawn of a brighter day.

⁽⁶⁾ The absence of conjunctions, and sudden change from the preterite to the future, lends a vividness to the picture.

"Raged heathen, tottered kingdoms
Gave with His voice (the signal) (and lo!)
Melts the earth."

⁽⁷⁾ **Lord of hosts.**—See Note on Ps. xxiv. 10.

Refuge.—Rightly in the margin with idea of height, as giving security.

⁽⁸⁾ **The Lord.**—Many MSS. read *Elohim* instead of "Jehovah."

Desolations . . .—Either, *silence of desolation*, "silence" being the primary sense of the word, or (as in Jer. xix. 8), *wonders*, which silence by their suddenness and marvel. So LXX. and Vulg., and this is confirmed by verse 10.

⁽⁹⁾ **He maketh.**—Comp. *Virg. Æn.*, iii. 560.

⁽¹⁰⁾ **I am God.**—The introduction of the Divine Protector Himself speaking just before the refrain is a fine touch of art.

XLVII.

This is one of those psalms that tantalise by seeming to tell the story of their origin, though on closer inspection the story refuses to be satisfactorily identified. Some public rejoicing for victory evidently gave it birth, but whether it was that of Jehoshaphat (2 Chron. xx.), or of Hezekiah (2 Kings xviii. 8), or of John Hyrcanus over the Idumæans (Jos., *Ant.*, xiii. 9, 1), must remain in the region of conjecture. The reading, "with the people," in verse 9 (see Note), would lend probability to the last of these queries. The occasion, whatever it was, seems to have led to a re-dedication of the Temple (verse 5), such as we read of 1 Macc. iv. 54. The rhythm is fine and varied.

Title.—See titles Pss. xlii. and iii.

⁽¹⁾ **Of triumph.**—Or, *of exultation*, as LXX. and Vulg. For the hand-clapping at a time of national rejoicing, such as the coronation of a king, see 2 Kings xi. 12 (comp. Ps. xcviii. 8); and for the "shout," comp. Num. xxiii. 21, "the shout of a king"; and 1 Sam. x. 24. With the Hebrews, as with our own English forefathers, this sign of popular assent,

"In full acclaim,
A people's voice,
The proof and echo of all human fame,"

played a large and important part.

⁽²⁾ **Most high.**—Or, possibly, a predicate, *is exalted*.

Terrible.—Literally, *feared.* (Comp. 2 Chron. xx. 29).

⁽³, ⁴⁾ **Shall subdue . . . shall choose.**—Rather, *subdues, chooses*, indicating a continued manifestation of the Divine favour.

⁽³⁾ **Our inheritance.**—The LXX. read, "his inheritance," suggesting that originally the passage may have run, *He chooses us for His inheritance*, an even commoner thought in the Hebrew mind than that of the present text, that Jehovah chose Canaan as an inheritance for Israel.

⁽⁴⁾ **The excellency of Jacob.**—This phrase, which literally means *the loftiness of Jacob*, is used in Nah. ii. 2 of the national glory, in Ezek. xxiv. 21 of the Temple, but in Amos vi. 8 has a bad sense, "the pride of Jacob." Here, as the text stands, it is to be understood of the country. (Comp. Isa. xiii. 19.)

(5) God is gone up with a shout, the LORD with the sound of a trumpet. (6) Sing praises to God, sing praises: sing praises unto our King, sing praises. (7) For God is the King of all the earth: sing ye praises ¹with understanding. (8) God reigneth over the heathen: God sitteth upon the throne of his holiness. (9) ²The princes of the people are gathered together, *even* the people of the God of Abraham: for the shields of the earth *belong* unto God: he is greatly exalted.

1 Or, *every one that hath understanding.*

2 Or, *The voluntary of the people are gathered unto the people of the God of Abraham.*

3 Or, *of.*

PSALM XLVIII.

A Song *and* Psalm ³ for the sons of Korah.

(1) Great *is* the LORD, and greatly to be praised in the city of our God, *in* the mountain of his holiness. (2) Beautiful for situation, the joy of the whole earth, *is* mount Zion, *on* the sides of the north, the city of the great King. (3) God is known in her palaces for a refuge.

(4) For, lo, the kings were assembled, they passed by together. (5) They saw *it, and* so they marvelled; they were troubled, *and* hasted away. (6) Fear took

---

(5) **Is gone up.**—Not, as in Gen. xvii. 22, Judg. xiii. 20, to heaven, but, as in Psa. xxiv., to the Temple, as is shown by the public acclaim accompanying the ark to its resting-place after victory. (Comp. 2 Chron. xx. 28; Ps. lxviii. 17; Amos ii. 2.)

(6) **Sing praises.**—Better, *Strike the harp.*

(7) **With understanding.**—Rather, *play a fine tune.* (See title Ps. xxxii.) Or perhaps as LXX., and Vulg. adverbially, *play with skill.*

(9) **The shields of the earth**—*i.e.,* the princes just mentioned, as in Hos. iv. 18; so LXX. and Vulg. ("strong ones"), which, however, they make the subject of the verb—"have been mightily exalted."

XLVIII.

Jerusalem has been in great peril from some coalition either of neighbouring monarchs or of the tributary princes of one of the great world-powers, and has been delivered through some unexplained sudden panic. With this event the poet of this psalm is contemporary. So much is clear from verses 4—8 (see Notes); but on what precise event we are to fix is not so clear. There are resemblances to the deliverance of Jehoshaphat (2 Chron. xx. 25), resemblances to the fate of Sennacherib's host (2 Kings xix.), resemblances to other signal changes of fortune in later times of Israel's history.

But if we can enter into the spirit of blended piety and patriotism which makes the poem so expressive of the whole better feeling of the best times of the nation, the recovery of the precise date of its production is immaterial.

The rhythm is remarkable. In no poem is the rapid lyric movement more striking.

Title. See Ps. xli.

(1) **To be praised.**—See Ps. xviii. 3, Note.

(2) **Situation.**—Heb., *nôph.* A word only found here, but explained from a cognate Arabic word to mean *elevation.* And this feature is quite distinctive enough of Jerusalem to lend confirmation to this explanation—"Its elevation is remarkable." (See Stanley, *Sinai and Palestine,* p. 170.)

On the other hand, an adverbial use—*highly beautiful* or *supremely beautiful* (comp. Lam. ii. 15, "The perfection of beauty, the joy of the whole earth") may be all that the poet intends.

Sides of the north.—A common phrase, generally taken to mean the quarter or region of the north (see Ezek. xxxviii. 6, 15; xxxix. 2; Isa. xiv. 13), but which, from the various uses of two words making it up, might mean *northern recesses* or *secret recesses,* according as we adopt the derived or the original meaning of *tsâphôn.*

With the former of the two meanings we should see a reference to the relative position of the Temple and its precincts to the rest of the city. For the identification of the ancient Zion (not to be confounded with the modern Zion) with the hill on which the Temple stood, see Smith's *Bib. Dict.,* art. "Jerusalem." (Comp. Stanley, *Sinai and Palestine,* p. 171.)

If, on the other hand, we elect to render *secret,* or *hidden,* or *secure recesses,* we have a figure quite intelligible of the security and peace to be found in God's holy city:

Beautiful for elevation,
The whole earth's joy;
Mount Zion, a secure recess,
City of the great King.

And the thought is taken up in the word *refuge* in the next verse. (Comp. Ezek. vii. 22, where the Temple is actually called "Jehovah's *secret* place.")

(3) **Refuge.**—See Note, Ps. xlvi. 1. Prominence should be given to the idea of security from *height.* We might render, "God among her castles is known as a high and secure tower."

(4) **The kings.**—With the striking picture of the advance and sudden collapse of a hostile expedition that follows, comp. Is. x. 28—34; possibly of the very same event.

The kings.—Evidently known to the writer, but, alas! matter of merest conjecture to us. Some suppose the kings of Ammon, Moab, and Edom, who attacked Jehoshaphat (2 Chron. xx. 25); others, the tributary princes of Sennacherib. In his annals, as lately deciphered, this monarch speaks of setting up tributary kings or viceroys in Chaldæa, Phœnicia, and Philistia, after conquering these countries. (See *Assyrian Discoveries,* by George Smith, p. 303.) Others again, referring the psalm to the time of Ahaz, understand Pekah and Rezin (2 Kings xv. 37). The touches, vivid as they are, of the picture, are not so historically defined as to allow a settlement of the question.

Assembled.—Used of the muster of confederate forces (Josh. xi. 5).

Passed by—*i.e.,* marched by. So, according to the true reading, the LXX. A frequent military term (Judg. xi. 29; 2 Kings viii. 21; Isa. viii. 8). Others, "passed away," but it is doubtful if the verb can have this meaning.

Together.—Notice the parallelism, *they came together, they passed by together.*

(5) **They saw.**—A verse like Ps. xlvi. 6, vivid from the omission of the conjunctions, wrongly supplied by

The Glory of God   PSALMS, XLIX.   *in Mount Zion.*

hold upon them there, *and* pain, as of a woman in travail. ⁽⁷⁾ Thou breakest the ships of Tarshish with an east wind. ⁽⁸⁾ As we have heard, so have we seen in the city of the LORD of hosts, in the city of our God: God will establish it for ever. Selah.

⁽⁹⁾ We have thought of thy lovingkindness, O God, in the midst of thy temple. ⁽¹⁰⁾ According to thy name, O God, so *is* thy praise unto the ends of the earth: thy right hand is full of righteousness.

⁽¹¹⁾ Let mount Zion rejoice, let the daughters of Judah be glad, because of thy judgments. ⁽¹²⁾ Walk about Zion, and go round about her: tell the towers thereof. ⁽¹³⁾ ¹ Mark ye well her bulwarks, ² consider her palaces; that ye may tell *it* to the generation following.

⁽¹⁴⁾ For this God *is* our God for ever and ever: he will be our guide *even* unto death.

PSALM XLIX.

To the chief Musician, A Psalm ³ for the sons of Korah.

⁽¹⁾ Hear this, all *ye* people; give ear,

Marginal notes:
1 Heb., *Set your heart to her bulwarks.*
2 Or, *raise up.*
3 Or, *of.*

---

the Authorised Version. It has reminded commentators of Cæsar's *Veni, vidi, vici.*

They *looked, even so were terrified, bewildered, panic-struck.*

Hasted away.—Or, *sprung up in alarm.*

(7) **Breakest.**—It is natural at first sight to connect this verse immediately with the disaster which happened to the fleet of Jehoshaphat (1 Kings xxii. 48, 49; 2 Chron. xx. 36). And that event may indeed have supplied the figure, but a figure for the dispersal of a *land army.* We may render:

> With a blast from the east
> Thou breakest (them as) Tarshish ships.

Or,

> With a blast from the east
> (Which) breaketh Tarshish ships (thou breakest them),

according as we take the verb, second person masculine, or third person feminine.

Shakspere, in *King John,* compares the rout of an army to the dispersion of a fleet—

> "So, by a roaring tempest on the flood,
> A whole Armada of convicted sail
> Is scattered and disjoined from fellowship."

This is preferable to the suggestion that the seaboard tribes were in the alliance, whose break-up the psalm seems to commemorate, and that the sudden dispersion of their Armada ruined the enterprise. Tarshish ships, a common term for large merchantmen (comp. *East Indiamen*), from their use in the Tarshish trade, are here symbols of a powerful empire. Isaiah, in chap. xxxiii., compares Assyria to a gallant ship. For the "east wind," proverbially destructive and injurious, and so a ready weapon of chastisement in the Divine hand, see Job xxvii. 21; Isa. xxvii. 8; and Ezek. xxvii. 26, where its harm to shipping is especially mentioned.

(8) **As we have heard.**—The generations of a religious nation are "bound each to each by natural piety." Probably here the ancient tale of the overthrow of Pharaoh and his host recurred to the poet's mind.

God will establish it.—Better, *God will preserve her for ever, i.e., the holy city.* This forms the refrain of the song, and probably should be restored between the parts of verse 3.

(9) **Thy temple.**—This verse seems to indicate a liturgic origin for the psalm.

(10) **According to thy name . . .**—"Name" here has plainly the meaning we give it in the phrase, "name and fame." God's praise was up to the reputation His great deeds had won. (Comp. Ps. cxxxviii. 2.)

Thy right hand is full of righteousness.—Not like Jove's, as heathen say, full of thunderbolts, but of justice.

(11) **Daughters of Judah.**—Not the maidens of Jerusalem, but the towns and villages of Judah.

Judgments.—Perhaps here, as in Ps. cxix. 132, with prominent idea of God's *customary* dealings with His people.

(12) **Walk about Zion.**—Notice here the strong patriotic feeling of Hebrew song. The inhabitants of the city are invited to make a tour of inspection of the defences which, under God's providence, have protected them from their foes. We are reminded of the fine passage in Shakspere's *Cymbeline,* which gratefully recalls "the natural bravery" of our own island home, or of the national songs about our "wooden walls." Comparison has also been drawn between this passage and a similar burst of patriotic sentiment from the lips of a Grecian orator (Thuc. ii. 53); but while the Greek thinks only of the men who made Athens strong, the Hebrew traces all back to God.

(12) **Tell**—*i.e., count.* So in Milton, "Every shepherd *tells* his tale," *i.e.,* counts his sheep.

(13) **Consider.**—The Hebrew word is peculiar to this passage. The root idea seems to be *divide,* and the natural sense of *divide her palaces* is, *take them one by one and regard them.*

(14) **Unto death.**—The words (*'al mûth*) are proved by the ancient versions and various readings to be really a musical direction, either placed at the end instead of the beginning, as in Hab. iii. 19, or shifted back from the title of the next psalm. See Ps. ix. title, '*alamôth.*

XLIX.

This psalm, though didactic, does not altogether belie the promise of lyric effort made in verse 4. Not only is it cast in a lyrical form, with an introduction and two strophes, ended each by a refrain (see Note, verse 12), but it rises into true poetry both of expression and feeling. Indeed, it is not as a philosophical speculation that the author propounds and discusses his theme, but as a problem of personal interest (verses 15, 16); hence throughout the composition a strain of passion rather than a flow of thought.

Title.—See titles Pss. iv., xlii.

(1) **Hear this.**—For the opening address, comp. Deut. xxxii. 1; Micah i. 2; Ps. l. 7; Isa. i. 2.

World.—As in Ps. xvii. 14; properly, *duration.* (Comp. our expression, "the things of time.")

The Vanity of   PSALMS, XLIX.   *Earthly Advantages.*

all *ye* inhabitants of the world : ⁽²⁾ both low and high, rich and poor, together. ⁽³⁾ My mouth shall speak of wisdom; and the meditation of my heart *shall be* of understanding. ⁽⁴⁾ ^a I will incline mine ear to a parable : I will open my dark saying upon the harp. ⁽⁵⁾ Wherefore should I fear in the days of evil, *when* the iniquity of my heels shall compass me about? ⁽⁶⁾ They that trust in their wealth, and boast themselves in the multitude of their riches; ⁽⁷⁾ none *of them* can by any means redeem his brother, nor give to God a ransom for him : ⁽⁸⁾ (for the redemption of their soul *is* precious, and it ceaseth for ever :) ⁽⁹⁾ that he should still live for ever, *and* not see corruption.

⁽¹⁰⁾ For he seeth *that* wise men die, likewise the fool and the brutish person perish, and leave their wealth to others. ⁽¹¹⁾ Their inward thought *is*, that their houses *shall continue* for ever, *and* their dwelling places ¹ to all generations; they

<small>a Ps. 78. 2 ; Matt. 13. 35.</small>

<small>¹ Heb., *to generation and generation.*</small>

⁽²⁾ **Both high and low.**—The two Hebrew expressions here used, *benê-ádam* and *benê-îsh*, answer to one another much as *homo* and *vir* in Latin. The LXX. and Vulg., taking *ádam* in its primary sense, render " sons of the soil and sons of men." Symmachus makes the expressions stand for *men in general* and men as *individuals*.

Shall be of understanding.—The copula supplied by the Authorised Version is unnecessary. The word rendered meditation may mean, from its etymology, " muttered thoughts," and it is quite consistent to say, *my musings speak of understanding.* So LXX. and Vulgate.

⁽⁴⁾ **I will incline mine ear.**—The psalmist first *listens*, that he may himself catch the inspiration which is to reach others through his song. It was an obvious metaphor in a nation to whom God's voice was audible, as it was to Wordsworth, for whom nature had an audible voice :

> " The stars of midnight shall be dear
>   To her ; and she shall *lend her ear*
>   In many a secret place,
>   Where rivulets dance their wayward round,
>   And beauty, born of murmuring sound,
>   Shall pass into her face."

Parable.—Heb. *máshal*, root idea, *similitude*. It is the term used of Balaam's prophecies, and of the eloquent speeches of Job. Hence here *proverb-song* (Ewald), since the psalmist intends his composition for musical accompaniment.

Dark saying.—Either from a root meaning *to tie*, and so " a knotty point;" or to *sharpen*, and so a *sharp, incisive* saying. The LXX. and Vulgate have " problem," " proposition."

To open the riddle is not to *solve* it, but to *propound* it, as we say to " open a discourse." (Comp. St. Paul's phrase, " opening and alleging.") The full phrase is probably found in Prov. xxxi. 26, " She openeth her mouth with wisdom.'"

⁽⁵⁾ **Should I fear?**—Here the problem is stated not in a *speculative*, but *personal* form. The poet himself *feels* the pressure of this riddle of life.

When the iniquity of my heels.—The Authorised Version seems to take " heels" in the sense of footsteps, as Symmachus does, and " when the evil of my course entangles me," is good sense, but not in agreement with the context. Render rather, *when iniquity dogs me at the heels*, i.e., when wicked and prosperous men pursue him with malice. This is more natural than to give the word *heel* the derived term of *supplanter*; the sense, too, is the same. There is no direct reference to Gen. iii. 15, though possibly the figure of the *heel* as a vulnerable part, and of wickedness lying like a snake in the path, may have occurred to the poet. The Syriac, however, suggests a different reading, " malice of my oppressors."

⁽⁶⁾ **They that**—*i.e.*, the rogues implied in the last verse.

⁽⁷⁾ **None of them can.**—Brother is here used in the wide sense of Lev. xix. 17, Gen. xiii. 11 (where rendered " the one "). The sense is the same whether we make it nominative or accusative. Death is the debt which all owe, and which each must pay for himself. No wealth can buy a man off. God, in whose hand are the issues of life and death, is not to be bribed; nor, as the next verse says, even if the arrangement were possible, would any wealth be sufficient.

⁽⁸⁾ **For.**—This verse is rightly placed in a parenthesis. " Soul " is the animal life, as generally, and here necessarily from the context. There is no anticipation of the Christian scheme of redemption from sin. A ransom which could buy a man from death, as one redeems a debtor or prisoner, would be beyond the means of the wealthiest, even if nature allowed such a bargain.

It ceaseth for ever.—This is obscure. It may mean, either *the ransom utterly fails*, or *the life utterly perishes*, and so cannot be ransomed. Or, as in the Prayer Book version, the verb may be taken transitively, " he lets that alone for ever." The first of these is the simplest, and most agreeable to the context.

⁽⁹⁾ **That**—*i.e.*, in order that ; introducing the purpose of the imagined ransom in verse 7. Others connect it consecutively with verse 8, " He must give up for ever the hope of living for ever."

⁽¹⁰⁾ **For he seeth.**—The clauses are wrongly divided in the Authorised Version. Translate—

> " On the contrary he must see it (the grave),
>   Wise men must die . . .
>   Likewise the fool and the stupid must perish."

The wealth of the prudent will not avail any more for indefinite prolongation of life, than that of fools.

⁽¹¹⁾ **Their inward thought is, that their houses shall continue for ever.**—These eleven words represent three in the Hebrew, and, as the text stands, give its sense, which is intelligible and consistent :

> " They believe their houses will last for ever,
>   Their dwelling places from generation to generation ;
>   They call the lands by their own names."

The reading followed by the LXX., Chaldee, and Syriac, *kibram* for *kirbam* gives a different thought—

> " Their graves are their homes,
>   Their dwelling places for ever."

(Comp. " his long home," Eccles. xii. 5.)

The last clause, which literally runs, *they call in their names upon lands*, is by some explained (see

call *their* lands after their own names. ⁽¹²⁾ Nevertheless man *being* in honour abideth not: he is like the beasts *that* perish.

⁽¹³⁾ This their way *is* their folly: yet their posterity ¹approve their sayings. Selah.

⁽¹⁴⁾ Like sheep they are laid in the grave; death shall feed on them; and the upright shall have dominion over them in the morning; and their ²beauty shall consume ³in the grave from their dwelling. ⁽¹⁵⁾ But God will redeem my soul ⁴from the power of ⁵the grave: for he shall receive me. Selah.

⁽¹⁶⁾ Be not thou afraid when one is made rich, when the glory of his house is increased; ⁽¹⁷⁾ ᵃfor when he dieth he shall carry nothing away: his glory shall not descend after him. ⁽¹⁸⁾ Though ⁶while he lived he blessed his soul: and *men* will praise thee, when thou doest well to thyself. ⁽¹⁹⁾ ⁷He shall go to the generation of his fathers; they shall never see light.

⁽²⁰⁾ Man *that is* in honour, and understandeth not, is like the beasts *that* perish.

PSALM L.
A Psalm ⁸of Asaph.

⁽¹⁾ The mighty God, *even* the LORD,

---

1 Heb., *delight in their mouth.*
2 Or, *strength.*
3 Or, *the grave being an habitation to every one of them.*
4 Heb., *from the hand of the grave.*
5 Or, *hell.*
a Job 27. 19.
6 Heb., *in his life.*
7 Heb., *The soul shall go.*
8 Or, *for Asaph.*

Isa. xliv. 5) to mean, "they are celebrated in their lands," which suits the text followed by the LXX.

(12) **Abideth not.**—This verse gives the kernel and the thought of, as it also serves as a refrain to, the poem, thus vindicating the claim of a lyric tone for this didactic psalm. The reading of the LXX. and Vulg. ("without understanding" instead of "abideth not"), which brings verse 12 into exact correspondence with verse 20, is unquestionably to be adopted. The present text could not really express *permanence*, the Hebrew verb meaning to *lodge temporarily*.

The next verse, too, is hardly intelligible, unless we read here—

"Man, though in honour, without understanding,
Is like the beasts; they perish."

(13) **This their way**—*i.e.*, the folly mentioned in the (amended) preceding verse, and described in verse 11.

Is their folly—*i.e.*, is a way of folly.

(14) **Like sheep they are laid in the grave.**—Rather, *like a flock for sheol they are arranged; death is their shepherd.* While planning for a long life, and mapping out their estates as if for a permanent possession, they are but a flock of sheep, entirely at the disposal and under the direction of another, and this shepherd is death. Comp. Keble's paraphrase.

"Even as a flock arrayed are they
For the dark grave; Death guides their way,
Death is their shepherd now."

The rendering, "feed on them," is an error. The rest of the verse as it stands is quite unintelligible. Among the many conjectured emendations, the best is (Burgess) to point the verb as the future of *yârad*, and render, "and the upright shall go down to the grave amongst them (*i.e.*, amongst the ungodly) until the morning" (for the last words compare Deut. xvi. 4), when in contrast to the wicked they shall see light (verse 20).

Adopting this emendation, a new force is lent to the next two clauses, which have puzzled modern commentators, as they did the ancient translators (LXX., "their help shall grow old in hell from their glory.") By a slight change of points and accents, and taking *mizbul* as a derivative noun equivalent to *zebul* (so also Grätz), we get, "Their beauty (is) for corruption; sheol (is) its dwelling," *i.e.*, all, wise and unwise, good and bad, must descend to the under world (verse 11), so that the upright accompany the wicked thither, and it becomes the dwelling-place of their beauty, *i.e.*, their bodies.

(15) **But God will.**—Better, *But God shall redeem my life from the hand of sheol when it seizes me.* Taken by itself, this statement might only imply that when just at the point of death, the Divine favour would draw him back and rescue him. But taken with the rendering given above to the previous verse, we must see here the dim foreshadowing of a better hope, that death did not altogether break the covenant bond between Jehovah and His people, a hope to which, through the later psalms and the book of Job, we see the Hebrew mind feeling its way. (Comp. Ps. xvi. 10; and see Note to Ps. vi. 5.)

(16, 17) **After** expressing his own hopes of escaping from death, or being rescued from corruption, the psalmist recurs to the question of verse 5, and completes the answer to it. He need not fear, however prosperous and wealthy his adversaries become, for they will die, and, dying, can take none of their possessions with them.

(18) **Though, while he lived . . . .**—This is abundantly illustrated by our Lord's parable of the rich fool (Luke xii. 19; comp. Deut. xxix. 19).

And men will.—Rather, *and though men praise thee*, &c. "Although prosperity produces self-gratulation, and procures the homage of the world as well, yet," &c.

(19) **They shall never.**—Better, *who will never again look on the light*, *i.e.*, "never live again," implying, in contrast, a hope of a resurrection for the upright. (See Note verse 14.)

L.

The one great corruption to which all religion is exposed is its separation from morality, and of all religions that of Israel was pre-eminently open to this danger. It was one of the main functions of the prophetical office to maintain the opposite truth—the inseparable union of morality with religion. This psalm takes rank with the prophets in such a proclamation. It makes it under a highly poetical form, a magnificent vision of judgment, in which, after summoning heaven and earth as His assessors, God arraigns before Him the whole nation, separated into two great groups; sincere but mistaken adherents to form; hypocrites, to whom religious profession is but a cloak for sin. The rhythm is fine and fairly well sustained.

Title.—Asaph was a Levite, son of Berachiah, and one of the leaders of David's choir (1 Chron. vi. 39). He

God come to Judgment.   PSALMS, L.   *His Pleasure not in Ceremonies.*

hath spoken, and called the earth from the rising of the sun unto the going down thereof. ⁽²⁾ Out of Zion, the perfection of beauty, God hath shined.

⁽³⁾ Our God shall come, and shall not keep silence: a fire shall devour before him, and it shall be very tempestuous round about him. ⁽⁴⁾ He shall call to the heavens from above, and to the earth, that he may judge his people. ⁽⁵⁾ Gather my saints together unto me; those that have made a covenant with me by sacrifice. ⁽⁶⁾ And the heavens shall declare his righteousness: for God *is* judge himself. Selah.

⁽⁷⁾ Hear, O my people, and I will speak; O Israel, and I will testify against thee: I *am* God, *even* thy God. ⁽⁸⁾ I will not reprove thee for thy sacrifices or thy burnt offerings, *to have been* continually before me. ⁽⁹⁾ I will take no bullock out of thy house, *nor* he goats out of thy folds. ⁽¹⁰⁾ For every beast of the forest *is* mine, *and* the cattle upon a thousand hills. ⁽¹¹⁾ I know all the fowls of the mountains: and the wild beasts of the field *are* ¹mine. ⁽¹²⁾ If I were hungry, I would not tell thee: *a* for the world *is* mine, and the fulness thereof. ⁽¹³⁾ Will I eat the flesh of bulls, or drink the blood of goats?

1 Heb., *with me.*

a Ex. 19. 5; Deut. 10. 14; Job 41. 11; Ps. 24. 1; 1 Cor. 10. 26, 28.

---

was also by tradition a psalm writer (2 Chron. xxix. 30, Neh. xii. 46). It is certain, however, that all the psalms ascribed to Asaph (lxxiii.—lxxxiii.) were not by the same hand, or of the same time (see Introduction to Ps. lxxiv.); and, as in the case of the Korahite psalms, probably the inscription, "to Asaph," only implies the family of Asaph, or a guild of musicians bearing that name (1 Chron. xxv. 1; 2 Chron. xx. 14; Ezra ii. 41).

⁽¹⁾ **The mighty God, even the Lord.**—Heb., *El Elohim, Jehovah*, a combination of the Divine names that has been very variously understood. The Authorised Version follows the rendering of Aquila and Symmachus. But the Masoretic accents are in favour of taking each term as an appellative. Hitzig objects that this is stiff, but it is so on purpose. The poet introduces his vision of judgment in the style of a formal royal proclamation, as the preterite tenses also indicate. But as in this case it is not the earthly monarch, but the Divine, who is "Lord also of the whole earth," the range of the proclamation is not territorial, "from Dan even unto Beersheba," as in 2 Chron. xxx. 5, but is couched in larger terms, "from sunrise to sunset," an expression constantly used of the operation of Divine power and mercy. (Comp. Pss. ciii. 12; cxiii. 3; Isa. xli. 25, xlv. 6.)

⁽²⁾ **Perfection of beauty**—*i.e.*, Zion, because the Temple, the residence of Jehovah, was there. (Comp. Ps. xlviii. 2; Lam. ii. 15; 1 Macc. ii. 12.)

Hath shined.—Comp. Ps. lxxx. 1; Deut. xxxiii. 2. A natural figure of the Divine manifestation, whether taken from the dawn or from lighting.

⁽³⁾ **Our God shall come . . . shall devour . . . shall be.**—Better, *comes . . . devours . . . is*. The drama, the expected scene having been announced, now opens. The vision unfolds itself before the poet's eye.

⁽⁴⁾ **He shall call.**—Better, *He calls*. The poet actually hears the summons go forth calling heaven and earth as witnesses, or assessors (comp. Micah vi. 2), of the judgment scene. (Comp. Deut. iv. 26; xxxii. 1; Isa. i. 2; Micah i. 2; 1 Macc. ii. 37.)

Israel, politically so insignificant, must have been profoundly conscious of the tremendous issues involved in its religious character to demand a theatre so vast, an audience so august.

⁽⁵⁾ **My saints.**—This verse is of great importance, as containing a formal definition of the word *chasîdim*, and so a direction as to its interpretation wherever it occurs in the Hebrew hymn book. The "saints" are those in the "covenant," and that covenant was ratified by *sacrifices*. As often, then, as a sacrifice was offered by an Israelite, it was a witness to the existence of the covenant, and we are not to gather, therefore, from this psalm that outward acts of sacrifice were annulled by the higher spirit taught in it; they were merely subordinated to their proper place, and those who thought more of the rites that bore testimony to the covenant than of the moral *duties* which the covenant enjoined, are those censured in this part of the psalm.

⁽⁶⁾ **The heavens.**—Here is an exceedingly fine touch. In obedience to the Divine summons the heavens are heard acknowledging the right of God to arraign the nations before Him in virtue of His moral sway. Render the verb in the present: *And the heavens declare*. The verse is adapted to Ps. xcvii. 6.

In the language of modern thought, order and law in the physical world are an evidence of an ordered moral government, and the obedience of the unconscious stars to that sway which, as Wordsworth says, "preserves them from wrong," is a challenge to man to submit himself consciously to the same will.

⁽⁷⁾ **Hear.**—The actual judgment now opens, God asserting in impressive tones His right to preside: *God, thy God, I . . .* the Elohistic form of the more usual "Jehovah, thy God."

⁽⁸⁾ **I will not . . .**—Better, *Not on account of thy sacrifices do I reprove thee, nor thy burnt offerings, which are always before me*. This part of the nation is judged not for neglect of ritual, but for mistaken regard for it. (See *Introduction* to this psalm.)

As usual in such visions of judgment (comp. Matt. xxv. 32) the arraigned nation is separated into two classes when brought before the bar of the judge, and the better part is first reproved.

^(9—18) Notice the fine tone of irony that pervades this rebuke, the best weapon against ritualistic errors.

⁽¹⁰⁾ **A thousand hills.**—Literally, *mountains of a thousand*, an expression for which there is no analogy, but which might conceivably mean, "mountains where the cattle are by thousands;" but surely the LXX. and Vulg. are right here, in rendering "oxen" instead of "a thousand," and we should read "hills of oxen."

⁽¹¹⁾ **Wild beasts.**—Literally, *that which moveth*. (Comp. Ps. lxxx. 13.)

(14) Offer unto God thanksgiving; and pay thy vows unto the most High: (15) and call upon me in the day of trouble: I will deliver thee, and thou shalt glorify me. (16) But unto the wicked God saith, What hast thou to do to declare my statutes, or *that* thou shouldest take my covenant in thy mouth? (17) *a*Seeing thou hatest instruction, and castest my words behind thee. (18) When thou sawest a thief, then thou consentedst with him, and [1]hast been partaker with adulterers. (19) [2]Thou givest thy mouth to evil, and thy tongue frameth deceit. (20) Thou sittest *and* speakest against thy brother; thou slanderest thine own mother's son. (21) These *things* hast thou done, and I kept silence; thou thoughtest that I was altogether *such an one as* thyself: *but* I will reprove thee, and set *them* in order before thine eyes. (22) Now consider this, ye that forget God, lest I tear *you* in pieces, and *there* be none to deliver. (23) Whoso offereth praise glorifieth me: and to him [3]that ordereth *his* conversation *aright* will I shew the salvation of God.

a Rom. 2. 21, 22.
[1] Heb., *thy portion was with adulterers.*
[2] Heb., *Thou sendest.*
[3] Heb., *that disposeth his way.*
b 2 Sam. 11. 2, & 12. 1.

PSALM LI.

To the chief Musician, A Psalm of David, *b*when Nathan the prophet came unto him, after he had gone in to Bath-sheba.

(1) Have mercy upon me, O God, according to thy lovingkindness: according unto the multitude of thy tender mercies blot out my transgressions.

---

(14) **Offer.**—Gratitude, and the loyal performance of known duties, are the ritual most pleasing to God. Not that the verse implies the cessation of outward rites, but the subordination of the outward to the inward, the form to the spirit. (See Ps. li. 17—19.)

(16) **But.**—The psalm here turns to address a worse class, those who, while undisguisedly wicked, shelter themselves under the name of the covenant.

What hast thou to do?—*i.e.*, how darest thou?

(18) **Thou consentedst with him**—*i.e.*, hast pleasure in. (Comp. Job xxxiv. 9.)

(19) **Givest.**—Literally, *lettest loose.*

Frameth.—Literally, *weaves.* So LXX. To *weave snares* is a common figure in all languages. Comp.

"My brain, more busy than the labouring spider,
Weaves tedious snares to trap mine enemies."
SHAKSPERE: *2 Henry VI.* iii. 2.

(20) **Sittest.**—Rather, as in Pss. x. 8, xvii. 12, *lurkest.*

Slanderest.—Literally, *givest a thrust*; but, from the parallelism, used of *words* that often hurt more than *blows.*

Mother's son.—In a country where polygamy was practised, this marks a closer relationship than the more general "brother" would do. (See Song of Sol. i. 6, Note.)

(21) The forbearance of God (intended to give room for repentance, Rom. ii. 4) is misconstrued. Men come to think the Divine Being as indifferent to evil as themselves.

That I was altogether.—We might render, *that I was actually.*

And set them in order.—The insertion of "them," referring back to "these things," is rather confusing. Better supply *thine offences.* All the sins of the wicked are marshalled before them.

(23) **Offereth praise.**—Better, *sacrificeth thanksgiving*, as in verse 14; the poet here sums up what he has previously said. This clause must therefore be considered as addressed to the sincere *formalist*, the next to the *openly wicked.*

To him that ordereth . . .—Literally, as the text stands, *placeth his way*, which is hardly intelligible. The version of Symmachus suggests the reading *tam*, instead of *sam*, "to him who walks uprightly." But being plainly intended for the ungodly, we want in this clause some mention of amendment; and if the poet wrote *shab*, we get, literally, *him who has turned his way*, *i.e.*, who has changed his course of life.

LI.

This psalm has been so identified with David, that to surrender the tradition which ascribes it to him seems a literary crime. Indeed, the character of the man has been read so constantly through the medium of Pss. xxxii. and li., that we must admit that a personality, dear to all the religious world, recedes and becomes less distinct before the criticism which questions the genuineness of the Davidic authorship of either of them. Yet in the case before us we must either break this long cherished association, or admit the last two verses of the psalm to be a later addition for liturgical use.

But the question of authorship does not affect the estimation in which this psalm has always been held, and always will be held, in the Church, as the noblest expression of penitence. Even if it was not originally, directly, and exclusively the expression of an individual's repentance, but rather the voice of the people of Israel deploring, during the exile, its ancient errors and sins (the only conclusion which completely explains verse 4, see Note), and praying for a new lease of covenant-favour, yet the associations of the psalm with individual experience of sin and repentance from it are now far too close to be broken, and it must ever remain in the truest sense one of the penitential psalms, suited for private use as well as for that of the Church. It presents as has been rightly said, the Hebrew and Christian idea of repentance; not remorse, not mere general confession of human depravity, not minute confessions of minute sins dragged to light by a too impulsive casuistry, but change of life and mind; and, in the words of Carlyle, "all earnest souls will ever discern in it the faithful struggle of an earnest human soul towards what is good and best." The parallelism is distinct and well sustained.

Title.—See title Ps. iv.

(1) **Blot out.**—The figure is most probably, as in Exod. xxxii. 32, 33, taken from the custom of erasing a written record (comp. Num. v. 23; Ps. lxix. 28). So

David, confessing his Sin,   PSALMS, LI.   *prays for Forgiveness.*

⁽²⁾ Wash me throughly from mine iniquity, and cleanse me from my sin. ⁽³⁾ For I acknowledge my transgressions: and my sin *is* ever before me.

⁽⁴⁾ Against thee, thee only, have I sinned, and done *this* evil in thy sight: *a* that thou mightest be justified when thou speakest, *and* be clear when thou judgest.

⁽⁵⁾ Behold, I was shapen in iniquity; and in sin did my mother ¹ conceive me. ⁽⁶⁾ Behold, thou desirest truth in the inward parts: and in the hidden *part* thou shalt make me to know wisdom.

⁽⁷⁾ *b* Purge me with hyssop, and I shall be clean: wash me, and I shall be whiter than snow. ⁽⁸⁾ Make me to hear joy and gladness; *that* the bones *which* thou hast broken may rejoice. ⁽⁹⁾ Hide thy face from my sins, and blot out all mine iniquities.

a Rom. 3. 4

¹ Heb., *warm me.*

b Lev. 14. 6; Num. 19. 18.

LXX. and Vulg. Isaiah, however (Isa. xliv. 22) uses the same word in a different connection, "I will blot out thy sins as a cloud." A fine thought that the error and guilt that cloud the mind and conscience can be cleared off like a mist by a breath from heaven.

Transgressions.—See Ps. xxxii. 1. The word seems to imply a wilful throwing off of authority or restraint, perhaps here the breach of the covenant-relation irrespective of any particular sin by which the breach was brought about. Whether it is an individual or the community that speaks, the prayer is that Jehovah would act according to His *chesed* or covenant-favour towards the suppliant, and wipe out from His records whatever has intervened between the covenant parties.

⁽²⁾ **Wash me throughly.**—Literally, *Wash me much,* whether we follow the Hebrew text or the Hebrew margin. The two clauses of the verse are not merely antithetic. The terms *wash* and *cleanse* seem to imply respectively the *actual* and the *ceremonial* purification, the former meaning literally *to tread,* describing the process of washing clothes (as blankets are washed to this day in Scotland) by trampling them with the feet, the latter used of the formal declaration of cleanliness by the priest in the case of leprosy (Lev. xiii. 6—34). (For the *iniquity* and *sin,* see Ps. xxxii. 1.)

⁽³⁾ **For I.**—There is an emphatic pronoun in the first clause which we may preserve, at the same time noticing the difference between the violation of the covenant generally in the term *transgressions* in the first clause, and the *offence* which made the breach in the second. (See Note verse 1.) *Because I am one who is conscious of my transgressions, and* (or, possibly, *even*) *my offence is ever before me.*

The thought that he had been unfaithful to the covenant was an accusing conscience to him, keeping his sin always before his eyes, and until, according to his prayer in verses 1 and 2, he was received back into conscious relationship again, his offence must weigh upon his mind. This explanation holds, whether an individual or the community speaks.

⁽⁴⁾ **Against thee, thee only . . .**—This can refer to nothing but a breach of the covenant-relation by the nation at large. An individual would have felt his guilt against the nation or other individuals, as well as against Jehovah. The fact that St. Paul quotes (from the LXX.) part of the verse in Rom. iii. 4 (see Note, *New Testament Commentary*) has naturally opened up an avenue for discussion on the bearing of the words on the doctrines of free-will and predestination. But the immediate object of his quotation appears to be to contrast the *faithfulness* of the God of the covenant with the *falsehood* of the covenant people ("Let God be true, and every man a liar"). The honour of God, as God of the covenant, was at stake. It is this thought which appears in the last clauses of this verse.

That . . .—*So that* (or, *in order that*) *thou art* (or *mayest be*) *justified in thy cause, and clear in thy judgment.* The Hebrew, rendered in the Authorised Version *when thou speakest,* is often used of a cause or suit (see (Exod. xviii. 16—22, "matter," &c.), and it is here plainly used in this sense and is parallel to judgment. The clause seems to imply not only a sense of a breach of the covenant, but some manifest judgment from Jehovah in consequence; and, as usual, it is of its effect on the heathen that the psalmist thinks. The Divine honour would be justified when the suffering nation confessed that condemnation and punishment had been deserved. This was apparently the meaning read in the words by the LXX.

⁽⁵⁾ **Behold, I was shapen . . .**—Better, *Behold, I was born in iniquity.*

The later rabbis, combining this verse with the mystery hanging over the origin and name of David's mother, represent him as born in adultery. (See Stanley, *Jewish Church,* chap. ii., p. 46, Note.) The word rendered *conceived* is certainly one generally used of animal desire. (The marginal *warm me* is erroneous.) But the verse is only a statement of the truth of experience so constantly affirmed in Scripture of hereditary corruption and the innate proneness to sin in every child of man. The argument for a personal origin to the psalm from this verse seems strong; but in Ps. cxxix. 1, and frequently, the community is personified as an individual growing from youth to age, and so may here speak of its far-back idolatrous ancestry as the mother who conceived it in sin.

⁽⁶⁾ **Truth.**—Or, *faithfulness.*

Inward parts.—The Hebrew word is found only once besides (Job xxxviii. 36), where it is in parallelism with "heart."

The sincerity and true self-discernment which God requires can only come of spiritual insight, or, as the last clause states it, divine instruction.

⁽⁷⁾ **Hyssop.**—The mention of this connects this verse with the priestly ordinances concerning leprosy and contact with a dead body (Lev. xiv.; Num. xix.); but generally it is a repetition of the former prayer to have the breach made in the covenant-relationship healed. (Comp. Is. i. 18.)

⁽⁸⁾ **The bones which thou hast broken . . .**—Through his whole being the psalmist has felt the crushing weight of sin; to its *very fibres,* as we say, his frame has suffered.

⁽⁹⁾ **Hide thy face . . .**—*i.e.,* thy angry look. (See Ps. xxi. 9.) More usually the expression is used in the opposite sense of hiding the *gracious* look. As long as Jehovah kept the *offences* before Him the breach in the covenant must continue.

(10) Create in me a clean heart, O God; and renew ¹ a right spirit within me. (11) Cast me not away from thy presence; and take not thy holy spirit from me. (12) Restore unto me the joy of thy salvation; and uphold me *with thy* free spirit.
(13) *Then* will I teach transgressors thy ways; and sinners shall be converted unto thee. (14) Deliver me from ² bloodguiltiness, O God, thou God of my salvation: *and* my tongue shall sing aloud of thy righteousness.
(15) O Lord, open thou my lips; and my mouth shall shew forth thy praise.
(16) For thou desirest not sacrifice; ³ else would I give *it*: thou delightest not in burnt offering. (17) ᵃ The sacrifices of God *are* a broken spirit: a broken and a contrite heart, O God, thou wilt not despise.
(18) Do good in thy good pleasure unto Zion: build thou the walls of Jerusalem.
(19) Then shalt thou be pleased with the sacrifices of righteousness, with burnt offering and whole burnt offering: then shall they offer bullocks upon thine altar.

PSALM LII.

To the chief Musician, Maschil, *A Psalm* of David, ᵇ when Doeg the Edomite came and told Saul, and said unto him, David is come to the house of Ahimelech.

(1) Why boastest thou thyself in mischief, O mighty man? the goodness of

¹ Or, *a constant spirit.*
² Heb., *bloods.*
³ Or, *that I should give* it.
a Isa. 57. 15, & 66. 2.
b 1 Sam. 22. 9.

---

(10) **Right spirit.**—So LXX. and Vulg.; but the *constant* of the margin is nearer the Hebrew, and better.

(11) **Cast me not away.**—This phrase is used of the formal rejection of Israel by the God of the covenant (2 Kings xiii. 23; xvii. 20; xxiv. 20; Jer. vii. 15). Its use here not only confirms the explanation of the notes above, but makes in favour of understanding the whole psalm of the community.

Take not thy holy spirit.—Commentators have discussed whether this means the spirit of *office* given to the king on his anointing (1 Sam. xvi. 13), or of *grace*, and Calvinists and Lutherans have made the text a battle-ground of controversy. Plainly, as the parallelism shows, the petition is equivalent to a prayer against rejection from the Divine favour, and is not to be pressed into any doctrinal discussion.

(12) **Joy of thy salvation.**—This again points to a sense of restoration of covenant privileges.

Thy free spirit.—Rather, *with a willing spirit*. Or we may render, *a willing spirit shall support me*.

(13) **Shall be converted.**—Better, *shall turn to thee*. (See Note Ps. l. 23.)

(14) **Bloodguiltiness . . .**—Literally, as in the margin, *bloods*. So in LXX. and in Vulg., but thus hardly making it clear whether the word implies the guilt of blood already shed or anticipated violence. The latter would rather have taken the form of Ps. lix. 2, "from men of blood." Probably we should read "from death," as in Ps. lvi. 13.

(15) **My lips.**—Comp. Ps. lxxi. 15. The sense of forgiveness is like a glad morning to song-birds.

(16) **Sacrifice.**—The rabbinical commentators on this verse represent *the penitence* of David as having taken the place of the *sin-offering* prescribed by the Law. In the mouth of an individual, language with such an intention would not have been possible. To the nation exiled and deprived of the legal rites, and by that very deprivation compelled to look beyond their outward form to their inner spirit, the words are most appropriate.

(18) **Do good.**—The last two verses have occasioned much controversy. They do not fit in well with the theory of Davidic authorship, Theodoret long ago saying that they better suited the exiles in Babylon. They seem at first sight to contradict what has just been asserted of sacrifice. On both grounds they have been regarded as a liturgical addition, such as doubtless the compiler made, without any sense of infringement of the rights of authorship. On the other hand, it is not only these two verses which harmonise with the feelings of the restored exiles, but the whole psalm, and the contradiction in regard to the worth of sacrifices is only apparent. While vindicating spiritual religion, the psalmist no more abrogates ceremonies than the prophets do. As soon as their performance is possible they will be resumed.

LII.

In this psalm the voice of the community of pious Israel plainly speaks. (See Note, verse 8.) The traditional title has not the slightest support in the contents or tone of the poem. (See Note, title.) The tyrant, or mighty man, who is addressed, is most probably one of those base time-servers who, against the national party, and against the religious sentiment, sold themselves to the foreign power that happened to be in the ascendant; and who, by lending themselves as the instruments of tyranny, became the means of rousing the patriotic spirit which at length, under the hand of Maccabæus, succeeded in shaking off the foreign yoke. The rhythm is varied and well sustained.

Title.—See title Pss. iv., xxxii. This is one of a series of three Elohistic psalms.

The historical reference in this inscription serves to cast discredit on the inscriptions generally, as showing on what insufficient grounds they could be received. There is not a syllable in the poem which conveniently applies to Doeg, or to the occurrence narrated in 1 Sam. xxii. 17; on the contrary, the accusation of lying (verses 1—3), the imputation of trust in riches (verse 7), as well as the general tone in which the psalm is couched, are quite against such an application.

(1) **Mighty man.**—Better, *hero*, used sarcastically. LXX. and Vulg., "a mighty one at mischief." (Comp. Isa. v. 22: "a hero at drinking.") The order of the Hebrew is, however, against this, and in favour of the English, *why dost thou exult in wickedness, O hero*, *i.e.*, perhaps, not only his own, but in the wickedness the people are led into by his means. This seems necessitated by the next clause. In spite of man's

The Doom of the Deceitful.   PSALMS, LIII.   *The Godless Fool.*

God *endureth* continually. ⁽²⁾ Thy tongue deviseth mischiefs; like a sharp razor, working deceitfully. ⁽³⁾ Thou lovest evil more than good; *and* lying rather than to speak righteousness. Selah. ⁽⁴⁾ Thou lovest all devouring words, ¹ O *thou* deceitful tongue.

⁽⁵⁾ God shall likewise ² destroy thee for ever, he shall take thee away, and pluck thee out of *thy* dwelling place, and root thee out of the land of the living. Selah.

⁽⁶⁾ The righteous also shall see, and fear, and shall laugh at him: ⁽⁷⁾ lo, *this is* the man *that* made not God his strength; but trusted in the abundance of his riches, *and* strengthened himself in his ³ wickedness.

⁽⁸⁾ But I *am* like a green olive tree in the house of God: I trust in the mercy of God for ever and ever. ⁽⁹⁾ I will praise thee for ever, because thou hast done *it*: and I will wait on thy name; for *it is* good before thy saints.

PSALM LIII.

To the chief Musician upon Mahalath, Maschil, *A Psalm* of David.

⁽¹⁾ The *a* fool hath said in his heart, *There is* no God. Corrupt are they, and have done abominable iniquity: *b* *there is* none that doeth good.

⁽²⁾ God looked down from heaven upon the children of men, to see if there were any that did understand, that did seek

---

Marginal notes:
1 Or, *and the deceitful tongue.*
2 Heb., *beat thee down.*
3 Or, *substance.*
a Ps. 10. 4, & 14. 1, &c.
b Rom. 3. 10.

---

folly and sin, God's *covenant favour endures all the day long.*

(2) **Working deceitfully.**—Better, *working guile.* (For the metaphor, see Pss. lv. 21, lvii. 4, &c.)

(4) **Devouring words.**—Literally, *words of swallowing,* such as swallow down (comp. Ps. v. 9, where the throat is called "an open sepulchre") a neighbour's life, honour, and goods.

(5) **Destroy.**—Better, *tear down,* as if of a building.

Take thee away.—Better, *lay hold of thee.* The Hebrew word is always used of taking a live coal from the hearth. Notice, however, that the exactly opposite is intended of our "pluck a brand from the burning." Here the idea is of pulling the house-fire to pieces, and so extinguishing domestic life.

(6) **Fear . . . laugh.**—The mingled feelings of awe at the tyrant's terrible fall, and exultation at his overthrow, are finely caught and described.

Dwelling-place.—Better, *tent.*

Root thee out.—This word, suggestive of rooting up a corrupt tree, becomes more forcible from the contrast in the figure of verse 8.

(8) **But I am like.**— The flourishing olive alternates with the vine, in Hebrew poetry, as an emblem of prosperous Israel. (See Jer. xi. 16; Hos. xiv. 6.) The epithet "green" hardly refers to the colour so much as the "vigour" of the tree, for the foliage of "wan grey olive wood" cannot be called verdant. But though the olive is scarcely, to our Western eyes, a beautiful tree, "to the Oriental the coolness of the pale-blue foliage, its evergreen freshness, spread like a silver sea along the slopes of the hills, speaks of peace and plenty, food and gladness" (Tristram, *Nat. Hist. of the Bible,* p. 374).

In the house of God.—Here and in the more elaborate simile (Ps. xcii. 13) the situation, "in the house of God," is added to show that the prophecy has come of religious trust. It is quite possible that trees were actually planted in the precincts of the Temple, as they are in the Haram area now, so that the rendering, "near the house of God," would express a literal fact. Or the whole may be figurative, as in the verse, "like the olive branches round about Thy table."

(9) **Because thou hast done it.**—Better, *because thou workest,* i.e., *for thy works,* but spoken in anticipation of future manifestations.

I will wait on thy name . . . .—Better, *I will wait for thy glory;* "name," here, after the mention of God's works in the last clause, being evidently, as so often, synonymous with "fame" and "reputation."

For it is good before thy saints.—This may mean that such a trustful expectation in the presence of the saints is good, or that it is pleasant in the eyes of the saints thus to wait, or we may take "name" as the subject.

The mention of the "saints" (*chasidím*) is by some supposed to indicate the Asmonean period as that of the composition of the Psalm.

LIII.

This Psalm is a variation from Psalm xiv. Which was the original, or whether both are not corruptions of some lost original, are questions involving minute comparisons and examinations of the Hebrew text, and possibly do not admit of satisfactory answers. Instead of "Jehovah" in Ps. xiv., Ps. liii. has *Elohim,* according to the style of this part of the collection. The other differences are discussed in the Notes. (See *Introduction* and Notes to Ps. xiv.)

Title.—See title, Ps. iv.

Upon Mahalath.—One of the most perplexing of the perplexing inscriptions. We have a choice of explanations from derivation between *upon a flute,* and *after the manner of sickness.* The word occurs again in the Title of Ps. lxxxviii., with the addition of "to sing." It is against the analogy supplied by other inscriptions to refer this to the sad nature of the contents of the Psalm, though in the case of Ps. lxxxviii. such an interpretation would be very appropriate and not inappropriate here. As in other cases, we look for some musical direction here, and if we take the root, meaning "sick" or "sad," we must render "to a sad strain," or "to the tune of a song beginning with the word 'sadness.'"

(1) **And.**—The conjunction is wanting in Ps. xiv. 1.

Iniquity.—Instead of the general term, "doings," in Ps. xiv., as if the adapter of the Psalm felt that a word applicable to good as well as evil was not strong enough to express the hideousness of the profanity.

God. ⁽³⁾ Every one of them is gone back: they are altogether become filthy; there is none that doeth good, no, not one.

⁽⁴⁾ Have the workers of iniquity no knowledge? who eat up my people as they eat bread: they have not called upon God. ⁽⁵⁾ There ¹ were they in great fear, *where* no fear was: for God hath scattered the bones of him that encampeth *against* thee: thou hast put *them* to shame, because God hath despised them.

⁽⁶⁾ ²Oh that the salvation of Israel *were* come out of Zion! When God bringeth back the captivity of his people, Jacob shall rejoice, *and* Israel shall be glad.

PSALM LIV.

To the chief Musician on Neginoth, Maschil, *A Psalm* of David, ^a when the Ziphims came and said to Saul, Doth not David hide himself with us?

⁽¹⁾ Save me, O God, by thy name, and judge me by thy strength. ⁽²⁾ Hear my prayer, O God; give ear to the words of my mouth. ⁽³⁾ For strangers are risen up against me, and oppressors seek after my soul: they have not set God before them. Selah.

⁽⁴⁾ Behold, God *is* mine helper: the Lord *is* with them that uphold my soul. ⁽⁵⁾ He shall reward evil unto ³mine enemies: cut them off in thy truth. ⁽⁶⁾ I will freely sacrifice unto thee: I will praise thy name, O Lord; for *it is* good. ⁽⁷⁾ For he hath delivered me out of all trouble: and mine eye hath seen *his desire* upon mine enemies.

PSALM LV.

To the chief Musician on Neginoth, Maschil, *A Psalm* of David.

⁽¹⁾ Give ear to my prayer, O God; and hide not thyself from my supplication.

Marginal notes:
1 Heb., *they feared a fear.*
2 Heb., *Who will give salvations, &c.*
a 1 Sam. 23. 19, & 26. 1.
3 Heb., *those that observe me.*

⁽³⁾ There are two unimportant variations from Ps. xiv. here: "every one," instead of "the whole," and "gone back" (*sag*) for "gone aside" (*sar*).

⁽⁴⁾ Notice the omission of the expressive "all" found in Ps. xiv.

⁽⁵⁾ **Where no fear was.**—This—the most interesting variation from Ps. xiv.—appears plainly to have been inserted to bring the Psalm into harmony with some circumstance belonging to the time for which it was adapted, but to which we have no clue. As to the choice among the various explanations that have been given of it, we must remark that the one which takes "fear" in a good sense ("Then were they in great fright where there was no fear of God") is excluded by the fact that the same word is employed in both clauses; and, as elsewhere *pâchad* is used of a "cause of terror," we may render, *There were they in great fear, where there was no cause for fear.*

Apparently, from the immediate context, this statement is made not of the enemies of Israel, but of Israel itself, and was so constantly applicable to a people supposed to be living under the immediate protection of God, and yet liable to sudden panics, that we need not try to recover the precise event referred to.

Of him that encampeth against thee.—Literally, *of thy besiegers*. The bones of the beleaguering host lie bleaching on the sand. But the text seems to have suffered. The LXX. and Vulg. have "the bones of them that please men," and a comparison with Ps. xiv. 5, 6 shows such a similarity of *letters*, with difference of *meaning*, that both texts look like different attempts to restore some faded MS. Many attempts have been made to restore the original, but none eminently satisfactory.

LIV.

If this Psalm is the outcome of individual feeling, the traditional title will suit it as well as any that conjecture can supply. But it reads more like the cry of a people in distress, an oppressed race, powerless except in its religious hope. A stanza of five lines, with marked and elegant rhythm is followed by eight loosely connected lines.

Title.—See Notes to titles of Pss. iv., xxxii.; and comp. 1 Sam. xxiii. 19, xxvi. 1.

⁽¹⁾ **By thy name.**—See Note, Ps. xx. 1. (Comp. Isa. xxx. 27.)

Judge me by thy strength—*i.e.*, in Thy power see that justice is done me.

⁽³⁾ **For strangers.**—This verse, with some variations, occurs again (Ps. lxxxvi. 14); some MSS. even reading here "proud," instead of "strangers." With the received reading we must understand by the word "foreign oppressors"—though, doubtless, the inscription of the Psalm may be defended by taking the word in a derived sense of those Israelites who have degenerated, and so deserve the name "aliens."

⁽⁴⁾ **With them . . .**—Better, *is a supporter of my life.* So LXX. and Vulgate.

⁽⁵⁾ **Cut them off.**—Or, *put them to silence.*

In thy truth.—Or, *according to thy faithfulness.*

⁽⁶⁾ **I will freely sacrifice.**—Better, *I will offer a willing* (or *freewill*) *sacrifice.*

For it is good.—Comp. Ps. lii. 9.

⁽⁷⁾ This verse does not actually state what has happened, but, according to a well-known Hebrew idiom should be rendered, *When he shall have delivered, &c.*

Hath seen his desire.—Or, *hath gloated on*. The Hebrews use the words *seeing* and *looking* very expressively, making the simple verb do almost what the *eye* itself can do: show *hatred, love, triumph, defeat, wistfulness, disgust, &c.* (See Pss. xxxv. 21, lii. 6, lix. 10, xcii. 11; Song of Sol. vi. 13; &c.)

LV.

This is one of the most passionate odes of the whole collection—bursts of fiery invective alternating with the most plaintive and melancholy reflections: it has supplied to Christianity and the world at least two expressions of intense religious feeling, the one (verses 6, 7) breathing despair, the other (verse 22) the most restful hope.

Its date and authorship must be left in the region of mere conjecture. The traditional ascription to David cannot on any ground be maintained. That

A Prayer for the Psalmist PSALMS, LV. *in his Distress.*

⁽²⁾ Attend unto me, and hear me: I mourn in my complaint, and make a noise; ⁽³⁾ because of the voice of the enemy, because of the oppression of the wicked: for they cast iniquity upon me, and in wrath they hate me.

⁽⁴⁾ My heart is sore pained within me: and the terrors of death are fallen upon me. ⁽⁵⁾ Fearfulness and trembling are come upon me, and horror hath ¹ overwhelmed me.

⁽⁶⁾ And I said, Oh that I had wings like a dove! *for then* would I fly away, and be at rest. ⁽⁷⁾ Lo, *then* would I wander far off, *and* remain in the wilderness. Selah. ⁽⁸⁾ I would hasten my escape from the windy storm *and* tempest.

⁽⁹⁾ Destroy, O Lord, *and* divide their tongues: for I have seen violence and strife in the city. ⁽¹⁰⁾ Day and night they go about it upon the walls thereof: mischief also and sorrow *are* in the midst of it. ⁽¹¹⁾ Wickedness *is* in the midst thereof: deceit and guile depart not from her streets.

⁽¹²⁾ For *it was* not an enemy *that* reproached me; then I could have borne *it*: neither *was it* he that hated me *that* did magnify *himself* against me; then I would have hid myself from him: ⁽¹³⁾ but *it was* thou, ² a man mine

¹ Heb., *covered me.*

² Heb., *a man according to my rank.*

Ahitophel is the subject of verses 12—14, 20, 21, is contrary to all we know of the history of the rebellion of Absalom, for the poet describes himself as obliged to support the outrages of his quondam friend in the same city with him, when he would gladly fly if he could. Such a situation could not have been David's; for if he had had such full knowledge of the plots preparing against him he would, as he easily might, have crushed it in its early stages. And it must be noticed that the Psalm does not represent the author as the victim of a *revolution*, but of *oppression* (verses 3, 4). The frightful picture of disorder arising from disorganisation of the government, given in verses 9—11, is most inapplicable to the state of Jerusalem in David's reign.

In the absence of any definite historic indication, it is better to give up all attempts to recover the individual singled out for everlasting infamy in verses 12—14, 20, 21. The rest of the poem speaks of enemies in the plural, and the individual on whom the poet especially turns may only be the representative of a class—the class of perfidious Israelites who, forsaking national and religious traditions, sided with the foreign oppressors, and, as usual in such cases, carried their animosity to the party they had betrayed to the bitterest end. The rhythmical structure is not fairly marked, but the epithetic parallelism predominates.

Title.—See title, Ps. iv.

⁽²⁾ **I mourn.**—A verb found in this form only in three other passages, always with the idea of *restlessness*—*e.g.*, Gen. xxvii. 40, of the roving life of a Bedouin; Jer. ii. 31, of moral restlessness; Hos. xii. 1, of political instability. Here it may either indicate that bodily restlessness which often serves as an outlet of grief:

"Hard mechanic exercise,
Like dull narcotics, numbing pain,"

or the distracted state of the mind itself.

And make a noise.—Better, *and must roar*, the form of the verb expressing the compulsion which the sufferer feels to give vent to his feelings in groans and murmurs. (See Note on Ps. xlii. 5.)

⁽³⁾ **Oppressor.**—This meaning of a rare word is secured from Amos ii. 13.

Cast iniquity.—Better, *roll mischief.* The figure seems to be drawn from the practice of rolling stones down on an enemy from a height. In Ps. cxl. 10 the same verb is used of rolling burning coals on a foe.

Hate me.—Better, *persecute me.*

⁽⁴⁾ **Is sore pained.**—Better, *writhes with pain.*

Terrors of death—*i.e.*, terrors caused by death, a horror of death.

⁽⁶⁾ **Oh that I had.**—Literally, *who will give me?*—The bird that was in the psalmist's thought was doubtless the Rock Pigeon (*Columba livia*), which selects for its nesting the lofty cliffs and deep ravines far from the neighbourhood of man. (Comp. Song of Sol. ii. 14, Note.)

Be at rest.—So the LXX. and Vulg., and the reading is consecrated by long use; but the parallelism seems to require the more literal *dwell* or *abide*.

⁽⁷⁾ **Remain.**—Better, *lodge.*

⁽⁹⁾ **Destroy.**—Literally, *swallow up.* So the LXX., forcibly, "drown in the sea." The object *them* must be supplied.

This sudden change from plaintive sadness to violent invective is one of the marked features of this poem. Some think there has been a transposition of verses, but in lyric poetry these abrupt transitions of tone are not uncommon nor unpleasing.

Divide their tongues—*i.e.*, cause division in their councils. "Divide their voices" would be almost English, being exactly the opposite of Shakspere's "a joint and corporate voice."

For I have seen.—With the sense, *and see still.*

⁽¹⁰⁾ **They go.**—It is quite in keeping with the Hebrew style to suppose *mischief* and *strife* personified here as the ancient versions do, and not only occupying the *city* as inhabitants, but prowling about its walls. So in the next verse *corruption* (see Ps. v. 9, Note), *deceit*, and *guile* are personified. Comp. Virgil's

"ubique
Luctus, ubique Pavor, et plurima mortis imago."

⁽¹¹⁾ **Deceit.**—Rather, *oppression*, or *violence.*

Streets.—Rather, *squares*, the open space at the gate of an Oriental city where public business was conducted. It is a miserable picture of misgovernment; in the very seat of justice is nothing but oppression and guile.

⁽¹²⁾ **For.**—The ellipse must be supplied from verse 9, *I invoke destruction for*, &c.

Then I could . . .—Better, *then* (or *else*) *I might bear it.*

⁽¹³⁾ **But it was . . .**—Better, *But thou art a man of my own standing.* The word *erek* is used (Exod.

equal, my guide, and mine acquaintance. (14) ¹ We took sweet counsel together, *and* walked unto the house of God in company.

(15) Let death seize upon them, *and* let them go down quick into ² hell: for wickedness *is* in their dwellings, *and* among them.

(16) As for me, I will call upon God; and the LORD shall save me. (17) Evening, and morning, and at noon, will I pray, and cry aloud: and he shall hear my voice.

(18) He hath delivered my soul in peace from the battle *that was* against me: for there were many with me. (19) God shall hear, and afflict them, even he that abideth of old. Selah. ³ Because they have no changes, therefore they fear not God. (20) He hath put forth his hands against such

as be at peace with him: ⁴ he hath broken his covenant. (21) *The words* of his mouth were smoother than butter, but war *was* in his heart: his words were softer than oil, yet *were* they drawn swords.

(22) ᵃ Cast thy ⁵ burden upon the LORD, and he shall sustain thee: he shall never suffer the righteous to be moved. (23) But thou, O God, shalt bring them down into the pit of destruction: ⁶ bloody and deceitful men ⁷ shall not live out half their days; but I will trust in thee.

PSALM LVI.

To the chief Musician upon Jonath-elem-rechokim, ⁸ Michtam of David, when the ᵇ Philistines took him in Gath.

(1) Be merciful unto me, O God: for man would swallow me up; he fighting

---

1 Heb., *Who sweetened counsel.*
2 Or, *the grave.*
3 Or, *With whom also there be no changes, yet they fear not God.*
4 Heb., *he hath profaned.*
a Ps. 37. 5; Matt. 6. 25; Luke 12. 22; 1 Pet. 5. 7.
5 Or, *gift.*
6 Heb., *men of bloods and deceit.*
7 Heb., *shall not half their days.*
8 Or, *A golden Psalm of David.*
b 1 Sam. 21. 11.

---

xl. 23) of the row of loaves constituting the shewbread, and the cognate verb means "to arrange." Here it may denote *rank*, but more probably the expression is *man of my assessment*, and so of the same importance in society. (Comp. Lev. v. 15; 2 Kings xii. 4.) The LXX. and Vulgate have "of one soul with me." Symmachus, "of like disposition." This sense may be implied, though not expressed in the Hebrew.

Guide.—So the old versions: the Hebrew word does denote the head of a tribe or family (Gen. xxxvi. 15, &c., "duke"), but that meaning seems excluded here by the previous description. Render, *companion*.

(14) **And walked . . .**—*i.e.*, joined the great public processions to the temple. (Comp. Ps. xliv. 4.) The word rendered "company" occurs again (Ps. lxiv. 2. Authorised Version, "insurrection." Comp. the same root, Ps. ii. 1.) The intimacy of these former friends was public as well as private.

(15) **Let death.**—According to the written text we should render *desolations upon them*. Here we have another sudden outburst of overmastering feeling.

Quick—*i.e.*, alive, perhaps with reminiscence of the fate of Korah. (Comp. Prov. i. 12.)

Hell.—*Sheôl*. (See Note Ps. vi. 5.)

And among them.—The conjunction is unnecessary. Render, *in their dwellings, in their very midst.*

(18) **He hath delivered.**—The Targum rightly makes this the petition just mentioned, "Deliver," &c.

(18) **From the battle.**—The reading of the LXX. is preferable, "from these drawing near to me."

For there were many with me.—This is only intelligible if we insert the word *fighting*. "For there were many fighting with me," *i.e.*, "against me." But the text seems corrupt.

(19) **God shall hear.**—Render this verse,

God shall hear and afflict them,
He abideth of old;
One in whom are no changes,
And yet they fear not God.

(Comp. James i. 17, "with whom is no variableness, neither shadow of turning.") As the text stands, for *afflict* we should have *answer*; but the LXX. and Vulg. have the true reading. The Selah must be removed as plainly out of place. The plural pronoun is used poetically for the singular. The word *changes*, *chalipôth*, is used of troops relieving guard (Job xiv. 14), of servants taking their turn of work, of a change of clothing, &c. Here generally *variableness*. The rendering of the Authorised Version does not suit the context. The reason of the assertion that, in spite of his invariableness, the wicked do not fear God, appears in the next verse. Instead of respecting those in covenant with one who does not change, they have not feared to attack and oppress them.

(20) **He hath.**—As in verse 12, the individual specially prominent in the traitorous crew is here singled out, and his treachery exposed.

He hath broken . . .—Literally, *he perforated*. In a note in his work on the Creed, referring to Col. ii. 14, Bishop Pearson says one mode of cancelling a bond was to drive a nail through it.

(21) **The words of his mouth.**—The ancient versions and the grammatical anomalies point to a corruption of the text. Read, *Smoother than butter is his face*. The reading *face* for *mouth* is suggested by the LXX., though their version has wandered far from the text even thus amended.

Drawn swords.—The comparison of the tongue to a sword is frequent; that of the words themselves not so usual, but apt. We may compare Shakspere's

"I will speak daggers to her, but use none."—*Hamlet.*

(22) **Burden.**—A word peculiar to this passage, probably meaning "gift," hence "lot" or "condition." The Talmud, however, uses the word as meaning "burden" and the LXX. by rendering "care" have prepared the way for the Christian consolation in 1 Peter v. 7.

LVI.

If the title referring to an imprisonment of David at Gath is to be defended, it must be from 1 Sam. xxi. 10—15, on the supposition that the feigned madness did not succeed in its object, although the narrative gives reason to suppose that it did. The alternative of rejecting the inscription appears less objectionable. We have

The Psalmist's Confidence   PSALMS, LVI.   *in God's Protection.*

daily oppresseth me. ⁽²⁾ ¹ Mine enemies would daily swallow *me* up: for *they be* many that fight against me, O thou most High. ⁽³⁾ What time I am afraid, I will trust in thee. ⁽⁴⁾ In God I will praise his word, in God I have put my trust; I will not fear what flesh can do unto me. ⁽⁵⁾ Every day they wrest my words: all their thoughts *are* against me for evil. ⁽⁶⁾ They gather themselves together, they hide themselves, they mark my steps, when they wait for my soul. ⁽⁷⁾ Shall they escape by iniquity? in *thine* anger cast down the people, O God.

¹ Heb., *Mine observers.*

⁽⁸⁾ Thou tellest my wanderings: put thou my tears into thy bottle: *are they* not in thy book? ⁽⁹⁾ When I cry *unto thee,* then shall mine enemies turn back: this I know; for God *is* for me. ⁽¹⁰⁾ In God will I praise *his* word: in the LORD will I praise *his* word. ⁽¹¹⁾ In God have I put my trust: I will not be afraid what man can do unto me. ⁽¹²⁾ Thy vows *are* upon me, O God: I will render praises unto thee. ⁽¹³⁾ For thou hast delivered my soul from death: *wilt* not *thou deliver* my feet from falling, that I may walk before God in the light of the living?

---

no clue, however, either to the person of the author or his time (beyond the general picture of danger and hostility), and the language rather gives the idea of large combined forces than of individual foes, especially in the prayer of verse 7. Probably the speaker is here again only the mouthpiece of oppressed and suffering Israel. The poetical form is irregular, but is plainly marked by the refrain in verses 3 and 11.

Title.—See Pss. iv., xvi., Title.

Upon Jonath-elem-rechokim—*i.e., upon a silent dove of distant (places).* Of the conjectures on the meaning of this Title it is in accordance with the conclusions accepted in other cases to take the one which makes it the first words of some well-known song to the tune of which this psalm might be sung.

⁽¹⁾ **Man . . .**—Heb., *enôsh,* either as in Psalm ix. 19, "mortal man," or, contemptuously, "a rabble, a multitude."

⁽²⁾ **Swallow me up.**—The root idea of the Hebrew word so rendered is by no means clear. In many passages where it is used the meaning given here by the LXX., "trample on," will suit the context quite as well as, or even better than, the meaning, "pant after," given in the Lexicons. (See Job v. 5; Isa. xlii. 14; Eccles. i. 5; Amos ii. 7, viii. 4.) And this sense of bruising by trampling also suits the cognate verb, *shûph,* used only three times (Gen. iii. 15; Job ix. 17; Ps. cxxxix. 11). Symmachus also here has "bruise," or "grind." On the other hand in Ps. cxix. 131; Job vii. 2, &c., we want the idea of "haste" or "desire." Possibly the original meaning of "trample" may have passed through the sense of physical haste to that of passion. Or we may even get the sense of "greedily devouring" by the exactly similar process by which we come to talk of devouring the road with speed. The same verb is used in the next verse with an object.

Fighting.—Better, *devouring.* (Comp. Ps. xxxv. 1.)

O thou most High.—Heb., *marôm,* which is here not a vocative, but an adverbial accusative, "proudly," in pride.

⁽³⁾ **What time.**—Heb., *yôm,* apparently with same meaning as *beyôm* in verse 10, "in the day."

I am afraid . . .—No doubt the right reading is, "I cry."

⁽⁴⁾ **In God.**—This verse, which forms the refrain (verses 11 and 12 are wrongly separated), is as it stands hardly intelligible, and the text is rendered suspicious by the fact that the LXX. read "my words," instead of "his word," and by the omission of the suffix altogether in verse 11, where the first clause of the refrain is doubled. The obvious treatment of the verse is to take the construction as in Ps. xliv. 8, "I praise God with my word," *i.e.,* in spite of all my enemies I find words to praise God.

I will not.—Rather, *I fear not. What can flesh do?*

⁽⁵⁾ **Wrest.**—Properly, *afflict;* and so some, "injure my cause." But "torture my words" is intelligible.

⁽⁶⁾ **They hide themselves.**—Better, *they set spies.*

Mark my steps.—Literally, *watch my heels.* (See Pss. xlix. 5, lxxxix. 51.)

⁽⁷⁾ **Shall they . . .**—Literally, *upon iniquity escape to them;* the meaning of which is by no means clear. The ancient versions do not help us. If we adopt a slight change of reading, viz., *palles* for *pallet,* the meaning will be clear, *for iniquity thou wilt requite them.*

⁽⁸⁾ **Wanderings.**—Rather, in the singular, *wandering,* which, from the parallelism with "tears," must mean "mental restlessness," the "tossings to and fro of the mind." Symmachus, "my inmost things."

Put thou my tears into thy bottle.—There is a play of words in the original of "bottle," and "wandering." We must not, of course, think of the *lachrymatories,* as they are called, of glass, which have been found in Syria (see Thomson, *Land and Book,* page 103). If these were really in any way connected with "tears," they must have formed part of funeral customs. The LXX., "Thou hast put my tears before thee," and Symmachus and Jerome, "put my tears in thy sight," suggest a corruption of the text; but, in any case, the poet's feeling here is that of Constance in Shakspeare's *King John*—

"His grandam's wrongs, and not his mother's shames,
Draw these heaven-moving pearls from his poor eyes,
Which heaven shall take in nature of a fee;
Ay, with those crystal beads Heaven shall be brib'd
To do him justice and revenge on you."

Book.—As in Ps. cxxxix. 16. Some prefer "calculation."

⁽¹²⁾ **Thy vows**—*i.e.,* vows made *to Thee,* but the form is most unusual. For the thought comp. Ps. xxii. 25. l. 14.

I will render—*i.e.,* in fulfilment of the vows.

⁽¹³⁾ **Wilt thou not deliver?**—Better, *hast thou not delivered?*

From falling.—Literally, *from a thrust.*

PSALM LVII.

To the chief Musician, [1] Al-taschith, Michtam of David, [a] when he fled from Saul in the cave.

(1) Be merciful unto me, O God, be merciful unto me: for my soul trusteth in thee: yea, in the shadow of thy wings will I make my refuge, until *these* calamities be overpast. (2) I will cry unto God most high; unto God that performeth *all things* for me.

(3) He shall send from heaven, and save me [2] *from* the reproach of him that would swallow me up. Selah. God shall send forth his mercy and his truth.

(4) My soul *is* among lions: *and* I lie even among them that are set on fire, *even* the sons of men, whose teeth *are* spears and arrows, and their tongue a sharp sword.

(5) Be thou exalted, O God, above the heavens; *let* thy glory *be* above all the earth.

(6) [b] They have prepared a net for my steps; my soul is bowed down: they have digged a pit before me, into the midst whereof they are fallen *themselves*. Selah.

(7) [c] My heart is [3] fixed, O God, my heart is fixed: I will sing and give praise. (8) Awake up, my glory; awake, psaltery and harp: I *myself* will awake early. (9) I will praise thee, O Lord, among the people: I will sing unto thee among the nations. (10) [d] For thy mercy *is* great unto the heavens, and thy truth unto the clouds.

(11) Be thou exalted, O God, above the heavens: *let* thy glory *be* above all the earth.

PSALM LVIII.

To the chief Musician, [4] Al-taschith, Michtam of David.

(1) Do ye indeed speak righteousness, O congregation? do ye judge uprightly.

---

[1] Or, *Destroy not*.
[a] 1 Sam. 24. 1.
[2] Or, *he reproacheth him that would swallow me up*.
[b] Ps. 7. 16, & 9. 15.
[c] Ps. 108. 1, &c.
[3] Or, *prepared*.
[d] Ps. 36. 5, & 108. 4.
[4] Or, *Destroy not, A golden Psalm of David*.

LVII.

This psalm offers a good example of the way in which hymns were sometimes composed for the congregation. It is plainly the work of a man with a fine poetic sense. The imagery is striking, and the versification regular and pleasing. A refrain divides it into two equal pieces, each falling into two stanzas of six lines. Yet it is plainly a composition from older hymns. (Comp. especially Pss. xxxvi. 5, 6, lvi. 2, 3, vii. 15, ix. 15.) The second part has itself in turn been used by another compiler. (See Ps. cviii.)

Title.—See Pss. iv., xvi., title, and comp. titles of Pss. lviii., lix., and lxv.

Al-taschith—*i.e., destroy not*, the first words of some song to the tune of which this was to be sung.

(1) **Trusteth.**—Better, *has taken refuge*. The future of the same verb occurs in the next clause.

Shadow of thy wings.—See Note, Ps. xvii. 8.

Until these calamities.—*Danger of destruction* gives the feeling of the Hebrew better than "calamities."

(2) **Performeth all things for me.**—Literally, *completes for me*, which may be explained from the analogy of Ps. cxxxviii. 8. But as the LXX. and Vulg. have "my benefactor" (reading *gomēl* for *gomēr*) we may adopt that emendation.

(3) **He shall send . . .**—The *selah* in the middle of this verse is as much out of place as in Ps. lv. 19. The LXX. place it after verse 2. The marginal correction of the second clause is decidedly to be adopted, the word "reproach" is here being used in the sense of "rebuke." For the verb "send," used absolutely, comp. Ps. xviii. 16.

(4) **Them that are set on fire.**—Rather, *greedy ones* (literally, *lickers*) in apposition to *lions*. The verse expresses the insecurity of the poet, who, his dwelling being in the midst of foes, must go to sleep every night with the sense of danger all round him. (See LXX.)

How grandly the refrain in verse 8 rises from such a situation.

(6) **A net.**—For this image, so common in Hebrew hymns, see Ps. ix. 15, &c., and for that of the *pit*, Ps. vii. 15, &c.

My soul is bowed down.—The verb so rendered is everywhere else transitive. So LXX. and Vulg. here, "And have pressed down my soul." Despite the grammar, Ewald alters "my soul" into "their soul." But no conjecture of the kind restores the parallelism, which is here hopelessly lost. We expect,

> They have prepared a net for my steps;
> They are caught in it themselves.

(7) **Fixed.**—Better, *steadfast*. (See Ps. li. 10, Note.)

(8) **My glory.**—See Note, Ps. vii. 5.

I myself will awake early.—Perhaps, rather, *I will rouse the dawn*. Comp Ovid. Met. xi. 597, where the cock is said *evocare Auroram*; and Milton, still more nearly:

> "Oft listening how the hounds and horn,
> Cheerily *rouse the slumbering morn*."—*L'Allegro*.)

LVIII.

After a challenge to certain corrupt magistrates, the poet in this piece shows his detestation of the wicked, and anticipates their fate. There is nothing in the contents of the psalm to bear out the traditional title; but neither is there anything to help us to fix on any other author or date. The same complaints of the maladministration of justice often meet us in the prophetic books, and there is therefore no need to bring the composition of the psalm down to a very late age, especially when the vivacity of the language, and the originality of the imagery, indicate the freshness and power of an early and vigorous age of literary activity. The rhythm is elegant and sustained.

Title.—See title to last psalm.

(1) **Congregation.**—This rendering comes of a mistaken derivation of the Hebrew word *élem*, which

The Unjust are   PSALMS, LVIII.   *Cradled in Wickedness.*

O ye sons of men? (2) Yea, in heart ye work wickedness; ye weigh the violence of your hands in the earth. (3) The wicked are estranged from the womb: they go astray [1] as soon as they be born, speaking lies. (4) Their poison is [2] like the poison of a serpent: *they are* like the deaf [3] adder *that* stoppeth her ear; (5) which will not hearken to the voice of charmers, [4] charming never so wisely. (6) Break their teeth, O God, in their mouth: break out the great teeth of the young lions, O LORD. (7) Let them melt away as waters *which* run continually: *when* he bendeth *his* bow to

[1] Heb., *from the belly.*
[2] Heb., *according to the likeness.*
[3] Or, *asp.*
[4] Or, *be the charmer never so cunning.*

---

offers some difficulty. As pointed, it must mean *silence* (comp. Ps. lvi. title, the only other place it occurs); and some, regardless of sense, would render, "do ye truly in silence speak righteousness." Of the many conjectures on the passage, we may choose between reading *elim* (short for *elim = gods*), and here, as in Exod. xxi. 6, xxii. 8; Ps. lxxxii. 6, applied to the *judges*) and *ulam* (with the LXX., Syriac, and Arabic, in the sense of *but*. To speak righteousness is, of course, *to pronounce a just judgment.* If we prefer the former of these (with most modern scholars), it is best to take *sons of men* in the accusative rather than the vocative, *do ye judge with equity the sons of men.*

(2) **In heart . . . in the earth** (or, better, *in the land*).—These in the text are in antithesis. The mischief conceived in the heart is weighed out, instead of justice, by these unjust magistrates. The balance of justice is thus turned into a means of wrong-doing. But, perhaps, we should rather arrange as follows:

Nay! with your heart ye work wickedness in the land,
With your hands you weigh out violence.

(3) **The Wicked.**—The poet passes from his indignant challenge to the unjust judges to speak of the wicked generally. He finds that such maturity of vice points to very early depravity. Such hardened sinners must have been cradled in wickedness.

(4) **Their poison . . .**—Better, *they have a venom like*, &c. The term for serpent is the generic *nāchash*.

The most forcible images of determined wickedness, and of the destruction it entails, now follow. The first is supplied by the serpent, the more suggestive from the accumulated evil qualities of which that animal has from the first been considered the type. Here the figure is heightened, since the animal is supposed to have been first tamed, but suddenly darts forth its fangs, and shows itself not only untamed, but untameable.

Adder.—Heb., *pethen*, translated *asp* in Deut. xxxii. 33; Job xx. 14; Isa. xi. 8 (and here by the LXX.). In the *Bible Educator* iv. 103, the *pethen* is identified with the Egyptian *cobra*, the species upon which the serpent charmers practise their peculiar science.

Deaf.—So Jer. viii. 17 refers to various kinds of serpents that "will not be charmed." Here, however, it would seem as if the poet were thinking of some individual of a species, generally tractable, that obstinately resists the spells and incantations of the charmer.

The image of the *deaf adder* was a favourite with Shakspeare, who, no doubt, derived it from this psalm.

"Pleasure and revenge
Have ears more deaf than adders to the voice
Of any true decision."   *Troilus and Cressida*, iii. 2.

(Comp. 2 Hen. VI., iii. 2.)

(5) **Charmers.**—Heb., *melachashim*, a word undoubtedly formed from the sound made by the charmer in imitating the snake, in order to entice it from its hole. Lane, in *Modern Egyptians*, describing a snake charmer at his task, says: "He assumes an air of mystery, strikes the walls with a short palm stick, whistles, makes a *clacking noise* with his tongue." The art of serpent charming, and the magic connected with it, was of great antiquity in Egypt, and passed thence to surrounding countries.

Charming never so wisely.—Literally, *one tying knots wisely*, i.e., *a most skilful charmer.*

(6) **Break their teeth.**—The change is abrupt from the image of obstinacy deaf to all charms, to that of violence that must be tamed by force.

Great teeth.—Literally, *biters, grinders.*

(7, 8) After the types of obstinate and fierce malignity, come four striking images of the fatuity of the wicked man's projects, and his own imminent ruin. The first of these compares him to water, which, spilt on a sandy soil, sinks into it and melts away. (Comp. 2 Sam. xiv. 14.) Perhaps a phenomenon, often described by travellers, was in the poet's mind, the disappearance of a stream which, after accompanying the track for some time, suddenly sinks into the sand. The words *which run continually*, even if the Hebrew can bear this meaning, only weaken the figure. The verb is in the reflexive conjugation, and has "to" or "for themselves" added, and seems to be exactly equivalent to our, *they walk themselves off.* This certainly should be joined to the clause following. Here, too, we must suppose that the sign of comparison, *khemô*, was dropped out by the copyist in consequence of the *lāmô* just written, and afterwards being inserted in the margin, got misplaced. We must bring it back, and read:

They are utterly gone, as when
One shoots his arrows.

This figure thus becomes also clear and striking. The arrow once shot is irrevocably gone, probably lost, fit emblem of the fate of the wicked. For the ellipse in *bend* (literally, *tread*, see Ps. vii. 12), comp. Ps. lxiv. 3, where also the action properly belonging to the *bow* is transferred to the *arrow.*

The words, "Let them be as cut in pieces," must be carried on to the following verse, which contains two fresh images: *So they are cut off* (LXX., "are weak") *as shablûl melts*; (*as*) *the abortion of a woman passes away without seeing the sun.* The word *shablûl*, by its derivation (*bālal* = to pour out) may mean any *liquid* or *moist* substance. Hence some understand *a watercourse*, others (LXX. and Vulg.) *wax*. The first would weaken the passage by introducing a bald repetition of a previous image. The second is quite intelligible. But the Talmud says *shablûl* is a *slug* or *shelless snail*, and there may be a reference in the passage to the popular notion derived from the slimy track of the creature, that the slug dissolves as it moves, and eventually melts away. Dr. Tristram, however (*Nat. Hist. Bib.*, p. 295), finds scientific support for the image in the myriads of snail shells found in the Holy Land, still adhering, by the calcareous exudation round the orifice, to the surface of the rock, while the animal itself is utterly shrivelled and wasted. The last image

shoot his arrows, let them be as cut in pieces. (8) As a snail *which* melteth, let *every one of them* pass away: *like* the untimely birth of a woman, *that* they may not see the sun. (9) Before your pots can feel the thorns, he shall take them away as with a whirlwind, ¹both living, and in *his* wrath.

(10) The righteous shall rejoice when he seeth the vengeance: he shall wash his feet in the blood of the wicked. (11) So that a man shall say, Verily there is ²a reward for the righteous: verily he is a God that judgeth in the earth.

1 Heb., *as living, as wrath.*

2 Heb., *fruit of the, &c.*

3 Or, *Destroy not, A golden Psalm of David.*

a 1 Sam. 19. 11.

4 Heb., *set me on high.*

5 Heb., *to meet me.*

PSALM LIX.

To the chief Musician, ³ Al-taschith, Michtam of David; ᵃ when Saul sent, and they watched the house to kill him.

(1) Deliver me from mine enemies, O my God: ⁴defend me from them that rise up against me. (2) Deliver me from the workers of iniquity, and save me from bloody men.

(3) For, lo, they lie in wait for my soul: the mighty are gathered against me; not *for* my transgression, nor *for* my sin, O LORD. (4) They run and prepare themselves without *my* fault: awake ⁵ to help me, and behold.

(5) Thou therefore, O LORD God of

---

presents no difficulty either in language or form, except that the form of the noun *woman* is unusual.

That they may not.—That this refers to the abortion which *passed away without seeing the sun*, is certain. The grammatical difficulty of want of concord may be got over by taking *abortion* as a collective noun.

(9) **Before.**—The figure in this difficult verse is generally intelligible, though the text as it stands resists all attempts to translate it. As in the preceding images, it must convey the idea of abortive effort and sudden ruin, and, as has generally been understood, some experience of eastern travel undoubtedly supplied the figure which accident or a copyist's error has rendered so obscure. The Hebrew literally runs, *Before (shall) understand your pots a bramble as* (or so) *living as* (or so) *heat sweeps them off*. The ancient versions mostly render *thorns* instead of *pots*, and make the simile to lie in the destruction of the bush before growing to maturity. The English versions have undoubtedly caught the figure more correctly. But it is doubtful if the Hebrew word rendered *feel* could be used of inanimate objects, and even if a kettle might be said to *feel* the *fire*, we should hardly speak of its *feeling* the *fuel*. Some change in the text must be made. A very slight change in one letter gives excellent sense to the first clause. *Before thorns* (taking the word *ātad* which in Judg. ix. 14, 15 is translated *bramble* collectively) *make your pots ready*. But the second clause remains very difficult. Even if (with Grätz) we read *charôl* (Job xxx. 7; Prov. xxiv. 31, "nettles") for *charôn*, and render *thorny bush*, the words *as living* still offer a puzzle. And even if with the Prayer Book we might render *raw* instead of *living*, yet *burning heat* could not stand for *cooked meat*. Apparently the poet intends to compare the sudden overthrow of the wicked before their arms could succeed, to the disappearance of the fuel before it had time to heat the cooking-pot; and it is quite possible that he compressed all this into a condensed expression, which we must expand: "As, before the brambles make the pots ready, they are consumed, so He will whirl them (*i.e.*, the wicked) away alive, as the fierce heat consumes the thorns." Hebrew poetry is always more satisfactory with metaphor than with simile, and here, as often, seems to falter between the two, and so becomes obscure.

(10) **Wash his feet.**—So in Ps. lxviii. 23. "Wading deep in blood" is the picture suggested.

LIX.

The fascinating conjecture of Ewald which connects this psalm with the Scythian irruption into Judæa in the reign of Josiah is not easily surrendered. Some wild nomad tribe supporting itself by pillage, terrifying the inhabitants of a beleaguered city with an outlandish gesture and speech, seems indicated by the recurring simile of the "dogs" (verses 6, 14, 15). And, again, the mode in which the heathen are spoken of in verse 8, and the effect to be produced far and wide by the evidence of Jehovah's power (verse 13) seems to point to a foreign invasion. But, on the other hand, the prominence given to the *utterances* of this poet's foes (verses 7, 12), seems to indicate that his danger was rather from calumnious and false accusations than from hostile violence. Was he merely the mouthpiece of the righteous part of the community, whom a hostile or renegade party is trying to devour, body and soul, character and substance, as the gaunt scavenger dogs devour in an Eastern city? At first sight an apparent double refrain (verses 6, 14; 9, 17) promises a regular poetical form, but the strophes are unequal and the parallelism loose.

Title.—See titles, Pss. iv., lvii., xvi., and see *Introduction*.

(1) **Defend me.**—Literally, *set me on high, i.e.*, place me on some lofty and secure height.

(3) **For, lo, they lie in wait . . .**—Better, *for look, they have laid an ambush.*

Mighty.—Perhaps with the idea of insolence in their strength.

Not for my transgression . . .—Better, *Without transgression or fault of mine*, as in next verse.

(4) **They run and prepare.**—These words might both be taken in a military sense. For "run," see Ps. xviii. 29; Job xv. 26, xvi. 14.

Help me.—Literally, as in margin, *meet*. It is found in a hostile sense, and never in the sense of helping. A suggested emendation, "Awake to my *calling*, and behold," removes the difficulty.

(5) **Therefore . . .**—Better, *Yea, even Thou . . .* Not only is there an emphatic "thou," but the passion of prayer cannot exhaust itself without piling up all the customary names of the Divine Being.

God of Israel.—This is added so emphatically because of the "heathen," against whom aid is invoked.

hosts, the God of Israel, awake to visit all the heathen : be not merciful to any wicked transgressors. Selah.

(6) They return at evening : they make a noise like a dog, and go round about the city. (7) Behold, they belch out with their mouth : swords *are* in their lips : for *a* who, *say they*, doth hear?

(8) But thou, O Lord, shalt laugh at them ; thou shalt have all the heathen in derision.

(9) *Because of* his strength will I wait upon thee : for God *is* ¹my defence. (10) The God of my mercy shall prevent me : God shall let me see *my desire* upon ²mine enemies.

(11) Slay them not, lest my people forget : scatter them by thy power ; and bring them down, O Lord our shield.

(12) *For* the sin of their mouth *and* the words of their lips let them even be taken in their pride : and for cursing and lying *which* they speak. (13) Consume *them* in wrath, consume *them*, that they *may* not *be* : and let them know that God ruleth in Jacob unto the ends of the earth. Selah. (14) And at evening let them return ; *and* let them make a noise like a dog, and go round about the city. (15) Let them wander up and down ³for meat, ⁴and grudge if they be not satisfied.

(16) But I will sing of thy power ; yea, I will sing aloud of thy mercy in the morning : for thou hast been my defence and refuge in the day of my trouble. (17) Unto thee, O my strength, will I sing : for God *is* my defence, *and* the God of my mercy.

a Ps. 10. 11 & 73. 11, & 94. 7.

1 Heb., *my high place.*

2 Heb., *mine observers.*

3 Heb., *to eat.*

4 Or, *if they be not satisfied, then they will stay all night.*

All the heathen ... wicked transgressors.—These two terms are not synonymous, but contrasted. There were not only foreign, but domestic foes, viz., the party who, pretending to be loyal Israelites, were yet intriguing with the foreigners. The literal "coverers of wickedness" implies concealment and treachery.

(6) **A dog.**—This comparison to the gaunt half-starved wild dogs of an Eastern town has met us before (Ps. xxii. 16). The verbs should be rendered as futures here and in verse 15.

Make a noise.—Better, *howl.* (See Note Ps. lv. 7.)

An English traveller has described the noise made by the dogs of Constantinople: "The noise I heard then I shall never forget. The whole city rang with one vast riot. Down below me at Tophane ; over about Stamboul ; far away at Scutari ; the whole 60,000 dogs that are said to overrun Constantinople appeared engaged in the most active extermination of each other without a moment's cessation. The yelping, howling, barking, growling, and snarling were all merged into one uniform and continuous even sound" (Albert Smith, *A Month at Constantinople,* quoted from Spurgeon's *Treasury of David*).

(7) **Behold.**—Without question this word should, as Mr. Burgess suggests, be emended to "spears" (*chanith* instead of *hinneh*), to give—

"Spears they pour out with their mouths,
Swords with their lips."

(Comp. Ps. lvii. 5, and

"She speaks poniards."—*As You Like It.*

(8) **Laugh.**—Comp. Ps. ii. 4, Note. Probably the same contrast is intended in these clauses as in verse 5.

(9) **His strength.**—This gives no intelligible meaning, and verse 17 shows that the ancient versions (and some MSS.) are right in reading "my strength" (vocative). The first two words of the next verse must also be brought back to this : "My strength, on Thee let me wait. For God is my fortress, God of my grace (or mercy)," *i.e.,* my gracious or merciful God.

(10) **Prevent**—*i.e.,* come to meet. (See Ps. xxi. 3, Note.)

See my desire.—See Note, Ps. liv. 7. (Comp. Ps. xcii. 11.)

(11) **Slay them not, lest my people forget ...**—The Spartans refused to allow the destruction of a neighbouring city, which had often called forth their armies, saying, "Destroy not the whetstone of our young men." Timon, in the play, is made to say—

"Live loath'd and long
You smiling smooth detested parasites,"

that the ruin of Athens might be complete, if deferred. National feeling, too, has often insisted on extreme modes of punishment, partly from vindictive feeling, partly for deterrent purposes. Witness the sequel to the Indian mutiny. But where is the parallel to the feeling that seems uppermost in the Psalmist's mind, viz., a wish for protracted retribution on the nations for the moral benefit of Israel?

Scatter them.—Better, *make them wander :* a word applied to Cain and to the Israelite wanderings in the wilderness.

(12) **For the sin ...**—As the text stands, it runs : *Sin of their mouth, word of their lips, and they are taken in their pride, and cursing and lying they say ;* where some would supply a copula, "The sin of their mouth is the word of their lips," which seems tautological nonsense. But, perhaps, we should take the accusative as adverb of instrument : *By the sin of their mouth, by the word of their lips, let them even be taken in their pride.*

And for cursing and lying which they speak.—That is, let their own malignant slanders, their blasphemous lies, recoil on their own heads ; a frequent thought in the Psalms.

(13) **That they may not be.**—Better, *That they may be no more.* These words are to be taken closely together. The signal overthrow of the poet's foes is to be a proof to the ends of the world of the sovereign rule of the God of Jacob.

(15) **Let them wander.**—This verse is variously understood. The margin gives the rendering of most modern scholars; but what does it mean by "They will pass the night"? To say they will not go away unsatisfied seems poor. Ewald's conjecture, "They will satisfy themselves forsooth, and remain," *i.e.,* die, seems strained. The slightest change in the vowel-points gives the interpretation adopted by the LXX., Vulg., Jerome, Luther, &c. : "If not satisfied they will *growl*," which admirably suits the context.

PSALM LX.

To the chief Musician upon Shushan-eduth, [1] Michtam of David, to teach; *a* when he strove with Aram-naharaim and with Aram-zobah, when Joab returned, and smote of Edom in the valley of salt twelve thousand.

(1) O God, *b* thou hast cast us off, thou hast [2] scattered us, thou hast been displeased; O turn thyself to us again. (2) Thou hast made the earth to tremble; thou hast broken it: heal the breaches thereof; for it shaketh. (3) Thou hast shewed thy people hard things: thou hast made us to drink the wine of astonishment. (4) Thou hast given a banner to them that fear thee, that it may be displayed because of the truth. Selah.

(5) *c* That thy beloved may be delivered; save *with* thy right hand, and hear me.

(6) God hath spoken in his holiness; I will rejoice, I will divide Shechem, and mete out the valley of Succoth.

---

[1] Or, *A golden Psalm.*
a 2 Sam. 8. 3, 13; 1 Chron. 18. 3.
b Ps. 44. 9.
[2] Heb., *broken.*
c Ps. 108. 6, &c.

LX.

This psalm is composite; certainly two (verses 1—5, 6—12), probably three, independent pieces (verses 1—5, 6—8, 9—12) compose it.

Verses 5—12 appear again at Psalm cviii. The fact that the compiler of that psalm began his adaptation with verse 5, and not where the ancient original piece begins (verse 6), as well as the trifling variations, show that this psalm was in its present state when the later arrangement was made. Most scholars agree in thinking that the oracular verses, 6—8, are Davidic, or belong to a period as old as David's; and the inscription no doubt refers us to the series of events which this part of the poem reflects.

There is nothing to guide conjecture as to the time when the ancient oracular promise of victory was embodied in a poem, which evidently reflects a period of national depression, either from some crushing defeat by a foreign enemy, or from civil strife, in which the pious part of the community had suffered. The poetical form is necessarily irregular.

Title.—See title, Pss. iv., xvi.

Upon Shushan-eduth (comp. Ps. lxxx., and Ps. xlv., title)—*i.e., upon a lily of testimony;* which has been variously explained to mean, "Upon lily-shaped bells," "A harp with six strings," &c. After the analogy of other titles, it is better to take it as the beginning of some hymn, to the tune of which this psalm was to be sung.

To teach.—This recalls 2 Sam. i. 18: "To teach the sons of Judah the [song of the] bow." This psalm, like the elegy over Saul and Jonathan, was possibly used to kindle the martial ardour of youthful Israel.

When he strove with . . . .—The allusion to "Aram-naharaim"—*i.e.,* Aram of the two rivers—and "Aram-zobah" are to be explained by the events narrated in 2 Sam. viii. and x. The English rendering of 2 Sam. viii. 13 reads as if Syrians, and not Edomites, were then slain in the valley of salt; but the Hebrew seems rather to be, "And David gat him a name in the valley of salt [eighteen thousand], when he returned from smiting the Syrians." This still leaves a discrepancy in the numbers; but it may be noticed that the mode of the introduction of the number in the history looks suspiciously like a gloss which may have been made from memory and afterwards crept into the text.

(1) **Hast scattered us.**—Literally, *hast broken us.* A word used of a wall or fence, Ps. lxxx. 12, but in 2 Sam. v. 20 applied to the rout of an army, an event which gave its name to the locality, "plain of breaches." So in English:

"And seeing me, with a great voice he cried,
They are broken, they are broken."—
TENNYSON: *Elaine.*

On the other hand, the two succeeding verses seem to refer to a *political* convulsion rather than a *military* defeat, and it has been conjectured that the *breach* between the two kingdoms is here indicated. (See the use of *perez*=*breach,* in Judg. xxi. 15.)

(2) **Earth.**—Rather, *land;* since, though the image is drawn from an earthquake, in which the solid ground trembles and buildings totter and fall (comp. Isa. xxx. 13), the convulsion described is *political,* not *physical.*

(3) **Hard things**—*i.e.,* a hard fate.

Wine of astonishment.—Literally, either *wine of reeling*—*i.e.,* an intoxicating draught—or *wine as reeling*—*i.e.,* bewilderment like wine, or wine, which is not wine, but bewilderment, according as we take the construction.

In any case the figure is the same which meets us often in Hebrew poetry (comp. Ps. lxxv. 8, 9; Isa. li. 17, 22; Jer. xxv. 15, &c.) expressing that infatuation which the heathen proverb so well describes:—

"Quem Deus vult perdere prius dementat."

(4) **Thou hast given.**—Amid the uncertainty attaching to this verse, one thing is certain, that the Authorised Version rendering of its second clause must be abandoned. Instead of *koshet* (truth), we must read with the LXX. and Symmachus *kesheth* (a bow). It is more than doubtful if the preposition rendered *because of* can have that meaning. Nor can the rendering of the verb, *that it may be displayed,* be defended. Render, *Thou hast given Thy fearers a banner, that they may rally to it from before the bow,* and comp. Isa. xiii. 2.

(5) From this verse onward the psalm appears again, with some variations noticed there, in Ps. cviii. 6—13.

(6, 7, 8) These three verses, forming the centre of the poem, are, plainly by their style, of different age and authorship from the beginning. Possibly, indeed, they formed an original poem by themselves, an ancient oracular saying descriptive of the relations of Israel to the tribes bordering on her territory, and were then employed by the compilers of this psalm and Ps. cviii., to rouse the drooping spirits of the race in some less fortunate time. (See *Introduction.*) The speaker is God Himself, who, according to a familiar prophetic figure, appears in the character of a warrior, the captain of Israel, proclaiming the triumphs won through His might by their arms. (Comp. Isa. lxiii. 1—6.) Here, however, the picture is rather playful than terrible—rather ironic than majestic. The conqueror is return-

The Leader of   PSALMS, LXI.   *the Hosts of Israel.*

(7) Gilead *is* mine, and Manasseh *is* mine; Ephraim also *is* the strength of mine head; Judah *is* my lawgiver; (8) Moab *is* my washpot; over Edom will I cast out my shoe: Philistia, ¹ triumph thou because of me.
(9) Who will bring me *into* the ² strong city? who will lead me into Edom?
(10) *Wilt* not thou, O God, *which* ᵃ hadst cast us off? and *thou*, O God, *which* didst not go out with our armies?
(11) Give us help from trouble: for vain *is* the ³ help of man.
(12) Through God we shall do valiantly: for he *it is that* shall tread down our enemies.

¹ Or, *triumph thou over me:* (by an irony.)
² Heb., *city of strength.*
ᵃ Ps. 44. 9, & 108. 11.
³ Heb., *salvation.*

PSALM LXI.

To the chief Musician upon Neginah, A Psalm of David.

(1) Hear my cry, O God; attend unto my prayer. (2) From the end of the

---

ing, as in the passage of Isaiah referred to above, from the battle, but he is not painted "glorious in his apparel, travelling in the greatness of his strength." The fury of the fight, the carnage, the bloodstained garments are all implied, not described. Instead of answering a challenge, as in Isaiah, by a description of the fight, here the champion simply proclaims the result of his victory as he proceeds to disarm and prepare for the bath—figures expressing the utmost contempt for the foe so easily subdued.

(6) **In his holiness . . .**—The LXX. and Vulg. have "in his sanctuary" which suits the utterance of an oracle.

I will rejoice . . .—Rather, *I will raise a shout of triumph.*

I will divide Shechem . . .—Rather, *I may divide,* &c., implying unquestioned right of ownership. Shechem and Succoth appear to be named as a rude indication of the whole breadth of the country, from west to east. The fact that Dr. Robinson and Vandervelde have identified one Succoth on the right bank of Jordan, does not at all weaken the evidence for the existence of another on the east of that river. See Gen. xxxiii. 17; Judg. viii. 5 *seq.*; Josh. xiii. 17 (where *ēmek* is used for valley, as here).

(7) Gilead and Manasseh on the east of Jordan, and Ephraim and Judah on the west, are employed to denote the whole dominion.

Strength of mine head . . .—*i.e.*, the helmet, or possibly with reminiscence of the patriarchal blessing on Joseph, Deut. xxxiii. 17.

Lawgiver.—In Hebrew a participle of verb meaning to *cut* or *engrave*, and is applied as here to the lawmaker (comp. Deut. xxxiii. 21), or to the *staff or sceptre* which was the emblem of law, Gen. xlix. 10, Num. xxi. 18. The LXX. and Vulg. have "my king."

(8) **Moab is my washpot**—*i.e.*, probably the *footbath*, a figure expressing great contempt, which receives illustration from the story told of Amasis (Herod. ii. 172) and the golden footpan, which he had broken to pieces and made into an image of one of the gods—from base use made divine—as allegorical of his own transformation from a private person to a king. Others explain, from analogy of Arabic proverbs, that the conqueror would as it were wash his face white, *i.e.*, acquire renown in Moab.

Possibly the comparison of Moab to a bath was suggested by its proximity to the Dead Sea, which might be said to be at the foot of Israel.

Over Edom . . .—The most natural explanation of this figure is that Edom is disgraced to the character of the slave to whom the conqueror tosses his sandals (*na'al* is collective), that they may be cleaned. (Comp. Matt. iii. 11). The symbolic action of Ruth iv. 7 had a different meaning, the transfer of a right of ownership, and so cannot be employed in illustration.

Of the "shoe," as a figure of what is vilest and most common, Dr. J. G. Wetzstein quotes many Arabic proverbs. A covering for the feet would naturally draw to it such associations. (Comp. the use of footstool repeatedly in the Psalms, and Shakespeare's use of foot,

"What my foot my tutor!"—*Tempest.*)

But the custom which Israel brought from Egypt (Exod. iii. 3), of dropping the sandals outside the door of a temple, and even of an ordinary house, must have served still more to fasten on that article of dress, ideas of vileness and profanation.

Philistia, triumph thou because of me . . .—This cannot be the meaning intended by the clause, since it is quite out of keeping with the context, and in Ps. cviii. we have the very opposite, "over Philistia will I triumph." We must therefore change this reading so as to get, *over Philistia is my triumph,* or render the text as it stands, from analogy with Isa. xv. 4: *Upon* (*i.e., because of*) *me, Philistia, raise a mournful wail.*

The LXX. and Vulg. indicate this meaning while translating the proper name, "the foreigners have been subdued to me."

(9) **Who will . . .**—*i.e.*, how can this ancient Divine oracle be fulfilled now in present circumstances? This is the poet's question. He may be a king himself eager for triumph, or more probably Israel personified. (See the plural in verses 10, 11, 12.) Edom is the particular foe in view, and as the difficulties of the undertaking present themselves, misgivings arise and the assurance gained from the triumphs of olden time turns into prayer, half plaintive, half confident, that the Divine favour and power may be once more on the side of the chosen people.

The strong city.—As in the Hebrew the article is wanting, any strongly fortified city might be intended, were it not for the parallelism. Here it must stand for *Selah* or *Petra*, the capital of Edom. For its impregnable position (see Note Obad. 3). The question, "Who will lead me into Petra?" is explained by the fact that there are only two possible approaches to the city, each a long narrow tortuous defile, and that the place itself is so buried in its ravines that it cannot be seen from any spot in its neighbourhood far or near.

LXI.

Here we have the prayer of an Israelite living at a distance from his country, and declaring in the simplest possible manner that in spite of this banishment he does not feel remote from God nor deprived of the Divine protection. It is a forecast of the great principle of spiritual worship which Jesus Christ was to proclaim.

The Psalmist declares God   PSALMS, LXII.   *his Strength and Protector.*

earth will I cry unto thee, when my heart is overwhelmed: lead me to the rock *that* is higher than I.

(3) For thou hast been a shelter for me, *and* a strong tower from the enemy. (4) I will abide in thy tabernacle for ever: I will ¹trust in the covert of thy wings. Selah. (5) For thou, O God, hast heard my vows: thou hast given *me* the heritage of those that fear thy name.

(6) ² Thou wilt prolong the king's life: and his years ³ as many generations. (7) He shall abide before God for ever: O prepare mercy and truth, *which* may preserve him. (8) So will I sing praise unto thy name for ever, that I may daily perform my vows.

PSALM LXII.
To the chief Musician, to Jeduthun, A Psalm of David.

(1) ⁴ Truly my soul ⁵ waiteth upon God: from him *cometh* my salvation. (2) He only *is* my rock and my salvation; he *is* my ⁶defence; I shall not be greatly moved.

(3) How long will ye imagine mischief against a man? ye shall be slain all of you: as a bowing wall *shall ye be, and*

---

1 Or, *make my refuge.*

2 Heb., *Thou shalt add days to the days of the king.*

3 Heb., *as generation and generation.*

4 Or *Only.*

5 Heb., *is silent.*

6 Heb., *high place.*

Tradition assigns this exquisite little song, with its fine spiritual discernment, to David. The repetition of the imagery of the high tower is in the Davidic style, but many critics think it breathes rather of the time of the captivity. Three equal stanzas of six short lines and elegant rhythm compose the poem.

Title.—See title Ps. iv.

Neginah, properly *neginath*, probably an error for *neginôth*, as in Ps. iv., as the LXX. and Vulg. ("in hymns") evidently read it. Or it may be an anomalous form of *neginah*, which, in Job xxx. 9, means a satirical song.

(2) **From the end of the earth . . .**—A hyperbolic expression for a great distance. Isaiah (v. 26) uses the expression of Assyria, and it would be natural in an exile's mouth, but must not be pressed to maintain any theory of the psalm's date.

When my heart is overwhelmed.—Literally, *in the covering of my heart*, the verb being used (Ps. lxv. 13) of the valleys covered with corn, and metaphorically, as here, of "the garment of heaviness," which wraps a sad heart (Ps. cii. title; Isa. lvii. 16). (Comp. Tennyson's "muffled round with woe.")

Lead me to the rock . . .—Literally, *upon the rock lead me*, which is probably a *constructio prægnans* for *lead me to the rock too high for me to climb by myself, and place me there*. The elevated rock is a symbol of security, which cannot be obtained without the Divine help. Others take the expression as figurative for a difficulty which it needs God's help to surmount.

(3) **A strong tower.**—Comp. Prov. xviii. 10.

(4) **I will abide.**—Rather, *Let me be a guest in*, etc. (Comp. Pss. xv. 1; xxvii. 4.)

Thy tabernacle. . .—It is difficult to decide whether this indicates the Mosaic tabernacle, and so may be used as an index of the date of the poem; or whether the tent is a general figure for the protection of God, wherever it may be found. It certainly recalls Ps. xxiii. 6.

For ever.—Literally, for *ages* or *æons*. For the same plural, see Ps. cxlv. 13.

I will trust . . .—Rather, *let me find refuge under the shelter of thy wings*. (For the image, see Note Ps. xvii. 8.)

(5) **Heritage.**—As the Authorised Version runs, the *heritage* is length of days, one promised generally to those who fear Jehovah (Prov. x. 27, xix. 23), and particularly to Israel (Deut. vi. 2) and its kings (Deut. xvii. 19, 20, which passage may have been in the psalmist's mind). But the LXX. and Vulg. read, "to them that fear thy name," meaning, of course, by the heritage, Canaan.

(6) See margin, and render as a prayer.

(7) **He shall abide.**—Better, *may he sit enthroned*.

Prepare.—Rather, *appoint*. But the LXX. had a different reading, and an ingenious emendation has been suggested from a comparison with Ps. xl. 11, viz., "let mercy and truth continually preserve him."

LXII.

The many close resemblances between this psalm and Ps. xxxix. lead to the inference that it belongs to the same time, and is even from the same pen. The author and his age are, however, alike unknown; and there is no indication to guide to their discovery. The psalm records an experience common in every age, of the vanity of those objects on which man is apt to set his affections; but an experience particularly likely to find expression in days such as so many of the psalms reflect, when there was open conflict between the national sentiment and the ruling classes. The poet's is a voice raised in behalf of pious Israel suffering under tyranny. A refrain (verses 1, 2, 5—7) marks the rhythmical structure, but the form is irregular.

Title.—See titles, Pss. iv., xxxix.

(1) **Waiteth upon God.**—Literally, *unto God (is) silence my soul*. (Comp. Pss. xxii. 2, xxxix. 2, lxv. 1.) The LXX. and Vulg., "shall be in subjection to," which no doubt gives one side of the feeling; but another may be illustrated by Wordsworth's—

"The holy time is *quiet* as a nun
Breathless with adoration."

(2) **Defence.**—Properly, *high tower*, as so often. The metaphor is important here from the contrast with the *tottering wall* of next verse.

Shall not be greatly moved . . .—*i.e.* (as in Ps. xxxvii. 24), shall not be made to totter or fall.

(3) **Imagine mischief.**—This is the Rabbinical rendering of a word that occurs only here. The LXX. have "fall upon"; Vulg., "rush upon," a meaning supported by an Arabic root meaning to *storm* or *assault*, and is so far preferable to Aquila's and Jerome's "plot against," and Symmachus' "labour in vain," or Syriac, "act foolishly."

Ye shall be slain.—The reading varies, the Tiberian school reading the verb *passive*, the Babylonian,

as a tottering fence. ⁽⁴⁾ They only consult to cast *him* down from his excellency: they delight in lies: they bless with their mouth, but they curse ¹inwardly. Selah.

⁽⁵⁾ My soul, wait thou only upon God; for my expectation *is* from him. ⁽⁶⁾ He only *is* my rock and my salvation: *he is* my defence; I shall not be moved. ⁽⁷⁾ In God *is* my salvation and my glory: the rock of my strength, *and* my refuge, *is* in God.

⁽⁸⁾ Trust in him at all times; *ye* people, pour out your heart before him: God *is* a refuge for us. Selah.

⁽⁹⁾ Surely men of low degree *are* vanity, *and* men of high degree *are* a lie: to be laid in the balance, they *are* ²altogether *lighter* than vanity. ⁽¹⁰⁾ Trust not in oppression, and become not vain in robbery: if riches increase, set not your heart *upon them*.

⁽¹¹⁾ God hath spoken once; twice have I heard this; that ³power *belongeth* unto God.

⁽¹²⁾ Also unto thee, O Lord, *belongeth* mercy: for ᵃ thou renderest to every man according to his work.

PSALM LXIII.

A Psalm of David, when he was in the wilderness of Judah.

⁽¹⁾ O God, thou *art* my God; early will I seek thee: my soul thirsteth for thee, my flesh longeth for thee in a dry and ⁴thirsty land, ⁵where no water is; ⁽²⁾ to see thy power and thy glory, so *as* I have seen thee in the sanctuary.

¹ Heb., *in their inward parts.*
² Or, *alike.*
³ Or, *strength.*
ᵃ Job 34. 11; Pro. 24. 12; Jer. 32. 19; Ezek. 7. 27; Matt. 16. 27; Rom. 2. 6; 2 Cor. 5. 10; Eph. 6. 8; Col. 3. 25; 1 Pet. 1. 17; Rev. 22. 12.
⁴ Heb., *weary.*
⁵ Heb., *without water.*

---

active. The latter is supported by the ancient versions. The primary meaning is given *to break*, and we get:

How long will ye assault a man?
(How long) will ye try to break him down,
As if he were a bowing wall, a tottering fence.

The metaphor of the falling wall is common in Eastern proverbs. "The wall is bowing," is said of a man at the point of death. "By the oppression of the headman, the people of that village are *a ruined wall*."

⁽⁴⁾ **Their mouth.**—Literally, *his mouth. They bless each with his mouth,* &c.

Excellency.—Rather, *height*, carrying on the metaphor of preceding verse.

⁽⁵⁾ As in verse 1. *Truly to God, be silence my soul.* The state of resignation is one which can only be preserved by prayer. We may *say, I will*, but can only *feel* it through prayer.

⁽⁷⁾ **In God.**—Literally, *upon God,* as in Ps. vii. 10.

⁽⁹⁾ **Are vanity.**—Or, *mere breath.*

To be laid in the balance.—Literally, *in the balances to go up,* which may mean *in the scales they must go up, i.e.,* kick the beam. But a slight change in one letter gives the more probable, *when weighed in the scales.*

⁽¹⁰⁾ **If riches increase.**—Even if by honest means you grow rich, distrust your wealth.

⁽¹¹⁾ **Once; twice.**—The usual Hebrew mode of emphasising a numerical statement, and one growing naturally out of the structure of the verse, which loves a climax. (Comp. Prov. vi. 16—19.) The union of power and love is proved to the poet by the fairness and justice mentioned in the last clause.

LXIII.

The figure of the first verse misunderstood (see Note) led to the inscription referring this psalm to the wandering period of David's life, a reference entirely out of keeping with the contents of the poem, even if it were Davidic. The conjecture is far more probable which makes it the sigh of an exile for restoration to the sacred scenes and institutions of his country, now cherished in memory; and so truly does it express the sentiments which would be common to all the pious community of Israel, that we need not vex ourselves with an enquiry, for which the data are so insufficient, into the precise individual or even the precise time to which it first refers. The last verse seems to carry us back to the troubled times immediately before the destruction of Jerusalem, when the existence of monarchy was trembling in the balance, and when some of those already in exile might be supposed to be watching its fortunes with feelings in which hope contended with misgiving, and faith with fear. The poetical form is irregular.

⁽¹⁾ **Early will I seek thee.**—LXX. and Vulgate, "to thee I wake early," *i.e.*, my *waking* thoughts are toward thee, and this was certainly in the Hebrew, since the verb here used has for its cognate noun the *dawn*. The *expectancy* which even in inanimate nature seems to await the first streak of morning is itself enough to show the connection of thought. (Comp. the use of the same verb in Song of Sol. vii. 12; and comp. Luke xxi. 28, *New Testament Commentary.*)

Soul . . . flesh.—Or, as we say, *body and soul.* (Comp. Ps. lxxxiv. 2, "my heart and my flesh.")

Longeth.—Heb., *khâmah*, a word only occurring here, but explained as cognate with an Arabic root meaning *to be black* as with *hunger* and *faintness*.

In.—Rather, *as*. (Comp. Ps. cxliii. 6.) This is the rendering of one of the Greek versions quoted by Origen, and Symmachus has "*as in,*" &c.

Thirsty.—See margin. *Fainting* is perhaps more exactly the meaning. (See Gen. xxv. 29, 30, where it describes Esau's condition when returning from his hunt.) Here the land is imagined to be *faint* for want of water. The LXX. and Vulgate have "pathless." The parched land thirsting for rain was a natural image, especially to an Oriental, for a devout religious soul eager for communion with heaven.

⁽²⁾ **To see thy power . . .**—The transposition of the clauses in the Authorised Version weakens the sense. Render, *So (i.e., in this state of religious fervour) in the sanctuary have I had vision of thee in seeing thy might and glory.* The psalmist means, that while he saw with his eyes the outward signs of Divine glory, he had a spiritual vision (the Hebrew word is that generally used of prophetic vision) of God.

(3) Because thy lovingkindness *is* better than life, my lips shall praise thee. (4) Thus will I bless thee while I live: I will lift up my hands in thy name. (5) My soul shall be satisfied as *with* ¹marrow and fatness; and my mouth shall praise *thee* with joyful lips: (6) when I remember thee upon my bed, *and* meditate on thee in the *night* watches. (7) Because thou hast been my help, therefore in the shadow of thy wings will I rejoice. (8) My soul followeth hard after thee: thy right hand upholdeth me. (9) But those *that* seek my soul, to destroy *it*, shall go into the lower parts of the earth. (10) ²They shall fall by the sword: they shall be a portion for foxes. (11) But the king shall rejoice in God; every one that sweareth by him shall glory: but the mouth of them that speak lies shall be stopped.

1 Heb., *fatness.*
2 Heb., *They shall make him run out like water by the hands of the sword.*

PSALM LXIV.
To the chief Musician, A Psalm of David.

(1) Hear my voice, O God, in my prayer: preserve my life from fear of the enemy. (2) Hide me from the secret counsel of the wicked; from the insurrection of the workers of iniquity: (3) ᵃ who whet their tongue like a sword, *and* bend *their bows to shoot* their arrows, *even* bitter words: (4) that they may shoot in secret at the perfect: suddenly do they shoot at him, and fear not. (5) They encourage themselves

a Ps. 11. 2.

---

(3) **Because.**—Such a sense of the blessedness of Divine favour—here in its peculiar sense of covenant favour—that it is better than life itself, calls for gratitude displayed all through life. "Love is the ever-springing fountain" from which all goodness proceeds, and a sense of it is even more than the happy sense of being alive. The following lines convey in a modern dress the feeling of this part of the psalm:—

"So gazing up in my youth at love,
As seen through power, ever above
All modes which make it manifest,
My soul brought all to a single test—
That He, the Eternal, First and Last,
Who in His power had so surpassed
All man conceives of what is might,
Whose wisdom too showed infinite—
Would prove as infinitely good."
R. BROWNING: *Christmas Eve.*

Thus—*i.e.*, in the spirit in which he now speaks. For the attitude of the uplifted hands, see Note, Ps. xxviii. 2.

(5) **Satisfied.**—This image of a banquet, which repeats itself so frequently in Scripture, need not be connected with the sacrificial feasts.

(6) **Remember.**—Better, *remembered.*

Bed.—Literally, *beds.*

Night watches.—According to the Jewish reckoning, the night was divided into three watches: the "beginning," or head (*rôsh*); the "middle" (*tikhôn*, Judg. vii. 19); and the "morning" (*boker*, Exod. xiv. 24).

(7) **Because . . .**—Better, *For thou hast been my helper; and under the shadow*, &c. (For the image see Pss. xvii. 8; xxxvi. 7; lvii. 1; lxi. 4.)

(8) **My soul . . .**—Literally, *my soul cleaved after thee*, combining two ideas. (Comp. Jer. xlii. 16.) The English phrase, "hung upon thee" (comp. Prayer-Book version), exactly expresses it.

For "depths," or "abysses of the earth," comp. Ps. cxxxix. 15; Eph. iv. 9. It means the under world of the dead.

(10) **Shall fall.**—See margin. But more literally, *they shall pour him on to the hands of the sword*, where the suffix *him* is collective of the enemy, and the meaning is, "they shall be given over to the power of the sword." (Comp. Jer. xviii. 21; Ezek. xxxv. 5.)

Foxes . . .—Rather, *jackals.* Heb., *shualim.* (See Note, Song of Sol. ii. 15.)

(12) **Sweareth by him.**—This is explained as meaning, "swear allegiance to him as the king," on the analogy of Zeph. i. 5. And this suits the context. On the other hand, the natural way to understand the phrase, "swear by" or "in him," is to refer it to the only oath allowed to the Israelite, "by the name of Jehovah" (Deut. vi. 13; Isa. lxv. 16; comp. Amos viii. 14), in which case we must explain by Deut. x. 20, 21, "Swear by his (Jehovah's) name; He is thy praise." Those who are loyal to Jehovah, who appeal to Him in all troubles, will find this promise true, "They shall glory," while the unfaithful and false, not daring to make the solemn appeal, will have their mouth stopped. (Comp. Rom. iii. 19.)

LXIV.

The situation indicated in this psalm is one that frequently occurs in Israel's hymn-book. A prey to calumny, the poet for himself, or, more probably, for the community, implores the protection of God, and then suddenly takes up the prophetic strain—persuaded, from the known order of Providence, that retribution must come—and foretells the sudden dissipation of the deeply-laid schemes of those who vex and oppress God's chosen people.

The last couplet is probably a liturgical addition, and not part of the original poem, which without it divides into three regular stanzas of seven lines.

Title.—See title, Ps. iv.

(1) **My prayer.**—Rather, *my cry, complaint*, as in Ps. lv. 2.

(2) **Secret counsel . . . insurrection.**—Better, *secret league* (*sôd*) . . . *noisy gathering* (*rigshah*). For *sôd* see Ps. xxv. 14, and for *rigshah* see Note to Ps. ii. 2.

(3) For the figure in this and the following verse, see Pss. x. 7, xi. 2, lii. 2, lvii. 4, lix. 7.

"'Tis slander,
Whose edge is sharper than the sword."
SHAKSPEARE.

For the ellipse in "they bend (literally, *tread*) their arrows," see Ps. lviii. 7.

(4) **And fear not.**—These are utterly unscrupulous, fearing neither God nor man.

(5) **They encourage themselves.**—Literally, *they strengthen for themselves an evil thing* (or

God's Sudden Vengeance.   PSALMS, LXV.   God Hears the Prayers of All.

in an evil ¹ matter: they commune ² of laying snares privily; they say, Who shall see them? ⁽⁶⁾ They search out iniquities; ³ they accomplish ⁴ a diligent search: both the inward *thought* of every one *of them*, and the heart, *is* deep. ⁽⁷⁾ But God shall shoot at them *with* an arrow; suddenly ⁵ shall they be wounded. ⁽⁸⁾ So they shall make their own tongue to fall upon themselves: all that see them shall flee away. ⁽⁹⁾ And all men shall fear, and shall declare the work of God; for they shall wisely consider of his doing.

⁽¹⁰⁾ The righteous shall be glad in the LORD, and shall trust in him; and all the upright in heart shall glory.

PSALM LXV.

To the chief Musician, A Psalm *and* Song of David.

⁽¹⁾ Praise ⁶ waiteth for thee, O God, in Sion: and unto thee shall the vow be performed.
⁽²⁾ O thou that hearest prayer, unto thee shall all flesh come.
⁽³⁾ ⁷ Iniquities prevail against me: *as*

Marginal notes:
1 Or, *speech*.
2 Heb., *to hide snares*.
3 Or, *we are consumed by that which they have throughly searched*.
4 Heb., *a search searched*.
5 Heb., *their wound shall be*.
6 Heb., *is silent*.
7 Heb., *Words, or, Matters of iniquities*.

"word," margin, LXX., and Vulg.,) which evidently means that they take their measures carefully, and are prepared to carry them out resolutely.

They commune . . .—Better, *they calculate how they may lay snares privily*. The conspirators carefully and in secret go over every detail of their plot.

Who shall see them?—Literally, *who shall look to them?* which seems at first glance to mean, "who will see the snares?" but this is weak. It may be equivalent to, "who is likely to see us?" the question being put indirectly. But in 1 Sam. xvi. 7, the expression, "looketh on," implies "regard for," which may possibly be the meaning here, "who careth for them?"

⁽⁶⁾ **They search out iniquities** — *i.e.*, they plan wicked schemes.

They accomplish a diligent search.—See margin, which indicates the difficulty in this clause. The versions and some MSS. also suggest a corruption of the tent. Read "They have completed their subtle measures" (literally, *the planned plan*).

⁽⁷, ⁸⁾ The meaning of these verses is clear. In the moment of their imagined success, their deeply-laid schemes just on the point of ripening, a sudden Divine retribution overtakes the wicked, and all their calumnies, invented with such cunning, fall back on their own heads. But the construction is most perplexing. The text presents a tangled maze of abrupt clauses, which, arranged according to the accents, run: *And God shoots an arrow, sudden are their wounds, and they make it* (or *him*) *fall on themselves their tongue*. The last clause seems to pronounce the law which obtains in Divine judgment. While God orders the retribution it is yet the recoil of their own evil on the guilty. In these cases,

"We still have judgment here, that we but teach
Bloody instructions, which, being taught, return
To plague the inventor; this evenhanded justice
Commends the ingredients of our poisoned chalice
To our own lips."   SHAKSPEARE: *Macbeth*.

Flee away.—The verb (*nādad*) properly means *to flutter the wings like a bird* (Isa. x. 14).

⁽⁹⁾ **For they shall wisely consider.**—Rather, *And they understand his work*.

⁽¹⁰⁾ **Shall glory.**—Or, perhaps, *shall shine forth clear, i.e.*, shall have their cause acknowledged just. The LXX. and Vulg. seem to have understood it so: "shall be praised."

LXV.

The feeling pervading this psalm is indicated by the initial words *quiet* and *praise*. The attitude of Israel towards God is one of silent expectation, or expressed thankfulness—it waits hopeful of blessing to be vouchsafed in history and nature, and then bursts forth, like the refreshed and renewed earth, into a loud song of praise. There is only one direct indication of the probable date of the poem—the mention of the Temple, which sets aside the traditional ascription to David. Some have seen reference to a great national deliverance, such as that from Sennacherib, and to an abundant harvest following it. Others, even as early as some MSS. of the LXX. (see Note to title), date the psalm during the exile. The language of the latter part certainly recalls the glowing pictures of the blessings of the Return painted by the later Isaiah. But we can afford to leave undiscovered the author and date of a poem which is perennially fresh and true—a harvest song for the whole world and for all time. The parallelism is symmetrical throughout, but in form the psalm is an ode without regularity of stanza.

Title.—See titles to Pss. iv., xlv.

The Vulgate and some MSS. of the LXX. add to the word song, "of Jeremiah or Ezekiel, for the people of the dispersion, as they were about to return home."

⁽¹⁾ **Praise waiteth . . .**—Literally, *To thee silence praise*, which recalls Ps. lxii. 1 (see Note), but must be differently explained. To say, *Praise is silence to thee*, is hardly intelligible. The LXX. and Vulg. read differently, "praise is comely." Better supply a conjunction, *To thee are quiet and praise, i.e.*, submissive expectation till the deliverance come (Ps. lxii. 1), and then exulting praise.

Shall the vow.—Better, *Is the vow paid, i.e.*, by the praise just mentioned.

⁽²⁾ **Unto thee shall all flesh come.**—This has usually, and most truly, been taken as prophetic of the extension of the true religion to the Gentiles. But we must not let what was, in the Divine providence, a fulfilment of the psalmist's words, hide their intention as it was conscious to himself. The psalm shows us the exclusiveness of Hebrew belief, and, at the same time, the nobler and grander feelings which are from time to time found struggling against it. The peculiar privilege of Israel has been stated in the first verse. Silent, yet confident, waiting for Jehovah's blessing, and then exultant praise for it (*Tehillah*). In this the other nations have no part; but all flesh may approach Jehovah in prayer (*Tephillah*). (Compare verse 5.)

⁽³⁾ **Iniquities.**—Literally, *Words* (or, *things*) *of iniquities, i.e.*, details of crime, or instances of wickedness. (Comp. Pss. xxxv. 20, cv. 27, cxlv. 5.)

for our transgressions, thou shalt purge them away.

(4) Blessed *is the man whom* thou choosest, and causest to approach *unto thee, that* he may dwell in thy courts: we shall be satisfied with the goodness of thy house, *even* of thy holy temple.

(5) *By* terrible things in righteousness wilt thou answer us, O God of our salvation; *who art* the confidence of all the ends of the earth, and of them that are afar off *upon* the sea: (6) which by his strength setteth fast the mountains; *being* girded with power: (7) which

¹ Or, *to sing*.

² Or, *after thou hadst made it to desire rain*.

³ Or, *thou causest rain to descend into the furrows thereof*.

⁴ Heb., *thou dissolvest it*.

stilleth the noise of the seas, the noise of their waves, and the tumult of the people. (8) They also that dwell in the uttermost parts are afraid at thy tokens: thou makest the outgoings of the morning and evening ¹ to rejoice. (9) Thou visitest the earth, and ² waterest it: thou greatly enrichest it with the river of God, *which* is full of water: thou preparest them corn, when thou hast so provided for it. (10) Thou waterest the ridges thereof abundantly: ³ thou settlest the furrows thereof: ⁴ thou makest it soft with showers: thou

---

Prevail.—Better, *have prevailed, have overcome me, been too much for me.* No doubt, though the pronoun is singular, we are to think of Israel at large here, confessing, by the mouth of the poet, its unworthiness of that Divine communion for which still (see next verse) God had chosen them. This is more in keeping with the general tone of the psalm than to refer the confession to an individual. The LXX. and Vulg. give the pronoun in the plural.

There appears in this verse an antithesis between *iniquity* and *transgression.* The latter certainly sometimes seems to be applied in distinction to the violation of the covenant, and possibly the distinction is present here. The frailty and sin common to all flesh has not exempted Israel; but the chosen people have to mourn besides transgressions of their own law. These, however, will be by sacrifice purged away, and then, brought back into full covenant privilege, the offenders will approach the earthly dwelling-place of the Divine, and dwell there.

(4) **Blessed.**—The ellipse of the relative is common enough (see Ps. xxxiv. 8, &c.), but here the antecedent is wanting as well. Perhaps we ought to read, *He whom thou choosest and bringest near shall dwell,* &c.

Courts.—From a root meaning *to wall round;* especially applied to the open space within the outer fence of the Tabernacle, or to the different courts of the Temple (Exod. xxvii. 9; 1 Kings vi. 36, vii. 12).

We shall be satisfied.—Better, *Let us be refreshed.*

Thy holy temple.—Literally, *The holy of thy temple,* which might mean "the holiness of thy temple."

(5) **By terrible things.**—Rather, *wondrously,* a noun used adverbially.

Wilt thou answer us.—Better, *Thou dost answer us;* describing the usual course of God's providence. The LXX. and Vulg. make it a prayer: "Hear us."

The conviction that God, the God of Israel's salvation or deliverance, would answer wonderfully in *righteousness,* was, of course, based on the whole experience of the Divine dealings. Righteousness was recognised as the foundation on which the moral order rested.

The confidence of all the ends of the earth. —This might refer to Israel in exile; but it seems more in accordance with the general tenor of the psalm to give the words their widest range. Consciously or unconsciously the whole world rests in God.

Of them that are afar off upon the sea.— Literally, *of the sea of those at a distance, i.e.,* of the farthest seas. (Comp. Isa. xi. 11: "of the islands of the sea.")

(6) **Girded.**—We see the Divine Architect of the world, girt for his labours in the Oriental fashion (see Note, Ps. xviii. 32), setting the mountains firm on their bases (comp. Ps. lxxv. 3), the poet evidently thinking at the same time how empires, as well as mountains, owe their stability to God.

(7) **Tumult.**—Here we see the literal passing into the figurative. From the raging seas the poet's thought goes to the anarchies arising from the wild passions of men, for which in all literature the ocean has furnished metaphors. (Comp. Isa. xvii. 12.) In a well-known passage, the Latin poet Virgil reverses the simile, likening the sudden calm which succeeds the storm that wrecked Æneas to the effect produced by a leader of men in a seditious city. (Virgil, *Æn.* i. 148.)

(8) **They also . . .**—Or, *So they.*

The outgoings . . .—A pregnant expression for the *rising of the morning and setting of the evening sun.* East and west.

To rejoice.—Better, *to sing for joy.* The whole earth from one utmost bound to the other is vocal with praise of the Creator and Ruler of the universe. So the morning stars sang together at the creation (Job xxxviii. 7).

(9) **Thou visitest . . .**—Better, *Thou hast visited.* Even if there is not reference to some particular season of plenty, yet with a glance back on the memory of such. Instead of "earth," perhaps, here, "land."

Waterest.—Or, *floodest.* The river of God stands for the rain. There is a Arabic proverb, "When the river of God comes, the river Isa (in Bagdad) ceases." The Rabbins say, "God has four keys which He never entrusts to any angel, and chief of these is the key of the rain." (Comp. Job xxvi. 8; xxviii. 26; xxxviii. 28.) The expression "river" for rain is very appropriate of the downpour of a country that has its rainy season. (Comp. "the rushing of the river rain," Tennyson's *Vivien.*)

Thou preparest . . .—The Authorised Version misses the sense, which is, *thou preparest their corn when thou hast prepared it* (the land) *so*—*i.e.,* in the manner now to be described. Thus LXX. and Vulgate.

(10) **Thou waterest . . . settlest.**—Better, *by watering . . . settling.*

Ridges . . . furrows.—These terms would be better transposed since by "settling" (literally, *pressing down*) is meant the softening of the ridges of earth between the furrows. The LXX. and Vulgate have "multiply its shoots."

blessest the springing thereof. (11) Thou crownest ¹ the year with thy goodness; and thy paths drop fatness. (12) They drop upon the pastures of the wilderness: and the little hills ² rejoice on every side. (13) The pastures are clothed with flocks; the valleys also are covered over with corn; they shout for joy, they also sing.

PSALM LXVI.

To the chief Musician, A Song or Psalm.

(1) Make a joyful noise unto God, ³ all ye lands: (2) sing forth the honour of his name: make his praise glorious. (3) Say unto God, How terrible *art thou* in thy works! through the greatness of thy power shall thine enemies ⁴ ⁵ submit themselves unto thee. (4) All the earth shall worship thee, and shall sing unto thee; they shall sing *to* thy name. Selah.

(5) Come and see the works of God: *he is* terrible *in his* doing toward the children of men. (6) He turned the sea into dry *land*: they went through the flood on foot: there did we rejoice in him. (7) He ruleth by his power for ever; his eyes behold the nations: let not the rebellious exalt themselves. Selah.

(8) O bless our God, ye people, and make the voice of his praise to be heard: (9) which ⁶ holdeth our soul in life, and suffereth not our feet to be moved.

(10) For thou, O God, hast proved us: thou hast tried us, as silver is tried.

---

1 Heb., *the year of thy goodness.*

2 Heb., *are girded with joy.*

3 Heb., *all the earth.*

4 Or, *yield feigned obedience.*

5 Heb., *lie.*

6 Heb., *putteth.*

Showers.—Literally, *multitudes* (of drops).

(11) **Thou crownest.**—Better, *hast crowned*. We generally connect the idea of *completion* with this metaphor, but the original thought in the Hebrew word, as in the Greek στέφω, is probably to *encompass*. Comp. the Latin *corono* in Lucretius, ii. 802—

"Sylva coronat aquas ingens nemus omne."

All "the circle of the golden year" had been attended by Divine goodness. The meaning seems to be that God had made a year which was naturally prosperous still more abundant.

Paths.—The root from which the Hebrew word is formed means *to roll*, or *revolve*, and it often means the track made by a wheel. This idea may be present since God is often represented in Hebrew poetry as riding on a chariot of clouds, generally with the association of wrath and destruction (Pss. xviii. 10; lxviii. 4), but here, with the thought of plenty and peace following on His track, as in the Latin poet—

"Te fugiunt venti, te nubila cœli
Adventumque tuum, tibi suaves dœdala tellus
Submittit flores, tibi rident æquora ponti
Placatumque ridet diffuso lumine cœlum."
LUCRETIUS, i. 6.

But it is more natural to give the word the meaning *revolutions*, and to think of the blessings brought by the "seasons as they roll."

Fatness.—A cognate accusative to the word "drop" used absolutely in the next verse. (Comp. Prov. iii. 20.)

(12) **They drop upon.**—Supply "fatness" from the last verse.

And the little hills.—See margin. The freshness and beauty of plant life, which suddenly, as by a miracle, in Eastern lands clothes the hill-sides, resembles a fair mantle thrown round their shoulders, as if to deck them for some festival.

LXVI.

The compilers of the Psalter found no tradition of authorship attached to this Psalm, and did not themselves conjecture one, nor have we any guide towards the time of its composition beyond the tone of innocence assumed in the last part, which marks that part as belonging to a period subsequent to the captivity, when persecution and suffering were no longer regarded as punishment for national disloyalty to the covenant. The poetical form is uncertain, but there is a marked change in the rhythm at verse 13, and some commentators regard the psalm as composite.

Title.—See titles, Pss. iv., xlviii.

Here there is a peculiarity in the absence of any author's name after the double title *song, psalm*. (Comp. Ps. lxvii., where the words are reversed.)

(1) **Make a joyful noise.**—Better, *sing aloud*, or *shout*.

All ye lands.—The margin is better.

(2) **Sing forth.**—Literally, *play on the harp*.

Make his praise glorious.—So the LXX., but the construction is dubious. Literally, *put glory his praise*, meaning perhaps, in parallelism with the first clause, "make the Divine glory the subject of your praise." But the opening words of the next verse, "say unto God, how," &c., are so bald that a suspicion arises as to the arrangement of the text. Perhaps by bringing back the initial words of verse 3 we get the true sense, "ascribe glory (and) speak praise to God."

(6) **Flood.**—Hebrew, *nâhar*, which generally stands for the Euphrates, but here, as in Ps. lxxiv. 15, for either the Jordan or the Red Sea.

There did we rejoice.—The verb is properly optative—*there* (*i.e.*, in those works) *let us rejoice*, and thus rendered is more in keeping with the first verses of the psalm. The LXX. and Vulg. have the future, "There we will rejoice in him."

(7) **His eyes behold.**—Better, *his eyes keep watch on the nations*. God is, as it were, Israel's outpost, ever on the alert to warn and defend them against surrounding nations.

Let not . . .—Literally, *the rebellious, let them not exalt for themselves*, where we may supply "horn" as in Ps. lxxv. 4, 5, or "head" as in iii. 3, cx. 7. For *the rebellious*, comp. Ps. lxviii. 6.

(9) **Which holdeth . . .**—The LXX. literally, *which putteth our soul into life*, *i.e.*, keeps us alive, as the parallelism shows.

Praise for Deliverance.   PSALMS, LXVII.   *The People Called to Praise God.*

(11) Thou broughtest us into the net; thou laidst affliction upon our loins. (12) Thou hast caused men to ride over our heads; we went through fire and through water: but thou broughtest us out into a ¹ wealthy *place*. (13) I will go into thy house with burnt offerings: I will pay thee my vows, (14) which my lips have ² uttered, and my mouth hath spoken, when I was in trouble. (15) I will offer unto thee burnt sacrifices of ³ fatlings, with the incense of rams; I will offer bullocks with goats. Selah.
(16) Come *and* hear, all ye that fear God, and I will declare what he hath done for my soul. (17) I cried unto him with my mouth, and he was extolled with my tongue.
(18) If I regard iniquity in my heart, the Lord will not hear *me:* (19) *but* verily God hath heard *me;* he hath attended to the voice of my prayer.
(20) Blessed *be* God, which hath not turned away my prayer, nor his mercy from me.

PSALM LXVII.

To the chief Musician on Neginoth, A Psalm *or* Song.

(1) God be merciful unto us, and bless us; *and* cause his face to shine ⁴ upon us; Selah. (2) That thy way may be known upon earth, thy saving health among all nations. (3) Let the people praise thee, O God; let all the people praise thee.
(4) O let the nations be glad and sing for joy: for thou shalt judge the people righteously, and ⁵ govern the nations upon earth. Selah. (5) Let the people praise thee, O God; let all the people praise thee.
(6) *Then* shall the earth yield her increase; *and* God, *even* our own God, shall bless us. (7) God shall bless us; and all the ends of the earth shall fear him.

1 Heb., *moist.*
2 Heb., *opened.*
3 Heb., *marrow.*
4 Heb., *with us.*
5 Heb., *lead.*

---

(11) **Net.**—The Hebrew in Ez. xii. 13 certainly means "net," as LXX. and Vulg. here. But Aquila, Symmachus, and Jerome prefer the usual meaning, "stronghold" (2 Sam. v. 7, &c.), which is more in keeping with the other images of violence and oppression. The fortress, the hard labour, the subjection as by foes riding over the vanquished, the passage through fire and water, all raise a picture of the direst tyranny.

(12) **Ride over our heads.**—For the figure comp. Isa. li. 23.

We went through fire and water.—A figure of extreme danger. (Comp. Isa. xliii. 2.)

A wealthy place.—The LXX. and Vulg., "to refreshment," which is certainly more in keeping with the figures employed, and may perhaps be got out of the root-idea of the word, "overflow." But a slight change gives the frequent figure "a broad place."

(14) **Uttered.**—Literally, *opened.*

(15) **I will offer.**—Such a holocaust could hardly have been vowed by a single person. It is the community that speaks. Besides, the ram was not a sacrifice for any individual, but particularly enjoined for the high priest (Lev. ix. 2), the head of a tribe (Num. vii.), or a Nazarite (Num. vi. 14). Incense is here the ascending smoke of the sacrifice.

(16) **Come.**—Refers back to verse 9.

(17) **And he . . .**—Literally, *exaltation (i.e., praise) was under my tongue,* apparently a Hebrew idiom akin to our "on the tip of the tongue," *i.e.,* ready at any moment for utterance.

(18) **If I regard . . .**—Rather, *if I had seen evil* (*i.e.,* had had it purposely in view) *in my heart, the Lord would not have heard me.* One may not "be pardoned and retain the offence." The reference may be either to the forming of wicked schemes, or to the complacent view of wickedness in others.

The protestation of innocence in this verse, being made by or for the community at large, marks a late period for the composition. (See Introduction, and Ps. xliv., Introduction and Notes.)

(20) **Who hath not turned . . .**—*i.e.,* he found himself able to pray, was not silenced. Notice the *zeugma.* God had not *rejected* his prayer nor *withdrawn* His grace.

LXVII.

This is a noble hymn of praise, which for its fine and free expression of grateful dependence on the Divine grace was worthy to become, as it has become, a Church hymn for all time. The last two verses connect the hymn immediately with harvest, and it would look as if this allusion had actually been added for some special occasion to what was a general song of praise, since the refrain in verse 5, besides marking its choral arrangement, indicates what appears to be the proper ending of the psalm.

Title.—See titles, Pss. iv. and lxvi.

(1) This verse is an adaptation of the priestly benediction (Num. vi. 24—26).

Upon us.—Rather, *with,* or *among* us; a variation from the formal benediction.

(2) **Saving health.** — The Hebrew word is that generally rendered "salvation," but often better rendered "help," or "deliverance." By "health" the translators meant "healing power," as in Shakspeare, *King John,* Act V., Scene 2:—

"For the health and physick of our right."

(3) **Praise.**—Better, *give thanks.*

(4) **For thou shalt judge.**— Better, *for thou judgest.*

And govern . . . .—Better, *and dost lead.* The word is used in Ps. xxiii. 3 of the "pastoral" care of God.

(6) **Then shall the earth yield her increase.**—It seems more in keeping with the expression of thanks to render here with the LXX. and Vulg., "The land hath yielded her increase."

The Discomfiture of the Wicked.   PSALMS, LXVIII.   *The Joy of the Righteous.*

PSALM LXVIII.

To the chief Musician, A Psalm *or* Song of David.

(1) Let ^a God arise, let his enemies be scattered: let them also that hate him flee ¹ before him. (2) As smoke is driven away, *so* drive *them* away: as wax melteth before the fire, *so* let the wicked perish at the presence of God. (3) But let the righteous be glad; let them rejoice before God: yea, let them ² exceedingly rejoice.

(4) Sing unto God, sing praises to his name: extol him that rideth upon the heavens by his name JAH, and rejoice before him. (5) A father of the fatherless, and a judge of the widows, *is* God in his holy habitation. (6) God setteth the solitary ³ in fami-

<small>*a* Num. 10 35.

¹ Heb., *from his face.*

² Heb., *rejoice with gladness.*

³ Heb., *in a house.*</small>

LXVIII.

"It is no easy task," writes Hitzig of this psalm, "to become master of this Titan." The epithet is apt. The psalm is Titanic not only in its unmanageable resistance to all the powers of criticism, but also in its lyric force and grandeur. It scales too, Titan-like, the very divinest heights of song.

In the case where there is still room for so many contradictory theories, it is best to confine an introduction to certainties. Ps. lxviii. will no doubt remain what it has been called, "the cross of critics, the reproach of interpreters;" but it tells us some facts of its history and character that are beyond question.

1. The mention of the Temple in verse 29, in a context which does not allow of the interpretation sometimes possible, *palace,* or *heavenly abode,* brings down the composition to a period certainly subsequent to Solomon.

2. The poet makes free use of older songs. Indeed M. Renan calls the psalm "an admirable series of lyric fragments" (*Langues Sémitiques,* p. 123). Most prominent among these references are those to Deborah's magnificent ode (Judg. v.) which is with the writer throughout, inspiring some of his finest thoughts.

3. The ode, while glancing ever and anon back over Israel's ancient history, is yet loud and clear with the "lyric cry" of the author's present. See verses 4, 5, 6, 7, 21, (where there is probably a veritable historic portrait), 22, 30 *seqq.*

4. The interest of this present, though we lack the key to its exact condition, centred, as far as the poet was concerned, in the Temple, which is represented as the object of the reverence and regard of foreign powers, who bring gifts to it.

5. Notwithstanding the warlike march of the poem, and the martial ring of its music, it appears from verses 5, 10, 19, 20, not to have been inspired by any immediate battle or victory, but by that general confidence in the protection of God which Israel's prophets and poets ever drew from the history of the past.

These few features, obvious on the face of the poem, lend probability to the conjecture which sees in this psalm a processional hymn of the second Temple. That Temple needed gifts and offerings from the Persian monarchs, and was rising into completion at a time when Israel could boast of no military greatness, but found its strength only in religion. The poetical form is irregular, varying with the subject and tone.

Title.—See titles, Pss. iv. and lxvi.

(1) **Let God arise.**—A reminiscence of the battle-cry raised as the ark was advanced at the head of the tribes (Num. x. 35). For interesting historical associations with this verse, see Gibbon (chap. lviii.), and Carlyle, *Cromwell's Letters and Speeches* (Vol. II., 185).

(2) **Smoke.**—The figure of the vanishing smoke has occurred before (see Ps. xxxvii. 20); for that of the melting wax see Ps. xcvii. 5. Both figures are too obvious to need reference to the cloud and fire of the ancient encampment.

(4) **Sing praises . . .**—Better, *play on the harp.*

Extol him that rideth upon the heavens. —Rather, *cast up a highway for him that rideth on the steppes.* (Comp. Isa. xl. 3, of which this is apparently an echo.) The poet's voice is the herald's who precedes the army of God to order the removal of all obstructions, and the formation of cairns to mark the road. Isa. lvii. 14, lxii. 10, are passages alluding to the same custom.

The translation, "upon the heavens," rests on a rabbinical interpretation of '*arabôth.*

By derivation it means "a dry sandy region," a "steppe." The singular of the noun forms with the article a proper name designating the Jordan valley. (In the poetical books, however, any wild tract of country is called '*Arabah*—Isa. xxxv. 1, 6.) The plural often designates particular parts of this region, as the plains of Moab or Jericho (2 Kings xxv. 4, 5). Such a restricted sense is quite in keeping with the allusions to the early history which make up so much of the psalm.

By his name JAH.—Better, *his name is Jah.* This abbreviated form of Jehovah is first found in Exod. xv. 2. No doubt the verse is a fragment of a song as old as the Exodus.

It may be noticed here that the dependence of this psalm on older songs is nowhere more conspicuous than in the very various use of the Divine names, *Elohim, Adonai, El, Shaddai, Jehovah, Jah.*

(5) The LXX. and Vulg. prefix to this verse, "They shall be troubled by the face of Him who is," &c., which seems to indicate that the abrupt introduction of this description of God is due to some loss in the text.

A father of the fatherless, and a judge of the widows.—These epithets of God seem to have become at a very early period almost proverbial.

(6) **Solitary . . .**—This might refer to the *childless* (comp. Ps. cxiii. 9), but it is better, in connection with the next clause, to think of the exiles scattered and dispersed, and who are by the Divine arm brought home.

With chains.—The Hebrew word is peculiar to this passage, and is derived by the Rabbis from a root meaning *to bind.* Modern scholars give "to prosper" as the meaning of the root, and render, *he bringeth the captives into prosperity.*

But.—Literally, *only.*

Rebellious.—As in Ps. lxvi. 7; *stubborn, refractory.*

In a dry land.—Or, *desert.*

It is natural, remembering the connection between the imagery of verse 4 and parts of the great prophet of the Return, to refer its expressions to those who

The Mighty Works of God   PSALMS, LXVIII.   *for His People.*

lies: he bringeth out those which are bound with chains: but the rebellious dwell in a dry *land*.

⁽⁷⁾ O God, when thou wentest forth before thy people, when thou didst march through the wilderness; Selah: ⁽⁸⁾ The earth shook, the heavens also dropped at the presence of God: *even Sinai itself was moved* at the presence of God, the God of Israel. ⁽⁹⁾ Thou, O God, didst ¹ send a plentiful rain, whereby thou didst ² confirm thine inheritance, when it was weary.

⁽¹⁰⁾ Thy congregation hath dwelt therein: thou, O God, hast prepared of thy goodness for the poor. ⁽¹¹⁾ The Lord gave the word: great *was* the ³ company of those that published *it*. ⁽¹²⁾ Kings of armies ⁴ did flee apace: and she that tarried at home divided the spoil.

⁽¹³⁾ Though ye have lien among the pots, *yet shall ye be as* the wings of a

1 Heb., *shake out.*
2 Heb., *confirm it.*
3 Heb., *army.*
4 Heb., *did flee, did flee.*

---

were left behind in Babylon when the restoration took place.

(7—10) We come now to the first of three unmistakable historic retrospects—the rescue from Egypt, the conquest of Canaan, and the establishment of Jerusalem as the political and religious capital. In these patriotic recollections the poet is naturally inspired by the strains of former odes of victory and freedom. The music especially of Deborah's mighty song (Judges v.), which, directly or indirectly, coloured so much of later Hebrew poetry (see Deut. xxxiii. 2; Hab. iii.) is in his ears throughout.

Wentest forth . . . didst march.—The parallel clauses as well as the words employed have, in the sound and sequence, a martial tread. The latter word, "didst march," is peculiar to Judges v., Hab. iii., and this psalm.

Even Sinai itself.—Better, *this Sinai.* (See Note, Judges v. 5, where the clause completing the parallelism, here omitted, is retained, and shows us that the predicate to be supplied here is *melted.*)

"The mountain melted from before Jehovah,
This Sinai from before Jehovah, God of Israel."

The demonstrative "this Sinai" appears more natural if we suppose the verse, even in Deborah's song, to be an echo or fragment of some older pieces contemporary with the Exodus itself. Such fragments of ancient poetry actually survive in some of the historical books —*e.g.*, Num. xxi. 17, 18; Exod. xv. 1—19.

⁽⁹, ¹⁰⁾ **Thou, O God . . .**—The text of these two verses literally runs, *A rain of gifts thou shakest out, O God, on thine inheritance, and when exhausted didst refresh it. Thy living creatures dwell therein; thou makest provision of thy goodness for the afflicted, O God.* The rain of gifts has been variously explained as *actual showers, blessings of prosperity, outpourings of the Holy Spirit.* Both the latter might no doubt be implied in the expression, but some particular material blessing seems indicated, and in connection with the desert wanderings the *rain of manna* suggests itself. By *thine inheritance* we understand God's *people,* as in Deut. iv. 20; Ps. xxviii. 9, &c. The "living creatures" in the next verse will then probably be the *quails;* and a slight emendation, lately suggested, carries conviction along with it. It consists in bringing "thy living creatures" into verse 9, and, by the insertion of a letter, to read instead of "they dwell therein"—*they are satisfied with it* (comp. Ps. lxxviii. 24, 25). This gives the rendering, *and when it was exhausted thou didst refresh it with thy living creatures; they are satisfied therewith.* (Burgess.)

⁽¹⁰⁾ **Thy congregation.**—See above. If the emendation there adopted seems unnecessary, we may render here, *Thy life dwells in her, i.e.,* in the people of Israel. (Comp. Ps. cxliii. 3.) The vigour consequent on the heavenly food might be called the Divine life, and conceal a higher application.

(11—14) These verses refer to the conquest of Canaan, the long history of which is, however, here crowded into one supreme and crowning moment: a word from God, and all was done.

⁽¹¹⁾ **The Lord gave . . .**—Literally, *The Lord gives a word.* Of the women who bring the news, the host is great. The Hebrew for *a word* is poetical, and used especially of a Divine utterance (Pss. xix. 4, lxxvii. 8; Hab. iii. 9). Here it might mean either the *signal* for the conflict, or the *announcement* of victory. But the custom of granting to bands of maidens the privilege of celebrating a triumph (Exod. xv. 20, 21; Judges v., xi. 34; 1 Sam. xviii. 6; 2 Sam. i. 20), here evidently alluded to, makes in favour of the latter.

By the "great company," or *host,* we are apparently to think, not of one large body of women celebrating some one particular victory, but successive and frequent tidings of victory following rapidly on one another—

"Thick as tale
Came post with post."—*Macbeth.*

The LXX. and Vulg. renderings have been the source of the erroneous view which makes this verse prophetic of a numerous and successful Christian ministry: "The Lord shall give the word to them that evangelise with great might."

⁽¹²⁾ **Kings of armies did flee apace.**—Better, *Kings of armies flee, flee.* This and the two next verses wear the air of being a fragment of those ancient battle-songs sung by the women after the defeat of the foe. The fact that they have thus been torn from their original context accounts for the great obscurity which hangs over them.

And she that tarried . . .—*i.e.,* the woman keeping the house; so the Hebrew. (Comp. Judges v. 24, " Women of the tent;" and the fond anticipations of Sisera's mother, verse 29.) So the Greeks called the mistress of the house οἰκουρός. (Eur. *Herc. Fur.* 45.)

Though this sense thus gives a general description of war, and the women waiting eagerly for the victorious home-coming is a picture true to life, yet the next verse indicates that we must suppose a latent reference to some tribe or party who shirked the dangers of battle, and played the part of the stay-at-home.

(13, 14) The agreement of the ancient versions in rendering these difficult verses shows that their obscurity does not arise, as in the case of so many passages of the Psalms, from any corruptions in the text, but from the fact that they are an adaptation of some

dove covered with silver, and her feathers with yellow gold. ⁽¹⁴⁾ When the Almighty scattered kings ¹in it, it was *white* as snow in Salmon.

⁽¹⁵⁾ The hill of God *is as* the hill of Bashan; an high hill *as* the hill of Bashan. ⁽¹⁶⁾ Why leap ye, ye high hills? *this is* the hill *which* God desireth to dwell in; yea, the LORD will dwell *in it* for ever. ⁽¹⁷⁾ The chariots of God *are* twenty thousand, ²*even* thousands of angels: the Lord *is* among them, as in

¹ Or, *for her, she was.*

² Or, *even many thousands.*

---

ancient war-song to circumstances to which we have no clue. If we could recover the allusions, the language would probably appear clear enough.

"Why rest ye among the sheepfolds?"
"A dove's wings are (now) covered with silver, and her feathers with the sheen of gold."
"When the Almighty scattered kings there,
It was snowing on Tsalmon."

Even in our ignorance of these allusions we at once recognise in the first member of this antique verse the scornful inquiry of Judges v. 16, addressed to the inglorious tribe that preferred ease at home to the dangers and discomforts of battle.

The word here rendered "sheepfolds" (in the Authorised Version *pots*, a meaning which cannot represent the Hebrew word or its cognates in any other place) is cognate to that used in Judges v. 16, and occurs in its present form in Ezek. xl. 43, where the margin renders, "andirons, or two hearthstones." The derivation from *to set* would allow of its application to any kind of *barrier*.

Whether Reuben, as in Deborah's song, or Issachar, as in Gen. xlix. 14, where a cognate word occurs ("burdens"), were the original stay-at-home, does not matter. The interest lies in the covert allusion made by the psalmist in his quotation to some cowardly or recreant party now playing the same disgraceful game.

The next clause, which has caused so much trouble to commentators, appears perfectly intelligible if treated as the answer made to the taunting question, and as simply a note of time:—they stayed at home because all nature was gay and joyous with summer. There is no authority for taking the rich plumage of the dove as emblematic of peace or plenty. The dove appears, indeed, in the Bible as a type, but only, as in all other literature, as a type of love (Song of Sol. ii. 14); whereas the appearance of this bird was in Palestine, as that of the swallow with us, a customary mark of time. (See Note, Song of Sol. ii. 12, 14.) And a verse of a modern poet shows how naturally its full plumage might indicate the approach of summer:—

"In the spring a lovelier iris changes on the burnished dove."—TENNYSON: *Locksley Hall.*

This reply calls forth from the first speaker a rejoinder in companion terms. The inglorious tribe plead summer joys as an excuse for ease. The reply tells of the devotion and ardour of those who, even amid the rigour of an exceptional winter, took up arms for their country: *When the Almighty scattered kings there, it was snowing on Tsalmon.* (For the geography of Tsalmon, see Judges ix. 48.) Whether intentionally or not, the sense of the severity of the snowstorm—rare in Palestinian winters—is heightened by the contrast implied in the name "Dark" or "Shadow Hill."

The peculiarity of the position of the locative *there* (literally, *in it*), coming before the mention of the locality itself, is illustrated by Isa. viii. 21.

(15—18) A third retrospect follows—the third scene in the sacred drama of Israel's early fortunes. It sets forth the glory of God's chosen mountain. A finer passage could hardly be found. The towering ranges of Bashan—Hermon with its snowy peaks—are personified. They become, in the poet's imagination, envious of the distinction given to the petty heights of Judæa. (Perhaps a similar envy is implied in Ps. cxxxiii. 3.) The contrast between the littleness of Palestine and the vast extent of the empires which hung upon its northern and southern skirts, is rarely absent from the minds of the prophets and psalmists. (See Isa. xlix. 19, 20.) Here the watchful jealousy with which these powers regarded Israel is represented by the figure of the high mountain ranges watching Zion (see Note below) like hungry beasts of prey ready to spring. And what do they see? The march of God Himself, surrounded by an army of angels, from Sinai to His new abode.

⁽¹⁵⁾ **The hill of God is . . .**—Better,
"Mountain of God, mount Basan;
Mountain of peaks, mount Basan."

Even if the range of Hermon were not included, the *basalt* (*basanite*, probably from the locality) ranges, always rising up before the eyes of those looking eastward from Palestine, must have been doubly impressive from their superior height, and the contrast of their bold and rugged outlines with the monotonous rounded forms of the limestone hills of Judæa. And it is quite possible that, in a poetic allusion, the term "mountains of Bashan" might include all the heights to the eastward of Jordan, stretching southward as well as northward. There would then be an additional propriety in their introduction as jealously watching the march of Israel from Sinai to take possession of the promised land. Why these trans-Jordanic ranges should be styled "mountains of God" has been much discussed. Some explain the term to denote ancient seats of religious worship; others take it simply as a general term expressing grandeur—"a ridge of god-like greatness."

⁽¹⁶⁾ **Why leap ye?**—The verb occurs only here, but is explained by Delitzsch, by comparison with an Arabic root, to express the attitude of a beast crouching down for a spring on its prey; a fine image: the jealous hills lying, like panthers, ready to spring on the passing Israelites. Or does the old feeling of jealousy of the tribes on the other side of Jordan still show itself lurking in this verse? Browning has an image somewhat similar:—

"Those two hills on the right
Crouched like two bulls."

Others make the meaning simply "to look enviously on." The older versions have caught the sense, "Why watch with suspicion?" We may translate the verse, *Why, mountains of many peaks, glare ye at the mountain which God hath desired for a residence? Yea, Jehovah will dwell there for ever.*

⁽¹⁷⁾ **The chariots.**—As the text stands, this verse can only be brought into harmony with the context by a certain violence to grammar. Its literal reading is, *God's chariots, two myriads of thousands, and again myriads of thousands* (literally, *of repetition*), *the Lord among them, Sinai in holiness*; which, by strict rule, must

Sinai, in the holy *place*. ⁽¹⁸⁾ ᵃ Thou hast ascended on high, thou hast led captivity captive: thou hast received gifts ¹for men; yea, *for* the rebellious also, that the Lord God might dwell *among them*.

⁽¹⁹⁾ Blessed *be* the Lord, *who* daily loadeth us *with benefits, even* the God of our salvation. Selah. ⁽²⁰⁾ *He that is* our God *is* the God of salvation; and unto God the Lord *belong* the issues from death.

⁽²¹⁾ But God shall wound the head of his enemies, *and* the hairy scalp of such an one as goeth on still in his trespasses.

⁽²²⁾ The Lord said, I will bring again from Bashan, I will bring *my people* again from the depths of the sea: ⁽²³⁾ that thy foot may be ²dipped in the blood of *thine* enemies, *and* the tongue of thy dogs in the same.

⁽²⁴⁾ They have seen thy goings, O God; *even* the goings of my God,

a Eph. 4. 8.

¹ Heb., *in the man.*

² Or, *red.*

---

mean: "God's chariots are innumerable, and the Lord rides in them to Sinai, into the holy place." But this rendering is quite against the whole tenor of the passage, which is descriptive of a march *from*, not *to*, Sinai. Hence some suggest the rendering, "The Lord is among them—a Sinai in holiness," meaning that Zion has become *Sinai*, a common enough figure in poetry (comp. *In medio Tibure Sardinia est*—Mart. iv. 60), but only discovered here by a roundabout process. There can hardly be a question as to the propriety of the emendation suggested by Dr. Perowne, *The Lord is with them; He has come from Sinai into the holy place.* (Comp. Deut. xxxii. 2, which was undoubtedly in the poet's mind.)

Of angels.—This rendering arose from a confusion of the word which means *repetition* with a word which means *shining*. LXX., "of flourishing ones"; Vulg., "of rejoicing ones." But the mistake is a happy one, and Milton's sonorous lines have well caught the feeling and music of the Hebrew:—

"About His chariots numberless were poured
Cherub and seraph, potentates and thrones,
And virtues, winged spirits and chariots winged,
From the armoury of God, where stand of old
Myriads."   *Paradise Lost*, vii. 196.

⁽¹⁸⁾ **Thou hast ascended on high.**—Or, *to the height*, i.e., Mount Zion, as in Ps. xxiv. (Comp. Jer. xxxi. 12; Ezek. xx. 40.)

Captivity captive. — Or, *captives into captivity.* (See Judg. v. 12, Note.)

For men.—This rendering is inadmissible. Literally, *in man*, which is equivalent to our *of men. Gifts of men* are therefore *captives* or *hostages*, viz., the *rebellious* in the next clause, i.e., the *heathen*, whom the poet describes as subjected to Jehovah, and their land made His dwelling-place. (For St. Paul's citation of this verse, or its original, see Note, Eph. iv. 8, *New Testament Commentary*.)

⁽¹⁹⁻²³⁾ The abrupt transition from the scene of triumph just described to the actual reality of things which the psalmist now for the first time faces, really gives the key to the intention of the poem. It is by God's favour and might, and not by the sword, that deliverance from the enemies actually threatening the nation is to be expected.

⁽¹⁹⁾ The verb, as the italics of the Authorised Version show, is of somewhat indefinite use. It appears to have both an active and passive sense, meaning to *lay a burden*, or to *receive a burden*. Here the context seems to require the latter: *who daily takes our burden for us*, i.e., either the burden of trial or of sin. (Comp. a somewhat similar passage, Ps. xcix. 8, "thou art a God who liftest for us," i.e., as Authorised Version, "forgivest us.") But it is quite possible to render, *if any put a burden on us, God is our help.*

⁽²⁰⁾ **He that is.**—The insertion is unnecessary. Render, *God unto us* (i.e., *our God*) *is a God of salvation*.

Issues from death.—Literally, *for death goings out*. The same word rendered *issues* in Prov. iv. 23, there means *sources*. Here it will mean *sources of death*, or *escapes from death* as we connect the clause with what precedes or follows; Jehovah would provide an *issue out of death* for Israel, but a *source of death* to Israel's enemies. The LXX. and Vulgate apparently take it in the former connection.

⁽²¹⁾ **Hairy scalp.**—Literally, *crown*, or *top*, or *head of hair*. The word is rendered "pate" in Ps. vii. 16. This is probably a portrait of some historical person hostile to Israel. Others take it as a type of pride and arrogance, comparing the use of the Greek verb κομᾶν. The word "scalp," properly *shell* (comp. "skull"), was a word in common use at the time of the translation of the English Bible—

"White beards have armed their thin and hairless scalps
Against thy majesty."
    SHAKSPERE: *Richard II.*

⁽²²⁾ **I will bring.**—The meaning of this verse is very obscure. It is plainly another fragment of some ancient song quoted, we can hardly doubt, with reference to the return from captivity. "Bashan" and the "depths of the sea" (comp. Amos. ix. 1—10) may, in the quotation, only stand generally for *east* and *west*, the sea being here the Mediterranean. But most probably the original verse referred to the passage of the Red Sea and the contest with the king of Bashan.

⁽²³⁾ **That thy foot.**—This makes an unnecessary transposition of a very involved sentence. The image is perfectly clear, though the syntax, as often happens in all languages, goes tripping itself up. The conqueror, after wading in the blood of his enemies, is met by the dogs, who lick his gory feet. With a change of one letter we may render, "That thou mayest wash thy foot in blood—yea, the tongue of thy dogs in (the blood of) thine enemies.

⁽²⁴⁻²⁷⁾ These hopes of national deliverance are kept alive in the worship of the sanctuary, which the poet now proceeds to describe. A solemn procession advances to the Temple, and we have a description of it by one evidently as interested in this ritual as familiar with it.

⁽²⁴⁾ **Goings.** — Better, *processions*. (Comp. Ps. xlii. 4.)

In the sanctuary.—Rather, *into the sanctuary*.

my King, in the sanctuary. (25) The singers went before, the players on instruments *followed* after; among *them were* the damsels playing with timbrels.

(26) Bless ye God in the congregations, *even* the Lord, [1] from the fountain of Israel.

(27) There *is* little Benjamin *with* their ruler, the princes of Judah [2] *and* their council, the princes of Zebulun, *and* the princes of Naphtali. (28) Thy God hath commanded thy strength: strengthen, O God, that which thou hast wrought for us.

(29) Because of thy temple at Jerusalem shall kings bring presents unto thee. (30) Rebuke [3] the company of spearmen, the multitude of the bulls, with the calves of the people, *till every one* submit himself with pieces of silver: [4] scatter thou the people *that* delight in war. (31) Princes shall come out of Egypt; Ethiopia shall soon stretch out her hands unto God.

(32) Sing unto God, ye kingdoms of the earth; O sing praises unto the Lord; Selah:

(33) To him that rideth upon the heavens of heavens, *which were* of old; lo, he doth [5] send out his voice, *and that* a mighty voice. (34) Ascribe ye strength unto God: his excellency *is* over Israel, and his strength *is* in the [6] clouds.

(35) O God, *thou art* terrible out of thy holy places: the God of Israel *is* he that giveth strength and power unto *his* people. Blessed *be* God.

[1] Or, ye that are of the fountain of Israel.
[2] Or, with their company.
[3] Or, the beasts of the reeds.
[4] Or, he scattereth.
[5] Heb., give.
[6] Or, heavens.

---

(25) **Players**—*i.e.*, harpers.
Playing with timbrels.—Or, *beating the tambourine*. For this instrument (Heb., *tôph*) see Exod. xv. 20, and comp. Judges xi. 34.

(26) **Bless ye.**—Apparently these words are part of the processional hymn. But in Judges v. 9 a similar outburst of praise appears to come from the poet.
From the fountain of Israel.—A comparison with Isa. xlviii. 1; li. 1, certainly allows us to understand this *in the congregations sprung from the head waters* (as we say) *of the races*, *i.e.*, the patriarchal ancestors. At the same time if there were any mode of taking the words literally instead of figuratively it would be preferable.

(27) **There is . . . .**—The procession is apparently a representative one, and the conjecture is probable which refers the selection of Zebulun and Naphtali to their prominence in Deborah's song. Benjamin may owe its position to the fact that it gave the nation its first king, and Judah would naturally figure in the pomp as the tribe of David. But other considerations besides may have had weight. The selection may have been made as representative of the two kingdoms.
Their ruler.—The Hebrew word has always a sense of a high-handed conqueror's rule, with the possible exception of Jer. v. 31. There is probably still a reference to Saul and his conquests—" little Benjamin who conquered for thee," or, possibly, here Benjamin takes the victor's place as leader of the procession.
Their council.—The reading must certainly be changed in accordance with Ps. lv. 14. Their *crowd*, or *company*.

(28) **Thy God hath commanded.**—Rather, with LXX. and the ancient versions generally, *Ordain, O God, thy strength*.

(29) **Kings.**—This verse is a strong argument for referring the psalm either to the time of the rebuilding of the Temple, or its re-dedication after the pollution by Antiochus Epiphanes.

(30) **Rebuke . . .**—See margin, which (if we change *beasts* to *beast*) gives the right rendering. So LXX. and Vulgate. The *beast of the reed* is undoubtedly symbolical of Egypt, whether it be the *crocodile* or the *hippopotamus*.

Bulls . . . calves.—These are possibly emblems respectively of the *strong* and the *weak*—the *princes* and the *common people*. (Comp., for a somewhat similar description of the Egyptians, Ps. lxxvi. 5, 6.) But a slight emendation suggested by Grätz gives *the herd of bulls despisers of the people*, a reading quite in keeping with the ordinary use of this figure. (See Ps. xxii. 12; Jer. l. 11.) The figure in connection with the *bull-worship* of Egypt is especially significant.

Till every one submit.—This clause still waits for a satisfactory explanation. The Authorised Version is intelligible, but grammatically indefensible. The LXX. are undoubtedly right in taking the verb as a contracted infinitive preceded by a negative particle (comp. Gen. xxvii. 1), and not as a participle. The meaning *submit* or *humble* (Prov. vi. 3) is only with violence deduced from the original meaning of the verb, which (see Dan. vii. 7) means to *stamp* like a furious animal. One cognate is used (Ezek. xxxiv. 18) of a herd of bulls fouling the pasture with their feet, and another means to *tread*. The form of the verb here used might mean *to set oneself in quick motion*, which is the sense adopted by the LXX. in Prov. vi. 3. Hence we get *rebuke . . . from marching for pieces of silver*, the meaning being that a rebuke is administered not only to Egypt, but also to those Jews who took the pay of Egypt as mercenaries, and oppressed the rest of the community, a sense in keeping with the next clause.

Scatter.—The verb, as pointed, means *hath scattered*, but the LXX. support the alteration to the imperative which the context demands.

(31) **Princes.**—Or, *magnates*.
Ethiopia.—Literally, *Cush shall make to run his hands to God*, an idiom easily intelligible, expressing hasty submission.

(32—35) A noble doxology, worthy of the close of one of the finest Hebrew hymns.

(32) **Sing praises . . .**—Better, *play and sing*. The Selah, as in some other cases, is introduced where to our sense of rhythm it is quite out of place.

(35) **Out of thy holy places**—*i.e.*, *out of Zion*. The plural "places" occurs also in Ps. lxiii. 17 (Heb.).

PSALM LXIX.

To the chief Musician upon Shoshannim, A Psalm of David.

(1) Save me, O God; for the waters are come in unto my soul. (2) I sink in ¹deep mire, where *there is* no standing: I am come into deep waters, where the floods overflow me.

(3) I am weary of my crying: my throat is dried: mine eyes fail while I wait for my God. (4) They that hate me without a cause are more than the hairs of mine head: they that would destroy me, *being* mine enemies wrongfully, are mighty: then I restored *that* which I took not away.

(5) O God, thou knowest my foolishness; and my ³sins are not hid from thee.

(6) Let not them that wait on thee, O Lord GOD of hosts, be ashamed for my sake: let not those that seek thee be confounded for my sake, O God of Israel. (7) Because for thy sake I have borne reproach; shame hath covered my face.

(8) I am become a stranger unto my brethren, and an alien unto my mother's children. (9) ᵃ For the zeal of thine house hath eaten me up; ᵇ and the reproaches of them that reproached thee are fallen upon me.

1 Heb., *the mire of depth.*
2 Heb., *depth of waters.*
3 Heb., *guiltiness.*
a John 2. 17.
b Rom. 15. 3.

LXIX.

If we cannot identify the author of this psalm with any other known individual, we must certainly set aside the traditional ascription to David. Verses 10, 11, 12, cannot by any ingenuity be worked into his known history. Verse 20 does not give a picture of David's condition at any time, for he always found a Nathan or a Barzillai even in his darkest hour. The conclusion (see Note verse 33), if not, as some think, a liturgical addition of a later date than the rest of the psalm, speaking as it does the language of past exile times, is another argument against the inscription. It also makes against an opinion shared by many critics, that refers this, together with Ps. x., &c., to Jeremiah. The real author is lost in the general sufferings of these victims of religious persecution (verse 9), for whom he speaks (verse 6). The expression of this affliction is certainly figurative—and never has grief found a more copious imagery—and therefore we cannot fix the precise nature of the persecution. There appear, however, to have been two parties in Israel itself, one zealous for the national religion, the other indifferent to it, or even scornful of it (verses 9—13). It is on the latter that the fierce torrent of invective that begins with verse 22 is poured—an invective we can best appreciate, if we cannot excuse it, by remembering that it was the outcome, not of personal hatred, but of religious exclusiveness. Except Ps. xxii., no other hymn from ancient Israel supplied more for quotation and application to the young Christian community, when searching deep into the recognised sacred writings of their nation to prove that the despised and suffering one was the Christ. That in so doing they fastened on accidental coincidences, and altogether ignored the impassable distance between one who could be the mouthpiece of such terrible curses and Jesus Christ, need not blind us to the illustration which is thrown on Him and His life by the suffering and endurance of this, as of all martyrs in a right cause. The psalm falls into stanzas, but not all of equal length. The parallelism is varied by triplets.

Title.—See title Pss. iv., xlv.

(1) **The waters . . .**—For this common and obvious figure of a "sea of troubles" comp. Pss. xviii. 4, 16, xxxii. 6, xlii. 7.

(3) **Crying.**—Better, *calling*, *i.e.*, on God in prayer. For a similar picture of utter dejection comp. xxii. 15.

The following English lines have caught the feeling of these verses:

> "How have I knelt with arms of my aspiring
> Lifted all night in irresponsive air,
> Dazed and amazed with overmuch desiring,
> Blank with the utter agony of prayer."
> *St. Paul*, by F. Myers.

(4) **They that would destroy me . . .**—Properly, *my exterminators*. It seems a piece of hypercriticism to object to this as too strong a word. It is a very allowable prolepsis. At the same time the parallelism would be improved by adopting, as Ewald suggests, the Syriac reading "my enemies without are more numerous than my bones," and the construction would be the same as in Ps. xl. 12.

Wrongfully.—Better, *without cause*. Comp. Ps. xxxv. 19.

Then I restored.—Rather, *what I did not steal I must then restore*, possibly a proverbial saying to express harsh and unjust treatment. Comp. Ps. xxxv. 11; Jer. xv. 10.

(5) **My foolishness.**—This does not conflict with a true Messianic application of the Psalm, but is fatal to that which would see in the author not an imperfect type, but a prophetic mouthpiece of Christ.

(6) **Let not them.**—We again meet the feeling so common in the Psalms (see especially xliv. 17—22), that the sufferings of any member of Israel must bring dishonour on the name of Jehovah and on His religion. Here, however, it seems to touch a higher chord of feeling and to approach the true Churchmanship—the *esprit de corps* of the Kingdom of Heaven—which attaches a greater heinousness to the sin because it may harm the brethren. Not only would Jehovah be dishonoured in the sight of the heathen if He seemed to be disregarding His part of the covenant, but for an Israelite to have violated his part brought shame on all Israel.

(7) **Because.**—Better, *for*.

For thy sake.—It is plain from verse 9 that these words can only mean that the reproach under which the psalmist (or the community of which he was the spokesman) laboured was borne in the cause of religion. (Comp. Jer. xv. 15.)

(8) **Mother's children.**—See Note Song of Sol. i. 6.

(9) **Of thine house**—*i.e.*, *for* thine house. Hos. viii. 1, shows that house might stand for congregation, but very probably we are to understand zeal for the restoration or repair of the Temple, or more likely

Prayer for Help and for   PSALMS, LXIX.   *the overthrow of the Wicked.*

(10) When I wept, *and chastened* my soul with fasting, that was to my reproach. (11) I made sackcloth also my garment; and I became a proverb to them. (12) They that sit in the gate speak against me; and I *was* the song of the ¹ drunkards.

(13) But as for me, my prayer *is* unto thee, O LORD, *in* an acceptable time: O God, in the multitude of thy mercy hear me, in the truth of thy salvation.

(14) Deliver me out of the mire, and let me not sink: let me be delivered from them that hate me, and out of the deep waters. (15) Let not the waterflood overflow me, neither let the deep swallow me up, and let not the pit shut her mouth upon me.

(16) Hear me, O LORD; for thy lovingkindness *is* good: turn unto me according to the multitude of thy tender mercies. (17) And hide not thy face from thy servant; for I am in trouble:

² hear me speedily. (18) Draw nigh unto my soul, *and* redeem it: deliver me because of mine enemies.

(19) Thou hast known my reproach, and my shame, and my dishonour: mine adversaries *are* all before thee. (20) Reproach hath broken my heart; and I am full of heaviness and I looked *for some* ³ to take pity, but *there was* none; and for comforters, but I found none. (21) They gave me also gall for my meat; *ᵃ* and in my thirst they gave me vinegar to drink.

(22) *ᵇ* Let their table become a snare before them: and *that which should have been* for *their* welfare, *let it become* a trap. (23) Let their eyes be darkened, that they see not; and make their loins continually to shake. (24) Pour out thine indignation upon them, and let thy wrathful anger take hold of them. (25) Let ⁴ their habitation be desolate; *and* ⁵ let none dwell in their tents.

Notes: 1 Heb., *drinkers of strong drink.*   2 Heb., *make haste to hear me.*   3 Heb., *to lament with me.*   ᵃ Matt. 27. 34, 48; Mark 15. 23; John 19. 29.   ᵇ Rom. 11. 9, 10.   4 Heb., *their palace.*   5 Heb., *let there not be a dweller.*

---

regard for its purity and honour. So at least one applied the words long after, John ii. 17 (where see Note in *New Testament Commentary*).

And the reproaches.—See St. Paul's application of these words Rom. xv. 3. If the author had been thinking chiefly of his sin as the cause of the reproach of God, surely he would have said "the reproaches of these that reproach *me* are fallen upon *Thee*." The intention seems to be that though in his own eyes a very insignificant and unworthy member of the community, yet being one who burnt with zeal for it, he felt as personally directed against himself all the taunts aimed at Jehovah and His religion.

(10) **When I wept . . .**—The expression *I wept* (or *lamented*) *my soul with fasting* is hardly intelligible, though perhaps we might say *I wept out my soul with fasting*. The LXX. and Ps. xxxv. 13 suggest an emendation to "I humbled my soul with fasting."

To my reproach.—Quite literally and better, *a reproach to me.* Those who made light of the covenant altogether, who were in heart apostates both in faith and patriotism, would naturally treat with contempt those outward signs by which an erring Israelite owned his offence and sought reconciliation.

(12) **In the gate . . .**—The place of public resort where justice was administered. (See Ps. ix. 14 Note.)

And I was the song.—Literally, *and songs of those drinking strong drink*, but we must supply the pronoun.

(13) **But.**—A better arrangement of the clauses of this verse is:

    But as for me my prayer (is) to Thee
    Jehovah in a time of grace,
    God in the abundance of Thy (covenant) mercy
    Hear me with the faithfulness of Thy help.

For the favourable or gracious time comp Isa. xlix. 8.

Whatever the sin of verse 5, &c., it had not cut the offender off from the sense of the blessings of the covenant, or he had been by pardon restored to it.

(15) **Pit.**—Properly, *well.* A stone usually covered the wells (Gen. xxix. 10), which explains the phrase,

"shut her mouth." Is this merely figurative; or have we here a reminiscence of some terrible crime, analogous to that of Cawnpore?

(20) **I am full of heaviness.**—Rather, *I am sick.* The word here used (with its cognates), as well as that rendered *pity* in the next clause, are favourite words with Jeremiah, as also are the figures of the next verse. (See Jer. viii. 14, ix. 15, xxiii. 15.)

(21) **Gall.**—Heb., *rôsh, i.e., head.* (Comp. *poppy heads.* See Deut. xxxii. 32.) In Hos. x. 4 it is translated *hemlock*, but is most probably the *poppy* (*papaver arenarium*), which grows everywhere in Palestine, and answers all the conditions. The rendering, *gall*, comes from the LXX.

Vinegar.—Sour wine would not be rejected as unpalatable (see Note Ruth ii. 14). It was forbidden to Nazarites as a luxury (Num. vi. 3). Was the author of the psalm possibly a Nazarite? or are the expressions in the psalm merely figurative? Comp.

    "The banquet where the meats became
    As wormwood."—TENNYSON: *Elaine.*

(22) **Let their table.**—The form of this imprecation is, of course, suggested by the figurative language immediately preceding. Life had been made bitter by rancour and enmity, and the psalmist hurls back his curses, couched in the terms which had arisen to his lips to express his own misery.

And that which.—Rather, *and to them in peace a noose.* Seated at the banquet, amid every sign of peace, and every means of enjoyment, let their surroundings of security and pleasure become their snare and ruin. (Comp. 1 Thess. v. 3. See St. Paul's citation, Rom. xi. 9, *New Testament Commentary.*)

(23) **Their eyes.**—The darkened eyes and trembling limbs (comp. Nahum ii. 10; Dan. v. 6) are expressive of terror and dismay.

(25) **Habitation.**—The derivation is from a word meaning *circle*, and a better rendering is therefore *encampment* or *village.* Nomadic tribes pitch their tents in an enclosed ring. The derivation of the English

Praise acceptable to God.   PSALMS, LXX.   *Prayer for Help.*

(26) For they persecute *him* whom thou hast smitten; and they talk to the grief of ¹those whom thou hast wounded.

(27) Add ²iniquity unto their iniquity: and let them not come into thy righteousness. (28) Let them be blotted out of the book of the living, and not be written with the righteous.

(29) But I *am* poor and sorrowful: let thy salvation, O God, set me up on high. (30) I will praise the name of God with a song, and will magnify him with thanksgiving. (31) *This* also shall please the LORD better than an ox *or* bullock that hath horns and hoofs. (32) The ³humble shall see *this, and* be glad: and your heart shall live that seek God. (33) For the LORD heareth the poor, and despiseth not his prisoners.

(34) Let the heaven and earth praise him, the seas, and every thing that ⁴moveth therein. (35) For God will save Zion, and will build the cities of Judah: that they may dwell there, and have it in possession. (36) The seed also of his servants shall inherit it: and they that love his name shall dwell therein.

1 Heb., *thy wounded*
2 Or, *punishment of iniquity.*
3 Or, *meek.*
4 Heb., *creepeth.*
a Ps. 40. 13, &c.
5 Heb., *to my help.*
b Ps. 35. 4, & 71. 13.

PSALM LXX.

To the chief Musician, *A Psalm* of David, to bring to remembrance.

(1) *Make haste,* ᵃO God, to deliver me; make haste ⁵to help me, O LORD. (2) ᵇLet them be ashamed and confounded that seek after my soul: let them be turned backward, and put to confusion, that desire my hurt. (3) Let them be turned back for a reward of their shame that say, Aha, aha.

(4) Let all those that seek thee rejoice and be glad in thee: and let such as love thy salvation say continually, Let God be magnified.

(5) But I *am* poor and needy: make haste unto me, O God: thou *art* my help and my deliverer; O LORD, make no tarrying.

---

town is precisely similar. The desolation of his homestead was, to the Arab, the most frightful of calamities. (Comp. Job xviii. 15. For St. Peter's use of this verse, combined with Ps. cix. 8, see Acts i. 20, and Note, *New Testament Commentary*.)

(26) **They talk . . .**—Better, *and respecting the pain of thy pierced ones, they talk.* (For the construction of this verb *talk*, see Ps. ii. 7.) We naturally think of Isa. liii. 4, and of the Cross.

(27, 28) It is doubtful whether these verses give the talk of the enemies just mentioned, or whether the psalmist himself, after a pause, resumes his imprecations. The former supposition certainly adds a fresh force to the prayer of verse 29; and it is more natural to suppose that the string of curses, once ended, should not be taken up again. On the other hand, would the apostates, against whom the psalm is directed, have put their animosity into the shape of a wish to have names blotted out of God's book? If so, it must be in irony.

(27) **Add iniquity.**—This may be understood in two different senses: (1) *Let sin be added to sin in thy account, till the tale be full.* (2) *Add guilt for guilt, i.e., for each wrong committed write down a punishment.*

And let them not . . —*i.e.*, let them not be justified in thy sight; not gain their cause at thy tribunal.

(28) **Book of the living**—or **life.**—This image, which plays so great a part in Christian poetry (Rev. iii. 5, xiii. 8, xxi. 27. Comp. Phil. iv. 3; Luke x. 20), is derived from the civil lists or registers of the Jews. (Exod. xxxii. 32; Jer. xxii. 30; Ezek. xiii. 9.) At first erasure from this list only implied that a man was dead, or that a family was extinct (see references above); but as death was thought to deprive of all benefit of the covenant (see Note, Ps. vi. 5), such erasure came to imply exclusion from all the rights and privileges of the Theocracy, and therefore from the glory of participating in the promised deliverance and restoration of the race, and so gradually, as eschatological ideas developed, from the resurrection to eternal life. Dan. xii. 1 marks a stage in this development. In the psalmist's mouth the words would correspond to the ideas current when he wrote. From the next clause, *Let them not be written with the righteous*, it might be argued that the idea had already appeared which limited the resurrection to the righteous—an idea current at the date of 2 Macc. vii. 14, but probably familiar to some minds much sooner.

(29) **Set me up on high.**—Or, *lift me up, i.e.*, into a secure place out of the reach of enemies.

(31, 32) The pre-eminence of *praise* above *sacrifice* is not infrequent in the Psalms. (Comp. Ps. l. 14.)

(31) **That hath . . .**—Literally, *showing horns and dividing the hoofs*, marking at once *clean* animals, and those of fit age for sacrifice.

(32) **Humble.**—Rather, *afflicted.*

And your heart . . .—Better, *may your heart live.* (See Ps. xxii. 5.)

(33) **For the Lord.**—This and the following verses evidently bring the psalm within the circle of literature, of which Isa. lxv. 17 *seq.*, is the noblest example—the literature inspired by the hope of the restoration and of the rebuilding of Jerusalem.

LXX.

For this detached fragment, broken off even in the middle of a clause, see Ps. xl. 13—17.

Title.—See titles Pss. iv., xxxviii.

(2) There are two omissions here from Ps. xl. 14, "together" and "to destroy it."

(4) **For a reward of . . .**—Ps. xl. 14, "and put to shame." The change is probably a copyist's error.

(5) **Make haste unto me, O God.**—In Ps. xl. 18, "The Lord (*Adonai*) thinketh on me."

God the Hope of the Righteous   PSALMS, LXXI.   *from Youth to Age.*

PSALM LXXI.

(1) In ^a thee, O LORD, do I put my trust: let me never be put to confusion. (2) Deliver me in thy righteousness, and cause me to escape: incline thine ear unto me, and save me. (3) ² Be thou my strong habitation, whereunto I may continually resort: thou hast given commandment to save me; for thou *art* my rock and my fortress.

(4) Deliver me, O my God, out of the hand of the wicked, out of the hand of the unrighteous and cruel man. (5) For thou *art* my hope, O Lord GOD: *thou art* my trust from my youth.

(6) By thee have I been holden up from the womb: thou art he that took me out of my mother's bowels: my praise *shall* be continually of thee.

(7) I am as a wonder unto many; but thou *art* my strong refuge. (8) Let my mouth be filled *with* thy praise *and with* thy honour all the day.

(9) Cast me not off in the time of old age; forsake me not when my strength faileth. (10) For mine enemies speak against me; and they that ³ lay wait for my soul take counsel together, (11) saying, God hath forsaken him: persecute and take him; for *there is* none to deliver *him*. (12) O God, be not far from me: O my God, make haste for my help. (13) Let them be confounded *and* consumed that are adversaries to my soul; let them be covered *with* reproach and dishonour that seek my hurt.

(14) But I will hope continually, and will yet praise thee more and more. (15) My mouth shall shew forth thy righteousness *and* thy salvation all the day; for I know not the numbers *thereof*. (16) I will go in the strength of the Lord GOD: I will make mention of thy righteousness, *even* of thine only.

(17) O God, thou hast taught me from my youth: and hitherto have I declared

a Ps. 31. 1.

1 Heb., *Be thou to me for a rock of habitation.*

2 Heb., *watch,* or, *observe.*

LXXI.

The Palestinian collectors of the sacred songs of Israel found no traditional inscription to this psalm, and left it without conjecture of its authorship. In Alexandria it appears to have been attributed to David, but with the addition that it had some peculiar connection with the son of Jonadab and the first exiles. This connection, together with the resemblance between this psalm and Jeremiah's writings, has led many critics to ascribe it to that prophet, a conjecture also borne out by the fact that it is, in great part, an adaptation of other psalms, chiefly xxii., xxxi., xxxv., and xl., since such dependence on older writings is a prominent feature in Jeremiah. His life of danger and adventure, his early consecration to his office, the high position which he took at one time in the councils of the nation, all agree with what the author of this psalm says of himself. (Comp. verse 6, with Jer. i. 5, and see Note, verse 21.) Still it is quite as likely that we have here another of those hymns composed, or, more properly speaking, in this case, arranged, to express not individual feeling and experience, but that of suffering Israel. (See Note, verses 6 and 20.) In a cento of passages from older compositions the rhythm is necessarily irregular.

(1—3) These verses are borrowed, with some verbal alterations, from Ps. xxxi. 1—3, where see Note.

(3) **Rock.**—Better, *cliff* (Hebrew *selah*), to distinguish it from *tsûr,* above.

(4—6) These verses are manifestly founded on Ps. xxxi. 8—10; but the variations are more marked than usual, and indicate a definite purpose of adaptation rather than copying.

(5) **My hope.**—Comp. Jer. xiv. 8, l. 7. Also in *New Testament*, 1 Tim. i. 1, "The Lord Jesus Christ our hope." Shakspere, with his fine ear for scriptural expressions, caught this.

"And God shall be my *hope,* my stay."
"God, our *hope,* shall succour us."—*2 Henry VI.*

(6) **Took me out.**—Comp. Ps. xxii. 10. The Hebrew is not the same, but the Authorised Version renders by the same word, treating it as a transitive participle of a word that elsewhere only means *to go through,* a doubtful expedient. The LXX. (and Vulg.) have "protector," σκεπαστής, which is probably an error for ἐκσπαστής (following xxii. 10, ἐκσπάσας), which would support the rendering, "he that severed me," a rendering for other reasons probable.

This allusion to birth and retrospect of life from the earliest infancy, is not unsuitable to Israel personified as an individual, or rather it suits both the individual and the community of which he is the mouthpiece. So it has often been in application treated as an epitome of the history of the Christian Church.

(7) **A wonder**—*i.e.,* not a miracle of preservation, but a *monster.* Though men point at him as something to be avoided or mocked, God is his refuge.

(9—11) This piece may be compared with Ps. xli. 6—8. The formal "saying" (verse 11), introducing a quotation, is an indication of a late date, the early literature employing no signs of quotation. (See, *e.g.,* Ps. lxviii. 12, 26.)

(12, 13) These verses recall Pss. xxii. 11, xxxv. 4, 26, xxxviii. 21, 22, xl. 13, 14.

(13) **Hurt.**—Literally, *evil.*

(15) Comp. Ps. xl. 5, which indicates the meaning here. Mere reminiscence must give place to actual calculation, which too must fail before the sense of Divine interference in his favour.

(16) **I will go . . .**—Rather, *I will come with the Lord Jehovah's mighty deeds, i.e.,* come with the tale of them (as last verse) and praise of them into the Temple. (Comp. Ps. v. 7, lxvi. 13.)

thy wondrous works. (18) Now also ¹when I am old and grey-headed, O God, forsake me not; until I have shewed ² thy strength unto *this* generation, *and* thy power to every one *that* is to come.

(19) Thy righteousness also, O God, *is* very high, who hast done great things: O God, who *is* like unto thee!

(20) *Thou*, which hast shewed me great and sore troubles, shalt quicken me again, and shalt bring me up again from the depths of the earth. (21) Thou shalt increase my greatness, and comfort me on every side.

(22) I will also praise thee ³ with the psaltery, *even* thy truth, O my God: unto thee will I sing with the harp, O thou Holy One of Israel. (23) My lips shall greatly rejoice when I sing unto thee; and my soul, which thou hast redeemed. (24) My tongue also shall talk of thy righteousness all the day long: for they are confounded, for they are brought unto shame, that seek my hurt.

1 Heb., *unto old a,e and grey hairs.*
2 Heb., *thine arm.*
3 Heb., *with the instrument of psaltery.*
4 Or, *of.*

PSALM LXXII.

A Psalm ⁴ *for Solomon.*

(1) Give the king thy judgments, O God, and thy righteousness unto the king's son.

---

(18) **Now also when.**—Literally, *yea, even to old age and grey hairs.* Ps. cxxix. 1 shows that this may be a national as well as an individual prayer.

Thy strength.—Literally, *thine arm,* the symbol of power. (Comp. Isa. lii. 10, liii. 1, &c.)

Unto this generation.—Literally, *to a generation,* explained by the next clause to mean, *to the coming generation.*

(19) **Very high.**—Literally, *to the height, i.e.,* to the heavens, as in Pss. xxxvi. 5, lvii. 10. The clauses should be arranged, *Thy righteousness also, O God, to the height—Thou who doest great things—God, who is like unto thee ?* (Comp. Exod. xv. 11.)

(20) **Quicken me.**—According to the written text, *quicken us,* an indication that the psalm is a hymn for congregational use. As for the change from singular to plural, that is common enough.

Depths . . .—Abysses, properly of water. (See Ps. xxxiii. 7.) Perhaps here with thought of the waters on which the earth was supposed to rest. If so, the image is the common one of a "sea of trouble."

(21) **Comfort me on every side.**—Literally, either *thou wilt compass with comfort,* or *wilt turn with comfort.* The LXX. adopts the latter.

(22) **With the psaltery.**—See Ps. lvii. 8, Note.

(23) **My lips shall . . .**—Rather, *my lips shall sing while I play to thee, i.e.,* a hymn should accompany the harp. There is, therefore, no thought of the union of the bodily and spiritual powers in praise of God, though it is natural the verse should have suggested such an interpretation to the Fathers; and indeed the thought of the poet, if we read the whole psalm, with its retrospect of life, is a wish—

" That mind and soul according well,
 May make one music as before,
 But vaster."

(24) **My tongue.**—Comp. this with the conclusion of Ps. xxxv.

LXXII.

At the first glance this psalm looks like one that would readily yield up not only its meaning, but its purpose and authorship. Odes in honour of royalty generally tell their own tale, and here we certainly have a prayer for a king, the son of a king, who is to be at once glorious and good, renowned and just, in whose reign peace is to "lie like a line of light from verge to verge," plenty is to crown the year with happiness, and the empire is to be as wide abroad as the government is righteous and beneficent at home. But, making every allowance for poetical exaggeration, it is impossible to find any monarch of Israel whose reign the poem exactly describes. The name of Solomon is naturally the first to suggest itself, as it did to those who prefixed the inscription. Undoubtedly the memory of his imperial greatness inspired the song. The psalmist looks for deliverance not to the sword, but to a wise and understanding heart. He prays that the king may be animated by the spirit which dictated Solomon's choice to discern between good and evil; and he perceives that the only solid foundation for national prosperity is a just administration. Internal justice, external power and prosperity, would go hand in hand. All this might have been breathed as a prayer at Solomon's succession; but the tone (verses 12–14) is hardly such as we should expect at the close of David's reign. These verses read rather like the hope of one who had seen the nation sunk in distress, and who hailed the advent of a young prince as bearing promise of restoration and renewal of power and glory. Josiah has been suggested by Ewald, as meeting these conditions; a foreign prince, Ptolemy Philadelphus, by Hitzig and Reuss. But the view which regards the psalm as *Messianic, i.e.,* descriptive of the peace and plenty and power anticipated under a prince as yet unborn and unknown, who was to come of David's line to restore the ancient glory of the theocracy, best suits its general tone. The verse is easy and graceful, with a regular parallelism, but an uncertain division of stanzas.

Title.—According to usage, this inscription can mean only *of Solomon,* denoting *authorship.* (See *Introduction.*)

(1, 2) The order of the words should be noticed —" judgments," " righteousness," " righteousness," " judgment "—as offering a good instance of introverted parallelism. With regard to the meaning of the words we are placed on *practical* ground; they refer to the faculty of judging in affairs of government, of coming to a great and fair decision. In fact, whether Solomon be the intended subject of the poem or not, the prayer made in his dream at Gibeon (1 Kings iii. 9) is the best comment on these verses. (Comp. Isa. xi. 4, xxxii. 1.)

(1) **The king . . . the king's son.**—The article is wanting in the Hebrew.

The King's Beneficent   PSALMS, LXXII.   *and Glorious Reign:*

(2) He shall judge thy people with righteousness, and thy poor with judgment. (3) The mountains shall bring peace to the people, and the little hills, by righteousness. (4) He shall judge the poor of the people, he shall save the children of the needy, and shall break in pieces the oppressor.

(5) They shall fear thee as long as the sun and moon endure, throughout all generations.

(6) He shall come down like rain upon the mown grass: as showers *that* water the earth. (7) In his days shall the righteous flourish; and abundance of peace [1] so long as the moon endureth. (8) He shall have dominion also from sea to sea, and from the river unto the ends of the earth. (9) They that dwell in the wilderness shall bow before him; and his enemies shall lick the dust.

(10) The kings of Tarshish and of the isles shall bring presents: the kings of Sheba and Seba shall offer gifts. (11) Yea, all kings shall fall down before him: all nations shall serve him.

(12) For he shall deliver the needy when he crieth; the poor also, and *him* that hath no helper. (13) He shall spare the poor and needy, and shall save the souls

[1] Heb., *till there be no moon*.

---

(3) **The mountains . . .**—Better, literally, *Let the mountains and the hills bring forth to the people peace in* (or *by*) *righteousness*. This imperative sense, instead of the future, is by most modern commentators preserved throughout the psalm. The LXX. give it here and in verse 17, but else use the future.

The verb here employed (properly meaning "lift up") is used in Ezek. xvii. 8, for "bearing fruit," and in Isa. xxxii. 17 peace is described as the natural work or fruit of righteousness. (Comp. Ps. lxxxv. 10.) For the same prominence given to its hills as the characteristic feature of Palestine, a land which is "not only mountainous, but a heap of mountains," comp. Joel iii. 18.

(5) **They shall . . .**—Literally, *may they fear Thee* (coevally) *with the sun, and in the face of the moon, generation of generation*. For the preposition, "coevally with," see Dan. iii. 33; (Hebrew) and comp. the Latin use of *cum*—

"Cum sole et luna semper Aratus erit."
             OVID: *Amor.*, xv. 16.

The phrase "in the presence of the moon" (see the same expression, verse 17, and compare Job viii. 16), means, not by the moonlight, but as long as the moon shines. (Comp. verse 7.) On the other hand, our phrase "under the moon" refers to space. With this passage Ps. lxxxix. 36, 37, alone in Hebrew poetry exactly compares, or may perhaps have been borrowed from here.

Whether God or the king is the object of the "fear" spoken of in this verse is a question that must remain unanswered.

(6) **He shall come down.**—The rule of the monarch is to be beneficent as the rain refreshing the earth, and covering it with blessings as with verdure. Under a similar image, David's last words (2 Sam. xxiii. 4) describe a good government.

Mown grass.—The Hebrew word means "a shearing," and is used of a fleece (Judg. vi. 37; so here, LXX., Vulg., and Prayer Book version); of a hay crop (Amos vii. 1). The reference here may be either to a "mown field," on which a shower would cause fresh grass to sprout, or to meadow grass ready for mowing.

(7) **Flourish**—*i.e.*, spring up and grow like vegetation after rain.

Endureth.—See margin, and comp. Job xiv. 12, "till the heavens be no more."

(8) **He shall have . . . .**—The original is more poetical, recalling the root idea of the verb, "may he tread down (the nations) from sea to sea."

That the river in the next clause is the Euphrates there can be no question, but are we, therefore, to see precise geographical limits in the expression "from sea to sea" (from the Mediterranean to the Red Sea), as in Exod. xxiii. 31, or is it merely poetical for a wide extent of empire? The vague and general expression, "ends of the earth," which takes the place of the definite "desert," in the passage of Exodus, makes in favour of the latter view. So, too, do the hyperbolic expressions in verses 5, 11, 17. On the other hand, verse 10 mentions particular places. The same phrase in Zech. ix. 10 describes the Messianic kingdom, and is certainly poetical, but whether that or this passage is the original is doubtful.

(9) **They that dwell in the wilderness . . . .**—The Hebrew word in other places is used of "wild animals" (Ps. lxxiv. 14; Isa. xxiii. 13). Here apparently it refers to the nomad tribes wandering over the desert. The LXX. and ancient versions generally have "Æthiopians."

Lick the dust.—The allusion is to the Eastern etiquette of prostration before a sovereign.

(10) **Tarshish.**—The question of the identity of this place (or district) with the "Tartessus" of the Greeks is too long for a note. (See Jonah i. 3.) But plainly the mention here of "the isles," *i.e.*, islands and coasts of the Mediterranean (comp. Dan. xi. 18; Isa. xi. 11), is in favour of the identity.

Bring presents.—Literally, *return presents*, but not in the sense of an interchange of royal gifts (as 1 Kings x. 13) but of "payment of tribute." The expression is illustrated by the words "revenue," "custom-house returns," &c. (Comp. the Latin, *reditus*.)

Sheba.—The Joktanide kingdom, embracing the greater part of Yemen or Arabia Felix, and so here representing Arabia, (the LXX. and Vulg. have "kings of Arabians") while "Seba" (or "Saba"), which was Cushite, and was by Josephus (*A. J.*, ii. 10, s. 2), identified with "Meroë," represents Africa. (See Gen. x. 7, 28, and Smith's *Bible Dictionary*, articles "Sheba" and "Seba.")

(11) **Yea, all kings shall . . .**—Better, as before, *Let all kings*.

(12) **For he shall deliver.**—Here the verb must be present, "for he delivereth" giving the reason of the wide sway asked for this monarch. The prayer is based on the justice and beneficence of his reign ("to him that hath shall be given"), in which the weak and poor find their lives safe from violence, and their property protected against fraud. The verse is almost word for word the same as Job xxix. 12.

Poor.—Rather, *afflicted*.

of the needy. (14) He shall redeem their soul from deceit and violence: and precious shall their blood be in his sight. (15) And he shall live, and to him ¹shall be given of the gold of Sheba: prayer also shall be made for him continually; *and* daily shall he be praised. (16) There shall be an handful of corn in the earth upon the top of the mountains; the fruit thereof shall shake like Lebanon: and *they* of the city shall flourish like grass of the earth. (17) His name ²shall endure for ever: ³his name shall be continued as long as the sun: and *men* shall be blessed in him: all nations shall call him blessed. (18) Blessed *be* the LORD God, the God of Israel, who only doeth wondrous things. (19) And blessed *be* his glorious name for ever: and let the whole earth be filled *with* his glory; Amen, and Amen. (20) The prayers of David the son of Jesse are ended.

1 Heb., *one shall give.*
2 Heb., *shall be.*
3 Heb., *shall be as a son to continue his father's name for ever.*
4 Or, *A Psalm for Asaph.*
5 Or, *Yet.*
6 Heb., *clean of heart.*

Book III.
PSALM LXXIII.
⁴ A Psalm of Asaph.

(1) ⁵ Truly God *is* good to Israel, *even* to such as are ⁶ of a clean heart.

---

(14) **And precious . . .**—The parallelism shows the meaning. The life of his people is dear to the king, and he therefore protects them from violence.

(15) **And he shall . . .**—Literally, *And he shall live, and shall give him of the gold of Sheba, and pray for him continually; every day shall he bless him.* This can only refer to the man whose protection from harm and redemption from fraud and violence is mentioned in the last verse. The subject under the just government of the monarch will *live,* and will bring to his benefactor daily blessing, as well as rich gifts, with the gold of Sheba, and "with true prayers that shall be up at heaven, and enter there."

The Prayer Book version, "prayer shall be made to him," is quite inadmissible.

Gold of Sheba—*i.e.* (see verse 10), of Arabia (as in Prayer-Book). A Greek historian (Agatharchides), writing of the Sabæans, gives an admiring account of the quantity of gold used in adorning and furnishing their houses. This wealth was probably acquired by commerce with India.

(16) **An handful.**—Rather, *abundance,* from a root meaning *spread.* The clauses, as arranged in the text, evidently miss the intention of the writer. Render,

"Let there be abundance of corn on the earth;
On the top of the mountains let it wave like Libanus,"

i.e., like the cedars of Libanus. The word rendered "wave" elsewhere is used of "earthquakes" or "violent storm," and suggests here rather a violent agitation than the quiet waving of a sunny cornfield, as if the very mountains were under cultivation, and their crowning woods that sway to and fro in the breeze were suddenly changed to grain. (Comp. Ps. xcii. 13.) The images suggested by the LXX. and Vulg., of the corn in the lowlands growing high enough to overtop Lebanon, is grotesque.

And they of the city . . .—Better, *and let them (men) spring forth from the city like grass from the earth.* (As images of large population, comp. Ps. xcii. 7; Job v. 25.) But probably we ought to transpose a letter and read, "and let *cities* spring up like grass from the earth."

(17) **Shall be continued.**—Rather, *have issue.* Literally, *send out new shoots.*

As long as the sun.—See Note on verse 5.

Shall be blessed in him.—Or, *bless themselves in him.* The meaning is clear, though the Hebrew is rather vague. The monarch will himself be a source of blessing to his people, who will never tire of blessing him. The psalmist's prayer finds a genuine echo in the noble dedication of *In Memoriam:*

"May you rule us long,
And leave us rulers of your blood
As noble, till the latest day!
May children of our children say,
'She wrought her people lasting good.'"

For the doxology closing the second book, and for the note apparently appended by the collector of this book, "the prayers of David the son of Jesse are ended," see *General Introduction.*

Book III.
LXXIII.

The motive of this psalm shows itself clearly in verse 3—perplexity at the sight of the prosperity of the wicked. Two psalms have already dealt with the question at some length, viz., Pss. xxxvii. and xlix. (See *Introduction* to those psalms.) The problem is stated here more fully, the poet trying to account not only for one, but for both sides of the paradox, the troubles that beset the righteous as well as the good fortune that befalls the ungodly. The solution, however, on the first side falls short of that reached in Ps. xlix. The author contents himself with the thought that the wicked stand in slippery places, and may at any moment come to ruin. On the other hand, he is beginning to feel the way towards a higher truth than was discerned before, the truth that while the success of evil is apparent and momentary, that of good is real and final; he even catches a glimpse of the still higher truth revealed in the pages of Job, that communion with God is itself a bliss above happiness, and that the consciousness of possessing this gives a joy with which the pleasures of mere temporary prosperity are not to be compared. The versification is almost regular.

Title.—See *Title* to Ps. l.

(1) **Truly.**—See Note, Ps. lxii. 2. This particle often, like the Latin *at,* introduces a rejoinder to some supposed statement.

Dryden's lines express the feeling of this opening—

"Yet sure the gods are good! I would fain think so,
If they would give me leave!
But virtue in distress, and vice in triumph,
Make atheists of mankind."

The question arises whether the second clause of the verse limits, or only repeats, the first. No doubt in

(2) But as for me, my feet were almost gone; my steps had well nigh slipped. (3) ᵃ For I was envious at the foolish, *when* I saw the prosperity of the wicked.
(4) For *there are* no bands in their death: but their strength *is* ¹ firm. (5) They *are* not ² in trouble *as other* men; neither are they plagued ³ like *other* men. (6) Therefore pride compasseth them about as a chain; violence covereth them *as* a garment. (7) Their eyes stand out with fatness: ⁴they have more than heart could wish. (8) They are corrupt, and speak wickedly *concerning* oppression: they speak loftily. (9) They set their mouth against the heavens, and their tongue walketh through the earth. (10) Therefore his people return hither: and waters of a full *cup* are wrung out to them. (11) And they say, How doth God know? and is there knowledge in the most High?
(12) Behold, these *are* the ungodly, who

ᵃ Job 21. 7; Ps. 37. 1; Jer. 12. 1.

¹ Heb., *fat.*

² Heb., *in the trouble of* other men.

³ Heb., *with.*

⁴ Heb., *they pass the thoughts of the heart.*

theory God was understood to be good to Israel generally, but the very subject of the psalm seems to require a limitation here. The poet sees that a moral correspondence with their profession is necessary, even in the chosen people—the truth which St. Paul stated with such insistance, "For they are not all Israel which are of Israel."

(2) **Slipped.**—Literally, *were poured out.* This metaphor for weakness and instability is obvious. Comp.

"Dissolvuntur enim tum demum membra *fluuntque.*"
LUCRETIUS, iv. 920.

(3) **Foolish.**—Better, *arrogant.*

When I saw.—Perhaps the conjunction is wrongly supplied, and the word "saw" here is synonymous with "envied" in the first clause. (Comp. Latin *invideo.*)

(4) **For there are no bands in their death.**—This is quite unintelligible, and does not fairly render the Hebrew, which gives, *For there are no bands to their death.* And by analogy of the derivation of *tormenta* from *torqueo,* we might give the Hebrew word *bands* the sense of *pangs,* rendering, "they have a painless death," if such a statement about the wicked were not quite out of keeping with the psalm. The ancient versions give us no help. Some emendation of the text is absolutely necessary. In the only other place it occurs (Isa. lviii. 6) the word means specially the *bands of a yoke;* hence a most ingenious conjecture, which, by only a change of one letter, gives *there are no bands to their yoke,* i.e., they are "chartered libertines," men of *libido effrenata et indomita,* a description admirably in keeping with that of the animal grossness in the next clause, "*fat* is their belly," (Comp. the image of an animal restive from over-feeding, Deut. xxxii. 15; Burgess, *Notes on the Hebrew Psalms.*)

Strength.—The word is curious, but explained by Arabic cognates to mean *belly,* possibly from its *roundness* ("a fair round belly with good capon lined"); from root meaning *roll.*

(6) **Therefore.**—Better,

"Therefore pride is their necklace,
And violence their mantle."

The first metaphor might have been suggested either by the fact that the rich lavished large sums on jewellery, especially necklaces (see Note, Song of Sol. i. 10), or possibly from the usual description of the proud as "stiffnecked."

(7) **Stand out with fatness.**—Literally, *go out from fat.* Which, if referring to the appearance, is exactly the opposite to what we should expect. *Sunken in fat* would express the idea of gross sensuality. The *eyes* and *heart* are evidently used as in Jer. xxii. 17, the *eyes* as giving the outward index of what the *heart* wishes; and if we take the *eyes* here to mean not the organs of sight, but, by metonymy, the *looks* (comp. Song of Sol. iv. 9), "they look out of fatness," the expression is intelligible enough. Or we might perhaps take the *eyes* to stand for the countenance. (See Gesenius, *sub voc.*), *their countenance stands out because of fatness.* Or, by taking this clause in direct parallelism with the following, we might understand that restless looking about for fresh excitement which comes of satiety. The following lines illustrate the whole verse:

"Triumphant plenty, with a cheerful grace,
Basks in their eyes, and sparkles in their face;
How sleek they look, how goodly is their mien,
When big they strut behind a double chin."—DRYDEN.

They have more.—See margin. Or the verb may be intransitive: *the imaginations of their hearts overflow.*

(8) **They are corrupt . . .**—This, which is the Rabbinical rendering, is now universally abandoned in favour of another derivation of the verb. The Masoretic arrangement of the clauses may be also improved on:

"They scoff and speak of wickedness,
Of violence from their eminence they speak,"

where the first clause means, *they speak mockingly of wickedness,* or *make a jest of sin.*

(9) **They set.**—The last clause is repeated here under a figure more defined:

"They have set their mouth in [*not against*] the heavens,
While their tongue walketh through the earth."

an image very expressive of a towering pride, vaunting itself to the skies, and trumpeting its own praises through the world.

(10) **Therefore.**—The Prayer Book version has undoubtedly caught the meaning here. It plainly describes the popularity gained (the surest way) by the self-applause described in the preceding verse. This version depends on the Hebrew margin, *Therefore do the people turn hither* (i.e., to them), *and full waters* (i.e., a cup full of adulation and flattery) *are sucked out by them.*

(11–14) The mutual relation of these verses has been the subject of many conflicting opinions. The following is the arrangement that seems preferable—

"And people say, How shall God know?
And does the Most High take notice of it?
Lo! there are wicked men,
And yet, always at ease, they amass riches.
It is in vain then that I have kept my heart pure,
And washed my hands in innocence;
For I have been plagued every day,
And my punishments (come) every morning."

—this reflection being put into the mouth of the public who are onlookers at the career of these timeservers.

prosper in the world; they increase *in* riches.

(13) Verily I have cleansed my heart *in* vain, and washed my hands in innocency. (14) For all the day long have I been plagued, and ¹chastened every morning. (15) If I say, I will speak thus; behold, I should offend *against* the generation of thy children.

(16) When I thought to know this ²it *was* too painful for me; (17) until I went into the sanctuary of God; *then* understood I their end.

(18) Surely thou didst set them in slippery places: thou castedst them down into destruction. (19) How are they *brought* into desolation, as in a moment! they are utterly consumed with terrors. (20) As a dream when *one* awaketh; *so*, O Lord, when thou awakest, thou shalt despise their image.

(21) Thus my heart was grieved, and I was pricked in my reins. (22) So foolish *was* I, and ³ignorant: I was *as* a beast ⁴before thee.

(23) Nevertheless I *am* continually with thee: thou hast holden *me* by my right hand. (24) Thou shalt guide me with thy counsel, and afterward receive me *to* glory.

(25) Whom have I in heaven *but thee?* and *there is* none upon earth *that* I desire beside thee. (26) My flesh and my heart faileth: *but* God *is* the ⁵strength of my heart, and my portion for ever.

(27) For, lo, they that are far from thee shall perish: thou hast destroyed all them that go a whoring from thee. (28) But *it is* good for me to draw near to God: I have put my trust in the Lord God, that I may declare all thy works.

PSALM LXXIV.

⁶ Maschil of Asaph.

(1) O God, why hast thou cast *us* off

---

1 Heb., *my chastisement was.*
2 Heb., *it was labour in mine eyes.*
3 Heb., *I knew not.*
4 Heb., *with thee.*
5 Heb., *rock.*
6 Or, *A Psalm for Asaph to give instruction.*

But the poet immediately goes on to disclaim it for himself.

(15) **If I say . . .**—Or, *If, thought I, I should reason thus, I should be faithless to the generation of thy sons.* Or, perhaps, *if it ever occurred to my mind to speak thus*, the Hebrew often using two finite verbs to express one thought. (See, *e.g.*, verses 8, 19.)

(16) **When I thought . . .**—*i.e., when I reflected in order to know this*—when I tried to think the matter out, get at the bottom of it. (For the sense of the verb, comp. Ps. lxxviii. 5; Prov. xvi. 9.)

It was too painful.—See margin.

(17) **Then understood I . . .**—Rather, *I considered their end.* The Temple service, with its blessings on righteousness, and stern warnings against wickedness, as they were read from the Book of the Law or from one of the prophets, or were chanted from some ancient song, gave the needed turn to the psalmist's speculations. He began to think not of the present, but the future; not of the advantages of sin, but its consequences—but still consequences in *this* world, the thought of a hereafter not having established itself sufficiently to have an ethical force.

(19) **In a moment.**—Literally, *in a wink.* (Comp. "In the twinkling of an eye.")

(20) **As a dream.**—Better,

"As a man on waking (despises) his dream,
So, O Lord, on rousing thyself, thou wilt
Despise their shadow."

an image of the result of the Divine judgment on the vain and boastful tyrants, which may be illustrated by Henry V.'s rising with his royalty to self-respect:—

"I have long dreamt of such a kind of man,
So surfeit-swell'd, so old, and so profane;
But, being awake, I do despise my dream."

(21) **Grieved.**—Literally, *grew sour*; or, as we say, "was soured."

(22) **Foolish.**—Better, *brutish.*

(24) **To glory.**—Better, *With honour*, as LXX. and Vulg.; or *achar* may be taken as a preposition: *Lead me after honour*, *i.e.*, in the way to get it.

The thought is not of a reward after death, but of that true honour which would have been lost by adopting the views of the worldly, and is only to be gained by loyalty to God.

(25) **And there . . .**—Or, *Besides thee I have no delight on earth.*

(28) **Works.**—Not God's doings, but *works* prescribed to the psalmist, messages entrusted to him; no doubt here the conclusions he had come to, or the truths that had been revealed to him, in contrast with the false opinions from which he had been freed.

LXXIV.

Two periods only in the history of the Jews offer possible place for the composition of this psalm—that immediately after the Chaldæan invasion, and that of the persecution under Antiochus Epiphanes (B.C. 167). Against the former of these is the statement in verse 9 (see Note), which could not have been spoken while Jeremiah was alive. Hence, with a certainty allowed by no other of the psalms, this, with Psalm lxxix., can be referred to the year before the patriotic rise of the Asmoneans. Indeed, as Delitzsch remarks, their contents coincide with the prayer of Judas Maccabæus preserved in 2 Macc. viii. 1—4. The only argument of any weight against this conclusion is the expression in verse 3, "ruins," which appears at first sight too strong a term for the mischief wrought by the Syrians at the command of Antiochus. But we must allow at such a crisis a little licence to patriotism and poetry; and, unless the words must be limited to the sanctuary (which is not absolutely necessary: see Note), the picture given in the Book of Maccabees of the state of the Holy City, is such as to bear out the psalm. The poetical form is irregular.

Title.—See titles, Pss. xxxii., 1.

(1) **Why hast . . .**—Better, *why hast thou never ceased abandoning us?*

Anger.—Literally, *nostril*, as in Ps. xviii. 8, "there went a smoke from his nostril."

for ever? *why* doth thine anger smoke against the sheep of thy pasture? (2) Remember thy congregation, *which* thou hast purchased of old; the ¹rod of thine inheritance, *which* thou hast redeemed; this mount Zion, wherein thou hast dwelt. (3) Lift up thy feet unto the perpetual desolations; *even all that* the enemy hath done wickedly in the sanctuary.

(4) Thine enemies roar in the midst of thy congregations; they set up their ensigns *for* signs. (5) *A man* was famous according as he had lifted up axes upon the thick trees. (6) But now they break down the carved work thereof at once with axes and hammers. (7) ²They have cast fire into thy sanctuary, they have defiled *by casting down* the dwelling place of thy name to the ground. (8) They said in their hearts, Let us ³destroy them toge-

1 Or, *tribe.*

2 Heb., *They have sent thy sanctuary into the fire.*

3 Heb., *break.*

The sheep of thy pasture.—An expression peculiar to the Asaphic psalms and Jer. xxiii. 1.

(2) **Purchased.**—Or, as in LXX., *acquired.* This word, together with the word "redeemed" in the next clause, and "right hand" in verse 11, show that Exod. xv. was in the writer's mind. (See especially verses 12, 13, 16 of that chapter.)

The word "congregation" here, as in the Mosaic books, presents the people in its religious aspect, as the expression "rod (or, *tribe*) of thine inheritance" presents it in its political character.

The rod of . . .—Better, *which thou hast redeemed as the tribe of thine inheritance, i.e.,* as thine own tribe.

The expression, "rod of thine inheritance," comes from Jer. x. 16, li. 19. (Comp. Isa. lxiii. 17.) It refers not to the shepherd's crook, but to the *sceptre*, or *leading staff*, of the prince of a tribe, and so passes into a term for the tribe itself (Exod. xxviii. 21; Judges xx. 2).

(3) **Lift up thy feet.**—Better, *Lift thy steps.* A poetical expression. God is invoked to hasten to view the desolation of the Temple. A somewhat similar expression will be found in Gen. xxix. 1 (margin).

Perpetual desolations.—The word rendered "desolations" occurs also in Ps. lxxiii. 18, where it is rendered "destruction." Here, perhaps, we should render *ruins which must be ever ruins*, or *complete ruins*, or possibly, taking the first meaning of *netsach, ruins of splendour.* Isa. xi. 4 does not offer a parallel, since the Hebrew is different, and plainly refers to the long time the places have been in ruins.

Even all . . .—Better, *the enemy hath devastated all in the holy place.* 1 Macc. i. 38—40, iii. 45 ("Now Jerusalem lay void as a wilderness") give the best explanation of the verse, descriptive, as it is, of the condition of the whole of Zion.

(4) **Thine enemies . . .**—As the text stands, render, *Thine enemies have roared in the midst of thine assembly*, but many MSS. have the plural as in verse 8, where see Note for the meaning of the word.

For "roared," see Ps. xxii. 1, Note, and comp. Lam. ii. 7, where a similar scene is described. Instead of the voices of priest and choir, there have been heard the brutal cries of the heathen as they shouted at their work of destruction like lions roaring over their prey; or if, as some think, the reference in the next clause is to military ensigns, we have a picture of a wild soldiery exulting round the emblem of their triumph.

They set up their ensigns for signs.—The Hebrew for *ensigns* and *signs* is the same. Possibly the poet meant to have written some word meaning *idols,* but avoids it from dislike of mentioning the abominable things, and instead of *places their idols as signs,* writes, *places their signs as signs.*

(5) The Authorised Version, with the ancient versions, has entirely mistaken the meaning of this verse, though, unlike the LXX. and Vulgate, it has the merit of being intelligible. Literally the words run, *he* (or *it*) *is known like one causing to come in on high against the thicket of trees axes,* which is generally understood, *it seems as if men were lifting up axes against a thicket of trees.* The ruthless destroyers go to work like woodcutters in a forest—the carved pillars are no more than so many trees to fell. But though this is intelligible, it does not read like Hebrew, and the contrast apparently intended between the *signs* of the heathen and the *signs* of Israel in verse 9 is not preserved. If, with the LXX., we read the verb in the plural, *are known* instead of *is known,* and supply the subject from the last clause, we get this contrast clearly brought out:

"They have set up their idols as signs,
They (these signs) are known in the lifting up on high."

"These visible idols are easily seen and recognised as soon as set up, but (verse 9) we see not our signs."

According as . . .—We have now, as so frequently, to supply the sign of comparison, and this clause with the next verse runs plainly enough—

"As in a thicket of trees with axes,
So now they break down all the carved work thereof with axes and hammers."

The "carved work" of Solomon's Temple represented *palm-trees* and flowers (1 Kings vi. 29), and possibly these were imitated in the second Temple; if so, the image is very appropriate.

(7) **They have cast fire into.**—Literally, *They have cast into fire thy sanctuary.* Probably a hyperbolic expression, and purporting to express the vastness of the conflagration. Others compare with the English "set on fire," and French *mettre à feu.* We learn from 1 Macc. iv. 38, and Josephus, *Antt.* xii., vii. 6, that Judas Maccabæus, in coming to restore the Temple, found that the gates had been burnt.

(8) **All the synagogues of God in the land.**—This expression excludes from *moed* either of the meanings possible for it in verse 4, "the Temple" or "the assembly." Buildings, and these places of worship, must be meant, and it is implied that they are scattered over the land, and can therefore mean nothing but synagogues. The "high places" would not be called God's, nor would Bethel and Dan have been so called being connected with irregular and unorthodox worship. Thus we have a clear note of time, indicating a period not only later than the rise of the synagogue in Ezra's time, but *much* later, since it takes time for a new institution to spread over a country. Aquila and Symmachus actually render "synagogues." Possibly the LXX. are right in putting the latter clause into the mouth of the enemies, "let us burn," &c.

ther: they have burned up all the synagogues of God in the land. (9) We see not our signs: *there is* no more any prophet: neither *is there* among us any that knoweth how long.

(10) O God, how long shall the adversary reproach? shall the enemy blaspheme thy name for ever? (11) Why withdrawest thou thy hand, even thy right hand? pluck *it* out of thy bosom.

(12) For God *is* my King of old, work-ing salvation in the midst of the earth. (13) ᵃ Thou didst ¹ divide the sea by thy strength: thou brakest the heads of the ² dragons in the waters. (14) Thou brakest the heads of leviathan in pieces, *and* gavest him *to be* meat to the people inhabiting the wilderness. (15) ᵇ Thou didst cleave the fountain and the flood: ᶜ thou driedst up ³ mighty rivers. (16) The day *is* thine, the night also *is* thine: thou hast prepared the light and the sun.

ᵃ Ex. 14. 21.
¹ Heb., *break*.
² Or, *whales*.
ᵇ Ex. 17. 5; Num. 20. 11.
ᶜ Josh. 3. 13.
³ Heb., *rivers of strength*.

---

(9) **We see not our signs . . .**—It is natural to take this statement in direct contrast to what verse 4 (see Note) says of the heathen signs. While these abominations—rallying points of savage profanity—were visibly set up, the tokens of the invisible God's presence, His wonders wrought for Israel, are no more seen.

There is no more any prophet.—This was the constant lament of the Maccabæan period (1 Macc. iv. 46, ix. 27, xiv. 41), and suits no earlier time—at least none into which the rest of the psalm would fit. During the exile period Jeremiah and Ezekiel were prophesying, and the complaint took quite a different form then and probably for some time afterwards (Lam. ii. 9; Ezek. vii. 26). The full desolation of the situation is told in "Song of the Three Children," verse 15: "Neither is there at this time prince, or prophet, or leader, or burnt offering, or sacrifice, or oblation, or incense, or place to sacrifice before Thee or find mercy."

Neither is there among us any that knoweth how long.—This, too, carries us on past the time of Jeremiah, who had given an exact date for the termination of the exile. Probably (if the arrangement of the words is right) we have here another expression of a widely-spread feeling—a feeling which inspired the apocalyptic literature, which had for its object partly to answer this question, how long? But it has been suggested, as more in the Hebrew style, to end the clause with the word *know*, and make it directly parallel with the preceding ("there is neither a prophet nor one who knows"), and carry on the interrogative to the next verse, where its repetition would add much to the force of the question there put. (Burgess.)

(10–15) In the true prophetic spirit, as Moses brought the cries of distress "by reason of their bondage" from the oppressed Israelites to God (Exod. v. 22), so this poet carries to the same God the pathos of this later cry, *How long? how long?* In answer, the deliverances of old rush into his mind. He recalls the right hand once stretched out to save (now thrust in inaction into the bosom), the wonders at the Red Sea, and all the long-continued providential guiding. Surely the same God will do the same wonders now!

(11) **Why withdrawest thou.**—Literally, *returnest*, *i.e.*, into the ample folds of the Eastern robe. The poet is thinking of Exod. iv. 7.

Pluck it out of thy bosom.—Literally, *out of the midst of thy bosom consume.* For the same absolute use of this verb comp. Ps. lix. 13. The clause is an instance of pregnant construction (comp. verse 7), and is plainly equivalent to, *Why dost thou not pluck out thy right hand to consume?*

(12) **For.**—Better, *and*, or *and yet*.

My king.—The poet speaks for Israel. (Comp. Ps. xliv. 4; Hab. i. 12.)

In the midst of the earth.—Or, as we might say, "on the great theatre of the world." Certainly we must not render here *land* instead of *earth*, since the wonders of Egypt, &c., are the theme.

(13) **Thou.**—Verse after verse this emphatic pronoun recurs, as if challenging the Divine Being to contradict.

Divide.—Literally, *break up*.

Dragons.—Hebrew, *tanninim*, not to be confounded with *tannim* (Ps. xliv. 19, where see Note). It is the plural of *tannin*, which always indicates some aquatic monster. In Gen. i. 21 it is translated *whale*, so here by Symmachus. The LXX. (comp. Vulgate) have rendered this word and leviathan (in the next verse) by δράκων, and, indeed, the parallelism indicates monsters of a similar, if not the same, kind. About *leviathan* the minute and faithful description of the *crocodile* in Job xli. does not leave a doubt, and therefore we conclude that the *tannin*, here as in Ezek. xxix. 3, xxxii. 2 (margin), Isa. xxvii. 1, li. 9 (where it is also, as here, joined with *leviathan*), an emblem of Egypt, was some great saurian, perhaps the alligator. The derivation from a root implying *extend*, favours this explanation. (Tristram, *Nat. Hist. of the Bible*, pp. 260, 261.) Besides its abundance, another fact leading to the crocodile becoming an emblem of Egypt, was the adoration paid to it. (See Herod., ii. 69.)

In the waters.—Literally, *on the waters*.

(14) **Leviathan.**—See last note.

And gavest him . . .—The crocodile was eaten by the people of Elephantine (Herod. ii. 69), but there is no allusion here to that custom, nor to the *Ichthyophagi* mentioned by Agatharchides, nor to the Æthiopians (as in the LXX.). It is the Egyptian corpses thrown up by the Red Sea that are to be devoured (comp. Ezek. xxix. 3–5) by the "wild beasts," called here "people," as the ants and conies are (Prov. xxx. 25, 26).

(15) **Thou didst cleave . . .**—Another pregnant expression for "thou didst cleave the rock, and a fountain came forth."

Flood.—Better, *brook*. Heb., *nāchal*.

Mighty rivers.—See margin. But, perhaps, rather, *rivers of constant flow*, that did not dry up in summer like the "brooks." The same word is used of the sea (Exod. xiv. 27), to express the return to the regular flow of the tide.

The verb "driest up" is that used (Josh. ii. 10) of the Red Sea, and chaps. iv. 23, v. 1 of the Jordan.

(16–18) An appeal from the God of history to the God of nature. Not only did He work wonders, but even the universe is the work of His hand

Prayer for Divine Aid   PSALMS, LXXV.   *against the Enemy*

(17) Thou hast set all the borders of the earth: thou hast ¹made summer and winter.

(18) Remember this, *that* the enemy hath reproached, O LORD, and *that* the foolish people have blasphemed thy name.

(19) O deliver not the soul of thy turtle-dove unto the multitude *of the wicked*: forget not the congregation of thy poor for ever. (20) Have respect unto the covenant: for the dark places of the earth are full of the habitations of cruelty. (21) O let not the oppressed return ashamed: let the poor and needy praise thy name.

(22) Arise, O God, plead thine own cause: remember how the foolish man reproacheth thee daily. (23) Forget not the voice of thine enemies: the tumult of those that rise up against thee ²increaseth continually.

PSALM LXXV.

To the chief Musician, ³Al-taschith, A Psalm *or* Song ⁴ of Asaph.

(1) Unto thee, O God, do we give thanks, *unto thee* do we give thanks: for *that* thy name is near thy wondrous works declare.

(2) ⁵ When I shall receive the congregation I will judge uprightly.

(3) The earth and all the inhabitants thereof are dissolved: I bear up the pillars of it. Selah.

Marginal notes:
1 Heb., *made them.*
2 Heb., *ascendeth.*
3 Or, *Destroy not.*
4 Or, *for Asaph.*
5 Or, *When I shall take a set time.*

---

(16) **The light and the sun.**—Evidently from Gen. i. 14, 16, where the same word occurs for the heavenly luminary generally, and then for the sun as chief.

(17) **All the borders of the earth**—*i.e.*, earth in all directions, and to its utmost bounds; as we say, "from pole to pole."

(18) **Remember this.**—Emphatical; the object of the enemy's reproach is the Being who has done all these mighty works, and is the author of all this wonderful world.

(19) **O deliver.**—To guide to the meaning of this verse, the word *chayyah* occurs in each clause, and it is presumable in the same sense (unless there is a purposed play on words). It may have one of three meanings: "life," "animal," "troop." Ps. xvii. 9 suggests that *chayyath nephesh* go together in the sense of "greedy band," and we get—

"Deliver not to the greedy band thy dove;
Forget not the band of the afflicted for ever."

(20) **Habitations.**—The word thus rendered is so consistently used of the "quiet resting-places" of God's people that it seems quite impossible that the psalmist should have used the expression, "resting-places of cruelty." A slight change in the text gives, "Look upon the covenant, for they have filled (Thy) land with darkness, Thy quiet dwelling with violence" (Burgess, *Notes on the Hebrew Psalms*).

(21) **Oppressed.**—Literally, *crushed*. (See Ps. ix. 9, x. 18.)

(22, 23) These verses show that the psalm was actually composed amidst the dark days it describes. It ends in expostulatory prayer, with as yet no brighter gleam of hope than prayer itself implies—and that when seemingly directed to deaf ears.

LXXV.

The note of despair in the last psalm is succeeded here by one of mingled expectancy and exultation. It is as if the pathetic question, "How long?" had suddenly and unexpectedly been answered by the appearance of a deliverer, sent, like one of the judges of old, exactly at the needful moment. East and west and south and north the eyes of Israel had been turned, and lo! in their midst is raised up one to save. No period in the history suits this attitude like the early days of the Asmonean successes. Mattathias and his sons are those whom God "setteth up." The "horn" that is to be cut off is Antiochus Epiphanes, who in the Book of Daniel is described as "a little horn, which waxed exceeding great towards the south, and towards the east, and towards the pleasant land" (Dan. viii. 9).

The psalm, whatever period produced it, is almost throughout inspired by the ancient song of Hannah (1 Sam. ii.), but borrows its most prominent image, that of the cup of wrath, from the prophetic books. It is not, therefore, original, but, at the same time, is not wanting in lyric power, nor deficient in rhythm. It opens with a couplet of praise, and then, with an abruptness which gives a dramatic turn, introduces God pronouncing the restoration of right and order. At verse 6 the poet resumes in his own person, but concludes with another Divine utterance.

Title.—See titles Pss. iv., lvii., lviii.

(1) **For that . . .**—The wonders just wrought for Israel have repeated the old conviction that God's name, a word of power to save (comp. Pss. xxxiv. 18, cxlv. 18), is near. (Comp. Ps. cv. 1.)

(2) **When I.**—Rather, *When I have chosen my time, I will judge uprightly*. This sense: "my time" being shown by the emphatic "I" of the Hebrew. (Comp. Acts xvii. 31.) The word rendered in the Authorised Version "congregation" (*moed*), has plainly here its first derivative sense of a set time, or "occasion." (Comp. Ps. cii. 13; Hab. ii. 3.) So LXX. and Vulg. here; but Symmachus gives "synagogue."

It is quite clear that the speaker of these words is God Himself, who suddenly, as in Ps. xlvi. 10, breaks in with the announcement of judgment. But how far the Divine utterance extends in the psalm is not quite clear. Some end it with verse 3; others with verse 5.

(3) **The earth . . .**—Better—

"Are earth and all its inhabitants dissolved?
It was I adjusted its pillars."

(See Hannah's song, 1 Sam. ii. 8.) Though the crisis be such that all is confusion and anarchy (comp. Isa. xxiv. 19, 20 for the figure), there is no cause for fear; there is still a Ruler in heaven, He who built up the edifice which now seems to totter to its fall. The verb rendered in the Authorised Version "bear up," is used in Job xxviii. 15, Isa. xl. 12 in the sense of "weighing" or "measuring;" but with the same allu-

⁽⁴⁾ I said unto the fools, Deal not foolishly: and to the wicked, Lift not up the horn: ⁽⁵⁾ lift not up your horn on high: speak *not with* a stiff neck. ⁽⁶⁾ For promotion *cometh* neither from the east, nor from the west, nor from the ¹ south. ⁽⁷⁾ But God *is* the judge: he putteth down one, and setteth up another.

⁽⁸⁾ For in the hand of the Lord *there is* a cup, and the wine is red; it is full of mixture; and he poureth out of the same: but the dregs thereof, all the wicked of the earth shall wring *them* out, *and* drink *them*.

⁽⁹⁾ But I will declare for ever; I will sing praises to the God of Jacob. ⁽¹⁰⁾ All the horns of the wicked also will I cut off; *but* the horns of the righteous shall be exalted.

1 Heb., *desert*.

2 Or, *for Asaph*.

PSALM LXXVI.

To the chief Musician on Neginoth, A Psalm *or* Song ² of Asaph.

⁽¹⁾ In Judah *is* God known: his name *is* great in Israel. ⁽²⁾ In Salem also is

---

sion to the creative work of God. Here it plainly means, so to adjust the pillars as to make them equal to the weight they have to bear.

The "pillars" are the "mountains," as in Job xxvi. 11. (See Note, Ps. xxiv. 2.) Comp. Shelley—

"Sunbeam proof, I hang like a roof,
The mountains its columns are."

⁽⁴⁾ **Fools ... foolishly.**—Better, *arrogant ... arrogantly.* See Ps. lxxiii. 3. (Comp. 1 Sam. ii. 3.)

⁽⁵⁾ **Lift not up your horn.**—The "horn" is a symbol of *honour* (Ps. cxii. 9); of *strength* (Micah iv. 13; Deut. xxxiii. 17). The figure is taken from horned animals. (See 1 Sam. ii. 1, 10.)

With a stiff neck.—Better, *with the neck proudly or wantonly raised.*

⁽⁶⁾ **For promotion . . .**—The Authorised Version has here rightly set aside the pointing of the text, which, as the LXX. and Vulg., reads—

"For not from the east, nor from the west,
Nor from the wilderness of mountains,"

a sentence which has no conclusion. The recurrence also of parts of the verb "to lift up" in verses 4, 5, 7, makes in favour of taking *harim* as part of the same verb here, instead of as a noun, "mountains." That the word *midbar* (wilderness) might be used for "south," receives support from Acts viii. 26.

Ewald thinks the four points of the compass should be completed by inserting a conjunction, and taking the "desert" and "mountains" to represent respectively the *south* and *north*. He then supplies the conclusion of the sentence from the following verse:—

"For neither from east nor west,
Neither from desert nor mountains,
Cometh judgment; but God is Judge."

This agrees with 1 Sam. ii. 10; but it is hardly needful to expect such scientific accuracy as to the points of the compass in Hebrew poetry.

⁽⁸⁾ **A cup.**—The figure of the cup of Divine fury is developed, as Psalm xi. 6 compared with Psalm xvi. 5 shows, from the more general one which represents life itself as a draught which must be drunk, bitter or sweet, according to the portion assigned. It appears again in Psalm lx. 3, and is worked out in prophetic books, Isa. li. 17; Hab. ii. 16, &c.; Ezek. xxiii. 32—34, and frequently in Jeremiah. The mode of its introduction here, after the statement that God "putteth down one and setteth up another," shows that the poet, in speaking of a "mixture," thinks of the *good* and *bad* commingled in the cup, which are, of course, poured out to those whose portion is to be *happiness* and *misery* in Israel; while for the heathen, the "wicked of the earth" (possibly including apostate Jews), only the *dregs* are left to be drained. There are, however, many obscure expressions.

Is red.—Better, *foameth*, from the rapid pouring out.

Mixture.—Heb., *mesekh*; which, like *mezeg*, may properly denote aromatic wine (wine mixed with spices), but here seems rather to imply the blending of the portions destined for the good and bad in Israel.

Wring.—Better, *drain*. (See Ps. lxxiii. 10.)

The LXX. and Vulg. seem to have had a slightly different text before them, and one which still more distinctly points to the interpretation given above: "Because in the hand of the Lord a cup of unmixed wine, full of mixture, and he turned it from this side to that, but its dregs were not emptied, all the sinners of the earth shall drink of them." The text has "poureth from this;" the word, "to that," may have dropped out.

⁽¹⁰⁾ **Will I cut.**—The Divine speaker again abruptly takes up the word in this verse. (For the abruptness, comp. Isa. xlviii. 15.) The "cutting off of the horns" recalls Zech. i. 18 *seq.*; Lam. ii. 3.

LXXVI.

The LXX. (followed by the Vulgate) have added to the Hebrew inscription of this psalm the words "to the Assyrian," indicating that at an early period it was, as it is still by many modern scholars, connected with the overthrow of Sennacherib. Certainly the verses 5 and 6 are most suitable to that event. On the other hand, the phrase in verse 9, "all the afflicted of the land," breathes of a time of national oppression, and suggests a later date. Verses 8 and 9 compared with verses 7, 8 of Ps. lxxv. lead to the conclusion that both were inspired by the Song of Hannah and may both refer to the same circumstances. And some critics not only bring it into the Maccabæan age, but fix on the victory of Judas over Seron (1 Macc. iii.) as the actual event celebrated in this poem. The versification is quite regular.

Title.—See title Pss. iv., l., lxv.

⁽¹⁾ **Judah ... Israel.**—A comparison with Ps. cxiv. 1, 2, leads to the conclusion that these names are introduced here in this order, simply for the rhythm. (Comp. "Salem" and "Sion" in the next verse, and notice that the four names offer an instance of introversion, the more restricted terms, Judah, Sion, occupying the first and last clauses, the more general Israel, Salem, the middle ones.)

⁽²⁾ **Salem.**—The LXX. and Vulgate translate "his place was in peace," and possibly the poet may use the

his tabernacle, and his dwelling place in Zion. (3) There brake he the arrows of the bow, the shield and the sword, and the battle. Selah.

(4) Thou *art* more glorious *and* excellent than the mountains of prey. (5) The stouthearted are spoiled, they have slept their sleep: and none of the men of might have found their hands. (6) At thy rebuke, O God of Jacob, both the chariot and horse are cast into a dead sleep.

(7) Thou, *even thou*, *art* to be feared: and who may stand in thy sight when once thou art angry? (8) Thou didst cause judgment to be heard from heaven; the earth feared, and was still, (9) when God arose to judgment, to save all the meek of the earth. Selah.

(10) Surely the wrath of man shall praise thee: the remainder of wrath shalt thou restrain.

(11) Vow, and pay unto the LORD your God: let all that be round about him bring presents [1] unto him that ought to be feared. (12) He shall cut off the spirit of princes: *he is* terrible to the kings of the earth.

PSALM LXXVII.

To the chief Musician, to Jeduthun, A Psalm [2] of Asaph.

(1) I cried unto God with my voice,

[1] Heb., *to fear*.

[2] Or, *for Asaph*.

---

word *Salem* with the thought in his mind of the peace won by God for Judah, or, again, it may be only a poet's preference for an ancient over a modern name; but the identification of the Salem of Gen. xiv. 18 with Jerusalem is too doubtful to allow much weight to this view. (See the whole question discussed in Sir G. Grove's article on "Salem," in Smith's *Bibl. Dict.*)

Tabernacle ... dwelling-place.—These renderings quite obliterate the image, which is that of a beast of prey crouching ready for its spring. Translate,

"In Salem is his covert,
And his lair in Sion."

and for these meanings of the Hebrew words *sokh* and *meónah* comp. Ps. x. 9; Jer. xxv. 38; Ps. civ. 22; Amos iii. 4.

(3) **There.**—This word in Ps. xiv. 5 does not appear to have a strictly definite local sense; and here may refer to time, possibly to some event, which we are not able with certainty to recover.

Arrows.—Literally, *flashes*. (See Note, Song of Sol. viii. 6.) The image may be derived from the lightning speed of the flight of arrows, or from the custom of shooting bolts tipped with flame (see Note, Ps. vii. 13), or the connection may be from the metaphor in Ps. xci. 5, 6, since the Hebrew word here used denotes pestilence in Hab. iii. 5.

The shield, the sword, and the battle—Hos. ii. 18 is the original of this. (Comp. Ps. xlvi. 9.) Notice the fine poetic touch in the climactic use of battle to sum up all the weapons of war.

(4) **Thou art ...**—Better, *Splendid art thou, glorious one, from the mountains of prey*. The construction is somewhat doubtful and favours Hupfeld's emendation (*nora, i.e., to be feared*, as in verses 8 and 13, instead of *noar, i.e., glorious*). Certainly the comparative of the Authorised Version is to be abandoned. The poet's thought plainly proceeds from the figure of verse 2. The mountains are the *mountains of prey* of the Lion of Judah. True, a different image, as so frequently in Hebrew poetry, suddenly interrupts and changes the picture. The hero appears from the battle shining in the spoils taken from the foe.

(5) **Are spoiled.**—Literally, *have let themselves be spoiled*. The picture is of men rendered powerless, at a glance, a word, from God.

Slept their sleep.—Better, *have sunk into a deep sleep*.

None of the men of might have found their hands.—This expression for powerlessness naturally grew into an idiom in a language that used the word *hand* as a synonym for *strength*. (Comp. Josh. viii. 20, margin; Exod. xiv. 31, margin; Deut. xxxii. 36, margin.) Delitzsch quotes a Talmudic phrase, "We did not find our hands and feet in the school house." We may compare the Virgilian use of *manus* (*Æn.* vi. 688), and Shakspeare's "a proper fellow of my hands," and for the use of "find" compare the common phrase "find one's tongue."

(6) **Are cast into a deep sleep.**—The same Hebrew expression is used of Sisera's profound slumber (Judges iv. 21). Deborah's Song and Exod. xv. are in the poet's mind, as they were to the author of Isa. xliii. 17, and as they have inspired the well-known lines of Byron's "Sennacherib."

(9) **Of the earth.**—Or, *of the land*.

(10) **Surely.**—The text of this verse as it stands is unintelligible—

"Surely the wrath of man shall praise Thee;
The residue of wrath Thou shalt gird Thyself with."

But the LXX. and Vulg. suggest the necessary emendation—

"Surely the wrath of man shall praise Thee,
And the residue of wraths do Thee honour,"

where the residue of wrath, like Virgil's *reliquiæ Danaum* (*Æn.* i. 30), means those that escape the enemies' rage, *i.e.*, the Israelites. Possibly we should render, " and those who remain from their wrath shall celebrate a festival," since the suggested emendation is the word used in that sense. And we must therefore think of the escape of Israel from Egypt (see above), and the festival which was so repeatedly announced to Pharaoh, as the purpose of their exodus. (See Burgess, *Notes on the Hebrew Psalms*.)

(11) **Vow, and pay ...**—This clause seems to be addressed to the Israelites, the next to the heathen.

(12) **He shall cut off ...**—Literally, *lop off*, as a vinedresser prunes a vine. For the image see Joel iii. 13; Isa. xviii. 5; Rev. xiv. 17 *seq*.

Spirit—*i.e.*, the life.

LXXVII.

The affliction out of which the mournful cry of this psalm rises is presented in such general terms that there is no single indication by which to refer it to one period more than another. As the consolation is sought entirely in the history of national deliverance,

even unto God with my voice; and he gave ear unto me. (2) In the day of my trouble I sought the Lord: ¹ my sore ran in the night, and ceased not: my soul refused to be comforted. (3) I remembered God, and was troubled: I complained, and my spirit was overwhelmed. Selah.

(4) Thou holdest mine eyes waking: I am so troubled that I cannot speak. (5) I have considered the days of old, the years of ancient times. (6) I call to remembrance my song in the night: I commune with mine own heart: and my spirit made diligent search.

(7) Will the Lord cast off for ever? and will he be favourable no more? (8) Is his mercy clean gone for ever? doth *his* promise fail ² for evermore? (9) Hath God forgotten to be gracious? hath he in anger shut up his tender mercies? Selah.

(10) And I said, This *is* my infirmity: *but I will remember* the years of the right hand of the most High. (11) I will remember the works of the LORD:

1 Heb., *my hand.*

2 Heb., *to generation and generation.*

---

and not in any display of divine goodness toward the author individually, it is safe to conclude that the troubles described are also national rather than personal. At all events, for the time the poet's individuality is entirely merged in the sense of public calamity. The question whether the psalm, or Hab. iii. 10—15, which at its close it resembles, is the original, would, if it could be decided, be some guide in ascertaining the date of the composition. But there appear arguments equally strong on both sides of this question. There is a striking change of rhythm at verse 16, otherwise the structure is regular.

Title.—See title Pss. iv., xxxix.

(1) **I cried . . .**—Better, following the Hebrew literally,

"My voice to God—and let me cry;
My voice to God—and He hears me."

The Authorised Version has followed the LXX. and Vulg. in neglecting the striking changes in mood running through this psalm. Soliloquy and narrative alternate as the poet's mood impels him—now to give vent to his feelings in sobs and cries, now to analyse and describe them.

(2) **My sore ran . . .**—The text of this verse is evidently faulty. As it stands it is unintelligible. *My hand was poured out and grew not dull* (like a corpse). The LXX. and Vulg. have, "with my hands against Him, and I was not deceived," pointing to a different reading. Symmachus has, however, "my hand was stretched out," which may be a possible meaning of the Hebrew, though a comparison with Lam. iii. 49 (comp. chap. ii. 18) suggests that *eye* was written instead of *hand.* The Authorised Version's *sore* comes from the Rabbins, who thought of the hand beating the breast, and rendered, "my blows were poured out." Though the probable text may be beyond recovery, the feeling of the verse is quite palpable. It expresses the anguish of the poet's soul—

"His vows in the night, so fierce and unavailing,
Stings of his shame and passion of his tears."

(3) **I remembered.**—Better,

"If I remember God I must sigh;
I meditate, and my spirit faints."

Or,

"Let me remember God, and sigh;
I must complain, and my spirit faints."

The word rendered *overwhelmed* (comp. Pss. cxlii. 3, cxliii. 4) means properly *covers itself up.* In Ps. cvii. 5 it is translated *fainted.*

(4) **Thou holdest mine eyes waking.**—Rather, *Thou hast closed the guards of my eyes*—i.e., my eyelids. The Authorised Version mistakes the noun, *guards,* for a participle, and mistranslates it by the *active* instead of the *passive.* For the verb *hold* in the sense of *shut,* see Nehem. vii. 3, and Job xxvi. 9, where God is described as veiling His throne in cloud, and so shutting it up, as it were, from the access of men.

I am so troubled.—The verb is used elsewhere of the *awestruck* state into which the mind is thrown by a mysterious dream (Gen. xli. 8; Dan. ii. 1, 3), and once (Judges xiii. 25) of inspiration, such as impelled the judges of old to become the liberators of their country. The parallelism here shows that it is used in the first connection. The poet has been *struck dumb* (the verb is rendered *strike* in the Lexicons) by a mysterious dream; he is too overawed to speak.

(6) **I call to remembrance.**—Better,

"Let me recall my harpings in the night;
Let me complain in my own heart,
And my spirit questions and questions."

(7—9) The self-questionings here follow as they rise sigh after sigh in the poet's heart. God's silences have always been more appalling to the human spirit than even the most terrible of His manifestations. To the pious Israelite, to whom the past history of his race appeared one scene of opportune interpositions to save at the moment when distress became too intolerable, it seemed as if the divine protection was altogether withdrawn when the misery was protracted and the sign of help withheld.

(10) **And I said . . .**—The word rendered "infirmity" may, by derivation, mean "wounding" or "piercing." So Symmachus, "my wound;" Aquila, "my sickness." Gesenius says, "that which makes my sickness." If we keep this meaning we must understand mental sickness or "madness," and understand the poet to say that to indulge in despairing cries is mere madness (comp. King Lear's, "Oh! that way madness lies"), he will recall God's ancient deliverances, and so re-establish his faith. But it seems more natural to take a sense which the cognate verb very commonly bears (Lev. xix. 8; Ezek. xxxvi. 22; Pss. lxxiv. 7, lxxxix. 39), and render, "I said this (such despair) is on my part profanation, profanation of the years of the right hand of the Most High." To despair of continued help from One who had been so gracious in the past is a kind of blasphemy. The word "profanation" must be understood as repeated for the sake of the grammar.

(11) **I will remember.**—The written text is, "I will celebrate." The intention is the same in both cases. Instead of continuing to despair, the poet re-

and His Deliverances PSALMS, LXXVIII. *of His People.*

surely I will remember thy wonders of old. ⁽¹²⁾ I will meditate also of all thy work, and talk of thy doings.

⁽¹³⁾ Thy way, O God, *is* in the sanctuary: who *is so* great a God as *our* God? ⁽¹⁴⁾ Thou *art* the God that doest wonders: thou hast declared thy strength among the people. ⁽¹⁵⁾ Thou hast with *thine* arm redeemed thy people, the sons of Jacob and Joseph. Selah.

⁽¹⁶⁾ The waters saw thee, O God, the waters saw thee; they were afraid: the depths also were troubled. ⁽¹⁷⁾ ¹ The clouds poured out water: the skies sent out a sound: thine arrows also went abroad. ⁽¹⁸⁾ The voice of thy thunder *was* in the heaven: the lightnings lightened the world: the earth trembled and shook. ⁽¹⁹⁾ Thy way *is* in the sea, and thy path in the great waters, and thy footsteps are not known.

⁽²⁰⁾ ᵃ Thou leddest thy people like a flock by the hand of Moses and Aaron.

¹ Heb., *the clouds were poured forth with water.*

ᵃ Ex. 14. 19.

² Or, *A Psalm for Asaph to give instruction.*

PSALM LXXVIII.

² Maschil of Asaph.

⁽¹⁾ Give ear, O my people, *to* my law: incline your ears to the words of my mouth.

---

solves on seeking encouragement for his faith in grateful praise of God for past mercies, and especially for the ancient deliverance from Egypt, which occupies the prominent place in his thoughts; "works" and "wonders" should be in the singular, referring to this one mighty deliverance.

⁽¹³⁾ **In the sanctuary.**—Rather, *with the holy, i.e.,* with "Israel," the "saint" of God.

(16—20) The prominence given to Joseph is a feature common to the Asaphic psalm. With this magnificent lyric of the passage of the Red Sea comp. Hab. iii. 10, 11. The narrative in Exodus says nothing of a storm, but Josephus has preserved the tradition (*Ant.,* ii. 16. 3). Philo also mentions the storm.

⁽¹⁶⁾ **The waters saw thee.**—Possibly alluding to the "look" which troubled the Egyptians (Exod. xiv. 24).

Were afraid.—Better, *writhed,* as in travail pains.

Went abroad—*i.e.,* darted hither and thither. The arrows are the lightnings.

⁽¹⁸⁾ **In the heavens.**—Literally, *in the vault.* The Hebrew, *galgal,* from *gālal,* "to roll," has the same derivation as "vault" (*volutum,* from *volvo*). It is strange that this rendering, which so well suits the parallelism, should have been set aside by modern scholars in favour of "whirlwind" or "rolling chariot wheels." The LXX. and Vulg. have 'wheel," but possibly with reference to the apparent revolution of the sky. The word, where it occurs in Isa. xvii. 13, means something rolled by the whirlwind, not the whirlwind itself.

⁽¹⁹⁾ **Are not known.**—"We know not, they knew not, by what precise means the deliverance was wrought; we know not by what precise track through the gulf the passage was effected. We know not; we need not know. The obscuring, the mystery, here as elsewhere, was part of the lesson. . . . All that we see distinctly is, that through this dark and terrible night, with the enemy pressing close behind, and the driving sea on either side, He led His people like sheep by the hand of Moses and Aaron" (Stanley, *Jewish Church,* i. 128).

To some minds the abruptness of the conclusion of the psalm marks it as unfinished. But no better end could have been reached in the poet's perplexity than that to which he has been led by his musings on the past, the thought of the religious aids ready to his hand, in the faith and worship left by Moses and Aaron. We are reminded of him who recalled the thoughts of the young man, searching for a higher ideal of duty, back to the law and obedience. Or if the psalm is rather an expression of the feeling of the community than of an individual, there is a pointed significance in the conclusion given to all the national cries of doubt and despair—the one safe course was to remain loyal and true to the ancient institutions.

LXXVIII.

This is the first and the longest specimen in the Hebrew hymn-book of a species of composition peculiar to it, and indeed peculiar to the literature of the Jews, as combining narrative with instruction. It has been rightly called "epi-didactic." It does not tell the story of the past with any view of celebrating heroic ancestors, or exalting conspicuous national virtues. On the contrary, it is a long confession of national failings. The Biblical conception of history is always religious, and, therefore, practical, and here the utmost prominence is given to those lapses from loyalty to Jehovah, against which the poet is covertly warning his own generation.

But while it thus expresses the pious feelings of the writer and his age, it is entirely characteristic in giving equal emphasis to their exclusiveness, and that not the exclusiveness of a nation only, or a religion, but of one tribe of a nation, and one doctrine of the religion. It is impossible to resist the conclusion that the author is quite as much concerned to establish the Divine purpose in rejecting Ephraim in favour of Judah, as in choosing Israel as a nation in distinction from the heathen. At the very outset, as soon as the faithlessness and perversity of the nation have been mentioned, Ephraim is singled out as the chief and typical example of disloyalty (verse 9). The conclusion of the psalm from verse 67 dwells with genuine satisfaction on the rejection of the northern tribes, and on the exclusive choice as the seat of the theocracy of the southern tribe, Judah. This prominence given to the disruption has led some critics to date the poem at the time of that event. But other considerations enter into the question. The "high places" are mentioned (verse 58) as one of the causes of the Divine wrath, a sentiment that only entered into the religious feeling of even the better minds about the time of Hezekiah. (See Kuenen's *Religion of Israel,* i. 79, 80, Eng. trans.) The poetical form is very irregular.

Title.—See Ps. xxxii. 1.

⁽¹⁾ For the formal opening see Ps. xlix. 1, Note.

My people.—An expression pointing to a position of weight and authority.

My law.—Here, rather *instruction,* or *doctrine.*

201

(2) *a* I will open my mouth in a parable: I will utter dark sayings of old: (3) which we have heard and known, and our fathers have told us. (4) We will not hide *them* from their children, shewing to the generation to come the praises of the LORD, and his strength, and his wonderful works that he hath done. (5) For he established a testimony in Jacob, and appointed a law in Israel, which he commanded our fathers, *b* that they should make them known to their children: (6) that the generation to come might know *them,* even the children *which* should be born; *who* should arise and declare *them* to their children: (7) that they might set their hope in God, and not forget the works of God, but keep his commandments: (8) and might not be as their fathers, a stubborn and rebellious generation; a generation ¹ *that* set not their heart aright,

and whose spirit was not stedfast with God. (9) The children of Ephraim, *being* armed, *and* ² carrying bows, turned back in the day of battle. (10) They kept not the covenant of God, and refused to walk in his law; (11) and forgat his works, and his wonders that he had shewed them. (12) Marvellous things did he in the sight of their fathers, in the land of Egypt, *in* the field of Zoan. (13) *c* He divided the sea, and caused them to pass through; and he made the waters to stand as an heap. (14) *d* In the daytime also he led them with a cloud, and all the night with a light of fire. (15) *e* He clave the rocks in the wilderness, and gave *them* drink as *out of* the great depths. (16) He brought streams also out of the rock, and caused waters to run down like rivers.

a Ps. 49. 4; Matt. 13. 35.
b Deut. 4. 9, & 6. 7.
¹ Heb., *that prepared not their heart.*
² Heb., *throwing forth.*
c Ex. 14. 21.
d Ex. 13. 21, & 14. 21.
e Ex. 17. 6; Num. 20. 11; Ps. 105. 41; 1 Cor. 10. 4.

(2, 3) **I will open.**—A difficulty is started by the fact that the psalm deals with history, and is neither a proverb (*māshal*) nor riddle (*chidah*). But the Divine rejection of the northern tribes may be the covert meaning which the poet sees to have been wrapped up in all the ancient history. The word *māshal* is also sometimes used in a wide, vague sense, embracing prophetic as well as proverbial poetry. (See Num. xxi. 27.)

For "dark sayings," literally, *knotty points,* see Num. xii. 8. In Hab. ii. 6 the word seems to mean a *sarcasm.*

For the use of this passage in Matt. xiii. 35, see Note, *New Testament Commentary.*

(5) **For he . . .**—Better, taking the relative of time (comp. Deut. xi. 6; Ps. cxxxix. 15), *For he established (it as) a testimony in Jacob and (as) a law appointed (it) in Israel when he commanded our forefathers to make them* (the "*wonderful works*" of last verse) *known to their children.* For the custom see reference in margin.

(8) **Stubborn.**—*Refractory.*

That set not their heart aright.—Literally, *did not establish their heart,* which preserves the parallelism better.

(9) **Armed, and carrying bows.**—Following Jer. iv. 29, and from analogy with Jer. xliv. 9 ("handle and bend the bow") we get as literal rendering of the Hebrew here, *drawing and shooting with the bow.* LXX. and Vulgate, "bending and shooting with the bow." But a close comparison of this verse with verse 57 of this psalm, and with Hos. vii. 16, has suggested to a recent commentator a much more satisfactory explanation, *The sons of Ephraim (are like men) drawing slack bowstrings which turn back in the day of battle.* "Both the disappointment on the day of battle and the cause of the disappointment, which are mentioned in the text, will be appreciated by the English reader who remembers that the result of the battle of Crecy was determined at the outset by a shower of rain which relaxed the strings of our enemy's bows" (Burgess, *Notes on the Hebrew Psalms.*)*

By taking this sense of a comparison of the general character of Ephraim to a bow with a relaxed string that fails at the moment it is wanted (a figure made more expressive by the fact that archery was a practice in which Ephraim excelled), we are freed from the necessity of conjecturing a particular incident to account for this verse, which seems to break the sequence of thought. The whole historical retrospect is intended to lead up to the rejection of the northern kingdom (represented by Ephraim), but the poet is unable to keep back his climax, and thrusts it in here almost parenthetically.

(12) **Field of Zoan.**—See Num. xiii. 22. It is the classical "Tanis," merely a corruption of *Tsoan, i.e.,* low country (LXX. and Vulgate). Tanis is situated on the east bank of what was formerly called the Tanitic branch of the Nile. Between it and Pelusium, about thirty miles to the east, stretched a rich plain known as "the marshes," or "the pastures," or "the field" of Zoan.

The psalm now turns to the adventures in the wilderness, postponing the marvels in Egypt till verse 43.

(13) **As an heap.**—See Note, Ps. xxxiii. 7.

(15) **And gave . . .**—Literally, *and gave them to drink as it were a great deep,* or as we might say, "oceans of drink"—a poetical exaggeration; or are we rather to think of the gift of water as produced by striking or boring through the rock to the great ocean on which the earth was supposed to rest?

(16) **Rock.**—Rather, *cliff — sela,* the word always used of the event that took place at Kadesh (Num. xx. 8—11), as *tsûr* is of the rock in Horeb. The plural of this latter word in verse 15 is poetical and general.

---

* This translation assumes that the primitive meaning of the verb *rāmah* is *was slack.* Certainly the root idea of the word (comp. the cognate *rāphah* and the meaning of the derivation in Prov. x. 4, xii. 24) seems to have been *relaxation.* That *turned back,* both here and in verse 57, refers to the *recoil* of a bow, seems indubitable.

in their Journey.   PSALMS, LXXVIII.   *through the Wilderness.*

(17) And they sinned yet more against him by provoking the most High in the wilderness. (18) And they tempted God in their heart by asking meat for their lust. (19) ᵃ Yea, they spake against God; they said, Can God ¹ furnish a table in the wilderness? (20) ᵇ Behold, he smote the rock, that the waters gushed out, and the streams overflowed; can he give bread also? can he provide flesh for his people?

(21) Therefore the LORD heard *this*, and was wroth: so a fire was kindled against Jacob, and anger also came up against Israel; (22) because they believed not in God, and trusted not in his salvation: (23) though he had commanded the clouds from above, and opened the doors of heaven, (24) ᶜ and had rained down manna upon them to eat, and had given them of the corn of heaven.

(25) ² Man did eat angels' food: he sent them meat to the full. (26) He caused an east wind ³ to blow in the heaven: and by his power he brought in the south wind. (27) He rained flesh also upon them as dust, and ⁴ feathered fowls like as the sand of the sea: (28) and he let *it* fall in the midst of their camp, round about their habitations. (29) So they did eat, and were well filled: for he gave them their own desire; (30) they were not estranged from their lust. But ᵈ while their meat *was* yet in their mouths, (31) the wrath of God came upon them, and slew the fattest of them, and ⁵ smote down the ⁶ chosen *men* of Israel.

(32) For all this they sinned still, and believed not for his wondrous works. (33) Therefore their days did he consume in vanity, and their years in trouble. (34) When he slew them, then they sought him: and they returned and enquired early after God. (35) And they remembered that God *was* their rock, and the high God their redeemer. (36) Nevertheless they did flatter him with their mouth, and they lied unto him with their tongues. (37) For their heart was not right with him; neither were they stedfast in his covenant. (38) But he, *being* full of compassion, forgave *their* iniquity, and destroyed *them* not: yea, many a time turned he his anger away, and did not stir up all his wrath. (39) For he remembered that they *were but* flesh; a wind that passeth away, and cometh not again.

(40) How oft did they ⁷ provoke him in the wilderness, *and* grieve him in the desert! (41) Yea, they turned back and tempted God, and limited the Holy One of Israel. (42) They remembered not his hand, *nor* the day when he delivered them ⁸ from the enemy. (43) How he

---

a Num. 11. 4.

¹ Heb., *order.*

b Ex. 17. 6; Num. 20. 11.

c Ex. 16. 14; John 6. 31.

² Or, *Every one did eat the bread of the mighty.*

³ Heb., *to go.*

⁴ Heb., *fowl of wing.*

d Num. 11. 33.

⁵ Heb., *made to bow.*

⁶ Or, *young men.*

⁷ Or, *rebel against him.*

⁸ Or, *from affliction.*

---

(17) **They sinned yet more and more.**—This implies the discontent which had already shown itself before the miraculous supply of water.

(19, 20) A comparison of these verses with the references in the margin shows how the ancient narratives fared under poetical treatment.

Furnish a table.—Comp. Ps. xxiii. 5, Note
Gushed out.—Comp. Ps. cv. 41.

(21) See references in margin.

(25) **Angels' food.**—See margin, and comp. Wisd. xvi. 20. LXX. and Vulgate, "angels' bread." Some explain, after Job xxiv. 22, xxxiv. 30, *lordly* food, such as *nobles* eat—here, *quails*. But in connection with "food from heaven," the popular idea of angels' food which poetry reluctantly gives up may be retained.

(26) **East wind ... south wind.**—Probably the very winds that brought the flights of quails, and not merely poetical details. (See Smith's *Biblical Dictionary*, art. "Quails.")

(27) No doubt there is poetical hyperbole here, but for the enormous numbers of quails that are now caught, see the article quoted above.

(29) **Desire.**—See Num. xi. 34, margin.

(30, 31) Evidently from Num. xi. 33, *They did not yet loath in consequence of their lusts, the meat was yet in their mouths when*, &c. For the expression, comp. the Latin *alienari ab aliqua re*, "to be disinclined to a thing, and our own "stranger to fear," &c.

(31) **Slew the fattest.**—This may mean either the *strongest* or the *noblest*.

(32–33) For the allusion see Num. xiv. 11—12, 28—35.

(35) **Rock.**—A reminiscence of Deut. xxxii. 15—18.

(38) The verbs in the first clause should be in the present, *But he, the compassionate, forgives iniquity, and doth not destroy, and many a time he turned away,* &c.

(39) "And what's a life? A blast sustained with clothing:
    Maintained with food, retained with vile self-loathing;
    Then, weary of itself, away to nothing."—
                               QUARLES: *Emblems.*

(40) **How oft.**—Ten instances of murmuring are actually recorded in Exodus and Numbers.

(41) **Limited.**—A verb used in Ezek. ix. 4 for putting a mark on the forehead, which has been very variously explained. Some render *branded* or *cast a stigma on*—*i.e.,* brought discredit on the Divine name. The LXX. and Vulg. have "exasperated," and so some moderns "crossed," "thwarted." Grätz emends to "asked signs from," but perhaps the ideas of marking something that has been *tried*, and that of *trying* or *tempting* are sufficiently near to allow us to render *tempted*.

(42) The reminiscence of the plagues that follows is not a complete enumeration, and does not proceed in the order of the historic narrative.

The Deliverance of Israel PSALMS, LXXVIII. *and their Punishments.*

had ¹ wrought his signs in Egypt, and his wonders in the field of Zoan: ⁽⁴⁴⁾ ᵃ and had turned their rivers into blood; and their floods, that they could not drink. ⁽⁴⁵⁾ ᵇ He sent divers sorts of flies among them, which devoured them; and frogs, which destroyed them. ⁽⁴⁶⁾ ᶜ He gave also their increase unto the caterpiller, and their labour unto the locust. ⁽⁴⁷⁾ ᵈ He ² destroyed their vines with hail, and their sycomore-trees with ³ frost. ⁽⁴⁸⁾ ⁴ He gave up their cattle also to the hail, and their flocks to ⁵ hot thunderbolts. ⁽⁴⁹⁾ He cast upon them the fierceness of his anger, wrath, and indignation, and trouble, by sending evil angels *among them*. ⁽⁵⁰⁾ ⁶ He made a way to his anger; he spared not their soul from death, but gave ⁷ their life over to the pestilence; ⁽⁵¹⁾ ᵉ and smote all the firstborn in Egypt; the chief *of their* strength in the tabernacles of Ham: ⁽⁵²⁾ but made his own people to go forth like sheep, and guided them in the wilderness like a flock. ⁽⁵³⁾ And he led them on safely, so that they feared not: but the sea ᶠ ⁸ overwhelmed their enemies. ⁽⁵⁴⁾ And he brought them to the border of his sanctuary, *even to* this mountain, *which* his right hand had purchased. ⁽⁵⁵⁾ He cast out the heathen also before them, and ᵍ divided them an inheritance by line, and made the tribes of Israel to dwell in their tents.

⁽⁵⁶⁾ Yet they tempted and provoked the most high God, and kept not his testimonies: ⁽⁵⁷⁾ but turned back, and dealt unfaithfully like their fathers: they were turned aside like a deceitful bow. ⁽⁵⁸⁾ ʰ For they provoked him to anger with their high places, and moved him to jealousy with their graven images.

⁽⁵⁹⁾ When God heard *this*, he was wroth, and greatly abhorred Israel: ⁽⁶⁰⁾ ⁱ so that he forsook the tabernacle of Shiloh, the tent *which* he placed among men; ⁽⁶¹⁾ and delivered his strength into captivity, and his glory into the enemy's hand. ⁽⁶²⁾ He gave his people over also unto the sword; and was wroth with his inheritance. ⁽⁶³⁾ The fire consumed their young men; and their maidens were not ⁹ given to marriage. ⁽⁶⁴⁾ Their priests fell by the sword; and their widows made no lamentation.

⁽⁶⁵⁾ Then the Lord awaked as one out

---

1 Heb., *set.*
ᵃ Ex. 7. 20.
ᵇ Ex. 8. 6, 24.
ᶜ Ex. 10. 13.
ᵈ Ex. 9. 23.
2 Heb., *killed.*
3 Or, *great hailstones.*
4 Heb., *He shut up.*
5 Or, *lightnings.*
6 Heb., *He weighed a path.*
7 Or, *their beasts to the murrain;* Ex. 9. 3.
ᵉ Ex. 9. 3, & 12. 29.
ᶠ Ex. 14. 27, & 15. 10.
8 Heb., *covered.*
ᵍ Josh. 13. 7.
ʰ Deut. 32. 21.
ⁱ 1 Sam. 4. 11.
9 Heb., *praised.*

⁽⁴⁵⁾ **Divers sorts of flies.**—Better, simply *flies.* See Note Exod. viii. 21.

Frogs.—See Exod. viii. 2, and *Bib. Ed.,* iv. 145.

⁽⁴⁶⁾ **Caterpillar.**—Heb., *chasil.* (See 1 Kings viii. 37.) Probably the *locust* in the *larva* or *pupa* state. For *locust* see Exod. x. 4 *seq.,* and *Bib. Ed.,* iv. 292. The LXX., Vulg., and Symmachus have "blight," but in 2 Chron. vi. 28 "cockchafer," as Aquila and Jerome here.

⁽⁴⁷⁾ **Vines.**—In the history of the plagues (Exod. ix. 13—25) no mention is made either of vines or sycamores or of fig-trees, as in Ps. cv. 33, and some consider that the poem reflects a Palestinian rather than an Egyptian point of view. But besides Num. xx. 5 and Joseph's dream there is abundance of evidence of the extensive cultivation of the vine in Egypt. The mural paintings contain many representations of vineyards. Wine stood prominent among the offerings to the gods, and a note on a papyrus of Rameses II. speaks of rations of wine made to workmen.

Sycamore.—See 1 Kings x. 27.

Frost.—The Hebrew word is peculiar to this place. The LXX. and Vulg. have "hoar-frost," Aquila "ice," Symmachus "worm." The root of the word appears to mean *to cut off,* so that by derivation any *devastating* force would suit the word.

⁽⁴⁸⁾ **Hail.**—Some copies read "pestilence," which from its association with *resheph,* as in Hab. iii. 5, a word there denoting some contagious malady (comp. Deut. xxxii. 24; see Note Ps. lxxvi. 3), is probably to be preferred here though the authority of the LXX. is against it. If so, we must refer this verse to the *murrain* that came on the cattle.

⁽⁴⁹⁾ **Evil angels.**—So LXX. and Vulg., but in the Hebrew *angels* (or *messengers*) *of ills* (so Symmachus), with evident reference to the destruction of the firstborn.

⁽⁵⁰⁾ **Made a way.**—Literally, *levelled a path.* So Symmachus.

⁽⁵⁴⁾ **This mountain**—*i.e.,* Zion, though from its apposition to *border* some prefer to take it of all the mountain country of Judæa.

Purchased.—Rather, *acquired.*

⁽⁵⁷⁾ **Turned aside . . .**—Better, *turned like a relaxed bow.* (See Note to verse 9.) The bows of the Hebrews, like those of other ancient nations, were probably, when unstrung, bent the reverse way to that assumed when strung, which makes the figure more expressive of the disposition which cannot be relied upon in the moment of need.

⁽⁶⁰⁾ **Forsook.**—The reference is of course to the disastrous defeat by the Philistines (1 Sam. iv). See especially verse 21 in connection with glory or *ornament* as applied here to the Ark. For *strength* in the same connection see Ps. cxxxii. 8.

⁽⁶³⁾ **Were not given.**—See margin. The desolation and misery were marked by the absence of the glad nuptial song.

⁽⁶⁴⁾ **And their widows . . .**—Undoubtedly referring to the fact that the wife of Phinehas died in premature labour, and so could not attend the funeral of her husband with the customary lamentations, which in Oriental countries are so loud and marked. The Prayer-Book version, therefore, gives the right feeling—"there were no widows to make lamentations."

⁽⁶⁵⁾ **That shouteth . . .**—For the boldness of the image which likens God to a giant warrior exhilarated

of sleep, *and* like a mighty man that shouteth by reason of wine. ⁽⁶⁶⁾ And he smote his enemies in the hinder parts: he put them to a perpetual reproach.

⁽⁶⁷⁾ Moreover he refused the tabernacle of Joseph, and chose not the tribe of Ephraim: ⁽⁶⁸⁾ but chose the tribe of Judah, the mount Zion which he loved. ⁽⁶⁹⁾ And he built his sanctuary like high *palaces,* like the earth which he hath ¹ established for ever.

⁽⁷⁰⁾ *^a* He chose David also his servant, and took him from the sheepfolds: ⁽⁷¹⁾ ² *^b* from following the ewes great with young he brought him to feed Jacob his people, and Israel his inheritance.

⁽⁷²⁾ So he fed them according to the integrity of his heart; and guided them by the skilfulness of his hands.

PSALM LXXIX.

A Psalm ³ of Asaph.

⁽¹⁾ O God, the heathen are come into thine inheritance; thy holy temple have they defiled; they have laid Jerusalem on heaps. ⁽²⁾ The dead bodies of thy servants have they given *to be* meat unto the fowls of the heaven, the flesh of thy saints unto the beasts of the earth. ⁽³⁾ Their blood have they shed like water round about Jerusalem; and *there was* none to bury *them*. ⁽⁴⁾ *^c* We are become a reproach to our neighbours, a scorn and derision to them that are round about us.

⁽⁵⁾ *^d* How long, LORD? wilt thou be angry for ever? shall thy jealousy burn like fire?

⁽⁶⁾ *^e* Pour out thy wrath upon the heathen that have not known thee, and upon the kingdoms that have not called upon thy name. ⁽⁷⁾ For they have devoured Jacob, and laid waste his dwelling place.

⁽⁸⁾ *^f* O remember not against us ⁴ former iniquities: let thy tender mercies speedily prevent us: for we are

---

1 Heb., *founded.*
a 1 Sam. 16. 11; 2 Sam. 7. 8.
2 Heb., *From after.*
b 2 Sam. 5. 2; 1 Chron. 11. 2.
3 Or, *for Asaph.*
c Ps. 44. 13.
d Ps. 89. 46.
e Jer. 10. 25.
f Isa. 64. 9.
4 Or, *the iniquities of them that were before us.*

---

with wine we may range this with the picture in Ps. lx. (See Notes.)

⁽⁶⁶⁾ **He smote.**—Possibly an allusion to 1 Sam. v. 9, or else to the repeated defeats of the Philistines under Saul and David.

⁽⁶⁹⁾ **He built.**—The first clause is vague, but evidently the poet is drawing attention to the grandeur and solidity of the Temple. Perhaps, *high as heaven—firm as earth.*

⁽⁷¹⁾ **Ewes great with young**—So also in Isa. xl. 11; but properly, *ewes with lambs.* Literally, *giving suck.*

LXXIX.

The relation of this psalm to Ps. lxxiv. is so close, notwithstanding some points of difference, that commentators are almost unanimous in assigning them to the same period, if not the same author. Verse 1, indeed, by itself seems to point to a *profanation* of the Temple, such as that by Antiochus, and not a *destruction* like Nebuchadnezzar's. To one of these events the psalm must refer. Great importance is attached to the similarity of verses 6, 7, with Jer. x. 25, and it certainly looks as if the latter were an adaptation and expansion of the psalmist. Again, verse 3 (see Note) appears to be quoted in 1 Macc. vii. 17. On the other hand, every one allows that the best commentary on the psalm is the 1st chapter of 1 Maccabees. A Maccabæan editor may have taken a song of the Captivity period and slightly altered it to suit the events before his eyes. The psalter affords other instances of such adaptation. (See, *e.g.*, Ps. lx.) The verse flows smoothly, now in triplets, now in couplets.

Title.—See Title, Ps. l.

⁽¹⁾ **Inheritance.**—Probably intended to embrace both *land* and *people.* (Exod. xv. 17; Ps. lxxiv. 2, &c.)

Heaps—*i.e., ruins.* (Comp. Micah iii. 12; Jer. xxvi. 18; and in singular, Micah i. 6.)

⁽²⁾ In addition to references in Margin see Deut. xxviii. 26.

Saints.—Heb., *chasîdîm.* (See Note, Ps. xvi. 10.) Here with definite allusion to the *Assdœans* of 1 Macc. vii.

⁽³⁾ **Their blood.**—In 1 Macc. vii. 17, we read "The flesh of thy saints and their blood have they shed round about Jerusalem, and there was none to bury them," introduced by " according to the word which he wrote." This is evidently a free quotation from this psalm, and seems to imply a reference to a contemporary.

None to bury.—For this aggravation of the evil comp. Jer. xiv. 16; xxii. 18, 19.

⁽⁴⁾ This verse occurs Ps. xliv. 13. Also possibly a Maccabæan psalm. (See Introduction to that psalm.)

The scenes still witnessed by travellers at the Jews' wailing-place offer a striking illustration of the foregoing verses, showing, as they do, how deepseated is the love of an ancient place in the Oriental mind. (See a striking description in Porter's *Giant Cities of Bashan.*)

⁽⁵⁾ **How long, Lord?**—The dominant cry of the Maccabæan age. (See Ps. lxxiv. 9.)

^(6–7) The poet prays in prophetical strain, that the fire of indignation may be turned from Israel and directed against the heathen oppressors. (For the relation to Jer. x. 25, see Introduction.)

⁽⁷⁾ **Dwelling place.**—Literally, *pasture,* as in Jer. xxiii. 3, xlix. 20, l. 19. The figure is a favourite one in the Asaphic group of psalms.

Former iniquities.—Better, *iniquities of former ones, i.e., of ancestors.* (Comp. Lev. xxvi. 45, "covenant of their ancestors," and for the thought Exod. xx. 5; Lev. xxvi. 39.)

Prevent.—Better, *come to meet.* Daniel ix. 16 seems to combine the language of this verse and verse 4.

Prayer against the Heathen. PSALMS, LXXX. *The Shepherd of Israel.*

brought very low. ⁽⁹⁾ Help us, O God of our salvation, for the glory of thy name: and deliver us, and purge away our sins, for thy name's sake.

⁽¹⁰⁾ Wherefore should the heathen say, Where *is* their God? let him be known among the heathen in our sight *by* the ¹ revenging of the blood of thy servants *which is* shed.

⁽¹¹⁾ Let the sighing of the prisoner come before thee; according to the greatness of ² thy power ³ preserve thou those that are appointed to die; ⁽¹²⁾ and render unto our neighbours sevenfold into their bosom their reproach, wherewith they have reproached thee, O Lord.

⁽¹³⁾ So we thy people and sheep of thy pasture will give thee thanks for ever: we will shew forth thy praise ⁴ to all generations.

PSALM LXXX.

To the chief Musician upon Shoshannim-Eduth, A Psalm ⁵ of Asaph.

⁽¹⁾ Give ear, O Shepherd of Israel, thou that leadest Joseph like a flock; thou that dwellest *between* the cherubims, shine forth. ⁽²⁾ Before Ephraim and Benjamin and Manasseh stir up thy strength, and ⁶ come *and* save us.

⁽³⁾ Turn us again, O God, and cause thy face to shine; and we shall be saved.

---

1 Heb., *vengeance.*
2 Heb., *thine arm*
3 Heb., *reserve the children of death.*
4 Heb., *to generation and generation.*
5 Or, *for Asaph.*
6 Heb., *come for salvation to us.*

⁽⁹⁾ **Purge away.**—Rather, *put a cover on.* So Cicero speaks of political crimes being *covered* by the plea of friendship.

Our sins.—How is this to be taken in connection with verse 8? Does the psalmist admit guilt in his own generation, as well as in those of former times? Or is he thinking only of the inherited guilt and punishment? The general tone of post-exile psalms inclines towards the latter view.

⁽¹⁰⁾ **Wherefore.**—Taken from Joel ii. 17.

Let him be known.—Better, *Let it be known,* i.e., where God is. Let the answer to the question be given in vengeance, and let us see it.

⁽¹¹⁾ **Appointed to die.**—See margin. This expression, as well as the "sighing of the prisoners," occurs, Ps. cii. 20, of the sufferers in the Captivity.

⁽¹²⁾ **Neighbours.**—The sharpest pang of the suffering came from the taunts of "neighbours." (See verse 4.)

Sevenfold.—As in Gen. iv. 15. We naturally contrast the law of Christian forgiveness.

Into their bosom.—The deep folds of the Eastern dress were used as a pocket. (Comp. Ruth iii. 15; Isa. lxv. 7; Jer. xxxii. 18; Luke vi. 38, &c.)

⁽¹³⁾ "The last word of the psalm is *Tehillah;* the one crowning privilege of God's people; the exulting and triumphant confidence in God, which only His chosen can entertain and express. It is here placed in splendid contrast with the reproach of the heathen, and of the malicious neighbours mentioned in the preceding verse. *Let them curse so long as thou dost bless*" (Burgess, *Notes on the Hebrew Psalms*).

LXXX.

That this plaintive cry for restoration to a state which should be indicative of the Divine favour, arose from Israel when groaning under foreign oppression which it was powerless to resist, is plain and incontestable. And if, with the almost unanimous consent of critics, we are right in rendering verse 6, "Thou makest us an object of strife to our neighbours," we should be able to approximate very nearly to the date of the poem. For there are only two periods when Palestine became an object of dispute between rival powers: when Assyria and Egypt made it their battleground; and, at a much later date, when it was the apple of discord between the Ptolemies and the Seleucidæ. But at the earlier of these two periods the language of the poet descriptive of utter prostration and ruin (verse 16) would hardly have been suitable. We hear, too again, in verse 4, the pathetic "how long?" of the Maccabæan age. No argument for date or authorship can safely be drawn from the mode in which the tribes are mentioned and arranged in verse 2. (See Note.) The refrain at verses 3, 7, and 19 indicates the structure of the poem.

Title.—See Pss. xlv., lx., and comp. title of Ps. lxix.

⁽¹⁾ The reference to the shepherd, so characteristic of the Asaphic psalms, is, no doubt, here chosen especially in recollection of Gen. xlviii. 15, xlix. 24. "Shepherd" and "Rock" were Jacob's especial names for God, as the "Fear" was that of Isaac, and the "Mighty" that of Abraham; but in the blessing of Joseph the patriarch seems to have made more than usually solemn pronunciation of it. It is, therefore, very doubtful whether we must press the selection of Joseph here as a distinct and intended reference to the northern tribes or kingdom, in distinction to Judah or the southern kingdom.

Dwellest.—Rather, *sittest* (enthroned). (Comp. Ps. xcix. 1.) That this is not a merely poetical idea drawn from clouds (as possibly in Ps. xviii. 10), but is derived from the throne, upheld by the wings of the sculptured cherubim in the Temple, is proved by Exod. xxv. 22. (Comp. Num. vii. 89. Comp. also "chariot of the cherubim," 1 Chron. xxviii. 18; Eccles. xlix. 8; also Isa. vi. 1, xxxvii. 16; Ezek. i. 26.)

⁽²⁾ **Before Ephraim . . .**—The tribes named from Joseph's sons and his uterine brother naturally range together; they encamped side by side on the west of the Tabernacle, and when the ark moved forward they took their places immediately behind it to head the procession. The preposition "before" would alone show that this ancient arrangement, and no recent political event, determines the manner in which the poet introduces the tribes. It is used of a funeral procession (2 Sam. iii. 31; Job xxi. 33).

⁽³⁾ **Turn us again**—i.e., "restore us," not necessarily with reference to the Captivity, but generally, *restore us to our pristine prosperity.*

Cause thy face to shine.—The desert encampment and march is still in the poet's thought. As in Ps. lxvii. 1 (see Note) we have here a reminiscence of the priestly benediction.

The Vine brought out of Egypt   PSALMS, LXXX.   *Cut Down and Burnt.*

(4) O LORD God of hosts, how long ¹wilt thou be angry against the prayer of thy people? (5) Thou feedest them with the bread of tears; and givest them tears to drink in great measure. (6) Thou makest us a strife unto our neighbours: and our enemies laugh among themselves.

(7) Turn us again, O God of hosts, and cause thy face to shine; and we shall be saved.

(8) Thou hast brought a vine out of Egypt: thou hast cast out the heathen, and planted it. (9) Thou preparedst room before it, and didst cause it to take deep root, and it filled the land. (10) The hills were covered with the shadow of it, and the boughs thereof *were like* ²the goodly cedars. (11) She sent out her boughs unto the sea, and her branches unto the river.

(12) Why hast thou *then* broken down her hedges, so that all they which pass by the way do pluck her? (13) The boar out of the wood doth waste it, and the wild beast of the field doth devour it.

(14) Return, we beseech thee, O God of hosts: look down from heaven, and behold, and visit this vine; (15) and the vineyard which thy right hand hath planted, and the branch *that* thou madest strong for thyself. (16) *It is* burned with fire, *it is* cut down: they perish at the rebuke of thy countenance.

(17) Let thy hand be upon the man of

¹ Heb., *wilt thou smoke?*
² Heb., *the cedars of God.*

Saved.—Or, *helped*. This verse constitutes the refrain.

(4) **How long wilt thou be angry?**—Literally, *until when hast thou fumed?* A pregnant construction combining two clauses. Thou hast been long angry; how long wilt thou continue to be angry? (Comp. Ps. xiii. 2, Note, and Exod. x. 3.) Others say the preterite here has the sense of a future perfect, which comes to the same thing: "How long wilt thou have fumed?" (See Müller's *Syntax*, § i. 3, rem. (a), Prof. Robertson's trans.)

Against the prayer.—Literally, *in*, i.e., *during the prayer*. The smoke of the Divine anger is, perhaps, conceived of as a cloud through which the prayer (often symbolised by an ascending incense) cannot penetrate.

(5) **Bread of tears.**—See Ps. xlii. 3.

In great measure.—Heb., *shalish*, i.e., a third part. (Comp. Isa. xl. 12, Margin.) Probably meaning a third part of an ephah. (See Exod. xvi. 36; Isa. v. 10, LXX.) But here evidently used in a general way, as we say "a peck of troubles."

(6) **A strife**—i.e., an object of contention. In no other sense could Israel be a strife to neighbouring nations. For the bearing of this on the date of the psalm see its Introduction.

Laugh among themselves.—Literally, *for themselves*. But LXX. and Vulg. read, "at us."

(8) **Thou hast brought.**—The verb is to be taken as a historic present, "Thou bringest." It is a verb used both of horticulture (Job xix. 10) and, like the word "planted" in the next clause, of breaking up and removing a nomadic encampment, "pulling out the tent-pins, and driving them in."

The vine (or vineyard), as an emblem of Israel, is so natural and apt that we do not wonder to find it repeated again and again in the Old Testament, and adopted in the New. Probably Isa. v. 1—7 was the parent image, unless the Patriarchal benediction on Joseph (Gen. xlix. 22) suggested that song.

(9) **Thou preparedst room.**—The reference is, of course, to the casting out of the heathen in verse 8.

Didst cause . . .—Rather, *it struck its roots deep*; literally, *rooted its roots*.

(10) **Goodly cedars.**—Literally, *cedars of God*. The branches of the vine are to grow to resemble the luxuriance of the most magnificent of all forest trees.

(11) **The sea . . . the river**—i.e., the Mediterranean and the Euphrates, the limits of the Solomonic empire. (See Deut. xi. 24; comp. Gen. xxviii. 14; Josh. i. 4.)

(12) **Pluck.**—For the same image of the broken fence, and the fruit gathered by the passers by, see Ps. lxxxix. 40, 41.

(13) **Boar.**—This is the sole mention of the *wild* boar in Scripture. But it must not therefore be inferred that it was rare in Palestine. (See Tristram's *Nat. Hist. Bib.*, p. 54.) The writer gives a sad picture of the ravage a herd of them will make in a single night. Comp.—

"In vengeance of neglected sacrifice,
On Oencus' fields she sent a monstrous boar,
That levell'd harvests and whole forests tore."
HOMER: *Iliad* (Pope's Trans.).

Wild beast.—It seems natural, at first, to take this beast as the emblem of some particular power or oppressor, as the crocodile is of Egypt, the lion of Assyria, &c. But the general term—literally, *that moving in the field* (see Ps. l. 11)—makes against such an identification.

(15) **And the vineyard which . . .**—Most modern scholars follow the LXX. and Vulg. in making the word rendered *vineyard* an imperative of a verb, meaning *protect: And protect what thy right hand hath planted*. This makes a good parallelism.

(16) **It is burned.**—This verse would certainly be far more intelligible, and also fit better into the rhythm, if it followed immediately after verse 13. The poet, while complaining that God fumed with anger while Israel prayed, would scarcely speak of themselves as perishing under His rebuke, which, in Psalm lxxvi. 6, is used of His attitude towards foes actually contending against Him. But if we read verses 13 and 16 together, we avoid this:—

"The boar out of the wood doth waste it
And the wild beast of the field doth devour it:
It is burned with fire, it is cut down:
Let them (the beasts) perish at the rebuke of thy countenance."

(See also Note to next verse.)

(17) **Man of thy right hand.**—This is manifestly a continuation of verse 15, and should follow it:—

"Protect what thy right hand hath planted,
The branch which thou hast made strong for thyself:
Let thy hand be over the man of thy right hand,
Over the son of man whom thou madest strong for thyself."

Prayer for Grace.   PSALMS, LXXXI.   *A Psalm of Praise.*

thy right hand, upon the son of man *whom* thou madest strong for thyself. ⁽¹⁸⁾ So will not we go back from thee: quicken us, and we will call upon thy name.

⁽¹⁹⁾ Turn us again, O LORD God of hosts, cause thy face to shine; and we shall be saved.

PSALM LXXXI.
To the chief Musician upon Gittith, A Psalm ¹ of Asaph.

⁽¹⁾ Sing aloud unto God our strength: make a joyful noise unto the God of Jacob. ⁽²⁾ Take a psalm, and bring hither the timbrel, the pleasant harp with the psaltery. ⁽³⁾ Blow up the trumpet in the new moon, in the time appointed, on our solemn feast day. ⁽⁴⁾ For this *was* a statute for Israel, *and* a law of the God of Jacob. ⁽⁵⁾ This he ordained in Joseph *for* a testimony, when he went out through ² the land of Egypt: *where* I heard a language *that* I understood not.

1 Or, *for Asaph.*

2 Or, *against.*

A fine instance of the mode in which the thought can pass naturally from the figurative to the literal. The *man of God's right hand* is evidently the man protected by the right hand, but the expression introduces such a tautology that we suspect a misreading.

In the words "son," "son of man," some see a reference to the Messiah. But the parallelism and context show that the poet is thinking of Israel as a community, of which the vine is the emblem.

⁽¹⁹⁾ **Turn us.**—By a fine gradation in the style of the address to God, the refrain has at last reached its full tone, expressive of the completest trust—

> "God's ways seem dark, but soon or late
> They touch the shining hills of day.
> The evil cannot brook delay;
> The good can well afford to wait."
>   WHITTIER.

LXXXI.

This is plainly a festival song, but by no means one of that jubilant class of festival songs that conclude the Psalter. The poet is in the truest sense a prophet, and, while calling on all the nation to join in the music of the feast, he tries to convince them of the sad lapse in religion from the ideal which the appointed feasts were intended to support. By a poetic turn of high order, he represents himself as catching suddenly, amid the blare of trumpets and clash of drums, the accents of a strange, unknown voice. He listens. It is God Himself speaking and recalling, by a few brief incisive touches, the history of the ancient deliverance from Egypt. The servitude, the storm passage of the Red Sea, the miraculous supply of water, with the revelation it made of the faithlessness of the people; the covenant at Sinai, the Decalogue, by its opening commandment—are all glanced at; and then comes the sad sequel, the stubbornness and perversity of the nation for which all had been done.

But the psalm does not end with sadness. After the rebuke comes the promise of rich and abundant blessing, upon the condition of future obedience.

The particular festival for which the psalm was composed, or which it celebrates, has been matter of controversy. The arguments in favour of the Feast of Tabernacles will be found stated in the Note to verse 3. But the mode of treatment would equally well suit any of the great Israelite feasts. They were at once memorials of God's goodness and witnesses of the ingratitude and perverseness which, with these significant records continually before them, the nation so sadly displayed. After the prologue the poem falls into two nearly equal strophes.

Title.—See Titles, Pss. iv., viii. 1.

⁽²⁾ **Take a psalm.**—Rather, *Strike up a tune* (with voice and harp).

Bring hither the timbrel.—Literally, *Give a timbrel* (or, *drum*), which evidently means "sound the timbrel," and may, perhaps, be explained by a phrase sometimes found in Hebrew—"Give a voice," *i.e.*, speak. Such phrases as "Let them have the drum," "Give them the drum," may illustrate the expression. (For the instrument, *tôph*, see Exod. xv. 20, and consult *Bible Educator*, ii. 214 *seq.*)

Harp . . . psaltery.—See Note, Ps. xxxiii. 2.

⁽³⁾ **Trumpet.**—Heb., *shôphar*. (See Exod. xix. 16; Ps. xlvii. 5.) In connection with this festival psalm the mention of the *shôphar* is especially interesting as being the only ancient Hebrew instrument of which the use is still on solemn occasions retained. (See *Bible Educator*, Vol. ii. 242.)

In the new moon.—Standing by itself this might mean the beginning of every month (comp. Num. x. 10), and so many scholars are inclined to take it here. Others render "in this month." But see next Note.

In the time appointed.—This is the rendering given of the Hebrew *kĕseh* by a long array of authorities. But in Prov. vii. 20, the only other place where the word is found, the Vulg. gives "after many days;" and while the English margin has "new moon" Aquila and Jerome give "full moon." This latter meaning is supported by the fact that the Syrian version gives *keso* for the 15th day of the month (1 Kings xii. 32). But in 2 Chron. vii. 10 the same word is used for the 23rd day; hence, it is supposed to denote the whole time of the moon's waning from the full. It seems, therefore, hardly possible that *keseh* as well as *chadesh* can mean *new moon* here as some think, though it is strange to find both the *new* and the *full* moon mentioned together. Some remove the difficulty by reading with the Syriac, Chaldee, and several MSS. *feast-days* in the plural, but the authority of the LXX. is against this reading. But apparently the festival in question was the Feast of Tabernacles. The word *chag* here used is said by Gesenius to be in the Talmud used pre-eminently of this feast, as it is in 2 Chron. v. 3; 1 Kings viii. 2 (comp. Ps. xlii. 4), and the Jews, always tenacious of ancient tradition, regularly use this psalm for the office of the 1st day of Tisri. Thus the new moon is that of the seventh month, which in Num. xxix. 1 is called especially "a day of trumpet blowing" (see Note verse 1), and the full moon denotes this feast. (See Num. xxix. 12; Lev. xxiii. 24.)

⁽⁴⁾ **For this.**—Better, *for it is a statute.* Referring either to the feast itself or to the mode of celebrating it.

Law.—Literally, *judgment*, as LXX. and Vulg.

⁽⁵⁾ **Joseph.**—The prominence given to this name indicates, according to some critics, that the author belonged to the northern kingdom: but when a poet

(6) I removed his shoulder from the burden: his hands ¹were delivered from the pots.

(7) Thou calledst in trouble, and I delivered thee; I answered thee in the secret place of thunder: I ᵃproved thee at the waters of ²Meribah. Selah.

(8) Hear, O my people, and I will testify unto thee: O Israel, if thou wilt hearken unto me; (9) there shall no strange god be in thee; neither shalt thou worship any strange god. (10) I am the LORD thy God, which brought thee out of the land of Egypt: open thy mouth wide, and I will fill it.

(11) But my people would not hearken to my voice; and Israel would none of me. (12) ᵇ So I gave them up ³unto their own hearts' lust: and they walked in their own counsels. (13) Oh that my people had hearkened unto me, and Israel had walked in my ways! (14) I should soon have subdued their enemies, and turned my hand against their adversaries. (15) The haters of the LORD should have ⁴ ⁵ submitted themselves unto him: but their time should have endured for ever. (16) He should have fed them also ⁶with the finest of the wheat: and with honey out of the rock should I have satisfied thee.

PSALM LXXXII.
A Psalm ⁷of Asaph.

(1) God standeth in the congregation of the mighty; he judgeth among the gods.

---

¹ Heb., *passed away.*
ᵃ Ex. 17. 6.
² Or, *Strife.*
ᵇ Acts 14. 16.
³ Or, *to the hardness of their hearts,* or, *imaginations.*
⁴ Or, *yielded feigned obedience.*
⁵ Heb., *lied.*
⁶ Heb., *with the fat of wheat.*
⁷ Or, *for Asaph.*

---

was wishing to vary his style of speaking of the whole people—the names *Israel* and *Jacob* have just been used—the name *Joseph* would naturally occur, especially with the mention of Egypt, where that patriarch had played such a conspicuous part.

Through the land of Egypt.—The Hebrew means either *upon, over,* or *against,* but none of these meanings will suit with *Israel* as the subject of the verb. Hence, the LXX., in disregard of use, give "out of Egypt." But *God* is doubtless the subject of the verb, and we may render, *over the land of Egypt,* in allusion to Exodus xii. 23, or *against the land of Egypt,* in reference to the Divine hostility to Pharaoh.

Where I heard . . .—The insertion of the relatival adverb, *where,* makes this refer to the Egyptian tongue (comp. Ps. cxiv. 1), giving an equivalent for, "when I was in a foreign country." So apparently the LXX. and Vulg. But the expression, *words unknown to me I heard,* when followed by an apparent quotation, most naturally introduces that quotation. The poet hears a message, which comes borne to him on the festival music, and this he goes on to deliver.

(6) **Pots.**—Deriving from a root *to boil,* and with allusion to *potteries,* which, probably, together with the *brick-kilns,* formed the scene of the forced labour of Israel. The LXX. and Vulg. have "slaved in the basket," but the basket, which is represented on Egyptian monuments, is doubtless meant by the *burden* of the last clause.

(7) **Thou calledst.**—The recital of God's past dealings with the people usual at the Feast of the Tabernacles (Deut. xxxi. 10—13; Neh. viii. 18) appears to follow here as if the feast were actually in progress and the crowd were listening to the psalmist.

I answered thee in the secret place of thunder.—Mr. Burgess is undoubtedly right in taking the verb as from *ānan,* "to cover," instead of *ānah,* "to answer." *I sheltered thee in the thundercloud,* with plain allusion to the "cloudy pillar." The same verb is used in Ps. cv. 39, "He spread out the cloud for a covering."

(8) **Hear, O my people.**—The Divine voice here repeats the warnings so frequently uttered during the desert-wandering.

(9) **Open . . .**—A condensed statement of God's gracious promise (Deut. vii. 12, 13, viii. 7, 9, xi. 13, 16, &c.). It is said to have been a custom in Persia, that when the king wishes to do a visitor especial honour he desires him to open his mouth wide, and the king then crams it full of sweetmeats, and sometimes even with jewels. And to this day it is a mark of politeness in Orientals to tear off the daintiest bits of meat for a guest, and either lay them before him, or put them in his mouth. (See Thomson, *Land and Book,* p. 127.)

(12) **Lust.**—Rather, *stubbornness,* or *perversity,* from root meaning "to twist."

(13, 14) **Hearken . . . subdue.**—The verbs should be taken in a future sense, "Oh that my people would hearken . . . I should soon subdue," &c. The poet changes from reminiscences of the past to the needs of the present.

(15) **Submitted.**—See Note, Ps. xviii. 44.

Him — *i.e,* Israel; Jehovah's enemies being also Israel's enemies.

Their time — *i.e.,* Israel's. One of the sudden changes of number so frequent in Hebrew poetry. As a nation Israel would continue to live and prosper.

(16) **Finest of the wheat.**—See margin, and comp. Ps. cxlvii. 14. The construction of this verse is matter of difficulty. Properly we should render, *And he fed them with the finest of the wheat, and with honey out of the rock satisfied thee.* The change of person is harsh, though perhaps it may be illustrated by Ps. xxii. 27, &c., but the past tense seems out of keeping with the context. The conclusions of Pss. lxxvii. and lxxviii. are hardly analogous. The pointing should be slightly changed to give, "And I would feed them also," &c.

LXXXII.

This psalm represents the conviction which was so profoundly fixed in the Hebrew mind, that Justice is the fundamental virtue of society, and that its corruption implies total disorganisation and ruin. The mode in which this conviction is presented is also distinctively Hebrew. We have here once more a vision of judgment. But it is not the whole nation of the Jews, or the nations of the world generally, that are here arraigned before the Divine tribunal; nor are there introduced any of those elements of grandeur and awe which generally accompany a theophany. God is not here driving across the heavens on His storm-chariot, and calling on the mountains to bear evidence of earth's sin. But

God is Judge PSALMS, LXXXII. *of the Earth.*

(2) How long will ye judge unjustly, and *accept the persons of the wicked? Selah.
(3) ¹Defend the poor and fatherless: do justice to the afflicted and needy.
(4) ᵇ Deliver the poor and needy: rid *them* out of the hand of the wicked.
(5) They know not, neither will they understand; they walk on in darkness:

all the foundations of the earth are ² out of course.
(6) ᶜ I have said, Ye *are* gods; and all of you *are* children of the most High.
(7) But ye shall die like men, and fall like one of the princes.
(8) Arise, O God, judge the earth: for thou shalt inherit all nations.

a Deut. 1. 17.
1 Heb., *Judge.*
b Prov. 24. 11.
2 Heb., *moved.*
c John 10. 34.

---

with a calm dignity, which is by contrast the more striking, the Divine arbiter comes to take His place as presiding Judge among the magistrates themselves, and depose them. In a few incisive words He pronounces them indifferent to justice, neglectful of their duties, venal, and unscrupulous, and warns them of the ruin they are bringing on society, and of their own certain downfall, however secure and inviolable their position appears.

Then the poet himself, with a wider sweep of view, that takes in not only the administrators of law, but the political situation of his nation, makes appeal to the "judge of all the earth," who in the conviction of Israel must do right.

The date of such a poem, if it could be recovered, would crown its interest; but it is in vain to discuss the conjectures, which range from the Davidic to the Macedonian age. The histories do not reveal anything in the early monarchy to indicate such abuses in the judicature as the psalm describes. The poetical form is irregular.

Title.—See title, Ps. l.

(1) **Standeth.**—In the Hebrew a *participle*, with an official ring about it. (See Isa. iii. 13.) It is used to designate departmental officers (1 Kings iv. 5, 7, 27, ix. 23. Comp. 1 Sam. xxii. 9; Ruth ii. 5, 6). Thus the psalm opens with the solemn statement that God had taken His official place as president of the bench of judges.

Congregation of the mighty.—Rather, *assembly of God*, or *divine assembly*; elsewhere, "the congregation of Jehovah" (Num. xxvii. 17, xxxi. 16; Josh. xxii. 16—18), *i.e.*, "Israel in its religious character."

He judgeth among the gods—*i.e.*, He is among the judges as presiding judge. For "gods," applied to men delegated with office from God, see Exod. xxi. 6, and, possibly, xxii. 8, 9. (See also Note, Ps. viii. 5, and comp. Exod. iv. 16, vii. 1.) The custom of designating God's vicegerents by the Divine name was a very natural one. The whole point of verse 6 lies in the double meaning the word can bear. (See Note.)

(2—4) These verses contain the rebuke addressed by the supreme judge to those abusing the judicial office and function.

(2) **How long?**—What a terrible severity in this Divine *Quousque tandem!*

> "The gods
> Grow angry with your patience; this their care,
> And must be yours, that guilty men escape not;
> As crimes do grow, justice should rouse itself."
> BEN JONSON.

Judge unjustly.—Literally, *judge iniquity*. For the opposite expression see Ps. lviii. 1. Lev. xix. 15, which lays down the great principle of strictly fair and unbribable justice is evidently in the poet's mind, as is shown by the use of the next clause.

Accept the persons.—Literally, *lift up the faces*. An expression arising from the Eastern custom of prostration before a king or judge. The accepted suitor is commanded to "lift up his face," *i.e.*, to arise. (Comp. Prov. xviii. 5, and Jehoshaphat's address to the judges, 2 Chron. xix. 7.) This fine sense of the majesty of incorruptible justice attended Israel throughout its history. (See Ecclus. vii. 6.)

(3) **Poor.**—Rather, *miserable*. (See Ps. xli. 1.) This verse recalls the solemn curse in Deut. xxvii. 19.

(4) **The poor and needy.**—Better, *The miserable* (as in verse 8) *and poor*, a different word from "needy" in verse 3.

(5) Here we imagine a pause, that interval between warning and judgment which is God's pity and man's opportunity; but the expostulation falls dead without a response. The men are infatuated by their position and blinded by their pride, and the poet, the spectator of this drama of judgment, makes this common reflection. The perversion of judgment strikes him, as it could not fail to do, as an indication of total anarchy and a dissolution of society, a convulsion like an earthquake.

They know not.—Comp. Ps. lviii. 4, "They have no knowledge;" there, too, of judges corrupted by the moral blindness which, as in the case of Lord Bacon, sometimes so strangely darkens those in whom intellectual light is most keen.

They walk on in darkness.—Or, better, *They let themselves walk in darkness*; the conjugation implying that inclination or will, and not circumstance, brings this dullness to the dictates of justice and right.

All the foundations . . .—The very existence of society is threatened when the source of justice is corrupt.

> "Back flow the sacred rivers to their source,
> And right and all things veer around their course;
> Crafty are men in council, and no more
> God-plighted faith abides as once of yore."
> EUR. *Med.*, 409.

(6) **I have said.**—Again the Divine voice breaks the silence with an emphatic *I*. "From me comes your office and your honoured title, *gods*; now from *me* hear your doom. *Princes though ye be, ye will die as other men: yea, altogether will ye princes perish.*" (For the rendering "altogether," literally, *like one man*, see Ezra ii. 64, iii. 9, &c.)

It is interesting to notice that verses 1 and 6 were quoted by Constantine at the opening of the council of Nicæa, to remind the bishops that their high office should raise them above jealousy and party feeling. (For the interest gained by the passage from our Lord's use of it to rebut the charge of blasphemy brought against Him by the scribes, see Note, *New Testament Commentary*, John x. 34.)

(8) **Arise.**—The psalm would have been incomplete had not the poet here resumed in his own person, with an appeal to the Supreme Judge to carry His decrees into effect against the oppressors of Israel. Here, at least, if not all through it, the affliction of the community, and the perversion of justice by foreign rulers, are

PSALM LXXXIII.

A Song or Psalm[1] of Asaph.

(1) Keep not thou silence, O God: hold not thy peace, and be not still, O God. (2) For, lo, thine enemies make a tumult: and they that hate thee have lifted up the head.[3] (3) They have taken crafty counsel against thy people, and consulted against thy hidden ones. (4) They have said, Come, and let us cut them off from *being* a nation; that the name of Israel may be no more in remembrance. (5) For they have consulted together with one [2] consent: they are confederate against thee: (6) the tabernacles of Edom, and the Ishmaelites; of Moab, and the Hagarenes; (7) Gebal, and Ammon, and Amalek; the Philistines with the inhabitants of Tyre; (8) Assur also is joined with them: [3]they have holpen the children of Lot. Selah.

(9) Do unto them as *unto* the *a*Midianites; as to *b*Sisera, as to Jabin, at the

[1] Or, *or Asaph*.
[2] Heb., *heart*.
[3] Heb., *they have been an arm to the children of Lot*.
a Judg. 7. 22.
b Judg. 4. 15, 24.

---

the motives of the song. It is as if, despairing of the amendment of the corrupt magistrates, the poet, pleading for Israel, takes his case out of their hands, as Cranmer in the play takes his case out of the hands of the council, and entrusts it to the Great Judge of the world, to whom, as a special inheritance, Israel belonged, but who was also to show His claim to the submission and obedience of all nations.

LXXXIII.

The array of proper names in this poem seems, at first sight, to promise an easy identification with some definite historical event. But our records nowhere speak of a confederation composed of all the tribes enumerated here; so that if we are to be governed by literal exactness, it is impossible to refer the psalm to any known period of Israelite history.

We must therefore, in any case, refer the mention of so many hostile tribes as combined in one confederacy to poetical exaggeration, and look for other indications which may guide us to the event most probable as the origin of the poem. This is the period of which we have a detailed and graphic account in 1 Macc. v. Before this there is no period at which, even poetically, Tyre could be enumerated among the active enemies of Israel, while the first words of this chapter are just a prose statement of what we have here poetically described. In the fact, too, that after his victorious progress Judas Maccabæus reviewed his troops in the great plain which had witnessed the slaughter of Sisera's host, and in the comparison drawn between the conduct of the city of Ephron (1 Macc. v. 46—49) with that of Succoth and Penuel, towards Gideon (Judges viii. 4—9), we have enough to account for the selection of examples from the times of the judges rather than from later history. The difficulty of the mention of Assyria, in verse 8, as occupying a subordinate part in a confederacy with Moab and Ammon, is no greater if the psalm is referred to this period than to any other. *Syria* (even if we discard the derivation of the name by abbreviation from *Assyria*) might yet poetically bear the name of the older power, and "auxiliaries out of Syria," of whom Josephus speaks in connection with the Maccabæan wars, would be not unnaturally in poetry described as "Assur, an arm to the children of Lot." The poem has a regular rhythmic form.

Title.—See title, Pss. xlviii. and l.

(1) **Keep not thou silence, O God.**—Literally, *God, not silence to thee.* (Comp. Isa. lxii. 7; and see Note, Ps. xxviii. 1.)

(2) **Make a tumult.**—Literally, *roar like the sea.* So (correctly) LXX. and Vulg. (See Ps. xlvi. 3.)

(3) **They have taken crafty counsel.**—Literally, *They have made their plot crafty*; or, as we say, "They have laid a deep plot."

Hidden ones—*i.e.*, those under God's close protection, as in Pss. xvii. 8, xxvii. 5, xxxi. 20.

(4) For this attack against, not only the independence, but even the continued existence of Israel as a nation, compare Esth. iii. 6, 9; Jer. xi. 19, xxxi. 36, xlviii. 2; Isa. vii. 8.

(5) **They are confederate.**—Literally, *they have cut a covenant*, from the custom described in Gen. xv. 17. (Comp. the Greek ὅρκια τέμνειν.)

Against thee.—God and "His hidden ones" are one, a truth preparing the way for that grander truth of the identification of the Son of man with all needing help or pity in Matt. xxv.

(6—8) In the enumeration of the confederate powers, the psalmist seems to follow a geographical order. He first glances southwards and eastwards, then turns to the west, and, finally, to the north.

(6) **The tabernacles**—*i.e.*, the tents of the nomad tribes.

Hagarenes.—A tribe mentioned in 1 Chron. v. 10, 19 (Hagarites), where see Note.

(7) **Gebal.**—If this is a noun, as generally supposed, and as printed in the text, we must take it as a synonym of Edom (the *Gebalene* of Eusebius). The Gebal of Ezek. xxvii. 9 is not to be thought of; but it is most likely a verb:

"Both Ammon and Amalek are joined together,
The Philistines (are joined) with the men of Tyre."

(8) **Assur.**—For the more usual *Ashur*, Assyria. Some, however, think the Syria is here intended, that name being, in the view of the Greek writers, a corruption of Assyria. ("The Greeks call them Syrians, but the Barbarians Assyrians."—Herod. vii., 63.) And even if etymologically incorrect, the error of the Greeks may have been consciously or unconsciously shared by the Jews, and the kingdom of the Seleucidæ be honoured by the name of the grander and more ancient power.

They have holpen.—See margin. And for the importance of the form of the statement see Introduction.

Children of Lot.—Ammon and Moab, who thus appear as the leaders of the confederacy.

(9—12) For the historical allusion see references in margin. The splendid victories of Barak and Gideon were the constant theme of poets and prophets when trying to encourage their own generation by the examples of the past. (See Isa. ix. 4; x. 26; Hab. iii. 7.)

brook of Kison: (10) which perished at En-dor: they became as dung for the earth. (11) Make their nobles like ªOreb, and like Zeeb: yea, all their princes as Zebah, and as Zalmunna: (12) who said, Let us take to ourselves the houses of God in possession.

(13) O my God, make them like a wheel; as the stubble before the wind.

(14) As the fire burneth a wood, and as the flame setteth the mountains on fire; (15) so persecute them with thy tempest, and make them afraid with thy storm. (16) Fill their faces with shame; that they may seek thy name, O LORD. (17) Let them be confounded and troubled for ever; yea, let them be put to shame, and perish:

(18) That men may know that thou, whose name alone is JEHOVAH, art the most high over all the earth.

ª Judg. 7. 25, & 8. 21.

¹ Or, of.

PSALM LXXXIV.

To the chief Musician upon Gittith, A Psalm ¹ for the sons of Korah.

(1) How amiable are thy tabernacles, O LORD of hosts! (2) My soul longeth, yea, even fainteth for the courts of the LORD: my heart and my flesh crieth out for the living God. ³) Yea, the sparrow hath found an house, and the swallow a nest for herself, where she

---

(10) **En-dor.**—This place, for which see 1 Sam. xxviii., is not mentioned in Judges iv., but is in the battle-field not far from the Taanach and Megiddo of Deborah's song. (Robinson, iii., 224.)

(12) **Houses.**—Rather, *pastures*. (See Ps. lxxix. 7.)

(13) **A wheel.**—Heb., *galgal*. (See Note, Ps. lxxvii. 18, and comp. Isa. xvii. 13, where the Authorised Version has literally *rolling thing*, the margin "thistle down," and the LXX., "dust of a wheel.") Sir G. Grove (Smith's *Bibl. Dict.*, art. Oreb) says, "like the spherical masses of dry weeds which course over the plains of Esdraelon and Philistia." He possibly refers to the wild artichoke, which struck Mr. Thomson so forcibly as the origin of the psalmist's figure. He describes them as vegetable globes, light as a feather, which, when the parent stem breaks, become the sport of the wind. "At the proper season thousands of them come suddenly over the plain, rolling, leaping, bounding with vast racket, to the dismay both of the horse and rider." To this day the Arabs, who call it *'akhûb*, employ it in the same figurative way:—

"May you be whirled like *'akhûb* before the wind!"
THOMSON: *Land and Book*, 563.

(14, 15) These verses are rightly taken together. The figure occurs in Isa. x. 17, 18 (comp. Zech. xii. 6), but there as a metaphor; here as a simile. "Before the rains came the whole mountain side was in a blaze. Thorns and briars grow so luxuriantly here that they must be burned off always before the plough can operate. The peasants watch for a high wind, and then the fire catches easily, and spreads with great rapidity" (Thomson, *Land and Book*, p. 341). The mountains are pre-eminently the *pastures*. (Comp. Pss. l. 10, cxlvii. 8.)

(16) **Thy name, O Lord.**—Rather, *thy name (which is) Jehovah*. The nations were to seek Him not only as God, but as Jehovah God of Israel. This is proved by verse 18. No doubt the thought uppermost in the verse is the submission of the heathen to Jehovah's power. But we may, looking back, read in it a nobler wish and a grander hope—the prophetic hope of a union of nations in a belief in the common fatherhood of God.

LXXXIV.

By an almost complete agreement of commentators this psalm is descriptive of a caravan of Israelites either returning from exile to Jerusalem or on its way up to one of the regular feasts. It has so many points of resemblance to Pss. xlii. and xliii. that it has been ascribed to the same author and referred to the same events. (See Notes to those psalms.) The singer, whether he speaks in his own name or that of Israel generally, is undoubtedly at present unable (see verse 2) to share in the Temple services which he so rapturously describes. The poetical structure is uncertain.

Title.—See titles Pss. iv., viii., xlii.

(1) **How amiable.**—Better, *How loved and how lovable*. The Hebrew word combines both senses.

Tabernacles.—Better, perhaps, *dwellings*. (Comp. Ps. xliii. 3.) The plural is used poetically, therefore we need not think of the various courts of the Temple.

(2) **Longeth.**—From root meaning to *grow pale*, expressing one effect of strong emotion—*grows pale with longing*. So the Latin poets used *pallidus* to express the effects of passionate love, and generally of any strong emotion :

"Ambitione mala aut argenti pallet amore."
HOR., *Sat.* ii. 3, 78.

Or we may perhaps compare Shakspeare's

"Sicklied o'er with the pale cast of thought."

For a similar fervid expression of desire for communion with God, comp. Ps. lxiii. 1.

Fainteth.—Or more properly, as LXX., *faileth*.

Courts.—This, too, seems, like tabernacles above, to be used in a general poetical way, so that there is no need to think of the court of the priests as distinguished from that of the people.

The living God.—Comp. Ps. xlii. 2, the only other place in the Psalms where God is so named.

(3) **Sparrow.**—Heb., *tsippôr*, which is found upwards of forty times in the Old Testament, and is evidently used in a very general way to include a great number of small birds. "Our common house-sparrow is found on the coast in the towns, and inland its place is taken by a very closely-allied species, *Passer Cisalpina*" (Tristram, *Nat. Hist. of the Bible*, p. 202).

Swallow.—Heb. *derôr*, which by its etymology implies a bird of rapid whirling flight. (See Prov. xxvi. 2, where this characteristic is especially noticed.) The ancient versions take the word as cognate with "turtle-dove." In an appendix to Delitzsch's Commentary on the Psalms, Dr. J. G. Wetzstein, identifies the *tsippôr* with the *ôsfur* of the Arabs, a generic name for small chirping birds, and *derôr* with *dûri*, which is specific of the *sparrow*.

Even thy altars.—Better, *at* or *near thine altars*, though even if taken as in the Authorised Version the

The Joy of Worship   PSALMS, LXXXIV.   *in the House of God.*

may lay her young, *even* thine altars, O LORD of hosts, my King, and my God. ⁽⁴⁾ Blessed *are* they that dwell in thy house: they will be still praising thee. Selah.

⁽⁵⁾ Blessed *is* the man whose strength *is* in thee; in whose heart *are* the ways of them. ⁽⁶⁾ Who passing through the valley ¹of Baca make it a well; the rain also ²filleth the pools. ⁽⁷⁾ They go ³from strength to strength, *every one of them in* Zion appeareth before God. ⁽⁸⁾ O LORD God of hosts, hear my prayer: give ear, O God of Jacob. Selah.

⁽⁹⁾ Behold, O God our shield, and look upon the face of thine anointed. ⁽¹⁰⁾ For a day in thy courts *is* better than a thousand. ⁴ I had rather be a doorkeeper in the house of my God, than to dwell in the tents of wickedness. ⁽¹¹⁾ For the LORD God *is* a sun and shield: the LORD will give grace and glory: ᵃno

---

¹ Or, *of mulberry trees make him a well*, &c.
² Heb., *covereth.*
³ Or, *from company to company.*
⁴ Heb., *I would choose rather to sit at the threshold.*
ᵃ Ps. 34. 9, 10.

---

meaning is the same. There is no real occasion for the great difficulty that has been made about this verse. It is absurd indeed to think of the birds actually nesting on the altars; but that they were found in and about the Temple is quite probable, just as in Herodotus (i. 159) we read of Aristodicus making the circuit of the temple at Branchidæ, and taking the nests of young sparrows and other birds. (Comp. the story in Ælian of the man who was slain for harming a sparrow that had sheltered in the temple of Æsculapius.) Ewald gives many other references, and among them one to Burckhardt showing that birds nest in the Kaaba at Mecca.

The Hebrew poetic style is not favourable to simile, or the psalmist would have written (as a modern would), "As the birds delight to nest at thine altars, so do I love to dwell in thine house."

(5—7) In these verses, as in the analogous picture (Isa. xxxv. 6—8; comp. Hosea ii. 15, 16), there is a blending of the real and the figurative; the *actual* journey towards Sion is represented as accompanied with ideal blessings of peace and refreshment. It is improbable that the poet would turn abruptly from the description of the swallows in the Temple to what looks like a description of a real journey, with a locality, or at all events a district, which was well known, introduced by its proper name, and yet intend only a figurative reference. On the other hand, it is quite in the Hebrew manner to mix up the ideal with the actual, and to present the spiritual side by side with the literal. We have, then, here recorded the actual experience of a pilgrim's route. But quite naturally and correctly has the world seen in it a description of the pilgrimage of life, and drawn from it many a sweet and consoling lesson.

(5) **Blessed is the man.**—Or collective, *men*, as the suffix, *their* hearts, shows.

Ways.—From a root meaning *to cast up*—and so *highways* marked by the heaps of stone piled up at the side (Isa. lvii. 14³). In Jer. xviii. 15 mere *footways* or *bypaths* are contrasted, and so the *highway* lends itself as a metaphor *for the way of peace and righteousness* (Prov. xii. 28), as it is taken here by the Chaldee and some modern expositors. But this moral intention is secondary to the actual desire to join the pilgrim band towards Sion, and this the verse describes in words which are echoed exactly in our own Chaucer:

"So pricketh hem Nature in her corages (in their hearts)
Than longen folk to go on pilgrimages."

The well-known and deeply loved route to the sacred shrine is in their minds, their hearts are set upon it.

(6) **Who passing through the valley of Baca.**—All the ancient versions have "valley of weeping," which, through the Vulg. *vallis lacrymosa*, has passed into the religious language of Europe as a synonym for life. And *Baca* (*bâkha*) seems to have this signification, whatever origin we give the word. The valley has been variously identified—with the valley of *Achor* (Hosea ii. 15; Josh. vii. 24); the valley of *Rephaim* (2 Sam. v. 22)—a valley found by Burckhardt in the neighbourhood of Sinai; and one, more recently, by Renan, the last station of the present caravan route from the north to Jerusalem. Of these, the valley of Rephaim is most probably in the poet's mind, since it is described (Isa. xvii. 5) as sterile, and as the text stands, we think of some place devoid of water, but which the courage and faith of the pilgrims treats as if it were well supplied with that indispensable requisite, thus turning adversity itself into a blessing. He either plays on the sound of the word (*Baca*, and *becaîm*) or the exudations of the *balsam* shrub gave the valley its name.

The rain also filleth the pools.—That *rain* is the right rendering of the Hebrew word here appears from Joel ii. 23. The rendering *pools* follows the reading, *berechôth*; but the text has *berachôth*, "blessings," as read by the LXX. and generally adopted now. Render *yea, as the autumn rain covers (it) with blessings*, i.e., just as the benign showers turn a wilderness into a garden, so resolution and faith turn disadvantage to profit. (Comp. Isa. xxxv. 6—8, xliii. 18 *seq.*)

(7) **They go from strength to strength**—i.e., each difficulty surmounted adds fresh courage and vigour.

"And he who flagg'd not in the earthly strife,
From strength to strength advancing, only he
His soul well knit, and all his battles won,
Mounts, and that hardly, to eternal life."
          MATTHEW ARNOLD.

The marginal "from company to company" follows the alternative meaning of the Hebrew word, and suggests a picture of the actual progress of the various bands composing a caravan. But the expression in either sense is hardly Hebrew, and the text is suspicious. It emends easily to "They go to the Temple of the Living God, to see the God of gods in Zion" (Grätz).

(9) **Shield . . . anointed.**—These are here in direct parallelism. So in Ps. lxxxix. 18. (See Note, and comp. Ps. xlvii. 9, Note.)

(10) **I had rather be a doorkeeper.**—Better, *I had rather wait on the threshold*, as not worthy (LXX. and Vulgate, "be rejected in scorn") to enter the precincts. The idea of "doorkeeper," however, though not necessarily involved in the Hebrew word, is suggested in a Korahite psalm, since the Korahites were "keepers of the gates of the tabernacle, and keepers of the entry." Compare with this wish the words

good *thing* will he withhold from them that walk uprightly.

⁽¹²⁾ O LORD of hosts, ᵃblessed *is* the man that trusteth in thee.

PSALM LXXXV.

To the chief Musician, A Psalm ¹for the sons of Korah.

⁽¹⁾ Lord, thou hast been ²favourable unto thy land : thou hast brought back the captivity of Jacob. ⁽²⁾ ᵇ Thou hast forgiven the iniquity of thy people, thou hast covered all their sin. Selah.

⁽³⁾ Thou hast taken away all thy wrath : ³ thou hast turned *thyself* from the fierceness of thine anger.

⁽⁴⁾ Turn us, O God of our salvation, and cause thine anger toward us to cease. ⁽⁵⁾ Wilt thou be angry with us for ever? wilt thou draw out thine anger to all generations ? ⁽⁶⁾ Wilt thou not revive us again : that thy people may rejoice in thee ? ⁽⁷⁾ Shew us thy mercy, O LORD, and grant us thy salvation.

⁽⁸⁾ I will hear what God the LORD will speak : for he will speak peace unto his people, and to his saints : but let them not turn again to folly.

⁽⁹⁾ Surely his salvation *is* nigh them that fear him ; that glory may dwell in our land.

⁽¹⁰⁾ Mercy and truth are met together ; righteousness and peace have kissed *each other*. ⁽¹¹⁾ Truth shall spring out of the earth ; and righteousness shall look down from heaven. ⁽¹²⁾ Yea, the LORD shall give *that which is* good ; and our land shall yield her increase. ⁽¹³⁾ Righteousness shall go before him ; and shall set *us* in the way of his steps.

a Ps. 2 12.
1 Or, *of*.
2 Or, *well pleased*.
b Ps. 32 1.
3 Or, *thou hast turned thine anger from waxing hot.*

---

which a Greek poet puts into the mouth of his hero, who sweeps the threshold of Apollo's temple :

> "A pleasant task, O Phœbus, I discharge,
> Before thine house in reverence of thy seat
> Of prophecy, an honoured task to me."
> EURIPIDES, *Ion*, 128.

LXXXV.

There is more than the statement of its first verse (see Note) to connect this psalm with the post-exile period. Its whole tone belongs to that time. The attitude with regard to national sin explains itself only by this reference. The punishment had fallen, and in the glad return Israel had seen a proof that God had covered her guilt, and taken away her sin. But the bright prospect had quickly been overclouded. The troubles that succeeded the return perplexed those who had come back, as they felt purified and forgiven. Hence many such pathetic cries as those of this psalm. In this particular instance, the cry, as we gather from verse 12, arose from the dread of famine, which was always regarded as a judgment on national sin. But, even as he utters his lament, the prophet (for the psalm has a true prophetic ring, and is in the highest sense Messianic) sees the clouds break, and hails the promise of abundant harvest, as he watches the sunshine of prosperity and peace once more strike across the land. The rhythm arrangement is uncertain.

Title.—See title, Pss. iv. and xlii.

⁽¹⁾ **Thou hast brought back.**—See Pss. xiv. 7, lxviii. 18. The expression might only imply generally a return to a state of former prosperity, as in Job xlii. 10, but the context directs us to refer especially to the return from exile. (See *Introduction*.)

⁽²⁾ **Forgiven.** — Rather, *taken away*. (See Ps xxxii. 1.)

⁽⁴⁾ **Turn us.**—Here equivalent to *restore us once more*. If, the poet felt, the captivity had taught its lesson, why, on the restoration, did not complete freedom from misfortune ensue? It is this which supplies the motive of his song.

⁽⁸⁾ **Speak peace** . . .—This word "peace" comprehends all that the nation sighed for :

> "Peace,
> Dear nurse of arts, plenties, and joyful truth."

To Christians the word has a higher meaning still, which directed the choice of this psalm for Christmas Day.

Folly.—See Pss. xiv. 1, xlix. 13. Here it most probably implies *idolatry*.

⁽⁹⁻¹¹⁾ The exquisite personification of these verses is, it has been truly remarked, exactly in Isaiah's manner. (See Isa. xxxii. 16 *seq*., xlv. 8, lix. 14.) It is an allegory of completed national happiness, which, though presented in language peculiar to Hebrew thought, is none the less universal in its application. Nor does it stop at material blessings, but lends itself to the expression of the highest truths. The poet sees once more the *glory* which had so long deserted the land come back—as its symbol, the ark, once came back—and take up its abode there. He sees the covenant *favour* once more descend and meet the divine *faithfulness* of which, lately, perplexed minds were doubting, but which the return of prosperity has now proved sure. Righteousness and peace, or prosperity, these inseparable brothers, kiss each other, and fall lovingly into each other's arms.

⁽¹⁰⁾ **Met together.**—The word is used of those who should be friends, but whom circumstances have sundered (Prov. xxii. 2).

⁽¹¹⁾ **Truth,** or "faithfulness," is here depicted as springing out of the earth, because the renewal of fertility has re-established the conviction of the faithfulness of Jehovah towards His people, which had been shaken.

Look down.—Used of bending forwards as from a window or battlement (Song of Sol. vi. 10, Note).

This "righteousness" (here in direct parallelism with *faithfulness*) had, as it were, been hidden like the sun behind a cloud, but now is seen showing its benign face once more in the skies.

⁽¹³⁾ **Righteousness shall . . .**—Better, *Righteousness shall walk in front of Him, and follow in His steps*.

Nothing is more instructive than the blending in verses 12 and 13 of material and moral blessings. They do go together, as experience, especially national

PSALM LXXXVI.

[1] A Prayer of David.

(1) Bow down thine ear, O LORD, hear me: for I *am* poor and needy. (2) Preserve my soul; for I *am* [2]holy: O thou my God, save thy servant that trusteth in thee.

(3) Be merciful unto me, O Lord: for I cry unto thee [3]daily. (4) Rejoice the soul of thy servant: for unto thee, O Lord, do I lift up my soul.

(5) *a* For thou, Lord, *art* good, and ready to forgive; and plenteous in mercy unto all them that call upon thee. (6) Give ear, O LORD, unto my prayer; and attend to the voice of my supplications. (7) In the day of my trouble I will call upon thee: for thou wilt answer me.

(8) Among the gods *there is* none like unto thee, O Lord; *b* neither *are there* any *works* like unto thy works. (9) All nations whom thou hast made shall come and worship before thee, O Lord; and shall glorify thy name. (10) For thou *art* great, and doest wondrous things: *c* thou *art* God alone.

(11) *d* Teach me thy way, O LORD; I will walk in thy truth: unite my heart to fear thy name. (12) I will praise thee, O Lord my God, with all my heart: and I will glorify thy name for evermore.

(13) For great *is* thy mercy toward me: and thou hast delivered my soul from the lowest [4]hell.

(14) O God, the proud are risen against me, and the assemblies of [5]violent *men* have sought after my soul; and have not set thee before them. (15) *e* But thou, O Lord, *art* a God full of compassion, and gracious, longsuffering, and plenteous in mercy and truth.

(16) O turn unto me, and have mercy upon me; give thy strength unto thy servant, and save the son of thine handmaid. (17) Shew me a token for good; that they which hate me may see *it*, and be ashamed: because thou, LORD, hast holpen me, and comforted me.

---

[1] Or, *A Prayer, being a Psalm of David.*
[2] Or, *one whom thou favourest.*
[3] Or, *all the day.*
a Joel 2. 13.
b Deut. 3. 24.
c Deut. 6. 4, & 32. 39; Isa. 37. 16, & 44. 6; Mark 12. 29; 1 Cor. 8. 4; Ephes. 4. 6.
d Ps. 25. 4, & 119. 33.
[4] Or, *grave.*
[5] Heb., *terrible.*
e Ex. 34. 6; Num. 14. 18; Ps. 103. 8, & 130. 4, & 145. 8.

---

testifies. In the same spirit is Wordsworth's well-known *Ode to Duty*:

> "Stern Law-giver! Yet thou dost wear
> The Godhead's most benignant grace,
> Nor know we anything so fair
> As is the smile upon thy face.
> Flowers laugh before thee on their beds,
> And fragrance in thy footing treads;
> Thou dost preserve the stars from wrong,
> And the most ancient heavens through Thee are fresh and strong."

LXXXVI.

This psalm is mainly composed of a number of sentences and verses from older compositions, arranged not without art, and, where it suited the adapter, so altered as to present forms of words peculiar to himself. (See Notes on verses 5, 6.) There is also evidence of design in the employment of the Divine names, Adonai being repeatedly substituted for Jehovah.

Title.—See end of Psalm xlii. and Introduction above.

(2) **For I am holy.**—Rather, in order to reproduce the feeling, *for I am one of the chosen ones; one of Thy saints,* &c. He pleads the covenant relation as a claim to the blessing. (See, on *chasid*, Note, Ps. l. 5.)

(5) **For thou.**—Up to this time the psalmist has only put forward his needs in various aspects as a plea for God's compassion. Now, not without art, he clenches his petition by an appeal to the nature itself of the Divine Being. The originals of the expressions in this verse will be found in Exod. xx. 6, xxxiv. 6—9; Num. xiv. 18, 19.

Ready to forgive.—The Hebrew word occurs nowhere else in the form found here. Etymologically it means *remitting*. The LXX. have ἐπιεικής, a word for which perhaps our *considerate* is the nearest equivalent, implying that legal right is overlooked and suspended in consideration of human weakness. Wisdom xii. 18 gives a good description of this Divine attribute.

(6) **Give ear.**—Here the petition takes a new starting-point.

(8) For the sources of this verse see marginal reference and Exod. xv. 11. After expressing his conviction of God's *willingness* to hear prayer, the psalmist goes on to his confidence in Divine power to save.

(9) For this wide prospect of Divine dominion see Ps. xxii. 31; Isa. xliii. 7.

(11) A reminiscence of older psalms. In addition to the marginal references, see Ps. xxvi. 3.

Unite my heart—*i.e.*, unite all my powers and concentrate them on Thy service. No doubt with recollection of Deut. vi. 5, x. 12. Comp. also Jer. xxxii. 39, on which apparently the expression is directly based. An undivided will is in morals and religion equally essential.

(12, 13) Comp. Pss. lvi. 13, lvii. 9, 10.

(13) **Lowest hell.**—Literally, *sheôl, beneath,* a fuller expression for the usual *sheôl, underworld.* (See Note, Ps. vi. 5.) There is no comparison implied as in the Authorised Version. It is evident from the next verse that what is meant is *danger of death from violence.*

(14) See Note, Ps. liv. 3, whence the verse is taken.

(16) **Servant . . . son of thine handmaid.**—Comp. Ps. cxvi. 16. The combined expressions imply a *homeborn slave.* (Comp. Gen. xiv. 14; Jer. ii. 14.)

(17) **A token for good**—*i.e.*, some sign of continued or renewed providential care and love, such, indeed, as an Israelite under the old covenant saw, and every pious heart under the new sees, in what to others is an every-day occurrence. The expression *for good* is a favourite one with Nehemiah (chap. v. 19, xiii. 31) and Jeremiah (chap. xxiv. 5, 6, and comp. Rom. viii. 28, &c.).

PSALM LXXXVII.

A Psalm *or* Song [1] for the sons of Korah.

⁽¹⁾ His foundation *is* in the holy mountains. ⁽²⁾ The LORD loveth the gates of Zion more than all the dwellings of Jacob. ⁽³⁾ Glorious things are spoken of thee, O city of God. Selah. ⁽⁴⁾ I will make mention of Rahab and Babylon to them that know me: behold Philistia, and Tyre, with Ethiopia; this *man* was born there. ⁽⁵⁾ And of Zion it shall be said, This and that man was born in her: and the highest himself shall establish her. ⁽⁶⁾ The LORD shall count, when he writeth up the people, *that* this *man* was born there. Selah.

[1] Or, *of.*

LXXXVII.

According to the common interpretation of this obscure psalm, it is unique not only in the Psalter but in Hebrew literature. Not even in Isaiah is Jewish exclusiveness so broken down. A nameless poet goes beyond the prophetic visions of the forceful submission of the Gentile world to anticipate the language of the Gospels and the spirit of St. Paul. Zion becomes in his song the "mother of us all"—Gentiles as well as Jews.

How far such a splendid hope really appears in the psalm may be gathered from the Notes. Here it is necessary to observe that a first glance at the song sees in it little more than a grand eulogy on the Holy City as a birthplace, which is declared dear to Jehovah not only above heathen countries, but above any city of Jacob—a city in which to have been born is a privilege and a boast far above what the fondest patriotism of a Philistine, a Tyrian, nay, even an Egyptian or Babylonian can claim. Possibly, after all, *exclusiveness* even more rigid than usual appears here, and we must see in the poem the exultation of a native of Jerusalem over all other Israelites, or of a Palestinian Hebrew over those who share the same blood but have the misfortune to date their birth from some Jewish colony rather than Jerusalem.

As to the time of composition the suggestion ventured on above would of itself bring it down to a very late date, a supposition supported in some degree by the fact that not Assyria but Babylon is mentioned in verse 4. The parallelism is very lax, and the structure uncertain.

Title.—See Title, Ps. xlii.

⁽¹⁾ **His foundation.**—This abrupt commencement with a clause without a verb has led to the conjecture that a line has dropped away. But this is unnecessary if we neglect the accents, and take *gates of Zion* in apposition with *His foundation:*

His foundation on the holy hill
Loveth Jehovah, (even) Zion's gates,
More than all Jacob's dwellings.

Here *His foundation* is equivalent to *that which He hath founded*, and the gates are put by metonymy for the city itself. (Comp. Jer. xiv. 2.)

With regard to the plural, *mountains*, it is probably only poetical, though geographically it is correct to speak of Jerusalem as situated on hills. Dean Stanley speaks of "the multiplicity of the eminences" which the city "shares, though in a smaller compass, with Rome and Constantinople" (*Sinai and Palestine,* p. 177).

⁽³⁾ The meaning of this verse is obvious in spite of its many grammatical difficulties. The praise of Zion had found many tongues, but the poet implies that he is going to swell the chorus.

⁽⁴⁾ This verse may be paraphrased—

I will mention to my intimates Rahab and Babylon; (I will say) look at Philistia and Tyre—yes, and even Ethiopia. So-and-so was born there.

The last clause is literally *this was born there*, and on its reference the whole meaning of the verse and the whole intention of the psalm turn. Now immediately after the mention of a place, *there* must surely refer to that place, and not to a place mentioned in the previous verse and there too addressed as in the second person. The demonstrative *this*, is evidently used in a general way. (Comp. the fuller form, Judg. xviii. 4, &c.) The poet begins his special addition to the praises of Zion, by enumerating various renowned nations much in the same way as Horace's

"Laudabunt alii claram Rhodon, aut Mitylenen,"

only instead of leaving them as a theme to others he tells us what he himself in ordinary conversation might say of these places, and of the estimation in which their natives were held. It is hardly possible to escape from the conclusion that the Palestinian Jew is here implying his superiority to those of his race who were born abroad, a spirit shown so strongly in the relations of the Hebrews to the Hellenistic Jews in the New Testament.

Rahab undoubtedly stands for *Egypt*, but the exact origin of the term and of its connection with Egypt is much disputed. Most probably it is a term (possibly Coptic) for some large sea or river monster symbolic of Egypt. (Comp. the word "dragons," Ps. lxxiv. 13, and see Job ix. 13, xxvi. 12.)

Ethiopia.—Heb., *Khûsh* (in Authorised Version *Cush*). (See Gen. x. 6; 2 Kings xix. 9.)

There is no need with our explanation to look for emblematic reasons for the choice of names in this verse—as Egypt for antiquity; Babylon, strength; Tyre, wealth, &c. There is no one of the districts where Jews of the Dispersion might not have been found, but no doubt in his enumeration the poet takes care to mention countries near and far, as Philistia and Ethiopia. There appears, however, to have been a district in Babylonia known to the Hebrews as *Khûsh* (Lenormant, *Origines de l'Histoire;* and see a paper on the site of Eden, in the *Nineteenth Century* for October, 1882). The parallelism would be improved by this reference here.

⁽⁵⁾ **And of Zion . . .**—This verse must be taken as antithetical to the preceding. The poet claims a prouder boast for natives of Jerusalem, because it was established by the Most High. Render, *But of Zion it is said, "This man and that* (literally, *man and man) was born in her, and her the Most High established."*

⁽⁶⁾ The proud boast of the preceding verse is repeated here with allusion to the census or birth-register of citizens. (See Ezek. xiii. 9; Isa. iv. 3; Ps. lxix. 28, Note.) No doubt these lists were often produced or appealed to in triumph to mark the superiority of a native of Jerusalem over those born at a distance.

A Prayer of   PSALMS, LXXXVIII.   *Grievous Complaint.*

(7) As well the singers as the players on instruments *shall be there*: all my springs *are* in thee.

PSALM LXXXVIII.

A Song *or* Psalm [1] for the sons of Korah, to the chief Musician upon Mahalath Leannoth, [2] Maschil of Heman the Ezrahite.

(1) O LORD God of my salvation, I have cried day *and* night before thee: (2) let my prayer come before thee: incline thine ear unto my cry; (3) for my soul is full of troubles: and my life draweth nigh unto the grave. (4) I am counted with them that go down into the pit: I am as a man *that hath* no strength: (5) free among the dead, like the slain that lie in the grave, whom thou rememberest no more: and they are cut off [3] from thy hand. (6) Thou hast laid me in the lowest pit, in darkness, in the deeps. (7) Thy wrath lieth hard upon me, and thou hast afflicted *me* with all thy waves. Selah.

(8) Thou hast put away mine acquaintance far from me; thou hast made me an abomination unto them: *I am* shut up, and I cannot come forth. (9) Mine

[1] Or, *of.*

[2] Or, *A Psalm of Heman the Ezrahite, giving instruction.*

[3] Or, *by thy hand.*

---

(7) The literal sense of this most obscure verse is—

"And singers as trumpeters
All my springs in Thee,"

which we may paraphrase, keeping in the same line with the rest of the psalm, *For such an one* (celebrating his birthday, Gen. xl. 20, Matt. xiv. 6) *the singers and musicians will sing* (to Zion), "*All my offspring is in Thee.*" Not only is it a boast to have been born in Zion, but in the genuine Hebrew spirit the boast is continued into the future generations, and the Hebrew of the Hebrews exults in addressing the sacred city as the cradle of his family.

For this figurative application of the word "springs" to posterity, comp. Ps. lxviii. 26; Isa. xlviii. 1; Prov. v. 16.

LXXXVIII.

"If you listen," says Lord Bacon, "to David's harp, you will hear as many hearse-like airs as carols." But even among these this psalm stands alone and peculiar for the sadness of its tragic tone. From beginning to end—with the one exception of the word "salvation" in the first line—there is nothing to relieve its monotony of grief. If this wail of sorrow is the expression of individual suffering there is no particular interest in ascertaining its date, unless we could also fix on its author. Uzziah when in "the separate house" of leprosy" (see Note on verse 5), Hezekiah in his sick-room, Jeremiah in his pit, Job on his dunghill, have each in turn been suggested. But the very fact that the tone of the psalm suits any one of these as well, and no better, than another, warns us of the uselessness of such suggestions.

Indeed it is extremely doubtful whether the psalm is a picture of individual sorrow at all, and not rather a figurative description of national trouble. There is a want of distinctness in the cause of the mourning. The battle-field, sickness, flood, imprisonment, each in turn is employed to represent it; and while at one time speaking of himself as at the point of death (verse 3), the poet goes on now to picture himself as actually *in the grave*, in *sheôl* itself. The expression in verse 15, "from my youth up," is not in any way against the reference of the psalm to the community. (See Ps. cxxix. 1, where it is expressly said "Israel" may use the expression.) The poetical form is almost regular.

Title.—See titles, Pss. xlii., xlviii.

Upon Mahalath Leannoth.—See title, Ps. liii., where "Mahalath" occurs alone. Render, *Upon the sickness of distress, i.e.*, upon a sickening distress, and understand it, as in other cases, as the name of a tune or first words of a hymn associated with music suitable to this melancholy effusion.

For "Maschil" see title, Ps. xxxii.

Heman the Ezrahite—*i.e.*, of the family of Zerah, the letters having been transposed; not the Heman of 1 Chron. vi. 33, but of 1 Kings iv. 31; 1 Chron. ii. 6.

This long inscription is really made up of two: "A song or psalm for the sons of Korah," and "To the chief musician," &c.

(3) **Grave.**—*Sheôl.* Here, as in Pss. vi. 4, 5, xxxiii. 19; Isa. xxxviii. 10, 11, there comes into prominence the thought that death severs the covenant relation with God, and so presents an irresistible reason why prayer should be heard now before it is too late.

(4) **As a man...**—Rather, *like a hero whose strength is gone.*

(5) **Free among the dead...** — So the old versions without exception, taking *chaphshi* as an adjective, as in Job iii. 19 (where used of *an emancipated slave*); 1 Sam. xvii. 25 (*free from public burdens*). So of the *separate* house for lepers, who were *cut off* from society (2 Kings xv. 5). Hence some refer the psalm to Uzziah. The Targum explains, "freed from legal duties." But plainly the meaning is here exactly that of *defunctus.* The verse offers an instance of introverted parallelism, and this clause answers to "they are cut off from thy hand." Gesenius, however, makes the Hebrew word a noun (comp. Ezek. xxvii. 20), and renders, *among the dead is my couch.*

Whom thou.—The dead are "clean forgotten, out of mind" even to God.

From thy hand—*i.e.*, from the guiding, helping hand which, though stretched out for living men, does not reach to the grave.

(6) **Lowest pit.**—See Note, Ps. lxxxvi. 13.

(7) **And thou hast afflicted.**—Literally, *And thou hast pressed (me) down with all thy breakers*, supplying the object, and taking the accusative in the text as the instrument, as in Ps. cii. 23, where the same verb is used (Authorised Version, "weakened").

(8) **I am shut up.**—Not necessarily an actual imprisonment or incarceration on account of leprosy, but another figurative way of describing great trouble. Job xix. 8 seems to have been before the poet.

(9) **Mourneth.**—Rather, *fadeth*, or *pineth.* So a Latin poet of the effects of weeping:—

"Mæsta neque assiduo tabescere lumina fletu,
Cessarent, tristique imbre madere genæ."
CATULLUS: xxviii. 55.

eye mourneth by reason of affliction: LORD, I have called daily upon thee, I have stretched out my hands unto thee.

(10) Wilt thou shew wonders to the dead? shall the dead arise *and* praise thee? Selah. (11) Shall thy lovingkindness be declared in the grave? *or* thy faithfulness in destruction? (12) Shall thy wonders be known in the dark? and thy righteousness in the land of forgetfulness? (13) But unto thee have I cried, O LORD; and in the morning shall my prayer prevent thee.

(14) LORD, why castest thou off my soul? *why* hidest thou thy face from me? (15) I *am* afflicted and ready to die from *my* youth up: *while* I suffer thy terrors I am distracted. (16) Thy fierce wrath goeth over me; thy terrors have cut me off. (17) They came round about me ¹daily like water; they compassed me about together. (18) Lover and friend hast thou put far from me, *and* mine acquaintance into darkness.

PSALM LXXXIX.

² Maschil of Ethan the Ezrahite.

(1) I will sing of the mercies of the LORD for ever: with my mouth will I make known thy faithfulness ³ to all genera-

¹ Or, *all the day.*

² Or, *A Psalm for Ethan the Ezrahite, to give instruction.*

³ Heb., *to generation and generation.*

(10—12) These verses probably contain the prayer uttered with the "stretched-out hands."

(10) **Shall the dead arise? . . .**—These words are not to be taken in the sense of a final resurrection as we understand it. The hope of this had hardly yet dawned on Israel. The underworld is imagined as a vast sepulchre in which the dead lie, each in his place, silent and motionless, and the poet asks how they can rise there to utter the praise of God who has forgotten them (verse 5). That this is meant, and not a coming forth again into a land of living interests, is shown in the next two verses. (See Notes.)

Dead.—Heb., *rephaim,* a word applied also to the gigantic races of Palestine (Deut. ii. 11, 20, &c.), but here evidently (as also in Prov. ii. 18, ix. 18, xxi. 16; Isa. xiv. 9; xxvi. 19) meaning the *dead.*

All the passages cited confirm the impression got from this psalm of the Hebrew conception of the state of the dead. They were languid, sickly shapes, lying supine, cut off from all the hopes and interests of the upper air, and even oblivious of them all, but retaining so much of sensation as to render them conscious of the gloomy monotony of death. (Comp. Isa. xxxviii. 18; Eccles. xvii. 27, 28; Baruch ii. 17.)

(11, 12) In these verses appear three prominent features of the Hebrew conception of the underworld. It is a place of "destruction" (comp. Job xxvi. 6; xxviii. 22), of "darkness" (comp. verse 6), and of "forgetfulness," which may imply not only that the dead are forgotten, both of God and men (comp. Ps. xxxi. 12 with verse 5), but that they themselves have, to borrow the heathen figure, drunk of the water of Lethe. (Comp. Pss. vi. 5, xxx. 9, and for both ideas combined Eccles. ix. 5—10.)

(11) **Lovingkindness.**—Better here, *covenant grace.* The grave knew nothing of this. Death severed the covenant relationship. So "faithfulness," "wonders," "righteousness" are all used in their limited sense as determined by the covenant.

(13) **But unto Thee . . .**—Better, *But as for me, I,* &c. The pronoun is emphatic. The speaker has *not* gone down to the land where all is silent and forgotten, and can therefore still cry to God, and send his prayer to meet (prevent, *i.e.* go to meet; see Ps. xvii. 13) the Divine Being who still has an interest in him. And this makes the expostulation of the next verses still stronger. Why, since the sufferer is still alive, is he forsaken, or seemingly forsaken, by the God of that covenant in which he still abides?

(14) **Castest thou off.**—The idea is that of throwing away something with loathing. (Comp. Ps. xliii. 2.)

(15) **Terrors.**—Another of the many expressions which connect this psalm with the book of Job. (See Job vi. 4, ix. 34, &c.)

Distracted.—The Hebrew word is peculiar to the place. The ancient versions all agree in taking it as a verb, and rendering it by some general term denoting "trouble." But the context evidently requires a stronger word, and possibly connecting with a cognate word meaning "wheel," we may get, "I turn giddy." A change of a stroke in one letter would give "I grow frigid." (Comp. Ps. xxxviii. 8.)

(16) **Have cut me off.**—Or, *extinguished me.* The form of the verb is very peculiar, and is variously explained. All that is certain is that it is intensive, expressing the hopeless and continued state of prostration of the sufferer. The LXX., "have frightened."

(17) **They**—*i.e.*, the terrors or horrors, now likened to a flood, a figure of frequent occurrence. (See Ps. xviii. 16, &c.)

(18) **And mine acquaintance into darkness.**— This is an erroneous rendering. Rather, *My acquaintance is darkness,* or, *darkness is my friend,* having taken the place of those removed. The feeling resembles Job xvii. 14; or we may illustrate by Tennyson's lines:—

"O sorrow, wilt thou live with me,
No casual mistress, but a wife,
My bosom friend, and half my life?
As I confess it needs must be."

LXXXIX.

This long psalm comes evidently from a time of great national depression and trouble. The idolatries that led to the Captivity, and the Captivity itself, are already in the past, and the poet can think only of the splendid promises of God to the race, and the paradox that while made by a God of truth and faithfulness, they have yet been broken; for Israel lies prostrate, a prey to cruel and rapacious foes, and the cry, "How long?" goes up in despair to heaven. The "servant" and "anointed" (verses 38 and 39) need not necessarily be a prince of the house of David—Rehoboam or Jehoiachim, or another; but the whole nation individualised and presented in the person of one of the Davidic princes, as in that of David himself (Ps. cxxxii. 17). The time of the persecution of Antiochus Epiphanes suits best all the conditions presented by the psalm.

tions. (2) For I have said, Mercy shall be built up for ever: thy faithfulness shalt thou establish in the very heavens. (3) I have made a covenant with my chosen, I have ᵃsworn unto David my servant, (4) Thy seed will I establish for ever, and build up thy throne ¹to all generations. Selah. (5) And the heavens shall praise thy wonders, O LORD: thy faithfulness also in the congregation of the saints. (6) For who in the heaven can be compared unto the LORD? who among the sons of the mighty can be likened unto the LORD? (7) God is greatly to be feared in the assembly of the saints, and to be had in reverence of all *them that are* about him.

(8) O LORD God of hosts, who *is a* strong LORD like unto thee? or to thy faithfulness round about thee? (9) Thou rulest the raging of the sea: when the waves thereof arise, thou stillest them. (10) Thou hast broken ²Rahab in pieces, as one that is slain; thou hast scattered thine enemies ³with thy strong arm. (11) ᵇThe heavens *are* thine, the earth also *is* thine: *as for* the world and the fulness thereof, thou hast founded them. (12) The north and the south thou hast created them: Tabor and Hermon shall rejoice in thy name.

(13) Thou hast ⁴a mighty arm: strong is thy hand, *and* high is thy right hand. (14) Justice and judgment *are* the ⁵habitation of thy throne: mercy and truth shall go before thy face.

Marginal notes:
ᵃ 2 Sam. 7. 11, &c.
¹ Heb., *to generation and generation.*
² Or, *Egypt.*
³ Heb., *with the arm of thy strength.*
ᵇ Gen. 1. 1; Is. 24. 1, & 50. 12.
⁴ Heb., *an arm with might.*
⁵ Or, *establishment.*

The poetical form is nearly regular, and the parallelism well marked.

Title.—For "Maschil" see title, Ps. xxxii.
Ethan the Ezrahite.—Probably to be identified with the man mentioned (1 Kings iv. 31) as among the celebrated sages surpassed by Solomon, and called Ezrahites, as being of the family of Zerah (1 Chron. ii. 6; see Note to title to last psalm). Probably when the titles were prefixed this sage had become confused with Ethan (or Jeduthun), the singer.

(1) **I will sing.**—This lyric purpose soon loses itself in a dirge.
For ever.—The Hebrew ('ôlam) has properly neither the abstract idea of negation of time, nor the concrete (Christian) idea of eternity, but implies indefiniteness, and looks either backwards or forwards.
With my mouth—*i.e.*, aloud, or loudly.

(2) **Mercy . . . faithfulness.**—These words, so often combined, express here, as commonly in the psalms, the attitude of the covenant God towards His people. The art of the poet is shown in this exordium. He strikes so strongly this note of the inviolability of the Divine promise only to make the deprecation of present neglect on God's part presently more striking.
Shall be built up for ever.—Better, *is for ever being built up.* Elsewhere figured as a "place of shelter," a "tower of refuge," God's faithfulness is here presented as an edifice for ever rising on foundations laid in the heavens. (Comp. Ps. cxix. 89.) The heavens are at once the type of unchangeableness and of splendour and height. Mant's paraphrase brings out the power of the verse:—

"For I have said, Thy mercies rise,
A deathless structure, to the skies:
The heavens were planted by Thy hand,
And as the heavens Thy truth shall stand."

And Wordsworth has sung of Him:—

"Who fixed immovably the frame
Of the round world, and built by laws as strong
The solid refuge for distress,
The towers of righteousness."

(Comp. Ps. xxxvi. 6.)

(3) **I have sworn.**—The prophetic passage (2 Sam. vii. 12, *seq.*) is in the poet's mind.

(5) **The heavens.**—Having repeated the Divine promise, the poet appeals to nature and history to confirm his conviction of the enduring character of the truth and grace of God. The heavens are witnesses of it as in Pss. l. 4, 6, xcvii. 6.
Shall praise.—The present tense would be better.
Wonders.—In the original the word is singular, perhaps as summing up all the covenant faithfulness as one great display of wonder.
Saints.—Here, apparently, not spoken of Israel, but of the hosts above. (See next verse; comp. Job iv. 18, xv. 15 for the same term, "holy ones," for angels.)

(6) **Sons of the mighty.**—Rather, *sons of God*—*i.e.*, angels. (Comp. Ps. xxix. 1.)

(7) It is better to take this verse in apposition with the foregoing:

"God sublime in the council of the holy ones,
And terrible among those surrounding him."

For a picture of the court of heaven see Job i. 6.

(8—13) Not only is God incomparable in heaven, He is also the only mighty and lofty one in nature or history.

(8) **O Lord.**—The Hebrew marches more grandly than the Authorised Version:

"Jehovah, God of Hosts,
Who as Thou is mighty, Jah?
And Thy faithfulness surrounds Thee."

Or the last clause may be rendered, *and what faithfulness is like that round about thee?* We must either think of the attendant throngs of loyal angels, or of God clothed as it were with faithfulness.

(10) **Rahab.**—See Note, Ps. lxxxvii. 4. The mention of the sea has carried the poet's thoughts to the Red Sea and the deliverance from Egypt, which is represented as some huge monster conquered and crushed.

(12) **Tabor and Hermon.**—Introduced not only as standing roughly for west and east, but for their prominence and importance in the landscape. (Comp. Hos. v. 1.)
Shall rejoice.—Better, *sing for joy.*

(13) **High is thy right hand.**—The strong hand is supposed raised to strike. (Comp. verse 42.)

(14) **Habitation.** — Rather, *foundation*, or *pillars*. Righteousness and judgment support God's throne, and mercy and truth ("those genii of sacred history") precede (*present* tense, not *future*) Him as forerunners precede a king.

God's Favour to   PSALMS, LXXXIX.   *the House of David.*

(15) Blessed *is* the people that know the *a* joyful sound: they shall walk, O LORD, in the light of thy countenance. (16) In thy name shall they rejoice all the day: and in thy righteousness shall they be exalted. (17) For thou *art* the glory of their strength: and in thy favour our horn shall be exalted. (18) For [1] the LORD *is* our defence; and the Holy One of Israel *is* our king. (19) Then thou spakest in vision to thy holy one, and saidst, I have laid help upon *one that is* mighty; I have exalted *one* chosen out of the people. (20) *b* I have found David my servant; with my holy oil have I anointed him: (21) with whom my hand shall be established: mine arm also shall strengthen him. (22) The enemy shall not exact upon him; nor the son of wickedness afflict him. (23) And I will beat down his foes before his face, and plague them that hate him. (24) But my faithfulness and my mercy *shall be* with him: and in my name shall his horn be exalted. (25) I will set his hand also in the sea, and his right hand in the rivers. (26) He shall cry unto me, Thou *art* my father, my God, and the rock of my salvation. (27) Also I will make him *my* firstborn, higher than the kings of the earth. (28) My mercy will I keep for him for evermore, and my covenant shall stand fast with him. (29) His seed also will I make *to endure* for ever, and his throne as the days of heaven. (30) If his children forsake my law, and walk not in my judgments; (31) if they [2] break my statutes, and keep not my commandments; (32) then will I visit their transgression with the rod, and their iniquity with stripes. (33) Nevertheless my lovingkindness [3] will I not utterly take from him, nor suffer my faithfulness [4] to fail. (34) My covenant will I not break, nor alter the thing that is gone out of my lips. (35) Once have I sworn by my holiness [5] that I will not lie unto David. (36) *c* His

a Num. 10. 6.

[1] Or, *our shield is of the* LORD, *and our king is of the Holy One of Israel.*

b 1 Sam. 16. 12.

[2] Heb., *profane my statutes.*

[3] Heb., *I will not make void from him.*

[4] Heb., *to lie.*

[5] Heb., *if I lie.*

c 2 Sam. 7. 16; Luke 1. 33; John 12. 34.

---

(15) **That know the joyful sound**—*i.e.*, that are familiar with the shouting and music that accompanied the feasts of Israel.

They shall walk.—Better in the present; and so of the verb in the next verse. The light of Jehovah's countenance of course means His favour.

(17) **Glory.**—Better, *ornament.* The crown of a nation's strength is not the triumphs it wins, nor the prosperity it secures, but the spirit in which these are used. Humility, and not pride, acknowledgment of God, and not conceit in her wealth or power, was the ornament of Israel's strength, and made her greatness in her best days.

Our horn shall be exalted.—See Note, Ps. cxxxii. 17. Modern Eastern proverbs, such as "What a fine horn he has!" spoken of a great man, still preserve the figure.

(18) **For the Lord.**—Or, rather—

"For of Jehovah is our shield,
And of Israel's Holy One our king,"

"shield" and "king" being in synonymous parallelism. Jehovah is the source of the theocratic power.

(19) The mention of the king allows the poet to bring still more into prominence the special promises made to Israel. The piece, which is couched in oracular language, is introduced by a prose statement recalling the sentences in Job which introduce a fresh speaker.

Holy one.—See Note, Ps. xvi. 10. Some MSS. (comp. LXX. and Vulg.) have the plural. The singular is correct, referring no doubt to Nathan, as is seen from 2 Sam. vii. 17; 1 Chron. xvii. 15. The oracular piece that follows (verses 19—37) is like Ps. cxxxii. 11—12, founded on this old prophetic passage; but while the original reference is to Solomon, here it is extended to all David's posterity.

I have . . .—Better, *I have placed help in a hero*—*i.e.*, I have chosen a hero as a champion for Israel.

(22) **Exact.**—This meaning is possible, and is supported by the LXX. and Vulgate, "shall not get profit." There may be an allusion to Deut. xv. 6, but perhaps it is better to take the verb in the same sense as the Hebrew margin of Ps. lv. 15, "shall not surprise him;" Symmachus has, "lead him astray."

(23) **Beat down.**—Probably *bray*, as in a mortar.

Plague.—Or, *smite.*

(24) **Faithfulness and mercy**, represented in verse 14 as God's attendants, are here commissioned to act as a guard to David and his house.

(25) **In the sea.**—A reference, as in Pss. lxxii. 8, lxxx. 11, to the limits of the Solomonic kingdom, the Mediterranean and the Euphrates. For the figure we may compare a saying attributed by Curtius to some Scythian ambassadors, who addressed Alexander in these terms: "If the gods had given thee a body as great as thy mind, the whole world would not be able to contain thee. Thou wouldst reach with one hand to the east, and with the other to the west."

(26) **He shall cry.**—This verse is interesting in view of the theological development in the psalter. We might think that the poet was referring to an actual psalm of David, with whom the expression, "My God, the rock of my salvation," was familiar (see Ps. xviii. 1, 2, &c.), were it not for the word "Father," a title for the Divine Being which the national religion did not frame till the exile period (Jer. iii. 4, 19; Isa. lxiii. 16).

(27) **Firstborn.**—Jesse's youngest son became the firstborn, the favourite son of God. Here, of course, the epithet is extended to all the Davidic succession.

(29) **Days of heaven.**—Deut. xi. 21. (Comp. Ps. lxxii. 5; and see below, verse 36.)

(30—33) An elaboration of 2 Sam. vii. 14, 15, and evidently made with a purpose. The poet acknowledges the sin of Israel in past times, but also regards the sufferings of the exile as having been the punish-

seed shall endure for ever, and his throne as the sun before me. (37) It shall be established for ever as the moon, and *as* a faithful witness in heaven. Selah.

(38) But thou hast cast off and abhorred, thou hast been wroth with thine anointed. (39) Thou hast made void the covenant of thy servant: thou hast profaned his crown *by casting it* to the ground. (40) Thou hast broken down all his hedges; thou hast brought his strong holds to ruin. (41) All that pass by the way spoil him: he is a reproach to his neighbours. (42) Thou hast set up the right hand of his adversaries; thou hast made all his enemies to rejoice. (43) Thou hast also turned the edge of his sword, and hast not made him to stand in the battle. (44) Thou hast made his ¹glory to cease, and cast his throne down to the ground. (45) The days of his youth hast thou shortened: thou hast covered him with shame. Selah.

(46) How long, LORD? wilt thou hide thyself for ever? shall thy wrath burn like fire? (47) Remember how short my time is: wherefore hast thou made all men in vain? (48) What man *is he that* liveth, and shall not see death? shall he deliver his soul from the hand of the grave? Selah.

(49) Lord, where *are* thy former lovingkindnesses, *which* thou ᵃswarest unto David in thy truth? (50) Remember, Lord, the reproach of thy servants; *how* I do bear in my bosom *the reproach of* all the mighty people; (51) wherewith thine enemies have reproached, O LORD; wherewith they have reproached the footsteps of thine anointed.

(52) Blessed *be* the LORD for evermore. Amen, and Amen.

¹ Heb., *brightness.*

ᵃ 2 Sam. 7. 15.

---

ment foretold by them. Hence the sin has been expiated, and the perplexity arises why Israel is still afflicted.

(37) **And as a faithful witness in heaven.**—Rather, *and there is a faithful witness in heaven*, which the parallelism shows to be the *moon*, just mentioned. The moon (see Ps. lxxxi. 3) was to the Jews—as to the ancients generally—the "arbiter of festivals," and the festivals were signs of the covenant, consequently that luminary might well be called "a witness in heaven."

(38) **But thou.**—The poem takes a new departure here. God is reproached for violating the covenant, and the contrast between the actual condition of things in Israel at present, and the glorious destiny promised, is feelingly set forth.

The boldness of this expostulation has scandalised the Jewish expositors. But see exactly similar language, Ps. xliv. 9, 22. The point of the poem, indeed, is gone if we soften down these expressions. The stronger the conviction of the inviolability of God's promises, the more vehement becomes the sense of right to expostulate at their seeming violation, the delay of the fulfilment of the covenant. We may illustrate by the Latin poet's

"Hic pietatis honos, sic nos in sceptra reponis?"
VIRGIL: *Æn.* i. 25.

(39) **Made void.**—Better, *cast off*, as the word is rendered in Lam. ii. 7, the only other place where it occurs. There the LXX. have "shook off;" here, "turned upside down."

Thou hast profaned.—Comp. Ps. lxxiv. 7.

(43) **Edge of his sword.**—The Hebrew is *tsûr, i.e., rock*, and a comparison with Josh. v. 2 (margin) suggests that we have here a reminiscence of the "stone age." The word "flint" for the edge of a weapon might easily survive the actual use of the implement itself. So we should still speak of "a foeman's steel" even if the use of chemical explosives entirely abolished the use of sword and bayonet. This is one of the cases where the condition of modern science helps us in exegesis of the Bible. The ancient versions, who knew nothing of the stone or iron ages, paraphrase, by "strength," or "help."

(44) **Thou hast . . .**—Literally, *Thou hast made to cease from his brightness—i.e.*, the brightness of the sun, promised in verse 36.

To the ground.—From being as the sun in heaven.

(46) **How long.**—With this persistent cry of the Maccabæan age (see Ps. lxxiv. 10), the poet shows that faith is not extinct, though it has a sore struggle with despair.

(47) **Remember.**—The text of this clause runs, *Remember I how duration*, which might possibly be an incoherent sob, meaning *remember how quickly I pass.* But since the transposition of a letter brings the clause into conformity with Ps. xxxix. 4, "how frail I am," it is better to adopt the change.

Wherefore hast thou . . .—Literally, *for what vanity hast thou created all men?*

"Count all the joys thine hours have seen,
Count all the days from anguish free,
And know, whatever thou hast been,
'Twere something better not to be."—BYRON.

(48) **What man.**—Rather, *What hero*, or *champion*, or *great man*. The word is used of a king (Jer. xxii. 30; comp. Isa. xxii. 17). The verse repeats a common poetic theme :—

"Pallida mors æquo pulsat pede pauperum tabernas,
Regumque turres."—HORACE, I. *Od.* iv.

The hand of the grave.—Rather, *of the underworld*, "hand" being used for "power."

(50) The phrase, "bear in my bosom," is explained by Ps. lxxix. 12.

(51) **Footsteps . . .**—Every step taken by Israel was the subject of reproach. Rabbinical writers connect the verse with the delay of the Messiah, since it brings reproach on those who wait for him in vain.

The Eternity of God   PSALMS, XC.   *and the Frailty of Man.*

Book IV.

PSALM XC.

¹ A Prayer of Moses the man of God.

(1) Lord, thou hast been our dwelling place ² in all generations. (2) Before the mountains were brought forth, or ever thou hadst formed the earth and the world, even from everlasting to everlasting, thou *art* God. (3) Thou turnest man to destruction; and sayest, Return, ye children of men. (4) ᵃ For a thousand years in thy sight are but as yesterday ³ when it is past, and as a watch in the night. (5) Thou carriest them away as with a flood; they are *as* a sleep: in the morning *they are* like grass *which* ⁴ groweth up. (6) In the morning it flourisheth, and groweth up; in the evening it is cut down, and withereth.

Marginal notes:
1 Or, *A Prayer, being a Psalm of Moses.*
2 Heb., *in generation and generation.*
a 2 Pet. 3. 8.
3 Or, *when he hath passed* them.
4 Or, *is changed.*

Book IV.

XC.

Notwithstanding the unanimous rejection of the Mosaic title of this psalm by the ancient and mediæval Christian commentators, it has found supporters among modern critics. It is urged that the transitoriness of human life was a theme peculiarly suited to the leader of a race doomed to wander in the wilderness till the sinful generation had died out, and that the general train of thought and feeling is worthy of Moses standing on the threshold of hopes he was not to be allowed to realise. It is a slender thread to support what, if we must regard it as more than a rabbinical conjecture, was probably the vaguest of traditions. (See *General Introduction* on the titles.) The subject of the brevity and vanity of life has occupied reflective minds in all periods and countries. Only a Hebrew could have handled it as it is handled here; but the contrast drawn between human frailty and Divine immutability is more suited to a later age of Israel than an early one. The very first verse seems to take a far more extended retrospect than was possible to Moses, while the pathetic cry, "How long?" in verse 13, suggests, as we have seen in the case of other psalms, even the Maccabæan age (but see title).

In one view it would be a misfortune to be able to fix on the precise moment when this poem was composed, and the voice that first spoke it. For it is what it has been well called "the funeral hymn of the world," and it belongs not to one race or age, but to the sorrows and the hopes of all the successive generations, who at the open grave have derived, or shall derive, consolation and faith from its Divine words. There is no definite verse structure. The rhythm is subordinated to the feeling.

Title.—Moses is called "the man of God," as in Deut. xxxiii. 1; Josh. xiv. 6; 1 Chron. xxiii. 14; 2 Chron. xxx. 16; Ezra iii. 2.

The Mosaic authorship is a question depending in a great measure on the view held as to the date of the later part of Deuteronomy, to which there are resemblances in many points of style and some points of detail. Those who bring the composition of that work down to the eighth century before Christ will unhesitatingly refer this psalm to a date as late, if not later. (For more, see *Introduction.*)

(1) **Dwelling place.**—LXX. and Vulg., "refuge," possibly reading *maôz* (as in Ps. xxxvii. 39) instead of *maôn*. So some MSS. But Deut. xxxiii. 17 has the feminine of this latter word, and the idea of a *continued abode* strikes the key-note of the psalm. The short duration of each succeeding generation of men on the earth is contrasted with the eternity of God and the permanence given to Israel as a race by the covenant that united them with the Eternal. But we may give extension to the thought. Human history runs on from generation to generation (so the Hebrew; comp. Deut. xxxii. 7); one goes, another comes; but in relation to the unchanging God, who rules over all human history, even the transient creatures of an hour may come to feel secure and at home.

(2) **Before the mountains.**—Render either,

"Before the mountains were born,
Or ever the earth and world were brought forth,"

in synonymous parallelism, or, better, in progressive,

"Before the mountains were born,
Or ever the earth and world brought forth"—

i.e., before vegetation or life appeared. (Comp. Job xv. 7.) "Mountains" are a frequent symbol of antiquity, as well as of enduring strength. (See Gen. xlix. 26; Prov. viii. 25.) The expression, "earth and the world," may be taken as meaning the earth, as distinguished from either heaven or the sea, and the habitable globe (LXX., οἰκουμένη). (Comp. Prov. viii. 31.)

From everlasting to everlasting—*i.e.*, from an indefinite past to an indefinite future (literally, *from hidden time to hidden*).

(3) **Thou turnest . . .**—Probably we must render, *Thou turnest man to dust; and sayest, Turn, sons of Adam*—*i.e.*, one generation dies and another succeeds (see Ps. civ. 29, 30), the continuance of the race being regarded as distinctly due to Divine power as the Creation, to which there is probably allusion.

The LXX. suggest as the true reading, "Turn not man to dust, but say rather," &c.

(4) **A thousand years.**—This verse, which, when Peter II. was written (see *New Testament Commentary*), had already begun to receive an arithmetical treatment, and to be made the basis for Millennarian computations, merely contrasts the unchangeableness and eternity of the Divine existence and purpose with the vicissitudes incident to the brief life of man. To One who is from the infinite past to the infinite future, and Whose purpose runs through the ages, a thousand years are no more than a yesterday to man:

"And all our yesterdays have lighted fools
The way to dusty death;"

or even as a part of the night passed in sleep:

"A thousand years, with Thee they are no more
Than yesterday, which, ere it is, is spent.
Or, as a watch by night, that course doth keep,
And goes and comes, unwares to them that sleep."
                      FRANCIS BACON.

The exact rendering of the words translated in the Authorised Version, "when it passeth," is doubtful. The LXX. have, "which has passed;" and the Syriac supports this rendering. For the "night watches," see Note, Ps. lxiii. 6.

(5, 6) The following is suggested as the most satisfactory rendering of these verses: *Time* (literally, a

The Frailty and Brevity   PSALMS, XC.   *of Human Life*

(7) For we are consumed by thine anger, and by thy wrath are we troubled.

(8) Thou hast set our iniquities before thee, our secret *sins* in the light of thy countenance.

(9) For all our days are ¹passed away in thy wrath: we spend our years ²as a tale *that is told*. (10) ³The days of our years *are* threescore years and ten; and if by reason of strength *they be* fourscore years, yet *is* their strength labour and sorrow; for it is soon cut off, and we fly away. (11) Who knoweth the power of thine anger? even according to thy fear, *so is* thy wrath. (12) So teach *us* to number our days, that we may ⁴apply *our* hearts unto wisdom.

(13) Return, O LORD, how long? and

¹ Heb., *turned away*.
² Or, *as a meditation*.
³ Heb., *As for the days of our years, in them are seventy years*.
⁴ Heb., *cause to come*.

---

year; but the root-idea is the *repetition* or *change of the seasons*) *carries them away with its flood; they are in the morning like grass sprouting; in the morning it flourishes and sprouts, in the evening it is cut down and withered.*

This is obtained by taking the verb as third feminine instead of second masculine, and slightly changing the vowels of the noun rendered in Authorised Version *sleep*. The confusion of the metaphor is thus avoided, and immediately on the mention of the *stream of time* is suggested the image of the vegetation springing into life at the first touch of rain, and dying in a day—an image so natural to an Oriental. The verb, *carries away with its flood*, is found only here and in Ps. lxxvii. 17 ("the clouds poured out water"), but the cognate noun is frequent for a heavy rainfall (Isa. iv. 6, &c.), such as in the East in a few moments causes a flood. This interpretation is partly supported by the LXX. and Vulg.: "Their years shall be nothingness;" and many commentators have felt that the image of the "stream of time" was required here. For the rendering *cut down*, comp. Job xxiv. 24. Some prefer "fades." The general force of the figure is the same whether we think of the generations dropping away like withered grass or cut down and dried like hay.

(7) **We.**—The change to the first person plural shows that the poet was not merely moralising on the brevity of human life, but uttering a dirge over the departed glory of Israel. Instead of proving superior to vicissitude the covenant race had shared it.

Troubled.—Comp. Ps. xlviii. 5. Better here, *frightened away*.

(8) **Our secret sins.**—Or, to keep the singular of the original, *our secret* (character).

The expression, "light of God's countenance," usually means "favour." But here the word rendered light is not the usual one employed in that expression, but rather means a body of light: "the sun (or eye) of Thy countenance." Comp.:

"Then Seeva opened on the accursed one
His eye of anger."
        SOUTHEY: *Curse of Kehama*.

(9) **Are passed away.**—Better, *are declining*.

A tale.—Rather, *a murmur*. (See Note, Ps. i. 2.) Probably, from the parallelism with *wrath*, a moan of sadness. So in Ezek. ii. 10, "a sound of woe." Since the cognate verb often means "meditate," some render here *thought*. Theognis says,

"Gallant youth speeds by like a thought."

(10) **Yet is their strength . . .**—The LXX. (and so Vulg.) appear to have had a slightly different reading, which gives much better sense: "Yet their additional years are but labour and sorrow." The old man has no reason to congratulate himself on passing the ordinary limit of life.

For it is soon cut off.—This seems hardly to give, as it professes to do, a reason for the fact that the prolongation of life beyond its ordinary limit brings trouble and sorrow, and we are compelled to see if the words can convey a different meaning. Literally the clause is, *for* (or *thus*) *passeth haste, and we fly away* (like a bird), which may be rendered, *thus there comes a haste that we may fly away*; *i.e.*, even though we may have prayed for an extension of life, it brings with it such weariness that we long at last to escape—a fact sufficiently true to experience.

"Yet are these feet, whose strengthless stay is numb,
Unable to support this lump of clay,
Swift winged with desire to get a grave."
        SHAKSPEARE.

(11) **Who knoweth . . .**—Better,

Who regardeth Thine anger
And—in a measure due to reverence—Thy wrath?

Who (no doubt with thought of Israel's enemies) *has that just terror of Thy wrath which a truly reverential regard would produce?* It is only the persons who have that fearful and bowed apprehension of His Majesty, and that sacred dread of all offence to Him, which is called the "fear of God." And this is not inconsistent with a child-like trust and love, and a peaceful security ("Of whom, then, shall I be afraid?"). On the other hand, those who scoff against religion often become the victims of wild and base terror.

(12) **Number our days.**—This verse as it stands literally gives *to allot*, or *in allotting* (see Isa. lxv. 12), *our days, so teach, and we will cause to come the heart wisdom*. The last clause, if intelligible at all, must mean "that we may offer a wise heart," and the natural way to understand the verse is to make God, not man, as in the Authorised Version, the reckoner of the days. "In allotting our days thus make us know (*i.e.*, make us know the power of Thine anger), in order that we may present a wise heart."

The verse must evidently be taken in close connection with the preceding, or the point of the petition is lost, and though the ordinary rendering, "Teach us to number our days," has given birth to a number of sayings which might be quoted in illustration, it is neither in itself very intelligible, nor, except by one instance in later Hebrew, can it be supported as a rendering of the original.

(13) **Return.**—Better, *turn*, either from anger (Exod. xxxii. 12), or merely as in Ps. vi. 4, "turn to thy servant."

Plainly we have here the experience of some particular epoch, and a prayer for Israel. From his meditation on the shortness of human existence the poet does not pass to a prayer for a prolonged life for himself, like Hezekiah, but for some intervention in relief of the suffering community of which he forms part.

How long?—See Note, Ps. lxxiv. 9.

Let it repent thee.—Better, *have pity on*. (See Deut. xxxii. 36.)

The Lord a Refuge   PSALMS, XCI.   *from the Pestilence.*

let it repent thee concerning thy servants. ⁽¹⁴⁾ O satisfy us early with thy mercy; that we may rejoice and be glad all our days. ⁽¹⁵⁾ Make us glad according to the days *wherein* thou hast afflicted us, *and* the years *wherein* we have seen evil. ⁽¹⁶⁾ Let thy work appear unto thy servants, and thy glory unto their children. ⁽¹⁷⁾ And let the beauty of the LORD our God be upon us: and establish thou the work of our hands upon us; yea, the work of our hands establish thou it.

PSALM XCI.

⁽¹⁾ He that dwelleth in the secret place of the most High shall ¹abide under the shadow of the Almighty.

⁽²⁾ I will say of the LORD, *He is* my refuge and my fortress: my God; in him will I trust.

⁽³⁾ Surely he shall deliver thee from the snare of the fowler, *and* from the noisome pestilence. ⁽⁴⁾ He shall cover thee with his feathers, and under his wings shalt thou trust: his truth *shall be thy* shield and buckler. ⁽⁵⁾ Thou shalt not be afraid for the terror by night; *nor* for the arrow *that* flieth by day; ⁽⁶⁾ *nor* for the pestilence *that* walketh in darkness; *nor* for the destruction *that* wasteth at noonday. ⁽⁷⁾ A thousand shall fall at thy side, and ten thousand at thy right hand; *but* it shall not come nigh thee. ⁽⁸⁾ Only with thine eyes shalt thou behold and see the reward of the wicked.

⁽⁹⁾ Because thou hast made the LORD, *which is* my refuge, *even* the most High, thy habitation; ⁽¹⁰⁾ there shall no evil befall thee, neither shall any plague come nigh thy dwelling.

1 Heb., *lodge.*

⁽¹⁴⁾ **Early**—*i.e.,* in the morning of new hope and courage after the night of affliction is spent. (See Ps. xlvi. 5.)

⁽¹⁵⁾ A prayer that prosperity may follow, proportionate to the mercy that has been endured.

⁽¹⁷⁾ **Beauty.**—Or, *pleasantness.* The Hebrew word, like the Greek χάρις, and our "grace," seems to combine the ideas of "beauty" and "favour."

XCI.

There are no data for ascertaining either the author or the date of this psalm. The variety of the figures employed seems to indicate a general view of life and its possible perils. It may have been a time when both war and pestilence were raging, but we cannot recover it. Whoever first breathed these words of trust, thousands have found them a source of strength and faith in the hour of trial and danger. Stier mentions that some years ago an eminent physician in St. Petersburg recommended this psalm as the best preservative against the cholera. It will also occur to every one that the psalm is the Hebrew, or, perhaps, rather the religious, expression of Horace's ode,

"Integer vitæ scelerisque purus."

The parallelism is fine and sustained.

(1, 2) **He ... I.**—The especial difficulty of this psalm, its abrupt changes of person, meets us at the outset. The text literally rendered, runs : "*He sitting in the hiding place of the Most High; In the shadow of the Almighty he lodgeth, I say to Jehovah, My refuge and my fortress, My God, I trust in Him.*" The change in the last clause presents no particular difficulty, as many similar instances occur; but that from the *third* person, in the first verse, to the *first,* in the second, is very awkward, and many shifts have been adopted to get out of it. The best is to supply the word *blessed* : "Blessed is he that," &c.* The different names for God employed here should be noticed. By their accumulation the poet makes the sum of assurance doubly sure.

(3) **Snare of the fowler.**—The image of the net has occurred frequently before. (See Ps. x. 15, &c.)

Here, as in Eccles. ix. 12, it is used generally of any unexpected peril to life.

Noisome pestilence.—Literally, *pestilence of calamities, i.e.,* fatal. (See Ps. lvii. 1, where the same word "calamities" occurs.)

(4) **Feathers ... wings ...**—For this beautiful figure, here elaborated, see Ps. xvii. 8, Note.

(5) **Terror by night.**—Possibly a night attack by an enemy. (Comp. Song of Sol. iii. 8; Prov. iii. 23—26.) Comp. Milton :—

"To bless the doors from nightly harm."

In this case the arrow flying by day would refer to dangers of actual battle. But it is quite possible that the latter may be merely the Oriental expression for the pestilence, since it is still so called by Arabians. "I desired to remove to a less contagious air. I received from Solyman the emperor this message : that the emperor wondered what I meant in desiring to remove my habitation. *Is not the pestilence God's arrow, which will always hit his mark ?*"—Quoted in Spurgeon's *Treasury of David,* from Busbequin's *Travels.*

(6) **Darkness ... noonday.**—Night and noon are, in Oriental climates, the most unwholesome, the former from exhalations, the latter from the fierce heat.

Destruction.—From a root meaning "to cut off;" here, from parallelism, "deadly sickness."

(7) **It shall not come nigh thee.**—*It, i.e.,* no one of the dangers enumerated. The pious Israelite bears a charmed life. Safe under Divine protection, he only sees the *effect* of perils that pass by him harmless.

(9) **Thou ... my.**—The difficulty of the change of person is avoided by the Authorised Version, but only with violence to the text, which runs, "For thou, Jehovah, my refuge; thou hast made the Most High thy habitation." It is best to take the first line as a kind of under-soliloquy. The poet is assuring himself of the protection which will be afforded one who trusts in God; and he interrupts his soliloquy, as it were, with a comment upon it : "Yes, this is true of myself, for Thou Jehovah art indeed my refuge." (For the Most High as a dwelling place, see Ps. xc. 1.)

(10) **Dwelling.**—Literally, *tent :* an instance in which the patriarchal life became stereotyped, so to speak, in

---

* The omission of this word by a copyist would be very natural, from its confusion with the numerical heading of the psalm and the initial letter of the word that now begins it.

The Faithfulness and   PSALMS, XCII.   *Majesty of God.*

(11) ^a For he shall give his angels charge over thee, to keep thee in all thy ways. (12) They shall bear thee up in *their* hands, lest thou dash thy foot against a stone. (13) Thou shalt tread upon the lion and ¹ adder: the young lion and the dragon shalt thou trample under feet.

(14) Because he hath set his love upon me, therefore will I deliver him: I will set him on high, because he hath known my name. (15) He shall call upon me, and I will answer him: I *will be* with him in trouble; I will deliver him, and honour him. (16) With ² long life will I satisfy him, and shew him my salvation.

PSALM XCII.

A Psalm or Song for the sabbath day.

(1) It is a good thing to give thanks unto the LORD, and to sing praises unto thy name, O most High: (2) to shew forth thy lovingkindness in the morning, and thy faithfulness ³ every night, (3) upon an instrument of ten strings, and upon the psaltery; ⁴ upon the harp with ⁵ a solemn sound. (4) For thou, LORD, hast made me glad through thy work: I will triumph in the works of thy hands.

(5) O LORD, how great are thy works! *and* thy thoughts are very deep. (6) A brutish man knoweth not; neither doth a fool understand this.

(7) When the wicked spring as the grass, and when all the workers of iniquity do flourish; *it is* that they shall be destroyed for ever: (8) but thou, LORD, *art* most high for evermore. (9) For, lo, thine enemies, O LORD, for, lo, thine enemies

a Matt. 4. 6; Luke 4. 10.

¹ Or, *asp.*

² Heb., *length of days.*

³ Heb., *in the nights.*

⁴ Or, *upon the solemn sound with the harp.*

⁵ Heb., *Higgaion.*

---

the language. (See Note, Ps. civ. 3.) Even we speak of "pitching our tent."

(11) **Angels.**—The idea of a special guardian angel for each individual has possibly been favoured by this verse, though it had its origin in heathen belief:

"By every man, as he is born, there stands
A spirit good, a holy guide of life."
                             MENANDER.

Here, however, it is not one particular individual, but all who have fulfilled the conditions of verses 9 and 10 who are the objects of angelic charge. (Comp. Ps. xxxiv. 7.) (For the well-known quotation of this and verse 12 in the Temptation, see Matt. iv. 6; Luke iv. 10, 11; with Notes in *New Testament Commentary*.)

(12) **In their hands.**—Literally, *on*, as a nurse a child. There is a Spanish proverb, expressive of great love and solicitude : "They carry him on the palms of their hands."

(13) **Lion . . . adder . . . young lion.**—These are used no doubt, emblematically for the various obstacles, difficulties, and danger which threatens life. (For "adder," see Note, Ps. lviii. 4; "dragon," Ps. lxxiv. 13.)

(14—16) Another abrupt change of person. The conclusion of the psalm comes as a Divine confirmation of the psalmist's expression of confidence. (Comp. Ps. l. 15, 23, with these verses.)

(14) **Set his love upon me.**—Or, *clung to me.*

(16) **Long Life.**—The promise of a long life, while in accordance with the general feeling of the Old Testament, is peculiarly appropriate at the close of this psalm, which all through speaks of protection from danger that threatened life.

XCII.

In this psalm we seem to have the Sabbath musings (see Note to Title) of one who had met the doubt born of the sight of successful wickedness, and struggled through it to a firm faith in "the Rock in whom is no unrighteousness," though sometimes on earth iniquity seems to flourish and prevail. It is difficult to determine whether the psalm simply expresses the religious feelings of Israel generally after the restoration, or whether it owes its origin to any special event. In 1 Macc. ix. 23 there is an evident echo of, or quotation from, the Greek version of verse 7. The versification is regular.

Title.—A psalm or song; more properly, *a lyric psalm*, *i.e.*, one specially intended for singing.

For the sabbath day.—The Talmud confirms this, saying that this psalm was sung on the morning of the Sabbath at the drink offering which followed the sacrifice of the first lamb (Num. xxviii. 9).

(2) **Lovingkindness . . . faithfulness.**—The two most prominent features in the display of the covenant relation of God towards His people. The connection of *lovingkindness* or *grace* with the morning, and *faithfulness* or *truth* with the evening, is only a result of the Hebrew poetic style; and yet there is a fitness in the association. Love breaks through the clouds of doubt as the morning light rises on the night; and thoughts of God's unerring and impartial justice best suit the evening—the trial time of the day.

(3) **Ten strings.**—See Note, Ps. xxxiii. 2.

Upon the harp with a solemn sound.—Rather, *with music of the harp*. For the Hebrew word, see Note, Ps. ix. 16.

(4) The Vulgate rendering of this verse is quoted by Dante in a beautiful passage descriptive of the happiness which flows from delight in the beauty of the works of God in *nature*. But the reference is to the works *in history*, not in *nature*. The psalmist is really expressing his gladness at God's wonders wrought for Israel. (Comp. Ps. xc. 15, 16, "Make us glad . . . let thy work appear unto thy servants.)

(5) **Thoughts.**—Better, *plans*, or *purposes*. (Comp. in addition to references in margin, Ps. xxxvi. 6.)

(6) **A brutish man.**—The Hebrew is apparently from a root meaning "to eat," and so refers to the man of mere animal nature, who lives for his appetites.

Fool.—From root meaning "fat," hence "gross," "stupid."

In the one case the moral sense has not come into play at all, in the other it is overgrown by sensuality, so that spiritual discernment, insight into the glories of the Divine mind, is impossible.

(7) This verse apparently introduces the statement of the truth which the sensualist does not understand, viz., that the prosperity of the wicked is only momen-

shall perish; all the workers of iniquity shall be scattered. ⁽¹⁰⁾ But my horn shalt thou exalt like *the horn of* an unicorn: I shall be anointed with fresh oil. ⁽¹¹⁾ Mine eye also shall see *my desire* on mine enemies, *and* mine ears shall hear *my desire* of the wicked that rise up against me.

⁽¹²⁾ *ᵃThe righteous shall flourish like the palm tree: he shall grow like a cedar in Lebanon. ⁽¹³⁾ Those that be planted in the house of the LORD shall flourish in the courts of our God. ⁽¹⁴⁾ They shall still bring forth fruit in old age; they shall be fat and ¹flourishing; ⁽¹⁵⁾ to shew that the LORD *is* upright: *he is* my rock, and *there is* no unrighteousness in him.

a Hos. 14. 5.

1 Heb., *green.*

2 Heb., *from then.*

3 Heb., *to length of days.*

PSALM XCIII.

⁽¹⁾ The LORD reigneth, he is clothed with majesty; the LORD is clothed with strength, *wherewith* he hath girded himself: the world also is stablished, that it cannot be moved. ⁽²⁾ Thy throne *is* established ²of old: thou *art* from everlasting.

⁽³⁾ The floods have lifted up, O LORD, the floods have lifted up their voice; the floods lift up their waves. ⁽⁴⁾ The LORD on high *is* mightier than the noise of many waters, *yea,* than the mighty waves of the sea.

⁽⁵⁾ Thy testimonies are very sure: holiness becometh thine house, O LORD, ³for ever.

---

tary, and will render their destruction all the more impressive. The Authorised Version is incorrect in introducing the second conjunction "when." Literally, *In the springing of the wicked like grass, flourish all the workers of iniquity to be destroyed for ever, i.e.,* the prosperity of an evil class or community gives an impulse to evil, and apparently for a time iniquity seems to have the upper hand, but it is only that the inevitable destruction may be more signal. For the emblematic use of vegetable life in the psalter see Note, Ps. i. 3, 4.

⁽¹⁰⁾ **Unicorn.**—Better, *buffalo.* (See Num. xxiii. 22; Ps. xxii. 21.)

⁽¹¹⁾ **Mine eye also.**—Better, *And my eye looked upon* (was able to look without fear) *my insidious foes, and for their rising against me as villains my ears listened* (without alarm).

⁽¹²⁾ **Palm tree.**—This is the only place where the palm appears as an emblem of moral rectitude and beauty of character, yet its aptness for such comparison has often been noticed. (See Tristram's *Natural History of the Bible,* p. 384.; and comp. Thomson's *The Land and the Book,* p. 49.)

A moral use was more often made of the cedar. Emblem of kingly might, it also became the type of the imperial grandeur of virtuous souls. (See *Bible Educator,* iii. 379.)

The contrast of the palm's perennial verdure, and the cedar's venerable age, an age measured not by years, but by centuries, with the fleeting moments of the brief day of the grass, to which the wicked are compared (verse 7), is very striking, as striking as that in Ps. i. between the empty husk and the flourishing fruit-tree.

⁽¹³⁾ (See Note, Pss. lii. 8, and Stanley's *Jewish Church,* ii. 207.)

⁽¹⁴⁾ **They shall still bring forth.**—Literally, *Still shall they sprout in hoary age, sappy and green shall they be,* alluding to the great fruitfulness of the date palm, and to the fact that to the very last this fruitfulness continues.

XCIII.

There is a power in the very brevity of this song. God is King, and all the rage and unrest of the world are impotent before that fact. It may have been inspired by some particular event, which it is hopeless to seek to recover, but it expresses a general truth. The angry tumult of men beats as vainly against the granite firmness of His righteous will as the waves against the shore. The tempests of history subside and pass as the tempest of the sea, but His laws remain for ever fixed and sure. The poetical form is regular.

⁽¹⁾ **The Lord reigneth.**—Comp. Pss. xcvii. 1, xcix. 1. Better, *Jehovah has become king:* the usual term for ascending the throne (2 Sam. xv. 10; 1 Kings i. 11, 13; 2 Kings ix. 13); used in Isaiah of the re-establishment of the State after the Captivity (Isa. xxiv. 23, lii. 7); and by the latest of Israel's poets, in that prophetic strain which looks beyond time and this world (Rev. xix. 6). The robing and girding with the sword were part of the ceremony of inauguration of a monarch's reign. (See Note, Ps. xlv. 3.)

The Lord is clothed . . .—These clauses run better: *majesty he has put on: Jehovah has put* (it) *on: with strength has girded himself.*

For the same representation of Jehovah as a warrior arranging himself for battle, compare Isa. lix. 17, lxiii. 1; or as a monarch robed in splendour, Psalm civ. 1.

The world also is established.—This would better begin verse 3. That the earth should be solidly seated in its hidden foundation, is itself a marvel; but this wonder is mentioned only to bring into greater relief the thought of the next verse, that the throne of God, to which the earth is only as a footstool (Isa. lxvi. 1), has its foundation firm and everlasting, free from the vicissitudes which beset earthly monarchies.

⁽³⁾ **Waves.**—Better, for the parallelism, *roaring:* but literally, *breaking of the waves on the shore.*

Floods, here poetically for the sea, as in Ps. xxiv. 2.

Lift up.—The repetition of the verb the third time in a different tense adds to the force. In LXX. and Vulgate this clause is "from the voices of many waters."

⁽⁴⁾ **Sea.**—Whether this description of a raging sea is to be taken literally, or as emblematic of war and its horrors, is doubtful.

⁽⁵⁾ **Thy testimonies.**—This statement must be taken in close connection with that of the preceding verse. The permanence of the covenant, and of the outward signs that attest it, is to the Israelite proof of the superiority of the Divine power over the forces of nature. We may extend the thought, and say that the moral law is a truer evidence of the existence of God than the uniformity of natural laws.

PSALM XCIV.

(1) O LORD [1]God, to whom vengeance belongeth; O God, to whom vengeance belongeth, [2]shew thyself. (2) Lift up thyself, thou judge of the earth: render a reward to the proud.

(3) LORD, how long shall the wicked, how long shall the wicked triumph?

(4) *How long* shall they utter *and* speak hard things? *and* all the workers of iniquity boast themselves?

(5) They break in pieces thy people, O LORD, and afflict thine heritage. (6) They slay the widow and the stranger, and murder the fatherless. (7) *a* Yet they say, The LORD shall not see, neither shall the God of Jacob regard *it*.

(8) Understand, ye brutish among the people: and *ye* fools, when will ye be wise? (9) *b* He that planted the ear, shall he not hear? he that formed the eye, shall he not see? (10) he that chastiseth the heathen, shall not he correct? he that teacheth man knowledge, *shall not he know?* (11) *c* The LORD knoweth the thoughts of man, that they *are* vanity.

(12) Blessed *is* the man whom thou chastenest, O LORD, and teachest him out of thy law; (13) that thou mayest give him rest from the days of adversity, until the pit be digged for the wicked.

(14) For the LORD will not cast off his people, neither will he forsake his inheritance. (15) But judgment shall return

---

[1] Heb., *God of revenges.*
[2] Heb., *shine forth.*
a Ps. 10. 11, 13.
b Ex. 4. 11; Prov. 20. 12.
c 1 Cor. 3. 20.

XCIV.

Verses 5 and 14, and, by implication, verse 10, show that this psalm was the expression, not of individual, but of national, sense of wrong and injustice. Yet the poet must, in his own person, have experienced the bitterness of the trouble, from the reference he makes, towards the close, to his own experiences. Apostate Jews may have been joined with the heathen oppressors. (See Note, verse 6.) There is no indication on which to found a conjecture as to date or authorship. The poetical form is regular.

(1) The original is far more striking in its conciseness. *God of retributions, Jehovah, God of retributions shine forth.* The emphatic repetition of a phrase is a feature of this psalm. (See verses 3, 23.)

(2) **Lift up thyself**—*i.e.*, either be exalted, or rise to give sentence.

(4) **How long . . . and.**—It is better to omit the italics, and render: *They speak out of utter impudence: all evil-doers boast.* The word rendered "boast" is by modern scholars connected with the Arabian title *Emir*, a "commander." They make themselves out to be persons of distinction, or, perhaps, *lord it* over God's people.

(5) **Break in pieces.**—Or, *crush*. (See Isa. iii. 15, where the word is in parallelism with "grind the faces of the poor.")

(6) **Stranger.**—The mention of the stranger as one friendless and helpless (Exod. xxii. 21), under the tyranny of the great, seems to imply that domestic, and not foreign oppression, is the grievance.

(7) **The Lord.**—In original, "Jah." This carelessness of heaven to injustice and crime, which, in the mouth of the heathen (or, perhaps, of apostate Jews), appeared so monstrous to the Hebrews, was a doctrine of the philosophy of ancient times. It appears in the saying of Seneca: "*Stoicus deus nec cor nec caput havet.*" And in the Homeric hymn to Demeter men are represented as only *enduring* the gifts of the gods because they are stronger, and give only grudgingly. (Comp. Lucretius, i. 45.) The feeling has been well caught in Tennyson's *Lotus Eaters*:

"Let us swear an oath, and keep it with an equal mind,
In the hollow Lotus-land to live and lie reclined,
On the hills like gods together, careless of mankind."

(8—10) The reality of a Divine Providence is proved both from nature and history—from the physical constitution of man and the moral government of the world. The psalmist's question is as powerful against modern atheism, under whatever philosophy it shelters itself, as against that of his day. Whatever the source of physical life or moral sense, their *existence* proves the prior existence of an original mind and will.

(10) **He that chastiseth.**—Or, *He who instructeth*. The thought to some extent anticipates St. Paul's teaching about the divine education of the heathen, in Romans i.

(11) **That they are vanity.**—The literal rendering, "for they are breath," referring not to thoughts, but to man collectively, gives equally good sense, and would, notwithstanding the order of the words, be natural, since the masculine pronoun is used. But the LXX. stands as the Authorised Version, and is so quoted by St. Paul (1 Cor. iii. 20), with the substitution of *wise men* for *men*.

(12, 13) **Blessed.**—A far higher note than one of mere complaint, or even of trust in God, is struck here. The beatitude of suffering could not be made altogether plain in the Old Testament, though in Job the spirit of it is nearly reached. Here the poet sees thus far, that he who is the victim of misfortunes may be congratulated if he may stand aside and calmly watch the course of Divine Providence involving evil men in punishment. What he has himself endured has chastened him, and *caused him to be quiet from the evil days*—*i.e.*, has calmed him in viewing evil circumstances. It would, however, but for the next clause, be more natural to understand, "shall deliver him from evil days."

Pit.—Comp. Ps. ix. 15.

(15) **But.**—Better, *For*; literally, *for to righteousness judgment shall turn, and after it all upright in heart*—*i.e.*, there shall no longer be the seeming contradiction in things. God's righteousness will triumph over the injustice under which Israel groans; His ways will be vindicated, so that all the upright in heart will acknowledge that "there is a reward for the righteous, a God who judges in the earth" (Ps. lviii. 11). Luther's fine paraphrase, "For Right must, whatever happens, remain Right," expresses the feeling; but, better still, the question, "Shall not the Lord of all the earth do right?" The phrase, "shall after it," is a common one for expressing attachment and adherence to a party or cause (Exod. xxiii. 2; 2 Sam. ii. 10; Ps. xlix. 13), and

unto righteousness: and all the upright in heart ¹shall follow it. ⁽¹⁶⁾ Who will rise up for me against the evil-doers? *or* who will stand up for me against the workers of iniquity? ⁽¹⁷⁾ Unless the LORD *had been* my help, my soul had ²almost dwelt in silence. ⁽¹⁸⁾ When I said, My foot slippeth; thy mercy, O LORD, held me up. ⁽¹⁹⁾ In the multitude of my thoughts within me thy comforts delight my soul.

⁽²⁰⁾ Shall the throne of iniquity have fellowship with thee, which frameth mischief by a law? ⁽²¹⁾ They gather themselves together against the soul of the righteous, and condemn the innocent blood. ⁽²²⁾ But the LORD is my defence; and my God *is* the rock of my refuge. ⁽²³⁾ And he shall bring upon them their own iniquity, and shall cut them off in their own wickedness; *yea,* the LORD our God shall cut them off.

PSALM XCV.

⁽¹⁾ O come, let us sing unto the LORD: let us make a joyful noise to the rock of our salvation. ⁽²⁾ Let us ³come before his presence with thanksgiving, and make a joyful noise unto him with psalms.

⁽³⁾ For the LORD *is* a great God, and a great King above all gods. ⁽⁴⁾ ⁴In his hand *are* the deep places of the earth:

1 Heb., *shall be after it.*
2 Or, *quickly.*
3 Heb., *prevent his face.*
4 Heb., *In whose.*

---

specially of adherence to Jehovah (1 Sam. xii. 14; 1 Kings xiv. 8).

⁽¹⁶⁾ **Rise up.**—Stand up—*i.e.*, as *champion.* (Comp. 2 Sam. xxiii. 11, of the exploit of Shammah, the son of Agee the Hararite; comp. Ps. ii. 2.)

⁽¹⁷⁾ **In silence**—*i.e.*, of the grave, as in Ps. xxxi. 17.

⁽¹⁹⁾ **Thoughts.**—Properly, dividing—*i.e.*, "perplexing" or "anxious" thoughts. (See Job iv. 13, xx. 2.) LXX. and Vulg., "griefs."

We may compare the Virgilian "animum nunc huc celerem, nunc dividit illuc," imitated by Tennyson:

> This way and that dividing his swift mind, In act to throw."

Delight.— Literally, *stroke,* and so *soothe.* The Hebrew word is used in Isa. lxvi. 11 of a mother quieting her child with the breast, and in Jer. xvi. 7 of the cup of consolation given to mourners at funerals.

⁽²⁰⁾ **Throne of iniquity.**—This is an apt expression for an oppressive and unjust government. The word rendered "iniquity" might mean "calamity" or "destruction" (see Ps. lvii. 1, and comp. Ps. xci. 3: "noisome"), but in Prov. x. 3 it seems to mean "lawless desire," which best suits this passage.

Have fellowship—*i.e., be associated in the government.* Could the theocracy admit to a share in it, not merely imperfect instruments of justice, but even those who perverted justice to evil ends?

Which frameth mischief by a law?—*i.e., making legislation a means of wrong.* Others, however, render, "against the law." But the former explanation best suits the next verse.

⁽²¹⁾ **They gather**—*i.e.*, possibly, *They crowd into the courts of law to take part in the unjust condemnation of the just,* or more generally, "They attack the life of the righteous." LXX., "they hunt." (Comp. Ps. xxxv. 15.)

XCV.

The LXX. prefix a title ascribing this psalm to David, and in quoting it the Epistle to the Hebrews (chap. iv. 7) uses the expression "in David." This, however, is only a mode of saying "in the Psalms." We may conjecture, from the contents, that some danger to religion was observed by the author, since the disobedience and perversity of the early history of the race are recalled. Beyond this we only perceive that the psalm was composed for the congregational use.* From earliest times it has played the part of an invitatory psalm in the Christian Church, as it does in the English morning service now. The rhythm is fine and varied.

⁽¹⁾ **O come.**—The invitation is general, and may be contrasted with the heathen warning to the uninitiated, *procul este profani.* This exhortation to worship God, not with penitence, but with loud thanksgiving, is, as Perowne notes, the more remarkable considering the strain in which the latter part of the psalm is written.

Make a joyful noise.—There is no one English expression for the full burst of instrumental and vocal music which is meant by the Hebrew word here applied to the Temple service. Vulg., *jubilemus.*

Rock of our salvation.—As in Ps. lxxxix. 26. (Comp. "rock of refuge," Ps. xciv. 22.)

⁽²⁾ **Come before.**—Literally, *go to meet.* It is the word rendered "prevent" in Ps. xviii. 5, where see Note.

⁽³⁾ **Above all gods.** — Not here angelic beings, but the gods of surrounding tribes, as accurately explained in Ps. xcvi. 4, 5. (Comp. Exod. xv. 11, xviii. 11.) Commentators vex themselves with the difficulty of the ascription of a real existence to these tribal deities in the expression, "King above all gods." But how else was Israel constantly falling into the sin of worshipping them? It was in the inspired rejection of them as possessing any sovereign power, and in the recognition of Jehovah's supremacy shown by the psalmists and prophets, that the preservation of Israel's religion consisted.

⁽⁴⁾ **Deep places.**—From a root meaning "to search," perhaps by digging. Hence either "mines" or "mineral wealth."

Strength of the hills.—The Hebrew word rendered "strength" is rare, found only here and Num. xxiii. 22, xxiv. 8 ("strength of an unicorn"), and Job xxii. 25 ("plenty of silver;" margin, "silver of strength"). The root to which the word is usually assigned means "to be weary," from which the idea of strength can only be derived on the *lucus a non lucendo*

---

* Psalms xcv.—c. appear to form a group (to which xciii. is also closely related) of songs composed for the celebration of the Return from Exile. (See the coincidences of thought and expression pointed out in the Notes, and comp. the Introduction to Ps. xcviii.)

¹the strength of the hills *is* his also. ⁽⁵⁾ ²The sea *is* his, and he made it : and his hands formed the dry *land*.

⁽⁶⁾ O come, let us worship and bow down : let us kneel before the LORD our maker. ⁽⁷⁾ For he *is* our God ; and we *are* the people of his pasture, and the sheep of his hand.

ᵃTo day if ye will hear his voice, ⁽⁸⁾ harden not your heart, ᵇas in the ³provocation, *and* as *in* the day of temptation in the wilderness : ⁽⁹⁾ when your fathers tempted me, proved me, and saw my work.

⁽¹⁰⁾ Forty years long was I grieved with *this* generation, and said, It *is* a people that do err in their heart, and they have not known my ways : ⁽¹¹⁾ unto whom I sware in my wrath ⁴that they should not enter into my rest.

PSALM XCVI.

⁽¹⁾ O ᶜ sing unto the LORD a new song : sing unto the LORD, all the earth. ⁽²⁾ Sing unto the LORD, bless his name ; shew forth his salvation from day to day. ⁽³⁾ Declare his glory among the heathen, his wonders among all people. ⁽⁴⁾ For the LORD *is* great, and greatly to be praised : he *is* to be feared above all gods.

⁽⁵⁾ For all the gods of the nations *are* idols : but the LORD made the heavens. ⁽⁶⁾ Honour and majesty *are* before him : strength and beauty *are* in his sanctuary.

Margin notes:
1 Or, *the heights of the hills* are *his.*
2 Heb., *Whose the sea is.*
a Heb. 3. 7, & 4. 7.
b Ex. 17. 2, 7 ; Num. 14. 22, &c.
3 Heb., *contention.*
4 Heb., *if they enter into my rest.*
c 1 Chron. 16. 23.

---

principle. Keeping the usual derivation, we may, with many critics, give the word the sense of "mines" or "treasures," because of the labours of extracting metal from the earth. This suits Job xxii. 25, and makes a good parallelism. But the LXX. and Vulg. have "heights," and by another derivation the Hebrew may mean shining, and so "sunny summit." With this agrees the rendering of the LXX. in Num. xxiii. 22, xxiv. 8, and the rhythm is preserved by an antithetic parallelism, as in next verse.

⁽⁶⁾ **Worship.**—Properly, *prostrate ourselves.*

Kneel.—The practice of kneeling low in the East, only used in moments of deep humiliation, is first mentioned in 2 Chron. vi. 13. It was also Daniel's practice (Dan. vi. 10).

⁽⁷⁾ **To-day if . . .**—In joining this clause with verses 8 and 9 the Authorised Version follows the LXX. The Masoretic text connects it with the preceding part of the verse, and there seems no good reason for departing from that arrangement. Indeed, the change from the third person, "his voice," to the first, "tempted me," in the same sentence is intolerable even in Hebrew poetry. Nor is there any necessity to suppose the loss of a line. Render : "For He is our God, and we are the people of his pasture, the sheep of his hand. To-day would that ye would hearken to his voice." The Oriental custom of leading flocks by the voice is doubtless alluded to, as in John x. 4. Notice the resemblance in verses 6, 7 to Ps. c. 3, 4.

⁽⁸⁾ The mention of the guiding voice suggests to the poet to make God Himself address His people, and with this verse the Divine warning begins.

Provocation . . . temptation.—It is better to keep here the proper names *Meribah* and *Massah* (Exod. xvii. 1—7 ; Num. xx. 13 ; comp. Deut. xxxiii. 8.)

⁽⁹⁾ **Proved me.**—Properly, of trying metals. This term is used of man's attitude towards Providence, both in a good and bad sense (Mal. iii. 10, 15).

And saw my work.—Better (as in Isa. xlix. 15), *Yea, they saw my works*, watched, that is, God's dealings with ever the same readiness to murmur and repine, and try the Divine patience.

⁽¹⁰⁾ See Notes, Heb. iii. 17, New Testament Commentary.

I grieved.—Better, *I loathed.*

A people that do err.—Literally, *a people of wanderers in heart.* They are morally astray through ignorance of God's paths.

⁽¹¹⁾ **I sware.**—Num. xiv. 21—27.

Rest.—This is, of course, the Promised Land, as the context unmistakably shows. The freedom taken with the passage by the author of the Epistle to the Hebrews, in order to make the psalm point us to a "future" rest, was such as Jewish doctors ordinarily used, and of which other instances occur in the New Testament—notably St. Paul's argument in Gal. iii. 16.

XCVI.

This "new song," breathing indeed aspirations and hopes which were not wholly new to Israel, but ideal, and still waiting for their complete fulfilment, most probably dates, according to the conjecture of the LXX., from the rebuilding of the Temple after the Captivity. No one can miss the points of resemblance with the literature of that period, especially the evidence of deeper sympathy with nature, and extended interest in mankind. The outward world has become instinct with emotion, while the barrier of faith and feeling beween Israel and other races is gradually breaking down.*

⁽¹⁾ **A new song.**—See Note, Ps. xxxiii. 3. It appears to have been a kind of national and religious "lyric cry" after the Restoration. (Comp. Isa. xlii. 10.)

⁽⁵⁾ **Idols.**—Literally, *nothings* ; Heb., *elilim*, with a play on the word *el*, God. This plainly shows that by *Gods*, in verse 4, the heathen deities, and not angels, are meant. (See Note, Ps. xcv. 3.) The LXX. sometimes renders the Hebrew word "idols," sometimes "vanities," but here "demons." Symmachus "non-existences."

But the Lord made the heavens.—*Nothings* could not do that, but only Jehovah.

⁽⁶⁾ **Honour . . .** The whole universe displays Jehovah's majesty, but chiefly his sanctuary in Israel, where it is typified by the costly splendour of the building and its rites. So the version of Apollinaris, "Pureness and stately glory fit his shrine." The chronicler having

---

* The LXX. inconsistently go on to ascribe the Psalm to David, probably because of its insertion in 1 Chron. xvi.

Righteousness of the   PSALMS, XCVII.   *Divine Government.*

(7) Give unto the LORD, O ye kindreds of the people, give unto the LORD glory and strength. (8) Give unto the LORD the glory ¹ *due unto* his name: bring an offering, and come into his courts. (9) O worship the LORD ² in the beauty of holiness: fear before him, all the earth. (10) Say among the heathen *that* ª the LORD reigneth: the world also shall be established that it shall not be moved: he shall judge the people righteously. (11) Let the heavens rejoice, and let the earth be glad; let the sea roar, and the fulness thereof. (12) Let the field be joyful, and all that *is* therein: then shall all the trees of the wood rejoice (13) before the LORD: for he cometh, for he cometh to judge the earth: he shall judge the world with righteousness, and the people with his truth.

PSALM XCVII.

(1) The LORD reigneth; let the earth rejoice; let the ³ multitude of isles be glad *thereof.* (2) Clouds and darkness *are* round about him: ᵇ righteousness and judgment *are* the ⁴ habitation of his throne. (3) A fire goeth before him, and burneth up his enemies round about. (4) His lightnings enlightened the world: the earth saw, and trembled. (5) The hills melted like wax at the presence of the LORD, at the presence of the Lord of the whole earth. (6) The heavens declare his righteousness, and all the people see his glory.

Marginal notes: 1 Heb., *of his name.*   2 Or, *in the glorious sanctuary.*   a Ps. 93. 1, & 97. 1.   3 Heb., *many, or, great isles.*   b Ps. 89. 14.   4 Or, *establishment.*

---

adopted this psalm as suitable for the occasion when the ark was brought to Zion by David, has substituted "strength and gladness are in his *place*," possibly because the Temple was not built at that time.

(7—9) These verses are a relic of Ps. xxix. 1, 2, where see Notes, but instead of being addressed to the angels it is, in accordance with the world of new ideas and feelings in which Israel lived after the Captivity, addressed to all the people of the world. A truly Messianic character is thus impressed on the psalm.

(8) **Offering.**—The *minchah*, or sacrifice of fine flour.

(9) **O worship the Lord in the beauty of holiness.**—Better, *Bow before Jehovah in holy attire.* But the LXX. and Vulgate have as in margin.

Fear before him.—Or literally, *let all the earth be moved before his face.*

(10) **Say among the heathen.**—The watchword of the Restoration, "Jehovah has become King" (see Ps. xciii. 1, note, and comp. Isa. lii. 7), is an Evangel not only for Jerusalem but for the world at large. But to it is added (see the difference of arrangement in 1 Chron. xvi. 29—31) the further statement of the stability of the world, emblem of the stability and justice of the Divine Government.

(11—13) Magnificent progress of the Divine Judge through His realm. There is only one thought, that of the inauguration of a righteous sway for all nations: at its advent, as in Isaiah's glorious visions (see Isa. xxxv. 1, 2, xlii. 10, xliv. 23, lv. 12), all nature seems to join the chorus of gladness.

(12) **Then shall all the trees . . .**—Comp.—

> "His praise, ye winds that from four quarters blow,
> Breathe soft or loud, and wave your tops ye pines,
> With every plant in sign of worship wave."—MILTON.

(13) **For he cometh, for he cometh.**—Notice the striking repetition, the natural expression of gladness.

XCVII.

Though in a very great measure a compilation from earlier writings (see Notes passim), this psalm, by more than one fine touch, proves itself the product not only of a thoughtful, but of a truly poetic mind. (Notice especially verses 2, 10, 11, and see Notes.) The rhythm is regular.

(1) **The Lord reigneth.**—For the thought and imagery comp. Ps. xcvi. 10, 11.

Multitude of the isles.—Literally, *isles many.* This wide glance to the westward embracing the isles and coasts of the Mediterranean (Ps. lxxii. 10), possibly even more distant ones still, is characteristic of the literature of post-exile times. (Comp. Isa. xlii. 10, 11, li. 15.)

(2) **Clouds and darkness.**—Comp. Ps. xviii. 10—12. The imagery in the first instance is borrowed from the Theophany at Sinai. (Exod. xix. 9, 16, xx. 21; Deut. iv. 11, v. 22, 23.)

Are the habitation.—Better, *are the foundation,* or *pillars.* (See margin.) This reappears from Ps. lxxxix. 14, but the connection with "clouds and darkness" is peculiar to this poet, and is striking. The immediate effect on the Hebrew mind, of the awful manifestation of the Divine power in nature, is not fear, but a sublime sense of safety in the established right and truth of God. They knew that it is one and the same power

> "Which makes the darkness and the light,
> And dwells not in the light alone,
> But in the darkness and the cloud,
> As over Sinai's peaks of old,
> While Israel made them gods of gold,
> Although the trumpet blew so loud."
>   TENNYSON: *In Memoriam.*

(3) This is an echo of Ps. l. 3. (Comp. also Ps. xviii. 8; Hab. iii. 4, 5.)

(4) See Ps. lxxvii. 17, 18, from which this is taken.

(5) **The hills melted.**—Comp. Ps. lxviii. 8, Note: Micah i. 4.

The Lord of the whole earth.—An expression first met with exactly in Josh. iii. 11—13, though Abraham speaks of God as judge of the whole earth (Gen. xviii. 25). (Comp. Micah iv. 13; Zech. iv. 10, vi. 5.) Though Jehovah was the tribal God, yet in marked distinction to surrounding tribes Israel regarded Him as having universal dominion.

(6) **All the people.**—Rather, *all the peoples.* At length the world at large is convinced, by visible manifestations, of what Israel had recognised through the veil

(7) *ᵃ* Confounded be all they that serve graven images, that boast themselves of idols: worship him, all *ye* gods. (8) Zion heard, and was glad; and the daughters of Judah rejoiced because of thy judgments, O Lord. (9) For thou, Lord, *art* high above all the earth: thou art exalted far above all gods. (10) Ye that love the Lord, *ᵇ* hate evil: he preserveth the souls of his saints; he delivereth them out of the hand of the wicked. (11) Light is sown for the righteous, and gladness for the upright in heart. (12) Rejoice in the Lord, ye righteous; and give thanks ¹ at the remembrance of his holiness.

PSALM XCVIII.

A Psalm.

(1) O sing unto the Lord a new song; for he hath done marvellous things: his right hand, and his holy arm, hath gotten him the victory. (2) *ᶜ* The Lord hath made known his salvation: his righteousness hath he ² openly shewed in the sight of the heathen. (3) He hath remembered his mercy and his truth toward the house of Israel: all the ends of the earth have seen the salvation of our God. (4) Make a joyful noise unto the Lord, all the earth: make a loud noise, and rejoice, and sing praise. (5) Sing unto the Lord with the harp; with the harp, and the voice of a psalm. (6) With trumpets and sound of cornet make a joyful noise before the Lord, the King. (7) Let the sea roar, and the fulness thereof; the world, and they that dwell therein. (8) Let the floods clap *their* hands: let the hills be joyful together (9) before the Lord;

ᵈ For he cometh to judge the earth:

ᵃ Ex. 20. 4; Lev. 26. 1; Deut. 5. 8; Heb. 1. 6.

ᵇ Ps. 34. 14; Amos 5. 15; Rom. 12. 9.

¹ Or, *to the memorial.*

ᶜ Isa. 52. 10.

² Or, *revealed.*

ᵈ Ps. 96. 13.

---

of darkness and cloud,—the eternal righteousness of which all the splendours of the storm have been a witness. (See Note, Ps. lxxxix. 6.)

(7) **Confounded**—*i.e.*, ashamed (Isa. xlii. 17; Jer. x. 14). The same idea is conveyed by the very word "idols" in Hebrew—empty, worthless things, *shaming* those who worship them.

It is doubtful whether the verbs here are to be taken as imperatives. So LXX., Vulgate, and Authorised Version. Probably a fact is stated.

All ye gods.—Not "angels," as in LXX. (See Note, Ps. viii. 5.) Here, however, the term is directly intended to include among superhuman beings the agencies worshipped by heathen nations as deities. The quotation Heb. i. 6 (see Note, *New Testament Commentary*) is made from the LXX. of Deut. xxxii. 43.

(8) **Zion heard.**—See Ps. xlviii. 11, Note.

(9) For the first clause see Ps. lxxxiii. 18; for the second Ps. xlvii. 2—10.

(10) **Ye that love the Lord.**—Notwithstanding certain points of similarity between this verse and Pss. xxxiv. 10—20, xxxvii. 28, and between verse 12 and Ps. xxxii. 11, the psalmist shows himself at the close more than a compiler—a true poet.

Hate evil.—It is better to point for the indicative, *They who love Jehovah, hate evil*, in order to avoid the awkward transition in the next clause. This practical test of true religion can never be obsolete. Love of God implies the hatred of all He hates. A heathen writer has expressed this in a striking way. Philosophy, holding a dialogue with Lucian, is made to say, "To love and to hate, they say, spring from the same source.' To which he replies, "That, O Philosophy, should be best known to you. My business is to hate the bad, and to love and commend the good, and that I stick to."

(11) **Light is sown**—*i.e.*, scattered. The metaphor must not be pressed so as to think of a harvest to come. The image is an obvious and common one.

"Sol etiam summo de vertice dissipat omnes
Ardorem in partes, et lumine conserit arva."
Lucretius.

And Milton, while enriching its metaphor, doubtless had the psalm in his mind:—

"Now morn, her rosy steps in the Eastern clime
Advancing, sow'd the earth with orient pearl."

XCVIII.

This psalm plainly belongs to that cycle of literature produced by the joy of the Restoration, and is in fact little more than a compilation from Isa. xl., xxvi., and from other psalms, especially Ps. xcvi. The psalm is irregular in form.

Title.—This is the only hymn of the whole collection with the bare inscription "a psalm."

(1) **Victory.**—The word more commonly rendered "salvation," as, indeed, in next verse.

(4) **Make a joyful noise.**—Better, *Break out into songs and music.*

(5) **Sing . . .**—Rather, *Play to Jehovah on a harp, on a harp, and with melodious sound of music.*

(6) **Trumpets . . cornet.**—(See Num. x. 2; Exod. xix. 16; and *Bible Educator*, ii. 231, 232.) This is the only place in the psalm where the *chatsotsereh*, or "straight trumpet" is mentioned.

(7) See Ps. xcvi. 11.

"Listen! the mighty Being is awake
And doth with His eternal motion make
A sound like thunder everlastingly."
Wordsworth.

(8) **Clap their hands.**—This expression, descriptive of the lapping sound of waves, occurs also in Isa. lv. 12.

Let the hills be joyful together.—

"Far along,
From peak to peak, the rattling crags among,
Leaps the live thunder! Not from one long cloud,
But every mountain now hath found a tongue,
And Jura answers through her misty shroud,
Back to the joyous Alps who call to her aloud."
Byron: *Childe Harold*, canto iii.

(9) See Ps. xcvi. 13.

with righteousness shall he judge the world, and the people with equity.

PSALM XCIX.

(1) The LORD reigneth; let the people tremble: he sitteth *between* the cherubims; let the earth ¹ be moved. (2) The LORD *is* great in Zion; and he *is* high above all the people. (3) Let them praise thy great and terrible name; *for it is* holy.

(4) The king's strength also loveth judgment; thou dost establish equity, thou executest judgment and righteousness in Jacob. (5) Exalt ye the LORD our God, and worship at his footstool; *for* ² he *is* holy.

(6) Moses and Aaron among his priests, and Samuel among them that call upon his name; they called upon the LORD, and he answered them. (7) He spake unto them in the cloudy pillar: they kept his testimonies, and the ordinance *that* he gave them.

(8) Thou answeredst them, O LORD our God: thou wast a God that forgavest them, though thou tookest vengeance of their inventions. (9) Exalt the LORD our God, and worship at his holy hill; for the LORD our God *is* holy.

PSALM C.

A Psalm of ³ praise.

(1) Make a joyful noise unto the LORD, ⁴ all ye lands. (2) Serve the LORD with gladness: come before his presence with singing.

(3) Know ye that the LORD he *is* God:

1 Heb., *stagger.*
2 Or, *it is holy.*
3 Or, *thanksgiving.*
4 Heb., *all the earth.*

XCIX.

This psalm plainly belongs to a group (see Ps. xcv., Introduction) to be referred to the post-exile times, when the renewed worship and nationality made it possible for the poet to compare his age with that of the greatest saints and heroes of old. The short refrain marks the poetical form.

(1) **The Lord reigneth.**—See Note, Ps. xciii. 1.
Tremble.—LXX. and Vulg., "be angry." The optative in this and the following clause is after the LXX.; but the Hebrew is in the ordinary present, *the peoples tremble, the earth staggers.*
He sitteth.—In original a participle.
Between the cherubims . . . — See Notes on Ps. lxxx. 1.

(3) **Great and terrible name.**—The rabbins see here the mystic tetragrammaton, whose pronunciation was kept so secret.
For it is holy.—This is grammatically possible, but as verses 5 and 9 repeat the expression, evidently as a refrain, and there it needs the masculine, it is better to read here, "Holy is He."
In this way, too, we avoid an awkward construction in the next verse, which should be joined closely with this: *Let them praise Thy great and terrible name* (saying), "Holy is He, and mighty, a king that loveth justice."

(5) **Worship at his footstool.**—*Prostrate yourselves at His footstool.* The earth is called the "footstool" of God (Isa. lxvi. 1; comp. Matt. v. 35); in other places the expression is used of the sanctuary (Ps. cxxxii. 7; comp. Isa. lx. 13; Lam. ii. 1). In 1 Chron. xxviii. 2 it seems to refer to the ark. No doubt here, after mentioning the throne above the cherubims, we must think of the ground on which the ark stood, or of the ark itself.

(6) **Moses.**—Better, *a Moses and an Aaron among his friends, and a Samuel among them that call upon his name; calling upon the Lord, and he answers them; in the pillar of cloud he speaks unto them.* The poet is enhancing the sacred character of the services of his own day by likening the priests and ministers to the sacred heroes of the past, as we might distinguish a period of great scientific achievement by saying, "We have a Newton or a Bacon among us." To make it a mere historical reference, "Moses and Aaron were," &c., would be altogether too abrupt and inaccurate, since Moses was not a *khohen*, nor did God speak to Samuel in the cloudy pillar. It is true that the present tense is changed in verse 7 to the preterite, but it is quite natural that the psalmist should glide into the narrative style after the mention of the historical name. The Son of Sirach also makes special reference to the prayer of Samuel (Ecclus. xlvi. 16). Possibly, too, there is an allusion to the meaning of his name, "asked," or "heard of God."

(8) **Thou tookest vengeance of their inventions** (or, *works*).—This does not refer to the personages just mentioned but to the people at large. The train of thought is as follows:—"There are great saints among us, as in olden time, but, as then, their prayers, while often procuring forgiveness, could not altogether avert punishment for sin; so the present community must expect retribution when sinful, in spite of the mediation of the better part of the nation." The Hebrew style did not favour similes, and hence the poet omits the signs of comparison, and leaves his inference to be drawn by his readers.

C.

This liturgic psalm, which as a hymn is so universally known and loved, is composed of four verses of triplets. Even when performed in the Temple, amid the exclusive notes of Judaism, its opening words must have inspired something of that catholic sentiment which pervades a congregation when singing what we know as the "Old Hundredth."

Title.—**Of praise.**—Better, *for thanks*, or, possibly *for the thankoffering*, *i.e.*, especially adapted for that particular ceremony. At all events it is a liturgical direction. LXX., "for (Vulg., *in*) confession."

(1) **Make a joyful noise.**—See Ps. xcviii. 4.
All ye lands.—Or, *all the earth.*

(3) **And not we ourselves.**—Most commentators now prefer the reading "His we are," as keeping the parallelism better, besides having great MS. support. The concluding part of the verse is an echo of Ps. xcv. 7.

it is he *that* hath made us, ¹ and not we ourselves; *we are* his people, and the sheep of his pasture. (4) Enter into his gates with thanksgiving, *and* into his courts with praise: be thankful unto him, *and* bless his name. (5) For the LORD *is* good; his mercy *is* everlasting; and his truth *endureth* ² to all generations.

¹ Or, *and his we are.*
² Heb., *to generation and generation.*

PSALM CI.
A Psalm of David.

(1) I will sing of mercy and judgment: unto thee, O LORD, will I sing. (2) I will behave myself wisely in a perfect way. O when wilt thou come unto me? I will walk within my house with a perfect heart. (3) I will set no ³ wicked thing before mine eyes: I hate the work of them that turn aside; *it* shall not cleave to me. (4) A froward heart shall depart from me: I will not know a wicked *person*. (5) Whoso privily slandereth his neighbour, him will I cut off: him that hath an high look and a proud heart will not I suffer.

³ Heb., *thing of Belial.*

CI.

The best comment on this psalm lies in the number of interesting associations that it has gathered to itself. It has been called a "mirror for princes," "a mirror for magistrates," and "the householders' psalm;" and many anecdotes are told of its use. Eyring, in his *Life of Ernest the Pious* (Duke of Saxe-Gotha), relates that he sent an unfaithful minister a copy of the 101st Psalm, and that it became the proverb in the country, when an official had done anything wrong, "He will certainly soon receive the prince's psalm to read" (Delitzsch). "When Sir George Villiers became the favourite and prime minister of King James, Lord Bacon, in a beautiful letter of advice, counselled him to take this psalm for his rule in the promotion of courtiers. It would have been well, both for the philosopher and favourite, if they had been careful to walk by this rule" (Note in Spurgeon's *Treasury of David*). "The 101st Psalm was one beloved by the noblest of Russian princes, Vladimir Monomachos; and by the gentlest of English reformers, Nicholas Ridley" (Stanley's *Jewish Church*, ii. 89). "But," adds this writer, "it was its first leap into life that has carried it so far into the future. It is full of stern exclusiveness, of a noble intolerance. But not against theological error; not against uncourtly manners; not against political insubordination;—but against the proud heart; the high look; the secret slanderer; the deceitful worker; the teller of lies. *These* are the outlaws from king David's court; *they* alone are the rebels and heretics whom he would not suffer to dwell in his house or tarry in his sight." Tradition may, indeed, well have been right in ascribing such a noble vow to David. And very possibly this connection led to the insertion of the first verse as suited to the "sweet singer," and also as giving the vow more the character of a hymn. That it did not form part of the original composition seems sufficiently certain from the unpoetical character of the psalm, which only in its parallelism preserves any features of poetry.

Title.—See Introduction.

(1) **Mercy and judgment**—or, as some render, *grace and right*—are the especially requisite attributes of a good monarch, or of magistrates generally. (See Matt. xxiii. 23, where the failure to practise them is charged on the ruling class in Judæa at that time, though, of course, also required in the conduct of every man; Micah vi. 8.) Here, no doubt, as almost all commentators have seen, they are first regarded ideally as attributes of the Divine King.

"And earthly power doth then show likest God's,
When mercy seasons justice."

Will I sing.—Better, *will I play.*

On the question of the connection of this verse with the rest of the psalm, see Introduction.

(2) **Behave myself wisely.**—Literally, *I will look to a guileless way.* The root "to look" is that from which *maskil* (Ps. xxxii., title) comes; hence some here see a reference to music, or song. But the Authorised Version is probably right, since the analogy of such words as "provident," "circumspect," shows how the idea of caution and then wisdom arises from that of looking. The English idiom, "look to your ways," illustrates the Hebrew here.

O when wilt thou come unto me?—This clause is so awkward, however translated, that some critics go the length of pronouncing it spurious. In the Old Testament, with the exception of Exod. xx. 24, the coming of God to a person is associated with the idea of punishment or inquisition (Ps. xvii. 3); and to see a reminiscence of 2 Sam. vi. 9 ("How shall the ark of the Lord come to me?") seems far-fetched. It is better, therefore, to take the verb as the third person feminine instead of second masculine, with "perfect way" as its subject. The only difficulty in the way of this rendering is the interrogative; but, as in Prov. xxiii. 22, it becomes a simple adverb of time, we may treat it so here: "I will give heed to a guileless way when it comes to me," *i.e.*, whenever a course of action arises, presenting an alternative of a *right* and *wrong*, or a *better* and *worse*, I will choose the *better*.

I will walk within my house.—This vow of an *Eastern* monarch should be read with the thought of the palace of a caliph at Bagdad, or a sultan at Constantinople, before the mind. But it is a reflection of universal application, that piety should begin at home, and religion show itself in the household as much as at church.

(3) **I will set no. . . . .**—Mark the wisdom of the resolve in a despotic monarch, who has only to speak to effect whatever he has looked on with desire.

Wicked thing.—*Thing* (or, *word*) *of Belial*. (See Note on Ps. xli. 8.)

I hate the work of them that turn aside.—Or, *I hate the doing of false things*, according as we take the word in the concrete or abstract.

It shall not cleave to me.—Such conduct shall not be mine.

(4) **Froward.**—See Note, Ps. xviii. 26.

(5) **Whoso . . .**—The "informer" and the "haughty favourite" are no unknown characters in an Oriental court.

A Prayer for   PSALMS, CII.   *Comfort in Affliction.*

(6) Mine eyes *shall be* upon the faithful of the land, that they may dwell with me: he that walketh [1] in a perfect way, he shall serve me. (7) He that worketh deceit shall not dwell within my house: he that telleth lies [2] shall not tarry in my sight. (8) I will early destroy all the wicked of the land; that I may cut off all wicked doers from the city of the LORD.

PSALM CII.

A Prayer [3] of the afflicted, when he is overwhelmed, and poureth out his complaint before the LORD.

(1) Hear my prayer, O LORD, and let my cry come unto thee. (2) Hide not thy face from me in the day *when* I am in trouble; incline thine ear unto me: in the day *when* I call answer me speedily. (3) For my days are consumed [4] like smoke, and my bones are burned as an hearth. (4) My heart is smitten, and withered like grass; so that I forget to eat my bread. (5) By reason of the voice of my groaning my bones cleave to my [5] skin. (6) I am like a pelican of the wilderness: I am like an owl of the desert. (7) I watch, and am as a sparrow alone upon the house top.

[1] Or, *perfect in the way.*
[2] Heb., *shall not be established.*
[3] Or, *for.*
[4] Or, (as some read) *into smoke.*
[5] Or, *flesh.*

Proud heart.—Literally, *broad*, that is, extended with pride. (Comp. Prov. xxi. 4.) But LXX. and Vulg., "insatiable."

Will not I suffer.—In Hebrew a simple and expressive "I cannot," to which we can supply "bear," from Jer. xliv. 22. (Comp. Isa. i. 13: "I cannot away with.")

(7) **Tarry in my sight**—*i.e.*, stand as a courtier in the royal presence. Comp. Homer:

"Hateful to me as gates of hell is he
Who hides one thing within his mind and speaks another."

(8) **Early.**—Literally, *in the morning*: referring, as Perowne observes, to the Oriental custom of holding courts of law in the early morning (Jer. xxi. 12; 2 Sam. xv. 2; Luke xxii. 66; John xviii. 28).

City of the Lord.—For similar expressions, see Pss. xlvi. 4, xlviii. 2, 8. The city must bear out its name in its character.

CII.

This psalm is peculiar for its title, which stands quite alone among the inscriptions. It is neither historical nor musical in its reference; but describes the character of the psalm, and the circumstances amid which it would be found useful. That it was, therefore, affixed at a late time, when the collection had come to be employed, not merely for liturgical purposes and in public worship, but in private devotion, there can be little doubt. But the composition of the psalm must be referred to national rather than individual feeling. It is true the suppliant speaks from personal experience of distress actually pressing upon him; but this distress has not an individual character, but is of that general kind which is felt under national calamity and misfortunes. It is natural, from verses 14 and 15, to refer the composition to the exile period. With this also agree the many points of coincidence with the prophecies of the second part of Isaiah. But it must be remarked that the causes which the prophets of the exile assign to the national captivity or catastrophe do not appear here. There is no expression of repentance or contrition; nor yet of the deeper insight which, towards the end of the exile, brought into prominence the doctrine of vicarious suffering. Those in whose name the psalmist writes are the servants of Jehovah, and have never been anything else. He does not distinguish them as an exception to the mass of the people, who are guilty and deserve the destruction in which the whole universe is to be involved. For this reason many critics bring the psalm down to the Antiochean period, when Jerusalem suffered so much, and at one time presented a desolation like that mourned in the psalm (1 Macc. i. 38, 39). The verse-structure is irregular.

Title.—See Introduction.

(1) **Prayer.**—Like love and all emotion, prayer has its own language, and this assumes here the forms of expression that meet us in other psalms. (See, *e.g.*, in addition to the reference in margin, Ps. xxxi. 2, xxxix. 12, lvi. 9, lix. 16, cxliii. 7.)

(2) This verse may be better arranged, *Hide not . . . in the day of my trouble. Incline . . . in the day when I call. Answer me speedily.*

(3) **Like smoke.**—Or, *in smoke*. (See margin. Comp. Ps. xxxvii. 20.)

Hearth.—Better, a *brand* or *fuel*; so LXX. and Vulgate, Aquila, and this meaning suits Isa. xxxiii. 14. (For the image see Ps. xxii. 15, xxxi. 10, xxxii. 3.)

(4) **Smitten.**—As by the sun. Exactly as in Hos. ix. 16.

So that I forget.—Better, *for I have forgotten*, &c. For this mark of deep sorrow comp. 1 Sam. i. 7, xx. 34, &c. (Comp. Homer, *Iliad*, xxiv. 129.)

(5) **Skin.**—See margin. In Lam. iv. 8, more correctly, "my skin cleaveth to my bones;" a picture of emaciation, the result of fasting.

(6) **Pelican.**—See Lev. xi. 18. "It has been objected that the pelican is a water-bird, and cannot, therefore, be the *kâath* of the Scriptures—'the pelican of the wilderness'—as it must of necessity starve in the desert; but a *midbar* (wilderness) is often used to denote a wide open space, cultivated or uncultivated, and is not to be restricted to barren spots destitute of water; moreover, as a matter of fact, the pelican after filling its capacious pouch with fish, molluscs, &c., often does retire to places far inland, where it consumes what it has captured. Thus, too, it breeds on the great sandy wastes near the mouths of the Danube. The expression 'pelican in the wilderness,' in the psalmist's pitiable complaint, is a true picture of the bird as it sits in apparently melancholy mood with its bill resting on its breast" (*Bible Educator*, iv. 8).

Owl.—Heb., *khôs*. (See Lev. xi. 17.) The bird is identified with the "owl" by the Hebrew in this passage, which should be rendered, "owl of the *ruins*." Some, however, would identify this bird with the pelican, since *khôs* means "cup," rendering "the pelican, even the pouch-bird." (See *Bible Educator*, ii. 346.) LXX., Aquila, Theodotion, all have "screech-owl;" Symmachus, the "hoopoe."

(7) **I watch**—*i.e.*, am sleepless.

The Unchangeableness and PSALMS, CII. *Faithfulness of God.*

(8) Mine enemies reproach me all the day; *and* they that are mad against me are sworn against me. (9) For I have eaten ashes like bread, and mingled my drink with weeping, (10) because of thine indignation and thy wrath: for thou hast lifted me up, and cast me down.

(11) *a* My days *are* like a shadow that declineth; and I am withered like grass. (12) But thou, O Lord, shalt endure for ever; and thy remembrance unto all generations.

(13) Thou shalt arise, *and* have mercy upon Zion: for the time to favour her, yea, the set time, is come. (14) For thy servants take pleasure in her stones, and favour the dust thereof. (15) So the heathen shall fear the name of the Lord, and all the kings of the earth thy glory. (16) When the Lord shall build up Zion, he shall appear in his glory.

(17) He will regard the prayer of the destitute, and not despise their prayer. (18) This shall be written for the generation to come: and the people which shall be created shall praise the Lord. (19) For he hath looked down from the height of his sanctuary; from heaven did the Lord behold the earth; (20) to hear the groaning of the prisoner; to loose ¹those that are appointed to death; (21) to declare the name of the Lord in Zion, and his praise in Jerusalem; (22) when the people are gathered together, and the kingdoms, to serve the Lord.

(23) He ²weakened my strength in the way; he shortened my days. (24) I said, O my God, take me not away in the midst of my days: thy years *are* throughout all generations.

(25) *b* Of old hast thou laid the foundation of the earth: and the heavens *are*

a Isa. 40. 6; Jam. 1. 10.

1 Heb., *the children of death.*

2 Heb., *afflicted.*

b Heb. 1. 10.

Sparrow.—See Note, Ps. lxxxiv. 3. Here render, *like a lonely bird.* Some MSS. read, "a wandering bird."

(8) **Sworn against me.**—Rather, *swear by me, i.e.,* make his name a byeword of execration, to be explained by Isa. lxv. 15; Jer. xxix. 22. LXX. and Vulg., "were swearing against me."

(9) **Ashes like bread.**—Lam. iii. 16. A figurative expression, like "dust shall be the serpent's meat" (Isa. lxv. 25; comp. Gen. iii. 14). With the last clause comp. Ps. xlii. 3, "tears have been my meat day and night." So too, as an emblem of disappointment, a modern poet:—

"But even while I drank the brook, and ate
The goodly apples, all these things at once
Fell into dust, and I was left alone."
                    TENNYSON: *Holy Grail.*

(10) **Indignation and thy wrath.**—Comp. Ps. xc. 7. The last part of the clause is a figure taken from the action of a whirlwind. (Comp. Job xxvii. 20, 21, xxx. 22.)

(11) **A shadow that declineth.**—Rather, *a lengthening shadow,* growing longer as the day declines, and therefore soon to vanish altogether. (Comp. Ps. cix. 23.)

"And now the sun had stretched out all the hills."
                    MILTON: *Lycidas.*

See also Note, Song of Sol. ii. 17.

(12) **For ever.**—The eternity of God, which must survive the world itself, is a pledge of the truth of the national hopes, in spite of the vicissitudes of individuals, and the swift succession of generations. For the word "remembrance," see Ps. xxx. 4. It is explained by Exod. iii. 15, "This is my name for ever, and this is my memorial through all generations." The generations come and go, and the memory of man perishes, but the name "Jehovah" endures still, the object of adoration and praise.

(13—16) The prospect (Isa. xl. 1—5) that the restoration of Jerusalem will take place simultaneously with the coming of Jehovah in glory, is here re-echoed from the prophet in a lyric form. "The set time" must not be rigidly explained by the "seventy years" of Jer. xxv. 11. The expression is general: "The hour is come." (Comp. Isa. xl. 2.)

(14) **Stones . . dust.**—This touching description of the devotion of the Jews to their ruined city is best illustrated by the actual history in Neh. iii., iv., and by the scenes so often described by travellers at the "wailing place" in modern Jerusalem.

(15) **Heathen.**—The same result of the restoration of the Holy City, viz., the recognition of Jehovah's power and glory by the heathen, occupies the great prophecy, Isa. xl.—xlvi.

(17) **The destitute.**—Literally, *the naked one.* Here the exiled people, *stripped* of home and religious rites. The word is only found once more, in Jer. xvii. 6 (comp. Jer. xlviii. 6 for a kindred form), where it is translated "heath," and in Arabic it is to this day the name of a stunted bush that grows in Palestine.

(18) **Written.**—This is interesting as being the only place in the Psalms where the memory of great events is said to be preserved in writing. Oral tradition is mentioned in Pss. xxii. 30, xliv. 1, lxxviii. 2.

Shall be created.—See Ps. xxii. 31, "a people that shall be born"—the coming generation (as the parallelism shows) for whom the world will be regenerated.

(20, 21) Comp. Isa. lxi. 1, 2, and generally the whole magnificent cycle of prophetic songs at the close of Isaiah.

Appointed to death.—See margin. LXX. and Vulg., "the sons of the slain."

(23) **In the way**—*i.e., in the course of life.* Others render, "by reason of the way," but the meaning is the same. The clause is exactly parallel to "shortened my days."

(24) **Take me not away.**—The fear of not living to see the restoration of his race prompts the psalmist to this prayer to the God whose years are not, like man's, for one generation, but endure from age to age.

(25) Comp. Isa. xliv. 24, xlviii. 13.

the work of thy hands. (26) They shall perish, but thou shalt ¹endure: yea, all of them shall wax old like a garment; as a vesture shalt thou change them, and they shall be changed: (27) but thou *art* the same, and thy years shall have no end.

(28) The children of thy servants shall continue, and their seed shall be established before thee.

PSALM CIII.

A Psalm of David.

(1) Bless the LORD, O my soul: and all that is within me, *bless* his holy name.

(2) Bless the LORD, O my soul, and forget not all his benefits: (3) who forgiveth all thine iniquities; who healeth all thy diseases; (4) who redeemeth thy life from destruction; who crowneth thee with lovingkindness and tender mercies; (5) who satisfieth thy mouth with good *things; so that* thy youth is renewed like the eagle's.

(6) The LORD executeth righteousness and judgment for all that are oppressed.

(7) He made known his ways unto Moses, his acts unto the children of Israel.

(8) *a* The LORD *is* merciful and gracious, slow to anger, and ²plenteous in mercy.

(9) He will not always chide: neither will he keep *his anger* for ever.

(10) He hath not dealt with us after

Marginal notes:
1 Heb., *stand.*
a Ex. 34. 6, 7; Num. 14. 18; Deut. 5. 10; Neh. 9. 17; Ps. 86. 15; Jer. 32. 18.
2 Heb., *great of mercy.*

---

(26) **Perish.**—Compared with man, the victim of incessant change and visible decay, the fixed earth and the uplifted mountains are often employed as symbols of endurance and perpetuity, but compared with God's eternal existence, they are but like a vesture that wears out. The source of the image is Isa. li. 6. (Comp. Isa. xxxiv. 4.) For the use made of the passage in Heb. i. 10, 12, see *New Testament Commentary.* The terms employed for "garment" and "vesture" (*beged, lebûsh*) are synonyms for the outer cloak worn by the Jews. The imagery of the text no doubt supplied Goëthe with the thought in his fine lines

"'Tis thus at the roaring loom of time I ply,
And weave for God the garment thou seest Him by!"

which in turn suggested to Carlyle the "Philosophy of Clothes." "Why multiply instances? It is written, the heavens and the earth shall fade away like a vesture, which, indeed they are—the time vesture of the Eternal."—*Sartor Resartus,* I. xi.

It is interesting to think how the science of geology confirms the image of the psalmist, showing how time has been literally changing the so solid-seeming earth, stripping off the robe that covers the hills, to fold it down at some river mouth, or at the bottom of the ocean bed.

(28) **Continue.**—Rather, *dwell,* i.e., in the land of Canaan. (Comp. Pss. xxxvii. 22, lxix. 36.)

CIII.

This psalm has been compared to a stream which, as it flows, gradually acquires strength and volume till its waves of praise swell like those of the sea. The poet begins by invoking his own soul to show its gratitude for the Divine favour, and, by a highly artistic touch, makes the psalm, after rising to sublime heights, end with the same appeal to personal experience. But national mercies fill much the larger space in his thought, and he speaks throughout as much in the person of the community as his own. Beyond one probable Aramaism in verse 3, and a possible dependence in one passage on the Book of Job (comp. verse 16 with Job xvii. 10), there is nothing to indicate the time of the psalm's composition. The rhythm is varied, and the form irregular.

(2) **Benefits.**—Literally, *actions,* whether good or bad (Judges ix. 16; Prov. xii. 14). But what a significance in the restricted meaning "benefits." God's *acts* are all *benefits.*

(3) **Forgiveth.**—The first "benefit" to one who aims at the higher life is the knowledge of the Divine readiness to forgive and renew, and this, as Augustine remarks, implies a quick moral sense: "God's benefits will not be before our eyes unless our sins are also before our eyes."

Diseases.—Here chiefly in a moral sense, as the parallelism "iniquity" shows, even if the next verse, taken literally, implies an allusion to physical suffering as well.

(4) **Destruction.**—Rather, *pit,* or *grave,* as in Ps. xvi. 10.

Crowneth.—A metaphor drawn from the common custom of wearing wreaths and garlands on festive occasions (Ecclus. xxxii. 2). Comp. Ps. viii. 5.

(5) **Mouth.**—On the Hebrew word thus rendered, see Ps. xxxii. 9. The word there adopted ("trappings," or "ornaments") would commend itself here, from the evident allusion in the next clause to the moulting of the bird, and its appearance in new plumage, if the expression "to satisfy ornament with good" were in any way intelligible. The LXX. and Vulg. have "desire;" the Syriac "body;" but the Chaldee, "age," which is supported (Gesenius) by the derivation, gives the best sense:—

Who satisfieth thine age with good, so that
Thy youth renews itself like the eagle.

The eagle's.—Heb., *nesher;* properly, the *griffon,* or *great vulture.* See Exod. xix. 4; and Note to Obadiah 4.

The rendering of the Prayer Book, "like the eagle's," follows the LXX. The idea that the eagle renewed its youth formed the basis of a Rabbinical story, and no doubt appears also in the myth of the Phœnix. But the psalmist merely refers to the fresh and vigorous appearance of the bird with its new plumage.

(6) **Oppressed.**—From individual the poet passes to national mercies, and goes back to the memorable manifestations of Divine favour vouchsafed to Moses.

(7) **Moses.**—A direct reference to Exod. xxxiii. 13.

(8) **Merciful and Gracious.**—The original confession (Exod. xxxiv. 6) had become a formula of the national faith. In addition to the marginal references, see Joel ii. 13, Ps. cxlv. 8.

(9, 10) This reflection naturally follows after the last quotation from Exodus.

our sins; nor rewarded us according to our iniquities. (11) For ¹as the heaven is high above the earth, *so great is his mercy toward them that fear him.* (12) As far as the east is from the west, *so far hath he removed our transgressions from us.*

(13) Like as a father pitieth *his* children, *so the* LORD *pitieth them that fear him.* (14) For he knoweth our frame; he remembereth that we *are* dust.

(15) *As for man, his days are as grass:* as a flower of the field, so he flourisheth. (16) For the wind passeth over it, and ²it is gone; and the place thereof shall know it no more. (17) But the mercy of the LORD *is* from everlasting to everlasting upon them that fear him, and his righteousness unto children's children;

¹ Heb., *according to the height of the heaven.*

² Heb., *it is not.*

a Deut. 7. 9.

³ Heb., *mighty in strength.*

(18) ᵃ to such as keep his covenant, and to those that remember his commandments to do them.

(19) The LORD hath prepared his throne in the heavens; and his kingdom ruleth over all.

(20) Bless the LORD, ye his angels, ³that excel in strength, that do his commandments, hearkening unto the voice of his word. (21) Bless ye the LORD, all ye his hosts; *ye* ministers of his, that do his pleasure. (22) Bless the LORD, all his works in all places of his dominion: bless the LORD, O my soul.

PSALM CIV.

(1) Bless the LORD, O my soul. O LORD my God, thou art very great; thou art clothed with honour and ma-

---

(11) **So great is his mercy toward.**—Literally, *Strong is his mercy upon* (or, *over*). (Comp. Ps. cxvii. 2.) The comparison in the first clause, and the use of this expression in Gen. xlix. 26 and 2 Sam. xi. 23, suggests as the right rendering here

For as the heaven is higher than the earth,
So far (above what was expected) for them fearing him prevails his mercy.

(For the same comparison, see Isa. lv. 7—9; and comp. Isa. xxxviii. 17; Micah vii. 19.)

(13) **Father.**—This anticipation of Christ's revelation of the paternal heart of God, is found also in the prophets.

(14) **Frame.**—Rather, *fashioning*; referring to Gen. ii. 7, or possibly to the image so common in the prophecy of the potter's vessel.

(16) **The wind**—*i.e.*, the hot, scorching blast, as in Isa. xl. 7. Even in our humid climate, it may be said of a flower—

"If one sharp wind sweep o'er the field,
It withers in an hour."

But the pestilential winds of the East are described as bringing a heat like that of an oven, which immediately blasts every green thing.

Know it no more.—Comp. Job vii. 10. Man vanishes away without leaving a trace behind. The pathos of the verse has been well caught in the well-known lines of Gray:—

"One morn I missed him on the accustomed hill,
Along the heath, and near his favourite tree:
Another came, nor yet beside the rill,
Nor up the lawn, nor at the wood was he."

(19) **Prepared.**—Rather, *established.*

(20) Just as in the highest revelation made by Jesus Christ the angels in heaven rejoice over the repentant sinner, so in the psalmist's view the mercy of Jehovah to his faithful people is cause for high acclaim among the hosts around the throne.

(21) **Hosts.**—There are apparently in the psalmist's thought three grades of beings in the hierarchy of praise:—

1. High angels around the throne.
2. Angelic powers, such as *winds, lightnings*, &c., specially commissioned to do God's behests, as in Ps. civ. 4.
3. Creation generally. (Comp. Ps. cxlviii.)

(22) **All his works.**—Not only the heavens and their hosts, but

"Earth with her thousand voices praises God."

Nor can the psalmist himself remain silent, but must repeat the self-dedication with which he began his song.

CIV.

This psalm touches the highest point of religious poetry. It is the most perfect hymn the world has ever produced. Even as a lyric it has scarcely been surpassed; while as a lyric inspired by religion, not only was all ancient literature, except that of the Hebrews, powerless to create anything like it, but even Christian poetry has never succeeded in approaching it. Milton has told the story of Creation, taking, as the psalmist does, the account in Genesis for his model; but the seventh book of the *Paradise Lost*, even when we make allowance for the difference between the narrative and lyric styles, is tame and prolix—seems to want animation and fire—by the side of this hymn.

At the very opening of the poem we feel the magic of a master inspiration. The world is not, as in Genesis, created by a Divine decree. It springs into life and motion, into order and use, at the touch of the Divine presence. Indeed, the pervading feeling of the hymn is the sense of God's close and abiding relation to all that He made; the conviction that He not only originated the universe, but dwells in it and sustains it: and this feeling fastens upon us at the outset, as we see the light enfolding the Creator as His robe, and the canopy of heaven rising over Him as His tent. It is not a lifeless world that springs into being. There is no void, no chaos; even the winds and clouds are not for this poet without denizens, or they themselves start into life and people the universe for his satisfaction. He cannot conceive of a world at any time without life and order. Nor has any poet, even of our modern age, displayed a finer feeling for nature, and that not in her tempestuous and wrathful moods—usually the source of Hebrew inspiration—but in her calm, everyday temper. He is the Wordsworth of the ancients, penetrated with a love for nature, and gifted with the insight that springs from love. This majestic hymn is anonymous in the Hebrew. The LXX. have ascribed it to David. Its

jesty. ⁽²⁾ Who coverest *thyself* with light as *with* a garment: who stretchest out the heavens like a curtain: ⁽³⁾ who layeth the beams of his chambers in the waters: who maketh the clouds his chariot: who walketh upon the wings of the wind: ⁽⁴⁾ ᵃ who maketh his angels spirits; his ministers a flaming fire: ⁽⁵⁾¹*who* laid the foundations of the earth, *that* it should not be removed for ever.

a Heb. 1. 7.

1 Heb., *He hath founded the earth upon her bases.*

---

close connection with Psalm ciii., and an Aramaic word in verse 12, indicate a post-exile date for its composition. The verse shows every variety of rhythm.

⁽¹⁻⁴⁾ First and second days of Creation. Instead, however, of describing the *creation* of light, the poet makes a sublime approach to his theme by treating it as a symbol of the Divine majesty. It is the vesture of God, the tremulous curtain of His tent, whose supporting beams are based, not on the earth, but on those cloud-masses which form an upper ocean. This curtain is then, as it were, drawn aside for the exit of the Monarch attended by His throng of winged messengers.

⁽¹⁾ **Clothed.** — For the same metaphor see Ps. xciii. 1.

⁽²⁾ **Who coverest.**—Perhaps better with the participles of the original retained:

Putting on light as a robe;
Spreading the heavens as a curtain.

The psalmist does not think of the formation of light as of a single past act, but as a continued glorious operation of Divine power and splendour. Not only is light as to the modern poet,

"Nature's resplendent robe,
Without whose vesting beauty all were wrapt
In unessential gloom,"

but it is the dress of *Divinity*, the "ethereal woof" that God Himself is for ever weaving for His own wear.

Curtain.—Especially of a *tent* (see Song of Sol. i. 5, &c.), the tremulous movement of its folds being expressed in the Hebrew word. Different explanations have been given of the figure. Some see an allusion to the curtains of the Tabernacle (Exod. xxvi., xxvii.). The associations of this ritual were dear to a religious Hebrew, and he may well have had in his mind the rich folds of the curtain of the Holy of Holies. So a modern poet speaks of

"The arras-folds, that variegate
The earth, God's ante-chamber."

Herder, again, refers the image to the survival of the nomadic instinct. But there is no need to put a limit to a figure so natural and suggestive. Possibly images of palace, temple, and tent, all combined, rose to the poet's thought, as in Shelley's "Ode to Heaven":—

"Palace roof of cloudless nights!
Paradise of golden lights!
  Deep immeasurable vast,
Which art now, and which wert then;
  Of the present and the past,
Of the Eternal where and when,
  Presence-chamber, temple, home,
  Ever-canopying dome
Of acts and ages yet to come!"

⁽³⁾ **Layeth the beams.**—Literally, *maketh to meet.* The meaning of the Hebrew word, which is an exact equivalent of the Latin *contignare*, is clear from Neh. ii. 8, iii. 3, 6, and from the meaning of the derived noun (2 Kings vi. 2, 5; Song of Sol. i. 17).

Chambers.—Literally, *lofts* or *upper stories.* (See 2 Kings iv. 10; Jer. xxii. 13, 14.)

In the waters.—The manner of this ethereal architecture is necessarily somewhat difficult to picture. The pavilion which God rears for His own abode appears to rest on a floor of rain-clouds, like a tent spread on a flat eastern roof. (See Ps. xviii. 11; Amos ix. 6, 7.) Southey's description of the Palace of Indra may perhaps help the imagination:—

"Built on the lake, the waters were its floor;
And here its walls were water arched with fire,
And here were fire with water vaulted o'er;
  And spires and pinnacles of fire
  Round watery cupolas aspire,
And domes of rainbow rest on fiery towers."
Curse of Kehama.

Who maketh the clouds His chariot.—See Ps. xviii. 10, probably the original of this verse; *chariot* (*rekhûb*) here taking the place of *cherub*.

Walketh upon the wings of the wind.—Doubtless the metaphor is taken from the clouds, which, in a wind-swept sky, float along like "the drifted wings of many companies of angels." The clause is thus in direct parallelism with the description of the *cloud* chariot. The figure has passed into modern song:

"Every gust of rugged *wings*
That blows from off each beaked promontory."
MILTON: *Lycidas.*

"No *wing of wind* the region swept."
TENNYSON: *In Memoriam.*

⁽⁴⁾ **Who maketh . . .**—Rather,

Who maketh winds His messenge
A flaming fire His ministers.

Or, keeping the order of the Hebrew,

Who maketh His messengers of winds,
And His ministers of flaming fire.

This is plainly the meaning required by the context, which deals with the use made by the Divine King of the various forms and forces of Nature. Just as He makes the clouds serve as a chariot and the sky as a tent, so he employs the winds as messengers and the lightnings as servants.

Taken quite alone, the construction and arrangement of the verse favours the interpretation of the author of the Epistle to the Hebrews (Heb. i. 7, Note, *New Testament Commentary*). This was the traditional Jewish interpretation, and on it were founded various theories of angelic agency.

But not only do the exigencies of the context set aside this interpretation, but Hebrew literature offers enough instances to show that the order in which a poet arranged his words was comparatively immaterial. Indeed, Dean Perowne has adduced two instances (Isa. xxxvii. 26, lx. 18) of precisely similar inversion of the natural order of immediate object and predicate. (See *Expositor*, December, 1878.) And no difficulty need be made about the change of number in *flame of fire* and *ministers*, since even if the former were not synonymous with *lightnings*, its predicate might be plural. (See Prov. xvi. 14, "The *wrath* of a king is *messengers* of death.")

⁽⁵⁻¹⁸⁾ The work of the third day of Creation in its two great divisions. (1) The separation of the land and water (verses 5—9); (2) the clothing of the earth with grass, herbs, and trees (verses 10—18). The poet, however, ranges beyond the Mosaic account, and already

The Wonderful   PSALMS, CIV.   *Providence of God.*

(6) Thou coveredst it with the deep as *with* a garment: the waters stood above the mountains. (7) At thy rebuke they fled; at the voice of thy thunder they hasted away. (8) ¹ They go up by the mountains; they go down by the valleys unto the place which thou hast founded for them. (9) Thou hast set a bound that they may not pass over; that they turn not again to cover the earth.

(10) ² He sendeth the springs into the valleys, *which* ³ run among the hills. (11) They give drink to every beast of the field: the wild asses ⁴ quench their thirst. (12) By them shall the fowls of the heaven have their habitation, *which* ⁵ sing among the branches. (13) He watereth the hills from his chambers: the earth is satisfied with the fruit of thy works. (14) He causeth the grass to grow for the cattle, and herb for the service of man: that he may bring forth food out of the earth; (15) and *ᵃ* wine *that* maketh glad the heart of man, *and* ⁶ oil to make *his* face to shine, and bread *which* strengtheneth man's heart.

(16) The trees of the LORD are full *of sap;* the cedars of Lebanon, which he hath

---

1 Or, *The mountains ascend, the valleys descend.*
2 Heb., *Who sendeth.*
3 Heb., *walk.*
4 Heb., *break.*
5 Heb., *give a voice.*
a Judges 9. 13.
⁶ Heb., *to make his face shine with oil,* or, *more than oil.*

---

peoples the earth with the living creatures of the fifth day. "It is not a picture of still life like that of Genesis, but a living, moving, animated scene" (Perowne).

(5) **Who laid . . .**—Better, *He fixed the earth on its foundations.* (Comp. Job xxxviii. 4—6; Prov. viii. 29.)

The inconsistency of this with Job xxvi. 7, "He laid the earth upon nothing," need not cause difficulty. Both treatments are poetical, not scientific. The word *foundations* implies stability and endurance (comp. Ps. lxxxii. 5), as in Shakspeare's

"The frame and huge foundation of the earth."

The verse has a historical interest from having supplied the Inquisition with an argument against Galileo.

(6) **The deep.**—The water-world is first considered as a vast garment wrapped round the earth, so that the mountain-tops are covered. But here it is beyond its right, and the Divine rebuke forces it to retire within narrower limits. It is noticeable that the idea of a chaos finds no place in the poetic conception of the world's genesis. The primitive world is not formless, but has its mountains and valleys already existing, though merged beneath the sea.

(8) **They go up.**—This translation is grammatically possible, but is inconsistent with the preceding description. It is better therefore to take the clause parenthetically, and to make hills and valleys the subjects. *Hills rise, valleys sink,* an interesting anticipation of the disclosures of geology, which, though in a different sense, tells of the upheaval of mountains and depression of valleys. Two passages in Ovid have been adduced in illustration (*Met.* i. 43, 344). And Milton, no doubt with the psalm as well as Ovid in his mind, wrote

"Immediately the mountains huge appear Emergent," &c.—*Paradise Lost,* book vii.

(9) **A bound.**—It is striking to observe what a deep impression their little line of coast, the barrier which beat off the waves of the Mediterranean, made on the Hebrew mind. The sea was an object of dread. Or if dread passes into reverent wonder, as in verses 25, 26, it ends there; the Jew never took *delight* in the sea. Hence, the coast has for him only one purpose and suggestion. It is not for enjoyment or recreation, or even for uses of commerce. It is simply the defence set by God against the hostile waters.

(10) **Springs.**—The account in Genesis goes on abruptly from the appearance of the dry land to speak of the vegetation which covers it, apparently without any physical means for its production. But a poet, especially an Oriental poet, thinks first of the springs and rivers on which fertility and life depend. And such is his sympathy with nature that in disregard of the original record he hastens at once to people his world with creatures to share the Creator's joy in its beauty and goodness.

Valleys—*i.e.,* the torrent beds, the "wadys" as the Arabs now call them.

Which run.—Better, *they flow between the hills.* The LXX. supply the subject "waters."

(11) **Wild asses.**—See Job xxxix. 5—8.

(12) **By them.**—Better, *above them, i.e.,* in the trees and bushes growing on the bank of the stream. Translate by the present, *have their homes.*

(13) **Chambers**—*i.e.,* of cloud, as in verse 3.

Thy works.—If we go by the parallelism, this means the "rain," here called God's works, as in Ps. lxv. 9 (see Note), his "river." Others prefer to see a general reference to the operations of nature which produce fruit.

(14) **For the service of man**—*i.e.,* for his use (so Gesenius). But some deny this meaning to the Hebrew, which properly means "labour" or "office." (In 1 Chron. xxvii. 26; Neh. x. 37, it means "agriculture," "tillage.") Hence they render, "And herbs for man's labour in bringing them forth from the earth," alluding to his task of cultivating the soil. Standing by itself the clause would indeed naturally require this sense, but the parallelism is against it, and in 1 Chron. xxvi. 30, "service of a king," we have a near approach to the meaning "use."

That he may.—Better, *bringing food out of the earth,* taking the verb as gerund instead of infinitive absolute.

(15) **And wine that . . .**—Better, *and wine gladdens man's heart, making his face shine more than oil* (see margin. The alternative follows the LXX. and Vulg., and suggests the anointing with oil at a banquet), *and bread man's heart sustains.*

Oil.—For oil and its uses see Ps. cxxxiii. 2, cxli. 5.

Strengtheneth.—Properly, *props* or *supports.* (Comp. "the staff of bread," Ps. cv. 16), and our "staff of life," and for the same phrase Gen. xviii. 5; Judg. xix. 5).

(16) **The trees . . .**—Better, *Jehovah's trees are satisfied.* The parallelism shows what are Jehovah's trees. The cedar of Lebanon (see 1 Kings iv. 33) was the grandest and fairest tree known to the Hebrew; and like lightning and the tropical rain, is honoured by the epithet most expressive of grandeur. (See *Bible Educator,* IV., 359.) Such trees the poet feels must have been planted by the Divine hand itself—man

God's Care for PSALMS, CIV. *His Creatures.*

planted; (17) where the birds make their nests: *as for* the stork, the fir trees *are* her house. (18) The high hills *are* a refuge for the wild goats; *and* the rocks for the conies.

(19) He appointed the moon for seasons: the sun knoweth his going down. (20) Thou makest darkness, and it is night: wherein ¹ all the beasts of the forest do creep *forth*. (21) The young lions roar after their prey, and seek their meat from God. (22) The sun ariseth, they gather themselves together, and lay them down in their dens.

(23) Man goeth forth unto his work and to his labour until the evening.

(24) O LORD, how manifold are thy works! in wisdom hast thou made them all: the earth is full of thy riches. (25) *So is* this great and wide sea, wherein *are* things creeping innumerable, both small and great beasts. (26) There go the ships: *there is* that leviathan, *whom* thou hast ² made to play therein.

(27) ª These wait all upon thee; that thou mayest give *them* their meat in due season. (28) *That* thou givest them they

1 * Heb., *all the beasts thereof do trample on the forest.*

2 Heb., *formed.*

a Ps. 145. 15.

---

could grow herbs, but not cedars—and here, as a proof of the lavish provision made by the Creator for the fertility of the earth, he states that even these monarchs of the wood have enough.

(17) **Stork.**—The LXX. give "heron," but Dr. Tristram has shown that there is no need to prefer "heron" here, on account of "the nesting in fir trees," since if near its feeding-grounds the stork readily selects a fir as the tallest and most convenient tree for its nest (*Nat. Hist. of the Bible*, p. 244).

"The eagle and the stork
On cliffs and cedar-tops their eyries build."—MILTON.

(18) **Wild goats.**—Heb., *climbers*, and so at home on the "high hills." (See 1 Sam. xxiv. 2, "the rocks of the wild goats.") "This animal, which is a relation of the Swiss ibex or steinbock, is now called the beden or jaela" (*Bible Educator*, II., 104).

Conies.—Heb., *shăphan*, *i.e.*, "hider." (Comp. Lev. xi. 5, and *Bible Educator*, II., 201.) Naturalists know it as the *hyrax Syriacus*. The LXX., Vulg., and Aquila have "hedgehogs."

(19) **The moon for seasons.**—See Ps. lxxxix. 37, Note. The mention of the inferior luminary first is no doubt partly due to its importance in fixing the calendar, but partly also to the diurnal reckoning, "the evening and the morning" as making the day.

The sun knoweth.—So Job xxxviii. 12 of the dawn. The sun is no mere mechanical timepiece to the Israelite poet, but a conscious servant of God. How beautifully this mention of sunset prepares the way for the exquisite picture of the nocturnal landscape, as the sunrise in verse 22 does for the landscape of the day.

In Genesis the creation of the "heavenly bodies"—the fourth day's work—is related in, so to speak, a scientific manner. But the poet, as in the former part of his treatment of the subject, at once goes to the influence of these phenomena on animated being. In Genesis the lamps of heaven are, as it were, hung out at God's command; in the poem they seem to move to their office of guiding the seasons and illuminating the earth like living things who are conscious of the glorious function they have to perform.

(20) **Creep forth.**—The word "forth" is better omitted. The Hebrew verb is that especially used of crawling animals and reptiles, and here, no doubt, is chosen to express the stealthy motion of the beasts when on the track of their prey. (See verse 25; comp. Job xxxvii. 8, xxxviii. 40.)

(22) **Lay them down.**—With sunrise all is changed. The wild animals, with their savage instincts, give way to man with his orderly habits and arranged duties. The curse of labour, on which the account in Genesis dwells, is here entirely out of sight, and instead there appears the "poetry of labour." And if all sense of the primal curse has disappeared, the later curse, which lies so heavy on the modern generations of overworked men,

"Who make perpetual moan,
Still from one labour to another thrown,"

has not appeared. The day brings only healthy toil, and the evening happy rest.

(24) **Riches.**—LXX., "creation;" Aquila, Symmachus, and the Vulg., "possession." The MSS. vary between singular and plural. *Creatures* will perhaps best express the sense here.

There is something as fine in art as true in religion in this sudden burst of praise—the "evening voluntary" of grateful adoration—into which the poet bursts at the mention of the day's close. Weariness leaves the soul, as it is lifted from contemplation of man's toil to that of God. Athanasius remarked on the sense of rest and refreshment produced by this change of strain.

(25) **So is . . .**—Better, *Yonder is the sea great and broad*. For a moment the poet, "lost in wonder, love and praise," has forgotten his model, the Mosaic account of creation. But suddenly, as his eye catches sight of the sea—we imagine him on some hill-top, commanding on the one hand the range of Lebanon, on the other the Mediterranean—the words recur to him, "Let the waters bring forth abundantly," &c.

Creeping.—See verse 20. Perhaps here, "swarming."

(26) **Ships.**—The poet writes like one who had been accustomed to see the navies of Phœnicia, one of the indications which leads to the hypothesis that he belonged to the northern part of Palestine. And here for once we seem to catch a breath of enthusiasm for the sea—so rare a feeling in a Jew.

Leviathan.—See Ps. lxxiv. 14. In Job (xli.) it is the crocodile, but here evidently an animal of the sea, and probably the *whale*. Several species of *cetacea* are still found in the Mediterranean, and that they were known to the Hebrews is clear from Lam. iv. 3. Various passages from classic authors support this view.

Whom Thou . . .—This clause is rendered by some "whom Thou hast made to play with him" (so LXX. and Vulg.), referring to Job xli. 5. It is a rabbinical tradition that Leviathan is God's plaything.

gather: thou openest thine hand, they are filled with good. ⁽²⁹⁾ Thou hidest thy face, they are troubled: thou takest away their breath, they die, and return to their dust. ⁽³⁰⁾ Thou sendest forth thy spirit, they are created: and thou renewest the face of the earth. ⁽³¹⁾ The glory of the LORD ¹ shall endure for ever: the LORD shall rejoice in his works. ⁽³²⁾ He looketh on the earth, and it trembleth: he toucheth the hills, and they smoke.

⁽³³⁾ I will sing unto the LORD as long as I live: I will sing praise to my God while I have my being. ⁽³⁴⁾ My meditation of him shall be sweet: I will be glad in the LORD. ⁽³⁵⁾ Let the sinners be consumed out of the earth, and let the wicked be no more. Bless thou the LORD, O my soul. Praise ye the LORD.

PSALM CV.

⁽¹⁾ O ^a give thanks unto the LORD; call upon his name: make known his

1 Heb., *shall be.*

a 1 Chron. 16. 8; Isa. 12. 4.

---

(29) **Thou hidest Thy face.**—Elsewhere an image of displeasure, here only of withdrawal of providential care. (See Ps. xxx. 7, where the expression "troubled" also occurs.)

Thou takest away their breath.—Not only is the food which sustains animal life dependent on the ceaseless providence of God, but even the very breath of life is His, to be sent forth or withdrawn at His will. But to this thought, derived of course from Genesis (comp. Ps. xc. 3, Note), the poet adds another. The existence of death is not a sorrow to him any more than it is a mystery. To the psalmist it is only the individual that dies; the race lives. One generation fades as God's breath is withdrawn, but another succeeds as it is sent forth.

(30) **Spirit.**—Rather, *breath*, as in verse 29. We must not here think of the later theological doctrine of the Holy Spirit. The psalmist evidently regards the breath of God only as the vivifying power that gives matter a distinct and individual, but transient, existence. Even in the speculative book of Ecclesiastes, the idea of a human soul having a permanent separate existence does not make its appearance. At death the dust, no longer animate, returns to the earth as it was, and the breath, which had given it life, returns to God who gave it—gave it as an emanation, to be resumed unto Himself when its work was done. Still less, then, must we look in poetry for any more developed doctrine.

(31) **The Lord shall rejoice.**—The poet still follows Genesis in representing God as looking on His finished work with pleasure, but he says nothing of a sabbath. But it is possible that the thought of the sabbath hymns of praise led him to join man with the Divine Being in celebrating the glory and perfection of creation.

(32) **Trembleth.**—With the praise is united something of awe and fear, since the majesty and power of Him who made the world is so great. Its very existence is dependent on His will, and a glance, a touch from Him would be enough to shake it to its foundations and consume it. For "the smoky mountain tops," comp. Ps. cxliv. 5, and see Note, Ps. cxlviii. 8.

(34) **My meditation.**—Rather, *my singing* or *my poetry.*

(35) **Sinners be consumed.**—This imprecation, which comes in at the close of this otherwise uniformly glad hymn, has been variously excused. The truth seems to be that from a religious hymn of Israel, since religion and patriotism were one, the expression of the national feeling against heathen oppressors and apostates who sided with them could not well be absent, whatever its immediate subject and tone. But the poet touches even a profounder truth.* The harmony of creation was soon broken by sin, and the harmony of the song of creation would hardly be complete, or rather, would be false and unreal, did not a discord make itself heard. The form such a suggestion would take was conditioned by the nationality of the poet; the spirit of it brings this ancient hymn at its close into accord with the feeling of modern literature, as reflected in Wordsworth's well-known "Verses Written in Early Spring":—

"I heard a thousand blended notes,
While in a grove I lay reclined,
In that sweet mood when pleasant thoughts
Bring sad thoughts to the mind.
To her fair works did Nature link
The human soul that through me ran.
And much it grieved my heart to think
What Man has made of Man."

Bless thou the Lord.—This is the first *hallelujah* in the psalter. Outside the psalter it is never found, and was therefore a liturgical expression coined in a comparatively late age. It is variously written as one or two words.

CV.

The motive of this historical psalm is plainly declared in verses 44 and 45, and the scope which the author allowed himself in the survey of the past appears in verse 11. He wishes this generation to remember that the continued possession of the Promised Land is contingent on obedience to the covenant God. In fact, the psalm is an elaboration of the charge so often repeated in the Book of Deuteronomy: "For the Lord thy God shall greatly bless thee in the land which the Lord thy God giveth thee for an inheritance to possess it, only if thou carefully hearken unto the voice of the Lord thy God to observe to do all these commandments which I command thee this day" (Deut. xv. 4, 5).

The psalm dates from a time prior to the composition of the first Book of Chronicles, for it forms part of the compilation of song in chapter xvi.; but there is no other indication by which to assign date or authorship. The conjecture is probable that it was compiled for liturgic use soon after the re-settlement in the country after the Captivity. The parallel structure, which is of the synthetic kind, alone gives it a claim to rank with poetry.

(1) **Call upon his name.**—Literally, *on* (or, *with*) *his name* (comp. verse 3, "glory in"), with idea of

---

* In reality the power of sin to interfere with God's pleasure in His universe is present as an undercurrent of thought in Ps. ciii., as well as civ. In the former it is implied that forgiveness and restoration are requisite before the harmony of the universe (verses 20—22) can become audible. The two psalms are also closely related in form.

deeds among the people. (2) Sing unto him, sing psalms unto him: talk ye of all his wondrous works. (3) Glory ye in his holy name: let the heart of them rejoice that seek the LORD.

(4) Seek the LORD, and his strength: seek his face evermore. (5) Remember his marvellous works that he hath done; his wonders, and the judgments of his mouth; (6) O ye seed of Abraham his servant, ye children of Jacob his chosen.

(7) He *is* the LORD our God: his judgments *are* in all the earth. (8) He hath remembered his covenant for ever, the word *which* he commanded to a thousand generations. (9) *a* Which *covenant* he made with Abraham, and his oath unto Isaac; (10) and confirmed the same unto Jacob for a law, *and* to Israel *for* an everlasting covenant: (11) *b* saying, Unto thee will I give the land of Canaan, ¹ the lot of your inheritance: (12) when they were *but* a few men in number; yea, very few, and strangers in it.

(13) When they went from one nation to another, from *one* kingdom to another people; (14) he suffered no man to do them wrong: yea, he reproved kings for their sakes; (15) *saying*, Touch not mine anointed, and do my prophets no harm. (16) Moreover he called for a famine upon the land: he brake the whole staff of bread. (17) He sent a man before them, *c even* Joseph, *who* was sold for a servant: (18) *d* whose feet they hurt with fetters: ² he was laid in iron: (19) until the time that his word came: the word of the LORD tried him. (20) *e* The king sent and loosed him; *even* the ruler of the people, and let him go free. (21) *f* He made him lord of his house, and ruler of all his ³ substance: (22) to bind his princes at his pleasure; and teach his senators wisdom.

(23) *g* Israel also came into Egypt; and Jacob sojourned in the land of Ham. (24) And he increased his people greatly; and made them stronger than their enemies. (25) *h* He turned their heart

---

a Gen. 17. 2 & 22. 16, & 26. 3 & 28.13, & 35. 11; Luke 1. 73; Heb. 6. 17.

b Gen. 13. 15, & 15. 18.

1 Heb., *the cord.*

c Gen. 37. 28.

d Gen. 39. 20.

2 Heb., *his soul came into iron.*

e Gen. 41. 14.

f Gen. 41. 40.

3 Heb., *possession.*

g Gen. 46. 6.

h Ex. 1. 8.

---

proclamation as well as *invocation*. Symmachus has "proclaim his name." This verse, which is found word for word in Isaiah xii. 4, is apparently one of the recognised doxologies of the Hebrew Church.

(2) **Sing psalms.**—Rather, *play, sing unto Him, play unto Him;* the usual choral direction.

(4) **Seek the Lord.**—Better, *Enquire after Jehovah and his power.* The congregation is directed to the historical survey which follows. This sense seems settled by Ps. cxi. 2: "The works of Jehovah are great, enquired into by all those who take delight in them." And hence the word "strength" must be understood as used generally of the manifestation of Divine power in the wondrous deeds now to be mentioned.

(7—11) First cause of praise; the ancient covenant.

(8) **Commanded.**—Better, *appointed,* or *conferred.*

(9) **Made.**—Literally, *cut;* the usual word for making a covenant (*icere fœdus*). The word is therefore here a synonym for "league," as in Haggai ii. 5.

(10) **Law . . . covenant.**—In Hebrew, *chok* and *berith,* which here seem to be used as synonyms. (Comp. the use of the former word in Ps. ii. 7.)

(11) This verse marks the scope of the psalm, to show how the promise made to Abraham was fulfilled.

(14) **Wrong.**—The allusion is doubtless to the incidents connected with Sarah and Rebekah at the courts of Egypt and Philistia. (See Gen. xxvi. 11.)

(15) **Anointed.**—In the plural, "my anointed ones." As referring to the patriarchs, the expression is not technical, since they were never, like priests, prophets, and kings in later times, actually *anointed.* But the terms being sometimes applied to the covenant people as a whole (see Ps. lxxxix. 38, 51), its application to the founders of the race, especially those to whom the "promises came," is very just.

As to the term "prophet," the poet found it expressly conferred on Abraham in Gen. xx. 7.

(16) **Called for a famine.**—Comp. 2 Kings viii. 1; and in Ezek. xiv. we see how famine, with war and pestilence and noisome beasts, were regarded as Divine emissaries to be summoned and sent on His missions.

Staff of bread.—Lev. xxvi. 26. (See, too, Note on Ps. civ. 15.)

(17) Repeats Joseph's own explanation, twice given, of the ways of Providence in his life (Gen. xlv. 5, l. 20).

(18) **He was laid in iron.**—The Prayer Book Version, "the iron entered into his soul," has established itself so firmly among expressive proverbial sayings, that the mind almost resents the Authorised Version. The grammar of the clause does not decide its sense with certainty; for its syntax is rather in favour of the Prayer Book Version, though the feminine form of the verb makes in favour of the marginal rendering. Symmachus has, "his soul came into iron;" the LXX., "his soul passed through iron." The Vulg., however, has the other Version, "the iron passed through his soul"—first found in the Targum. The parallelism is in favour of the Authorised Version.

(19) **Until the time that his word came**—*i.e.,* until his (Joseph's) interpretation of the dreams was fulfilled (Gen. xli. 12). (For the expression "his word came," equal to "came to pass," comp. Judges xiii. 12.)

Word of the Lord.—As a different Hebrew word from that in the previous clause is used, better render, *saying* (or, *oracle*) *of Jehovah.*

Tried him.—Better, *purified him, i.e.,* proved him innocent of the charge for which he was imprisoned. (For this sense of the verb, see Pss. xvii. 3, xviii. 30; Prov. xxx. 5, margin.) The psalmist means that by enabling him to foretell the dreams of Pharaoh's servants, God brought about the proof of his innocence.

(25) **Turned their heart.**—So the hardening of Pharaoh's heart is throughout the historical narrative

The Rescue of   PSALMS, CVI.   *Israel from Bondage.*

to hate his people, to deal subtilly with his servants. (26) *a* He sent Moses his servant; and Aaron whom he had chosen. (27) *b* They shewed [1] his signs among them, and wonders in the land of Ham. (28) *c* He sent darkness, and made it dark; and they rebelled not against his word. (29) *d* He turned their waters into blood, and slew their fish. (30) Their land brought forth frogs in abundance, in the chambers of their kings. (31) *f* He spake, and there came divers sorts of flies, *and* lice in all their coasts. (32) *g* [2] He gave them hail for rain, *and* flaming fire in their land. (33) He smote their vines also and their fig trees; and brake the trees of their coasts. (34) *h* He spake, and the locusts came, and caterpillars, and that without number, (35) and did eat up all the herbs in their land, and devoured the fruit of their ground. (36) *i* He smote also all the firstborn in their land, the chief of all their strength.

(37) *j* He brought them forth also with silver and gold: and *there was* not one feeble *person* among their tribes. (38) *k* Egypt was glad when they departed: for the fear of them fell upon them. (39) *l* He spread a cloud for a covering; and fire to give light in the night. (40) *m The people* asked, and he brought quails, and satisfied them with the bread of heaven. (41) *n* He opened the rock, and the waters gushed out; they ran in the dry places *like* a river.

(42) For he remembered his holy promise, *and* Abraham his servant. (43) And he brought forth his people with joy, *and* his chosen with [3] gladness: (44) *o and* gave them the lands of the heathen: and they inherited the labour of the people; (45) that they might observe his statutes, and keep his laws. Praise ye the LORD.

PSALM CVI.

(1) [4] Praise ye the LORD. O *p* give

---

a Ex. 3. 10.
b Ex. 7. 9.
[1] Heb., *words of his signs.*
c Ex. 10. 22.
d Ex. 7. 20.
e Ex. 8. 6.
f Ex. 8. 17, 24.
g Ex. 9. 23.
[2] Heb., *He gave their rain hail.*
h Ex. 10. 4.
i Ex. 12. 29.
j Ex. 12. 35.
k Ex. 12. 33.
l Ex. 13. 21.
m Ex. 16. 12.
n Ex. 17. 6; Num. 20. 11; 1 Cor. 10. 4.
[3] Heb., *singing.*
o Josh. 13. 7; Deut. 6. 10, 11.
[4] Heb., *Hallelujah.*
p Ps. 107. 1 & 118. 1, & 136. 1.

---

ascribed to Jehovah. (Comp. Isa. vi. 9, 10; Mark iv. 12, &c.)

Deal subtilly.—The reference is to the murdering of the male children (Exod. i. 10: "Come and let us deal wisely with them").

(27) **They shewed.**—Literally, *They placed, i.e.,* did.

His signs.—Literally (as in margin), *the words of his tokens*; but it may also be rendered, "the details of his signs." (Comp. Ps. lxv. 3: "matters of iniquity," or, "details of sin.") So here, "details of signs," *i.e.*, signs in detail or sequence, sign after sign.

(28) **Darkness.**—The enumeration of the plagues omits the fifth and sixth, and begins with the ninth, and appends a clause which, from the first, has troubled translators. Of whom is it said, "They rebelled not against his words"? Of the Egyptians it is not true; and to refer the words to Moses and Aaron, in contrast with their resistance to the Divine command at Massah and Meribah, is feeble. The LXX. and the Syriac solved the difficulty by rejecting the negative. (Comp. the Prayer Book Version.)

The simplest explanation is to take the verb as imperfect subjunctive: "He sent darkness, and made it dark, that they might not rebel against his word."

But this fails to supply a reason for the position in the list of the ninth plague, and the suggested emendation of Mr. Burgess is so satisfactory in this respect, that it almost by itself carries conviction with it. By a very slight change, he obtains: "He sent darkness, and darkened them, that they might not discern his tokens;" taking *deber* in the same sense that it bears in verse 27.

Thus the plague of darkness is, by a slight device of the poet, made to symbolise the moral blindness displayed by the Egyptians throughout.

(29) For the various terms used in describing the plagues, see Notes to the historical account in Exodus.

(34) **Caterpillars.**—To the locust, *'aarbeh,* alone mentioned in Exodus, the psalmist adds, as a poetical synonym to suit his parallelism, caterpillar (*yelek*), a word occurring in Joel i. 4, ii. 25; Nahum iii. 15; Jer. li. 14, 27. By derivation the word means "licker" (comp. Num. xxii. 4), and is possibly used in a wide or general sense for insects of the locust kind. (See *Bible Educator,* IV. 294.)

(36) See Ps. lxxviii. 51.

(37) **Feeble person.**—Literally, *stumbling.* (Comp. Isa. v. 27: "None shall be weary or *stumble* among them," *i.e.*, none unfit for the march and military duty.)

(39) **Cloud.**—As in Isa. iv. 5. The reason assigned for the cloud in the historical books is lost sight of. Instead of a pillar marking the line of march, or as a protection against the pursuing foe, it is a canopy for protection from the sun. Sir Walter Scott expresses the same idea in Rebecca's hymn.

(41) **Rock.**—The Hebrew *tsûr* refers us to the miracle at Horeb.

(43) **Gladness.**—Better, *singing.* Alluding, possibly, to Miriam's song on the shore of the Red Sea.

CVI.

The motive of this historical psalm differs from that of the last as it does from that of Psalm lxxviii. Its survey of the past is neither hymnic nor didactic, but penitential. Though the first of the series of "Hallelujah" psalms, it is closely related to these long liturgical confessions of national sins which are distinctly enjoined in Deut. xxvi., where the type form of them is given, and of which the completest specimen is retained in Neh. ix.

But this example sprang from particular circumstances. It evidently dates from the exile period, and may well, both from its spirit and from its actual correspondence of thought and language in some of the verses, have been composed by Ezekiel, to encourage that feel-

A General Confession   PSALMS, CVI.   *of Disobedience.*

thanks unto the LORD; for *he is* good: for his mercy *endureth* for ever.

(2) Who can utter the mighty acts of the LORD? *who* can shew forth all his praise?

(3) Blessed *are* they that keep judgment, *and* he that doeth righteousness at all times.

(4) Remember me, O LORD, with the favour *that thou bearest unto* thy people: O visit me with thy salvation; (5) that I may see the good of thy chosen, that I may rejoice in the gladness of thy nation, that I may glory with thine inheritance.

(6) We have sinned with our fathers, we have committed iniquity, we have done wickedly. (7) Our fathers understood not thy wonders in Egypt; they remembered not the multitude of thy mercies; *a* but provoked *him* at the sea, *even* at the Red sea. (8) Nevertheless he saved them for his name's sake, that he might make his mighty power to be known.

(9) He rebuked the Red sea also, and it was dried up: so he led them through the depths, as through the wilderness. (10) And he saved them from the hand of him that hated *them*, and redeemed them from the hand of the enemy. (11) *b* And the waters covered their enemies: there was not one of them left. (12) *c* Then believed they his words; they sang his praise.

(13) *d* 1 They soon forgat his works; they waited not for his counsel: (14) *e* but 2 lusted exceedingly in the wilderness, and tempted God in the desert. (15) *f* And he gave them their request; but sent leanness into their soul.

(16) *g* They envied Moses also in the camp, *and* Aaron the saint of the LORD. (17) *h* The earth opened and swallowed up Dathan, and covered the company of Abiram. (18) *i* And a fire was kindled in

a Ex. 14. 11, 12.
b Ex. 14. 27, & 15. 5.
c Ex. 14. 31, & 15. 1.
d Ex. 15. 24, & 16. 2.
1 Heb., *They made haste, they forgat.*
e Num. 11. 4; 1 Cor. 10. 6.
2 Heb., *lusted a lust.*
f Num. 11. 31.
g Num. 16. 1, &c.
h Num. 16. 31; Deut. 11. 6.
i Num. 16. 35, 46.

---

ing of penitence from which alone a real reformation and restoration of the nation could be expected. The verse is mostly synthetic.

(1—5) These verses form an introduction to the psalm, and make it evident that while the writer spoke as one of a community, and for the community, he still felt his *personal* relation to Jehovah.

(1) This formula of praise in the Jewish Church occupied, as a choral refrain, a similar position to the *Gloria Patri* in Christian worship. The precise date of its first appearance cannot be ascertained. The chronicler includes it in the compilation from different psalms, which he introduces as sung when the Ark was brought to Zion (1 Chron. xvi. 34); and represents it not only as chanted by the procession of priests and Levites, but as bursting spontaneously from the lips of the assembled multitudes at the dedication of Solomon's Temple (2 Chron. vii. 3). He mentions it also in connection with Jehoshaphat's revival of choral music. And it is probable that he was not guilty of any great anachronism in giving it this early existence; for Jeremiah speaks of it as a refrain as familiar as those customary at weddings (Jer. xxxiii. 11), and, indeed, foretells its revival as of a practice once common, but long disused. But the fact that it is found in four liturgical hymns, besides Ps. cxxxvi., where it becomes a refrain after every verse, as well as its express mention in Ezra iii. 11 as used at the dedication of the second Temple, shows that its use became more general after the Captivity; and it was in use in the Maccabæan period (1 Macc. iv. 24).

(2) **Praise.**—*Tehillah*, a term that has become technical for a liturgic hymn. (*Tehillim* is the general Hebrew word for the psalter. See Gen. Introduction.) The psalmist asks in this verse who is worthy or privileged to sing a *tehillah*, and replies himself that loyalty to the covenant confers this privilege.

(5) The tone of this verse indicates a prospect of a speedy advent of good; and serves itself to give a probable date to the psalm.

(6) **We.**—Regard must be paid to the fact that the confession includes the speaker and his generation, as well as the ancestors of the race. The psalm proceeds from the period of the Captivity, when the national conscience, or at all events that of the nobler part of the nation, was thoroughly alive to the sinfulness of idolatry.

(7) **At the sea.**—LXX., "going up to the sea."

(12) An epitome of Exod. xiv. 31 and xv.

(13—33) These twenty verses cover the desert wanderings, beginning with the discontented spirit mentioned in Exod. xv. 23.

(13) **They waited not . . .**—They could not *wait* for the natural and orderly outcome of the counsel of God.

(14) **Lusted.**—See margin.

(15) **Leanness.**—The LXX., Vulg., and Syriac read "satiety." As Mr. Burgess points out, by accepting this reading, and giving *nephesh* its very usual signification of "lust" (comp. Ps. lxxviii. 18, where also the word rendered "request" occurs) we get two exact synthetical clauses:—

"And he gave them their request,
And sent satiety for their lust."

(16—18) The poet has Numb. xvi., xvii. in his mind.

(16) **Saint.**—The holy one. The complaint of the disaffected party was that Moses and Aaron usurped this title, which belonged to all the congregation (Num. xvi. 3—5).

(17) The omission of Korah is in keeping with the historical accounts, which indicate a difference both in the attitude of Korah and his family from that of Dathan and Abiram, and also a difference of fate. (Comp. Num. xvi. 23, *seqq.*; Deut. xi. 6; Num. xxvi. 10.)

The Story of   PSALMS, CVI.   *Israel's Rebellions.*

their company; the flame burned up the wicked.

⁽¹⁹⁾ ^a They made a calf in Horeb, and worshipped the molten image. ⁽²⁰⁾ Thus they changed their glory into the similitude of an ox that eateth grass. ⁽²¹⁾ They forgat God their saviour, which had done great things in Egypt; ⁽²²⁾ wondrous works in the land of Ham, *and* terrible things by the Red sea.

⁽²³⁾ ^b Therefore he said that he would destroy them, had not Moses his chosen stood before him in the breach, to turn away his wrath, lest he should destroy *them.*

⁽²⁴⁾ Yea, they despised ¹ the pleasant land, they believed not his word: ⁽²⁵⁾ ^c but murmured in their tents, *and* hearkened not unto the voice of the Lord. ⁽²⁶⁾ Therefore he lifted up his hand against them, to overthrow them in the wilderness: ⁽²⁷⁾ ² to overthrow their seed also among the nations, and to scatter them in the lands.

⁽²⁸⁾ ^d They joined themselves also unto Baalpeor, and ate the sacrifices of the dead. ⁽²⁹⁾ Thus they provoked *him* to anger with their inventions: and the plague brake in upon them. ⁽³⁰⁾ ^e Then stood up Phinehas, and executed judgment: and *so* the plague was stayed. ⁽³¹⁾ And that was counted unto him for righteousness unto all generations for evermore.

⁽³²⁾ ^f They angered *him* also at the waters of strife, so that it went ill with Moses for their sakes: ⁽³³⁾ because they provoked his spirit, so that he spake unadvisedly with his lips.

⁽³⁴⁾ They did not destroy the nations, ^g concerning whom the Lord commanded them: ⁽³⁵⁾ ^h but were mingled among the heathen, and learned their works. ⁽³⁶⁾ And they served their idols: which were a snare unto them. ⁽³⁷⁾ Yea, they

a Ex. 32. 4.
b Ex. 32. 10.
¹ Heb., *a land of desire.*
c Num. 14. 2.
² Heb., *To make them fall.*
d Num. 25. 3.
e Num. 25. 7.
f Num. 20. 13.
g Deut. 7. 2.
h Judges 1. 21.

⁽¹⁹⁾ **In Horeb.**—This expression, which is Deuteronomic (see Deut. iv. 15, v. 2, &c.), shows that Deut. ix. 8—12, as well as Exod. xxxii., was before the poet.

⁽²⁰⁾ **Their glory**—*i.e.*, Jehovah, as shown by Jer. ii. 11.

Similitude.—This is also a Deuteronomic word (Deut. iv. 16, 18), meaning originally "structure," from a root meaning "to build," and so "form," "model."

⁽²¹⁾ **Forgat God their saviour.**—With evident allusion to Deut. vi. 12.

⁽²²⁾ **Land of Ham.**—A synonym for Egypt, peculiar to the historic psalms (Pss. lxxviii. 51, cv. 23, 27).

⁽²³⁾ **Stood before him in the breach . . .**—This is generally explained after Ezek. xxii. 30, where undoubtedly it is an image taken from the defence of a besieged town. (Comp. Ezek. xiii. 5.) But it is possible that we should render, "Had not Moses stood before him (*i.e.*, submissively; see Gen. xli. 46; Deut. i. 38) in the breaking forth (of his anger)," since the verb from which the substantive here used comes is the one employed (Exod. xix. 22), "lest the Lord break forth upon them." So the LXX. seem to have understood the passage, since they render here by the same word, which in verse 30 does duty for "plague." (Comp. Vulg., *refractio*.)

(24—27) The rebellion that followed the report of the spies.

⁽²⁶⁾ **Lifted up his hand.**—Not to strike, but to give emphasis to the oath pronounced against the sinners. (See Exod. vi. 8, margin; Deut. xxxii. 40; comp. Ps. cxliv. 8.) The substance of the oath here referred to is given in Num. xiv. 28—35.

⁽²⁷⁾ **Overthrow.**—This verse is evidently copied from Ezek. xx. 23, but the psalmist has either intentionally or accidentally changed the prophet's verb "scatter" into "overthrow," just used in verse 26. The error, if an error, is as old as the LXX. version.

(28—31) The licentious character of the cult of Baalpeor in Num. xxv. is expressed in the word "joined," better, *yoked.* LXX. and Vulg., "were initiated," *i.e.*, by prostitution.

⁽²⁸⁾ **Ate the sacrifices of the dead**—*i.e.*, the sacrifices of a *dead* divinity. Num. xxv. 2, "and they called the people unto the sacrifices of their gods," shows that here we must not see any allusion to necromantic rites, such as are referred to in Deut. xviii. 11; Isa. viii. 19, and the parallelism shows that the "god" in question is Baal-peor.

Carcases of idols.—This phrase is actually used in Lev. xxvi. 30; here no doubt the plural is used poetically for the singular.

⁽³⁰⁾ **Executed judgment.**—The Prayer Book has "prayed," following the Chaldee and Syriac. The LXX. and Vulg. have "appeased."

(32, 33) The insurrection against Moses and Aaron at Meribah Kadesh, entailing on the Lawgiver the forfeiture for himself of entering into Canaan. (See references in the margin.)

⁽³³⁾ **They provoked his spirit.**—The natural interpretation is to take this of Moses' spirit. So LXX. and Vulg., "they embittered his spirit." The usage of the phrase is, however, in favour of referring the words to the temper of the people towards God, "they rebelled against His spirit."

Spake unadvisedly.—Compare the same verb with the same addition, "with the lips," in Lev. v. 4. This interpretation of the fault of Moses is partial. A comparison of all the historical narratives shows that it was rather for a momentary lapse into the despairing spirit of the people, than for addressing them as rebels, that Moses was excluded from the Promised Land.

(34—39) The national sin after the settlement in Canaan.

⁽³⁷⁾ **Devils.**—Literally, *lords*, meaning, of course, the false deities. The word is, no doubt, chosen to represent the meaning of the heathen gods' names

God's Forbearance   PSALMS, CVII.   *towards the Israelites.*

sacrificed their sons and their daughters unto devils, (38) and shed innocent blood, *even* the blood of their sons and of their daughters, whom they sacrificed unto the idols of Canaan: and the land was polluted with blood. (39) Thus were they defiled with their own works, and went a whoring with their own inventions.

(40) Therefore was the wrath of the Lord kindled against his people, insomuch that he abhorred his own inheritance. (41) And he gave them into the hand of the heathen; and they that hated them ruled over them. (42) Their enemies also oppressed them, and they were brought into subjection under their hand.

(43) *a* Many times did he deliver them; but they provoked *him* with their counsel, and were ¹brought low for their iniquity.

(44) Nevertheless he regarded their affliction, when he heard their cry:

a Judges 2. 16.

¹ Or, *impoverished,* or, *weakened.*

b Lev. 26. 41, 42.

c Ps. 106. 1 & 118. 1, & 136. 1.

(45) *b* and he remembered for them his covenant, and repented according to the multitude of his mercies. (46) He made them also to be pitied of all those that carried them captives.

(47) Save us, O Lord our God, and gather us from among the heathen, to give thanks unto thy holy name, *and* to triumph in thy praise. (48) Blessed *be* the Lord God of Israel from everlasting to everlasting: and let all the people say, Amen. Praise ye the Lord.

Book V.

PSALM CVII.

(1) O *c* give thanks unto the Lord, for *he is* good: for his mercy *endureth* for ever.

(2) Let the redeemed of the Lord say so, whom he hath redeemed from the hand of the enemy; (3) and gathered them out of the lands, from the east, and

---

Ba'alim, Adonim. For the same Hebrew word, see Deut. xxxii. 17 (Judges ii. 11, Baalim).

The Arabic equivalent of the Hebrew word became in Spain *the Cid*, and exists still in the Moorish *sidi*, i.e., "my lord."

(38) **Innocent blood.**—Human sacrifice, and especially that of *children*, was a Canaanite practice. It seems to have been inherent in Phœnician custom, for Carthage was, two centuries after Christ, notorious for it. (See Sil. Ital., iv. 767.)

(40—43) Having made review of the sinful past, the poet briefly but impressively describes the punishment which once and again had fallen on the nation. But as his purpose is to make his generation look on the Captivity as a supreme instance of this punishment, and to seek for deliverance by repentance, he mentions only the judgments inflicted by foreign foes.

(46) **Made them also to be pitied.**—Literally, *gave them for companions*, a phrase found in Solomon's prayer (1 Kings viii. 50, and also in Dan. i. 9, Heb.).

(47) **Save us.**—For this prayer the whole psalm has prepared the way.

(48) **Blessed . . .** — The doxology, which is only slightly altered from that at the end of the second book, is quoted as part of the psalm in 1 Chron. xvi. 36—an indication that by that time this book was complete, if not the whole collection.

Book V.

CVII.

Two widely different accounts have been given of this psalm; one, that it describes historically the dangers and sufferings of the return from captivity, and the Divine power and guidance which brought the redeemed safely through them; the other, that it presents a general picture or group of pictures of the vicissitudes of human life and the interposition of Divine Providence. The true explanation probably lies intermediate between these two. Verses 2 and 3 leave no room for question that the poet had the Return primarily in his mind. Indications in the same direction are supplied by the many expressions and figures taken from the later chapters of Isaiah, among which is prominent the phrase "the redeemed of Jehovah." But, on the other hand, the series of vivid pictures of which the greater part of the poem is composed are not directly historical, notably the sea-piece (verses 23—32).

While, therefore, the psalm may properly be regarded as a lyric embodiment of the lessons of the Captivity, it applies these lessons to the human lot generally, and travels over the whole experience of human life for the pictures under which it presents them. The fortunes of his own race were uppermost in the psalmist's mind, but the perils depicted are typical of the straits into which men of all lands and all times are driven; and he had learnt that the goodness and wisdom which at the cry of prayer come to extricate and save are not confined to one race, but are universal and continuous.

Critics unite in assigning a late date for the composition of this poem, and no one doubts that it was intended for liturgic use. The beautiful double refrain marks the division of its somewhat irregular versification.

Of the unity of the poem there is considerable doubt. The piece beginning at verse 33 is not only in form very different from the first, but bears marks of greatly inferior poetical power. (See Note to verse 33.)

(1) For this doxology see Note, Ps. cvi. 1.

(2) **Redeemed of the Lord.**—See for this grand expression, for which so high a destiny was prepared, Isa. lxii. 12; and comp. chaps. lxiii. 4, xxxv. 9.

(3) **Gathered them.**—The usual prophetic word for the Restoration. (See references in margin, and with the verse comp. Isa. xlix. 12.)

From the south.—See margin. The sea here can hardly be any sea but the Mediterranean, and therefore ought, according to general use (see Gen. xii. 8, &c.), to stand for the *west*. But as this makes the enumeration

from the west, from the north, and ¹from the south. ⁽⁴⁾ They wandered in the wilderness in a solitary way; they found no city to dwell in. ⁽⁵⁾ Hungry and thirsty, their soul fainted in them. ⁽⁶⁾ Then they cried unto the LORD in their trouble, *and* he delivered them out of their distresses. ⁽⁷⁾ And he led them forth by the right way, that they might go to a city of habitation.

⁽⁸⁾ Oh that *men* would praise the LORD *for* his goodness, and *for* his wonderful works to the children of men! ⁽⁹⁾ For he satisfieth the longing soul, and filleth the hungry soul with goodness.

⁽¹⁰⁾ Such as sit in darkness and in the shadow of death, *being* bound in affliction and iron; ⁽¹¹⁾ because they rebelled against the words of God, and contemned the counsel of the most High: ⁽¹²⁾ therefore he brought down their heart with labour; they fell down, and *there was* none to help. ⁽¹³⁾ Then they cried unto the LORD in their trouble, *and* he saved them out of their distresses. ⁽¹⁴⁾ He brought them out of darkness and the shadow of death, and brake their bands in sunder.

⁽¹⁵⁾ Oh that *men* would praise the LORD *for* his goodness, and *for* his wonderful works to the children of men! ⁽¹⁶⁾ for he hath broken the gates of brass, and cut the bars of iron in sunder.

⁽¹⁷⁾ Fools because of their transgression,

¹ Heb., *from the sea.*

---

of the points of the compass imperfect, several emendations have been proposed, the best of which is *yamin* (the "right hand," and so "south") for *yam*.

Or is the text right, and instead of looking for a complete compass, ought we to connect this general statement with the four tableaux of misery presently painted, and so take "out of the sea" literally in reference to verses 23—30?

(4—9) The wanderers.

(4) **They.**—It seems more natural to understand the subject of the verb *wandered* from the preceding clauses, than to supply a general subject, *they*; but this is by no means a certain interpretation. It depends on the view we take of the poem. (See Introduction.)

A solitary way.—Better, *in a desert track.* (Comp. Acts viii. 26.) There is a grammatical difficulty, but this does not affect the general intention of the verse. Whether it represents an historical fact, or merely draws an imaginary picture, the reference to the dangers of Eastern travel is equally clear and distinct.

City to dwell in.—Literally, *city of habitation,* as rendered in verse 7.

"Boundless and bare
The lone and level sands stretch far away."—SHELLEY.

(5) **Fainted.**—Literally, *let itself be covered.* (See Ps. lxxvii. 3.)

(7) **By the right way.**—Better, *in a straight way.* Even in the pathless wilderness "there is a hand that guides."

(8) **Oh that men.**—The subject is rather to be supplied from the preceding clauses, "let them praise," &c. Some, however, render "they praise," &c.

On the other hand, the insertion of "for" in each clause of the Authorised Version is correct (so LXX. and Vulg.).

(9) **Longing soul.**—Or, *thirsty,* as in Isa. xxix. 8. (Comp. verse 5.) The word originally applies to an animal running up and down in search of food or water. (See Joel ii. 9; Prov. xxviii. 15.)

(10—16) The prisoners.

(10) **In darkness.**—A common synonym for a dungeon. (See Isa. xlii. 7, xlix. 9, both of the exiles in Babylon; comp. Micah vii. 8.)

This description, applicable to prisons in all ages but the most modern, was especially suitable for those of the ancients, who admitted no light at all; *e.g.,* the Mamertine prison at Rome. Comp. Virgil, *Æn.* vi. 734:

"Neque auras
Dispiciunt clausæ tenebris et carcere cæco."

In affliction and iron.—Both words are found also in Ps. cv. 18, but distributed into the two clauses of the verse—*hurt, iron.* (Comp., too, Job xxxvi. 8, "bound in fetters and holden in cords of affliction.") The LXX. and Vulg. have "in poverty and in iron."

(11) **Contemned.**—This word is an old Mosaic designation for the *provocation* offered by the chosen people (Num. xiv. 11, 23), as well as for the *abhorrence* shown by Jehovah for their sin (Deut. xxxii. 19). Certainly this verse is more closely applicable to violation of the Theocratic relations of Israel to Jehovah than of heathen opposition to God.

(12) **Brought down.**—Literally, *made them bend.*
Fell down.—Better, *stumbled.*

The whole verse presents a picture of men staggering under the forced labour which was the usual fate of captives under the great Oriental monarchies.

(14) **Break their bands in sunder.**—See Ps. ii. 3.

(15) **Oh that . . .**—The subject is the participle in verse 10, "such as sit," a fact which bears upon the proper subject in verse 8.

(16) Isa. xlv. 2 was present to the poet's mind.

Virgil's picture of the shrine of war (*Æn.* vii. 607) has been compared to this.

(17—22) The sick.

(17) **Fools**—*i.e., infatuated in wickedness.* (Comp. the noun *foolishness* in Ps. xxxviii. 5 with the same ethical sense; and comp. Job v. 3 and the frequent connection of folly with sin in the book of Proverbs.) Another Hebrew word is used in the same way (Ps. xiv. 1).

Because of their transgressions.—Better more literally, *because of way of transgression,* or, *their course of sin,* indicating a settled habit.

Are afflicted . . .—Properly, *brought* (or *bring*) *affliction on themselves.* LXX. and Vulgate, "were humbled;" and some understand "afflict themselves" —*i.e.,* grieve for their sins. This would explain the distaste for food in the next verse equally well as actual sickness. But the analogy of the other stanzas is not in favour of indicating repentance before the emphatic "then they cry," &c.

and because of their iniquities, are afflicted. (18) ᵃTheir soul abhorreth all manner of meat; and they draw near unto the gates of death. (19) Then they cry unto the LORD in their trouble, and he saveth them out of their distresses. (20) He sent his word, and healed them, and delivered *them* from their destructions. (21) Oh that *men* would praise the LORD *for* his goodness, and *for* his wonderful works to the children of men! (22) and let them sacrifice the sacrifices of thanksgiving, and declare his works with ¹rejoicing.

(23) They that go down to the sea in ships, that do business in great waters; (24) these see the works of the LORD, and his wonders in the deep. (25) For he commandeth, and ²raiseth the stormy wind, which lifteth up the waves thereof. (26) They mount up to the heaven, they go down again to the depths: their soul is melted because of trouble. (27) They reel to and fro, and stagger like a drunken man, and ³are at their wit's end. (28) Then they cry unto the LORD in their trouble, and he bringeth them out of their distresses. (29) He maketh the storm a calm, so that the waves thereof are still. (30) Then are they glad because they be quiet; so he bringeth them unto their desired haven. (31) Oh that *men* would praise the LORD *for* his goodness, and *for* his wonderful works to the children of men! (32) Let them exalt him also in the congregation of the people, and praise him in the assembly of the elders.

(33) He turneth rivers into a wilderness, and the water-springs into dry ground; (34) a fruitful land into ⁴barrenness, for the wickedness of them that dwell therein. (35) ᵇHe turneth the wilderness into a standing water, and dry ground into watersprings. (36) And there he maketh the hungry to dwell, that they may prepare a city for habitation; (37) and sow the fields, and plant vineyards, which may yield fruits of increase. (38) He blesseth them also, so that they are multiplied greatly; and suffereth not their cattle to decrease.

(39) Again, they are minished and brought low through oppression, affliction, and sorrow. (40) ᶜHe poureth contempt upon princes, and causeth them

a Job 33. 20.

1 Heb., *singing*.

2 Heb., *maketh to stand*.

3 Heb., *all their wisdom is swallowed up*.

4 Heb., *saltness*.

b Isa. 41. 18.

c Job 12. 21.

---

(18) **Soul.**—The Hebrew word for *soul* is very commonly used for *strong appetite* (see verse 9), so that we might paraphrase, "their appetite is turned to loathing." Comp. this verse with Job xxxiii. 20.

(20) **He sent His word.**—In history (see Ps. cv. 19), as in the natural world (Ps. cxlvii. 18), God's word is His messenger. (Comp. Isa. lv. 10, 11.)

Destructions.—This follows the LXX., who derive as in Ps. ciii. 4. A better derivation, however, gives "pits," either with metaphorical allusion to the "depths" of suffering, or literally, of the "graves" to which the sufferers had drawn near.

(23—32) Storm-tossed mariners.

(23) **They that go down to the sea.**—An expression so exactly opposite to the ancient equivalent for *embarking* that we feel we have the very Hebrew feeling. From the high lands of Judæa it was a literal descent to the shores of the Mediterranean. So Jonah *went down* to Joppa (Jonah i. 3). (Comp. Isa. xlii. 10.)

Do business.—Probably with allusion to commercial enterprise.

(25) **He commandeth.**—Literally, *He speaks*. The Almighty fiat, as in Genesis i.

(26) **They mount up.—**

"Tollimur in cœlum curvato gurgite, et idem
Subducta ad Manes imos desedimus unda."
VIRGIL: Æn. iii. 564.

Their soul is melted.—The recollection of sea-sickness is the best comment on this and the next verse.

(27) **Reel to and fro.**—Or more exactly, *spin round and round*.

Are at their wit's end.—An admirable paraphrase of the Hebrew, "all their wisdom swalloweth itself up." The poet, from the expressions employed, is possibly writing under the influence of Ps. xxii. 14; but he has evidently himself been to sea and experienced the dangers and discomforts he so graphically describes. Ovid (*Trist*. i. 2) has been quoted in illustration:

"Me miserum, quanti montes volvuntur aquarum
Jamjam tacturos sidera summa putes.
Quantæ diducto subsidunt æquore valles:
Jamjam tacturas Tartara nigra putes
Rector in incerto est, nec quid fugiatve petatve
Invenit: *ambiguis ars stupet ipsa malis*."

See on this passage Addison in *Spectator*, No. 489.

(28) **Then they cry.**—There is a saying,

"Qui nescit orare, discat navigare."

(32) **Let them exalt.**—The addition of this to the refrain, as of 22 to that of the last stanza, clearly points to a liturgical use in the psalm.

(33) The change in character and style of the psalm at this point is so marked as to suggest an addition by another hand. It is not only that the artistic form is dropped, and the series of vivid pictures, each closed by a refrain, succeeded by changed aspects of thought, but the language becomes harsher, and the poet, if the same, suddenly proclaims that he has exhausted his imagination.

(34) **Barrenness.**—Better, *a salt marsh*, as in LXX. and Vulg. (See Job xxxix. 6.)

(35) **Standing water.**—Or, *a pool of water*. (See Isa. xxxv. 7, xli. 18, 19, xlii. 15.)

The dependence of this psalm on these passages in Isaiah is indubitable. But the images are employed in a different manner. The prophet only thinks of the

to wander in the ¹wilderness, *where there is* no way. ⁽⁴¹⁾ ᵃYet setteth he the poor on high ²from affliction, and maketh *him* families like a flock.

⁽⁴²⁾ ᵇThe righteous shall see *it*, and rejoice: and all iniquity shall stop her mouth. ⁽⁴³⁾ Whoso *is* wise, and will observe these *things*, even they shall understand the lovingkindness of the LORD.

¹ Or, *void place.*

a 1 Sam 2. 8; Ps. 113. 7, 8.

² Or, *after.*

PSALM CVIII.

A Song *or* Psalm of David.

⁽¹⁾ O God, my heart is fixed; I will sing and give praise, even with my glory. ⁽²⁾ Awake, psaltery and harp: I *myself* will awake early. ⁽³⁾ I will praise thee, O LORD, among the people: and I will sing praises unto thee among the nations.

⁽⁴⁾ For thy mercy *is* great above the heavens: and thy truth *reacheth* unto the ³clouds. ⁽⁵⁾ Be thou exalted, O God, above the heavens: and thy glory above

b Job 5. 16, & 22. 19.

³ Or, *skies.*

c Ps. 60. 5.

all the earth. ⁽⁶⁾ ᶜThat thy beloved may be delivered: save *with* thy right hand, and answer me.

⁽⁷⁾ God hath spoken in his holiness; I will rejoice, I will divide Shechem, and mete out the valley of Succoth. ⁽⁸⁾ Gilead *is* mine; Manasseh *is* mine; Ephraim also *is* the strength of mine head; Judah *is* my lawgiver; ⁽⁹⁾ Moab *is* my washpot; over Edom will I cast out my shoe; over Philistia will I triumph.

⁽¹⁰⁾ Who will bring me into the strong city? who will lead me into Edom? ⁽¹¹⁾ *Wilt* not *thou*, O God, *who* hast cast us off? and wilt not thou, O God, go forth with our hosts? ⁽¹²⁾ Give us help from trouble: for vain *is* the help of man. ⁽¹³⁾ Through God we shall do valiantly: for he *it is that* shall tread down our enemies.

PSALM CIX.

To the chief Musician, A Psalm of David.

⁽¹⁾ Hold not thy peace, O God of my

---

joy of returning Israel (verses 39—41). But here the thought is that in the reverses of fortune, which even the chosen nation must be prepared for, God will intervene to protect and save. But the construction is very awkward, owing to the mode in which, in verse 40, two clauses from Job xii. 21 and 24 are introduced.

(41) **Like a flock.**—This figure of a rapid increase of population is also borrowed from Job xxi. 11.

(42) Again the dependence on the book of Job is seen. (See marginal reference.)

(43) The psalm ends in the style, and almost in the very words, of the prophecy of Hosea. (Comp. Hos. xiv. 9.)

CVIII.

This psalm is taken with some variations from Pss. lvii. and lx., verses 1—5 being from Ps. lvii. 7—11; verses 6—13 being from Ps. lx. 7—14, where see Notes.

The principal variations are in verse 3, *Jehovah* for *Adonai.*

In verse 6 the construction is changed to suit the new arrangement and the variation in verse 10, on which see Note, Ps. lx. 8. For the authorship of the parts of which the psalm is composed, see their Introductions. The ascription of the composite production to David furnishes a strong presumption against the historical value of the inscriptions.

CIX.

The peculiar horror of the imprecations in this extraordinary psalm does not lie in the dreadful consequences they invoke. Shakspeare puts curses equally fierce and terrible into Timon's mouth:

"Piety, and fear,
Religion to the gods, peace, justice, truth,
Domestic awe, night-rest, and neighbourhood,
Instruction, manners, mysteries, and trades,
Degrees, observances, customs, and laws,
Decline to your confounding contraries,
And let confusion live!"

Nor is this horror due to the fact, assuming it to be a fact, that these imprecations are not general in their direction, like the misanthrope's curses, but are levelled at a single individual, for the passions of revenge and hatred intensify by contraction of their range. The whole difficulty of the psalm lies in the fact that it was, as the inscription shows, actually, if not primarily, intended for use in the public service of the sanctuary.

But this very use at once divests the psalm of one of the greatest sources of difficulty, its personal character. Whatever its origin, whoever the original object of the imprecations, it is certain that they became public, ecclesiastical, national.

It is quite possible that from the first the writer spoke in the name of the persecuted nation against some oppressive heathen prince, such as Antiochus Epiphanes. Certainly, when sung by the congregation it expressed not an individual longing for revenge, but all the pent-up feeling—religious abhorrence, patriotic hatred, moral detestation—of the suffering community.

The continuance of its recitation in Christian churches opens up another question, and has, in a great measure, been the motive for the various apologetic explanations that have been started for the psalm. It is strange that even yet the old theory, which justifies the language of the imprecations as prophetically the language of Christ, should find advocates. The "quotation" theory is noticed in the Notes. On the quotation of the imprecations by St. Peter, see Notes, *New Testament Commentary,* Acts i. 20, 21. The parallelism is synthetic.

Title.—" To the chief musician." (See Note to title of Ps. iv.)

(1) **God of my praise.**—That is, God to whom as covenant God it was a privilege to make *tehillah.* (See Deut. x. 20, 21, where Jehovah is said to be "the praise" of those who "swear by His name." Comp. also Ps. cvi. 2, 3, and Note, and Ps. xxxiii. 1. Perhaps "God of my glory or boast" would more nearly give

The Psalmist complains   PSALMS CIX.   *of His Enemies.*

praise; (2) for the mouth of the wicked and the ¹mouth of the deceitful ²are opened against me: they have spoken against me with a lying tongue. (3) They compassed me about also with words of hatred; and fought against me without a cause. (4) For my love they are my adversaries: but I *give myself unto prayer.* (5) And they have rewarded me evil for good, and hatred for my love.

(6) Set thou a wicked man over him: and let ³Satan stand at his right hand. (7) When he shall be judged, let him ⁴be condemned: and let his prayer become sin. (8) Let his days be few; *and* ᵃlet another take his ⁵office. (9) Let his children be fatherless, and his wife a widow. (10) Let his children be continually vagabonds, and beg: let them seek *their bread* also out of their desolate places. (11) Let the extortioner catch all that he hath; and let the strangers spoil his labour. (12) Let there be none to extend mercy unto him: neither let there be any to favour his fatherless children. (13) Let his posterity be cut off; *and* in the generation following let their name be blotted out. (14) Let the iniquity of his fathers be remembered with the LORD; and let not the sin of

1 Heb., *mouth of deceit.*
2 Heb., *have opened themselves.*
3 Or, *an adversary.*
4 Heb., *go out guilty,* or, *wicked.*
ᵃ Acts 1. 20.
5 Or, *charge.*

---

the force of the original. The psalmist prays that Jehovah's silence may not make his confident glorifying in the covenant promises vain.

(2) **Of the deceitful.**—Properly, as in margin, *of deceit;* consequently, to make the two expressions alike, it is proposed to read, instead of "mouth of the wicked" (properly, *of a wicked man*), "mouth of wickedness." In any case the best English equivalent will be, "a wicked mouth and a deceitful mouth." "A blow with a word strikes deeper than a blow with a sword" (*Whichcote*).

Spoken against me.—Rather (comp. Ps. xii. 3), *talked with me.*

(4) **For my love** . . .—*i.e., in return for my love I give myself unto prayer.* For a concise expression of the same kind as "I prayer," see Ps. cxx. 7, "I peace." Of course the psalmist means, that in the face of all the taunts and reproaches of his maligners, he simply and naturally has recourse to prayer, and, as the context seems to indicate, prayer *for them.*

(6) **Set thou a wicked man over him.**—This rendering is abundantly confirmed by Lev. xxvi. 16; Num. iv. 27, xxvii. 16; Jer. xv. 3, li. 27, against Hitzig's proposed "Pronounce against him—guilty," which also would only anticipate verse 7. (Comp., too, the noun "office" in verse 8, from the same verb.) The wish expressed is that the persons indicated may fall into the hands of an unscrupulous judge. If, however, we are to think of the divine judgment, then this clause must be taken as exactly parallel to the next: "Appoint a wicked man against him." Here the imprecatory part of the psalm begins, and it has been ingeniously argued that the whole of it (verses 6—20) is a quotation, giving, not the psalmist's curse on his foes, but theirs on *him.* Such quotations, without any introductory words, are common, and the theory is tenable, but improbable.

Satan.—By no means here a proper name, though the LXX. and Vulg. have *diabolus.* The use of the same word in verses 4, 20, 29 is decisive on giving it the general meaning, "adversary" (as in margin) here; even though without the article. Satan is used for the tempting angel in 1 Chron. xxi. 1, and in Zech. iii. 1 we find the same post, "at the right hand," assigned to the accuser. An unscrupulous judge and an adversary as accuser, these are the substance of this imprecation.

(7) **When he shall be judged.**—Literally, *in his being judged.* (See margin.) The meaning is, "may he go out of court a condemned man."

Let his prayer become sin.—If this clause stood by itself, the most natural way would be to give "prayer" and "sin" their usual sense, and see in it the horrible hope that the man's prayer to God for mercy would be reckoned as "sin." That such was the result of the performance of religious rites by a wicked man was, it is true, a thought familiar to the Hebrew. (See, in addition to the marginal reference, Prov. xv. 8, xxi. 27.) But the judgment just spoken of is that of an earthly tribunal. Hence we must render here, *let his prayer be an offence,* that is, instead of procuring him a mitigation of his sentence, let it rather provoke the unscrupulous judge to make it heavier. For sin in this sense of offence, see Eccles. x. 4, and comp. 1 Kings i. 21.

(8) **Office.**—See Note, verse 6. Evidently some post of power and influence.

(9) **Children . . . wife.**—It is one of the sadly peculiar features of this series of curses that the resentment of the imprecator cannot satisfy itself on the *person* of his foe, but fastens also on his innocent descendants. To invoke a speedy death does not content him; he must feast his anger with the thought of the fatherless children and desolate widow.

(10) **Be continually vagabonds.**—"Wander and wander about" would better reproduce the original.

Desolate places.—Rather, *ruins.* They are imagined creeping out of the ruins of their homes to beg. But there was a different reading, followed by the LXX. and Vulg., "let them be driven out of their homes." This reading involves but a slight literal change. Comp.,

"Worse evil yet I pray for on my spouse;
Let him still live, through strange towns roam in want,
Exiled, suspected, cowering, with no home."
                    SENECA: *Med.,* i. 19.

(11) **Let the extortioner.**—Better, *let the usurer lay traps to catch all that he hath.* So Timon:

"Let prisons swallow them,
Debts wither them to nothing."

(13) **Posterity.**—The Hebrew theory of the Divine government was, that if ruin did not overtake the sinner himself, it would fall on his posterity; his name would be forgotten, and his race extinct.

(14) **Fathers.**—The sweet of vengeance lies in its completeness. The curse must strike backwards as well as forwards, and the root as well as the branch be destroyed. Undoubtedly the Mosaic Law, which proclaimed that the "iniquity of the fathers should be visited on the children," suggested the form of the imprecation.

his mother be blotted out. ⁽¹⁵⁾ Let them be before the LORD continually, that he may cut off the memory of them from the earth. ⁽¹⁶⁾ Because that he remembered not to shew mercy, but persecuted the poor and needy man, that he might even slay the broken in heart.

⁽¹⁷⁾ As he loved cursing, so let it come unto him: as he delighted not in blessing, so let it be far from him. ⁽¹⁸⁾ As he clothed himself with cursing like as with his garment, so let it come ¹into his bowels like water, and like oil into his bones. ⁽¹⁹⁾ Let it be unto him as the garment *which* covereth him, and for a girdle wherewith he is girded continually. ⁽²⁰⁾ *Let* this *be* the reward of mine adversaries from the LORD, and of them that speak evil against my soul.

⁽²¹⁾ But do thou for me, O GOD the Lord, for thy name's sake: because thy mercy *is* good, deliver thou me. ⁽²²⁾ For I *am* poor and needy, and my heart is wounded within me. ⁽²³⁾ I am gone like the shadow when it declineth: I am tossed up and down as the locust. ⁽²⁴⁾ My knees are weak through fasting; and my flesh faileth of fatness. ⁽²⁵⁾ I became also a reproach unto them: *when* they looked upon me they shaked their heads.

⁽²⁶⁾ Help me, O LORD my God: O save me according to thy mercy: ⁽²⁷⁾ that they may know that this *is* thy hand; *that* thou, LORD, hast done it.

⁽²⁸⁾ Let them curse, but bless thou: when they arise, let them be ashamed; but let thy servant rejoice. ⁽²⁹⁾ Let mine adversaries be clothed with shame, and let them cover themselves with their own confusion, as with a mantle.

⁽³⁰⁾ I will greatly praise the LORD with my mouth; yea, I will praise him among the multitude. ⁽³¹⁾ For he shall stand at the right hand of the poor, to save him ²from those that condemn his soul.

PSALM CX.

A Psalm of David.

⁽¹⁾ The *ᵃ*LORD said unto my Lord, Sit

1 Heb., *within him.*
2 Heb., *from the judges of his soul.*
a Matt. 22. 44; Mark 12. 36; Luke 20. 42; Acts 2. 34; 1 Cor. 15. 25; Heb. 1. 13.

Sin of his mother.—Is the necessity of the parallelism sufficient to account for this mention of the mother, or is some definite circumstance in the poet's thought? The theory which makes this portion of the psalm (verses 6—20), a quotation of curses really uttered by Shimei against David, finds an allusion to the Moabitish descent on the mother's side. (Comp. the Rabbinical explanation of Ps. li. 5.)

⁽¹⁶⁾ **Poor.**—The Hebrew word thus rendered, viz., '*ani*, has suggested a reference to the murder of the high priest Onias (2 Macc. iv. 34—36).

^(17, 18) **Let.**—The optatives in the English are wrong. These verses express facts, and the imprecation follows in verse 19. Render—

> He loved cursing; and it comes;
> He delighted not in blessing; and it departs;
> Yea, he clothed himself in cursing as with his cloak,
> And it came like water into his bowels,
> And like oil into his bones;
> May it be, &c.

Comp. the proverb, "Curses, like chickens, always come home to roost."

The fabled shirt of Nessus, which ate into the mighty form of Hercules, has suggested itself to commentators in illustration of this image. In a good sense the same figure is a favourite one with the Hebrews. (See Isa. xi. 5.)

Verse 19 has struck most commentators as an anti-climax, and the quotation theory is supported by this fact. But imprecations show their impotence in this way; the angry soul can never be quite "unpacked with curses;" the language of passion exhausts itself too soon, and a violent speech often dies away in unintelligible mutterings or even gestures of rage.

⁽²⁰⁾ **Reward.**—Either "work" or "wages." The LXX. and Vulg. take it in the former sense, "This is their work who," &c.

⁽²¹⁾ **Do thou for me.**—It is almost impossible in English to retain the emphasis of this appeal, made still more emphatic by the sudden change from imprecation on an enemy to prayer for mercy towards self.

⁽²³⁾ **Shadow when it declineth.**—Literally, *a lengthened shade.* (Comp. Ps. cii. 11, and see Note, Song of Sol. ii. 17.) When the day declines the shadow lengthens, it becomes longer and longer, till it vanishes in the universal darkness. Thus does the life of the suffering generation pass away.

Tossed up and down.—Better, *tossed* or *shaken out*, as from the lap. So LXX. and Vulg. (See Neh. v. 13, where the same verb is three times used.) The grasshopper was an emblem of timidity (Job xxxix. 20).

⁽²⁴⁾ **Faileth of fatness.**—Literally, *has failed me from fat*, i.e., has dwindled away.

^(28—31) It is impossible not to notice the anti-climax in these verses, if they are spoken by the same person as verses 16—20, and directed against the same enemies, of whom the one there singled out is the prominent figure. It is not only that the effect is weakened by the change back to the plural number, but the same imprecations are repeated in a diluted and modified form. But perhaps in verse 28 we should drop the *optative*, and read, "they will curse, but thou dost bless."

⁽²⁹⁾ **Mantle.**—Heb., *meil*, which was also a garment worn over the tunic.

⁽³¹⁾ **For he . . .**—Jehovah is the poor man's advocate, just as an adversary was the wicked man's accuser.

CX.

At the first sight the authorship and purpose of this psalm are, for a Christian expositor, not only placed beyond the necessity of conjecture, but even removed from the region of criticism, by the use made of its first verse by our Lord, and the emphatic manner in which He quotes it as the Divinely inspired utterance of

thou at my right hand, until I make thine enemies thy footstool. (2) The LORD shall send the rod of thy strength out of Zion: rule thou in the midst of thine enemies.

(3) Thy people *shall be* willing in the

David (Matt. xxii. 41—45; Mark xii. 35—37; Luke xx. 41—44). But it is now, even among the most orthodox, an admitted fact that, in matters of literature and criticism, our Lord did not withdraw Himself from the conditions of His time, and that the application He made of current opinions and beliefs does not necessarily stamp them with the seal of Divine authorisation.

The prominent thought in the psalm is the *formal* union in one person of the royal dignity and the priesthood. Now all the kings of Israel and Judah at times assumed priestly functions, but only twice in the history can the offices be said to have been *formally* combined—in the person of Joshua son of Josedech (Zech. xi. 12, 13), and in that of the Asmonean Jonathan and his successors (1 Macc. xi. 57). The latter reference is preferable. The impression left by the psalm is exactly in accordance with the history of the Asmoneans. One whom Jehovah has declared by solemn oath a priest; one, *i.e.*, in whom the priesthood was indubitably and firmly fixed, is exalted at Jehovah's right hand as a king, and, as a warrior, rides on with Jehovah to triumph. And the choice of Melchizedek, as type (see Note, verse 4), does not arise from any idea of contrasting his *order* with that of Aaron, but from the necessity of going back to him for an instance of actual and formal priesthood combined in the same person, with kingly rank. In 1 Macc. xiv. 41 the very expression of the psalm, "high priest for ever," is used of Simon.

The abrupt ending of this short psalm has led many critics to regard it as a fragment. The parallelism is very lax.

(1) **The Lord said** . . .—The usual prophetic phrase, generally translated, "Thus saith," &c. (See Note, Ps. xxxvi. 1.)

The psalmist may possibly be quoting an old prophetic saying, but, according to the usual way in which the expression is used, it marks an immediate inspiration.

My Lord.—Heb., *adoni*, an address of honour to those more noble than the speaker, or superior in rank: to a father, Gen. xxxi. 35; to a brother, Num. xii. 11; a royal consort, 1 Kings i. 17, 18; to a prince, 1 Kings iii. 17; with addition of the royal title, "my Lord, O king," 2 Sam. xiv. 19.

The question of the person here intended is, of course, closely bound up with the general question of the authorship and meaning of the psalm. Here the various views that have been held are briefly enumerated:—

(1) The Messiah; and, if so, with a prophetic consciousness of His Divinity, or, at least, His superiority as a Prince over all other princes. (2) David himself: this is, of course, inconsistent with the Davidic *authorship* of the psalm. (3) Solomon. (4) Hezekiah. (5) Joshua son of Josedech. (6) One of the priest-kings of the Asmonean dynasty.

We now come to the words of the oracle: "Sit thou at my right hand, till I make thine enemies thy footstool."

Commentators have sought in the customs of Arabia, and even in the mythology of the Greek poets, for proof that this expression denotes viceroyalty or co-partnership in the throne. If this meaning could be established from Hebrew literature, these parallels would be confirmatory as well as illustrative; but the nearest approach to be found in the Old Testament only makes the seat at the king's right hand a mark of extreme honour. (See the case of Bath-sheba, 1 Kings ii. 19; of the queen consort of Ps. xlv. 9; of Jonathan, 1 Macc. x. 63.)

Nothing more can be assumed, therefore, from the words themselves than an invitation to sit at Jehovah's right hand to watch the progress of the victorious struggle in which wide and sure dominion is to be won for this Prince. But even this is obscured by the concluding part of the psalm (see verse 5), where Jehovah is said to be at the right hand of the person addressed, and is beyond question represented as going out with him to battle. Hence, we are led to the conclusion, that the exact position ("at the right hand") i not to be pressed in either case, and that no more is intended than that, with Jehovah's help, the monarch who is the hero of the poem will acquire and administer a vast and glorious realm.

Footstool.—The imagery of the footstool (literally *a stool for thy feet*) is no doubt taken from the custom mentioned in Josh. x. 24.

(2) **Send.** — The verb should be here rendered *stretch*, as in Gen. xxii. 10, xlviii. 14, and frequently of stretching out the hand, often with hostile intent. The poet here speaks in his own person, addressing the King, to whom the oracle has just been announced.

Rod of thy strength—*i.e.*, the sceptre, which is the emblem of royal power and sway. (See Jer. xlviii. 17.) The word "staff" is different from that rendered "rod," in Ps. ii. 9; and the image is not, as there, necessarily of a weapon of destruction, but only of kingly rule, as in Ps. xlv. 6.

Rule thou . . .—It is better to take these words as a quotation, and understand them as spoken of Jehovah. In the picture before us the Divine King seats the earthly monarch by His side, and taking his sceptre from his hand, stretches it in token of the wide empire he is to administer from Zion, where they sit enthroned, over the surrounding nations, and bids him assume the offered sway, in spite of the foes that surround him at present. The expression "in the midst," instead of "over," implies the condition under which the sovereignty was to be assumed, as also does the rest of the psalm, proceeding to describe the wars by which ultimate triumph over the hostile tribes would be secured.

(3) This difficult verse runs, literally, *Thy people willingnesses* (or, *willing offerings*) *in the day of thy force in holy attire, from the womb of morning dew of thy youth.*

The first clause is tolerably clear. The word rendered *force* means either "strength" or "an army;" and the noun *willingnesses* appears as a verb in Judges v. 9, to express the alacrity with which the northern clans mustered for battle. We may therefore translate: *Thy people will be willing on thy muster-day.*

As to the next two words there is a variation in the text. Many MSS. read, by the slightest change of a Hebrew letter, "on the holy mountains" (this was also, according to one version, the reading of Symmachus and Jerome), and, adopting the reading, we have a

The Judgment to come   PSALMS, CXI.   *upon the Heathen.*

day of thy power, in the beauties of holiness ¹ from the womb of the morning: thou hast the dew of thy youth.

⁽⁴⁾ The LORD hath sworn, and will not repent, ᵃThou *art a priest for ever after* the order of Melchizedek. ⁽⁵⁾ The Lord at thy right hand shall strike through kings in the day of his wrath. ⁽⁶⁾ He shall judge among the heathen, he shall fill *the places* with the dead bodies; he shall wound the heads over ²many countries. ⁽⁷⁾ He shall drink of the brook in the way: therefore shall he lift up the head.

Marginal notes:
1 Or, *more than the womb of the morning: thou shalt have*, &c.
a Heb. 5. 6, & 7. 17.
2 Or, *great*.
3 Heb., *Hallelujah*.

PSALM CXI.

⁽¹⁾ ³Praise ye the LORD. I will praise the LORD with *my* whole heart, in the

---

picture of the people mustering for battle with alacrity on the mountains round Zion, under the eye of Jehovah Himself, and in obedience to the outstretched sceptre.

The second clause is not so clear. By themselves the words "from the womb of morning dew of thy youth," would naturally be taken as a description of the vigour and freshness of the person addressed: "thine is the morning dew of youth." With the image compare—

"The meek-eyed morn appears; *mother of the dews.*"
                                              THOMSON.

(Comp. Job xxxviii. 28.)

But the parallelism directs us still to the gathering of the army, and the image of the *dew* was familiar to the language as an emblem at once of *multitude* (2 Sam. xvii. 11, 12), of *freshness* and *vigour* (Ps. cxxxiii. 3; Hosea xiv. 5), and was especially applied to Israel as a nation in immediate relation to Jehovah, coming and going among the nations at His command (Micah v. 7). Here there is the additional idea of brightness—the array of young warriors, in their bright attire, recalling the multitudinous glancing of the ground on a dewy morning: *thy young warriors come to thee thick and bright as the morning dew.*

Milton has the same figure for the innumerable hosts of angel warriors:—

          "An host
Innumerable as the stars of night
Or stars of morning, dewdrops, which the sun
Impearls on every leaf and every flower."

⁽⁴⁾ **After the order of Melchizedek.**—This follows the LXX. and Vulg. Better, *after the manner of*, since there could have been with the psalmist no intention of contrasting this priesthood with that of Aaron, as there naturally was when the Aaronic order had come to an end or was visibly doomed to extinction.

The previous history of Israel itself offered no example of the formal union of kingly and priestly offices in one person. It first appears in idea in Zech. vi. 12, 13; in actual fact in the pontificate of Jonathan (1 Macc. x. 21). It is true that the royal and priestly *functions* were sometimes united, especially in the case of David, and in 2 Sam. viii. 18, David's sons are called "priests" (in English version, "chief rulers;" margin, or *princes*). It was therefore necessary to go back to Melchizedek, in whom history recognised this sanctioned and formal union (Gen. xiv. 18). For the various points brought out in the Epistle to the Hebrews vi., vii., see *New Testament Commentary.*

⁽⁵⁾ **The Lord at thy right hand.**—We are naturally tempted to understand this as still of the king whom the first verse placed at Jehovah's right hand. But the word for Lord here is *Adonai*, which is nowhere else used except of God. Moreover, God throughout has as yet appeared as the active agent. It is He who stretched out the sceptre and conferred the office of priest; and hitherto the king has been the person addressed. It is therefore necessary still to consider him as addressed, and suppose that the change of position of Jehovah from the king's right hand to his left is simply due to the usage of the language. To *sit at the right hand* was an emblem of honour, *to stand at the right hand* was a figure of protecting might (Pss. xvi. 8, cix. 31); and the imagery of a battle into which the song now plunges caused the change of expression.

⁽⁶⁾ **He shall judge.**—Comp. Ps. ix. 8, &c.

He shall fill.—The construction is peculiar, and in the Hebrew for *heathen* and *corpses* there is a play on words. A slight change in the vowel pointing gives a better construction than is obtained by understanding any word as the Authorised Version does, and critics generally: *He judges among the heathen fulness of corpses.* At first the poet meant to write, "He judges among the heathen fulness of judgment" (comp. Job xxxvi. 17), but, for the sake of the play on the sound, changed his words to "fulness of corpses."

He shall wound the heads.—Literally, *crushes a head over a vast land,* where "head" means, as in Judges vii. 16, 20, a band or host of men. The picture is of a vast battle-field with heaps of slain. Others understand, "the chief or master of a wide land." (Comp. Hab. iii. 14, "head of his villages.")

⁽⁷⁾ **Drink . . . lift up.**—The victorious leader, "faint yet pursuing" (Judges viii. 4), pauses at the stream that crosses his path, and then refreshed, with head once more erect, continues his pursuit of the foe. Such is undoubtedly the meaning of this verse, and we need not suppose a sudden change of subject, as some critics do, as if the picture representing a thirsty warrior were unworthy of Jehovah. Poetry knows nothing of such timidity, and with the grand scene of Isa. lxiii. 1—6, of the hero stained with blood, we need not hesitate to admit this further detail so true to life, even if we had not in Pss. lx. and cviii. images of a still more homely type.

CXI.

Psalms cxi. and cxii. should be read closely together, the one being a pendant of the other. They are both acrostics of at once the simplest and most perfect construction, each clause (not, as usual, each verse of two or more clauses) exhibiting the alphabetical arrangement. There are therefore exactly twenty-two clauses, nearly of three words each. In order to limit the number of verses to ten—considered a perfect number—the last two verses in each psalm are arranged as triplets.

The close relation of the two psalms is also exhibited in their subject. The first exhibits Jehovah in covenant with man; the second, man in covenant with Jehovah. The one sings the Divine praise in view of the kindness God has shown to Israel; in the second, the feeling of the just man—*i.e.,* the Israelite faithful to the covenant, is

assembly of the upright, and *in* the congregation. ⁽²⁾ The works of the LORD *are* great, sought out of all them that have pleasure therein. ⁽³⁾ His work *is* honourable and glorious: and his righteousness endureth for ever. ⁽⁴⁾ He hath made his wonderful works to be remembered: the LORD *is* gracious and full of compassion. ⁽⁵⁾ He hath given ¹meat unto them that fear him: he will ever be mindful of his covenant. ⁽⁶⁾ He hath shewed his people the power of his works, that he may give them the heritage of the heathen. ⁽⁷⁾ The works of his hands *are* verity and judgment; all his commandments *are* sure. ⁽⁸⁾ They ²stand fast for ever and ever, *and are* done in truth and uprightness. ⁽⁹⁾ He sent redemption unto his people: he hath commanded his covenant for ever: holy and reverend *is* his name. ⁽¹⁰⁾ ^aThe fear of the LORD *is* the beginning of wisdom: ³a good understanding have all they ⁴that do *his* commandments: his praise endureth for ever.

PSALM CXII.

⁽¹⁾ ⁵Praise ye the LORD. Blessed *is* the man *that* feareth the LORD, *that* delighteth greatly in his commandments. ⁽²⁾ His seed shall be mighty upon earth: the generation of the upright shall be blessed. ⁽³⁾ Wealth and riches *shall be* in his house: and his righteousness endureth for ever. ⁽⁴⁾ Unto the upright there ariseth light in the darkness: *he is* gracious, and full of compassion, and righteous. ⁽⁵⁾ A good man sheweth favour, and lendeth: he will guide his affairs with ⁶discretion. ⁽⁶⁾ Surely he shall not be moved for ever: the righteous shall be in everlasting remembrance. ⁽⁷⁾ He shall not be

Marginal notes:
3 Heb., *are stablished.*
a Job 28. 28; Prov. 1. 7, & 9. 10; Eclus. 1. 16.
3 Or, *good success.*
4 Heb., *that do them.*
5 Heb., *Hallelujah.*
b Heb., *judgment.*

---

the subject. In both we discover the strength of these religious convictions, which, in spite of the contradictions experienced in actual life, persist in maintaining the grand principle of Divine justice, and declaring that the cause of virtue will triumph, and success and wealth never fail the faithful.

The close relation of the two psalms is marked by the echo in the second, of phrases applied in the first to Jehovah. (Comp. *e.g.*, Pss. cxi. 3, with cxii. 3, 9; cxi. 4, with cxii. 4, 6.)

⁽¹⁾ **Praise ye the Lord.**—This short doxology does not strictly form part of the psalm. The alphabetical arrangement begins with "I will praise," &c.

Assembly.—See Note on Ps. xxv. 14.

⁽²⁾ **Sought out**—*i.e.*, they are the object of meditation and enquiry. (See Note, Ps. cv. 4.) The psalmist was no doubt thinking of historical proofs of Jehovah's goodness to the chosen race, but his words are capable of a wide range. The best illustration of them may be found in the writings in which Mr. Ruskin warns this generation against the danger of insensibility to natural beauty.

⁽⁴⁾ **He hath made . . .**—Literally, *He hath made a memorial for His wonderful works*, as in Josh. iv. 7, &c.

⁽⁵⁾ **He hath given.**—Better, *He gave.*

Meat.—The word often means "prey," from its being torn as by a wild beast, but it is used in Prov. xxxi. 15, Mal. iii. 10, in the simple sense of *food.* (Comp. also the verb, Prov. xxx. 8.) There need not therefore be any allusion to the spoils taken in the Canaanitish wars, though the next verse makes this exceedingly probable. (See Sir G. Grove's remarks; article "Meat" in Smith's *Bible Dictionary.*)

⁽¹⁰⁾ **A good understanding . . .**—Better, *a good estimation have all they that do them.* The parallelism here, as the context of Prov. iii. 4, decides for this rendering against that of the margin, "a good success." Not only is piety the beginning of wisdom, but righteousness wins good esteem. For by *his praise* we must certainly understand the praise of the good man.

CXII.

⁽²⁾ **Mighty.**—In the sense of *wealthy*, as in Ruth ii. 1.

⁽³⁾ **His righteousness endureth for ever.**—The parallelism in verse 9, where the same clause is repeated, seems to require for righteousness the limited sense which the Talmud gives the word—viz., *liberality* or *beneficence.* See also Dan. iv. 27, in the LXX. Still the saying is true in its widest sense. "There is nothing, no, nothing, innocent or good, that dies or is forgotten; let us hold to that faith, or none" (Dickens).

⁽⁴⁾ **Ariseth . . .**—The Hebrew verb is commonly used of the sunrise. (Comp. Ps. xcvii. 11; Isa. lviii. 8.) For the good man the darkest night of trouble and sorrow will have a dawn of hope.

He is gracious . . .—The Authorised Version is right in making this a description of the upright man's character. The construction certainly at first appears strange, since "the upright" is in the plural, while the epithets in this clause resume the singular of verse 3. This may be best explained by treating the first clause of this verse as a familiar proverbial saying, which the poet introduces, as a quotation, without changing the number to suit his own construction.

⁽⁵⁾ **A good man.**—Rather, *happy is the man who gives and lends*, good being here not used in a moral sense, but meaning *prosperous.*

He will guide . . .—Rather, *he will gain his cause in (the) judgment.* So apparently the LXX. and Vulg. Others, "he will sustain his affairs by justice." The verb primarily means "to measure," but in the conjugation here used has the sense of "sustains." (See Gen. xlv. 11, xlvii. 12, l. 21, where the Authorised Version has "nourish.") The meaning is confirmed by the parallelism of the next verse.

⁽⁶⁾ See Ps. xv. 5; Prov. x. 7.

⁽⁷⁾ The story of Job, when the messengers of ill succeeded one another so fast, is an illustration of the

afraid of evil tidings: his heart is fixed, trusting in the LORD. (8) His heart *is* established, he shall not be afraid, until he see *his desire* upon his enemies. (9) ª He hath dispersed, he hath given to the poor; his righteousness endureth for ever; his horn shall be exalted with honour.

(10) The wicked shall see *it*, and be grieved; he shall gnash with his teeth, and melt away: the desire of the wicked shall perish.

PSALM CXIII.

(1) ¹ Praise ye the LORD. Praise, O ye servants of the LORD, praise the name of the LORD. (2) ᵇ Blessed be the name of the LORD from this time forth and for evermore. (3) ᶜ From the rising of the sun unto the going down of the same the LORD'S name *is* to be praised. (4) The LORD *is* high above all nations, *and* his glory above the heavens. (5) Who *is* like unto the LORD our God, who ² dwelleth on high, (6) who humbleth *himself* to behold *the things that are* in heaven, and in the earth! (7) ᵈ He raiseth up the poor out of the dust, *and* lifteth the needy out of the dunghill; (8) that he may set *him* with princes, *even* with the princes of his people. (9) He maketh the barren woman ³ to keep house, *and to be* a joyful mother of children. Praise ye the LORD.

PSALM CXIV.

(1) When Israel went out of Egypt, the house of Jacob from a people of

a 2 Cor. 9. 9.
1 Heb., *Hallelujah.*
b Dan. 2. 20.
c Mal. 1. 11.
2 Heb., *exalteth himself to dwell.*
d 1 Sam. 2. 8; Ps. 107. 41.
3 Heb., *to dwell in an house.*
e Ex. 13. 3.

---

truth of this verse. "A good conscience before God" is the best "armour against fate."

"Virtue is bold, and goodness never fearful."—
SHAKSPERE: *Measure for Measure.*

(8) **Until he see.**—See Note, Ps. lix. 10, and comp. Ps. cxii. 8.

(9) **He hath dispersed.**—The conjugation of the verb indicates a *frequent* and *customary* action.

For St. Paul's use of this verse, see *New Test. Com.* 2 Cor. ix. 9.

His horn.—For the image of the exalted horn see Note, Ps. lxxv. 5.

(10) **Gnash.**—See Ps. xxxv. 16.

Melt away.—As we say, "Consume with vexation."

CXIII.

This psalm begins the *Hallel*, or as sometimes called, *the great Hallel*—though that name more properly is confined to Ps. cxxxvi.—recited at the great Jewish feasts. It is partly modelled on Hannah's song. Its form is regular.

(1) **Ye servants of the Lord**—*i.e.*, Israel. (See Ps. lxix. 36.)

(4) Comp. Ps. viii. 1, &c.

(6) **Humbleth himself.**—Contrast this condescension with the *indifference* to human joys and sorrows which heathen deities were said to show.

(7–8) See 1 Sam. ii. 8, from which the verses are taken; and comp. Luke i. 52.

So the heathen poet sang of Jove (Hor.: *Odes* i., xxxiv., xxxv.).

(7) **Dunghill.**—Literally, *a heap of rubbish.* "Before each village in Hauran there is a place where the household heap up the sweepings of their stalls, and it gradually reaches a great circumference and a height which rises far above the highest buildings of the village." "The *mezbela* serves the inhabitants of the district as a watch-tower, and on close oppressive evenings as a place of assembly, because there is a current of air on the height. There the children play about the whole day long; there the forsaken one lies who, having been seized with some horrible malady, is not allowed to enter the dwellings of men, by day asking alms of the passers by, and at night hiding himself among the ashes which the sun has warmed."—Delitzsch's *Commentary on the Book of Job*, ii. 152, with Note by Wetzstein. It was on the *mezbela* that, according to tradition, Job sat.

(9) **He maketh.**—See margin. Motherhood alone assured the wife of a fixed and dignified position in her husband's house. The quotation from Hannah's song suggested the allusion to her story. We are no doubt right in taking this joyful mother as emblematic of the nation itself restored to prosperity and joy.

CXIV.

This psalm is among the most artistic in the whole collection. Though ending so abruptly as to suggest that it may be a fragment (the LXX., Syriac, Arabic versions, and some MSS. capriciously join it to the following psalm) it is in form perfect. The versification is regular, and the stanzas as complete and finished as in a modern hymn, consisting each of four lines, and presenting each a perfect example of synthetic parallelism. (See Introduction, § 5.) But a higher art displays itself here. The reserve with which the Divine name is withheld, till everything is prepared for its utterance, and the vivid manner in which each feature of the rapid scene is flashed upon us by a single word, so that a whole history is accurately presented in a few graphic touches, achieve a dramatic and a lyric triumph of the most remarkable kind. Besides the historic interest of the psalm as part of the Hallel, and of the hymn sung with Christ before His passion, it has a new interest from Dante, who makes it the passage song of the spirits into Purgatory:—

"Upon the storm stood the celestial pilot;
Beatitude seemed written in his face,
And more than a hundred spirits sat within.
'In Exitu Israel de Egypto'
They chanted all together in one voice,
With whatso in that psalm is after written."—
Purg. 45 (LONGFELLOW).

(1) **When Israel went out.**—LXX., in "the Exodus of Israel."

A people of strange language.—LXX., rightly, "a barbarous people." Since the Hebrew word, like the

God's Power over Nature.   PSALMS, CXV.   *The Folly of Idolatry.*

strange language; ⁽²⁾ Judah was his sanctuary, *and* Israel his dominion.

⁽³⁾ ^a The sea saw *it*, and fled: ^b Jordan was driven back. ⁽⁴⁾ The mountains skipped like rams, *and* the little hills like lambs.

⁽⁵⁾ What *ailed* thee, O thou sea, that thou fleddest? thou Jordan, *that* thou wast driven back? ⁽⁶⁾ Ye mountains, *that* ye skipped like rams; *and* ye little hills, like lambs?

⁽⁷⁾ Tremble, thou earth, at the presence of the Lord, at the presence of the God of Jacob; ⁽⁸⁾ ^c which turned the rock *into* a standing water, the flint into a fountain of waters.

PSALM CXV.

⁽¹⁾ Not unto us, O Lord, not unto us, but unto thy name give glory, for thy mercy, *and* for thy truth's sake. ⁽²⁾ Wherefore should the heathen say, ^d Where *is* now their God? ⁽³⁾ ^e But our God *is* in the heavens: he hath done whatsoever he hath pleased.

⁽⁴⁾ ^f Their idols *are* silver and gold, the work of men's hands. ⁽⁵⁾ They have mouths, but they speak not: eyes have they, but they see not: ⁽⁶⁾ they have ears, but they hear not: noses have they, but they smell not: ⁽⁷⁾ they have hands, but they handle not: feet have they, but they walk not: neither speak they through their throat. ⁽⁸⁾ They that make them are like unto them; so *is* every one that trusteth in them.

⁽⁹⁾ O Israel, trust thou in the Lord: he *is* their help and their shield. ⁽¹⁰⁾ O house of Aaron, trust in the Lord: he

a Ex. 14. 21.

b Josh. 3. 13.

c Ex. 17. 6; Num. 20. 11.

d Ps. 42. 10, & 79. 10.

e Ps. 135. 5.

f Ps. 135. 11.

Greek, implies a certain scorn or ridicule, which ancient races generally had for those speaking another language. To this day the Russians call the Germans "dumb."

⁽²⁾ **Judah was.**—Better, *became*. The feminine verb shows that the country is intended, and not the tribe, and the parallelism directs us to think not of the territory of the tribe of Judah alone, but of the whole country. Notice the art with which the name of God is reserved, and the simple pronoun, His, used. (Comp. Exod. xix. 6.)

⁽³⁾ **Fled.**—The Authorised Version weakens the effect by rendering "it was driven back." (See Josh. iii. 16.) The scene presented is of the "descending stream" (the words employed seem to have a special reference to that peculiar and most significant name of the "Jordan") not parted asunder, as we generally fancy, but, as the psalm expresses it, "turned backwards" (Stanley, *Jewish Church*, i. 229).

⁽⁴⁾ **Skipped.**—The Hebrew word thus rendered is translated "dance" in Eccles. iii. 4. (See Ps. xviii. 7.) Exodus xix. 18 was no doubt in the poet's thought, but the leaping of the hills formed part of every theophany.

⁽⁷⁾ **Tremble.**—Literally, *be in travail*. This answer to his question is introduced with consummate art. Well may the mountains tremble, when it is the Lord of all the earth, the God of Jacob, who is present. Notice that till now the mention of the Divine power which wrought the deliverance was kept in suspense.

CXV.

That this is a late liturgical psalm all commentators agree, but the precise period of its composition cannot be ascertained. The belief that death cut the Hebrew off from all the privileges of the covenant seems to forbid so late a date as the Maccabæan age, though a psalm so priestly in its character, and which apparently celebrates some martial success, would else be appropriately ascribed to the Asmonean period. The psalm has a historic interest for Englishmen, having been chanted by order of Henry V. after the battle of Agincourt. The choric arrangement is indicated by the change of address.

⁽¹⁾ **Not unto us . . .**—This rejection of all self-praise is implied in all Hebrew poetry.

Mercy . . . truth . . .—Both a distinct reference to the covenant. Both these covenanted blessings were assailed by the heathen taunt, "Where is now their God?"

It is difficult for us to reproduce in imagination the apparent triumph, which the idolater, who could point to *his* deity, felt he had over the worshipper of the invisible God, when outward events seemed to be going against the latter. But we may estimate the strength of the conviction, which even under the apparent withdrawal of Divine favour, could point to the heavens as the abode of the Invisible, and to misfortune itself as a proof of the existence and power of One who could in everything do what pleased him.

^(4—8) This passage cannot compare with the magnificent irony of Isa. xliv. 9—20, but there is still a noticeable vein of sarcasm running through it, visible even more in the original than in the English. (Comp. Ps. cxxxv. 15—18.)

⁽⁷⁾ **Neither speak they.**—The Hebrew implies not only the want of articulate speech, but of utterance at all.

⁽⁸⁾ **Every one that trusteth . . .**—

"Who moulds in gold or stone a sacred face
Makes not the god; but he who asks his grace."

⁽⁹⁾ **O Israel.**—There is consummate art in this sudden change of address. It is like the pointed application of some general truth in a sermon. It is possible that in the liturgic use a change in the music was made here, the Levites and choir turning to the people with a loud burst of song.

He is their help and their shield.—The original form of this motto of trust appears in Ps. xxxiii. 20. Here the change of person suggests some musical arrangement. Apparently one part of the choir, or, it may be, one officiating priest, addressed successively the whole congregation with the charge, "trust in Jehovah," and each time the full choir took up the refrain, "He is their helper and shield," repeating to the priest the ground on which he urged confidence and loyalty. Then in verses 12 and 13 congregation and choir join, changing to the *first* person.

is their help and their shield. ⁽¹¹⁾ Ye that fear the LORD, trust in the LORD: he *is* their help and their shield.

⁽¹²⁾ The LORD hath been mindful of us: he will bless *us;* he will bless the house of Israel; he will bless the house of Aaron. ⁽¹³⁾ He will bless them that fear the LORD, *both* small [1] and great. ⁽¹⁴⁾ The LORD shall increase you more and more, you and your children. ⁽¹⁵⁾ Ye *are* blessed of the LORD which made heaven and earth.

⁽¹⁶⁾ The heaven, *even* the heavens, *are* the LORD'S: but the earth hath he given to the children of men. ⁽¹⁷⁾ The dead praise not the LORD, neither any that go down into silence. ⁽¹⁸⁾ *a* But we will bless the LORD from this time forth and for evermore. Praise the LORD.

PSALM CXVI.

⁽¹⁾ I love the LORD, because he hath heard my voice *and* my supplications.

[1 Heb., *with*.]
a Dan. 2. 20.
[2 Heb., *in my days*.]
b Ps. 18. 5, 6.
[3 Heb., *found me*.]
c 2 Cor. 4. 13.
d Rom. 3. 4.

⁽²⁾ Because he hath inclined his ear unto me, therefore will I call upon *him* [2] as long as I live.

⁽³⁾ *b* The sorrows of death compassed me, and the pains of hell [3] gat hold upon me: I found trouble and sorrow. ⁽⁴⁾ Then called I upon the name of the LORD; O LORD, I beseech thee, deliver my soul.

⁽⁵⁾ Gracious *is* the LORD, and righteous; yea, our God *is* merciful. ⁽⁶⁾ The LORD preserveth the simple: I was brought low, and he helped me. ⁽⁷⁾ Return unto thy rest, O my soul; for the LORD hath dealt bountifully with thee. ⁽⁸⁾ For thou hast delivered my soul from death, mine eyes from tears, *and* my feet from falling.

⁽⁹⁾ I will walk before the LORD in the land of the living. ⁽¹⁰⁾ *c* I believed, therefore have I spoken: I was greatly afflicted: ⁽¹¹⁾ I said in my haste, *d* All men *are* liars.

⁽¹³⁾ **Them that fear the Lord**—*i.e.*, all Israel.

⁽¹⁴⁾ **The Lord shall increase.**—More literally,

"Jehovah shall heap blessings on you,
On you and on your children."

^(17, 18) The connection of these verses with the rest of the psalm is far from plain. Why the psalmist should suddenly be struck with the dreadful thought that death broke the covenant relationship, and silenced prayer and praise, is not easy to see. Was the psalm first chanted after some victory? and was this suggested by the sight of the slain, who, though they had helped to win the triumph, could yet have no share in the praises that were ascending to Jehovah?

⁽¹⁷⁾ **Silence.**—The land of silence is, of course, Sheôl, the under-world. (So the LXX., "Hades.")

CXVI.

The late date of composition of this psalm is shown both by the presence of Aramaic forms and the use made of earlier portions of the psalter. It was plainly a song of thanksgiving, composed to accompany the offerings made after some victory. The most important question arising from it is whether it is personal or the voice of the community. As we have seen in other cases a strong individual feeling does not exclude the adaptation of a psalm to express the feelings of the people of Israel as a whole. The rhythm is unequal.

⁽¹⁾ **I love the Lord.**—Besides this rendering, where *Jehovah* is supplied as an object, this poet being given to use verbs without an object (see verses 2, 10), there are two other possible translations.

1. *I have longed that Jehovah should hear,* &c.—For this meaning of the verb *to love* see Jer. v. 31, Amos iv. 5; and for the construction see Ps. xxvii. 4, 5, 6. So the Syriac and Arabic versions.

2. *I am well pleased that Jehovah hears* (or *will hear*).—So LXX. and Vulg.

⁽²⁾ If we take translation (1) of verse 1 this verse will state the ground of the longing to pray. "I have longed for Jehovah to hear me now, for He, as in past times, inclines His ear to me." The latter clause of the verse offers some difficulty. The literal rendering of the text, given by the LXX. and Vulg., is, "and in my days I will call (for help). But there is none." 2 Kings xx. 19 does not, as suggested, confirm the explanation "all the days of my life." It would seem more natural to take the text as an equivalent of the common phrase "in the day when I call" (Pss. lvi. 10, cii. 3, &c.), and render the verse:

For He inclines His ear to me,
And that in the day when I call.

⁽³⁾ **The pains of hell.**—Or, *oppressions of Sheôl,* if we retain the text. But a very slight change in a single letter brings the clause into closer correspondence with Ps. xviii. 5, 6, whence it is plainly borrowed, *the nets of Sheôl*. We may reproduce the original more exactly by using, as it does, the same verb in the last two clauses of the verse:

Nets of Sheôl caught me,
Trouble and sorrow I catch.

⁽⁶⁾ **The simple.**—Inexperienced, in a good sense, as often in Proverbs. LXX. and Vulg., "babes."

Brought low.—See Note, Ps. xxx. 2.

⁽⁷⁾ **Return . . .**—In a very different spirit from the fool's address to his soul in the parable. The psalmist's repose is not the worldling's serenity nor the sensualist's security, but the repose of the quiet conscience and the trusting heart.

⁽⁸⁾ **Falling.**—Or, *stumbling*. (See Ps. lvi. 13, the original of this passage.)

^(10, 11) **I believed, therefore have I spoken.**—This is the rendering of LXX. and Vulg., and it has become almost proverbial from St. Paul's adaptation of it (2 Cor. iv. 13; see *New Testament Commentary*). And no doubt this is the sense of the words, though the particle *khî* has been taken in a wrong connection. Mr. Burgess has certainly given the true explanation of the use of this particle. It sometimes *follows* instead

Gratitude to God. PSALMS, CXVII.—CXVIII. *The Eternity of His Mercy.*

(12) What shall I render unto the LORD *for* all his benefits toward me? (13) I will take the cup of salvation, and call upon the name of the LORD. (14) I will pay my vows unto the LORD now in the presence of all his people. (15) Precious in the sight of the LORD *is* the death of his saints. (16) O LORD, truly I *am* thy servant; I *am* thy servant, *and* the son of thine handmaid: thou hast loosed my bonds. (17) I will offer to thee the sacrifice of thanksgiving, and will call upon the name of the LORD. (18) I will pay my vows unto the LORD now in the presence of all his people, (19) in the courts of the LORD'S house, in the midst of thee, O Jerusalem. Praise ye the LORD.

a Rom. 15. 11.

b 1 Chron. 16. 8; Ps. 106. 1 & 107. 1, & 136. 1.

1 Heb., *out of distress.*

PSALM CXVII.

(1) O *a* praise the LORD, all ye nations: praise him, all ye people. (2) For his merciful kindness is great toward us: and the truth of the LORD *endureth* for ever. Praise ye the LORD.

PSALM CXVIII.

(1) O *b* give thanks unto the LORD; for he is good: because his mercy *endureth* for ever. (2) Let Israel now say, that his mercy *endureth* for ever. (3) Let the house of Aaron now say, that his mercy *endureth* for ever. (4) Let them now that fear the LORD say, that his mercy *endureth* for ever.

(5) I called upon the LORD ¹in distress:

---

of *preceding* the verb affected by it. We must render, *It is because I believed that I spoke* (of God's graciousness, &c.). What follows then comes in as an antithesis. *I was in great trouble; I said in my pain,* "*All men are untrustworthy or deceitful.*" Or (LXX.), *In an ecstasy of despair I said,* "*The whole race of mankind is a delusion.*" The meaning of the whole passage may be thus put: It is through trust in God that I thus speak (as above—viz., of God being glorious and righteous, and of His preserving the souls of the simple). It was not always so. Once in distrust I thought that God did not care for man, and that the whole of humanity was a failure. The word *chăphez*, rendered in Authorised Version *haste*, more properly *alarm*, is in Job xl. 23 contrasted with *trust*, as it is here with *faith*. For the sense *failure* or *vanity* for the word rendered in Authorised Version *liars*, see Isa. lviii. 11 ("fail;" margin, "lie or deceive").

(13) **I will take.**—Or, *lift up.*

Cup of salvation.—The *drink offering* or *oblation* which accompanied festival celebrations (Num. xxix. 19, &c.). Others think of the Passover cup mentioned Matt. xxvi. 27, when this psalm as part of the Hallel was sung. Others, again, take the figurative sense of cup—*i.e.*, portion, lot, as in Ps. xvi. 5.

(15) **Precious . . .**—This is only another form of the statement in Ps. lxxii. 14. But again we have to ask why the thought of death should intrude upon the psalmist at this moment. (See Note, Ps. cxv. 17.) The answer is that, as in verse 8, a recent deliverance from death is spoken of. It is natural to take this psalm as a thanksgiving song for the safety, perhaps victory, of the survivors in some battle, but then the grateful community naturally and dutifully remember the dead.

(16) **Thy servant, and the son of Thine handmaid.**—Comp. Ps. lxxxvi. 16. Not only himself but his family were in the covenant, and, as very commonly in the East, the mother is selected for mention instead of the father.

CXVII.

This, shortest of all the psalms, might well be called *multum in parvo*, for in its few words it contains, as St. Paul felt (Rom. xv. 11), the germ of the great doctrine of the universality of the Messianic kingdom. That it was intended for liturgical use there can be no doubt, and possibly it is only one of the many varieties of the Hebrew Doxology. What is also very noticeable, is the ground on which all the world is summoned to join in the praise of Jehovah—His covenant kindness and the fulfilment of His promises to Israel. The idea latent under this is shown in the second word rendered *praise*; properly, *to soothe*. The nations are imagined coming to make their peace with Israel's God after seeing His display of power for their sakes; but a wider and nobler truth emerged out of this.

CXVIII.

The character of this psalm as a Temple song of thanksgiving is stamped on every line of it. The marked divisions with the refrains (verses 1—4, 8—9) have induced commentators to arrange it in parts, supposed to have been sung in turn by the full choir, the congregation, and the priests. It is not, however, by any means certain to what particular event or time the psalm is to be assigned. Many incidents in connection with the rebuilding of the second Temple have been fixed upon in connection with verses 22, 23. Others have gone to the Maccabæan period for the occasion of the thanksgiving. Several expressions seem to allude to a particular feast, with its peculiar prayers and sacrifices (verses 24—27), and there can be little doubt that this was the Feast of Tabernacles. The words of verse 25 were, we know, sung on one of the days—called the Great Hosanna (*Save now*)—of the feast; a name given also to the boughs carried and waved in the sacred procession. If verses 19—23 imply the completion of the Temple, it is natural to fix on the first complete celebration of the Feast of Tabernacles after the Return (Neh. viii. 14 *seq.*).

(1—4) Comp. Ps. cxv. 9—13, where a similar choral arrangement is found.

(5) **I called.**—Better, *out of the straitness I cried to Jah; answered me, with freedom, Jah.* The meaning of the last clause (literally, *with room.* Comp.: "Ay, marry, now my soul has elbow-room"—*King John*) is determined by the parallelism of Ps. xviii. 19. The versions read "freedom of Jah," *i.e.,* boundless freedom."

the LORD answered me, *and set me* in a large place. (6) *"The LORD is* ¹on my side; I will not fear: what can man do unto me? (7) The LORD taketh my part with them that help me: therefore shall I see *my desire* upon them that hate me.

(8) *It is* better to trust in the LORD than to put confidence in man. (9) *ᵇIt is* better to trust in the LORD than to put confidence in princes.

(10) All nations compassed me about: but in the name of the LORD will I ²destroy them. (11) They compassed me about; yea, they compassed me about: but in the name of the LORD I will ³destroy them. (12) They compassed me about like bees; they are quenched as the fire of thorns: for in the name of the LORD I will ³destroy them.

(13) Thou hast thrust sore at me that I might fall: but the LORD helped me. (14) *ᶜThe LORD is* my strength and song, and is become my salvation.

(15) The voice of rejoicing and salvation *is* in the tabernacles of the righteous: the right hand of the LORD doeth valiantly. (16) The right hand of the LORD is exalted: the right hand of the LORD doeth valiantly.

(17) I shall not die, but live, and declare the works of the LORD. (18) The LORD hath chastened me sore: but he hath not given me over unto death.

(19) Open to me the gates of righteousness: I will go into them, *and* I will praise the LORD: (20) this gate of the LORD, into which the righteous shall enter. (21) I will praise thee: for thou hast heard me, and art become my salvation.

(22) *ᵈThe stone which* the builders refused is become the head *stone* of the corner. (23) ⁴This is the LORD's doing; it *is* marvellous in our eyes. (24) This *is* the day *which* the LORD hath made; we will rejoice and be glad in it.

(25) Save now, I beseech thee, O LORD: O LORD, I beseech thee, send now prosperity.

(26) *ᵉBlessed be* he that cometh in the

---

a Ps. 56. 4, 11; Heb. 13. 6.

¹ Heb., *for me.*

b Ps. 146. 3.

² Heb., *cut them off.*

³ Heb., *cut down.*

c Ex. 15. 2; Isa. 12. 2.

d Matt. 21. 42; Mark 12. 10; Luke 20. 17; Acts 4. 11; 1 Pet. 2. 4.

⁴ Heb., *This is from the LORD.*

e Matt. 21. 9.

---

(6) A reminiscence of Ps. lvi. 9—11.

(7) Made up of Ps. liv. 4—7, where see Notes.

(9) **Trust.**—The word constantly used of the security the Israelite found in his relation to Jehovah. The meaning here is apparently, "Fidelity to the covenant is better than alliance with foreign princes," though, of course, the larger sense, in which the words are applicable to all men, may be read into the words.

(11) **But in the name . . .**—Or, more emphatically, *It is in Jehovah's name that,* &c.

(12) **Like bees.**—The image of the "bees" may be derived from Deut. i. 44 (comp. Isa. vii. 18), but the LXX. suggest that the poet employed an original and far more expressive image, for they read, "as bees surround the comb." Possibly the word *comb* dropped out of the Hebrew text, because the copyist was thinking of Deut. i. 44.

The fire of thorns.—See Ps. lviii. 9, Note. The rapidity with which a fire made of thorns burns gives the point of the comparison. The LXX. and Vulg. gave this more plainly by rendering, "they burnt out like a fire in thorns." Shakespeare may have had this verse in his thought when he wrote :

"Shallow jesters and rash bavin (*i.e.,* brushwood) wit,
Soon kindled and soon burnt."—*King Henry IV.*

(14) **Thou hast.**—Better, *Thou didst thrust and thrust at me.* This sudden change of person and challenge of the foes themselves is very dramatic.

(15) **In the tabernacles of the righteous.**—Whether we are to see an allusion here to an actual encampment, as the context seems to indicate, or whether tents are put poetically for dwellings, depends on the view taken of the date and occasion of the psalm.

(16) **Is exalted.**—Here evidently the attitude of a warrior. The hand is *lifted up to strike.*

(17) **I shall not die, but live.**—It is Israel, and not an individual, who thus claims a continuance of life for the display of God's glory. But as so often we find, the hope is so expressed as to suit not only the community for whom the psalm was composed and sung, but each member of it individually.

(19) **The gates of righteousness.**—This is explained by the next verse as the gate of the Temple, where the righteous, *i.e.,* Israel alone, entered. There does not seem the least reason for taking the words here in any but this literal sense, though doubtless they are capable of endless spiritual applications. We must imagine a procession chanting the triumphal song as in Ps. xxiv., and summoning the gates to open on its approach.

(22) **The stone.**—Better, *a stone.* There is no article. Israel is, of course, this stone, rejected as of no account in the political plans of those who were trying to shape the destinies of the Eastern nations at their own pleasure, but in the purpose of God destined to a chief place in the building up of history. The image is developed by Isa. xxviii. 16, 17, and prepared, by the Messianic hope poured into it, for the use of Christ Himself and the repeated applications of it to Him by the apostles (Matt. xxi. 42—44; Acts iv. 11; 1 Pet. ii. 7; Eph. ii. 20; see *New Testament Commentary*).

(23) **The Lord's doing.**—This change of destiny, which made Israel of sudden political importance, is to be ascribed to none but Jehovah Himself.

(24) **This is the day.**—Either the festival for which the psalm was composed (Feast of Tabernacles ?) or more generally the day of triumph won by Jehovah, as in preceding verse.

(25) **Save now.**—This is not the adverb of time. Render, *Save, we pray.* (See Matt. xxi. 9.)

(26) **Blessed . . .**—These words of welcome are probably spoken by the Levite in charge, to the procession approaching the gates. According to Rabbinical writings, pilgrim caravans were thus welcomed on their arrival at Jerusalem.

name of the LORD: we have blessed you out of the house of the LORD. (27) God *is* the LORD, which hath shewed us light: bind the sacrifice with cords, *even* unto the horns of the altar. (28) Thou *art* my God, and I will praise thee: *thou art* my God, I will exalt thee.

(29) O give thanks unto the LORD; for *he is* good: for his mercy *endureth* for ever.

PSALM CXIX.

ALEPH.

(1) Blessed *are* the ¹undefiled in the way, who walk in the law of the LORD. (2) Blessed *are* they that keep his testimonies, *and that* seek him with the whole heart. (3) They also do no iniquity: they walk in his ways. (4) Thou hast commanded *us* to keep thy precepts diligently. (5) O that my ways were directed to keep thy statutes! (6) Then shall I not be ashamed, when I have respect unto all thy commandments. (7) I will praise thee with uprightness of heart, when I shall have learned ² thy righteous judgments. (8) I will keep thy statutes: O forsake me not utterly.

BETH.

(9) Wherewithal shall a young man cleanse his way? by taking heed *thereto* according to thy word.

1 Or, *perfect, or, sincere.*

2 Heb., *judgments of thy righteousness.*

---

(27) **Shewed us light . . .**—Whether this is literal or figurative is difficult to decide. If *literal*, it may be a repetition of verse 24; or if there is a particular reference in this psalm to the Feast of Tabernacles, Mr. Burgess's suggestion, which connects the light with the pillar of cloud and fire, of which that feast was very probably specially commemorative, is most worthy of notice. Figuratively the words would, of course, mean "the light of salvation and hope," as so frequently in the Psalms. It is also possible there may be allusion to the priestly benediction (Num. vi. 25), where the verb is the same.

Bind the sacrifice . . .—This cannot well be, "tie the victim to the horns of the altar," for the Hebrew is "as far as to," and no satisfactory explanation is possible of binding animals as far as the altar, unless we are to translate "bind and lead." But the Hebrew word rendered *victim* might by derivation ("to go round") easily mean a *circlet* or *crown*, and by supplying the verb *go* we get *bind on a crown, go with garlands even to the horns of the altar.* The ancient versions, LXX., Vulg., Aquila, Symmachus, all point to this rendering.

CXIX.

An acrostic must wear an artificial form, and one carried out on the elaborate plan set himself by this author could not fail to sacrifice logical sequence to the prescribed form. Why the number eight was selected for each group of verses, or why, when the author succeeded, in all but two of the 176 verses, in introducing some one synonym for the law, he failed in two, verses 122 and 132, we must leave to unguided conjecture. The repetition of the name Jehovah, occurring exactly twenty-two times, could hardly have been without intention, but in the change rung on the terms that denote the Law there is no evidence of design. That the aphorisms in which the praise of the Law is thus untiringly set forth were not collected and arranged as a mere mnemonic book of devotion appears from the under-current of feeling which runs through the psalm, binding the whole together. At the same time, it is quite inconsistent with the ordinary history of literary work to suppose that such a mechanical composition could owe its origin to the excitement of any one prominent occurrence; rather it is the after reflection of one, or more likely of many, minds on a long course of events belonging to the past, but preserved in memory, reflections arranged in such a way as not only to recall experiences of past days, but to supply religious support under similar trials. The same mode of viewing the psalm finds room for the apparent inconsistency which makes one author assign it to a young man (verses 9, 99, 100), another to a man of mature if not advanced age (verses 33, 52, 96, &c.). And if there is a monotony and sameness in the ever-recurring phrases, which under slightly different expressions state the same fact, the importance of that fact, not only to a Jew, but to a Christian also, cannot be exaggerated. "It is strange," writes Mr. Ruskin, "that of all the pieces of the Bible which my mother taught me, that which cost me most to learn, and which was to my child's mind chiefly repulsive, the cxixth psalm, has now become of all most precious to me in its overflowing and glorious passion of love for the law of God."

ALEPH.

(1) **Undefiled.**—Better, *blameless* or *perfect.*

Way.—See the same use without a qualifying epithet in Ps. ii. 12. There was only one way of safety and peace for an Israelite, here by the parallelism defined as "the law of Jehovah." But even heathen ethics bore witness to the same truth: "Declinandum de viâ sit modo ne summa turpitudo sequatur" (Cic., *De Amicitia*, xvii.).

(5) **Directed . . .**—So LXX. and Vulg. The Hebrew is perhaps slightly different, *established*, or settled. (See Prov. iv. 26.)

(6) **Have respect unto.**—Literally, *look upon*, or *into*, as in a mirror. (Comp. James i. 23.) The Divine Law is as a mirror, which shows man his defects; the faithful, in looking in it, have no cause to blush.

Judgments.—Not here in common sense of visitations for sin, but only one of the change of synonyms for *law*. (See this use in Exod. xxi. 1, xxiv. 3, &c.)

BETH.

(9) **Wherewithal.**—There can be little question that the right rendering of this verse is, *By what means can a young man purify his way, so as to keep it according to Thy word?* but from Josh. vi. 18 we might render *keep himself*. The English rendering, which follows the LXX. and Vulg. is, of course, possible, but the other is more natural and more in accordance with the general drift of the psalm. The answer is supposed, or rather left to be inferred, from the whole

The Wondrousness and Beauty   PSALMS, CXIX.   *of God's Law.*

(10) With my whole heart have I sought thee: O let me not wander from thy commandments. (11) Thy word have I hid in mine heart, that I might not sin against thee. (12) Blessed *art* thou, O LORD: teach me thy statutes. (13) With my lips have I declared all the judgments of thy mouth. (14) I have rejoiced in the way of thy testimonies, as *much as* in all riches. (15) I will meditate in thy precepts, and have respect unto thy ways. (16) I will delight myself in thy statutes: I will not forget thy word.

GIMEL.

(17) Deal bountifully with thy servant, *that* I may live, and keep thy word. (18) ¹Open thou mine eyes, that I may behold wondrous things out of thy law. (19) ᵃI *am* a stranger in the earth: hide not thy commandments from me. (20) My soul breaketh for the longing *that it hath* unto thy judgments at all times. (21) Thou hast rebuked the proud *that are* cursed, which do err from thy commandments. (22) Remove from me reproach and contempt; for I have kept thy testimonies. (23) Princes also did sit *and* speak against me: *but* thy servant did meditate in thy statutes. (24) Thy testimonies also *are* my delight *and* ²my counsellors.

DALETH.

(25) My soul cleaveth unto the dust: quicken thou me according to thy word.

¹ Heb., *Reveal.*

ᵃ Gen. 47. 9; 1 Chron. 29. 15; Ps. 39. 12; Heb. 11. 13.

² Heb., *men of my counsel.*

---

tenor of the psalm, which is that men, and especially young men, whose passions and temptations are strong in proportion to their inexperience, can do nothing of themselves, but are dependent on the grace of God. The omission of a direct answer rather strengthens than impairs the impression on the reader.

We must not, from the mention of youth, conclude that this psalm was written in that period of life. Perhaps, on the contrary, it is one who, like Browning's Rabbi ben Ezra, while seeking how best to spend old age, looks back on youth, not with remonstrance at its follies, but with the satisfaction that even then he aimed at the best he knew.

(10) **With my whole heart . . .**—The self-mistrust of the second clause is a proof of the reality of the first. "Lord, I believe; help thou my unbelief," is another form of this.

(11) **Thy word.**—A different term to that in verse 9. The two are interchanged throughout the psalm.

Hid . . .—As the Oriental hid treasures. (Comp Matt. xiii. 44.)

In mine heart, that I might not sin against thee.—The best comment on this is contained in our Lord's words (Matt. xv. 19).

(13) **With my lips.**—He has not kept his hidden treasure to himself, but, like the good householder of the Gospels, has brought out things new and old.

GIMEL.

(17) **Deal bountifully . . . that I may live.**—Comp. Pss. xiii. 3, 6, and cxvi. 7, 8, where we see, as here, the same connection between this Hebrew word and preservation from death. *Life* is connected with obedience to the Divine law throughout the Bible (Lev. xviii. 5; Deut. vi. 24; Ps. xli. 1, 2; Luke x. 28).

(18) **Open.**—Literally, *uncover* (see margin), as if without Divine grace the eyes were veiled to the wonder and beauty of the moral law. (Comp. 2 Cor. iv. 18.)

(19) **I am a stranger.**—A comparison of verse 54 with Gen. xlvii. 9 (comp. Ps. xxxix. 12) shows that the general transitory condition of life, and not any particular circumstance of the psalmist's history is in view. Human intelligence does not suffice to fathom the will of God. The mortal is a stranger on the earth; both time and strength are wanting to attain to knowledge which only Divine wisdom can teach.

(20) **Breaketh.**—The Hebrew is peculiar to this place and Lam. iii. 16. The LXX., Vulg., and Aquila have "greatly desired;" Symmachus, "was perfect;" Theodotion, "had confidence;" Jerome, "longed," all which point either to a different reading or to a different sense from that which is given in the lexicons to the word.

(21) LXX. and Vulg. divide the verse: "Thou hast rebuked the proud; cursed are they," &c. This is preferable.

(22) **Remove.**—Some render "roll," with allusion to Josh. v. 9. But it is more probably the same word as that rendered "open" in verse 18 (see Note) which may have for object the covering taken off (Isa. xxii. 8; Nahum iii. 5), or of the thing from which the covering is taken, as in verse 18.

(23) **Speak.**—Comp. Ps. l. 20 for the same implied sense in this verb. This verse reads as if Israel, and not a mere individual, were the subject of the psalms.

(24) **Counsellors.**—See margin. Instead of taking the princes of verse 23 into counsel, he takes God's testimonies.

DALETH.

(25) **Cleaveth to the dust.**—The same figure is used in Pss. xxii. 29, xliv. 25, in the former of death, in the latter of deep degradation and dishonour.

The prayer, "make me live," suggests that the dust of death is here prominently in view, as in Tennyson's "Thou wilt not leave us in the dust." Else we might rather think of the dryness of summer dust as a type of despondency and spiritual depression.

"A wicked whisper came, and made
My heart as dry as dust."—COLERIDGE.

It was this verse which the Emperor Theodosius recited when doing penance at the door of Milan Cathedral for the massacre of Thessalonica (Theodoret, v., 18).

Quicken thou me according to thy word. —See verses 88, 107, 145, 154, 156. This reiterated prayer, with its varied appeal to the Divine truth, lovingkindness, constancy, must certainly be regarded as the petition of Israel for revived covenant glory,

A Prayer for   PSALMS, CXIX.   *the Wisdom of Obedience.*

(26) I have declared my ways, and thou heardest me: *a* teach me thy statutes. (27) Make me to understand the way of thy precepts: so shall I talk of thy wondrous works. (28) My soul [1] melteth for heaviness: strengthen thou me according unto thy word. (29) Remove from me the way of lying: and grant me thy law graciously. (30) I have chosen the way of truth: thy judgments have I laid *before me.* (31) I have stuck unto thy testimonies: O LORD, put me not to shame. (32) I will run the way of thy commandments, when thou shalt enlarge my heart.

HE.

(33) Teach me, O LORD, the way of thy statutes; and I shall keep it *unto* the end. (34) Give me understanding, and I shall keep thy law; yea, I shall observe it with *my* whole heart. (35) Make me to go in the path of thy commandments; for therein do I delight. (36) Incline my heart unto thy testimonies, and not to covetousness.

(37) [2] Turn away mine eyes from beholding vanity; *and* quicken thou me in thy way. (38) Stablish thy word unto thy servant, who *is devoted* to thy fear. (39) Turn away my reproach which I fear: for thy judgments *are* good. (40) Behold, I have longed after thy precepts: quicken me in thy righteousness.

VAU.

(41) Let thy mercies come also unto me, O LORD, *even* thy salvation, according to thy word. (42) [3] So shall I have wherewith to answer him that reproacheth me: for I trust in thy word. (43) And take not the word of truth utterly out of my mouth; for I have hoped in thy judgments. (44) So shall I keep thy law continually for ever and ever. (45) And I will walk [4] at liberty: for I seek thy precepts.

(46) I will speak of thy testimonies also before kings, and will not be ashamed. (47) And I will delight myself in thy commandments, which I have

a Ps. 25. 4, & 27. 11, & 86. 11.

1 Heb., *droppeth*.

2 Heb., *Make to pass*.

3 Or, *So shall I answer him that reproveth me in a thing*.

4 Heb., *at large*.

---

though, at the same time, it offers a wide and rich field of application to individual needs.

(26) **I have declared.**—Or, *recounted*.
My ways.—Or, as we should say, my *courses*, my *past life*, including, as the context shows, confession of sins and prayer for pardon.

(27) **Make me to understand.**—Only the Israelite truly loyal to the covenant was considered worthy to enquire into the marvels of the dealings of God. (See Ps. cvi. 2, Note.) Perhaps we might extend the thought so far as to say that a true historical insight is possible only to one whose moral sense is rightly trained and directed.

(28) **Melteth**—The Hebrew word is used in Eccles. x. 18 of a dripping roof of a house; in Job xvi. 20 of weeping. The LXX. and Vulg. have "slumbered," which suits far better with the next clause, which is literally, *make me rise up*. Symmachus has "distils."

(29) **Way of lying.**—Not of falsehood to men so much as insincerity and unfaithfulness towards God, the opposite of the truth and faithfulness of verse 30.
Grant me.—Rather, *be gracious to me according to thy law*. This is the persistent cry of the psalm.

(32) **Run the way.**—Plainly the psalmist means that he will not only be able to walk in the Divine way, but even to run in it when certain restraints are removed which now confine and check him. Hence we may understand, by the *enlargement of the heart*, not so much the expansion of the faculties as deliverance from oppressing fears, &c., as Pss. iv. 1, xviii. 36, and render "when thou hast set my heart at large." So the Prayer Book Version, "set my heart at liberty."

HE.

(33) **To the end.**—See verse 112. This word, used adverbially, is peculiar to this psalm.

(35) **Path.**—From root to *tread, the trodden way*, plain with the track of all the pious pilgrims' feet of past times.

(36) **Covetousness.**—Literally, *rapine, prey.* In Ps. xxx. 9 simply, "gain."

(37) **From beholding vanity.**—Perhaps *from looking on idols.*

(38) **Who is devoted to thy fear.**—This is an improbable explanation of this elliptical expression. There are two renderings, each in accordance with the general drift of the psalm: (1) *Stablish to Thy servant Thy word, which leads to fear of Thee*; or, more likely, (2) *Stablish to Thy servant Thy promise which is to those who fear Thee*, as apparently the LXX.

(39) **My reproach which I fear.**—The word for fear is an unusual one, used in Deut. ix. 19, xxviii. 60, for very strong dread. The reproach may be either the disgrace in God's sight of violating His commands, or, as the context (verse 42) suggests, a reproach from men for keeping God's law.

(40) **Quicken me in thy righteousness**—*i.e.,* Let the sense of thy eternal justice give me vigour and life. Or the thought may be of the invigorating influence of a complete surrender to a righteous law, as in Wordsworth's *Ode to Duty*:—

"I myself commend
Unto thy guidance from this hour.
Oh let my weakness have an end!
Give unto me, made lowly, wise,
The spirit of self-sacrifice,
The confidence of reason give,
And in the light of truth thy bondsman let me live."

VAU.

(42) **So shall I have.**—Better literally, *as the LXX. and Vulg., and I shall answer my reviler a word, for I trust in Thy word, i.e.,* when reproached it will be enough to pronounce God's promise. The repetition of *davar* here and in verse 43 makes for this explanation in preference to that of the margin.

(45) **At liberty.**—See margin. Literally, in *a large place.* (See verse 32; comp. Prov. iv. 12.)

(46) The Vulgate (which in the tenses follows the LXX.) of this verse was the motto of the Augsburg

loved. (48) My hands also will I lift up unto thy commandments, which I have loved; and I will meditate in thy statutes.

ZAIN.

(49) Remember the word unto thy servant, upon which thou hast caused me to hope. (50) This *is* my comfort in my affliction: for thy word hath quickened me. (51) The proud have had me greatly in derision: *yet* have I not declined from thy law. (52) I remembered thy judgments of old, O LORD; and have comforted myself. (53) Horror hath taken hold upon me because of the wicked that forsake thy law. (54) Thy statutes have been my songs in the house of my pilgrimage. (55) I have remembered thy name, O LORD, in the night, and have kept thy law. (56) This I had, because I kept thy precepts.

CHETH.

(57) *Thou art* my portion, O LORD: I have said that I would keep thy words. (58) I intreated thy ¹favour with *my* whole heart: be merciful unto me according to thy word. (59) I thought on my ways, and turned my feet unto thy testimonies. (60) I made haste, and delayed not to keep thy commandments. (61) The ²bands of the wicked have robbed me: *but* I have not forgotten thy law. (62) At midnight I will rise to give thanks unto thee because of thy righteous judgments. (63) I *am* a companion of all *them* that fear thee, and of them that keep thy precepts. (64) The earth, O LORD, is full of thy mercy: teach me thy statutes.

TETH.

(65) Thou hast dealt well with thy servant, O LORD, according unto thy word. (66) Teach me good judgment and knowledge: for I have believed thy commandments. (67) Before I was afflicted I went astray: but now have I kept thy word. (68) Thou *art* good, and doest good; teach me thy statutes. (69) The proud have forged a lie against me: *but* I will keep thy precepts with *my* whole heart. (70) Their heart is as fat as grease; *but* I delight in thy law. (71) *It is* good for me that I have been

1 Heb., *face.*

2 Or, *companies.*

Confession, *Et loquebar in testimoniis tuis in conspectu regum, et non confundebar.*"

(48) **My hands.**—See Ps. xxviii. 2. The expression here is elliptical: "I will lift my hands in prayer for power to observe Thy commands."

ZAIN.

(50) **Comfort.**—As in Job vi. 10, where the same noun occurs, its only other use. We might render, "This is my comfort, that thy word quickeneth me."

(53) **Horror.**—Rather, *violent indignation*, a storm of rage, hot and fierce as the simoon. For the word, see Ps. xi. 6, Note.

(54) **Songs.**—Or, *Thy statutes were my music in the house of my sojournings.* Possibly with reference to the exile (comp. Ps. cxxxvii. 4), but with comparison with verse 9 (see Note), more probably the reference is to the transitoriness of human life. In connection with the next verse comp. Job xxxv. 10.

(56) **This I had, because . . .** — Literally, *This was to me*, &c., *i.e.*, this consoling recollection of the mercies of God, of His covenant grace, was to him, happened, or came to him, in consequence of his habitual obedience. Virtue is indeed then most its own reward, in times of quiet reflection, like the night, when to the guilty come remorse and apprehension, but to the good man " calm thoughts regular as infant's breath."

CHETH.

(57) **Thou art my portion, O Lord.**—This rendering is in accordance with Pss. xvi. 5, lxxiii. 26. But, even with these passages in view, a better rendering would be—

"This is my portion, O Lord, I said (it),
To keep Thy words."

(58) **I intreated.**—See Ps. xlv. 12.

(59) **I thought on.**—The Hebrew implies repeated and frequent meditation.

(61) **The bands . . .**—Rather, *cords of the wicked surrounded me.* (See Ps. xviii. 5, 6.) So all ancient versions except the Targum.

(62) **Midnight.**—See verse 55.

TETH.

(66) **Good judgment.**—More exactly, *good taste.* Here, however, in a moral, not æsthetic sense. Perhaps *tact* or *delicate moral perception* represents it. We may compare St. Paul's use of the Greek words, ἐπίγνωσις and αἴσθησις in Phil. i. 9.

(67) That there is allusion here to the Babylonian exile, and its moral and religious effect on the nation, there can be little doubt.

(68) It is characteristic of this psalm that the higher the conception of the Divine nature, the more earnest becomes the prayer for knowledge of His will in relation to conduct.

(69) **Have forged.**—Rather, *patched.* The verb occurs twice besides (Job xiii. 4, xiv. 17). Gesenius compares the Greek, δόλον ἅπτειν, and the Latin, *suere dolos.* Comp. also

"You praise yourself by laying defects of judgment to me;
but you patched up your excuses."
Antony and Cleopatra: Act ii., Scene 2.

(70) **As fat as grease.**—For this emblem of pride and insensibility, see Pss. xvii. 10, lxxiii. 7; Isa. vi. 10.

(71) **It is good . .** .—See verse 67. Probably the result of discipline on the nation is intended, though the "sweet uses of adversity" were long ago a truism of moralists. See Æsch., *Agam.*, 172:

"Who guideth mortals to wisdom, maketh them grasp lore
Firmly through their pain."

Prayers, Praises, and   PSALMS, CXIX.   *Vows of Obedience*

afflicted; that I might learn thy statutes. ⁽⁷²⁾ ^a The law of thy mouth *is* better unto me than thousands of gold and silver.

JOD.

⁽⁷³⁾ Thy hands have made me and fashioned me: give me understanding, that I may learn thy commandments. ⁽⁷⁴⁾ They that fear thee will be glad when they see me; because I have hoped in thy word. ⁽⁷⁵⁾ I know, O LORD, that thy judgments *are* ¹right, and *that* thou in faithfulness hast afflicted me. ⁽⁷⁶⁾ Let, I pray thee, thy merciful kindness be ²for my comfort, according to thy word unto thy servant. ⁽⁷⁷⁾ Let thy tender mercies come unto me, that I may live: for thy law *is* my delight. ⁽⁷⁸⁾ Let the proud be ashamed; for they dealt perversely with me without a cause: *but* I will meditate in thy precepts. ⁽⁷⁹⁾ Let those that fear thee turn unto me, and those that have known thy testimonies. ⁽⁸⁰⁾ Let my heart be sound in thy statutes; that I be not ashamed.

CAPH.

⁽⁸¹⁾ My soul fainteth for thy salvation: *but* I hope in thy word. ⁽⁸²⁾ Mine eyes fail for thy word, saying, When wilt thou comfort me? ⁽⁸³⁾ For I am become like a bottle in the smoke; *yet* do I not forget thy statutes. ⁽⁸⁴⁾ How many *are* the days of thy servant? when wilt thou execute judgment on them that persecute me? ⁽⁸⁵⁾ The proud have digged pits for me, which *are* not after thy law. ⁽⁸⁶⁾ All thy commandments *are* ³faithful: they persecute me wrongfully; help thou me. ⁽⁸⁷⁾ They had almost consumed me upon earth; but I forsook not thy precepts. ⁽⁸⁸⁾ Quicken me after thy lovingkindness; so shall I keep the testimony of thy mouth.

LAMED.

⁽⁸⁹⁾ For ever, O LORD, thy word is settled in heaven. ⁽⁹⁰⁾ Thy faithfulness *is* ⁴unto all generations: thou hast established the earth, and it ⁵abideth. ⁽⁹¹⁾ They continue this day according to thine ordinances: for all *are* thy servants. ⁽⁹²⁾ Unless thy law *had been* my delights, I should then have perished in mine affliction. ⁽⁹³⁾ I will never forget thy precepts: for with them thou hast quickened me. ⁽⁹⁴⁾ I *am* thine, save me; for I have sought thy precepts. ⁽⁹⁵⁾ The wicked have waited for me to destroy me: *but* I will consider thy

Marginal notes: a Ps. 19. 10; Prov. 8. 11. — 1 Heb., *righteousness.* — 2 Heb., *to comfort me.* — 3 Heb., *faithfulness.* — 4 Heb., *to generation and generation.* — 5 Heb., *standeth.*

---

(72) **Better unto me**—*i.e.*, better for me.
Thousands of.—We must supply *shekels* or *pieces*.

JOD.

(73) **Fashioned.**—Literally, *fixed, established.*

(74) **They . . . will be glad.**—The great truth of spiritual communion, and the mutual help and consolation derived from it, is latent here. In its primary sense, that the preservation and deliverance of the righteous, who are victims of persecution, afford comfort and joy to all truly good, the verse has been amply confirmed by history. Matt. v. 16, "Let your light so shine," &c.

(75) See verses 67—71.

(78) **Dealt.**—Better, *wronged me*; literally, *bent me.*

CAPH.

(81) **Fainteth.**—The same Hebrew word as *fail* in the next verse.

(82) **Mine eyes fail.**—The *failing* of the eyes is here evidently to be understood of the effort of straining to catch or keep sight of a distant object, not, as so frequently in the Psalms (see Ps. vi. 7, &c.), from sickness or even grief. Comp.

"I would have broke my eye-strings, cracked them, but
To look upon him."—SHAKESPEARE: *Cymbeline.*

(83) **A bottle in the smoke.**—The insertion of *yet* by our translators shows that they understood this as a figure of abject misery. The wine-skin would, of course, shrivel, if hung above a fire, and would afford an apt image of the effect of trouble on an individual or community. "As wine-skin in the smoke my heart is sere and dried." Some think that as a bottle hung up anywhere in an ancient house would be in the smoke, nothing more is implied than its being set aside; but this is too weak.

We find in the ancient poets allusion to the custom of mellowing wine by heat:

"Prodit fumoso condita vina cado."—OVID: *Fast.* v. 517.

(Comp. Hor. *Ode* iii. 8, 9, 10). And so some understand the image here of the good results of the discipline of suffering. The LXX. and Vulg., instead of *smoke*, have "hoar-frost." The Hebrew word has this meaning in Ps. cxlviii. 8, but in the only other place where it occurs (Gen. xix. 28) it is *smoke*. The possibility of rendering *hoar-frost* here suggests another explanation. The word *nôd* (bottle) may be used of a *cloud*, and as the psalmist has just spoken of his eyes failing, we may have here only another expression for weeping.

(84) As in Ps. lxxxix. 47, 48, the psalmist here utters what was the dread of each generation of Israel, a dread lest it should have passed away before the day of deliverance should arrive.

(85) **Which.**—Better, *who.* Its antecedent, of course, the *proud*, not the *pits*.

(87) **Upon earth.**—Rather, *on the land.* (Comp. Ps. lviii. 2.)

LAMED.

(89, 90) See Ps. lxxxix. 2.

(91) **They** (the heavens and the earth) **continue to this day according to Thine ordinances: for all** (*i.e.*, all creation) **are Thy servants.**—In Hebrew *the all*, *i.e.*, the universe. The parallelism is in this way preserved, while in the alternative, "as for Thy judgments, Thy," &c., it is lost.

Prayers, Praises, and   PSALMS, CXIX.   *Vows of Obedience*

testimonies. ⁽⁹⁶⁾ I have seen an end of all perfection: *but* thy commandment *is* exceeding broad.

MEM.

⁽⁹⁷⁾ O how love I thy law! it *is* my meditation all the day. ⁽⁹⁸⁾ Thou through thy commandments hast made me wiser than mine enemies: for ¹they *are* ever with me. ⁽⁹⁹⁾ I have more understanding than all my teachers: for thy testimonies *are* my meditation. ⁽¹⁰⁰⁾ I understand more than the ancients, because I keep thy precepts. ⁽¹⁰¹⁾ I have refrained my feet from every evil way, that I might keep thy word. ⁽¹⁰²⁾ I have not departed from thy judgments: for thou hast taught me. ⁽¹⁰³⁾ ª How sweet are thy words unto my ²taste! *yea, sweeter* than honey to my mouth! ⁽¹⁰⁴⁾ Through thy precepts I get understanding: therefore I hate every false way.

NUN.

⁽¹⁰⁵⁾ Thy word *is* a ³lamp unto my feet, and a light unto my path. ⁽¹⁰⁶⁾ I have sworn, and I will perform *it*, that I will keep thy righteous judgments. ⁽¹⁰⁷⁾ I am afflicted very much: quicken me, O LORD, according unto thy word. ⁽¹⁰⁸⁾ Accept, I beseech thee, the freewill offerings of my mouth, O LORD, and teach me thy judgments. ⁽¹⁰⁹⁾ My soul *is* continually in my hand: yet do I not forget thy law. ⁽¹¹⁰⁾ The wicked have laid a snare for me: yet I erred not from thy precepts. ⁽¹¹¹⁾ Thy testimonies have I taken as an heritage for ever: for they *are* the rejoicing of my heart. ⁽¹¹²⁾ I have inclined mine heart ⁴to perform thy statutes alway, *even unto* the end.

SAMECH.

⁽¹¹³⁾ I hate *vain* thoughts: but thy law do I love. ⁽¹¹⁴⁾ Thou *art* my hiding place and my shield: I hope in thy word. ⁽¹¹⁵⁾ ᵇDepart from me, ye evildoers: for I will keep the commandments of my God. ⁽¹¹⁶⁾ Uphold me according unto thy word, that I may live: and let me not be ashamed of my hope. ⁽¹¹⁷⁾ Hold thou me up, and I shall be safe: and I will have respect unto thy statutes continually. ⁽¹¹⁸⁾ Thou hast trodden down all them that err from thy statutes: for their

---

1 Heb., *it is ever with me.*
a Ps. 19. 10.
2 Heb., *palate.*
3 Or, *candle.*
4 Heb., *to do.*
b Matt. 7. 23.

---

(96) **I have seen.**—The exact thought of the psalmist here is doubtful, and it offers such a wide application, embracing so many truths of experience, that possibly he had more than one meaning in his mind. Keeping as close to the context as possible, the meaning will be: "To all perfection (or apparent perfection) a limit is visible, but the Divine Law is boundless alike in its scope and its requirements." This, translated into the language of modern ideas, merely says that the actual can never correspond with the ideal:

"Who keeps a spirit wholly true
To that ideal which he bears?"

But in the word *end* in Hebrew, as in English, there is a limitation in time, as in space (see Job xxvi. 10, xxviii. 3; comp. Symmachus, "I have seen the end of all settled things"), and the Prayer Book version may really give the psalmist's thought as indicating the difference between mere change and progress.

"The old order changeth, yielding place to new,
And God fulfils Himself in many ways,
Lest one good custom should corrupt the world."
TENNYSON: *Morte d'Arthur.*

MEM.

(98) Better, *Thy commandments make me wiser than my enemies.* The same correspondence of wisdom with loyal obedience to the Law is found in the Book of Proverbs.

(99) **More understanding . . .**—The Rabbinical writers disliked the idea of a scholar professing wisdom above his teachers, and rendered, "from all my teachers I got wisdom," which was certainly far more in keeping with the process by which the Talmud grew into existence.

(100) **Ancients.**—Or, more probably, as the LXX. and Vulg., and the old versions generally took it, *old men.*

NUN.

(105) See Prov. vi. 23.
So Wordsworth calls Duty:

"A light to guide."

(106) **Perform.**—The same verb as in verse 28—*strengthen*; often used in Esther for *confirm.*

(108) **Freewill offerings of my mouth** — *i.e.*, thanks and praise.

(109) **My soul.**—For this figure of peril see Judges xii. 3; 1 Sam. xix. 5, &c.

SAMECH.

(113) **I hate vain thoughts.**—Rather, *I hate men who halt between two opinions,* following 1 Kings xviii. 21, where the cognate noun from the same root, *to divide,* appears. Probably we are to think of those among the Jews who were for political reasons favourably inclined towards foreign customs and ideas, and who would not throw in their lot frankly and courageously with the national party.

(114) **My shield.**—For this expression see Pss. iii. 3, vii. 10.

(115) **For.** — Better, *and.* The presence of the wicked was a hindrance to religion. It is Israel trying to purify itself from the leaven of evil influence that speaks. The first clause is from Ps. vi. 8.

(118) **Trodden down.**—Better, *thou despisest.* So LXX. and Vulg. Aquila, "Thou hast impaled." Symmachus, "Thou hast convicted." Literally the word seems to mean *to weigh* or *value,* but, from the habit of the buyer beating down the price by depre-

deceit *is* falsehood. (119) Thou ¹puttest away all the wicked of the earth *like* dross: therefore I love thy testimonies. (120) My flesh trembleth for fear of thee; and I am afraid of thy judgments.

AIN.

(121) I have done judgment and justice: leave me not to mine oppressors. (122) Be surety for thy servant for good: let not the proud oppress me. (123) Mine eyes fail for thy salvation, and for the word of thy righteousness. (124) Deal with thy servant according unto thy mercy, and teach me thy statutes. (125) I *am* thy servant; give me understanding, that I may know thy testimonies. (126) *It is* time for *thee*, LORD, to work: *for* they have made void thy law. (127) *a*Therefore I love thy commandments above gold; yea, above fine gold. (128) Therefore I esteem all *thy* precepts concerning all *things to be* right; *and* I hate every false way.

PE.

(129) Thy testimonies *are* wonderful: therefore doth my soul keep them. (130) The entrance of thy words giveth light; it giveth understanding unto the simple. (131) I opened my mouth, and panted: for I longed for thy commandments. (132) Look thou upon me, and be merciful unto me, ²as thou usest to do unto those that love thy name. (133) Order my steps in thy word: and let not any iniquity have dominion over me. (134) Deliver me from the oppression of man: so will I keep thy precepts. (135) Make thy face to shine upon thy servant; and teach me thy statutes. (136) Rivers of waters run down mine eyes, because they keep not thy law.

TZADDI.

(137) Righteous *art* thou, O LORD, and

---

1 Heb., *causest to cease.*

a Ps. 19. 10; Prov. 8. 11.

2 Heb., *according to the custom towards those,* &c.

---

ciating, comes to have a sense of this kind. Mr. Burgess aptly quotes Prov. xx. 14. We may compare the English word *cheapen*, which originally only meant to *buy*.

For their deceit is falsehood.—Rather, as the parallelism indicates, *for their tricks are in vain;* or perhaps, to bring out the full intention of the Hebrew, we must paraphrase: "for their wiles are as fruitless as they are deceitful." So Symmachus: "all their craft is vain."

(119) **Thou puttest away.**—For this common Scriptural figure comp. Jer. vi. 28—30; Ezek. xxii. 18—20. This is indeed a process which is continually going on, and it is one test of the true religious character that it can discern it at work under the seeming contradictions of the world. Where apparently vice succeeds and prospers it is really marked out for expulsion,

"To those who
All treasures and all gain esteem as dross;
And dignities and powers, all but the Highest."
MILTON.

(120) **Trembleth.**—The original is far stronger. Better, as in Job iv. 15, *the hair of my flesh stands up*. So Symmachus.

AIN.

(122) **Be surety.**—Just as Judah became surety for the safety of Benjamin (Gen. xliii. 9), so the psalmist asks God to be answerable for the servant who had been faithful to the covenant, and stand between him and the attacks of the proud. So Hezekiah (Isa. xxxviii. 14) asks God to "undertake" for him against the threat of death. There is also, no doubt, the further thought that the Divine protection would vindicate the profession which the loyal servant makes of his obedience, as in Job xvii. 3, where God is summoned as the only possible guarantee of the sufferer's innocence. This and verse 132 are the only verses not actually mentioning, under one of its terms, the Law.

(123) See verse 82.

(126) **They have made void thy law.**—Some treat the verse as parenthetical, but is it not that the irreligion of the wicked makes the Law even more dear to the psalmist? What they reject is to him priceless,

"Faithful found;
Among the faithless, faithful only he."

(128) **Therefore I esteem.**—As the text stands, this verse literally runs, *Therefore all precepts of all I make straight. Every path of falsehood I hate.* The LXX. and Vulg. have, "Therefore to all Thy commandments I was being directed. Every unjust path I hated," which only necessitates a slight change in the reading of one word. It is true that the expression, *all precepts of all*, may be explained as a strengthened form of *all precepts*—as we say, "all and every"—though the passages (Ezek. xliv. 30; Num. viii. 16) generally adduced are not strictly analogous. But the Lexicons supply no authority for taking the verb *yāshar* in the sense of "esteem right," and the figure of the path in the next clause seems here plainly to fix its meaning. Translate, therefore, *Therefore after all Thy precepts I direct (my way). Every false way I detest.*

PE.

(130) **Entrance.**—Literally, *opening,* which the LXX. and Vulg. better represent by "manifestation," "declaration." (Comp. "opening and alleging," Acts xvii. 3.)

(131) Comp. Job xxix. 23.

(132) **As . . . name.**—See margin. But the absence of the suffix is against this correction, as it is against the Authorised Version itself. Rather, *according to the right of*. It was not only theirs by custom, but by right of the covenant.

(133) **Have dominion.**—Or, *get the mastery*. The Arabic root cognate with the Hebrew of the word appears in the title *sultan*.

TZADDI.

(137) **And upright.**—For an interesting historical association with this verse see Gibbon's account of the death of the Emperor Maurice (chap xlvi.).

upright *are* thy judgments. (138) Thy testimonies *that* thou hast commanded *are* ¹righteous and very ²faithful. (139) ᵃ My zeal hath ³consumed me, because mine enemies have forgotten thy words. (140) Thy word *is* very ⁴pure: therefore thy servant loveth it. (141) I *am* small and despised: *yet* do not I forget thy precepts. (142) Thy righteousness *is* an everlasting righteousness, and thy law *is* the truth. (143) Trouble and anguish have ⁵taken hold on me: *yet* thy commandments *are* my delights. (144) The righteousness of thy testimonies *is* everlasting: give me understanding, and I shall live.

KOPH.

(145) I cried with *my* whole heart; hear me, O LORD: I will keep thy statutes. (146) I cried unto thee; save me, ⁶and I shall keep thy testimonies. (147) I prevented the dawning of the morning, and cried: I hoped in thy word. (148) Mine eyes prevent the *night* watches, that I might meditate in thy word. (149) Hear my voice according unto thy lovingkindness: O LORD, quicken me according to thy judgment. (150) They draw nigh that follow after mischief: they are far from thy law. (151) Thou *art* near, O LORD; and all thy commandments *are* truth. (152) Concerning thy testimonies, I have known of old that thou hast founded them for ever.

RESH.

(153) Consider mine affliction, and deliver me: for I do not forget thy law. (154) Plead my cause, and deliver me: quicken me according to thy word. (155) Salvation *is* far from the wicked: for they seek not thy statutes. (156) ⁷ Great *are* thy tender mercies, O LORD: quicken me according to thy judgments. (157) Many *are* my persecutors and mine enemies; *yet* do I not decline from thy testimonies. (158) I beheld the transgressors, and was grieved; because they kept not thy word. (159) Consider how I love thy precepts: quicken me, O LORD, according to thy lovingkindness. (160) ⁸Thy word *is* true *from* the beginning: and every one of thy righteous judgments *endureth* for ever.

SCHIN.

(161) Princes have persecuted me without a cause: but my heart standeth in awe of thy word. (162) I rejoice at thy word, as one that findeth great spoil.

---

¹ Heb., *righteousness.*
² Heb., *faithfulness.*
ᵃ Ps. 69.9; John 2.17.
³ Heb., *cut me off.*
⁴ Heb., *tried, or, refined.*
⁵ Heb., *found me.*
⁶ Or, *that I may keep.*
⁷ Or, *Many.*
⁸ Heb., *The beginning of thy word is true.*

---

(138) **Thy testimonies.**—Better, *Thou hast commanded Thy testimonies in righteousness and very faithfulness.* But unquestionably another arrangement of the text of these two verses is correct. It takes the verb *commandest* with verse 137, and gets the simple and obvious "righteous art Thou, O Lord, and upright in the judgments which Thou hast commanded. Thy testimonies are righteous, and faithful to the uttermost" (Burgess). (See Ps. vii. 6 and verse 144.)

(140) **Pure.**—More literally, *purged by trial.* LXX. and Vulg., "fired." It is not only the excellence, but the *proved* excellence, of the Divine Word, which is the object of love and adoration here.

(141) These words are hardly applicable to an individual, while to the struggling Israel, in relation to the great Eastern Powers, they are peculiarly suitable.

(142) **Thy . . .**—Better, *Thy righteousness is right for ever, and Thy law is truth.*

KOPH.

(147) **Prevented.**—See Pss. xviii. 5, lxxix. 8. The Authorised Version gives the sense, *I was up before the morning.*

Dawning of the morning.—The Hebrew word means literally "breath," and is used of the fresh breeze that blows both at sunset (Job xxiv. 15; Prov. vii. 9) and sunrise (Job vii. 4). Generally in our version rendered "twilight."

(149) **According to Thy judgment.**—See Note, verse 132. We must certainly here give the Hebrew noun the meaning of a "custom," which it bears there. (Comp. Prayer Book version, "according as Thou art wont.")

(150, 151) **Near.**—Notice the antithesis. *They, the wicked,* are *near* with their temptation to sin and their hindrances to virtue. *Thou* art near with the aid and support of Thy law.

(152) The more obvious rendering of this verse is, *Of old I was instructed out of Thy testimonies, for*—not for a brief time, but for ever—*Thou didst found them,* where *for ever* expresses indefinite past as well as indefinite future.

RESH.

(158) **Transgressors.**—Better, *the faithless* (or, *traitors*).

Was grieved.—The Hebrew is a far stronger word, and the sense is intensified by the rare conjugation: *was filled with loathing at; sickened with disgust.*

"The recreants I survey,
And loathing turn away."—KEBLE.

(160) **Beginning.**—Heb., *head*; but here, as in Ps. cxxxix. 17, it might be rendered *sum.* (Comp. Prov. i. 7.) The translation "*from* the beginning," of the Authorised Version must at all events be abandoned.

SCHIN.

(161) **Princes.**—Here again we have an indication of the national character of the psalm. It was the whole community which suffered from the intrigues and violence of princes.

(162) Comp. Isa. ix. 3.

(163) I hate and abhor lying: *but* thy law do I love. (164) Seven times a day do I praise thee because of thy righteous judgments. (165) Great peace have they which love thy law: and ¹nothing shall offend them.

(166) LORD, I have hoped for thy salvation, and done thy commandments. (167) My soul hath kept thy testimonies; and I love them exceedingly. (168) I have kept thy precepts and thy testimonies: for all my ways *are* before thee.

TAU.

(169) Let my cry come near before thee, O LORD: give me understanding according to thy word. (170) Let my supplication come before thee: deliver me according to thy word.

(171) My lips shall utter praise, when thou hast taught me thy statutes. (172) My tongue shall speak of thy word: for all thy commandments *are* righteousness.

(173) Let thine hand help me; for I have chosen thy precepts. (174) I have longed for thy salvation, O LORD; and thy law *is* my delight. (175) Let my soul live, and it shall praise thee; and let thy judgments help me.

(176) I have gone astray like a lost sheep; seek thy servant; for I do not forget thy commandments.

PSALM CXX.

A Song of degrees.

(1) In my distress I cried unto the LORD, and he heard me.

(2) Deliver my soul, O LORD, from lying lips, *and* from a deceitful tongue. (3) ²What shall be given unto thee? or what shall be ³done unto thee, thou

---

1 Heb., *they shall have no stumbling block.*

2 Or, *What shall the deceitful tongue give unto thee? or, what shall it profit thee?*

3 Heb., *added.*

---

(164) **Seven times.**—Some commentators think the number is used here only in a general way for "often," "repeatedly;" but the number seven evidently had some sacred association for the Hebrews. (Comp. Lev. xxvi. 18; Prov. xxiv. 16; Matt. xviii. 21, &c.) No doubt the seven canonical hours were partly derived from this verse. Elsewhere we find three times as the stated occasions of prayer (Ps. lv. 17).

(165) **Nothing shall offend them.**—See margin. Perhaps the verse should take the form of a wish: *great peace to the lovers of Thy law; no stumbling-block to them.* Or, it may be, *great peace have they who love Thy word and who find no hindrance.* It was not the fact that the faithful did *not* stumble.

TAU.

(171) **Shall utter.**—Better, preserving the metaphor of the Hebrew, *pour forth a stream of praise.*

(172) **My tongue shall speak of Thy word.**—Rather, *My tongue shall make response to Thy word, that all Thy commandments are true.*

(176) **I have gone astray like a lost sheep.**—It would be in accordance with a true religious character that even at the end of a long protestation of obedience to the Divine law the psalmist should confess his weakness and sin. But while this may be a legitimate application of the close of this remarkable composition, and while the LXX. suggest a comparison with our Lord's parable by their rendering (comp. Matt. xviii. 11; Luke xix. 10), this could hardly have been the intention of the words of this verse. More likely there is a reference to the condition of the community, for the word rendered "lost" (literally, *perishing*) is used in Isa. xxvii. 13 of the exiled Hebrews, and is rendered "outcasts;" the emphatic "I do not forget Thy commandments," which is the real close of the psalm, seems to make this view imperative.

CXX.

This is the first of the fifteen "songs of degrees," as the title appears in our version ("of steps" in the LXX. and Vulg.; literally, *of goings up*). The probable meaning of this strange inscription is discussed in the General Introduction. That the Psalms so entitled formed a collection made with some definite intention can hardly be questioned. But whatever that intention, the position of this psalm in the collection is unaccountable. Even if the title denotes a rhythmical peculiarity—a kind of climactic progress in the verse—it is only just observable here, while there is not the slightest touch in the poem, which can be brought into peculiar connection or association with a pilgrimage to Jerusalem, or with the return from the captivity. One thing is clear; we are again, after the long gnomic cxixth Psalm, in the region and air of lyric song, this fragment, for it is nothing more, being bright and intense with passion and fire. If the poem is personal, it records an experience which every phase of life in all ages presents, the mischief arising from slander. If—the more probable conjecture—it is national, then we must look for its motive in the complications which would naturally arise when Israel had to struggle amid foreign powers and influences to maintain its religious and national existence. The "enemy to peace" (verse 6; comp. Ps. cxxix. 5; Ezra iv. 1) has been most plausibly identified with the *Samaritans.* (See 2 Kings xvii. 24 *seq.*, and Josephus, *Ant.* xi., ii. 1.)

Title.—"Song of degrees." Rather, *lyric song of goings up,* or *ascents.*

(2) **Deliver . . .**—This is the cry for help of which mention has just been made. The thought is one we have met frequently. Of all the elements of bitterness which made up the lot of Israel under foreign dominion, taunts and calumnies seem to have made the deepest wound, and left the most lasting scar. This was "the torture prolonged from age to age," under which we hear psalmist after psalmist raising his cry for deliverance.

(3) **What shall . . ?**—Literally, *What will he give to thee,* and *what will he add to thee, deceitful tongue?* where it is better, as in the Authorised Version, to take the subject as indefinite, and so render by the passive. Thus we get in substance the following question: "What more can be added to thee (*i.e.*, in the way of epithet), besides *lying* and *false, thou deceitful tongue?*" the answer is given by suggesting the usual metaphors of malicious speech, "the warrior's sharpened arrows" (Jer. ix. 8; Ps. lvii. 4); "fire" (James iii. 6). Only

false tongue? ⁽¹⁾ Sharp arrows of the mighty, with coals of juniper.

⁽⁵⁾ Woe is me, that I sojourn in Mesech, *that* I dwell in the tents of Kedar! ⁽⁶⁾ My soul hath long dwelt with him that hateth peace. ⁽⁷⁾ I *am*

1 Or, *It is as the sharp arrows of the mighty man, with coals of juniper.*
2 Or, *a man of peace.*
3 Or, *Shall I lift up mine eyes to the hills? whence should my help come?*

²*for* peace: but when I speak, they *are* for war.

PSALM CXXI.
A Song of degrees.

⁽¹⁾ ³I will lift up mine eyes unto the

---

here both images are elaborated. For the Hebrew word *give* with the sense of comparison, see 1 Sam. i. 16, "Count (Heb., *give*) not thine handmaid for a daughter of Belial." Gesenius compares the use of the Greek τιθέναι, instead of νομίζειν. So, too, the word "add" has a similar sense (1 Kings x. 7; see margin).

⁽⁴⁾ **Sharp.**—Better, *sharpened, whetted*, as if for a purpose.

Juniper.—Properly, *broom*. Hebrew, *rothem*, a plant identical with the Arabian *retem* and Algerian *retama*. (See 1 Kings xix. 4, 5.) Doctor Tristram mentions the employment of this bush for fuel. "It is ruthlessly uprooted by the Arabs, wherever it is tolerably abundant, for the manufacture of charcoal, which is considered of the finest quality, and fetches a higher price at Cairo than any other kind. Several travellers have mentioned their meeting with Bedouins employed in conveying *retem* charcoal to the Egyptian markets" (*Nat. Hist. of the Bible*, p. 360; see also *Bible Educator* iv. 194). Burckhardt and Robinson also both noticed this trade.

Wonderful stories are told both by Jerome and the rabbis, how travellers, having cooked their food by fires made of the juniper wood, which they suppose to be the wood here meant, and returning a year after to the same spot, still found the embers alive.

⁽⁵⁾ **Mesech.**—This name is generally identified with *Moschi*, mentioned by Herodotus (iii. 94), a tribe on the borders of Colchis and Armenia. It appears again in the prophet Ezekiel xxvii. 13, xxxviii. 3, xxxix. 1. The only reason for suspecting the accuracy of this identification is the remoteness from *Kedar*, who were a nomad tribe of Arabia. (See Gen. xxv. 13; Song of Sol. i. 5.) But in the absence of any other indication of the motive for the mention of these tribes here, this very remoteness affords a sufficiently plausible one; or they may be types of savage life, selected the one from the north, and the other from the south, as poetry dictated. It is quite possible that the circumstances amid which the poet wrote made it necessary for him to veil in this way his allusion to powerful tribes, from whose violence the nation was suffering. At all events, the two concluding verses leave no doubt that some troubled state of affairs, in which the choice of courses was not easy, and affecting the whole nation, not an individual, is here presented.

⁽⁷⁾ **I am for peace.**—For the pregnant, "I peace," see Note, Ps. cix. 3. Both pronouns, *I* and *they*, are emphatic. No doubt these verses are intended to indicate the nature of the malicious speeches mentioned in verses 2 and 3. We imagine Israel in peculiarly difficult political relations under the Persians, possibly very soon after the Return, trying to keep in favour and peace with the ruling powers, but continually drawn into trouble by the jealousy and bitterness of other subject tribes. (See Introduction.)

CXXI.

This simple but exquisite little hymn of four four-line verses, dwells almost exclusively on the sleepless guardianship of His people by the God who made the world. An implied contrast with the idols of the heathen, "peradventure sleeping," while their votaries pray (1 Kings xviii. 27), is felt in every verse. (See Note verse 1.) But it is only implied. The poet seems to want nothing to heighten his truthful confidence, neither vivid colouring nor elaborate imagery, nothing save the repetition again and again of the one word *keep*. (See Notes.) What a history were that, if it could be written, of the countless thousands of Christians who have been consoled in trouble or sickness by this psalm! Among others, it was read at the death-bed of Julius Hare. It is in this psalm that the step-like progression of the rhythm is most plainly marked.

Title.—The Hebrew, in many editions, presents a variation from the usual "song *of* degrees." Here, "a song *for* the degrees"—a variation which has been claimed in support of two rival theories, since it favours equally the view which make these hymns pilgrim songs, and that which sees in them a reference to the actual *steps* leading up to the Temple.

⁽¹⁾ **Whence.**—Our version is certainly incorrect in following the LXX. and Vulg. in making *whence* a relative. The Hebrew word is always interrogative; even in Josh. ii. 4 it is indirectly interrogative. But the margin is hardly right in making the whole verse interrogative. Render, *I will lift up mine eyes to the hills. Whence comes my help?* The hills are those on which Jerusalem is built, the plural being understood, as in Ps. lxxxvii. 1. (See Note.) This gaze of hope does not absolutely decide the standpoint of the poet. He might have been like Ezekiel (vi. 2) when bidden to turn "towards the mountains of Israel" in the distant plain of Mesopotamia; or he may have been close on the end of the pilgrim journey, and actually under the sacred hills. But wherever he stands, this question is not one of doubt; he knows, as in Pss. iii. 4, xiv. 7, that help will come from God's holy hill "out of Zion." He puts the question for the sake of the emphatic answer in the next verse. Possibly, as suggested by the marginal rendering and reference, the poet may in his mind have been contrasting the confidence with which a worshipper of Jehovah might look up to the sacred city on the crest of the holy hill with that superstition and idolatry which was associated with so many hills and high places in Canaan. If this is so, the best commentary, both on the poetry and the religion of the psalm, is to be found in Mr. Ruskin's fascinating discourses on mountains in "Modern Painters," their influence on the ancient, mediæval, and modern mind, and the part they have played alike in the mythology of the pagan times and the religion of the Christian world. There must also be added, in connection with the feeling of the Jew, the part his mountains played as a barrier of defence (Ps. cxxv. 2), and as heights of observation from which to watch for the messengers of peace (Isa. lii. 7; Nah. i. 15).

"In the mountains did he feel his faith
. . . . and there his spirit shaped
Her prospects."—WORDSWORTH.

hills, from whence cometh my help. ⁽²⁾ ^aMy help *cometh* from the LORD, which made heaven and earth.

⁽³⁾ He will not suffer thy foot to be moved: he that keepeth thee will not slumber. ⁽⁴⁾ Behold, he that keepeth Israel shall neither slumber nor sleep. ⁽⁵⁾ The LORD *is* thy keeper: the LORD *is* thy shade upon thy right hand. ⁽⁶⁾ The sun shall not smite thee by day, nor the moon by night. ⁽⁷⁾ The LORD shall preserve thee from all evil: he shall preserve thy soul. ⁽⁸⁾ The LORD shall preserve thy going out and thy coming in from this time forth, and even for evermore.

a Ps. 124. 8.

PSALM CXXII.

A Song of degrees of David.

⁽¹⁾ I was glad when they said unto me, Let us go into the house of the LORD.
⁽²⁾ Our feet shall stand within thy gates, O Jerusalem.
⁽³⁾ Jerusalem is builded as a city that

⁽²⁾ **My help cometh . . .**—Not as the superstition of the Canaanite said, from the sacred summits themselves, but from their Creator's Lord. It is noticeable that the style, "maker of heaven and earth," is a peculiarity of psalms which are certainly post-exile, and show how strongly the contrast with heathenism impressed the creative power of God on the Hebrew mind. When the idolater, pointing to his visible god, taunted the Israelite with having no god, the reply, that He made the heavens, and the earth, and all things, and that these were the proofs of His being, was most natural. (See Jer. x. 11.)

⁽³⁾ **He will not.**—The LXX. and Vulg. rightly, "may He not suffer," &c. The Hebrew cannot be a simple negative. That it is Israel which is addressed the next verse seems to prove.

⁽⁴⁾ **Slumber nor sleep.**—This repetition, with the addition of a synonym, offers a very good instance of the *step-like* style supposed by many critics to give their name to these psalms. But it must be carefully noticed that there is no climax in the force of the two words, the first, if anything, being the stronger. It is used of the sleep of death (Ps. lxxvi. 5).

⁽⁵⁾ **Thy keeper.**—Notice again how the prominent word is caught up from the preceding verse and amplified, and then again repeated, and again amplified in verses 7, 8, where *preserve* is an unfortunate substitution by the Authorised Version.

Shade.—An image of protection, and one peculiarly attractive to the Oriental. (See Num. xiv. 9, margin; Ps. xci. 1; Isa. xxv. 4, xxxii. 2.)

Upon thy right hand.—Some commentators combine this expression with the figure of the shadow, supposing the psalmist, in the phrase "right hand," to allude to the *south* or *sunny* side. But this is prosaic. No doubt there is here, as so often, a confused combination of metaphors. We have several times met with the figure of the right-hand comrade in war, a protection to the unshielded side (Pss. xvi. 8, cix. 31, &c.).

⁽⁶⁾ **Smite thee.**—The mention of shade leads to the amplification of the figure. The evil effects of *sunstroke* are too well known to need comment. They are often mentioned in the Bible (2 Kings iv. 18, 20; Jonah iv.; Judith viii. 3).

Nor the moon by night.—Possibly there is allusion to the belief, so common in old times, of the harmful influence of the moon's light—a belief still recalled in the word lunacy. It is a fact that temporary blindness is often caused by moonlight. (See authorities referred to by Ewald and Delitzsch.) Others, again, think that the injurious cold of the night is here placed in antithesis to the heat of the noonday sun (comp. Gen. xxxi. 40; Jer. xxxvi. 30), the impression that intense cold *burns* being common in the East, as indeed everywhere. Tennyson speaks of the moon being "keen with frost." But it is also possible that the generally harmful effects of night air are intended.

^(7—8) Instead of *preserve*, read *keep*, the persistent dwelling on this one word making one of the chief beauties of this hymn.

⁽⁸⁾ **Thy going out and thy coming in.**—A common Hebrew expression to denote the whole of life. (See Deut. xxviii. 6, &c.; comp. St. Paul's prayer, 1 Thess. v. 23.)

CXXII.

It is on this psalm chiefly that the theory of the *pilgrim odes* is based. It tells its design in almost so many words, and actually refers to the ordinance which directed every male Israelite to visit the holy city three times a year. The poet stands in imagination or memory at the gates of Jerusalem. The journey is done, and at this moment the excitement and joy with which it was commenced are lovingly recalled. Then follow the impressions produced in the caravan of country strangers by the aspect of the city, the throngs of pilgrims pouring in at the several gates, the royal residences and courts of justice. At this moment the feelings of patriotic admiration and reverence get the better of mere wonder. The thought of the capital—capital political and religious—excites other emotions; and, as in so many instances of other pilgrims in connection with Jerusalem and of Rome, the prayer for the city's welfare rises to the poet's lips—a prayer which is none the less real because it reproduces literally the formal Oriental greetings which at such a time would be passing to and fro among the excited groups. The psalm, which shows only very slightly the step-like rhythm, is best arranged in couplets.

Title.—The addition of *David* is plainly a gratuitous conjecture. The LXX. knew nothing of it.

⁽¹⁾ **Let us go.**—Or, *we will go*. This verse is inscribed over the portico of St. Paul's Cathedral.

⁽²⁾ **Our feet shall stand.**—Rather, *Our feet have been, and are now, standing.* "Here we stand at last at thy gates, O Jerusalem." We must imagine the pilgrims arresting their steps to gaze about them as they reach the gates.

⁽³⁾ This verse is somewhat perplexing. It is explained to refer either to the rebuilding of the city and reuniting of the parts which had been disconnected in the destruction, or, which is far better (see Introduction), is taken as a rustic's impression on first seeing a compact city after being accustomed to straggling villages. The astonishment of Virgil's shepherd is aptly compared: "Urbem quam dicunt Romam, Melibœe

is compact together: ⁽⁴⁾ whither the tribes go up, the tribes of the LORD, unto the testimony of Israel, to give thanks unto the name of the LORD. ⁽⁵⁾ For there ¹are set thrones of judgment, the thrones of the house of David. ⁽⁶⁾ Pray for the peace of Jerusalem: they shall prosper that love thee. ⁽⁷⁾ Peace be within thy walls, *and* prosperity within thy palaces. ⁽⁸⁾ For my brethren and companions' sakes, I will now say, Peace *be* within thee. ⁽⁹⁾ Because of the house of the LORD our God I will seek thy good.

¹ Heb., *do sit.*

PSALM CXXIII.
A Song of degrees.

⁽¹⁾ Unto thee lift I up mine eyes, O thou that dwellest in the heavens. ⁽²⁾ Behold, as the eyes of servants *look* unto the hand of their masters, *and* as the eyes of a maiden unto the hand of her mistress; so our eyes *wait* upon the LORD our God, until that he have mercy upon us. ⁽³⁾ Have mercy upon us, O LORD, have mercy upon us: for we are exceedingly filled with contempt. ⁽⁴⁾ Our soul is exceedingly filled with the scorning of those that are at ease, *and* with the contempt of the proud.

PSALM CXXIV.
A Song of degrees of David.

⁽¹⁾ If *it had not been* the LORD who

---

putavi, Stultus ego, huic nostræ similem." But a far more satisfactory meaning is suggested by the LXX. They (comp. Symmachus) take the word rendered *compact* as a noun, meaning *union*. The verse then may run: *Jerusalem, the (one) built like a city, union is in it together*, i.e., it is the rallying point of all the tribes. (See next verse.)

⁽⁴⁾ **Unto the testimony.**—This is erroneous. The words are parenthetical: "Thither go (or, must and shall go) the tribes, the tribes of Judah (it is an ordinance for Israel) to praise the name of Jehovah." (See Ex. xxiii. 17, Deut. xvi. 16, to this regulation.)

⁽⁵⁾ **Thrones.**—Jerusalem, at first a cause of wonder as a city, is now to the pilgrims a cause of admiration as the *capital*. The mention of the "House of David" itself disposes of the title, but does not prove that the monarchy was still in existence, since even the Sanhedrim might be said to administer justice from the throne of the house or successors of David. The administration of justice was the original and principal duty of a monarch in time of peace (1 Kings iii. 11, *seq.*). The marginal "do sit" gives the literal rendering of the Hebrew, which in this use of *sit*, where we should say in English *stand*, is exactly the provincial Scotch.

⁽⁶,⁷⁾ It is impossible in English to reproduce the effect of the original in these references to the usual greetings of the East, since at the same time they contain alliterations and a play on the name of Jerusalem. There is first the challenge to the body of pilgrims to give the customary salutation, and then it is taken up in a threefold wish, varied each time. Then follows the reason of this unanimous and hearty prayer: "Ask for the peace of the city of peace; prosperity be to thy lovers, peace within thy walls, prosperity in thy palaces."

⁽⁸⁾ **Peace be within thee.**—Here the formal greeting actually appears, that which greets every traveller in the East (John xx. 19). (Comp. Luke x. 5.) The full form appears in 1 Sam. xxv. 6.

⁽⁹⁾ **Because . .**—Now for the first time the religious motive of the pilgrimage appears, rendered all the more emphatic by being kept for the concluding verse.

CXXIII.

This psalm has been beautifully called *Oculus Sperans* (the Eye of Hope). That it reflects the feelings of Israel under foreign oppression there is no doubt, but there is no indication of precise time, unless we are to adopt the Hebrew margin, and see in the concluding word a reference to the *Ionians*, which would bring the psalm within the Macedonian period. The step-like rhythm is not very marked; but the psalm so abounds in assonance that it has been called the "Rhyming Psalm."

⁽¹⁾ **O thou that dwellest.**—*O thou throned one.*

⁽²⁾ **Eyes.**—As the eyes of the slave are fixed on the *hand* of the master or mistress, waiting for a sign or direction, so Israel waits, expectant of the hint of Divine interference to deliver from the tyrant. The picture will be so familiar to readers of Oriental stories as hardly to need actual illustration; but Savary's (*Letters on Egypt*, p. 135, quoted by Perowne) description exactly reproduces the intention of the poet: "The slaves stand silent at the bottom of the rooms, with their hands crossed over their breasts. *With their eyes fixed upon their master*, they seek to anticipate every one of his wishes." Comp. "Cave oculos a meis oculis quoquam demoveas" (Ter. *Adelph*. ii. 1, 16).

⁽³⁾ **Exceedingly filled.** — Or, *sated more than enough.*

⁽⁴⁾ **The scorning.**—The Hebrew offers a rare use of the article—probably it should be reproduced by our demonstrative, *this scorning*. The LXX., however, have, "The scorn for those at ease, and the contempt for the proud," which requires only the substitution of a letter, removes an anomaly in construction, and gives a better sense: "Let our desire be satisfied to the full with the scorn for those at ease, and the same contempt for the proud." Notice how the figure is retained. The oppressors are the *masters and mistresses*, living in luxury, while the slaves wait. Gesenius quotes Sallust (*secundis rebus ferox*) in illustration of the wantonness of secure and luxurious power. As we read the verse, we seem to feel

"The whips and scorns of time,
The oppressor's wrong, the proud man's contumely."

CXXIV.

In this psalm we have a reminiscence of a catastrophe so tremendous, that all the combined images under which the poets of past times had figured the many

was on our side, now may Israel say; ⁽²⁾ If *it had not been* the LORD who was on our side, when men rose up against us: ⁽³⁾ then they had swallowed us up quick, when their wrath was kindled against us: ⁽⁴⁾ then the waters had overwhelmed us, the stream had gone over our soul: ⁽⁵⁾ then the proud waters had gone over our soul.

⁽⁶⁾ Blessed *be* the LORD, who hath not given us *as* a prey to their teeth. ⁽⁷⁾ Our soul is escaped as a bird out of the snare of the fowlers: the snare is broken, and we are escaped.

⁽⁸⁾ ᵃOur help *is* in the name of the LORD, who made heaven and earth.

ᵃ Ps. 121. 2.

¹ Heb., *wickedness*.

PSALM CXXV.
A Song of degrees.

⁽¹⁾ They that trust in the LORD *shall be* as mount Zion, *which* cannot be removed, *but* abideth for ever. ⁽²⁾ *As* the mountains *are* round about Jerusalem, so the LORD *is* round about his people from henceforth even for ever. ⁽³⁾ For the rod of ¹the wicked shall not rest upon the lot of the righteous; lest the righteous put forth their hands unto iniquity.

⁽⁴⁾ Do good, O LORD, unto *those that be* good, and to *them that are* upright in their hearts. ⁽⁵⁾ As for such as turn aside unto their crooked ways, the LORD shall lead them forth with the workers of iniquity: *but* peace *shall be* upon Israel.

---

vicissitudes of Israel appear insufficient. Nothing but the total ruin of the city and Temple, and the captivity of the nation, could have left an impression so deep and lasting. It is the restored remnant that thus ascribe to Jehovah their escape—so marvellous, so miraculous, that the older deliverance from Egypt colours the language in which it is described. The Aramaisms of the poem leave no room for upholding the ascription to David. The rhythm is finely varied.

Title.—"Of David." The LXX. know nothing of this addition. The imagery recalls Davidic poems, and possibly suggested the inscription. (See *Introduction.*)

(2) **If it had not been.**—For this motto of the covenant, see Ps. xciv. 17.

Men.—Better, *man.* In this use of the general term, we must, as Reuss points out, see an indication of the time of composition of the psalm. One who could so speak of the whole world as separated into two parts (*Jews* and *heathen*), discloses a sense of isolation and exclusiveness which brings us far down from the time of the prophets. They, indeed, spoke of it as the ideal of the future. This psalmist regards it as an accomplished fact.

(3) **Then.**—Critics are at issue both as to the form and meaning of the word—whether it is an archaism or an aramaism, expressing *time* or logical sequence.

Swallowed . . . quick (alive).—No doubt an allusion to the fall of Korah (Num. xvi. 32, 33), where the same verb and adjective occur together. (See also Ps. lv. 15.)

(4) **Waters.**—The sudden transition in the imagery from the earthquake to the flood is characteristic of Hebrew poetry. (For the flood, see Pss. xviii. 4, 16, lxix. 14, cxliv. 7.)

Stream.—The torrent swollen with the winter rain. (Comp. Isa. viii. 7, 8.)

(5) **Proud.**—The Hebrew presents a rare form, which is considered indicative of later composition. For the epithet, comp. Æschylus, *Prom. Vinct.* 717:

"And you will reach the scornful river—well it deserves the name."

(7) **Snare.**—Another rapid transition to a favourite figure, that of the hunter's net. (Comp. Ps. x. 9, &c.)

(8) **Who made.**—See Note on Ps. cxxi. 2.

CXXV.

This psalm brings prominently out the danger to which Israel was subjected from heathen rule—a danger of being forced or seduced away from the political and religious principles of the restored nation. From this danger the poet believes those who keep faithful to the religion of Jehovah are secured, as Jerusalem itself is secured by the strength of its geographical situation. Neither the parallelism nor the step-like rhythm is marked.

(2) **As the mountains.**—In the first verse, the *stability* of the faithful is compared to that of Mount Zion; here their *security* to that of the city girt by its hills. (On the geographical reference, see Dean Stanley, *S. and P.*, pp. 174, 175.) Robinson's description is—"The sacred city lies upon the broad and high mountain range, which is shut in by the two valleys, Jehoshaphat and Hinnom. All the surrounding hills are higher: in the east, the Mount of Olives; on the south, the so-called Hill of Evil Counsel, which ascends from the valley of Hinnom; on the west, the ground rises gently to the border of the great wadi, as described above; while on the north the bend of a ridge which adjoins the Mount of Olives limits the view to the distance of about a mile and a half." In Zech. ii. 4, 5, the protecting care of Jehovah is likened to a wall round the city, instead of to the rampart of mountains, as here.

(3) **Rod.**—The imagery of this unusually long verse is peculiar. The "rod of the wicked," or "of wickedness," is the *heathen sceptre*, and the righteous are the Israelites who hold fast to the religion of their fathers. This sceptre now rests—a word expressing the presence of tyranny—upon the Holy Land; but this is not for a continuance. God will not suffer the tyranny to last, lest the righteous should be seduced or forced into connivance with practices which religion unites with patriotism to condemn.

(5) **Turn aside unto their crooked ways.**—Or, *bend their crooked ways, i.e.,* pursue evil courses.

But peace.—Better, as an innovation on the customary form, *peace be in Israel.* (See Note on Ps. cxxii. 6, and comp. Ps. cxxviii. 6.)

A Gladsome Retrospect.   PSALMS, CXXVI.—CXXVII.   *A Joyful Forecast.*

PSALM CXXVI.
A Song of degrees.

(1) When the LORD [1] turned again the captivity of Zion, we were like them that dream. (2) Then was our mouth filled with laughter, and our tongue with singing: then said they among the heathen, The LORD [2] hath done great things for them. (3) The LORD hath done great things for us; *whereof* we are glad. (4) Turn again our captivity, O LORD, as the streams in the south. (5) They that sow in tears shall reap in [3] joy. (6) He that goeth forth and weepeth, bearing [4] precious seed, shall doubtless come again with rejoicing, bringing his sheaves *with him.*

Marginal notes:
[1] Heb., *returned the returning of Zion.*
[2] Heb., *hath magnified to do with them.*
[3] Or, *singing.*
[4] Or, *seed basket.*
[5] Or, *of Solomon.*

PSALM CXXVII.
A Song of degrees [5] for Solomon.

(1) Except the LORD build the house,

CXXVI.

The two stanzas, marked so plainly by the changes of tense and tone, of this exquisite little poem, though telling with the distinctness of actual description the nature of the circumstances amid which it was written, give no indication of an exact date. All we can see with certainty is that the psalm is post-exile. The recollection of the exuberant burst of joy at the first news of the return from the Captivity, enables the psalmist to anticipate a similar change from gloom to gladness now. The words of the song are too deeply enshrined in the heart of the whole world to make us very anxious to recover the precise time which gave expression to the nameless poet's feelings. The rhythm is fine and varied.

(1) **When the Lord . . .**—Literally, *In turning by Jehovah the turning of Zion.* The phrase is not precisely the same as that in verse 4, which is usual, and offers no difficulty. Here the form of the noun "turning" presents some difficulty; but, after the analogy of a few other words, it can bear the concrete meaning "returned:" *when Jehovah brought back the returned of Zion.*

Like them that dream.—The LXX. and Vulg. have "as if consoled." The Hebrew word primarily means "to be fat," or "fleshy," and in Isa. xxxviii. 16 is rendered "recover"—a meaning that would give a good sense here, and which is adopted by the Chaldean paraphrases: "We were like unto such men who have recovered." On the other hand, the usual rendering suggests that the news of the restoration appeared too good to be true. "Surely you are dreaming" is a common saying. An illustration has been aptly produced in Livy's description of the feelings of the Greeks when they heard at the Isthmian games (B.C. 196), after the defeat of the Macedonians by T. Flaminius, the proclamation of the herald that they should, by the free gift of the Roman people, retain their liberty. "The joy was too great for men to take it all in. None could well believe that he had heard aright, and they looked on one another in wonder, like the empty show of a dream" (*Livy*, xxxiii. 32).

(2) **Singing.**—As frequently of the restoration in Isaiah—xlii. 11, xliv. 23, liv. 1, &c.

Hath done.—See margin, and comp. Joel ii. 21.

(4) **Captivity.**—Here there is a change. The joy of the great Return was too great not to last on through many vicissitudes. But the poet now thinks of the many exiles still dispersed among the nations, and prays for another manifestation of Divine favour and power.

The streams in the south.—Rather, *the channels in the south.* The allusion is to the sudden filling of the dry torrent-beds of the southern district of Palestine in the rainy season. So the poet prays that *torrents* of the returned may pour into the desolate and deserted country. (Comp. Isa. xlix. 18 for the same feeling, but under a different figure.) The LXX. have "in the south wind," evidently thinking of the melting of a frozen stream, instead of the filling of a dry river-bed.

(5) **Joy.**—Rather, *singing,* as in verse 2. The harvest-home songs are contrasted with the anxiety of the seed-time. Probably the poet found the proverbial saying already current, but he has touched it with the consecrating hand till it has become only less precious than the saying of Divine lips, "Blessed are they that mourn, for they shall be comforted."

(6) The original is very expressive, by the idiom of infinitive combined with finite verb.

> "He shall walk, and walk and weep,
> Bearing the handful of seed:
> He shall come, and come with singing,
> Bearing his sheaves,"

where we must certainly see an extension and not a mere repetition of the former figure, for the very form of the expression suggests the long patient labour of the sower, and the reward which patience and perseverance always bring—a harvest in proportion to the toil and trouble of seed-time. The words of the prophet Haggai (chaps. i. 10, 11, ii. 19), contemporary with the Return, should be compared. The word rendered "precious" in the Authorised Version may be correctly represented by "handful." Its meaning is "drawing;" and from Amos ix. 13 (see margin) we see that the sower was called "the drawer of seed," no doubt from the hand being repeatedly drawn out for the cast from the bag or basket containing the seed. Others render "seed-basket" here. The contrast so beautifully painted in this verse was certainly realised when "the priests and Levites, and the rest of the children of the captivity, kept the dedication of the house of God with joy" (Ezra vi. 16; comp. vi. 22; Neh. xii. 42).

CXXVII.

Man's toil, and skill, and care would be all unavailing were there not a "Divinity shaping our ends." This is the thought common in Hebrew literature (see Notes), now so expressed as to include not only the greater purposes of human activity, but even the homeliest duty of every-day life. All fall under the same benign and watchful surveillance. The smallest details, as the largest concerns of life, are objects of the Divine regard; and in little things, as well as great, the great lesson to learn is that man cannot of himself command success, though it awaits the weakest who has the Divine blessing. If any particular set of circumstances must be sought for this expression of a truth so firmly planted in Israel, it is natural to look for them during the troubles and anxieties which accompanied

Human Dependence   PSALMS, CXXVII.   *upon God.*

they labour in vain ¹ that build it: except the LORD keep the city, the watchman waketh *but* in vain. ⁽²⁾ *It is* vain for you to rise up early, to sit up late, to eat the bread of sorrows: *for* so he giveth his beloved sleep.

⁽³⁾ Lo, children *are* an heritage of the LORD: *and* the fruit of the womb *is his* reward. ⁽⁴⁾ As arrows *are* in the hand of a mighty man; so *are* children of the youth. ⁽⁵⁾ Happy *is* the man that ²hath his quiver full of them: they shall not

¹ Heb., *that are builders of it in it.*
² Heb., *hath filled his quiver with them.*

---

the restoration and rebuilding of Jerusalem. Possibly the haste to rebuild the private houses before the public necessities were supplied (comp. Haggai i. 2, 4) may have given the motive of the poem, though it is but in the most delicate way, and under figures universally applicable, that the people are reminded that home, and family, and property alike depend on God. The rhythm is fine and varied.

Title.—"For Solomon." The rendering is wrong even if the inscription be admitted. Rather, *of Solomon*, which is the usual form of ascribing authorship. It is not difficult to account for this addition to the usual title, "Song of degrees," an addition wanting in the LXX. Not only was it natural to think of Solomon, the great *builder*, in connection with the opening of the psalm, but in the words "his beloved" there was to Jewish ears a suggestion of the name "Jedidiah," and the resemblance to the Book of Proverbs, both in form and sentiment, is marked. See, for example, Prov. x. 22, which sums up the prevailing thought of the psalm.

⁽¹⁾ **House.**—*A house*, any house, not the Temple. The thought is a general one. Even in the common labours of men, it is the Divine blessing which contributes the success. *An Gottes Segen ist alles gelegen.*

Waketh.—Perhaps better, *watcheth.* The house that has been built with such toil, the city which has been planned with such skill, may suddenly fall before the midnight attack of the robber or the enemy, in spite of the strictest police, unless God's vigilant providence preserve it.

⁽²⁾ **It . . . sleep.**—This verse, of the literal rendering of which there is no question, has met with many different interpretations. About the first clause there is no difference. Early rising, to pursue the business of the day, is vain without the Divine blessing on the labour. The next two clauses admit two different interpretations. Some connect the sitting down with the meal: "delaying to sit down and eat the bread of cares" (or sorrow), *i.e.*, so immersed in business as to allow hardly time for meals. But it seems far more natural to take the Hebrew in its more extended sense of resting, and so explain, nearly as the Authorised Version:—

"It is in vain to rise early;
To delay the hour of rest,
To eat the bread that has been won by toil;
At His pleasure He giveth to His beloved (in) sleep."

As to the last clause, it seems right, from its use in Gen. i., "it was so," to give *so* the sense "at His pleasure," this being also indicated by the general drift of the psalm. The word "sleep" may be either the direct object, as in the LXX. and Vulg., or the accusative used adverbially, "in sleep," "while they sleep." That the latter suits the context best there can be no question. The whole intention of the psalm is to assert the truth which the Book of Proverbs sums up in one sentence (chap. x. 22): "The blessing of Jehovah maketh rich, and toil can add nothing thereto," the truth which was so impressively taught in the Sermon on the Mount, by the contrast of man's restless ambition with the unconscious dependence on the Divine

bounty of birds and flowers. To say that what others toil for from morning till night in vain, God gives to His beloved without all this anxiety and exertion, *while they sleep*, puts this truth forcibly, and with that disregard of apparent paradox which was natural to a Hebrew, and which appears so prominently in our Saviour's treatment of the subject. Labour is decried as unnecessary neither here nor in the Sermon on the Mount, but "carking care" is dismissed as unworthy those who, from past experience, ought to trust the goodness of the great Provider. The Greek proverb, "The net catches while the fisher sleeps," and the German, "God bestows His gifts during the night," bring common expressions to confirm this voice of inspiration, which was, in almost so many words, recalled in our Lord's parable (Mark iv. 27). But old association pleads for the equally true and equally beautiful rendering which makes sleep the gift of God. If there is one thing which seems to come more direct from Heaven's bounty than another, that in its character is more benign, in its effects more akin to the nature of God, it is the blessing of sleep. In all times men have rendered thanks to Heaven for this boon. The ancients not only spoke of sleep as "most grateful of known gifts," but made itself a god. The psalmist unconsciously, but most truly, teaches us the further lesson that it is not only a Divine blessing, but a proof of Divine love:

"Of all the thoughts of God that are
Borne inward unto souls afar,
Across the psalmist's music deep,
Now tell me if that any is
For gift or grace surpassing this—
He giveth His beloved sleep."
                  MRS. BROWNING.

⁽³⁾ **Children.**—With the true patriarchal feeling of the blessing of a numerous offspring, the poet here directly alludes to Gen. xxx. 2. "Heritage of Jehovah" is, of course, "heritage from Jehovah," *i.e.*, a promise granted by Him, just as Israel itself was a possession He made for Himself.

⁽⁴⁾ **Children of the youth**—*i.e.*, the offspring of an early marriage. Aquila, "sons of young and vigorous parents." The young man, with his numerous family around him, is like the vigorous warrior with his quiver full of arrows.

⁽⁵⁾ **They.**—Not the *sons.* There is here one of the sudden changes of number in which Hebrew poetry abounds. (See especially Ps. cvii. 43.) Parents who have large families of sons are evidently intended. From the figure of the warrior and the arrows we should expect here, too, a martial image. They shall not be discomfited, but they shall challenge their enemies in the gates. In illustration may be quoted:

"Therefore men pray to have around their hearth,
Obedient offspring, to requite their foes
With harm, and honour whom their father loves;
But he whose issue is unprofitable,
Begets what else but sorrow to himself,
And store of laughter to his enemies?"
                  SOPH.: *Antig.*, 641

On the other hand, it is the habit of Hebrew poetry to accumulate metaphors, and the *gate* is so commonly spoken of as the place of public resort, where legal

be ashamed, but they ¹shall speak with the enemies in the gate.

PSALM CXXVIII.
A Song of degrees.

⁽¹⁾ Blessed *is* every one that feareth the LORD; that walketh in his ways. ⁽²⁾ For thou shalt eat the labour of thine hands: happy *shalt* thou *be*, and *it shall be* well with thee. ⁽³⁾ Thy wife *shall be* as a fruitful vine by the sides of thine house: thy children like olive plants round about thy table.

⁽⁴⁾ Behold, that thus shall the man be blessed that feareth the LORD. ⁽⁵⁾ The LORD shall bless thee out of Zion: and thou shalt see the good of Jerusalem all the days of thy life. ⁽⁶⁾ Yea, thou shalt see thy children's children, *and* peace upon Israel.

PSALM CXXIX.
A Song of degrees.

⁽¹⁾ ²Many a time have they afflicted me from my youth, may Israel now say: ⁽²⁾ Many a time have they afflicted me

1 Or, *shall subdue,* as Ps. 18. 47, or, *destroy.*

2 Or, *Much.*

---

cases were decided (Isa. xxix. 21; Amos v. 12, &c.), that it is quite as likely that the allusion here is to the support which a man's just cause would receive when evidently backed up by a long retinue of stalwart sons. This view certainly receives support from Job v. 4, where we have the very opposite picture of a tyrant's sons, not only unable to support their father, but themselves "crushed in the gate;" and the phrase "speak with their enemies" in this same verse may be illustrated from Josh. xx. 4; Jer. xii. 1.

CXXVIII.

The last psalm taught in a homely way the great lesson of cheerful content, and this, while announcing the promises attached to fidelity to Jehovah, still confines itself to the domestic circle—with the implied truth that national prosperity is bound closely up with domestic happiness, and depends on the cultivation of domestic virtues. And what an idyllic picture is here of peace and happiness!—the natural effects of that spirit of simple piety which often preserves itself through many generations under a humble roof. We see the father of the family, working hard no doubt, but recompensed for all his pains by an honourable competence, and the mother, instead of seeking distraction outside her home, finding all her pleasures in the happiness of her numerous children, who, fresh and healthy as young saplings, gather daily round the simple but ample board. Happy the family, poor or rich, whose annals tell such a tale! But the happiness could not be real or sincere which did not look beyond the home circle, to the prosperity of the larger circle of the nation of which it forms part; and so, like Burns' famous poem, which, in telling the story of the Scottish peasant's home-life, has caugh the very spirit of the old Hebrew song, the psalmist ends with a patriotic prayer. The parallelism is here and there perfect.

⁽²⁾ **For thou.**—The Hebrew by the position of the particle is more emphatic:

"For it is the labour of thine hands thou shalt eat."

(See Note, Ps. cxvi. 10.) This picture of a successful and peaceful husbandry, which itself throws a whole flood of light on the condition of Palestine and of the people, now not nomadic but agricultural, is rendered still more emphatic by references to the numerous passages where it is foretold that enemies would devour the harvests (Deut. xxviii. 30—33; Lev. xxvi. 16).

Happy.—The same word translated *blessed* in verse 1.

⁽³⁾ **By the sides.**—No doubt the *inner part* of the house is meant (see Ps. xlviii. 2)—the *gynecæum* or woman's quarter—or perhaps the sides of the inner court or quadrangle. This is no more out of keeping with the figure of the *vine* than the table is with that of olive plants. Though the Hebrews had not yet developed the fatal habit of secluding their women, as later Orientals have done, still there was a strict custom which allotted a more private tent (Gen. xviii. 9) or part of a house to them. And doubtless we are here also to think of the good housewife who is engaged within at the household duties, and is not like the idle gossip, sitting "at the door of her house on a seat in the high places of the city" (Prov. ix. 14). The *vine* and *olive* are in Hebrew poetry frequent symbols of fruitfulness and of a happy, flourishing state. (See Ps. lii. 8; Jer. xi. 16.) The comparison of children to the healthy young shoots of a tree is, of course, common to all poetry, being indeed latent in such expressions as "scion of a noble house." (Comp. Euripides, *Medea* 1,098: "a sweet young shoot of children.")

⁽⁴⁾ **Behold, that.**—Better, *Look! for thus,* &c. The poet calls attention to the charming picture he has drawn of domestic bliss and then points his moral.

⁽⁵⁾ **Shall . . . shalt.**—Here and in the next verse the optative is plainly required: "May Jehovah," &c.; "mayst thou see," &c. The patriotic sentiment could not wait long for expression in such a psalm. No people ever perceived more strongly than the Jews the connection between the welfare of the state and that of the family.

⁽⁶⁾ **Children's children.**—Dr. Perowne illustrates from Virgil: "adspicies . . . natos natorum et qui nascentur ab illis." (Comp. Zech. viii. 4, 5.)

And peace . . .—The conjunction spoils the passage. The psalm concludes with the prayer, "Peace upon Israel." (Comp. Ps. cxxv. 5.)

CXXIX.

Out of some deadly peril Israel looks for deliverance to the righteousness of Jehovah, which from the childhood of the race has repeatedly manifested itself in help and deliverance. As the cord of bondage was cut in Egypt so will it be cut again, and the same shame and confusion overtake the present oppressors which fell upon the Pharaohs. But of the precise time and occasion there is no indication. The two stanzas into which the poem falls would be perfectly similar but for the last line, which looks suspiciously like an after addition of some copyist to bring the harvest scene into exact correspondence with the picture in Ruth. (See Note to verse 8.)

⁽¹⁾ **Many a time.**—Or more literally, *much*. (See margin.)

from my youth: yet they have not prevailed against me. ⁽³⁾ The plowers plowed upon my back: they made long their furrows. ⁽⁴⁾ The LORD *is* righteous: he hath cut asunder the cords of the wicked.

⁽⁵⁾ Let them all be confounded and turned back that hate Zion. ⁽⁶⁾ Let them be as the grass *upon* the housetops, which withereth afore it groweth up: ⁽⁷⁾ wherewith the mower filleth not his hand; nor he that bindeth sheaves his bosom. ⁽⁸⁾ Neither do they which go by say, The blessing of the LORD *be* upon you: we bless you in the name of the LORD.

PSALM CXXX.

A Song of degrees.

⁽¹⁾ Out of the depths have I cried unto thee, O LORD.

⁽²⁾ Lord, hear my voice: let thine ears be attentive to the voice of my supplications. ⁽³⁾ If thou, LORD, shouldest mark iniquities, O Lord, who shall stand? ⁽⁴⁾ But *there is* forgiveness with thee, that thou mayest be feared.

From my youth.—Here, of course, not the youth of a person, but of the nation. The poet glances back even to the Egyptian bondage. (See Hosea ii. 15, "as in the days of her youth, and as in the days when she came up out of the land of Egypt;" comp. Ezek. xxiii. 3; Jer. ii. 2, xxii. 21, recalling all the long series of oppressions suffered by the race.)

May Israel now say.—There is in the original no adverb of *time*: "let Israel say."

(3) **Furrows.**—The Hebrew word only occurs once besides, in 1 Sam. xiv. 14, where the margin renders as here, *furrow*—a rendering which plainly *there* is not intelligible. "Half a furrow of an acre of land," as a space in which twenty men were killed, gives no clear idea to the mind. But Dr. J. G. Wettstein, in his excursus at the end of Delitzsch's Commentary, explains the *ma'an* to be the strip of ground which the ploughman takes in hand at one time, and round which consequently at the end of each furrow the plough turns. Delitzsch's "furrow-strip," therefore, more exactly reproduces the word, though here doubtless it is used with a poetic freedom and may be translated *furrow*. The double image, suggesting the lash given to a slave, and at the same time the actual and terrible imprints of oppression left on the country as well as the race, is as striking as poetry ever produced. It, in fact, combines two separate prophetic figures, Isa. l. 6 and li. 23.

(4) **The Lord is righteous.**—This expression of faith, introduced without any conjunction, is itself a revelation of the deeply-rooted religion of Israel.

Cords.—Literally, *cord*. As in Ps. cxxiv. 7, the net was broken and the bird escaped, so here the cord binding the slave (comp. Ps. ii. 3) is severed and he goes free.

(6) **Which withereth afore it groweth up.**—This clause, with its Aramaic colouring, probably contains a textual error. The context seems certainly to require the meaning "before it is plucked up," and many scholars get this meaning out of the Hebrew verb used elsewhere of "plucking off a shoe" and "drawing a sword." They give, which is no doubt legitimate, an impersonal sense to the active verb, "which withereth before one pulls it up." The LXX. (received text), the Vulg., Theodotion, and the Quinta favour this rendering. On the other hand, the image of grass withering before it comes to maturity is exactly what we should expect here, growing as it does without soil (comp. the "seed on the rock" in the parable of the sower), and suggests a more complete and sudden destruction of the enemies, who perish before the abortive plans of evil can be carried out. The rendering of the Authorised Version is therefore to be retained, and is actually supported by Aquila, Symmachus, the Sexta, and in various readings of the LXX. A thatched cottage in our country might present the picture suggested by the verse, but it was much more familiar where the housetops were flat and plastered with a composition of mortar, tar, ashes, and sand, which, unless carefully rolled, would naturally become covered with weeds. Indeed, in many cases, especially on the poorest sort of houses, the roof would be little better than hard mud. For similar allusions comp. 2 Kings xix. 26 and Isa. xxxvii. 27.

(8) This harvest scene is exactly like that painted in Ruth ii. 4, and the last line should be printed as a return greeting from the reapers.

CXXX.

It is the soul of the people which here throws itself on the Divine forgiveness, waiting for deliverance as one waiteth for the dawn. Verses 7 and 8, which are evidently taken up by the full choir, leave no doubt of the national character of the psalm. But the strong *personal* feeling breathed into it has made it even more the *de profundis* of individuals than of churches or nations. Luther's fondness for this psalm is well known. The progressive or step-like parallelism is well marked.

(1) **Out of the depths.**—A recurrent image for overwhelming distress (Pss. xviii. 16, lxxxviii. 7; also lxix. 2, where the same Hebrew word occurs). It is used literally in Isa. li. 10 for the sea.

(3) **If thou.**—The word rendered "mark" is "watch" in verse 6. If "Jah" were to watch for men's lapses, as one watches for the dawn, nothing but signal punishment could follow. So Job (Job x. 14, xiv. 16) actually believed God did watch; while the prophets Jeremiah (Jer. iii. 5) and Amos (Amos i. 11) use the word of the strict care taken that the consequences should follow the sin. It is a fact worthy of attention, that misfortune provokes at this crisis, in this people so profoundly religious, not murmurings against the Divine dealings, but a sense of deep contrition.

(4) **But.**—Rather, *for*, marking an ellipse easily supplied. Israel's sense of Jehovah's readiness to forgive was too deep to need expression, it was understood; "Thou wilt not mark, &c., for . . ."

Forgiveness.—The article in the original may be more than that common with abstract nouns. "The forgiveness we need."

That thou mayest be feared.—Either that the forgiven ones may become more profoundly reli-

Waiting for the Lord.   PSALMS, CXXXI.—CXXXII.   *Humility and Patience.*

(5) I wait for the LORD, my soul doth wait, and in his word do I hope. (6) My soul *waiteth* for the Lord more than they that watch for the morning: [1] *I say, more than* they that watch for the morning. (7) Let Israel hope in the LORD: for with the LORD *there is* mercy, and with him *is* plenteous redemption. (8) And he shall redeem Israel from all his iniquities.

PSALM CXXXI.
A Song of degrees of David.

(1) LORD, my heart is not haughty, nor mine eyes lofty: neither do I [2] exercise myself in great matters, or in things too [3] high for me. (2) Surely I have behaved and quieted [4] myself, as a child that is weaned of his mother: my soul *is* even as a weaned child. (3) Let Israel hope in the LORD [5] from henceforth and for ever.

PSALM CXXXII.
A Song of degrees.

(1) LORD, remember David, *and* all his

[1] Or, *which watch unto the morning.*
[2] Heb., *walk.*
[3] Heb., *wonderful.*
[4] Heb., *my soul.*
[5] Heb., *from now.*

---

gious, or perhaps, rather, that the manifestation of Divine mercy to Israel may strike fear in the heathen.

(5) **I wait.**—The Hebrew expresses, *I have been waiting, and still wait.* Mark the earnestness in the repetition, *I wait, my soul waits.*

(6) **Watch for the morning.**—Comp. Ps. cxxiii. 2 for another figure of the same earnest upward gaze. In the "watcher for the dawn" there may be an allusion to the Levite-sentinel whose duty it was to signal the first ray of dawn, and the moment for commencing the sacred rites of the Temple (Ps. cxxxiv. 1), but the figure if general, as marking the impatience of a deeply agitated soul—a sufferer waiting for relief, a contrite sinner for forgiveness—is as striking as graceful. (See Deut. xxviii. 67.)

(7) **Let Israel.**—Rather (as in Prayer-Book), *Hope Israel in Jehovah.* It is the watchword of faith addressed to the nation. (Comp. Ps. cxxxi. 3 for a rarer form of it.)

(8) **He.**—Emphatic. He and only He. The redemption must not be limited to the *consequences* of *iniquity*, though including these. The psalm belongs to the age of true national contrition, when nothing would satisfy but deliverance from sin, as well as from its punishment. This appears decisively from a comparison with Ps. xxv. 22, where the expression is "from all his *troubles.*" Thus, this psalm was prepared to be what it has become, one of the penitential psalms of the world.

CXXXI.

The most perfect and sincere resignation breathes through this short poem. It is so plain from the last verse, that not an individual, but Israel, is here represented, that we need not stay to discuss the addition to the inscription, which makes David its author (probably with recollection of 2 Sam. vi. 22), or to conjecture whether Nehemiah or Simon Maccabæus, or any other particular person, has left here an expression of his feelings.

1) " Pride has its seat in the heart, looks forth at the eyes, and expresses itself in the actions."

Do I exercise.—Rather, *have I been in the practice of*; literally, *have walked in* (see Vulg.) or *gone into.* The conjugation denotes repeated action, and the past is used, as so frequently, with notion of continuance into the present.

(2) **Surely.**—This seems the best way of rendering the phrase, which literally is *if not*, and is plainly elliptical, being commonly used to express strong asseveration after an oath.

I have behaved . . .—The figure here is plain. It is taken from a baby's first real sorrow when he not merely feels pain, but is allowed no access to that which was his solace hitherto. He moans, and frets, and sobs, but at last is quieted by the love which is powerful to soothe, even when it must deny. So, as George Herbert says of man, "If goodness lead him not, then weariness may toss him to God's breast." But the exact rendering is matter of difference and difficulty. The verb rendered "behave" means *to make equal or like.* This is its meaning, even in Isa. xxxviii. 13, which is the only place referred to by Gesenius in support of his translation here "calmed." We cannot, therefore, render, as many critics, "I calmed and quieted my soul." But, as in Hebrew, it is common to express one idea by the combination of two verbs, so "I made like, and I quieted my soul," is really an idiomatic way of saying "I made as quiet as." The redundancy of the sign of comparison *as* after verbs of likening may be illustrated by Ps. xlix. 12, as well as by the passage in Isaiah referred to above. We thus get: "Surely I made my soul as quiet as a weaned child upon his mother, as a weaned child upon me, my soul." Instead of fretting after what is too great for him, he quiets his ambition, and his spirit lies calm and gentle, like a child in its mother's arms, that after the first trouble of weaning is over is soothed and lulled by the maternal caress. Perhaps the opposite idea, expressed by the common phrase, "to *nurse* ambitious thoughts," may serve to illustrate this somewhat unwonted image. For Israel as a "weaned child," comp. Isa. xxviii. 9.

CXXXII.

This psalm, at first sight, seems from comparison with 2 Chron. vi. to be a hymn of Solomon's, or of his age, in commemoration of the completion and dedication of the Temple. What, however, makes such an obvious conjecture at once suspicious is that David, and not Solomon himself, should figure as the founder and builder of the Temple. Beyond question the psalm is ideal in its treatment of the history, and it is just conceivable that Solomon, who in 2 Chron. vi. is so careful to draw a contrast between his father's project and his own accomplishment of that project, might in a poem have been entirely silent as to his share in the work. A poet of his court would hardly have been so reticent. It is, however hardly credible that Solomon would have blended incidents belonging only to the history of the ark with those relating to the building of his own Temple. Altogether verse 6 clears up only as we take a more and more distant standpoint from the incidents it notes. A very late poet might easily refer the Temple

afflictions: ⁽²⁾ how he sware unto the LORD, *and* vowed unto the mighty *God* of Jacob; ⁽³⁾ surely I will not come into the tabernacle of my house, nor go up into my bed; ⁽⁴⁾ I will not give sleep to mine eyes, *or* slumber to mine eyelids, ⁽⁵⁾ until I find out a place for the LORD, ¹an habitation for the mighty *God* of Jacob.

⁽⁶⁾ Lo, we heard of it at Ephratah: we found it in the fields of the wood. ⁽⁷⁾ We will go into his tabernacles: we will worship at his footstool. ⁽⁸⁾ ᵃArise, O LORD, into thy rest; thou, and the ark of thy strength. ⁽⁹⁾ Let thy priests be clothed with righteousness; and let thy saints shout for joy.

1 Heb., *habitations.*

a Num. 10. 35; 2 Chron. 6. 41.

---

altogether to David, and see in the removal of the ark a step in a prepared design. Other indications, pointing to the Asmonean dynasty as that in whose honour the poem was composed, are alluded to in the notes. The parallelism is very marked, and well sustained.

⁽¹⁾ **Afflictions.**—The word so rendered is the infinitive plural of a verb, which in its first sense means to *declare* or *tell*. It is better to keep this meaning here, "Lord, remember David and all his declarations."

⁽²⁾ **How he sware.**—Literally, *who sware.* The expression "Mighty One of Jacob" is taken from the patriarch himself (Gen. xlix. 24; comp. Isa. i. 24, &c.).

⁽³⁻⁵⁾ It is vain to search the historical accounts for this vow. It may be implied from 2 Sam. vii. 2, and from the persistent purpose which David certainly nourished. The LXX. and Vulg. give the vow in even greater detail, adding, "and rest to my temples."

⁽³⁾ **Tabernacle.**—We have in the mention of *tent* either a reminiscence of the old nomadic times of the race, or an allusion to David's own wandering and warlike habits.

⁽⁴⁾ **I will not.**—For this proverbial expression see Prov. vi. 4.

⁽⁶⁾ **Lo, we heard.**—This verse has been pronounced inexplicable, and yet the general intention is clear. The vow in which David declared his purpose has just been quoted, and that which is now said to have been heard and found can hardly be anything else than this purpose. In fact, the *feminine* suffix to the verbs points directly back to the word rendered *afflictions* in verse 1, which is really a feminine form. This being settled, we need not go from the plain direction of such places as Gen. xxxv. 19, xlviii. 7; Ruth iv. 11; Micah v. 2, which pronounce the identity of Ephratah with Bethlehem, to seek any other locality which might possibly be so called. David's purpose would naturally be connected—especially after a long lapse of time—with the birthplace of his family. But though taking this poetical licence, the psalm keeps sufficiently close to history as to recognise in the discovery of the Ark at Kirjath-jearim an important, nay, a decisive step in the project of building the Temple. Though his purpose may not have been even dimly defined to David when he moved the Ark, history justly sees in that momentous change the initial step in the grander undertaking. That "the fields of the wood" (Heb., *sedey-yā'ar*) is one designation of Kirjath-jearim (city of Yaarim, which went by so many names: Jer. xxvi. 20; Ezra ii. 25; Josh. xv. 10, 11) there can be little doubt. We must not, of course, think here of David's contemporaries, but of those of the psalmist, who poetically are represented as taking important part in the early plans for building the Temple—just as we might say, speaking of our old cathedrals, "we built fine churches in those days." The poet makes them say, identifying themselves with the people of those distant times, while naturally the historical correctness suffers, "We heard his project at Bethlehem; we found out *its* meaning (saw it take shape) at Kirjath-jearim." For *mātsâ*, in the sense of "finding out the meaning or discerning," see Judges xiv. 12, "of a riddle." This sentence reminds one of a riddle by its form.

⁽⁷⁾ **We will.**—*Let us go*, &c.

Tabernacles.—Better, *habitation*, as in verse 5, where the same word is used. The plural occurs also in Ps. lxxxiv. 1. These words do not, as the last verse, recall an incident of the past, but express the determination of the present. The result of David's project is that the present generation have a place of worship. It does not detract from this explanation to refer the psalm to post-exile times, and to the second Temple, since the fact of the existence of a temple at any time could be poetically ascribed to David.

His footstool.—See on Ps. xcix. 5.

⁽⁸⁻¹⁰⁾ These are the words which the chronicler (2 Chron. vi. 41, 42) puts into Solomon's mouth at the dedication of the Temple. Some think that they are there only as a quotation from this psalm, but the mode in which the words are here introduced points the other way. The psalmist does not at his distance from the events distinguish between David and Solomon. He merges the executor of the work in the projector; and in honour of the second Temple it is as natural for him to take up words used at the actual dedication of the first as it was to refer to the original purpose in David's mind. All is blended together in the long perspective of poetry. As to the form of the words, they are of course themselves a reminiscence of the ancient battle-cry of the nation when the Ark set forward on the march. (See Ps. lxviii. 1, Note.) The mention of the Ark does not definitely dispose of the Maccabæan theory of this psalm, though it doubtless must weigh against it. The quotation may have been adopted generally without meaning literal correspondence between all the circumstances—just as the battle-cry had become merely a *religious* formula—or, as Lightfoot and Prideaux suggest (see Prideaux, *Connection*, i. 141), there may have been an ark made for the second Temple in imitation of the original.

⁽⁸⁾ **Ark of thy strength.**—See the reference in Chronicles. The expression occurs nowhere else but in Ps. lxxviii. 61, where the word *strength* by itself denotes the *ark*. The technical word *ark* nowhere else occurs in the psalms. For *strength* the LXX. and Vulg. have "sanctification."

⁽⁹⁾ **Clothed with righteousness.**—The original is "salvation," as below in verse 16, though the Hebrew word is slightly varied. This variation, however, is an almost positive proof that the psalmist, not the chronicler, is adopting words for his own purpose.

(10) For thy servant David's sake turn not away the face of thine anointed. (11) The LORD hath sworn *in* truth unto David; he will not turn from it; *a* Of the fruit of ¹thy body will I set upon thy throne. (12) If thy children will keep my covenant and my testimony that I shall teach them, their children shall also sit upon thy throne for evermore. (13) For the LORD hath chosen Zion; he hath desired *it* for his habitation. (14) This *is* my rest for ever: here will I dwell; for I have desired it. (15) I will ²abundantly bless her provision: I will satisfy her poor with bread. (16) I will also clothe her priests with salvation: and her saints shall shout aloud for joy. (17) *b* There will I make the horn of David to bud: I have ordained a ³lamp for mine anointed. (18) His enemies will I clothe with shame: but upon himself shall his crown flourish.

a 2 Sam. 7. 12; 1 Kings 8. 25; 2 Chron. 6. 16; Luke 1. 69; Acts 2. 30.

1 Heb., *thy belly.*

2 Or, *surely.*

b Luke 1. 69.

3 Or, *candle.*

PSALM CXXXIII.

A Song of degrees of David.

(1) Behold, how good and how pleasant

Possibly the priestly garments are mentioned, not only as symbolic of righteousness, but also as investing whoever possessed them, with supremacy political as well as religious. This is rendered more probable by the express mention of the *diadem* below (verse 18, see Note). "Whoever had these, the priestly paraphernalia, in his possession, had virtually the appointment to the office (high priest)" (Stanley, *J. C.* iii. 353). But if so, the Vulgate of the verse, in the form it has passed from the Breviary into Anglican worship, has amply recovered for the verse its larger and deeper spiritual intention: "Endue Thy ministers with righteousness, and make Thy chosen people joyful."

Saints—*chasidim.* Here very possibly technical of the party so called in the Maccabæan period. (See Note, Ps. xvi. 10.)

(10) The most obvious construction of this verse is that which makes it an intercession, on the ground of the Divine partiality for David, in behalf of another prince—one of his successors—by the people at large. In the original (2 Chron. vi. 42) it is of course Solomon who prays for himself; here (see *Introduction*) we must naturally think of one of the Asmonean princes. The expression "to turn away the face," of a suppliant, instead of "turning from him," is borrowed from court etiquette. (Comp. 1 Kings ii. 16, margin.)

(11) **In truth.**—This is a possible rendering, but it is more impressive to render, *Jehovah hath sworn unto David. It is a true oath; He will not depart from it.* (Comp. Ps. cx. 4.) The substance of the oath which follows is taken from 2 Sam. vii.

(13) **Zion.**—The dynasty of David and the location of the sanctuary at Zion are intimately associated, as in Ps. lxxviii. 67, 68. (Comp. Ps. cxxii. 4, 5.)

(17) **Horn of David.**—The sprouting or growing horn is an image of young, vigorous life. (See Note, Ps. lxxv. 5.) The Messianic application of this prediction comes out in Zechariah's song (Luke i. 69).

I have ordained a lamp.—Or, *I have trimmed a lamp;* the word used in connection with the sacred lights, under the express charge of Aaron and his sons (Exod. xxvii. 21; Lev. xxiv. 2, 3). But with this distinctly sacerdotal allusion we must also combine the special allusion to the Davidic dynasty, according to the promise (1 Kings xi. 36): "That David my servant may have a light (or, *lamp,* as here) always before me in Jerusalem."

(18) **Crown** (*nezer*).—As the distinctive use of this word in Israel—by its derivation meaning *mark of separation*—was for the golden plate, inscribed "Holiness to the Lord," worn on the high priest's mitre (see Exod. xxix. 6, xxxix. 30), we cannot be wrong in seeing here a special allusion to the same. This allusion is rendered more probable by the use of the word rendered "flourish" (properly, *shine*), a cognate to which was the technical name given to this golden plate. (See the reference in Exod. xxix., above.) It is also possibly alluded to in Ps. lxxxix. 39, the only other place in the psalms where the word occurs, though as the word is used of the royal crown in 2 Sam. i. 10, &c., the allusion is not certain. But if the Maccabæan hypothesis is correct, the use of the word, instead of the more usual word for "crown," is interesting. "One relic of the ancient insignia has been preserved which was probably prized as the most precious of all. It was the golden plate affixed to the turban, inscribed 'Holiness to Jehovah,' which was believed to have come down from the time of Aaron, and which, treasured through all the vicissitudes of the Jewish state, was carried to Rome by Titus, and seen there by the great Jewish Rabbi, in the time of Hadrian" (Stanley, *J. C.* iii. 353).

CXXXIII.

The unity, which is in a manner so truly Oriental, eulogised in this poem, is not mere brotherhood, not political or even religious union *generally,* but *unity at Zion,* as the last clause of the beautiful little poem convincingly proves. Nor is it, as most commentators assume, the gathering of the pilgrims at the yearly feast, appropriate though the song would be for such a gathering, and adapted, or at all events arranged, as it doubtless was, for it. The "blessing" (see verse 3), the covenant blessing, which rested on Zion, where was the centre both of the political and religious life of the nation, is the subject of this psalm. For determining the date of the poem, there is not the slightest indication. The inscription may be dismissed as a Rabbinical conjecture. Perhaps we may conjecture that if the psalm had been composed before the exile, when the sacred oil was still in existence, the consecration of the reigning high priest, instead of that of Aaron, might have been selected. The step-like rhythm is just audible.

(1) **In unity.**—Better, *altogether.* The Hebrew particle *gam,* here used with the word "together," is in our version sometimes rendered "yea," when it plainly should be taken with the adjective to intensify it exactly like our "all." (See, for instance, Ps. xxv. 3; 2 Sam. xix. 30.) The common idiom, *gam shenayim,* "all two" (*i.e.,* both), exactly like the French *tous deux,* and the German *alle beide,* decides this. Many commentators, rendering *also together,* see an emphasis on the gathering for the yearly feasts: "How good and

| *The Excellence* | PSALMS, CXXXIV. | *and Pleasantness of Unity.* |

it is for brethren to dwell ¹together in unity! ⁽²⁾ *It is* like the precious ointment upon the head, that ran down upon the beard, *even* Aaron's beard: that went down to the skirts of his garments; ⁽³⁾ as the dew of Hermon, *and as the dew* that descended upon the mountains of Zion: for there the LORD commanded the blessing, *even* life for evermore.

¹ Heb., *even together.*

PSALM CXXXIV.

A Song of degrees.

⁽¹⁾ Behold, bless ye the LORD, all *ye*

---

pleasant for those who are by race and religion brothers to unite for a sacred purpose." The allusion may be there, but the conjecture and purpose of the psalm, and not the form of the expression, suggest it. To a Hebrew, political and religious sentiment were always combined; and Jerusalem was the centre towards which their thoughts and eyes always turned. The translation of the LXX., "to the same place," though not exactly rendering the Hebrew, perhaps brings out the thought, for the poet was plainly thinking of "unity at Zion." This verse was quoted by the Roman legate at the meeting of Anselm and William II. at Windsor, Whitsunday, 1095. It was read at the reception of a new member into the brotherhood of the Knights Templars, and is by St. Augustine quoted as the Divine authority for monastic life.

⁽²⁾ **It is like.**—The italics of the Authorised Version are wrongly inserted. *Unity* could not be said to *flow down.* The other term of the simile is implied in verse 3. (See Note.) Literally, *Like the oil, the good oil, on the head descending upon the beard, Aaron's beard, which (was) descending to the mouth of his robes.* Oil meets us as the standing symbol of joy and festivity. (See Ps. xlv. 7, Note; Isa. lxi. 3.) It is also brought closely into connection with *love* (Song of Sol. i. 3). But while this association, as also the pleasure derived from the fragrance of the oil, would be present here as always in the truly Oriental image, its elaboration in this passage points to a further purpose. It is the holy oil, that whose composition is described in Exod. xxx. 22, 23, that the poet alludes to. This, while the garments of all the priests were *sprinkled* with it (Exod. xxix. 21; Lev. viii. 30), was *poured* on the head of Aaron (Exod. xxix. 7; Lev. viii. 12, xxi. 10), so that the description of the psalm, unpleasing as it is to Western ideas, of the saturation, not only of his head, but of face and beard, was actually true. It would run down his neck to the *collar* of the priestly robe. That this is the meaning of "mouth" here is plain from the actual description of the sacerdotal garments (Exod. xxviii. 31, 32): "And thou shalt make the robe of the ephod all of blue. And there shall be a *mouth* in the top of it, in the midst thereof: and it shall have a binding of woven work round about the *mouth* of it, as it were the *mouth* of a habergeon, that it be not rent." (Comp. Exod. xxix. 23; and Job xxx. 18, where Authorised Version has "collar.") To the ideas of "joy" and "fragrance," therefore, must also be added that of "consecration." But the point of the comparison does not lie even here; nor is it in the *freshness* of the dew, in the next verse, or its *abundance,* though dew suggests both of these (see Note, Ps. cx. 3), but in the word three times repeated—*descending.* Our version unfortunately obscures this point, by rendering this recurrent participle each time by a different word, missing, at the same time, the marked peculiarity of the rhythm of these psalms. The oil descends from Aaron's head over his face and beard; the dew of Hermon descends on Zion—low in actual measurement, but exalted by the Divine favour above the loftiest hills. It is not *unity,* then, in itself which is the subject of the poem, but the unity of the *covenant* under which all blessings *flowed down* from above, rested on Mount Zion. and took outward shape and form there in the political and religious constitution.

⁽³⁾ **As the dew** . . .—Better, keeping the same word as in verse 2. *like the dew of Hermon, which descended on the Mount Zion.* This statement of the dew of a mountain in the *north* descending on a mountain in the *south,* appears so strange and impossible that our version inserted the words, "and as the dew." But the sentence is constructed in exactly the same form as verse 2, and the *dew* on Mount Zion must be as clearly the same dew as that on Mount Hermon, as the oil running down to the beard was the same as that poured on the head. Nor may we take "the mountains of Zion" in a general way for the mountains of the country lying round Hermon like spurs, as Van de Velde does in the passage from his *Travels,* quoted by Delitzsch. Mount Zion itself is intended (comp. Ps. cxxi. 1, cxxv. 2, for this plural) as the last clause, "there Jehovah commanded the blessing," clearly shows. Delitzsch says on the passage, "This feature of the picture is taken from the natural reality, for an abundant dew, when warm days have preceded, might very well be diverted to Jerusalem by the operation of the cold current of air, sweeping down from the north over Hermon. We know, indeed, of our own experience how far a cold air coming from the Alps is perceptible and produces its effects." But setting aside the amount of scientific observation required for such a perception of fact, would any one speak of the dew of Mont Blanc descending on the Jura?

We must evidently take "the dew of Hermon" as a poetical synonym for "choice dew." No doubt the height of Hermon, and the fact of its being so conspicuous, determined the expression. This choice dew, from its freshness, abundance, and its connection with life and growth, is a symbol, as the sacred oil also is, of the covenant blessing in its *nature.* The descent of the moisture offered itself, as the flowing down of the oil did, as an emblem of the *operation* of the blessing. But the conclusion of the simile is only implied. No doubt the poet intended to write, "As the oil poured on Aaron's head flowed down to his beard, and as the dew of Hermon flowed down on Mount Zion, so the covenant blessing descended on Jehovah's people;" but at the mention of Mount Zion he breaks off the simile, to make the statement, "for there Jehovah," &c. Hebrew poetry did not greatly favour the simile, and often confuses it with metaphor. (See Notes, Ps. lviii. 9; Song of Sol. viii. 12.)

CXXXIV.

This little song, with its appeal and its response, fitly closes the Songs of the Steps. It is a challenge to the Levites going on duty for the night to praise Jehovah, as others have already done by day. For the importance of this psalm in deciding the date of the close of the Psalter, see *General Introduction.*

servants of the LORD, which by night stand in the house of the LORD. (2) Lift up your hands ¹*in* the sanctuary, and bless the LORD. (3) The LORD that made heaven and earth bless thee out of Zion.

PSALM CXXXV.

(1) Praise ye the LORD. Praise ye the name of the LORD; praise *him*, O ye servants of the LORD. (2) Ye that stand in the house of the LORD, in the courts of the house of our God, (3) praise the LORD; for the LORD *is* good: sing praises unto his name; for *it is* pleasant. (4) For the LORD hath chosen Jacob unto himself, *and* Israel for his peculiar treasure. (5) For I know that the LORD *is* great, and *that* our Lord *is* above all gods. (6) Whatsoever the LORD pleased, *that* did he in heaven, and in earth, in the seas, and all deep places. (7) *ᵃ*He causeth the vapours to ascend from the ends of the earth; he maketh lightnings for the rain; he bringeth the wind out of his treasuries.

(8) *ᵇ*Who smote the firstborn of Egypt, ²both of man and beast. (9) *Who* sent tokens and wonders into the midst of thee, O Egypt, upon Pharaoh, and upon all his servants. (10) *ᶜ*Who smote great nations, and slew mighty kings; (11)Sihon king of the Amorites, and Og king of Bashan, and all the kingdoms of Canaan: (12) *ᵈ*and gave their land *for* an heritage, an heritage unto Israel his people. (13) Thy name, O LORD, *endureth* for ever; *and* thy memorial, O LORD, ³throughout all generations. (14) For the LORD will judge his people, and he will repent himself concerning his servants. (15) *ᵉ*The idols of the heathen *are* silver and gold, the work of men's hands. (16) They have mouths, but they speak not; eyes have they, but they see not; (17) they have ears, but they hear not; neither is there *any* breath in their mouths. (18) They that make them are like unto them: *so is* every one that trusteth in them. (19) Bless the LORD, O house of Israel:

---

1 Or, *in holiness.*

a Jer. 10. 13.

b Ex. 12. 29.

2 Heb., *from man unto beast.*

c Num. 21. 24, 25, 26, 34, 35.

d Josh. 12. 7.

3 Heb., *to generation and generation.*

e Ps. 115. 4, 5, 6, 7, 8.

---

(1) **All ye servants.**—We learn from 1 Chron. ix. 33 that there were Levites whose duties brought them to the Temple by night. Moreover, the word *'âmad*, "stand," is the customary word for sacerdotal service (Deut. x. 8, xviii. 7; 1 Chron. xxiii. 30, &c.).

(2) **Lift up your hands** (see Note, Ps. xxviii. 2) (in) **the sanctuary.**—The usual meaning would be *to the sanctuary* (see reference above), but since the servants of Jehovah are here addressed as standing *in* the sanctuary, this direction seems unreasonable. Render, therefore, *in holiness*, and comp. "lifting up holy hands" (1 Tim. ii. 8).

(3) **Made heaven and earth.**—For this style, as frequent in this group of psalms, see Ps. cxxi. 2.

CXXXV.

This psalm is a mosaic from older writings, and was plainly put together for liturgic use. It pretends to no originality, and shows very little art or care in the composition. The date must be very late.

(1) The psalm opens with an adaptation and expansion (comp. Ps. cxvi. 19) of Ps. cxxxiv. 1. As there, the priestly class is addressed. Some, however, think that the addition, "courts of the house of our God," as well as verse 19, make the application to all these standing in covenant relation to Jehovah. This is possible, but not proved by the evidence adduced.

(3) **Sing praises.**—Rather, *play.*

For it is pleasant—*i.e.*, thus to sing hallelujah. (See Ps. cxlvii. 1; Prov. xxii. 18. Others take *name* as the subject, and the Prayer-Book version suggested to Crashaw the beautiful hymn beginning "Come lovely name," &c.

(4) **Peculiar treasure.**—A special covenant-name for Israel (Exod. xix. 5; Deut. vii. 6, &c.), and of private **property** (1 Chron. xxix. 3; Eccles. ii. 8).

(5, 6) Adapted from Ps. cxv. 3.
(7) Adapted from Jer. x. 13, li. 16.

Causeth the vapours to ascend.—Mr. Burgess is undoubtedly right in referring this to the *mist* which went up from the earth, and watered the whole face of the ground "before the useful trouble of the rain" (Gen. ii. 6), since the original passage in Genesis has a plain reference to the story of the Creation, and the *rain* is immediately mentioned as coming into existence after the *vapours*. That a different term is used in Genesis does not make against this since the Hebrew term here is a general one derived from the verb "to ascend."

Lightnings for the rain—*i.e.*, "to bring rain." Such was the Oriental notion, see Zech. x. 1 and compare 1 Sam. xii. 17. Both of these places refer to showers out of the ordinary rainy season, such as thunder-storms in the harvest season. The sudden downfall of sheets of rain after a flash and peal is even in this climate sufficiently striking to make such a notion as the dependence of rain on lightning quite conceivable, how much more in tropical countries, and where, except in the due rainy season, it would never probably fall without thunder and lightning.

Wind out of his treasuries.—Comp. the Greek and Latin ideas of the "caves" of the winds.

(8) **Egypt.**—This abrupt change from the miracles of nature to the marvels of history is apparently copied from the next psalm, where see Note, verse 10.

(12) Ps. cv. 44, cxi. 6.
(13) This verse is from Exod. iii. 15.
(14) From Deut. xxxii. 36.

Judge—*i.e.*, see them righted.

(15, 16) With slight variations from Ps. cxv. 4—8.

(19, 21) From Ps. cxv. 9—11, with the addition, "O house of Levi."

bless the LORD, O house of Aaron: ⁽²⁰⁾ bless the LORD, O house of Levi: ye that fear the LORD, bless the LORD. ⁽²¹⁾ Blessed be the LORD out of Zion, which dwelleth at Jerusalem. Praise ye the LORD.

PSALM CXXXVI.

⁽¹⁾ O ^agive thanks unto the LORD; for he is good: for his mercy *endureth* for ever. ⁽²⁾ O give thanks unto the God of gods: for his mercy *endureth* for ever. ⁽³⁾ O give thanks to the Lord of lords: for his mercy *endureth* for ever.
⁽⁴⁾ To him who alone doeth great wonders: for his mercy *endureth* for ever. ⁽⁵⁾ ^bTo him that by wisdom made the heavens: for his mercy *endureth* for ever. ⁽⁶⁾ ^cTo him that stretched out the earth above the waters: for his mercy *endureth* for ever. ⁽⁷⁾ ^dTo him that made great lights: for his mercy *endureth* for ever: ⁽⁸⁾ the sun ¹to rule by day: for his mercy *endureth* for ever: ⁽⁹⁾ the moon and stars to rule by night: for his mercy *endureth* for ever.
⁽¹⁰⁾ ^eTo him that smote Egypt in their firstborn: for his mercy *endureth* for ever: ⁽¹¹⁾ ^fand brought out Israel from among them: for his mercy *endureth* for ever: ⁽¹²⁾ with a strong hand, and with a stretched out arm: for his mercy *endureth* for ever.
⁽¹³⁾ ^gTo him which divided the Red sea into parts: for his mercy *endureth* for ever: ⁽¹⁴⁾ and made Israel to pass through the midst of it: for his mercy *endureth* for ever: ⁽¹⁵⁾ ^hbut ²overthrew Pharaoh and his host in the Red sea: for his mercy *endureth* for ever.
⁽¹⁶⁾ ⁱTo him which led his people through the wilderness: for his mercy *endureth* for ever. ⁽¹⁷⁾ To him which smote great kings: for his mercy *endureth* for ever: ⁽¹⁸⁾ ^jand slew famous kings: for his mercy *endureth* for ever: ⁽¹⁹⁾ ^kSihon king of the Amorites: for his mercy *endureth* for ever: ⁽²⁰⁾ ^l and Og the king of Bashan: for his mercy *endureth* for ever: ⁽²¹⁾ ^mand gave their land for an heritage: for his mercy *endureth* for ever: ⁽²²⁾ even an heritage unto Israel his servant: for his mercy *endureth* for ever.
⁽²³⁾ Who remembered us in our low estate: for his mercy *endureth* for ever: ⁽²⁴⁾ and hath redeemed us from our enemies: for his mercy *endureth* for ever. ⁽²⁵⁾ Who giveth food to all flesh: for his mercy *endureth* for ever.
⁽²⁶⁾ O give thanks unto the God of heaven: for his mercy *endureth* for ever.

⁽²¹⁾ **Out of Zion.**—As in Ps. cxxviii. 5, Jehovah blesses the covenant people out of Zion, so here they bless him out of Zion—that is the place where the reciprocal relation is best and chiefly realised. This localisation is made more emphatic by the addition of the name Jerusalem to Zion. (Comp. Pss. lxxvi. 2, cxxv. 1, 2.)

CXXXVI.

The recurrence in this psalm of the ancient liturgic refrain (see Notes, Pss. cvi. 1, cxviii. 1), not after every verse, but after every clause, marks clearly the peculiarity of its choral use, and shows that it was composed expressly for the Temple service. It is invariably allowed to be one of the latest hymns in the collection. It has generally been known among the Jews as the Great Hallel, a designation, however, at other times given to the series Pss. cxx.—cxxxvi. (according to others Pss. cxxxv. 4—cxxxvi.).

^(2, 3) **God of gods . . . Lord of Lords.**—From Deut. x. 17.

⁽⁴⁾ Ps. lxxii. 18.

⁽⁵⁾ **By wisdom.**—From Ps. civ. 24, Prov. iii. 19, or Jer. x. 12.

⁽⁶⁾ While this section in many points recalls the account of creation in Genesis, it employs terms from other parts of Scripture.

Stretched out.—A word and idea peculiar to Isaiah and this psalm (Isa. xlii. 5, xliv. 24); properly to beat out with the feet, then to overlay with a plate of metal (Isa. xl. 12). The earth is regarded as a flat plate that has been beaten out and spread on the face of the waters, whereas in Genesis it is pictured as emerging out of the waters.

⁽⁷⁾ **Lights.**—An unusual word, meaning *light* itself, and not *luminaries*. But possibly the poet wished in one phrase to combine Gen. i. 3 and 14, 15.

⁽¹⁰⁾ **For his mercy.**—Here the refrain, after the mention of the destruction of the Egyptian first-born, and subsequently after that of war and slaughter, sounds harsh to Christian ears. But the word mercy (*khesed*) in the Hebrew motto implies distinctly *covenant grace*, that special favour of Jehovah in which the heathen did not share, and which was often most signally shown in their destruction.

⁽¹⁹⁾ **Sihon.**—Literally, *to Sihon*. Evidently the composer, after beginning so many verses with the preposition, placed it here inadvertently, whence it was copied in Ps. cxxxv. 11.

⁽²⁴⁾ **Redeemed.**—Better, as in original, *snatched us from*. (Comp. Ps. vii. 2, used of a lion suddenly seizing his prey.)

⁽²⁵⁾ **All flesh.**—Here apparently the word *mercy* takes a wider image and applies to all men. But only apparently so. Israel could think of Jehovah providing for the bodily wants of all as He was the creator of all, but the covenant grace was for them alone.

⁽²⁶⁾ **God of heaven.**—See Neh. i. 4, ii. 4. This title, though implied in Ps. xi. 4 and similar passages, was not used before the exile. Away from Zion and

The Sorrows of   PSALMS, CXXXVII.   *the Captivity.*

PSALM CXXXVII.

(1) By the rivers of Babylon, there we sat down, yea, we wept, when we remembered Zion. (2) We hanged our harps upon the willows in the midst thereof. (3) For there they that carried us away captive required of us ¹a song; and they that ²wasted us *required of us* mirth, *saying,* Sing us *one* of the songs of Zion.

(4) How shall we sing the LORD's song in a ³strange land?

(5) If I forget thee, O Jerusalem, let my right hand forget *her cunning.* (6) If I do not remember thee, let my tongue cleave to the roof of my mouth; if I prefer not Jerusalem above ⁴my chief joy.

(7) Remember, O LORD, *ᵃ*the children of Edom in the day of Jerusalem; who said, ⁵Rase *it,* rase *it, even* to the foundation thereof. (8) O daughter of Babylon, who art to be ⁶destroyed; happy *shall he be,* ⁷that rewardeth thee as thou hast

---

Marginal notes:
1 Heb., *the words of a song.*
2 Heb., *laid us on heaps.*
3 Heb., *land of a stranger?*
4 Heb., *the head of my joy.*
a Obad. 10, &c.
5 Heb., *Make bare.*
6 Heb., *wasted.*
7 Heb., *that recompenseth unto thee thy deed which thou didst to us.*

---

the visible token of the Divine presence, the hearts of the faithful began more and more to dream of their God as

    "One that His mansion hath on high
    Above the reach of mortal eye."

At the end the Vulgate repeats verse 3. (See Prayer Book.)

CXXXVII.

This fine song, blended as it is of tears and fire, with its plaintive opening and its vindictive close, is one of the clearest records left in Hebrew literature of the captivity, but whether it dates immediately from it, or looks back with a distant though keen and clear gaze, is difficult to decide. Babylon may only have been on the verge of its doom, or she may already have fallen. (See Note on verse 8.) It is possible that just as long afterwards another great power was symbolised under the name, so here the ruin of the Persian or Grecian dominion may be covertly invoked under the symbol "daughter of Babylon." The rhythm characteristic of the "songs of degrees" reappears here.

The LXX. prefix a curious title "To David of Jeremiah;" Vulg., "Psalmus David Jeremias," which has been explained "a David-like song by Jeremiah."

(1) **By the rivers . . .**—Mentioned as the characteristic feature of the country, as we say "among the mountains of Wales." The canals which irrigated Babylonia made it what an ancient writer called it, the greatest of "cities of river places."

(2) **Willows.**—It is perhaps not necessary to attempt to identify the trees mentioned in this verse, since the touching picture may only be a poetical way of expressing the silence during the exile of all the religious and festal songs. The '*ereb*' is certainly not the *willow*, a tree not found in Babylonia, but the *poplar* (*Populus Euphraticus*).

(3) **A song.**—See margin. The expression is generally regarded as pleonastic, but may be explained as in Ps. cv. 27, where see Note. Perhaps "some lyric thing" would express the original. No doubt it is a Levite who is requested to sing.

They that wasted us.—A peculiar Hebrew word which the LXX. and Vulg. take as synonymous with the verb in the first clause. The modern explanation, "they that make us howl," is far preferable. Those whose oppression had raised the wild Oriental scream of lamentation, now asked for mirth.

Songs of Zion—or, as in the next verse, *songs of Jehovah*, were of course the liturgical hymns. Nothing is more characteristic than this of the Hebrew feeling. The captors asked for a national song, as the Philistines asked for sport from Samson, to amuse them.

The Hebrew can think only of one kind of song, that to which the genius of the race was dedicated.

(4) **Strange land.**—The feeling expressed in this question is too natural to need any such explanation as that it was contrary to the Law to sing a sacred song in a strange land. Nehemiah's answer (Neh. ii. 2, 3) offers a direct illustration.

Of Jerusalem's choir in Babylon it might truly be said:

    "Like strangers' voices here they sound,
    In lands where not a memory strays,
    Nor landmark breathes of other days,
    But all is new unhallowed ground."
                  TENNYSON: *In Memoriam.*

(5) **Her cunning**—*i.e.,* the skill of playing on the harp. If at such a moment the poet can so far forget the miserable bondage of Jerusalem as to strike the strings in joy, may his hand for ever lose the skill to touch them.

(7) **Remember . . .**—*Remember, Jehovah, for the children of Edom the day of Jerusalem.* The prophecy of Obadiah gives the best comment on this verse: "For thy violence against thy brother Jacob shame shall cover thee, and thou shalt be cut off for ever. In the day that thou stoodest on the other side, in the day that the strangers carried away captive his forces, and foreigners entered into his gates and cast lots upon Jerusalem, even thou wast as one of them. But thou shouldest not have looked on the day of thy brother in the day that he became a stranger; neither shouldest thou have rejoiced over the children of Judah in the day of their destruction; neither shouldest thou have spoken proudly in the day of distress" (Obadiah, verses 10—12.) (See Excursus on the date and authorship of that book.)

Rase . . .—Literally, *make naked or bare.* (Comp. a similar use of another verb, Micah i. 6.) The LXX. and Vulg. have "empty out, empty out."

Thereof.—Literally, *in it.*

(8) **Daughter of Babylon**—*i.e.,* Babylon itself. (See Ps. ix. 14, Note.)

Who art to be destroyed.—Considerable doubt attaches to the meaning of the Hebrew word here. Our version is that of Theodotion. Aquila and Jerome have "wasted" (comp. Prayer Book version); Symmachus, "robber;" the LXX. and Vulg., "wretched."

As pointed, the word is a passive participle, and must be rendered as by Aquila, "wasted" or "destroyed," but with the recollection that a Hebrew would thus speak proleptically of a doom foreseen though not accomplished. Delitzsch quotes an Arab saying: "Pursue the caught one"—*i.e.,* sure to be caught.

The "luxury of revenge" is well expressed in this beatitude, pronounced on him who can carry out to all its bitter end the *lex talionis*. Commentators have

served us. (9) Happy *shall he be*, that taketh and ^adasheth thy little ones against ¹the stones.

PSALM CXXXVIII.

A Psalm of David.

(1) I will praise thee with my whole heart: ^bbefore the gods will I sing praise unto thee. (2) I will worship toward thy holy temple, and praise thy name for thy lovingkindness and for thy truth: for thou hast magnified thy word above all thy name.

(3) In the day when I cried thou answeredst me, *and* strengthenedst me *with* strength in my soul.

(4) All the kings of the earth shall praise thee, O LORD, when they hear the words of thy mouth. (5) Yea, they shall sing in the ways of the LORD: for great *is* the glory of the LORD.

(6) Though the LORD *be* high, yet hath he respect unto the lowly: but the proud he knoweth afar off. (7) Though I walk in the midst of trouble, thou wilt revive me: thou shalt stretch forth thine hand against the wrath of mine enemies, and thy right hand shall save me.

(8) The LORD will perfect *that which* concerneth me: thy mercy, O LORD, *endureth* for ever: forsake not the works of thine own hands.

a Isa. 13. 16.

¹ Heb., *the rock*.

b Ps. 119. 46.

---

in turn tried to disguise and justify the expression of passion. Happily the Bible allows us to see men as they were without taking their rules of feeling and conduct as ours. "The psalm is beautiful as a poem—the Christian must seek his inspiration elsewhere."

(9) **Little ones.**—Literally, *sucklings*.

Stones.—Better, *cliff* or *rock*.

For this feature of barbarous cruelty with which ancient war was cursed see 2 Kings viii. 12; Isa. xiii. 16; Hosea x. 14, &c.; and comp. Homer, *Iliad*, xxii. 63:

"My bleeding infants dashed against the floor."

CXXXVIII.

The suggestion contained in the last addition made to the Hebrew inscription by the LXX., "Of Haggai and Zechariah," brings this psalm within the post-exile period, the most likely time of its composition. The tone and tenor are what we should look for if Zerubbabel or Nehemiah were its author. Some great success had evidently just been gained (verses 1—5); but trouble still pressed on the community for whom the poet speaks—some work of pressing need was impeded, and Jehovah's strong hand could alone bring it to completion. This would suit the times of Ezra and Nehemiah.

On the other hand, the achievement already performed may have been of a military kind, and the psalm may breathe the hopes of the Maccabæan period. The poetical form is nearly regular and the rhythm stately, as suits the subject.

(1) **Before the gods.**—Undoubtedly, as in Ps. lxxxii. 1: "before the great" or "mighty." (Comp. Ps. cxix. 46, "before kings.")

Sing praise.—Rather, *play*.

(2) Notice that "loving-kindness" and "truth" are joined as inseparable attributes of Jehovah in His relation to the chosen race.

For thou hast magnified—*i.e.*, the promise made for help and deliverance has been fulfilled, and more than fulfilled. The psalmist often speaks of *Jehovah's name*, or *reputation*, or *honour* being at stake. Here the poet can say that the praise won is even beyond what might have been expected. It is true this would have been expressed more in accordance with our expectation by "Thou hast magnified Thy Name above Thy promise;" but comp. Ps. xlviii. 10 for a similar thought, and for the language comp. Tennyson's :

"I am become a name."

The LXX. and Vulg. felt the difficulty too great, and render "Thy holy one," instead of "Thy word."

(3) **Strengthenedst me with strength.**—Or, *encouragest me strongly*. (See Note to Song of Sol. vi. 5, where the same Hebrew form occurs.)

In my soul.—Or, *at my desire*.

(4, 5) The general sense of these verses is plain, though there are slightly different ways of understanding the expressions. The psalmist imagines that the word or *promise*, which has been so abundantly fulfilled, will, by its performance, convince all the kings of the earth, and bring them in confession and praise to Jehovah. For a Hebrew the expression "hear the words of Thy mouth," referring in this instance immediately back to verse 2, was synonymous with "see Thy wonders," since for them "God spoke and it was done."

(5) **In the ways.**—Rather, *of the ways*, this preposition being so used frequently after verbs of speaking praising (comp. Pss. xx. 7, xliv. 8, lxxxvii. 3, cv. 2), though there is no parallel instance of such a use with this particular verb *sing*.

For *ways* used of God's mighty works in creation see Job xxvi. 14, xl. 19; of His action in history, Ps. xviii. 30; Deut. xxxii. 4. It seems against the parallelism to understand literally that the heathen kings would come to walk in God's ways—*i.e.*, in righteousness, and so praise Him, as in Micah iv. 2. The meaning is that heathen monarchs will be compelled to acknowledge the glory of Jehovah.

(6) **Knoweth afar off.**—Or, *recognises from afar*. From His exaltation Jehovah looks down alike on the lowly and on the proud, but it is to show a gracious interest in the former, while the latter are merely marked as persons to be kept at a distance. "Lowliness and humility are the court dress of God; he who wears them will please Him well."

(7) This verse echoes Pss. xxiii. 4, xxx. 3, lxxi. 20.

Against the wrath. — Or perhaps, *upon the wrath*.

(8) **Perfect that which concerneth me.**—Or, as in the analogous phrase (Ps. lvii. 2), *will complete for me*—*i.e.*, either "all my undertakings," or, as in Phil. i. 6, "what he has begun in and for me."

Forsake not.—Better, *the works of Thine hands; do not leave them unfinished.* (See for the same verb Neh. vi. 3; Prov. iv. 13: "let her not go.")

PSALM CXXXIX.

To the chief Musician, A Psalm of David.

(1) O Lord, thou hast searched me, and known me. (2) Thou knowest my downsitting and mine uprising, thou understandest my thought afar off. (3) Thou ¹compassest my path and my lying down, and art acquainted *with* all my ways. (4) For *there is* not a word in my tongue, *but*, lo, O Lord, thou knowest it altogether. (5) Thou hast beset me behind and before, and laid thine hand upon me. (6) *Such* knowledge *is* too wonderful for me; it is high, I cannot *attain* unto it. (7) Whither shall I go from thy spirit? or whither shall I flee from thy presence? (8) ᵃIf I ascend up into heaven, thou *art* there: if I make my bed in hell, behold, thou *art there*. (9) If I take the wings of the morning, *and* dwell

¹ Or, *winnowest*.

ᵃ Amos 9. 2, 3, 4.

The special intention of the prayer depends on the origin of the psalm. If it arose out of the troubles of rebuilding Jerusalem and reconstituting the state, it is intelligible and expressive. Or the reference may be to all Jehovah's gracious intentions for Israel.

CXXXIX.

This psalm falls into four strophes unequal in length, but clearly marked. Had it ended at the third it could have been easily described as a poem on the omniscience and omnipresence of God, and though many of the expressions that have been used about this psalm would seem extravagant if repeated, yet it would be acknowledged by all as one of the sublimest in the whole collection. In its tone it is personal and reflective rather than speculative, and yet some of the profoundest metaphysical questions are touched, or at least suggested, and as we read we feel at every moment that we stand on the verge of the discovery of weighty truths concerning God's nature and his relation to man. But suddenly, as only a Hebrew poet could do, the writer breaks away from the subject, to denounce ungodly men with a storm of indignation nowhere surpassed. For the explanation of this see Note to verse 19.

The superscription ascribing the psalm to David must be abandoned in the face not only of the strong Aramaic colouring of the psalm, but also of the development of its eschatology, which marks a late epoch. It is certainly as late as the latest in the collection. Though not sustained throughout, the parallelism is exceptionally fine.

Title.—See Title, Ps. iv.

The Codex Alex. of the LXX. adds, "of Zechariah," and a later hand, "on the dispersion."

(1) **Searched . . .**—Comp. Ps. xliv. 21, "shall not God search this out." The word is used of mining operations, Job xxviii. 3; of exploring a country, Judges xviii. 2.

(2) **Down-sitting and uprising**—as in Deut. vi. 7, to denote the whole daily life—business and rest.

Thought.—An Aramaic form found nowhere else, but, from one possible derivation ("companion"), meaning the thoughts which are inseparable companions, *most intimate thoughts.* Comp. *Macbeth* iii. 2:

"How now, my lord? Why do you keep alone,
Of sorriest fancies your companions making?"

Afar off.—Exactly as in Ps. cxxxviii. 6. Jehovah notes and recognises the proud from afar off, so here though He has His home in heaven He knows what are the thoughts and feelings amid which a man habitually lives. (Comp. Job xxii. 12, 13.) The Hebrew expression literally means, *thou hast intelligence as to my thought from afar,* an Aramaic expression.

(3) **Compassest.**—There is some obscurity about this word. The Hebrew verb means first *to scatter,* and is used of throwing corn about to winnow it (Isa. xxx. 24; Jer. iv. 11; Ruth iii. 2). Hence by an easy metaphor it may mean *to sift* or *search out.* The LXX. and Theodotion, followed by the Vulg., have *traced, investigated.* Jerome has *winnowed.* The Authorised Version rendering appears to come from a mistaken etymology.

A most plausible suggestion connects the verb with *zûr, to lodge,* which makes a perfect parallelism with the verb *to dwell,* in the next clause. Literally,

About my path and bed thou art a guest,
In all my ways thou dwellest;

i.e., art as familiar with all my life as one inhabiting the same house could be.

My path.—Literally, *my going.*

(4) **For there is not . . .**—This has been understood in two ways:—

My tongue cannot utter a word which thou dost not altogether know.

or,

Before my tongue can utter a word thou knowest it altogether.

(5) **Beset**—as a beleaguered city from which there is no escape.

(6) **Such . . .**—God's omniscience is for man at once *transcendent, unattainable, impossible.* Possibly the article has dropped away, and we should read *this knowledge.* LXX. and Vulg. have "thy knowledge."

For the thought comp. verses 17, 18, and Romans xi. 33.

(7) **Spirit.**—If this clause stood alone we should naturally understand by God's *Spirit* His creative and providential power, from which nothing can escape (comp. Ps. civ. 30). But taken in parallelism with *presence* in the next clause the expression leads on to a thought towards which the theology of the Old Testament was dimly feeling, which it nearly reached in the Book of Wisdom. "The Spirit of the Lord filleth the world," but which found its perfect expression in our Saviour's announcement to the woman of Samaria.

(8) **If I make my bed in hell.**—Literally, *If I make Sheôl my bed.* (For the thought see Amos ix. 2, and comp. Prov. xv. 11; Job xxvi. 6.)

This conviction that the underworld was not exempt from the vigilance and even from the visitation of Jehovah makes an advance in thought from Ps. vi. 5 (where see Note), &c., where death is viewed as cutting off the Hebrew altogether from his relation to the Theocracy.

(9) **If . . .**—Literally,

I lift wings of dawn
I dwell in the end of the sea.

in the uttermost parts of the sea; (10) even there shall thy hand lead me, and thy right hand shall hold me. (11) If I say, Surely the darkness shall cover me; even the night shall be light about me. (12) Yea, ªthe darkness ¹hideth not from thee; but the night shineth as the day: ²the darkness and the light *are* both alike *to thee.*

(13) For thou hast possessed my reins:

ª Job 26. 6; Heb. 4. 13.
¹ Heb., *darkeneth not.*
² Heb., *as is the darkness, so is the light.*
³ Heb., *greatly.*
⁴ Or, *strength, or, body.*

thou hast covered me in my mother's womb. (14) I will praise thee; for I am fearfully *and* wonderfully made: marvellous *are* thy works; and *that* my soul knoweth ³right well. (15) My ⁴substance was not hid from thee, when I was made in secret, *and* curiously wrought in the lowest parts of the earth. (16) Thine eyes did see my substance, yet being unper-

The wings of the morning.—This exquisite image suggesting not only the pinions of cloud that seem often to lift the dawn into the sky, but also the swift sailing of the light across the world, may be compared to the "wings of the sun" in Mal. iv. 2, and the "wings of the wind" in Ps. xviii. 10.

The uttermost parts of the sea—*i.e.*, to a Hebrew *the extreme west.* The poet imagines himself darting from east to farthest west, with the rapidity of light.

(10) **Even there . . .**—The expressions "lead me," "hold me," are elsewhere used of the protecting and guiding providence of God (Pss. v. 8, xxiii. 3, xxvii. 11, lxxiii. 24). And yet the psalmist speaks here as if he were a guilty being trying to escape from the Divine notice. The truth is a profound one. Even when God discovers and overtakes those who guiltily try to hide from Him, it is to take them under His loving care.

(11) **If I say . . .**—Rather,

I say only let darkness crush me,
And light become night around me.

Commentators have mostly been frightened by the metaphor in the first line, though it has been preserved both by the LXX. and Vulg., and can only be avoided either by forcing the meaning of the verb from what it bears in Gen. iii. 15, Job ix. 17, or altering the text. Yet the Latins could speak even in prose of a region "oppressed by darkness" (Sen. *Ep.* 82); and when night was used as figurative of death, *nocte premi* was a common poetical figure. Indeed, the word rendered *darkness* here is actually, in Ps. lxxxviii. 6, used of *death*, and if we understood this figure here we might render the word *trample*, illustrating by Horace

"Jam te premet nox fabulæque Manes."

Such a view would suit the thought to which the poet immediately passes—to God the darkness of death and the nothingness before birth are alike. On the other hand, as the main thought is that nowhere is there escape from God's sight in height, or depth, or distance so to exhaust the possibilities we seem to need, *darkness*.

The second clause does not begin the apodosis: it is in synthetic parallelism with the first.

(12) **Hideth not.**—Better to keep as near as possible to the original *maketh not dark.* Others render *cannot be too dark for thee.* The highest development of the psalmist's thought is of course to be found in St. John's declaration, "God is light and in Him is no darkness at all."

Shineth.—Or, *giveth* light.

The darkness . . .—Literally, *as darkness, so light.*

"God is the light which, never seen itself, makes all things visible, and clothes itself in colours."—RICHTER.

(13) **For . . .**—The mystery of birth regarded as one of the greatest mysteries (see Eccl. xi. 5), is a proof of God's omniscience.

Possessed.—The context seems to require *formed, fashioned*, as, according to Gesenius, in Deut. xxxii. 6, (Authorised Version "bought") (Comp. Gen. xiv. 19, where *maker* should be read for possessor.)

For "reins" see Ps. xvi. 7.

Covered me.—Most critics render here *didst weave me.* (Comp. Job x. 11.) But the usual sense of the word *cover* or *protect*, suits equally well. The prime thought is that every birth is a divine creation.

(14) **For I am . . .**—Literally, *because I am fearfully separated* or *distinguished* (see Note on Pss. xxvi. 7, xl. 5), which might mean *separated from the womb, i.e., born.* (Comp. Gal. i. 15; Ps. xxii. 10.) Or if the reference is national rather than individual, it would imply, as so frequently, the choice of Israel by Jehovah in distinction to other races.

(15) **Substance.**—Aquila "bones," LXX. and Vulg. "bone," Symmachus "strength." Perhaps, generally, *body.* But the common Hebrew word for bone differs only in the pointing.

In secret.—Comp. Æsch. *Eum.* 665.

Curiously wrought.—From the use of the verb in Exod. xxvi. 36, xxvii. 16, it plainly refers to some kind of tapestry work, but whether of the nature of weaving or embroidery is matter of controversy. The English sufficiently suggests the figure.

In the lowest parts of the earth.—This figurative allusion to the womb is intended no doubt to heighten the feeling of mystery attaching to birth. There may also be a covert allusion to the creation from dust as Ecclus. xl. 1, "From the day that they go out of their mother's womb, till the day that they return to the mother of all things." This allusion falls in with the view which meets us in other parts of the Old Testament, that the creation of Adam is repeated at every birth (Job xxxiii. 6, and see above, verse 13).

Others, since the expression "lowest places of the earth" is used of the unseen world (Ps. lxiii. 9; comp. lxxxvi. 13), see here a confirmation of the view that the state before birth and after death are in this poem regarded as the dark void of night, with all the recesses of which, however, God is acquainted. (Comp. the expressions "Womb of Sheôl," "Belly of hell," Jonah ii. 2; Ecclus. li. 5.)

(16) This difficult verse, rendered word for word, gives—

"My fœtus (literally, *rolled*) saw thine eyes,
And on thy book all of them were written;
Days were formed, and not (or, as the Hebrew margin, *to him*) one in them."

The reading "substance yet being imperfect" of the Authorised Version follows the LXX. and Vulg., and (Symmachus, "shapeless thing") periphrastically de-

God's Thoughts Precious.   PSALMS, CXXXIX.   *Denunciation of the Wicked.*

fect; and in thy book ¹ all *my members* were written, ²*which* in continuance were fashioned, when *as yet there was* none of them. ⁽¹⁷⁾ ᵃ How precious also are thy thoughts unto me, O God! how great is the sum of them. ⁽¹⁸⁾ *If* I should count them, they are more in number than the sand: when I awake, I am still with thee.

⁽¹⁹⁾ Surely thou wilt slay the wicked, O God: depart from me therefore, ye bloody men. ⁽²⁰⁾ For they speak against thee wickedly, *and* thine enemies take *thy name* in vain. ⁽²¹⁾ Do not I hate them, O LORD, that hate thee? and am not I grieved with those that rise up against thee? ⁽²²⁾ I hate them with perfect hatred: I count them mine enemies. ⁽²³⁾ Search me, O God, and know my heart: try me, and know my thoughts: ⁽²⁴⁾ And see if *there be any* ³wicked way in me, and lead me in the way everlasting.

---

1 Heb., *all of them.*
2 Or, *what days they should be fashioned.*
ᵃ Ps. 40. 5.
3 Heb., *way of pain, or, grief.*

---

notes the *embryo*, which the Hebrew word—literally, *rolled*, or *wrapped*, used in 2 Kings ii. 8, " of a mantle," in Ezekiel xxvii. 24, " bales " (Authorised Version, " clothes; " margin, " foldings ")—almost scientifically describes. (Comp. Job x. 8—12; 2 Macc. vii. 22.)

Others take it of the ball of the threads of destiny; but this is not a Hebrew conception. By inserting the word *members*, the Authorised Version suggests a *possible*, but not a probable, interpretation. The Hebrew language likes to use a pronoun before the word to which it refers has occurred (see Note, Ps. lxviii. 14); and, in spite of the accents, we must refer *all of them* to "days" (Authorised Version, "in continuance").

" Thine eyes beheld my embryo,
And in thy book were written
All the days, the days
Which were being formed,
When as yet there were none of them."

But a much more satisfactory sense is obtained by adopting one slight change and following Symmachus in the last line—

" The days which are all reckoned, and not one of them is wanting."

All the ancient versions make that which is written in God's book either the days of life, or men born in the course of these days, each coming into being according to the Divine will.

⁽¹⁷⁾ **Precious.**—Rather, *weighty*, the first meaning of the word. The parallelism requires this, as also the peculiar word for "thoughts," for which see verse 2. We have here the antithesis to that verse: while the Divine penetration discovers the most intimate thought of man, man finds God's secrets incomprehensible.

⁽¹⁸⁾ **If I should . . .**—The original is more expressive:—

" Let me count them—more than the sand they are many:
I have awaked—and still with thee."

With the countless mysteries of creation and providence the poet is so occupied, that they are his first waking thought; or, perhaps, as the Hebrew suggests, his dreams are continued into his early thoughts.

" Is not the vision He? (ho' He be not that which He seems?
Dreams are true while they last; and do we not live in dreams?"
               TENNYSON: *Higher Pantheism.*

⁽¹⁹⁾ **Slay the wicked.**—This abrupt transition from a theme so profound and fascinating to fierce indignation against the enemies of God, would certainly be strange anywhere but in the Psalms. And yet, perhaps, philosophically regarded, the subject of God's omniscience must conduct the mind to the thought of the existence of evil, and speculation on its origin and development. But the Hebrew never speculated for speculation's sake. The practical concerns of life engaged him too intensely. Where a modern would have branched off into the ever-recurring problem of the entrance of evil into the world, the Israelite turned with indignation on those who then and there proved the existence of sin in concrete act.

Surely . . .—Or, rather—

" O that thou wouldest slay, O God, the wicked,
And that ye bloody men would depart from me."

We get the last clause, which is better than an abrupt change to the imprecations, by a slight change of reading.

⁽²⁰⁾ **For they speak.**—Better, *Who rebel against thee.* This is actually the reading of the fifth of the Greek translations preserved by Origen, and entails only a change of the vowel pointing.

And thine enemies.—The state of the text is unsatisfactory. The subject to the verb must be that of the last clause, and the rendering "enemies" of a word properly meaning *cities* is very doubtful, in spite of 1 Sam. xxviii. 16 (but Aquila has "rivals," and Symmachus "adversaries"), where there is also a textual correction required.

Of the various proposed emendations, the simplest produces

" And rise up *against them* in vain."

⁽²¹⁾ **Do not I . . .**—Better—

" Must I not hate thy haters, Jehovah,
And feel loathing for thy assailants?"

⁽²²⁾ **With perfect hatred.**—Literally, *with perfection of hatred.* Comp. Tennyson's

" Dowered with the hate of hate."

⁽²³⁾ **Search.**—The same word with which the psalm opens. The inevitable scrutiny of the Divine Being is invited.

Thoughts.—As in Ps. xciv. 19; a word meaning (Ezek. xxxi. 5) *branches*, and so expressing the *ramifications* of thought.

⁽²⁴⁾ **Wicked way.**—The Hebrew may mean (after 1 Chron. iv. 9; Isa. xiv. 3) *way of sorrow*, or (after Isa. xlviii. 5) *way of an idol, i.e.,* idolatry, which is preferable.

Way everlasting.—Rather, here as in Jer. vi. 16, xviii. 15, of the old, *i.e.,* the true, religion, *in the ancient way.* The word rendered "everlasting" merely expresses *indefinite* time, whether past or future.

Prayer for Deliverance from   PSALMS, CXL.   *the Snares of the Wicked.*

PSALM CXL.

To the chief Musician, A Psalm of David.

(1) Deliver me, O LORD, from the evil man: preserve me from the ¹violent man; (2) which imagine mischiefs in *their* heart; continually are they gathered together *for* war. (3) They have sharpened their tongues like a serpent; *adders'* poison *is* under their lips. Selah.

(4) Keep me, O LORD, from the hands of the wicked; preserve me from the violent man; who have purposed to overthrow my goings. (5) The proud have hid a snare for me, and cords; they have spread a net by the wayside; they have set gins for me. Selah.

(6) I said unto the LORD, Thou *art* my God: hear the voice of my supplications, O LORD. (7) O GOD the Lord, the strength of my salvation, thou hast covered my head in the day of battle. (8) Grant not, O LORD, the desires of the wicked: further not his wicked device; ²*lest* they exalt themselves. Selah.

(9) *As for* the head of those that compass me about, let the mischief of their own lips cover them. (10) Let burning coals fall upon them: let them be cast

---

1 Heb., *man of violences.*

a Ps. 58. 4; Rom. 3. 13.

2 Or, *let them not be exalted.*

CXL.

The date of its composition is in no way indicated in this psalm. Its resemblance to Psalms lviii. and lxiv. hardly needs to be pointed out. "The close of all three psalms sounds much alike; they agree in the use of rare forms of expression, and their language becomes fearfully obscure in style and sound, when they are directed against the enemies." Besides the conjecture of Davidic authorship by the Rabbins, further developed by the addition in the Syriac, "when Saul threw the spear," Manasseh's reign, the immediate post-exile times, and the Maccabæan age, have all been selected for the situations out of which the psalm sprang. It is most in harmony with its feeling to suppose Israel speaking as a community, or an individual who identifies his own fortunes entirely with that of the better part of the nation. Heathen oppressors and foreign influences are undoubtedly attacked in the poem, and the blessings attending a loyal adherence to the religious and national traditions supply the cheerful and confident tone in which it ends. The rhythm is fine and varied.

Title.—See Ps. iv.

(1) **Evil man.**—The singular of the object in this verse must not lead us to think the psalm is an expression of personal feeling against one enemy, for it is immediately changed to the plural.

Violent man.—See Margin.

(2) **Imagine . . .**—Or, *contrive, plot.*

Gathered together.—This translation follows the analogy of Ps. lvi. 6. Others render, "dwell with wars." But it is preferable to derive from a root meaning *to incite*: "They are continually stirring up wars." It is the situation described in Ps. cxx. 7 and frequently; Israel would be at peace, but within and without are those ever trying to involve her in troubles.

(3) Comp. Pss. lxiv. 3, lviii. 4, lii. 2, x. 7.

Adders.—The Hebrew word is peculiar to this place, and is explained by Gesenius to be a compound of two words, to represent "that which rolls itself up and lies in ambush." "Besides the cobra and the cerastes, several other species of venomous snakes are common in Syria, and we may apply the name, either generically or specifically, to the vipers. Two species, *Vipera ammodytes* and *Vipera euphratica*, we found to be very common. The former of these was known to Linnæus as inhabiting Palestine. They are plainly-coloured serpents, with broad flat heads and suddenly-contracting tails" (Tristram, *Nat. Hist. of the Bible*, p. 275). The LXX. and Vulg. read "asp." (Comp. Rom. iii. 13.)

(4) **Overthrow my goings.**—Literally, *thrust aside my steps.* The verse is a repetition, with variation, of verse 1.

(5) **Net.**—An elaboration of the favourite image of the net. (Ps. ix. 15.) The frequent occurrence of this figure well indicates the dangers to which Israel was subjected through the leaning of many of the nation itself to foreign influences.

(7) **In the day of battle.**—Literally, *in the day of arms*, *i.e.*, when he was arming for fight. God covered the warrior's head, *i.e.*, provided the "helmet of salvation" (Isa. lix. 17). (Comp. also Ps. lx. 9: "Strength of my head.") Others, however, follow the LXX. and Authorised Version in understanding by "day of arms" the *day of battle.*

(8) **Desires.**—The form of the Hebrew word is anomalous, but the meaning certain. The LXX. and Vulg. give the first clause thus: "Give me not over to the enemy, by reason of their own desire;" which may possibly have been in St. Paul's mind in Rom. i. 24.

Further not.—The text of this clause has undoubtedly suffered. The Authorised Version follows the LXX. and Vulg. in inserting a negative before the last word. These versions also take the word rendered "wicked devices" as a verb, not finding a noun of the form anywhere else: "They have plotted against me: desert me not, lest they exalt themselves." So also Symmachus, and another Greek version quoted by Origen.

As the text at present stands, we must render: *his plot do not further—they lift up.* Looking on to the next verse, "the head of those surrounding me," the suggestion at once arises that the verb *lift up* properly belongs to this clause:

"His plot do not further.
They lift the head, these surrounding me."

This arrangement disregards the "selah," and also obliges us to suspect that a clause has dropped out after the first clause of verse 9—a suspicion confirmed by the rhythm.*

(9) **Head.**—Ewald, who keeps to the text, takes *rôsh* in the sense of poison (see Ps. lxix. 22, Note):—

"The poison of those encircling me,
Let them be covered with the perdition of their lips."

This brings verses 8, 9 into harmony with verse 4. But the emendation given above is better.

(10) In this verse too there is a grammatical difficulty, which the margin, "Let there fall on them," instead of

---

* Mr. Burgess amends to "Further not his plot to his exaltation."

288

God's Regard for the Righteous.   PSALMS, CXLI.   *A Prayer in Temptation.*

into the fire; into deep pits, that they rise not up again. ⁽¹¹⁾ Let not ^{1 2}an evil speaker be established in the earth: evil shall hunt the violent man to overthrow *him*.

⁽¹²⁾ I know that the LORD will maintain the cause of the afflicted, *and* the right of the poor. ⁽¹³⁾ Surely the righteous shall give thanks unto thy name: the upright shall dwell in thy presence.

¹ Heb., *a man of tongue.*

² Or, *an evil speaker, a wicked man of violence, be established in the earth: let him be hunted to his overthrow.*

³ Heb., *directed.*

PSALM CXLI.
A Psalm of David.

⁽¹⁾ LORD, I cry unto thee: make haste unto me; give ear unto my voice, when I cry unto thee. ⁽²⁾ Let my prayer be ³ set forth before thee *as* incense; *and* the lifting up of my hands *as* the evening sacrifice.

⁽³⁾ Set a watch, O LORD, before my mouth; keep the door of my lips.

"Let them bring upon them," does not remove, since the subject of the next verb is third person *singular*. The first verb is usually taken impersonally, as by the LXX., which version is actually to be followed in rendering *coals of fire* (literally, *coals accompanied with fire*, or, *coals as fire*), and we get the somewhat awkward, but intelligible—

"Let them bring upon them coals of fire;
Let him cast them into pits that they rise not again.'

But a very slight change gives a plain grammatical sentence with the subject carried on from the last verse:

"Let it (mischief) bring even upon themselves coals of fire;
Let it cast them into pits, so that they rise no more."
(Burgess.)

The word "pits" is peculiar to the passage. Gesenius, deriving from a root meaning "to boil up," renders, "whirlpools," which, as in Ps. lxvi. 12, combines "water" with "fire," as joint emblems of *perils* that cannot be escaped. But Symmachus, Theodotion, and Jerome render "ditches," which is supported by a Rabbinical quotation, given by Delitzsch: "first of all they burned them in pits; when the flesh was consumed they collected the bones, and burned them in coffins."

⁽¹¹⁾ **An evil speaker.**—Literally, as in LXX. and Vulg., *a man of tongue*; (Comp. Ecclus. viii. 3; Job xi. 2.) margin, "man of lips." It is hardly possible to resist the suggestion that some particular person, noted for the loudness or violence of his speech, was intended.

Evil shall hunt . . .—Comp. Prov. xiii. 21 and Horace, *Odes* iii. 2, Conington's translation :

"Though vengeance halt, she seldom leaves
The wretch whose flying step she hounds.'

To overthrow.—The Hebrew is a noun, formed from a root meaning "to thrust," and literally means either *to destruction* or *with hasty pursuit*. Some render "with successive thrusts;" but this is hardly a hunting figure.

⁽¹²⁾ Comp. Ps. ix. 4, 16.

⁽¹³⁾ **Surely.**—Or, perhaps here, *only,* the primary meaning of the particle.

Dwell.—For the thought comp. Pss. xi. 7, xvi. 11. After the peril and seeming abandonment God again proves the covenant promise true, and those whom the heathen would have chased from the land find in it a sure dwelling-place in the light of the presence and favour of Jehovah.

CXLI.

This is one of the most obscure psalms in the whole psalter, hardly a clause of verses 5, 6, 7 offering anything more than a conjectural meaning. The author appears from verse 2 to be a priest or Levite, being so familiar with the rites of the sanctuary as to use them as metaphors. From verses 3 and 4 we gather that he (or as verse 7 indicates, the community for which he speaks) is under a temptation to betray the cause of Jehovah and true religion, either by pronouncing some blasphemy, or indulging in some license forbidden by a high covenant ideal. The reference to the unlawful *dainties* in verse 4 (if we adopt that rendering) naturally suggests either idolatrous feasts (comp. Ps. xvi. 4) or banquets connected with the games and other foreign innovations against which, when introduced under Grecian influence, the stricter Jews so bitterly protested. Can the allusion in verse 3 be to the *musical* gifts and accomplishments of the Levites, which the apostate part of the nation wished to enlist on the side of these Greek customs, but which the poet declines to exhibit, praying for support in his pious resolution? Or does verse 6 rather indicate a judicial position for the author; and is he afraid of being himself led into the perversion of justice, which he so strongly denounces, by the promise of popular favour?

The Davidic inscription cannot be for a moment maintained. There is no period of David's life which the psalm could represent. The overthrow of some oppressive and persecuting court party, such as existed at Jerusalem either in the Persian or Grecian period, is surely indicated in verse 6. The rhythm is fine, and fairly sustained.

⁽²⁾ **Set forth . . .**—See margin; but more literally, *be erected,* suggesting the pillar of smoke (comp. Tennyson's "Azure pillars of the hearth") continually rising to heaven. Some think the *incense* refers to the morning sacrifice, so that the verse will mean, "let my prayer rise regularly as morning and evening sacrifice." But this is hardly necessary.

Sacrifice—*i.e.,* the offering of flour and oil, which followed the burnt offering both at morning and evening (Lev. ii. 1—11; in Authorised Version, "meat offering "), and here probably associated specially with evening, because the prayer was uttered at the close of the day. (See Note, verse 3.)

For the "lifted hands," here, from the parallelism, evidently only a symbol of prayer, and not a term for oblation, see Ps. xxviii. 2, Note.

"For what are men better than sheep or goats,
That nourish a blind life within the brain,
If, knowing God, they lift not hands of prayer,
Both for themselves, and those that call them friend."
TENNYSON : *Morte d'Arthur.*

⁽³⁾ **Watch.**—The image drawn from the guard set at city gates at night seems to indicate the evening as the time of composition of the psalm.

Door of my lips.—Comp. "doors of thy mouth" (Micah vii. 5), and so in Euripides, πύλαι στόματος. For the probable motive of the prayer, see Introduction. The poet's feeling is that of Xenocrates: " I have often repented of having spoken, but never of having been silent."

(4) Incline not my heart to *any* evil thing, to practise wicked works with men that work iniquity: and let me not eat of their dainties.

(5) ¹Let the righteous smite me; *it shall be* a kindness: and let him reprove me; *it shall be* an excellent oil, *which* shall not break my head: for yet my prayer also *shall be* in their calamities.

(6) When their judges are overthrown in stony places, they shall hear my words; for they are sweet.

(7) Our bones are scattered at the grave's mouth, as when one cutteth and cleaveth *wood* upon the earth. (8) But mine eyes *are* unto thee, O God the Lord: in thee is my trust; ²leave not my soul destitute. (9) Keep me from the snares *which* they have laid for me, and the gins of the workers of iniquity.

¹ Or, *Let the righteous smite me kindly, and reprove me; let not their precious oil break my head*, &c.

² Heb., *make not my soul bare.*

---

(4) **To practise wicked works . . .**—The Vulg., *ad excusandas excusationes,* following the LXX., not only preserves the expressive assonance of the original, but probably conveys its meaning better than the somewhat tame English version. Evidently the danger to be guarded against was not so much a sinful act as a sinful utterance, and the expression "to make pretexts or excuses" may possibly refer to the casuistries by which some of the laxer Jews excused their participation in heathen rites or licentious banquets. Symmachus has, "to devise wicked devices."

Dainties.—The word is peculiar to this passage, but derived from a root meaning "pleasant." The LXX. and Vulg. refer it to persons instead of things. But the use of the same root in verse 6, "for they are *sweet,*" where the reference is to "words," suggests a meaning here different both from the English and the ancient versions. "I will not taste of their sweets" may mean "I will not listen to their allurements: what finds favour with them shall not tempt me." On the other hand, if we retain the English allusion to the dainties of a feast (so Symmachus), the word in verse 6 will be used metaphorically in contrast. The words of condemnation he utters, though bitter to these feasters, are in reality sweet with the sweetness of truth.

(5) The difficulties of the psalm thicken here. Render, *Let a righteous man smite me, it is a kindness; and let him reprove me, it is oil for the head: my head shall not refuse it though it continue; yet my prayer is against their wickedness.*

The word rendered "smite" is that used of Jael's "hammer strokes" (Judg. v. 26). (Comp. Isa. xli. 7.) The Hebrew for "reprove" is probably used in a judicial sense, as in Gen. xxxi. 37; Isa. ii. 4; Prov. xxiv. 25, &c. The greatest obscurity attaches to the word rendered above "refuse," but in the Authorised Version "break," probably because in Ps. xxxiii. 10 ("bring to none effect") it is in parallelism with "break." The LXX. and Vulg. take it as meaning "anoint," rendering (from a different text to ours) "let not oil of a wicked man anoint my head." If we might adopt this reading it would remove the difficulty of this part of the verse, and give an excellent parallelism: "A righteous man may smite me in mercy and reprove me, but let not a wicked man's oil anoint my head;" *i.e.,* I would welcome reproof from the righteous, but reject even the festive oil offered by the wicked. For the rendering "wickednesses," instead of "calamities," comp. Job xx. 12; Ps. xciv. 23. For the sense of "although" given to the conjunction, see Exod. xiii. 17. The suffix "their" refers back, of course, to the *ungodly* in verse 4. The "oil for the head" (comp. Ps. xlv. 7) is a natural emblem of festivity, and the whole sentiment of the passage is tolerably clear. Rather than join in the wicked mirth of a profane banquet, the poet would be the object of continued rebuke and chastisement from one of the godly—his prayer meanwhile still rising for protection against the allurements held out to tempt him. We probably have sketched here the actual condition of many a Levite between the apostate and the loyal part of the nation.

(6) This verse again is full of obscurities. The first clause probably should be rendered, *Let their judges be broken to pieces by the force* (literally, *hands*) *of the rock;* or, *let their judges be cast down by the sides of the cliff—i.e.,* hurled down the precipitous face of the ravine (See 2 Chron. xxv. 12, and notice that the word here is "Selaʽ," the name of the capital of Edom; comp. Hosea x. 14; Ps. cxxxvii. 9, where, however, the expression is "against the cliff.")

They shall . . .—Better, *then shall they hear my words; how dainty they are,* &c. The expression is ironical. The ungodly party, when their power is broken, instead of being entertained by the poet at a licentious banquet, will listen indeed to his words—shall hear a "dainty song" from him—viz., "a song of triumph."

(7) **Our bones.**—The literal rendering of this verse is: *As when one cutteth and cleaveth in the earth our bones are scattered at the mouth of Sheôl.*

The reading "our bones" necessarily makes this an abrupt transition from the fate of the unjust judges in the last verse to that of the afflicted people, but in a correction by a second hand in the Codex Alex. of the LXX. we find the much easier and more satisfactory "their bones"—a reading confirmed by the Syriac, Ethiopic, and Arabic versions; as also by the fact that the word here rendered "cleave" is that employed in 2 Chron. xxv. 12 (see reference above, verse 6) of the Edomites thrown from the cliff. But the abrupt transition is not unlikely in Hebrew poetry, and the more difficult reading is according to rule to be preserved.

The figure is mistaken in the Authorised Version. The reference is not to the ground strewn with the logs left by a woodcutter, but to the clods of earth left by the plough. Keeping the present text, and making the figure refer to the righteous, we should naturally compare Ps. cxxix. 3, where ploughing is used as an image of affliction and torture, as "harrowing" is with us. The verse might be paraphrased: "We have been so harrowed and torn that we are brought to the brink of the grave," the image being, however, heightened by the recollection of some actual massacre.

(8, 9) Comp. Ps. xxv. 15.

(9) **From the snare.**—The original idiom is far more forcible: "from the hands (or, 'clutches') of the snare." (See above, verse 6, "in the hands of the cliff.")

A Prayer of David   PSALMS, CXLII.—CXLIII.   *in Extremity.*

(10) Let the wicked fall into their own nets, whilst that I withal ¹escape.

PSALM CXLII.

²Maschil of David: A Prayer when he was in the cave.

(1) I cried unto the LORD with my voice; with my voice unto the LORD did I make my supplication. (2) I poured out my complaint before him; I shewed before him my trouble. (3) When my spirit was overwhelmed within me, then thou knewest my path. In the way wherein I walked have they privily laid a snare for me. (4) ³I looked on *my* right hand, and beheld, but *there was* no man that would know me: refuge ⁴failed me; ⁵no man cared for my soul.

1 Heb., *pass over.*
2 Or, A Psalm of David, giving instruction.
3 Or, Look on the right hand, and see.
4 Heb., *perished from me.*
5 Heb., *no man sought after my soul.*

(5) I cried unto thee, O LORD: I said, Thou *art* my refuge *and* my portion in the land of the living. (6) Attend unto my cry; for I am brought very low: deliver me from my persecutors; for they are stronger than I. (7) Bring my soul out of prison, that I may praise thy name: the righteous shall compass me about; for thou shalt deal bountifully with me.

PSALM CXLIII.
A Psalm of David.

(1) Hear my prayer, O LORD, give ear to my supplications: in thy faithfulness answer me, *and* in thy righteousness. (2) And enter not into judgment with thy servant: for *a*in thy sight shall no man living be justified.

a Ex. 34. 7; Rom. 3. 20; Gal. 2. 16.

---

(10) Comp. Ps. vii. 15.

Withal.—Probably, *altogether* ("whilst I altogether escape"), which some join with the previous clause, "Let the wicked fall into their own nets together, whilst I escape."

CXLII.

This is one of the eight psalms assigned by their inscriptions to the time of David's persecution by Saul. There is nothing in the contents either to support or controvert the title, unless the recurrence of expressions found in Pss. xlii., lxi., lxxvii., marks dependence on them. But such dependence would not detract from the originality of the poem before us, an originality shown rather in the passion and play of feeling than in the poetic figure and expression. The parallelism is varied.

Title.—Maschil. (See Title Ps. xxxii.) For the rest of the inscription see *Introduction.*

(1) **I cried . . .**—See Ps. iii. 4, &c.

(2) **I poured out.**—See the same verb used in similar sense, Pss. xlii. 4, lxii. 8; and with the second clause comp. Ps. cvii. 6.

(3) **When my spirit.**—Literally, *in the muffling upon me of my spirit.* When my spirit was so wrapped in trouble and gloom, so "muffled round with woe" that I could not see the path before me, was distracted and unable to chose a line of conduct, *Thou* (emphatic) knewest my path. (Comp. for the same verb Pss. lxi. 2, lxxvii. 3.)

(4) **I looked.**—The Authorised Version follows the ancient versions in turning the Hebrew imperatives into historic tenses. But they are easily intelligible if taken rhetorically, and indeed the psalm loses in liveliness by missing them:

"On the path by which I must walk they have laid a trap for me;
    Look to the right and see,
    Not a friend is in sight.
    Failed has refuge from me,
    There is none who careth for my soul."

To the "right," because according to the regular Hebrew metaphor it was on the "right hand" that the protector would stand. (See Note Ps. xvi. 8, &c.; and comp. Pss. cix. 6, 31, cx. 5, cxxi. 5.)

(5) With this verse comp. Pss. xxxi. 3, xxii. 8, xvi. 5, &c.

(7) **Out of prison.**—This expression, which must certainly be figurative of distress (comp. Ps. cxliii. 11), probably led to the inscription.

Compass me about.—The Hebrew word here employed is used in a hostile sense in Ps. xxii. 12; Judges xx. 43; Hab. i. 4. It is better, therefore, to follow the LXX. and render:

"In my case the righteous are waiting
    Till," &c.

This sense "waiting for," besides being favoured by the construction, suits well the passage, Prov. xiv. 18.

"The simple inherit folly,
But the prudent *wait for* knowledge,

and is Aquila's rendering there of the word as it is here.

CXLIII.

This psalm is chiefly interesting as an instance of the way in which the deeper religious life of the post-exile times was upheld and cherished by the experience of past times and the faith of older generations as it had found expression in prophecy and song. For, as the Notes will show, there is hardly a phrase which is not derived from some older source—a fact which at once disposes of the inscription.

Probably it is not an individual, but the community, which thus under affliction confesses its sin and comforts itself with reflections on the past.

(1) **Faithfulness . . . righteousness.**—The first word recalls the covenant promise, the second the faith, expressed so frequently, on which the covenant rested, that the Judge of all the world must do right. St. John founds the appeal for forgiveness on the same pair of Divine qualities (1 John i. 9; comp. Ps. lxv. 5.)

(2) **And enter not.**—The Divine justice has just been invoked, and now the appellant suddenly seems to deprecate it. These verses really sum up the apparent paradox of the Book of Job, as also the expressions recall that Book. (See Job iv. 17, ix. 2, 32, xiv. 3, *seq.*, xv. 14, xxii. 4, &c.) In one breath Job frequently pours forth pathetic protestations of his innocence, and dread lest God should take him at his word

David Prays for   PSALMS, CXLIV.   *Deliverance and Quickening.*

(3) For the enemy hath persecuted my soul; he hath smitten my life down to the ground; he hath made me to dwell in darkness, as those that have been long dead. [1 Or, *for I am become like*, &c.] (4) Therefore is my spirit overwhelmed within me; my heart within me is desolate. (5) I remember the days of old; I meditate on all thy works; I muse on the work of thy hands. (6) I stretch forth my hands unto thee: my soul *thirsteth* after thee, as a thirsty land. Selah. [2 Heb., *hide me with thee.*] (7) Hear me speedily, O LORD: my spirit faileth: hide not thy face from me, [1] lest I be like unto them that go down into the pit. (8) Cause me to hear thy lovingkindness in the morning; for in [3 Heb., *my rock.*] thee do I trust: cause me to know the way wherein I should walk; for I lift up my soul unto thee. (9) Deliver me, O LORD, from mine enemies: I [2] flee unto thee to hide me.

(10) Teach me to do thy will; for thou *art* my God: thy spirit *is* good; lead me into the land of uprightness. (11) Quicken me, O LORD, for thy name's sake: for thy righteousness' sake bring my soul out of trouble. (12) And of thy mercy cut off mine enemies, and destroy all them that afflict my soul: for I *am* thy servant.

PSALM CXLIV.

A Psalm of David.

(1) Blessed *be* the LORD [3] my strength,

---

and arraign him for trial. Man, in his desire to have his character vindicated before man, appeals to the just Judge, but instantly falls back with a guilty sense that before that tribunal none can stand :

"For merit lives from man to man,
And not from man, O Lord, to Thee.

Shall . . . be justified.—This follows the LXX. Better, *is just.*

(3) This verse explains the last. The affliction under which the psalmist suffers is evidence that God is visiting for sin.

He hath made . . .—See Lam. iii. 6; and comp. Ps. lxxxviii. 5, 6.

Long dead.—Literally, either *dead of old*, or *dead for ever*, according as we take *'ôlam* of past or future time. LXX., νεκροὺς αἰῶνος; Vulg., *mortuos sæculi.*

(4) See Ps. cxlii. 3, and Notes.

Is desolate.—Or, more literally, as in Isa. lix. 16, lxiii. 5, &c., *wondered*; literally, *fills itself with astonishment.*

(5) See Ps. lxxvii. 5, 6.

(6) With the first clause comp. Ps. xliv. 20.

Thirsty land.—See Ps. lxiii. 1, which explains this elliptical sentence. As our Lord taught, God is even more ready to send the refreshing spiritual shower than man's heart to receive it.

(7) With the first clause comp. Ps. lxix. 17, with the second, Ps. cii. 2,

This dependence on former psalms does not detract from the reality of the feeling expressed by means of these ancient sobs and cries. The contrast of the present with former times (verse 5) with the recollection of God's dealings then, joined to thoughtful contemplation of the reality of His power as displayed in His works, makes the psalmist's anguish the more intense, his longing the more consuming, his supplication the more urgent.

(8) **In the morning.**—Comp. Ps. xc. 14. The expression either means "early," or is figurative of the dawn of hope and salvation.

The way wherein I should walk—*i.e.*, the way at once of duty and safety.

I lift up my soul.—Or, *my desire.*

(9) **I flee . . .**—Literally, *unto thee have I hidden.* A phrase which has been variously explained—(1) to Thee I have confided my troubles: (2) and, better, as in the Authorised Version, *to Thee I* (*have fled and*) *hid* (*myself*). The reflexive use of the Hebrew verb is sufficiently established by Gen. xxxviii. 14; Deut. xxii. 12 (Jonah iii. 6 is doubtful).

(10) **Thy spirit is good; lead me.**—Or, rather, *let thy good spirit lead me.* (For the omission of the article with the adjective after the determinative noun, comp. Gen. xxxvii. 2.)

Land of uprightness.— Better, *level land* (Deut. iv. 43, "plain country;" comp. Jer. xlviii. 21), here metaphorically of tranquillity and happiness. (Comp. Isa. xxvi. 10; Ps. xxvii. 11.)

(11, 12) The last two verses are made of reminiscences of former psalm experiences. The verbs should be in the future, not the imperative.

For thy name's sake.—Comp. Ps. xxiii. 3, &c.

(11) **Quicken me, O Lord.**—Comp. Pss. cxxxviii. 7 and cxix. frequently.

Out of trouble.—Comp. Pss. xxxiv 17, cxlii. 7.

(12) Comp. Pss. xviii, 40, liv. 7.

CXLIV.

There is nothing more curious in the composition of the psalter than the union of the two entirely dissimilar pieces which compose this psalm. Verses 1—11 are a mere cento from former psalms, the xviiith furnishing the greater number of expressions and figures, and must from this circumstance be regarded as one of the latest in the collection, whereas verses 12—15 are composed of a fragment of some ancient song, whose beginning is lost, and which has neither grammatical nor logical connection with the medley of quotations that precedes it. (See Note to verse 12). This interesting fragment gives, unfortunately, no indication of its date or authorship. We can imagine it, however, chanted at harvest, at festivals, or as "the help tune" of the reapers:

"their wine song, when hand
Grasps at hand, eye lights eye in good friendship,
and great hearts expand,
And grow one in the sense of this world's life."
R. BROWNING: *Saul.*

The progressive rhythm of the latter part is very fine.

(1) **Strength.**—Rather, *rock.* Comp. Ps. xviii. 2, 46. LXX. and Vulg., "my God."

*which teacheth my hands ¹to war, *and my fingers to fight*: ⁽²⁾ ᵇ²my goodness, and my fortress; my high tower, and my deliverer: my shield, and *he* in whom I trust; who subdueth my people under me.

⁽³⁾ ᶜLord, what *is* man, that thou takest knowledge of him! or the son of man, that thou makest account of him! ⁽⁴⁾ ᵈMan is like to vanity: his days *are* as a shadow that passeth away.

⁽⁵⁾ Bow thy heavens, O Lord, and come down: touch the mountains, and they shall smoke. ⁽⁶⁾ ᵉCast forth lightning, and scatter them: shoot out thine arrows, and destroy them. ⁽⁷⁾ Send thine ³hand from above; rid me, and deliver me out of great waters, from the hand of strange children; ⁽⁸⁾ whose mouth speaketh vanity, and their right hand *is* a right hand of falsehood.

⁽⁹⁾ I will sing a new song unto thee, O God: upon a psaltery *and* an instrument of ten strings will I sing praises unto thee. ⁽¹⁰⁾ *It is he* that giveth ⁴salvation unto kings: who delivereth David his servant from the hurtful sword. ⁽¹¹⁾ Rid me, and deliver me from the hand of strange children, whose mouth speaketh vanity, and their right hand *is* a right hand of falsehood:

⁽¹²⁾ That our sons *may be* as plants grown up in their youth; *that* our daughters *may be* as corner stones, ⁵polished

---

a 2 Sam. 22. 35.

1 Heb., *to the war, &c.*

b 2 Sam. 22. 2, 3, 40.

2 Or, *My mercy.*

c Job 17. 7; Ps. 8. 4; Heb. 2. 6.

d Job 14. 2; Ps. 39. 5.

e Ps. 18. 13, 14.

3 Heb., *hands.*

4 Or, *victory.*

5 Heb., *cut.*

Which teacheth.—See Ps. xviii. 34. More literally,

"Who traineth my hands for war,
 My fingers for fight."

⁽²⁾ **My goodness.**—Or, *my lovingkindness*, or *my grace*, a shortened form of "God of my grace" (Ps. lix. 10, 17). The expression is exactly analogous to the term "grace," applied to kings as the source of grace or mercy. For the other epithets, see Ps. xviii. 2.

Who subdueth.—Ps. xviii. 47; but the verb is different (cognate with 2 Sam. xxii. 48), and here the singular, "my people," instead of "my peoples." Some MSS. indeed have the plural here, and the Syriac and Chaldee followed them, or changed to suit Ps. xviii. If we had the historical incidents out of which the psalm sprung we might account for the change.

⁽³⁾ See Ps. viii. 4.

⁽⁴⁾ **Vanity . . . shadow.**—See Pss. xxxix. 5, 6, cii. 11. The occasion of the introduction of these sentiments here is not quite clear. It may be the humility of the warrior who ascribes all success to God instead of to human prowess, or it may be a reflection uttered over the corpses of comrades, or, perhaps, a blending of the two.

⁽⁵⁾ **Come down.**—The theophany for which the psalmist prays is described in the classic language for such manifestations taken from Ps. xviii. 9, 13, 16, 17, 43, 45, with reminiscences of Ps. civ. 32; Exod. xix. 18. But there are touches of originality, as in the next clause.

⁽⁶⁾ **Cast forth lightning.**—Literally, *lighten lightning*, the verb being quite peculiar to this place.

⁽⁷⁾ **Rid.**—The Hebrew verb means "to tear asunder," and is used of the gaping of the mouth (Ps. xxii. 13). The meaning here is got from the cognate Arabic, and Syriac.

Strange children.—Literally, *sons of the stranger.*

⁽⁸⁾ **Right hand of falsehood.**—Most probably with allusion to the custom (see Ps. cvi. 26) of raising the right hand in taking an oath.

⁽⁹⁾ See Ps. xxxiii. 2, 3.

O God.—The only instance of *Elohim* in the last two books of the psalter with the exception of Ps. cviii., which is a compilation from two older songs.

⁽¹⁰⁾ **David his servant.**—See Ps. xviii. 50.

⁽¹²⁾ **That our sons.**—This rendering of the relative, which so strangely begins this fragment, would be possible after Gen. xi. 7, xiii. 16, &c., if a finite verb instead of participles followed; or it might mean "because," as in Gen. xxx. 18, &c., but for the same anomalous construction; or it might, as by the LXX., be rendered *whose*, if any antecedent for it could be discovered. But all these devices are plainly impossible, and there is nothing for it but to treat the passage which it introduces as a fragment of another poem quite unconnected with the previous part of the psalm. Render, *we whose*.

As plants.—The Hebrew word seems always to denote a young, vigorous tree lately planted. (See especially Job xiv. 9, aptly translated by the LXX. νεόφυτον. (For the comparison, comp. Isa. v. 7; Pss. i. 3, Note, cxxviii. 3.)

Grown up in their youth.—The form here used is peculiar, but in another conjugation the verb is frequently used of *bringing* up children (see 2 Kings x. 6; Isa. i. 2, xxiii. 4, &c.), as it is of the rain nourishing young plants (Isa. xliv. 14). Here the poet must mean *grown tall beyond their age*, or the figure is somewhat tame. A suggestion to read, "reproductive in their youth," *i.e.*, though young themselves, bringing up families, improves the poetry, and suits well the intention of this fragment of song and the general feeling of the Hebrew race. Comp. especially Ps. cxxvii. 4, "sons of youth" (Burgess).

Corner stones.—The word only occurs once besides, in Zech. ix. 15, where it is used of the corners of the altar. The derivation is from a root meaning *to conceal*, as is also the word rendered *garners*, in the next verse. Aquila and Symmachus, "angles."

Polished.—The Hebrew word means *to hew*, used, with one exception, of wood for fuel, but is cognate with a word used of *stones*, and in Isa. li. 1 in the passive participle of a cave hewn in a rock. The exception is Prov. vii. 16, where the word is applied to tapestry.

After the similitude of a palace—*i.e.*, like a large and stately building. There seems no reason to confine the reference to the Temple, as the LXX. and Vulg. do, though the absence of the article is not insuperably against this (Isa. xliv. 28).

The explanations usually given of this passage make the resemblance to be either to caryatides carved at the angles of a palace, or to carved or variegated wood pillars in the corners of a spacious room. For the former there seems to be no authority in Scripture or known Hebrew usage. The latter has the support of Dr. J. G. Wetzstein, but seems far-fetched. It is far

after the similitude of a palace : ⁽¹³⁾ *that* our garners *may be* full, affording ¹all manner of store : *that* our sheep may bring forth thousands and ten thousands in our streets : ⁽¹⁴⁾ *that* our oxen *may be* ²strong to labour; *that there be* no breaking in, nor going out; that *there be* no complaining in our streets.

⁽¹⁵⁾ *ᵃHappy is that* people, that is in such a case : *yea, happy is that* people, whose God *is* the LORD.

PSALM CXLV.

David's Psalm of praise.

⁽¹⁾ I will extol thee, my God, O king : and I will bless thy name for ever and ever. ⁽²⁾ Every day will I bless thee; and I will praise thy name for ever and ever.

⁽³⁾ Great *is* the LORD, and greatly to be praised; ³and his greatness *is* unsearchable. ⁽⁴⁾ One generation shall praise thy works to another, and shall declare thy mighty acts.

⁽⁵⁾ I will speak of the glorious honour of thy majesty, and of thy wondrous ⁴works. ⁽⁶⁾ And *men* shall speak of the might of thy terrible acts : and I will ⁵declare thy greatness. ⁽⁷⁾ They shall abundantly utter the memory of thy

---

1 Heb., *from kind to kind.*
2 Heb., *able to bear burdens,* or, *loaden with flesh.*
a Ps. 33. 12, & 65. 4.
3 Heb., *and of his greatness there is no search.*
4 Heb., *things,* or, *words.*
5 Heb., *declare it.*

---

more according to Hebrew feeling to render the words simply, *like hewn angles, the building of a palace;* an image suggestive, like that of "the wall" in Song of Sol. viii. 9 (see Note), of unassailable chastity and virtue. Perhaps the phrase "women of strength or of a strong fortification," in Ruth iii. 11, may imply the same figure. Grätz alters to "daughters of a palace."

⁽¹³⁾ **All manner of store.**—See margin, *all kinds of corn.*

Thousands and ten thousands. — Literally, *thousands multiplied.*

Streets.—Rather, *outplaces,* i.e., pastures, fields, as in Job v. 10 (where see margin).

⁽¹⁴⁾ This verse is full of obscurities. The words rendered "oxen, strong to labour," can hardly bear this meaning with the present pointing, since the participle is passive, and there is no authority for rendering *oxen bearing burdens.* The words have been rendered *oxen laden,* either with the produce of the land, or with their own fat (so apparently the LXX.), or with young, *pregnant*—all open to the objection that the passive of *to bear* must mean "to be borne," and the latter to the further objection that the words are in the masculine. But since *allûphim* elsewhere means "heads of families" (Jer. xiii. 21, &c.) or "princes," and the noun cognate with the verb is used of a post connected with the revenue (1 Kings xi. 28; comp. the connection between the Greek φορός and φέρτερος), the participle passive may easily here mean "honoured," or "high in office." Or, from the use of the cognate Chaldee form in Ezra vi. 3, "strongly laid," we might render, *our princes firmly established;* and this is the best explanation of the passage.

No breaking in.—Heb., a "breach," *i.e.,* in the town walls. LXX. and Vulg., "no falling of the fence." Others refer to the folds for cattle. (See Ps. lx. 2.) Ewald, however, connecting closely with the mention of "pregnant oxen," renders *no abortion.* So Syriac : " Our cattle are great (with young), and there is not a barren one among them."

Nor going out—i.e., either to war, or into *captivity* (Prayer Book version), or the breaking out of cattle. The first is the more probable.

Complaining.—Rather, *outcry, cry of sorrow,* as in Jer. xiv. 2; or possibly, *cry of battle.*

Streets.—Better, *squares.*

⁽¹⁵⁾ **Happy.**—It is only a narrow and one-sided religion that can see anything out of place in this beatitude of plenty and peace. If we could rejoice with the psalms, fully and without misgiving, in the temporal blessings bestowed by Heaven, we should the more readily and sincerely enter into the depths of their spiritual experience. And the secret of this lies in the full comprehension and contemplation of the beautiful and pleasant as the gift of God.

CXLV.

This alphabetical psalm recalls in many expressions and phrases the thoughts and feelings of older songs. It has been identified with the "New Song" promised in Ps. cxliv. 9. Possibly some thought of the kind may have led to its following it. The song, though abounding in familiar psalm expressions, deserves the claim of originality from the insistance of its conviction of the Divine love and pity and care for all the world and all creatures.

The acrostic arrangement is incomplete (see Note, verse 13), thus supplying only twenty-one instead of twenty-two stanzas. The parallelism is well sustained.

Title.—This is the only psalm inscribed *tehillah,* though the whole collection is, in Hebrew, called *Tehillîm,* or *Tillim.* (See General Introduction.) It is possibly from verse 21; or perhaps this distinction is due to the early rise of the custom of repeating it daily at the noonday repast. So it would be called "Praise," just as we speak of "the grace" before and after meat.

⁽¹⁾ The psalm opens with familiar psalm strains. (Comp. openings of Pss. xxx., xxxiv.)

For ever and ever.—In contemplation of the greatness and majesty of God time ceases to be. The poet vows a homage indefinitely prolonged.

⁽³⁾ **Greatly to be praised.**—See Ps. xviii. 3 and comp. Ps. xlviii. 1.

And his greatness.—Literally, more expressive, *and for his greatness no search.* (Comp. Isa. xl. 28; Job xi. 7.)

⁽⁴⁾ **Shall praise.**—Or, *praises,* with idea of indefinite continuance; and so in the following verses.

⁽⁵⁾ **I will speak.**—Or, perhaps, *sing.* The verb is often rendered *meditate* (Pss. lxxvii. 12, cxix. 15, &c.) :

Thy wondrous works.—Rather, as in Ps. cv. 27 (see Note; comp. Ps. lxv. 3), *the details of thy wonders.* In psalms like cv., cvi., &c., is the detailed fulfilment of this purpose.

⁽⁶⁾ **Thy greatness.**—Or, according to the written text, *greatnesses.* So Aquila and Jerome. The parallelism is decidedly in favour of the plural.

⁽⁷⁾ **Abundantly utter.**—Literally, *pour forth in a stream,* as in Pss. xix. 2, lxxviii. 2.

great goodness, and shall sing of thy righteousness.

(8) ᵃ The LORD *is* gracious, and full of compassion; slow to anger, and ¹of great mercy. (9) The LORD *is* good to all: and his tender mercies *are* over all his works.

(10) All thy works shall praise thee, O LORD; and thy saints shall bless thee. (11) They shall speak of the glory of thy kingdom, and talk of thy power; (12) to make known to the sons of men his mighty acts, and the glorious majesty of his kingdom. (13) Thy kingdom *is* ²an everlasting kingdom, and thy dominion *endureth* throughout all generations.

(14) The LORD upholdeth all that fall, and raiseth up all *those that be* bowed down. (15) The eyes of all ³wait upon thee; and thou givest them their meat in due season. (16) Thou openest thine hand, and satisfiest the desire of every living thing.

(17) The LORD *is* righteous in all his ways, and ⁴holy in all his works. (18) The LORD *is* nigh unto all them that call upon him, to all that call upon him in truth. (19) He will fulfil the desire of them that fear him: he also will hear their cry, and will save them. (20) The LORD preserveth all them that love him: but all the wicked will he destroy.

(21) My mouth shall speak the praise of the LORD: and let all flesh bless his holy name for ever and ever.

PSALM CXLVI.

(1) ⁵ Praise ye the LORD. Praise the LORD, O my soul. (2) While I live will I praise the LORD: I will sing praises unto my God while I have any being.

ᵃ Ex. 34. 6, 7; Num. 14. 18; Ps. 86. 5, 15 & 103. 8.

1 Heb., great in mercy.

2 Heb., a kingdom of all ages.

3 Or, look unto thee.

4 Or, merciful, or, bountiful.

5 Heb., Hallelujah.

---

(8) Comp. Pss. lxxxvi. 15, ciii. 8, cxi. 4.

(9, 10) **All.**—This wide outlook over the world as the object, with all that it contains, of the Divine pity and love, is a noble anticipation of our Lord's teaching in the Sermon on the Mount and is introduced in a similar manner. Just as the subjects of the kingdom of heaven should exceed the heathen in kindness and goodness, because they know the universal and impartial grace of the Father, so here the *saints, the members of the covenant*, are to *bless* Jehovah, who shows them peculiar favour, but also lets His tender mercies flow in an unchecked stream over all His works. All Jehovah's works confess Him, but His saints *bless* Him.

(11, 12) It is the privilege of the *saints* to impress the less favoured natures with the glory of the Divine kingdom, which the theocratic relation has displayed in and to them.

(12) **To make.**—Or, *by making known*.

(13) See margin, and comp. Dan. iv. 3, 34. But it is not necessary to see any dependence between the passages because of the recurrence of phrases which must have been of daily use in the theocracy.

The *nun* stanza, which should come after verse 13, has most probably dropped away. The LXX. and Vulg., Syriac, and Ethiopic have here a variation of verse 17, which would, in Hebrew, give a verse beginning with the required letter; but it is unknown to the other ancient versions, is rejected by the Jewish writers, and, though found in one Hebrew MS., is apparently suspicious there. But these arguments can hardly weigh against the improbability that, in an artificial composition, one letter (and that an easy one for the purpose) should have been either purposely or accidentally omitted in the original draft, especially when we reflect how extremely unlikely it was that the LXX. should trouble themselves to supply a verse in order to keep up an arrangement of which they took no notice, perhaps even hardly observed it.

(14) **The Lord.**—Comp. Ps. xxxvii. 24. It marks a grand step in theology when the first instance of majesty of the Divine Being is sought in His condescension to human weakness and pity for frailty and want. The heathen had seen that this was *king-like*—

"Regia (crede mihi) res est succurrere lapsis."
OVID: *Ep. de Ponto II*., 9, 11.

But they had hardly seen that it was also *god-like*.
For "raiseth" and "bowed down," see Ps. cxlvi. 8.

(15, 16) These verses are adapted from Ps. civ. 27, 28

(18) **The Lord is nigh . . .**

"Closer is He than breathing, and nearer than hands and feet."
TENNYSON: *Higher Pantheism*.

(20) **Preserveth . . . destroy.**—Notice this recurrent thought, that the guardianship of the good implies the destruction of the wicked.

(21) **Holy name.**—As in Pss. xxxiii. 21, ciii. 1, cv. 3.

CXLVI.

This liturgical hymn, beginning and ending with the familiar "Hallelujah," is the first of the series of five which are sometimes called the "Greek"—in distinction to the "Egyptian"—Hallel. It was evidently composed for a time of great national depression, when the community, sick of dependence on the favour of foreign princes, turned more and more to the thought of the eternal righteousness and faithfulness of Jehovah.

The recurrence in a slightly changed form of verse 4 in 1 Macc. ii. 63 shows that the psalm was in existence when that book was written, and also serves to confirm the impression that it belongs to the Maccabæan age. The rhythm is varied.

(1, 2) **Praise.**—Following Pss. ciii. 1, 22, civ. 33, "praise" being substituted for "bless."

(3, 4) **Princes**—The thought of Ps. cxviii. 8, 9 is here elaborated, with distinct allusion to Gen. ii. 7 and iii. 19 (Comp. 1 Macc. ii. 63.) The verse, no doubt, was in Shakespeare's mind when he made Wolsey say:

"Oh, how wretched
Is that poor man that hangs on princes' favours!"

as it was quoted by Strafford when the news reached him that Charles I. had given the royal assent to the bill of attainder against him. But in the psalm it is

Man's Fickleness and   PSALMS, CXLVII.   *God's Faithfulness.*

(3) *a*Put not your trust in princes, nor in the son of man, in whom *there is* no ¹help. (4) His breath goeth forth, he returneth to his earth; in that very day his thoughts perish. (5) Happy *is he* that *hath* the God of Jacob for his help, whose hope *is* in the LORD his God: (6) Which made heaven, and earth, the sea, and all that therein *is:* which keepeth truth for ever: (7) Which executeth judgment for the oppressed: which giveth food to the hungry. The LORD looseth the prisoners: (8) the LORD openeth *the eyes of* the blind: the LORD raiseth them that are bowed down: the LORD loveth the righteous: (9) The LORD preserveth the strangers; he relieveth the fatherless and widow: but the way of the wicked he turneth upside down. (10) *b*The LORD shall reign for ever. even thy God, O Zion, unto all generations. Praise ye the LORD.

a Ps. 118. 8, 9.

1 Or, *salvation.*

b Ex. 15. 8.

2 Heb., *griefs.*

PSALM CXLVII.

(1) Praise ye the LORD: for *it is* good to sing praises unto our God; for *it is* pleasant; *and* praise is comely. (2) The LORD doth build up Jerusalem: he gathereth together the outcasts of Israel. (3) He healeth the broken in heart, and bindeth up their ²wounds. (4) He

---

not the caprice of princes, as in these notable instances, but their frailty as men that is declared untrustworthy.

(4) **In that very day . . .**—Comp. Antony's words:
"But yesterday the word of Cæsar might
Have stood against the world; now lies he there,
And none so poor to do him reverence."
       SHAKSPEARE, *Julius Cæsar.*

Thoughts.—The Hebrew word is peculiar to this passage. "Fabrications" would reproduce its etymological meaning.

(5) For the different aspects of the Divine nature and character inspiring trust see Introduction. With this verse comp. Pss. xxxiii. 12, cxliv. 15.

Hope.—The Hebrew word is rare in the psalter, expressing earnest "looking for," or "waiting for." (See Pss. civ. 27, cxix. 166.)

(6) **Truth.**—Or, *faithfulness.* The connection of this feature of the Divine character with the creative act is worthy of notice. That act alone was for the universe a promise and pledge, just as the covenant was a peculiar promise to Israel. Tennyson has put the same thought into verse:
"Thou madest man, he knows not why;
He thinks he was not made to die;
And Thou hast made him: *Thou art just.*"
       In Memoriam.

(7) Comp. Pss. ciii. 6, civ. 27, cvii. 9, cxxxvi. 25; Isa. lv. 1.

Here follow five lines, each beginning with the Divine name, and each consisting of three words, the rhythm prominent in the book of Job.

(8) **Openeth.**—Here, and through the verse, the verbs are participles. The elliptical "open the blind" is easily understood.

Blindness is sometimes figurative of distress and helplessness (Deut. xxviii. 29; Isa. lix. 9, &c.), sometimes of want of mental or spiritual discernment, as Isa. xxix. 18, xlii. 7, &c. Here, most probably, the former.

Raiseth.—See Ps. cxlv. 14.

(9) The stranger, the widow, and the orphan are constantly presented in the Law as objects of compassion and beneficence. The orphan and widow are mentioned as under God's care (Ps. lxviii. 5).

Relieveth.—Or rather, *restoreth,* by taking up their cause and seeing justice done. Certain forms of the verb are used of bearing witness, and possibly here there is allusion to a court of justice, in which God appears as witnessing on the side of the weak and defenceless.

Turneth upside down.—Rather, *bends aside.* The same word in Ps. cxix. 78 is rendered "dealt perversely." The idea seems in both cases to be that of interference, to thwart and impede a course of action. In Ps. cxix. it is an evil-disposed person who interferes with the righteous. Here it is the Divine providence which, when the wicked man has laid out his plans, and looks as it were along a plain and level road of prosperity, bends the prosperous course aside; makes the path crooked, instead of straight; full of trouble and calamity, instead of prosperous and sure.

(10) Comp. Exod. xv. 18; Ps. xcix. 1.

CXLVII.

Composed of three pieces, without any regular rhythmical structure, and only loosely connected by the same general thought and method of expression, this psalm yet deserves to rank high in the poetry of the Bible. While freely using existing materials, especially Pss. xxxiii., civ.; Isa. xl.; and the book of Job, the author gives proof of his own powers in the keenness of his observation of nature, and in his sympathy with the life and movement of the world, as well as by the free play of his fancy round each phenomenon that attracts him.

The evident allusion to a rebuilding of Jerusalem has been referred both to the great restoration under Nehemiah and to the repairs and fortifications of Hyrcanus (1 Macc. xvi. 23).

(1) Ps. cxxxv. 3 is plainly before the poet in this verse; and yet, since Ps. xxxiii. is in other respects his model, it is extremely doubtful whether we ought to change the reading, so as to make a complete correspondence between the verses, or suppose that the alteration was intentional, in accordance with " praise is comely for the upright" in Ps. xxxiii. 1. (See Notes on both the passages; comp. also Ps. xcii. 1.)

(2) **Build up**—*i.e.,* of course, "rebuild." The word "outcasts," which is that used in Isa. xi. 12 and lvi. 8, shows that the rebuilding after the captivity is intended. The LXX. and Vulg. have "dispersion;" Symmachus, "those thrust out."

(3) **Broken in heart.**—As in Ps. xxxiv. 18. (Comp. Isa. lxi. 1.)

Wounds.—See margin, and comp. Job ix. 28; Prov. xv. 13.

(4) **Stars.**—This proof of God's power to help, by reference to the stars of heaven, which are beyond man's

God's Tenderness and Greatness. PSALMS, CXLVIII. *His Delight in His Children.*

telleth the number of the stars; he calleth them all by *their* names. ⁽⁵⁾ Great *is* our Lord, and of great power: ² his understanding *is* infinite. ⁽⁶⁾ The LORD lifteth up the meek: he casteth the wicked down to the ground.

⁽⁷⁾ Sing unto the LORD with thanksgiving; sing praise upon the harp unto our God: ⁽⁸⁾ who covereth the heaven with clouds, who prepareth rain for the earth, who maketh grass to grow upon the mountains. ⁽⁹⁾ ^aHe giveth to the beast his food, *and* to the young ravens which cry. ⁽¹⁰⁾ He delighteth not in the strength of the horse; he taketh not pleasure in the legs of a man. ⁽¹¹⁾ The LORD taketh pleasure in them that fear him, in those that hope in his mercy.

⁽¹²⁾ Praise the LORD, O Jerusalem; praise thy God, O Zion. ⁽¹³⁾ For he hath

Marginal notes:
1 Heb., *of his understanding there is no number.*
a Job 38. 41; Ps. 104. 27, 28.
2 Heb., *Who maketh thy border peace.*
3 Heb., *fat of wheat.*
4 Heb., *his words.*
5 Heb., *Hallelujah.*

strengthened the bars of thy gates; he hath blessed thy children within thee. ⁽¹⁴⁾ ²He maketh peace *in* thy borders, *and* filleth thee with the ³finest of wheat. ⁽¹⁵⁾ He sendeth forth his commandment *upon* earth: his word runneth very swiftly. ⁽¹⁶⁾ He giveth snow like wool: he scattereth the hoarfrost like ashes. ⁽¹⁷⁾ He casteth forth his ice like morsels: who can stand before his cold? ⁽¹⁸⁾ He sendeth out his word, and melteth them: he causeth his wind to blow, *and* the waters flow.

⁽¹⁹⁾ He sheweth ⁴his word unto Jacob, his statutes and his judgments unto Israel. ⁽²⁰⁾ He hath not dealt so with any nation: and *as for his* judgments, they have not known them. Praise ye the LORD.

PSALM CXLVIII.

⁽¹⁾ ⁵Praise ye the LORD. Praise ye the

---

power to count, much more to name, but which the Almighty both numbers and names, seems rather abruptly introduced, but the train of thought is clear. To assemble the dispersed of Israel, however numerous and scattered, was easy to the ruler of the hosts of heaven. The original promise to Abraham was, of course, in the poet's mind, but still more Isa. xl. 26—28, from which the expression may have been taken. The dramatic "Lift your eyes on high and behold" supplies the link needed in the abrupt entrance of the thought of the psalm.

⁽⁵⁾ **Of great power.**—Literally, *abounding in power.*

Infinite.—Literally, *without number.* (See Note, Ps. cxlv. 3, and Isa. xl. 28; that prophetic passage being still in the poet's mind, though the expression is changed.)

⁽⁶⁾ **The meek.**—Or, *the afflicted.* (See Note Ps. xxii. 26.)

⁽⁷⁾ **Sing.**—Literally, *answer,* which some think suggests an antiphonal arrangement. Though the strophic arrangement is only loosely marked, the psalm takes a new departure here, with a fresh invocation to praise, going on to fresh proofs from nature of the Almighty Power.

⁽⁹⁾ Comp. Pss. civ. 14, cxlv. 15; Job xxxviii. 41; Luke xii. 24.

The proper attitude towards one who is thus "great to grant as mighty to make," is not conceit of wisdom and strength, but humble dependence and trust.

⁽¹⁰⁾ **Strength of the horse . . . legs of a man.** —This somewhat strange antithesis has been explained to refer to cavalry and infantry, but the much more expressive passage, Ps. xxxiii. 16, 17, which was plainly before this poet, would hardly have been altered so strangely. The horse as a type of strength and endurance was of course common. (Comp. especially Job xxxix. 19—25.) And we have before seen that Eastern nations naturally select fleetness of foot as the typical quality in a vigorous warrior. (See Ps. xviii. 33.)

The constant epithet "swift-footed Achilles," suggests the best explanation of the second clause of the verse. (Comp. 2 Sam. ii. 18).

⁽¹²⁾ **Praise.**—For this verb, properly *stroke,* or *soothe,* see Ps. lxiii. 5.

⁽¹³⁾ **For he hath strengthened.**—An allusion to the new fortifications of the restored city is probable, though the expression is plainly figurative of security and peace.

With the second clause comp. Isa. lx. 17, 18.

⁽¹⁴⁾ **Maketh peace.**—Or, *placing as thy border peace.*

Finest of the wheat.—Literally, *fat of wheat.* (See Ps. lxxxi. 16.)

⁽¹⁵⁾ Ps. xxxiii. is still in the poet's thought, and verses 6, 7 especially; but some extraordinary season of frost seems to have kindled his inspiration, so that he not only elaborates but improves on his model. The word of God is personified as a messenger who runs swiftly forth to do his bidding, at first in binding the earth and sheaves up with frost, and then (verse 18) in suddenly thawing and releasing them.

⁽¹⁶⁾ **Like wool.**—Both in whiteness and fleecy texture. "The snow falls in large flakes, equal in size to a walnut, and has more resemblance to locks of wool than it has in our country" (Niven, *Biblical Antiq.,* p. 21).

"Aspice quam densum tacitarum vellus aquarum
Defluat.   MART., *Ep.* iv. 3.

⁽¹⁷⁾ **Morsels.**—Or, *crumbs.* (Gen. xviii. 5; Judges xix. 5.) Doubtless the allusion is to hail.

⁽¹⁹⁾ **Jacob . . . Israel.**—As in the other two pieces into which the psalm divides (verses 6—11), the thought passes from the grandeur of God revealed in nature to the divine protection and favour accorded to Israel.

⁽²⁰⁾ **Any nation.**—This boast in Israel's peculiar and exclusive privilege may be compared with Deut. iv. 7, xxxii. 32—41.

Judgments.—Here plainly not manifestations of wrath; but, as so frequently in Ps. cxix., the display of righteousness towards Israel.

CXLVIII.

This glorious anthem, as it has been the model of countless hymns of praise, is best appreciated and understood by comparison with some of these. The

LORD from the heavens: praise him in the heights. (2) Praise ye him, all his angels: praise ye him, all his hosts. (3) Praise ye him, sun and moon: praise him, all ye stars of light. (4) Praise him, ye heavens of heavens, and ye waters that *be* above the heavens.

(5) Let them praise the name of the LORD: for he commanded, and they were created. (6) He hath also stablished them for ever and ever: he hath made a decree which shall not pass.

(7) Praise the LORD from the earth, ye dragons, and all deeps: (8) fire, and hail; snow, and vapours; stormy wind fulfilling his word: (9) mountains, and all hills; fruitful trees, and all cedars:

"song of the three children," found in the LXX. version of Daniel, is no doubt an imitation, but in its elaboration and its artificial style loses much of the lyric fire of the original. And of the rest, Isaac Taylor truly says: "It is but feebly and as afar off, that the ancient liturgies—except so far as they merely copied their originals—came up to the majesty and wide compass of the Hebrew worship, such as it is indicated in the cxlviiith Psalm. Neither Andrews, nor Gregory, nor the Greeks, have reached or approached this level. And in tempering the boldness of their originals by admixtures of what is more Christian and spiritual, the added elements sustain an injury which is not compensated by what they bring forward of a purer or less earthly kind: feeble, indeed, is the tone of these anthems of the ancient church; sophisticated or artificial is their style."

The motive of the psalm, too, is quite different from that sympathetic feeling for nature which enters so largely and powerfully into modern poetry. Not that this feeling was entirely unknown to the Hebrew mind. It makes itself felt elsewhere; but here it is not because the poet wants nature to join him in praise that he summons the universe to his choir, but that he may, in the last verse, enhance the glory and privilege of Israel. All nature has reason to praise the Creator who called it into being, and gave it its order so fair and so established, and poetically the universe may be imagined full of adoring creatures, but in reality, praise as a privilege belongs only to Israel. It is not here a contrast between inanimate and animate, rational and irrational creation. Still less does there show itself the feeling that motives Keble's

"All true, all faultless, all in tune."

On the contrary, it is the covenant people that alone possess the privilege. Expression is piled on expression to establish this fact. "His people," "His saints," "a people near unto Him."

The immediate occasion of the psalm may very probably have been some victory, but conjecture cannot recover it.

(1) **From the heavens . . . in the heights.**—Some would render *ye of the heavens*, but the parallelism is in favour of the Authorised Version. "Heavens" and "heights" in this verse, and "angels" and "hosts" in the next, are analogously parallel. The heights contain the heavens (comp. Job xvi. 19, xxv. 2), as the hosts embrace the angels or messengers of God (Josh. v. 14); the larger term being in such case placed synthetically last. The prepositions thus keep their full meaning. *From* the heavens, or *from* a choir in the heights, comes the burst of angelic praise.

(4) **Heavens of heavens.**—See Ps. lxviii. 33, and references. Before passing downwards to the earth the invocation pauses to combine all the heights, which have been before addressed in the expression which denotes their position relatively to the earth; the highest heaven of all, and then the world of water which, in the Hebrew conception of the Cosmos, was supposed to be the foundation, while itself rests on the firmament or heavenly vault. (See Ps. civ. 3.)

(6) **Stablished.**—Literally, *made to stand, i.e.,* set them up.

He hath made . . .—Rather, *he hath made an ordinance, and will not transgress it.* This is more obvious and natural than to supply a new subject to the second verb, "and none of them transgress it." This anticipates, but only in form, the modern scientific doctrine of the inviolability of natural order. It is the imperishable faithfulness of God that renders the law invariable. See the remarkable passages, Jer. xxxi. 36, xxxii. 20, from which we conclude that a covenant was supposed to have been made between God and nature as between Jehovah and Israel, the one being as imperishable as the other. A comparison of the two passages referred to shows that the Hebrew words *ordinance* and *covenant* might be used synonymously. The Authorised Version, which, following the LXX. and Vulg., makes the ordinance itself imperishable, violates the usage of the Hebrew verb.

(7) **Earth.**—The invocation now passes downwards, and the first sound of terrestrial praise is to come, according to the order of Creation in Gen. i., from the sea-monsters (for which see Note, Pss. lxxiv. 13, xci. 13), the "deeps" being added to include all great waters in which such creatures are found.

(8) **Fire.**—*Lightning,* as in Pss. xviii. 12, cv. 32, where it is also found with "hail."

Vapours.—The same Hebrew word in Gen. xix. 28 and Ps. cxix. 83 is rendered "smoke," and from the use of the cognate verb is certainly connected with "burning." Hence we probably have here the figure *chiasmus* (*fire* and hail, snow and *smoke*), the smoke answering to the fire, as the snow to the hail. On the other hand, from Pss. xviii. 8, clxiv. 5, it is plain that the driving mists of a storm were regarded as smoke. (Comp.

"The smoky mountain tops."—TENNYSON.)

This invocation of the powers of the air is a fine poetic touch, and shows the freedom of lyric treatment of the story of Creation, which in Genesis passes at once from the monsters of the deep to the land and its creatures. To the poet there is another region of life and power; other voices, which, though wild and fierce, may yet join in the grand anthem of praise.

Stormy wind.—As in Ps. cvii. 25. This, to us, free and uncontrollable agent is yet but a messenger of Jehovah, fulfilling his word (Ps. civ. 4).

(9) **Mountains, and all hills.**—The invocation now alights on the crests of the highest mountains, and passes downward to the lower hills where vegetable life begins.

God's Name Excellent. PSALMS, CXLIX. *A New Song.*

(10) beasts, and all cattle; creeping things, and ¹flying fowl: (11) kings of the earth, and all people; princes, and all judges of the earth: (12) both young men, and maidens; old men, and children: (13) let them praise the name of the LORD: for his name alone is ²excellent; his glory *is* above the earth and heaven.

(14) He also exalteth the horn of his people, the praise of all his saints; *even* of the children of Israel, a people near unto him. Praise ye the LORD.

PSALM CXLIX.

(1) ³Praise ye the LORD. Sing unto the LORD a new song, *and* his praise in the congregation of saints.

(2) Let Israel rejoice in him that made him: let the children of Zion be joyful in their King. (3) Let them praise his name ⁴in the dance: let them sing praises unto him with the timbrel and harp.

(4) For the LORD taketh pleasure in his people: he will beautify the meek with salvation. (5) Let the saints be joyful in glory: let them sing aloud upon their beds.

(6) *Let* the high *praises* of God *be* ⁵in their mouth, and a twoedged sword in

1 Heb., *birds of wing.*
2 Heb., *exalted.*
3 Heb., *Hallelujah.*
4 Or, *with the pipe.*
5 Heb., *in their throat.*

Fruitful trees.—Rather, *fruit trees;* the fruit-bearing tree being representative of one division of the vegetable world, planted and reared by man, the cedars of the other, which are (Ps. civ. 16) of God's own plantation.

(10) So here we have *wild* animals and *domesticated* animals. (See Note, Ps. l. 10.)

Creeping things.—This seems to include all the smaller creatures that move on the ground, in contrast with the birds that fly above it.

(11) **All people.**—And now the whole animate and inanimate universe having been summoned, man takes his place as leader of the choir; and here the poet's language is couched so as to include all, all ranks and nations, of every age, and each sex.

(13) **Excellent.**—Rather, *exalted.* As in Isa. xii. 4. So LXX. and Vulg.

Above the earth and heaven.—There is a fine artistic touch in the order of the words in this. All *heaven* and *earth* have been summoned to the chorus of praise, of Him who is now declared to be above *earth* and *heaven.*

(14) **He hath . . .**—Render, *and he hath raised a horn for his people. Praise is for all His saints, for the sons of Israel, a people near Him.*

The raising of the horn evidently implies some victory, or assurance of victory, which, no doubt, gave the first impulse for this song of praise. (See Introduction.) For the figure see Note, Ps. lxxv. 4, 5.

The verse is a repetition of a frequent statement of the Psalms. While poetically all the universe, inanimate as well as animate, all men, heathen as well as Hebrews, can be called to sing "hallelujah," it remains as it has ever been, the covenant privilege of Israel. This explanation disposes at once of the charge which has been brought against this verse of narrowing a grand universal anthem, and ending the psalm with an anti-climax.

CXLIX.

History supplies a terrible comment on this psalm. "Under the illusion that it might be used as a prayer without any spiritual transmutation, Ps. cxlix. has become the watchword of the most horrible errors. It was by means of this psalm that Caspar Scloppius, in his *Classicum Biblicæ Sacræ*, which, as Bakius says, is written, not with ink but with blood, inflamed the Roman Catholic princes to the thirty years' religious war; and in the Protestant Church Thomas Monzen stirred up the war of the peasants by means of this psalm" (Delitzsch).

So the fanaticism and cruelty of times that should have been more enlightened have been fed by the record the Jews have left of their blended religious and patriotic zeal. The age when such a psalm was most likely to be produced was undoubtedly that of the Maccabees, and the coincidence between verse 6 of the psalm and 2 Macc. xv. 27 may indicate the very series of events amid which, with hymns of praise in their throats, and a two-edged sword in their hand, the *chasidim* in battle after battle claimed and won the honour of executing vengeance on Jehovah's foes. The synthetic parallelism is finely marked.

(1) **A new song.**—See Ps. xxxiii. 3.

The congregation.—Apparently the psalm puts us in the Maccabæan age, when the *chasidim* was become a regular title for the patriotic party.

(3) **In the dance.**—Rather, as margin, *with the pipe.* The use of the word *machôl* in what was evidently a list of all the orchestral instruments used in the Temple in the next psalm, would alone be almost decisive of the meaning. But one possible derivation is certainly in favour of this rendering, as also the translation in the Syriac version by the name of a flute still found in Syria. Its connection, too, with the *timbrel* or *drum* (comp. our pipe and tabor), just as a cognate, *chalîl*, is connected in 1 Sam. x. 5; Isa. v. 12, points the same way. (See *Bible Educator*, i. p. 70, and Note to Song of Sol. vi. 13.)

Timbrel.—See Exod. xv. 20; *Bible Educator*, i. 314.

Harp.—See Ps. xxxiii. 2.

(4) **He will beautify the meek . . .**—Rather, *He adorns the oppressed with salvation.* Not only is the victory which achieves the deliverance of the afflicted people a relief to them, but the honour won in the sight of the world is like a beautiful robe, a figure no doubt suggested by the actual triumphal dresses of the victors, or the spoils in which they appeared after the battle. (Comp. Isa. lv. 5, lx. 7; lxi. 3; Judges v. 30.)

(5) The two clauses are directly parallel:

"Let the *chasidîm* raise a cry in glory:
Let them sing aloud upon their couches."

Either the rejoicing is carried far into the night, and when retired to rest the happy people burst out anew into singing; or (see Hosea vii. 14), the couches may rather be the divans where feasts were held.

(6) **High praises.**—Literally, *exaltations of celebration, i.e.*, hymns of praise.

their hand; ⁽⁷⁾ to execute vengeance upon the heathen, *and* punishments upon the people; ⁽⁸⁾ to bind their kings with chains, and their nobles with fetters of iron; ⁽⁹⁾ *a* to execute upon them the judgment written: this honour have all his saints. Praise ye the LORD.

PSALM CL.

⁽¹⁾ ¹ Praise ye the LORD. Praise God in his sanctuary: praise him in the firmament of his power.

a Deut. 7. 1.

1 Heb., *Hallelujah.*

2 Or, *cornet.*

3 Or, *pipe.*

⁽²⁾ Praise him for his mighty acts: praise him according to his excellent greatness.
⁽³⁾ Praise him with the sound of the ² trumpet: praise him with the psaltery and harp. ⁽⁴⁾ Praise him with the timbrel and ³ dance: praise him with stringed instruments and organs. ⁽⁵⁾ Praise him upon the loud cymbals: praise him upon the high sounding cymbals.
⁽⁶⁾ Let every thing that hath breath praise the LORD. Praise ye the LORD.

Mouth.—Rather, *throat.*

⁽⁷⁾ **Heathen . . . people.**—Rather, *nations . . . peoples.*

⁽⁹⁾ **The judgment written.**—If we knew the exact circumstance which produced the psalm, and had the names of the nobles and princes taken prisoners, we should easily guess at the contents of the "judgment written," which was, perhaps, some special order, the carrying out of which is celebrated here; or we may think of the judgments against the nation registered here and there in the sacred books, and so by prescription made legitimate, such as that of the Canaanites, Amalekites, &c.; or we may give the phrase a still more general sense, as in Isa. lxv. 6: "Behold, it is written before me: I will not keep silence, but will recompense, even recompense into their bosom." Ought we not, however, to read the verse: *To execute judgment upon them. It is written, This honour have all his saints.*

This honour.—Israel is here regarded as the instrument of God's righteous judgments on the heathen.

CL.

In the place of the short doxology, such as concludes each of the former books of the psalter, this psalm was fitly composed or selected to close the whole collection. It has been well called "the finale of the spiritual concert," and no doubt afforded a good musical display, music performed with full orchestra and choir, every kind of instrument known to the Hebrews, *wind, string,* and *percussion,* being mentioned, and in the last verse all who had breath and voice being invited to join. The form of the invocation embracing heaven and earth, and putting forward as the object of praise both Jehovah's majesty and His great works wrought for Israel, is also exactly suited for a conclusion to the great collection of Israelite song. The parallelism is perfect.

⁽¹⁾ **Sanctuary**—That is, the temple. Some take it in direct parallelism with firmament, and understand the "heavenly palace," or "Temple" (comp. Ps. xi. 4); but, as in Ps. cxlviii., the invocation to praise includes heaven and earth; so here, but in the reverse order, the earthly sanctuary first, and the sublime things done on earth (verse 2), then heaven and the exalted greatness there.

⁽²⁾ **Mighty acts . . . excellent greatness.**—The one displayed on earth, the other manifested in heaven. (See preceding Note.)

⁽³⁾ **Trumpet.**—Heb., *shôphar.* (See Pss. lxxxi. 3, xcviii. 6. LXX., σάλπιγξ.) It was the crooked horn, sometimes also called *keren.* (*Bible Educator,* ii. 231.)

Psaltery and harp.—See Note, Ps. xxxiii. 2.

⁽⁴⁾ **Timbrel and dance.**—See Ps. cxlix. 3.

Stringed instruments. — *Minnim.* Literally, *parts,* so *threads,* so here, as in LXX. and Vulg., "with" or "on strings." (See Note, Ps. xlv. 9.)

Organs.—Heb., *'ugab,* which has been variously identified with the *syrinx,* or Pan's pipes, of the Greeks, with the "bagpipe," and even with a rude instrument embodying the principle of the modern organ. (See *Bible Educator,* ii. 70, 183, 229.)

⁽⁵⁾ **Cymbals.**—Heb., *tseltselim* (2 Sam. vi. 5), a word evidently formed to express the sound of the instrument. Two kinds are evidently indicated in this verse, the "loud" cymbals (literally, *cymbals of hearing*), and "high-sounding" (literally, *of tumult*). As the Arabs use at present a larger and smaller instrument (see *Bible Educator,* ii., 211, 311), it is possible that the same distinction is made here, but which would be the larger instrument it is impossible from the Hebrew to determine.

⁽⁶⁾ **Everything that hath breath. — LXX.** "every breath;" Vulg., "every spirit;" literally, *all breath.* We naturally wish to give these words their largest intent, and to hear the psalter close with an invocation to "the earth with her thousand voices" to praise God. But the psalm so distinctly and positively brings us into the Temple, and places us among the covenant people engaged at their devotions, that we are compelled to see here a hymn specially suited to close the collection of hymns of the covenant, as the first and second were to begin it. It is, therefore, not all breathing beings, but only all assembled in the sanctuary, that are here addressed; and the loud hallelujah with which the collection of psalms actually closes rises from Hebrew voices alone.

THE PROVERBS

INTRODUCTION
TO
THE PROVERBS

The contents of this book cover a wider space of ground than its English title would lead anyone to expect; for the Hebrew word *māshāl*, translated "Proverbs" in our version, while, indeed, it bears this sense, includes also several other meanings. Originally, it would seem, it signified a "figure" or "comparison," and we find it used in Holy Scripture for (1) "a parable," such as those in the Gospels, inculcating moral or religious truth, in which the figure and the thing signified by it are kept distinct from each other. Examples of this are to be found in the parables of the two eagles and vine, in Ezek. xvii., and of the boiling pot, in Ezek. xxiv. It is also used (2) for "a short pointed saying," in which, however, a comparison is still involved: for instance, Prov. xxv. 25, "As cold waters to a thirsty soul, so is good news from a far country." Hence it passed into the sense of (3) "a proverb," in which a comparison may still be implied, though it is no longer expressed, such as Ezek. xviii. 2, "The fathers have eaten sour grapes, and the children's teeth are set on edge." Lastly, the sense of comparison or figure being lost, it became equivalent to (4) an "instructive saying," such as Prov. xi. 4, "Riches profit not in the day of wrath, but righteousness delivereth from death." The form of this might be lengthened till it became equivalent to (5) "a didactic poem," such as Ps. xlix. 4, "I will incline mine ear to a parable," &c. Of this kind were the prophecies of Balaam, in Num. xxiii. and xxiv., in which he is said to have "taken up his parable." In certain cases this form of parable might become equivalent to "satire," as in the prophet's song of triumph over fallen Babylon, in Isa. xiv. Of these various forms of the *māshāl*, it would seem that (1) and (3) do not occur in the Proverbs, (5) is largely employed in chaps. i.–ix., while (2) and (4) are frequent in the later chapters of the book.

As to the poetical form which the *māshāl* of Solomon assumes, the thought of the writer is most generally completed in the *distich*, or verse of two lines. But the relation of the two lines to each other may vary in different cases. Sometimes (1) the idea contained in the first is repeated in the second with slightly altered form, so as to be brought out more fully and distinctly, as in chap. xi. 25, "The liberal soul shall be made fat, and he that watereth shall be watered also himself." Or (2) the second line may illustrate the first by presenting the contrast to it, as in chap. x. 1, "A wise son maketh a glad father: but a foolish son is the heaviness of his mother." Or, again, (3) a distinct truth may be presented to the reader in each line, with little apparent connection between them, as in chap. x. 18, "A cloak of hatred are lying lips, and he that spreadeth slander is a fool." Many distichs contain entire parables in themselves, a resemblance to the lesson inculcated being drawn from every-day life, as chap. x. 26, "As vinegar to the teeth, and as smoke to the eyes, so is the sluggard to them that send him." In all these cases it will be noticed that the distich is complete in itself, without any further explanation being required. But sometimes the subject extends to four (chap. xxv. 4, 5), six (chap. xxiii. 1—3), and eight (chap. xxiii. 22—25) lines, or, it may be, to three (chap. xxii. 29), five (chap. xxiii. 4, 5), or seven (chap. xxiii. 6—8). It may even be prolonged beyond these limits to an indefinite number of verses, as in the acrostic (chap. xxxi. 10, *sqq.*) in praise of a virtuous wife.

As to the general contents of the Book of Proverbs, it will be noticed on examination that they do not form one harmonious whole, but that they naturally fall into several clearly marked divisions, each of them distinguished by peculiarities of style. They are as follows:

(1) Chap. i. 1—6, an introduction, describing the purpose of the book.

(2) Chaps. i. 7—ix. 18, comprising fifteen didactic poems—not single unconnected verses, like most of the book—exhorting to the fear of God and the avoidance of sin. Many of these are addressed to "my son"; in others Wisdom is introduced as pleading to be heard, and setting forth the blessings she brings with her.

(3) Chaps. x. 1—xxii. 16, the second great division of the book; these are headed by a new title, "The proverbs of Solomon." They consist of 375 separate distichs, quite unconnected with each other, the sense being completed in each verse of the English Version; in the first six chapters of this collection the antithetic form of proverb chiefly prevails, but the other forms mentioned above as employed in this book are also represented.

(4) To this course of distichs follows an introduction (chap. xxii. 17—21), containing an exhortation to "hear the words of the wise"; the style of this is not unlike section (2). This serves as a heading to the (5) appendix of chaps. xxii. 22—xxiv. 22, in which every form of the *māshāl* may be found, from the distich up to the lengthened didactic poem, such as was frequent earlier in the book.

(6) Next comes a second appendix (chap. xxiv. 23—34), beginning, "These also belong to the wise" (*i.e.*, as their authors), containing proverbs of various lengths which resemble chaps. i. 7—ix. 18, and the Book of Ecclesiastes.

(7) This is followed by the third great division of the book (chaps. xxv.—xxix.), with the title, "These are also proverbs of Solomon, which the men of Hezekiah king of Judah copied out." It differs from the previous collection (chaps. x.—xxii. 16) in this respect: that the verses are chiefly parabolic, not antithetic, in their character, and the sense, instead of being completed in a distich, extends to five lines, or even further.

(8) At this point the proverbs of Solomon are ended, for the rest of the book does not profess to have been composed by him. It consists of three appendices:

PROVERBS.

(*a*) chap. xxx. "The words of Agur the son of Jakeh," an unknown author, supposed by Rabbinical writers, against all probability, to be Solomon himself; (*b*) "The words of King Lemuel," also unknown (chap. xxxi. 1—9); and (*c*) the acrostic in praise of a good wife (chap. xxxi. 10, *sqq.*).

There is another noticeable feature in the Book of Proverbs: that it contains many repetitions, the same thought being often expressed for a second time in similar or identical terms. Thus the Hezekiah collection (7) contains many repetitions of proverbs which have already appeared in part (3); and in some cases it even repeats itself, as does part (5) also; and this is very frequently the case in part (3) as well.

These various features which distinguish the book—viz., the difference in the style of the several parts, the separate headings which occur, and the frequent repetitions—would seem to render it certain that the whole book cannot have originally made its appearance in its present shape at any one time. It rather bears the mark of having been, like the Psalms, collected at various times, and by various persons. Thus, each editor of the five books which compose the Psalter appears to have brought together as many psalms of David or the sons of Korah or Asaph, or other writers, as he could find. Many which had escaped the notice of an earlier editor were afterwards incorporated by a successor into a later book. Thus the first book (Pss. i.—xli.) consists almost entirely of psalms of David, yet others also ascribed to him are found in the second (Pss. xlii.—lxxii.), fourth (Pss. xc.—cvi.), and fifth (Pss. cvii.—cl.) books; the second similarly contains many by the sons of Korah, but there is a further collection of theirs to be found in the third; one psalm by Asaph appears in the second book, and several more in the third, and so on. It seems probable that in the same way each of the three great collections of proverbs which are attributed to Solomon may be due to the care of different collectors, each of whom incorporated into his own book such materials as he met with. In so doing, he was not always careful to omit what had been set down before, and even occasionally admitted a proverb twice into his own collection. But we find parallels to this in the Psalter. Psalm lxx., for instance, is a repetition of the latter end of Ps. xl., Ps. liii. of Ps. xiv., Ps. cviii. of Pss. lvii. and lx.

As to the authorship of the book, there seems on the whole to be no good reason for casting doubt on the tradition which ascribes chaps. i.—xxix. to King Solomon. How eminently unsatisfactory the attempts are which have been made to settle the date and circumstances under which each portion of the book was composed, may be seen by the very opposite conclusions arrived at by critics who have attempted to solve the problem. When we find authors of eminence differing by, it may be, two centuries in their estimate of the age of a passage, and unable to agree as to which part of the book was written first, it is clear that little importance can be attached to the internal evidence upon which such theories are based.

It should also be noticed that, in spite of the reasons alleged above, which might have led us to ascribe the various sections of the book to different authors, yet there is still so strong a likeness between Prov. i.—xxix., Ecclesiastes, and Canticles, as to render it highly probable that all three had only one author, and if so, that he was Solomon. For it would be difficult to find anyone else to whom they might with any show of probability be ascribed.

Although some objections have been at times taken to the book, on the score of the supposed contradictions contained in it, yet it has always held its place in the Hebrew Canon of Scripture. How great its influence upon the Jewish mind has been, may be seen from the imitations of it which are still extant, the Books of Wisdom and Ecclesiasticus. Among Christians it has always been held in the highest esteem. It is frequently quoted in the New Testament. By the Fathers it was named the "All-excellent Wisdom." The description of wisdom which it contains was universally interpreted by them as declaratory of the work of Christ, as Creator of the world and Redeemer of mankind: an interpretation borne out by our Lord's own words and the teaching of St. Paul.*

Lists of the principal commentaries which have been written upon Proverbs may be found in Keil's Introduction to the Old Testament (translated in Clark's *For. Theol. Library*, 1871), and in the article on Proverbs in Smith's *Dictionary of the Bible*. Of all those which have come in my way, I must chiefly express my obligations to the works of Rosenmüller and Delitzsch. The commentary of Bishop Wordsworth is noticeable as containing many references to the works of the Fathers bearing upon the interpretation of the book.

---

* See Note on chap. i. 20.

THE PROVERBS.

CHAPTER I.—⁽¹⁾ The proverbs of Solomon the son of David, king of Israel;
⁽²⁾ To know wisdom and instruction; to perceive the words of understanding; ⁽³⁾ to receive the instruction of wisdom, justice, and judgment, and ¹equity; ⁽⁴⁾ to give subtilty to the simple, to the young man knowledge and ²discretion.

⁽⁵⁾ A wise *man* will hear, and will increase learning; and a man of understanding shall attain unto wise counsels: ⁽⁶⁾ to understand a proverb, and ³the interpretation; the words of the wise, and their dark sayings.

⁽⁷⁾ ^aThe fear of the LORD *is* ⁴the beginning of knowledge: *but* fools despise wisdom and instruction. ⁽⁸⁾ My son,

---

B.C. written cir. 1000.

1 Heb., *equities.*
2 Or, *advisement.*
3 Or, *an eloquent speech.*
a Job 28. 28; Ps. 111. 10; ch. 9. 10.
4 Or, *the principal part.*

1.—INTRODUCTION DESCRIBING THE PURPOSE OF THE BOOK (verses 1—6).

⁽¹⁾ **Proverbs.**—For the various senses of the Hebrew *māshāl* thus translated, see Introduction.

Solomon.—The absolute quiet and prosperity of the reign of Solomon (the man of peace), as described in 1 Kings iv. 20, *sqq.*, would naturally be conducive to the growth of a sententious philosophy; whereas the constant wars and dangerous life of David had called forth the impassioned eloquence of the Psalms.

⁽²⁾ **To know.**—That is, they are written that one may know. The writer in this and the following verses heaps up synonyms with which to bring out the wide purpose of the instruction he offers.

Wisdom (*chokhmah*).—The original meaning of this word is "firmness," "solidity," having an opinion based upon sound reasons; the opposite state of mind to being "carried about with every wind of doctrine" (Eph. iv. 14).

Instruction (*mûsār*).—Or rather, *discipline,* the knowledge how to keep oneself under control. (Comp. 2 Pet. i. 6: "Add to your knowledge temperance," or self-control.)

To perceive the words of understanding.—Comp. Heb. v. 14: "To have the senses exercised to discern both good and evil." (Comp. also Phil. i. 10.) The opposite condition to this is having the heart made "fat" (Isa. vi. 10) by continuance in evil, so that it can no longer understand.

⁽³⁾ **To receive the instruction of wisdom.**—To take in, or appropriate, the "discipline" which results in "prudence" (*haskēl*) or practical wisdom; so David "behaved himself wisely" (1 Sam. xviii. 5).

Equity.—Literally, *what is straight,* so true, honest.

⁽⁴⁾ **Subtilty** (*'Ormah*).—Used in a bad sense (Exod. xxi. 14) for "guile." For the meaning here, comp. Matt. x. 16: "Be ye wise as serpents;" comp. also the reproof of Luke xvi. 8, that "the children of this world are in their generation wiser than the children of light;" and St. Paul's advice to "redeem the time" (Eph. v. 16), *i.e.*, seize opportunities for good.

Simple.—Literally, *those who are open* to good impressions and influences, but who also can be easily led astray. (Comp. chap. viii. 5 and xiv. 15.)

Young man.—The Hebrew term is used of any age from birth to about the twentieth year.

Discretion.—Or rather, *thoughtfulness;* a word also used in a bad sense in chap. xii. 2, and there translated "wicked devices."

⁽⁵⁾ **A wise man will hear.**—That is, if he listen to these proverbs. (Comp. chap. ix. 9.) It is not the young only who will derive profit from them.

A man of understanding.—Or rather, *of discernment.*

Wise counsels.—Literally, *arts of seamanship:* *i.e.,* guiding himself and others aright through the "waves of this troublesome world."

⁽⁶⁾ **Interpretation.**—Or an obscure thing which needs interpretation, so corresponding to "dark sayings."

Dark sayings.—Literally *knots,* intricate sayings, like Samson's riddle (Judges xiv. 12).

2.—FIFTEEN DIDACTIC POEMS, OR DISCOURSES ON VARIOUS SUBJECTS (chaps. i. 7—ix. 18).

(*a*) *First Discourse:*—*Against Companionship in Robbery* (chap. i. 7—19).

⁽⁷⁾ **The fear of the Lord is the beginning of knowledge.**—The first discourse is prefaced by a distich, which serves as a key-note to all the teaching of the book. This expression, "the fear of the Lord," occurs thirteen times in the Proverbs, and plays a prominent part throughout the Old Testament.

"When God of old came down from heaven,
In power and wrath He came."

That law which was given amid "blackness, and darkness, and tempest" was enforced by the threat, "Cursed is every one that continueth not in all things which are written in the book of the law to do them" (Gal. iii. 10). Men had to be taught how hateful sin was to God, and the lesson was for the most part instilled into them by the fear of immediate punishment. (Comp. Deut. xxviii.) But when the lesson had been learnt, and when mankind had found by experience that they were unable to keep the law of God by their own strength, then the new covenant of mercy was revealed from Calvary, even free justification "by God's grace, through the redemption that is in Christ Jesus" (Rom. iii. 24). And with this new message a new motive to obedience was preached. The "fear of the Lord" was now superseded by the higher duty of the "love of God," and of man, for His sake. "The love

The Enticements of Sinners   PROVERBS, I.   *to be Resisted.*

hear the instruction of thy father, and forsake not the law of thy mother: ⁽⁹⁾ for they *shall be* ¹ an ornament of grace unto thy head, and chains about thy neck.

⁽¹⁰⁾ My son, if sinners entice thee, consent thou not. ⁽¹¹⁾ If they say, Come with us, let us lay wait for blood, let us lurk privily for the innocent without cause: ⁽¹²⁾ let us swallow them up alive as the grave; and whole, as those that go down into the pit: ⁽¹³⁾ we shall find all precious substance, we shall fill our houses with spoil: ⁽¹⁴⁾ cast in thy lot among us; let us all have one purse: ⁽¹⁵⁾ my son, walk not thou in the way with them; refrain thy foot from their path: ⁽¹⁶⁾ ^a for their feet run to evil, and make haste to shed blood. ⁽¹⁷⁾ Surely in vain the net is spread ⁷ in the sight of any bird. ⁽¹⁸⁾ And they lay wait for their *own* blood; they lurk privily for their *own* lives. ⁽¹⁹⁾ So *are* the ways of every one that is greedy of gain; *which* taketh away the life of the owners thereof.

⁽²⁰⁾ ³ ^b Wisdom crieth without; she uttereth her voice in the streets: ⁽²¹⁾ she crieth in the chief place of concourse, in the openings of the gates: in the city she uttereth her words, *saying*, ⁽²²⁾ How long, ye simple ones, will ye love simplicity? and the scorners delight in their

---

Marginal notes: 1 Heb., *an adding.*   *a* Isa. 59. 7; Rom. 3. 15.   2 Heb., *in the eyes of everything that hath a wing.*   3 Heb., *Wisdoms, that is, excellent wisdom.*   *b* ch. 8. 1.

---

of Christ constraineth us," says St. Paul. "We love Him because He first loved us," writes St. John. Now, it was seen that, although the "fear of the Lord" may be the "beginning of wisdom," yet something better still may be aimed at: that "he that feareth is not made perfect in love;" and so the teaching of St. John, the last New Testament writer, is summed up in the words, "If God so loved us, we ought also to love one another" (1 John iv. 11).

Fools (*'evilim*).—Self-willed, headstrong persons, who will listen to no advice.

⁽⁸⁾ **My son.**—The address as of a master to his pupil. This phrase only occurs twice again in Proverbs, excepting in sections (2) and (4).

Law.—Rather, *teaching*. (Comp. chap. iii. 1.)

⁽⁹⁾ **Ornament of grace.**—Given by Wisdom. (Comp. chap. iv. 9.)

Chains about thy neck.—The reward of Joseph (Gen. xli. 42) and of Daniel (Dan. v. 29).

⁽¹⁰⁾ **If sinners entice thee.**—A warning against taking part in brigandage, a crime to which Palestine was at all times peculiarly exposed, from the wild character of its formation, and from its neighbourhood to predatory tribes, who would invade the country whenever the weakness of the government gave them an opening. The insecurity to life and property thus occasioned would provide a tempting opportunity for the wilder spirits of the community to seek a livelihood by plunder.

⁽¹¹⁾ **Without cause.**—To be taken with "lurk." Though he has done us no harm.

⁽¹²⁾ **Alive.**—Comp. the death of Dathan and Abiram (Numb. xvi. 30).

⁽¹⁶⁾ **For their feet . . .**—The first reason against taking part with them: the horrible nature of the crime they are committing.

⁽¹⁷⁾ **Surely in vain . . .**—The second reason: their folly in so doing, for God will bring punishment upon them; in the "same net which they hid privily will their foot be taken" (Ps. ix. 15). Even birds are wiser than they. It is useless to spread a net in the sight of any bird.

⁽¹⁸⁾ **And they lay wait.**—Yet they cannot see that in truth they are laying wait, not for the innocent, but for themselves, as God will deliver him, and bring the mischief they designed for him upon their own head.

⁽¹⁹⁾ **So are the ways . . .**—The conclusion of the discourse. The same phrase occurs in Job viii. 13.

Which taketh away . . .—That is, covetousness takes away the life of him who has this vice in his heart, who is, according to the Hebrew idiom, the "owner" of it. (Comp. similar expressions in chaps. xxii. 24, xxiii. 2, where an "angry" man and a man "given to appetite" are literally an *owner* of anger and appetite.)

(*b*) *Second Discourse:—Wisdom Addresses her Despisers* (chap. i. 20—33).

⁽²⁰⁾ **Wisdom.**—The form of the Hebrew term (*chokhmôth*) has been taken for an abstract singular noun, but probably it is the plural of *chokhmah* (chap. i. 2), signifying the multiform excellences of wisdom. It is possible that Solomon may have originally meant in this passage only to describe, in highly poetic language, the influence and work in their generation of those in whom "the fear of the Lord" dwells. So, too, many of the Psalms (Ps. xlv., for example), in the first instance it would seem, are intended to describe the excellence of some earthly saint or king, yet they are completely fulfilled only in the Son of man, the ideal of all that is noblest and best in man. And thus the description of Wisdom in her manifold activity, as represented in chaps. i., viii., ix., so closely corresponds to the work of our Lord, as depicted in the New Testament, that from the earliest times of Christianity these passages have been held to be a prophecy of Him; and there is good reason for such a view. For a comparison of Luke xi. 49 ("Therefore also said the wisdom of God, Behold, I send," &c.) with Matt. xxiii. 34 (where He says, "Behold, I send") would seem to show that He applied the title to Himself. St. Paul in like manner speaks of Him as the "Wisdom of God" (1 Cor. i. 24); says He has been "made unto us wisdom" (1 Cor. i. 30); and that in Him "are hid all the treasures of wisdom" (Col. ii. 3). For passages from the Fathers embodying this view, see references in Bishop Wordsworth on this chapter.

⁽²¹⁾ **Crieth.**—She cannot bear to see sinners rushing madly on their doom. (Comp. Christ's weeping over Jerusalem, Luke xix. 41; and Rom. ix. 2, *sqq.*; Phil. iii. 18, *sqq.*)

⁽²²⁾ **How long . . .**—Three classes of persons are here addressed: (1) *simple* ones, open to good influences, but also to evil (chap. i. 4); (2) *scorners* (*lētsim*), men who despised what was holy, priding themselves on their cleverness in so doing (chap. xiv. 6), who avoided the wise, and held themselves above their

The Fate of those   PROVERBS, II.   *who Despised Wisdom*

scorning, and fools hate knowledge? (23) turn you at my reproof: behold, I will pour out my spirit unto you, I will make known my words unto you. (24)ᵃ Because I have called, and ye refused; I have stretched out my hand, and no man regarded; (25) but ye have set at nought all my counsel, and would none of my reproof: (26) I also will laugh at your calamity; I will mock when your fear cometh; (27) when your fear cometh as desolation, and your destruction cometh as a whirlwind; when distress and anguish cometh upon you. (28)ᵇ Then shall they call upon me, but I will not answer; they shall seek me early, but they shall not find me: (29) for that they hated knowledge, and did not choose the fear of the LORD: (30) they would none of my counsel: they despised all my reproof. (31) Therefore shall they eat of the fruit of their own way, and be filled with their own devices. (32) For the ¹turning away of the simple shall slay them, and the prosperity of fools shall destroy them. (33) But whoso hearkeneth unto me shall dwell safely, and shall be quiet from fear of evil.

CHAPTER II.—(1) My son, if thou wilt receive my words, and hide my commandments with thee; (2) so that thou incline thine ear unto wisdom, *and* apply thine heart to understanding; (3) yea, if thou criest after knowledge, *and* ²liftest up thy voice for understanding;
(4) ᶜ If thou seekest her as silver, and searchest for her as *for* hid treasures; (5) then shalt thou understand the fear of the LORD, and find the knowledge of God.

a Isa. 65. 12, & 66. 4; Jer. 7. 13; Ezek. 8. 18.

b Job 27. 9; Isa. 1. 15; Jer. 11. 11, & 14. 12; Mic. 3. 4.

1 Or, *ease of the simple.*

2 Heb., *givest thy voice.*

c Matt. 13. 44.

advice (chap. xv. 12), proud, arrogant men (chap. xxi. 24). The name first appears at the time of Solomon, when the prosperity of the nation was favourable to the growth of religious indifference and scepticism. Isaiah had to deal with them in his day, too (Isa. xxviii. 14). (3) *Fools* (*khesîlîm*), dull, stupid persons, stolidly confident in their own wisdom.

(23) **I will pour out my spirit unto you.**—Comp. the prophecy of Joel ii. 28, promised by our Lord (John vii. 38, 39), and fulfilled at Pentecost (Acts ii. 17).

I will make known my words unto you.—For a similar promise that God's will shall be revealed to those who fear and follow Him, comp. Ps. xxv. 14: "The secret of the Lord is with them that fear him;" and Christ's promise: "If any man will do God's will, he shall know of the doctrine," &c. (John vii. 17).

(24) **Because I have called.**—Wisdom's call having been rejected, she now changes her tone from "mercy" to "judgment" (Ps. ci. 1). (Comp. Rom. x. 21: "All day long I have stretched forth my hands," &c.)

(26) **I also will laugh . . . I will mock.**—For expressions like this, comp. Pss. ii. 4, xxxvii. 13, lix. 8, where the same actions are attributed to God. They are not to be taken literally, of course, for the sight of human folly can give no pleasure to Him. They signify that He will act as if He mocked when He refuses to hear their cry. Similar expressions, imputing human actions to the Almighty, are Gen. xi. 5, 7; 2 Chron. xvi. 9; Ps. xviii. 9; human feelings, Gen. vi. 6.

(28) **Then shall they call upon me.**—They did not call upon Him in an "acceptable time," in "a day of salvation" (Isa. xlix. 8), while He was "near" (Isa. lv. 6); so at last the master of the house has "risen up, and shut-to the door" (Luke xiii. 25), and will not listen to their cries.

They shall seek me early.—As God had done, " daily rising up early," and sending the prophets unto them (Jer. vii. 25).

(32) **The turning away of the simple . . .**—*i.e.*, from God. (Comp. Jer. ii. 19.)

Prosperity of fools—*i.e.*, the security, apathy of dull, stupid people (*khesîlîm*), who cannot believe that God will fulfil His threatenings. (Comp. Ps. lxxiii. throughout.)

(33) **Shall dwell safely . . .**—Comp. Ps. xxxvii. throughout for similar promises.

Shall be quiet from fear of evil.—Comp. Ps. cxii. 7 : " He shall not be afraid of any evil tidings," &c.

II.

(c) *Third Discourse:—An Exhortation to follow after Wisdom* (chap. ii.).

(1) **Hide**—*i.e.*, store up. (Comp. verse 4.)
(4) **If thou seekest her as silver.**—That the process of mining was understood long before the time of Solomon, is proved by the remains of copper mines discovered in the peninsula of Sinai, and the gold mines in the Bisháree desert of Egypt. Rock inscriptions have been found near the former, dating from a great age, in the opinion of Lepsius from 4000 B.C. (See the article "Mines," in Smith's *Dictionary of the Bible;* comp. also the description in Job xxviii. 1—11.) Silver was brought to Solomon from Arabia (2 Chron. ix. 14) and Tarshish (2 Chron. ix. 21), probably Tartessus, in Spain.

Searchest for her as for hid treasures.—From the great insecurity of life and property in Eastern countries, the hiding of treasures in the earth has always been of frequent occurrence. It would often, no doubt, happen that the owner would die without disclosing the place of concealment to any one else, and the treasure thus be lost. Hunting after such hoards has in consequence been always of the keenest interest to Orientals, and as such furnishes the groundwork for one of our Lord's parables (Matt. xiii. 44).

(5) **Find the knowledge of God.**—It is the highest of all gifts, even eternal life itself, to know God, the Giver of all good things. It was to bestow this knowledge upon man that Christ came into the world (John xvii. 3). He promises (chap. xiv. 21) the manifestation of Himself as the reward of obedience and love. And yet our highest knowledge of God in this life must be so imperfect, in comparison with the knowledge of Him hereafter, when we shall see Him "face to face" (1 Cor. xiii. 12), that St. Paul (Gal. iv.

(6) ᶜFor the LORD giveth wisdom: out of his mouth *cometh* knowledge and understanding. (7) He layeth up sound wisdom for the righteous: *he is a* buckler to them that walk uprightly. (8) he keepeth the paths of judgment, and preserveth the way of his saints. (9) Then shalt thou understand righteousness, and judgment, and equity; *yea,* every good path. (10) When wisdom entereth into thine heart, and knowledge is pleasant unto thy soul; (11) discretion shall preserve thee, understanding shall keep thee: (12) to deliver thee from the way of the evil *man,* from the man that speaketh froward things; (13) who leave the paths of uprightness, to walk in the ways of darkness; (14) who rejoice to do evil, *and* delight in the frowardness of the wicked; (15) whose ways *are* crooked, and *they* froward in their paths: (16) to deliver thee from the strange woman, ᵇ even from the stranger *which* flattereth with her words; (17) which forsaketh the guide of her youth, and forgetteth the covenant of her God. (18) For her house inclineth unto death, and her paths unto the dead. (19) None that go unto her return again, neither take they hold of the paths of life. (20) That thou mayest walk in the way of good *men,* and keep the paths of the righteous. (21) ᶜFor the upright shall dwell in the land, and the perfect shall remain in it. (22) ᵈBut the wicked shall be cut off from the earth, and the transgressors shall be ¹rooted out of it.

CHAPTER III.—(1) My son, forget not my law; ᵉbut let thine heart keep my commandments: (2) for length of days, and ²long life, and peace, shall

a James 1. 5; 1 Kings 3. 9.

b ch. 5. 3, & 7. 5.

c Ps. 37. 29.

d Job 18. 17; Ps. 104. 35.

¹ Or, *plucked up.*

e Deut. 8. 1, & 30. 16.

² Heb., *years of life.*

---

9) describes our relation to Him now as better expressed by "being known of Him:" *i.e.,* recognised, acknowledged by Him as His children, rather than by "knowing" Him.

(6) **For the Lord giveth wisdom.**—As St. James (chap. i. 5) expresses it, He gives it to every man "liberally, and upbraideth not:" *i.e.,* blames him not for asking it.

(7) **Sound wisdom.**—Literally, *furtherance, advancement.* (Comp. "Whosoever hath, unto him shall be given, and he shall have more abundance," Matt. xiii. 12.)

(8) **He keepeth the paths of judgment**—*i.e.,* protects those who walk in them.

His saints.—Or rather, *His ardent worshippers* (*chasidim*), a term used in the Pentateuch (Deut. xxxiii. 8) of the tribe of Levi, for their zeal in God's service (Exod. xxxii.), and of very frequent occurrence in the Psalter. The word "saint" rather implies dedication to God, as Israel was a "holy nation" (Exod. xix. 6) to God, and Christians (Phil. i. 1) are now in the same position. The term *chāsid,* at the time of the Maccabees, was assumed by such "as were voluntarily devoted to the law" (1 Macc. ii. 42), in opposition to those who favoured the Greek religion and culture.

(10) **When wisdom . . .**—Rather to be taken as an explanation of the preceding, *For wisdom will enter,* &c.

(12) **Froward things.**—(Heb., *tahpŭkhôth*), *i.e.,* misrepresentations, distortions of the truth.

(14) **Delight in the frowardness of the wicked.**—This positive taking pleasure in evil is mentioned by St. Paul (Rom. i. 32) as the last stage of degradation.

(16) **To deliver thee from the strange woman.**—Another work of wisdom, to save from profligacy. Of the two epithets here used, "strange" (*zārah*) and "stranger" (*nokhriyyah*), the first implies that she belonged to another family, the second to another nation. It would seem as if the evil example of Solomon (1 Kings xi. 1), in marrying foreign women, had become common in Israel, and that they, by their vicious lives, had become a deadly source of corruption. Brought up in the lax views of morality which prevailed among heathen nations at this time, they would not consider themselves bound by the high standard of purity which was enjoined upon Hebrew women by the Law.

(17) **The guide of her youth.**—Or rather, *friend with whom she has lived in intimacy:* that is, the husband of her youth; in other words, her first love. Jeremiah uses the same phrase (chap. iii. 4). (Comp. "wife of thy youth," Prov. v. 18; Mal. ii. 14.)

Forgetteth the covenant of her God—*i.e.,* the marriage covenant, made in the presence of God. (Comp. "wife of thy covenant," Mal. *l.c.*)

(18) **For her house inclineth . . .**—Rather, *she sinks down with her house:* house and all, like Dathan and Abiram.

Unto the dead.—In Hebrew *the Rephāim.* The word may signify those "at rest" (comp. Job iii. 17: "There the weary are at rest"); or the "weak." (Comp. Isa. xiv. 10: "Art thou also become weak as we?")

(16—19) Besides the literal sense of this passage, as given above, commentators have very generally found in it a spiritual meaning, a warning against idolatry and apostasy. The union of Israel to God is so frequently spoken of in the prophets under the figure of a marriage, and their rejection of Him for idols as adultery, that the passage may well bear this further sense, especially as Jeremiah (chap. iii. 4) has borrowed this very phrase, "guide of her youth," for a passage in which he is reproving the Jews for their faithlessness. The figure is also very common in the New Testament, as descriptive of the union of Christ and the Church.

(21) **The upright shall dwell in the land**—*i.e.,* of Canaan, according to the old promise made to Abraham, renewed in the fifth commandment, and constantly repeated in the prophets.

III.

(*d*) *Fourth Discourse:—Exhortation to Various Virtues* (chap. iii. 1—18).

(2) **Long life.**—That is, a life worth living, fit to be called "life"; whereas "length of days" only implies

Exhortation to Trust   PROVERBS, III.   *The Preciousness of Wisdom.*

they add to thee. ⁽³⁾ Let not mercy and truth forsake thee: *ᵃ*bind them about thy neck; write them upon the table of thine heart: ⁽⁴⁾ *ᵇ*so shalt thou find favour and ¹good understanding in the sight of God and man.

⁽⁵⁾ Trust in the LORD with all thine heart; and lean not unto thine own understanding. ⁽⁶⁾ *ᶜ*In all thy ways acknowledge him, and he shall direct thy paths. ⁽⁷⁾ *ᵈ*Be not wise in thine own eyes: fear the LORD, and depart from evil. ⁽⁸⁾ It shall be ²health to thy navel, and ³marrow to thy bones.

⁽⁹⁾ *ᵉ*Honour the LORD with thy substance, and with the firstfruits of all thine increase: ⁽¹⁰⁾ *ᶠ*so shall thy barns be filled with plenty, and thy presses shall burst out with new wine.

⁽¹¹⁾ *ᵍ*My son, despise not the chastening of the LORD; neither be weary of his correction: ⁽¹²⁾ for whom the LORD loveth he correcteth; even as a father the son *in whom* he delighteth.

⁽¹³⁾ Happy *is* the man *that* findeth wisdom, and *ʰ*the man *that* getteth understanding. ⁽¹⁴⁾ *ⁱ*For the merchandise of it *is* better than the merchandise of silver, and the gain thereof than fine gold. ⁽¹⁵⁾ She *is* more precious than rubies: and all the things thou canst desire are not to be compared unto her. ⁽¹⁶⁾ Length of days *is* in her right hand; *and* in her left hand riches and honour. ⁽¹⁷⁾ Her ways *are* ways of pleasantness, and all her paths *are* peace. ⁽¹⁸⁾ She *is* a tree of life to them that lay hold upon her: and happy *is* every one that retaineth her.

⁽¹⁹⁾ The LORD by wisdom hath founded the earth; by understanding hath he ⁵established the heavens. ⁽²⁰⁾ By his knowledge the depths are broken up, and the clouds drop down the dew. ⁽²¹⁾ My son, let not them depart from thine eyes: keep sound wisdom and discretion: ⁽²²⁾ so shall they be life unto thy soul, and grace to thy neck. ⁽²³⁾ *ⁱ*Then

---

a Ex. 13. 9; Deut. 6. 8.
b Ps. 111. 10.
1 Or, *good success.*
c 1 Chron. 28. 9.
d Rom. 12. 16.
2 Heb., *medicine.*
3 Heb. *watering,* or, *moistening.*
e Ex. 23. 19, & 34. 26; Deut. 26. 2, &c.; Mal. 3. 10, &c.; Luke 14. 13.
f Deut. 28. 8.
g Job 5. 17; Heb. 12. 5, Rev. 3. 19.
4 Heb., *the man that draweth out understanding.*
h Job 28. 15, &c.; Ps. 19. 10; ch. 8. 11, 19. & 16. 16.
5 Or, *prepared.*
i Ps. 37. 24, & 91. 11.

---

extension of life, the reward promised for obedience to parents.

⁽³⁾ **Mercy.**—Or rather, *love*, shown by God to man (Exod. xxxiv. 7), by man to God (Jer. ii. 2), and to his fellow man (Gen. xxi. 23); "truth," or rather, *faithfulness*, especially in keeping promises, is similarly used both of God (Ps. xxx. 10) and man (Isa. lix. 14). The two are often joined, as in this place. They are the two special attributes by which God is known in His dealings with men (Exod. xxxiv. 6, 7), and as such must be imitated by man (Matt. v. 48).

Bind them about thy neck . . .—These directions resemble the figurative orders with regard to the keeping of the Law in Exod. xiii. 9 and Deut. vi. 8, the literal interpretation of which led to the use of prayer-fillets and phylacteries among the Jews. Certain texts of Scripture were copied out, enclosed in a leather case, and tied at the time of prayer on the left arm and forehead.

Table.—Rather, *tablet* (Luke i. 63; comp. Jer. xxxi. 33).

⁽⁴⁾ **Favour and good understanding.**—Particularly noted as distinguishing the childhood of our Lord (Luke ii. 52).

⁽⁷⁾ **Fear the Lord, and depart from evil.**—The same result is reached by Job also (chap. xxviii. 28) in his inquiry after wisdom.

⁽⁸⁾ **Navel.**—As being the centre, and so the most important part of the body. (Comp. the epithet applied to Delphi, "navel of the earth.")

Marrow.—Literally, *watering*: *i.e.*, refreshing. (Comp. Job xxi. 24.) For the opposite condition, "dryness" of the bones, comp. chap. xvii. 22.

⁽¹⁰⁾ **Presses.**—Or *vats*, into which the newly pressed juice flowed: the "winefat" of Mark xii. 1. (Comp. the promise to follow upon payment of tithes, Mal. iii. 8—12.)

⁽¹¹⁾ **Despise not the chastening of the Lord . . .**—Comp. Job v. 17. A wonderful advance beyond the teaching of the Pentateuch: *e.g.*, Deut. xxviii., in which the Jews had to be treated as children, and punishment or reward follow as the immediate consequence of bad or good behaviour. Under such a discipline misfortune could only be regarded as a punishment, a sign of God's displeasure; but now a further manifestation of His dealings with man is made. When He sends trouble upon His children, He is no longer to be regarded as an offended father punishing their faults, but as one who in love is correcting them. Even the New Testament quotes these words with approval, and without adding anything to their teaching (Heb. xii. 5—13). There it is shown how all God's children must, without exception, submit to this discipline.

⁽¹⁵⁾ **Rubies.**—The meaning of the Hebrew *penînîm* is doubtful. Lam. iv. 7 shows the colour to have been red; "coral" is a probable rendering; that of "pearls" is unlikely. For the thought, comp. Job xxviii. 15—19.

⁽¹⁷⁾ **Peace.**—The highest reward of the New Testament for the life of thankful dependence upon God (Phil. iv. 6, 7).

⁽¹⁸⁾ **A tree of life.**—Evidently an allusion to Gen. ii. and iii. No mention is made of it except in Proverbs (chaps. xi. 30, xiii. 12, xv. 4) and Revelation (chaps. ii. 7, xxii. 2).

(*e*) *Fifth Discourse:—Wisdom as Creator and Protector* (chap. iii. 19—26).

⁽¹⁹⁾ **The Lord by wisdom . . .**—A passage anticipatory of the doctrine of John i. 3. (Comp. Pss. civ. 24, and cxxxvi. 5.) A further advance towards the personality of the Creator is made in chap. viii. 27, *sqq.*

⁽²⁰⁾ **Are broken up.**—Or, *burst forth*: the word used in Gen. vii. 11 of the breaking forth of the waters from the interior of the earth at the flood. (Comp. Job xxxviii. 8.)

Drop down the dew.—Of great importance in countries where for months together there is no rain.

shalt thou walk in thy way safely, and thy foot shall not stumble. (24) When thou liest down, thou shalt not be afraid: yea, thou shalt lie down, and thy sleep shall be sweet. (25) Be not afraid of sudden fear, neither of the desolation of the wicked, when it cometh. (26) For the LORD shall be thy confidence, and shall keep thy foot from being taken.

(27) Withhold not good from ¹them to whom it is due, when it is in the power of thine hand to do *it*. (28) Say not unto thy neighbour, Go, and come again, and to morrow I will give; when thou hast it by thee. (29) ²Devise not evil against thy neighbour, seeing he dwelleth securely by thee. (30) Strive not with a man without cause, if he have done thee no harm. (31) ᵃEnvy thou not ³the oppressor, and choose none of his ways.

(32) For the froward *is* abomination to the LORD: ᵇ but his secret *is* with the righteous. (33) ᶜThe curse of the LORD *is* in the house of the wicked: but he blesseth the habitation of the just. (34) ᵈSurely he scorneth the scorners: but he giveth grace unto the lowly. (35) The wise shall inherit glory: but shame ⁴shall be the promotion of fools.

CHAPTER IV.—(1) Hear, ye children, the instruction of a father, and attend to know understanding. (2) For I give you good doctrine, forsake ye not my law. (3) For I was my father's son, ᵉ tender and only *beloved* in the sight of my mother. (4) ᶠHe taught me also, and said unto me, Let thine heart retain my words: keep my commandments, and live. (5) Get wisdom, get understanding: forget *it* not; neither decline from the words of my mouth. (6) Forsake her not, and she shall preserve thee: love her, and she shall keep thee. (7) Wisdom *is* the principal thing; *therefore* get wis-

---

1 Heb., *the owners thereof.*
2 Or, *Practise no evil.*
a Ps. 37. 1.
3 Heb., *a man of violence.*
b Ps. 25. 14.
c Mal. 2. 2.
d James 4. 6; 1 Pet. 5. 5.
4 Heb., *exalteth the fools.*
e 1 Chron. 29. 1.
f 1 Chron. 28. 9.

---

(25) **Desolation of the wicked.**—That is, the storm which overwhelms them.

(*f*) *Sixth Discourse:—Exhortation to Charity, Peace, Contentment* (chap. iii. 27—35).

(27) **Them to whom it is due**—*i.e.*, the poor and needy. An exhortation to us to make to ourselves "friends of the mammon of unrighteousness" (uncertain riches, Luke xvi. 9), remembering that we are not absolute owners, but "stewards of the manifold grace of God" (1 Pet. iv. 10), so that when we "fail," *i.e.*, die, "they," the friends we have made by our liberality, may welcome us to heaven.

(32) **His secret is with the righteous**—*i.e.*, He holds confidential intercourse with them. (Comp. Ps. xxv. 14, and the reward of love and obedience to Christ, that both Father and Son will "come" unto the believer, and "make their abode with him," through the indwelling Spirit, John xiv. 23.)

(33) **He blesseth the habitation of the just.**—The word rendered "habitation" often signifies "pasture," "sheepfold," and this is a relic of the time when the Israelites led a nomad life and had no fixed habitations; so the cry, "To your tents, O Israel!" (1 Kings xii. 16) was still in use long after the settlement in Canaan. By some there is thought to be a distinction intended between the well-built "house" of the wicked and the slightly constructed cottage of the humble just man, no better than a shepherd's hut.

(34) **Surely he scorneth the scorners.**—Rather, *If*, or, *Although he scorns the scorners, yet to the lowly he giveth grace.* Another form of the teaching of chap. i. 24—33. If man rejects God's offers of mercy, they will in time be withdrawn from him. And so, as man deals with God, will God at last deal with him. (Comp. Lev. xxvi. 23, 24; Pss. xviii. 25, 26, lxxxi. 11, 12; Rom. i. 24—26.) The verse is quoted in Jas. iv. 6 and 1 Pet. v. 5.

(35) **Shame shall be the promotion of fools.**—That is, dull, stupid people, who despise God's threatenings (chap. i. 32), are distinguished from others by what is a disgrace to them (Phil. iii. 19), and so are noticeable only as examples to be shunned by others. (See Note on chap. xiv. 29.)

IV.

(*g*) *Seventh Discourse:—Recollections of his Father's Instructions* (chaps. iv. 1—v. 6).

(1) **A father.**—That is, of me, your teacher.

(3) **For I was ... son ...**—It is not only his own advice that he has to offer; he can tell his disciples of the excellent discipline and teaching he received from his parents in his old home. It may be remarked that the notices of Solomon's early years which occur in this and the following verses harmonise well with what we know of him from the historical books of the Bible.

Tender.—The epithet applied to Solomon by his father (1 Chron. xxix. 1).

Only beloved.—The word *yāchîd* originally signified an "only" (son), as in Zech. xii. 10. Then it came to mean "beloved as an only son," and that appears to be the sense of it in Gen. xxii. 2, as applied to Isaac (for Ishmael was then living), and to Solomon here (for Bath-sheba had other children by David, 1 Chron. iii. 5). In Greek translations it is rendered "only-begotten" and "well-beloved," epithets applied in their highest sense to Christ (John i. 14; Matt. iii. 17).

In the sight of my mother.—Implying her affection, as Gen. xvii. 18.

(4) **He taught me also.**—Comp. David's advice to Solomon (1 Chron. xxviii. 9, 10).

(5) **Get wisdom, get understanding.**—Like the pearl of great price (Matt. xiii. 46).

(7) **Wisdom is the principal thing...**—This may also be translated, *The beginning of wisdom is Get* (or, *to get,* comp. chap. xvi. 16) *wisdom: and with* (*i.e.*, at the price of) *all thou hast gotten* (thy possessions) *get understanding.*

dom: and with all thy getting get understanding. (8) Exalt her, and she shall promote thee: she shall bring thee to honour, when thou dost embrace her. (9) She shall give to thine head *an ornament of grace: ¹a crown of glory shall she deliver to thee. (10) Hear, O my son, and receive my sayings; and the years of thy life shall be many. (11) I have taught thee in the way of wisdom; I have led thee in right paths. (12) When thou goest, thy steps shall not be straitened; ᵇand when thou runnest, thou shalt not stumble. (13) Take fast hold of instruction; let *her* not go: keep her; for she *is* thy life.

(14) ᶜEnter not into the path of the wicked, and go not in the way of evil men. (15) Avoid it, pass not by it, turn from it, and pass away. (16) For they sleep not, except they have done mischief; and their sleep is taken away, unless they cause *some* to fall. (17) For they eat the bread of wickedness, and drink the wine of violence. (18) But the path of the just *is* as the shining light, that shineth more and more unto the perfect day. (19) The way of the wicked *is* as darkness: they know not at what they stumble.

(20) My son, attend to my words; incline thine ear unto my sayings. (21) Let them not depart from thine eyes; keep them in the midst of thine heart. (22) For they *are* life unto those that find them, and ²health to all their flesh. (23) Keep thy heart ³with all diligence; for out of it *are* the issues of life. (24) Put away from thee ⁴a froward mouth, and perverse lips put far from thee. (25) Let thine eyes look right on, and let thine eyelids look straight before thee. (26) Ponder the path of thy feet, and ⁵let all thy ways be established. (27) ᵈTurn not to the right hand nor to the left: remove thy foot from evil.

CHAPTER V. — (1) My son, attend unto my wisdom, *and* bow thine ear to my understanding: (2) that thou mayest regard discretion, and *that* thy lips may keep knowledge.

(3) ᵉFor the lips of a strange woman drop *as* an honeycomb, and her ⁶mouth *is* smoother than oil: (4) but her end is bitter as wormwood, sharp

---

a ch. 1. 9.

1 Or, *she shall compass thee with a crown of glory.*

b Ps. 91. 11.

c Ps. 1. 1, ch. 1. 10, 15.

2 Heb., *medicine.*

3 Heb., *above all keeping.*

4 Heb., *frowardness of mouth, and perverseness of lips.*

5 Or, *all thy ways shall be ordered aright.*

d Deut. 5. 32.

e ch. 2. 16, & 6. 24.

6 Heb., *palate.*

---

(8) **Exalt her, and she shall promote thee.**—Comp. 1 Sam. ii. 30, "Them that honour me I will honour."

(13) **For she is thy life.**—Comp. 1 John v. 12, "He that hath the Son hath life."

(16) **For they sleep not . . .**—The practice of evil has become as it were a second nature to them, they cannot live without it.

(17) **The bread of wickedness.**—*i.e.*, acquired by wickedness, as (chap. x. 2) "treasures of wickedness."

(18) **But the path of the just . . .**—The just have the Lord for their light (Ps. xxvii. 1), on them the "Sun of righteousness" has arisen (Mal. iv. 2), as "the light of the morning, even a morning without clouds" (2 Sam. xxiii. 4), and this light, that is, their knowledge of God, will become clearer and clearer till the "perfect day," when they shall see Him as He is (1 John iii. 2). (Comp. Job xi. 17; and Notes on chap. vi. 23.)

(19) **The way of the wicked is as darkness.**—By refusing to "walk in the light" of God's Word, and conscience (1 John i. 7), the light that was in them has become darkness (Matt. vi. 23); they know not whither they are going (John xii. 35), and stumble (chap. xi. 10) over difficulties which in the light they might have avoided.

(22) **For they are life . . .**—Comp. 1 Tim. iv. 8, "Godliness is profitable unto all things, having the promise of the life that now is, (the highest happiness that man can attain to now, peace of mind,) and of that which is to come," the assurance of a joyful resurrection.

(23) **Keep thy heart with all diligence.**—Rather, *above all things that are to be guarded.*

For out of it are the issues of life.—That is, from it comes life (and also death). From it proceed "all holy desires, all good counsels, and all just works," signs of the life with God within the soul; or, "evil thoughts, murders," &c. (Matt. xv. 19), "the end of which things is death" (Rom. vi. 21).

(24) **A froward mouth.**—Heb. *'iqqeshûth*, literally, *distortion*, or twisting of the truth, not the same word as in chap. ii. 12, 14.

Perverse lips—*i.e.*, that "turn aside" from the truth.

(25) **Let thine eyes look right on.**—Comp. the advice of Ecclus. vii. 36, "Whatsoever thou takest in hand, remember the end," and of Heb. xii. 2, to look "unto Jesus, the author and finisher of our faith."

(26) **Ponder the path of thy feet.**—Rather, *make it smooth, level: take all obstacles out of it which may prevent thy going in the way God is leading thee.* Comp. the directions to cut off even the hand or the foot that offends (Matt. xviii. 8). This verse is quoted in Heb. xii. 13.

Let all thy ways be established.—Or, *directed aright;* see that they lead straight to the end (Ps. cxix. 5).

(27) **Turn not aside . . .**—Comp. the direction of Josh. i. 7, and the praise accorded to David (1 Kings xv. 5).

V.

(3) **Her mouth is smoother than oil.**—The experience of David also with Ahitophel (Ps. lv. 21).

(4) **Bitter as wormwood.**—The *absinthium* of Rev. viii. 11, where, apparently, it is considered as a poison. So God's message to St. John (Rev. x. 10),

Warnings against   PROVERBS, V.   *the Strange Woman.*

as a twoedged sword. ⁽⁵⁾ ^aHer feet go down to death; her steps take hold on hell. ⁽⁶⁾ Lest thou shouldest ponder the path of life, her ways are moveable, *that* thou canst not know *them.* ⁽⁷⁾ Hear me now therefore, O ye children, and depart not from the words of my mouth. ⁽⁸⁾ Remove thy way far from her, and come not nigh the door of her house: ⁽⁹⁾ lest thou give thine honour unto others, and thy years unto the cruel: ⁽¹⁰⁾ lest strangers be filled with ¹thy wealth; and thy labours *be* in the house of a stranger; ⁽¹¹⁾ and thou mourn at the last, when thy flesh and thy body are consumed, ⁽¹²⁾ and say, How have I hated instruction, and my heart despised reproof; ⁽¹³⁾ and have not obeyed the voice of my teachers, nor inclined mine ear to them that instructed me! ⁽¹⁴⁾ I was almost in all evil in the midst of the congregation and assembly. ⁽¹⁵⁾ Drink waters out of thine own cistern, and running waters out of thine own well. ⁽¹⁶⁾ Let thy fountains be dispersed abroad, *and* rivers of waters in the streets. ⁽¹⁷⁾ Let them be only thine own, and not strangers' with thee. ⁽¹⁸⁾ Let thy fountain be blessed: and rejoice with the wife of thy youth. ⁽¹⁹⁾ *Let her be as* the loving hind and pleasant roe; let her breasts ²satisfy thee at all times; and ³be thou ravished always with her love. ⁽²⁰⁾ And why wilt thou, my son, be ravished with a strange woman, and embrace the bosom of a stranger? ⁽²¹⁾ ^bFor the ways of man *are* before the eyes of the Lord, and he pondereth all his goings. ⁽²²⁾ His own iniquities

a ch. 7. 27.

¹ Heb., *thy strength.*

² Heb., *water thee.*

³ Heb., *err thou always in her love.*

b Job 31. 4, & 34. 21; ch. 15. 3; Jer. 16. 17, & 32. 19.

---

was in his mouth sweet as honey (comp. Ps. xix. 10), but made his belly bitter; that is, he met with much sorrow and trouble in making it known to men, but through this "much tribulation" (Acts xiv. 22) he "entered into the kingdom of heaven."

⁽⁵⁾ **Take hold on hell.**—They lead straight to it.

⁽⁶⁾ **Lest thou shouldest ponder . . .**—The meaning of the English version appears to be, "To prevent thy choosing the path of life, she leads thee by devious paths that thou knowest not where thou art." It may also be rendered, "Far from smoothing for herself the path of life, her steps wander without her observing it." By these words is described the reckless career of a vicious woman, who at last dares not think whither her steps are leading her, but as it were with eyes shut, totters on till she falls to rise no more.

(*h*). *Eighth Discourse:—Against Adultery, and in Praise of Marriage* (chap. v. 7—23).

⁽⁷⁾ **Hear me now therefore, O ye children.**—In this verse Solomon apparently ceases to report the words of his father, and resumes his speech in his own person.

⁽⁸⁾ **Remove thy way . . .**—The great safeguard in such temptations, as all moralists with one mouth advise, is flight.

⁽⁹⁾ **Thine honour.**—Rather, *freshness, vigour.*

Thy years.—The best years of thy life.

Unto the cruel.—That is the temptress herself, or her hangers-on and associates, whose sole idea is plunder.

⁽¹¹⁾ **When thy flesh and thy body are consumed.**—Ruin of health has followed ruin of property.

⁽¹²⁾ **How have I hated instruction.**—The last stage of misery is the remorse which comes too late. (Comp. Matt. xxv. 30.)

⁽¹⁴⁾ **I was almost in all evil . . .**—Rather, *I had almost fallen into every sin: I was so infatuated that I might have committed any sin, and that openly before all.* Or, *I might have been visited with extremest punishment at the hands of the congregation, death by stoning* (Lev. xx. 10, John viii. 5). The offender's eyes are now opened, and he shudders at the thought of the still greater troubles into which he might, in his infatuation, have fallen.

^(15—20) **Drink waters out of thine own cistern . . .**—In these verses Solomon urges his disciples to follow after purity in the married life; he pictures in vivid terms the delights which it affords as compared with the pleasures of sin.

Out of thine own cistern.—The "strange woman," on the other hand, says, "Stolen waters are sweet" (chap. ix. 17). The same figure is employed in Cant. iv. 15, where a wife is compared to "a fountain of gardens, a well of living waters, and streams from Lebanon." In Jer. ii. 13 God compares Himself to a "fountain of living waters," and complains that Israel had deserted Him, and hewed out for themselves "broken cisterns that can hold no water." This passage in Proverbs has in like manner often been interpreted as an exhortation to drink deeply from the living waters of the Holy Spirit given in the Word and Sacraments (John vii. 37).—For reff. see Bishop Wordsworth.

⁽¹⁸⁾ **Let thy fountain . . .**—As a reward for purity of life, the blessing of a numerous offspring is invoked. (Comp. Ps. cxxviii. 3, where the wife is a "fruitful vine," and the children numerous and flourishing like olive-branches.)

⁽¹⁷⁾ **Let them be only thine own.**—The deepest joys and sorrows of each heart are sacred, and cannot be shared with others (chap. xiv. 10), and so it is with the various relations of family life also, strangers have no part in them.

⁽¹⁹⁾ **Loving hind and pleasant roe.**—The deer and chamois, from their grace and speed and lustrous eyes, have always been chosen by the Oriental poets as figures of human strength and beauty. (Comp. Cant. ii. 9, 17, vii. 3, viii. 14; Ps. xviii. 33.) Both these animals are said to be remarkable for their affection to their young.

⁽²¹⁾ **For the ways of man . . .**—Another reason for avoiding sin is the certainty of detection by the Judge, whose "eyes run to and fro through the whole earth" (2 Chron. xvi. 9), comp. Ps. xi. 4.

^(22, 23) **His own iniquities . . .**—The final scene in the life of the profligate is here described. He has

shall take the wicked himself, and he shall be holden with the cords of his ¹sins. ⁽²³⁾ He shall die without instruction; and in the greatness of his folly he shall go astray.

CHAPTER VI.—⁽¹⁾ My son, if thou be surety for thy friend, *if* thou hast stricken thy hand with a stranger, ⁽²⁾ thou art snared with the words of thy mouth, thou art taken with the words of thy mouth. ⁽³⁾ Do this now, my son, and deliver thyself, when thou art come into the hand of thy friend; go, humble thyself, ²and make sure thy friend. ⁽⁴⁾ Give not sleep to thine eyes, nor slumber to thine eyelids. ⁽⁵⁾ Deliver thyself as a roe from the hand *of the hunter*, and as a bird from the hand of the fowler. ⁽⁶⁾ Go to the ant, thou sluggard;

¹ Heb., *sin*.

² Or, *so shalt thou prevail with thy friend.*

a ch. 24. 33.

b ch. 13. 4, & 20. 4.

³ Heb., *casteth forth.*

consider her ways, and be wise: ⁽⁷⁾ which having no guide, overseer, or ruler. ⁽⁸⁾ provideth her meat in the summer, *and* gathereth her food in the harvest. ⁽⁹⁾ ᵃHow long wilt thou sleep, O sluggard? when wilt thou arise out of thy sleep? ⁽¹⁰⁾ *Yet* a little sleep, a little slumber, a little folding of the hands to sleep: ⁽¹¹⁾ ᵇ so shall thy poverty come as one that travelleth, and thy want as an armed man.

⁽¹²⁾ A naughty person, a wicked man, walketh with a froward mouth. ⁽¹³⁾ He winketh with his eyes, he speaketh with his feet, he teacheth with his fingers; ⁽¹⁴⁾ frowardness *is* in his heart, he deviseth mischief continually; he ³soweth discord. ⁽¹⁵⁾ Therefore shall his calamity come suddenly; suddenly shall he be broken without remedy.

---

sinned so long that he is "tied and bound," hand and foot, with the "chain of his sins," and cannot get free even had he the wish to do so.

(23) **He shall die without instruction.**—Rather, *for want of discipline*, because he would not control himself, "he shall die," and "for the greatness of his folly (self-will) he shall go astray," and "wander where there is no way" (Job xii. 24).

VI.

(*i*). *Ninth Discourse:—Against Suretyship* (chap. vi. 1—5).

(1) **If thou be surety for thy friend.**—When the Mosaic Law was instituted, commerce had not been taken up by the Israelites, and the lending of money on interest for its employment in trade was a thing unknown. The only occasion for loans would be to supply the immediate necessities of the borrower, and the exaction of interest under such circumstances would be productive of great hardship, involving the loss of land and even personal freedom, as the insolvent debtor and his family became the slaves of the creditor (Neh. v. 1—5). To prevent these evils, the lending of money on interest to any poor Israelite was strictly forbidden (Lev. xxv. 35—7); the people were enjoined to be liberal, and lend for nothing in such cases. But at the time of Solomon, when the commerce of the Israelites had enormously developed, and communications were opened with Spain and Egypt and (possibly) with India and Ceylon, while caravans penetrated beyond the Euphrates, then the lending of money on interest for employment in trade most probably became frequent, and suretyship also, the pledging of a man's own credit to enable his friend to procure a loan. And when the wealth that accompanied this development of the national resources had brought luxury in its train, borrowing and suretyship would be employed for less worthy purposes, to supply the young nobles of Jerusalem with money for their extravagance. Hence possibly the emphatic language of the text and chaps. xx. 16, and xxvii. 13.

Stricken thy hand.—That is, as we should say, "shaken hands on the bargain."

With a stranger.—Or rather, *for another*, i.e., thy friend.

(3) **When thou art come. . .**—Rather, *for thou hast come under the power of thy friend*; thou hast made thy freedom and property dependent on him for whom thou hast become surety.

Humble thyself.—Literally, *let thyself be trampled on, humbly sue.*

Make sure.—Rather, *assail impetuously, importune.*

(5) **Of the hunter.**—This, or some such phrase (perhaps, the hand "that held him"), must be supplied here.

(*j*). *Tenth Discourse:—Against Sloth* (chap. vi. 6—11)

(7) **Guide.**—Properly, *judge* (the Arabic *cadi*), then *leader, prince.*

(11) **As one that travelleth.**—The form of the Hebrew is intensive, "one who moves swiftly," as in Ps. civ. 3, it is applied to God's "moving upon the wings of the wind." While the sluggard sleeps, poverty is coming on apace.

As an armed man.—Against whom the sleeper will be defenceless. Verses 10 and 11 are repeated in chap. xxiv. 33, 34.

(*k*). *Eleventh Discourse:—Against Deceit and Malice* (chap. vi. 12—19).

(12) **A naughty person.**—According to its original meaning, a "worthless" person, Heb. *a man of Belial.*

Froward mouth.—Comp. chap. iv. 24.

(13) **He winketh with his eyes . . .**—A picture, taken from the life, of a malicious tattler and scandalmonger, who fills out his lying tale with winks and signs, whereby even more is suggested than he says, to the blasting of his neighbour's character.

(15) **Suddenly shall he be broken.**—Shattered as a potter's vessel (Isa. xxx. 14), without hope of recovery. This character of a malicious mischief-maker would seem to be especially hateful to God; it is described in like terms in Ps. lxiv. and a similar

(16) These six *things* doth the LORD hate: yea, seven *are* an abomination ¹unto him: (17) ²a proud look, a lying tongue, and hands that shed innocent blood, (18) an heart that deviseth wicked imaginations, ᵃfeet that be swift in running to mischief, (19) a false witness *that* speaketh lies, and he that soweth discord among brethren.

(20) ᵇMy son, keep thy father's commandment, and forsake not the law of thy mother: (21) bind them continually upon thine heart, *and* tie them about thy neck. (22) When thou goest, it shall lead thee; when thou sleepest, it shall keep thee; and *when* thou awakest, it shall talk with thee. (23) ᶜFor the commandment *is* a ³lamp; and the law *is* light; and reproofs of instruction *are* the way of life: (24) ᵈto keep thee from the evil woman, from the flattery ⁴of the tongue of a strange woman.

(25) ᵉLust not after her beauty in thine heart; neither let her take thee with her eyelids. (26) For by means of a whorish woman *a man is brought* to a piece of bread: and ⁵the adulteress will hunt for the precious life. (27) Can a man take fire in his bosom, and his clothes not be burned? (28) Can one go upon hot coals, and his feet not be burned? (29) So he that goeth in to his neighbour's wife; whosoever toucheth her shall not be innocent. (30) *Men* do not despise a thief, if he steal to satisfy his soul when he is hungry; (31) but *if* he be found, he shall restore sevenfold; he shall give all the substance of his house. (32) *But* whoso committeth adultery with a woman lacketh ⁶understanding: he *that* doeth it destroyeth his own soul. (33) A wound and dishonour shall he get; and his reproach shall not be wiped away. (34) For jealousy *is* the rage of a man: therefore he will not spare in the day of vengeance. (35) ⁷He will not regard any ransom; neither will he rest content, though thou givest many gifts.

CHAPTER VII.— (1) My son, keep my words, and lay up my commandments with thee. (2) Keep my commandments, and live; and my law as

Marginal notes:
1 Heb., *of his soul.*
2 Heb., *Haughty eyes.*
ᵃ Rom. 3. 15.
ᵇ ch. 1. 8.
ᶜ Ps. 19. 8, & 119. 105.
3 Or, *candle.*
ᵈ ch. 2. 16 & 5. 3, & 7. 5.
4 Or, *of the strange tongue.*
ᵉ Matt. 5. 28.
5 Heb., *the woman of a man,* or, *a man's wife.*
6 Heb., *heart.*
7 Heb., *He will not accept the face of any ransom.*
ᶠ Deut. 6. 8, & 11. 18; ch. 3. 3.

---

fate foretold of it; in verse 19 also it is held up as the very worst of the seven detestable things there mentioned.

(16) **These six things doth the Lord hate . . .**—Rather, *six are the things which He hateth.* It is a sort of climax:—He hates six things, but the seventh worse than all. This numerical form of proverb, to which the name of *middah* is given by later writers, is found also in chap. xxx. 15, 16, 18, 19, 21—23, 29—31; Job v. 19; Amos i. 3—ii. 1; Ecclus. xxiii. 16, xxv. 7, xxvi. 5, 28; and in all these instances the number first named is increased afterwards by one. This peculiarity is absent from the instances occurring in chap. xxx. 7—9, 24—28; Ecclus. xxv. 1, 2.

(17) **A proud look.**—Hateful to God, because rendering men unfit to receive grace. Till they acknowledge their weakness, they will not seek for His strength, and without it they can make no progress in holiness. (Comp. 1 Pet. v. 5, and Christ's commendation of the "poor in spirit," Matt. v. 3.)

(18) **Feet that be swift in running to mischief.**—Who do not yield to temptation after a struggle against it, but give themselves up as willing slaves to their lusts.

(*l*). *Twelfth Discourse:—Against Adultery* (chap. vi. 20—35).

(21) **Bind them continually upon thine heart.**—See above on chap. iii. 3.

(23) **For the commandment is a lamp . . .**—Comp. Pss. xix. 8, and cxix. 98—100, 104, 105. The servant of God may often feel much perplexity as to his duty, darkness may seem to have settled down upon his path. But there is always some "commandment," or positive order, about which he can have no doubt, calling for his immediate obedience; there is always some "law," or rather "instruction" in God's Word offering itself as his guide; there are always some "reproofs of discipline," that is, he knows he has certain things to shun, others to follow, for the purpose of self-discipline. It is by following out these parts of his duty that he does know, which are, as it were, a "light shining in a dark place" (2 Pet. i. 19), that man prepares himself for more light and clearer vision; then God "opens his eyes" that he may "behold wondrous things out of His law" (Ps. cxix. 18); because he has some knowledge of God's will and desire to do it, more is given unto him (Matt. xiii. 12), and his path becomes continually clearer, shining "more and more unto the perfect day" (chap. iv. 18).

(29) **Shall not be innocent.**—That is to say, *unpunished.*

(30) **Men do not despise a thief . . .**—A man who is driven to theft by poverty is more worthy of pity than disdain; not so the adulterer. Again, the thief can make retribution, while the adulterer can have none to offer.

(31) **But if he be found, he shall restore sevenfold.**—Rather, *And if he be found, he may restore sevenfold, he may give up all the wealth of his house.* The law only required a two—or four—or five-fold compensation (Exod. xxii.); he may do even more. "Sevenfold" signifies full restitution. (Comp. Gen. iv. 24; Lev. xxvi. 28.)

(34) **For jealousy is the rage of a man.**—That is jealousy is furious, and cannot be appeased by bribes.

the apple of thine eye. (3) ᶠBind them upon thy fingers, write them upon the table of thine heart. (4) Say unto wisdom, Thou *art* my sister; and call understanding *thy* kinswoman: (5) ᵃthat they may keep thee from the strange woman, from the stranger which flattereth with her words.

(6) For at the window of my house I looked through my casement, (7) and beheld among the simple ones, I discerned among ¹the youths, a young man void of understanding, (8) passing through the street near her corner; and he went the way to her house, (9) in the twilight, ²in the evening, in the black and dark night: (10) and, behold, there met him a woman *with* the attire of an harlot, and subtil of heart. (11) ᵇ(She *is* loud and stubborn; her feet abide not in her house: (12) Now *is she* without, now in the streets, and lieth in wait at every corner.) (13) So she caught him, and kissed him, *and* ³with an impudent face said unto him, (14) ⁴*I have* peace offerings with me; this day have I payed my vows. (15) Therefore came I forth to meet thee, diligently to seek thy face, and I have found thee. (16) I have decked my bed with coverings of tapestry, with carved *works*, with fine linen of Egypt. (17) I have perfumed my bed with myrrh, aloes, and cinnamon. (18) Come, let us take our fill of love until the morning: let us solace ourselves with loves. (19) For the goodman *is* not at home, he is gone a long journey: (20) He hath taken a bag of money ⁵with him, *and* will come home at ⁶the day appointed.

(21) With her much fair speech she caused him to yield, with the flattering of her lips she forced him. (22) He goeth after her ⁷straightway, as an ox goeth to the slaughter, or as a fool to the correction of the stocks; (23) till a dart strike through his liver; as a bird hasteth to the snare, and knoweth not that it *is* for his life.

(24) Hearken unto me now therefore, O ye children, and attend to the words of my mouth. (25) Let not thine heart decline to her ways, go not astray in her paths. (26) For she hath cast down many wounded: yea, many strong *men* have been slain by her. (27) ᶜHer house *is* the way to hell, going down to the chambers of death.

a ch. 5. 3.
1 Heb., *the sons*.
2 Heb., *in the evening of the day*.
b ch. 9. 13.
3 Heb., *she strengthened her face, and said*.
4 Heb., *Peace offerings are upon me*.
5 Heb., *in his hand*.
6 Or, *the new moon*.
7 Heb., *suddenly*.
c ch. 2. 18, & 5. 5.

VII.

(m). Thirteenth Discourse:—Also Against Adultery
(chap. vii.).

(3) Bind them upon thy fingers.—See above on chap. iii. 3. The thong of the phylactery or fillet for the left arm was wound seven times round it, and as many times round the middle finger.

(7) Among the simple ones.—He was not yet vicious, only empty-headed.

(8) And he went the way . . .—The word is used of the slow step of a religious procession (2 Sam. vi. 13), here of the sauntering of the idle youth up and down the street within view of the temptress's house.

(9) In the twilight . . .—He has no excuse of sudden temptation to offer; from twilight till dark night he had trifled with danger, and now at last his "calamity comes" (chap. vi. 15).

(10) Subtil of heart.—Feigning love to her husband and devotion to her lovers, yet caring for none, only to satisfy her own passions.

(11) Her feet abide not in her house.—She is not a "keeper at home," as St. Paul (Titus ii. 5) would have Christian matrons to be.

(14) I have peace offerings with me.—Rather, *upon me, i.e.,* I had vowed them. and to-day I have accomplished my vow. The peace-, or thank-offering as it is also rendered, was purely voluntary, in token of thanksgiving for some mercy. The breast and right shoulder of the victim were given to the priest, and the rest belonged to the offerer, who was thus admitted, as it were, to feast with God (Lev. iii., vii.), profanation of this privilege being punished with death. Peace-offerings were accordingly offered on occasions of national rejoicing, as at the inauguration of the covenant (Exod. xxiv. 5), at the accession of Saul (1 Sam. xi. 15), and at the bringing up of the ark to Zion (2 Sam. vi. 17), &c. This turning of what should have been a religious festival for the family into an occasion for license, is paralleled by the desecration of the Agapæ at Corinth (1 Cor. xi. 20 *sqq.*) and the history of Church-feasts among ourselves. (For the spiritual interpretation of this passage as symbolising false doctrine, see Bishop Wordsworth; and also Notes on chap. ii. 16—19 above.)

(16) Carved works.—Rather, *with coloured or striped coverlets.* For another notice of the extravagance of the women of Jerusalem, see Isa. iii., and for a description of the trade of Tyre, the great supplier of foreign luxuries, see Ezek. xxvii. Myrrh is said to be a natural product of Arabia, aloes and cinnamon of the east coast of Africa and Ceylon.

(19) The goodman.—Literally, *the man;* she does not even call him "my husband."

At the day appointed.—Rather, *at the full moon,* a fortnight later, as now it would seem to have been new moon, when the nights are dark.

(22) Or as a fool to the correction of the stocks.—This sense is only gained by a transposition of the original. It has been attempted to translate it literally "and as if in fetters to where one corrects fools," *i.e.,* to prison.

(23) Till a dart strike through his liver.—These words must be taken in a parenthesis.

That it is for his life.—*i.e.,* at the cost of it, when "his flesh and body are consumed," and remorse has seized upon him (chap. v. 11).

The Cry of Wisdom.   PROVERBS, VIII.   *Her Praises*

CHAPTER VIII.—(1) Doth not *a*wisdom cry? and understanding put forth her voice? (2) She standeth in the top of high places, by the way in the places of the paths. (3) She crieth at the gates, at the entry of the city, at the coming in at the doors. (4) Unto you, O men, I call; and my voice *is* to the sons of man. (5) O ye simple, understand wisdom: and, ye fools, be ye of an understanding heart. (6) Hear; for I will speak of excellent things; and the opening of my lips *shall be* right things. (7) For my mouth shall speak truth; and wickedness *is* ¹an abomination to my lips. (8) All the words of my mouth *are* in righteousness; *there is* nothing ²froward or perverse in them. (9) They *are* all plain to him that understandeth, and right to them that find knowledge. (10) Receive my instruction, and not silver; and knowledge rather than choice gold.

(11) *b*For wisdom *is* better than rubies; and all the things that may be desired are not to be compared to it. (12) I wisdom dwell with ³prudence, and find out knowledge of witty inventions. (13) The fear of the LORD *is* to hate evil: pride, and arrogancy, and the evil way, and the froward mouth, do I hate. (14) Counsel *is* mine, and sound wisdom: I *am* understanding; I have strength. (15) By me kings reign, and princes decree justice. (16) By me princes rule, and nobles, *even* all the judges of the earth. (17) I love them that love me; and those that seek me early shall find me. (18) *c*Riches and honour *are* with me; *yea,* durable riches and righteousness. (19) *d*My fruit *is* better than gold, yea, than fine gold; and my revenue than choice silver. (20) I ⁴lead in the way of righteousness, in the midst of the paths of judgment: (21) that I may cause those that love me

a ch. 1. 20.

1 Heb., *the abomination of my lips.*

2 Heb., *wreathed.*

b Job 28. 15; Ps. 19. 10; ch. 3. 15, & 16. 16.

3 Or, *subtilty.*

c ch. 3. 16.

d ch. 3. 14.

4 Or, *walk.*

VIII.

(n). *Fourteenth Discourse:—The Praise of Wisdom* (chap. viii.)

(1) **Doth not wisdom cry?**—See above on chap. i. 20. In contrast with the secret allurements of Vice under the cover of night, is here represented the open invitation of Wisdom. (Comp. John xviii. 20: "I spake openly to the world . . . and in secret have I said nothing.")

(2) **She standeth in the top of high places.**—*i.e.*, in the higher parts of the city, where her voice will best be heard.

By the way . . .—She goes everywhere where she may find the greatest concourse of people, "God not being willing that any should perish, but that all should come to repentance" (2 Pet. iii. 9). So the apostles made large centres of population such as Antioch, Ephesus, or Corinth, the headquarters of their missionary enterprise.

(4) **O men**—*i.e.*, "great ones;" "sons of man" are those of inferior rank; comp. the Hebrew of Isa. ii. 9, where the same words are translated "great man," and "mean man." Comp. the generality of the invitation of Ps. xlix. 2.

(5) **O ye simple.**—See above on chap. i. 4 for an explanation of "simple," as also of "wisdom" (*'ormah*) there translated "subtilty."

Ye fools.—(*khesîlim*), see above on chap. i. 22.

(6) **The opening of my lips shall be right things.**—That is, *I will open my mouth to speak them.*

(8) **Froward.**—That is, *twisted,* or *crooked.*

(9) **They are all plain . . .**—Because "the secret of the Lord is (only) with them that fear Him" (Ps. xxv. 14), and God reveals such things unto them by His Spirit (1 Cor. ii. 10), while the "natural man receiveth not the things of the Spirit of God, for they are foolishness unto him" (*ibid.*, verse 14).

(11) **Rubies.**—See above on chap. iii. 15.

(12) **Dwell with prudence.**—(*'ormah*), literally, *inhabit* it, have settled down and taken up my abode with it, am at home there.

Witty inventions.—Literally, *well thought out plans* (*mezimmôth*) translated "discretion" (chap. i. 4).

(13) **The fear of the Lord is to hate evil.**—Because there can never be any truce between the kingdoms of light and darkness (Matt. vi. 24), so if we are the friend of one, we must be the enemy of the other.

Pride and arrogancy . . . do I hate.—See above on chap. vi. 17.

(14) **Sound wisdom.**—See above on chap. ii. 7.

Strength.—Comp. Eccles. vii. 19. For these various gifts of wisdom, comp. Isa. xi. 2.

(15) **Princes.**—Literally, *men of weight,* or, *importance.*

(16) **All the judges of the earth.**—By the aid of heavenly wisdom only can they give right and just judgments, and so fulfil the high office delegated to them by God Himself, from the possession of which they are themselves termed "gods" (Exod. xxii. 28; Ps. lxxxii. 1). For the same reason kings, as ruling by His authority, have the same title accorded to them (Ps. xlv. 6).

(17) **I love them that love me.**—Comp. John xiv. 21: he that loveth me . . . . I will love him.

(18) **Riches and honour are with me.**—"If this passage is taken in a material sense, Ps. cxii. 3 and the promises in the Pentateuch of wealth as the reward of obedience might be compared with it. But doubtless the "true riches" (Luke xvi. 11) are here alluded to, the consciousness of possessing God's honour and favour, called in Eph. iii. 8 the "unsearchable riches of Christ."

(19) **My fruit . . . . my revenue.**—*i.e.*, the gain and profit which come from possessing me.

(20) **I lead in the way of righteousness.**—Comp. Ps. xxxvii. 23; also a prayer for such guidance, Ps. cxix. 33, cxliii. 8; and a promise of it Isa. xxx. 21

(21) **That I may cause those that love me to inherit substance.**—The work which each one by

to inherit substance; and I will fill their treasures. (22) The LORD possessed me in the beginning of his way, before his works of old. (23) I was set up from everlasting, from the beginning, or ever the earth was. (24) When *there were* no depths, I was brought forth; when *there were* no fountains abounding with water. (25) Before the mountains were settled, before the hills was I brought forth: (26) while as yet he had not made the earth, nor the ¹fields, nor ²the highest part of the dust of the world. (27) When he prepared the heavens, I *was* there: when he set ³a compass upon the face of the depth: (28) when he established the clouds above: when he strengthened the fountains of the deep: (29) *a* when he gave to the sea his decree, that the waters should not pass his commandment: when he appointed the foundations of the earth: (30) then I was by him, *as* one brought up *with him*: and I was daily *his* delight, rejoicing always before him; (31) rejoicing in the habitable part of his earth; and my delights *were* with the sons of men.

1 Or, *open places.*
2 Or, *the chief part.*
3 Or, *a circle.*
a Gen. 1. 9, 10; Job 38. 10, 11; Ps. 104. 9.

---

my help shall do will be stored up for him in heaven (Matt. vi. 20), it will be as "gold tried in the fire" (Rev. iii. 18), which will abide the trial of "the day" (1 Cor. iii. 13).

(22) **The Lord possessed me in the beginning of his way.**—The Hebrew word translated "possessed" in this passage (*qānah*) seems originally to have signified to "set up" or "establish," and is applied (1) to the "forming" of the heavens (Gen. xiv. 19) and the "begetting" of a son, (Deut xxxii. 6); next it signifies (2) to "acquire" (Gen. iv. 1), (3) to "purchase" (Gen. xxv. 10), and (4) to "own," as in Isa. i. 3. From the fact that "set up" and "brought forth" are used just after as synonyms to it, it is most likely that (1) is the proper meaning of the word here, and that the sense of the passage is that Wisdom was "formed" or "begotten" before the Creation, comp. Pss. civ. 24; cxxxiv. 5. This agrees with the rendering of the most important Greek translation, the Septuagint (ἔκτισε). When in Christian times it was observed how well the description of Wisdom in Job and Proverbs harmonised with that of God the Son in the New Testament, such passages as this were universally applied to Him, and the present one was rightly interpreted as describing His eternal generation from the Father. Such was the view, for instance, of Justin Martyr, Irenaeus, and Tertullian. But when the Arian controversy arose, this phrase was seized upon by the opponents of our Lord's Divinity, and claimed as teaching that He was, though the highest of created beings, still only a creature. The Catholics then changed their ground, some standing up for the rendering of Aquila, ἐκτήσατο ("acquired" or "possessed"), others applying the term ἔκτισε to Christ's Incarnation (comp. "first-begotten among many brethren," Rom. viii. 29), or to His being appointed to be the first principle or efficient cause of His creatures, the "beginning of the creation of God" (Rev. iii. 14). For references to the Fathers see Bishop Wordsworth's note, and, for a like variation in the rendering of "first-begotten of every creature," comp. Bishop Lightfoot's note on Col. i. 15.

In the beginning of his way.—That is, His way of acting, His activity in the Creation. But the preposition "in" does not occur in this passage, and from a comparison of Job xl. 19, where *behemōth* (the hippopotamus) is termed the "beginning of the ways of God," *i.e.*, chief of His works, it is probable that this verse should be translated, "He brought me forth as the beginning of His way, as the earliest of His works from of old," *i.e.*, before the depths, and mountains, and hills, &c.

(23) **I was set up.**—An unusual word; also applied to our Lord in Ps. ii. 6 when "set" as King on Zion.

(24) **I was brought forth.**—*i.e.*, born. The same word is used in Ps. li. 5 (7), and Job xv. 7.

(26) **The earth.**—*i.e.*, the cultivated and enclosed part of it.

The fields.—The open country.

The highest part of the dust of the world. Literally, "the head of the dusts of the fertile earth" *i.e.* the heaps of the clods of arable land, or better perhaps, "the sum of the atoms of dust." Some refer to Gen. ii. 7, and interpret the words of man, as formed out of the dust.

(27) **When he set a compass upon the face of the depth**—*i.e.*, when He stretched the vault of heaven over it: the same expression is used in Job xxii. 14. It is also interpreted of the circle of the horizon.

(28) **When he established the clouds above.** —Literally, *made firm*; comp. Gen. i. 6.

When he strengthened the fountains of the deep.—More probably, *when they flowed forth with strength*.

(29) **When he gave to the sea his decree . . .** —Compare the same thoughts in Job xxxviii. 4, 10, 11.

(30) **As one brought up with him**—*i.e.*, his foster child; as Mordecai "brought up" Esther (Esth. ii. 7). But the word may also bear the sense of "artificer." It probably occurs in this meaning in Jer. lii. 15 (though translated "multitude," in accordance with 2 Kings xxv. 11), and in a slightly different form, Cant. vii. 1. This meaning is much more suitable, and harmonises with Pss. civ. 24, cxxxvi. 5, and Heb. i. 2.

I was daily his delight.—The pronoun "his" does not occur in the Hebrew, which is, literally, *I was delights*, *i.e.*, all joy, delight, as Ps. cix. 4: "I am prayer," *i.e.*, give myself wholly to it. The words express the joy with which Wisdom carried out the work of God.

Rejoicing always before him.—The same expression is used in 2 Sam. vi. 21 by David (there translated "play"), to describe his "leaping and dancing before the Lord."

(31) **Rejoicing in the habitable part of his earth.**—Rather, *the fertile part.* (Comp. Gen. i. 31, where the satisfaction of God with His creation is described; and Ps. civ. 31.)

My delights were with the sons of men.— Or rather, *in them.* (Comp. Gen. iii. 8, where it would seem that the "Lord God" had been in the habit of assuming human form, and admitting man to His pre-

(32) Now therefore hearken unto me, O ye children: for ᵃblessed *are they that* keep my ways. (33) Hear instruction, and be wise, and refuse it not. (34) Blessed *is* the man that heareth me, watching daily at my gates, waiting at the posts of my doors. (35) For whoso findeth me findeth life, and shall ¹obtain favour of the LORD. (36) But he that sinneth against me wrongeth his own soul: all they that hate me love death.

CHAPTER IX. — (1) Wisdom hath builded her house, she hath hewn out her seven pillars: (2) she hath killed ²her beasts; she hath mingled her wine; she hath also furnished her table. (3) She hath sent forth her maidens: she crieth upon the highest places of the city, (4) whoso *is* simple, let him turn in hither: *as for* him that wanteth understanding, she saith to him, (5) Come, eat of my bread, and drink of the wine *which* I have mingled. (6) Forsake the foolish, and live; and go in the way of understanding.

(7) He that reproveth a scorner getteth to himself shame: and he that rebuketh a wicked *man getteth* himself a blot. (8) ᵇReprove not a scorner, lest he

---

a Ps. 119. 1, 2, & 128. 1; Luke 11. 28.

1 Heb., *bring forth.*

2 Heb., *her killing.*

b Matt. 7. 6.

---

sence.) Such appearances as this, and that to Abraham in Gen. xviii., and to Joshua in Josh. v., were supposed by the Fathers to have been anticipations of the Incarnation of God the Son, who is here described under the name of Wisdom.

(32) **Now therefore hearken**—*i.e.*, now that ye know how great my power is, and what love I have to you, in that I rejoice in you, and call you my sons. (Comp. 1 John iii. 1.)

(34) **Watching daily at my gates.**—A figure taken from an ardent scholar waiting till the doors of the school are opened, and he can begin his studies. Or it represents a courtier expecting the appearance of his sovereign, or a lover that of his mistress. (Comp. Wisd. viii. 2.)

(35) **Whoso findeth me findeth life.**—Comp. 1 John v. 12; John viii. 51; and above, chap. iii. 18, where Wisdom is described as a "tree of life."

(36) **He that sinneth against me.**—Rather, *He that misses me does not find me.* So in Greek, sin (ʼαμαρτία) is a "missing" of the true object of life.

IX.

(*o*). *Fifteenth Discourse: the Invitations of Wisdom and Folly* (chap. ix.).

(1) **Wisdom hath builded her house**—*i.e.*, in preparation for the feast to which she is about to invite her guests. It is not an unusual custom in the Old Testament to describe intimate communion with God, and the refreshment which the soul of man thereby receives, under the figure of a festival. Thus in Exod. xxiv. 11, when the elders of Israel were admitted to the vision of the Almighty, they "did eat and drink." The same idea occurs frequently in the prophets also (as Isa. xxv. 6, lxv. 13; Zeph. i. 7, 8); and is brought out in the New Testament with great fulness in the parables of the great supper (Luke xiv.) and the marriage of the king's son (Matt. xxii.). Christ, the supreme Wisdom, has "builded His house" by taking man's flesh at His Incarnation, and thus rearing for Himself a "temple of the Holy Ghost" (John ii. 19); and also by building for Himself a "spiritual house" (1 Pet. ii. 5), "the house of God, which is the church of the living God" (1 Tim. iii. 15). (For references to the Fathers, see Bishop Wordsworth.) In the previous chapter Christ's work as Creator was described; now He is set forth as Regenerator of mankind.

She hath hewn out her seven pillars.—Suggestive of the sevenfold gifts of the Spirit (Isa. xi. 2; Rev. i. 4), typified by the seven-branched candlestick of the Tabernacle (Exod. xxv. 37).

(2) **She hath killed her beasts.**—Comp. Matt. xxii. 4.

She hath mingled her wine—*i.e.*, probably, flavoured it with spices, to improve the flavour. (Comp. chap. xxiii. 30.) But the wine used at the Passover (Matt. xxvi. 29, &c.) was mingled with water to decrease its strength.

She hath also furnished her table.—"Christ hath furnished His own Table, exhibiting His precious and spotless Body and Blood, which are daily celebrated at that mystic and divine board, being sacrificed in commemoration of that ever-to-be-remembered original table of that mystic and divine supper."—S. Hippolytus (ed. Lagarde, p. 199), quoted by Wordsworth.

(3) **She hath sent forth her maidens.**—Wisdom being here described under the figure of a woman, is properly represented as attended by her maidens, whom she sends forth to summon the guests. But the King (Matt. xxii.) despatches His servants for the same work, viz., His prophets and wise men and scribes (Matt. xxiii. 34), whom from age to age He sends forth as His messengers.

She crieth upon the highest places of the city—so that all may hear. (Comp. our Lord's command to proclaim His message "upon the housetops," Matt. x. 27).

(4) **Whoso is simple . . . as for him that wanteth understanding.**—So God does not call many "wise men after the flesh, not many mighty, not many noble" (1 Cor. i. 26); but chooses the "foolish," "weak," and "base," whom man might overlook; not being willing that any should perish (2 Pet. iii. 9), especially His "little ones" (Matt. xviii. 14), who are liable to fall through their inexperience and want of judgment.

(5) **Come, eat of my bread . . .**—Comp. the invitations of Isa. lv. 1 and John vi. 35.

(6) **Forsake the foolish.**—Rather, *the simple;* be no longer counted among the weak, who can be "carried about with every wind of doctrine" (Eph. iv. 14), but "stand fast in the faith, quit you like men, be strong" (1 Cor. xvi. 13).

(7) **He that reproveth a scorner . . .**—Wisdom does not address the scoffer, nor the godless: this would be "giving that which is holy unto the dogs, and casting pearls before swine" (Matt. vii. 6). (Comp. our Lord's own plan of teaching by parables, that His hearers might not understand (Luke viii. 10).

hate thee: rebuke a wise man, and he will love thee. ⁽⁹⁾ Give *instruction* to a wise *man*, and he will be yet wiser: teach a just *man*, and he will increase in learning. ⁽¹⁰⁾ ^aThe fear of the LORD *is* the beginning of wisdom: and the knowledge of the holy *is* understanding. ⁽¹¹⁾ ^bFor by me thy days shall be multiplied, and the years of thy life shall be increased. ⁽¹²⁾ If thou be wise, thou shalt be wise for thyself: but *if* thou scornest, thou alone shalt bear *it*.

⁽¹³⁾ ^cA foolish woman *is* clamorous: she *is* simple, and knoweth nothing. ⁽¹⁴⁾ For she sitteth at the door of her house, on *a* seat in the high places of the city, ⁽¹⁵⁾ to call passengers who go right on their ways: ⁽¹⁶⁾ whoso *is* simple, let him turn in hither: and *as for* him that wanteth understanding, she saith to him, ⁽¹⁷⁾ stolen waters are sweet, and bread ¹*eaten* in secret is pleasant. ⁽¹⁸⁾ But he knoweth not that the dead *are* there; *and that* her guests *are* in the depths of hell.

CHAPTER X.—⁽¹⁾ The proverbs of Solomon. ^dA wise son maketh a glad father: but a foolish son *is* the heaviness of his mother. ⁽²⁾ ^eTreasures of wickedness profit nothing: but righteousness delivereth from death. ⁽³⁾ ^fThe LORD will not suffer the soul of the righteous to famish: but he casteth away ²the substance of the wicked. ⁽⁴⁾ ^gHe becometh poor that dealeth *with*

a Job 28. 28; Ps. 111. 10; ch. 1. 7.
b ch. 10. 27.
c ch. 7. 11.
1 Heb., *of secrecies.*
d ch. 15. 20.
e ch. 11. 4.
f Ps. 37. 25.
2 Or, *the wicked for their wickedness.*
g ch. 12. 24.

Getteth to himself shame.—Or, *insult*.

⁽⁹⁾ **Give instruction to a wise man.**—Comp. Matt. xiii. 12 and xxv. 29.

⁽¹⁰⁾ **The fear of the Lord . . .**—Comp. Isa. xi. 2, where the "spirit of knowledge" and of the "fear of the Lord" is counted as the gift of God. (For the general sense of the passage, see above, on chap. i. 7.)

Knowledge of the holy—*i.e.*, "the Holy One," as in chap. xxx. 3.

⁽¹¹⁾ **For by me thy days shall be multiplied . . .**—The connection of this verse with the preceding one is as follows:—It is true wisdom to fear and know God, for thus length of years and life that is worth living are to be gained. (Comp. chap. iii. 2.)

⁽¹²⁾ **Thou shalt be wise for thyself**—*i.e.*, to thine own benefit. (Comp. 1 Cor. iii. 8.)

Thou alone shalt bear it — *i.e.*, its penalty. (Comp. Gal. vi. 5.)

⁽¹³⁾ **A foolish woman.** — Rather, *the Foolish woman*; Folly personified, in opposition to Wisdom described above.

Clamorous.—Not of dignified mien, as her rival.

Simple.—Heb., *simplicity*, *i.e.*, she is simplicity itself.

And knoweth nothing.—And so leaves room for all evil to enter in and dwell with her (Matt. xii. 45); thus she perishes, like Israel, for "lack of knowledge" (Hosea iv. 6).

⁽¹⁴⁾ **She sitteth at the door of her house.**—She does not care, like Wisdom, to send forth her maidens "to seek and to save that which was lost" (Luke xix. 10); she contents herself with sitting at ease, just outside her own door, and calling to the passers-by.

⁽¹⁶⁾ **Whoso is simple . . .**—She imitates Wisdom closely in her address: Satan, too, transforms himself into an "angel of light" (2 Cor. xi. 14). Folly attracts those undecided characters who are in the right track, but have not the constancy to persevere in it; who, "in time of temptation, fall away."

⁽¹⁷⁾ **Stolen waters are sweet.** — See above, on chap. v. 15.

Bread eaten in secret.—The same figure is used in chap. xxx. 20.

⁽¹⁸⁾ **The dead are there.**—Comp. on chap. ii. 18.

X.

3. A COLLECTION OF 375 SEPARATE VERSES ON VARIOUS SUBJECTS, MARKED BY A NEW HEADING (chaps. x. 1—xxii. 16).

⁽¹⁾ **The proverbs of Solomon.**—The new title and different style of composition mark a new collection of proverbs. (See above, in the *Introduction*.) Each verse is distinct and complete in itself; but the collector appears to have endeavoured to throw together such as touched on the same subject. For instance, chap. x. 4, 5, show why one man fails and another succeeds; verses 6 and 7, how blessings and curses follow different persons. But the connection is sometimes so slight as to be difficult to catch.

⁽²⁾ **Treasures of wickedness** — *i.e.*, gained by wrong-doing.

Righteousness delivereth from death.—The Hebrew word translated "righteousness" has a much wider meaning than its English equivalent, which generally bears the sense only of deciding fairly, being especially applied to judges. But a "righteous" man in Hebrew is one who "renders to all their due," whether to God, as Noah, who was "just and perfect" before Him (Gen. vi. 9, vii. 1; comp. Eccles. vii. 20), or to man. To his fellow-men his "justice" will show itself in liberality (Ps. xxxvii. 21), mercy (chap. xii. 10), carefulness of speech (chap. xv. 28), truthfulness (chap. xiii. 5), and wisdom (chap. ix. 9). He is considerate to animals also (chap. xii. 10). So in the sermon on the Mount our Lord (Matt. vi. 1) says, "Take heed that ye do not your 'righteousness' [so the best MSS. read] before men;" and then specifies it under the heads of almsgiving, prayer, and fasting. In this passage it forms a contrast to riches gained by wrong, and therefore would seem particularly to signify "almsgiving," as its Greek equivalent does in 2 Cor. ix. 10. It is often rendered so by the LXX., and it is the most usual sense of the word in late Hebrew. It is so interpreted also in Tobit iv. 10 and xii. 9, where this passage is quoted. (Comp. Ecclus. iii. 30, xxix. 12, and our Lord's advice, Luke xvi. 9.) It "delivers from death," as being a sign of the divine life within, which is "hid with Christ in God" (Col. iii. 3).

⁽³⁾ **The Lord will not suffer the soul of the righteous to famish.**—Comp. David's experience

Moral Virtues and   PROVERBS, X.   *their contrary Vices.*

a slack hand: but the hand of the diligent maketh rich. ⁽⁵⁾ He that gathereth in summer *is* a wise son: *but* he that sleepeth in harvest *is* a son that causeth shame.

⁽⁶⁾ Blessings *are* upon the head of the just: but *ᵃ*violence covereth the mouth of the wicked. ⁽⁷⁾ *ᵇ*The memory of the just *is* blessed: but the name of the wicked shall rot. ⁽⁸⁾ The wise in heart will receive commandments: but ¹a prating fool ²shall fall. ⁽⁹⁾ *ᶜ*He that walketh uprightly walketh surely: but he that perverteth his ways shall be known. ⁽¹⁰⁾ *ᵈ*He that winketh with the eye causeth sorrow: but a prating fool ³shall fall.

⁽¹¹⁾ *ᵉ*The mouth of a righteous *man is* a well of life: but violence covereth the mouth of the wicked. ⁽¹²⁾ Hatred stirreth up strifes: but *ᶠ*love covereth all sins. ⁽¹³⁾ In the lips of him that hath understanding wisdom is found: but a rod *is* for the back of him that is void of ⁴understanding. ⁽¹⁴⁾ Wise *men* lay up knowledge: but the mouth of the foolish *is* near destruction.

⁽¹⁵⁾ *ᵍ*The rich man's wealth *is* his strong city: the destruction of the poor *is* their poverty. ⁽¹⁶⁾ The labour of the righteous *tendeth* to life: the fruit of the wicked to sin. ⁽¹⁷⁾ He *is in* the way of life that keepeth instruction: but he that refuseth reproof ⁵erreth. ⁽¹⁸⁾ He that hideth hatred *with* lying lips, and he that uttereth a slander, *is* a fool. ⁽¹⁹⁾ In the multitude of words there wanteth not sin: but he that refraineth his lips *is* wise. ⁽²⁰⁾ The tongue of the just *is as* choice silver: the heart of the wicked *is* little worth. ⁽²¹⁾ The lips of the righteous feed many: but fools die for want ⁶of wisdom.

a ver. 11.
b Ps. 112. 6.
1 Heb., *a fool of lips.*
2 Or, *shall be beaten.*
c Ps. 23. 4.
d ch. 6. 13.
3 Or, *shall be beaten.*
e ch. 13. 14.
f 1 Cor. 13. 4; 1 Pet. 4. 8.
4 Heb., *heart.*
g ch. 18. 11.
5 Or, *causeth to err.*
6 Heb., *of heart.*

(Ps. xxxvii. 25), and the great promise of our Lord to those who "seek first the kingdom of God and his righteousness" (Matt. vi. 33). (Comp. also below, chap. xiii. 25.)

He casteth away the substance of the wicked.—Rather, *He repels* (the word is used in 2 Kings iv. 27, of Gehazi "thrusting away" the Shunammite) *the eager, passionate desire of the wicked.* However much they long for it, they get it not, "because they ask amiss" (James iv. 3).

⁽⁶⁾ **Violence covereth the mouth of the wicked.**—Curses and deeds of violence have proceeded from his mouth, but God frustrates them, they "return unto him void" (Isa. lv. 11), and, as it were, stop his mouth, reducing him to silence.

⁽⁸⁾ **A prating fool** (*'evil*). (See above, on chap. i. 7.)

⁽⁹⁾ **Walketh surely.**—He has no cause to fear lest anything to his discredit should come out, but can trust quietly in the Lord (Ps. cxii. 7); while he that goeth by crooked paths will be found out (Matt. x. 26), and the fear of this gives him perpetual uneasiness. Or the meaning may be that he will be "instructed," *i.e.*, punished by misfortune, as Jer. xxxi. 19.

⁽¹⁰⁾ **Causeth sorrow** to the person who is the butt of his ridicule, or against whom his malice is directed.

⁽¹¹⁾ **Violence covereth the mouth of the wicked.**—If these words are to be taken as in verse 6, then the first line must mean that the righteous man speaks to his own profit. But perhaps it will be better here to interpret the second line in the sense of "the mouth of the godless hideth violence," *i.e.*, it conceals under deceitful words the mischief intended for others. With God is the "well of life" (Ps. xxxvi. 9; Rev. xxii. 17); and in like manner the "mouth of the righteous" brings comfort and refreshment to the weary and heavy laden.

⁽¹²⁾ **Hatred stirreth up strifes . . .**—Hatred rakes up again old feuds which have slumbered, but love covers up and refuses to look at any wrong done to it. A similar expression occurs in 1 Peter iv. 8 and James v. 20, though probably in a somewhat different sense. (See the note on the former passage.)

⁽¹⁴⁾ **The mouth of the foolish is near destruction**—*i.e.*, is a near, ever-threatening calamity; one never knows what awkward or dangerous thing he will not say next: whereas wise men store up knowledge, and bring it forth as it is wanted (Matt. xiii. 52).

⁽¹⁵⁾ **The rich man's wealth is his strong city**—*i.e.*, an actual protection to him against his enemies, for by it he can get aid; or (as chap. xviii. 11) it gives him the consciousness of power, courage: whereas poverty drags a man down, and prevents his advance in life, or makes him timid, and unable to defend himself.

⁽¹⁶⁾ **The labour of the righteous tendeth to life.**—For the gains of his honest toil have the blessing of God upon them, and so bring him satisfaction of mind and the power of performing his duties in life; whereas all that the wicked man acquires only helps him to sin yet more, by enabling him to indulge his evil passions.

⁽¹⁷⁾ **Erreth.**—Literally, *committeth error.* This is probably the true sense, and harmonises better with being "in the way of life," which occurs just before, than the marginal rendering, "causeth to err." The word occurs in a similar sense in Jer. xlii. 20 (there translated, "ye have dissembled").

⁽¹⁸⁾ **He that hideth hatred . . .**—This would be more correctly translated, "He that hideth hatred is a mouth of falsehood: he that spreadeth slander is a fool" (*khesîl*: chap. i. 22). (For the construction, "he . . . is a mouth of falsehood," comp. note on chap. viii. 30; and for the sentiment, David's complaint, Ps. xli. 6).

Is a fool.—For he does mischief to his neighbour, and only gets ill-will for himself.

⁽¹⁹⁾ **In the multitude of words there wanteth not sin,** for they are sure to fail in truthfulness, or charity, or opportuneness, and will come under the condemnation of Matt. xii. 36, as being the outcome of a careless heart.

⁽²¹⁾ **The lips of the righteous feed many**—*i.e.*, sustain them by words of counsel, encouragement, and comfort, giving to each one his "meat in due season" (Matt. xxiv. 45).

Moral Virtues and   PROVERBS, XI.   *their contrary Vices.*

(22) The blessing of the LORD, it maketh rich, and he addeth no sorrow with it. (23) *ᵃIt is* as sport to a fool to do mischief: but a man of understanding hath wisdom. (24) The fear of the wicked, it shall come upon him: but the desire of the righteous shall be granted. (25) As the whirlwind passeth, so *is* the wicked no *more:* but the righteous *is* an everlasting foundation. (26) As vinegar to the teeth, and as smoke to the eyes, so *is* the sluggard to them that send him. (27) ᵇThe fear of the LORD ¹prolongeth days: but the years of the wicked shall be shortened. (28) The hope of the righteous *shall be* gladness: but the ᶜexpectation of the wicked shall perish. (29) The way of the LORD *is* strength to the upright: but destruction *shall be* to the workers of iniquity. (30) ᵈThe righteous shall never be removed: but the wicked shall not inhabit the earth. (31) The mouth of the just bringeth forth wisdom: but the froward tongue shall be cut out. (32) The lips of the righteous know what is acceptable: but the mouth of the wicked *speaketh* ²frowardness.

CHAPTER XI.—(1) A ᵉ³false balance *is* abomination to the LORD: but ⁴a just weight *is* his delight. (2) *ᶠWhen* pride cometh, then cometh shame: but with the lowly *is* wisdom. (3) ᵍThe integrity of the upright shall guide them: but the perverseness of transgressors shall destroy them. (4) ʰRiches profit not in the day of wrath: but righteousness

a ch. 14. 9.
b ch. 9. 11.
1 Heb., *addeth.*
c Job 8. 13, & 11. 20; Ps. 112. 10.
d Ps. 37. 22, & 125. 1.
2 Heb., *frowardnesses.*
e Lev. 19. 36; Deut. 25. 15 : ch. 16. 11, & 20. 10, 23.
3 Heb., *Balances of deceit.*
4 Heb., *a perfect stone.*
f ch. 15. 33 & 16. 18, & 18. 12.
g ch. 13. 6.
h ch. 10. 2; Ezek. 7. 19; Zeph. 1. 18.

Fools.—Headstrong, obstinate persons (chap. i. 7).

For want of wisdom.—Or it may be translated, "Through one who is destitute of wisdom." As one righteous man will guide many aright, so one unwise man will lead many fools to ruin.

(22) **And he addeth no sorrow with it**—whereas riches without God's blessing bring only trouble with them. Or the passage may mean, "And labour adds nothing thereto." (Comp. Ps. cxxvii. 2, where God is said to give to His beloved while they sleep all that others toil early and late for in vain.)

(23) **But a man of understanding hath wisdom.**—Rather, *But wisdom (is sport) to a man of understanding,* i.e., one rejoices in mischief, the other (comp. chap. viii. 30) in wise thoughts and deeds.

(24) **The fear of the wicked**—*i.e.,* that of which he is afraid. (Comp. Isa. lxvi. 4; Heb. x. 27.)

The desire of the righteous shall be granted.—For they submit their will to the will of God, and pray for what He sees best for them, which accordingly He grants; moreover, the Holy Spirit also aids them, making intercession for them "according to the will of God" (Rom. viii. 27).

(25) **As the whirlwind passeth.**—Better, *when the whirlwind,* &c. (Comp. Wisd. v. 14, 15; Job xxi. 18; Matt. vii. 24, *ff.*) Death is ruin to the wicked, and gain to the righteous (2 Tim. i. 12).

(27) **The fear of the Lord prolongeth days.**—The special Old Testament blessing for obedience (comp. chap. ix. 11), often fulfilled now, too, in the case of those who live on to old age, in the quiet fulfilment of duty; while others are shortening their lives by excessive anxieties, or the pursuit of pleasure.

(29) **The way of the Lord**—*i.e.,* in which He has directed men to walk. (Comp. Ps. xxv. 12; Matt. xxii. 16; Acts ix. 2.) It is a strong protection to the righteous, for no harm can happen to them while they follow it (1 Peter iii. 13); *but it is destruction* (not, there is destruction) *to the workers of iniquity,* because the fact of their having rejected the teaching of God will be their condemnation. (Comp. 2 Cor. ii. 15, 16.)

(30) **The righteous shall never be removed.**—See above on chap. ii. 21, and Psalm xxxvii. 29.

But the wicked shall not inhabit the earth.—Rather, *The godless abide not in the land.* They often have to become vagabonds, like Cain, for their crimes. This, too, was the great punishment threatened by Moses and all the prophets, which at last fell upon the Jews, and is still in force.

(31) **Bringeth forth wisdom.**—As the fields their "increase" (Deut. xxxii. 13); hence words are termed the "fruit of the lips" (Isa. lvii. 19).

The froward tongue.—See above on chap. ii. 12.

Shall be cut out.—Comp. Christ's warning (Matt. xii. 36). Sins of the tongue will be severely judged, because, besides doing mischief to others, they are signs of an evil mind within (*ib.* v. 34).

(32) **What is acceptable.**—To God and man. (Comp. the gracious words which proceeded out of Christ's lips, Luke iv. 22.)

Speaketh frowardness.—Rather, *is mere falsehood, misrepresentation.* (See above on chap. viii. 30.)

XI.

(1) **A false balance is abomination to the Lord.**—A similar proverb is found in chap. xx. 23, and praise of just weights, chap. xvi. 11, xx. 10. The repetition suggests that this form of cheating had become common in the time of Solomon, when the commerce of Israel began to develop. If so, there would be good reason for these frequent warnings, for it would have been useless to raise the superstructure of a religious life, as is the intention of this book, without first laying the foundation of common honesty between man and man.

A just weight.—Literally, *stone,* stones having been used for weights from early times. (Comp. Lev. xix. 36.) A standard weight, "the king's stone," seems to have been kept by David (2 Sam. xiv. 26).

(2) **Then cometh shame.**—For they have not the grace of God to keep them from falling. (See above on chap. vi. 17.)

(3) **The perverseness of transgressors shall destroy them.**—Fraudulent persons (literally, *those who "cover" a matter up*) pervert the truth, thereby ruining their own characters (inasmuch as in time they can hardly distinguish right from wrong), and losing the favour of Almighty God.

(4) **In the day of wrath.**—Riches profit in no day of wrath when God "visits" His people to take

delivereth from death. (5) The righteousness of the perfect shall ¹direct his way: but the wicked shall fall by his own wickedness. (6) The righteousness of the upright shall deliver them: but ᵃtransgressors shall be taken in *their own* naughtiness.

(7) When a wicked man dieth, *his* expectation shall perish: and the hope of unjust *men* perisheth. (8) ᵇThe righteous is delivered out of trouble, and the wicked cometh in his stead. (9) An ᶜhypocrite with *his* mouth destroyeth his neighbour: but through knowledge shall the just be delivered. (10) When it goeth well with the righteous, the city rejoiceth: and when the wicked perish, *there is* shouting. (11) By the blessing of the upright the city is exalted: but it is overthrown by the mouth of the wicked.

(12) He that is ²void of wisdom despiseth his neighbour: but a man of understanding holdeth his peace. (13) ³A talebearer revealeth secrets: but he that is of a faithful spirit concealeth the matter. (14) ᵈWhere no counsel *is*, the people fall: but in the multitude of counsellors *there is* safety.

(15) He that is surety for a stranger ⁴shall smart *for it*: and he that hateth ⁵suretiship is sure. (16) A gracious woman retaineth honour: and strong *men* retain riches. (17) The merciful man doeth good to his own soul: but *he that is* cruel troubleth his own flesh. (18) The wicked worketh a deceitful work: but to him that soweth righteousness *shall* be a sure reward. (19) As righteousness tendeth to life: so he that pursueth evil *pursueth it* to his own death.

(20) They that are of a froward heart *are* abomination to the LORD: but *such as are* upright in *their* way *are* his delight. (21) *Though* hand *join* in hand, the wicked shall not be unpunished: but the seed of the righteous shall be delivered.

(22) *As* a jewel of gold in a swine's snout, *so is* a fair woman which ⁶is

1 Heb., *rectify.*
ᵃ ch. 3. 22.
ᵇ ch. 21. 18.
ᶜ Job 8. 13.
2 Heb., *destitute of heart.*
3 Heb., *He that walketh, being a talebearer.*
ᵈ 1 Kings 12. 1.
4 Heb., *shall be sore broken.*
5 Heb., *those that strike* hands.
6 Heb., *departeth from.*

---

account of their evil doings; much less will they avail in "the day" (1 Cor. iii. 13).

Righteousness delivereth from death.—See above on chap. x. 2.

(5) **Shall direct his way.**—Or, *make smooth*, as chap. iii. 6. The just man by his exact performance of all duty both towards God and man receives more and more light, and therefore continually sees more clearly how to avoid the difficulties that beset his path. The wicked darkens his conscience more and more by the commission of evil, till he stumbles as in the night (John xi. 9), and at last falls, and rises not again.

(6) **In their own naughtiness.**—Rather, *passionate desire*, as at chap. x. 3. Their own strong passions are their ruin.

His expectation.—What he hoped for, worldly prosperity. (Comp. Wisd. v. 14.)

(8) **The righteous is delivered out of trouble . . .**—That is, misfortunes pass by the righteous and fall upon the wicked. (Comp. chap. xxi. 18.) Or, it may mean that the righteous "is taken away from the evil to come" by death (Isa. lvii. 1), the wicked lives on to suffer in his place.

(9) **An hypocrite.**—Rather, *the impure, profane.*

Through knowledge.—The just, by the knowledge given them by God, shall see through the fraud.

(11) **By the blessing of the upright.**—Especially by their prayers, which, like Abraham (Gen. xviii. 23, *sqq.*), and the Jews of the captivity (Jer. xxix. 7; Ezra vi. 10) they offer for those with whom they live.

By the mouth of the wicked—*i.e.*, by the "cursing, deceit, and fraud" with which his mouth is filled (Ps. x. 7).

He that is void of wisdom despiseth his neighbour.—A warning against rash judgments (Matt. vii. 1, 2). It displays a want of intelligence, very noticeable in uneducated people, not to be able to understand other people's difficulties; but "a man of understanding holdeth his peace," not being rash to condemn, as well knowing that he may be mistaken in his estimate of another, and of the wisest course to be pursued.

(14) **In the multitude of counsellors there is safety**—*i.e.*, where there are plenty to guide the state.

(15) **He that is surety for a stranger.**—Rather, *for another*, as chap. vi. 1.

Is sure.—Rather, *is in quiet*, undisturbed by the anxieties described in chap. vi. 3—5.

(16) **A gracious woman retaineth honour . . .**—Each sex has its own power. A woman by her attractiveness wins and retains favour, a man by his strength and riches.

(17) **The merciful man.**—Rather, *one who shows love.* (See above on chap. iii. 3.) Our good and evil deeds return to us in blessings or curses. (Comp. verse 25.)

(18) **Worketh a deceitful work**—*i.e.*, which ends in nothing, deceiving his hopes. (Comp. verse 7.)

But to him that soweth righteousness shall be a sure reward.—Rather, *he that soweth righteousness* (worketh) *a sure reward for himself.* (For "righteousness," see above on chap. x. 2.)

(19) **As righteousness tendeth to life.**—Rather, *genuine righteousness tendeth to life.*

(21) **Though hand join in hand.**—For this sense comp. Isa. xxviii. 15, *sqq.* The passage may also mean "hand to hand," *i.e.*, from one generation to another; or, what is most probable, "the hand to it," *i.e.*, assuredly. For the general sense of the verse, comp. Ps. xxxvii.

(22) **As a jewel of gold in a swine's snout.**—Rather, *a nose-ring* run through the right nostril and hanging down over the mouth; a female ornament used from the earliest times (Gen. xxiv. 47; Isa. iii. 21; Ezek. xvi. 12), and still worn in the East.

without discretion. (23) The desire of the righteous *is* only good: *but* the expectation of the wicked *is* wrath. (24) There is that scattereth, and yet increaseth; and *there is* that withholdeth more than is meet, but *it tendeth* to poverty. (25) *a* ¹ The liberal soul shall be made fat: and he that watereth shall be watered also himself.

(26) He that withholdeth corn, the people shall curse him: but blessing *shall be* upon the head of him that selleth *it*. (27) He that diligently seeketh good procureth favour: *b* but he that seeketh mischief, it shall come unto him. (28) He that trusteth in his riches shall fall: but *c* the righteous shall flourish as a branch. (29) He that troubleth his own house shall inherit the wind: and the fool *shall be* servant to the wise of heart. (30) The fruit of the righteous *is* a tree of life; and he that ² winneth souls *is* wise. (31) *d* Behold, the righteous shall be recompensed in the earth: much more the wicked and the sinner.

CHAPTER XII.—(1) Whoso loveth instruction loveth knowledge: but he that hateth reproof *is* brutish. (2) A good *man* obtaineth favour of the LORD: but a man of wicked devices will he condemn. (3) A man shall not be established by wickedness: but the *e* root of the righteous shall not be moved. (4) *f* A virtuous woman *is* a crown to her husband: but she that maketh ashamed *is* as rottenness in his bones. (5) The thoughts of the righteous *are* right: *but* the counsels of the wicked *are* deceit. (6) *g* The words of the wicked *are* to lie in wait for blood: but the mouth of the upright shall deliver them. (7) *h* The wicked are overthrown, and *are* not: but the house of the righteous shall stand. (8) A man shall be commended according to his wisdom: but

a 2 Cor. 9. 9.
¹ Heb., *The soul of blessing.*
b Ps. 7. 15, 16 & 9. 15, 16, & 10. 2 & 57. 6.
c Ps. 1. 3, & 92. 12, &c.; Jer. 17. 8.
² Heb., *taketh.*
d 1 Pet. 4. 18.
e ch. 10. 25.
f 1 Cor. 11. 7.
g ch. 1. 11, 18.
h Ps. 37. 37; ch. 11. 21.

---

(23) **The desire of the righteous is only good,** and therefore it, being in accordance with the will of God, is granted to them.

The expectation of the wicked is wrath. —Rather, *presumption*; they do not ask in the way or for the things which God wills they should (Jas. iv. 3), and therefore it is mere presumption on their part to expect the fulfilment of their desires.

(24) **There is that scattereth**—*i.e.,* with bounteous hand (comp. Ps. cxii. 9), "and yet increaseth" in wealth and blessings (comp. chap. xix. 17, and the old epitaph, "What we spent, we had; what we saved, we lost; what we gave, we have.")

(26) **He that withholdeth corn** till it has reached an exorbitant price, "the people shall curse him: but blessing shall be upon the head of him that selleth it" at a fair price. The truth of this is not affected by the fact that the dealer's selfishness is in the long run beneficial to the community by limiting consumption in consequence of the rise in the price of corn.

(27) **Procureth favour.**—By the very act of striving after good, he is seeking for the favour of both God and man.

(28) **He that trusteth in his riches shall fall.** —Because of their uncertainty, and because they prevent his trusting in the living God (1 Tim. vi. 17).

(29) **He that troubleth his own house.**—Possibly by his niggardliness and avarice, as chap. xv. 27.

Shall inherit the wind.—Will get nothing for his pains.

The fool (*'evil*).—The self-willed, who will listen to no advice, and so comes to ruin.

(30) **The fruit of the righteous is a tree of life.**—The righteous, by the performance of his duty to his neighbours, brings, as it were, life and healing (Rev. xxii. 2) to them, and "the wise man winneth souls," attracts them to himself, and induces them to follow his example.

(31) **Behold the righteous shall be recompensed in the earth.**—That is, even he shall be punished for his misdeeds, as were Jacob, Moses, David; how much more shall "the wicked and the sinner." The LXX. translates freely, "If the righteous scarcely be saved, where shall the ungodly and the sinner appear?" a rendering adopted in 1 Peter iv. 18.

XII.

(1) **Whoso loveth instruction loveth knowledge.**—Rather, *he that loveth knowledge loveth discipline,* i.e., to put himself in the place of a learner; while "he that hateth reproof," who will not take advice, is "brutish," "nourishing a blind life within the brain," like the animals who are incapable of improvement.

(2) **A good man.**—The corresponding phrase, "a man of wicked devices," *i.e.,* who plots against his neighbour, fixes the sense of "good" as signifying "benevolent" (comp. Ps. lxxiii. 1); and for the sentiment, Luke vi. 35.

(4) **A virtuous woman.**—Literally, *of power, i.e.,* of ability and character, like the wife described in chap. xxxi., or the "able" men of Exod. xviii. 21.

(5) **The thoughts of the righteous are right.** —Or, *justice*. (Comp. Matt. xii. 35.)

(6) **The words of the wicked are to lie in wait for blood**—*i.e.,* are calculated for this end.

The mouth of the upright shall deliver them—*i.e.,* those for whom the wicked lie in wait.

(7) **The wicked are overthrown.**—By the righteous judgments of God (Ps. xxxvii. 35, 36), or by the storms of temptation and trouble, which, when they come, overwhelm the house built on the sand of earthly hopes, and not on the "Rock of ages." (Isa. xxvi. 4; Matt. vii. 24, *sqq.*)

(8) **According to his wisdom**—*i.e.,* intelligent observance of the ends to be pursued in life, and the best means of attaining to them; in other words, finding out the will of God and how to fulfil it.

Shall be despised.—Comp. 1 Sam. ii. 30.

Moral Virtues and PROVERBS, XII. *their contrary Vices.*

he that is ¹of a perverse heart shall be despised. ⁽⁹⁾ *He that is* despised, and hath a servant, *is* better than he that honoureth himself, and lacketh bread. ⁽¹⁰⁾A righteous *man* regardeth the life of his beast : but the ²tender mercies of the wicked *are* cruel. ⁽¹¹⁾ ᵃHe that tilleth his land shall be satisfied with bread : but he that followeth vain *persons is* void of understanding. ⁽¹²⁾ The wicked desireth ³the net of evil *men* : but the root of the righteous yieldeth *fruit.* ⁽¹³⁾⁴ᵇThe wicked is snared by the transgression of *his* lips : but the just shall come out of trouble. ⁽¹⁴⁾ ᶜA man shall be satisfied with good by the fruit of *his* mouth : and the recompence of a man's hands shall be rendered unto him. ⁽¹⁵⁾ᵈThe way of a fool *is* right in his own eyes : but he that hearkeneth unto counsel *is* wise. ⁽¹⁶⁾ A fool's wrath is ⁵presently known : but a prudent *man* covereth shame. ⁽¹⁷⁾ᵉ*He that* speaketh truth sheweth forth righteousness : but a false witness deceit. ⁽¹⁸⁾ᶠThere is that speaketh like the piercings of a sword : but the tongue of the wise *is* health. ⁽¹⁹⁾ The lip of truth shall be established for ever : but a lying tongue *is* but for a moment. ⁽²⁰⁾ Deceit *is* in the heart of them that imagine evil : but to the counsellors of peace *is* joy. ⁽²¹⁾ There shall no evil happen to the just : but the wicked shall be filled with mischief. ⁽²²⁾ Lying lips *are* abomination to the LORD : but they that deal truly *are* his delight. ⁽²³⁾ᵍ A prudent man concealeth knowledge : but the heart of fools proclaimeth foolishness. ⁽²⁴⁾ ʰThe hand of the diligent shall bear rule : but the ⁶slothful shall be under tribute. ⁽²⁵⁾ⁱHeaviness in the heart of man maketh it stoop : but a

1 Heb., *perverse of heart.*
2 Or, *bowels.*
a ch. 28. 19.
3 Or, *the fortress.*
4 Heb., *The snare of the wicked is in the transgression of lips.*
b ch. 18. 7.
c ch. 13. 2.
d ch. 3. 7.
5 Heb., *in that day.*
e ch. 14. 5.
f Ps. 57. 4, & 59. 7.
g ch. 13. 16, & 15. 2.
h ch. 10. 4.
6 Or, *deceitful.*
i ch. 15. 13.

⁽⁹⁾ **He that is despised.**—That is, lowly in his eyes and those of others, as David (1 Sam. xviii. 23); if "he hath a servant," that is, if he be in easy circumstances. It has been remarked that "the first necessity of an Oriental in only moderate circumstances is a slave."

He that honoureth himself.—Boasts of his pedigree, it may be, and is all the while starving.

⁽¹⁰⁾ **Regardeth the life of his beast.**—Rather, *knows their feelings* (comp. Exod. xxiii. 9), and so can feel for them. God's own care for the brute creation (Jon. iv. 11) was shown in the merciful provisions of the Law, by which cattle shared the rest of the Sabbath, and had their portion of the corn as it was being trodden out (Deut. xxv. 4).

Tender mercies.—What the wicked calls tenderness and kind treatment is really cruelty, as he takes no thought for the comfort of his beast.

⁽¹¹⁾ **Vain persons.**—Or, *things,* such as "searching for hid treasures" (chap. ii. 4).

⁽¹²⁾ **The wicked desireth the net of evil men** —*i.e.,* to enrich himself by prey as they do; but the "root of the righteous yieldeth fruit," by their own exertion they gain all they require without injuring others.

⁽¹³⁾ **The wicked is cursed by the transgression of his lips.**—For his words, the product of his evil heart, while designed to injure others, often bring the offender himself into trouble (Ps. vii. 16), and moreover, as being the true index of the inner life of the soul, are being stored up as a witness against him at the day of judgment" (Matt. xii. 37). The "just man," on the contrary, avoids all this "trouble."

⁽¹⁴⁾ **A man shall be satisfied with good by the fruit of his mouth . . .**—Even in this life the wise counsels and kindly deeds by which others are aided, the "bread cast upon the waters" (Eccles. xi. 1), return to the giver in the shape of love and respect, and, it may be, of similar aid; while the full recompense, "good measure, pressed down, and shaken together, and running over," will come later, at the great day of retribution.

⁽¹⁶⁾ **A fool's wrath is presently known.**— He cannot contain himself if he thinks himself slighted or injured; the "prudent man," on the other hand, "covereth shame," not noticing an insult at the time, but waiting for a convenient opportunity of telling the offender of his fault and bringing him to a better mind (Matt. xviii. 15).

⁽¹⁸⁾ **There is that speaketh.** — Rather, *that babbleth,* like the piercing of a sword, that chatters on, not noticing or caring how he may wound the feelings of others by his inconsiderate remarks.

The tongue of the wise is health. — Or, *healing;* soothing the wounds made by the other's indiscriminate chatter.

⁽¹⁹⁾ **A lying tongue is but for a moment.**— Being detected and silenced by the providence of God, (Comp. Ps. lxiv. 7, 8.)

⁽²⁰⁾ **Deceit is in the heart . . .**—Those who plot and devise evil against others begin by deceiving them, and end by deceiving themselves also; whereas the "counsellors of peace," who seek the good of their neighbours, bring joy to them and to themselves also through the satisfaction derived from a good conscience.

⁽²¹⁾ **There shall no evil happen to the just.**— Comp. our Lord's promise as to temporal matters for those who "seek the kingdom of God" (Matt. vi. 33) and for God's care in spiritual matters, 1 Cor. x. 13.

⁽²³⁾ **A prudent man concealeth knowledge.**— Till the right opportunity for bringing it forth presents itself; while "the heart of fools proclaimeth foolishness," cannot help blurting out and displaying its ignorance and folly, which it mistakes for wisdom.

⁽²⁴⁾ **Under tribute.**—Like the descendants of the Amorites and other former inhabitants of Canaan, by whose forced labour Solomon executed his great works (1 Kings ix. 20, 21). A Hebrew from poverty might be reduced to slavery (Lev. xxv. 39).

⁽²⁵⁾ **Heaviness in the heart of man maketh it stoop.**—But, as this is not favourable to the spiritual life, we have warnings against excessive anxiety (Matt.

Moral Virtues and   PROVERBS, XIII.   *their contrary Vices.*

good word maketh it glad. (26) The righteous *is* more ¹excellent than his neighbour: but the way of the wicked seduceth them. (27) The slothful *man* roasteth not that which he took in hunting: but the substance of a diligent man *is* precious. (28) In the way of righteousness *is* life; and *in* the pathway *thereof there is* no death.

CHAPTER XIII.—(1) A wise son heareth his father's instruction: but a scorner heareth not rebuke. (2) *ᵃ* A man shall eat good by the fruit of *his* mouth: but the soul of the transgressors *shall* eat violence. (3) He that keepeth his mouth keepeth his life: *but* he that openeth wide his lips shall have destruction. (4) The soul of the sluggard desireth, and *hath* nothing: but the soul of the diligent shall be made fat. (5) A righteous *man* hateth lying: but a wicked *man* is loathsome, and cometh to shame. (6) *ᵇ* Righteousness keepeth him that is upright in the way: but wickedness overthroweth ²the sinner. (7) There is that maketh himself rich, yet *hath* nothing: *there is* that maketh himself poor, yet *hath* great riches. (8) The ransom of a man's life *are* his riches: but the poor heareth not rebuke. (9) The light of the righteous rejoiceth: *ᶜ* but the ³lamp of the wicked shall be put out. (10) Only by pride cometh contention: but with the well advised *is* wisdom. (11) *ᵈ* Wealth *gotten* by vanity shall be diminished: but he that gathereth ⁴ by labour shall increase. (12) Hope deferred maketh the heart sick: but *when* the desire cometh, *it is* a tree of life. (13) Whoso despiseth the word shall be destroyed: but he that feareth the commandment ⁵ shall be rewarded. (14) *ᵉ* The law of the wise *is* a

1 Or, *abundant.*
ᵃ ch. 12. 14.
ᵇ ch. 11. 3, 5, 6.
2 Heb., *sin.*
ᶜ Job 18. 6, & 21. 17.
3 Or, *candle.*
ᵈ ch. 10. 2, & 20. 21.
4 Heb., *with the hand.*
5 Or, *shall be in peace.*
ᵉ ch. 14. 27.

---

vi. 34), and exhortations to cast all our care upon God (1 Pet. v. 7; Ps. xxxvii. 5) as a religious duty, that trusting in Him, and so having from Him the "peace which the world cannot give," our hearts may be "set to obey" His commandments.

(26) **The righteous is more excellent than his neighbour.**—Though, perhaps, inferior to him in worldly advantages. Or, it may signify, the just man is a guide to his neighbour, showing him "the way wherein he should walk;" the wicked, on the other hand, so far from guiding others, himself helplessly wanders.

(27) **The slothful man roasteth not that which he took in hunting.**—Or, *does not net,* (*i.e.,* secure) *his prey; but a valuable possession to a man is diligence.*

(28) **In the way of righteousness is life.**—Comp. above on chap. x. 2, "Righteousness delivereth from death."

XIII.

(1) **A wise son heareth his father's instruction.**—Or, *is his father's instruction,* i.e., the result and embodiment of it.

A scorner.—See above on chap. i. 22.

(2) **A man shall eat good by the fruit of his mouth.**—See above on chap. xii. 14.

Shall eat violence.—Comp. chaps. i. 31, xxvi. 6.

(3) **He that keepeth his mouth keepeth his life.**—Comp. above, on chaps. iv. 23 and xii. 13.

(5) **A wicked man is loathsome, and cometh to shame.**—Or it may signify, "disgraceth and putteth to shame" (by his calumnies), or "acts basely and shamefully."

(6) **Righteousness keepeth him that is upright in the way.**—See above on chap. xi. 5.

(7) **There is that maketh himself rich, yet hath nothing.**—Comp. Luke xii. 21, and the advice given in Rev. iii. 17.

There is that maketh himself poor.—Comp. Luke xii. 33.

(8) **The ransom of a man's life are his riches.**—In times of trouble he may have to give them all to save his life. For the spiritual sense comp. Luke xvi. 9.

But the poor heareth not rebuke.—Or, *threatening.* (Comp. Job iii. 18, xxxix. 7.) He has no need to regard it; his poverty and insignificance are his protection.

(9) **The light of the righteous rejoiceth**—*i.e.,* burns joyously, as the sun "rejoiceth as a giant to run his course" (Ps. xix. 5). A distinction may be drawn between the "light" of the righteous and "lamp" of the wicked. The one walks in the "light" of God's truth, and so his path becomes continually more plain (see above on chap. vi. 23); the other walks by the glimmer of his own "lamp," the "fire" and "sparks" of his own kindling (Isa. l. 11), the fancies of his own devising, and so his end is darkness. But this distinction is not always observed (comp. Job xviii. 5, 6, where "light" and "lamp" are both applied to the wicked.)

(10) **Only by pride cometh contention.**—Rather, *by pride cometh nothing but contention.* A man who is too proud to receive counsel is sure to fall out with others; they are wise who suffer themselves to be advised.

(11) **Wealth gotten by vanity.**—As we should say, "in an unsatisfactory manner," that is to say, by dishonesty.

(12) **A tree of life.**—See above, on chap. xi. 30.

(13) **Shall be destroyed.**—Literally, *brings ruin on himself.* Or the sense may be, "is (still) bound to it," even although he may contemptuously neglect it. Comp. the advice (Matt. v. 25), to "agree with our adversary quickly," that is, satisfy the requirements of the law of God while there is time, lest it appear as our adversary at the day of judgment.

(14) **The law of the wise.**—Or, rather, *his instruction.* (Comp. chap. x. 11.)

Snares of death.—Set by the devil (2 Tim. ii. 26).

fountain of life, to depart from the snares of death. (15) Good understanding giveth favour: but the way of transgressors *is* hard. (16)ᵃ Every prudent *man* dealeth with knowledge: but a fool ¹layeth open *his* folly. (17) A wicked messenger falleth into mischief: but a faithful ambassador *is* health. (18) Poverty and shame *shall be to* him that refuseth instruction: but he that regardeth reproof shall be honoured. (19) The desire accomplished is sweet to the soul: but *it is* abomination to fools to depart from evil. (20) He that walketh with wise *men* shall be wise: but a companion of fools ²shall be destroyed. (21) Evil pursueth sinners: but to the righteous good shall be repayed. (22) A good *man* leaveth an inheritance to his children's children: and the ᵇwealth of the sinner *is* laid up for the just. (23) ᶜMuch food *is in* the tillage of the poor: but there is *that is* destroyed for want of judgment. (24) ᵈHe that spareth his rod hateth his son: but he that loveth him chasteneth him betimes. (25) ᵉThe righteous eateth to the satisfying of his soul: but the belly of the wicked shall want.

CHAPTER XIV.— (1) Every wise woman buildeth her house: but the foolish plucketh it down with her hands. (2) He that walketh in his uprightness feareth the LORD: ᶠbut *he that is* perverse in his ways despiseth him. (3) In the mouth of the foolish *is* a rod of pride: but the lips of the wise shall preserve them. (4) Where no oxen *are*, the crib *is* clean: but much increase *is* by the strength of the ox. (5) ᵍA faithful witness will not lie: but a false witness will utter lies. (6) A scorner seeketh wisdom, and *findeth it* not: but ʰknowledge *is* easy unto him that understandeth. (7) Go from the presence of a foolish man, when thou

a ch. 12. 23, & 15. 2.
1 Heb., *spreadeth*.
2 Heb., *shall be broken*.
b Job 27. 17.
c ch. 12. 11.
d ch. 23. 13.
e Ps. 34. 10, & 37. 3.
f Job 12. 4.
g Ex. 20. 16, & 23. 1; ch. 6. 19, & 12. 17.
h ch. 8. 9.

---

(15) **Good understanding giveth favour.**—Comp. the union of "wisdom" and "favour with God and man" (Luke ii. 52).
The way of transgressors is hard.—Rough and barren as the valley described in Deut. xxi. 4, in contrast to the green "pastures" and "waters of comfort" of Ps. xxiii. 2.
(17) **Falleth into mischief.**—And brings those also who sent him into trouble; but "a faithful messenger is health" both to himself and his employers.
(19) **But it is abomination to fools . . .**—That is, though their clinging to evil prevents the attainment of such objects as are worth desiring. If the verse be interpreted "therefore it is abomination," &c., the sense will be, "because the satisfaction of desire is pleasant, therefore fools will not give up anything, though evil, on which they have set their minds."
(20) **Shall be destroyed**—*i.e.*, morally ruined.
(21) **Evil pursueth sinners.**—The "snares, fire, and brimstone," of Ps. xi. 6; while the "good measure, pressed down, shaken together, and running over" (Luke vi. 38), awaits the righteous.
(22) **A good man.**—As this corresponds to the "just" man in the next line, who is one who "renders to all their due" (see above on chap. x. 2), it probably has the meaning here of "liberal," "unselfish;" such a one gains the promise given in chap. xi. 25.
(23) **Tillage.**—Properly, *the newly-made field*, on which much labour has been expended. The poor hardworking man, by God's blessing, gains an abundant living, while many (rich persons) are ruined for their neglect of what is right.
(24) **Betimes.**—While he may yet be influenced rightly, and before faults are rooted in him.
(25) **The righteous eateth to the satisfying of his soul**—*i.e.*, has enough for his wants. (See above on chap. x. 3.)

XIV.

(1) **Every wise woman buildeth her house.**—This should be rendered, "*The wisdom* (literally, *wisdoms*; see above on chap. i. 20; *chokhmôth* should probably be read here, as there, not *chakhmôth*) *of women buildeth* (for each) *her house, but* (their) *folly plucketh it down,*" &c.
Buildeth her house.—Each person and each good work throughout the household grows, as it were, under her fostering hand. (Comp. Eph. ii. 21.)
(2) **He that walketh in his uprightness feareth the Lord.**—Rather, *He who fears the Lord walketh in his uprightness.* (Comp. John xiv. 21.) And likewise, "he that despiseth Him is perverse in his ways." The fear of God and its absence are clearly seen in the outward conduct.
(3) **In the mouth of the foolish** (self-willed) **is a rod of pride.**—He has to smart for his ill-judged sayings; or, he punishes others with them. But this does not agree so well with what follows.
But the lips of the wise shall preserve them (the wise) from the difficulties into which the foolish come by their rash talk.
(4) **Where no oxen are, the crib is clean . . .**—A proverb which may be taken in various ways. Some have seen in it an exhortation to kindness towards animals in consideration of their great usefulness. Others, that labour has its disagreeable aspect, but also brings its reward, whether material prosperity ("much increase") or a more enduring reward. (Comp. Gal. vi. 9.)
(6) **A scorner seeketh wisdom, and findeth it not.**—Because "God resisteth the proud" (1 Peter v. 5), and none can give wisdom but He who alone has it (1 Cor. ii. 11); but He teaches him that "feareth the Lord" (Ps. xxv. 11).
(7) **Go from the presence of a foolish man** —(*khesîl*)—*i.e.*, a dull, stupid one, when the time

perceivest not *in him* the lips of knowledge. (8) The wisdom of the prudent *is* to understand his way: but the folly of fools *is* deceit. (9) *a*Fools make a mock at sin: but among the righteous *there is* favour. (10) The heart knoweth [1] his own bitterness; and a stranger doth not intermeddle with his joy. (11) The house of the wicked shall be overthrown: but the tabernacle of the upright shall flourish. (12) *b*There is a way which seemeth right unto a man, but the end thereof *are* the ways of death. (13) Even in laughter the heart is sorrowful; and the end of that mirth *is* heaviness. (14) The backslider in heart shall be *c*filled with his own ways: and a good man *shall be satisfied* from himself. (15) The simple believeth every word: but the prudent *man* looketh well to his going. (16) A wise *man* feareth, and departeth from evil: but the fool rageth, and is confident. (17) *He that is* soon angry dealeth foolishly: and a man of wicked devices is hated. (18) The simple inherit folly: but the prudent are crowned with knowledge. (19) The evil bow before the good; and the wicked at the gates of the righteous. (20) *d*The poor is hated even of his own neighbour: but [2]the rich *hath* many friends. (21) He that despiseth his neighbour sinneth: *e*but he that hath mercy on the poor, happy *is* he. (22) Do they not err that devise evil? but mercy and truth *shall be* to them that devise good. (23) In all labour there is profit: but the talk of the lips *tendeth* only to penury. (24) The crown of the

---

a ch. 10. 23.
[1] Heb., *the bitterness of his soul.*
b ch. 16. 25.
c ch. 1. 31.
d ch. 19. 7.
[2] Heb., *many are the lovers of the rich.*
e Ps. 112. 9.

---

comes that you see you can do him no good; for "evil communications corrupt good manners." Thus Samuel "came no more to see Saul," when he saw that remonstrances were unavailing with him, though he continued to "mourn" for him, remembering from what high estate he had fallen.

(8) **The wisdom of the prudent is to understand his way.**—To look to it carefully that it is such as God would have it; but "the folly of fools [stupid persons, as verse 7], is deceit;" it shows itself in trying to cheat others, though they are sure to be detected at last.

(9) **Fools make a mock at sin.**—Rather, perhaps, *sin mocks fools* (they miss the gratification they expected from it); or, *the sin-offering mocks them.* God does not accept it, and so they have the trouble and cost of offering it for nothing; "but among the upright there is favour." God is well pleased with them.

(10) **The heart knoweth his own bitterness . . .**—None can perfectly sympathise with the sorrows or joys of others, except the ideal Son of Man, who came to "bear our griefs and carry our sorrows" (comp. Heb. iv. 15), yet could join in the marriage-feast at Cana.

(11) **The house of the wicked shall be overthrown.**—Observe the contrast between the "house" and "tabernacle" (tent); the slighter one shall stand, while the more strongly built one shall perish. (Comp. chap. iii. 33.)

(12) **There is a way which seemeth right unto a man,** and yet he will be punished if he follows it, for his perverted conscience may arise from his desertion of God, and his refusal of the light He offered. (Comp. Rom. i. 28, *sqq.*)

(13) **Even in laughter the heart is sorrowful.**—By this God would teach us that nothing can satisfy the soul of man but Himself, and so would urge us to seek Him, who is the only true object of our desires. (Comp. Ps. xxxvi. 8.)

(14) **The backslider in heart**—*i.e.,* who turns away from God. (Ps. xliv. 19.)

Shall be filled with his own ways.—(Comp. chap. i. 31, and Matt. vi. 2, &c.: "They have their reward.") They get to the full what they look for, though it is but swine's husks, instead of food fit for God's children.

A good man.—See above on chap. xiii. 22.

Shall be satisfied from himself.—His own work. (Comp. Isa. iii. 10.)

(15) **The simple.**—See above on chap. i. 22.

Believeth every word.—And so, having no fixed principles by which to go, often takes a wrong step; while the prudent man considers well (verse 8) whither each step will lead, and therefore does not go astray.

(16) **A wise man feareth.**—(Comp. chap. iii. 7.)

The fool rageth.—Gives way to passionate excitement, and "is confident" in his own wisdom; he has no "quietness and confidence" (Isa. xxx. 15) in God.

(17) **Dealeth foolishly.**—Does silly things, and makes himself an object of ridicule, but not of hatred; whereas the "man of (wicked) devices" is hated for his cold-blooded malice.

(18) **The simple inherit folly.**—As weeds spring up in unoccupied soil, so "simple" (chap. i. 22) persons, whose minds are unoccupied with good, often become self-willed; while the knowledge which the "prudent" gain by looking well to their steps (verse 15) adorns them as a crown.

(19) **The evil bow before the good.**—(Comp. 1 Sam. ii. 36.) That this final retribution is certain is implied by the tense employed, though it may be long delayed till the "awakening" (Ps. lxxiii. 20) of God and man to judgment. (Comp. Wisd. v. 1, *sqq.*)

(20) **The poor is hated even of his own neighbour.**—This sad experience of life is repeated in chap. xix. 7. The following verse serves as a corrective of this selfish tendency of mankind.

(22) **Do they not err that devise evil?**—Comp. Wisd. v. 6, 7.

Mercy and truth.—God will be merciful, and also fulfil His promises of protection and reward to them (Wisd. iii. 9).

(24) **The crown of the wise is their riches.**—They adorn and set off the wisdom of the wise, and bring it more prominently into notice; but the "foolishness of fools" remains folly. The rich fool only displays his folly all the more from being set in a conspicuous position.

wise *is* their riches: *but* the foolishness of fools *is* folly. (25) *a*A true witness delivereth souls: but a deceitful *witness* speaketh lies. (26) In the fear of the LORD *is* strong confidence: and his children shall have a place of refuge. (27) *b*The fear of the LORD *is* a fountain of life, to depart from the snares of death. (28) In the multitude of people *is* the king's honour: but in the want of people *is* the destruction of the prince. (29) *He that is* slow to wrath *is* of great understanding: but he that is ¹hasty of spirit exalteth folly. (30) A sound heart *is* the life of the flesh: but envy the rottenness of the bones.

(31) *c*He that oppresseth the poor reproacheth his Maker: but he that honoureth him hath mercy on the poor. (32) The wicked is driven away in his wickedness: but the righteous hath hope in his death. (33) Wisdom resteth in the heart of him that hath understanding: but *that which is* in the midst of fools is made known. (34) Right-eousness exalteth a nation: but sin *is* a reproach ²to any people. (35) The king's favour *is* toward a wise servant: but his wrath is *against* him that causeth shame.

CHAPTER XV.—(1) A *d*soft answer turneth away wrath: but grievous words stir up anger. (2) The tongue of the wise useth knowledge aright: *e*but the mouth of fools ³poureth out foolishness. (3) *f*The eyes of the LORD *are* in every place, beholding the evil and the good. (4) ⁴A wholesome tongue *is* a tree of life: but perverseness therein *is* a breach in the spirit. (5) *g*A fool despiseth his father's instruction: but he that regardeth reproof is prudent.

(6) In the house of the righteous *is* much treasure: but in the revenues of the wicked is trouble. (7) The lips of the wise disperse knowledge: but the heart of the foolish *doeth* not so. (8) *h*The sacrifice of the wicked *is* an abomination to the LORD: but the

a ver. 5.
b ch. 13. 14.
¹ Heb., *short of spirit.*
c ch. 17. 5; Matt. 25. 40.
² Heb., *to nations.*
d ch. 25. 15.
e ch. 12. 23, & 13. 16; ver. 28.
³ Heb., *belcheth,* or, *bubbleth.*
f Job 34. 21; ch. 5. 21; Jer. 16. 17, & 32. 19; Heb. 4. 13.
⁴ Heb., *The healing of the tongue.*
g ch. 10. 1.
h ch. 21. 27; Isa. 1. 11, & 66. 3; Jer. 6. 20, & 7. 22; Amos 5. 22.

---

(26) **His children.**—Either, the children of the man who fears the Lord, as the blessing of Abraham (Gen. xvii. 7, 8) and David (Jer. xxxiii. 20, 21) descended to their children; or the pronoun may refer to God's children, *i.e.*, those who look up to Him as a father, an expression which occurs in the Old Testament (*e.g.*, Ps. lxxiii. 15), but is brought forward more prominently in the New Testament.

(27) **Fountain of life.**—Comp. chap. xiii. 14 and John iv. 14.

(28) **In the multitude of people is the king's honour.**—Not in ambitious wars. In these words speaks the "man of rest" (1 Chron. xxii. 9). (Comp. the description of Solomon's kingdom in the days of his prosperity; 1 Kings iv. 20.)

(29) **He that is hasty of spirit exalteth folly**—*i.e.*, brings it into view, or shows himself highly foolish. Or it may signify, "he takes up and carries away folly as his portion," as chap. iii. 35 may be translated, "fools receive shame for their portion."

(30) **A sound heart**—*i.e.*, one in healthy condition, of which the passions and emotions are under control.

(31) **Reproacheth his Maker.**—For having placed him in such a lowly condition. The equality of all men, as being all of them the work of God, is taught by Gen. i. 27; Job xxxi. 15; Prov. xxii. 2. The duty of aiding the poor is in Matt. xxv. 40 based on the still higher ground of the union of Christ with His people, which makes Him regard good done to them as done to Himself.

But he that honoureth him . . .—This would be better rendered, *but he that hath mercy on the poor honoureth Him.*

(32) **The wicked is driven away in his wickedness.**—Or, *is overthrown in his misfortune,* *i.e.*, when it comes upon him (comp. Ps. xxxiv. 21), for he has none to aid or comfort him.

But the righteous hath hope in his death.—Comp. Job's confidence (Job xiii. 15 and Ps. xxiii. 4). The gravest troubles do not terrify him.

(33) **But that which is in the midst of fools is made known.**—"Wisdom" is the subject of this as of the former half of the verse. "Wisdom rests in the heart of him that hath understanding;" he does not care to drag it out and exhibit it, but the fool cannot keep to himself anything which he thinks he knows.

(34) **Righteousness.**—See above, on chap. x. 2.

XV.

(2) **Useth knowledge aright.**—Brings it forth at the proper time and place.

(3) **Beholding the evil and the good.**—Waiting till the iniquity of the one is full (Gen. xv. 16), watching to aid the other (Ps. xxxiv. 15, 17).

(4) **A wholesome tongue.**—One which heals and soothes by its gentleness and judicious words. (Comp. chap. xii. 18.)

A tree of life.—Comp. chaps. iii. 18, xi. 30.

Perverseness.—Distortion of the truth. (Comp. chap. xi. 3.)

A breach in the spirit—*i.e.*, deeply wounds another's spirit.

(5) **A fool** (*'evil*).—See above, on chap i. 7.

(6) **In the house of the righteous is much treasure.**—For God's blessing (chap. iii. 33) is upon it; while the wicked, from his recklessness in the pursuit of gain, brings trouble (verse 27) upon himself and his family.

(7) **But the heart of the foolish doeth not so.**—Or, *disperseth that which is not right.*

(8) **The sacrifice of the wicked is an abomination to the Lord.**—And their prayers also (Isa. i. 11). The worthlessness of sacrifice without obedience (comp. 1 Sam. xv. 22) may be here especially men-

prayer of the upright *is* his delight. ⁽⁹⁾ The way of the wicked *is* an abomination unto the LORD: but he loveth him that followeth after righteousness. ⁽¹⁰⁾ ¹Correction *is* grievous unto him that forsaketh the way: *and* he that hateth reproof shall die. ⁽¹¹⁾ ᵃHell and destruction *are* before the LORD: how much more then the hearts of the children of men?

⁽¹²⁾ A scorner loveth not one that reproveth him: neither will he go unto the wise. ⁽¹³⁾ ᵇA merry heart maketh a cheerful countenance: but by sorrow of the heart the spirit is broken. ⁽¹⁴⁾ The heart of him that hath understanding seeketh knowledge: but the mouth of fools feedeth on foolishness. ¹⁵⁾ All the days of the afflicted *are* evil: but he that is of a merry heart *hath* a continual feast. ⁽¹⁶⁾ ᶜBetter *is* little with the fear of the LORD, than great treasure and trouble therewith. ⁽¹⁷⁾ ᵈBetter *is* a dinner of herbs where love is, than a stalled ox and hatred therewith. ⁽¹⁸⁾ ᵉA wrathful man stirreth up strife: but *he that is* slow to anger appeaseth strife. ⁽¹⁹⁾ The way of the slothful *man is* as an hedge of thorns: but the way of the righteous ²*is* made plain.

⁽²⁰⁾ ᶠA wise son maketh a glad father: but a foolish man despiseth his mother. ⁽²¹⁾ ᵍFolly *is* joy to *him that is* ³destitute of wisdom: but a man of understanding walketh uprightly. ⁽²²⁾ ʰWithout counsel purposes are disappointed: but in the multitude of counsellors they are established. ⁽²³⁾ A man hath joy by the answer of his mouth: and a word *spoken* ⁴in due season, how good *is it!*

⁽²⁴⁾ ⁱThe way of life *is* above to the wise, that he may depart from hell beneath. ⁽²⁵⁾ ᵏThe LORD will destroy the house of the proud: but he will establish the border of the widow. ⁽²⁶⁾ ˡThe thoughts of the wicked *are* an abomination to the LORD: but *the words* of the pure *are* ⁵pleasant words.

⁽²⁷⁾ He that is greedy of gain trou-

Marginal notes:
1 Or, *Instruction.*
a Job 26. 6.
b ch. 17. 22.
c Ps. 37. 16; ch. 16. 8; 1 Tim. 6. 6.
d ch. 17. 1.
e ch. 26. 21, & 29. 22.
2 Heb., *is raised up as a causey.*
f ch. 10. 1.
g ch. 10. 23.
3 Heb., *void of heart.*
h ch. 11. 14.
4 Heb., *in his season.*
i Phil. 3. 20; Col. 3. 1, 2.
k ch. 12. 7, & 14. 11.
l ch. 6. 18.
5 Heb., *words of pleasantness.*

---

tioned, because men are apt to think that what involves cost and trouble must be pleasing to God, even when not accompanied with what alone He cares for, a loving heart.

The prayer of the upright is his delight.—Even when offered by itself, without sacrifice.

⁽¹⁰⁾ **Correction is grievous.**—Rather, *There is a grievous correction for him that forsaketh the* (right) *way*; first of all, punishment for the sake of "correction" (Lev. xxvi. 14, *sqq.*), and then, lastly, in the case of obstinate hatred of "reproof," death (*Ibid.* verse 33).

⁽¹¹⁾ **Hell and destruction.**—"Hell" is here the general name for the unseen world (*Hades*) beyond the grave, so called, according to one derivation, from its always "asking" for more victims, and never being satisfied. (Comp. chap. xxvii. 20.) "Destruction" (*Abaddon*) is the lowest hell, corresponding to the "abyss" of Luke viii. 31; Rev. ix. 1, 11; the abode of evil spirits and the lost. (For the thought, comp. Job xxvi. 6, and Ps. cxxxix. 8.)

⁽¹²⁾ **A scorner.**—See above on chap. i. 22.

⁽¹³⁾ **By sorrow of heart the spirit is broken.**—See above on chap. xii. 25.

⁽¹⁵⁾ **All the days of the afflicted are evil.**—Another caution against over-anxiety. The "afflicted" here evidently means, not one who has to bear great misfortunes, but one who makes the worst of everything, to whom the "clouds return after the rain" (Eccl. xii. 2); while one who is "of a merry heart" does just the contrary.

⁽¹⁶⁾ **Trouble.**—The "disquiet" (Ps. xxxix. 6) which attends the pursuit and care of riches, in contrast to the "peace" which they have who love God's law. (Ps. cxix. 165.)

⁽¹⁹⁾ **As a hedge of thorns.**—Every difficulty in his path serves as an excuse for inaction (comp. chap. xxii. 13); while the upright man, who does his duty as in the sight of God, goes "from strength to strength" (Ps. lxxxiv. 7), along the path of life smoothed for him (Isa. xxvi. 7), performing the "just works" appointed for him to do.

⁽²¹⁾ **Folly.**—Shown in wasted opportunities, and the commission of evil (chap. x. 23), while the "man of understanding" directs his way in accordance with the will of God.

⁽²³⁾ **A man hath joy by the answer of his mouth.**—So much mischief is done by the tongue, and its slips are so many, that when a man makes a suitable reply, he may well rejoice and look upon it as the gift of God (chap. xvi. 1).

⁽²⁴⁾ **The way of life is above to the wise.**—These words sound like a faint echo of such passages as Phil. iii. 20; Col. iii. 1, 2, though the writer's meaning may only have been that the wise man who fears the Lord (chap. i. 7) is rewarded with long life on earth (chap. iii. 16), and escapes death and hell (chap. ii. 18, 19). Comp. Isa. xxxviii. 18, 19.

⁽²⁵⁾ **The proud**—who trust in their own strength; while He will "establish the border," or landmark, of the helpless widow, who has none to cry to but Him. The frequently threatened punishment against one who removes his neighbour's landmark, shews the offence to have been a common form of oppression. (Comp. Deut. xix. 14, xxvii. 17; Prov. xxii. 28; Job xxiv. 2; Hos. v. 10.)

⁽²⁶⁾ **The thoughts of the wicked.**—Rather, *thoughts of evil, wicked designs.*

But the words of the pure are pleasant words.—Rather, *pleasant words* (*i.e.*, kindly meant, soothing words; comp. chap. xvi. 24) *are pure* in God's sight; accepted by Him as coming from a well-meaning heart.

⁽²⁷⁾ **He that is greedy of gain.**—Ill-gotten gain, especially bribes, as is seen in the next line.

Troubleth his own house.—The word used of Achan (Josh. vii. 25).

Moral Virtues and   PROVERBS, XVI.   *their Contrary Vices.*

bleth his own house; but he that hateth gifts shall live. (28) The heart of the righteous studieth to answer: but the mouth of the wicked poureth out evil things. (29) ^aThe LORD *is* far from the wicked: but he heareth the prayer of the righteous. (30) The light of the eyes rejoiceth the heart: *and* a good report maketh the bones fat.

(31) The ear that heareth the reproof of life abideth among the wise. (32) He that refuseth ¹instruction despiseth his own soul: but he that ²heareth reproof ³getteth understanding. (33) The fear of the LORD *is* the instruction of wisdom; and ^bbefore honour *is* humility.

CHAPTER XVI.—The ^{c 4}preparations of the heart in man, and the answer of the tongue, *is* from the LORD. (2) ^dAll the ways of a man *are* clean in his own eyes; but the LORD weigheth the spirits. (3) ^{e 5}Commit thy works unto the LORD, and thy thoughts shall be established. (4) The LORD hath made all *things* for himself: ^fyea, even the wicked for the day of evil. (5)^gEvery one *that is* proud in heart *is* an abomination to the LORD: *though* hand *join* in hand, he shall not be ⁶unpunished. (6) By mercy and truth iniquity is purged: and by the fear of the LORD *men* depart from evil. (7) When a man's ways please the LORD, he maketh even his enemies to be at peace with him.

(8) ^hBetter *is* a little with righteousness than great revenues without right. (9) ⁱA man's heart deviseth his way: but the LORD directeth his steps. (10) ⁷A divine sentence *is* in the lips of the king: his mouth transgresseth not in

---

a Ps. 34. 16, & 145. 18.
1 Or, *correction.*
2 Or, *obeyeth.*
3 Heb., *possesseth an heart.*
b ch. 18. 12.
c ver. 9; ch. 19. 21, & 20. 24; Jer. 10. 23.
4 Or, *disposings.*
d ch. 21. 2.
e Ps. 37. 5, & 55. 22; Matt. 6. 25; Luke 12. 22; 1 Pet. 5. 7.
5 Heb., *Roll.*
f Job 21. 30.
g ch. 6. 17, & 8. 13.
6 Heb., *held innocent.*
h Ps. 37. 16; ch. 15. 16.
i ver. 1.
7 Heb., *Divination.*

Gifts.—Bribes taken by a judge. (Eccl. vii. 7.)

(28) **The heart of the righteous studieth to answer**—*i.e.,* aright, knowing how much good and evil is caused by words. (Comp. Jas. iii. 5, *sqq.*)

(29) **He heareth the prayer of the righteous.** —For they desire above all things to do His will, and so their petitions to this effect are heard by Him.

(30) **The light of the eyes . . .** —It does the heart good to see one whose eyes are sparkling with happiness.

A good report.—Good news, affecting either oneself or others.

(31) **The ear that heareth the reproof of life**—*i.e.,* one which does not refuse reproof, or instruction, which leads to life. (Comp. chap. vi. 23.) The "ear" is put for the person, as in Job xxix. 11.

(33) **The fear of the Lord is the instruction of wisdom.**—Or, *a discipline which leads to wisdom.* (Comp. chap. i. 7.)

Before honour is humility.—Humility leads to it. (Comp. Luke i. 52.)

XVI.

(1) **The preparations of the heart in man . . .** —Rather, *To man belong the counsels of the heart.* He may turn over in his mind what is the right thing to be said on any occasion, "but from the Lord is the answer of the tongue." (Comp. chap. xv. 23.)

(2) **All the ways of a man are clean in his own eyes.**—Yet that does not excuse his faults in God's sight. (Comp. 1 Cor. iv. 4.) So much the more reason is there for anxious self-examination and testing the conduct by God's word, and, when this has been done to the best of our power, still to pray for cleansing from faults which have escaped our notice. (Ps. xix. 12.)

(3) **Commit thy works unto the Lord.**—Literally, *roll them upon Him*, as a burden too heavy to be borne by thyself. "Thy works" signify all that thou hast to do. (Comp. Ps. xxxvii. 5.) God provides such works for us. (Comp. Eph. ii. 10.)

And thy thoughts shall be established.—Thy plans shall prosper, for they will be undertaken according to the will of God, and carried out by His aid. (Comp. 1 Cor. iii. 9; 2 Cor. vi. 1.)

(4) **The Lord hath made all things for himself**—*i.e.,* to serve His own purposes, that His wisdom, goodness, &c., may be thereby revealed. Or the passage may be translated, "hath made all for its own end or purpose." The assertion that "He has made the wicked for the day of evil," does not mean that He created any one for punishment—*i.e.,* predestined him for destruction. It only teaches that even the wicked are subservient to God's eternal purposes; that Pharaoh, for instance, by his rebellion could not change God's plans for the deliverance of His people, but only gave Him an occasion for showing forth His power, justice, goodness, and longsuffering. The "day of evil," *i.e.,* punishment, at last overtook Pharaoh in accordance with the law and purpose of God that the wicked, if unrepentant, shall be punished, and thereby serve as a warning to others; but God by his long-suffering shewed that He was "not willing" that he should "perish," but rather that he "should come to repentance" (2 Pet. iii. 9). This appears to be also the teaching of St. Paul in Rom. ix. 17, *sqq.*

(5) **Though hand join in hand.**—See Note on chap. xi. 21.

(6) **Mercy and truth.**—See above on chap. iii. 3. Mercy and truth cannot, of course, in themselves "purge iniquity," only so far as they are signs of the "faith which worketh by love" (Gal. v. 6), which accepts the salvation offered by God (Rom. i. 16, 17). (Comp. the statement with regard to charity, 1 Pet. iv. 8.)

By the fear of the Lord men depart from evil.—Or, rather, *escape misfortune.* (Comp. Ps. xxxvii. throughout.)

(7) **When a man's ways please the Lord . . .** —Comp. Gen. xxvi. 28; 2 Chron. xvii. 10, 11.

(9) **A man's heart deviseth his way . . .** —"Man proposeth, God disposeth." (See below on chap. xx. 24.)

(10) **His mouth transgresseth not in judgment.**—Or, *should not transgress,* as being the representative of God upon earth, and so distinguished by the

Moral Virtues and PROVERBS, XVI. *their Contrary Vices.*

judgment. ⁽¹¹⁾ ^aA just weight and balance *are* the LORD's: ¹all the weights of the bag *are* his work. ⁽¹²⁾ *It is* an abomination to kings to commit wickedness: for the throne is established by righteousness. ⁽¹³⁾ Righteous lips *are* the delight of kings; and they love him that speaketh right. ⁽¹⁴⁾ The wrath of a king *is as* messengers of death: but a wise man will pacify it. ⁽¹⁵⁾ In the light of the king's countenance *is* life; and ^bhis favour *is* as a cloud of the latter rain.

⁽¹⁶⁾ ^cHow much better *is it* to get wisdom than gold! and to get understanding rather to be chosen than silver! ⁽¹⁷⁾ The highway of the upright *is* to depart from evil: he that keepeth his way preserveth his soul. ⁽¹⁸⁾ ^dPride goeth before destruction, and an haughty spirit before a fall. ⁽¹⁹⁾ Better *it is* to be of an humble spirit with the lowly, than to divide the spoil with the proud.

⁽²⁰⁾ ²He that handleth a matter wisely shall find good: and whoso ^etrusteth in the LORD, happy *is* he. ⁽²¹⁾ The wise in heart shall be called prudent: and the sweetness of the lips increaseth learning. ⁽²²⁾ ^fUnderstanding *is* a wellspring of life unto him that hath it: but the instruction of fools *is* folly. ⁽²³⁾ The heart of the wise ³teacheth his mouth, and addeth learning to his lips. ⁽²⁴⁾ Pleasant words *are as* an honeycomb, sweet to the soul, and health to the bones.

⁽²⁵⁾ ^gThere is a way that seemeth right unto a man, but the end thereof *are* the ways of death. ⁽²⁶⁾ ⁴He that laboureth laboureth for himself; for his mouth ⁵craveth it of him. ⁽²⁷⁾ ⁶An ungodly man diggeth up evil: and in his lips *there is* as a burning fire. ⁽²⁸⁾ ^hA froward man ⁷soweth strife: and a whisperer separateth chief friends. ⁽²⁹⁾ A violent man enticeth his neighbour, and leadeth him into the way *that is* not good. ⁽³⁰⁾ He shutteth his eyes to devise froward things: moving his lips he bringeth evil to pass. ⁽³¹⁾ The hoary head *is* a crown of glory, *if* it be found in the way of righteousness. ⁽³²⁾ *He that is* slow

---

a Lev. 19. 36; ch. 11. 1.
¹ Heb., *all the stones.*
b ch. 19. 12.
c ch. 8. 11.
d ch. 11. 2, & 18. 12.
² Or, *He that understandeth a matter.*
e Ps. 2. 12 & 34. 8, & 125. 1; Isa. 30. 18; Jer. 17. 7.
f ch. 13. 14.
³ Heb., *maketh wise.*
g ch. 14. 12.
⁴ Heb., *The soul of him that laboureth.*
⁵ Heb., *boweth unto him.*
⁶ Heb., *A man of Belial.*
h ch. 6. 14, 19 & 15. 18, & 26. 21, & 20. 22.
⁷ Heb., *sendeth forth.*

---

title of "God" himself (Ps. lxxxii. 6). This verse recalls the days of Solomon's youth, when it was his highest aspiration to judge his people righteously (1 Kings iii. 9). Comp. David's noble words (2 Sam. xxiii. 3).

⁽¹¹⁾ **A just weight and balance are the Lord's.**—See above on chap. xi. 1.

⁽¹²⁾ **It is an abomination to kings . . . .**—This and the following verse are, like verse 10, descriptive of the ideal king who, above all things, loves truth and justice. Ps. lxxii. works out the thought more fully. How feebly the character was fulfilled by Solomon or the best of his successors the history of Israel shews. It was too high a conception for man to carry out, and was fulfilled only in the person of David's Son, who is "King of kings, and Lord of lords" (Rev. xix. 16).

⁽¹⁵⁾ **A cloud of the latter rain.**—This fell at the end of March, maturing the barley and wheat crops before the harvest in April. It was eagerly looked for as of great importance. (Comp. Ps. lxxii. 6 for the same figure.)

⁽¹⁷⁾ **The highway of the upright is to depart from evil.**—This is the plain way of duty, which lies right before him, which cannot be mistaken, whatever other difficulties he may have. (See above on chap. vi. 23.)

He that keepeth his way.—That looks well to it.

⁽¹⁸⁾ **Pride goeth before destruction.**—In contrast to the blessing promised to humility in chap. xv. 33.

⁽²⁰⁾ **He that handleth a matter wisely.**—Or, perhaps, *he that attendeth to the word* of God. (Comp. chap. xiii. 13.)

⁽²¹⁾ **The sweetness of the lips increaseth learning.**—Power to express the thoughts in graceful language adds greatly to the value of learning.

⁽²²⁾ **The instruction of fools is folly.**—While understanding is "a fountain of life" (chap. x. 11) giving health and refreshment and vigour both to the possessor and his friends, the discipline given by fools is worse than useless, being folly itself. Or it may mean, "the discipline which fools have to endure is folly." If they will not be taught by wisdom, their own folly will serve as a rod to correct them.

⁽²³⁾ **Addeth learning to his lips.**—His wisdom and learning do not remain hidden in his heart, but continually rise to his lips, like the waters of an everflowing fountain, for the instruction of others.

⁽²⁴⁾ **Pleasant words.**—Comp. chap. xv. 26.

Health to the bones.—Comp. 1 Sam. xiv. 27.

⁽²⁶⁾ **He that laboureth laboureth for himself.**—Rather, *the desire*, or *hunger, of the labourer laboureth for him, for his mouth urges him on*; the feeling that he is supplying his own needs gives him strength for his work.

⁽²⁷⁾ **Diggeth up evil.**—Digs, as it were, a pit for others by his malicious plottings and slanders (Ps. vii. 15).

In his lips there is as a burning fire.—"Set on fire of hell" (James iii. 6).

⁽²⁸⁾ **A froward man.**—Who distorts the truth.

⁽²⁹⁾ **A violent man enticeth his neighbour . . . .**—Comp. chap. i. 10, *sqq.*

⁽³⁰⁾ **He shutteth his eyes . . . .**—By the movement of eyes and lips he gives the signal for mischief to his confederates. (Comp. chap. vi. 13.)

⁽³¹⁾ **If it be found in the way of righteousness.**—Rather, *it is found*; old age being promised as the reward of obedience. (Comp. chaps. iii. 1, 2, 16, iv. 10, ix. 11, x. 27.)

⁽³²⁾ **He that is slow to anger . . . .**—For victory over self is the hardest of all victories. (Comp. 1 Cor. ix. 27.)

Moral Virtues and   PROVERBS, XVII.   *their Contrary Vices.*

to anger *is* better than the mighty; and he that ruleth his spirit than he that taketh a city. (33) The lot is cast into the lap; but the whole disposing thereof *is* of the LORD.

CHAPTER XVII.—(1) Better *is* a dry morsel, and quietness therewith, than an house full of ¹sacrifices *with* strife. (2) A wise servant shall have rule over a son that causeth shame, and shall have part of the inheritance among the brethren. (3) *b*The fining pot *is* for silver, and the furnace for gold: but the LORD trieth the hearts. (4) A wicked doer giveth heed to false lips; *and* a liar giveth ear to a naughty tongue. (5) *c*Whoso mocketh the poor reproacheth his Maker: *and* he that is glad at calamities shall not be ²unpunished. (6) *d*Children's children *are* the crown of old men; and the glory of children *are* their fathers.

(7) ³Excellent speech becometh not a fool: much less do ⁴lying lips a prince. (8) *e*A gift *is as* a ⁵precious stone in the eyes of him that hath it: whithersoever it turneth, it prospereth. (9) *f*He that covereth a transgression ⁶seeketh love; but he that repeateth a matter separateth *very* friends. (10) ⁷A reproof entereth more into a wise man than an hundred stripes into a fool. (11) An evil man seeketh only rebellion: therefore a cruel messenger shall be sent against him. (12) Let a bear robbed of her whelps meet a man, rather than a fool in his folly. (13) Whoso *g*rewardeth evil for good, evil shall not depart from his house.

(14) The beginning of strife *is as* when one letteth out water: therefore leave

a ch. 15.17.
1 Or, *good cheer.*
b Ps. 26. 2; ch. 27. 21; Jer. 17. 10; Mal. 3. 3.
c ch. 14. 31.
2 Heb., *held innocent.*
d Ps.127.3, & 128.3.
3 Heb., *a lip of excellency.*
4 Heb., *A lip of lying.*
e ch. 18. 16
5 Heb., *stone of grace.*
f ch. 10. 12.
6 Or, *procureth.*
7 Or, *A reproof aweth more a wise man, than to strike a fool an hundred times.*
g Rom. 12. 17; 1 Thess. 5. 15; 1 Pet. 3. 9.

---

(33) **The lot is cast into the lap . . . .**—In other words, much that we attribute to chance is due to the providence of God. (Comp. Matt. x. 29, 30.) This should be an encouragement to trust in Him.

XVII.

(1) **A house full of sacrifices.**—Possibly the same as the "peace offerings" of chap. vii. 14 (where see note). The consumption of these may have at times degenerated into licence (comp. 1 Sam. i. 13), and quarrelling have ensued.

(2) **A wise servant shall have rule over a son that causeth shame . . . .**—This was strikingly exhibited in the case of Ziba, who by his timely succour to David (2 Sam. xvi.), first gained all the property of his master, Mephibosheth (*i.e.,* the "man of shame"), and was later confirmed in the possession of half of it. Slaves, especially those "born in the house," often rose to a position of great trust. (Comp. Gen. xxiv. 2, xxxix. 4—6.) Eliezer would have been Abraham's heir had not Isaac been born (Gen. xv. 3).

(3) **The fining pot is for silver.**—See above on chap. ii. 4.

The Lord trieth the hearts.—By allowing sorrows and temptations to assail them, in order that they may come out of the trial as pure gold (Rev. iii. 18; 1 Pet. i. 7; 1 Cor. iii. 13; Mal. iii. 3), purged of earthly infirmities.

(5) **Whoso mocketh the poor reproacheth his Maker.**—See above on chap. xiv. 31.

He that is glad at calamities.—Of enemies. (Comp. chap. xxiv. 18; Job xxxi. 29.)

(6) **Children's children are the crown of old men.**—Comp. Ps. cxxvii. and cxxviii.

The glory of children are their fathers.—And, as such, to be honoured by them. For the blessing which parents bring to children, comp. 1 Kings xi. 13, xv. 4; Jer. xxxiii. 21.

(7) **Excellent speech becometh not a fool.**—Rather, perhaps, *Superfluous* or *pretentious words become not a vile person* (*nâbhâl*), such as is described in Isa. xxxii. 6. (Comp. 1 Sam. xxv. 25.)

Much less do lying lips a prince.—Or, *liberal person* (Isa. xxxii. 8): *noblesse oblige.*

(8) **A gift is as a precious stone . . .**—A description of the influence of bribery:—*A bribe is as a jewel in the eyes of him that receives it; whithersoever he turns he prospers:* all his energies are called out by the prospect of gain, so that he carries out successfully all that he sets his hand to. The constant warnings against this form of corruption, from the time of Moses (Exod. xxiii. 8) to that of the prophets (Amos v. 12; Isa. i. 23, &c.), show the prevalence of the evil in Israel.

(9) **He that covereth a transgression seeketh love**—*i.e.,* one who does not notice, but rather conceals and excuses, anything done against him; that man "follows after charity" (1 Cor. xiv. 1). (Comp. chap. x. 12.)

He that repeateth a matter, who is always returning to old grievances, "alienates (even his) chief friend."

(11) **An evil man seeketh only rebellion.**—Or, *A rebellious man* (literally, *rebellion;* comp. Ezek. ii. 7) *seeketh only evil.*

A cruel messenger.—Such as the "chief of the executioners" (margin of Gen. xxxvii. 36), who was always ready to carry out the bidding of an Oriental king. (Comp. 1 Kings ii. 34, 46.) The ministers of the Divine wrath against impenitent sinners appear as "tormentors" in Matt. xviii. 34. (For the office of the angels in the same work, comp. Rev. viii. 6, *sqq.*)

(12) **A bear robbed of her whelps.**—Proverbially dangerous then (2 Sam. xvii. 8; Hos. xiii. 8). (See also 1 Kings ii. 24.)

A fool (*khesîl*).—Comp. chap. i. 32.

(14) **The beginning of strife is as when one letteth out water.**—The drops which ooze through a tiny hole in the bank of a reservoir soon swell into an unmanageable torrent; so from insignificant beginnings arise feuds which cannot be appeased. Solomon constructed large pools (Eccles. ii. 6) beyond Bethlehem, and is supposed to have brought the water from these by an aqueduct into Jerusalem.

Before it be meddled with.—The same expression is used at chaps. xviii. 1, xx. 3. It probably means

Moral Virtues and   PROVERBS, XVIII.   *their Contrary Vices.*

off contention, before it be meddled with. ⁽¹⁵⁾ *^a*He that justifieth the wicked, and he that condemneth the just, even they both *are* abomination to the LORD. ⁽¹⁶⁾Wherefore *is there* a price in the hand of a fool to get wisdom, seeing *he hath* no heart *to it?* ⁽¹⁷⁾ *^b*A friend loveth at all times, and a brother is born for adversity. ⁽¹⁸⁾ *^c*A man void of ¹understanding striketh hands, *and* becometh surety in the presence of his friend. ⁽¹⁹⁾ He loveth transgression that loveth strife: *and* he that exalteth his gate seeketh destruction. ⁽²⁰⁾ ²He that hath a froward heart findeth no good: and he that hath a perverse tongue falleth into mischief. ⁽²¹⁾ *^d*He that begetteth a fool *doeth it* to his sorrow: and the father of a fool hath no joy. ⁽²²⁾ *^e*A merry heart doeth good ³like a medicine: but a broken spirit drieth the bones. ⁽²³⁾A wicked *man* taketh a gift out of the bosom to pervert the ways of judgment. ⁽²⁴⁾ *^f*Wisdom *is* before him that hath understanding; but the eyes of a fool *are* in the ends of the earth. ⁽²⁵⁾ *^g*A foolish son *is* a grief to his father, and bitterness to her that bare him. ⁽²⁶⁾Also to punish the just *is* not good, *nor* to strike princes for equity. ⁽²⁷⁾ *^h*He that hath knowledge spareth his words: *and* a man of understanding is of ⁴an excellent spirit. ⁽²⁸⁾ *ⁱ*Even a fool, when he holdeth his peace, is counted wise: *and* he that shutteth his lips *is* esteemed a man of understanding.

CHAPTER XVIII.—⁽¹⁾ ⁵Through desire a man, having separated himself, seeketh *and* intermeddleth with all wisdom. ⁽²⁾ A fool hath no delight in understanding, but that his heart may discover itself. ⁽³⁾ When the wicked cometh, *then* cometh also contempt, and with ignominy reproach. ⁽⁴⁾ *^k*The words of a man's mouth *are as* deep waters, *and* the wellspring of wisdom *as* a flowing brook.

a Ex. 23. 7; ch. 24. 24; Isa. 5. 23.
b ch. 18. 24.
c ch. 6. 1, & 11. 15.
1 Heb., *heart.*
2 Heb., *The froward of heart.*
d ch. 10. 1.
e ch. 12. 25, & 15. 13.
3 Or, *to a medicine.*
f Eccles. 2. 14, & 8. 1.
g ch. 10. 1 & 15. 20, & 19. 13.
h James 1. 19.
4 Or, *a cool spirit.*
i Job 13. 5.
5 Or, *He that separateth himself seeketh according to his desire, and intermeddleth in every business.*
k ch. 20. 5.

---

before (men) *show their teeth*, a metaphor from an angry dog.

⁽¹⁵⁾ **He that justifieth the wicked**—*i.e.*, acquits. The perversion of justice was a fruitful source of evil in Israel, and a constant topic of reproach in the mouth of the prophets (1 Sam. viii. 3; Ps. lxxxii. 2; Isa. v. 7).

⁽¹⁶⁾ **Wherefore is there a price ...**—He will still remain a fool, though he has paid high for instruction, if he has no capacity for taking it in.

⁽¹⁷⁾ **A friend loveth at all times ...**—Rather, *The (true) friend loveth at all times, and (as) a brother is born for adversity.*

⁽¹⁸⁾ **In the presence of his friend.**—Or, *With his neighbour.* (For the same warning, comp. chap. vi. 1, *sqq.*)

⁽¹⁹⁾ **He that exalteth his gate.**—Builds himself a sumptuous house.

⁽²⁰⁾ **He that hath a froward heart findeth no good.**—For he is an abomination to God (chap. xi. 20), and so gains no blessing from Him.

⁽²¹⁾ **He that begetteth a fool** (*khesîl*).—See above, on chap. i. 32.

The father of a fool (*nâbâl*).—See above, on verse 7.

⁽²²⁾ **A merry heart doeth good like a medicine.**—Or rather, *Makes good a recovery.* (For the duty of religious gladness, in gratitude for the love of God towards us, comp. Phil. iii. 1, iv. 4.)

⁽²³⁾ **A wicked man taketh a gift out of the bosom.**—Or rather, *receives it.* "From the bosom" signifies the folds of the dress in which the bribe was concealed, ready to be slipped into the judge's hand whose favour was to be bought.

⁽²⁴⁾ **Wisdom is before him that hath understanding**—*i.e.*, he can easily find her.

But the eyes of a fool are in the ends of the earth.—He is looking for her everywhere, while all the time she lies straight before him. (For the thought, comp. Deut. xxx. 11—14.)

⁽²⁶⁾ **Also.**—Among other evil things. The subject of perversion of justice is again taken up.

To punish.—Especially by fining.

To strike—*i.e.*, scourge. (Comp. Deut. xxv. 1—3.)

For equity—*i.e.*, when they have acted uprightly.

⁽²⁷⁾ **He that hath knowledge ...**—This verse will better be rendered, *He that restrains his words hath knowledge, and one who is cool of temper is a man of understanding.* The avoidance of rash speech and hasty temper is here advised.

XVIII.

⁽¹⁾ **Through desire a man, having separated himself ...**—This should probably be rendered, *The separatist seeketh after his own desire, against all improvement he shows his teeth.* The man of small mind is here described, who will only follow his own narrow aims, who holds himself aloof from men of wider views than his own, and will not join with them in the furtherance of philanthropic or religious plans, but rather opposes them with all his power, as he can see nothing but mischief in them. (For his temper of mind, comp. John vii. 47—49.)

Intermeddleth.—See above on chap. xvii. 14.

Wisdom.—See above on chap. ii. 7.

⁽²⁾ **But that his heart may discover itself**—*i.e.*, unless his cleverness can be displayed thereby; he does not prize understanding for itself, apart from his own interests.

⁽³⁾ **When the wicked cometh, then cometh also contempt.**—Comp. the whole burden of Ps. cvi., that sorrow and shame follow sin.

⁽⁴⁾ **The words of a man's mouth are as deep waters ...**—*i.e.*, the words of a "man," properly so called, are as deep waters which cannot be easily fathomed; they are a copious stream, which flows from a never failing source; they are a fountain of wisdom which is never exhausted.

Moral Virtues and   PROVERBS, XVIII.   *their Contrary Vices.*

(5) *ᵃIt is* not good to accept the person of the wicked, to overthrow the righteous in judgment. (6) A fool's lips enter into contention, and his mouth calleth for strokes. (7) A *ᵇ* fool's mouth *is* his destruction, and his lips *are* the snare of his soul. (8) *ᶜ*The words of a ¹talebearer are ²as wounds, and they go down into the ³innermost parts of the belly. (9) He also that is slothful in his work is brother to him that is a great waster. (10) *ᵈ*The name of the LORD *is* a strong tower: the righteous runneth into it, and ⁴is safe. (11) *ᵉ*The rich man's wealth *is* his strong city, and as an high wall in his own conceit. (12) *ᶠ* Before destruction the heart of man *is* haughty, and before honour *is* humility. (13) He that ⁵answereth a matter before he heareth *it*, it *is* folly and shame unto him. (14) The spirit of a man will sustain his infirmity; but a wounded spirit who can bear? (15) The heart of the prudent getteth knowledge; and the ear of the wise seeketh knowledge. (16) *ᵍ* A man's gift maketh room for him, and bringeth him before great men. (17) *He that is* first in his own cause *seemeth* just; but his neighbour cometh and searcheth him. (18) The lot causeth contentions to cease, and parteth between the mighty. (19) A brother offended *is harder to be won* than a strong city: and *their* contentions *are* like the bars of a castle. (20) *ʰ* A man's belly shall be satisfied with the fruit of his mouth; *and* with the increase of his lips shall he be filled. (21) Death and life *are* in the power of the tongue: and they that love it shall eat the fruit thereof. (22) *ⁱWhoso* findeth a wife findeth a good *thing*, and obtaineth favour of the LORD. (23) The poor useth intreaties; but the rich answereth *ᵏ*roughly. (24) A man *that* hath friends must shew himself friendly: *ˡ*and there is a friend *that* sticketh closer than a brother.

a Lev. 19. 15; Deut. 1. 17, & 16. 19; ch. 24. 23.
b ch. 10. 14 & 12. 13, & 13. 3.
c ch. 12. 18, & 26. 22.
1 Or, *whisperer*.
2 Or, *like as when men are wounded*.
3 Heb., *chambers*.
d Ps. 18. 2 & 27. 1, & 144. 2.
4 Heb., *is set aloft*.
e ch. 10. 15.
f ch. 11. 2 & 15. 33, & 16. 18.
5 Heb., *returneth a word*.
g ch. 17. 8.
h ch. 12. 14, & 13. 2.
i ch. 19. 14.
k James 2. 3.
l ch. 17. 17.

---

(6) **His mouth calleth for strokes**, which he provokes by his insolence and quarrelsomeness.

(7) **A fool's mouth is his destruction.**—See above on chap. xii. 13.

(8) **The words of a talebearer are as wounds.** —Or, more probably, "as dainty morsels" that are eagerly swallowed, and "go down into the innermost parts of the belly," *i.e.*, are treasured up in the deepest recesses of the heart, to be remembered and brought out again when an opportunity for employing them occurs.

(9) **He also that is slothful in his work.**— Whatsoever it may be that is committed to his care, is "brother to him that is a great waster," or "destroyer"; neglect of duty causes almost as much mischief in life as active wickedness.

(10) **The name of the Lord is a strong tower.** —The "name of the Lord" signifies the titles by which He has made Himself known, descriptive of His attributes, as "merciful, gracious, longsuffering, abundant in goodness and truth," &c. (Exod. xxxiv. 5, 7); the righteous takes refuge in these, and finds himself in safety, lifted above the trouble which seemed ready to overwhelm him. The rich man's "strong city" and "high wall" are such only in "his own conceit," and fail him in the time of need. (Comp. chap. xxiii. 5.)

(13) **He that answereth a matter before he heareth it** . . .—Comp. Ecclus. xi. 8.

(14) **The spirit of a man.**—That is, one properly so called, who draws his strength from God, will "sustain his infirmity," help him to bear up against trouble; "but a wounded spirit" (not one crushed with the sense of sin, for that God will lift up, Isa. lxvi. 2; Ps. li. 17), which retires into itself and nurses its griefs, "who can bear" the wear of it?

(16) **A man's gift.**—Judicious liberality "maketh room for him," helps him to make his way through life. (Comp. Luke xvi. 9, and the advice there given so to use temporal riches as to gain those of heaven.)

(17) **He that is first in his own cause seemeth just.**—A man who tells his own story can make a good case for himself out of it, "but his neighbour" (*i.e.*, his adversary in the suit) "cometh and searcheth him," sifts his statements, and shows them to be untenable.

(18) **The lot causeth contentions to cease,** as being the judgment of God (chap. xvi. 33).

And parteth between the mighty, who would otherwise settle their differences by blows.

(19) **A brother offended.**—Or rather, *wronged*.

Their contentions.—Of such as have once been friends, "are like the bars of a castle," or palace, forming an almost impassable barrier to reconciliation. The bitterness of quarrels between friends is proverbial.

(20) **A man's belly shall be satisfied with the fruit of his mouth.**—See above on chap. xii. 14.

(21) **Death and life are in the power of the tongue.**—See above on chap. iv. 23, where much the same power is attributed to the heart as is here given to the tongue as being its exponent. (Comp. also chap. xii. 13.)

They that love it—*i.e.*, to use it.

(22) **Whoso findeth a wife** . . .—One who deserves the name of wife, as the one described in chap. xxxi. 10, *sqq*.

(23) **The rich answereth roughly.**—A warning against the hardening effect of riches. (Comp. Mark x. 23.)

(24) **A man that hath friends must shew himself friendly.**—Rather, *a man of many friends will suffer loss*, for he will impoverish himself by constant hospitality, and in trouble they will desert him (Ps. xli. 9); but "there is a friend," one in a thousand, "that sticketh closer than a brother." (Comp. chap. xvii. 17.)

CHAPTER XIX.—⁽¹⁾ ^a Better *is* the poor that walketh in his integrity, than *he that is* perverse in his lips, and is a fool. ⁽²⁾ Also, *that* the soul *be* without knowledge, *it is* not good; and he that hasteth with *his* feet sinneth. ⁽³⁾ The foolishness of man perverteth his way: and his heart fretteth against the LORD. ^{(4) b} Wealth maketh many friends; but the poor is separated from his neighbour. ^{(5) c} A false witness shall not be ¹ unpunished, and *he that* speaketh lies shall not escape. ⁽⁶⁾ Many will intreat the favour of the prince: and every man *is* a friend to ² him that giveth gifts. ^{(7) d} All the brethren of the poor do hate him: how much more do his friends go far from him? He pursueth *them with* words, *yet* they *are* wanting *to him*.

⁽⁸⁾ He that getteth ³ wisdom loveth his own soul: he that keepeth understanding shall find good. ^{(9) e} A false witness shall not be unpunished, and *he that* speaketh lies shall perish. ⁽¹⁰⁾ Delight is not seemly for a fool; much less *f* for a servant to have rule over princes. ^{(11) g} The ⁴ discretion of a man deferreth his anger; and *it is* his glory to pass over a transgression. ^{(12) h} The king's wrath *is* as the roaring of a lion; but his favour *is* as dew upon the grass.

^{(13) i} A foolish son *is* the calamity of his father: ^k and the contentions of a wife *are* a continual dropping. ⁽¹⁴⁾ House and riches *are* the inheritance of fathers: and *l* a prudent wife *is* from the LORD. ⁽¹⁵⁾ Slothfulness casteth into a deep sleep; and an idle soul ^m shall suffer hunger. ^{(16) n} He that keepeth the commandment keepeth his own soul; *but* he that despiseth his ways shall die. ^{(17) o} He that hath pity upon the poor lendeth unto the LORD; and ⁵ that which he hath given will he pay him again. ^{(18) p} Chasten thy son while there is hope, and let not thy soul spare ⁶ for his crying. ⁽¹⁹⁾ A man of great wrath shall suffer punishment: for if thou deliver *him*, yet thou must ⁷ do it again. ⁽²⁰⁾ Hear

---

a ch. 28. 6.
b ch. 14. 20.
c Ex. 23. 1.; Deut. 19. 16; ch. 6. 19, & 21. 28.
1 Heb., *held innocent.*
2 Heb., *a man of gifts.*
d ch. 14. 20.
3 Heb., *an heart.*
e ver. 5.
f ch. 30. 22; Eccles. 10. 6.
g ch. 14. 20.
4 Or, *prudence.*
h ch. 16. 15 & 20. 2. & 28. 15.
i ch. 10. 1 & 15. 20, & 17. 21, 25.
k ch. 21. 9, & 27. 15.
l ch. 18. 22.
m ch. 10. 4, & 20. 13.
n Luke 11. 28.
o Matt. 10. 42, & 25. 40; 2 Cor. 9. 6, 7.
5 Or, *his deed.*
p ch. 13. 24, & 23. 13.
6 Or, *to his destruction: or, to cause him to die.*
7 Heb., *add.*

XIX.

⁽¹⁾ **Perverse in his lips.**—One who distorts the truth; translated "froward" in chap. iv. 24. That a rich man is here intended appears likely from the parallel passage in chap. xxviii. 6.

⁽²⁾ **Also, that the soul be without knowledge is not good.**—Ignorance is bad, as well as folly.

He that hasteth with his feet sinneth.—Haste without knowledge misses the mark aimed at. (See above on viii. 36.)

⁽³⁾ **The foolishness of man perverteth his way.**—A man's own self-will (i. 7) overturns his way, stops his progress, whether in temporal or spiritual matters, and then, instead of blaming himself, "his heart fretteth against the Lord." (Comp. Isa. viii. 21; Rev. xvi. 10. 11.)

⁽⁴⁾ **The poor is separated from his neighbour.**—Or, *but the feeble, his friend separates himself (from him)*. It was just in order to counteract these selfish instincts of mankind that the merciful provisions of such passages as Deut. xv. 7. *sqq.*, and Luke xiv. 13, were laid upon God's people.

⁽⁷⁾ **He pursueth them with words, yet they are wanting to Him.**—The first half of a verse has apparently dropped out here. The sense may be, that the poor man hunts after words—*i.e.*, seeks to get promises of help from his friends, and these end in nothing—mere talk.

⁽⁸⁾ **He that getteth wisdom.**—Literally, *heart.* For that "wisdom," or "knowledge," that begins with the "fear of the Lord" (see above on chap. i. 7), and ends with loving Him, is not a matter of intellect only, but of the heart also—*i.e.*, the will and affections.

⁽¹⁰⁾ **Delight is not seemly for a fool.**—He is ruined by prosperity and luxury: much more is a slave unfit to rule over princes. The writer has in his mind the case of an emancipated slave being raised to high place by court favour, and then insolently trampling on those who were once far above him. (Comp. chap. xxx. 22; Eccl. x. 6. 7.)

⁽¹¹⁾ **It is his glory to pass over a transgression.**—In this he imitates a Greater. Comp. Mic. vii. 18; Rom. iii. 25; Matt. v. 45.)

⁽¹³⁾ **A continual dropping.**—As of the rain leaking through the flat roof of an eastern house on a wet day. (Comp. xxvii. 15.)

⁽¹⁵⁾ **Slothfulness casteth into a deep sleep.**—Or rather, *makes it fall upon a man*, as upon Adam (Gen. ii. 21).

⁽¹⁶⁾ **He that despiseth his ways**—*i.e.*, takes no heed to them, whether they please God or not.

Shall die.—Physically (comp. Exod. xii. 15; 1 Cor. xi. 30), spiritually (comp. Luke i. 79); a death to be completed hereafter (Rev. ii. 11).

⁽¹⁷⁾ **Lendeth unto the Lord.**—Who "for our sakes became poor, that we through his poverty might be rich" (2 Cor. viii. 9), and Who regards all done to one of his poor brethren as done unto Himself (Matt. xxv. 40).

⁽¹⁸⁾ **And let not thy soul spare for his crying.**—Or, *but set not thy soul on his destruction.* Do not go so far as to kill him in thy zeal for his good, or despair of his amendment. (Comp. Eph. vi. 4; Col. iii. 21.) It may also signify "do not let him perish for want of chastisement," as chap. xxiii. 13 is also explained.

⁽¹⁹⁾ **For if thou deliver him, yet thou must do it again.**—As St. Paul says (Gal. vi. 5), "Every man shall bear his own burden." We cannot shield wrong-headed people from the consequences of their want of self-control, however much we may pity them for the suffering they have brought on themselves.

⁽²⁰⁾ **That thou mayest be wise in thy latter end.**—That "though thy beginning might be small, yet that thy latter end should greatly increase" (Job viii. 7)

counsel, and receive instruction, that thou mayest be wise in thy latter end. ⁽²¹⁾ ^aThere are many devices in a man's heart; nevertheless the counsel of the LORD, that shall stand. ⁽²²⁾ The desire of a man *is* his kindness: and a poor man *is* better than a liar. ⁽²³⁾ The fear of the LORD *tendeth* to life: and *he that hath it* shall abide satisfied; he shall not be visited with evil. ⁽²⁴⁾ ^bA slothful man hideth his hand in *his* bosom, and will not so much as bring it to his mouth again. ⁽²⁵⁾ ^cSmite a scorner, and the simple ¹will beware: and reprove one that hath understanding, *and* he will understand knowledge. ⁽²⁶⁾He that wasteth *his* father, *and* chaseth away *his* mother, *is* a son that causeth shame, and bringeth reproach. ⁽²⁷⁾ Cease, my son, to hear the instruction *that causeth* to err from the words of knowledge. ⁽²⁸⁾ ²An ungodly witness scorneth judg-

a Job 23. 13; Ps. 33. 10, 11; ch. 16. 1, 9; Isa. 46. 10.

b ch. 15. 19, & 26. 13, 15.

c ch. 21. 11.

¹ Heb., *will be cunning.*

² Heb., *A witness of Belial.*

d ch. 16. 14, & 19. 12.

e ch. 10. 4.

³ Or, *winter.*

f ch. 18. 4.

⁴ Or, *bounty.*

ment: and the mouth of the wicked devoureth iniquity. ⁽²⁹⁾ Judgments are prepared for scorners and stripes for the back of fools.

CHAPTER XX.—⁽¹⁾ Wine *is* a mocker, strong drink *is* raging: and whosoever is deceived thereby is not wise. ⁽²⁾ ^dThe fear of a king *is* as the roaring of a lion: *whoso* provoketh him to anger sinneth *against* his own soul. ⁽³⁾ *It is* an honour for a man to cease from strife: but every fool will be meddling. ⁽⁴⁾ ^eThe sluggard will not plow by reason of the ³cold; *therefore* shall he beg in harvest, and *have* nothing. ⁽⁵⁾ ^fCounsel in the heart of man *is like* deep water; but a man of understanding will draw it out. ⁽⁶⁾ Most men will proclaim every one his own ⁴goodness: but a faithful man who can find? ⁽⁷⁾ The

---

⁽²¹⁾ **There are many devices** (or, *thoughts*) **in a man's heart.**—"He disquieteth himself in vain" (Ps. xxxix. 6), endeavouring to carry out his various plans in life, while the one unchangeable "counsel of the Lord," *that* shall stand—*i.e.*, abide in all its fulness. (Comp. Isa. xlvi. 10, 11; Ps. xxxiii. 11; Job xxiii. 13.)

⁽²²⁾ **The desire of a man is his kindness**—*i.e.*, what makes a man desired or beloved is his kindness. Or, the kindness of a man consists in—is shewn by—his good-will, even though he cannot carry it out.

And a poor man (who would do a kindness if he could) **is better than a liar.**—Than a rich man who could help another, but professes to be unable to do so.

⁽²³⁾ **The fear of the Lord tendeth to life.**—To life in this world, the reward of uprightness promised to the Israelites of old (Isa. xxxvii. 29); and to life in the next (Mark x. 30).

He shall not be visited with evil.—(Comp. Lev. xxvi. 6.) A higher blessing is promised in the New Testament; not immunity from trouble, for trouble may be needed for advance in holiness (Rom. viii. 28), but protection in it (1 Pet. iii 13; Rom. viii. 35, *sqq.*).

⁽²⁴⁾ **A slothful man hideth his hand in his bosom.**—Better, in the *dish* that stood in the middle of the table at an Oriental dinner, into which the guests dipped their hands to take out the food for themselves (Matt. xxvi. 23).

⁽²⁵⁾ **Smite a scorner, and the simple will beware.**—For "scorner" and "simple" see note on i. 22. Reproof is of no avail to turn the "scorner" from his evil way (ix. 7; xiii. 1; xv. 12), punishment will also do him no good; but it may make the "simple," whose character is not yet formed for good or evil, reflect and amend. So God at first punishes sinners for their good (Amos. iv. 6, *ff.*), afterwards, when they are obdurate, as a warning to others (*ibid.* 12; Deut. xxix. 21, *ff.*).

⁽²⁷⁾ **Cease, my son, to hear the instruction that causeth to err . . .**—Or the passage may mean, *Cease to hear instruction if you are only going to err afterwards*—Make up your mind what you are intending to do hereafter, and act now accordingly; better not know the truth than learn it only to desert it. (Comp. 2 Pet. ii. 21.)

⁽²⁸⁾ **An ungodly** (worthless) **witness scorneth judgment.**—Despises the orders of the Law to avoid perjury (Exod. xx. 16; Lev. v. 1). (Comp. 1 Kings viii. 31).

The mouth of the wicked devoureth iniquity.—As a dainty morsel. (Comp. xviii. 8.)

⁽²⁹⁾ **Judgments are prepared for scorners.**—(Comp. ver. 25.)

Fools.—See above on chap. i. 22.

XX.

⁽¹⁾ **Wine is a mocker, strong drink is raging**—*i.e.*, producing these effects in those who subject themselves to their power.

⁽²⁾ **The fear of a king is as the roaring of a lion,** *i.e.*, the dread which he casts upon others when he is becoming angry is a warning of approaching danger.

Sinneth against his own soul—*i.e.*, against his own life.

⁽³⁾ **But every fool.**—Self-willed person. (Comp. chap. i. 22.)

Will be meddling.—Or, rather, *shewing his teeth:* (Comp. chap. xvii. 14) thinking that his own personal dignity is at stake.

⁽⁵⁾ **Counsel in the heart of man is like deep water.**—The wise thoughts of a "man," fitly so-called (comp. chap. xviii. 4), may be hid deep in his breast, like the waters of a well, but a man of understanding knows how to draw them out as by a windlass and bucket (Exod. ii. 16).

⁽⁶⁾ **Most men will proclaim every one his own goodness.**—Will be full of his benevolent intentions, "but a faithful man," who carries out these promises, "who can find?"

⁽⁷⁾ **The just man.**—Comp. chap. x. 2.

His children are blessed after him.—Comp. 1 Kings xv. 4, Jer. xxxiii. 20, 21.

Moral Virtues and PROVERBS, XX. *their Contrary Vices.*

just *man* walketh in his integrity: *a*his children *are* blessed after him. (8) A king that sitteth in the throne of judgment scattereth away all evil with his eyes. (9) *b*Who can say, I have made my heart clean, I am pure from my sin? (10) *c*1Divers weights, *and* 2divers measures, both of them *are* alike abomination to the LORD. (11) Even a child is known by his doings, whether his work *be* pure, and whether *it be* right. (12) *d*The hearing ear, and the seeing eye, the LORD hath made even both of them. (13) *e*Love not sleep, lest thou come to poverty; open thine eyes, *and* thou shalt be satisfied with bread. (14) *It is* naught, *it is* naught, saith the buyer: but when he is gone his way, then he boasteth. (15) There is gold, and a multitude of rubies: but the lips of knowledge *are* a precious jewel. (16) *f*Take his garment that is surety *for* a stranger: and take a pledge of him for a strange woman. (17) *g* 3Bread of deceit *is* sweet to a man; but afterwards his mouth shall be filled with gravel. (18) *h*Every purpose is established by counsel: and with good advice make war. (19) *i*He that goeth about *as* a talebearer revealeth secrets: therefore meddle not with him that 4flattereth with his lips. (20) *k*Whoso curseth his father or his mother, his 5lamp shall be put out in obscure darkness. (21) An inheritance *may be* gotten hastily at the beginning; but the end thereof shall not be blessed. (22) *l*Say not thou, I will recompense evil; *but* wait on the LORD, and he shall save thee.

(23)*m*Divers weights *are* an abomination unto the LORD; and 6a false balance *is* not good. (24) *n*Man's goings *are* of the LORD; how can a man then understand his own way? (25) *It is* a snare to the man *who* devoureth *that which is* holy, and after vows to make enquiry. (26) *o*A

---

a Ps. 112. 2.
b 1 Kings 8. 46; 2 Chron. 6. 36; Job 14. 4; Ps. 51. 5; Eccles. 7. 20; 1 John 1. 8.
c Deut. 25. 13, &c.; ch. 11. 1, & 16. 11.
1 Heb., *A stone and a stone.*
2 Heb., *an ephah and an ephah.*
d Ex. 4. 11; Ps. 94. 9.
e ch. 12. 11, & 19. 15.
f ch. 27. 13.
g ch. 9. 17.
3 Heb., *Bread of lying,* or, *falsehood.*
h ch. 15. 22.
i ch. 11. 13.
4 Or, *enticeth.*
k Ex. 21. 17; Lev. 20. 9; Matt. 15. 4.
5 Or, *candle.*
l Deut. 32. 35; ch. 17. 13, & 24. 29; Rom. 12. 17; 1 Thess. 5. 15; 1 Pet. 3. 9.
m ver. 10.
6 Heb., *balances of deceit.*
n Ps. 37. 23; ch 16. 9; Jer. 10. 23.
o Ps. 101. 5, &c.; ver. 8.

---

(8) **A king that sitteth in the throne of judgment . . .**—See note on chap. xvi. 12.

(9) **Who can say, I have made my heart clean?**—Though we may have done our best by self-examination and confession, and repentance and trust in the atoning blood of Christ to obtain remission of sin, still the heart is so deceitful (Jer. xvii. 9), sins may so easily have escaped our notice (Ps. xix. 12, 1 Cor. iv. 4), that satisfaction with ourselves ought never to be allowed (Rom. xi. 20).

(10) **Divers weights and divers measures . . .** —See above on chap. xi. 1.

(11) **Even a child is known by his doings . . .** —The disposition soon shews itself; all the more reason, therefore, to train it betimes.

(12) **The Lord hath made even both of them.** —And, therefore, they are to be used as He would have them. (Comp. our Lord's constant warning, "He that hath ears to hear, let him hear.") The proverb may also remind us of the admonition in chap. xv. 3, and Ps. xciv. 9, to remember God's constant watchfulness over us.

(13) **Open thine eyes.**—Be up and stirring.

(14) **It is naught, saith the buyer.**—He cries down the goods he wants to purchase.

Then he boasteth.—How he has outdone the seller, and got the goods below their value. For other notices of cheating in trade see above on chap. xi. 1.

(15) **Rubies.**—See above on chap. iii. 15.

Lips of knowledge.—See above on chap. xviii. 4.

(16) **Take his garment that is surety for a stranger.**—Another warning against suretiship. (See above on chap. vi. 1.) If a man is rash enough to become surety for another, he must suffer for his imprudence, and learn wisdom by feeling the effects of his folly.

And take a pledge of him for a strange woman.—Rather, *take him as a pledge* (seize upon his person who has become surety) *for a strange woman,* (according to the margin) or, *for strangers* (as the text reads).

(19) **Flattereth with his lips.**—Rather, *is open with his lips,* cannot keep them shut.

(20) **His lamp shall be put out in obscure darkness.**—See above, on chap. xiii. 9.

(21) **The end thereof shall not be blessed.**—Comp. chap. xxviii. 20: the evil means by which he acquired the possession will, at the last, be visited upon him. Thus Jacob was punished severely for the selfishness by which he gained the birthright, and for the fraud by which he obtained the blessing belonging to his brother.

(22) **Wait on the Lord and he shall save thee.** —Do not look for vengeance on enemies (for they are to be forgiven), but for deliverance from their attacks; forget their malice, remember only God's love for thee, and trust in Him. (Comp. 1 Peter iii. 13, Rom. viii. 28.)

(24) **Man's goings are of the Lord.**—Comp. Jer. x. 23 and the collect, "O God, from whom . . . all just works do proceed."

How can a man then understand his own way?—*i.e.,* how he should go. So much the more reason for the prayer of Ps. xxv. 3, "Shew me thy ways, O Lord." (Comp. Ps. cxix. 33, *ff,* cxliii. 8.)

(25) **It is a snare to a man who devoureth that which is holy.**—Rather, *It is a snare for a man (i.e.,* gets him into trouble) *rashly to say,* "*It is dedicated*" (*i.e.,* when he thoughtlessly dedicates anything to God), *and after he has vowed to enquire* (whether he can keep his word). (Comp. Eccles. v. 2, 4—6.)

(26) **A wise king scattereth the wicked.**— Rather, *winnows* them.

And bringeth the wheel over them.—Comp. Isa. xxviii. 27. A sort of sledge or cart was driven over the stalks of corn spread upon the threshing-floor, by means of which the grain was separated from the husk. A wise king winnows out evil persons from among his people, thus putting an end to their corrupting influence. (Comp. Matt. iii. 12.)

wise king scattereth the wicked, and bringeth the wheel over them. ⁽²⁷⁾ The spirit of man *is* the ¹candle of the LORD, searching all the inward parts of the belly. ⁽²⁸⁾ ᵃMercy and truth preserve the king: and his throne is upholden by mercy. ⁽²⁹⁾ The glory of young men *is* their strength: and ᵇthe beauty of old men *is* the grey head. ⁽³⁰⁾ The blueness of a wound ²cleanseth away evil: so *do* stripes the inward parts of the belly.

CHAPTER XXI.—⁽¹⁾ The king's heart *is* in the hand of the LORD, *as* the rivers of water: he turneth it whithersoever he will. ⁽²⁾ ᶜEvery way of a man *is* right in his own eyes: but the LORD pondereth the hearts. ⁽³⁾ ᵈTo do justice and judgment *is* more acceptable to the LORD than sacrifice. ⁽⁴⁾ ᵉ³An high look, and a proud heart,

1 Or, *lamp.*
a Ps. 101. 1; ch. 20. 14.
b ch. 16. 31.
2 Heb., *is a purging medicine against evil.*
c ch. 16. 2.
d 1 Sam. 15. 22; ch. 15. 8; Isa. 1. 11; Hos. 6. 6; Mic. 6. 7, 8.
e ch. 6. 17.
3 Heb., *Haughtiness of eyes.*
4 ¹Or, *the light of the wicked.*
f ch. 10. 2, & 13. 11.
5 Heb., *saw them,* or, *dwell with them.*
g ch. 19. 13 & 25. 24, & 27. 15.
6 Heb., *a woman of contentions.*
7 Heb., *an house of society.*
h James 4. 5.
8 Heb., *is not favoured.*
i ch. 19. 25.

and ⁴the plowing of the wicked, *is* sin. ⁽⁵⁾ The thoughts of the diligent *tend* only to plenteousness; but of every one *that is* hasty only to want. ⁽⁶⁾ ᶠThe getting of treasures by a lying tongue *is* a vanity tossed to and fro of them that seek death. ⁽⁷⁾ The robbery of the wicked shall ⁵destroy them; because they refuse to do judgment. ⁽⁸⁾ The way of man *is* froward and strange: but *as for* the pure, his work *is* right. ⁽⁹⁾ ᵍIt *is* better to dwell in a corner of the housetop, than with ⁶a brawling woman in ⁷a wide house. ⁽¹⁰⁾ ʰThe soul of the wicked desireth evil: his neighbour ⁸findeth no favour in his eyes. ⁽¹¹⁾ ⁱWhen the scorner is punished, the simple is made wise: and when the wise is instructed, he receiveth knowledge. ⁽¹²⁾ The righteous *man* wisely

---

⁽²⁷⁾ **The spirit of man is the candle of the Lord.**—The spirit of man, breathed into him at first by the Creator (Gen. ii. 7), and afterwards quickened and illumined by the Divine Spirit, is the "candle of the Lord," given to man as an inward light and guide.

Searching all the inward parts of the belly.—That is, of the inmost heart of man; testing all his thoughts, feelings, desires, by God's law, approving some, condemning others, according as they agree with it or not. The word "belly" is equivalent to "heart" or "soul" in Job xv. 2, 15, xxxii. 19. (Comp. John vii. 38.)

⁽²⁸⁾ **Mercy and truth preserve the king.**—See above on chap. iii. 3. The love and faithfulness he shows to his subjects draw out the same qualities in them, and these are the safeguard of his throne. So (Ps. cxxx. 4) the mercy shown by God inspires man with a reverent fear of Him, while harshness might have made him a slave, or driven him through despair into rebellion. (Comp. Jer. xxxiii. 9.)

⁽²⁹⁾ **The beauty of old men is the grey head.**—As suggesting the possession of experience and wisdom. It is the fault of the aged, therefore, if they do not receive the honour due to them, and this arises from their not having so spent their youth and middle age as to make their old age venerable.

⁽³⁰⁾ **The blueness of a wound.**—Rather, *the stripes of a wound,* or wounds which cut into the flesh, cleanse away evil.

So do stripes the inward parts of the belly.—Better, *and blows* (which reach) *the inward parts of the belly, i.e.,* which are felt in the inmost recesses of the heart (comp. verse 27). Kindness is thrown away upon some people: they can only be touched by punishment.

XXI.

⁽¹⁾ **As the rivers of water.**—Channels for irrigation (comp. Ps. i. 3). He turns the heart of the king, whose favour is as the latter rain (chap. xvi. 15) and dew (xix. 12), now towards one suppliant and now towards another, as He thinks fit, for "the hearts of kings are in His rule and governance."

⁽²⁾ **Every way of a man is right in his own eyes.**—See above, on chap. xvi. 2.

⁽³⁾ **To do justice and judgment, &c.**—See above on chap. x. 2.

Is more acceptable than sacrifice.—See above on xv. 8.

⁽⁴⁾ **The plowing of the wicked.**—*i.e.,* their work, all they do; for it is not done to please God but themselves; nor carried on in His strength, but in reliance upon their own, and therefore it is "sin," not pleasing to Him. For the word here translated "plowing," see above on chap. xiii. 23, where it is rendered "tillage." It may also signify "lamp" (see above on xiii. 9).

⁽⁵⁾ **The thoughts of every one that is hasty tend only to want.**—This proverb is met with on all sides: "More haste, worse speed"; "Festina lente"; "Eile mit Weile."

⁽⁶⁾ **Is a vanity tossed to and fro of them that seek death.**—Rather, *is* (as) *the driven* (fleeting) *breath of those who are seeking death.* They are seeking in reality not riches, but death, and these riches will vanish like their own breath. (Comp. Wisd. v. 14; Ps. lxviii. 2).

⁽⁷⁾ **The robbery of the wicked.**—Or, *their violence.* See above on chap. i. 19. (Comp. Ps. ix. 15.)

⁽⁸⁾ **The way of man is froward and strange.**—The words may also mean "Tortuous is the way of a man who is laden with sin." (Comp. chap. ii. 15.)

⁽⁹⁾ **It is better to dwell in a corner of the housetop.**—Though there exposed to all the storms of heaven. The flat tops of houses were, in the East, used for exercise (2 Sam. xi. 2), sleeping, (1 Sam. ix. 26), devotion (Acts x. 9), and various domestic purposes (Jos. ii. 6).

⁽¹⁰⁾ **His neighbour findeth no favour in his eyes.**—The wicked must have whatever he has set his heart upon, however much trouble and sorrow he may cause to his neighbour thereby.

⁽¹¹⁾ **When the scorner is punished, the simple is made wise.**—See above on chap. xix. 25.

⁽¹²⁾ **The righteous man wisely considereth the house of the wicked.**—Rather, *A Righteous one* (God) *marks the house of the wicked and overthroweth*

considereth the house of the wicked: but God overthroweth the wicked for their wickedness. (13) *a*Whoso stoppeth his ears at the cry of the poor, he also shall cry himself, but shall not be heard. (14) *b* A gift in secret pacifieth anger: and a reward in the bosom strong wrath. (15) *It is* joy to the just to do judgment: but destruction *shall be* to the workers of iniquity. (16) The man that wandereth out of the way of understanding shall remain in the congregation of the dead. (17) He that loveth ¹pleasure *shall be* a poor man: he that loveth wine and oil shall not be rich. (18) *c*The wicked *shall be* a ransom for the righteous, and the transgressor for the upright. (19) *d It is* better to dwell ²in the wilderness, than with a contentious and an angry woman.

(20) *There is* treasure to be desired and oil in the dwelling of the wise; but a foolish man spendeth it up. (21) He that followeth after righteousness and mercy findeth life, righteousness, and honour. (22) *e* A wise *man* scaleth the city of the mighty, and casteth down the strength of the confidence thereof. (23) *f* Whoso keepeth his mouth and his tongue keepeth his soul from troubles. (24) Proud *and* haughty scorner *is* his name, who dealeth ³in proud wrath. (25) *g* The desire of the slothful killeth him; for his hands refuse to labour. (26) He coveteth greedily all the day long: but the *h* righteous giveth and spareth not. (27) *i* The sacrifice of the wicked *is* abomination: how much more *when* he bringeth it ⁴with a wicked mind? (28) *k* ⁵A false witness shall perish: but the man that heareth speaketh constantly. (29) A wicked man hardeneth his face: but *as for* the upright, he ⁶ directeth his way. (30) *l There is* no wisdom nor understanding nor counsel against the LORD. (31) *m* The horse *is* prepared against the day of battle: but *n* ⁷safety *is* of the LORD.

a Matt. 18. 30.
b ch. 17. 8, & 18. 16.
1 Or, *sport.*
c ch. 11. 8.
d ver. 9.
2 Heb., *in the land of the desert.*
e Eccles. 9. 14.
f ch. 12. 13, & 18. 21.
3 Heb., *in the wrath of pride.*
g ch. 13. 4.
h Ps. 112. 9.
i Ps. 50. 9; ch. 15. 8; Isa. 66. 3; Jer. 6. 20; Amos 5. 22.
4 Heb., *in wickedness.*
k ch. 19. 5, 9.
5 Heb., *A witness of lies.*
6 Or, *considereth.*
l Jer. 9. 23.
m Ps. 33. 17.
n Ps. 3. 8.
7 Or, *victory.*

---

the wicked for (their) *destruction.* He watches the evil to see whether they will repent (Luke xiii. 8), and if they will not, at last overthrows them when their iniquity has become full (Gen. xv. 16).

(13) **He also shall cry himself, but shall not be heard.**—Because he showed no mercy. (Comp. Matt. v. 7, xviii. 30; Jas. ii. 13.)

(14) **A gift in secret.**—Comp. Abigail and David (1 Sam. xxv. 18).

(15) **But destruction shall be to the workers of iniquity.**—This may also mean, "It is a terror to the workers of iniquity (to do right)." They are afraid to trust such promises as Matt. vi. 33. They think they will be ruined if they do not cheat their neighbours when they have an opportunity.

(16) **Shall remain in the congregation of the dead.**—Described in Isa. xiv. 9; he shall not take part in the resurrection of Isa. xxvi. 19. A prophecy of retribution after death.

(17) **Wine and oil.**—The accompaniments of a feast. The oil, or precious unguents, were poured over the head (comp. Ps. xxiii. 5). It was the excessive love and gratitude of the two Marys (Luke vii. 38; John xii. 3) which prompted them to anoint the Lord's feet. These perfumes were sometimes of great value, the "pound of ointment of spikenard" (John xii. 3) was worth "more than three hundred pence" (£10 12s. 6d.), the wages of a day labourer (Matt. xx. 2) for nearly a year.

(18) **The wicked shall be a ransom for the righteous.**—The righteous is "delivered out of trouble (chap. xi. 8; comp. Isa. lvii. 1), and the wicked cometh in his stead" to receive upon his own head God's descending punishment. So it was with Mordecai and Haman.

(21) **Righteousness and mercy.**—He who endeavours to give God and man their due (see above on x. 2), and to shew love to them (chap. iii. 3), will gain for himself length of days (chap. iii. 16) power to live more and more uprightly, and present honour from God and man for so doing. In a higher sense he will gain life eternal now and hereafter (John xvii. 3), righteousness, or the forgiveness of sins (Rom. ii. 13), and honour (Rom. viii. 30) at the last day, when he will be acknowledged as a true son of God (Rom. viii. 19).

(23) **Whoso keepeth his mouth and his tongue, &c.**—See above on chap. xii. 13.

(24) **Proud and haughty scorner is his name.**—See above on chap. i. 22.

(25) **The desire of the slothful killeth them.**—Their love for sloth and pleasure ruins them in soul and body and fortune.

(26) **He coveteth greedily all the day long,** that he may "consume it on his lusts" (Jas. iv. 3), while the righteous (verse 21) gives to all who need, remembering that he is a steward (Luke xvi. 9), not an owner, and that blessing will attend upon him for so doing (Acts xx. 35).

(27) **How much more when he bringeth it with a wicked mind?**—Plotting at the same time future wickedness, or thinking to make God, by the sacrifice, overlook his sin, and so become, as it were, his confederate.

(28) **But the man that heareth** (carefully, and repeats accurately) **speaketh constantly** (his testimony will live).—Comp., "he being dead yet speaketh," Heb. xi. 4.

(29) **A wicked man hardeneth his face.**—Is insensible to rebuke, and will not confess himself in the wrong, but "the upright directeth his way," as God would have him, or, as the margin implies, "looks well" to it, sees that it is in accordance with His commandments.

(30) **There is no wisdom . . . against the Lord.**—Comp. 1 Cor. iii. 19; Isa. liv. 17; Ps. ii. 4.

(31) **The horse is prepared against the day of battle.**—These had been imported largely from Egypt in Solomon's time, though this was in direct contravention of the Law (1 Kings iv. 26, and Deut. xvii. 16).

CHAPTER XXII.—⁽¹⁾ ^a *A good* name *is* rather to be chosen than great riches, *and* ¹loving favour rather than silver and gold. ⁽²⁾ ^b The rich and poor meet together: the LORD *is* the maker of them all. ⁽³⁾ ^c A prudent *man* foreseeth the evil, and hideth himself: but the simple pass on, and are punished. ⁽⁴⁾ ^{d 2} By humility *and* the fear of the LORD *are* riches, and honour, and life. ⁽⁵⁾ Thorns *and* snares *are* in the way of the froward: he that doth keep his soul shall be far from them. ⁽⁶⁾ ³ Train up a child ⁴ in the way he should go: and when he is old, he will not depart from it.

⁽⁷⁾ The rich ruleth over the poor, and the borrower *is* servant ⁵ to the lender. ⁽⁸⁾ ^e He that soweth iniquity shall reap vanity: ⁶ and the rod of his anger shall fail. ⁽⁹⁾ ^{f 7} He that hath a bountiful eye shall be blessed; for he giveth of his bread to the poor. ⁽¹⁰⁾ ^g Cast out the scorner, and contention shall go out; yea, strife and reproach shall cease. ⁽¹¹⁾ He that loveth pureness of heart, ⁸ *for* the grace of his lips the king *shall* be his friend. ⁽¹²⁾ The eyes of the LORD preserve knowledge, and he overthroweth ⁹ the words of the transgressor. ⁽¹³⁾ ^h The slothful *man* saith, There is a lion without, I shall be slain in the streets. ⁽¹⁴⁾ ⁱ The mouth of strange women *is* a deep pit: he that is abhorred of the LORD shall fall therein. ⁽¹⁵⁾ Foolishness *is* bound in the heart of a child; but ^k the rod of correction shall drive it far from him. ⁽¹⁶⁾ He that oppresseth the poor to increase his *riches*, *and* he that giveth to the rich, *shall* surely *come* to want.

⁽¹⁷⁾ Bow down thine ear, and hear the words of the wise, and apply thine heart unto my knowledge. ⁽¹⁸⁾ For *it is* a pleasant thing if thou keep them ¹⁰ within thee; they shall withal be fitted in thy lips. ⁽¹⁹⁾ That thy trust may be in the LORD, I have made known to thee this day, ¹¹ even to thee. ⁽²⁰⁾ Have not I written to thee excellent things in

a Eccles. 7. 1.
1 Or, *favour is better than*, &c.
b ch. 29. 13.
c ch. 27. 12.
d Ps. 112. 3.
2 Or, *The reward of humility*, &c.
3 Or, *Catechise.*
4 Heb., *in his way.*
5 Heb., *to the man that lendeth.*
e Job 4. 8; Hos. 10. 13.
6 Or, *and with the rod of his anger he shall be consumed.*
f 2 Cor. 9. 6.
7 *Good of eye.*
g Ps. 101. 5.
8 Or, *and hath grace in his lips.*
9 Or, *the matters.*
h ch. 26. 13.
i ch. 2. 16 & 5. 3, & 7. 5 & 23. 27.
k ch. 13. 24 & 19. 18, & 23. 13 & 29. 15, 17.
10 Heb., *in thy belly.*
11 Or, *trust thou also.*

XXII.

⁽¹⁾ **Loving favour.**—Or, *favour is better than silver and gold.* "Favour" may signify the grace which wins love, as well as the favour gained thereby.

⁽²⁾ **The rich and poor meet together.**—Are thrown together in the world in order to aid each other in the path through life, remembering that they are brethren, sons of one Father. (Comp. 1 Cor. xii. 27.)

⁽³⁾ **A prudent man foreseeth the evil, and hideth himself,** as the Israelites hid themselves within their houses from the destroying angel, Noah within the Ark, the Christians before the fall of Jerusalem (Luke xxi. 21) in Pella. (Comp. Isa. xxvi. 20.)

⁽⁴⁾ **By humility and the fear of the Lord.**—Rather, *by* (or, the reward of) *humility is the fear of the Lord.* He guides the humble and teaches them His fear. (Comp. Ps. xxv. 9.)

Honour, and life.—Comp. chap. xxi. 21.

⁽⁵⁾ **Thorns.**—Comp. note on chap. xv. 19.

⁽⁸⁾ **Vanity**—*i.e.,* calamity, trouble.

The rod of his anger shall fail.—When his time comes, and his iniquity is full, he shall himself suffer the punishment he brought on others, as Babylon did (Isa. xiv. 6), Assyria (*ibid.* xxx. 31).

⁽¹⁰⁾ **The scorner.**—See above on chap. i. 22.

⁽¹¹⁾ **For the grace of his lips.**—Rather, *who has grace of lips;* one who loves the truth and can speak it pleasantly.

⁽¹²⁾ **The eyes of the Lord preserve knowledge**—*i.e.,* men who know and speak the truth. (See above on chap. xxi. 28.)

He overthroweth the words of the transgressor—*i.e.,* the deceitful; He brings his lies to light.

⁽¹³⁾ **The slothful man saith, There is a lion without . . .**—No excuses are too absurd for him, he fears to meet a lion in the open country, or, he might be murdered in the streets.

⁽¹⁴⁾ **Strange women.**—See above on chap. ii. 16.

⁽¹⁵⁾ **Foolishness is bound in the heart of a child.**—Self-will is meant. (See above on chap. i. 7.) Children have to be taught to yield their wills to others.

⁽¹⁶⁾ **He that oppresseth the poor . . .**—Rather, *he that does so is* (thereby) *giving to the rich, only to* (his own) *loss.* That is, he shall be none the better for the act of oppression, but shall have to disgorge his prey to some one richer and more powerful than himself, and thereby be reduced to poverty.

4. AN INTRODUCTION, CONTAINING AN EXHORTATION TO "HEAR THE WORDS OF THE WISE," SERVING AS A HEADING TO chaps. xxii. 22—xxiv. 22 (chap. xxii. 17—21).

⁽¹⁷⁾ **Hear the words of the wise.**—Comp. chap i. 6. As "wise" is in the plural number, it would seem as if the following section contained proverbs written by others than Solomon, though they may have been collected by him. (Comp. chap. xxiv. 23.)

⁽¹⁸⁾ **They shall withal be fitted in thy lips.**—Rather, *if they be established* (dwell constantly) *upon thy lips.* They are to be as a watch, and "keep the door of his lips" against sin (Ps. cxli. 3), to teach him what to say in difficulty (Mark xiii. 11), how to speak without fear even before kings (Ps. cxix. 46); by them the "praises of God" will ever be in his mouth (Ps. cxlix. 6).

⁽¹⁹⁾ **I have made known to thee this day, even to thee** these counsels of the wise. The words, "this day," recall the warning of Heb. iii. 13, and the emphatic "to thee, even to thee," imply that the message of God, though it may be general in its form, yet is addressed to each individual soul among His people (comp., "Ho, every one that thirsteth," Isa.

counsels and knowledge, (21)that I might make thee know the certainty of the words of truth; that thou mightest answer the words of truth ¹to them that send unto thee?

(22) Rob not the poor, because he is poor: *a*neither oppress the afflicted in the gate: (23) *b*for the LORD will plead their cause, and spoil the soul of those that spoiled them. (24) Make no friendship with an angry man; and with a furious man thou shalt not go: (25)lest thou learn his ways, and get a snare to thy soul. (26) *c*Be not thou one of them that strike hands, or of them that are sureties for debts. (27) If thou hast nothing to pay, why should he take away thy bed from under thee? (28) *d*Remove not the ancient ²landmark, which thy fathers have set. (29) Seest thou a man diligent in his business? he shall stand before kings; he shall not stand before ³mean men.

CHAPTER XXIII.—(1) When thou sittest to eat with a ruler, consider diligently what is before thee: (2) and put a knife to thy throat, if thou be a man given to appetite. (3) Be not desirous of his dainties: for they are deceitful meat. (4) *e*Labour not to be rich: cease from thine own wisdom. (5) ⁴Wilt thou set thine eyes upon that which is not? for riches certainly make themselves wings; they fly away as an eagle toward heaven.

(6) Eat thou not the bread of him that hath an evil eye, neither desire thou his dainty meats: (7) for as he thinketh in his heart, so is he: Eat and drink, saith he to thee; but his heart is not with thee. (8) The morsel which thou hast eaten shalt thou vomit up, and lose thy sweet words. (9) Speak not in the ears of a fool: for he will despise the wisdom of thy words.

(10) *f*Remove not the old ⁵landmark; and enter not into the fields of the fatherless: (11) *g*for their redeemer is mighty; he shall plead their cause with thee.

Marginal notes:
1 Or, to those that send thee.
a Zech. 7. 10.
b Job. 31. 14; ch. 23. 11.
c ch. 6. 1, & 11. 15.
d Deut. 19. 14, & 27. 17; ch. 23. 10.
2 Or, bound.
3 Heb., obscure men.
e 1 Tim. 6. 9, 10.
4 Heb., Wilt thou cause thine eyes to fly upon.
f Deut. 19. 14, & 27. 17; ch. 22. 28.
5 Or, bound.
g Job 31. 21; ch. 22. 23.

---

lv. 1); each being well known, and an object of love on the part of his Redeemer.

(21) **That thou mightest answer the words of truth to them that send unto thee?**—This rendering is somewhat doubtful, but seems to give the best sense to the passage. The scholar is to be instructed not for his own profit alone, but in order that he may be able to teach others also. (Comp. 1 Pet. iii. 15.)

5. FIRST APPENDIX TO THE "PROVERBS OF SOLOMON" (chap. x. 1—xxii. 16), CONTAINING PROVERBS OF DIFFERENT LENGTHS, FROM THE DISTICH TO THE LENGTHENED DIDACTIC POEM (chaps. xxii. 22—xxiv. 22).

(22) **Neither oppress the afflicted in the gate.**—The place of business (Gen. xxxiv. 20) and of judgment (Deut. xxi. 19; Amos v. 15). (Comp. the title, "the Sublime Porte.") This, with the following verse 23, forms a tetrastich or verse of four lines, as do also verses 24 and 25.

(25) **Lest thou . . . get a snare to thy soul**—i.e., lose thy life.

(26) **Be not thou one of them that strike hands.**—Another warning against suretiship. (See above, on chap. vi. 1.)

(27) **Why should he take away thy bed from under thee?**—If the mantle was taken in pledge, it had to be restored before sundown for the poor man to sleep in; but this merciful provision of the Law was evidently evaded. (Comp. Ezek. xviii. 12.)

(28) **Remove not the ancient landmark.**—The stones marking the boundaries of the fields: evidently a not uncommon crime, from the earnestness with which it is forbidden. (Comp. chap. xxiii. 10; Deut. xix. 14, xxvii. 17.)

(29) **He shall stand before kings.**—Shall attend upon them as their minister. (Comp. Gen. xli. 46.) This verse is a tristich, containing three lines.

XXIII.

(1) **Consider diligently what is before thee.**—Rather, Who is before thee; that thy host is not an equal, but one who, if offended, might do thee deadly harm.

(2) **And put a knife to thy throat.**—Use the strongest methods to keep thine appetite in check, if thou art likely to give way to it, and then, overcome by meat and drink, to say or do anything to offend thy host.

(3) **Deceitful meat.**—Not offered out of friendship and love to thee; for an unguarded word spoken in the insecurity of the festive hour might bring ruin to thee.

(4) **Cease from thine own wisdom.**—Cleverness shewn in piling up wealth.

(5) **They fly away.**—Rather, As an eagle that flieth toward heaven, far beyond thy reach.

(6) **Him that hath an evil eye.**—A sordid, grudging temper.

(7) **For as he thinketh in his heart, so is he.**—He is not really friendly and hospitable, as his words would imply, but he grudges every morsel thou takest, calculating its cost.

(8) **Shalt thou vomit up.**—Shalt be disgusted at having partaken of hospitality which was not freely offered to thee.

And lose thy sweet words.—All thy civil speeches and thanks for the cold welcome thou hast had.

(9) **Speak not in the ears of a fool.**—Do not waste thy time in explaining matters to him.

A fool.—A dull, stupid person. (Comp. chap. i. 22.)

(10) **Remove not the old landmark.**—See above, on chap. xxii. 28.

(11) **Their redeemer is mighty.**—They may have no near kinsman (Lev. xxv. 25) to redeem their land,

(12) Apply thine heart unto instruction, and thine ears to the words of knowledge. (13) ᵃWithhold not correction from the child: for if thou beatest him with the rod, he shall not die. (14) Thou shalt beat him with the rod, and shalt deliver his soul from hell. (15) My son, if thine heart be wise, my heart shall rejoice, ¹even mine. (16) Yea, my reins shall rejoice, when thy lips speak right things.

(17) ᵇ Let not thine heart envy sinners: but be thou in the fear of the LORD all the day long. (18) ᶜFor surely there is an ²end; and thine expectation shall not be cut off. (19) Hear thou, my son, and be wise, and guide thine heart in the way. (20) ᵈBe not among winebibbers; among riotous eaters ³ of flesh: (21) for the drunkard and the glutton shall come to poverty: and drowsiness shall clothe a man with rags. (22) ᵉHearken unto thy father that begat thee, and despise not thy mother when she is old. (23) Buy the truth, and sell it not; also wisdom, and instruction, and understanding. (24) ᶠ The father of the righteous shall greatly rejoice: and he that begetteth a wise child shall have joy of him. (25) Thy father and thy mother shall be glad, and she that bare thee shall rejoice.

(26) My son, give me thine heart, and let thine eyes observe my ways. (27) ᵍFor a whore is a deep ditch; and a strange woman is a narrow pit. (28) ʰShe also lieth in wait ⁴as for a prey, and increaseth the transgressors among men.

(29) ⁱ Who hath woe? who hath sorrow? who hath contentions? who hath babbling? who hath wounds without cause? who hath redness of eyes? (30) They that tarry long at the wine; they that go to seek mixed wine. (31) Look not thou upon the wine when it is red, when it giveth his colour in the cup, when it moveth itself aright. (32) At the last it biteth like a serpent, and stingeth like ⁵an adder. (33) Thine eyes shall behold strange women, and thine heart shall utter perverse things. (34) Yea, thou shalt be as he that lieth down ⁶in the midst of the sea, or as he

a ch. 13. 24 & 19. 18, & 22. 15.
1 Or, *even I will rejoice.*
b Ps. 37. 1, & 73. 3; ch. 3. 31, & 24. 1.
c ch. 24. 14.
2 Or, *reward.*
d Rom. 13. 13; Eph. 5. 18.
3 Heb., *of their flesh.*
e ch. 1. 8.
f ch. 10. 1, & 15. 20.
g ch 22. 14.
h ch. 7. 12.
4 Or, *as a robber.*
i Isa. 5. 11.
5 Or, *a cockatrice.*
6 Heb., *in the heart of the sea.*

---

yet they have a mighty Deliverer (Exod. vi. 6), who will redress their wrongs.

(13) **He shall not die**—*i.e.*, a moderate correction, such as that advised in chap. xix. 18 (see note), will not injure him—quite the reverse.

(14) **And shalt deliver his soul from hell**—*i.e.*, Hades, the abode of the dead (Isa. xiv. 9), death being the punishment of sin, and long life the reward of well-doing (chap. iii. 2).

(16) **My reins shall rejoice.**—These being represented in Hebrew poetry as the seat of the deepest affections, answering to "heart" in verse 15. (Comp. Ps. vii. 9; Jer. xii. 2; Rev. ii. 23.)

(18) **An end**, which shall be peace (Ps. xxxvii. 37), corresponding to the "manifestation of the sons of God" (Rom. viii. 19), when we shall be "like" God (1 John iii. 2).

(19) **Hear thou, my son,** whatever others may do. (Comp. above, on chap. xxii. 19.)

Guide thine heart in the way.—That is, of God. (Comp. Isa. xl. 3, and note on Acts ix. 2.)

(21) **Drowsiness,** that follows after such debauches.

(23) **Buy the truth, and sell it not.**—The "truth" is here described under the three heads of wisdom, self-discipline, and understanding. (See above, on chap. i. 2.) All these are to be obtained from God (James i. 5), who gives to every man "liberally," "without money and without price," (Isa. lv. 1). (Comp. Rev. iii. 18, and the "treasure" and "pearl of great price" of Matt. xiii. 44—46.)

(26) **My son, give me thine heart.**—For that is the one gift alone worthy of acceptance which man can offer to God, and the only one which God will accept; an offering which man endeavours to keep for himself, substituting for it alms, unreal prayers, outward observances of religion, and obedience in matters of little moment. (Comp. Matt. xxii. 37.)

(27) **Strange woman** (*nokhriyyah*).—See above, on chap. ii. 16.

(28) **Increaseth the transgressors** (faithless) **among men.**—This vice being the fruitful source of faithlessness both towards man and God.

(29) **Wounds without cause?**—Which might have been avoided, and which serve no good end.

Redness of eyes?—Rather, *dimness.*

(30) **They that go to seek mixed wine.**—Or, *To test;* to see whether it is to their taste. The wines of the ancients were not generally drunk pure, but diluted with water or flavoured with spices. (See above on chap. ix. 2.)

(31) **When it giveth its colour.**—Or *sparkles.*

When it moveth itself aright.—Or, *when it glides easily* down the throat.

(33) **Thine eyes shall behold strange women.** —*i.e.*, look out for them, impurity being the constant attendant of drunkenness. Or, the word may be translated "strange things," referring to the strange fancies of a drunkard, the horrible and fantastic visions present to his disordered brain.

Perverse things.—His notions of right and wrong being completely distorted.

(34) **As he that lieth down in the midst of the sea.**—And so would inevitably be drowned if he trusted to its smooth, glassy appearance.

As he that lieth upon the top of a mast.—Whom every roll of the ship might hurl into the waves. The absolute insensibility of the drunkard to danger is here described. Or it may mean that everything round the drunkard and the ground on which he lies, seem to rock like the waves of the sea, or the masthead of a ship.

that lieth upon the top of a mast. (35) They have stricken me, *shalt thou say, and* I was not sick; they have beaten me, *and* ¹I felt *it* not: when shall I awake? I will seek it yet again.

CHAPTER XXIV.—(1) Be not thou envious against evil men, neither desire to be with them. (2) *b* For their heart studieth destruction, and their lips talk of mischief. (3) Through wisdom is an house builded; and by understanding it is established: (4) and by knowledge shall the chambers be filled with all precious and pleasant riches. (5) A wise man ² *is* strong; yea, a man of knowledge ³ increaseth strength. (6) *c* For by wise counsel thou shalt make thy war: and in multitude of counsellors *there is* safety. (7) Wisdom *is* too high for a fool: he openeth not his mouth in the gate. (8) He that deviseth to do evil shall be called a mischievous person. (9) The thought of foolishness *is* sin: and the scorner *is* an abomination to men. (10) *If* thou faint in the day of adversity, thy strength *is* ⁴ small. (11) *d* If thou forbear to deliver *them that are* drawn unto death, and *those that are* ready to be slain; (12) if thou sayest, Behold, we knew it not; doth not he that pondereth the heart consider *it?* and he that keepeth thy soul, doth *not* he know *it?* and shall *not* he render to *every* man *e* according to his works?

(13) My son, eat thou honey, because *it* is good; and the honeycomb, *which is* sweet ⁵ to thy taste: (14) *f so shall* the knowledge of wisdom *be* unto thy soul: when thou hast found *it*, *g* then there shall be a reward, and thy expectation shall not be cut off.

(15) Lay not wait, O wicked *man*, against the dwelling of the righteous; spoil not his resting place: (16) *h* for a just *man* falleth seven times, and riseth up again: but the wicked shall fall into mischief. (17) *i* Rejoice not when thine enemy falleth, and let not thine heart be glad when he stumbleth: (18) lest the LORD see *it*, and ⁶ it displease him, and he turn away his wrath from him.

(19) *j* ⁷ Fret not thyself because of evil men, neither be thou envious at the wicked; (20) for there shall be no reward to the evil *man*; *k* the ⁸ candle

---

(35) **They have stricken me, and I was not sick.**—The drunken man feels no blows or ill usage.

When shall I awake?—He longs to rouse himself from his slumber that he may return to his debauch.

XXIV

(3) **Through wisdom is an house builded.**—See above on chap. xiv. 1.

(4) **All precious and pleasant riches.**—Not only earthly wealth, but the "true riches" (Luke xvi. 11), the knowledge and love of God. (Comp. note on chap. xxiii. 23.)

(5) **A man of knowledge increaseth strength.**—For the spiritual sense, comp. 2 Peter iii. 18.

(6) **Wise counsel.**—See above on chap. i. 5. In the great spiritual fight also (Eph. vi. 12) we need wise counsel, to see the end to be aimed at, and the means of attaining it.

(7) **Wisdom is too high for a fool.**—For "wisdom" (literally, *wisdoms*), comp. note on chap. i. 20. He has been too self-willed to learn; so while others express their opinions when the business or justice of his city is being transacted (see above on chap. xxii. 22) he has to remain sheepishly silent.

(9) **The thought of foolishness is sin.**—Rather, *Sin is the contrivance (plotting) of self-will.* Sin is the "transgression of the law" of God (1 John iii. 4), when we desert the plain rule of duty, and plot how we can indulge our own self-will.

(10) **If thou faint in the day of adversity.**—And prove unable to help thyself or others; an exhortation to courage (comp. Heb. xii. 12). A "more excellent way" is shown in the following verse.

(11) **If thou forbear . . .**—Rather, *Deliver those that are taken to death, and those that are tottering to the slaughter, stop them!*

(12) **If thou sayest, Behold, we knew it not.**—Man being too much inclined to answer after the manner of Cain (Gen. iv. 9), "Am I my brother's keeper?" when he might give aid to those who need it.

(14) **So shall the knowledge of wisdom be unto thy soul.**—Rather, *Know* (or understand) *that wisdom is such* (equally sweet and good) *for thy soul.*

A reward.—Literally, *a future.* (Comp. chap. xxiii. 18.)

(16) **For a just man falleth seven times and riseth up again.**—That is, falls into trouble (not *sin*, as is often supposed). Therefore thy malice will be of no avail, for God's protection is about him. (Comp. Job v. 19; Ps. xxxiv. 19, and xxxvii. 24.)

Seven times—*i.e.*, frequently. (Comp. Matt. xviii. 21.)

(18) **And he turn away his wrath from him.**—Upon thee as having sinned more deeply than thine enemy in thus rejoicing at his misfortunes. (Comp. chap. xvii. 5.)

(19) **Fret not thyself because of evil men**—*i.e.*, at the sight of their prosperity, the same difficulty which occurred to the Psalmist (Ps. xxxvii. 1). (Comp. also Ps. lxxiii. 3 and Jer. xii. 1.)

(20) **For there shall be no reward.**—Literally, *future*, as in verse 15.

The candle of the wicked shall be put out.—See above on chap. xiii. 9.

Sundry Maxims and   PROVERBS, XXV.   *Observations of Solomon,*

of the wicked shall be put out. ⁽²¹⁾ My son, fear thou the LORD and the king: *and* meddle not with ¹them that are given to change: ⁽²²⁾ for their calamity shall rise suddenly; and who knoweth the ruin of them both?

⁽²³⁾ These *things* also *belong* to the wise. *^a It is* not good to have respect of persons in judgment. ⁽²⁴⁾ *^b*He that saith unto the wicked, Thou *art* righteous; him shall the people curse, nations shall abhor him: ⁽²⁵⁾ but to them that rebuke *him* shall be delight, and ² a good blessing shall come upon them. ⁽²⁶⁾ *Every man* shall kiss *his* lips ³ that giveth a right answer. ⁽²⁷⁾ Prepare thy work without, and make it fit for thyself in the field; and afterwards build thine house. ⁽²⁸⁾ Be not a witness against thy neighbour without cause; and deceive *not* with thy lips. ⁽²⁹⁾ *^c* Say not, I will do so to him as he hath done to me: I will render to the man according to his work.

⁽³⁰⁾ I went by the field of the slothful, and by the vineyard of the man void of understanding; ⁽³¹⁾ and, lo, it was all grown over with thorns, *and* nettles had covered the face thereof, and the stone wall thereof was broken down. ⁽³²⁾ Then I saw, *and* ⁴ considered *it* well: I looked upon *it, and* received instruction. ⁽³³⁾ *^d* Yet a little sleep, a little slumber, a little folding of the hands to sleep: ⁽³⁴⁾ so shall thy poverty come *as* one that travelleth; and thy want as ⁵ an armed man.

CHAPTER XXV.—⁽¹⁾ These *are* also proverbs of Solomon, which the men of Hezekiah king of Judah copied out. ⁽²⁾ *It is* the glory of God to conceal a thing: but the honour of kings *is* to search out a matter. ⁽³⁾ The heaven for height, and the earth for depth, and

Marginal notes:
1 Heb., *changers.*
^a Lev. 19. 15; Deut. 1. 17, & 16. 19; ch. 18. 5, & 28. 21; John 7. 24.
^b ch. 17. 15; Isa. 5. 23.
2 Heb., *a blessing of good.*
3 Heb., *that answereth right words.*
^c ch. 20. 22.
4 Heb., *set my heart.*
^d ch. 6. 9, &c.
5 Heb., *a man of shield.*

⁽²¹⁾ **Them that are given to change.**—Perhaps rather, *those who think differently.*

⁽²²⁾ **The ruin of them both**—*i.e.,* the rebels against God and the king.

6. SECOND APPENDIX TO "THE PROVERBS OF SOLOMON," CONTAINING PROVERBS OF VARIOUS LENGTHS, RESEMBLING chaps. i. 7—ix., AND THE BOOK OF ECCLESIASTES (chap. xxiv. 23—34).

⁽²³⁾ **These things also belong to the wise**—*i.e.,* have the wise for their authors. (Comp. chaps. i. 6, xxii. 17.)

⁽²⁶⁾ **Every man shall kiss his lips** . . . Rather, *He kisseth the lips that giveth right answers.* His words are as pleasant as if he had kissed the inquirer's lips.

⁽²⁷⁾ **Prepare thy work without** . . . —Method in work is here advised; first till the ground, and then build the house which will be maintained by the produce of the field. In the spiritual life, too, we should seek to "perceive and know what things we ought to do," if we are not to waste time and energy upon unsuitable and unattainable objects.

⁽²⁸⁾ **Without cause**—*i.e.,* do not mention thy neighbour's faults unless for some good reason, not for malice or love of gossip.

⁽²⁹⁾ **Say not, I will do so to him as he hath done to me.**—A wonderful anticipation this of New Testament teaching, very different from the spirit of Lev. xxiv. 19, 20. Comp. chap. xx. 22, and James ii. 13, "For he shall have judgment without mercy that shewed no mercy."

⁽³⁰⁾ **I went by the field of the slothful** . . . — The parable of the vineyard let out to husbandmen for them to render the fruits in due season (Matt. xxi. 33), and of the thorns which choked the word (*ibid.,* chap. xiii. 7), suggest a spiritual meaning for this passage. It warns us not to allow the weeds of evil habits to spring up in the garden of the soul through sloth, nor to suffer God's protecting care (the wall) to be withdrawn from us because we have not sought it constantly in prayer.

⁽³⁴⁾ **As one that travelleth.**—See above on chap. vi. 11.

XXV.

7. THE THIRD GREAT DIVISION OF THE BOOK; ANOTHER COLLECTION OF SOLOMONIC PROVERBS, CHIEFLY PARABOLIC IN CHARACTER (chaps. xxv.—xxix.).

⁽¹⁾ **These are also proverbs of Solomon, which the men of Hezekiah copied out.**—To this time they had existed, it may be, partly by oral tradition, partly in writing; but now Hezekiah, in his anxiety to preserve these sacred memorials of the past, had them copied out and formed into one collection. To his care we probably also owe the compilation of Books II. (Ps. xlii.—lxxii.) and III. (lxxiii.—lxxxix.) of the Psalter, in the former of which are included several psalms of David's which had not found a place in Book I., though this last-named book consists almost, if not entirely, of psalms ascribed to him. In the same manner the present book (chaps. xxv.—xxix.) contains proverbs of Solomon which apparently were not known to the compiler of the previous collection.

⁽²⁾ **It is the glory of God to conceal a thing.** —For the more we search into the mysteries of nature or revelation, the more do we discover depths of which we had no idea before. God has so ordered things that man may not presume to measure himself with his Maker, but may recognise his own insignificance. (Comp. Rom. xi. 33, *ff.*)

But the honour of kings is to search out a matter.—To see their way through political difficulties, and to unmask crime and fraud.

⁽³⁾ **The heart of kings is unsearchable.**—A warning, it may be, against presuming upon the favour of a king from thinking that one knows all that is in his mind. (Comp. chap. xxiii. 1. 2.)

the heart of kings ¹*is* unsearchable. ⁽⁴⁾Take away the dross from the silver, and there shall come forth a vessel for the finer. ⁽⁵⁾ ᵃTake away the wicked *from* before the king, and his throne shall be established in righteousness.

⁽⁶⁾ ²Put not forth thyself in the presence of the king, and stand not in the place of great *men:* ⁽⁷⁾ ᵇfor better *it is* that it be said unto thee, Come up hither; than that thou shouldest be put lower in the presence of the prince whom thine eyes have seen.

⁽⁸⁾ Go not forth hastily to strive, lest *thou know not* what to do in the end thereof, when thy neighbour hath put thee to shame. ⁽⁹⁾ ᶜDebate thy cause with thy neighbour *himself;* and ³discover not a secret to another: ⁽¹⁰⁾lest he that heareth *it* put thee to shame, and thine infamy turn not away.

⁽¹¹⁾A word ⁴fitly spoken *is like* apples of gold in pictures of silver. ⁽¹²⁾*As* an earring of gold, and an ornament of fine gold, *so is* a wise reprover upon an obedient ear. ⁽¹³⁾ᵈAs the cold of snow in the time of harvest, *so is* a faithful messenger to them that send him: for he refresheth the soul of his masters. ⁽¹⁴⁾Whoso boasteth himself ⁵of a false gift *is like* clouds and wind without rain. ⁽¹⁵⁾ᵉBy long forbearing is a prince persuaded, and a soft tongue breaketh the bone.

⁽¹⁶⁾ Hast thou found honey? eat so much as is sufficient for thee, lest thou be filled therewith, and vomit it. ⁽¹⁷⁾ ⁶Withdraw thy foot from thy neighbour's house; lest he be ⁷weary of thee, and *so* hate thee.

⁽¹⁸⁾ᶠA man that beareth false witness against his neighbour *is* a maul, and a sword, and a sharp arrow. ⁽¹⁹⁾ Confidence in an unfaithful man in time of trouble *is like* a broken tooth, and a foot out of joint. ⁽²⁰⁾*As* he that taketh away a garment in cold weather, *and as* vinegar upon nitre, so *is* he that singeth songs to an heavy heart.

⁽²¹⁾ᵍIf thine enemy be hungry, give him bread to eat; and if he be thirsty, give him water to drink. ⁽²²⁾For thou shalt heap coals of fire upon his head, and the LORD shall reward thee.

⁽²³⁾ ⁸The north wind driveth away

---

¹ Heb., *there is no searching.*
ᵃ ch. 20. 8.
² Heb., *Set not out thy glory.*
ᵇ Luke 14. 10.
ᶜ Matt. 5. 25, & 18. 15.
³ Or, *discover not the secret of another.*
⁴ Heb., *spoken upon his wheels.*
ᵈ ch. 13. 17.
⁵ Heb., *in a gift of falsehood.*
ᵉ Gen. 32. 4, &c.; 1 Sam. 25. 24, &c.; ch. 15. 1, & 16. 14.
⁶ Or, *Let thy foot be seldom in thy neighbour's house.*
⁷ Heb., *full of thee.*
ᶠ Ps. 120. 4; ch. 12. 18.
ᵍ Ex. 23. 4; Rom. 12. 20.
⁸ Or, *The north wind bringeth forth rain; so doth a backbiting tongue an angry countenance.*

⁽⁴⁾ **And there shall come forth a vessel for the finer.**—Or, *So there results a vessel to the refiner,* or silversmith. He is able to make one.

⁽⁵⁾ **His throne shall be established in righteousness**—whereas violence and wrong pull it down. (Jer. xxi. 12, xxii. 3, *sqq.*; Zech. vii. 9, *sqq.*)

⁽⁷⁾ **In the presence of the prince whom thine eyes have seen,** and whose place thou hast shamelessly taken. The same lesson was repeated by our Lord in Luke xiv. 10, *sqq.*, and enforced on the ground of His own example. (Matt. xx. 25, *sqq.*)

⁽⁸⁾ **When thy neighbour hath put thee to shame.**—Proved thee to be in the wrong, and won his cause against thee.

⁽⁹⁾ **Debate thy cause with thy neighbour.**—As our Lord says, "If thy brother trespass against thee, go and tell him his fault between thee and him alone" (Matt. xviii. 15). Or it may mean, "If you must go to law with another, do not drag others into the matter by disclosing their secrets in order to help your cause.

⁽¹⁰⁾ **Lest he that heareth it put thee to shame.**—Lest he cry shame upon thee for thy treachery, and thine infamy be not forgotten.

⁽¹¹⁾ **A word fitly spoken.**—Or, it may be, *at the proper time.* (Comp. chap. xv. 23.)

Apples of gold in pictures of silver.—Probably golden-coloured apples are meant, or fruit of the same tint, such as pomegranates, citrons, or oranges. "Pictures" of silver probably means "figures," *i.e.,* baskets or dishes of ornamental work.

⁽¹³⁾ **As the cold of snow in the time of harvest.**—Not a snowstorm, as this would be a calamity (chap. xxvi. 1), but snow employed to cool drinks in the summer heats. The use of this was probably familiar to Solomon in his summer palace at Lebanon (1 Kings ix. 19). The peasants of Lebanon are said now to store up snow in the clefts of the mountain, and convey it in summer to Damascus and the coast towns. For the opposite picture of the unfaithful messenger comp. chap. x. 26.

⁽¹⁴⁾ **Whoso boasteth himself of a false gift**—*i.e.,* talks loudly of what he is going to do for another, and then does nothing.

Clouds and wind.—Generally followed by heavy rain. (Comp. 1 Kings xviii. 45.)

⁽¹⁶⁾ **Hast thou found honey?**—A common occurrence in Palestine, where swarms of wild bees abounded in the woods. (Comp. Judg. xiv. 8; 1 Sam. xiv. 27.) Hence came the expression of a "land flowing with (milk and) honey."

⁽¹⁸⁾ **A maul**—*i.e., hammer,* connected with "malleus" and "mallet." A false witness is as mischievous as the most deadly weapons.

⁽²⁰⁾ **As vinegar upon nitre,** by which the nitre is rendered useless.

Is he that singeth songs to an heavy heart.—Not the true sympathy advised by St. Paul. (Rom. xii. 15.)

⁽²²⁾ **Thou shalt heap coals of fire on his head.**—Thou shalt make him burn with shame at the thought of the wrong he has done thee. Thus, to bring a sinner to repentance is well-pleasing to the Lord, who shall reward thee for it. This is better far than to indulge resentment, which must bring sorrow to oneself, punishment from God—whose prerogative of vengeance (Rom. xii. 19) has been usurped—and only serve to harden the offender in his hostility.

⁽²³⁾ **The north wind driveth away rain.**—The marginal rendering is probably more correct: "The

Sundry Maxims and   PROVERBS, XXVI.   *Observations of Solomon.*

rain: so *doth* an angry countenance a backbiting tongue. ⁽²⁴⁾ *^aIt is* better to dwell in the corner of the housetop, than with a brawling woman and in a wide house. ⁽²⁵⁾ *As* cold waters to a thirsty soul, so *is* good news from a far country. ⁽²⁶⁾ A righteous man falling down before the wicked *is as* a troubled fountain, and a corrupt spring. ⁽²⁷⁾ *It is* not good to eat much honey: so *for men* to search their own glory *is not* glory. ⁽²⁸⁾ *^b*He that *hath* no rule over his own spirit *is like* a city *that is* broken down, *and* without walls.

CHAPTER XXVI.—⁽¹⁾ As snow in summer, and as rain in harvest, so honour is not seemly for a fool. ⁽²⁾ As the bird by wandering, as the swallow by flying, so the curse causeless shall not come. ⁽³⁾ A *^c*whip for the horse, a bridle for the ass, and a rod for the fool's back. ⁽⁴⁾ Answer not a fool according to his folly, lest thou also be like unto him. ⁽⁵⁾ Answer a fool according to his folly, lest he be wise in ¹his own conceit. ⁽⁶⁾ He that sendeth a message by the hand of a fool cutteth off the feet, *and* drinketh ² damage. ⁽⁷⁾ The legs of the lame ³are not equal: so *is* a parable in the mouth of fools. ⁽⁸⁾ ⁴As he that bindeth a stone in a sling, so *is* he that giveth honour to a fool. ⁽⁹⁾ *As* a thorn goeth up into the hand of a drunkard, so *is* a parable in the mouth of fools. ⁽¹⁰⁾ ⁵The great *God* that formed

a ch. 19. 13, & 21. 9.
b ch. .6. 32.
c Ps. 32. 9; ch. 10. 13.
¹ Heb., *his own eyes.*
² Or, *violence.*
³ Heb., *are lifted up.*
⁴ Or, *As he that putteth a precious stone in an heap of stones.*
⁵ Or, *A great man grieveth all, and he hireth the fool, he hireth also transgressors.*

---

north wind bringeth forth rain;" but as this seems to be opposed to Job xxxvii. 22, it has been thought that the north-west, which is a rainy wind, must be intended here.

So doth an angry countenance a backbiting tongue.—Rather, *So doth a backbiting tongue (bring forth, or cause) troubled faces.*

⁽²⁴⁾ **It is better to dwell in the corner of the housetop.**—See above on chap. xxi. 9.

⁽²⁵⁾ **Good news from a far country.**—This is suggestive of the little communication which in old times took place between distant countries.

⁽²⁶⁾ **A righteous man falling down before the wicked . . .**—The mouth of the righteous was described (chap. x. 11) as a "well of life," from the comfort and refreshment it brings to the weary through the just and kindly counsel it offers. But if the righteous man yields to the pressure put upon him by the wicked, and through fear or favour gives up his principles, then he can no longer give forth counsel out of a pure heart; he becomes like a fountain which has been fouled by the feet of cattle drinking at it (Ezek. xxxiv. 18), and like a corrupted spring.

⁽²⁷⁾ **So for men to search their own glory is not glory.**—The sense of this passage is very doubtful. It may mean, "But to search into difficult matters is an honour." Self-indulgence and study are here contrasted.

⁽²⁸⁾ **Like a city that is broken down, and without walls.**—Exposed to the assault of every temptation.

XXVI.

⁽¹⁾ **As rain in harvest.**—This was very unusual in Palestine (comp. 1 Sam. xii. 17, *sqq.*), and of course very unsuitable for carrying on the work of harvest.

So honour is not seemly for a fool.—*i.e.*, for a dull person, confident in his own wisdom (chap. i. 22). It only confirms him in his good opinion of himself, making him less inclined than ever to learn.

⁽²⁾ **As the bird by wandering, as the swallow by flying.**—Rather, *As the bird* (any small one, especially the sparrow) *is made for wandering, and the swallow for flying* (where it pleases), *so the curse causeless* (*i.e.*, spoken without reason) *shall not come* (reach its destination). The Hebrew reads in the margin "to him," instead of "not," in the sense that a causeless curse, though it passes out of sight like a bird in its flight, yet returns "to him" who uttered it —an idea expressed in more than one English proverb. (Comp. Ps. cix. 17, 18; Isa. lv. 11.)

⁽⁴⁾ **Answer not a fool.**—Comp. chap. i. 22.

According to his folly.—Do not lower yourself by disputing or arguing with him; he will not take in your meaning, and will think he has got the better of you, perhaps will insult you. It is noticeable that our Lord never answered a question which should not have been asked Him, but always put it by (*e.g.*, Matt. xxi. 23, *sqq.*; Luke xiii. 23, 24; xxiii. 9; John xxi. 21, 22; Acts i. 6, *sqq.*).

⁽⁵⁾ **Answer a fool according to his folly.**— As his folly deserves, sharply and decisively, and in language suited to his comprehension.

⁽⁶⁾ **Cutteth off the feet.**—He wants his business done, but if he sends a fool to do it, he might as well cut off his messenger's legs, for the business will not be transacted; nay, worse than this, he will "drink damage," *i.e.*, suffer positive mischief from the blundering of his emissary.

⁽⁷⁾ **The legs of the lame are not equal.**—Better, perhaps, *The legs hang down from a lame man, and so is a parable* (useless) *in the mouth of fools*; they can make no more use of it for the guidance of themselves or others, than can a lame man use his legs. (Comp. Luke viii. 10.)

⁽⁸⁾ **As he that bindeth a stone in a sling . . .** —*i.e.*, the stone is soon gone from the sling and seen no more, so honour and a fool soon part company. This seems on the whole the most probable rendering of this verse.

⁽⁹⁾ **As a thorn goeth up into the hand of a drunkard.**—Rather, (*As*) *a thornbush* (*which*) *comes into the hand of a drunkard, so* (*is*) *a parable* (*which comes*) *into the mouth of fools*. They know not how to use it, and only do themselves and others harm by it. (Comp. 2 Pet. iii. 16.)

⁽¹⁰⁾ **The great God that formed all things both rewardeth the fool, and rewardeth transgressors.**—If this rendering of the passage could stand, Matt. vi. 2 might be quoted in illustration of it. If fools and transgressors will set their mind upon "husks" (Luke xv. 16) instead of the food God has

all *things* both rewardeth the fool, and rewardeth transgressors. (11) ᵃAs a dog returneth to his vomit, so a fool ¹returneth to his folly. (12) Seest thou a man wise in his own conceit? *There is* more hope of a fool than of him.

(13) ᵇThe slothful *man* saith, *There is* a lion in the way; a lion *is* in the streets. (14) *As* the door turneth upon his hinges, so *doth* the slothful upon his bed. (15) ᶜThe slothful hideth his hand in *his* bosom; ²it grieveth him to bring it again to his mouth. (16) The sluggard *is* wiser in his own conceit than seven men that can render a reason.

(17) He that passeth by, *and* ³meddleth with strife *belonging* not to him, *is like* one that taketh a dog by the ears. (18) As a mad *man* who casteth ⁴firebrands, arrows, and death, (19) so *is* the man *that* deceiveth his neighbour, and saith, Am not I in sport? (20) ⁵Where no wood is, *there* the fire goeth out: so ᵈwhere *there is* no ⁶talebearer, the strife ⁷ceaseth. (21) ᵉ*As* coals *are* to burning coals, and wood to fire; so *is* a contentious man to kindle strife.

(22) ᶠThe words of a talebearer *are* as wounds, and they go down into the ⁸innermost parts of the belly. (23) Burning lips and a wicked heart *are like* a potsherd covered with silver dross. (24) He that hateth ⁹dissembleth with his lips, and layeth up deceit within him; (25) when he ¹⁰speaketh fair, believe him not: for *there are* seven abominations in his heart. (26) *Whose* ¹¹ hatred is covered by deceit, his wickedness shall be shewed before the *whole* congregation. (27) ᵍWhoso diggeth a pit shall fall therein: and he that rolleth a stone, it will return upon him. (28) A lying tongue hateth *those that are* afflicted by it; and a flattering mouth worketh ruin.

CHAPTER XXVII.—(1) ʰBoast not thyself of ¹²to morrow; for thou knowest

---

a 2 Pet. 2. 22.
1 Heb., *iterateth his folly.*
b ch. 22. 13.
c ch. 19. 24.
2 Or, *he is weary.*
3 Or, *is enraged.*
4 Heb., *flames, or sparks.*
5 Heb., *Without wood.*
d ch. 22, 10.
6 Or, *whisperer.*
7 Heb., *is silent.*
e ch. 15. 18, & 29. 22.
f ch. 18. 8.
8 Heb., *chambers.*
9 Or, *is known.*
10 Heb., *maketh his voice gracious.*
11 Or, *hatred is covered in secret.*
g Ps. 7: 15, 16, & 9. 15; Eccles. 10. 8.
h James 4. 13, &c.
12 Heb., *to morrow day.*

---

provided for His children, He does not deny it to them; they have the reward they seek for. But the Hebrew can hardly yield this meaning. Of all the various renderings suggested, perhaps the most unobjectionable is as follows. *A master* (one skilled in his art), *produces everything* (by his own care and oversight he sees himself that it is properly done); *but a fool hires* (others to do his work), *and he hires passers by.*, *i.e.*, any casual person that comes in his way, whether skilled or not, and so the work is done badly.

(11) **So a fool returneth to his folly.**—Though he knows it to be folly, and ruinous to him: but vice has become to him a second nature, and he cannot, even if he would, escape from it. This is especially true of those who have given way to drink or impurity of life.

(12) **Seest thou a man wise in his own conceit.** —Comp. the warnings of Rom. xii. 16, and Rev. iii. 17, 18.

There is more hope of a fool than of him. —So the "publicans and harlots," who had foolishly strayed from God, yet returned to Him at the preaching of the Saviour, while the Pharisees and lawyers "rejected the counsel of God against themselves" (Luke vii. 30), thinking they had no need of it.

(13) **The slothful man saith, There is a lion in the way . . .**—See above on chap. xxii. 13.

(15) **The slothful hideth his hand in his bosom.**—See above on chap. xix. 24.

(16) **Seven men.**—A round number. (Comp. verse 25, vi. 31, xxiv. 16.)

That can render a reason—*i.e.*, give a sensible judgment on any matter submitted to them.

(17) **Meddleth with strife.**—Rather, *that is excited with strife.* If quarrelling and taking revenge on our own account are forbidden (Rom. xii. 18, 19), how much more is the mixing up of ourselves in the disputes of other persons.

Like one that taketh a dog by the ears.—Who deserves to be bitten for his pains, the usual result of interfering in quarrels.

(18) **Firebrands.**—Arrows to which some blazing material was attached, in order that they might set on fire whatever they touched.

(22) **The words of a tale-bearer are as wounds.**—See above on chap. xviii. 8.

(23) **Burning lips**—*i.e.*, burning with love, while there is an evil heart within.

A potsherd covered with silver dross.—Pottery glazed with dross of silver, a well-known method of ornamentation. For similar proverbs, comp. Matt. xxiii. 27; Luke xi. 39.

(25) **Seven abominations.**—See above on verse 16, and comp. "seven spirits" (Matt. xii. 45) and "seven devils" (Mark xvi. 9).

(26) **Whose hatred is covered by deceit.**—Rather, *hatred may cover itself by deceit* (but) *his wickedness* (*i.e.*, of the hater, implied in "hatred") *will be displayed in the congregation*, *i.e.*, openly, when a suitable opportunity for indulging his hatred occurs.

(27) **Whoso diggeth a pit shall fall therein.**—A simile taken from hunters making pits as traps for wild animals. The same doctrine of retribution being brought upon the sinner's head by God the righteous Judge is taught in Ps. vii. 11, *sqq.*

(28) **A lying tongue hateth those that are afflicted by it.**—As the remembrance of them calls up his own wickedness to the mind of the offender. This is one reason why "the carnal mind is enmity against God" (Rom. viii. 7), as being conscious of having rejected God's love, and so hating to be reminded of Him.

XXVII.

(1) **Boast not thyself of to-morrow.**—This is forbidden also in James iv. 13, *sqq.*; but there on the higher ground that it argues a want of submission to the will of Almighty God. This temper of mind, as well as the opposite one of too great anxiety for the morrow (Matt. vi. 34), proceed from the same cause,

Sundry Maxims and   PROVERBS, XXVII.   *Observations of Solomon,*

not what a day may bring forth. (2) Let another man praise thee, and not thine own mouth; a stranger, and not thine own lips (3) A stone is [1]heavy, and the sand weighty; but a fool's wrath is heavier than them both. (4) [2]Wrath is cruel, and anger is outrageous; but who is able to stand before [3]envy? (5) Open rebuke is better than secret love. (6) *a* Faithful are the wounds of a friend; but the kisses of an enemy are [4]deceitful.

(7) The full soul [5]loatheth an honeycomb; but *b* to the hungry soul every bitter thing is sweet. (8) As a bird that wandereth from her nest, so is a man that wandereth from his place. (9) Ointment and perfume rejoice the heart: so *doth* the sweetness of a man's friend [6]by hearty counsel. (10) Thine own friend, and thy father's friend, forsake not; neither go into thy brother's house in the day of thy calamity: *for c* better is a neighbour *that is* near than a brother far off.

(11) *d* My son, be wise, and make my heart glad, that I may answer him that reproacheth me. (12) *e* A prudent man foreseeth the evil, *and* hideth himself; but the simple pass on, *and* are punished. (13) *f* Take his garment that is surety for a stranger, and take a pledge of him for a strange woman. (14) He that blesseth his friend with a loud voice, rising early in the morning, it shall be counted a curse to him. (15) *g* A continual dropping in a very rainy day and a contentious woman are alike. (16) Whosoever hideth her hideth the wind, and the ointment of his right hand, *which* bewrayeth *itself*.

(17) Iron sharpeneth iron; so a man sharpeneth the countenance of his friend. (18) Whoso keepeth the fig tree shall eat

---

1 Heb., *heaviness.*
2 Heb., *Wrath is cruelty, and anger an overflowing.*
3 Or, *jealousy?*
a Ps.141.5.
4 Or, *earnest, or, frequent.*
5 Heb., *treadeth under foot.*
b Job 6.7.
6 Heb., *from the counsel of the soul.*
c ch. 17.17, & 18. 24.
d ch. 10.1, & 23. 24.
e ch. 22. 3.
f ch. 20. 16.
g ch. 19. 13.

---

too much dependence upon self, and are only to be met by learning to realise the love of God for His children (*ibid.*, 26, 30, 33), and looking up to Him daily for protection, guidance, and support.

(2) **Let another man** (*zar*) **praise thee . . . a stranger** (*nokhri*).—As to the difference between these words, see above on chap. ii. 16. A higher consideration than this is suggested in 2 Cor. x. 18.

(3) **But a fool's wrath is heavier than them both**—*i.e.*, harder to bear. (Comp. Ecclus. xxii. 15.) The "fool" here (*evil*) is the headstrong, self-willed person, who has never learned to control himself, but bursts out into the maddest rage when crossed.

(4) **But who is able to stand before envy?** —Rather, *jealousy*. (Comp. chap. vi. 34.) "Wrath" and "anger" rage for awhile like a storm, and then subside; but jealousy can never be completely set at rest.

(5) **Secret love**—*i.e.*, that never discloses itself in acts of kindness, not even in "open rebuke" when such is needed.

(6) **Faithful are the wounds of a friend**—*i.e.*, the "open rebuke" of the previous verse, the "smiting" and "reproof" of Ps. cxlii. 5.

The kisses of an enemy are deceitful.—Rather, *plentiful*, showered upon one, but all meaningless.

(7) **The full soul loatheth an honeycomb.**—So the moderate use of the good things of this life increases our enjoyment of them. But in spiritual things, the less we content ourselves with, the less hunger we feel, and less enjoyment do we derive from them.

(8) **A man that wandereth from his place.**—That wandereth forth as an exile that has lost his home. Comp. Gen. xii. 4, and, on the contrary, Job's hope that he would "die in his nest" (chap. xxix. 18). For the spiritual sense comp. Luke xv. 13, *sqq.*

(9) **Ointment and perfume.**—Comp. chap. vii. 17 and note on chap. xxi. 17.

(10) **Better is a neighbour that is near.**—See above on chap. xvii. 17 and xviii. 24. "Near" and "far off"—*i.e.*, in feeling.

(11) **My son.**—The address of a father to his son, or master to pupil.

That I may answer him that reproacheth me for having brought you up badly when he sees you ignorant or ill-behaved. So Christians are exhorted to let their "light so shine before men" that their Father in heaven may be thereby glorified (Matt. v. 16).

(12) **A prudent man foreseeth the evil.**—See above on xxii. 3.

(13) **Take a pledge of him for a strange woman.**—See above on xx. 16; and for "strange woman" comp. note on chap. ii. 16.

(14) **He that blesseth his friend with a loud voice . . .**—If gratitude is to be acceptable, the time, place, and manner of shewing it must all be well chosen. A man who is so eager to express his thanks that he begins early in the morning, and in so loud a voice as to draw upon his patron the attention of all the bystanders, is looked upon as a nuisance; any one would as soon be cursed as blessed by him. So God loves heartfelt gratitude offered in secret. (Comp. Matt. vi. 5, 6.)

(15) **A continual dropping in a very rainy day.** —See above on xix. 13.

(16) **Whosoever hideth her hideth the wind**— *i.e.*, you might as well try and stop the wind from blowing as seek to restrain her.

And the ointment of his right hand, which bewrayeth itself.—Rather, perhaps, *and oil meeteth his right hand*—*i.e.*, if he puts out his hand to stop her she slips through it like oil.

(17) **So a man sharpeneth the countenance of his friend**—*i.e.*, the play of wit with wit sharpens and brightens up the face.

(18) **Whoso keepeth the fig-tree**—*i.e.*, tends it carefully year after year, "shall eat the fruit thereof" when it has come to perfection.

So he that waiteth on his master—*i.e.*, attends to him, observes and follows out his wishes, "shall be honoured" for his good service. (Comp. Matt. xxv. 21.)

the fruit thereof: so he that waiteth on his master shall be honoured. (19) As in water face *answereth* to face, so the heart of man to man. (20) Hell and destruction are [1] never full; so *a* the eyes of man are never satisfied. (21) *b As* the fining pot for silver, and the furnace for gold; so *is* a man to his praise. (22) Though thou shouldest bray a fool in a mortar among wheat with a pestle, *yet* will not his foolishness depart from him.

(23) Be thou diligent to know the state of thy flocks, *and* [2] look well to thy herds. (24) For [3] riches *are* not for ever: and doth the crown endure [4] to every generation? (25) The hay appeareth, and the tender grass sheweth itself, and herbs of the mountains are gathered. (26) The lambs *are* for thy clothing, and the goats *are* the price of the field. (27) And *thou shalt have* goats' milk enough for thy food, for the food of thy household, and *for* the [5] maintenance for thy maidens.

CHAPTER XXVIII.—(1) The *c* wicked flee when no man pursueth: but the righteous are bold as a lion. (2) For the transgression of a land many *are* the princes thereof: but [6] by a man of understanding *and* knowledge the state *thereof* shall be prolonged. (3) A poor man that oppresseth the poor *is like* a sweeping rain [7] which leaveth no food. (4) They that forsake the law praise the wicked: but such as keep the law contend with them. (5) Evil men understand not judgment: but they that seek the LORD understand all *things*.

---

1 Heb., *not.*
a Eccles. 1. 8.
b ch. 17. 3.
2 Heb., *set thy heart.*
3 Heb., *strength.*
4 Heb., *to generation and generation.*
5 Heb., *life.*
c Lev. 26. 36.
6 Or, *by men of understanding and wisdom shall they likewise be prolonged.*
7 Heb., *without food.*

---

(19) **So the heart of man** (answereth) **to man.**—What is in our own hearts we find in others also. Whatever are the distinguishing features of our own characters we discover and elicit the same in others. The merciful, the generous, the devout, the pure, recognise the same qualities in others, and themselves feel and receive sympathy from such persons. So the evil, too, find themselves in harmony with those of like disposition.

(20) **Hell and destruction.**—See above on xv. 11.

The eyes of man are never satisfied.—Comp. Eccles. i. 8, iv. 8. God would thus teach us that in Himself only can man find complete satisfaction. (Comp. Ps. xxxvi. 8, 9; 1 Cor. ii. 9.)

(21) **So is a man to his praise**—*i.e.*, as the fining-pot and furnace test the metals put into them, so does that on which a man prides or boasts himself. Observe what this is—*e.g.*, wealth, or show, or popularity, or duty—and you will see what sort of a man he is. Or it may mean, praise—*i.e.*, popularity, is as great a trial to a man as the fining-pot to silver; he must be of good metal if he comes unhurt out of this. Or, again, it may signify, let a man test his praise—*i.e.*, examine by whom and for what he is praised, and be sure it is genuine and well deserved.

(22) **Though thou shouldest bray** (*i.e.*, pound) **a fool** (a self-willed, headstrong person) **in a mortar among wheat with a pestle.**—This would separate completely the husks from the wheat; but obstinacy has become a part of such a man's nature, and cannot be got rid of even by such violent measures.

(23) **Be thou diligent to know the state of thy herds . . .**—In the last five verses of this chapter the peace and security of the pastoral life are described as being far superior to the uncertainty attending other sources of wealth and the regal power. For the spiritual sense of this passage comp. 1 Pet. v. 2—4.

(24) **For riches are not for ever.**—Comp. chap. xxiii. 5. So it is well to have a sure source of income, like husbandry or cattle-feeding, upon which to fall back.

(25) **The hay appeareth.**—Or perhaps better, *is gone.* The quiet succession of the crops and seasons is here described.

Herbs of the mountains—*i.e.*, pasturage.

(26) **And the goats are the price of the field**—*i.e.*, you can purchase a field from the profit of your goats.

(27) **For the maintenance for thy maidens,** who tend the cattle.

XXVIII.

(1) **The wicked flee when no man pursueth.**—Comp. the curse pronounced upon Israel for disobedience (Lev. xxvi. 17, 36).

The righteous are bold as a lion.—Comp. Lev. xxvi. 8; 1 Sam. xvii. 32, *sqq.*; Ps. xci. 1, *sqq.*

(2) **For the transgression of a land many are the princes thereof.**—Comp. 1 Kings xv. 27, *sqq.*, and indeed the whole history of the kingdom of Israel as compared with the regular succession of the family of David in accordance with the promise of Ps. lxxxix. 33.

The state thereof shall be prolonged—*i.e.*, its settled condition. Or it may signify "right" (*i.e.*, authority) "continues."

(3) **A poor man that oppresseth the poor.**—If the recollection of his own former troubles has not softened his heart towards his poor neighbours, he will be rendered more callous to their sufferings.

Is like a sweeping rain which leaveth no food.—That sweeps away grain and soil, instead of bringing plenty with it.

(4) **They that forsake the law praise the wicked.**—The mark of extreme wickedness. (Comp. Rom. i. 32.)

But such as keep the law contend with them.—Just as the sight of ill-doing was the one thing which roused our Lord to wrath, while insults and wrongs offered to Himself were passed by unnoticed.

(5) **Evil men understand not judgment.**—Or, *what is right.* For God reveals Himself only to those who fear Him (Ps. xxv. 14, comp. 1 Cor. ii. 11; 1 John ii. 20); they, by following the light they have, are "guided into all truth" (John xvi. 13); the evil, by continually shutting their eyes to the light, at last cannot see it, even if they would (John xii. 39, *sqq.*).

(6) ᵃ Better *is* the poor that walketh in his uprightness, than *he that is* perverse *in his* ways, though *he be* rich. (7) ᵇ Whoso keepeth the law *is* a wise son: but he that ¹is a companion of riotous *men* shameth his father. (8) ᶜ He that by usury and ²unjust gain increaseth his substance, he shall gather it for him that will pity the poor. (9) He that turneth away his ear from hearing the law, even his prayer *shall be* abomination. (10) ᵈ Whoso causeth the righteous to go astray in an evil way, he shall fall himself into his own pit: but the upright shall have good *things* in possession. (11) The rich man *is* wise ³in his own conceit; but the poor that hath understanding searcheth him out. (12) ᵉ When righteous *men* do rejoice, *there is* great glory: but when the wicked rise, a man is ⁴hidden. (13) ᶠ He that covereth his sins shall not prosper: but whoso confesseth and forsaketh *them* shall have mercy. (14) Happy *is* the man that feareth alway: ᵍ but he that hardeneth his heart shall fall into mischief. (15) *As* a roaring lion, and a ranging bear; *so is* a wicked ruler over the poor people. (16) The prince that wanteth understanding *is* also a great oppressor: *but* he that hateth covetousness shall prolong *his* days. (17) ʰ A man that doeth violence to the blood of *any* person shall flee to the pit; let no man stay him. (18) ⁱ Whoso walketh uprightly shall be saved: but *he that is* perverse *in his* ways shall fall at once. (19) ʲ He that tilleth his land shall have plenty of bread: but he that followeth after vain *persons* shall have poverty enough. (20) A faithful man shall abound with blessings: ᵏ but he that maketh haste to be rich shall not be ⁵innocent. (21) ˡ To have respect of persons *is* not good: for, for a piece of bread *that* man will transgress. (22) ⁶ He that hasteth to be rich *hath*

a ch. 19. 1.
b ch. 29. 3.
1 Or, *feedeth gluttons.*
c ch. 13. 22; Eccles. 2. 26.
2 Heb., *by increase.*
d ch. 21. 27.
3 Heb., *in his eyes.*
e ch. 11. 10; ver. 28; Eccles. 10. 6.
4 Or, *sought for.*
f Ps. 32. 5; 1 John 1. 9, 10.
g Rom. 11. 20.
h Gen. 9. 6; Ex. 21. 14.
i ch. 10. 25.
j ch. 12. 11.
k ch. 13. 11, & 23. 4; 1 Tim. 6. 9.
5 Or, *unpunished.*
l ch. 18. 5, & 24. 23.
6 Or, *He that hath an evil eye hasteth to be rich.* Ver. 20.

---

(6) **Better is the poor that walketh . . .**—A variation of chap. xix. 1.

Perverse in his ways.—According to the pointing of the text the words signify, "perverse in two ways." That is, the sinner tries to "go two ways" (Ecclus. ii. 12); to follow his own way without entirely deserting God's; to "serve God and mammon;" he is "double-minded" (James i. 8), instead of setting before himself God's will as the guide of his life.

(8) **He that by usury . . . increaseth his substance.**—See above on chap. vi. 1.

He shall gather it for him that will pity the poor.—The "pound" is taken from him who knows not how to use it (Luke xix. 24), and given to one who does. (Comp. 1 Sam. xv. 28.)

(9) **Even his prayer shall be abomination.**—See above on chap. xv. 8.

(10) **He shall fall himself into his own pit.**—See above on chap. xxvi. 27.

(11) **The rich man is wise in his own conceit.**—For the blinding effect of wealth comp. Rev. iii. 17.

(12) **When righteous men do rejoice** — *i.e.*, prosper, or triumph.

There is great glory.—Men rejoice, and array themselves in their gayest attire.

A man is hidden.—Literally, *is sought for.* They hide themselves for fear (comp. verse 28), and must be sought for, in order to be found.

(13) **He that covereth his sins.**—As Adam and Eve did, when they had transgressed (1 Gen. iii. 8), as David did to his own loss (Ps. xxxii. 3).

Whoso confesseth and forsaketh them shall have mercy, and be at once completely forgiven; though he must still suffer the punishment due for his offences (2 Sam. xii. 14, *sqq.*), and will, for having yielded to temptation, be the less able to resist it when next assailed by it.

(14) **Happy is the man that feareth alway** lest he should fall, and so, distrusting himself, seeks heavenly aid (Phil. ii. 12).

He that hardeneth his heart.—(Comp. Exod. viii. 15, *sqq.*)

Shall fall into mischief.—As he will have lost the guidance and protection of God.

(15) **A ranging bear**—*i.e.*, wandering hungrily in great want of food.

Over the poor people—*i.e.*, a people too weak to resist him, over whom he can tyrannise without fear.

(16) **A prince that wanteth understanding is also a great oppressor.**—Thereby losing the love of his people, and at the same time impoverishing them; thus killing the goose that laid the golden eggs. He also by his misdeeds draws down upon himself God's anger in the shape of an early death. Comp. the woe pronounced upon Jehoiakim (Jer. xxii. 13, *sqq.*).

(17) **A man that doeth violence to the blood of any person.**—Rather, *that is burdened with his blood*, has wilfully murdered any one.

Shall flee to the pit.—Fulfilling the curse of Gen. ix. 6.

Let no man stay him—*i.e.*, attempt to rescue him from the punishment he has deserved.

(18) **He that is perverse in his ways.**—Literally, *two ways.* (Comp. note on verse 6.)

At once—*i.e.*, all of a sudden, without warning.

(19) **He that tilleth his land shall have plenty of bread.**—The curse of Gen. iii. 17—19 being, in God's mercy, turned into a blessing.

(20) **A faithful man,** who is true to God and man, "shall abound with blessings" from God and man. Comp. Job's description of his own blameless life and the blessings attending it (Job xxix.).

(21) **For, for a piece of bread.**—A thing proverbially of little value. (Comp. Ezek. xiii. 19.)

That man will transgress.—So degrading is the habit of servility.

(22) **Hath an evil eye.**—Envies others their prosperity, and keeps all he has for himself.

And considereth not that poverty shall come upon him.—For it is "the liberal soul" that

an evil eye, and considereth not that poverty shall come upon him. (23) *a* He that rebuketh a man afterwards shall find more favour than he that flattereth with the tongue. (24) Whoso robbeth his father or his mother, and saith, It is no transgression; the same is the companion of [1] a destroyer. (25) *b* He that is of a proud heart stirreth up strife: but he that putteth his trust in the LORD shall be made fat. (26) He that trusteth in his own heart is a fool: but whoso walketh wisely, he shall be delivered. (27) *c* He that giveth unto the poor shall not lack: but he that hideth his eyes shall have many a curse. (28) *d* When the wicked rise, men hide themselves: but when they perish, the righteous increase.

CHAPTER XXIX.—(1)[2] He, that being often reproved hardeneth *his* neck, shall suddenly be destroyed, and that without remedy. (2) *e* When the righteous are [3] in authority, the people rejoice: but when the wicked beareth rule, the people mourn. (3) *f* Whoso loveth wisdom rejoiceth his father: *g* but he that keepeth company with harlots spendeth *his* substance. (4) The king by judgment establisheth the land: but [4] he that receiveth gifts overthroweth it. (5) A man that flattereth his neighbour spreadeth a net for his feet. (6) In the transgression of an evil man *there is* a snare: but the righteous doth sing and rejoice. (7) *h* The righteous considereth the cause of the poor: *but* the wicked regardeth not to know *it.* (8) Scornful men [5] bring a city into a snare: but wise *men* turn away wrath. (9) *If* a wise man contendeth with a foolish man, whether he rage or laugh, *there is* no rest. (10) [6] The bloodthirsty hate

a ch. 27. 6.
1 Heb., *a man destroying.*
b ch. 15. 10.
c Deut. 15. 7, &c.; ch. 22. 9.
d ver. 12; ch. 29. 2.
2 Heb., *A man of reproofs.*
e ch. 11. 10, & 28. 28; Eccles. 10. 5.
3 Or, *increased.*
f ch. 10. 1 & 15. 20, & 27. 11.
g ch. 5 5, & 28. 7; Luke 15. 13.
4 Heb., *a man of oblations.*
h Job 29. 16.
5 Or, *set a city on fire.*
6 Heb., *Men of blood.*

"shall be made fat" (chap. xi. 25), not such as he, who can get no blessing from God.

(23) **He that rebuketh a man, afterwards shall find more favour . . .**—*i.e.*, when the man reproved comes to his senses, and finds how true a friend the reprover has been to him. Or, the words may perhaps mean, He that rebuketh a man (that is going) backwards. (Compare Jer. vii. 24, and Jas. v. 20.)

(24) **It is no transgression.**—Because all would in time come to him.

The companion of a destroyer.—Comp. chap. xviii. 9. Though the deed may be done secretly, yet he is no better than one who by open violence and wrong assails his neighbour.

(25) **He that is of a proud heart.**—Who thinks much of himself, "stirreth up strife" by his struggles with others for pre-eminence, and mostly gains only vexation and disappointment for his trouble; "but he that putteth his trust in the Lord shall be made fat," being richly rewarded with that "peace which passeth all understanding."

(26) **He that trusteth in his own heart,** is confident in his own wisdom (comp. 1 Cor. iii. 18, *sqq.*); he will perish in his folly.

But whoso walketh wisely.—Literally, *in wisdom,* which begins with the "fear of the Lord" (chap. ix. 10), "shall be delivered" from the trouble into which the "fool" is brought by his self-confidence.

(27) **He that giveth unto the poor shall not lack.**—See above on chap. xi. 24.

Shall have many a curse.—With this comp. Ecclus. iv. 5, 6.

XXIX.

(1) **Hardeneth his neck.**—And will not bear the "easy yoke" of God. (Comp. Matt. xi. 29, 30.)

Shall suddenly be destroyed.—Literally, *shattered,* like a potter's vessel that cannot be mended (Jer. xix. 11; Isa. xxx. 14).

And that without remedy.—For what more can be done for him, if he has despised God's warnings? (Comp. Heb. vi. 4, *sqq.*)

(3) **Whoso loveth wisdom . . .**—This verse is illustrated by the parable of the prodigal son (see Luke xv.).

(4) **By judgment.**—Upright decisions.

He that receiveth gifts.—To pervert justice (chap. xv. 27).

(6) **In the transgression of an evil man there is a snare.**—For he knows not how by repentance to escape God's wrath.

But the righteous doth sing and rejoice. —Being assured of God's mercy to those who repent, he rejoices because his conscience is clear, and the "peace of God" (Phil. iv. 7) keeps his heart.

(7) **The wicked regardeth not to know it.**— Literally, *understandeth not knowledge;* he does not know nor care to know anything about his poorer neighbour's affairs, so as to be able to help him. He cares as little about him as did Dives about Lazarus, though he saw him each time he went out of his own door.

(8) **Scornful men.**—See above on chap. i. 22.

Bring a city into a snare.—Rather, *excite the passions of;* literally, *fan,* as a flame.

Wise men turn away wrath.—By their gentle counsels.

(9) **Whether he rage or laugh**—*i.e.*, whether the wise man treat him with sternness or good temper, yet "there is no rest," the fool will not cease from his folly; or, the sense may be, "the fool rages and laughs;" he will not listen quietly to argument, by which he might be brought to wisdom, but is either violent or supercilious.

(10) **The bloodthirsty hate the upright.**—Or, *perfect man.* "for what fellowship hath righteousness with unrighteousness" (2 Cor. vi. 14); the life of the perfect man is a continual reproach to them.

But the just (or upright) seek his soul—*i.e.* care for the life of the perfect; their uprightness shows itself in active help-giving.

the upright: but the just seek his soul. ⁽¹¹⁾ A fool uttereth all his mind: but a wise man keepeth it in till afterwards. ⁽¹²⁾ If a ruler hearken to lies, all his servants are wicked. ⁽¹³⁾ ^a The poor and ¹ the deceitful man meet together: the LORD lighteneth both their eyes. ⁽¹⁴⁾ ^b The king that faithfully judgeth the poor, his throne shall be established for ever. ⁽¹⁵⁾ ^c The rod and reproof give wisdom: but ^d a child left to himself bringeth his mother to shame. ⁽¹⁶⁾ When the wicked are multiplied, transgression increaseth: ^e but the righteous shall see their fall. ⁽¹⁷⁾ ^fCorrect thy son, and he shall give thee rest; yea, he shall give delight unto thy soul. ⁽¹⁸⁾ Where there is no vision, the people ² perish: but he that keepeth the law, happy is he. ⁽¹⁹⁾ A servant will not be corrected by words: for though he understand he will not answer. ⁽²⁰⁾ Seest thou a man that is hasty ³ in his words? There is more hope of a fool than of him. ⁽²¹⁾ He that delicately bringeth up his servant from a child shall have him become his son at the length. ⁽²²⁾ ^gAn angry man stirreth up strife, and a furious man aboundeth in transgression. ⁽²³⁾ ^h A man's pride shall bring him low: but honour shall uphold the humble in spirit. ⁽²⁴⁾ Whoso is partner with a thief hateth his own soul: he heareth cursing, and bewrayeth it not. ⁽²⁵⁾ The fear of man bringeth a snare: but whoso putteth his trust in the LORD ⁴ shall be safe. ⁽²⁶⁾ ⁱ Many seek ⁵ the ruler's favour; but every man's judgment cometh from the LORD. ⁽²⁷⁾ An unjust man is an abomination to the just: and he that is upright in the way is abomination to the wicked.

a ch. 22. 2.
1 Or, the usurer.
b ch. 20. 28.
c ver. 17.
d ch. 10. 1, & 17. 21, 25.
e Ps. 37. 36 & 58. 10, & 91. 8.
f ch. 13. 24 & 22. 15, & 23. 13, 14.
2 Or, is made naked.
3 Or, in his matters?
g ch. 15. 18, & 26. 21.
h Job 22. 29; ch. 15. 33, & 18. 12; Matt. 23. 12; Luke 14. 11.
4 Heb., shall be set on high.
i ch. 19. 6.
5 Heb., the face of a ruler.

⁽¹¹⁾ **The fool** (khesil, chap. i. 22) **uttereth all his mind.**—Or, pours out all his wrath; but a wise man keepeth it in till afterwards, or keepeth it back.

⁽¹²⁾ **If a ruler hearken to lies, all his servants are wicked.**—If a ruler shows that he likes adulation and falsehood rather than unpleasant truths, his attendants will provide him with what he wishes. (Comp. Ecclus. x. 2.) So Jeremiah complains (chap. v. 31) that prophets, priests, and people were all wilfully deceiving each other.

⁽¹³⁾ **The poor and the deceitful man** (rather, oppressor) **meet together.**—A variation of chap. xxii. 2, on which see note.

The Lord lighteneth both their eyes.—Enlightens the eyes of both with the light of life (Ps. xiii. 4). To Him each owes life, so the one may remember that life with its sorrows will have an end, and the other, that He will take stern vengeance for oppression.

⁽¹⁴⁾ **His throne shall be established for ever.**—Comp. the promise made to Judah (Jer. xxii. 3, 4).

⁽¹⁵⁾ **A child left to himself.**—Allowed to wander unchecked as the wild ass (Job xxxix. 5).

Bringeth his mother to shame.—Whose foolish indulgence has ruined him.

⁽¹⁶⁾ **But the righteous shall see their fall** with joy (Ps. liv. 7), having long expected it (ibid. lxxiii. 18, sqq.).

⁽¹⁸⁾ **Where there is no vision.**—No revelation of God's will (Isa. i. 1), when God teaches none by His Spirit that they may instruct others. So it was in the evil days of Eli (1 Sam. iii. 1), and Asa (2 Chron. xv. 3).

The people perish.—Or, run wild. (Comp. Hosea iv. 6.)

But he that keepeth the law.—The teaching of those whom God has instructed. (Comp. Isa. i. 10.)

⁽¹⁹⁾ **A servant will not be corrected with words.**—A slave must be corrected by sterner means; it is only fear of punishment which will move him; "for though he understand, he will not answer," will not reply to your call, or render obedience to your command. The willing obedience of a son, and the grudging obedience of a slave, are contrasted in Rom. viii. 15.

⁽²⁰⁾ **There is more hope of a fool** (khesil) **than of him.**—The fool is a dull, self-satisfied person, but may learn better; the man who is hasty and ill-advised in his words has a harder task before him in governing his tongue. (Comp. James iii. 2 sqq.)

⁽²¹⁾ **Shall have him become his son at the last.**—Confidential slaves sometimes rose to be the heirs of their master's property. (See above on chap. xvii. 2.) But here the warning seems to be rather against spoiling a slave by over-indulgence, lest he at the last forget his position, just as old and petted servants are apt to become somewhat dictatorial.

⁽²²⁾ **Aboundeth in transgression.**—For what will he not say and do when overcome by anger?

⁽²³⁾ **Honour shall uphold the lowly in spirit.**—Rather, the lowly in spirit shall lay hold upon honour. (Comp. chap. xviii. 12.)

⁽²⁴⁾ **Hateth his own soul.**—See above on chap. i. 19.

He heareth cursing.—Rather, the oath or adjuration of the judge that anyone cognisant of the theft shall give information with regard to it. He hears and remains silent, and thus becoming the accomplice of the thief, he shares his punishment.

⁽²⁵⁾ **The fear of man bringeth a snare.**—Even, it may be, the loss of eternal life. (Comp. Matt. x. 28; John xii. 25.)

⁽²⁶⁾ **Many seek the ruler's favour.**—And to be advanced by him; but his approval is of little value, for "every man's judgment cometh from the Lord;" it is He who really decides each man's worth. (Comp. 1 Sam. xvi. 7; 1 Cor. iv. 5.)

CHAPTER XXX.—(1) The words of Agur the son of Jakeh, *even* the prophecy: the man spake unto Ithiel, even unto Ithiel and Ucal, (2) Surely I *am* more brutish than *any* man, and have not the understanding of a man. (3) I neither learned wisdom, nor ¹have the knowledge of the holy.

(4) ᵃWho hath ascended up into heaven, or descended?ᵇ who hath gathered the wind in his fists? who hath bound the waters in a garment? who hath established all the ends of the earth? what *is* his name, and what *is* his son's name, if thou canst tell?

(5) ᶜEvery word of God *is* ²pure: he *is* a shield unto them that put their trust in him. (6) ᵈAdd thou not unto his words, lest he reprove thee, and thou be found a liar.

(7) Two *things* have I required of thee; ³deny me *them* not before I die: (8) remove far from me vanity and lies: give me neither poverty nor riches; ᵉfeed me

¹ Heb., *know.*
ᵃ John 3. 13.
ᵇ Job 38. 4; Ps. 104. 3; Isa. 40. 12.
ᶜ Ps. 12. 6 & 18. 30, & 19. 8 & 119. 140.
² Heb., *purified.*
ᵈ Deut. 4. 2 & 12. 32; Rev. 22. 18, 19.
³ Heb., *withhold not from me.*
ᵉ Matt. 6. 11.

XXX.

8. THE PROVERBS OF SOLOMON END HERE. THE REST OF THE BOOK IS COMPOSED OF THREE APPENDICES: (*a*) THE WORDS OF AGUR; (*b*) THE WORDS OF KING LEMUEL; AND (*c*) THE PRAISE OF A GOOD WIFE (chaps. xxx., xxxi.).

APPENDIX (*a*).

(1) **The words of Agur the son of Jakeh, even the prophecy.**—Jewish interpreters have seen in these titles (but apparently without a shadow of reason) a designation of Solomon himself, the "convener" and instructor of assemblies (Eccles. i. 1; xii. 11), son of the "obedient" man after God's own heart. But they in all probability belong to some otherwise unknown sage, whose utterances were thought not unworthy of being joined with those of the wise King of Israel himself. In support of this view 1 Kings iv. 30 may be adduced as a proof of the estimation in which the wisdom of foreign nations was at this time held. The book of Job also, which possibly now was added to the canon of Scripture, is certainly of foreign, probably of Arabian, origin. Some light may be thrown upon the nationality of Agur by the words translated in the Authorised version "the prophecy" (*massâ*). This is the term constantly employed to express the "utterance," or, more probably, the message which a prophet "bore" to his hearers, often one of gloomy import (Isa. xiii. 1, etc.). But the term is not very appropriate to the contents of this chapter, nor to the "words of King Lemuel," in chap. xxxi., and the expression, "the prophecy," standing quite alone, with no other words to qualify it, is very singular. For these reasons it has been proposed to translate the beginning of the verse thus: "The words of Agur the son of Jakeh the Massan," *i.e.*, a descendant of the Massa mentioned in Gen. xxv. 14 as a son of Ishmael. This would place his home probably in North Arabia, and Lemuel would be king of the same tribe.

The man spake.—The word translated "spake" is most frequently used of the revelation of God to prophets, rarely (Num. xxiv. 3 and 2 Sam. xxiii. 1) of the utterances of inspired prophets; never of the words of ordinary men.

Unto Ithiel, even unto Ithiel and Ucal.—These most probably were disciples of his. As their names may mean "God with me," and "I am strong," a fanciful delineation of their characters, in the style of the "Pilgrim's Progress," has been attempted by some writers. And a mystical interpretation of them, "You must have God with you, if you are to be strong," may be found in Bishop Wordsworth's Commentary. It has been proposed also, as is possible with a slight change in the pointing, to translate these words thus: "I am weary, O God, I am weary, and am weak," or, "have made an end," and to make them an introduction to verse 2, which supplies the reason for this weariness, "For I am more brutish," etc. Thus is described, it has been thought, the sinking at heart of one who has sought after God, and the more he has realised the divine excellence, has become the more conscious of his own nothingness. But this rendering is unnecessary, as the Authorised version gives a good sense.

(2) **Surely I am more brutish than any man.**—Rather, *than that I can be called a man*, one "formed in the image of God." (Comp. Ps. lxxiii. 22.)

(3) **The knowledge of the holy**—*i.e.*, the Holy One, God. (Comp. chap. ix. 10.)

(4) **Who hath ascended up into heaven** . . .—The reason of Agur's sadness is here declared. he feels himself far off from possessing anything that may be called knowledge of God or of His works. (Comp. Gal. iv. 9; 1 Cor. xiii. 12.) The questions in this verse are intended to bring out the nothingness of man as compared with the might of the Creator of the Universe; they resemble Job xxxviii.—xli., and Isa. xl. 12 *sqq.*

Who hath bound the waters in a garment?—Stretching out the clouds as a "curtain" (Ps. civ. 2; Isa. xl. 22), to keep the rain from falling upon the earth. (Comp. Job xxvi. 8.)

What is his name?—We may call Him the Self-existing (Jehovah), Powerful (Shaddai), Strong (El), Awful (Eloah) Being; we may describe Him as merciful, gracious, etc. (Exod. xxxiv. 5 *sqq.*), but no words will describe Him adequately, for not till the next life shall we see Him as He is (1 John iii. 2), and He has been pleased to reveal Himself only partially to us.

What is his son's name?—See the description of wisdom in chap. viii. 22 *sqq.*, and the notes there.

(5) **Every word of God is pure.**—Comp. Ps. xix., where first (verses 1—6) the glories of God as revealed in nature are described, and then (verse 7 *sqq.*) the excellence of the revelation of Himself in His word is extolled. Every word of God is "pure," *i.e.*, tested and proved in the furnace of experience; *e.g.*, His promise to be a "shield" (Gen. xv. 1) to those that trust in Him. (Comp. Ps. xviii. 30.)

(6) **Lest he reprove thee.**—Or, *convict thee of thy falsehood.*

(7) **Two things have I required of thee.**—The commencement of a series of numerical proverbs. (See above on chap. vi. 16.)

Before I die—*i.e.*, while life lasts.

(8) **Vanity.**—Falsehood either towards God or man.

Food convenient for me.—Literally, *bread of my portion*, such as is apportioned to me as suitable by the care of the heavenly Father. Comp. "daily

with food ¹ convenient for me: ⁽⁹⁾ ᵃlest I be full, and ² deny *thee*, and say, Who *is* the LORD? or lest I be poor, and steal, and take the name of my God *in vain*.

⁽¹⁰⁾ ³ Accuse not a servant unto his master, lest he curse thee, and thou be found guilty.

⁽¹¹⁾ *There is* a generation *that* curseth their father, and doth not bless their mother. ⁽¹²⁾ *There is* a generation *that* are pure in their own eyes, and *yet* is not washed from their filthiness. ⁽¹³⁾ *There is* a generation, O how ᵇlofty are their eyes! and their eyelids are lifted up. ⁽¹⁴⁾ ᶜ *There is* a generation, whose teeth *are as* swords, and their jaw teeth *as* knives, to devour the poor from off the earth, and the needy from *among* men.

⁽¹⁵⁾ The horseleach hath two daughters, *crying*, Give, give. There are three *things that* are never satisfied, *yea*, four *things* say not, ⁴ *It is* enough: ⁽¹⁶⁾ the grave; and the barren womb; the earth *that* is not filled with water; and the fire *that* saith not, It *is* enough.

⁽¹⁷⁾ The eye *that* mocketh at *his* father, and despiseth to obey *his* mother, the ravens of ⁵ the valley shall pick it out, and the young eagles shall eat it.

⁽¹⁸⁾ There be three *things which* are too wonderful for me, yea, four which I know not: ⁽¹⁹⁾ the way of an eagle in the air; the way of a serpent upon a rock; the way of a ship in the ⁶ midst of the sea; and the way of a man with a maid. ⁽²⁰⁾ Such *is* the way of an adulterous woman; she eateth, and wipeth her mouth, and saith, I have done no wickedness.

⁽²¹⁾ For three *things* the earth is disquieted, and for four *which* it cannot bear: ⁽²²⁾ ᵈ for a servant when he reigneth; and a fool when he is filled with meat; ⁽²³⁾ for an odious *woman* when she is married; and an handmaid that is heir to her mistress.

⁽²⁴⁾ There be four *things which* are little upon the earth, but they *are* ⁷ exceeding wise: ⁽²⁵⁾ ᵉ the ants *are* a people not strong, yet they prepare their meat in the summer; ⁽²⁶⁾ the conies *are but* a feeble folk, yet make they their houses in the rocks; ⁽²⁷⁾ the locusts have no king, yet go they forth all of them ⁸ by bands; ⁽²⁸⁾ the spider taketh hold with her hands, and is in kings' palaces.

⁽²⁹⁾ There be three *things* which go well, yea, four are comely in going: ⁽³⁰⁾ a lion

---

Notes:
1 Heb., *of my allowance.*
a Deut. 32. 15.
2 Heb., *belie thee.*
3 Heb., *Hurt not with thy tongue.*
b ch. 6. 17.
c Job 29. 17. Ps. 52. 2, & 57. 4.
4 Heb., *Wealth.*
5 Or, *the brook.*
6 Heb., *heart.*
d ch. 19. 10.
7 Heb., *wise, made wise.*
e ch. 6. 6.
8 Heb., *gathered together.*

---

bread" (Matt. vi. 11) in the sense of "proper for our sustenance."

⁽⁹⁾ **Lest I be full, and deny thee.**—For "pride and fulness of bread" were among the sins which brought destruction on Sodom (Ezek. xvi. 49). (Comp. Job xxi. 14, 15.)

And take the name of my God in vain.—Literally, *handle it roughly, irreverently*; particularly in finding fault with His providence.

⁽¹⁰⁾ **Accuse not a servant**—*i.e.*, a slave, thus making his already hard life still more intolerable.

And thou be found guilty before God of having wronged him, and so have to bear the punishment.

⁽¹¹⁾ **There is a generation . . .**—The words "there is" are not in the Hebrew, so it is left in doubt what is the predicate of these four evil "generations," whether Agur means by them to describe the men of his own time, or to say that such are unbearable. (Comp. verse 21.) The same characters are to be found in the description of men of the "last days" (2 Tim. iii. 1 *sqq*).

⁽¹⁵⁾ **The horseleach hath two daughters, crying, Give, give.**—The word "crying" is not in the Hebrew. The leech is here chosen as the emblem of insatiable greed; if it could speak, its "daughters," *i.e.*, the words it would utter, would be "Give, give." So it forms an introduction to the quartette of "insatiable things" which follow.

⁽¹⁶⁾ **The grave.**—See above, on chap. xv. 11, where it is translated "hell."

⁽¹⁷⁾ **The ravens of the valley shall pick it out**—*i.e.*, the rebellious son shall die of a "grievous death" (Jer. xvi. 4). The propensity of ravens to attack the eyes is well known.

⁽¹⁸⁾ **Too wonderful for me.**—The wonder in Agur's eyes seems to be that none of the four leave any trace behind them. (Comp. Wisd. v. 10 *sqq*.) For a spiritual interpretation of these and other passages in this chapter, comp. Bishop Wordsworth's Commentary.

⁽²⁰⁾ **Such is the way of an adulterous woman.**—As there is no proof of her guilt, she flatly denies it.

⁽²²⁾ **For a servant when he reigneth.**—The mischief done by Oriental favourites at court, who often began life as slaves, was proverbial.

A fool (*nābhāl*).—See above, on chap. xvii. 7. It is only when he has to work hard for his living that he will behave himself decently; if he gets a little money, it will soon be wasted in idleness and self-indulgence.

⁽²³⁾ **For an odious woman when she is married.**—She pays off, with interest, the slights which she had formerly to endure from her married friends.

An handmaid that is heir to her mistress, and who is nervously anxious to preserve her newly-acquired dignity.

⁽²⁶⁾ **The conies are but a feeble folk,** being only about as big as a rabbit, with nails instead of claws, and weak teeth. Its Hebrew name (*shāphān*) signifies a "hider," from its habit of living in clefts of the rocks; its scientific name is *Hyrax Syriacus*. The translation "coney," *i.e.*, rabbit, is a mistake. In general appearance it resembles a guinea-pig or marmot.

⁽²⁸⁾ **The spider taketh hold with her hands.**—The lizard, rather than the spider, seems to be here intended. As each first line of these four verses is an expression of weakness, it has been proposed to trans-

which is strongest among beasts, and turneth not away for any; (31) a ¹ ² greyhound; an he goat also; and a king, against whom *there is* no rising up. (32) If thou hast done foolishly in lifting up thyself, or if thou hast thought evil, ᵃ *lay* thine hand upon thy mouth. (33) Surely the churning of milk bringeth forth butter, and the wringing of the nose bringeth forth blood: so the forcing of wrath bringeth forth strife.

CHAPTER XXXI.—(1) The words of king Lemuel, the prophecy that his mother taught him. (2) What, my son? and what, the son of my womb? and what, the son of my vows? (3) Give not thy strength unto women, nor thy ways to that which destroyeth kings. (4) *It is* not for kings, O Lemuel, *it is* not for kings to drink wine; nor for princes strong drink: (5) lest they drink, and forget the law, and ³ pervert the judgment ⁴ of any of the afflicted. (6) ᵇ Give strong drink unto him that is ready to perish, and wine unto those that be ⁵ of heavy hearts. (7) Let him drink, and forget his poverty, and remember his misery no more.

(8) Open thy mouth for the dumb in the cause of all ⁶ such as are appointed to destruction. (9) Open thy mouth, ᶜ judge righteously, and plead the cause of the poor and needy.

(10) ᵈ Who can find a virtuous woman?

---

1 Or, *horse.*
2 Heb., *girt in the loins.*
a Job 21. 5, & 40. 4.
3 Heb., *alter.*
4 Heb., *of all the sons of affliction.*
b Ps. 104. 15.
5 Heb., *bitter of soul.*
6 Heb., *the sons of destruction.*
c Lev. 19. 15; Deut. 1. 16.
d ch. 12. 4.

---

late thus: "The lizard thou canst catch with the hands, and yet," etc. (Comp. for this praise of wisdom, Eccles. ix. 14 *sqq.*)

(31) **A greyhound.**—It is very doubtful what animal is meant here as being "girt [*i.e.*, slender] in the loins." Several have been suggested, *e.g.*, the horse, zebra, cock; but the rendering of the Authorised Version is as probable as any.

A king, against whom there is no rising up.—Who marches with resistless force, trampling on his conquered foes. (Comp. the description of the march of the Assyrians, Isa. xxxvii. 24 *sqq.*; comp. also Isa. lxiii. 1 *sqq.* and Joel ii. 2 *sqq.*) It has been proposed to translate these words also as "a king with whom is [*i.e.*, followed by] his people," in much the same sense.

(32) **Lay thine hand upon thy mouth**—*i.e.*, be silent. Agur deprecates two things which may easily lead to a quarrel, arrogance and malice. He explains this in the next verse.

(33) **Surely the churning of milk bringeth forth butter . . . .**—The same word is used in the Hebrew for the three which appear in the Authorised Version, "churning," "wringing," and "forcing." The sense will be, "For (as) pressure on milk produces butter, and pressure on the nose produces blood, (so) pressure on wrath (violence towards a hot-tempered person) produces anger." (Comp. chap. xv. 1.)

XXXI.
APPENDIX (*b*).

(1) **The words of king Lemuel . . . .**—More probably this should be translated, "The words of Lemuel, king of Massâ." (See above on chap. xxx. 1.) "Lemuel," which most likely signifies (dedicated) "to God," has been, like Agur, supposed to be a designation of Solomon, but with no good reason.

The prophecy that his mother taught him.—Mothers were looked upon with great veneration in the East. (Comp. chap. i. 8, vi. 20.) The mothers of kings especially were treated with marked respect, receiving the title of "queen-mother." (Comp. 1 Kings ii. 19 and xv. 13.) This seems to be the reason why the mothers of Jewish kings are so constantly mentioned, *e.g.*, 1 Kings xiv. 31, xv. 2; 2 Kings xii. 1. At the present time the mother of the Khedive ranks before his principal wife.

(2) **What, my son?**—*i.e.*, what shall I say? The question, thrice repeated, shows her extreme anxiety to give good advice to this son, who was "tender, and only beloved in the sight of his mother."

The son of my vows.—Perhaps given, like Samuel, in answer to her prayers and vows.

(3) **Nor thy ways to that which destroyeth kings.**—A slight change in the punctuation will give a better sense, "to those that destroy kings," *i.e.*, women. Give not thy life to dissipation at their bidding. (Comp. chap. vi. 24, *sqq.*; 1 Kings xi. 1).

(4) **It is not for kings to drink wine.**—Another of the temptations of kings. (Comp. 1 Kings xvi. 9, xx. 16; Eccles. x. 17.) Perversion of justice as the result of revelry is also noted by Isaiah (chap. v. 22, 23). Comp. St. Paul's advice to "use this world so as not abusing," or rather "using it to the full" (1 Cor. vii. 31)

(6) **Give strong drink unto him that is ready to perish.**—For this is not waste, but an advantageous use of God's gift. (Comp. St. Paul's advice, 1 Tim. v. 23.) It was out of a merciful remembrance of this passage that the pious ladies of Jerusalem used to provide a medicated drink for criminals condemned to be crucified, in order to deaden their pain. This was offered to our Lord (Matt. xxvii. 34), but He would not drink it, as He wished to keep His mind clear to the last, and was willing to drink to the dregs the "cup which His Father had given Him."

(8) **Open thy mouth for the dumb.**—Who cannot from timidity or ignorance plead his own cause, and who would therefore be crushed by his antagonist.

Such as are appointed to destruction.—Certain to perish if left unaided. Comp. Job's account of his exertions for victims of high-handed oppression, an ever recurring evil under weak despotic governments (Job xxix. 12, *sqq.*).

APPENDIX (*c*).—THE PRAISE OF A GOOD WIFE.
(Chap. xxxi. 10, *sqq.*)

This is written in the form of an acrostic, the twenty-two verses composing it each commencing with a letter of the Hebrew alphabet. This may have been done, as in the case of several of the psalms, which are of a

for her price *is* far above rubies. ⁽¹¹⁾ The heart of her husband doth safely trust in her, so that he shall have no need of spoil. ⁽¹²⁾ She will do him good and not evil all the days of her life. ⁽¹³⁾ She seeketh wool, and flax, and worketh willingly with her hands. ⁽¹⁴⁾ She is like the merchants' ships; she bringeth her food from afar. ⁽¹⁵⁾ She riseth also while it is yet night, and giveth meat to her household, and a portion to her maidens. ⁽¹⁶⁾ She considereth a field, and ¹ buyeth it: with the fruit of her hands she planteth a vineyard. ⁽¹⁷⁾ She girdeth her loins with strength, and strengtheneth her arms. ⁽¹⁸⁾ ² She perceiveth that her merchandise *is* good: her candle goeth not out by night. ⁽¹⁹⁾ She layeth her hands to the spindle, and her hands hold the distaff. ⁽²⁰⁾ ³ She stretcheth out her hand to the poor; yea, she reacheth forth her hands to the needy. ⁽²¹⁾ She is not afraid of the snow for her household: for all her household *are* clothed with ⁴ scarlet. ⁽²²⁾ She maketh herself coverings of tapestry; her clothing *is* silk and purple. ⁽²³⁾ Her husband is known in the gates, when he sitteth among the elders of the land. ⁽²⁴⁾ She maketh fine linen, and selleth *it*: and delivereth girdles unto the merchant. ⁽²⁵⁾ Strength and honour *are* her clothing; and she shall rejoice in time to come. ⁽²⁶⁾ She openeth her mouth with wisdom; and in her tongue *is* the law of kindness. ⁽²⁷⁾ She looketh well to the ways of her household, and eateth not the bread of idleness. ⁽²⁸⁾ Her children arise up, and call her blessed; her husband *also*, and he praiseth her. ⁽²⁹⁾ Many daughters ⁵ have done virtuously, but thou excellest them all. ⁽³⁰⁾ Favour *is* deceitful, and beauty *is* vain: *but* a woman *that* feareth the LORD, she shall be praised. ⁽³¹⁾ Give her of the fruit of her hands; and let her own works praise her in the gates.

1 Heb., *taketh.*
2 Heb., *She tasteth.*
3 Heb., *She spreadeth.*
4 Or, *double garments.*
5 Or, *have gotten riches.*

---

didactic character (*e.g.*, xxv., xxxiv., xxxvii., cxix.), to render it more easy for committal to memory. By some writers the acrostic form has been supposed to argue a late date for the poem, but there is no evidence for this. One psalm, at all events, of which there seems no reason to doubt the Davidic authorship—the 9th—is cast in this form.

⁽¹⁰⁾ **Who can find a virtuous woman?**—Various mystical interpretations of the person here implied have been held at different times. She has been supposed to signify the Law, the Church, the Holy Spirit.

⁽¹¹⁾ **So that he shall have no need of spoil.**—Rather, *shall have no lack of gain.* His incomings constantly increase from the prudent care of his wife.

⁽¹³⁾ **And worketh willingly with her hands.**—Literally, *with the pleasure or willingness of her hands;* they, as it were, catch her willing spirit.

⁽¹⁴⁾ **She bringeth her food from afar.**—Looks for opportunities of buying cheaply at a distance from home, instead of paying a larger price on the spot.

⁽¹⁵⁾ **And giveth meat to her household, and a portion to her maidens.**—Gives out food for her household, and the allotted portion of provisions (comp. xxx. 8) or work (comp. Exod. v. 14) to her maidens.

⁽¹⁶⁾ **She considereth a field.**—Fixes upon a suitable one for purchase.

With the fruit of her hands.—With her savings she buys a vineyard and stocks it.

⁽²⁰⁾ **She stretcheth out her hand to the poor.**—Either in sympathy or with alms; "yea, she reacheth forth (both) her hands to the needy;" she is keenly alive to their sorrows, and pities them and aids them with all her power.

⁽²¹⁾ **She is not afraid of the snow.**—Not uncommon in winter-time in Palestine and the neighbouring countries. (Comp. 2 Sam. xxiii. 20; Ps. cxlvii. 16.)

All her household are clothed with scarlet, which by its very colour suggests warmth and comfort.

⁽²³⁾ **Her husband is known in the gates.**—See above on xxii. 22. Instead of being a hindrance to her husband's advancement, she furthers it. Her influence for good extends to him also. Having no domestic anxieties, he is set free to do his part in public life.

⁽²⁵⁾ **Strength and honour are her clothing.**—She never parts with them; they serve her, like clothing, for protection and ornament. (Comp. Ps. civ. 1.)

And she shall rejoice in time to come.—Rather, *smiles at the coming day*; does not fear the future.

⁽²⁶⁾ **She openeth her mouth with wisdom.**—She is not a mere household drudge, with no thought beyond providing food and clothing for her family. She cares for their higher interests, and knows how to guide them with her wisdom.

In her tongue is the law of kindness.—Kindness is the law by which she regulates all her words.

⁽²⁹⁾ **Many daughters**—*i.e.*, women (Gen. xxx. 13; Cant. vi. 9); a term of affection.

⁽³⁰⁾ **Favour is deceitful, and beauty is vain.**—Outward graces do not last; praise that will be real and enduring is for those only who fear the Lord, and, out of regard for Him, perform the duties of life as the "virtuous woman" here described.

⁽³¹⁾ **Give her of the fruit of her hands**—*i.e.*, honour her for her noble life, "and let her own works praise her in the gates;" let them be recounted when men meet together; the mere mention of them will be sufficient, as no words could add anything to her praise.

ECCLESIASTES: OR, THE PREACHER

INTRODUCTION
TO
ECCLESIASTES; OR, THE PREACHER

THE proofs have been given elsewhere that the collection of sacred writings which was held in reverence by the Jews of Palestine in the days of our Lord and His Apostles, consisted of twenty-two books, and that these included the Book of Ecclesiastes. The first preachers of Christianity appear to have been in complete agreement with their unconverted brethren as to the authority of their sacred books; and in point of fact, all the books of the Jewish Canon have always enjoyed unquestioned authority in the Christian Church. It is no disparagement to the authority of the Book of Ecclesiastes that no direct quotation from it is to be found in the New Testament. A few coincidences of thought or expression have been pointed out (for instance, Eccl. xi. 5 with John iii. 8, Eccl. ix. 10 with John ix. 4); but none of them is decisive enough to warrant our asserting with any confidence that the Old Testament passage was present to the mind of the New Testament writer. But there is no reason to imagine that any of the Apostles would have hesitated to appeal to the authority of any book of the Jewish Canon, if his subject had required such a reference.

In the Jewish schools there was controversy, about the end of the first century of our era, whether the Book of Ecclesiastes was one of those which "defile the hands;" that is to say, whether it was affected by certain ceremonial ordinances, devised in order to guard the sacred books from irreverent usage. We need not inquire what exact amount of authority might be conceded to the book by those who then placed it on a lower level than the rest; for the view which ultimately prevailed, recognised it as entitled to all the prerogatives of Canonical Scripture. It does not appear that the Solomonic authorship of the book was questioned in the course of these disputes. Thus in the Christian Church, Theodore of Mopsuestia, while accepting Solomon's authorship, supposed him to have written the book by human prudence, not Divine inspiration.

It is proper to mention that the place of the work in modern Hebrew Bibles is not the same as in English Bibles, where all the books ascribed to Solomon are placed together. In the Hebrew, after the Proverbs comes Job; then Song of Songs, Ruth, Lamentations, Ecclesiastes, and Esther. But the reason of this arrangement is that the last five books, called the five rolls, were written on separate rolls for use in synagogue worship on special festivals. They are arranged in the order in which these festivals occur, Ecclesiastes being fourth because the Feast of Tabernacles, on which it is read, is fourth in order. The Masoretic arrangement of these rolls was different; and in the oldest dated Hebrew MS. Ecclesiastes is third. It is very precarious to draw, as some have done, from this arrangement for liturgical purposes, a presumption against the acknowledgment of Solomon's authorship by the Jews. And, in fact, the order of our English Bibles may claim to be the older of the two, being the order both of the Septuagint and of the Talmud.

While we consider the canonical authority of the Book of Ecclesiastes as sufficiently guaranteed by the general sanction which the founders of the Christian Church gave to the Jewish Scriptures, we cannot find that any opinion as to the authorship of the book is entitled to claim apostolic authority. The book, as has been remarked, is not mentioned in the New Testament; and the ascription of canonical authority to a book determines nothing as to its authorship. Nothing was supposed to be known with certainty as to the authorship of some books, which, nevertheless, held an undisputed place in the Canon: for example, Joshua, Judges, Job.

In discussing the authorship of a book, internal evidence holds, relatively to external, a far higher place in the case of the Old than of the New Testament. In the latter case we have available the testimony of witnesses separated by a comparatively short interval from the time of the composition of the books. Thus when a question arises as to a various reading in the Apocalypse, Irenæus confirms the evidence of the best MSS. by an appeal to the testimony of persons who had seen the Apostle John. But the earliest witnesses from whom we can learn anything as to the composition of Old Testament books, are later by hundreds of years than the books of which they speak. Thus, though the belief that Solomon was the author of the Book of Ecclesiastes was for many centuries practically universal both among the Jews and in the Christian Church, yet the earliest period to which we can trace the belief is some centuries later than the age of Solomon; and the belief may easily have been generated by inference from the text itself, not by historical tradition. In the disputes concerning the Book of Ecclesiastes in the Jewish schools, which have been already mentioned, we cannot find that the topic of external evidence was employed on either side. The whole controversy turned on the contents of the book, concerning which we are as competent to form an opinion as were either of the opposing parties then. On the one side it was alleged that the book contained contradictory statements, and that it taught erroneous doctrine; on the other, explanations were given which were held to be satisfactory. It was pointed out that the book began and ended with words of the Law (chaps. i. 3 and xii. 13); and in particular, its statement as to the "conclusion of the whole matter," was regarded as removing all doubt as to the author's design.

Turning now to examine what we can learn of its authorship from the book itself, we find that the title runs, "The words of Kohéleth son of David, King in

ECCLESIASTES.

Jerusalem." We have here the difficulty that the name Kohéleth does not occur in the historical books as the name either of king or private person. If the words "son of David" be understood strictly, Solomon must be intended—the only one of David's sons who reigned in Jerusalem. If we were to suppose the words to have been used more loosely, we might think of any of the descendants of David who succeeded him on the throne; in particular, perhaps, of Manasseh, whose experience might well have made him feel the vanity of human life. But this latter view is supported by no authority, and the things attributed to Kohéleth agree too well with what is told of Solomon in the Book of Kings, to allow us to think that any one else is intended. Thus Kohéleth excels all his predecessors in wisdom (chap. i. 16; see 1 Kings iii. 12), and set in order many proverbs (chap. xii. 10; 1 Kings iv. 32). The description of his state (chap. ii.) corresponds with what is told of Solomon (1 Kings x.); while his unfavourable experience of women (chap. vii. 28) is what might be expected from Solomon (1 Kings xi.).

But if Solomon is intended, why is he called Kohéleth? This particular form is not found elsewhere in the Old Testament, but there are of frequent occurrence other forms of the same grammatical root, which have the sense of collecting or assembling. Thus it is this root which furnishes the ordinary name for the congregation or assembly of the children of Israel; while the corresponding verb is used of the gathering together of the congregation. These words are used in connection with Solomon (1 Kings viii.), where it is told (verses 1, 2) how Solomon "assembled" the children of Israel, and (verses 14, 22, 55, 65) how he blessed the "congregation." Accordingly, the LXX. translates Kohéleth by the name which we still use, "Ecclesiastes," which St. Jerome explains as one who gathers an assembly. It is less closely translated in our version "Preacher," or one who addresses an assembly; while the rendering which has been proposed, "debater in an assembly," is still more open to the objection that it imports a meaning not suggested by the word. According to our present Hebrew text, Kohéleth has in one place the article prefixed, indicating that it is not a proper name, but an official title. We accept the rendering of the LXX. as giving the best explanation of the word; and we reject the explanations: (*a*) that the word means a collector of sayings, for the Hebrew word is used of collecting persons, not things; (*b*) that it means the assembly itself, for all through the book the word is used as the name of a person; and, not to mention other explanations, (*c*) Renan's suggestion that the word Kohéleth has no meaning, and is only a mnemonic acrostic, formed, according to a custom of the later Jews, by putting together the first letters of the words of an unknown longer title.

The word Kohéleth, however, presents some grammatical anomalies. With one we need not trouble the English reader; but the most important is that the word is feminine in its form. In three places the verb which is in agreement is masculine; once, according to the present text, it is feminine, but so very slight a change of reading would bring this passage into conformity with the others, that we cannot feel sure that there is any real difference. A common explanation of the feminine form Kohéleth is that the speaker is Wisdom (in Hebrew a feminine noun) supposed to be incarnate in the person of Solomon. This interpretation, which connects the ideas of "wisdom" and "gathering together," has an attraction for the Christian reader when he remembers how one greater than Solomon, even the Wisdom of God, said, "How often would I have gathered thy children together." Yet the suggestion will not bear a close examination. In the Book of Proverbs, where Wisdom is introduced as speaking, no room is left for misunderstanding: here not the smallest hint is given that Wisdom is speaking, and on the contrary, several places are inconsistent with such a supposition. For instance, the speaker sets himself to "search and seek out wisdom," "turns himself to behold wisdom;" nay, when he said, "I will be wise," finds that "wisdom is far from him." We have no right to accuse the author of having failed to carry out a personification consistently, unless we first give some proof that he intended personification, and of such proof there is not a shadow.

We believe that no more recondite explanation of the use of the feminine form is to be looked for than that the usage of the language at the time permitted it. It is no uncommon thing that an abstract noun, though feminine in form, should come to be used as a noun appellative. In a modern language a man may have applied to him titles such as *majesté, grandeur, altesse,* with corresponding feminine pronouns. A similar use is found in Hebrew, especially in the later Hebrew. It is a feminine noun which denotes the office of governor borne by Nehemiah (Neh. xii. 26) and others; feminine names of form like Kohéleth—viz., Sophereth and Pochereth—occur in the lists (Ezra ii. 55, 57).

Having come to the conclusion that Kohéleth means Solomon, and that he is so called with special reference to that religious assembly of the people which he brought together and which he addressed, we have still to inquire whether the book purports to be written by Solomon. It certainly professes to record his words, but whether or not it professes that he himself is the writer is doubtful. The words of the Preacher appear to come to an end at chap. xii. 8, and then follows an epilogue in which he is spoken of in the third person. One possible explanation of this is that the book does not profess to have been written by Solomon, but only to contain the words of Solomon as recorded by another person, who in the epilogue speaks in his own name. Jewish tradition certainly refers to the time of Hezekiah not only the reduction of the Book of Proverbs to its present form (as stated in Prov. xxv. 1), but also in like manner the writing of the Book of Ecclesiastes.

Against the theory that Solomon himself was the writer the following arguments are urged: (*a*) Kohéleth says (chap. i. 12), "I was king over Israel in Jerusalem." We know Solomon was king till his death, therefore he who speaks of his reign in the past tense must be, not Solomon himself, but a later writer, who knew, moreover, that there were kings over Israel who did not reign in Jerusalem. That the tense used conveys to a Hebrew reader the impression that at the time of writing Solomon was king no longer, is evident from the Rabbinical legend which grew out of it. It was related that King Solomon, having displeased God, was deprived of the ring by which he ruled over the demons, whereupon Asmodeus their king assumed the form of Solomon and reigned in his place, while he himself was driven from door to door, and beaten by incredulous hearers to whom he told his story, and among whom he went about saying, "I am Kohéleth, who was king over Israel in Jerusalem." On the other hand, whatever the impression conveyed by the words, they cannot be absolutely inconsistent with Solomonic authorship; for even the writer of a fiction would not put into Solomon's mouth words which he could not

ECCLESIASTES.

have used. The tense used is the same as in the verbs which follow, "I gave my heart," "I communed with my own heart," &c. Solomon is speaking of his past; he is telling how he made trial what wealth and splendour could do for human happiness, and he properly uses the past tense in telling how when he made his experiment he had the advantage of being king. A similar argument against the Solomonic authorship is drawn from the comparison (chaps. i. 16, ii. 9) between Solomon and those who had reigned in Jerusalem before him; which admits of the reply that a later writer could not have used this language, since David was the only predecessor of Solomon whom the later Jews recognised as king, but that he himself might have had in his mind the Jebusite kings who had reigned in Jerusalem before its capture by David.

(b) Kohéleth speaks in the tone of a subject, not of a sovereign. Some passages of which this may be said can be paralleled by passages in the Book of Proverbs, but one class of passages is of a special character. Kohéleth complains (chap. iii. 16) that wickedness was in the place of judgment; (chap. iv. 6) he tells how, looking on the tears of the oppressed who had no comforter (for with their oppressors there was power), he deemed it better to be dead than to be alive; twice more (chaps. v. 8, vii. 7) he returns to the subject of the tyranny of the powerful and the corruption of the judges; he complains of the bad choice of rulers by the sovereign—"folly set in great dignity, and the rich sitting in low places." All is written in the tone of a man who looked on bad government as an infliction of Providence against which it was hopeless to contend, not of one who was personally responsible for the evil he failed to set right as he was bound to do. This argument makes a strong impression on me, and I am only imperfectly satisfied with the reply that the scene is laid in the old age of Solomon, after he had been persuaded by female influence to trust into unfit hands power which he was not afterwards strong enough to revoke.

In this connection it may be stated that even if the book be accepted as written by Solomon in his old age, there is no warrant for the common opinion that it was intended as an expression of penitence for the errors of his middle life. No such expression of penitence is to be found; his different experiments in search of happiness are recorded as failures, but without shame or repentance; and in particular not only is the sin of countenancing idolatry, with which he is charged in the Book of Kings, not deplored, but no warning against idolatry is given in the whole book.

The ascription of the work to the old age of Solomon has been made to answer other objections. For example, the general state of the nation appears to have been one of great misery. Death was thought better than life, and men looked with regret on the former days, which they pronounced to be better than the present. This is said to be inconsistent with the prosperity of Solomon's reign; but it is replied that the discontent which broke out so violently immediately after his death must have been growing, and not without cause, during the later years of his reign.

(c) The style of the book is strongly marked by the author's individuality, and is confessedly unlike that either of the Proverbs or the Song of Songs. But it is urged that there may be great differences of style between works written by the same man in his youth and in his old age. It is more important to observe that the Hebrew of the book is very different from that of the books known to be of early date. It is, in fact, much more like the Hebrew of the Talmud than is that of any other book in the Canon, so that, judged by this test alone, it will be pronounced one of the latest in the Bible. The references we give in the Notes will show that many words occur in this book which elsewhere occur only in those of the canonical books which are known to be the latest. The argument from the grammatical forms used in the book is not less strong, but the details cannot be given in a Commentary like the present. Concerning each particular instance discussed, there is room for controversy. Earlier parallels have been found for some of the instances brought forward as indications of modern date. In other cases it can be said that it is only the scantiness of the early literature which prevents such parallels from being found; and it has been sought, by tracing analogies in other Shemitic languages, to make it probable that the words objected to as modern might easily have been found in the early Hebrew literature, if we had larger remains of it. The force of the argument, however, is cumulative. It would be very precarious to condemn a book as modern because of its containing three or four words or phrases which have a modern ring. Any one who takes up an early English book will be startled at occasionally coming across phrases which he had not imagined to be so old; and yet no one can fail to recognise the reality of the difference of style between an early book and a recent one. The strength of the present argument altogether depends on the number of words and forms of expression for which an apology must be found if the antiquity of the book is to be maintained. Of those who are entitled to speak with authority as Hebrew scholars, a very great majority regard this argument alone as decisive against the Solomonic authorship; and I am myself so much impressed by the marks of lateness in the Hebrew that I do not venture to put forward a theory which otherwise has something to recommend it, viz., that the book was written in the days of the later Hebrew monarchy, as a record of traditions then preserved of the teaching of Solomon on the occasion of his great assembly.

The conclusion, then, at which I arrive is that, while there is not one of the arguments against the Solomonic authorship which might not be made to give way if convincing external testimony in favour of it were produced, the accumulated weight of the internal arguments would be decisive in the absence of such external proof. To some minds the unanimous consent of the Christian Church for many centuries is decisive external proof; and so the answers to arguments of the former class are easily accepted. Formal Church decision on the subject there has been none; and to me it appears that the weight which attaches to the opinions of Christian Fathers on a question of canonicity does not belong to their opinions on the authorship of Old Testament books. No one now has any difficulty in owning that many of the psalms are later than the time of David, yet not only does Augustine regard the mention of Babylon as made by David under prophetic inspiration, but Philaster counts in his list of heresies the denial that all the 150 psalms were David's. If an Old Testament book is not mentioned in the New Testament, we have no reason to suppose that any later revelation as to its authorship was made to the Christian Church. At the time of the formation of the Church, Jewish general belief ascribed the Book of Ecclesiastes to Solomon, and that opinion was naturally adopted by Christian critics. The fact just mentioned as to general Jewish belief in the first century of our era (and in all probability for a considerable time previously) is one entitled to great weight; but considering that the date to which we can trace that belief back is still at least 700 years later than Solomon, I cannot regard it as decisive; and in the face of the arguments on the other side, I find myself unable to assert Solomon's authorship. The case would be different if the alternative were that we should be obliged to impute deception to a book which we accept as canonical, and to suppose that the writer, who knew himself not to be Solomon, falsely tried to make his readers believe that he was. But accepting the view suggested by the epilogue, that a later writer professes to record the teaching of Solomon, we are at liberty to suppose either that he really does what he professes, oral teaching of Solomon having been preserved by a true tradition, or else that the whole is a dramatic fiction, a form of composition common enough among profane writers, and against the use of which by an inspired writer no reason can be assigned.

Those who reject the Solomonic authorship are far from being agreed among themselves as to the date which they will assign the work, from which it is reasonable to infer, not that Solomon after all must have written it, but that the data for any determination of the kind are insufficient. It has been attempted to discover historical references in different passages, such as chap. ix. 14; but none of these attempts inspires any strong conviction as to its success. Indeed, when we remember how scanty are our materials for a knowledge of Jewish history after the Captivity, we shall not be surprised if we find a difficulty in identifying historical allusions. Again, coincidences have been pointed out between the teaching of Kohéleth and that of different schools of Greek philosophy; and these have been regarded as proving indebtedness on the part of the former, and thus as establishing a very late date for the book. Yet these coincidences are after all but superficial. It would be equally easy to prove by them that Kohéleth was a Stoic or Epicurean; yet he certainly was neither, but one whose theism was thoroughly Hebrew. I have not been able, then, to convince myself that Kohéleth had studied a philosophy by which he is so little really influenced, or that the things which he has in common with it are other than thoughts which may have occurred independently to reflecting men of different nations. I prefer, therefore, not to put forward any theory as to the date of composition, not regarding any as sufficiently proved. Some considerations, however, must be mentioned which place certain limits on hypotheses.

(1) In the time of Herod the Great the book was old enough to be regarded as Scripture. We are told by Josephus that Herod used to go about in disguise in order to learn what was thought of his government, and a story in the Talmud relates that he went in this way to a leading rabbi who had been deprived of sight by his orders, and from whom he expected to draw some angry denunciation of the wrongs which he and his brethren had suffered at his hands. But the rabbi resisted every temptation to curse the king, quoting Eccles. x. 20; and the story goes on to tell that the king was moved to make atonement for these wrongs by rebuilding the Temple. In another Talmudical story, the scene of which is laid somewhat later, the celebrated Gamaliel is represented as depicting the miraculous results that would follow when, in the coming age of the Messiah, the curse should be removed from nature, and a contentious pupil (by whom it is imagined St. Paul is intended) objects, Is it not written, There is nothing new under the sun? Without overrating the amount of credence that these anecdotes deserve, we do not think that the stories could have originated or been accepted if the composition of the book had been within living memory in the reign of Herod.

(2) Ecclesiastes is more ancient than the apocryphal Book of Wisdom. It cannot reasonably be doubted that the author of the Book of Wisdom was acquainted with Ecclesiastes, the coincidences being such as cannot be ascribed to accident. In particular the whole passage (Wisdom ii. 1—10) is full of echoes of Ecclesiastes. There are several passages in the latter book which appear to teach Epicurean or pessimistic doctrine; and of these the explanation was offered long since, of which every interpreter is still bound to take account, that the writer is not giving his own conclusions, but stating the opinions of an infidel or objector. And this seems to be the view taken by the author of Wisdom, who introduces the passage with the preface, "The ungodly said, reasoning with themselves, but not aright." We need not suppose that the author of Wisdom rejected the authority of Ecclesiastes; he may have only sought to bring out more clearly what he believed to be its true meaning. Accordingly the solution of the problem of life afforded by the doctrine of future retribution, concerning the use of which made in Ecclesiastes there has been dispute, is in Wisdom taught with a distinctness which leaves no room for controversy. We do not gain much for the antiquity of Ecclesiastes in proving it to be older than Wisdom, the date of the latter book being uncertain. About 150 years before Christ is not an improbable determination.

(3) Ecclesiastes is more ancient than the apocryphal book, Ecclesiasticus, or Wisdom of the Son of Sirach. The proof of this seems to me sufficient, but it is far from being so cogent as in the case of the Book of Wisdom. It is a natural inference from the mention in the prologue of the threefold division of sacred books, "the Law, the prophets, and the rest of the books," that the Canon had been then closed. And that then, as now, it included Kohéleth is made probable by coincidences, some of which no doubt can be explained as indicating that both writers used a common source; for example, "he that diggeth a pit shall fall into it" (Ecclus. xxvii. 26, Eccles. x. 8), has probably its original in Prov. xxvi. 27; Ps. vii. 15. Other resemblances may be accidental, though we think the presumption is in favour of literary obligation, especially in the first instance (Ecclus. xii. 13, Eccles. x. 11; Ecclus. xiii. 25, 26, Eccles. viii. 1; Ecclus. xix. 16, Eccles. vii. 20—22; Ecclus. xx. 7, xxi. 25, 26, Eccles. x. 2, 3, 12, 14; Ecclus. xl. 4, Eccles. i. 7). Several others might be mentioned, and the argument gains much in strength from its cumulative force, it being unlikely that so many resemblances should be all accidental. The closest resemblance is in the passages (Ecclus. xxxiii. 13—15, xlii. 24, 25), which, on being carefully compared with Eccles. vii. 13—15, exhibit what must be pronounced to be more than chance agreement. Even when the Son of Sirach uses the Book of Proverbs he usually does not copy slavishly, so that we have no right to expect closer agreement in this case; and if borrowing has been established in any one instance, the coincidences in other cases are not likely to be accidental. The Book of Sirach is older than that of Wisdom, but concerning its date also there is much disagreement among critics.

(4) Ecclesiastes is anterior to the times of the Maccabees. Under the persecution of Antiochus Epiphanes many a Jew was forced to choose whether he would forsake the faith of his fathers or submit to tortures and death. It then passed from being a question debated by speculative theologians, to become one of the greatest

practical moment, whether if in obedience to God's command he gave up all the happiness of this life, there was any future life in which he might hope for compensation. And the affirmative answer was thenceforward embraced by pious Jews with an intensity of faith of which we find no trace in Ecclesiastes. Neither, again, have we in that book any indication of the strong patriotic feeling to which the Maccabean struggles gave rise.

The testimonies that we have produced as to the use of the Book of Kohéleth entitle us to say that it must have been composed more than two centuries before Christ. The absence of documentary evidence leaves still some centuries between the age of Solomon and the date we have named, for our choice among which we have no guide except what inferences we can draw from the book itself. But the importance of placing a lower limit on the date of the book is that it controls speculations founded on the character of its Hebrew. This has so many affinities with Talmudical Hebrew that some scholars have attempted to bring down the date almost to our Lord's time. The evidence as to the use of the book for a couple of centuries before that time shows that a certain reserve must be used in relying on the argument from language. A kindred argument has been built on the character of the Greek translation. At the beginning of the second century of our era, a Jew named Aquila published a new translation of the Old Testament, the chief characteristic of which was slavish literalness, even to the violation of Greek idiom. In particular he thought it necessary to represent by a Greek preposition a Hebrew particle which, as being a mere sign of the accusative case, previous versions had properly left untranslated. This peculiarity is found in the now extant Greek translation of Ecclesiastes. Yet the conclusion to which we are tempted, that this translation is the work of Aquila, is contradicted by the fact that a different translation, under the name of Aquila, was known to Origen. No proof being possible that the peculiarity in question was an invention of Aquila's, it would be rash to conclude, as some have done, that Kohéleth was not translated into Greek until his time. Nor can we even say with any certainty that the present Greek text has been interpolated from Aquila's translation. But we may, at least, add this to the presumptions against the Solomonic authorship; for if at the time the LXX. translation was made this book was regarded as Solomon's, it seems likely that we should now have a Greek translation of it not differing in character from that of the Book of Proverbs.

It may be stated here that there are some passages in the book which, notwithstanding all that commentators have done to explain them, remain so obscure that there is reason to suspect the difficulty arises from corruption in the Hebrew text. But the remedy of critical conjecture is so precarious that in this Commentary no attempt has been made to resort to it, and it has been preferred to confess inability to give any explanation commending itself as perfectly satisfactory.

The Book of Ecclesiastes contains some internal evidence of having been written in Palestine; not, like the Book of Wisdom, in Egypt. Thus (chaps. xi. 3, xii. 2) the clouds full of rain are spoken of. The writer lives near the Temple (chap. v. 1); and "the city" (chaps. viii. 10, x. 15) is, to all appearance, Jerusalem. It may be doubted, however, whether, if the writer's residence had been exclusively in Palestine, he could have gained that familiarity with royal courts which he more than once exhibits.

Great as has been the diversity of opinion as to the authorship and date of the Book of Ecclesiastes, there has been fully as great as to its interpretation, and even as to its whole plan and object. We may set aside one system of interpretation, although it found favour in the Christian Church for centuries: that, namely, in which this Old Testament book was made to teach New Testament doctrine from one end to the other, and the most unlikely verses were forced to prophesy of Christ.* We need not inquire whether, when this style of comment was introduced, anything more was meant than to make the words of the Old Testament book the occasion for edifying practical observations; it is only for such purpose that comment of this sort would be likely to be used now. But even interpreters who, looking at the book solely from its human side, set themselves to discover the intention with which the author wrote, are found unable to agree in any conclusion. The cause of this disagreement is that different utterances of the book unquestionably contradict each other, and in such wise as to leave room for controversy which of them express the author's real sentiments. Indeed, we are told that it was on account of these self-contradictions that the authority of the book was impugned in the Rabbinical schools. The following are a few of the examples of these contradictions given by a Jewish commentator: that in one place (chap. viii. 15) Kohéleth praises mirth, in another (chap. ii. 2) he condemns it as unprofitable; that in one place (chap. ii. 13) he owns that wisdom has an advantage over folly, in another (chap. ii. 13) he denies that there is any; the state of the dead is said to be better than that of the living (chap. iv. 2), and the contrary (chap. ix. 4). We are told (chap. viii. 12) that it shall be well with those who fear God, and (chap. vii. 13) that it shall not be well with the wicked, and that he shall not prolong his days; and yet (chap. vii. 15) that there is a wicked man who does prolong his days in his wickedness, and (chap. viii. 14) that there are wicked to whom it happens according to the doings of the righteous.

Dismissing, however, discrepancies between what may be regarded as incidental statements, we find that the book has suggested opposite answers to the inquiry, what was the main lesson which the author designed to teach? He defines his subject plainly enough in the words which strike the key-note of his work, "vanity of vanities; all is vanity." His theme is the nothingness of human life; the unsatisfying character of its pleasures, the profitless result of its pursuits, the uncertainty whether the best human prudence can gain any real happiness. But as to the practical conclusion which the writer means to recommend, his readers have formed different opinions. Some have imagined that he inculcates an ascetic with-

---

* For example, "There is one alone, and there is not a second, yet he hath neither child nor brother; yet is there no end of all his labour, neither is his eye satisfied with riches: neither saith he, For whom do I labour and bereave my soul of good?" This is the Saviour who descended alone, and without companion, to save the world. There is no end of His labour in bearing our sins and grievances for us; His eye will not be satisfied with riches while He ever desires our salvation. "If two lie together, then they have heat; but how can one be warm alone? And if one prevail against him, two shall withstand him, and a threefold cord is not quickly broken." If one should sleep—that is, be dissolved in death—and have Christ with him, he is warmed, and comes to life again. If the devil come with attacks too strong for a man to bear alone, he nevertheless will have who has Christ for his companion. And if Father, Son, and Holy Spirit come, that triple cord is not easily broken, &c.

drawal from earthly pleasures, which have been proved to be worthless; some, that he gives his disciples the Epicurean counsel to enjoy life while they can, not knowing how long its happiness may last; some, that he teaches a sceptical despair of regulating conduct in a world where all is ruled by chance or fate. And we find ourselves perplexed by different answers when we inquire what solution the writer offers of the difficulties arising from the imperfections of the retribution which conduct meets in this world. He has complained that "all things come alike to all; there is one event to the righteous and the wicked; to the good and to the clean, and to the unclean; to him that sacrificeth, and to him that sacrificeth not; as is the good so is the sinner; and he that sweareth, as he that feareth an oath." Does he then remove the difficulty by the Christian solution that there will be a future life in which the imperfections of earthly retribution will be adjusted, and the Divine justice fully vindicated? There are passages which would seem to indicate that Kohéleth had no such idea, and that he regarded the end of this mortal existence as the absolute end of all our joys and sorrows. "That which befalleth the sons of men befalleth beasts; even one thing befalleth them; as the one dieth, so dieth the other; yea, they have all one breath, so that a man hath no pre-eminence above a beast, for all is vanity. All go unto one place; all are of the dust and all turn to dust again." "The living know that they shall die, but the dead know not anything, neither have they any more a reward, for the memory of them is forgotten, also their love, and their hatred, and their envy, is now perished; neither have they any more a portion for ever in anything that is done under the sun." "Whatsoever thy hand findeth to do, do it with thy might; for there is no work, nor device, nor knowledge, nor wisdom, in the grave whither thou goest." Yet the passages here cited are balanced by another chain of passages running through the book, professing the same belief in future judgment and retribution, which is declared in the formal conclusion at the end. "I said in my heart, God shall judge the righteous and the wicked, for there is a time there for every purpose and for every work." "Though a sinner do evil a hundred times, and his days be prolonged, yet surely I know that it shall be well with them that fear God, which fear before him: but it shall not be well with the wicked, neither shall he prolong his days, which are as a shadow, because he feareth not before God." "Rejoice, O young man, in thy youth, and let thy heart cheer thee in the days of thy youth, and walk in the ways of thine heart, and in the sight of thine eyes; but know thou that for all these things God will bring thee into judgment." And the conclusion of the whole is, "God shall bring every work into judgment, with every secret thing, whether it be good or whether it be evil." It has been proposed to account for these seeming inconsistencies by the hypothesis that the book represents, not the sentiments of a single person, but the debates of an "assembly"; yet I cannot regard any attempt as successful which has been made to throw the book into the form of a dialogue, in which different speakers take their part. But the form of the book suggests that its contradictory utterances express the sentiments, not of different persons, but of the same person at different times, and that as Kohéleth relates his various experiments of life, so he tells also the opinions which he formed, but which subsequent experience compelled him to modify. According to this view we should regard the conclusion last stated (chap. xii. 14) as that in which he finally acquiesced, and which overrules any previous expressions that may be inconsistent with it.

Some have attempted to evade the argument drawn from the last verse by the suggestion that in this passage only a judgment in this life is referred to. But we have no experience in this life of a judgment in which every secret thing is brought to light and receives retribution, and the whole tenor of the book forbids us to imagine that the author asserts that anything of the kind takes place here. The only other way of escaping the necessity of interpreting the book by its formal conclusion, is to assert that the epilogue is not by the same author as the rest of the book. The assertion is easy to make, but difficult to prove. There would be justification for it if the doctrine of the epilogue contradicted that of the rest of the book; but in truth the epilogue does no more than give emphatic adoption to a solution which has been indicated already. Delitzsch (pp. 206, 430, Eng. Trans.) has found in the language of the epilogue, indications that it proceeded from the same author as the rest of the book, far more numerous than one could beforehand have expected to find in so short a passage. Certain it is that when the authority of the book was discussed in the Jewish schools, no doubt was entertained that the epilogue formed an integral part of the book; for it was the orthodoxy of the conclusion which banished doubts raised by some earlier passages. At the time, then, of these discussions the epilogue must have been of immemorial antiquity; and, if added by a different hand, then at the time when it was added the book of Kohéleth must have been of undisputed authority, and we may reasonably believe must have been received as Solomon's. For the hypothesis assumes that the sentiments of the author of the epilogue are at variance with those of the writer of the book itself; and there would have been nothing to prevent him from doing as later Jews were tempted to do, and rejecting the book altogether, if its traditional authority at the time had not been too strong for him; and how, in that case, he could have succeeded in getting universal acceptance for his addition, as if it had been part of the original tradition, is not easy to explain.

To many a modern Christian reader it will seem strange that it should be a question admitting of debate whether or not a canonical Old Testament book recognises the doctrine of a future life.

To such a reader we offer the following considerations :—

(1) In the dispensation of God's providence, the communication of religious knowledge has been progressive, like "light shining more and more unto the perfect day." Prophets of old earnestly desired to look into those things which are exposed to the view of the least in the Gospel dispensation, and searched diligently into the meaning of dark sayings of their own which the light of subsequent revelations enables us with ease to interpret (1 Peter i. 10).

(2) If we admit this principle, we have no cause for surprise if we find in the earlier portions of God's revelation intimations rather than express declarations of those great truths which in the fulness of time were plainly disclosed. Each sacred writer was only empowered to communicate those truths which God had revealed to him. Each could say, "The word that God putteth in my mouth, that will I speak." We do not derogate from the inspiration of any Old Testament writer if we refuse to force his words so as to make

ECCLESIASTES.

them convey a more express declaration of Gospel truth than their natural meaning suggests.

(3) Now, it must be owned that the doctrine of future retribution did not occupy in the minds of pious men of the old dispensation the same place among unquestioned truths which it holds in our own convictions. The proof of this assertion does not depend so much on particular texts as on the fact that the stumbling-block which, more than any other speculative difficulty, caused the feet of those of old time wellnigh to slip, was that "they were envious of the foolish when they saw the prosperity of the wicked." Many of the psalms, as well as portions of the Book of Job, resemble the Book of Ecclesiastes in exhibiting the perplexity caused to thoughtful men of old by the frequent distribution of temporal happiness and misery, apparently, irrespective of the deserts of men, or even contrary to what we conceive it ought to be. We hear nothing of these difficulties in the New Testament. The disciples saw their enemies in possession of temporal power, and themselves at the extreme of earthly wretchedness, yet they never dreamed of questioning the ways of God's providence, but counted that their "light affliction, which was but for a moment," was working for them a "far more exceeding and eternal weight of glory." But in the case of the Old Testament writers referred to, the conclusion that it shall surely in the end be well with them that fear the Lord, is one which they seem to have arrived at by an effort of faith in the power, goodness, and justice of God as generally known to them, rather than on any more distinct revelation of the way in which He will make His cause to triumph.

(4) If to the reader it seem strange that the Bible should contain a detailed record of perplexities which a later revelation has removed, let him remember that the Bible contains an inspired account of the external history of God's people, including the story of the sins and follies of many of them, and that we have all cause to own that this history contains valuable lessons for our learning. In an age when the trials of many are from speculative difficulties more than from the allurements of vice, can we pronounce it unfitting that the sacred volume should also contain for our instruction an inspired account of the internal history of a pious man of old, should make known to us his doubts and difficulties, and let us see how, apparently without being in possession of any such satisfactory solution of his difficulties as could content his intellect, his heart taught him that surely it shall be well with them that fear God, and that the conclusion of the whole matter is that to fear God and keep His commandments is the whole duty of man? The contradictions of the Book of Ecclesiastes spring out of the conflict between the writer's faith and his experience—his faith that the world is ordered by God, and his experience that events do not fall out as he would have expected God should have ordered them. He seems to have lived in that darkest hour, the hour before dawn, when, through brooding on the imperfections of earthly retribution, many minds were prepared for the reception of the fuller revelation that was coming. The writer of Ecclesiastes takes a gloomy view of life, but he is at the opposite pole from the atheistic pessimists of modern times. The whole book is pervaded by belief in the God who rules the world, though it may be in a way incomprehensible to man.

It is plain, then, what instruction we may derive from the inspired history of the mental struggles of one perplexed by difficulties of which we know the solution. We, too, have our intellectual difficulties, and we must sometimes decide to hold fast to certain great truths of faith, notwithstanding objections which we do not know how satisfactorily to remove. In such a case we may be comforted by the study of the history of one who, in old time, passed through a similar experience, and by observing how, while his understanding was wandering perplexed, his heart by a shorter way arrived at the goal.

ECCLESIASTES; OR, THE PREACHER

CHAPTER I.—⁽¹⁾ The words of the Preacher, the son of David, king in Jerusalem.

⁽²⁾ ^aVanity of vanities, saith the Preacher, vanity of vanities; all *is* vanity. ⁽³⁾ ^bWhat profit hath a man of all his labour which he taketh under the sun? ⁽⁴⁾ *One* generation passeth away, and *another* generation cometh: ^cbut the earth abideth for ever. ⁽⁵⁾ ^dThe sun also ariseth, and the sun goeth down, and ¹hasteth to his place where he arose. ⁽⁶⁾ The wind goeth toward the south, and turneth about unto the north; it whirleth about continually, and the wind returneth again according to his circuits. ⁽⁷⁾ ^eAll the rivers run into the sea; yet the sea *is* not full; unto the place from whence the rivers come, thither they ²return again. ⁽⁸⁾ All things *are* full of labour; man cannot utter *it*: ^fthe eye is not satisfied with seeing, nor the ear filled with hearing. ⁽⁹⁾ ^gThe thing that hath been, it *is that* which shall be; and that which is done *is* that which shall be done: and *there is* no new *thing* under

B.C. cir. 977.

a Ps. 39. 5, 6, & 62. 9, & 144. 4; ch. 12. 8.
b ch. 2. 22, & 3. 9.
c Ps. 104. 5, & 119. 90.
d Ps. 19. 6.
1 Heb., *panteth*.
e Job 38. 10; Ps. 104. 8, 9.
2 Heb., *return to go*.
f Prov. 27. 20.
g ch. 3. 15.

⁽¹⁾ **The words.**—The Book of Nehemiah begins similarly; so do the prophecies of Jeremiah and Amos, and of Agur and Lemuel (Prov. xxx., xxxi.).

The Preacher.—Rather, *convener* (see Introduction). This word (*Kohéleth*) occurs in this book, chaps. i. 1, 2, 12, vii. 27, where, according to our present text, it is joined with a feminine, being elsewhere used with a masculine; and chap. xii. 8, 9, 10, having the article in the first of these passages, and there only, being elsewhere used as a proper name.

⁽²⁾ **Vanity of vanities.**—This verse strikes the key-note of the whole work. In using this expression we mean to indicate the opinion that the unity of the book is rather that of a musical composition than of a philosophical treatise. A leading theme is given out and followed for a time. Episodes are introduced, not perhaps logically connected with the original subject, but treated in harmony with it, and leading back to the original theme which is never lost sight of, and with which the composition comes to a close (chap. xii. 8).

The word translated "vanity" (which occurs thirty-seven times in this book, and only thirty-three times in all the rest of the Old Testament) in its primary meaning denotes breath or vapour, and is so translated here in some of the Greek versions (comp. James iv. 4); so in Isaiah lvii. 13. It is the same word as the proper name Abel, on which see Note on Gen. iv. 2. It is frequently applied in Scripture to the follies of heathenism (Jer. xiv. 22, &c.), and also to the whole estate of men (Pss. xxxix. 5, 6, lxii. 9, cxliv. 4). The translation "vanity" is that of the LXX. We may reasonably believe that St. Paul (Rom. viii. 20) had this key-note of Ecclesiastes in his mind.

"Vanity of vanities" is a common Hebrew superlative, as in the phrases "Heaven of heavens," "Song of songs," "Holy of holies," "Lamentation of lamentations" (Micah ii. 4, margin).

Saith the Preacher.—Heb., *said*. The Hebrew constantly employs the preterite when English usage requires the present or perfect. In the case of a message the point of time contemplated in Hebrew is that of the giving, not the delivery, of the message. So "Thus said Benhadad," "Thus said the Lord" (1 Kings xx. 2, 5, 13 and *passim*) are rightly translated by the present in our version. In the present case this formula is one which might conceivably be employed if the words of Kohéleth were written down by himself; yet it certainly rather suggests that we have here these words as written down by another.

(3–11) Man is perpetually toiling, yet of all his toil there remains no abiding result. The natural world exhibits a spectacle of unceasing activity, with no real progress. The sun, the winds, the waters, are all in motion, yet they do but run a round, and nothing comes of it.

⁽³⁾ **What profit.**—The Hebrew word occurs ten times in this book (chaps. ii. 11, 13, iii. 9, v. 9, 16, vii. 12, x. 10, 11) and nowhere else in the Old Testament, but is common in post-Biblical Hebrew. The oft-recurring phrase "under the sun" is a peculiarity of this book. In other books we have "under heaven."

⁽⁴⁾ Comp. Ecclus. xiv. 19.

⁽⁵⁾ **Hasteth.**—Heb., *panteth*. The word is used of eager desire (Job vii. 2; Ps. cxix. 131).

Where he arose.—Better, *there to rise again*.

⁽⁶⁾ The order of the Hebrew words permits the first clause, "going towards the south and returning towards the north," to be understood in continuation of the description of the movements of the sun, and so some interpreters have taken them, but probably erroneously. The verse gains in liveliness if more literally rendered, "going towards the south and circling towards the north, circling, circling goes the wind, and to its circles the wind returns."

⁽⁷⁾ **Whence the rivers come.**—Better, *whither the rivers go*. (Comp. Ecclus. xl. 11.)

⁽⁸⁾ This verse is capable of another translation which would give the sense "other instances of the same kind might be mentioned, but they are so numerous that it would be wearisome to recount them." We abide by the rendering of our version.

⁽⁹⁾ **No new thing.**—Contrast Jer. xxxi. 22; Isa. xliii. 19, lxv. 17. Justin Martyr (*Apol.* i. 57) has what

the sun. (10) Is there *any* thing whereof it may be said, See, this *is* new? it hath been already of old time, which was before us. (11) *There is* no remembrance of former *things*; neither shall there be *any* remembrance of *things* that are to come with *those* that shall come after.

(12) I the Preacher was king over Israel in Jerusalem. (13) And I gave my heart to seek and search out by wisdom concerning all *things* that are done under heaven: this sore travail hath God given to the sons of man ¹ to be exercised therewith. (14) I have seen all the works that are done under the sun; and, behold, all *is* vanity and vexation of spirit. (15) *ᵃ That which is* crooked cannot be made straight: and ² that which is wanting cannot be numbered. (16) I communed with mine own heart, saying, Lo, I am come to great estate, and have gotten ᵇ more wisdom than all *they* that have been before me in Jerusalem: yea, my heart ³ had great experience of wisdom and knowledge. (17) ᶜ And I gave my heart to know wisdom, and to know madness and folly: I perceived that this also is vexation of spirit. (18) For ᵈ in much wisdom *is* much grief: and he that increaseth knowledge increaseth sorrow.

CHAPTER II.—(1) I said in mine heart, Go to now, I will prove thee with

Or, to afflict them.
a ch. 7. 13.
2 Heb., *defect.*
b 1 Kings 4. 30, & 10. 7, 23.
3 Heb., *had seen much.*
c ch. 1. 12, & 7. 23.
d ch. 12. 12.

---

looks like a reminiscence of this verse; but we cannot rely on it to prove his acquaintance with the book, the same idea being found in Grecian philosophy.

(10) **Of old time.**—The Hebrew word here is peculiar to Ecclesiastes, where it occurs eight times (chaps. ii. 12, 16, iii. 15, iv. 2, vi. 10, ix. 6, 7), but is common in later Hebrew.

(11) If anything appears new, this is only because its previous occurrence has been forgotten. So likewise will those of this generation be forgotten by those who succeed them.

KOHELETH RELATES HIS OWN EXPERIENCE.

(12) Having in the introductory verses stated the argument of the treatise, the writer proceeds to prove what he has asserted as to the vanity of earthly pursuits, by relating the failures of one who might be expected, if any one could, to bring such pursuits to a satisfactory result. Solomon, in this book called Kohéleth, pre-eminent among Jewish sovereigns as well for wisdom as for temporal prosperity, speaking in the first person, tells how, with all his advantages, he could secure in this life no lasting or satisfying happiness. He relates first how he found no satisfaction from an enlightened survey of human life. He found (verse 14) that it presented a scene of laborious exertion empty of profitable results. His researches (verse 15) only brought to light errors and defects which it was impossible to remedy; so that (verse 18) the more thought a man bestowed on the subject, the greater his grief. On the name Kohéleth, and the phrase "was king," see Introduction.

Over Israel.—King *of* Israel is the usual phrase in the earlier books, but there are examples of that here employed (1 Sam. xv. 26; 2 Sam. xix. 23; 1 Kings xi. 37).

(13) **Gave my heart.**—The phrase occurs again in this book (verse 17, vii. 25, viii. 9, 16) and often elsewhere. (See Dan. x. 12; 2 Chron. xi. 16, &c.) The heart among the Hebrews is regarded as the seat, not merely of the feelings, but of the intellectual faculties, and so the word is constantly used in what follows. "I gave my heart" is the same as "I applied my mind."

To seek.—Deut. xiii. 14; Lev. x. 16.
Search out.—Numb. xiv. 36; 38; Eccles. vii. 25.
Travail.—The word occurs again in this book (chaps. ii. 23, 26, iii. 10, iv. 8, v. 3, 14, viii. 16) but nowhere else in the Old Testament, though kindred forms are common. The word itself is common in Rabbinical Hebrew, in the sense of business.

"To afflict them" (margin). This is too strong a translation; better, *to travail therein.*

(14) **Vexation.**—The word occurs only in this book (chaps. ii. 11, 17, 26, iv. 4, 6, vi. 9). The A. V. translation, "vexation of spirit," is difficult to justify. Very nearly the same phrase occurs in Hosea xii. 1, and is there translated "feeding on wind," for in Hebrew, as in some other languages, the name for "spirit" primarily denotes breath or wind. Accordingly many interpreters understand the phrase of the text "feeding on wind" (see Isa. xliv. 20). The same root, however, which means to "feast on a thing," has the secondary meaning to "delight in a thing," and so the corresponding noun in Chaldee comes to mean "pleasure" or "will." (Comp. Ezra v. 17, vii. 18.) Accordingly the LXX. and many modern interpreters understand the phrase of the text "effort after wind."

(15) **Made straight.**—The verb occurs only in this book (chaps. vii. 13, xii. 9, "set in order") and in Rabbinical Hebrew. So likewise "that which is wanting" is peculiar to this passage, and to later Hebrew.

(16) **Wisdom and knowledge.**—Isa. xxx. 6; Rom. xi. 33.

(17) **Madness and folly** are words we should not expect to find in this context, and accordingly some interpreters have attempted by variations of reading to substitute for them words of the same nature as "wisdom and knowledge," but see chaps. ii. 12, vii. 25. Taking the text as it stands, it means to know wisdom and knowledge fully by a study of their contraries. The word for "madness" is peculiar to this book, but the corresponding verb occurs frequently in other books.

(18) **Grief.**—Irritation.

II.

Kohéleth, having tried wisdom and philosophic investigation, proceeded next to see what cheerful enjoyment could do for human happiness.

(1) **In mine heart.**—*To* mine heart (Luke xii. 19; Ps. xlii. 11).
Go to now.—Num. xxii. 6; Judg. xix. 11.
Enjoy.—Heb., *see.*

mirth, therefore enjoy pleasure: and, behold, this also *is* vanity. (2) *I said of laughter, It *is* mad: and of mirth, What doeth it? (3) *I sought in mine heart ¹to give myself unto wine, yet acquainting mine heart with wisdom; and to lay hold on folly, till I might see what *was* that good for the sons of men, which they should do under the heaven ²all the days of their life. (4) I made me great works; I builded me houses; I planted me vineyards: (5) I made me gardens and orchards, and I planted trees in them of all *kind of* fruits: (6) I made me pools of water, to water therewith the wood that bringeth forth trees: (7) I got *me* servants and maidens, and had ³servants born in my house; also I had great possessions of great and small cattle above all that were in Jerusalem before me: (8) *I gathered me also silver and gold, and the peculiar treasure of kings and of the provinces: I gat me men singers and women singers, and the delights of the sons of men, as ⁴musical instruments, and that of all sorts. (9) So I was great, and increased more than all that were before me in Jerusalem: also my wisdom remained with me. (10) And whatsoever mine eyes desired I kept not from them, I withheld not my heart from any joy; for my heart rejoiced in all my labour: and *this was my portion of all my labour. (11) Then I looked on all the works that my hands had wrought, and on the labour that I had laboured to do: and, behold, all *was* *vanity and vexation of spirit, and *there was* no profit under the sun.

(12) And I turned myself to behold

a Prov. 14. 13; ch. 7. 6.

b ch. 1. 17.

1 Heb., *to draw my flesh with wine.*

2 Heb., *the number of the days of their life.*

3 Heb., *sons of my house.*

c 1 Kings 9. 28, & 10. 14.

4 Heb., *musical instrument and instruments.*

d ch. 3. 22, & 5. 18, & 9. 9.

e ch. 1. 3.

(2) Prov. xiv. 13.
Mad.—Ps. cii. 9.
(3) **Sought.**—The word translated "search out" (chap. i. 13).
"Draw," margin. There is no Biblical parallel for the use of the word in this sense. The general meaning is plain.
Acquainting.—Rather, *guiding.* The word is used of the driver of an animal or the shepherd of a flock (2 Sam. vi. 3; Ps. lxxx. 1; Isa. lxiii. 4). Kohéleth contemplated not an unrestrained enjoyment of pleasure, but one controlled by prudence.
All the days.—(See margin). This phrase occurs again in chaps. v. 17, vi. 12. We have "men of number" in the sense of "few"—*i.e.,* so few that they can be numbered (Gen. xxxiv. 30, and often elsewhere). So we may translate here "for their span of life."
(4) **Houses.**—1 Kings v. 11; 2 Chron. viii. 4.
Vineyards.—1 Chron. xxvii. 27; Cant. viii. 11.
(5) **Orchards.**—Rather, *parks.* The word, which occurs also in Cant. iv. 3, Neh. ii. 8, is originally Persian, and passed into the Greek and into modern languages in the form of "paradise" (Luke xxiii. 43; 2 Cor. xii. 4; and in LXX., Gen. ii, 10, xiii. 10; Num. xxiv. 6; Isa. i. 30; Ecclus. xxiv. 30; Susan. v. 4). Parks and trees giving, not only fruit, but shade from the hot Eastern sun, were an almost necessary part of kingly luxury. The king's garden is spoken of in 1 Kings xxi. 2; 2 Kings xxi. 18, xxv. 4; Neh. iii. 15.
(6) **Pools.**—In a place south of Bethlehem are still pointed out three gigantic reservoirs, known as the Pools of Solomon (Stanley's *Jewish Church,* ii. 197). The place is probably the same as that called Etham by Josephus in his description of Solomon's luxury (*Ant.* viii. 7. 3). Josephus speaks of another Pool of Solomon (*Bell. Jud.* v. 4. 2). Tanks are necessary for irrigation in a land where natural streams are few and are dried up in summer. The king's pool is mentioned in Neh. ii. 14.
(7) **Got me.**—The servants acquired by purchase are distinguished from those born in the house. (Concerning the number of Solomon's servants, see 1 Kings iv. 27, x. 5; and of his cattle, chaps. iv. 23, viii. 63.)

(8) **Peculiar treasure.**—The word is used of the Jewish people (Exod. xix. 9; Ps. cxxxv. 4; Mal. iii. 17; but generally 1 Chron. xxix. 3). That Solomon had tributary kings is stated (1 Kings iv. 21; 2 Chron. ix. 24; Ps. lxxii. 10; Ezra iv. 20). The word used for "provinces" here and in chap. v. 8, occurs in reference to the provinces of the Persian Empire repeatedly in the Book of Esther; Ezra ii. 1; Neh. vii. 6; Dan. viii. 2. (See also Lam. i. 1; Ezek. xix. 8.) The word is almost wholly absent from the earlier books, save that it occurs where the "princes of the provinces" are mentioned (1 Kings xx.).
Singers.—Music was regarded as a necessary accompaniment of feasts (Isa. v. 12; Amos vi. 5; Ecclus. xxxii. 5, xlix. 1). For David's employment of professional singers, see 2 Sam. xix. 35.
Delights.—Cant. vii. 6; Prov. xix. 10; Micah i. 16, ii. 9.
Musical instruments.—The Hebrew word here used occurs nowhere else, and commentators are reduced to look to the etymology for the explanation of it. Their guesses are so numerous that it would be wearisome to recount them. That adopted in our version is by no means one of the most probable. The interpretation "concubines" is most in favour with commentators, though they differ among themselves as to the grounds on which they justify this translation. And it does appear unlikely that this notorious feature of Solomon's court should be omitted in an enumeration of his luxury. It will be seen from the margin that the words "of all sorts" have nothing corresponding to them in the original, but are intended as an equivalent for a Hebrew idiom, in which a plural is intensified by prefixing a noun in the singular.

(9—11) Kohéleth carried out his plan of tempering his enjoyment with discretion, but while he took his fill of the pleasure that fell to his lot, he found in it no abiding profit. He goes on in the following paragraph to complain that the wisdom and other advantages he possessed in his search for happiness render his failure the more disheartening.

(12) This verse presents some difficulties of translation which need not be discussed here. The Authorised

wisdom, *a* and madness, and folly: for what *can* the man *do* that cometh after the king? ¹*even* that which hath been already done. ⁽¹²⁾ Then I saw ²that wisdom excelleth folly, as far as light excelleth darkness. ⁽¹⁴⁾ *ᵇ*The wise man's eyes *are* in his head; but the fool walketh in darkness: and I myself perceived also that *ᶜ*one event happeneth to them all. ⁽¹⁵⁾ Then said I in my heart, As it happeneth to the fool, so it ³happeneth even to me; and why was I then more wise? Then I said in my heart, that this also *is* vanity. ⁽¹⁶⁾ For *there is* no remembrance of the wise more than of the fool for ever; seeing that which now *is* in the days to come shall all be forgotten. And how dieth the wise *man?* as the fool. ⁽¹⁷⁾ Therefore I hated life; because the work that is wrought under the sun *is* grievous unto me: for all *is* vanity and vexation of spirit. ⁽¹⁸⁾ Yea, I hated all my labour which I had ⁴taken under the sun: because *ᵈ* I should leave it unto the man that shall be after me. ⁽¹⁹⁾ And who knoweth whether he shall be a wise *man* or a fool? yet shall he have rule over all my labour wherein I have laboured, and wherein I have shewed myself wise under the sun. This *is* also vanity. ⁽²⁰⁾ Therefore I went about to cause my heart to despair of all the labour which I took under the sun. ⁽²¹⁾ For there is a man whose labour *is* in wisdom, and in knowledge, and in equity; yet to a man that hath not laboured therein shall he ⁵leave it *for* his portion. This also *is* vanity and a great evil. ⁽²²⁾ *ᵉ*For what hath man of all his labour, and of the vexation of his heart, wherein he hath laboured under the sun? ⁽²³⁾ For all his days *are* ᶠsorrows, and his travail grief; yea, his heart taketh not rest in the night. This is also vanity.

⁽²⁴⁾ *ᵍ* There *is* nothing better for a man, *than* that he should eat and drink, and *that* he ⁶should make his soul enjoy good in his labour. This also I saw, that it *was* from the hand of God. ⁽²⁵⁾ For who can eat, or who else can hasten *hereunto*, more than I? ⁽²⁶⁾ For

---

Version gives the following very good sense: If the king has failed in his experiment, what likelihood is there that a private person should be more successful? Yet bearing in mind that in chap. v. 18 the "man that cometh after the king" means his successor, and also that the theme of the whole section is that in human affairs there is no progress, it is more simple to understand this verse: the king's successor can do no more than run the same round that has been trodden by his predecessor.

⁽¹³⁾ Wisdom surely has an advantage over folly, yet how full of "vanity" is that advantage. Let the wise man have done his best, soon death comes; the wise man is forgotten, and all he has gained by his labour passes, without labour, into the hands of one who may be no inheritor of his wisdom.

Excelleth.—There is profit in wisdom more than in folly. The same word "profit" is used as in chap. v. 11. (See Note on chap. i. 3.)

⁽¹⁴⁾ **Event.**—Translated "hap," or "chance" (Ruth ii. 13; 1 Sam. vi. 9, xx. 26).

⁽¹⁶⁾ It might be urged on behalf of the Solomonic authorship that Solomon himself might imagine that in the days to come he and his wisdom would be forgotten, but that such a thought does not become a long subsequent writer who had been induced by Solomon's reputation for wisdom to make him the hero of his work. It would seem to follow that the writer is here only giving the history of Solomon's reflections, and not his ultimate conclusions. Better to omit the note of interrogation after "wise man," and put a note of exclamation after "fool," the "how" being used as in Isa. xiv. 4; Ezek. xxvi. 17.

⁽¹⁷⁾ **Is grievous.**—Rather, *was.*

⁽¹⁸⁾ Eccles. ix. 19. There seems to be no special reference to Rehoboam, but only the assertion of the general principle that the wisest of men must leave all that his labour has gained to be enjoyed by another who may be destitute of wisdom. The thought is not so much that it is a hardship for the wise man to leave what he has gained, as that it is that he should have no advantage over the fool who enjoys the same without any merit.

⁽¹⁹⁾ **Have rule.**—The word occurs again in chaps. vi. 2, viii. 9; elsewhere only in Nehemiah and Esther, and in Ps. cxix. 133.

⁽²⁰⁾ **Went about.**—Chaps. vii. 25, ix. 14, xii. 5.

⁽²¹⁾ **Equity.**—Rather, *skill, success* (chaps. iv. 4, v. 7). The noun is peculiar to this book. The corresponding verb occurs in chaps. x. 10, xi. 6; Esther viii. 5.

⁽²³⁾ The fact that the wise man must surrender his acquisitions exhibits the inutility of the painful toil by which he has gained them.

⁽²⁴⁾ **Nothing better.**—"Not good" is the sense of the Hebrew as it stands, for it will be observed that the word "than" is in italics. But as this word might easily have dropped out by a transcriber's error, interpreters, taking in connection chaps. iii. 12, 22, v. 18, viii. 15, generally agree to modify the text so as to give it the meaning of our version, according to which the sense is: "Seeing the uncertainty of the future, the only good a man can get from his labour is that present pleasure which he can make it yield to himself; and whether he can even enjoy so much as this depends on God." If the text be not altered, the sense is: "It is not good for a man to eat, &c., seeing it depends on God whether or not that is possible."

⁽²⁵⁾ **Hasten.**—Hab. i. 8.

More than I.—There is a various rendering, which has the authority of the LXX., and which has every appearance of being right: "without Him."

⁽²⁶⁾ On the doctrine that the wicked amass wealth for the righteous, see marginal references.

God giveth to a man that *is* good ¹ in his sight wisdom, and knowledge, and joy: but to the sinner he giveth travail, to gather and to heap up, that *ᵃ* he may give to *him that is* good before God. This also *is* vanity and vexation of spirit.

CHAPTER III.—⁽¹⁾ To every *thing there is* a season, and a *ᵇ* time to every purpose under the heaven: ⁽²⁾ a time ³ to be born, and a *ᶜ* time to die; a time to plant, and a time to pluck up *that which is* planted; ⁽³⁾ a time to kill, and a time to heal; a time to break down, and a time to build up; ⁽⁴⁾ a time to weep, and a time to laugh; a time to mourn, and a time to dance; ⁽⁵⁾ a time to cast away stones, and a time to gather stones together; a time to embrace, and *ᵈ* a time ³ to refrain from embracing; ⁽⁶⁾ a time to ⁴ get, and a time to lose; a time to keep, and a time to cast away; ⁽⁷⁾ a time to rend, and a time to sew; *ᵉ* a time to keep silence, and a time to speak; ⁽⁸⁾ a time to love, and a *ᶠ* time to hate; a time of war, and a time of peace.

⁽⁹⁾ *ᵍ* What profit hath he that worketh in that wherein he laboureth? ⁽¹⁰⁾ I have seen the travail, which God hath given to the sons of men to be exercised in it. ⁽¹¹⁾ He hath made every *thing* beautiful in his time: also he hath set the world in their heart, so that *ʰ* no man can find out the work that God maketh from the beginning to the end. ⁽¹²⁾ I know that *there is* no good in them, but for *a man* to rejoice, and to do good in his life. ⁽¹³⁾ And also *ⁱ* that every man should eat and drink, and enjoy the good of all his labour, it *is* the gift of God. ⁽¹⁴⁾ I know that, whatsoever God doeth, it shall be for ever: nothing can be put to it, nor any thing taken from it: and God doeth *it*, that *men* should fear before him. ⁽¹⁵⁾ *ʲ* That which hath been is now; and that which is to be hath already been; and God requireth ⁵ that which is past.

⁽¹⁶⁾ And moreover I saw under the sun the place of judgment, *that* wickedness *was* there; and the place of righteous-

---

1 Heb., *before him.*
a Job 27. 17; Prov. 28. 8.
b ver. 17; ch. 8. 6.
2 Heb., *to bear.*
c Heb. 9. 27.
d Joel 2. 16; 1 Cor. 7. 5.
3 Heb., *to be far from.*
4 Or, *seek.*
e Amos 5. 13.
f Luke 14. 26.
g ch. 1. 3.
h ch. 8. 17; Rom. 11. 33.
i ch. 2. 24.
j ch. 1. 9.
5 Heb., *that which is driven away.*

III.

The thought expressed at the end of the last chapter is developed in this chapter, which treats of the supremacy of God. Man can have no enjoyment except as He is pleased to bestow it. He has pre-ordained the times and seasons of all human events, and success cannot be obtained except in conformity with His arrangement.

⁽¹⁾ **A season.**—The word is only found in later Hebrew (Neh. ii. 6; Esther ix. 27, 31), and in the Chaldee of Daniel and Ezra.

Purpose.—The use of the word here and in chaps. iii. 17, v. 8, viii. 6, in the general sense of "a matter," belongs to later Hebrew. The primary meaning of the word is "pleasure" or "desire," and it is so used in this book (chaps. v. 4; xii. 1, 10).

⁽²⁾ The list of times and seasons is ranged in Hebrew MSS. and printed books in two parallel columns.

A time to die.—Job xiv. 5.

⁽⁴⁾ **Mourn.**—This is the ordinary word used for noisy funeral lamentations (Jer. iv. 8; 1 Sam. xxv. 1).

⁽⁵⁾ **Gather stones.**—As the collecting of stones for building purposes is included in verse 4, it is thought that what is here referred to is the clearing or marring of land (Isa. v. 2, lxii. 10; 2 Kings iii. 19, 25).

⁽⁶⁾ **To lose.**—Elsewhere this word means to destroy, but in the later Hebrew it comes to mean to lose, like the Latin "perdere."

⁽¹¹⁾ **In his time.**—In modern English, "its."

The world.—The word here translated "world" has that meaning in post-Biblical Hebrew, but never elsewhere in the Old Testament, where it occurs over 300 times. And if we adopt the rendering "world," it is difficult to explain the verse so as to connect it with the context. Where the word occurs elsewhere it means "eternity," or "long duration," and is so used in this book (chaps. i. 4, 10, ii. 16, iii. 14, ix. 6, xii. 5). Taking this meaning of the word here (the only place where the word is used with the article), we may regard it as contrasted with that for "time," or season, immediately before. Life exhibits a changing succession of weeping alternating with laughing, war with peace, and so forth. For each of these God has appointed its time or season, and in its season each is good. But man does not recognise this; for God has put in his heart an expectation and longing for abiding continuance of the same, and so he fails to understand the work which God does in the world.

So that no.—The connecting phrase here employed is rendered "because none" (Deut. ix. 28; 2 Kings vi. 3, &c.), "so that none" (Jer. ix. 10; Zeph. iii. 6, &c.).

End.—Chaps. vii. 2, xii. 13; Joel ii. 20; 2 Chron. xx. 16. A word belonging to the later Hebrew.

⁽¹²⁾ **I know.**—Literally, *I knew: i.e.,* I came to know. The writer is relating the conclusions at which he successively arrived.

To do good.—This phrase is always used elsewhere in a moral sense: "to act rightly." When enjoyment is meant, the phrase used is, as in the next verse, "to see good;" but the context seems to require that this sense should be given to the phrase in this verse also.

(13, 14) Ecclus. xi. 17, xviii. 6.

⁽¹⁵⁾ **Is now.**—Rather, *was long ago.*

Requireth.—*Seeketh again : i.e.,* recalleth the past. The writer has not been speaking of the bringing of the past into judgment, but of the immutable order of the universe, which constantly repeats itself. But it would seem that the word suggesting the thought of seeking for the purpose of judgment leads on to the next topic.

⁽¹⁶⁾ This verse introduces the consideration of the difficulty arising from the imperfection of moral retri-

ness, *that* iniquity *was* there. (17) I said in mine heart, "God shall judge the righteous and the wicked: for *there is* ᵇ a time there for every purpose and for every work.

(18) I said in mine heart concerning the estate of the sons of men, ¹ that God might manifest them, and that they might see that they themselves are beasts. (19) ᶜ For that which befalleth the sons of men befalleth beasts; even one thing befalleth them: as the one dieth, so dieth the other; yea, they have all one breath; so that a man hath no preeminence above a beast: for all *is* vanity. (20) All go unto one place; ᵈ all are of the dust, and all turn to dust again. (21) Who knoweth the spirit ² of man that ³ goeth upward, and the spirit of the beast that goeth downward to the earth? (22) ᵉ Wherefore I perceive that *there is* nothing better, than that a man should rejoice in his own works; for that *is* his portion: for ᶠ who shall bring him to see what shall be after him?

CHAPTER IV.—(1) So I returned, and considered all the ᵍ oppressions that are done under the sun: and behold the tears of *such as were* oppressed, and they had no comforter; and on the ⁴ side of their oppressors *there was* power; but they had no comforter. (2) ʰ Wherefore I praised the dead which are already dead more than the living which are yet alive. (3) ⁱ Yea, better *is he* than both they, which hath not yet been, who hath not seen the evil work that is done under the sun.

(4) Again, I considered all travail, and ⁵ every right work, that ⁶ for this a man is envied of his neighbour. This *is* also vanity and vexation of spirit. (5) ʲ The fool foldeth his hands together, and eateth his own flesh. (6) ᵏ Better *is* an handful *with* quietness, than both the hands full *with* travail and vexation of spirit.

(7) Then I returned, and I saw vanity under the sun. (8) There is one *alone*, and *there is* not a second; yea, he hath neither child nor brother: yet *is there* no end of all his labour; ˡ neither is his eye satisfied with riches; neither *saith he*, For whom do I labour, and bereave my

---

a Rom. 2. 6, 8; 2 Cor. 5. 10; 2 Thess. 1. 6.
b ver. 1.
¹ Or, *that they might clear God, and see*, &c.
c Ps. 49. 12, & 73. 22; ch. 2. 16.
d Gen. 3. 19; ch. 12. 7.
² Heb., *of the sons of man*.
³ Heb., *is ascending*.
e ch. 2. 24, & 5. 18.
f ch. 6. 12, & 8. 7, & 10. 14.
g ch. 3. 16, & 5. 8.
⁴ Heb., *hand*.
h Job 3. 17, &c.
i Job 3. 11, 16, 21; ch. 6. 3.
⁵ Heb., *all the rightness of work*.
⁶ Heb., *this* is the *envy of a man from his neighbour*.
j Prov. 6. 10, & 24. 33.
k Prov. 15. 16, & 16. 8.
l Prov. 27. 20; 1 John 2. 16; Ps. 39. 6.

---

bution in this life. Other places where the iniquity of judges is mentioned are chaps. iv. 1, v. 8, vi. 7, viii. 9, 10.

(17) **A time there**—viz., with God. In this verse a judgment after this life is clearly spoken of, but not yet asserted as a conclusion definitely adopted, but only as a belief of the writer's conflicting with the doubts expressed in the following verses. "I said in mine heart," with which verses 17, 18 both begin, conveys the idea, "I thought," "and yet again I thought." The writer returns again to speak of the punishment of the wicked in chaps. viii. 15, xi. 9.

(19) **That which befalleth.**—The word translated "event" in chap. ii. 13 (where see Note).

Breath.—The same word as "spirit" (verse 21; Gen. vii. 15; Ps. civ. 30).

(21) The LXX., followed by a great body of interpreters, ancient and modern, translate, "Who knoweth whether the spirit of man goeth upward?" &c., and this agrees better with the context of this paragraph. The sceptical thought is, "We see that death resolves into dust (Gen. iii. 19; Eccles. xii. 7; see also Ecclus. xli. 10) the bodies of men and animals alike; and if it be alleged that there is a difference as to what becomes of their spirits, can this be asserted with the certainty of knowledge?" The writer here seems to have read both Ps. xlix. 14 and Prov. xv. 24.

IV.

(1) Having dwelt on the instability of human happiness, the Preacher now turns to contemplate the actual misery of which the world is full.

Oppressions.—Job xxxv. 9; Amos iii. 9.

No comforter.—If Solomon were the writer, one asks, What was the king about? Could he do nothing but express helpless despair?

(2) **I praised the dead.**—Job iii. 11; Exod. xxxii. 32; 1 Kings xix. 4; Jer. xx. 14; Jonah iv. 3. The word which is translated "yet" in this verse belongs to later Hebrew, and does not occur elsewhere in the Old Testament.

(4) **Right work.**—Rather, *skilful*. (See Note on chap. ii. 21.)

(5) **Eateth his own flesh.**—Interpreters have usually taken these words metaphorically, as in Ps. xxvii. 2; Isa. xlix. 26; Micah iii. 3, and understood them as a condemnation of the sluggard's conduct as suicidal. But it has been proposed, taking the verse in connection with that which precedes and those which follow, to understand them literally, "eats his meat;" the sense being that, considering the emulation and envy involved in all successful exertion, one is tempted to say that the sluggard does better who eats his meat in quiet. There is, however, no exact parallel to the phrase "eats *his* flesh;" and I think that if the latter were the meaning intended, it would have been formally introduced in some such way as, "Wherefore I praised the sluggard." Adopting, then, the ancient interpretation, we understand the course of conduct recommended to be the golden mean between the ruinous sloth of the fool and the vexatious toil of the ambitious man.

(7) **Then I returned.**—The vanity of toil is especially apparent in the case of a solitary man. It is possible, as has been suggested (see chap. ii. 18), that this may have been the writer's own case. The following verses, which speak of the advantages of

Advantages of Friendship and Unity. ECCLESIASTES, V. *Vanities in Divine Service.*

soul of good? This *is* also vanity, yea, it *is* a sore travail.

⁽⁹⁾ Two *are* better than one; because they have a good reward for their labour. ⁽¹⁰⁾ For if they fall, the one will lift up his fellow: but woe to him *that is* alone when he falleth; for *he hath* not another to help him up. ⁽¹¹⁾ Again, if two lie together, then they have heat: but how can one be warm *alone?* ⁽¹²⁾ And if one prevail against him, two shall withstand him; and a threefold cord is not quickly broken.

⁽¹³⁾ Better *is* a poor and a wise child than an old and foolish king, ¹ who will no more be admonished. ⁽¹⁴⁾ For out of prison he cometh to reign; whereas also *he that is* born in his kingdom becometh poor. ⁽¹⁵⁾ I considered all the living which walk under the sun, with the second child that shall stand up in his stead. ⁽¹⁶⁾ *There is* no end of all the people, *even* of all that have been before them: they also that come after shall not rejoice in him. Surely this also *is* vanity and vexation of spirit.

CHAPTER V.—⁽¹⁾ Keep thy foot when thou goest to the house of God, and be more ready to hear, *ᵃ* than to give the sacrifice of fools: for they consider not that they do evil. ⁽²⁾ Be not rash with thy mouth, and let not thine heart be hasty to utter *any* ² thing before God: for God *is* in heaven, and thou upon earth: therefore let thy words be *ᵇ* few. ⁽³⁾ For a dream cometh through the multitude of business; and a fool's voice *is known* by multitude of words. ⁽⁴⁾ *ᶜ* When thou vowest a vow unto God, defer not to pay it; for *he hath* no pleasure in fools: *ᵈ* pay that which thou hast vowed. ⁽⁵⁾ *ᵉ* Better *is it* that thou shouldest not vow, than that thou shouldest vow and not pay. ⁽⁶⁾ Suffer not thy mouth to cause thy flesh to sin; neither *ᶠ* say thou before the angel, that it *was* an error: wherefore should

Marginal references:
1 Heb., *who knoweth not to be admonished.*
a 1 Sam. 15. 22; Ps. 50. 8; Prov. 15. 8, & 21. 27.
2 Or, *word.*
b Prov. 10. 19; Matt. 6. 7.
c Num. 30. 2; Deut. 23. 21.; Ps. 50. 14, & 76. 11.
d Ps. 66. 13, 14.
e Prov. 20. 25; Acts 5. 4.
f 1 Cor. 11. 10.

---

friendship and unity, are of a more cheerful tone than the rest of the book.

⁽¹⁰⁾ **Woe.**—The word occurs only here and in chap. x. 16, but is common in post-Biblical Hebrew.

⁽¹¹⁾ **They have heat.**—The nights in Palestine were often very cold, and it would seem (Exod. xxii. 26) that it was common to sleep without any cover but the ordinary day garment; though see Isa. xxviii. 20.

⁽¹³⁾ The section commencing here presents great difficulties of interpretation, in overcoming which we have little help from the context, on account of the abruptness with which, in this verse, a new subject is introduced.

Poor.—The word occurs again in this book (chap. ix. 15, 16), but not elsewhere in the Old Testament: kindred words occur in Deut. viii. 9; Isa. xl. 20. No confidence can be placed in the attempts made to find a definite historical reference in this verse and the next.

⁽¹⁴⁾ **Becometh.**—Instead of this translation, it is better to render, *in his kingdom he was even poor;* but there is ambiguity in the Hebrew, as in the English, whether the antecedent of the "his" and the "he" is the old king or the new one.

⁽¹⁵⁾ **I considered.**—Heb., *I saw.* Most modern interpreters regard the "second child" as identical with the "young man" of verse 13, and understand the passage, "I saw him at the head of all his people; yet his great popularity was but temporary, and the next generation took no pleasure in him." It seems to me that by no stretch of rhetoric can "all the living which walk under the sun" be taken for the subjects of the sovereign in question. I am inclined to think that the Preacher reverts to the general topic, and considered all the living with the "second youth," *i.e.*, the second generation which shall succeed them. He saw the old generation hardened in its ways, and incapable of being admonished, and then displaced by a new generation, with which the next will feel equal dissatisfaction.

V.

⁽¹⁾ In the Hebrew division this is the last verse of the preceding chapter; but clearly here a new section begins, containing proverbs in the second person singular, which has not hitherto been used. There is no obvious connection with what has gone before; possibly the precepts here introduced were traditionally known to have been part of Solomon's teaching.

They consider not.—The most natural translation of this clause would be, "They know not how to do evil," *i.e.*, are incapable of doing evil. This would force us to understand the subject of the clause to be, not the fools, but those who are ready to hear. The Authorised Version exhibits one of the expedients resorted to in order to get a better meaning. Another is, "They are without knowledge, so that they do evil."

⁽²⁾ **Few.**—Ecclus. vii. 14, xviii. 22.

⁽⁴⁾ There is here a clear recognition of the passage in Deuteronomy. (See reff.; comp. Ecclus. xviii. 23.)

No pleasure in fools.—Comp. Isa. lxii. 4.

⁽⁶⁾ **The angel.**—It has been proposed to translate this word the "messenger," or ambassador of God, and understand "the priest" (see Mal. ii. 7); and it has been regarded as one of the notes of later date in this book that the word should be used in such a sense. But even in the passage of Malachi there is no trace that the word "angel" had then become an ordinary name for the priest, such as would be intelligible if used in that sense without explanation from the context. Neither, again, is there reason for supposing that the priest had power to dispense with vows alleged to have been rashly undertaken. The power given him (Lev. xxvii.) is of a different nature. I therefore adhere to the obvious sense, which suggests that the real vow is observed and recorded by a heavenly angel. It falls in with this view that the phrase is "*before* the angel." If an excuse pleaded to a priest was intended, we should have, "Say not thou *to* the priest."

God be angry at thy voice, and destroy the work of thine hands? (7) For in the multitude of dreams and many words *there are* also *divers* vanities: but *a* fear thou God.

(8) If thou seest the oppression of the poor, and violent perverting of judgment and justice in a province, marvel not ¹at the matter: for *b he that is* higher than the highest regardeth; and *there be* higher than they. (9) Moreover the profit of the earth is for all: the king *himself* is served by the field.

(10) He that loveth silver shall not be satisfied with silver; nor he that loveth abundance with increase: this *is* also vanity. (11) When goods increase, they are increased that eat them: and what good *is there* to the owners thereof, saving the beholding *of them* with their eyes? (12) The sleep of a labouring man *is* sweet, whether he eat little or much: but the abundance of the rich will not suffer him to sleep.

(13) There is a sore evil *which* I have seen under the sun, *namely*, riches kept for the owners thereof to their hurt.

(14) But those riches perish by evil travail: and he begetteth a son, and *there is* nothing in his hand. (15) *c* As he came forth of his mother's womb, naked shall he return to go as he came, and shall take nothing of his labour, which he may carry away in his hand. (16) And this also *is* a sore evil, *that* in all points as he came, so shall he go: and *d* what profit hath he that *e* hath laboured for the wind? (17) All his days also he eateth in darkness, and *he hath* much sorrow and wrath with his sickness.

(18) Behold *that* which I have seen: *f* ² *it is* good and comely *for one* to eat and to drink, and to enjoy the good of all his labour that he taketh under the sun ³ all the days of his life, which God giveth him: for it *is* his portion. (19) Every man also to whom God hath given riches and wealth, and hath given him power to eat thereof, and to take his portion, and to rejoice in his labour; this *is* the gift of God. (20) ⁴For he shall not much remember the days of his life: because God answereth *him* in the joy of his heart.

a ch. 12. 13.
1 Heb., *at the will, or, purpose.*
b Ps. 58. 11, & 82. 1.
c Job 1. 21; Ps. 49. 17; 1 Tim. 6. 7.
d ch. 1. 3.
e Prov. 11. 29.
f ch. 2. 24, & 3. 12, & v 7, & 11. 9.
2 Heb., *there is a good which is comely*, &c.
3 Heb., *the number of the days.*
4 Or, *Though he give not much, yet he remembereth*, &c.

Error.—The word is that which describes sins of *ignorance* (Num. xv.). The tacit assumption in this verse, that God interposes to punish when His name is taken in vain, clearly expresses the writer's real conviction, and shows that such a verse as chap. ix. 2 is only the statement of a speculative difficulty.

(7) This verse presents some difficulties of translation springing from corruption of text, but not affecting the general sense; according to which the many words which belong to the dreams and vanities of heathendom are contrasted with the fear of the only God.

(8) The interpretation of this verse depends on the sense we give to "marvel." There are some who take it of simple surprise. "You need not think it strange; the instances of oppression which you observe are only parts of a gigantic scheme of mutual wrong-doing, the oppressors of one being themselves oppressed in turn by their superiors." But instead of "Do not wonder," the meaning "be not dismayed" is preferable. (Comp. Ps. xlviii. 5; Job xxvi. 11; Isa. xiii. 8; Jer. iv. 9.) The verse then supplies the answer to the gloomy view of chap. iv. 4. In the view that the last clause speaks of the Divine rectification of earthly injustice, I am confirmed by observing that the author of this book delights in verbal assonances, and constantly links together words similar in sound. An English version might admit the meaning: "Over the high oppressor stands a higher, and over both, those who are higher still;" though even here there is the difficulty that the highest of all are spoken of in the plural number, of which it is a very awkward explanation that the "higher" is the king, and that the women and favourites who govern him are the "higher still."

But I cannot but think that the language of the Hebrew, that over the "*gebōh*" there be "*gebōhim*," is intended to suggest *Elohim* to the reader's mind.

On the word "province," see Note, chap. ii. 8; and on "matter," chap. iii. 1.

(9) **Is served by.**—Or, *is servant to.* Many eminent interpreters connect this verse with what precedes, and translate, "and on the whole the profit of the land is a king devoted to agriculture," an observation which it is hard to clear of the charge of irrelevance. I prefer, as in our version, to connect with the following verses, and the best explanation I can give of the connection of the paragraph is that it contains a consideration intended to mitigate the difficulty felt at the sight of riches acquired by oppression, namely, that riches add little to the real happiness of the possessors.

(13) **Sore evil.**—Chap. vi. 2; Jer. xiv. 17; Nah. iii. 19.

(14) **Evil travail.**—Unsuccessful business.

Nothing in his hand.—The same words occur in a literal sense in Judges xiv. 6.

(15) There is a clear use of Job i. 21. (See also Ps. cxxxix. 15.) And this passage itself is used in Ecclus. xl. 1.

(17) We pass without notice some variations of translation in this verse, which do not materially affect the sense.

(18) The Preacher is led back to the conclusion at which he had arrived (chaps. ii. 24, iii. 12, 22).

(20) "In the enjoyment of God's gifts he does not think much of the sorrows or brevity of life." This is the usual explanation; and though not satisfied with it, we cannot suggest a better.

CHAPTER VI.—(1) There is an evil which I have seen under the sun, and it *is* common among men: (2) a man to whom God hath given riches, wealth, and honour, so that he wanteth nothing for his soul of all that he desireth, yet *a* God giveth him not power to eat thereof, but a stranger eateth it: this *is* vanity, and it *is* an evil disease. (3) If a man beget an hundred *children*, and live many years, so that the days of his years be many, and his soul be not filled with good, and also *that* *b* he have no burial; I say, *that* *c* an untimely birth *is* better than he. (4) For he cometh in with vanity, and departeth in darkness, and his name shall be covered with darkness. (5) Moreover he hath not seen the sun, nor known *any thing*: this hath more rest than the other. (6) Yea, though he live a thousand years twice *told*, yet hath he seen no good: do not all go to one place? (7) *d* All the labour of man *is* for his mouth, and yet the ¹appetite is not filled. (8) For what hath the wise more than the fool? what hath the poor, that knoweth to walk before the living? (9) Better *is* the sight of the eyes ² than the wandering of the desire: this *is* also vanity and vexation of spirit. (10) That which hath been is named already, and it is known that it *is* man: *e* neither may he contend with him that is mightier than he. (11) Seeing there be many things that increase vanity, what *is* man the better? (12) For who knoweth what *is* good for man in *this* life, ³ all the days of his vain life which he spendeth as *f* a shadow? for who can tell a man what shall be after him under the sun?

CHAPTER VII.—(1) A *g* good name *is* better than precious ointment; and the day of death than the day of one's birth. (2) *It is* better to go to the house of mourning, than to go to the house of feasting: for that is the end of all men; and the living will lay *it* to his heart. (3) ⁴ Sorrow *is* better than laughter: for *h* by the sadness of the countenance the

a Luke 12. 20.

b 2 Kings 9. 35; Isa. 14. 19; Jer. 22. 19.

1 Heb., *soul*.

c Job 3. 16; Ps. 58. 8; ch. 4. 3.

d Prov. 25. 16.

2 Heb., *than the walking of the soul*.

e Job 9. 32; Isa. 45. 9.

3 Heb., *the number of the days of the life of his vanity*.

f Ps. 144. 4; James 4. 14.

g Prov. 15. 30, & 22. 1.

4 Or, *Anger*.

h 2 Cor. 7. 10.

VI.

(1) **Common among.**—Rather, *heavy upon*. In this section it is remarked how even when riches remain with a man to the end of his life they may fail to bring him any real happiness.

(2) **Riches, wealth, and honour.**—The three words are used together regarding Solomon (2 Chron. i. 11).

(3) That a man should be so occupied in the pursuit of riches as never to take any enjoyment from them is a common experience enough; but that the same man should have no sepulchre to preserve his name after him need not necessarily happen, so that one is tempted to think that the Preacher has some actual occurrence in his mind.

Untimely birth.—See references. We have just had another reminiscence of the Book of Job. (See chap. v. 15.)

(4) **He.**—Rather, *it*—viz., the untimely birth.

(6) **Though.**—The conjunction here used is only found again in Esther vii. 4.

(8) **That knoweth to walk.**—*Understands how to conduct himself.* But why this should be limited to the poor is not obvious.

(10) Of this difficult verse I prefer the translation, "What he is his name has been called long ago, and it is known that it is man; neither may he strive," &c.—*i.e.*, the name given long ago to man (Gen. ii. 7) indicates his weakness; neither can he contend with the Almighty. There may be a reference to Gen. vi. 3, where a kindred word is used.

Mightier.—The word here used is found only in the Chaldee books of the Bible and in later Hebrew.

(11) **Things.**—We might also translate "words."

(12) **As a shadow.**—Chap. viii. 13; Job xiv. 2.

VII.

In the sections immediately following, the continuity of the history of the Preacher's mental struggles is broken by the introduction of a number of proverbs, some of which have so little apparent relation to the context, that Renan even takes them to be intended as specimens of the "many words which increase vanity." But of any work, whether actually representing or intended to represent the teaching of Solomon, proverbs might be expected to form a necessary part. And though the ingenuity may not be successful which has been employed in trying to find a strict logical sequence in this part of the work, yet the thoughts are not unconnected with each other, nor out of harmony with the whole. The question with which the preceding chapter concludes, "Who knoweth what is good for a man?" is taken up in this, verses 1, 2, 3, 5, 8, 11, all beginning with the word "good." This characteristic would have been better kept up in translation if the first word of all these verses had been made "better." "Better is sorrow than laughter," &c.

(1) There is a play on words in the original (found also in Cant. i. 3), which Plumptre represents by "a good name is better than good nard." It was probably an older proverb, which the Preacher completes by the startling addition, "and so is the day of death better than that of birth." For the use of perfumes, see Ruth iii. 3; 2 Sam. xii. 20; Prov. vii. 17; Dan. x. 3.

(2) Comparing this verse with chap. ii. 24, it is plain that the Preacher does not in the latter place recommend reckless enjoyment, but enjoyment tempered by the fear of God, and looking to the end.

(3) **Sadness of the countenance.**—Gen. xl. 7; Neh. iii. 3. "Anger" (margin). This is the usual meaning of the word, and so in verse 9. It is accordingly

heart is made better. (4) The heart of the wise *is* in the house of mourning; but the heart of fools *is* in the house of mirth.

(5) *a It is* better to hear the rebuke of the wise, than for a man to hear the song of fools. (6) *b* For as the ¹ crackling of thorns under a pot, so *is* the laughter of the fool: this also *is* vanity. (7) Surely oppression maketh a wise man mad; *c* and a gift destroyeth the heart. (8) Better *is* the end of a thing than the beginning thereof: *and* the patient in spirit *is* better than the proud in spirit. (9) *d* Be not hasty in thy spirit to be angry: for anger resteth in the bosom of fools. (10) Say not thou, What is *the cause* that the former days were better than these? For thou dost not enquire ² wisely concerning this. (11) Wisdom ³ *is* good with an inheritance: and *by it there is* profit to them that see the sun.

(12) For wisdom *is* a ⁴ defence, *and* money *is* a defence: but the excellency of knowledge *is, that* wisdom giveth life to them that have it. (13) Consider the work of God: for *e* who can make *that* straight, which he hath made crooked? (14) *f* In the day of prosperity be joyful, but in the day of adversity consider: God also hath ⁵ set the one over against the other, to the end that man should find nothing after him.

(15) All *things* have I seen in the days of my vanity: there is a just *man* that perisheth in his righteousness, and there is a wicked *man* that prolongeth *his life* in his wickedness. (16) Be not righteous over much; neither make thyself over wise: why shouldest thou ⁶ destroy thyself? (17) Be not over much wicked, neither be thou foolish: *g* why shouldest thou die ⁷ before thy time? (18) *It is* good that thou shouldest take hold of this; yea, also from this withdraw not thine hand: for he that feareth God shall come forth of them all. (19) *h* Wisdom strengtheneth the wise more than ten mighty *men* which

---

a Ps. 141. 5; Prov. 13. 18, & 15. 31, 32.
b Ps. 118. 12; ch. 2. 2.
¹ Heb., *sound.*
c Ex. 23. 8; Deut. 16. 19.
d Prov. 14. 17, & 16. 32; James 1. 19.
² Heb., *out of wisdom.*
³ Or, *as good as an inheritance, yea, better too.*
⁴ Heb., *shadow.*
e ch. 1. 15.
f Deut. 28. 47.
⁵ Heb., *made.*
⁶ Heb., *be desolate.*
g Ps. 55. 23.
⁷ Heb., *not in thy time?*
h Prov. 21. 22, & 24. 5; ch. 9. 16.

---

adopted here by the older translators, but the rendering of our version is required by the context.

(6) There is again a play on words, which German translators represent by "the crackling of nettle under the kettle," and Plumptre "the crackling of stubble which makes the pot bubble." The reference plainly is to the quick blazing up and quick going out of the flame.

(7) **Surely.**—Rather, *For.* This change is required not only by literalness, but by the fact that the verse comes in a series of paragraphs, each commencing with the word "better," as does the next verse. This verse therefore cannot introduce a new subject, but must be connected with what has gone before. But it is so hard to do this satisfactorily, that Delitzsch conjectures that a line may have dropped out, and that this verse may have begun with "Better": *e.g.*, "Better is a little with righteousness, &c.," as in Prov. xvi. 8. If this be thought too strong a remedy, we may explain the connection, that by listening to faithful rebuke rather than to the flattery of fools, a ruler may be checked in a course of oppression or corruption which threatens to undermine his understanding. As we understand the passage, he becomes mad who commits, not who suffers, the oppression.

(8) **Thing.**—Here, as in chap. vi. 11 and elsewhere, we may also translate "word." Possibly the thought still is the advantage of bearing patiently "the rebuke of the wise."

(9) **Resteth.**—Prov. xiv. 33.

(10) **Concerning.**—This preposition is used after "enquire" only in later Hebrew (Neh. i. 2).

(11) **With.**—This is the ordinary meaning of the word, and accordingly is the rendering of the older translators, but the marginal "as good as," or "equally with," agrees so much better with the context, that the only question is whether the word will bear that meaning. And though in some places where it is translated "like," the rendering "with" may be substituted, yet the passages in Eccles. ii. 16, "no resemblance to the wise equally with the foolish," Job ix. 26, "my days have passed like the swift ships," seem to be decisive that it will.

Profit.—In defence of the marginal "yea, better," may be pleaded that the word is translated as an adverb (Esther vi. 6; and in this book (chap. ii. 16, vi. 8, 11, vii. 16, xii. 9, 12).

(12) **A defence.**—Literally, *a shadow* (Pss. xci. 1, cxxi. 5, &c.). This verse harmonises with the interpretation of the preceding verse, which we prefer, "Wisdom and riches alike confer protection, but the pre-eminence of wisdom is," &c.

(14) Ecclus. xiv. xxxiii. The first clause may be more closely rendered, "In the good day be of good cheer." As a consolation in time of adversity the thought Job ii. 10 is offered. The last clause connects itself with the first, the idea being that of chap. iii. 22; "take the present enjoyment which God gives, seeing that man cannot tell what shall be after him."

(15) **Days of my vanity.**—Chap. vi. 12.

(16) **Righteous over-much.**—The caution is against morbid scrupulosity and over-rigorism. We may illustrate by the case of the Jews, who refused to defend themselves against their enemies on the Sabbath day. The next verse is a necessary corrective to this: "Yet be cautious how thou disregardest the restraints of law."

(18) In the uncertainty of the issues of life, it is good for a man to make trial of opposite rules of conduct, provided he always restrain himself by the fear of God. (Comp. chap. xi. 6.)

(19) **Mighty men.**—The word is translated "governor" Gen. xlii. 6, and so see chap. x. 5; see also chap. viii. 8. The preacher returns to the topic of verse 12. Of the "For" in the next verse, only forced explanations have been given; the sentiment is Solomon's (1 Kings viii. 46).

The Difficulty of Wisdom. ECCLESIASTES, VIII. *The Duty of Loyalty.*

are in the city. (20) ^a For *there is* not a just man upon earth, that doeth good, and sinneth not. (21) Also ¹take no heed unto all words that are spoken; lest thou hear thy servant curse thee: (22) For oftentimes also thine own heart knoweth that thou thyself likewise hast cursed others.

(23) All this have I proved by wisdom: ^b I said, I will be wise; but it *was* far from me. (24) That which is far off, and exceeding deep, who can find it out? (25) ² I applied mine heart to know, and to search, and to seek out wisdom, and the reason *of things*, and to know the wickedness of folly, even of foolishness *and* madness: (26) ^c and I find more bitter than death the woman, whose heart *is* snares and nets, *and* her hands *as* bands: ³whoso pleaseth God shall escape from her; but the sinner shall be taken by her. (27) Behold, this have I found, saith the preacher, ⁴ *counting* one by one, to find out the account: (28) which yet my soul seeketh, but I find not: ^d one man among a thousand have I found; but a woman among all those have I not found.

(29) Lo, this only have I found, ^e that God hath made man upright; but they have sought out many inventions.

CHAPTER VIII.—(1) Who *is* as the wise *man*? and who knoweth the interpretation of a thing? ^f a man's wisdom maketh his face to shine, and ⁵ the boldness of his face shall be changed.

(2) I *counsel thee* to keep the king's commandment, and *that* in regard of the oath of God. (3) Be not hasty to go out of his sight: stand not in an evil thing; for he doeth whatsoever pleaseth him. (4) Where the word of a king *is, there is* power: and ^g who may say unto him, What doest thou? (5) Whoso

---

a 1 Kings 8. 46;
Prov. 20. 9;
John 1. 8.

1 Heb., *give not thine heart.*

b Rom. 1. 22.

2 Heb., *I and mine heart compassed.*

c Prov. 5. 3, & 22. 14.

3 Heb., *he that is good before God.*

4 Or, *weighing one thing after another, to find out the reason.*

d Job 33. 23.

e Gen. 1. 27.

f Prov. 4. 8, & 17. 24.

5 Heb., *the strength.*

g Job 34. 18.

---

(22) **Thine own heart knoweth.**—Chap. viii. 5; 1 Kings ii. 44; Prov. xiv. 10.

(23) The confession of failure to attain speculative knowledge gives energy to the preacher's next following enunciation of the practical lesson which he *has* learned from his experience.

(24) Rather translate, "That which is, is far off." The phrase, "that which is," or "hath been," to denote the existing constitution of the universe, occurs in chaps. i. 9, iii. 15, vi. 19. (See chap. viii. 17.)

(25) **The reason of things.**—The corresponding verb "to count" is common. This noun is almost peculiar to this book, where it occurs again in chaps. vii. 27, 29, ix. 10; save that in 2 Chron. xxvi. 15 we have the plural in the sense of military engines.

(26) Ecclus. ix. 3, xxvi. 23.

Snares.—See chap. ix. 12; used for siege works, chap. ix. 14.

Nets.—Hab. i. 15; Ezek. xxvi. 5.

Bands.—Judg. xv. 14.

(28) **One man among a thousand.**—See Job ix. 3, xxxiii. 23. The disparaging estimate of the female sex here expressed is common in countries where polygamy is practised. (See Ecclus. xxv. 24, xlii. 13.) It is credible enough that Solomon, with his thousand wives, did not find a good one among them; but see Prov. xviii. 22, xix. 14, xxxi. 10.

VIII.

(1) This verse in praise of wisdom can be connected either with what precedes or what follows. (See Hos. xiv. 9.)

Interpretation.—The word occurs elsewhere in the Chaldee parts of Daniel.

Boldness.—Impudence is removed from the countenance. See Prov. vii. 13, xxi. 29; Ecclus. xiii. 25.

(2) The unconnected "I" with which this verse begins, indicates that some word has early dropped out of the text. The italics with which our translators fill the gap no doubt give the right sense. It may be mentioned that Ecclesiastes is characterised by a superfluous use of the pronoun "I" after the verb, just as if in Latin we constantly had, instead of "dixi," "dixi ego." The counsels given here and chap. x. 4 are not what we should expect from Solomon, but rather from one who had himself lived under a despotism.

In regard of.—The words so translated are found again chaps. iii. 18, vii. 14; see also Pss. xlv. 5, lxxix. 9, cx. 4.

The oath of God.—Unsuccessful attempts have been made to find in these words a definite historic reference. It is idle to quote the fact recorded by Josephus that Ptolemy Lagus secured the allegiance of his Jewish subjects by exacting an oath from them. This book has no connection with Egypt, and we need not look beyond the Bible for proof that an oath of vassalage was imposed on the Jews by their foreign masters, and that the breach of such an oath was regarded by the prophets as sin (2 Chron. xxxvi. 13; Ezek. xvii. 13, 16, 18). And there is reason to think that similar pledges had been given to native kings (1 Sam. x. 3; 1 Chron. xxix. 24; 2 Chron. xxiii. 3).

Of God.—2 Sam. xxi. 7; 1 Kings ii. 43.

(3) I believe the rendering of our version to be correct, though some have taken it, "Be not hasty : go out of his sight." The best commentary on this verse is chap. x. 4, which gives the meaning, "When censured by the king, do not abandon the hope of retaining his favour, nor obstinately persist in what he condemns." I do not find adequate proof of the assertion of some commentators, that "go out of his sight" can mean "withdraw allegiance from him," and so that the "evil thing" means a rebellious conspiracy. The advice, "Be not hasty" to rebel, instead of "do not rebel," is inconsistent with the context.

(4) **Power.**—The word used here and chap. v. 8, only occurs again in the Chaldee part of Daniel. In the latter part of the Hebrew verse is one of the many reminiscences of the work of Job (Job ix. 12; see also Wisd. xii. 12).

keepeth the commandment ¹ shall feel no evil thing: and a wise man's heart discerneth both time and judgment. ⁽⁶⁾ Because to every purpose there is time and judgment, therefore the misery of man *is* great upon him. ⁽⁷⁾ For he knoweth not that which shall be: for who can tell him ² when it shall be? ⁽⁸⁾ *There is* ᵃno man that hath power ᵇover the spirit to retain the spirit; neither *hath he* power in the day of death: and *there is* no ³ discharge in *that* war; neither shall wickedness deliver those that are given to it. ⁽⁹⁾ ᶜAll this have I seen, and applied my heart unto every work that is done under the sun: *there is* a time wherein one man ruleth over another to his own hurt. ⁽¹⁰⁾ And so I saw the wicked buried, who had come and gone from the place of the holy, and they were forgotten in the city where they had so done: this *is* also vanity. ⁽¹¹⁾ ᵉBecause sentence against an evil work is not executed speedily, therefore the heart of the sons of men is fully set in them to do evil. ⁽¹²⁾ ᵈThough a sinner do evil an hundred times, and his *days* be prolonged, yet surely I know that ᵉit shall be well with them that fear God, which fear before him: ⁽¹³⁾ But it shall not be well with the wicked, neither shall he prolong *his* days, *which are* as a shadow; because he feareth not before God. ⁽¹⁴⁾ There is a vanity which is done upon the earth; that there be just *men*, unto whom it ᶠhappeneth according to the work of the wicked; again, there be wicked *men*, to whom it happeneth according to the work of the righteous: I said that this also *is* vanity. ⁽¹⁵⁾ ᵍThen I commended mirth, because a man hath no better thing under the sun, than to eat, and to drink, and to be merry: for that shall abide with him of his labour the days of his life, which God giveth him under the sun. ⁽¹⁶⁾ When I applied mine heart to know wisdom, and to see the business that is done upon the earth: (for also *there is that* neither day nor night seeth sleep with his eyes:) ⁽¹⁷⁾ Then I beheld all the work of God, that a man cannot find out the work that is done under the sun: because though a man labour to seek *it* out, yet ʰhe shall not find *it*; yea farther; though a wise *man* think to know *it*, yet shall he not be able to find *it*.

CHAPTER IX.—⁽¹⁾ For all this ⁴I

1 Heb., *shall know.*
2 Or, *how it shall be?*
a Ps. 49. 6, 7
b Job 14.
3 Or, *casting off weapons.*
c Ps. 10. 6, & 50. 21; Isa. 26. 10.
d Isa. 65. 20; Rom. 2. 5.
e Ps. 37. 11, 18, 19. Isa. 3. 10.
f Ps. 73. 14.
g ch. 3. 22.
h ch. 3. 11; Ps. 73. 16.
4 Heb., *I gave*, or, *set to my heart.*

⁽⁶⁾ The connecting particles here present difficulties which have not been satisfactorily solved; and it has even been conjectured that some words may have dropped out of the text. The first half of the verse repeats chap. iii. 1; the second almost verbally chap. vi. 1; on this account our translation "misery" is to be preferred to "wickedness" as some render it.

⁽⁸⁾ **Spirit.**—As has been remarked in similar cases, the translation "wind" is possible; but the rendering of the whole verse as given in our version seems to me as good as any that it has been proposed to substitute.

Discharge.—Elsewhere only (Ps. lxxviii. 49) where it is translated "sending."

⁽⁹⁾ **Own hurt.**—The Hebrew is ambiguous. We might omit "own," and understand the verse of the misery inflicted by a tyrant on his subject, not on himself. But the context speaks of the small gain from his oppressions to the tyrant himself.

⁽¹⁰⁾ **They had so done.**—An ambiguity in translation of this verse arises from the fact that the word translated "so" is rendered "well" (2 Kings vii. 9 and elsewhere). Consequently some understand the verse, "The wicked receive an honourable burial, while those who have acted well are driven away from the holy place (viz. Jerusalem, Isa. xlviii. 2; Neh. xi, 1, 18) and forgotten." But we prefer to translate the word "so" the second time, as well as the first, where it occurs in the verse; and to take the meaning to be that the oppressor's prosperity is but temporary, for soon comes death, burial, and forgetfulness of his honour.

⁽¹¹⁾ **Sentence.**—This is a Persian word only found in Esther i. 20, and in Chaldee parts of Ezra and Daniel.

⁽¹²⁾ **Though.**—Better, *Because*; the first part of this verse being in continuation of the preceding. The latter part of the verse states the faith which the writer holds in spite of apparent contrary experience.

⁽¹³⁾ **As a shadow.**—Chap. vi. 12; Wisd. ii. 5; see also Wisd. iv. 8.

⁽¹⁴⁾ **Happeneth.**—The word is used in this sense only in Esther ix. 26.

⁽¹⁵⁾ The writer returns to the sentiment expressed already (chaps. ii. 24, iii. 12, 22, v. 17).

Eat, and to drink, and to be merry.—The three words occur together 1 Kings iv. 20.

⁽¹⁶⁾ It would have been better if the new chapter had been made to begin here. The sentiment is that already expressed in chap. iii. 11.

Seeth sleep with his eyes.—Ps. cxxxii. 4; Prov. vi. 4; Gen. xxxi. 40. The identical expression occurs in Terence, *Heaut.* III. i. 82, "Somnum hercle ego hac nocte oculis non vidi meis."

IX.

⁽¹⁾ **No man knoweth.**—If this verse stood by itself we should understand, "Man cannot know whether he will experience marks of the Divine favour, or the reverse;" but taking verse 6 into account, we understand of a man's own love or hatred the objects of which he cannot tell beforehand.

considered in my heart even to declare all this, that the righteous, and the wise, and their works, *are* in the hand of God: no man knoweth either love or hatred *by all that is* before them. (2) *a* All *things* come alike to all: *there is* one event to the righteous, and to the wicked; to the good and to the clean, and to the unclean; to him that sacrificeth, and to him that sacrificeth not: as *is* the good, so *is* the sinner; *and* he that sweareth, as *he* that feareth an oath. (3) This *is* an evil among all *things* that are done under the sun, that *there is* one event unto all: yea, also the heart of the sons of men is full of evil, and madness *is* in their heart while they live, and after that *they* go to the dead. (4) For to him that is joined to all the living there is hope: for a living dog is better than a dead lion. (5) For the living know that they shall die: but the dead *b* know not any thing, neither have they any more a reward; for *c* the memory of them is forgotten. (6) Also their love, and their hatred, and their envy, is now perished; neither have they any more a portion for ever in any *thing* that is done under the sun.

(7) Go thy way, eat thy bread with joy, and drink thy wine with a merry heart; for God now accepteth thy works. (8) Let thy garments be always white; and let thy head lack no ointment. (9) 1 Live joyfully with the wife whom thou lovest all the days of the life of thy vanity, which he hath given thee under the sun, all the days of thy vanity: *d* for that *is* thy portion in *this* life, and in thy labour which thou takest under the sun. (10) Whatsoever thy hand findeth to do, do *it* with thy might; for *there is* no work, nor device, nor knowledge, nor wisdom, in the grave, whither thou goest.

(11) I returned, and saw under the sun, that *e* the race *is* not to the swift, nor the battle to the strong, neither yet bread to the wise, nor yet riches to men of understanding, nor yet favour to men of skill; but time and chance happeneth to them all. (12) For man also knoweth not his time: as the fishes that are taken in an evil net, and as the birds that are caught in the snare; so *are* the sons of men *f* snared in an evil time, when it falleth suddenly upon them.

(13) This wisdom have I seen also under the sun, and it *seemed* great unto me: (14) *There was* a little city, and few men within it; and there came a great king against it, and besieged it, and built great bulwarks against it: (15) now there was found in it a poor wise man, and he by his wisdom delivered the city; yet no man remembered that same poor man. (16) *g* Then said I, Wisdom *is* better than strength: nevertheless the poor man's wisdom *is* despised, and his words are not heard. (17) The words of wise *men* are heard in quiet more than the cry of him that ruleth among fools. (18) Wisdom *is* better than weapons of war: but *h* one sinner destroyeth much good.

CHAPTER X.—(1) Dead 2 flies cause

---

a Ps. 73. 3, 12, 13; Mal. 3. 15.
b Job 14. 21; Isa. 63. 16.
c Job 7. 10; Isa. 26. 14.
1 Heb., *See, or, enjoy life.*
d ch. 2. 24, & 3. 13, & 5. 18.
e Amos 2. 14; Jer. 9. 23.
f Prov. 29. 6; 1 Thess. 5. 3.
g Prov. 21. 22; ch. 7. 19.
h Josh. 7. 1.
2 Heb., *Flies of death.*

By all.—Rather, *all is before them.*

(2) **He that sweareth.**—Zech. v. 3.

(3) We have again the sentiments expressed in chap. ii. 14—16, iii. 19, v. 15, vi. 12.

(4) There is a various reading here in the Hebrew. Our translators, following the older translators, adopt the reading of the margin. That of the text gives, instead of "joined," a word signifying "chosen;" the best sense that can be given to which is to translate, "For who is excepted," joining it with the previous verse, beginning this one, "To all the living," &c. With regard to the statement of the following verses, comp. Ps. vi. 3 and the marginal references there given. The shepherd's dog is spoken of Job xxx. 1, and watchdogs Isa. lvi. 10. Elsewhere in the Old Testament the dog is an unclean animal living or dead.

(6, 7) **Now.**—Rather, *long ago.*

(7) **Accepteth.**—The thought has been expressed before (chap. ii. 24, viii. 15), that earthly enjoyment is to be received as given by God's favour.

(8) 2 Sam. xii. 20, xiv. 2; Ps. xlv. 8, civ. 14; Rev. vii. 9.

(10) **Thy hand findeth.**—Lev. xii. 8; Judg. ix. 33; and margin, *reff.*

The grave.—*Sheol* (John ix. 4).

(11) Rom. ix. 16.

Chance.—Elsewhere only in 1 Kings v. 4.

(12) Prov. vii. 23; Ezek. xii. 13; Hosea vii. 12.

(14) Idle attempts have been made to find a historic reference in this passage. What is here told is so like the story (2 Sam. xx.) of the deliverance of Abel-beth-Maachah by a wise woman, whose name, nevertheless, has not been preserved, that we cannot even be sure that the writer had any other real history in his mind.

X.

(1) **Dead flies.**—Literally, *flies of death,* which, according to a common Hebrew idiom, "weapons of death" (Ps. vii. 14); "snares of death" (Ps. xviii. 5) ought to mean death-giving or poisonous flies; but the existing translation yields so satisfactory a sense that we are unwilling to disturb it. (Comp. 1 Cor. v. 6.) There is a close connection with the last words of the

the ointment of the apothecary to send forth a stinking savour: *so doth* a little folly him that is in reputation for wisdom *and* honour. ⁽²⁾ A wise man's heart *is* at his right hand; but a fool's heart at his left. ⁽³⁾ Yea also, when he that is a fool walketh by the way, ¹ his wisdom faileth *him*, and he saith to every one *that* he *is* a fool.

⁽⁴⁾ If the spirit of the ruler rise up against thee, leave not thy place; for ᵃ yielding pacifieth great offences. ⁽⁵⁾ There is an evil *which* I have seen under the sun, as an error *which* proceedeth ²from the ruler: ⁽⁶⁾ folly is set ³in great dignity, and the rich sit in low place. ⁽⁷⁾ I have seen servants ᵇ upon horses, and princes walking as servants upon the earth.

⁽⁸⁾ ᶜ He that diggeth a pit shall fall into it; and whoso breaketh an hedge, a serpent shall bite him. ⁽⁹⁾ Whoso removeth stones shall be hurt therewith; *and* he that cleaveth wood shall be endangered thereby. ⁽¹⁰⁾ If the iron be blunt, and he do not whet the edge, then must he put to more strength: but wisdom *is* profitable to direct. ⁽¹¹⁾ Surely the serpent will bite without enchantment; and a ⁴ babbler is no better.

1 Heb., *his heart.*
a 1 Sam. 25. 24; Prov. 25. 15.
2 Heb., *from before.*
3 Heb., *in great heights.*
b Prov. 19. 10, & 30. 22.
c Ps. 7. 15; Prov. 26. 27.
4 Heb., *the master of the tongue.*

preceding chapter, which might better have been brought to a close at the end of verse 12.)

Apothecary.—Exod. xxx. 35.

Him that is in reputation for.—Substitute " is weightier than." The sense remains the same, viz., that a little folly undoes the effect of much wisdom.

⁽²⁾ **At his right hand.**—Perhaps better, *towards his right hand, i.e.,* leads him to go to the right hand. The thought is the same as chap. ii. 13, namely, that though the actual results of wisdom are often disappointing, the superiority of wisdom over folly is undeniable.

⁽³⁾ **That he is a fool.**—In Hebrew, as in English, the antecedent of "he" may be taken differently, and so the Vulg. and other authorities understand the verse as meaning that the fool in his self-conceit attributes folly to everyone else. But it is better, as well as more obvious, to take the verse of the self-betrayal of the fool (Prov. xiii. 16, xvii. 28, xviii. 2).

⁽⁴⁾ We return now to the thought of chap. viii. 3. For "spirit" in the sense of "anger," see Judg. viii. 3.

Rise up.—Ps. lxxviii. 21; 2 Sam. xi. 20.

Yielding.—Literally, *healing*. (See Prov. xv. 4.)

Pacifieth great offences.—Rather, probably, *quieteth great offences,* that is to say, not so much "puts an end to the offence felt by the ruler," as to the offences likely to be committed if he do not restrain himself.

⁽⁵⁾ **Error.**—The word is the same as at verse 6.

⁽⁷⁾ Considering that the importation of horses was a new thing in the reign of Solomon, we look on it as a mark of later age that a noble should think himself dishonoured by having to go on foot while his inferiors rode on horseback.

⁽⁸⁾ Commentators cannot be said to have been very successful in their attempts to trace a connection between the proverbs of this chapter. Perhaps nothing better can be said than that the common theme of these proverbs is the advantage of wisdom, and here in particular of caution in great enterprises. It is forcing the connection to imagine that the enterprise from which the writer seeks to dissuade, is that of rebellion against the ruler whose error is condemned (verse 5).

Diggeth a pit.—See Prov. xxvi. 27; Ecclus. xxvii. 26. The word here used for "pit" is found in later Hebrew, and nowhere else in the Old Testament.

An hedge.—Rather, *a stone wall,* in the crevices of which serpents often have their habitation. (Comp. Prov. xxiv. 31; Lam. iii. 9; Amos v. 19.) This verse admits of a curious verbal comparison with Isa. lviii. 12, "builder of the breach," in one, answering to "breacher of the building" in the other.

⁽⁹⁾ **Removeth.**—The nearest parallel is 1 Kings v. 17, where the word is used with regard to the quarryings, not the removing of stones. For the latter sense, however, there is countenance in 2 Kings iv. 4, where the word is translated "set aside."

Cleaveth wood.—Or, *cutteth down trees,* an operation not free from danger (Deut. xix. 5).

⁽¹⁰⁾ The wording of this verse in the original is very obscure; and we can only say of the rendering in the text that it seems to be preferred to any which it has been proposed to substitute for it. The mention of cutting wood in the preceding verse suggests the illustration from the axe, exemplifying how wisdom will serve instead of strength.

Iron.—2 Kings vi. 5; Isa. x. 34; Prov. xxvii. 17.

Whet.—Ezek. xxi. 21, where it is translated "make bright."

Edge.—Literally, *face*. We have often in Hebrew "mouth of the sword," for edge of the sword, but the only parallel for the expression "face" in that sense is in the highly poetical passage in Ezek. xxi. 16, just referred to.

Must he put to more strength.—"Make his strength mighty," the words being nearly the same as in the phrase "mighty men of strength" (1 Chron. vii. 5).

⁽¹¹⁾ This also is a difficult verse. Literally translated it is, *If the serpent bite for lack of enchantment, there is no advantage to the master of the tongue.* It seems best to follow the LXX. and other interpreters, and take the "master of the tongue" to mean the snake charmer, who possesses the "voice of the charmer" (Ps. lviii. 5). The whisperings of the snake charmer, so often described by Eastern travellers, are referred to also in Jer. viii. 17, and in a passage, probably founded on the present text (Ecclus. xii. 13), "Who will pity a charmer that is bitten with a serpent?" The mention of the serpent in verse 8 seems to have suggested another illustration of the advantage of wisdom in the different effects of snake-charming, as used by the expert or the unskilful. The phrase, "master of the tongue," seems to have been chosen in order to lead on to the following verses, which speak of the different use of the tongue by the wise man and the fool.

Enchantment.—According to the primary meaning "whispering" (2 Sam. xii. 19; Isa. xxvi. 16).

No better.—No advantage to. (See Note on chap. i. 3.)

The Blessedness of good Government. ECCLESIASTES, XI. *Kings and Rich Men not to be Cursed.*

(12) *a* The words of a wise man's mouth *are* ¹gracious; but the *b* lips of a fool will swallow up himself. (13) The beginning of the words of his mouth *is* foolishness: and the end of ² his talk *is* mischievous madness. (14) *c* A fool also ³ is full of words: a man cannot tell what shall be; and *d* what shall be after him, who can tell him? (15) The labour of the foolish wearieth every one of them, because he knoweth not how to go to the city.

(16) *e* Woe to thee, O land, when thy king *is* a child, and thy princes eat in the morning! (17) Blessed *art* thou, O land when thy king *is* the son of nobles, and *f* thy princes eat in due season, for strength, and not for drunkenness! (18) By much slothfulness the building decayeth; and through idleness of the hands the house droppeth through. (19) A feast is made for laughter, and *g* wine ⁴ maketh merry: but money answereth all *things*. (20) *h* Curse not the king, no not in thy ⁵ thought; and curse not the rich in thy bed-chamber: for a bird of the air shall carry the voice, and that which hath wings shall tell the matter.

CHAPTER XI.—(1) Cast thy bread 6 *h* upon the waters: for thou shalt find it after *i* many days. (2) *k* Give a portion to seven, and also to eight; for *l* thou knowest not what evil shall be upon the earth. (3) If the clouds be full of rain, they empty *themselves* upon the earth:

a Prov. 10. 32, & 12. 13.
1 Heb., *grace.*
b Prov. 10. 14, & 18. 7.
2 Heb., *his mouth.*
c Prov. 15. 2.
3 Heb., *multiplieth words.*
d ch. 3. 22, & 6. 12, & 8. 7.
e Isa. 3. 4. 5.
f Prov. 31. 4.
g Ps. 104. 15.
4 Heb., *maketh glad the life.*
h Ex. 22. 28; Acts 23. 5.
5 Or, *conscience.*
6 Heb. *upon the face of the waters.*
i Isa. 32. 20.
j Deut. 15. 10; Prov. 19. 17; Matt. 10. 42; Gal. 6, 9.
k Ps. 112. 9; Luke 6. 30; 1 Tim. 6. 18.
l Eph. 5, 16.

---

(14) **A man cannot tell.**—This thought occurs repeatedly in this book. (See *reff.*) The connection here would be better seen if the clause were introduced with "and yet." The fool's courageous loquacity is contrasted with the cautious silence which experience of his ignorance has taught the wise man.

(15) **To go to the city.**—Evidently a proverbial expression; "is not able to find his way on a plain road." (Comp. Isa. xxxv. 8.)

(16) **Woe.**—See Note on chap. iv. 10.

A child.—The Hebrew word has a wide range, being constantly translated *lad* or *young man*, and applied, for instance, to Solomon (1 Chron. xxix. 1), to Rehoboam (2 Chron. xiii. 7), and according to a usage common to many languages (*e.g.*, the Latin *puer*), it often means a servant (2 Sam. xvi. 1, &c.). Some take it in that sense here, contrasting it with the nobly-born king of the next verse. But comp. Isa. iii. 12.

In the morning.—Isa. v. 11; Acts ii. 15.

(18) **Droppeth**—*i.e.*, lets the rain drop through.

(19) I look on these verses as isolated proverbs, and believe that the obvious meaning suggested by the English of this verse is the right one. Those who strive to trace a continuity of thought take verse 18 as a figurative description of the ruin of an ill-governed land; verse 19 as describing the riot of those rulers who make feasts for merriment, and have money freely at their disposal; and (verse 20) as a warning to the subjects to beware how, notwithstanding all this misgovernment, they venture to rebel.

(20) **Thought.**—A word of later Hebrew, found only in Daniel and Chronicles.

That which hath wings.—Literally, *master of wings*; and so also Prov. i. 17. (Comp. "master of the tongue," verse 11.)

XI.

(1) In this section the preacher is drawing to a close, and he brings out practical lessons very different from those which views of life like his have suggested to others. From the uncertainty of the results of human effort, he infers that we ought the more diligently to make trial of varied forms of exertion, in order that this or that may succeed. From the instability of human happiness, he draws the lesson that we ought to enjoy freely such happiness as life affords, yet with a temperate and chastened joy, and mindful of the account we shall have to render. The most popular explanation of verse 1 is, that the figure is taken from the casting of seed on irrigated lands, as, for instance, in Egypt before the waters of the Nile have subsided; and that the duty of beneficence is here inculcated. We are to sow our benefits broadcast, and be assured we shall have a harvest of reward. It is easier to raise objections to this interpretation than to improve on it. That the word translated "bread" is sometimes used in the sense of seed corn, see Isa. xxviii. 28, xxx. 23; Ps. civ. 14. It is objected that the words "cast on the waters" are, literally, "send over the face of the waters," the word "send" being nowhere else used in the sense of sowing. It has been remarked that in the East bread is used in the shape of light cakes, which would float on water; and the text has been understood as directing the casting of such cakes into a running stream—an irrational proceeding, not likely to occur to any but one to whom this text might have suggested it, and not offering ground for expectation that he who so cast his bread would find it again. It has been less absurdly proposed to understand the text as advising maritime enterprise; but the word "bread" does not harmonise with this explanation. There is nothing else in the book according with such advice; and the next verse, about "the evil that shall be *upon the earth*," shows that the writer was not thinking of the dangers of the sea. I believe, therefore, that verse 6, which speaks distinctly of the sowing of seed, is the best commentary on the present verse, which means, cast thy seed, even though thou canst not see where it will fall. Possibly the application of the figure is not to be restricted to acts of beneficence; but the next verse may lead us to think that these are primarily intended, and to these especially the encouragement at the end of the verse applies; for in other cases this book gives a less cheerful view of the possible success of human plans.

(2) **To seven, and also to eight.**—Quite similar forms of expression occur in Job v. 19; Prov. xxx. 21; Amos i. 3; Micah v. 4. The numbers seven and eight are used indefinitely in the advice to multiply our modes of exertion, ignorant as we are which may miscarry.

(3) The world is ruled by fixed laws, the operation of which man has no power to suspend.

and if the tree fall toward the south, or toward the north, in the place where the tree falleth, there it shall be. (4) He that observeth the wind shall not sow; and he that regardeth the clouds shall not reap. (5) As thou knowest not what *is* the way of the spirit, nor *a* how the bones *do grow* in the womb of her that is with child: even so thou knowest not the works of God who maketh all. (6) In the morning sow thy seed, and in the evening withhold not thine hand: for thou knowest not whether ¹shall prosper, either this or that, or whether they both *shall be* alike good.

(7) Truly the light *is* sweet, and a pleasant *thing it is* for the eyes to behold the sun: (8) But if a man live many years, *and* rejoice in them all; yet let him remember the days of darkness; for they shall be many. All that cometh *is* vanity. (9) Rejoice, O young man, in thy youth; and let thy heart cheer thee in the days of thy youth, and *b* walk in the ways of thine heart, and in the sight of thine eyes: but know thou, that for all these *things* God will bring thee into judgment. (10) Therefore remove ²sorrow from thy heart, and *c* put away evil from thy flesh: for *d* childhood and youth *are* vanity.

CHAPTER XII.—(1) Remember *e* now thy Creator in the days of thy youth, while the evil days come not, nor the years draw nigh, *f* when thou shalt say, I have no pleasure in them; (2) while the sun, or the light, or the moon, or the stars, be not darkened, nor the clouds return after the rain: (3) In the day when the keepers of the house shall tremble, and the strong men shall bow themselves, and ³the grinders cease

a Ps. 139. 14.
1 Heb., *shall be right.*
b Num. 15. 39.
2 Or, *anger.*
c 2 Col. 7. 1; 2 Tim. 2. 21.
d Ps. 39. 5.
e Prov. 22. 6; Lam. 3. 27.
f 2 Sam. 19. 35.
3 Or, *the grinders fail, because they grind little.*

---

(4) But it is idle to try to guard against all possibilities of failure. To demand a certainty of success before acting would mean not to act at all.

(5) The wording of this passage leaves it ambiguous whether we have here two illustrations of man's ignorance, or only one; whether we are to understand the verse as declaring that we know neither the way of the wind nor the growth of the embryo, or whether, retaining the translation "spirit," we take the whole verse as relating to the latter subject. (Comp. John iii. 6.) The word for "her that is with child" occurs in that sense here only in the Old Testament, and in later Hebrew.

(6) **Prosper.**—The word is used again in chap. x. 10 and Esther viii. 5, and belongs to modern Hebrew. (Comp. Gal. vi. 7, 8.)

(8) **Days of darkness.**—Pss. lxxxviii. 12, cxliii. 3; Job x. 21. (Comp. also Ps. lvi. 13; Job xxxiii. 30.)

(9) The beginning of the last chapter would more conveniently have been placed here than where the division is actually made. It is hard to interpret the judgment spoken of in this verse of anything but future judgment, when we bear in mind how much of the book is taken up with the complaint that retribution does not take place in this life.

(10) **Sorrow.**—See Note on chap. vii. 3.

Youth.—The word occurs not elsewhere in the Old Testament; but nearly the same word is used of black hair in Lev. xiii. 37; Cant. v. 11.

XII.

(1) **Creator.**—This occurs as a Divine name in Isa. xl. 23, xliv. 15, and elsewhere. Here it is in the plural, like the Divine name Elohim. (See also Note on verse 8.) We have "thy Maker" in the plural in Job xxxv. 10; Ps. cxlix. 2; Isa. liv. 5; and "Holy One" in Prov. ix. 10, xxx. 3; Hosea xi. 12.

(2) Here the style rises, and we have a figurative description of the "evil days;" but, as sometimes happens in the case of highly wrought poetry, it is much easier to perceive the general effect intended than to account for all the words which produce it. English readers generally have been deeply impressed by verses 6, 7, in a general way understanding them as speaking of the dissolution of the noble structure of the bodily frame; and they scarcely gain anything by the efforts of commentators to explain to them what exactly is meant by the "silver cord" and the "golden bowl." After using all the help my predecessors have given me, I frankly own myself unable to give more than a vague account of the figures employed in this whole passage.

Darkened.—See chap. xi. 8. On darkness of the heavens as a symbol of calamity, comp. Isa. xiii. 10, 11; Jer. iv. 28, 29; Ezek. xxxii. 7—9; Joel ii. 1—10; Amos viii. 9, 10; and contrast Isa. xxx. 26, lx. 10.)

(3) In this verse we have a description of an afflicted and affrighted house: the servants below (keepers of the house; comp. 2 Sam. xx. 3) in consternation [the word for "tremble" occurs twice more in Biblical Hebrew (Esther v. 9; Habak. ii. 7), but is common in Aramæan]; the masters (men of might, translated "able men" Exod. xviii. 21, 25; comp. "mighty in power," Job xxi. 7) in equal distress; so also the grinding maids below, discontinuing their work (Exod. xi. 5; Isa. xlvii. 1, 2); the ladies, who look out at the lattices (Judges v. 8; 2 Sam. v. 16; Prov. vii. 6; 2 Kings ix. 30), forced to withdraw. (For the four classes, comp. Isa. xxiv. 2; Ps. cxxxii. 2.)

Expositors have generally understood the house here described as denoting the decaying body of the old man. To the English reader the "grinders" of our version suggest "teeth" in a way that the "grinding maidens" of the Hebrew does not; and the ladies looking out of the lattices can easily be understood of "the eyes." But when it is attempted to carry out the figure, and to find anatomical explanations of all the other images employed, the interpretation becomes so forced that some have preferred to understand verse 3 as only a general description of the consternation produced by such a tempest as is spoken of in verse 2. I cannot but think that the "house" does denote the bodily frame; but I regard as unsuccessful the attempts

The Creator to be Remembered in Youth. ECCLESIASTES, XII. *The Conclusion of the whole matter.*

because they are few, and those that look out of the windows be darkened, (4) and the doors shall be shut in the streets, when the sound of the grinding is low, and he shall rise up at the voice of the bird, and all the daughters of musick shall be brought low; (5) also *when* they shall be afraid of *that which is* high. And fears *shall be* in the way, and the almond tree shall flourish, and the grasshopper shall be a burden, and desire shall fail: because man goeth to ^ahis long home, and ^bthe mourners go about the streets: (6) Or ever the silver cord be loosed, or the golden bowl be broken, or the pitcher be broken at the fountain, or the wheel broken at the cistern. (7) ^cThen shall the dust return to the earth as it was: and the spirit shall return unto God ^dwho gave it. (8) ^eVanity of vanities, saith the preacher; all *is* vanity

(9) And ¹moreover, because the preacher was wise, he still taught the people knowledge; yea, he gave good heed, and sought out, and ^fset in order many proverbs. (10) The preacher sought to find out ²acceptable words: and *that which was* written *was* upright, *even* words of truth. (11) The words of the wise *are* as goads, and as nails fastened *by* the masters of assemblies, *which* are given from one shepherd. (12) And further, by these, my son, be admonished: of making many books *there is* no end; and ^gmuch ³study *is* a weariness of the flesh.

(13) ⁴Let us hear the conclusion of the whole matter: Fear God, and keep his commandments: for this *is* the whole duty of man. (14) For ^hGod shall bring every work into judgment, with every secret thing, whether *it be* good, or whether *it be* evil.

a Job 17. 13.
b Jer. 9. 17.
c Gen. 3. 19; Job 34. 15; Ps. 104. 29.
d Num. 27. 18; Job 34. 14; Zech. 12. 1.
e ch. 1. 2.
1 Or, *the more wise the preacher was, &c.*
f 1 Kings 4. 32.
2 Heb. *words of delight.*
g ch. 1. 18.
3 Or, *reading.*
4 Or, *The end of the matter, even all that hath been heard, is.*
h Rom. 2. 16, & 14. 10; 2 Cor. 5. 10.

---

which have been made to carry out this idea into its details.

(4) The first two clauses continue the description of the afflicted house; all communication with the outer world broken off: the double doors towards the street shut, the cheerful noise of grinding not heard without (Jer. xxv. 10, 11; Rev. xviii. 22). If a more minute explanation of the double doors is to be given, we may understand the verse as speaking of the closing of the lips on the falling away of the teeth. (See Job xli. 14; Ps. cxli. 3; Micah v. 7.)

He shall rise up.—No satisfactory explanation of this clause has been given. The following are three of the best interpretations that have been proposed: (1) The old man, whose state has been figuratively described before, is said to sleep so badly that the chirping of a bird will awake him. (2) His voice becomes feeble like the chirping of a bird (Is. xxix. 4, 32). (3) The bird of ill omen raises his voice (Ps. cii. 6, 7; Zeph. ii. 14). Each of these interpretations is open to serious objections, which I do not state at length, having myself nothing better to propose.

(5) The old man is beset with terrors; terrors from on high, terrors on the way: all in which he had taken delight before, has charms for him no longer; the almond causes loathing (for so may be translated the word rendered "flourished" in our version); the locust, in the East a favourite article of food, is now burdensome; the caper berry (translated "desire" in our version) fails; for man is going to his everlasting house, &c.

(6) **Golden bowl.**—Zech. iv. 3.

(7) The preacher has risen above the doubts of chap. iii. 21. (See also Gen. iii. 19.)

(9) In the introduction I have stated my conviction that the epilogue which here follows is an integral part of the book. If so, it seems to me clear that the writer, who has up to this recorded the words of Kohéleth, now speaks in his own name, and informs his readers that the preacher, whose teaching of the people he preserves, was also a writer, and the author of the well-known Proverbs.

Moreover.—This, the first word of the epilogue, is one of the specialties of the book of Ecclesiastes. (See chap. ii. 15.) So is also the word for "set in order" (chap. i. 15, vii. 13).

(11) **Words of the wise.**—In this and the next verse the weighty words of sages, such as was Kohéleth, are contrasted with the volubility of modern bookmakers. Though the general purpose of the verses is plain, the words used are enigmatical, and one cannot feel great confidence in assigning their precise meaning. The translation of our version fairly represents the original, if it is observed that the words "by" and "which," which determine the meaning, are in italics. With regard to the "nail," compare Ezra ix. 8; Isa. xxii. 23. The word "masters" we have had twice in this book already in the sense of possessor, "master of the tongue" (chap. x. 11), "master of wings" (chap. x. 20). "Assemblies" is a word not coming from the same root as that from which Kohéleth is derived. It might mean collections of sayings as well as of people. It is difficult to affix any meaning to the last clause, except that the sages, of whom the verse speaks, have been given for the instruction of the people by Israel's great Shepherd (Ps. lxxx. 1).

(12) **Study.**—The word occurs here only in the Old Testament; but is not a Talmudic word.

(13) **Whole duty of man.**—Rather, *the duty of every man.* The sacred writer practically anticipates the teaching of Rom. iii. 29.

(14) Considering that the book is filled with complaints of the imperfection of earthly retribution, this announcement of a tribunal, at which "*every* work," "*every secret* thing," shall be brought into judgment, cannot be reasonably understood of anything but a judgment after this life; so that this book, after all its sceptical debatings, ends by enunciating, more distinctly than is done elsewhere in the Old Testament, the New Testament doctrine of a day when God shall judge the secrets of men (Rom. ii. 16), shall bring to light the hidden things of darkness, and make manifest the counsels of the hearts (1 Cor. iv. 5).

THE SONG OF SOLOMON

INTRODUCTION
TO
THE SONG OF SOLOMON

The "Song of Songs"—from its Latin name, "canticum canticorum," known generally as Canticles—holds, without question, the first place among the puzzles of literature. Such uncertainty attaches to its subject, its purpose, its authorship, and even its form, that it would have occupied in any literature a place similar to that of Shakespeare's Sonnets in our own. Born on the sacred soil of Palestine, and appearing among the Holy Scriptures, it offers the greater difficulty of explaining its position. The history of the interpretation of the book from the earliest times has been a long apology to account for its place in the sacred Canon.

For from beginning to end there is not a single word in it which suggests any connection with religion. It presents itself as a page of secular literature that has become bound up with sacred. Of the rest of the Bible the forty-fifth Psalm is most naturally compared with it, since it has marriage for its theme, and is called in the inscription "A Song of Loves." But there in the space of seven verses the name of God occurs four times. Here it is not found at all. The word "Jah" indeed appears in the Hebrew (viii. 6), but only in its proverbial use as an expression of greatness. The forty-fifth Psalm, on the contrary, though on a secular subject, is as deeply religious in tone as any of those destined for Temple use. In the true Hebrew spirit everything is made subordinate to the master feelings of loyalty to the God Jehovah and reliance upon Him. In the Song of Songs not a trace of this feeling shows itself. There is not a single religious or spiritual sentiment of any kind, nor is there even the most distant allusion to any sacred rite or ordinance whatever. It is only by the cabalistic method of the Rabbis that reference to the Mosaic system can be forced into the book. The Law, the Temple, the Sacrifices, are unknown. There is not the faintest echo of the worship of the sanctuary. The priest and Levite are silent, and the voice of the prophet is not heard.

Yet the absence of direct religious allusion is not the only, is not the principal, distinction which sets the Canticles in contrast with other parts of the Old Testament. Rather it is the absence of the religious intention which everywhere else controls Hebrew poetry. The poem stands alone as an instance of what Hebrew poetic genius could do when released from the religious purpose. Nature is no longer, as in the rest of sacred song, the veil of the Divine, admired and loved as the vesture, the dwelling of the Most High. The breath of spring, the flowers of the valley, the woods and hills, are here loved for their own sake. The universe is not now filled with the angels of Jehovah, "fulfilling His word." The winds blowing from the north or the south, the streams flowing from the mountains, the lightning flash, "all are but ministers of love, and feed his sacred flame" (chaps. iv. 15, 16; viii. 6). The lessons of the lily, so dear to this poet, are not those of the Sermon on the Mount—it is to him only what the daisy was to Chaucer, a sweet emblem of the "truth of womanhede." The grass is a verdant couch for him (chap. i. 16), not, as to the author of Psalm civ., a suggestion of a wide and beneficent providence, or, as to Isaiah, an emblem of human frailty. It is not because God has planted them that he recalls the cedars of Lebanon, nor because their majestic beauty humbles human pride, but because their branches form a shady bower for meetings with his love. Had we the whole literature of Palestine, doubtless there would be found among it many other specimens of poetry which in distinction from that which is directly religious in tone we call profane. Israel must have given birth to "bards of passion and of mirth." Love and wine no doubt had their praises sung in the gathering of the vintage and at the harvest festivals. The strangeness lies in the fact of the admission of a specimen of amatory poetry into the sacred collection. How did the vigilance of those who watched the formation of the Canon allow it?

The allegorical and typical methods of interpretation which began with the Talmud, and have continued in favour till comparatively recent times, supply one answer to this question. Modern criticism for the most part substitutes a profound moral purpose for a concealed sacred meaning, as the *raison d'être* of the poem. This introduction will only set forth the plan and purpose of the book as it can be gathered, without hypothesis, from itself.

1. The subject of the book is the sentiment of love.

2. The language is like that of all love poetry, passionate, sensuous, voluptuous, in some cases with Oriental licence passing the bounds of the Western standards of sobriety and propriety.

3. The lovers whose mutual passion is sung are wedded. This is evident, not alone from the use of the word *khallah*—see note, chap. iv. 8—which, though its common employment is to designate a wife, might possibly in the language of love be employed (as sister in the same verse) as a term of strong endearment, but by quite a sufficient number of indications which, combined, leave no doubt on the point. (1) The deliberations of the heroine's family as to what shall be done with her when at a marriageable age are introduced in his own manner by the poet in one of the reminiscences of which the book is composed (viii. 8 *seq.*, *with note*), and such a turn given as to show beyond question that she married the man of her choice. (2) There is impressed on the whole poem a feeling of the superiority of wedded love over concubinage, and of monogamy over polygamy. (3) The glowing pictures of Solomon's marriage (iii. 6 *seq.*) are introduced evidently either as a foil, to set off the simpler yet greater happiness of the poet, or because this very marriage is the actual subject of the poem. (4) Lastly, the only class of literature with which the poem can be naturally compared is the epithalamium. Many points of analogy with compositions of this class are noticed in the notes, and the one conjecture which is almost irresistible is that first started by Bossuet,

that it was actually composed for such a purpose, and was a specimen of a species of literature common in Palestine.

4. Certain obstacles that lay in the way of this union, and which constancy and devotion succeeded in surmounting, furnish the incidents of the piece.

5. There is a kind of unity in the book. The lovers are the same throughout, but the unity is of feeling, not of form. The poem has the *appearance* of a collection of scattered pieces. Certain marks of division are self-evident; *e.g.*, at ii. 7, iii. 5, iv. 7, v. 1, and viii. 4. No commentator makes less than five breaks.

6. The poem does not consist of one continuous narrative, nor exhibit a plot progressively developed, but the *same* story of courtship is repeated again and again in different forms, with the same conclusion.* In one case the actual form is repeated with expansions (comp. iii. 1 *seq.* with v. 2 *seq.*). Descriptions, images, phrases, refrains, repeat themselves.

7. The story is varied by the use of dialogue. Different speakers can be plainly recognised; *e.g.*, a bridegroom in the character of a shepherd (whether real or assumed, as in so much pastoral poetry, is uncertain), a bride, the Shulamite, as a shepherdess, various maidens, the brothers of the bride. Others are conjectured, and the poem has frequently been arranged as a drama, with regular acts and scenes. All that is certain is that the author, as a matter of form, puts his sentiments into the mouth of different persons, instead of writing in his own person, and that his work is thoroughly dramatic in feeling.

These seven indications are clear and apparently beyond conjecture. Whether the writer had a concealed purpose beyond that of telling his story, whether it is his own passion which he paints so feelingly, or only an ideal representation of love, whether the scenes described are actual or imaginary, the characters historical or fictitious, all this will continue to be a matter of dispute; but it will never be questioned that there is in the Song of Solomon the delineation of a true and passionate love, a constancy tempted and tried, but triumphant over all obstacles, and proof against all seduction, "strong as death, inexorable as Hades," and that the representation is given in verse of such exquisite melody and poetry of such blended sweetness and power, that it must, apart from all other merits, rank by these alone among the highest lyric attempts of the world.

But it has assumed a place far higher. Not only has it a place in the sacred canon, but it has, in the mystic sense attached to it, been regarded as the most sacred book there. Its first commentator, R. Akiba, who lived in the first century of our era, said of it, "The whole world is not worthy of the day in which this sublime song was given to Israel; for all the Scriptures are holy, but this sublime Song is most holy." On the other hand, a recent commentator, E. Reuss (*Le Cantique des Cantiques dit de Salomon*, Paris, 1879), hesitates to include it in his commentary on the Bible, lest his readers should be shocked at a book so totally different from all the rest of Scripture, and conceived in a spirit, if not anti-religious, yet positively strange to all religious sentiments. It was no doubt the shock experienced by pious minds that first suggested the allegorical method of interpretation, which in spite of the uncompromising verdict of criticism will probably continue to keep its hold on the book. As Renan says, "the mystical sense is false philosophically, but it is true religiously. It corresponds to the great sanctification of love inaugurated by Christianity." Association consecrates no less than dedication. Words, though in themselves indifferent, when set to sublime music partake of its inspiration. So the Canticles can never, under any interpretation, altogether lose the sacred power impressed upon them by generations of pious minds. But apart from an assumed religious character, the poem has its proper place in the Bible. The passion of love is ennobling according as it partakes of the moral sentiment. There have been writers on the Song who have been unable to discover any trace of this controlling influence, "but from beginning to end only marks of folly, vanity, and looseness" (Whiston). Such a view loses sight of the Eastern origin of the poem, and neglects the undoubted contrast displayed throughout between the meretricious manners of the harem and the purity of a constant passion, between the evils of polygamy and the blessings attending the unalterable attachment of two loving souls. It is not a taint of voluptuousness that can rob of its principal worth such a representation of love as culminates in the magnificent description in verses 6 and 7 of chapter viii., and this representation is alone enough to justify the admission of the Song into the Canon; for, in the language of Bunsen, "There would be something wanting in the Bible, if there was not found there an expression of the deepest and the strongest of all human feelings."

---

* This may seem an arbitrary assumption in the face of the attempts of so many eminent scholars to present the poem as a regular drama, but the unsatisfactory nature of *all* such attempts is a sufficient testimony to the fact that they have overlooked the plain indications given by the book itself.

THE SONG OF SOLOMON

CHAPTER I.—⁽¹⁾ The song of songs, which *is* Solomon's.
⁽²⁾ Let him kiss me with the kisses of his mouth:
*For ¹ thy love *is* better than wine.
⁽³⁾ Because of the savour of thy good ointments
Thy name *is as* ointment poured forth,
Therefore do the virgins love thee.
⁽⁴⁾ *^b* Draw me, we will run after thee:
The king hath brought me into his chambers:
We will be glad and rejoice in thee,
We will remember thy love more than wine:
² The upright love thee.
⁽⁵⁾ I *am* black, but comely, O ye daughters of Jerusalem,
As the tents of Kedar, as the curtains of Solomon.

B.C. written cir. 1014.
a ch. 4. 10.
1 Heb., *thy loves.*
b John 6. 44.
2 Or, *they love thee uprightly.*

Verse 1 contains the title of the book: literally, *A song of the songs* (Heb., *Shîr hashîrim*), *which to Solomon, i.e., of which Solomon is author.* This has been understood as meaning "one of Solomon's songs," with allusion to the 1,005 songs (1 Kings iv. 32) which that monarch composed. But when in Hebrew a compound idea is to be expressed definitely, the article is prefixed to the word in the genitive. So here not merely "*a* song of songs" (comp. holy of holies), *i.e.*, "a very excellent song," but "*The* song of songs," *i.e.*, the most excellent or surpassing song. For the question of authorship and date of poem, see *Excursus* I.

⁽²⁾ **Love.**—Marg., *loves, i.e.*, caresses or kisses, as the parallelism shows. The LXX., followed by the Vulg., read *breasts* (probably *dadaï* instead of *dôdaï*), the origin of many fanciful interpretations: *e.g.*, the two breasts = the two Testaments which breathe love, the first promising, the second revealing Christ. The reading is condemned by the obvious fact that the words are not spoken *to* but *by* a woman, the change of persons, from second to third, not implying a change of reference or speaker, but being an enallage frequent in sacred poetry. (Comp. Deut. xxxii. 15; Isa. i. 29, &c.) Instead of "let him kiss me," many prefer the reading "let him give me to drink," which certainly preserves the metaphor (comp. chap. vii. 9), which is exactly that of Ben Jonson's:—

"Or leave a kiss but in the cup,
And I'll not ask for wine."

⁽³⁾ **Because of the savour.**—The general sense of this verse is plain, though grammatical difficulties render the literal translation doubtful. It should be divided into three clauses, not into two only, as in the Authorised Version: "Because of their odour (or, with regard to their fragrance) thy ointments (are) sweet." There is no authority for taking *riach* = sense of smell, or we should naturally translate "to the smell thy ointments are sweet." The rendering of the next clause, "thy name is (like) oil poured forth," is to be preferred, though it necessitates making either *shemen* = oil, or *shem* = name, feminine, for which there is no example, since the alternative, which takes *tûrak* = poured forth, second masculine instead of third feminine, is harsh: "Thou art poured forth like oil with regard to thy name." The image is an obvious one (comp. Eccles. vii. 1). There is a play on words in *shemen* and *shemka*.

Virgins.—Heb., *alamôth*; *young girls.* (See Note, chap. vi. 8.) Those who understand Solomon to be the object of the desire expressed in these verses understand by *alamôth* "the ladies of the harem." In the original these three verses plainly form a stanza of five lines.

⁽⁴⁾ **The king hath brought me.**—The dramatic theory of the poem (see *Excursus* II.) has been in a great measure built up on interpretations given to this verse. We understand it as a repetition, in another form, of the protestation of love made in verses 1–3. Like them, it forms a stanza of five lines. The clause, "the king hath brought," &c., is—in accordance with a common Hebrew idiom, where an hypothesis is expressed by a simple perfect or future without a particle (comp. Prov. xxii. 29, xxv. 16)—to be understood, "Even should the king have brought me into his chambers, yet our transport and our joys are for *thee* alone; even then we would recall thy caresses, those caresses which are sweeter than wine."

The upright love thee.—Marg., *they love thee uprightly*; Heb., *meysharim*, used in other places either (1) in the abstract, "righteousness," &c., Ps. xvii. 2, xcix. 4; Prov. viii. 6 (so LXX. here); or (2) adverbially, Ps. lviii. 2, lxxv. 3 (and chap. vii. 9 below; but there the *Lamed* prefixed fixes the adverbial use). The Authorised Version follows the Vulg., *Recti diligunt te*, and is to be preferred, as bringing the clause into parallelism with the concluding clause of verse 3: "Thou who hast won the love of all maidens by thy personal attractions, hast gained that of the sincere and upright ones by thy character and thy great name."

⁽⁵⁾ **As the tents of Kedar**—*i.e., Dark as the Kedareen tents of black goats' hair, beautiful as the royal pavilions with their rich hangings.* For a similar style of parallelism, comp. Isa. xv. 3: "On her housetops, and to her open streets, every one howleth, descendeth with weeping." For *Kedar*, see Gen. xxv. 13.

As the poet puts this description of the lady's complexion into her own mouth, we must understand it as a little playful raillery, which is immediately redeemed by a compliment. It also prepares the way for the reminiscence of an interesting passage in her early life. See next verse.

(6) Look not upon me, because I *am* black,
Because the sun hath looked upon me:
My mother's children were angry with me;
They made me the keeper of the vineyards;
But mine own vineyard have I not kept.
(7) Tell me, O thou whom my soul loveth, where thou feedest,
Where thou makest *thy flock* to rest at noon:
For why should I be ¹as one that turneth aside by the flocks of thy companions?
(8) If thou know not, O thou fairest among women,
Go thy way forth by the footsteps of the flock,
And feed thy kids beside the shepherds' tents.
(9) I have compared thee, O my love,
To a company of horses in Pharaoh's chariots.
(10) Thy cheeks are comely with rows *of jewels,*

¹ Or, *as one that is veiled.*

---

(6) **Look not . . .**—*i.e., with disdain,* as in Job xli. 34 (Heb. 26).
Black.—Literally, *blackish.*
The sun . . .—The word translated *looked upon* occurs only twice besides (Job xx. 9, xxviii. 7). The "all-seeing sun" is a commonplace of poetry; but here with sense of scorching. The heroine goes on to explain the cause of her exposure to the sun. Her dark complexion is accidental, and cannot therefore be used as an argument that she was an Egyptian princess, whose nuptials with Solomon are celebrated in the poem.
Mother's children—*i.e., brothers,* not necessarily *step*-brothers, as Ewald and others. (Comp. Ps. l. 20, lxix. 8.) The reference to the mother rather than the father is natural in a country where polygamy was practised.
Mine own vineyard . . .—The general sense is plain. While engaged in the duties imposed by her brothers, she had been compelled to neglect something—but what? Some think *her beloved,* and others *her reputation;* Ginsburg, literally, *her own special vineyard.* But the obvious interpretation connects the words immediately with the context. Her *personal appearance* had been sacrificed to her brothers' severity. While tending their vines she had neglected her own complexion.

(7) **Where thou feedest . . . thy flock . . . For why should I be . . ?**—The marginal reading, *that is veiled,* follows the LXX. in rendering the Hebrew literally. But it has been found somewhat difficult to assign a meaning to a literal translation. The suggestions = *unknown* (Ewald), *veiled as a harlot* (Delitzsch, &c.; comp. Gen. xxxviii. 15), *fainting* (Gesenius), seem all wide of the mark, since the question only refers to the danger of missing her beloved through ignorance of his whereabouts. A transposition of two letters would give a word with a sense required = *erring, wandering about,* a sense, indeed, which old Rabbinical commentators gave to this word itself in Isa. xxii. 16 (Authorised Version, *cover*); and probably the idea involved is the obvious one that a person with the head muffled up would not find her way easily, as we might say, "Why should I go about blindfold?"
The Rabbinical interpretation of this verse is a good instance of the fanciful treatment the book has received: "When the time came for Moses to depart, he said to the Lord, 'It is revealed to me that this people will sin and go into captivity; show me how they shall be governed and dwell among the nations whose decrees *are oppressive as the heat*; and wherefore is it they shall wander among the flocks of Esau and Ishmael, who make *them idols equal to thee as thy companions?*'"

(8) **If thou know not.**—With this verse one subsection of the poem plainly ends. Most of the supporters of the dramatic theory make verse 9 begin the second scene of Act I.; and many of them understand this reply to the heroine's question as an ironical allusion on the part of the court ladies to her low birth. We take it rather as one of the many playful ways in which the poet either recalls or arranges meetings with the object of his passion (comp. chap. ii. 10—14). In the first seven verses he imagines her sighing for him, and in his absence, fancying, as lovers do, causes which might keep them asunder or make him forsake her, such as the loss of her complexion, her abduction into a royal harem; and then in verse 8 shows how groundless her fears are by playfully suggesting a well-known way of finding him.

(9) **Company of horses.**—So Vulg., *equitatus,* but Heb. *susah* more properly = *mare,* as in LXX., τῇ ἵππῳ μου. The ground of the comparison is variously understood. Some, offended at the comparison of female beauty to that of a horse, think the rich trappings of a royal equipage suggested it, while on the other hand, the mention of the caparisoned steed may have suggested the reference to the lady's ornaments. But Anacreon (60) and Theocritus (Idyll xviii. 30, 31), and also Horace (Ode iii. 11), have compared female with equine beauty; and an Arab chief would not hesitate to prefer the points of his horse to the charms of his mistress.
Chariots.—The plural shows that the image is general, and with no reference to any one particular equipage. Pharaoh's teams are selected as pre-eminently fine by reputation. The supposition that there is a reference to some present from the Egyptian to the Israelite monarch is gratuitous. The kings of Israel bought their horses and chariots at a high price (1 Kings x. 29).

(10) **Rows.**—Heb., *tôrim,* from *tûr* = went round; hence = either circlets or strings of jewels, or the round beads themselves of which necklaces, &c., were made.
Chains.—Literally, *perforated, i.e.,* beads, or possibly coins strung together. "Arab ladies, particularly the married, are extravagantly fond of silver and gold ornaments, and they have an endless variety of chains, bracelets, anklets, necklaces, and rings. It is also quite common to see thousands of piastres, in various coins, round the forehead and suspended from the neck, and covering a system of network, called suffa, attached to the back of the head-dress, which spreads over the

	SOLOMON'S SONG, I.	
The Ornaments		*of Love.*

Thy neck with chains *of* gold.
(11) We will make thee borders of gold with studs of silver.
(12) While the king *sitteth* at his table, My spikenard sendeth forth the smell thereof.
(13) A bundle of myrrh *is* my wellbeloved unto me; He shall lie all night betwixt my breasts.
(14) My beloved *is* unto me *as* a cluster of ¹camphire in the vineyards of En-gedi.
(15) ᵃ Behold, thou *art* fair, ² my love; Behold, thou *art* fair; thou *hast* doves' eyes.
(16) Behold, thou *art* fair, my beloved, yea, pleasant: Also our bed *is* green.
(17) The beams of our house *are* cedar, and our ³ rafters of fir.

1 Or, *cypress.*
a ch. 4. 1; & 5. 12.
2 Or, *my companion.*
3 Or, *galleries.*

---

shoulders and falls down to the waist" (Thomson, *The Land and the Book*).

Olearius (quoted by Harmer) says:—"Persian ladies use as head-dress two or three rows of pearls, which pass round the head and hang down the cheeks, so that their faces seem set in pearls." Lady Mary Montague describes the Sultana Hafitan as wearing round her head-dress four strings of pearls of great size and beauty.

(11) **Borders.**—The same word translated *rows* in preceding verse. In the dramatic theory, this verse put into Solomon's mouth takes the form of a seductive offer of richer and more splendid ornaments to dazzle the rustic maiden; but no theory is necessary to explain a fond lover's wish to adorn the person of his beloved.

(12) **While the king sitteth.**—There is no need to imagine a scene where the monarch, having failed in his attempt to allure the shepherdess by fine offers, retires to his banquet, leaving her to console herself with the thoughts of her absent shepherd love. As in verse 2 the poet makes his mistress prefer his love to wine, so here she prefers the thought of union with him to all the imagined pleasures of the royal table.

Spikenard.—Heb., *nerd*—is exclusively an Indian product, procured from the *Nardostachys jatamansi*, a plant of the order *Valerianaceæ*. It was imported into Palestine at a very early period. The perfume is prepared by drying the shaggy stem of the plant (see Tristram's *Nat. Hist. of Bible*, pp. 484, 485). There is a sketch of the plant in Smith's *Bibl. Dict.*

(13) **A bundle of myrrh.**—The mention of perfumes leads the poet to a new adaptation of the language of flowers. For myrrh (Heb., *môr*), see Gen. xxxvii. 25. For various personal and domestic uses, see Ps. xlv. 8; Prov. vii. 17, v. 13. Ginsburg quotes from the Mischna to prove the custom, alluded to in the text, of wearing sachets, or bottles of myrrh, suspended from the neck. Tennyson's exquisite little song in *The Miller's Daughter* suggests itself as a comparison :—

"And I would be the necklace,
  And all day long to fall and rise
Upon her balmy bosom
  With her laughter or her sighs.
And I would lie so light, so light,
  I scarce should be unclasped at night."

(14) **Camphire.**—Marg., *cypress*; Heb., *côpher*. There is no doubt of the identity of this plant with the *Henna* of the Arabs, the *Lawsonia alba* or *inermis* of botanists. Robinson found it growing in abundance at En-gedi (where *alone* it is found), and suggested the identification (see his Note, *Researches*, ii. 211). Tristram describes it thus: "It is a small shrub, eight or ten feet high, with dark back, pale green foliage, and clusters of white and yellow blossoms of a powerful fragrance. Not only is the perfume of the flower highly prized, but a paste is made of the dried and pounded leaves, which is used by the women of all ranks and the men of the wealthier classes to dye the palms of the hands, the soles of the feet, and the nails" (*Nat. Hist. of the Bible*, p. 339). (Comp. also Thomson, *The Land and the Book*, p. 602, who, however, prefers to identify *côpher* with some specially favourite kind of grapes, but without giving any sufficient reason.) For En-gedi, see Josh. xv. 62. It is the only place in Southern Palestine mentioned in this poem, the other allusions (except Heshbon, chap. vii. 4, which is in Moab) being to northern localities.

(15) **Behold, thou art fair.**—The song is now transferred to a male speaker—the advocates for the dramatic theory cannot agree whether Solomon or the shepherd; and no wonder, since the poem gives no indication.

My love.—Marg., *companion*, LXX. πλησίον, in Heb. *rayati*, is used for the female, *dôdi* being her usual term for her lover. Beyond this the terms of endearment used cannot safely be pressed for any theory.

Thou hast doves' eyes.—Literally, *thine eyes are doves'*. The same image is repeated (chap. iv. 1), and adopted in return by the heroine (chap. v. 12). The point of the comparison is either quickness of glance or generally tenderness and grace. The dove, a favourite with all poets as an emblem of love, is especially dear to this bard. Out of about fifty mentions of the bird in Scripture, seven occur in the short compass of this book. For general account of the dove in Palestine, see Ps. lv. 6, and for particular allusions Notes below to chap. ii. 11, 12, 14. (Comp. Shakespeare's *Coriolanus*, v. 3 :—

"Or those doves' eyes
That can make gods forsworn."

Tennyson's *Maud* :—

"Do I hear her sing as of old,
My bird with the shining head,
My own dove, with her tender eye?")

(16) **Our bed is green.**—The heroine replies in similar terms of admiration, and recalls "the happy woodland places" in which they were wont to meet.

(17) **Rafters.**—Marg., *galleries* (comp. chap. vii. 5); LXX, φατνώματα; Vulg., *laquearia*; Heb., *rahit*, from *rahat* = run, flow: hence (1) *a gutter*, from the water running down (Gen. xxx. 38); (2) *a curl*, from its flowing down the neck (*infra*, vii. 5—Heb. 6); (3) here *rafters*, or roof beams, from their spreading overhead. "Our couch was the green grass, the arches of our bower the cedar branches, and its rafters the firs." Others read *rachitim*, which is explained as a transposition for *charitim* = turned work. But the thought is plainly connected with the woods, not with a gorgeous house. For cedar see 1 Kings iv. 33.

Fir.—Heb., *berûth* (Aramaic form of *berôsh*), a tree often mentioned in connection with *cedar* as an emblem

Emblems of True   SOLOMON'S SONG, II.   *and Tender Love.*

CHAPTER II.—⁽¹⁾ I am the rose of Sharon, *and* the lily of the valleys. ⁽²⁾ As the lily among thorns, so *is* my love among the daughters. ⁽³⁾ As the apple tree among the trees of the wood, So *is* my beloved among the sons. [1] I sat down under his shadow with great delight, And his fruit *was* sweet to my [2] taste. ⁽⁴⁾ He brought me to the [3] banqueting house,

[1] Heb., *I delighted and sat down*, &c.
[2] Heb., *palate*.
[3] Heb., *house of wine*.

---

of majesty, &c. (Ezek. xxxi. 8; Isa. xxxvii. 24, lx. 13). "The plain here has evidently been buried deep under sand long ages ago, precisely as at Beirût, and here are the usual pine forests growing upon it (Beirût is by some derived from *berôth*). These are the finest specimens we have seen in Palestine, though every sandy ridge of Lebanon and Hermon is clothed with them. In my opinion it is the Heb. *berôsh*, concerning which there is so much confusion in the various translations of the Bible . . . the generic name for the *pine*, of which there are several varieties in Lebanon. *Cypress* is rarely found there, but *pine* everywhere, and it is the tree used for beams and rafters" (Thomson, *The Land and the Book*, p. 511). The *Pinus maritima* and the *Aleppo pine* are the most common, the latter being often mistaken for the Scotch fir. (See Tristram, *Nat. Hist. of Bible*, p. 353, &c.)

II.

⁽¹⁾ **The rose.**—Heb., *chabatseleth*. The identification of this flower is a much vexed question. From its derivation, it should be a bulbous plant (*batsal*—a bulb), and it happens that the flower which for other reasons best satisfies the requirements is of this kind, viz., the Sweet-scented Narcissus (*Narcissus tazetta*). "Others have suggested the crocus, of which there are many species very common, but they are deficient in perfume, and there is no bulb more fragrant than the narcissus; it is, besides, one of which the Orientals are passionately fond. While it is in flower it is to be seen in all the bazaars, and the men as well as the women always carry two or three blossoms, at which they are continually smelling" (Tristram, *Nat. Hist. of Bible*, p. 477). Dr. Thomson prefers the *mallow*, from the fact that the Arabs call it khubbazey. In Isa. xxxv. 1, the only other place where *chabatseleth* occurs, the LXX., Vulg., and Chaldee render "lily," and many eminent moderns "autumn crocus." Here the LXX. and the Vulg. have *flower*.

Of Sharon.—Better, *of the plain*, as in the LXX. Here (as invariably except 1 Chron. v. 16) the Hebrew has the article before *sharon*, but without definite local allusion to the district north of Philistia. The verse is by many taken as a snatch of a song into which the heroine breaks in answer to the eulogies on her beauty. It is certainly spoken with modest and lowly intention: "I am a mere flower of the plain, a lily of the valley;" by no means like Tennyson's "Queen lily and rose in one."

Lily.—So the LXX. and Vulg.; Heb., *shôshanath* (fem. of *shôshan*, or *shûshan*; comp. name *Susan*), a word occurring seven times in the poem, three times in 1 Kings vii., and in the headings to Pss. xlv., lx., lxix., lxxx. The Arabs have the word, and apply it to any brilliantly coloured flower, as the tulip, anemone, ranunculus. Although many plants of the lily tribe flourish in Palestine, none of them give a predominant character to the flora. There are, however, many other plants which would in popular language be called lilies. Of these, the *Irises* may claim the first mention; and Dr. Thomson (*Land and Book*, p. 256) unhesitatingly fixes on one, which he calls *Huleh Lily*, or the Lily of the Gospel and of the Song of Songs. "Our flower," he says, "delights most in the valleys, but it is also found in the mountains. It grows among thorns, and I have sadly lacerated my hands while extricating it from them. . . . Gazelles still delight to feed among them, and you can scarcely ride through the woods north of Tabor, where these lilies abound, without frightening them from their flowery pasture." Tristram, however, prefers the Anemone (*A. coronaria*), "the most gorgeously painted, the most conspicuous in spring, and the most universally spread of all the treasures of the Holy Land" (*Nat. Hist. of Bible*, p. 464).

⁽²⁾ **Among the daughters**—*i.e.*, among other maidens.

⁽³⁾ **Apple tree.**—So the LXX. and Vulg.; Heb., *tappuach*. Out of the six times that the word is used, four occur in this book, the other two being Prov. xxv. 11—"apple of gold"—Joel i. 12, where it is joined with vine, fig, &c., as suffering from drought. It has been very variously identified. The quince, the citron, the apple, and the apricot have each had their advocates.

The *apple* may be set aside, because the Palestine fruit usually called the *apple* is really the *quince*, the climate being too hot for our apple. (But see Thomson, *The Land and the Book*, p. 546.) The requirements to be satisfied are (1) grateful shade, verse 3; (2) agreeable taste, verses 3—5; (3) sweet perfume, chap. vii. 8; (4) golden appearance, Prov. xxv. 11. The *quince* is preferred by many, as being by the ancients consecrated to love, but it does not satisfy (2), being astringent and unpleasant to the taste till cooked. The *citron* does not, according to Thomson and Tristram, satisfy (1); but according to Rev. W. Drake, in Smith's *Bible Dictionary*, "it is a large and beautiful tree, gives a deep and refreshing shade, and is laden with golden-coloured fruit." The *apricot* meets all the requirements, and is, with the exception of the fig, the most abundant fruit of the country. "In highlands and lowlands alike, by the shores of the Mediterranean and on the banks of the Jordan, in the nooks of Judæa, under the heights of Lebanon, in the recesses of Galilee, and in the glades of Gilead, the apricot flourishes, and yields a crop of prodigious abundance. Many times have we pitched our tents in its shade, and spread our carpets secure from the rays of the sun. . . . There can scarcely be a more deliciously-perfumed fruit; and what can better fit the epithet of Solomon, 'apples of gold in pictures of silver,' than its golden fruit as its branches bend under the weight, in their setting of bright yet pale foliage?" (Tristram, *Nat. Hist. of Bible*, p. 335).

Among the sons—*i.e.*, among other young men.

⁽⁴⁾ **Banqueting house.**—Marg., *house of wine*; not the cellar of the palace, nor the banqueting hall of Solomon, nor the vineyard, but simply the place of the delights of love. The comparison of love with wine is still in the thought. (Comp. Tennyson's "The new strong wine of love.")

The Spring-time   SOLOMON'S SONG, II.   *of Love.*

And his banner over me *was* love.
(5) Stay me with flagons, ¹comfort me with apples:
For I *am* sick of love.
(6) ᵃ His left hand *is* under my head,
And his right hand doth embrace me.
(7) ² ᵇ I charge you, O ye daughters of Jerusalem,
By the roes, and by the hinds of the field,
That ye stir not up, nor awake *my* love, till he please.
(8) The voice of my beloved! behold, he cometh

¹ Heb., *straw me with apples.*
ᵃ ch. 8. 3.
² Heb., *I adjure you.*
ᵇ ch. 3. 5; & 8. 4.
ᶜ ver. 17.
³ Heb., *flourishing.*

Leaping upon the mountains, skipping upon the hills.
(9) ᶜ My beloved is like a roe or a young hart:
Behold, he standeth behind our wall,
He looketh forth at the windows,
³ Shewing himself through the lattice.
(10) My beloved spake, and said unto me,
Rise up, my love, my fair one, and come away.
(11) For, lo, the winter is past, the rain is over *and* gone;
(12) The flowers appear on the earth;
The time of the singing *of birds* is come,

And his banner . . .—*i.e.,* "and there I felt the sweet sense of a tender protecting love."

(5) **Flagons.**—Heb., *ashishôth,* apparently a dried cake, but of what substance is uncertain. From the margin of Hosea iii. 1, possibly "grape cakes." In 2 Sam. vi. 19 it occurs as one of the gifts distributed by David at the removal of the ark, and is rendered by the LXX., *a cake from the frying-pan.* Here the LXX. have *sweet unguents,* and the Vulg. *flowers.* The Authorised Version, *flagons,* follows a Rabbinical interpretation.

Comfort.—The margin, *straw me with apples,* follows the LXX., the Hebrew word occurs in Job xvii. 3; Authorised Version, "make my bed"—*ibid.* xli. 30 (Heb. 22). Authorised Version, "spreadeth." Hence some translate here, "make me a bed of apple-leaves;" but the parallelism is against this, and the root idea in both the words translated "comfort" and "stay" is putting a prop or support under. Metaphorically = *refresh* or *sustain.*

(7) **Roes.**—Heb., *tsebi, tsebiyah;* undoubtedly the *ghazal* of the Arabs; the *gazelle.* (See 1 Chron. xii. 8.)

Hinds.—Heb., *ayyalah.* (See Gen. xlix. 21.) The LXX. strangely read, *by the powers and virtues of the field.*

My love.—Here almost certainly in the concrete, though there is no instance of such use except in this and the corresponding passages. The Authorised Version, "till he please," is a mistake in grammar. Read, *till she please.* The poet imagines his beloved sleeping in his arms, and playfully bids her companions keep from intruding on her slumbers. This verse (which is repeated in chaps. iii. 5 and viii. 4) marks natural breaks in the poem and adds to the dramatic effect. But there is no occasion to imagine a real stage, with actors grouped upon it. The "daughters of Jerusalem" are present only in the poet's imagination. It is his manner to fancy the presence of spectators of his happiness and to call on outsiders to share his bliss (comp. chaps. iii. 11, v. 16, vi. 13, &c.), and it is on this imaginary theatre which his love conjures up that the curtain falls, here and in other places, on the union of the happy pair. Like Spenser, in his *Epithalamium,* this poet "unto himself alone will sing;" but he calls on all things bright and beautiful in the world of nature and man to help him to solemnise this joyful rite, and now the moment has come when he bids "the maids and young men cease to sing."

(8) **The voice of my beloved.**—So here there is no need of the clumsy device of supposing the heroine in a dream. This most exquisite morsel of the whole poem falls quite naturally into its place if we regard it as a sweet recollection of the poet's, put into the mouth of the object of his affections. "The voice" (Heb., *kôl*), used to arrest attention = Hark! (Comp. Ps. xxix.) The quick sense of love discerns his approach a long way off. (Compare—

"Before he mounts the hill, I know
He cometh quickly."—Tennyson's *Fatima.*)

(9) **Wall.**—As an instance of the fertility of allegorical interpretation, the variety of applications of this passage may be quoted. The *wall* = (1) the wall between us and Christ, *i.e.,* our mortal condition; (2) "the middle wall of partition," the law; (3) the iniquities separating man from God, so that He does not hear or His voice cannot reach us; (4) the creatures behind whom God Himself stands speaking through them, and "si fas dicere, (5) the flesh of Christ itself spread over His Divinity, through which it sounds sweetly and alters its voice" (Bossuet).

Looketh forth.—Rather, *looking through,* as in next clause, where the same Hebrew particle occurs, and may = either *out* or *in,* as context requires. Here plainly *in at.*

Shewing himself.—Marg., *flourishing.* The primitive idea seems to be "to look bright." Hence the Hiphil conjugation = "to make to look bright;" here "making his eyes glance or twinkle as he peers in through the lattice."

(11) **Winter.**—Heb., *sethav,* only used here; probably from root = *to overcast:* the season of cloud and gloom.

The rain is over and gone.—Wordsworth uses this line in a description of an early spring in a very different climate.

(12) **The time of the singing**—Heb., *zamir*—may mean *pruning* (so LXX. and Vulg.), but parallelism requires *singing-time* (a meaning which analogy will certainly allow us to give to the Hebrew word *zamir*). Nor can the correctness of our version in inserting *of birds* be questioned, since from the context it is plainly "the untaught harmony of spring," and not the voices of men intended. It is true there is no authority for this beyond the context, and the allusions to the singing of birds are besides very few in Scripture; but travellers say that different species of warblers (*Turdidæ*), especially the *bulbul* and the *nightingale,* abound in the wooded valleys, filling the air in early spring with the rich cadence of their notes (Tristram's *Nat. Hist. of the Bible,* p. 160).

And the voice of the turtle is heard in our land;
(13) The fig tree putteth forth her green figs,
And the vines *with* the tender grape give a *good* smell.
Arise, my love, my fair one, and come away.
(14) O my dove, *that art* in the clefts of the rock, in the secret *places* of the stairs,
Let me see thy countenance, let me hear thy voice;
For sweet *is* thy voice, and thy countenance *is* comely.
(15) Take us the foxes, the little foxes, that spoil the vines:
For our vines *have* tender grapes.
(16) *a* My beloved *is* mine, and I *am* his: he feedeth among the lilies.
(17) *b* Until the day break, and the shadows flee away,
Turn, my beloved,

a ch. 6. 3; & 7. 10.

b ch. 4. 6.

c ch. 8. 14.

1 Or, *of division*.

And be thou like a roe or a young hart Upon the mountains ¹ of Bether.

CHAPTER III.—(1) By night on my bed I sought him whom my soul loveth:
I sought him, but I found him not.
(2) I will rise now, and go about the city
In the streets, and in the broad ways
I will seek him whom my soul loveth:
I sought him, but I found him not.
(3) The watchmen that go about the city found me:
To whom I said, Saw ye him whom my soul loveth?
(4) *It was* but a little that I passed from them,
But I found him whom my soul loveth:
I held him, and would not let him go,
Until I had brought him into my mother's house,
And into the chamber of her that conceived me.

Turtle.—Heb., *tôr* (*turtur*), from its plaintive note. Three species are found in Palestine, but the one intended is doubtless our own turtle-dove (*Turtur auritus*). It is migratory, and its advent marks the return of spring (Jer. viii. 7). "Search the glades and valleys even by sultry Jordan at the end of March, and not a turtle-dove is to be seen. Return in the second week of April, and clouds of doves are feeding on the clovers of the plain." "The turtle, immediately on its arrival, pours forth from every garden grove and wooded hill its melancholy yet soothing ditty from early dawn till sunset" (Tristram's *Nat. Hist. of the Bible*, p. 219).

(13) **The fig tree putteth forth her green figs.**—Literally, *has ripened its unripe figs.* Heb., *phag* (preserved in Bethphage); not the early fruit that appears before the leaves (Matt. xxiv. 31), but the green fruit that remains through the winter (Gesenius and Tristram).

The vines with the tender grape.—Literally, *the vines (are) blossoms,* i.e., are in blossom.

(14) **O my dove . . . in the clefts of the rock.**—The rock pigeon (*Columba livia*), the origin of the domestic races, invariably selects the lofty cliffs and deep ravines (comp. Jer. xlviii. 28; Ezek. vii. 16) for its roosting places, and avoids the neighbourhood of men. The modesty and shyness of his beloved are thus prettily indicated by the poet. For the expression "clefts of the rock," see Note, Obad. 3.

The stairs—*i.e.*, steep places (comp. Ezek. xxxviii. 20, margin), from root = *to go up*.

(15) **Take us the foxes.**—Possibly this is a verse of a familiar country song, introduced here from the suggestion of the "sweet voice" in the last verse; but more probably to be compared to the "avaunt" so commonly addressed by poets in Epithalamia and love songs to all mischievous and troublesome creatures. Thus in Spenser's *Epithalamium*, owls, storks, ravens, and frogs are warned off.

Foxes.—Comp. Judges xv. 4. Whether *our fox* or the *jackal* (Heb., *shual*), it is known to be equally destructive to vineyards. Theocritus (*Id.* v. 112) is often compared:—

"I hate those brush-tailed foxes, that each night
Spoil Micon's vineyards with their deadly bite."

In the allegorising commentators they stand for *heretics.*

(16) **He feedeth.**—Heb., *he that is feeding his flock—the pastor.*

(17) **Until the day break.**—Heb., *breathe,* i.e., becomes cool, as it does when the evening breeze sets in. The time indicated is therefore evening, "the breathing blushing hour" (Campbell). (Comp. Gen. iii. 8, "The cool of the day"—margin, *wind.* This interpretation is also fixed by the mention of the flying, i.e., lengthening shadows. Comp. Virg. *Ecl.* i. 84: "Majoresque cadunt altis de montibus umbræ;" and Tennyson, *The Brook*—

"We turned our foreheads from the falling sun,
And followed our own shadows, thrice as long
As when they followed us.")

Bether.—Marg., *of division*; LXX., *of ravines or hollows,* either as separating the lovers or as intersected by valleys. Gesenius compares Bethron (2 Sam. ii. 29).

III.

(1) A reminiscence (elaborated in chap. v. 2 seq.) of the intensity of their love before their union, put by the poet into his lady's mouth. She "arises from dreams" of him, and goes to find him.

(3) **The watchmen that go about the city.**—"Henceforward until morning the streets are deserted and silent, with only here and there a company returning from a visit, with a servant bearing a lantern before them. The city-guard creeps softly about in utter darkness, and apprehends all found walking in the streets without a light" (Thomson, *Land and Book,* p. 32—in description of Beirût).

(4) **I held him . . .**—Bossuet, following Bede,

The Espousals   SOLOMON'S SONG, IV.   *of the King.*

(5) *a* I charge you, O ye daughters of Jerusalem,
By the roes, and by the hinds of the field,
That ye stir not up, nor awake *my* love, till he please.
(6) *b* Who *is* this that cometh out of the wilderness like pillars of smoke,
Perfumed with myrrh and frankincense,
With all powders of the merchant?
(7) Behold his bed, which *is* Solomon's;
Threescore valiant men *are* about it, of the valiant of Israel.
(8) They all hold swords, *being* expert in war:
Every man *hath* his sword upon his thigh because of fear in the night.
(9) King Solomon made himself ¹a chariot of the wood of Lebanon.
(10) He made the pillars thereof *of* silver,
The bottom thereof *of* gold, the covering of it *of* purple,
The midst thereof being paved *with* love,
For the daughters of Jerusalem.
(11) Go forth, O ye daughters of Zion,
And behold king Solomon with the crown wherewith his mother crowned him
In the day of his espousals,
And in the day of the gladness of his heart.

CHAPTER IV.—(1) *c* Behold, thou *art* fair, my love; behold, thou *art* fair;
Thou hast doves' eyes within thy locks:
Thy hair *is* as a *d* flock of goats, ²that appear from mount Gilead.

a ch. 2. 7; & 8. 4.
b ch. 8. 5.
1 Or, *a bed.*
c ch. 1. 15; & 5. 12.
d ch. 6. 5, 6.
2 Or, *that eat of,* &c.

---

regards this as prophetic of Mary Magdalen (type of the Church) on the morning of the Resurrection.

(6) **Who is this that cometh.**—The dramatic feeling is decidedly shown in the passage introduced by this verse, but we still regard it as a scene passing only in the theatre of the fancy, introduced by the poet in his Epithalamium, partly from his sympathy with all newly-wedded people, partly (as chap. viii. 11) to contrast the simplicity of his own espousals, of which all the joy centred in true love, with the pomp and magnificence of a royal marriage, which was a State ceremony.

Wilderness.—Heb., *midbar.* The idea is that of a wide open space, with or without pasture: the country of nomads, as distinguished from that of a settled population. With the article (as here) generally of the desert of Arabia, but also of the tracts of country on the frontiers of Palestine (Josh. viii. 16; Judges i. 16; comp. Matt. iii. 1, &c.).. Here = *the country.*

Like pillars of smoke.—The custom of heading a cortége with incense is both very ancient and very general in the East: probably a relic of religious ceremonials where gods were carried in processions. For *Frankincense,* see Exod. xxx. 34.

(7) **Bed.**—Heb., *mitta.* Probably, from context, a litter.

(8) **Because of fear**—*i.e.*, because of the alarms common at night. For *fear* in the sense of object of fear, comp. Ps. xci. 5; Prov. iii. 25.

(9) **A chariot.**—Marg., *bed*; Heb., *appiryôn.* A word of very doubtful etymology. Its derivation has been sought in Hebrew, Persian, Greek, and Sanskrit. The LXX. render φορεῖον; Vulg., *ferculum*; and it seems natural, with Gesenius, to trace the three words to the root common in *parah,* φέρω, *fero, fahren,* bear, and possibly the sign of such a common origin in the Sanskrit *pargana* = *a saddle* (Hitzig). At all events, *appiryôn* must be a *palanquin,* or *litter,* both from the context, which describes the approach of a royal cortége, and from the description given of it, where the word translated *covering* suggests the notion of a movable litter, rather than of a State bed.

(10) **Bottom.**—Heb., *rephidah* = *supports.* Probably the back of the litter on which the occupant leaned.

The midst thereof . . .—Literally, *its interior paved love from the daughters of Jerusalem.* There are three possible renderings. (1) Its interior made bright by a lovely girl of, &c.; and (2) its interior paved in a lovely way by, &c.; (3) its interior tesselated as a mark of love by, &c. The last of these does the least violence to the text as it stands, but very possibly some words have dropped out between *ratzuph,* paved, and *ahabah,* love.

IV.

(1) **Locks.**—Heb., *tsammah,* only besides in chap. vi. 7 and Isa. xlvii. 2. The derivation, and the existence of cognate Arabic words, leave no doubt that it means *veil.* So, in Isa. xlvii. 2, the LXX. understood it, though here they have given the strange and meaningless translation, " out of thy silence," which the Vulg. has still further mystified into " from that which lies hid within," a rendering which has been a fruitful source of moral allusion to the more hidden beauties of the soul. If the veil was worn in ancient times in Palestine, as by Eastern ladies now, covering the lower part of the face, but allowing the eyes to be seen, the description is very appropriate.

That appear.—Marg., *that eat of;* Heb., *galash:* only here and in the corresponding passage, chap. vi. 5. The word has had a variety of most contradictory interpretations. The Authorised Version follows the LXX., and has the support of Ewald's great authority. The marginal *eat of* rests only on the existence of cognates in Syriac and Arabic = *obtained, collected* (see Lee's *Heb. Dict.*), which would rather point to such a rendering as, " which they obtain from mount Gilead." The Vulg., *quæ ascenderunt,* is followed by some commentators, though the bulk give the exactly opposite: " come down," or " run down," or " hang down from." In such a difficulty only the context can decide, and any translation suggesting the dark hair flowing in masses round the shoulders is allowable. At the same time, from a tendency of the author to accumulate, and sometimes to confuse, his figures (verses 12, 15, chap. v. 12, 13), probably here it is the long, soft, delicate, generally black hair of the Oriental goat which is compared to that of

Emblems of   SOLOMON'S SONG, IV.   *Beauty.*

(2) Thy teeth *are* like a flock *of sheep that are even* shorn, which came up from the washing;
Whereof every one bear twins, and none *is* barren among them.
(3) Thy lips *are* like a thread of scarlet, and thy speech *is* comely:
Thy temples *are* like a piece of a pomegranate within thy locks.
(4) Thy neck *is* like the tower of David builded for an armoury,
Whereon there hang a thousand bucklers, all shields of mighty men.

(5) *a* Thy two breasts *are* like two young roes that are twins,
Which feed among the lilies.
(6) *b* Until the day ¹ break, and the shadows flee away,
I will get me to the mountain of myrrh, and to the hill of frankincense.
(7) *c* Thou *art* all fair, my love; *there is* no spot in thee.
(8) Come with me from Lebanon, *my* spouse, with me from Lebanon:
Look from the top of Amana, from the top of Shenir *d* and Hermon,

a ch. 7. 3.
b ch. 2. 17.
¹ Heb., *breathe.*
c Eph. 5. 27.
d Deut. 3. 9.

---

the lady, as well as the general appearance presented by the whole flock suspended on the mountain side.

(2) **Thy teeth . . .**—*i.e., white as newly washed sheep.* The word translated *shorn* is only used as a synonym for *sheep*, as we see by comparison with chap. vi. 6. The only other place where it is found is 2 Kings vi. 6, where it is used of cutting wood.

Bear twins.—The Hebrew word means "to make double." But this may either be "to produce twins," as in the text, or "to make pairs," or "to occur in pairs," a rendering which gives far better sense. The perfect and regular rows of teeth are exactly paired, upper to lower, like the sheep coming two and two from the washing, not one being bereaved of its fellow.

(3) **Speech.**—Rather, *mouth*, as the parallelism shows.

Thy temples . . .—Rather, *like a piece of pomegranate thy cheeks behind thy veil.* (See Note to verse 1.) "The pomegranate brings to my mind the blushes of my beloved, when her cheeks are covered with a modest resentment" (Persian Ode, quoted by Ginsburg from Sir Wm. Jones). For the pomegranate see Exod. xxviii. 34. It naturally supplied to the Eastern poet the image for which the Western poet goes to the apple. "Her cheeks like apples which the sun hath rudded" (Spenser).

(4) **Tower of David.**—This is not likely to be identified, when even the towers of Phasaelus and Hippicus, minutely described by Josephus, cannot be found. The structure at the north-west angle, known since the Crusades as the "Tower of David," is Herodian. No clue would be given by the words in the text, "builded for an armoury," even were it certain that this is their right rendering. The LXX. regard the Heb. *thalpiôth* as a proper name. Rabbinical authority is in favour of "as a model for architects," but most modern commentators, though differing as to the etymology, agree in giving the sense of the English Version, which the context seems to require. (Comp. Ezek. xxvii. 11: "They hanged their shields upon thy walls round about; they have made thy beauty perfect.") The shields and targets made by Solomon for the house in the forest of Lebanon may have suggested this addition to an image which is repeated in chap. vii. 7, and, indeed, is too common to need remark. "Her snowy neck like a marble tower" (Spenser). "Her neck is like a stately tower" (Lodge).

(6) **Until the day break.**—See Note, chap. ii. 17. *Until the day breathe* = *when evening is come*. Commentators have tried to identify the *mountain of myrrh* and *hill of frankincense*, but these only carry on the thought of verse 5 under another figure. We have come to another break in the poem, the end of another day, and, as before, though the metaphor is changed, the curtain falls on the complete union of the bridegroom with his bride.

(8) **Come with me.**—Better, *to me*. LXX., *hither*; so Vulg. and Luther, reading *athi*, imperative of *athah*, instead of *itti* = *with me*, or more properly, *as regards me*. The reading involved only a difference of vowel points, and is to be preferred. We have here another reminiscence of the obstacles which had attended the union of the pair under another figure. The course of true love, which never yet, in East or West, ran smooth, is beset here by tremendous difficulties, symbolised by the rocks and snows of the range of Lebanon, which shut in the poet's northern home, and the wild beasts that haunted these regions. Like Tennyson's shepherd, he believes that "love is of the valleys," and calls to her to come down to him from her inaccessible heights. The word *Shûr*, translated in English Version *look*, has properly in the LXX. its primitive meaning, *come*. To suppose a literal journey, as some do, to these peaks of the mountain chain one after another, is absurd. They are named as emblems of height and difficulty. *Shenir* (Senir, 1 Chron. v. 23) is one of the peaks of Hermon. *Amana* has been conjectured to be a name for the district of Anti-Libanus in which the Abana (*Barada*) has its source, but nothing is certain about it. The appellative *spouse* first occurs in this verse. In Hebrew it is *khallah*, and is translated in the Authorised Version either "daughter-in-law," or "bride," or "spouse," according as the relationship, now made complete by marriage, is regarded from the point of view of the parents of the bridegroom or of himself (*e.g., daughter-in-law*, Gen. xi. 31, xxxviii. 11; Lev. xx. 22; Micah vii. 6, &c. &c.; *bride*, Isa. xlix. 18, lxi. 10, lxii. 5, &c. &c.). Its use does not by itself prove that the pair were united in wedlock, because in the next verse the word *sister* is joined to *spouse*, and it may, therefore, be only a stronger term of endearment, and in any case, when put into the lover's mouth while describing the difficulties in the way of union, it is *proleptic*; but its presence strongly confirms the impression produced by the whole poem, that it describes over and over again the courtship and marriage of the same couple. For *lion* see Gen. xlix. 9. The *leopard* was formerly very common in Palestine, as the name *Bethnimrah*, *i.e., house of leopards* (Num. xxxii. 36) shows. (Comp. Jer. v. 6, xlii. 23; Hosea xiii. 7.) Nor is it rare now. "In the forest of Gilead it is still so numerous as to be a pest to the herdsmen" (Tristram, *Nat. Hist. of Bibl.*, p. 113).

The LXX. translate *amana* by πίστις, and this has been turned into an argument for the allegorical treatment of the book. But it is a very common error

The Garden   SOLOMON'S SONG, V.   *of the Beloved.*

From the lions' dens, from the mountains of the leopards.
(9) Thou hast [1] ravished my heart, my sister, *my* spouse;
Thou hast ravished my heart with one of thine eyes,
With one chain of thy neck.
(10) How fair is thy love, my sister, *my* spouse!
a How much better is thy love than wine!
And the smell of thine ointments than all spices!
(11) Thy lips, O *my* spouse, drop *as* the honeycomb:
Honey and milk *are* under thy tongue;
And the smell of thy garments *is* like the smell of Lebanon.
(12) A garden [2] inclosed *is* my sister, *my* spouse;
A spring shut up, a fountain sealed.
(13) Thy plants *are* an orchard of pomegranates, with pleasant fruits;
[3] Camphire, with spikenard, (14) spikenard and saffron;
Calamus and cinnamon, with all trees of frankincense;
Myrrh and aloes, with all the chief spices:
(15) A fountain of gardens, a well of living waters,
And streams from Lebanon.
(16) Awake, O north wind; and come, thou south;
Blow upon my garden, *that* the spices thereof may flow out.
Let my beloved come into his garden,
And eat his pleasant fruits.

CHAPTER V.—(1) I am come into my garden, my sister, *my* spouse:
I have gathered my myrrh with my spice;
I have eaten my honeycomb with my honey;
I have drunk my wine with my milk:

1 Or, *taken away my heart.*
a ch. 1. 2.
2 Heb., *barred.*
3 Or, *cypress.*

---

of the LXX. to translate proper names. (Comp. chap. vi. 4.)

(9) **Ravished.**—Marg., *taken away*, whereas many (including Herder, Ewald, &c.) give an exactly opposite sense: "thou hast given me heart, emboldened me." The literal, "thou hast *hearted* (*libabtini*) me,".if we can so say, may mean either; the language of love would approve either *stolen my heart* or *given me thine*. But the reference to "chain"—*anak* (a form occurring also in Judges viii. 26; Prov. i. 9) seems to confirm the rendering of the Authorised Version. His heart has been caught, the poet playfully says, by the neck-chain. Tennyson's

"Thy rose lips and full-blown eyes
Take the heart from out my breast,"

gives the feeling of the passage.

(12) **A garden inclosed.**—Comp. with this passage verses 12—15; Prov. v. 15, 21. The closed or walled garden and the sealed fountain appear to have been established metaphors for the pure and chaste wife. For the latter, at least, there is not only the above passage in Proverbs, but a prayer still in use in Jewish marriages: "Suffer not a stranger to enter into the sealed fountain," &c.

(13) **Thy plants.**—Some have thought the offspring of the marriage intended here; but the poet is plainly, by a new adaptation of the language of flowers, describing the charms of the person of his beloved.

Orchard.—Heb. *pardes*; LXX. παράδεισος; found only elsewhere in Neh. ii. 8 (where see Note), Eccles. ii. 5. The *pomegranate* was perhaps an emblem of love, having been held sacred to the Syrian Venus. (See Tristram, *Nat. Hist. of Bible*, p. 389.)

Camphire.—See Note, chap. i. 14.

(14) **Spikenard.**—See Note, chap. i. 12. *Saffron*; Heb. *carchom*; only here. The Arabic name is still *kûrkûm* = *Crocus sativus*, a well-known bulb of the order *Iridaceæ*. The pistil and stigma, dried, form the saffron.

Calamus.—Heb. *kâneh*. (Comp. *kâneh bosem*=sweet calamus, Ex. xxx. 23; *k. hottôv*=sweet cane, Jer. vi. 20.) There are many sweet grasses in India and the East. *Andropogon calamus aromaticus* has been identified (Royle) with the "reed of fragrance" of Exodus, and Jeremiah's "good reed from a far country," but the identification is not to be implicitly accepted. (See *Bible Educator*, Vol. I., p. 245.)

Cinnamon.—Heb. *kinnamôn* probably included *Cinnamomum Zeylanicum* (cinnamon) and *Cinnamomum cassia* (*Cassia lignea*). (See *Bible Educator*, Vol. I., p. 245.) The rind of the plant is the "cinnamon" in use. The plant belongs to the family of laurels, and grows in Ceylon, on the Malabar coast, and in East Indian Islands. It attains a height of from twenty to thirty feet, having numerous boughs, bearing leaves of a scarlet colour when young, but changing to a bright green, and white blossoms.

Aloes.—See Note, Num. xxiv. 6.

With all the chief spices.—"That in thy sweet all sweets encloses" (H. Constable).

(16) **Blow upon my garden.**—After the description of his beloved's charms under these figures, the poet, under a companion figure, invokes the "airs of love" to blow upon the garden, that its perfumes may "flow out" for him—that the object of his affections may no longer keep herself reserved and denied to him. Tennyson's melodious lines are recalled which describe how, when a breeze of morning moves,

"The woodbine spices are wafted abroad,
And the musk of the roses blown."

Let my beloved . . .—This should form a separate verse, being the reply made to the appeal in the first part of the verse. The maiden yields to her lover's suit.

V.

(1) **I am come into my garden.**—This continues the same figure, and under it describes once more the complete union of the wedded pair. The only difficulty lies in the invitation, "Eat, O friends; drink, yea, drink abundantly, O beloved" (Marg., *and be*

Eat, O friends; drink, ¹yea, drink abundantly, O beloved.

⁽²⁾ I sleep, but my heart waketh:
It *is* the voice of my beloved that knocketh, *saying,*
Open to me, my sister, my love, my dove, my undefiled:
For my head is filled with dew,
And my locks with the drops of the night.

⁽³⁾ I have put off my coat; how shall I put it on?
I have washed my feet; how shall I defile them?

⁽⁴⁾ My beloved put in his hand by the hole *of the door,*
And my bowels were moved ²for him.

⁽⁵⁾ I rose up to open to my beloved;
And my hands dropped *with* myrrh,
And my fingers *with* ³sweet smelling myrrh,

Upon the handles of the lock.

⁽⁶⁾ I opened to my beloved;
But my beloved had withdrawn himself, *and* was gone:
My soul failed when he spake:
I sought him, but I could not find him;
I called him, but he gave me no answer.

⁽⁷⁾ The watchmen that went about the city found me,
They smote me, they wounded me;
The keepers of the walls took away my veil from me.

⁽⁸⁾ I charge you, O daughters of Jerusalem,
If ye find my beloved, ⁴that ye tell him,
That I *am* sick of love.

⁽⁹⁾ What *is* thy beloved more than *another* beloved, O thou fairest among women?

¹ Or, *and be drunken* with *loves.*
² Or (as some read), *in me.*
³ Heb., *passing,* or *running about.*
⁴ Heb., *what.*

---

drunken with loves). Some suppose an invitation to an actual marriage feast; and if sung as an epithalamium, the song might have this double intention. But the margin, "be drunken with loves," suggests the right interpretation. The poet, it has been already said (Note, chap. ii. 7), loves to invoke the sympathy of others with his joys, and the following lines of Shelley reproduce the very feeling of this passage. Here, as throughout the poem, it is the "new strong wine of love," and not the fruit of the grape, which is desired and drunk.

"Thou art the wine, whose drunkenness is all
We can desire, O Love! and happy souls,
Ere from thy vine the leaves of autumn fall,
Catch thee and feed, from thine o'erflowing bowls,
Thousands who thirst for thy ambrosial dew."
Prince Athanase.

⁽²⁾ **I sleep.**—This begins the old story under an image already employed (chap. iii. 1). Here it is greatly amplified and elaborated. The poet pictures his lady dreaming of him, and when he seems to visit her, anxious to admit him. But, as is so common in dreams, at first she cannot. The realities which had hindered their union reappear in the fancies of sleep. Then, when the seeming hindrance is withdrawn, she finds him gone, and, as before, searches for him in vain. This gives opportunity to introduce the description of the charms of the lost lover, and so the end of the piece, the union of the pair, is delayed to chap. vi. 3.

My head is filled with dew.—Anacreon, iii. 10 is often compared to this.

"'Fear not,' said he, with piteous din,
'Pray ope the door and let me in.
A poor unshelter'd boy am I,
For help who knows not where to fly:
Lost in the dark, and with the dews,
All cold and wet, that midnight brews.'"

(Comp. also Propert. i. 16—23; Ovid, *Amor.* ii. 19—21.)

⁽³⁾ **Coat.**—Heb. *cutoneth*=cetoneth; Gr. χίτων, tunic.

⁽⁴⁾ **By the hole**—*i.e.,* through (Heb. *min*), as in chap. ii. 9. The hole is the aperture made in the door above the lock for the insertion of the hand with the key. The ancient lock was probably like the one in use in Palestine now. It consists of a *hollow* bolt or bar, which passes through a staple fixed to the door and into the door-post. In the staple are a number of movable pins, which drop into corresponding holes in the bolt when it is pushed home, and the door is then locked. To unlock it, the key is slid into the hollow bolt, and the movable pins pushed back by other pins in it, corresponding in size and form, which fill up the holes, and so enable the bolt to be withdrawn. It is said that, in lieu of a proper key, the arm can be inserted into the hollow bolt and the pins be pushed up by the hand, if provided with some soft material, as lard or wax, to fill up the holes, and keep the pins from falling back again till the bolt is withdrawn. This offers one explanation of verse 5. Coming to the door and having no key, the lover is supposed to make use of some myrrh, brought as a present, in trying to open the door, and, not succeeding, to go away. The *sweet smelling* (Marg., *passing,* or *running about*) is the myrrh that drops from the tree naturally, before any incision is made in the bark, and is considered specially fine. Others explain verse 5 by comparison with the heathen custom alluded to in Lucretius iv. 1173:—

"At lacrimans exclusus amator limina sæpe
Floribus et sertis operit posteisque superbos
Unguet amaricino, et foribus miser oscula figit."

(Comp. Tibullus, i. 2—14.) Perhaps Prov. vii. 17 makes the comparison allowable, but the first explanation is preferable.

⁽⁶⁾ **When he spake.**—We can suppose an ejaculation of disappointment uttered by the lover as he goes away, which catches the ear of the heroine as she wakes.

⁽⁷⁾ **The watchmen.**—See Note on chap. iii. 3.

Veil.—Heb. *redíd*; LXX. θέριστρον. Probably a light summer dress for throwing over the person on going out in a hurry, like the *tsaiph* put on by Rebecca (Gen. xxiv. 65). Only elsewhere in Isa. iii. 23.

⁽⁹⁾ **What is thy beloved?**—This question, introducing the description of the bridegroom's person, raises almost into certainty the conjecture that the poem was actually sung, or presented as an epithalamium, by alternate choirs (or single voices) of maidens

Beauty of   SOLOMON'S SONG, VI.   *the Beloved.*

What *is* thy beloved more than *another* beloved, that thou dost so charge us? [1]
(10) My beloved *is* white and ruddy,
[1] The chiefest among ten thousand.
(11) His head *is as* the most fine gold,
His locks *are* [2] bushy, *and* black as a raven.
(12)[a] His eyes *are as the eyes* of doves by the rivers of waters,
Washed with milk, *and* [3] fitly set.
(13) His cheeks *are as* a bed of spices, *as* [4] sweet flowers:
His lips *like* lilies, dropping sweet smelling myrrh.
(14) His hands *are as* gold rings set with the beryl:
His belly *is as* bright ivory overlaid *with* sapphires.
(15) His legs *are as* pillars of marble, set upon sockets of fine gold:

His countenance *is* as Lebanon, excellent as the cedars.
(16)[5] His mouth *is* most sweet: yea, he *is* altogether lovely.
This *is* my beloved, and this *is* my friend, O daughters of Jerusalem.

CHAPTER VI.—(1) Whither is thy beloved gone, O thou fairest among women?
Whither is thy beloved turned aside? that we may seek him with thee.
(2) My beloved is gone down into his garden, to the beds of spices,
To feed in the gardens, and to gather lilies.
(3) [b] I *am* my beloved's, and my beloved *is* mine:
He feedeth among the lilies.

[1] Heb., *a standard bearer.*
[2] Or, *curled.*
[a] ch. 1. 15; & 4. 1.
[3] Heb., *sitting in fulness, that is, fitly placed, and set as a precious stone in the foil of a ring.*
[4] Or, *towers of perfumes.*
[5] Heb., *His palate*
[b] ch. 2. 16; & 7. 10.

---

and young men, as in the *Carmen Nuptiale* of Catullus, vying the one in praise of the bridegroom, the other of the bride. Mere love-poems contain descriptions of the charms of the fair one to whom they are addressed, but not of the poet himself.

(10) **Chiefest.** — Marg., *a standard bearer*; Heb. *dagúl*, participle of a word occurring in Ps. xx. 5, where the Authorised Version gives "we will set up our banners."

(11) **Bushy.**—Marg., *curled*; Heb., *taltallim*=flowing in curls, or heaped up, *i.e.*, thick, bushy, according as we derive from *talah* or *tel*. The LXX. (followed by the Vulg.) take *taltallim* for another form of *zalzallim* (Isa. xviii. 5, *sprigs* of the vine), and render palm-leaves.

(12) **Fitly set.**—Literally, *sitting in fulness*, which the Margin explains, according to one received method of interpretation, as beautifully set, like a precious stone in the foil of a ring. If the comparison were to the *eyes* of the dove, this would be a sufficient interpretation, the image being perfect, owing to the ring of bright red skin round the eye of the turtle-dove. But there is no necessity to have recourse to the figure *comparatio compendiana* here, since doves delight in bathing; and though there is a certain delicious haze of indistinctness in the image, the soft iridescence of the bird floating and glancing on the face of the stream might not too extravagantly suggest the quick loving glances of the eye. Keats has a somewhat similar figure:—

"To see such lovely eyes in *swimming search*
After some warm delight, that seems to perch
Dove-like in the dim cell lying beyond
Their upper lids;"

and Dr. Ginsburg aptly quotes from the *Gitagovinda*: "The glances of her eyes played like a pair of *waterbirds* of azure plumage, that sport near a full-grown lotus in *a pool* in the season of dew." The words *washed in milk* refer to the white of the eye, which swells round the pupil like the *fulness* of water, *i.e.*, the swelling wave round the dove. The parallelism is like that of chap. i. 5.

(13) **His cheeks are as a bed of spices.**—Probably with allusion to the beard perfumed (Marg., *towers of perfumes*), as in Ps. cxxxiii. 2.

Lilies.—Comp. "He pressed the *blossom* of his lips to mine" (Tennyson, *Œnone*).

(14) **His hands . . .**—*Galil*, translated *ring*, is more probably a *cylinder* (from *galal*, to roll), referring to the rounded arm, ending in a well-shaped hand with beautiful nails.

Beryl.—Heb. *tarshish*; LXX. θαρσίς. Possibly "stones of Tarshish," and if so, either chrysolite or topaz, both said to have been first found in Tartessus, an ancient city of Spain, between the two mouths of the Bœtis (Guadalquiver). Mentioned as one of the precious stones in the breastplate of the High Priest (Exod. xxviii. 20, xxxix. 13). The LXX. adopt the various renderings χρυσόλιθος, ἄνθραξ, λίθος ἄνθρακος, or, as here, keep the original word.

Bright ivory.—Literally, *a work of ivory*, *i.e.*, a *chef-d'œuvre* in ivory.

Sapphires.—It is doubtful whether the sapphire of Scripture is the stone so called now, or the lapis-lazuli. The former best suits Exod. xxviii. 18 and Job xxviii. 6, because lapis-lazuli is too soft for engraving. The comparison in the text either alludes to the *blue veins* showing through the white skin or to the colour of some portion of dress.

(15) **Marble.**—Heb. *shesh.* Here and in Esther i. 6.

(16) **His mouth is most sweet.** — Literally, *his palate* (see Margin) *sweetnesses*, *i.e.*, his voice is exquisitely sweet. The features have already been described, and *chek*, palate, is used of the organ of *speech* and *speech* itself (Job vi. 30; Prov. v. 3).

VI.

(1—3) **Whither is thy beloved gone . . .** By a playful turn the poet heightens the description of the lover's beauty by the impression supposed to be produced on the imaginary bystanders to whom the picture has been exhibited. They express a desire to share the pleasures of his company with the heroine, but she, under the figure before employed (chap. iv. 12—16), declares that her affections are solely hers, and that, so far from being at their disposal, he is even now hastening to complete his and her happiness in their union. Difficulties crowd on the dramatic theory at this passage. Most of its advocates have recourse to

Beauty of SOLOMON'S SONG, VI. *the Bride*

(4) Thou *art* beautiful, O my love, as Tirzah,
Comely as Jerusalem, terrible as *an army* with banners.
(5) Turn away thine eyes from me, for [1] they have overcome me:
Thy hair *is* *a* as a flock of goats that appear from Gilead.
(6) Thy teeth *are* as a flock of sheep which go up from the washing,
Whereof every one beareth twins, and *there is* not one barren among them.
(7) As a piece of a pomegranate *are* thy temples within thy locks.
(8) There are threescore queens, and fourscore concubines,
And virgins without number.

(9) My dove, my undefiled is *but* one;
She *is* the *only* one of her mother,
She *is* the choice *one* of her that bare her.
The daughters saw her, and blessed her;
Yea, the queens and the concubines, and they praised her.
(10) Who *is* she *that* looketh forth as the morning,
Fair as the moon, clear as the sun,
And terrible as *an army* with banners?
(11) I went down into the garden of nuts to see the fruits of the valley,
And to see whether the vine flourished, *and* the pomegranates budded.

[1] Or, *they have puffed me up.*

a ch. 4. 1, 2.

some arbitrary insertion, such as, "here the lovers are re-united," but they do not tell us how the distance from the harem at Jerusalem to the garden in the north was traversed, or the obstacles to the union surmounted. In the imagination of the poet all was easy and natural.

(4) **Beautiful . . . as Tirzah.**—There is no sufficient reason for the employment of Tirzah side by side with Jerusalem in this comparison but the fact that they were both capitals, the one of the northern, the other of the southern kingdom. This fixes the date of the composition of the poem within certain limits (see *Excursus* I.). Jeroboam first selected the ancient sanctuary of Shechem for his capital; but, from some unexplained cause, moved the seat of his government, first to Penuel, on the other side Jordan, and then to Tirzah, formerly the seat of a petty Canaanite prince. (See 1 Kings xii. 25, xiv. 17, xv. 21, 33, xvi. 6, 8, 15, 18, 23; Josh. xii. 24.) Robinson identified *Tirzah* with *Tellûzah*, not far from Mount Ebal, which agrees with Brocardus, who places *Thersa* on a high mountain, three degrees from Samaria to the east. Tirzah only remained the capital till the reign of Omri, but comes into notice again as the scene of the conspiracy of Menahem against Shallum (2 Kings xv. 14—16). The LXX. translate *Tirzah* by εὐδοκία, Vulg. *suavis*; and the ancient versions generally adopt this plan, to avoid, as Dr. Ginsburg thinks, the mention of the two capitals, because this made against the Solomonic authorship.

As Jerusalem.—See Lam. ii. 15. As to the idea involved in a comparison so strange to us, we notice that this author is especially fond of finding a resemblance between his love and familiar localities (see chaps. v. 15 and vii. 4, 5); nor was it strange in a language that delighted in personifying a nation or city under the character of a maiden (Isa. xlvii. 1), and which, ten centuries later, could describe the new Jerusalem as a bride coming down from heaven adorned for her husband (Rev. xxi. 9, *seqq.*).

An army with banners.—Heb. *nidgalôth*, participle of niphal conjugation = bannered. (Comp.—

"And what are cheeks, but ensigns oft,
That wave hot youth to fields of blood?")

(5) **Overcome.**—Marg., *puffed up*; Heb. *hiríbuni*, from the verb *rahab*, a word whose root-idea seems to be to show spirit against oppression or prejudice. (See Isa. iii. 5; Prov. vi. 3.) The *Hiphil* therefore = make me spirited, or bold. (Comp. Ps. cxxxviii. 3.) The LXX. and Vulg., however, followed by many moderns, take it in the sense of *scare* or *dazzle*.

For the rest of the description, see Note, chap. iv. 1, *seqq.*

(8) **There are threescore queens.**—Presumably a description of Solomon's harem (from comp. with chap. viii. 11, 12), though the numbers are far more sober than in 1 Kings xi. 3. Probably the latter marks a later form of the traditions of the grand scale on which everything at the court of the monarch was conducted, and this, though a poetic, is a truer version of the story of his loves. The conjunction of *alamôth* with concubines, *pilageshim* (comp. παλλακή, *pellex*), decides for translating it *puellæ* rather than *virgines*.

(9) **My dove . . . is but one.** — "While the monarch's loves are so many, *one* is mine, my dove, my perfect one: *one*, the delight of her mother, the darling of her who bore her." It is impossible not to see in this a eulogy on monogamy, which, in practice, seems always to have been the rule among the Jews, the exceptions lying only with kings and the very rich. The eulogy is made more pronounced by putting an unconscious testimony to the superiority of monogamy into the mouths of the "queens and concubines," who praise and bless this pattern of a perfect wife.

(10) **Who is she.**—This verse is supposed to be spoken by the admiring ladies. The paragraph mark in the English Version should rather be at the beginning of the next verse. (Comp.—

"But soft, what light through yonder window breaks?
It is the East, and Juliet is the sun!
Arise, fair sun," &c.—*Romeo and Juliet.*)

But the poet heightens his figure by combining both the great lights of heaven with the dawn, and putting the praise in the mouth of "the meaner beauties of the night," who feel their own inferiority "when the moon doth rise," still more before the "all paling" sun.

(11—13) **I went down into the garden . . .**—For a discussion on this obscure passage in its entirety, see *Excursus* III.

(11) **Nuts.**—Heb. *egôz*; only here. (Comp. Arabic *ghaus* = the walnut, which is at present extensively cultivated in Palestine.)

Fruits.—Heb. *ebi* = green shoots; LXX. ἐν γεννήμασι.

Valley.—Heb. *nachal*; LXX., literally, χειμάρρου. *the torrent-bed*. It is the Hebrew equivalent of the

SOLOMON'S SONG, VII.

The King's Daughter — *all glorious.*

(12) ¹ Or ever I was aware, my soul ² made me *like* the chariots of Ammi-nadib.
(13) Return, return, O Shulamite;
Return, return, that we may look upon thee.
What will ye see in the Shulamite?
As it were the company ³ of two armies.

CHAPTER VII.—(1) How beautiful are thy feet with shoes, O prince's daughter!

The joints of thy thighs *are* like jewels,
The work of the hands of a cunning workman.
(2) Thy navel *is like* a round goblet, *which* wanteth not ⁴ liquor:
Thy belly *is like* an heap of wheat set about with lilies.
(3) ᵃThy two breasts *are* like two young roes *that are* twins.
(4) Thy neck *is* as a tower of ivory;
Thine eyes *like* the fishpools in Heshbon, by the gate of Bath-rabbim:

1 Heb., *I knew not.*
2 Or, *set me on the chariots of my willing people.*
3 Or, *of Mahanaim.*
4 Heb., *mixture.*
a ch. 4. 5.

Arabic *wady.* Here the LXX. insert, "There I will give thee my breasts"; reading, as in chap. i. 2, *dadaï* (breasts) for *dôdaï* (caresses).

(12) **Or ever I was aware.**—Marg., *I knew not;* Heb. *Lo yadahti,* which is used adverbially (Ps. xxxv. 8), "at unawares." (Comp. Prov. v. 6; Jer. l. 24.) The LXX. read, "my spirit did not know."

Made me like . . .—Marg., *set me on the chariots;* but literally, according to the present Hebrew text, *set me chariots,* &c.

Ammi-nadib.—Marg., *of my willing people,* as though the reading were *ammi hanadib,* since the article ought to be present after a noun with suffix. For *ammi* = my fellow citizens, comp. Gen. xxiii. 11; Lam. ii. 11. A better interpretation, instead of taking the *yod* as the suffix *my,* treats it as an old genitival ending, and renders, *companions of a prince.* But this does not make the passage more intelligible.

(13) **O Shulamite.**—Heb. *hashulammît.* This vocative, with the article, indicates a Gentile name rather than a proper name (*Ges.,* § 108, Eng. Trans.), and no doubt the LXX., ἡ Σουναμῖτις, "the Shunamite" —that is, *maiden of Shunem*—is correct.

Shunem was discovered by Robinson in Sôlam, a village on the declivity at the western end of Little Hermon (Dûhy), and which answers to all the requirements of Shunem in 1 Sam. xxviii. 4, 2 Kings iv. 8 (comp. Josh. xix. 18), and with a slight correction as to distance with the *Sulem* which Eusebius (Onomasticon) and Jerome identify with *Sunem.* For the interchange of *n* and *l,* comp. *Zerin* = Jezreel; *Beitun* = Bethel; *lachats* = *nachats,* to burn.

The fact that Abishag was a *Shunamite,* and that Adonijah sought her in marriage (1 Kings i. 3), has given rise to the conjecture that these two are the heroine and hero of this poem.

From a comparison with chap. viii. 10, "then was I in his eyes as one that found favour" (Heb. *shalôm,* peace), arises the untenable theory that Shulamite is a feminine of Solomon = the graceful one: untenable, because the feminine of *Shelomah* would be *Shelomît.*

As it were the company of two armies.— Marg., *of Mahanaim;* LXX., "she coming like dances of the camps;" Vulg., "unless dances of camps;" Heb. *khimcholath hammachanaim. Mecholath* is fem. of *machol,* which (see Smith's *Bib. Dict.,* under "Dance") is supposed to be properly a musical instrument of percussion. The LXX. generally translate, as here, χορός; but in Ps. xxxii. 11 (Heb. x. 12) χαρά, joy; Jer. xxxi. 4, 14, συναγωγή, assembly. In Ps. cxlix. 3, cliv. 4, the Margin suggests *pipe* instead of *dance;* and many scholars derive it from *chal* = to bore (comp. *chalîl,* a flute). (See *Bible Educator,* Vol. II., p. 70.) Its associated meaning would naturally be *dance.*

Machanaim is either a regular dual = of two camps, or there is some reference, which we cannot recover, to local customs at the place of that name. To see any connection between this passage and Gen. xxxii. 2, and still more to think of *angelic dances,* borders on the absurd. But the connection between military sports and dancing has always been close in the East, and the custom now existing of performing a *sword-dance* at weddings possibly gives the clue to this curious passage.

Some conjectural interpretations will be found in the *Excursus,* but the whole passage is hopelessly obscure.

VII.

(1) **How beautiful . . .**—Literally, *How beautiful are thy feet* (or *thy steps*) *in the sandals.* This description of the beauty of the bride—

"From the delicate Arab arch of her feet
To the grace that, bright and light as the crest
Of a peacock, sits on her shining head"—

is plainly connected with the dance mentioned in the last verse, and possibly proceeds in this order, instead of from the head downwards, because the feet of a dancer would first attract attention. See end of *Excursus* III.

O prince's daughter! — Heb. *Bath-nadib* (the LXX. keep Ναδάβ)—evidently again suggested by *Ammi-nadib,* in chap. vi. 12. But as the allusion there cannot be recovered, nothing relating to the rank of the heroine can be deduced from the recurrence of *nadib* (= noble) here. The reference may be to character rather than descent, just as in the opposite expression, "daughter of Belial" (1 Sam. i. 16).

Joints.—Heb. *chamûk,* from *chamah* = went away, probably refers to the rapid movements in dancing, and the image is suggested by the graceful curves formed by a chain or pendulous ornament when in motion. Or the reference may be to the contour of the person.

(2) **Heap of wheat set about with lilies.**— Wetstein (quoted by Delitzsch in his Appendix) remarks that in Syria the colour of wheat is regarded as the most beautiful colour the human body can have; and after remarking on the custom of decorating the heaps of winnowed corn with flowers in token of the joy of harvest, says:—"The appearance of such heaps of wheat, which one may see in long parallel rows on the threshing-floors of a village, is very pleasing to a peasant; and the comparison of the Song (chap. vii. 5) every Arabian will regard as beautiful."

(4) **Fishpools in Heshbon.** — Literally, *pools.* The Authorised Version follows the Vulg. *piscinæ,* for which there is no authority. For *Heshbon,* see Note on Num. xxi. 26. The ruins still remain, with the same

Emblems	**SOLOMON'S SONG, VII.** *of tender Love.*

Thy nose *is* as the tower of Lebanon which looketh toward Damascus.

(5) Thine head upon thee *is* like ¹ Carmel,
And the hair of thine head like purple;
The king *is* ² held in the galleries.

(6) How fair and how pleasant art thou,
O love, for delights !

(7) This thy stature is like to a palm tree,
And thy breasts to clusters *of grapes.*

(8) I said, I will go up to the palm tree,
I will take hold of the boughs thereof:

Now also thy breasts shall be as clusters of the vine,
And the smell of thy nose like apples;

(9) And the roof of thy mouth like the best wine for my beloved, that goeth down ³ sweetly,
Causing the lips ⁴ of those that are asleep to speak.

(10) *a* I *am* my beloved's, and his desire *is* toward me.

(11) Come, my beloved, let us go forth into the field;
Let us lodge in the villages.

---

¹ Or, *crimson.*
² Heb., *bound.*
³ Heb., *straightly.*
⁴ Or, *of the ancient.*
a ch. 2. 16; & 6. 3.

---

name *Hesban,* in the Wady of that name (*Robinson,* p. 278). "There are many cisterns among the ruins; and towards the south, a few yards from the base of the hill, is a large ancient reservoir, which calls to mind the passage in Cant. vii. 4" (Smith's *Bib. Dict.*). Captain Warren took a photograph of "the spring-head of the waters of Hesban," published by the Palestine Exploration Fund. In regard to the image, comp.—

"Adspicies oculos tremulo fulgore micantes
Ut sol a liquida sœpe refulget aqua."
Ovid. Art. Am., ii. 722.

Comp. also Keats :—

"Those eyes, those passions, those supreme pearl springs."

The gate of Bath-rabbim.—Doubtless the name of an actual gate, so called from the crowds of people streaming through it: *daughter of multitudes.*

(5) **Carmel.**—Marg., *crimson,* from reading *charmîl,* which preserves the parallelism with the next clause better. But the whole passage deals in the author's favourite figures from localities; and certainly the comparison of a finely-set head to a mountain is at least as apt as that in the preceding verse, of the nose to a "tower in Lebanon." Besides, there may be a play on words, which in turn may have suggested the allusion to *purple* in the next clause, or possibly the vicinity of *Carmel* to *Tyre* may have led to the thought of its famous dyes.

Hair.—Heb. *dallath,* most probably = flowing tresses. For comparison—

"Carmine purpurea est Nisi coma."
"Et pro purpureo dat pœnas Scylla capillo."

(Comp. πορφύρεος πλόκαμος in Lucian., and πορφυραῖ χαῖται in Anacreon.) So Collins :—

"The youths whose locks divinely spreading,
Like vernal hyacinths in sullen hue."
Ode to Liberty.

The king is held (Marg., *bound*) **in the galleries.** —For *galleries,* see Note on chap. i. 17. Translate "A king caught and bound by thy tresses," *i.e.,* they are so beautiful that a monarch would be caught by them. (Comp.—

"When I lie tangled in her hair
And fettered in her eye.")

(7) **This thy stature.**—Comp. Ecclus. xxiv. 14. Not only was the tall and graceful palm a common figure for female beauty, but its name, *tamar,* was common as a woman's name (Gen. xxxviii. 6; 2 Sam. xiii. 1, &c.).

Clusters of grapes.—The italics were probably added by the English Version to bring the verse into agreement with "clusters of the vine" in the next verse; but no doubt the rich clusters of dates are at the moment in the poet's thought.

(8) **Boughs.**—Heb. *sansan;* only here. Probably a form derived from the sound, like *salsal, zalzal,* &c., denoting the waving of the long feathery branches of the palm.

Smell of thy nose—*i.e.,* "fragrance of thy breath," *ap* = nose being used apparently because of the resemblance of its root, *anap* = breathe, with that of *tappuach* = apple.

(9) **Causing the lips.**—The text in this verse has evidently undergone some change. The LXX., instead of *siphthei yesheynim,* lips of sleepers, read *sephathaim veshinnayim,* χείλεσί μου καὶ ὀδοῦσι. The Marg., instead of *yesheynim,* sleepers, reads *yeshanim,* the ancient, which Luther adopts, translating "of the previous year." *Ledôdi,* for my beloved, is evidently either an accidental insertion of the copyist, the eye having caught *dôdi* in the next verse, or more probably is wrongly vowelled. The verse is untranslatable as it stands; but by reading *ledôdai,* "to my caresses" (comp. chaps. i. 2, iv. 10, vii. 12), we get a sense entirely harmonious with the context, and this is a change less violent than to reject *ledôdi* altogether. It is the old figure, comparing kisses to wine (comp. chaps. i. 2, ii. 4, v. 1). "The roof of the mouth" (comp. chap. v. 16), or palate, is put by metonymy for the mouth generally. *Dôbeb* is either from the root *dôb,* cognate with *zôb* = flow gently, and means *suffusing,* in which case we translate "Thy mouth pours out an exquisite wine, which runs sweetly down in answer to my caresses, and suffuses (LXX. ἱκανούμενος, *accommodating itself to*) our lips as we fall asleep "— or, according to the Rabbinical interpretation, followed by the Authorised Version (which connects *dôbeb* with *dabab,* a Talmudic word = speaking), there may be in it the idea of a dream making the lips move as in speech. In this case the lines of Shelley suggest the meaning :—

"Like lips murmuring in their sleep
Of the sweet kisses which had lulled them there."
Epipsychidion.

(10) **I am my beloved's.**—This verse ends a section, not, as in the Authorised Version, begins one.

(11) **Forth into the field.**—Comp. chaps. ii. 10, vi. 11. The same reminiscence of the sweet courtship in the happy "woodland places." It has been conjectured that this verse suggested to Milton the passage beginning, "To-morrow, ere fresh morning streak the East," &c. (*P. L.* iv. 623, &c.)

⁽¹²⁾ Let us get up early to the vineyards;
Let us see if the vine flourish, *whether* the tender grape ¹ appear,
And the pomegranates bud forth:
There will I give thee my loves.
⁽¹³⁾ The ^a mandrakes give a smell,
And at our gates *are* all manner of pleasant *fruits*, new and old,
Which I have laid up for thee, O my beloved.

CHAPTER VIII.—⁽¹⁾ O that thou *wert* as my brother, that sucked the breasts of my mother!
When I should find thee without, I would kiss thee;
Yea, ² I should not be despised.
⁽²⁾ I would lead thee, *and* bring thee into my mother's house, *who* would instruct me:
I would cause thee to drink of ^b spiced wine of the juice of my pomegranate.
^{(3) c} His left hand *should be* under my head, And his right hand should embrace me.
^{(4) d} I charge you, O daughters of Jerusalem, ³ That ye stir not up, nor awake *my* love, until he please.
^{(5) e} Who *is* this that cometh up from the wilderness, leaning upon her beloved?
I raised thee up under the apple tree:
There thy mother brought thee forth:
There she brought thee forth *that* bare thee.
⁽⁶⁾ Set me as a seal upon thine heart,
As a seal upon thine arm:
For love *is* strong as death;
Jealousy *is* ⁴ cruel as the grave:
The coals thereof *are* coals of fire,
Which hath a most vehement flame.

Marginal notes:
¹ Heb., *open.*
a Gen. 30. 14.
² Heb., *they should not despise me.*
b Prov. 9. 2.
c ch. 2. 6.
d ch. 2. 7; & 3. 5.
³ Heb., *why should ye stir up, or why,* &c.
e ch. 3. 6
⁴ Heb., *hard.*

---

(12) Tender grape appear.—Literally, *vine blossoms open.* (See Note on chap. ii. 13.)
My loves—*i.e.*, caresses. LXX., as before, read "breasts."

(13) Mandrakes.—Heb. *dûdaim* = love-apples. Suggested probably by the word *loves* immediately preceding, as well as the qualities ascribed to the plant, for which see Note, Gen. xxx. 14.

VIII.

(1) O that thou wert as my brother.—The poet makes his beloved recall the feelings she had for him before the obstacles to their union were removed. She dared not then avow her affection for him as a lover, and wished that their relationship had been such as to allow of their meeting and embracing without reproach. Marg., "They (*i.e.*, her family and friends) should not *despise* (*i.e., reproach*) me."

(2) Juice of my pomegranate.—"The Orientals," says Dr. Kitto, "indulge largely in beverages made of fresh juice of various kinds of fruits. Among these, sherbet made of pomegranate juice is particularly esteemed; and from its agreeable and cooling acidity, the present writer was himself accustomed to prefer it to any other drink of this description." The meaning of the verse is explained by chaps i. 2, v. 1, vii. 9.

(4) I charge you.—See Note, chap. ii. 6, 7.

(5) Who is this that cometh.—This begins a new section, which contains the most magnificent description of true love ever written by poet. The dramatic theory encounters insuperable difficulties with this strophe. Again we presume that the theatre and the spectators are imaginary. It is another sweet reminiscence, coming most naturally and beautifully after the last. The obstacles have been removed, the pair are united, and the poet recalls the delightful sensations with which he led his bride through the scenes where the youth of both had been spent, and then bursts out into the glorious panegyric of that pure and perfect passion which had united them.

Leaning upon her beloved . . .—The LXX. add here *shining white,* and the Vulgate, *flowing with delights.*

I raised thee up.—Literally, *aroused: i.e.,* I inspired thee with love. For this sense of exciting a passion, given to the Hebrew word, compare Prov. x. 12; Zech. ix. 13. Delitzsch restores from the Syriac what must have been the original vowel-pointing, making the suffixes feminine instead of masculine.

There thy mother . . .—Not necessarily *under* the apple-tree, which is commemorated as the scene of the betrothal, but near it. The poet delights to recall these early associations, the feelings with which he had watched her home and waited her coming. The Vulg. has here *ibi corrupta est mater tua, ibi violata est genetrix tua,* which savours of allegory. So in later times the *tree* has been taken to stand for the *Cross,* the individual excited to love under it the *Gentiles* redeemed at the foot of the Cross, and the deflowered and corrupted mother the *synagogue of the Jews* (the mother of the Christian Church), which was corrupted by denying and crucifying the Saviour.

(6) Seal.—See Jer. xxii. 24; Hag. ii. 23, &c. A symbol of something especially dear and precious.

Jealousy.—*Strong passion,* from a word meaning *to be red with flame*; not in a bad sense, as the parallelism shows:—

"Strong as death is love,
Inexorable as Sheol is ardent passion."

Grave.—Heb. *sheôl.* Perhaps, as in the LXX., *Hades,* with its figurative gates and bars (Ps. vi. 5, Note).

Coals.—Heb. *resheph*; in Ps. lxxviii. 48, *hot thunderbolts* (comp. Hab. iii. 5); in Job v. 7, *sparks*; Marg., *sons of the burning*; Deut. xxxii. 24, *burning heat* of the burning fever of the plague.

A most vehement flame.—Literally, *a flame of Jah,* the only place where a sacred name occurs in the book, and here, as in the Authorised Version, adverbially, to express something superlatively great and strong. Southey's lines are a faint echo of this:—

"But love is indestructible,
Its holy flame for ever burneth,
From heaven it came, to heaven returneth."

⁽⁷⁾ Many waters cannot quench love,
  Neither can the floods drown it:
  If a man would give all the substance
    of his house for love,
  It would utterly be contemned.
⁽⁸⁾ We have a little sister, and she hath
    no breasts:
  What shall we do for our sister in the
    day when she shall be spoken for?
⁽⁹⁾ If she *be* a wall, we will build upon her
    a palace of silver:
  And if she *be* a door, we will inclose
    her with boards of cedar.
⁽¹⁰⁾ I *am* a wall, and my breasts like
    towers:
  Then was I in his eyes as one that
    found ¹favour.
⁽¹¹⁾ Solomon had a vineyard at Baal-hamon;
  He let out the vineyard unto keepers;
  Every one for the fruit thereof was to
    bring a thousand *pieces* of silver.

¹ Heb. *peace*.

⁽⁷⁾ **It would utterly be contemned.**—Better, *he would be*, &c., and literally, *to despise, they would despise him*; infinitive absolute before finite verb expressing intensity. (Comp. 1 Sam. xx. 6; Amos ix. 8, &c.)

This fine passage, with its reference to the invincible might and untempted constancy of true love, hardly leaves a doubt that the poem, while an ideal picture of the passion, is also a reminiscence of an actual history of two hearts that had been tried and proved true both against difficulties and seductions.

⁽⁸⁾ **We have a little sister.**—Commentators are almost all at one in the feeling that the poem properly ends with verse 7. Those who construct the poem on the plan of a drama can find no proper place for what follows (unless as a meaningless epilogue), and the want of cohesion with the main body of the work is so evident that many scholars have rejected it as a later addition; others have tried to find a place for it by re-arranging the whole poem. But if the various sections are, as above explained, only a succession of different presentments of the same story of courtship and marriage, made without any regard to order, but simply as they occurred to the memory of the poet, this conclusion presents no difficulty, either from its position or its meaning. With a view to artistic form, we might wish it away or in some other part of the poem; but the author had no regard to artistic form, or not the same conception of it as we have.

A little sister . . .—The recollection is carried back to the childhood of the bride. Her brothers are supposed to be debating how to deal with her when an offer of marriage should be made for her.

In the day when she shall be spoken for? —*i.e.*, asked in marriage (comp. 1 Sam. xxv. 29). At present she is unmarriageable.

⁽⁹⁾ **If she be a wall.**—The *wall* and *door* are emblems of chastity and its opposite. The *palace of silver* some commentators explain by reference to the custom (among the Druses) of wearing an ornament like a horn on the head. But this is unlikely. The metaphors of the *wall* and *door* are naturally expanded. If the maiden grows up virtuous and inaccessible to seduction *we will build upon her a palace of silver, i.e.*, we will so provide for her in marriage that from her may spring an illustrious house; but if otherwise, *we will enclose her with boards of cedar, i.e.*, the strongest precautions shall be taken to guard her honour. This passage is one of the strongest arguments for the theory that chaste wedded love is the theme of this book, the poet going on in verse 10 to put into the heroine's mouth a protestation of purity; and by which virtuous disposition, even more than by her beauty, she had won her husband's love: "I have grown up to virtuous womanhood, and I have found favour in his eyes."

⁽¹⁰⁾ **I am a wall . . .**—The heroine interrupts with a protestation of her purity, and of her right to marry, being of age, and conscious of being beloved.

^(11, 12) **Solomon had a vineyard . . .**—Here the poet repeats the sentiment of chap. vi. 8, 9—the contrast of his love for one chosen bride with the state of feeling and morality fostered by polygamy. But while in the former passage the contrast lay in number only, here it lies also in the *value* which comes to be set on the possession. Any one member of the harem of Solomon is no dearer to him than one of his many vineyards, which has to be cultivated by hirelings (perhaps with allusion to the eunuchs who guard the seraglio), and is valued only for the return it yields. But the one wedded wife is a vineyard tended by the owner, loved for its own sake as well as valued. A certain obscurity arises from the abrupt transition from simile to metaphor. Long similes, so common in classical poetry, are almost unknown in that of the Hebrews. Complete, the simile would have run, " As Solomon, who possesses so many vineyards, does not keep any one, even the choicest, in his own hands, but entrusts it to keepers and only enjoys an annual rent, so, with such a large and costly establishment of wives, he has none that is to him what my *one*, my sole possession, is to me." But after the first member of it in verse 11, he breaks abruptly into metaphor, so much more natural to him, " My vineyard," &c. For the figure comp. iv. 12, 13.

Baal-hamon.—Many are the conjectures hazarded as to the locality of this place. It has been identified (1) with Baal-gad, or Heliopolis (Rosenmüller); (2) with Hammon, a place in the tribe of Asher (Josh. xix. 28, Ewald); (3) with Balamo (LXX. Βελαμών), a place mentioned in the Book of Judith, chap. viii. 3, in connection with Dothaim, which (if the same as Dothan) has possibly been discovered to the south of the valley of Esdraelon.—*Recovery of Jerusalem*, p. 463 (1871). (Comp. Judith iv. 10, iii. 9; Meier, Hitzig, &c.) But no identification is necessary. If the poet had any definite place in his mind he merely used it for the play on words (*Baal-hamon*=lord of multitude). The correct translation is " a vineyard was to Solomon *as* lord of a multitude." The particle *be* often has this force. Ex. vi. 3: " I appeared as God Almighty." Comp. Prov. iii. 26; Isa. xl. 10; 1 Chron. ix. 33, &c. We further note that *Baal*, as *lord* with us, often means *husband*, and *Baal-hamon* has a covert allusion to the polygamy of the king.

A thousand pieces of silver.—Supply *shekels*. The substantives denoting weight, measure, or time are frequently omitted (Gen. xx. 16). (Comp. Isa. vii. 23: *a thousand silverlings*, whence we see that it was customary to portion off vineyards into sections containing a certain number of vines.) For worth of shekel, see Gen. xxiii. 15.

⁽¹²⁾ My vineyard, which *is* mine, *is* before me:
Thou, O Solomon, *must have* a thousand,
And those that keep the fruit thereof two hundred.
⁽¹³⁾ Thou that dwellest in the gardens,
The companions hearken to thy voice:
Cause me to hear *it*.
⁽¹⁴⁾ ¹Make haste, my beloved,
And be thou like to a roe or to a young hart
Upon the mountains of spices.

¹ Heb., *Flee away.*

⁽¹²⁾ **Thou, O Solomon . . .**—*i.e.,* "Let Solomon keep and enjoy his possessions (his harem of mercenary beauties), which cost so much to obtain and keep; I am happier in the secure love of my one true wife." The mention of "two hundred to the keepers of the fruit" seems added to show the cost of a polygamous establishment on a great scale.

⁽¹³⁾ **Thou that dwellest.**—In verse 13 we have another brief reminiscence of the early days of courtship, when the lover envied every one near the maiden, the companions who could see and hear her, and sighed for tokens of affection which she lavished on them.

⁽¹⁴⁾ **Make haste, my beloved.**—Verse 14 recalls the answer made at last to the sighs. It repeats the metaphor of chap. ii. 17, where we see that the Authorised Version, *make haste,* is more correct than the margin. Thus the poem ends with two short verses that compress into them all that has been over and over again related under different figures: the wooing and the wedding of two happy souls.

EXCURSUS ON NOTES TO SONG OF SOLOMON

EXCURSUS I.—ON THE DATE AND AUTHORSHIP OF THE SONG.

THE title and Rabbinical tradition are in favour of the Solomonic Authorship. But the value of the evidence of the title is not greater than that of the titles of the Psalms, which need the confirmation of internal evidence before they are accepted as authority. Beyond this there is no external evidence whatever.

INTERNAL EVIDENCE:—I. For the Solomonic Authorship.

(1) The knowledge displayed of plants and animals, and other productions of nature, which is in accordance with 1 Kings iv. 33.

(2) The evidence of wide acquaintance with foreign things, products of the East, &c., such as we know Solomon possessed; add to this the decidedly secular tone and feeling, a tone and feeling belonging only to this age.

(3) Similarity with certain parts of the Book of Proverbs. Comp. chap. v. 6, with Prov. i. 28—chap. iv. 12, with Prov. v. 15—chap. iv. 5, with Prov. v. 19—chap. viii. 7, with Prov. vi. 34, 35—chap. vi. 9, with Prov. xxxi. 28; also for analogies of diction comp. in the Hebrew, chap. iv. 9, with Prov. i. 9—chap. iv. 11, with Prov. v. 3—chap. i. 2, with Prov. xxvii. 6—chap. vii. 2, with Prov. xxv. 12—chap. iv. 14, with Prov. vii. 17.

(4) The language is such as we should expect from the Solomonic age. It belongs to the flourishing period of the Hebrew tongue. Highly poetical, vigorous and fresh, it has no traces of the decay which manifested itself in the declining period of Israel and Judah. All the Aramean colouring it has can be explained by the hypothesis of a northern origin (see below).

No one of these indications is conclusive, and all together amount to no more than a strong probability in favour of a date not far removed from the Solomonic era. They certainly make against the extreme view of Grätz, who finding, as he thinks, in the book, a number of words of Greek origin, brings its date down to the third or second century before our era. Others, also on linguistic grounds, have referred it to the post-exile times.

II. The view most generally accepted at present is that the poem was the work of a poet in the northern kingdom, composed not long after the separation of the two kingdoms, probably about the middle of the tenth century before Christ.

The following are among the chief reasons for accepting such a view.

(1) In evidence of its northern birthplace, are the frequent and almost exclusive mention of localities in the north; the author's strongly expressed dislike of the luxury and expense of Solomon's court, which necessitated the exactions that so contributed to the schisms between the two kingdoms (1 Kings xii. 4, seq.; 2 Chron. x. 1, seq.); the entire absence of all allusions to the temple and its worship; the exaltation of Tirzah to an equal place with Jerusalem as a type of beauty (vi. 4); dialectical peculiarities, which can only be accounted for on this hypothesis, or on the untenable one of an extremely late composition; the comparison with Hosea, undoubtedly a northern writer, which shows that the two authors "lived in the same circle of images, and that the same expressions were familiar to them" (Renan, *Le Cantique des Cantiques*, p. 112, referring to Hitzig, *Das Hohelied*, pp. 9, 10).

This fact of a northern origin established, it follows almost inevitably that the date of the poem must be placed somewhere in the middle of the tenth century, for it was only during the period from 975 to 924 B.C. that Tirzah occupied the position of northern capital (see Note *ad loc.*); and the whole tone and spirit of the book, together with its treatment of Solomon, is what we should expect at a time not far removed from the rupture of the two kingdoms. As yet tradition had not exaggerated the splendour of the Solomonic era: in the references to Solomon's guard, his harem, and his arsenal, the figures are not extravagant, as in the comparatively late accounts in Kings and Chronicles. A crowd of smaller indications point the same way, *e.g.*, the mention of Heshbon, which had ceased to be an Israelitish town by Isaiah's time (Isa. xv. 8). The mention of the Tower of David, as still possessing a garrison (vii. 4, and iv. 4), the allusion to Pharaoh's equipages have a similar tendency; while it is almost inconceivable that Solomon himself or any author, while that monarch was alive, and his rule all-powerful, could have represented him and his court in such an unfavourable light as they appear in the song. But it is exactly the representation we should look for in a poet of the northern kingdom in the early years after it revolted against the tyranny of the Davidic dynasty.

EXCURSUS II.—ON THE FORM AND PURPOSE OF THE POEM.

The dramatic feeling was not altogether strange to the Hebrews, as we see from the Book of Job, the sixty-third chapter of Isaiah, the concluding chapters of Micah, and certain of the Psalms. And there is undoubtedly a great deal of the dramatic element in the "Song of Songs." Two characters at least speak, a bride and a bridegroom, and as early as the Alexandrian codex of the LXX. translation the dramatic character was recognised, the words "bride" and "bridegroom" being in many instances prefixed to denote the persons speaking. Following out the suggestions thus given by the poem itself, a great many commentators have arranged it as a regular drama, and suppose that it may actually have been put on the stage, but this hypothesis can only be supported by a long succession of other hypotheses. M. Renan, for example, thinks that all the actors must have been present on the stage at once, but always unobservant of what was going on outside their own rôle.

SOLOMON'S SONG.

And in fact the almost infinite diversity of conjecture hazarded in support of the dramatic theory and the tremendous liberties taken with the text by its advocates go far to disprove it altogether. But it is not necessary, on the other hand, to have recourse to a theory like Herder's, that the Song is a collection of different love-poems selected and arranged by Solomon. The pieces have a certain unity of subject and style. This is now generally admitted, but they are so loosely connected that they might easily be detached, and a new arrangement made without altering the sense and purpose. Indeed various suggestions of such alterations have at times been made.

The division we accept gives the following lyrical pieces, which we regard not, strictly speaking, as separate poems, but as stanzas of the same poem, somewhat loosely strung together, and not arranged after any definite artistic method.

{ I. chap. i. 2—8.
{ II.   "   i. 9—II. 7.
  III.   "   ii. 8—17.
  IV.   "   iii. 1—5.
  V.   "   iii. 6—11.
{ VI.   "   iv. 1—7.
{ VII.   "   iv. 8—11.
{ VIII.   "   iv. 12—V. 1.
  IX.   "   v. 2—VI. 3.
  X. chap. vi. 4—9.
  XI.   "   vi. 10—13.
  XII.   "   vii. 1—10.
  XIII.   "   vii. 11—viii. 4.
  XIV.   "   viii. 5—7.
  XV.   "   viii. 8—10.
  XVI.   "   viii. 11—12.
  XVII.   "   viii. 13, 14.

The break at the end of II., IV., and XIII. is marked by the formula, "I charge thee," &c.; at the end of III. and VI. by another formula, expressing the return of night, "until the day breaks," &c., properly "until the day cools," *i.e.*, the evening. Similarly the emphatic declaration, "I am my beloved's," &c., which ends the pieces IX. and XII. An abrupt change of situation sometimes indicates the beginning of a new stanza, as at end of I., VI., and XIV., or a question marks a new departure, as at the beginning of V. and XI. Some of the pieces, as indicated by the brackets, are more closely related than others. But in every case, without exception, there is described, or at least implied, under figures transparent enough, the complete union of the wedded pair. In fact each piece has exactly, whether short or long, whether more or less elaborate, the same general character and *dénoûment*. Each tells from one or other point of view the story of a courtship, ending in the complete and happy union of the lovers. The book is a series of love-poems, written, or supposed to be written, by a husband for or to his own wife, to recall to her, in the midst of their perfect union, the difficulties their love had encountered, the obstacles thrown in its way, its devoted constancy on both sides, and ultimate conquest over every hindrance.

There is a further conjecture which the form of the poem suggests, it is that these love-poems, by whomsoever originally composed, were arranged and adapted for the celebration of marriages, since, as pointed out in the Notes, maidens and young men vie in praising, these the bridegroom's beauty, those the bride's. But whether arranged for any one particular marriage or to be used at such events generally, there is no indication. The daughters of Jerusalem and the friends of the bridegroom may actually have been introduced to sing these praises, or they may have only been present in fancy; we have no positive indication to guide us. Bossuet is really to be credited with this suggestion, though his division into seven portions to suit a period of seven days, the ordinary duration of an Eastern wedding, is somewhat too arbitrary. His conjecture in its general outline is accepted by Renan as well as by our own scholar Lowth; the former even finds confirmation of the Epithalamium hypothesis in the expression of Jer. vii. 34, and xxv. 10, "the voice of the bridegroom and the voice of the bride." The analogy of modern Eastern weddings is a still stronger confirmation of this conjecture, that the Song was employed as an Epithalamium, if not composed in that character. It also helps to explain what else would seem extravagant in the poem and bordering on the licentious. The manners of many countries allow at weddings a relaxation of the ordinary rules of propriety. It was so in Palestine. "The evening feast was one of boisterous merriment, almost amounting to rioting. There were regular joke-makers; anything however false might be said of the bride, and to make the gravest Rabbi, even the President of the Sanhedrim, sing or dance, seemed a special object of delight" ("Marriage among the Ancient Hebrews," by the Rev. Dr. Edersheim, *Bible Educator*, Vol. IV., p. 270). In the remarks on the Song of Songs, by Dr. J. J. Wetstein, given by Delitsch in an Appendix to his Commentary, many illustrations of the poem are adduced from modern Bedouin customs, among others, that of the Wasf, or a description of the personal perfections and beauty of the young couple, of which a specimen is actually given, very analogous in character and imagery to vii. 2—6. But it is not only the East which offers analogy. Love and its language are necessarily the same all the world over. Spenser's famous Epithalamium helps us to understand the Song of Solomon.

As to the versification of the Song of Songs, it contains examples of almost all the different forms of *parallelism*, the name given to indicate that balance of clause against clause, either in regard to construction or sense, which constitutes the chief element of Hebrew rhythm. But the greater part of it is free even of the very lax rules which seem to have guided the poets of Israel. We may compare them to those irregular measures in which so many modern poets love to express their sweet and wayward fancies, in which the ear alone is the metrical law. Had the Song but the completeness given by rhyme, it would want nothing of the richness of sound of the finest pieces of Tennyson's *Maud*. (See *Bible Educator*, Vol. III., p. 48.)

EXCURSUS III.—ON THE PASSAGE, CHAP. VI. 11—13.

Translated word for word this passage runs as follows:—"Into the garden of nuts I descended to see the verdure of the valley, to see if the vine was shooting, if the pomegranates flourished. I did not know,—my soul,—put me,—chariots of my people—noble. Come back, come back the Shulamite. Come back, come back, in order that we may see thee. What do you see in Shulamite? Like the dance of two camps."

This the LXX. translate:—"Into the garden of nuts I descended to see among the vegetation of the torrent bed, to see if the vine flourished, if the pomegranate sprouted, *there I will give thee my breasts*. My soul did not know, the chariots of Amminadab put me—return, return, Shunamite, return, return, and we will contemplate thee. What will you see in the Shunamite? She that cometh like choruses of the camps."

The Vulgate does not insert the promise of love, and reads: "and I did not know, my soul troubled me on account of the four-horsed chariots of Amminadab. Return, return, Shulamite, that we may look at thee. What wilt thou see in the Shulamite; if not the chorus of camps."

A comparison of the above seems to show—

(1) That the Hebrew text has not come down to us in its integrity.

(2) That the Greek translators had before their eyes another text.

(3) That neither they nor St. Jerome understood the text which came to them already incomplete.

Yet this impossible passage, "the rags of a text irremediably corrupt," has become for many scholars the key to the entire book. *The heroine in a moment of bewilderment strays into the midst of a cortége of King Solomon, who instantly falls in love with her; or perhaps into the midst of a detachment of his troops, who capture her for the royal harem, after a comparison of her simple country style of dancing with that of the trained court ladies.* This, or some similar device, is resorted to by most of those who construct an elaborate drama out of this series of love-lyrics, the whole structure falling to pieces when we see that on this, the centre, the only passage giving a possible incident on which to hang the rest, no reliance whatever can be placed, since it is so obviously corrupt.

The following are a few of various suggested translations of this piece:—

"My heart led me—I know not how—far from the troop of my noble people. Come back, come back, they cry, that we may see thee, Shulamite. What do you see in me, a poor Shulamite?"

"My desire made of me, so to speak, a chariot of my noble people," &c.

"My desire brought me to a chariot, a noble one," &c.

"Suddenly I was seized with fright,—chariots of my people, the Prince!"

As to "the dance of Mahanaim," even if by itself intelligible, as a reference to an old national dance, as we say "Polonaise," "Scotch dance," or as a dance performed by two choirs or bands (see Note *ad loc.*) the connection with the context is almost inexplicable. The only suggestion which seems worthy of consideration, connects the words not with what precedes but with what immediately follows. If a word or words leading to the comparison, "like," &c., have dropped out, or if "like a dance of Mahanaim" may be taken as a kind of stage direction, to introduce the choric scene, the passage will become clear in the light thrown on it by the analogy of the modern Syrian marriage customs.

The question, "What do you see in Shulamite?" may be understood as a challenge to the poet to sing the customary "wasf" or eulogy on the bride's beauty, which accordingly follows in the next chapter. But before it began, a dance after the manner of the sword dance that forms at present a customary part of a Syrian wedding, would in due course have to be performed, and the words "(dance) like the dance of Mahanaim" would be a direction for its performance. See end of *Excursus* II. on the form of the Poem.

THE BOOK OF THE PROPHET
ISAIAH

INTRODUCTION
TO
THE BOOK OF THE PROPHET
ISAIAH

I. **Life of Isaiah.**—(1) We cannot write the life of Isaiah as we can write that of St. Paul. We have no contemporary notices of him by other writers, and only a few dim traditions as to any facts of his life and death. His writings, containing, as they do, the messages which he had to give to men from God, are as far as possible from being intentionally autobiographical. We know less of his home-life than we do of Hosea's; less of the manner in which he was treated by priests and princes and rival prophets, than we do of the manner in which Jeremiah was treated by his contemporaries. All that we can do, in the dearth of this information from without, is to look to the prophet's writings, and see what they tell us of the man, to draw inferences more or less legitimate from acknowledged facts, to trace out hints scattered here and there by chance, to supply a theory based upon some phenomena and explaining others, and so to construct what I have elsewhere called an "Ideal Biography of Isaiah." *

(2) Of the father of Isaiah we know nothing but the name which he bore himself, and that which he gave his son. The former, Amoz, is probably a shortened form of Amaziah ("strong is Jehovah"), and if we were to accept the Rabbinic maxim, that where the name of a prophet's father is given it is because the father also was a prophet, we might infer that Isaiah was trained in early youth for the work that lay before him. The name Isaiah ("*Jah*," or "*Jehovah, saves*") would seem to indicate that he who gave it was a man whose belief in the Lord God of Israel was strong and living, perhaps that he dedicated his child to be a witness of the truth which the name implies. Isaiah's practice of giving symbolic and suggestive names to his children may have been inherited from his father. It may be inferred, without much risk of error, from the circumstances of Isaiah's call (chap. vi. 1), that he was a priest. The vision which he saw was from the court which none might enter but the sons of Aaron. The reformer of the ceremonial hypocrisy that had defiled the sanctuary (chaps. i. 11—14, xxviii. 7), was to come, as in the instances of Jeremiah, the Baptist, Savonarola, Luther, from the sanctuary itself. The character of a man's mother may always in some measure be inferred from that of the man himself. In Isaiah's case we have, besides this, suggestive allusions to a mother's care for her children (chap. xlix. 15). The tenderness with which she comforts her son is the type of the pitying love of Jehovah for His chosen, which remembers even when that natural tenderness forgets (chap. lxvi. 12, 13). We may feel sure that she presented rather the older pattern of the godly matrons of Israel than the life of frivolous luxury sketched by her son in such vivid colours in chap. iii. 16—23. Looking to the fact that from twenty-five to thirty was the normal age at which priest or Levite entered on his functions, and that Isaiah does not plead his youth, as Jeremiah did (Jer. i. 6), as a reason for shrinking back from his calling as a prophet, we may fix his birth at from B.C. 788—783, and accordingly we have to think of the boy as growing up during the latter half of the reign of Uzziah. His education was naturally grounded on the sacred books of his country, as far as they then existed. Allusive references to Eden and Noah (chaps. li. 3, liv. 9), to Abraham and Sarah (chaps. xli. 8, li. 1, 2), to Jacob and Moses (chaps. xli. 8, lxiii. 11, 12), to Sodom and Gomorrah (chaps. i. 9, xiii. 19), show that these books must have included the substance of Genesis and Exodus. The Book of Judges supplied the memories of the day of Midian (chaps. ix. 4, x. 26). The Proverbs of Solomon, then, as always, prominent in Jewish education, furnished him with an ethical and philosophical vocabulary (chaps. xi. 1, 3, xxxiii. 5, 6), and with the method of parabolic teaching (chap. xxviii. 23—29), and taught him to lay the foundations of morality in the "fear of the Lord." As he advanced to manhood, the Book of Job met him, with its bold presentations of the problems of the universe, and gave the training which he needed for his work as the great poet-prophet of Israel. (See Cheyne's "Isaiah," ii. 226, and essay on "Job and the Second Part of Isaiah," ii. 243.)

(3) The Psalms which were then in use in the Temple supplied emotions, imagery, culture of another kind, which bore fruit in the "songs" or "hymns" which Isaiah actually incorporated in the collection of his writings (chaps. v. 1—7, xii. xxvi. 1—4), perhaps, also in the Psalms of the sons of Korah, some, at least, of which belong to the same period (Pss. xliv.—xlviii), and bear traces of parallelism of thought. The instances of a like parallelism between the language of Isaiah and that of Deuteronomy,* are not sufficient to settle the question as to the date and authorship of that book, but they may be at least considered as contributing to its solution. Side by side with this religious education there are signs of a wider culture, of training in the medical science of the time (chaps. i. 6, xxxviii. 21), of some knowledge of the history and religion of the great empires which were contending for the sovereignty of the East (chaps. xviii. 2, xix. 11—13, xxiii. 12, 13, xlvi. 1). The prosperous reign of Uzziah revived the commerce of Jerusalem, and from the men of Tyre and others he heard of the far-off voyages of the ships of

---

* See a series of papers with this title in the *Expositor*, Second Series, 1883.

* See Dr. Kay, in the *Speaker's Commentary*, Note on Isaiah, chap. i.

ISAIAH.

Tarshish to the isles of Chittim (chaps. ii. 16, xxiii. 1, 14, lx. 9), of the distant Shinar, and Media, and Elam (chaps. xi. 11, xiii. 17, xxi. 2, xxii. 6), and of the isles of the sea (chap. xi. 11), even of the land of Sinim (China) (chap. xlix. 12). His knowledge of Egypt, of Zoan, and Noph, and Pathros (chap. xix. 11), of the rivers of Ethiopia, and the seven streams of the Delta (chap. xi. 11, 15), of Dibon and Nebo, and other Moabite cities (chaps. xv. 2, xvi. 9), implies, if not actual travel, much intercourse with travellers, in those countries. He may have learnt the Aramaic of the northern provinces of Syria, and so been able, like Hezekiah's ministers, to converse even with Assyrians (chap. xxxvi. 11), and have known more than his fellows of their names and titles, and the organisation of their armies, as in the Sargon and the Tartan of chap. xx. 1. He may have watched with his own eyes the art of the metallurgist (chap. i. 25), of the sculptor, of the painter, which he describes so vividly (chap. xliv. 12).

(4) Two facts in the reign of Uzziah would seem to have impressed themselves on the mind of the young prophet: (1) the earthquake which is mentioned by Amos (chap. i. 1), and Zechariah (chap. xiv. 5), and which has left many traces of its influence as a type of Divine judgments in Isaiah's writings (chaps. ii. 19, xxiv. 19, 20); and (2) the leprosy which came on the king as a punishment for the sacrilegious usurpation of the functions of the priesthood (2 Chron. xxvi. 20, 21), and which may well have suggested the terrible question whether he himself, and the whole nation of which he was a member, were not tainted with a like spiritual uncleanness, which yet he felt powerless to remedy (chaps. i. 6, vi. 5).

(5) The theophany of chap. vi. was the answer to these questionings and misgivings. He entered on a new stage of life, with new powers, and the sense of a new vocation. The touch of the burning coal upon his lips was, as it were, an instantaneous purgatory, cleansing his iniquity. But the work on which he entered was, beyond that of any other prophet, an arduous and a terrible one. He had to be a herald of devastation, and defeat, and exile; of messages the immediate effect of which would be to increase the spiritual deafness and blindness of his hearers (chap. vi. 10). The one gleam of hope in the thick darkness was that which told of the "remnant" in which the true Israel should at last revive, of the young scion which should rise out of the decayed tree, the branches of which had been lopped off as by the axe of the Divine judgments (chap. vi. 13).

(6) Isaiah does not seem, however, to have entered at once upon the public exercise of a prophet's calling. His first work was to study the present and the future in the volume of the past, and in his history of the reign of Uzziah (2 Chron. xxvi. 22), with its material prosperity, its national arrogance, its formalism and hypocrisy, its luxuries and its pomp, its corruption and its cruelty, we may well believe that he probed to the quick the ulcerous sores which were eating into the nation's life, as he did afterwards in the "great indictment," with which his collected writings open. To this period of his life, under Jotham, we may also assign his marriage with a woman like-minded with himself, not without her own share of prophetic gifts (chap. viii. 3), and the birth of the son whose name, Shear-jashub ("remnant returns"), embodying, as it did, at once the terror and the hope of his great vision, made him, even in his infancy, "a sign and a wonder" to the people (chap. viii. 18).

(7) There are signs, however, that Isaiah was recognised as a prophet before the close of the reign of Jotham. At the beginning of that of Ahaz he had disciples, who gathered round him and took notes of his teaching (chap. viii. 16). He would seem to have been on terms of intimacy with Zechariah, the father of the wife of Ahaz, the mother of Hezekiah, and with the high priest Urijah (chap. viii. 2; 2 Chron. xxix. 1). The tone of authority in which he speaks to Ahaz (chap. vii. 4, 13), might almost seem to suggest that the education of the young prince had been entrusted to his care, as that of Solomon had been to Nathan. If the result, as far as Ahaz was concerned, was disappointing, the influence which he began to exercise on the mind of his future successor, born when Ahaz himself was scarcely out of the age of tutelage, must have been abundant compensation. The fact that Hezekiah's mother was the daughter or granddaughter of one who had understanding in the visions of God (2 Chron. xxvi. 5) suggests the inference that she may have been chosen by Jotham, under Isaiah's guidance, as a wife for the young king, and that the devotion and purity of Hezekiah's character were mainly due to her influence, as directed by him. Anyhow, the events of that reign, the invasion of Rezin and Pekah, the conquests of Pul, the intervention of Tiglath-pileser, the rise of the Ethiopian dynasty of the Pharaohs, represented by So, or Sabaco, the wars with the Philistines, and other neighbouring nations, must have given many occasions, over and above those recorded in his writings, for the exercise of his gifts of insight as a prophet and a statesman, seeing the secret workings that lay below the surface of things, and proclaiming the righteous government of Jehovah, as disposing and ordering all. During this period also we may rightly think of the influence of contemporary prophets such as Hosea and Amos, in the northern kingdom, and above all Micah, his friend and contemporary in Judah, as working upon his mind, enlarging his thoughts, completing the training which fitted him for the higher and more commanding position which he was to occupy in the reign of Hezekiah. To Micah especially we can trace his visions of the restored Temple (chap. ii. 2—4; Micah iv. 1), his protests against greed and drunkenness (Micah ii. 1—11), his hopes of a Prince of Peace rising out of the house of David (Micah v. 2, 5).

(8) At the commencement of that reign, Isaiah must have been over sixty. The king whom he had trained, and whose mother was under his direction, was only twenty-five, and in the whole opening policy of his reformation, the restoration of the worship of the Temple, with its psalmody and music, the effort after a renewed unity shown in his invitation to Ephraim and Manasseh, Issachar and Zebulun, to keep the passover at Jerusalem, the conversion of the heathen and their admission, as proselytes, into fellowship with Israel, (2 Chron. xxix.—xxxii.), we can trace, without the shadow of a doubt, the influence of his instructor. If the prophet did not identify the king with the ideal ruler, the Prince of Peace of his earlier utterances (chap. ix. 6), he must have seen in him the pledge and earnest of the possibilities of a future like that of the stem and branch of Jesse in chap. xi. 1. It was a time of joy such as the nation had not seen since the days of Solomon (2 Chron. xxx. 26). The king himself assumed the office of a teacher, and "spake comfortably" to the hearts of priests and laity, and appeared almost as a priest interceding for the ignorant and erring (2 Chron. xxx. 18), in words which must have been, in greater or less measure, the echo of Isaiah's teaching. He added to the sacred books of Israel by collecting the Proverbs of Solomon that had been floating in the

ISAIAH.

minds of men, though, as yet they had not been put together, and in which, as dealing largely with the duties and the faults of rulers, Isaiah may well have found the "ideal of a patriot king" which he hoped to see realised in his pupil (Prov. xxv.—xxix.). It was not long, however, before the bright dawn was overcast. There were perils from without and from within. The successive invasions of Shalmaneser, Sargon, Sennacherib, the conquest of Samaria, and the captivity of the Ten Tribes threw the people of Judah into a state of restless agitation. Some of the king's counsellors trusted in the prospect of an alliance with the Ethiopian dynasty ruling in Egypt, represented by Sabaco and Tirhakah (chaps. xviii. 2, xx. 3, xxx. 2). Some thought it more prudent to acknowledge the suzerainty of the Assyrian king and to pay a moderate tribute. Some fell back on new fortifications which were to make Jerusalem impregnable, and gave themselves up to a boastful and defiant revelry (chap. xxii. 9—13). The aged prophet stood almost alone as he told men, now in speech and now in strange and startling acts (chap. xx. 2), that their one way of safety was to repent and to seek the kingdom of God and His righteousness (chaps. xxii. 12, xxvi. 8, 9, xxviii. 16), and not to weave their webs of diplomacy and intrigue (chap. xxx. 1). They mocked at his iterated utterances in the name of the Holy One of Israel (chaps. xxviii. 9—14, xxx. 11). They, for their parts, would none of Him. The king himself fell away from the bright promise of his early reign. The chief place among his counsellors was given to Shebna, of low or foreign extraction, ostentatious, arrogant, the chief advocate of a braggart and rollicking defiance (chap. xxii. 15—19). Among those counsellors Isaiah could count only on the support of the respectable Eliakim, and even he was tainted with the nepotism which is the besetting sin of Eastern rulers, and in which the prophet read the forecast of a future fall (chap. xxii. 20—25).

(9) The danger which had threatened Jerusalem from the armies of Sargon was averted by submission and the payment of tribute. He laid waste Judah, but left the capital untouched. Before long a danger of another kind threatened the frustration of Isaiah's hopes. The king, not yet thirty-five, and as yet without an heir, was sick unto death (chap. xxxviii. 1). In the words in which the prophet-physician announced the danger there was a sad significance. Men who read between the lines might trace in that "set thine house in order," the hint that there was disorder alike in the policy of the kingdom and in the inner habitation of the soul, that needed to be set right. As it was, the king's repentance and the prayer of faith prevailed, and fifteen years were added to his life. His marriage with Hephzibah (2 Kings xxi. 1) was probably determined by the counsels of the prophet, who saw in her very name ("my delight is in her"), an augury of good (chap. lxii. 4), and the name given to the child who was to succeed him, Manasseh ("forgetting"), bore witness that the king was following up his policy of conciliating the remnant of Ephraim and Manasseh, and of proclaiming an amnesty of all past animosities (2 Chron. xxx. 1—12). There was, however, even then a cloud upon the horizon. The king lent too willing an ear to the insidious proposals of Merodachbaladan, the rebel king of Babylon, against whom Sargon had been carrying on a long-continued warfare, and had in the weakness of his pride displayed the treasures of his palace and his arsenal, as if they, and not the living God, were the strength of Israel (chap. xxxix. 1—8; 2 Chron. xxxii. 31). Against that alliance the fiery zeal of the old prophet kindled into a white heat of indignation. It was full of untold evils in its immediate and remote consequences. It was in that burst of inspiration that Isaiah had his first clear vision of the Babylonian captivity, beyond which he was afterwards led to see the dawn of a brighter day of redemption and return.

(10) The danger which Isaiah had predicted soon drew near. Sargon was murdered in his palace, and his successor (Sennacherib) having in the first year of his reign crushed the Babylonian revolt, and driven Merôdachbaladan into the marshes of the lower Euphrates (see Notes on chap. xxxvi. 1), turned his arms to subdue the rebels of his southern provinces, and among others Hezekiah, who had attacked and imprisoned the Assyrian ruler of Ashdod, and demanded an exorbitant tribute, which could only be paid by emptying the treasure-house, that had been boastfully shown to the Babylonian envoys, and stripping even the Temple of its gold (2 Kings xviii. 14—16). Even this, however, did not avail. The Assyrian king, suspecting probably that negotiations were going on between Hezekiah and Tirhakah, tore up the treaty, led his armies against Jerusalem, and sent Rabshakeh and his companions to demand an unconditional surrender (2 Kings xviii. 17 —27). We need not now follow the history of that mission. In its relation to Isaiah's life we may find in it the time of his crowning glory. At last mockers were silenced, and the people could "see their teachers" (chap. xxx. 20). King, priests, nobles, came in procession to the house of Isaiah in the sackcloth of supplication. Would he not once more intercede for them with the Holy One of Israel? The occasion was worthy of the grand burst of prophecy which was Isaiah's last public utterance.

(11) During the three or four years that remained of Hezekiah's reign, after the destruction of the Assyrian armies, the position of Isaiah was one of safety and of honour. It was probably during this period that he fell back upon the line of work with which he started, and wrote the history of the reign of Hezekiah, which manifestly served as the basis of 2 Chron. xxix.—xxxii. 32. But the time must also have been one of disappointment and of dark forebodings for the future. Hezekiah had only partially fulfilled the hopes with which Isaiah had hailed his accession to the throne. He must have seen that the boy prince, Manasseh, whom he was too old to educate himself, was likely to walk in the steps of his grandfather rather than his father. As soon as Hezekiah died his whole policy was reversed. The Shebna party were once more in the ascendant. Foreign alliances and foreign idolatries prevailed as they had done in the days of Ahaz. The disciples who had gathered round Isaiah during his long career entered an unavailing protest (2 Chron. xxxiii. 10), and were slain by Manasseh as the prophets of Jehovah had been slain of old by Jezebel and Ahab (2 Kings xxi. 16). According to a Jewish tradition, not in itself improbable, Isaiah himself perished in the persecution, being accused of blasphemy for having said that he had seen the Lord, as in chap. vi., and was condemned to die by being enclosed in the hollowed trunk of a tree, and then sawn asunder. The writer of the Epistle to the Hebrews is supposed to allude to this tradition in Heb. xi. 37. Of the sons of Isaiah we have nothing but the names; but it is well to remember that those names must have made them, as long as they lived, the representatives to the generation that came after them of all that was most characteristic in their father's teaching. Whether the prophet himself was engaged during the

ISAIAH.

later years of his life in providing for the perpetuation of his leading ideas in another form, is a question which will meet us farther on.

II. Arrangement of Isaiah's prophecies.—

(1) It is obvious that the writings of a man who has played a conspicuous part as a writer or a teacher may be brought together in very various ways. The writer may be his own editor, sifting and selecting from the MSS. of many years, and arranging them either in chronological order or else according to a method independent of that order, and determined by personal or ideal associations. Or the task of editing may be left to a friend, disciple, or secretary, acting as Baruch seems to have acted in relation to Jeremiah (Jer. xxxvi. 4, 18, 32). Or again, the papers may come in a loose and fragmentary state into the hands of the scribes, or men of letters, of a later generation, and they may exercise their functions with varying degrees of insight or of accuracy, editing with or without notes and glosses and interpolations. When we have no record as to which process was adopted, the problem is complicated by the possibility that all three processes may have mingled in varying and uncertain proportions. It is not to be wondered at that critics who are not content to assume that the arrangement which they find in the existing Hebrew text of the Old Testament can claim a Divine authority which could be claimed by no other, should come on these points to widely different conclusions, and be influenced by considerations more or less subjective. The task of a complete critical analysis lies beyond the limits within which the present writer has to work, and all that will be now attempted will be the endeavour to note the probable sequence of the chapters or other sub-sections of Isaiah's writings.

(2) It is tolerably plain, at the outset, that we have three chief divisions.

(*A*) Chaps. i.—xxxv. A collection, not necessarily a complete collection, of prophetic writings from the death of Uzziah to the closing years of Hezekiah.

(*B*) Chaps. xxxvi.—xxxix. An historical appendix to that collection, connected with the most memorable passage in Isaiah's life.

(*C*) Chaps. xl.—lxvi. A complete and systematically arranged collection, manifestly having a unity of its own, and having for its central subject the restoration of the Jews from Babylon.

It remains to examine the arrangement of the sections in each group.

(*A*) Chap. i. A general introduction to the whole, probably written in the latter part of the reign of Jotham, embodying the results of Isaiah's study of the reign of Uzziah, possibly retouched under Hezekiah.

Chaps. ii.—v. A further denunciation of the sins of Israel, and the judgments coming on them, coloured in part by reminiscences of the earthquake under Uzziah, and painting the social evils of that period. Mingling with the prophecies of judgment are visions of a future restoration (chaps. ii. 2, iv. 2—6), shared by Isaiah with his contemporary Micah. Chaps. i.—v. may be considered as deliberately placed before chap. vi., as showing the state of things which preceded the call there narrated.

Chaps. vii.—x. 4. Narrative mingled with prophecies belonging to the early years of Ahaz. First definite prediction of the Assyrian invasion, and of an ideally righteous king (chap. ix. 6, 7); the witness of the names of Isaiah's children; the true Immanuel.

Chaps. x. 5—xii. 6. Clearer announcement of the Assyrian invasion of Tiglath-pileser (?), Salmaneser (?), or Sargon (?). Renewed vision of the return of the remnant (the true Shear-Jashub), and of the true Immanuel, or righteous King (chap. xi. 1—16), coloured probably by the virtues of the young Hezekiah, and the captivity of the ten tribes.

Chaps. xiii.—xxiii. Obviously in its form an independent collection of "burdens" or oracles, bearing on the history of Jerusalem and the neighbouring nations, all probably written under Hezekiah, and in some cases as an answer to ambassadors who came to consult the prophet as to the future of the people who sent them (chap. xiv. 32). "The burden of Babylon" (chaps. xiii., xiv.), assuming it to be Isaiah's, was probably among the latest, written after the mission of Merôdach-baladan had directed the prophet's mind to that city, as almost equally with Nineveh the capital of the Assyrian empire, and destined for a time to take its place as the great world-power (chap. xiv. 25), but is placed first, as the Epistle to the Romans stands in the New Testament at the head of St. Paul's epistles, on account of its importance. Chaps xviii.—xx. are connected with the plans of an Egypto-Ethiopian alliance; chap. xxi. with the future destruction of Babylon; chap. xxii. with Sargon's or Sennacherib's (?) attack on Judah.

Chaps. xxiv.—xxvii. The four poems seem grouped together, not necessarily as having been written continuously, but as having for their common subject "the day of the Lord," which brings at once judgment and redemption. The recurrence of the phrase "in that day," in chaps. xxvi. 1, xxvii. 1, 12, connects them with chap. iv. 1; the glory of the "mountain of the Lord," in chap. xxv. 6, with chap. ii. 2. With the exception of the passing reference to Moab in chap. xxv. 10, the group is less definitely historical than any other.

Chaps. xxviii.—xxxii., like the "burdens" of chaps. xiii.—xxiii., have an outward unity in the opening formula of "Woe to" (chaps. xxviii. 1, xxix. 1, xxx. 1, xxxi. 1, xxxiii. 1), in which the prophet falls back upon the model of one of his earlier writings (chap. v. 8, 11, 18, 20). The whole group belongs to the time when the march of Sargon's (?) or Sennacherib's (?) armies was striking terror into the people, and leading them once again to projects of foreign alliances. The picture of the ideally righteous king, in chap. xxxii. 1—8, reminding us of chaps. ix. 6, 7, xi. 1—9, is suggestive. Hezekiah had not fulfilled the ideal. It was still in the distant future; but the hopes of the prophet were inextinguishable.

Chaps. xxxiii.—xxxv. The close of the first great collection, historically turning mainly on Sennacherib's invasion, and the part taken by the Edomites in his attack on Judah (chap. xxxiv. 5, 6), but ending in a vision of the restoration of all things which transcends all history (chap. xxxv. 1—10). They would have been fitting "last words" for the aged prophet, when his work seemed all but over. They were, perhaps, a stepping stone to the greater and more connected work which, more than anything else, was to make his name immortal, in chaps. xl.—lxvi.

(*B*) Chaps. xxxvi.—xxxix. Probably, looking to the difference of style, not written by Isaiah, but appended, perhaps by some disciple, perhaps by a scribe-editor, in the time of Ezra, as embodying what could be gathered of the prophet's closing work, and his almost greatest utterance, and based, perhaps, upon the prophet's history of Hezekiah (2 Chron. xxxii. 32). In chronological order, chaps. xxxviii., xxxix. should come first, as dealing with events prior to the destruction of Sennacherib's army.

(*C*) The question of the arrangement of chaps. xl.—

ISAIAH.

lxvi. will be considered here independently of its authorship. A tripartite division is apparently indicated by the recurrence of the burden, "There is no peace, saith my God, to the wicked," in chaps. xlviii. 22, lvii. 21, as follows:—

(1) Chaps. xli.—xlviii. 22, open with the proclamation of the return of the exiles, and pass on to the contrast between the greatness of Jehovah and the nothingness of the gods of the heathen. Cyrus appears as the central figure, the ideally righteous man, the anointed of the Lord (chaps. xliv. 26—xlv. 7); but the Servant of the Lord, afterwards so prominent, appears also in chap. xlii. 1—7.

(2) Chaps. xlix. 1—lvii. 21 are occupied chiefly with the Servant of the Lord, thought of now in his personal, now in his collective, unity, in whom the prophet is taught to see even more than he had seen in Hezekiah or Cyrus, the instrument by which God's work for Israel and for mankind was to be accomplished, by the victory, not of power only or chiefly, but of vicarious suffering (chaps. xlix. 4—7, l. 6, lii. 13—liii. 12).

(3) Chaps. lviii.—lxvi. 24. This portion ends with an expansion of the thought of the "no peace" of the two previous sections. It is remarkable as gathering up, and developing to their highest point, what had been throughout the prominent thoughts of Isaiah's work as a teacher—his condemnation of his people's sins (chaps. lxv. 2—12, lxvi. 3, 4); his visions of a new world of righteousness and peace (chaps. lx., lxi. lxv. 17—25); of a redeemed Israel fulfilling its ideal (chap. lxvi. 10—14); of one in whom the ideas of the righteous King and the Servant of the Lord are strangely blended (chap. lxi. 1—3); of the ultimate overthrow of all the enemies of God (chap. lxvi. 15, 24). Not a few critics have gone farther than this, and have traced an elaborate tripartite division of three sections in each part; and again a further grouping of three sub-sections under each of the nine thus formed, the structure of the whole book being, on this view, as elaborately planned as Dante's *Commedia*, on the basis of the mystic number three thus squared and cubed.* It may be questioned, however, whether this arrangement is not too artificial, at variance with the character of Isaiah's mind, and embarrassing rather than helpful in tracing, what it is in any case difficult to trace, the sequence and continuity of thought. A more natural explanation seems to be, that the writer's mind, dwelling now on one great idea, now on another, wrote now this and now that section, often with a considerable interval between them, so that we have not a book after modern fashion, with beginning, middle, and end, but rather a series of detached pieces, connected mainly by subtle links of association, like the *Pensées* of Pascal, the *Meditations* of Marcus Aurelius, or Wordsworth's *Ecclesiastical Sonnets*. On the assumption of Isaiah's authorship, the whole of this second volume must be assigned, with scarcely the shadow of a doubt, to the closing years of the reign of Hezekiah or the opening years of that of Manasseh, and therefore to a very advanced period of the prophet's life. Of him, as of Moses, it might have been said, that "his eye was not dim nor his natural force abated." The old age of Isaiah must have been the counterpart, in its receptive and apocalyptic power, of the old age of St. John.

III. **The authorship of Isaiah xl.—lxvi.—**
(1) The limits within which I must confine myself do not admit of anything like an exhaustive treatment of this question. It may be well to begin by noting what it involves. Were the authorship of Isaiah disproved, it would not follow that we had a spurious book, a counterfeit and a forgery, or even, as in the case of the hypothesis of the later date of Ecclesiastes, a case of personated authorship without the *animus decipiendi*. All that would follow would be that some unknown writer, at or about the time of the return of the Jews from Babylon, had so imbued himself with the thoughts and even the style of Isaiah, that his work was accepted by his contemporaries, or by the scribes who were concerned in the completion of the Old Testament Canon under Ezra, as rounding off the cycle of that prophet's teaching. In regard to all the Messianic elements in it, its great argument against idolatry, and its visions of judgment and restoration, it would still retain all the dignity and authority of inspiration, and be entitled to the place which it occupies in the Hebrew Canon. Even its appeals to the foreknowledge of God, as manifested in prophetic announcements of the downfall of Babylon and the victories of Cyrus (chaps. xl. 13, xli. 26—28, xliii. 9, xlv. 21), would retain their force as referring to prophecies, like those of Jeremiah and Micah, which foretold a like downfall of the city on the Euphrates, and a like restoration of Jerusalem.

(2) The arguments which have led many recent critics to the conclusion that the authorship of Isaiah is disproved, are briefly these:—

(*a*) That the whole standpoint of the writer is that of one who was living at the time of the return of the Jews from the Babylonian captivity, and specially that the name of Cyrus was altogether beyond the horizon of Isaiah's knowledge.

(*b*) That the central thought of the Servant of the Lord, as made perfect through suffering and dying vicariously for the sins of his people, is entirely foreign to the teaching of the historical Isaiah.

(*c*) That the style and vocabulary of chaps. xl.—lxvi. are so different from those of chaps. i.—xxxix. as to imply diversity of authorship.

(3) On the other hand, it has been urged—

(*a*) That on the assumption of Isaiah's inspiration, he may have been led to place himself, as in an ecstatic vision, like that of Balaam and other prophets, in a time and country other than his own.

(*b*) That the name of Cyrus may have been within the limit of Isaiah's human knowledge, or may have been supernaturally revealed to him. See Note on chap. xliv. 28.

(*c*) That the knowledge of Babylon and its life and worship as shown in 2 Isaiah is not more than may be accounted for by the commerce of the time, the diplomatic intercourse with Merôdach-baladan, and other sources.

(*d*) That the forms of idolatry condemned in chaps. lvii. 5, 6, lxv. 3—5, 11, belong much more to the state of Palestine under Manasseh than to that of the Babylonian exiles, either before or after their return.

(*e*) That the reference to Hephzibah and Azubah, the names of the mothers of Manasseh and Jehoshaphat, in chap. lxii. 4, 12, is more natural in one living under the former king than it would be in a writer a century and a half later.

(*f*) That the local colouring of the book, as seen in the "clifts of the rocks" in chap. lvii. 5, the trees of chaps. xli. 19, xliv. 14, lv. 12, the "tents" of chap. liv. 2, the references to Midian, Kedar, Nebaioth, Lebanon, in chap. lx. 6—13, is Palestinian rather than Mesopotamian.

---

* See Delitzsch's *Isaiah*, on chaps. xl.—lxvi. in Clark's *Foreign Theological Library*.

(g) That the idea of the Servant of the Lord was one which might have been developed by Isaiah's experience, from the failure of his earlier hopes, from teaching like that of the Book of Job, with which he was obviously familiar, and from the lesson thus learnt that in that apparent failure, in the suffering and death of every righteous servant, culminating in those of Him who was to fulfil the ideal, lay the secret of an eternal victory.

(h) That the ideal completeness of the restoration of Israel depicted in 2 Isaiah xl. 1—16, xli. 17—19, xliii. 2—6, xlix. 7—26, liv., lv., lviii. 8—14, is more natural in one contemplating the return of the exiles from a distance, than to one who, as a contemporary, watched the somewhat meagre results recorded in Ezra and Nehemiah, in Haggai and Zechariah.

(i) That on the assumption of the writer of 2 Isaiah having been a contemporary with the return, it is strange that there should be no trace of him in any one of the writers just mentioned, no reference in what he himself wrote to those who were contemporary actors on the stage of history, Zerubbabel and Joshua, or to the prophets who had preceded him, Jeremiah, Ezekiel, Daniel.

(j) That the resemblances of style and language between the two books—a resemblance closer than that between either of them and any other book of the Old Testament—preponderate over the diversities. The induction upon which this statement is based has been exhibited with much fulness by Dr. Kay, Mr. Birks, Mr. Cheyne, and others, in their respective Commentaries. The limits within which I have to confine myself prevent my entering on it. It will be enough to note one or two of the most striking instances :

(A) The dominance in both books of the name and the thought of the Holy One of Israel, fourteen times in each, and very rarely elsewhere.

(B) The recognition of the Spirit of the Lord as the source of the wisdom of the true king in chaps. xi. 1, 2, and lxi. 1.

(C) The formula "the Lord" or "the mouth of the Lord hath spoken," in chaps. i. 2, 20, xl. 5, lviii. 14, and of the peculiar Hebrew form for "saith the Lord," in chaps. i. 11, 18, xxxiii. 10, and in chaps. xli. 21, lxvi. 9, both peculiar, or all but peculiar, to Isaiah.

(D) The frequent recurrence of the word *tohu*, the "chaos" of Gen. i. 1, three times in 1 Isaiah, and seven times in 2 Isaiah, almost, as it were, the catchword of both books, much as some modern writers are characterised by their use of phrases like "the absolute" or "the eternities."

(E) The numerous traces in both books that the writers of each had received the same literary culture, and were cast in the same mould. Allusive references to Genesis, the Psalms, the Book of Job, Proverbs, are conspicuous in each. (See Cheyne, ii. *Appendix*, for details).

(4) It has to be remembered, however, that the inductive argument on either side is hardly more than tentative, and is uncertain in its results. A writer of genius, as he grows old, develops new thoughts, enlarges his vocabulary, varies his phraseology and style according to the occasion which leads him to write or the intensity of his own emotions. Many, if not most, New Testament students find no difficulty in accepting the Pastoral Epistles as written by St. Paul, in spite of the long list of words found in them which are not found in his other writings, and the peculiarities of style and thought which characterise them. On the other hand, the history of all literature shows that one writer may, either from pure reverence and love, or from a deliberate purpose of personation, so imbue his mind with the thoughts and language of another, adopt his phrases, reproduce the turns and tricks of his style, that it will not be easy even for an expert to distinguish between the counterfeit and the original. All that can be said as to the application of this inductive method to 1 and 2 Isaiah is, that the parallelisms and the peculiarities may fairly be left to balance each other. So far as I can judge, and I speak with the reserve of one who cannot claim the authority of an expert, there seems to me a slight preponderance in favour of the former.

(5) On this ground then, as well as on a review of the other elements of evidence, I adopt the hypothesis that we have in the two books that are placed in the Hebrew Canon of the Old Testament under the name of Isaiah, substantially the work of one and the same author. I admit in so doing that there is so strong a *primâ facie* case for the opposite hypothesis, that it would be simply impertinent and unfair to charge those who adopt it with irreverence, or haste, or prejudice. The second part of Isaiah would remain as a priceless treasure whoever wrote it, just as the worth of the Epistle to the Hebrews is unaffected by the question whether it was written by Paul or by Apollos, or some unknown writer; it would still have for us, as Christians, the incomparable attraction of having been in part, at least, the basis of the theology of Christendom. It was given to that book to revive, from time to time, the dormant Messianic hopes of Israel; to exercise a traceable influence on the minds of later prophets, such as Jeremiah, Haggai, Zechariah, and Malachi; to nourish the souls of those who were looking for consolation and redemption in Jerusalem (Luke ii. 25, 38); to contribute, if "the word be not too bold," to the education of Him who was to meet those longing expectations. There, as in the mirror of the Divine word, Jesus of Nazareth saw, in the Servant of the Lord, the guiltless Sufferer, the righteous King, that which He recognised as the archetype, after which His own life and death were to be fashioned (Mark x. 45). There the Baptist found that which defined his position in the kingdom of God, as a voice crying in the wilderness (John i. 23). There the publican Evangelist found the Christ delineated as he had seen Him in Jesus (Matt. viii. 17). There Peter, and Paul, and John, and Philip, found the foreshadowings of all that was most precious to them in the teaching of their Master, a witness to Jesus in His lowliness, His purity, His gentleness, His sufferings and death and victory (Acts viii. 35; 1 Pet. ii. 21—24), the ground of their hopes of the restoration of Israel (Rom. v. 15, 20), of the redemption of mankind, and of the restoration of all things, the vision of a new heaven and a new earth, wherein dwelleth righteousness (2 Pet. iii. 13), the apocalypse of the city of God, the heavenly Jerusalem (Rev. xxi., xxii.). There the souls of devout Christians, century after century, have found, more than in any other utterance of prophecy, the Evangel pre-evangelised, the exceeding great and precious promises which sustained them in their conflict with temptation, under the burden of their sins, and turned their sorrow and sighing into the songs of an everlasting joy.

IV. (1) It remains that I should acknowledge the debt of gratitude which I owe, in greater or less measure, to some of my forerunners. The list of commentators on Isaiah is a very long one, and it is probable, to use a phrase of the old Rabbis, that no one has ever entered into the House of the Interpreter with reverent footsteps without finding some treasure which he might make peculiarly his own. Of these I cannot claim to have consulted more than comparatively few. The circumstances under which I have had to write the notes that follow—a somewhat prolonged absence from England, and the pressure of other work on my return—have restricted my range of choice. The English student will scarcely complain if that limitation has led me to a more careful study of those whom I chose as the safest and most trustworthy guides. The limits within which I have had to work forbade my discussing the views of other commentators, and I have had to be content with giving results, apart from the processes which led to them. All the more is it right that I should, here at least, acknowledge my obligations to those to whom I am conscious that I am most largely indebted—to Ewald, here, as always, suggestive, bold, original; to Delitzsch, exhaustive and complete, with an almost more than Teutonic exhaustiveness; to my old Oxford instructor in Hebrew, Dr. Kay, looking into the spiritual significance of words and phrases, and investigating suggestive parallelisms with a microscopic minuteness; above all, to Mr. Cheyne, in whom the spirit of a wide and fearless research, and the vividness of historical imagination, are blended, in a measure rarely found elsewhere, with a spirit of devout reverence and insight which makes his Commentary on Isaiah wellnigh all that the scholar student can desire. It has been my effort, while reserving to myself the right of an independent judgment so far as I felt competent to exercise it, to follow, though with unequal steps, in the path in which these interpreters have gone before me, learning myself, according to the old adage, in the endeavour to teach others.

(2) I have further to acknowledge my many obligations to Mr. Sayce, M. Oppert, and the other Assyriologists whose labours, collected in the *Records of the Past* series, published by Mr. Bagster, have made the inscriptions which have thrown a new light on the writings of Isaiah accessible to the average English student. Looking to the class of readers for whom I write, I have thought it better, as a rule, to refer to that series than to books like Mr. George Smith's *Assyrian Discoveries* and *History of Sennacherib*; or Dr. Ginsburg's *Moabite Stone*, or Mr. Budge's *Esarhaddon*, or Schrader's *Keil-Inschriften*; or papers that lie buried as it were, in the *Transactions* of learned societies.

THE BOOK OF THE PROPHET
ISAIAH

CHAPTER I.—The vision of Isaiah the son of Amoz, which he saw concerning Judah and Jerusalem in the days of Uzziah, Jotham, Ahaz, *and* Hezekiah, kings of Judah.

(2) *a* Hear, O heavens, and give ear, O earth: for the LORD hath spoken, I have nourished and brought up children, and they have rebelled against me. (3) *b* The ox knoweth his owner, and the ass his master's crib: *but* Israel doth not know, my people doth not consider. (4) Ah, sinful nation, a people ¹laden with iniquity, a seed of evildoers, children that are corrupters: they have forsaken the LORD, they have provoked the Holy One of Israel unto anger, they are ²gone away backward. (5) Why should ye be stricken any more? ye will ³revolt more and more: the whole head

B.C. cir. 760

a Deut. 32. 1.
b Jer. 8. 7.
1 Heb., *of heaviness.*
2 Heb., *alienated, or, separated.*
3 Heb., *increase revolt.*

---

(1) **The vision of Isaiah the son of Amoz ...**—The term "vision," as descriptive of a prophet's work (1 Sam. iii. 1), is the correlative of the old term "seer," as applied to the prophet himself (1 Sam. ix. 9). The latter fell into disuse, probably because the pretenders to the clairvoyance which it implied brought it into discredit. The prophet, however, did not cease to be a "seer;" and to see visions was still one of the highest forms of the gift of the spirit of Jehovah (Joel ii. 28). It describes the state, more or less ecstatic, in which the prophet sees what others do not see, the things that are yet to come, the unseen working of the eternal laws of God. As compared with "the word of the Lord," it indicates a higher intensity of the ecstatic state; but the two terms were closely associated, and, as in chap. ii. 1, a man was said to *see* "the word of the Lord." Judah and Jerusalem are named as the centre, though not the limit, of the prophet's work.

(2) **Hear, O heavens, and give ear, O earth.**—The prophet opens the great indictment by calling the universe to listen to it. The words remind us of Deut. xxx. 19; xxxii. 1, but the thought was the common inheritance of Hebrew poets (Ps. l. 4; Jer. vi. 19, xxii. 29), and we can draw no inference from the parallelism as to the date of either book.

I have nourished and brought up children. The last word has in the Hebrew the emphasis of position: *Sons I have reared and brought up.* From those who had thus grown up under a father's care filial duty might have been expected; but it was not so. The sons had rebelled against their father's control. It is significant that the prophet starts from the thought of the fatherhood of God in His relation to Israel. The people might be unworthy of their election, but He had chosen them (Exod. iv. 22; Deut. xiv. 1; Hos. xi. 1).

(3) **The ox knoweth his owner . . .**—As in Exod. xx. 17; 1 Sam. xii. 3, the ox and the ass rather than, as with us, the horse and the dog, are the representative instances of the relation of domesticated animals to man. These know that relation, and act according to it; but Israel did not, or rather would not, know. So Jeremiah dwells, turning to a different region of animal life, on the instinct which leads the stork, the swallow, and the crane to fulfil the law of their being (Jer. viii. 7), while Israel "knew not"—*i.e.,* did not acknowledge—the law of Jehovah.

(4) **Ah, sinful nation . . .**—The Hebrew interjection is, like our English "Ha!" the expression of indignation rather than of pity.

A seed of evildoers, children that are corrupters.—The first phrase in the Hebrew idiom does not mean "the progeny of evil-doers," but those who, as a seed or brood, are made up of such. (Comp. chap. xiv. 20, lxv. 23.) The word "children" (better, as in verse 2, *sons*) once more emphasises the guilt of those who ought to have been obedient.

They have forsaken the Lord . . .—The three verbs paint the several stages of the growth in evil. Men first forsake, then spurn, then openly apostatise. (Comp. Luke xvi. 13). In the "Holy One of Israel" we have the Divine name on which Isaiah most delights to dwell, and which had been impressed on his mind by the *Trisagion,* which accompanied his first call to the office of a prophet (chap. vi. 3). The thought expressed by the name is that all ideas of consecration, purity, and holiness are gathered up in God. The term occurs fourteen times in the first part of Isaiah, and sixteen times in the second. A corrupt people needed to be reminded ever more and more of the truth which the name asserted.

(5) **Why should ye be stricken any more? ye will revolt more and more.**—Better, *by revolting more and more.* The prophet does not predict persistency in rebellion, but pleads against it. (Comp. "Why will ye die?" in Ezek. xviii. 31.)

The whole head is sick ....—Better, *every head .... every heart.* The sin of the people is painted as a deadly epidemic, spreading everywhere, affecting the noblest organs of the body (see Note on Jer. xvii. 9), and defying all the resources of the healing art. The description that follows is one of the natural parables of ethics, and reminds us of Plato's description of the souls of tyrants as being full of ulcerous sores (*Gorg.,* c. 80). The description may have connected itself with the prophet's personal expe-

is sick, and the whole heart faint. ⁽⁶⁾ From the sole of the foot even unto the head *there is* no soundness in it; *but* wounds, and bruises, and putrifying sores: they have not been closed, neither bound up, neither mollified with ¹ointment. ⁽⁷⁾ ªYour country *is* desolate, your cities *are* burned with fire: your land, strangers devour it in your presence, and *it is* desolate, ²as overthrown by strangers. ⁽⁸⁾ And the daughter of Zion is left as a cottage in a vineyard, as a lodge in a garden of cucumbers, as a besieged city. ⁽⁹⁾ ᵇExcept the LORD of hosts had left unto us a very small remnant, we should have been as ᶜSodom, *and* we should have been like unto Gomorrah.

⁽¹⁰⁾ Hear the word of the LORD, ye rulers of Sodom; give ear unto the

---

¹ Or, *oil.*
ª Deut. 28, 51, 52; ch. 5. 5.
² Heb., *as the overthrow of strangers.*
ᵇ Lam. 3. 22; Rom. 9. 29.
ᶜ Gen. 19. 24.

---

rience or training in the medicine and surgery of his time, or with the diseases which came as judgments on Jehoram (2 Chron. xxi. 18) and Uzziah (2 Chron. xxvi. 20). We find him in chap. xxxviii. 21 prescribing for Hezekiah's boil. It would seem, indeed, from 2 Chron. xvi. 12, that the prophets, as an order, practised the art of healing, and so were rivals of the "physicians," who depended chiefly on idolatrous charms and incantations. The picture of the disease reminds us of the language of Deut. xxviii. 22—35; Job ii. 7, and of the descriptions of like pestilences in the history of Florence, and of England. Every part of the body is tainted by the poison. We note a certain technical precision in the three terms used: "wounds" (literally, *cuts*, as inflicted by a sword or knife); "bruises," or *weals*, marks of the scourge or rod; "putrifying sores," wounds that have festered into ulcers. As the diagnosis is technical, so also are the therapeutic agencies. To "close" or "press" the festering wound was the process tried at first to get rid of the purulent discharge; then, as in Hezekiah's case (chap. xxxviii. 21), it was "bound up," with a poultice, then some stimulating oil or unguent, probably, as in Luke x. 34, oil and wine were used, to cleanse the ulcer. No such remedies, the prophet says, had been applied to the spiritual disease of Israel.

⁽⁷⁾ **Your country is desolate . . .**—It is natural to take the words as describing the actual state of things when the prophet wrote. There had been such invasions in the days of Ahaz, in which Israel and Syria (chap. vii. 1), Edom and the Philistines, had been conspicuous (2 Chron. xxviii. 17, 18); and the reign of Hezekiah already had witnessed that of Sargon (chap. xx. 1).

The Hebrew has no copulative verb, but joins subject and predicate together with the emphasis of abruptness: *Your land—a desolation,* and so on. The repetition of the word "strangers" is characteristic of Isaiah's style.

As overthrown by strangers.—Conjectural readings give (1) "as the overthrow of Sodom;" (2) "as the overthrow of (*i.e.*, wrought by) a rain-storm." The word rendered "overthrown" is elsewhere applied only to the destruction of the cities of the plain (Deut. xxix. 23; Amos iv. 11; Jer. xlix. 18). So taken, the clause prepares the way for the fuller comparison of verses 9, 10.

⁽⁸⁾ **The daughter of Zion.**—The phrase stands, as everywhere (Ps. xlv. 12; Lam. ii. 8; Micah iv. 10), for the ideal city personified.

Is left as a cottage in a vineyard . . .—The "hut," or "*booth*,"—in which the keeper of the vineyards dwelt, apart from other habitations, was an almost proverbial type of isolation, yet to such a state was Zion all but reduced. The second similitude is of the same character. Cucumbers and other plants of the gourd type (Jonah iv. 6) were largely cultivated in Judæa, and here, too, each field or garden, like the olive groves and vineyards of Italy, had its solitary hut.

As a besieged city.—The comparison of the besieged city to itself is at first startling. Rhetorically, however, it forms a climax. The city was not at this time actually besieged, but it was so hemmed in with perils, so isolated from all help, that this was what its condition practically came to. It was neither more nor less than "as a besieged city," or 'within a measurable distance' of becoming so.

⁽⁹⁾ **Except the Lord of hosts . . .**—This name also had been stamped on the prophet's mind at the time of his call (chap. vi. 3). The God of the hosts (or *armies*) of heaven (sun, moon and stars, angels and archangels) and of earth had not been unmindful of the people. The idea of the "remnant" left when the rest of the people perished is closely connected with the leading thought of chap. vi. 12, 13. It had, perhaps, been impressed on the prophet's mind by the "remnant" of Israel that had escaped from Tiglath-pileser or Sargon (2 Chron. xxx. 6; comp. Mic. v. 7).

We should have been as Sodom . . .—Here the prophet, continuing perhaps the thought of verse 7, speaks of the destruction, in the next verse of the guilt, of the cities of the plain. Both had passed into a proverb. So Ezekiel (xvi. 46—56) works out the parallelism; so our Lord speaks of the guilt of Sodom as being lighter than that of Capernaum (Matt. xi. 23); so the tradition has condensed itself in the Arabic proverb, quoted by Cheyne, "More unjust than a *kadi* of Sodom." (Comp. chap. iii. 9; Deut. xxxii. 32.)

⁽¹⁰⁾ **Hear the word of the Lord, ye rulers of Sodom.**—The Hebrew text, by leaving a space between the two verses, indicates the beginning of a new section. It is noticeable that the prophet does not address the king. It may be that he trusted him, but not his ministers. We have to remember that the rulers (better, *judges*; same word as *kadi*) thus addressed were probably those who were outwardly active in Hezekiah's work of reformation, or had taken part in the older routine worship under Uzziah. For princes and people alike that reformation was but superficial. The priestly writer of the Book of Chronicles might dwell only on the apparent good in either reign (2 Chron. xxvii. 2; xxix.—xxxi.); but the eye of Isaiah saw below the surface. In "the word of the Lord," and "the law of our God," we have two different aspects of the revelation of the Divine will, the first being the prophetic message of the prophet, the second pointing primarily, perhaps, to the law given by Moses, but including also, as in Pss. xix. 7, cxix. 1; Isa. xlii. 4, 24, li. 7, all forms of direct ethical teaching, especially, perhaps, such as were actually based upon the law or *Torah* as a text.

The Worthlessness of Outward Worship.   ISAIAH, I.   *The Call to Repentance.*

law of our God, ye people of Gomorrah. (11) To what purpose *is* the multitude of your *a* sacrifices unto me? saith the LORD: I am full of the burnt offerings of rams, and the fat of fed beasts; and I delight not in the blood of bullocks, or of lambs, or of [1] he goats. (12) When ye come [2] to appear before me, who hath required this at your hand, to tread my courts? (13) Bring no more vain oblations; incense is an abomination unto me; the new moons and sabbaths, the calling of assemblies, I cannot away with; it is [3] iniquity, even the solemn meeting. (14) Your new moons and your appointed feasts my soul hateth: they are a trouble unto me; I am weary to bear *them*. (15) And *b* when ye spread forth your hands, I will hide mine eyes from you: yea, when ye [4] make many prayers, I will not hear: your hands are full of *c* [5] blood. (16) Wash you, make you clean; put away the evil of your doings from before mine eyes; *d* cease to do evil; (17) learn to do well; seek judgment, [6] relieve the oppressed,

a Prov. 15. 8, & 21. 27; ch. 66. 3; Jer. 6. 20; Amos 5. 21.
[1] Heb., *great he goats.*
[2] Heb., *to be seen.*
[3] Or, *grief.*
b Prov. 1. 28; Jer. 14. 12; Mic. 3. 4.
[4] Heb., *multiply prayer.*
c ch. 59. 3.
[5] Heb., *bloods.*
d 1 Pet. 3. 11.
[6] Or, *righten.*

---

(11) **To what purpose is the multitude of your sacrifices?** . . .—Isaiah carries on the great *catena* of prophetic utterances as to the conditions of acceptable worship (1 Sam. xv. 22; Pss. xl. 6, l. 7—14, li. 16, 17). In Hosea vi. 6; Amos v. 21—24; Micah vi. 6—8 we have the utterances of contemporary prophets, who may have exercised a direct influence on his teaching. The description points primarily, perhaps, to the reign of Uzziah, but may include that of Hezekiah. The account of the sacrifices agrees with 2 Chron. xxix. 21—29.

Saith the Lord . . .—Here, as in verse 18, xxxiii. 10, xli. 21, lxvi. 9, the prophet uses the future instead of the familiar past tense. *This is what Jehovah will say, once and for ever.*

(12) **When ye come to appear before me.**—Literally, *before my face.* This is the meaning given by the present Hebrew text, and it is, of course, adequate. The Syriac version and some modern scholars (*e.g.*, Cheyne) adopt a reading which gives *to see my face.* In either case the implied thought is that the worshippers believed that they came into the more immediate presence of Jehovah when they entered the Temple courts. To "appear before God" was the normal phrase for visiting the Temple at the three great Feasts and other solemn occasions (Exod. xxxiv. 23; Pss. xlii. 3, lxxxiv. 7).

(13) **Bring no more vain oblations.**—These were of the *minchah* class, the "meat-offerings," or, more properly, *meal*-offerings of Lev. vii. 9—12. This, with its symbolic accompaniment of incense (chap. lxvi. 3), was the characteristic feature of the thank-offerings and peace-offerings.

Incense is an abomination.—The Hebrew word is not that usually translated "incense," and is found in Ps. lxvi. 15 ("incense," or *'*sweet smoke, "of rams"), in connection with animal sacrifice. There does not appear, however, any adequate reason why we should take the *minchah* in any but its usual sense of meal-offering. The prophet brings together all the chief ritual phrases without an elaborate attention to the details connected with them.

The new moons and sabbaths . . .—The classification agrees with that of 2 Chron. viii. 13: "sabbaths, new moons, and solemn feasts." (Comp. Hos. ii. 11). The term "convocation," or "assembly," was specially applied to the Passover, the Feast of Weeks, and the Feast of Tabernacles (Lev. xxiii. 7, 21, 27). The religious revival under Hezekiah brought all these into a fresh prominence (2 Chron. xxxi. 3). In Col. ii. 16 they appear together as belonging to the Judaising Essene Christians of the apostolic age.

It is iniquity, even the solemn meeting.—The Hebrew construction has the abruptness of indignation: "*The new moon and sabbaths, and calling of assemblies . . . iniquity with a solemn assembly I cannot bear.* This was what made the crowded courts of the Temple hateful to the messenger of Jehovah. "Iniquity" was there. The character of a ruling caste is not changed in a day, and the lives of rulers and judges were under Hezekiah as they had been in the days of Ahaz, or at least in those of Uzziah.

(14) **Your new moons and your appointed feasts.**—The latter word included the sabbaths (Lev. xxiii. 3). The words add nothing to what had been said before, but they come with all the emphasis of iteration.

My soul.—The words are in one sense anthropomorphic. With man the "soul" expresses the full intensity of life and consciousness, and so, in the language of the prophets, it does with God.

(15) **When ye spread forth your hands.**—The words point to the attitude of one who prays, as was the manner of Jews, Greeks, and Romans ("tenditque ad sidera palmas," Virg., *Æn.*, xii. 196), standing, and with hands stretched out toward heaven. (Comp. Luke xviii. 11—13.)

When ye make many prayers.—The Pentateuch contains no directions for the use of forms of prayer beyond the benediction of Num. vi. 23—26, and two forms connected with the Passover in Deut. xxvi. 5—10, 13—15. The "eighteen prayers" for daily use belong to the later Rabbinic stage of Judaism. It lies in the nature of the case, however, that first a real, and then an ostentatious devotion would show itself in the use of such forms, possibly, as in Ps. cxix. 164, "seven times a day." In Prov. xvii. 14, xxviii. 9, which belong to the reign of Hezekiah, and may, therefore, indirectly represent Isaiah's teaching, we have the warnings of the wise as to the right use of such forms.

Your hands are full of blood.—Literally, *bloods,* as implying many murderous acts. The words point to the guilt of judges and princes, such as that described in Hosea iv. 2. Life was sacrificed to greed of gain, or lust, or vindictiveness. To the prophet's eye those hands, stretched upwards in the Temple by some, at least, of the king's ministers and judges, were red with the blood of the slain. (Comp. chap. lix. 3.)

(16) **Wash you, make you clean . . .**—The words were probably as an echo of Ps. li. 7. Both psalmist and prophet had entered into the inner meaning of the outward ablutions of ritual.

Cease to do evil; (17) **learn to do well.**—Such words the prophet might have heard in his youth

The Promise of Forgiveness. ISAIAH, I. *Corruptio optimi pessima*

judge the fatherless, plead for the widow.

(18) Come now, and let us reason together, saith the LORD: though your sins be as scarlet, they shall be as white as snow; though they be red like crimson, they shall be as wool. (19) If ye be willing and obedient, ye shall eat the good of the land: (20) but if ye refuse and rebel, ye shall be devoured with the sword: for the mouth of the LORD hath spoken *it*.

(21) How is the faithful city become an harlot! it was full of judgment; righteousness lodged in it; but now murderers. (22) Thy silver is become dross, thy wine mixed with water: (23) thy princes *are* rebellious, and companions of thieves: every one loveth gifts, and followeth after rewards: they

---

from Amos (Amos v. 14, 15). What had then been spoken to the princes of the northern kingdom was now repeated to those of Judah.

(17) **Relieve the oppressed.**—More accurately, *correct the oppressor.* The prophet calls on the rulers not merely to acts of benevolence, but to the courageous exercise of their authority to restrain the wrong-doing of the men of their own order. We are reminded of what Shakespeare says of Time, that it is his work—
"To wrong the wronger till he render right."
(*Rape of Lucrece.*)

Judge the fatherless.—The words are still primarily addressed to men in office. They are told that they must be true to their calling, and that the "fatherless" and the "widow," as the typical instances of the defenceless, ought to find an advocate in the judge.

(18) **Come now, and let us reason together.**—The Authorised Version suggests the thought of a discussion between equals. The Hebrew implies rather the tone of one who gives an authoritative *ultimatum*, as from a judge to the accused, who had no defence, or only a sham defence, to offer (Micah vi. 2, 3). "Let us sum up the pleadings—that *ultimatum* is one of grace and mercy—'Repent, and be forgiven.'"

Though your sins be as scarlet.—The two colours probably corresponded to those now designated by the English words. Both words point to the dyes of Tyre, and the words probably received a fresh emphasis from the fact that robes of these colours were worn by the princes to whom Isaiah preached (2 Sam. i. 24). To the prophet's eye that dark crimson was as the stain of blood. What Jehovah promises is that the guilt of the past, deep-dyed in grain as it might be, should be discharged, and leave the character with a restored purity. Men might dye their souls of this or that hue, but to bleach them was the work of God. He alone could *transfigure* them that they should be "white as snow" (Mark ix. 3). Comp. the reproduction of the thought, with the added paradox that it was the crimson "blood of the lamb" that was to bleach and cleanse, in Rev. iii. 4, 5, vii. 14.

(19) **If ye be willing and obedient, ye shall eat the good of the land.**—The promise of temporal blessings as the reward of a true repentance, instead of the spiritual peace and joy of Ps. li. 8—12, fills us at first with a sense of disappointment. It has to be remembered, however, that the prophet spoke to those who were unjust and selfish, and who were as yet far from the broken and contrite heart of the true penitent. He was content to wake up in them the dormant sense of righteousness, and to lead them to recognise the moral government of God. In the long run they would not be losers by a change of conduct. The choice of eating or "being eaten" (the "devoured" of verse 20),

enjoying a blameless prosperity, or falling by the sword, was placed before those to whom the higher aspirations of the soul were little known. Such is, at all times, one at least of the methods of God's education of mankind.

(21) **How is the faithful city become an harlot! . . .**—The opening word, as in Lam. i. 1, is the key-note of an elegiac wail, which opens a new section. The idea of prostitution as representing apostasy from Jehovah was involved in the thought that Israel was the bride whom He had wooed and won (Hosea i.—iii.; Jer. ii. 2). The imagery was made more impressive by the fact that actual prostitution entered so largely into the ritual of many of the forms of idolatry to which the Israelites were tempted (Num. xxv. 1, 2). So Ezekiel (chap. xvi. 1—59) develops the symbolism with an almost terrible fulness. So our Lord spoke of the Pharisees as an "adulterous generation" (Matt. xii. 39). The fact that Hosea, an earlier contemporary, had been led to tell how he had been taught the truth thus set forth by a living personal experience, is not without significance in its bearing on the *genesis* of Isaiah's thoughts.

Righteousness lodged in it; but now murderers.—Better, *assassins.* The word implies not casual homicide, but something like the choice of murder and robbery as a profession. Hosea (vi. 9) had painted a like picture as true of Samaria. The traveller who sojourned in Jerusalem, the poor who lived there, were exposed to outrage and murder; and all this was passing before men's eyes at the very time when they were boasting, as it were, of their "glorious reformation."

(22) **Thy silver is become dross . . .**—The two images describe the degeneracy of the rulers to whose neglect this disorder was due. (See Notes on Jer. vi. 28—30.) Hypocrisy and adulteration were the order of the day. The coinage of judgment and justice was debased; the wine of spiritual life (Prov. ix. 5), of enthusiasm and zeal for good, was diluted till it had lost all power to strengthen and refresh. In "the salt that has lost its savour" of Matt. v. 13 we have a like symbolism.

(23) **Thy princes are rebellious.**—The Hebrew words present an alliterative paronomasia (*sārim, sōrerim*), which may be represented by "Thy rulers are rebels." Here, as before, we note the influence of Hosea (ix. 15), from whom the words are cited.

Companions of thieves.—We seem almost to be reading a report of the state of police in a provincial city under the government of Turkey as it is, or of Naples or Sicily as they were. The *kadi* himself is in secret partnership with the brigands who infest the highways. Nothing can be done without *baksheesh*, and the robbers who have the plunder can bribe more heavily than the man whom they have robbed. (Comp. Micah vii. 3.) To the complaints of the widow and the

The City of Righteousness. ISAIAH, I. *The Destruction of the Transgressors.*

a judge not the fatherless, neither doth the cause of the widow come unto them. (24) Therefore saith the Lord, the LORD of hosts, the mighty One of Israel, Ah, I will ease me of mine adversaries, and avenge me of mine enemies: (25) and I will turn my hand upon thee, and ¹ purely purge away thy dross, and take away all thy tin: (26) and I will restore thy judges as at the first, and thy counsellors as at the beginning: afterward thou shalt be called, The city of righteousness, the faithful city. (27) Zion shall be redeemed with judgment, and ² her converts with righteousness. (28) And the ᵇ³ destruction of the transgressors and of the sinners *shall be* together, and they that forsake the LORD shall be consumed. (29) For they shall be ashamed of the oaks which ye have desired, and ye shall be confounded for the gardens that ye have chosen. (30) For ye shall be as an oak whose leaf fadeth, and as a garden that hath no water. (31) And the strong shall be as tow, ⁴ and the maker of it as a spark, and they shall both burn together, and none shall quench *them*.

a Jer. 5. 28; Zech. 7. 10.

1 Heb., *according to pureness.*

2 Or, *they that return of her.*

b Job 31. 3; Ps. 1. 6, & 5. 6, & 73. 27, & 92. 9, & 104. 35.

3 Heb., *breaking.*

4 Or, *and his work.*

---

orphan the judges turned a deaf ear, and put off the hearing of their cause with indefinite procrastination. There is, perhaps, a touch of irony in the word for "bribes" (*shalmōnim*, as if "peace gifts"), which were sought after, instead of *shalōm*, the true peace itself.

(24) **Therefore saith the Lord.**—The word for "saith" (literally, *whisper*) is that which always indicates the solemn utterance of an oracle. The solemnity is emphasised by the exceptional accumulation of Divine names. He who speaks is the Eternal, the Lord of the armies of earth and heaven, the Hero, the Mighty One, of Israel. The latter name is found also in chap. xlix. 26, lx. 16; Gen. xlix. 24; Ps. cxxxii. 2, 5, and not elsewhere.

Ah, I will ease me of mine adversaries.—In bold, anthropomorphic language, which reminds us of Ps. lxxviii. 65, Jehovah is represented as waking out of slumber, and rising up to judgment. The words "ease" and "avenge" in the Hebrew have nearly the same sound (*nicham* and *niqqam*), and come from the same root, the primary thought being that of the deep breath which a man draws in the act of throwing off a burden. The weariness and impatience of verse 14, the long-suffering that waited, had come to an end at last (comp. chap. v. 11, 13), and the day of vengeance had come. The punishment was, however, to be reformatory, and not merely penal.

(25) **I will turn my hand upon thee.**—The phrase, like the English "visit," presents both a severe and a gracious aspect. Of the former we have instances in Ps. lxxxi. 14, Amos i. 8; of the latter in Zech. xiii. 7. The context here inclines to the latter meaning. Jehovah punishes that He may save, and smites that He may heal.

Purely purge away thy dross.—Better, *will smelt away thy dross with lye*, or *potash*, which was used in the smelting process. The imagery of verse 22 is resumed. The great Refiner can purify the debased metal. In Mal. iii. 2, 3, we have the same image expanded. The process involved, of course, the rejection of the dross—*i.e.*, in the interpretation of the parable, of the lead that *would* not let itself be turned to silver.

Tin.—Better, perhaps, *lead*. In either case Isaiah's knowledge of metallurgy was probably due to intercourse with the Phœnicians, who brought both lead and tin from Tarshish (*i.e.*, Spain).

(26) **I will restore thy judges as at the first.**—The prophet looks back to the good old days, the time probably of David, or the early years of Solomon (1 Kings x. 9)—as Englishmen look back to those of Elizabeth—when judges were faithful, and princes upright, and the people happy—to such an ideal polity as that of Pss. xv. and xxiv.

The city of righteousness, the faithful city. —The two nouns are not the same, and the second has rather the meaning of "citadel," the acropolis of Jerusalem. There is possibly an allusive reference to the idea embodied in the names of Melchizedek (Gen. xiv. 18; Heb. vii. 2) and Adonizedec (Josh. x. 3), as connected with Jerusalem. So in Jer. xxxiii. 16 the ideal city, no less than the ideal king, is to be called *Jehovah Tsidkenu* ("the Lord our righteousness").

(27) **Zion shall be redeemed with judgment . . .**—Better, *through justice*. The condition of the redemption which primarily proceeds from the compassion of Jehovah is found in the renewed righteousness of man to man described in the preceding verse. Without that no redemption was possible, for that was of its very essence.

Her converts.—Literally, *those that turn*. The conversion implied is obviously not that of Gentiles to the faith of Israel, but of Israelites who had gone astray. The word is the same as that which meets us in the name of Shear-jashub (*the remnant shall return*), and is prominent in the teaching of Jeremiah, "Turn ye, and live" (chaps. iii. 12, 14, iv. 1, *et al.*).

(28) **Of the transgressors and of the sinners.** —The first of the two words presents evil in its aspect of apostasy, the second in that of the open sin which may accompany the apostasy or exist without it.

(29) **They shall be ashamed of the oaks . . .**— Better, *terebinths*. The words point to the groves that were so closely connected with the idolatry of Canaan, especially with the worship of the *asherah*, and which the people had chosen in preference to the sanctuary of Jehovah (chaps. xvii. 8, lvii. 5, lxvi. 17; Deut. xvi. 21; 2 Kings xvi. 4; Jer. iii. 6). Greek worship presents the parallels of the groves of Daphne at Antioch, and those of Dodona and of the Eumenides at Colônos. The "gardens" were the precinct planted round the central tree or grove.

(30) **Ye shall be . . .**—Men were to think of the pleasant places that had tempted them, not as they had seen them, fresh and green, but as burnt up and withered, and then were to see in that desolation a parable of their own future. The word for "strong" occurs only in Amos ii. 9, where we find "strong as the oaks."

(31) **The maker of it as a spark.**—Better, *his work as a spark*. The sin itself becomes the instrument of destruction. The mighty and the proud, who were foremost in the work of idolatry, and who did not repent, should perish with their work—*i.e.*, with the idol

The Mountain of the Lord's House.   ISAIAH, II.   *Swords to be turned into Plowshares.*

CHAPTER II.—(1) The word that Isaiah the son of Amoz saw concerning Judah and Jerusalem. (2) And ᵃ it shall come to pass in the last days, *that* the mountain of the LORD's house shall be ¹ established in the top of the mountains, and shall be exalted above the hills; and all nations shall flow unto it. (3) And many people shall go and say, Come ye, and let us go up to the mountain of the LORD, to the house of the God of Jacob; and he will teach us of his ways, and we will walk in his paths; for out of Zion shall go forth the law, and the word of the LORD from Jerusalem. (4) And he shall judge among the nations, and shall rebuke many people: and they shall beat their swords into plowshares, and their spears into ²prun-

a Mic. 4. 1, &c.

1 Or, *prepared.*

2 Or, *scythes.*

---

which their hands had made. The tow and the spark are chosen as representing the most rapid form of combustion.

II.

(1) **The word that Isaiah the son of Amoz saw.**—On the relation of this chapter to chap. i., see *Introduction*. The moral and social state described in it points to an earlier date than the reformation of Hezekiah. The sins of the people are more flagrant; but there is not as yet with them the added guilt of a formal and ceremonial worship. The character of the king in chap. iii. 12 corresponds with that of Ahaz. The influence of the Philistines, traceable in verse 6, is probably connected with their invasion of Judah in that reign (2 Chron. xxviii. 18). The mention of "ships of Tarshish" in verse 16 points to a time when the commerce of the Red Sea (1 Kings ix. 26, xxii. 48) was still in the hands of Judah, and prior, therefore, to the capture of Elath by Rezin, king of Syria (2 Kings xvi. 6). We are able, therefore, with hardly the shadow of uncertainty, to fix the date of the whole section as belonging to the early years of the reign of Ahaz, with, perhaps, a backward glance at evils which belonged also to the reigns of Uzziah and Jotham. The title of the superscription unites in an exceptional form the two ideas of the prophet and of the seer. What follows is "the *word*" of Isaiah, but it is a word that he has *seen*.

(2) **It shall come to pass in the last days.**—The three verses that follow are found in almost identical form in Micah iv. 1—3, with the addition of a verse (Micah iv. 4) which describes the prosperity of Judah—every man sitting "under his vine and his fig-tree," as in the days of Solomon. Whether (1) Isaiah borrowed from Micah, or (2) Micah from Isaiah, or (3) both from some earlier prophet, or (4) whether each received an independent yet identical revelation, is a problem which we have no adequate data for solving. Micah prophesied, like Isaiah, under Ahaz, Jotham, and Hezekiah, and so either may have heard it from the other. On the other hand, the prophecy of the destruction of Jerusalem, on which these verses follow, in Micah iii. 12, appears from Jer. xxvi. 18 to have been spoken in the days of Hezekiah. On the whole, (3) seems to have most to commend it. (See *Introduction.*)

For "in the last days" read *latter* or *after days;* the idea of the Hebrew words, as in Gen. xlix. 1; Num. xxiv. 14, being that of remoteness rather than finality. For the most part (Deut. iv. 30, xxxi. 29) they point to the distant future of the true King, to the time of the Messiah.

The mountain of the Lord's house.—The prophet's vision of the far-off days sees, as it were, a transfigured and glorified Jerusalem. Zion, with the Temple, was to be no longer surrounded by hills as high as, or higher than, itself (Ps. cxxv. 2), scorned by other mountains (Ps. lxviii. 16, 17); but was to be to Israel as a Sinai or a Lebanon, as a Mount Meru, or an Olympus, "an exceeding high mountain" (Ezek. xl. 2), whose physical elevation should answer to its spiritual. (Comp. Zech. xiv. 10.) So in that vision of the future, the waters of Shiloah, that went softly, were to become a broad and rushing river (chap. xxxiii. 21; Ezek. xlvii. 3—12). So, when men had been taught by experience that this ideal was to be realised in no Jerusalem on earth, the seer of Patmos saw a yet more transcendent vision of the glories of the heavenly Jerusalem (Rev. xxi. 10—xxii. 5), and yet even these were but types and figures of divine and ineffable realities.

All nations shall flow unto it.—Better, *all the nations*—*i.e.*, the heathen as distinct from Israel. The prophet sees and welcomes the approach of pilgrims from all regions of the earth to the new sanctuary. Thus early in his work was Isaiah (half unconsciously as to the manner in which his vision was to be realised) the prophet of a universal religion, of which the truths of Judaism were the centre, and of a catholic Church. In the admission of proselytes, commemorated in Ps. lxxxvii. (probably written about this time), we may see what may either have suggested the prophecy, or have seemed as the first-fruits of its fulfilment.

(3) **Many people shall go and say . . .**—What was precious to the prophet's heart was the thought that these pilgrims from afar would not come as with a formal worship like that of chap. i. 10—15, but, like the queen of Sheba (1 Kings x. 1—10), as seekers after truth, desiring to be taught. (Comp. chap. lx. 3.) The "ways" and the "paths" are the great laws of righteousness, which lead to the eternal life. The verb for "teach" is the root of the Hebrew for "law," as the "teaching" of Jehovah.

Shall go forth the law . . .—In the preaching of the Christ, in the mission of the Twelve, in the whole history of the Apostolic Church, we have, to say the least, an adequate fulfilment of the promise. The language of St. Paul, however, suggests that there may be in the future a yet more glorious mission, of which Jerusalem shall once more be the centre (Rom. xi. 12—15).

(4) **He shall judge among the nations.**—For "rebuke" read *decide* or *arbitrate*. The ideal Divine King is to be all, and more than all, that Solomon had been (1 Kings x. 24). In reliance on His wisdom and equity, nations would refer their disputes to His decision instead of the arbitrament of war. Here again we have a partial fulfilment, it may be hoped, a "springing and germinant accomplishment," in the history of Christendom. So far as the teaching of Christ has influenced international polity and law, He has been the supreme arbitrator of their disputes.

inghooks: nation shall not lift up sword against nation, neither shall they learn war any more.

⁽⁵⁾ O house of Jacob, come ye, and let us walk in the light of the LORD. ⁽⁶⁾ Therefore thou hast forsaken thy people the house of Jacob, because they be replenished ¹from the east, and *are* soothsayers like the Philistines, and they ²please themselves in the children of strangers. ⁽⁷⁾ Their land also is full of silver and gold, neither *is there any* end of their treasures; their land is also full of horses, neither *is there any* end of their chariots: ⁽⁸⁾ their land also is full of idols; they worship the work of their own hands, that which their own fingers have made: ⁽⁹⁾ and the mean man boweth down, and the great man humbleth himself: therefore forgive them not.

⁽¹⁰⁾ Enter into the rock, and hide thee

¹ Or, *more than the east.*
² Or, *abound with the children, &c.*

And they shall beat their swords into plowshares.—The words invert the picture of an earlier prophet, who spoke of a time of war (Joel iii. 10). Isaiah must have known that prediction, and yet he proclaims (following Hosea ii. 18) that peace, not war, is the ideal goal towards which the order of the Divine government is tending. (Comp. Zech. ix. 10; Luke ii. 14.)

⁽⁵⁾ **O house of Jacob . . .**—The ideal of the future has been brought before Israel; but it is still far off, and the people must learn repentance, must themselves "walk in the light of the Lord," before they can be as light-bearers to other nations. (Comp. the lines of thought in Rom. xi. 11—15.)

⁽⁶⁾ **Therefore thou hast forsaken thy people . . .**—Better, *For Thou hast . . .* This was the sad, dark present, in contrast with the bright future. Jehovah "went not forth" with the armies of Judah (Ps. lxviii. 7); and the Syrians, Edomites, and Philistines, possibly the Assyrians also (2 Kings xvi. 9; 2 Chron. xxviii. 17—20), were laying the lands waste.

Because they be replenished from the east.—The disasters of the time are viewed as chastisements for sin, and the sin consisted in casting off their national allegiance to Jehovah. The "east," from which they were replenished, with which they filled their thoughts and life, was Syria and Mesopotamia, to whose influence they had yielded, and whose *cultus* Ahaz had adopted (2 Kings xvi. 10—12).

And are soothsayers like the Philistines.—Literally, *cloud-diviners.* The word points to the claim of being "storm-raisers," which has been in all ages one of the boasts of sorcerers. The conquests of Uzziah (2 Chron. xxvi. 6) had brought Judah into contact with the Philistines, and the oracles at Ekron and elsewhere (2 Kings i. 2) attracted the people of Judah. There was, as it were, a mania for divination, and the "diviners" of Philistia (1 Sam. vi. 2) found imitators among the people of Jehovah.

They please themselves in the children of strangers.—Literally, *they strike hands with,* as meaning, (1) they enter into contracts with, or (2) they make common cause with. The commerce of the people with foreign nations, which had expanded under Uzziah (2 Kings xiv. 22), was, from the prophet's point of view, the cause of much evil. It was probably conducted, as at an earlier date, chiefly by Phœnician sailors and merchants (1 Kings ix. 27), and thus opened the way to their impurity of worship and of life (Jonah i. 5). The sense of being a peculiar and separate people wore away. The pictures of the "strange woman" and the foreign money-lender of Prov. v. 3, vi. 1, present two aspects of this evil.

⁽⁷⁾ **Their land also is full of silver and gold.**—The long and prosperous reign of Uzziah, especially his trade with Ophir, had reproduced the wealth of the days of Solomon. Tribute came from the Arabians and Ammonites (2 Chron. xxvi. 8). The words point to an earlier date than that at which Ahaz was left "naked and distressed" (2 Chron. xxviii. 19). Even under Hezekiah, Sennacherib records in the inscription on the Taylor cylinder that the tribute paid by that king amounted to 30 talents of gold, and 800 talents of silver, besides wrought metal; and a like profusion of wealth, prior to Sennacherib's invasion, is shown in the account of Hezekiah's display of his treasures, in chap. xxxix. 2 (Cheyne, *in loc.*; *Records of the Past,* i. 38).

Their land is also full of . . . chariots.—Here also the reign of Uzziah was like that of Solomon (1 Kings x. 26—28). Chariots were used probably both for state pageants (Song of Sol. i. 9, iii. 9, 10) and as part of the *matériel* of war (2 Chron. i. 14, ix. 25). Isaiah here also agrees with Micah (i. 13) in looking on this as "the beginning of sin" (see Deut. xvii. 16; 1 Sam. viii. 11). For him, as for Zechariah (ix. 9), the true King was to come, not with chariots and horses, but riding, as the judges of Israel had ridden (Judg. v. 10, x. 4, xii. 14), on "a colt, the foal of an ass."

⁽⁸⁾ **Their land also is full of idols.**—The word which Isaiah chooses for "idols" (*elilim*—*i.e.,* vain, false, gods) seems intentionally contrasted with *elim* (gods, or mighty ones), and may fairly be rendered by *no-gods.* The reign of Ahaz was conspicuous from the first for this *cultus* (2 Chron. xxviii. 2, 3), but it had been prominent even under Jotham (2 Chron. xxvii. 2).

⁽⁹⁾ **And the mean man boweth down.**—The English gives adequately the significance of the two words for "man"—in Hebrew, *adam* and *ish.* The Authorised Version applies the words to the prostrations of the worshippers of idols, whether of low or high degree; others refer them to the punishment of that idolatry: *The mean man must be bowed down . . . the great man must be humbled.*

Therefore forgive them not.—As a prayer the words find a parallel in Pss. lxix. 27, cix. 14, but the rendering adopted by Cheyne and others, *And thou canst not forgive them,* is perhaps preferable. The sin is treated as "a sin unto death," for which it is vain to pray (chap. xxii. 14).

⁽¹⁰⁾ **Enter into the rock.**—The limestone caverns of Palestine were natural asylums in times of terror and dismay (Judg. vi. 2, xv. 8; 1 Sam. xiii. 6, xiv. 11, xxiv. 3; 1 Kings xviii. 4). Here, as in Micah i. 4, we may probably trace the impression left by the earthquake under Uzziah (Amos i. 1), when the people fled in terror from the city (Zech. xiv. 5). Isaiah foresees the recurrence of a like panic in the future.

in the dust, for fear of the LORD, and for the glory of his majesty. (11) The *a*lofty looks of man shall be humbled, and the haughtiness of men shall be bowed down, and the LORD alone shall be exalted in that day. (12) For the day of the LORD of hosts *shall be* upon every one *that is* proud and lofty, and upon every one *that is* lifted up; and he shall be brought low: (13) and upon all the cedars of Lebanon, *that are* high and lifted up, and upon all the oaks of Bashan, (14) and upon all the high mountains, and upon all the hills *that are* lifted up, (15) and upon every high tower, and upon every fenced wall, (16) and upon all the ships of Tarshish, and upon all ¹pleasant pictures. (17) And the loftiness of man shall be bowed down, and the haughtiness of men shall be made low: and the LORD alone shall be exalted in that day. (18) And ²the idols he shall utterly abolish. (19) And they shall go into the *b*holes of the rocks, and into the caves of ³the earth, for fear of the LORD, and for the glory of his majesty, when he ariseth to shake terribly the earth.

(20) In that day a man shall cast ⁴his idols of silver, and his idols of gold,

a ch. 5. 15.

1 Heb., *pictures of desire.*

2 Or, *the idols shall utterly pass away.*

b Hos. 10. 8; Luke 23. 30; Rev. 6. 16, & 9. 6.

3 Heb., *the dust.*

4 Heb., *the idols of his silver,* &c.

---

(11) **The lofty looks of man . . .**—Better, *the lofty looks of the mean man . . . the haughtiness of the great man.* The self-assertion which is the essential element of pride may be found at the opposite extremes of social life.

The Lord alone shall be exalted . . .—The verb, as in Ps. xlvi. 7, 11 (see margin and text of Authorised Version), implies the image of a rock-citadel, towering in its strength, and offering the one safe asylum in a time of danger. (Comp. also Ps. lxi. 2.)

(12) **The day of the Lord of hosts shall be . . .**—Literally, *the Lord of hosts hath a day . . .* As generally in the prophets, any time of special judgment or special mercy is as "a day of Jehovah." Man feels himself in the presence of a higher power, working in this way or in that for righteousness. The phrase had been specially prominent in the mouth of Isaiah's forerunner, Amos (viii. 9—13, ix. 11).

Upon every one that is proud and lofty . . .—The emphatic iteration of "lifted up" is noticeable as indicating that the prophet sees in that self-assertion the root-evil of his time, that which was most destructive of the fear of the Lord, and most surely brought down judgment on the offender. So the devout historian of Greece reads the teaching of the history which he tells. He saw the loftiest trees most exposed to the lightning-flash, the loftiest monarch most liable to the working of the Divine Nemesis (Herod., vii. 10).

(13) **Upon all the cedars of Lebanon . . .**—The words find a striking parallel in the passage from Herodotus just referred to. In that storm which is about to burst over the land, the cedars and the oaks, and, we may add, those who were as the cedars and the oaks, in their pride and glory, should all alike be shattered.

(14) **And upon all the high mountains.**—Possibly the prophet may have had in his mind the thunderstorm of Ps. xxix. 5—"the Lord breaketh the cedars of Lebanon." The oaks of Bashan were, like the cedars of Lebanon, proverbially types of forest greatness (chap. xxxiii. 9). Literally, the words must have found a fulfilment in the ravages of Sargon's and Sennacherib's armies.

(15) **Upon every high tower.**—Generic as the words are, they have a special reference to the fortifications which were the glory of Uzziah's reign, and were continued by his successors (2 Chron. xxvi. 9, 10, xxvii. 3, 4; Hosea viii. 14; Micah v. 11; comp. also chap. xxii. 8—11, Ps. xlviii. 13).

(16) **And upon all the ships of Tarshish.**—The words point to the commerce in the Red Sea carried on by the fleets of Uzziah and Jotham (1 Kings xxii. 48); perhaps also to that in the Mediterranean with Tarshish, or Tartessus (Spain), as in Jonah i. 3. The "ships of Tarshish" had come to be used generically for all ships of the class used in such commerce, whether crossing the Mediterranean to Spain, or circumnavigating Africa, or passing over the Persian Gulf to Ophir.

Upon all pleasant pictures.—Literally, *upon all imagery of delight.* (Comp. Lev. xxvi. 1; Num. xxxiii. 52.) The combination of the phrase with "the ships of Tarshish" suggests the inference that it includes the works of art which were brought by them from East and West. For these, it would seem, there was a mania among the higher classes in Jerusalem, like that which in later times has fastened upon china, or pictures, or carvings in ivory. So the ships of Solomon brought gold and silver, and "ivory and apes and peacocks" (1 Kings x. 22). The "ivory beds" of Amos vi. 4, the "gold rings set with the beryl," the "ivory overlaid with sapphires," the "pillars of marble set upon sockets of fine gold" of Song of Sol. v. 14, 15, the precious things in the treasury of Hezekiah (chap. xxxix. 2), may be taken as examples of this form of luxury. The æstheticism of the Roman Empire, of the *Renaissance* of the fifteenth century, of the age of Louis XIV., of our own time and country, presents obvious parallels.

(17) **And the loftiness of man shall be bowed down.**—Iteration is used as the most solemn form of emphasis. That was the burden of the prophet's song.

(18) **And the idols.**—Better, *The no-gods shall pass away.* The seven words of the English answer to three in the Hebrew. As with a profound sense, conscious or unconscious, of the power of rhythm, the prophet first condenses the judgment that is coming on the *no-gods*, and then expands it.

(19) **And they shall go into the holes of the rocks.**—The imagery of the earthquake in Uzziah's reign (see Note on verse 10) is still present to Isaiah's thoughts. (See Rev. vi. 15.)

When he ariseth to shake terribly the earth.—The Hebrew verb and noun have the emphasis of a paronomasia which cannot be reproduced in English, but of which the Latin "*ut terreat terram*" gives some idea.

(20) **A man shall cast his idols of silver . . .**—The picture of the earthquake is still continued. The

God's Greatness; Man's Littleness.　　ISAIAH, III.　　The Desolation of Jerusalem.

¹ which they made *each one* for himself to worship, to the moles and to the bats; ⁽²¹⁾ to go into the clefts of the rocks, and into the tops of the ragged rocks, for fear of the LORD, and for the glory of his majesty, when he ariseth to shake terribly the earth.

⁽²²⁾ Cease ye from man, whose breath *is* in his nostrils: for wherein is he to be accounted of?

1 Or, *which they made for him.*

2 Heb., *a man eminent in countenance.*

CHAPTER III.—⁽¹⁾ For, behold, the Lord, the LORD of hosts, doth take away from Jerusalem and from Judah the stay and the staff, the whole stay of bread, and the whole stay of water, ⁽²⁾ the mighty man, and the man of war, the judge, and the prophet, and the prudent, and the ancient, ⁽³⁾ the captain of fifty, and ²the honourable man, and the counsellor, and the cunning artificer,

---

men who have taken refuge in the caves fling away the idols, that they have found powerless to help them, to the moles and bats which had their dwelling there. It is perhaps significant that the animals thus named were proverbial for their blindness and love of darkness. Such, the prophet seems to say, were the fit custodians of the idols whom none could worship except those that hated the light and were spiritually blind.

Which they made each one for himself.— Better, *which they* (the carvers of the idol) *made for him* (the worshipper).

⁽²¹⁾ **To go into the clefts of the rocks . . .**— Comp. for the phrase, Exod. xxxiii. 22. The picture of verse 19 is reproduced, with some noticeable variations. As men feel shock after shock of the earthquake, and see the flashing fires, and hear the crash of the thunder, they leave the larger caverns in which they had at first sought shelter, and where they have left the idols that were once so precious, and fly to the smaller and higher openings, the "clefts of the rocks," and the *rents of the crags*, in their unspeakable panic.

⁽²²⁾ **Cease ye from man . . .**—The verse is wanting in some MSS. of the LXX. version, and is rejected by some critics, as of the nature of a marginal comment, and as not in harmony with the context. The first fact is the most weighty argument against it, but is not decisive. The other objection does not count for much. To "cease from man" as well as from "idols" is surely the natural close of the great discourse which had begun with proclaiming that men of all classes and conditions should be brought low. The words "whose breath is in his nostrils" emphasise the frailty of human life (Gen. ii. 7, vii. 22; Ps. cxlvi. 3, 4). Looking to that frailty, the prophet asks, as the psalmist had asked, "What is man?" (Ps. viii. 1). What is he to be valued at?" If it could be proved that the verse was not Isaiah's, it is at least the reflection of a devout mind in harmony with his.

III.

⁽¹⁾ **For, behold, the Lord, the Lord of hosts, doth take away from Jerusalem . . .**—From the general picture of the state of Judah as a whole, of the storm of Divine wrath bursting over the whole land, Isaiah turns to the Holy City itself, and draws the picture of what he saw there of evil, of that which would be seen before long as the punishment of the evil.

The stay and the staff . . .—In the existing Hebrew text the words receive an immediate interpretation, as meaning the two chief supports of life—bread and water. So we have the "staff of bread" in Lev. xxvi. 26; Ps. cv. 16; Ezek. iv. 16, v. 16. Possibly, however, the interpretation is of the nature of a marginal gloss, which has found its way into the text, and "the stay and staff" (in the Hebrew the latter word is the feminine form of the former) are really identified with the "pillars of the state," the great women as well as the great men who are named afterwards. On the other hand, verse 7 implies the pressure of famine, and the prophet may have intended to paint the complete failure of all resources, both material and political.

⁽²⁾ **The mighty man, and the man of war.**— The first word points to the aristocracy of landed proprietors, the latter to those who, whether of that class or not, had been prominent as leaders in the king's armies.

The judge, and the prophet.—Each is named as the representative of a class. The latter was that to which Isaiah himself belonged, but in which he found, as Jeremiah did afterwards, his chief opponents.

The prudent, and the ancient.—The former word has the more definite meaning of "diviners," those who had a real gift of wisdom, but who by their abuse of that gift had become as degenerate prophets. In the "ancient" we have the "elders" who were prominent in the municipal politics of the East, and formed at least the nucleus of the king's council (Ruth iv. 4; 2 Sam. xix. 11; 1 Kings xx. 7, xxi. 8; and elsewhere).

⁽³⁾ **The captain of fifty, and the honourable man.**—The first title implies a division like that of Exod. xviii. 21, of which "fifty" was all but the minimum unit. So we have the three "captains of fifty" in 2 Kings i. 9—15. The "honourable man" (literally, *eminent in countenance*) would seem to occupy a position in the civil service of the State analogous to that of the "captain of fifty" in the military.

The counsellor, and the cunning artificer.— From the modern stand-point the two classes seem at opposite extremes of the social order. The latter, however (literally, *masters in arts*), would seem to have occupied a higher position in the East, like that of military or civil engineers or artists with us. So in 2 Kings xxiv. 14, Jer. xxiv. 1, the "craftsmen and the smiths" are grouped with the "men of might" who were carried to Babylon by Nebuchadnezzar, and contrasted with the poor who were left behind. The military works of Uzziah had doubtless given a prominence to the "cunning men" who were employed on them (2 Chron. xxvi. 15). By some critics, however, the word is taken as equal to "magician."

The eloquent orator.—Literally, *skilled in speech.* The Authorised Version suggests the idea of the power of such skill in controlling the debates of popular assemblies. Here, however, the thought is rather that of one who says the right words at the right time; or possibly the enchanter who has his formulæ (the word implies the whisper of incantations, as in chap. viii. 19) ready at command for all occasions.

Tyranny and Anarchy.   ISAIAH, III.   *The Oppression of the Poor.*

and the ¹eloquent orator. (4) And I will give *ᵃchildren to be* their princes, and babes shall rule over them. (5) And the people shall be oppressed, every one by another, and every one by his neighbour: the child shall behave himself proudly against the ancient, and the base against the honourable. (6) When a man shall take hold of his brother of the house of his father, *saying,* Thou hast clothing, be thou our ruler, and *let* this ruin *be* under thy hand: (7) in that day shall he ²swear, saying, I will not be an ³healer; for in my house *is* neither bread nor clothing: make me not a ruler of the people.

(8) For Jerusalem is ruined, and Judah is fallen: because their tongue and their doings *are* against the LORD, to provoke the eyes of his glory. (9) The shew of their countenance doth witness against them; and they declare their sin as *ᵇ*Sodom, they hide *it* not. Woe unto their soul! for they have rewarded evil unto themselves.

(10) Say ye to the righteous, that *it shall be* well *with him:* for they shall eat the fruit of their doings. (11) Woe unto the wicked! *it shall be* ill *with him:* for the reward of his hands shall be ⁴given him.

(12) *As for* my people, children *are* their oppressors, and women rule over them. O my people, ⁵they which lead thee cause *thee* to err, and ⁶destroy the way of thy paths. (13) The LORD standeth up to plead, and standeth to judge the people. (14) The LORD will enter into judgment with the ancients of his people, and the princes thereof: for ye have ⁷eaten up the vineyard; the spoil of the poor *is* in your houses. (15) What mean ye *that* ye beat my people to pieces, and grind the faces of the poor? saith the Lord GOD of hosts.

(16) Moreover the LORD saith, Because

Marginal notes:
1 Or, *skil'ul of speech.*
a Eccles. 10. 16.
2 Heb., *lift up the hand.*
3 Heb., *binder up.*
b Gen. 13. 13, & 18. 21, & 19. 5.
4 Heb., *done to him.*
5 Or, *they which call thee blessed.*
6 Heb., *swallow up.*
7 Or, *burnt.*

---

(4) **I will give children to be their princes.**—Better, *youths.* The words may point obliquely to Ahaz, who had ascended the throne at the age of twenty (2 Chron. xxviii. 1). Manasseh was but twelve when he became king; Josiah but eight (2 Chron. xxxiii. 1, xxxiv. 1). In an Eastern monarchy the rule of a young king, rash and without experience, guided by counsellors like himself, was naturally regarded as the greatest of evils, and the history of Rehoboam had impressed this truth on the mind of every Israelite. (Comp. Eccles. x. 16.)

(5) **The people shall be oppressed . . .**—The words paint the worst form of the decadence of an Eastern kingdom. All is chaotic and anarchic; a fierce struggle for existence; the established order of society subverted; the experience of age derided by the petulance of youth. The picture of the corruption of a monarchy is as vivid and complete in its way as that which Thucydides (iii. 82—84) draws of the corruption of a democracy. It might seem to have been drawn from the Turkey or the Egypt of our own time.

(6, 7) **When a man shall take hold of his brother . . .**—Disorder was followed by destitution. The elder brother, the impoverished owner of the ruined dwelling, the head of a family or village, turns in his rags to the younger, whose decent garments seem to indicate comparative wealth, and would fain transfer to him the responsibilities of the first-born, though he has but a ruined tenement to give him. And instead of accepting what most men would have coveted (Gen. xxv. 31—33), the younger brother rejects it. He has enough bread and clothing (same word as in Exod. xxii. 27) for himself, and no more. It is not for him to bind up the wounds of others, or to try to introduce law where all is lawlessness. The supreme selfishness of a *sauve qui peut* asserts itself in his answer. In chap. iv. 1 we have another feature of the same social state.

(8) **For Jerusalem is ruined . . .**—The outward evils of the kingdom are traced to their true source. Men have provoked, in the prophet's bold anthropomorphic language, "the *eyes* of His glory," the manifestation of His being as All-knowing, Almighty, All-holy.

(9) **They declare their sin as Sodom.**—The comparison is, it should be remembered, of probably an earlier date than that in chap. i. 10. In the reign of Ahaz (perhaps the prophet, editing in his old age, thought also of that of Manasseh) there was not even the homage which vice pays to virtue by feigning a virtue which it has not. Men fell into an utter shamelessness, like that of the cities of the plain (Gen. xix. 5), generally in the luxury and profligacy of their lives (Ezek. xvi. 49), perhaps also with a more definite and horrible resemblance (1 Kings xiv. 24, xv. 12; 2 Kings xxiii. 7).

Woe unto their soul!—In the midst of the confusions of the times the prophet is bidden to proclaim that the law of a righteous retribution would be seen working even there.

(12) **Children are their oppressors . . .**—This points, as before (verse 4), to the youth and yet more the character of Ahaz. The influence of the queen-mother or of the seraglio was dominant in his counsels. Cowardly (chap. vii. 2), idolatrous, delighting in foreign worships and foreign forms of art (2 Kings xvi. 10), such was the king who then sat on the throne of Judah. And the evil worked downwards from the throne. Those who should have been the leaders of the people were quick only to *mislead.* Princes, priests, judges were all drifting with the current of debasement.

(13) **The Lord standeth up to plead . . .**—The people may think that the prophet is their censor. He bids them know that Jehovah is their true accuser and their judge. "Ye," he says, with all the emphasis of a sudden change of person, as if turning, as he spoke, to the nobles and elders, "*ye* have devoured the vineyard, *ye* have spoiled the poor." (Comp. chap. v. 1—8; Prov. xxx. 12—14.)

(16) **Because the daughters of Zion . . .**—From the princes that worked evil, Isaiah turns to their

The Pride of the Daughters of Zion.   ISAIAH, III.   *Their Dress and Ornaments.*

the daughters of Zion are haughty, and walk with stretched forth necks and [1]wanton eyes, walking and [2]mincing *as* they go, and making a tinkling with their feet: (17) therefore the Lord will smite with a scab the crown of the head of the daughters of Zion, and the LORD will [3]discover their secret parts. (18) In that day the Lord will take away the bravery of *their* tinkling ornaments about their feet, and *their* [4]cauls, and *their* round tires like the moon, (19) the [5]chains, and the bracelets, and the [6]mufflers, (20) the bonnets, and the ornaments of the legs, and the headbands, and the [7]tablets, and the earrings. (21) the rings, and nose jewels, (22) the changeable suits of apparel, and the mantles, and the wimples, and the crisping pins, (23) the glasses, and the fine

[1] Heb., *deceiving with their eyes.*
[2] Or, *tripping nicely.*
[3] Heb., *make naked.*
[4] Or, *networks.*
[5] Or, *sweet balls.*
[6] Or, *spangled ornaments.*
[7] Heb., *houses of the soul.*

---

wives, sisters, concubines, who were showing themselves degenerate daughters of Sarah and Rebecca. A like denunciation meets us in chap. xxxii. 9—12, but this is without a parallel in the minuteness of its detail. It is as though the prophet had gone into the boudoir of one of the leaders of the fashions of Jerusalem, and taken an inventory of what he found there. Possibly we may trace the influence of the prophetess-wife of Isaiah (chap. viii. 3), seeking to recall those of her own sex to a higher life. We note, on a smaller scale, a like teaching in the married apostle (1 Peter iii. 3, 4). Twenty-one distinct articles are mentioned. Their names for the most part appear to have a foreign stamp on them. Then, as at other times, luxury imported its novelties, and the women of Judah took up the fashions of those of Tyre or Damascus or Philistia. It is not without interest to compare the protests of Juvenal (*Sat.* vi.), Dante (*Purgat.* xxiii. 106—111), Chrysostom, and Savonarola against like evils.

With stretched forth necks . . .—The corruption which the prophet paints showed itself then, as it has done in later times, in the adoption by the decent classes of society of the gait and glances of the harlots of alien birth (comp. Prov. vii. 9—21), with, perhaps, the difference of a certain affectation of coyness.

Making a tinkling with their feet.—Small silver bells were fastened on the ankles, and so the beauties of Jerusalem carried, as it were, their music with them. The custom still exists in Syria and Arabia, though forbidden by the Koran. English nursery rhymes seem to recall a time when it was not unknown in Western Europe.

(17) **The Lord will smite with a scab . . .**—The words point partly to diseases, such as leprosy, causing baldness, engendered by misery and captivity, partly to the brutal outrage of the Assyrian invaders, stripping off the costly garments and leaving the wearers to their nakedness. (Comp. Ezek. xvi. 37; Nahum iii. 5.)

(18) **Tinkling ornaments.**—These were anklets, *i.e.*, rings of metal, with or without bells, which produced the tinkling of verse 16. The "cauls" were probably *wreaths*, or plaits of gold or silver net-work, worn over the forehead from ear to ear, but have been taken by some scholars as sun-like balls worn like a necklace.

Round tires like the moon.—The crescent ornaments which were hung on the necks of the camels of the Midianites in the time of Gideon (Judges viii. 21), and are still worn by Arabian women. It is not improbable that they were connected with the worship of Ashtaroth. Among modern Arabian women they are regarded as a charm against the evil eye. (See Note on Jer. xliv. 17—19.)

(19) **The chains.**—Better, as in Judg. viii. 26, where they are also ornaments of Midianite kings, *earrings*. These and the "bracelets" were probably of gold. The "mufflers" were the long flowing veil, or *mantilla*, worn so as to cover the head, as now in Spain, or Egypt, or Turkey.

(20) **The bonnets . . .**—The English word is, perhaps, too modern in its associations, and should be replaced by "diadems" (Exod. xxxix. 28; Isa. lxi. 10).

The ornaments of the legs.—These were chains connecting the anklets of verse 18, and so regulating the "mincing" or "tripping" motion of the wearer.

The headbands.—Better, *girdles*, always the most highly ornamented part of an Eastern dress, such as were worn by brides (Jer. ii. 32; Isa. xlix. 18).

The tablets.—Literally, *houses of the soul*—*i.e.*, of the spirit or essence of a perfume. These seem to have been of the nature of *scent-bottles*, or the modern vinaigrettes.

The earrings.—The noun is connected with the idea of enchantments. Better, *amulets* or *charms*, such as are worn in the East as safeguards against the evil eye.

(21) **The rings, and nose jewels.**—The first word points to the signet ring, worn both by men and women of wealth (Exod. xxxv. 22; Num. xxxi. 50; Esth. iii. 12, viii. 8; Jer. xxii. 24); the latter to the ornaments worn pendent from the nostrils as by modern Arabian women (Gen. xxiv. 22).

(22) **The changeable suits of apparel.**—Better, *state*, or *festal*, *dresses*. The word is used in Zech. iii. 4, of the high priest's garments, "gold and blue, and purple, and fine linen" (Exod. xxviii. 6).

The mantles.—Better, *tunics*. The uppermost of the two garments, commonly richly embroidered.

Wimples.—The obsolete English word describes accurately enough the large *shawl*, like a Scotch plaid, worn over the tunic, as in the "vail" worn by Ruth (Ruth iv. 15).

The crisping pins.—Better, *purses* (2 Kings v. 23), the small embroidered bags, or reticules, attached to the girdles. The girdle itself was used as a purse by men. This was a refinement of female luxury.

(23) **The glasses**—*i.e.*, the polished metal *mirrors* (as in Exod. xxxviii. 3; Job xxxvii. 18; 1 Cor. xiii. 12; James i. 23), which the Eastern lady carried in her hand, that she might adjust her toilet. The LXX. rendering, "Laconian [Spartan] garments," *i.e.*, indecently transparent, is curious enough to deserve notice, as throwing light on the social life of Alexandria, if not of Israel.

The fine linen—*i.e.*, the chemise worn under the tunic next the skin. The Heb. *sedin*, like the Greek σινδων (Mark xiv. 51), seems to imply a commerce with India; so our muslin (*mosul*) and calico (*calicut*) bear record of their origin. In Sanscrit, *sindhu* is the term for fine linen.

The hoods—*i.e.*, the *turbans* which completed the attire, and over which was thrown the "vail," or gauze

The Downfall of Pride.   ISAIAH, IV.   *The Branch of Jehovah.*

linen, and the hoods, and the vails. ⁽²⁴⁾ And it shall come to pass, *that* instead of sweet smell there shall be stink; and instead of a girdle a rent; and instead of well set hair baldness; and instead of a stomacher a girding of sackcloth; *and* burning instead of beauty. ⁽²⁵⁾ Thy men shall fall by the sword, and thy ¹ mighty in the war. ⁽²⁶⁾ And her gates shall lament and mourn; and she *being* ^{2 3} desolate shall sit upon the ground.

1 Heb., *might.*
2 Or, *emptied.*
3 Heb., *cleansed.*
4 Heb., *let thy name be called upon us.*
5 Or, *take thou away.*
6 Heb., *beauty and glory.*
7 Heb., *for the escaping of Israel.*

CHAPTER IV.—⁽¹⁾ And in that day seven women shall take hold of one man, saying, We will eat our own bread, and wear our own apparel: only ⁴ let us be called by thy name, ⁵ to take away our reproach.

⁽²⁾ In that day shall the branch of the LORD be ⁶ beautiful and glorious, and the fruit of the earth *shall be* excellent and comely ⁷ for them that are escaped of Israel. ⁽³⁾ And it shall come to pass, *that he that is* left in Zion, and *he that*

---

mantle. Jewish women, however, did not veil their faces after the manner of those of Turkey and Arabia. The prophet seems to have carried his eye upward from the feet to the head, as he catalogued with indignant scorn the long list of superfluities. We may compare the warnings of 1 Tim. ii. 9; 1 Pet. iii. 3. It is noticeable that stockings and handkerchiefs do not seem to have been used by the women of Judah.

⁽²⁴⁾ **And it shall come to pass.**—Now comes the terrible contrast of the day of destruction that is coming on all this refined luxury. Instead of the balmy perfume of the scent-bottles, there shall be the stench of squalor and pestilence; instead of the embroidered girdle (chap. xi. 5), not a "rent," but the *rope* by which they would be dragged in the march of their conquerors; instead of the plaited hair (1 Pet. iii. 3; 1 Tim. ii. 9), natural or artificial, the baldness of those who were cropped as slaves were cropped (comp. 1 Cor. xi. 5, 6); instead of the "stomacher" (better, *cloak*, or *mantle*), the scanty tunic of the coarsest sackcloth; instead of the elaborate beauty in which they had exulted, the burning, or *brand*, stamped on their flesh, often in the barbarism of the East on the forehead, to mark them as the slaves of their captors.

⁽²⁵⁾ **Thy men . . .** ⁽²⁶⁾ **her gates . . .**—The feminine pronoun in both verses points to the daughter of Zion as representing her many daughters. As in Lam. i. 1, and as in the JUDÆA CAPTA medals that commemorated the destruction of Jerusalem by Titus, she is represented as sitting on the ground desolate and afflicted.

IV.

⁽¹⁾ **And in that day seven women . . .**—The chapter division wrongly separates this verse from the foregoing. It comes as the climax of the chastisement of the daughters of Zion, as the companion picture to chap. iii. 6. As men sought eagerly, yet in vain, a protector, so women should seek for a husband. Those who had been wooed and courted, and had been proudly fastidious, should supplicate in eager rivalry (the seven women to one man implies a land depopulated by war, and so making polygamy natural) for the protection of marriage, and that not on the usual conditions of having food and clothing found for them (Exod. xxi. 10), but as working for their own livelihood.

To take away our reproach.—Better, as an imperative, *take thou away*. The reproach is that of being childless. From the Jewish standpoint that was not only the great sorrow, but the great shame, of womanhood, implying, as men thought, a sin of which it was the chastisement (Gen. xxx. 23; 1 Sam. i. 6; Luke i. 25).

⁽²⁾ **In that day . . .**—The dark picture of punishment is relieved by a vision of Messianic glory, like that of chap. ii. 1—4. The "day" is, as in chap. iii. 18, the time of Jehovah's judgments.

The branch of the Lord . . .—The thought of the "branch," though not the Hebrew word, is the same as in chap. xi. 1. The word itself is found in the Messianic prophecies of Jer. xxiii. 5, 6, xxxiii. 15; Zech. iii. 8, vi. 12. The two latter probably inherited both the thought and the word from this passage. Here, then, if we thus interpret the words, we have the first distinct prophecy in Isaiah of a personal Messiah. He is the "Branch of Jehovah," raised up by Him, accepted by Him. And the appearance of that Branch has as its accompaniment (the poetic parallelism here being that at once of a resemblance and of contrast) the restoration of outward fertility. That thought Isaiah had inherited from Ps. lxxii. 16; Hosea ii. 21, 22; Joel iii. 18; Amos ix. 13. He transmitted it to Ezek. xxxiv. 27; Zech. ix. 16, 17. The interpretation which takes "the branch [or growth] of the Lord" in its lower sense, as used collectively for "vegetation," and, therefore, parallel and all but synonymous with the "fruits of the earth," seems to miss the true meaning. Rabbinic exegesis may be of little weight, but the acceptance of the term as Messianic by Jeremiah and Zechariah is surely conclusive. It will be noted that the prophecy of the Branch (*tsemach*) here comes after a picture of desolation, just as that of the Branch (*netzer*) does in chap. xi. 1. The thought seems applied by our Lord to Himself in John xii. 24.

For them that are escaped of Israel.—These are, of course, identical with the "remnant" of chaps. i. 9, vi. 13, to whom the prophet had been taught to look as to the trusted depositaries of the nation's future.

⁽³⁾ **He that is left in Zion . . .**—The prophet turns from the Jerusalem that then was, with the hypocrisies and crimes of the men and the harlot fashions of its women, to the vision of a new Jerusalem, which shall realise the ideal of Pss. xv. and xxiv. There every one should be called "holy" (comp. 1 Cor. i. 2; 2 Cor. i. 1), and the name should be no unreal mockery (chap. xxxii. 5), but should express the self-consecration and purity of its inhabitants.

Every one that is written among the living. —Literally, *for life*. The idea is that of "the book" or "register" of life in which are written the names of those who are worthy of living in the heavenly city. It meets us as early as Exod. xxxii. 32, and appears in Pss. lvi. 8, lxix. 28; Ezek. xiii. 9.; Mal. iii. 16; Dan. xii. 1; Acts xiii 48; Phil. iv. 3; Rev. iii. 5, xiii. 8, xxi. 27. An examination of the passages, especially the first, will show that while it involves the idea of an election, it excludes that of an irreversible predestination, and that

The Cleansing of the Daughters of Zion. ISAIAH, V. *The Covert from Storm and Rain.*

remaineth in Jerusalem, shall be called holy, *even* every one that is written ¹among the living in Jerusalem: ⁽⁴⁾ when the Lord shall have washed away the filth of the daughters of Zion, and shall have purged the blood of Jerusalem from the midst thereof by the spirit of judgment, and by the spirit of burning. ⁽⁵⁾ And the LORD will create upon every dwelling place of mount Zion, and upon her assemblies, a

ᵃ cloud and smoke by day, and the shining of a flaming fire by night: for ² upon all the glory *shall be* ³ a defence. ⁽⁶⁾ And there shall be a tabernacle for a shadow in the daytime from the heat, and for a place of refuge, and for a covert from storm and from rain.

CHAPTER V.—⁽¹⁾ Now will I sing to my wellbeloved a song of my beloved touching his vineyard. My wellbeloved

1 Or, *to life.*
a Ex. 13. 21.
2 Or, *above.*
3 Heb., *a covering.*

---

the election has to be "made sure" by a life in harmony with it. (2 Pet. i. 10.)

⁽⁴⁾ **When the Lord shall have washed away the filth. . .**—This serves as the connecting link with chap. iii. 16—24. The prophet has not forgotten the daughters of Zion. Jehovah will wash away, as with the baptism of repentance, the "filth," the moral uncleanness, that lay beneath their outward show of beauty. The "blood of Jerusalem," in the next verse, has a wide range of meaning, from the "murders" of chap. i. 15, 21, to the Moloch sacrifices in which the women had borne a conspicuous part (Ps. cvi. 38; Isa. lvii. 5; Ezek. xxii. 2, 3).

By the spirit of judgment, and by the spirit of burning.—The word for "spirit" is better taken in its more literal meaning, as *breath* or *blast*, as in chaps. xxx. 27, 28, xl. 7. The words indicate that the prophet saw in the "blood" of which he speaks a greater enormity than that of the daughters of Zion. The one might be washed away. The other needed, as it were, the "fiery baptism" of the wrath of Jehovah. (Comp. chap. xxx. 27; Matt. iii. 11.) The Authorised Version "burning" represents the root-meaning of the word, but it is elsewhere (chap. vi. 13; Deut. xiii. 5, xvii. 7) used for "destruction" generally.

⁽⁵⁾ **And the Lord will create . . .**—The verb "create" has all the solemn force with which we find it in Gen. i. 1. It is one of Isaiah's favourite words. The word for "dwelling-place" is almost invariably used for the tabernacle or temple, and would seem to have that meaning here. This determines the character of the "assemblies." They are not the meetings of the people for counsel or debate, as in a Greek *ecclesia*, but their "gatherings," their "solemn assemblies," in the courts of the temple. The thoughts of the prophet travel back to the history of the Exodus, when the presence of Jehovah was manifested as a cloud by day and a pillar of fire by night (Exod. xiii. 21; Num. ix. 15, x. 34, xiv. 14). In that Presence there would be safety and peace. The image is a favourite one with Isaiah, possibly as connected with the vision of chap. vi. 4, for God's protection of His people.

Upon all the glory shall be a defence.—The phrase is almost startlingly abrupt. The thought seems to be that over the "glory" of the new Jerusalem, as just described, there shall be stretched the over-arching *canopy* of the Divine Love. The word for "defence" occurs in this sense in Ps. xix. 5, Joel ii. 16, and is still used by Jews of the "canopy" held over bride and bridegroom at a wedding. The "baldacchino" over the altar of an Italian church probably represents the image that was present to Isaiah's mind.

⁽⁶⁾ **And there shall be a tabernacle.**—Perhaps *It shall be . . .* The thought is that of Pss. xxvii. 5, xxxi. 20. In the manifested glory of Jehovah men would find, as the traveller finds in his tent, a protection against all forms of danger, against the scorching heat of noon, and against the pelting storm.

V.

⁽¹⁾ **Now will I sing to my wellbeloved.**—Literally, *Now let me sing.* The chapter bears every mark of being a distinct composition, perhaps the most elaborately finished in the whole of Isaiah. The parable with which it opens has for us the interest of having obviously supplied a starting-point for a later prophet (Jer. ii. 21), and for our Lord's teaching in the like parable of Matt. xxi. 33—41. Here, however, there is the distinctive touch of the irony of the opening verse. The prophet presents himself, as it were, in the character of a minstrel, ready to sing to his hearers one of the love-songs in which their culture delighted (Amos vi. 5.) In its language and rhythm it reminds us of the Song of Solomon. The very word "beloved" recalls Song of Sol. v. 1, 2; the description of the vineyards, that of Song of Sol. viii. 11—13. The probability that the parallelism was intentional is increased by the coincidence of chap. vii. 23, and Song of Sol. viii. 11, which will meet us further on. On this assumption Isaiah's words have a special interest as showing how early that poem lent itself to a mystical interpretation. One might almost conjecture that the prophet allured the people to listen by music as well as words, and appeared, as Elisha and other prophets had done, with harp or pipe in hand (2 Kings iii. 15; 1 Sam. x. 5, xvi. 23; chap. xxx. 29). The frequency of such hymns (chaps. xii., xxv., xxvi. 1—4) shows, at any rate, that the prophet had received the training of a psalmist. (See *Introduction.*)

A song of my beloved.—A slightly different reading adopted by some critics gives *A song of love.* The "beloved" is purposely not named, but appears afterwards as none other than Jehovah. The word, closely connected with the ideal name Jedediah (the beloved of Jehovah; 2 Sam. xii. 25), occurs in twenty-six passages of Song of Sol., and not elsewhere.

A very fruitful hill.—Literally, *a horn, the son of oil.* The combination "horn of oil" in 1 Sam. xvi. 1, 13, and 1 Kings i. 39, suggests the thought that the phrase is equivalent to "the horn of the anointed" (Kay). The term "horn" was a natural synonym for a hill. So we have Matterhorn, Aarhorn, &c., in the Alps. Oil was naturally symbolic of fertility. In Ps. lxxx. 8—16, we have a striking parallel. The "fruitful hill" was Canaan as a whole, with a special reference to Judah and Jerusalem. The "choicest vine"—literally, *vine of Sorek* (Gen. xlix. 11; Jer. ii. 21), bearing a small dark purple grape—pointed back to the fathers of the nation, who, idealised in the retrospect, were as the heroes of faith compared with the then present

The Song of the Vineyard.   ISAIAH, V.   *The Parable interpreted.*

hath a ᵃvineyard in ¹a very fruitful hill : ⁽²⁾ and he ²fenced it, and gathered out the stones thereof, and planted it with the choicest vine, and built a tower in the midst of it, and also ³made a winepress therein : and he looked that it should bring forth grapes, and it brought forth wild grapes. ⁽³⁾ And now, O inhabitants of Jerusalem, and men of Judah, judge, I pray you, betwixt me and my vineyard. ⁽⁴⁾ What could have been done more to my vineyard, that I have not done in it ? wherefore, when I looked that it should bring forth grapes, brought it forth wild grapes ? ⁽⁵⁾ And now go to ; I will tell you what I will do to my vineyard :

a Jer. 2. 21 ; Matt. 21. 33 ; Mark 12. 1 ; Luke 20. 9.

1 Heb., *the horn of the son of oil.*

2 Or, *made a wall about it.*

3 Heb., *hewed.*

4 Heb., *for a treading.*

5 Heb., *plant of his pleasures.*

6 Heb., *a scab.*

b Mic. 2. 2.

I will take away the hedge thereof, and it shall be eaten up ; *and* break down the wall thereof, and it shall be ⁴trodden down : ⁽⁶⁾ and I will lay it waste : it shall not be pruned, nor digged ; but there shall come up briers and thorns : I will also command the clouds that they rain no rain upon it. ⁽⁷⁾ For the vineyard of the LORD of hosts *is* the house of Israel, and the men of Judah ⁵his pleasant plant : and he looked for judgment, but behold ⁶oppression ; for righteousness, but behold a cry.

⁽⁸⁾ Woe unto them that join ᵇhouse to house, *that* lay field to field, till *there be* no place, that they may be placed alone in the midst of the earth !

---

generation. The picture which forms the parable might almost take its place among the *Georgics* of Palestine. The vineyard on the hillside could not be ploughed, and therefore the stones had to be taken out by hand. It was fenced against the beasts of the field. There was a tower for a watchman to guard it against the attacks of robbers. (Comp. Virg. *Georg.* ii. 399—419.) Each part has its own interpretation.

⁽²⁾ **And he fenced it.**—In the "fence" we may recognise the law and institutions of Israel which kept it as a separate people (Eph. ii. 14) ; in the "stones" that were gathered out, the removal of the old idolatries that would have hindered the development of the nation's life ; in the "tower" of the vineyard (comp. in a different context chap. i. 8), the monarchy and throne of David, or the watch-tower from which the prophets looked forth (Hab. ii. 1 ; Isa. xxi. 5—8) ; in the "winepress," the temple in which the fruits of righteousness were to issue in the wine of joy and adoration (Zech. ix. 17 ; Eph. v. 18). It was, we may note, one of the maxims of the Rabbis that the duty of a scribe was "to set a fence around the law" (*Pirke Aboth*, i. 1). In the last clause of the verse the pleasant song suddenly changes its tone, and the "wild grapes" (sour and hard, and not larger than bilberries) are types of deeds of harsh and cruel injustice on which the prophet proceeds to dwell.

⁽³⁾ **And now, O inhabitants of Jerusalem.**—"The song of the vineyard" comes to an end and becomes the text of a discourse in which Jehovah, as the "Beloved" of the song, speaks through the prophet. Those to whom the parable applies are invited, as David was by Nathan, to pass an unconscious judgment on themselves. (Comp. Matt. xxi. 40, 41, as an instance of the same method.)

⁽⁴⁾ **What could have been done more . . .**—The prophet cuts off from the people the excuse that they had been unfairly treated, that their Lord was as a hard master, reaping where he had not sown (Matt. xxv. 24). They had had all the external advantages that were necessary for their growth in holiness, yet they had not used them rightly. (Comp. the striking parallelism of Heb. vi. 4—8.)

⁽⁵⁾ **I will take away the hedge . . .**—This involved the throwing open of the vineyard to be as grazing land which all the wild bulls of Bashan—*i.e.*, all the enemies of Zion—might trample on (Ezek. xxxiv. 18). The interpretation of the parable implies that there was to be the obliteration, at least for some time and in some measure, of the distinctness and independence of the nation's life. (Comp. Hos. iii. 4, for a like sentence in another form.)

⁽⁶⁾ **There shall come up briers and thorns.**—The picture of desolation is still part of a parable. The "briers and thorns" (both the words are peculiar to Isaiah) are the base and unworthy who take the place of the true leaders of the people (Judges ix. 7—15). The absence of the pruning and the digging answers to the withdrawal of the means of moral and spiritual culture (John xv. 2 ; Luke xiii. 8). The command given to the clouds (comp. 2 Sam. i. 21, for the outward form of the thought) implies the cessation of all gracious spiritual influences.

⁽⁷⁾ **For the vineyard of the Lord of hosts.**—The words remind us of Nathan's "Thou art the man," to David (2 Sam. xii. 7), and of our Lord's words in Matt. xxi. 42, 43.

Behold oppression.—The Hebrew word carries with it the idea of *bloodshed*, and points to the crimes mentioned in chaps. i. 15, iv. 4. The "cry" is that of the victims who appeal to Jehovah when they find no help in man (Gen. iv. 10 ; Deut. xxiv. 15 ; James v. 4).

⁽⁸⁾ **Woe unto them that join house to house.**—The series of "Woes" which follows has no precedent in the teaching of earlier prophets. The form of Luke vi. 24—26 seems based upon it. The general indictment of chap. i. is followed by special counts. That which leads off the list was the destruction of the old village life of Palestine. The original ideal of the nation had been that it should consist of small proprietors ; and the Jubilee (Lev. xxv. 13, xxvii. 24), and the law of the marriage of heiresses (Num. xxvii. 1—11, xxxvi. xxxiii. 54) were intended as safeguards for the maintenance of that ideal. In practice it had broken down, and might had taken the place of right. Landmarks were removed (Deut. xix. 14, xxvii. 17 ; Prov. xxii. 28), the owners of small estates forcibly expelled (Micah ii. 2) or murdered as Naboth had been (1 Kings xxi. 16) ; the law of debt pressed against the impoverished debtor (Neh. v. 5), and the law of the Jubilee was practically set aside. In place of the small freeholders there rose up a class of large proprietors, often the *novi homines* of the state (*e.g.*, Shebna in chap. xxii. 16), while the original owners sank into slavery (Neh. v. 5) or became

The Woe of the Spoiler. ISAIAH, V. *The Woe of the Drunkard.*

(9) ¹ In mine ears *said* the LORD of hosts, ² Of a truth many houses shall be desolate, *even* great and fair, without inhabitant. (10) Yea, ten acres of vineyard shall yield one bath, and the seed of an homer shall yield an ephah.

(11) ᵃ Woe unto them that rise up early in the morning, *that* they may follow strong drink; that continue until night, *till* wine ³ inflame them! (12) And the harp, and the viol, the tabret, and pipe, and wine, are in their feasts: but they regard not the work of the LORD, neither consider the operation of his hands. (13) Therefore my people are gone into captivity, because *they have* no knowledge: and ⁴ their honourable men *are* famished, and their multitude dried up with thirst. (14) Therefore hell hath enlarged herself, and opened her mouth without measure: and their glory, and their multitude, and their pomp, and he that rejoiceth, shall descend into it. (15) And ᵇ the mean man shall be brought down, and the mighty man shall be humbled, and the eyes of the lofty shall be humbled: (16) but the LORD of hosts shall be exalted in judgment, and

---

1 Or, *This is in mine ears, saith the LORD, &c.*

2 Heb., *If not, &c.*

a Prov. 23. 29, 30.

3 Or, *pursue them.*

4 Heb., *their glory are men of famine.*

b ch. 2. 9, 11, 17.

---

tenants at will, paying exorbitant rents in kind or money, and liable at any moment to be evicted. Isaiah's complaint recalls the agrarian laws by which first Licinius and then the Gracchi sought to restrain the extension of the *latifundia* of the Roman patricians, and Latimer's bold protest against the enclosure of commons in the sixteenth century. The evil had been denounced before by Micah (ii. 2), and in a psalm probably contemporary with Isaiah (Ps. xlix. 11). The fact that the last year of Uzziah coincided with the Jubilee may have given a special point to Isaiah's protest.

(9) **In mine ears said the Lord.**—The italics show that there is no verb in the Hebrew, the text, if it be correct, giving the emphasis of abruptness; but it is rightly supplied in the Authorised Version. The sentence that follows is one of a righteous retribution: There shall be no profit or permanence in the property thus unjustly gained.

(10) **Ten acres.**—The disproportion was as great as that which we have seen in recent times in vine countries suffering from the *Phylloxera* or the *oidium*, or in the potato failures of Ireland. The *bath* was equal to seventy-two Roman sextarii (Jos. *Ant.* viii. 2—9), about seven and a half gallons, and this was to be the whole produce of ten acres, from which an average yield of 500 *baths* might have been expected. The Hebrew word for "acre" means primarily the ground that could be ploughed in a day by a yoke of oxen.

The seed of an homer shall yield an ephah. —Here also there is an all but total failure. The *homer* was a dry measure of thirty-two pecks, and the *ephah* was equal to one-tenth of a *homer* (Ezek. xlv. 11; Exod. xvi. 36). This scanty crop—Ruth's gleanings for a single day (Ruth ii. 17)—one-tenth of the seed sown, was to take the place of the "thirtyfold, sixty, and a hundredfold" (Gen. xxvi. 12; Matt. xiii. 8) of average or prosperous years.

(11) **Woe unto them that rise up early.**—The same class as in verse 8 meets us under another aspect. In Judah, as elsewhere, the oppressors were conspicuous for their luxury (Amos vi. 5, 6). They shocked public feeling by morning banquets (Eccles. x. 16, 17; Acts ii. 14). Not wine only, but the "strong drink" made from honey and from dates and other fruits (possibly including, as a generic term, the beer for which Egypt was famous) was seen on their tables. The morning feast was followed, perhaps with hardly a break, by an evening revel. (Comp. chaps. xxii. 13, xxviii. 7.)

(12) **The harp, and the viol.**—Here again the fashions of Judah followed those of Samaria, so closely indeed that Isaiah addresses the rulers of his own city as "the drunkards of Ephraim" (chap. xxviii. 1; Amos vi. 5). The list of instruments is fairly represented by the English words, but *lute* (or *hand-harp*), *cymbal*, *timbrel* (or *tambourine*), and *flute* would come somewhat closer to the Hebrew.

They regard not the work of the Lord.—The life of luxury was then, as ever, one of practical atheism. Those who so lived did not see, never do see, any Divine plan or order in the world around them. They anticipated, in their swine-like greed, the baser types of the school of Epicurus.

(13) **My people are gone into captivity.**— The great captivity of Judah lay as yet far off, but the prophet may be speaking of it as already present in his vision of the future. Probably, however, the disastrous wars of Ahaz had involved many captures of the kind referred to (2 Chron. xxviii. 5, 8, 17, 18).

Because they have no knowledge.—Better, *and they knew not*—*i.e.*, did not foresee that this must be the outcome of their conduct. The "honourable men" and the "multitude" are named as representing all classes of society.

(14) **Therefore hell hath enlarged herself.**— The Hebrew *Sheol*, or *Hades*, like "hell" itself in its original meaning, expressed not a place of torment, but the vast shadow-world of death, thought of as being below the earth (Pss. xvi. 10, xlix. 14). Here, as elsewhere (Jonah ii. 2; Prov. i. 12, xxx. 16), it is half-personified, as Hades and Death are in Rev. vi. 8, xx. 13, 14. In that unseen world there were, in the later belief of Judaism, the two regions of Gehenna and of Eden or Paradise. What the prophet says is that all the pomp and glory of the rich oppressors are on their way to that inevitable doom. The word for "glory" (as in 1 Sam. iv. 22) is the same as that for "honourable men" in verse 13, so that the original has all the emphasis of repetition.

(15) **The mean man shall be brought.**—The recurrence of the burden of chap. ii. 9, 11, 12, 17, connects chap. v. with the earlier portion of the introduction.

(16) **Shall be sanctified.**—Men had not recognised the holiness of Jehovah, and therefore He must manifest that holiness (in that sense "be sanctified") in acts of righteous severity. The "Holy One of Israel" was, we must remember, the name, of all Divine names, in which Israel most delighted, the ever-recurring burden of all the prophet's utterances.

The Catalogue of Woes.   ISAIAH, V.   *The Kindling of the Lord's Anger.*

¹ ² God that is holy shall be sanctified in righteousness. ⁽¹⁷⁾ Then shall the lambs feed after their manner, and the waste places of the fat ones shall strangers eat.

⁽¹⁸⁾ Woe unto them that draw iniquity with cords of vanity, and sin as it were with a cart rope: ⁽¹⁹⁾ that say, Let him make speed, *and* hasten his work, that we may see *it*: and let the counsel of the Holy One of Israel draw nigh and come, that we may know *it!*

⁽²⁰⁾ Woe unto them ³ that call evil good, and good evil; that put darkness for light, and light for darkness; that put bitter for sweet, and sweet for bitter!

⁽²¹⁾ Woe unto *them that are* ᵃ wise in their own eyes, and prudent ⁴ in their own sight!

⁽²²⁾ Woe unto *them that are* mighty to drink wine, and men of strength to mingle strong drink: ⁽²³⁾ which ᵇ justify the wicked for reward, and take away the righteousness of the righteous from him! ⁽²⁴⁾ Therefore as ⁵ the fire devoureth the stubble, and the flame consumeth the chaff, *so* their root shall be as rottenness, and their blossom shall go up as dust: because they have cast away the law of the LORD of hosts, and despised the word of the Holy One of Israel. ⁽²⁵⁾ Therefore is the anger of the LORD kindled against his people, and he hath stretched forth his hand against them, and hath smitten them: and the hills did tremble, and their carcases *were* ⁶ torn in the midst of the streets.

ᶜ For all this his anger is not turned away, but his hand *is* stretched out still.

Marginal notes:
1. Or, *the holy God.*
2. Heb., *holy.*
3. Heb., *that say concerning evil, It is good*, &c.
4. Heb., *before their face.*
5. Heb., *the tongue of fire.*
6. Or, *as dung.*

a Prov. 3. 7; Rom. 12. 16.
b Prov. 17. 15.
c ch. 9. 12, 17, 21, & 10. 4.

⁽¹⁷⁾ **Then shall the lambs feed after their manner.**—Better, *feed even as on their pasture.* The meaning is clear enough. The lands that have been gained by oppression shall, in the day of retribution, become common pasture ground instead of being reserved for the parks and gardens of the rich; and strangers—*i.e.*, invaders, Philistines, Assyrians, or nomadic tribes—shall devour the produce (chap. i. 7). Possibly, however, the "lambs" may stand for the poor and meek, as in contrast with the "fat ones" of the earth. The LXX. version follows a different reading in the second clause, and gives "kids" instead of "strangers."

⁽¹⁸⁾ **That draw iniquity with cords of vanity.**—The phrase is boldly figurative. Evil-doers are thought of as harnessing themselves as to the chariot of sin. The "cords of vanity"—*i.e.*, of *emptiness* or *ungodliness*—are the habits by which they are thus bound. The "cart ropes," thicker and stronger than the "cords," represent the extreme stage, when such habits become irresistibly dominant. Probably the words may point to some idolatrous procession, in which the chariot of Baal or Ashtaroth was thus drawn by their worshippers, like that of Demêter or Cybele in Greece, or Juggernâth in India.

⁽¹⁹⁾ **That say, Let him make speed.**—We have here, as in chap. xxviii. 10, and Jer. xvii. 15, the very words of the wealthy scoffers of Judah. Such taunts are not peculiar to any age or country. We find them in the speech of Zedekiah (1 Kings xxii. 24), in that of the mockers of 2 Pet. iii. 4. In the name of Isaiah's second son (chap. viii. 3) we may probably find an answer to the taunt. The words "the counsel of the Holy One of Israel" were obviously emphasised with a sneer at the name on which Isaiah dwelt so constantly. (Comp. chap. xxx. 11.)

⁽²⁰⁾ **Woe unto them that call evil good.**—The moral state described was the natural outcome of the sins condemned in the preceding verses. So Thucydides (iii. 82—84) describes the effects of the spirit of party in the Peloponnesian war. Rashness was called courage, and prudence timidity, and treachery cleverness, and honesty stupidity. That deliberate perversion is in all ages the ultimate outcome of the spirit that knows not God, and therefore neither fears nor loves Him, whether it shows itself in the licence of profligacy, or the diplomacy of Machiavellian statesmen, or the speculations of the worshippers of Mammon.

⁽²¹⁾ **Woe unto them that are wise in their own eyes.**—Here again the prophet would seem to have definite individual counsellors in his mind. For such men the ideal of statesmanship was a series of shifts and expedients, based upon no principle of righteousness. (Comp. chaps. xxix. 15, xxx. 1.)

⁽²²⁾ **Woe unto them that are mighty to drink . . . . strong drink.**—The words in part reproduce the "woe" of verses 11, 12, but with the distinctive feature that there the revellers were simply of the careless self-indulgent type, while here they are identified with the unjust and corrupt rulers. They were *heroes* and *valiant men* only in and for their cups. To such men it seemed a light matter to acquit the guilty and condemn the guiltless. The prophet dwells on the familiar truth, *Judex damnatur cum nocens absolvitur.* The Targum, it may be noticed, has "the mammon of falsehood" (comp. Luke xvi. 9), for the "reward" of the Hebrew.

⁽²⁴⁾ **Therefore as the fire devoureth.**—Literally, *the tongue of fire.* The scene brought before us is—(1) that of a charred and burnt-up field, horrible and hideous to look upon (comp. Heb. vi. 8); (2) that of a tree decayed and loathsome. The double imagery represents the end of the riotous mirth of the unjust judges.

⁽²⁵⁾ **The hills did tremble.**—We again trace the influence of the earthquake which was still fresh in the memories of men. (See Note on chap. ii. 10.)

Their carcases were torn.—Better, *were as sweepings,* or, *as refuse.* The words may point either to pestilence, or war, or famine. The stress laid on scarcity in verse 10 makes it probable that the last was prominent in the prophet's mind.

For all this his anger is not turned away.—The same formula meets us in chaps. ix. 12, 21, x. 4, xiv. 27, with a solemn knell-like iteration. It bids the people remember after each woe that this is not all. They do not as yet see the end of the chastisement through which God is leading them. "For all this"

The March of the Avengers.   ISAIAH, VI.   *The Vision in the Temple.*

⁽²⁶⁾ And he will lift up an ensign to the nations from far, and will hiss unto them from the end of the earth: and, behold, they shall come with speed swiftly: ⁽²⁷⁾ none shall be weary nor stumble among them; none shall slumber nor sleep; neither shall the girdle of their loins be loosed, nor the latchet of their shoes be broken: ⁽²⁸⁾ whose arrows *are* sharp, and all their bows bent, their horses' hoofs shall be counted like flint, and their wheels like a whirlwind: ⁽²⁹⁾ their roaring *shall be* like a lion, they shall roar like young lions: yea, they shall roar, and lay hold of the prey, and shall carry *it* away safe, and none shall deliver *it*. ⁽³⁰⁾ And in that day they shall roar against them like the roaring of the sea: and if *one* look unto the land, behold darkness *and* ¹sorrow, ²and the light is darkened in the heavens thereof.

CHAPTER VI.—⁽¹⁾ In the year that king Uzziah died I *saw also the Lord sitting upon a throne, high and lifted up, and ³his train filled the temple. ⁽²⁾ Above it stood the seraphims: each one

Marginal notes:
1 Or, *distress.*
2 Or, *when it is light, it shall be dark in the destructions thereof.*
a John 12. 41.
B.C. cir. 758.
3 Or, *the skirts thereof.*

---

may mean (1) because of all the sins, or (2) notwithstanding all the punishment already inflicted. (Comp. Lev. xxvi. 18, 23.)

⁽²⁶⁾ **And he will lift up an ensign.**—The banner on the summit of a hill indicated the meeting-place of a great army. In this case the armies are thought of as doing the work of Jehovah Sabaoth, and therefore as being summoned by Him. The same image meets us in chaps. xi. 10, 12, xiii. 2, xviii. 3, xlix. 22, lxii. 10.

Will hiss unto them.—The verb meets us in a like context in chap. vii. 18. It seems to describe the sharp shrill whistle which was to the ear what the banner was to the eye, the signal of a rendezvous. Possibly, as in chap. vii. 18, the idea of the bees swarming at the whistling of the bee-master is already in the prophet's thoughts.

From the end of the earth.—The words point to the Assyrians, the Euphrates being the boundary of Isaiah's political geography.

^(27—29) **None shall be weary . . .**—The three verses paint the progress of the invading army. Unresting, unhasting, in perfect order, they march onward. They do not loosen their girdle for repose. The latchet or *thong* which fastens their sandals is not "broken" or untied. The light-armed troops are there, probably the Medes and Elamites in the Assyrian army (chap. xiii. 18). The chariots of the Assyrians themselves are there, sweeping onward like a tempest. Their unshod hoofs (the practice of shoeing horses was unknown in the ancient East) are hard as flint. Comp. Homer's epithet of "brazen-footed" (*Il.* v. 329); and Amos vi. 12. The battle-cry is heard far off like the roaring of lions.

⁽³⁰⁾ **They shall roar against them.**—Literally, *there is a roaring over him.* The verb is the same as in the previous verse, and points therefore to the shout and tramp of the armies. It suggests the thought of the roaring of the sea, and this in its turn that of the darkness and thick clouds of a tempest; or possibly, as before, of an earthquake; or possibly, again, of an eclipse. The word for "heavens" is not that commonly used; better, *clouds.*

VI.

⁽¹⁾ **In the year that king Uzziah died.**—Probably before his death. Had it been after it, the first year of king Jotham would have been the more natural formula. The chapter gives us the narrative of the solemn call of Isaiah to the office of a prophet. It does not follow that it was written at that time, and we may even believe that, if the prophet were the editor of his own discourses, he may have designedly placed the narrative in this position that men might see what he himself saw, that all that was found in the preceding chapters was but the development of what he had then heard, and yet, at the same time, a representation of the evils which made the judgments he was commissioned to declare necessary. On the relation of the call to the prophet's previous life, see *Introduction.*

The date is obviously given as important, and we are led to connect it with the crisis in the prophet's life of which it tells. He had lived through the last twenty years or so of Uzziah's reign. There was the show of outward material prosperity. There was the reality of much inward corruption. The king who had profaned the holiness of the Temple had either just died or was dragging out the dregs of his leprous life in seclusion (2 Chron. xxvi. 21). The question, What was to be the future of his people ? must have been much in the prophet's thoughts. The earthquake that had terrified Jerusalem had left on his mind a vague sense of impending judgment. It is significant that Isaiah's first work as a writer was to write the history of Uzziah's reign (2 Chron. xxvi. 22). (See *Introduction.*)

I saw also the Lord sitting upon a throne. —Isaiah had found himself in the court of the Temple, probably in that of the priests. He had seen the incense-clouds rising from the censer of the priest, and had heard the hymns and hallelujahs of the Levites. Suddenly he passes, as St. Paul afterwards passed, under the influence of like surroundings (Acts xxii. 17), into a state of ecstatic trance, and as though the veil of the Temple was withdrawn, he saw the vision of the glory of the Lord, as Moses (Exod. xxiv. 10) and Micaiah of old had seen it (1 Kings xxii. 19), as in more recent times it had appeared to Amos (ix. 1). The King of kings was seated on His throne, and on the right hand and on the left were the angel-armies of the host of heaven, chanting their hymns of praise.

His train filled the temple.—The word for "temple" is that which expresses its character as the *palace* of the great King. (Comp. Ps. xi. 4, xxix. 9; Hab. ii. 20.) The "train" answers to the skirts of the glory of the Lord, who clothes Himself with light as with a garment (Exod. xxxiii. 22, 23). It is noticeable (1) that the versions (LXX., Targum, Vulg.) suppress the train, apparently as being too anthropomorphic, and (2) that to the mind of St. John this was a vision of the glory of the Christ (John xii. 41).

⁽²⁾ **Above it stood the seraphims . . .**—It is noticeable that this is the only passage in which the seraphim are mentioned as part of the host of heaven.

had six wings; with twain he covered his face, and with twain he covered his feet, and with twain he did fly. (3) And ¹ one cried unto another, and said, ᵃ Holy, holy, holy, *is* the LORD of hosts: ² the whole earth *is* full of his glory. (4) And the posts of the ³ door moved at the voice of him that cried, and the house was filled with smoke.

1 Heb., *this cried to this.*
a Rev. 4. 8.
2 Heb., *his glory is the fulness of the whole earth.*
3 Heb., *thresholds.*
4 Heb., *cut off.*
5 Heb., *and, in his hand a live coal.*

(5) Then said I, Woe *is* me! for I am ⁴ undone; because I *am* a man of unclean lips, and I dwell in the midst of a people of unclean lips: for mine eyes have seen the King, the LORD of hosts.

(6) Then flew one of the seraphims unto me, ⁵ having a live coal in his hand, *which* he had taken with the

---

In Num. xxi. 6, the word (the primary meaning of which is *the burning ones*) occurs as denoting the fiery serpents that attacked the people in the wilderness. Probably the brazen serpent which Hezekiah afterwards destroyed (2 Kings xviii. 4) had preserved the name and its significance as denoting the instruments of the fiery judgments of Jehovah. Here, however, there is no trace of the serpent form, nor again, as far as the description goes, of the animal forms of the cherubim of Ezek. i. 5—11, and of the "living creatures" of Rev. iv. 7, 8. The "burning ones" are in the likeness of men, with the addition of the six wings. The patristic and mediæval distinction between the seraphim that excel in love, and the cherubim that excel in knowledge, rests apparently on the etymology of the former word. The "living creatures" of Rev. iv. 7, 8, seem to unite the forms of the cherubim of Ezekiel with the six wings of the seraphim of this passage. Symbolically the seraphim would seem to be as transfigured cherubim, representing the "flaming fire" of the lightning, as the latter did the storm-winds and other elemental forces of nature (Ps. civ. 4).

Each one had six wings.—The thought seems to be that the human form was clothed as it were with six wings. One pair of wings covered the face in token of adoring homage (Ezek. i. 11); a second, the feet, including the whole lower part of the human form, while with the third they hovered as in the firmament of heaven above the skirts of the glory of the Divine Throne. It is noticeable that the monuments of Persepolis represent the Amshashpands (or ministers of God) as having six wings, two of which cover the feet.

(3) **And one cried unto another.**—So in Ps. xxix. 9, which, as describing a thunderstorm, favours the suggestion that the lightnings were thought of as the symbols of the fiery seraphim, we read, "in his temple doth every one *say, Glory.*" The threefold repetition, familiar as the *Trisagion* of the Church's worship, and reproduced in Rev. iv. 8 (where "Lord God Almighty" appears as the equivalent of Jehovah Sabaoth), may represent either the mode of utterance, first antiphonal, and then in full chorus, or the Hebrew idiom of the emphasis of a three-fold iteration, as in Jer. vii. 4, xxii. 29. Viewed from the standpoint of a later revelation, devout thinkers have naturally seen in it an allusive reference to the glory of Jehovah as seen alike in the past, the present, and the future, which seems the leading idea in Rev. iv. 8, or even a faint foreshadowing of the Trinity of Persons in the Unity of the Godhead. Historically we cannot separate it from the name of the Holy One of Israel, which with "the Lord of hosts" was afterwards so prominent in Isaiah's teaching.

(4) **The posts of the door.** — Better, *the foundations of the threshold.* The words seem to point to the prophet's position as in front of the Holy of holies.

The house was filled with smoke. — The vision had its prototype in "the smoke as of a furnace" on Sinai (Exod. xix. 18), in the glory-cloud of 1 Kings viii. 10, and possibly in its lurid fire-lit darkness represented the wrath of Jehovah, as the clear brightness of the throne did His love. So in Rev. xv. 8, the "smoke from the glory of God" precedes the outpouring of the seven vials of wrath. The parallelism of the clouds of incense-smoke as the symbol of adoring prayer (Rev. v. 8, viii. 4) suggests an alternative interpretation as possible; but in that case mention would probably have been made of the censers from which it rose. The incense-clouds of the Temple may in either case have been the starting-point of the mystic vision.

(5) **Then said I, Woe is me.** — The cry of the prophet expresses the normal result of man's consciousness of contact with God. So Moses "hid his face, for he was afraid to look upon God" (Exod. iii. 6). So Job "abhorred himself and repented in dust and ashes" (Job xlii. 6). So Peter fell down at his Lord's feet, and cried, "Depart from me, for I am a sinful man, O Lord" (Luke v. 8). Man at such a time feels his nothingness in the presence of the Eternal, his guilt in the presence of the All-holy. No man can see God and live. (Comp. also 1 Sam. vi. 20.)

I am a man of unclean lips. — The prophet's words present at once a parallel and a contrast to those of Moses in Exod. iv. 10. The Lawgiver feels only, or chiefly, his want of the *gift* of utterance which was needed for his work. With Isaiah the dominant thought is that his lips have been defiled by past sins of speech. How can he join in the praises of the seraphim with those lips from which have so often come bitter and hasty words, formal and ceremonial prayers? (Comp. James iii. 2, 9). His lips are "unclean" like those of one stricken, as Uzziah had been, by leprosy (Lev. xiii. 45). He finds no comfort in the thought that others are as bad as he is, that he "dwells in the midst of a people of unclean lips." Were it otherwise, there might be some hope that influence from without might work his purification. As it is, he and his people seem certain to sink into the abyss. To "have seen the King, the Lord of hosts," was in such a case simply overwhelming (Exod. xxxiii. 20).

(6) **Then flew one of the seraphims.** — In presenting the vision to our mind's eye we have to think of the bright seraph form, glowing as with fire, and with wings like the lightning-flash, leaving his station above the throne, and coming to where the prophet stood in speechless terror. The altar from which he took the "live coal"—literally, *stone*, and interpreted by some critics of the stones of which the altar was constructed — is commonly thought of as belonging, like that of Rev. viii. 5, ix. 13, to the heavenly Temple which was opened to the prophet's view. There seems, however, a deeper meaning in the symbolism if we

The Mission of the Prophet.   ISAIAH, VI.   *The Sentence of Judicial Blindness.*

tongs from off the altar: (7) and he ¹laid *it* upon my mouth, and said, Lo, this hath touched thy lips ; and thine iniquity is taken away, and thy sin purged.

(8) Also I heard the voice of the Lord, saying, Whom shall I send, and who will go for ᵃ us? Then said I, ²Here *am* I; send me. (9) And he said, Go, and tell this people, ᵇ Hear ye ³ ⁴ indeed, but understand not; and see ye indeed, but perceive not. (10) Make the heart of this people fat, and make their ears heavy, and shut their eyes; lest they see with their eyes, and hear with their ears, and understand with their heart, and convert, and be healed.

<small>1 Heb., *caused it to touch.*
a Gen. 1. 26.
2 Heb., *Behold me.*
b Matt. 13. 14; Mark 4. 12; Luke 8. 10; John 12. 40; Acts 28. 26; Rom. 11. 8.
3 Or, *without ceasing*, &c.
4 Heb., *hear ye in hearing*, &c.</small>

---

think of the seraph as descending from the height above the throne to the altar of incense, near which Isaiah actually stood. It was from that altar that the glowing charcoal was taken. What had seemed part of the material of a formal worship became quickened with a living power. The symbol became sacramental. So in Ps. li. 7, the prayer of the penitent is "Purge me with hyssop"—*i.e.*, make the symbol a reality. Fire, it need hardly be said, is throughout the Bible the symbol at once of the wrath and the love of God, destroying the evil and purifying the good (Num. xxxi. 23; Mal. iii. 2; Matt. iii. 11; 1 Cor. iii. 15; Heb. xii. 29; 1 Pet. i. 7). Isaiah passed, as it were, through the purgatory of an instantaneous agony.

(7) **And he laid it upon my mouth.**—So Jehovah "touched the mouth" of Isaiah's great successor (Jer. i. 9); but not in that case with a "coal from the altar." That prophet, like Moses (Exod. iv. 10), had felt only or chiefly the want of power ("Alas! I cannot speak"), and power was given him. Isaiah desired purity, and his prayer also was answered.

Thine iniquity is taken away, and thy sin purged.—The clauses express the two elements of the great change which men, according to their varying systems, have called Conversion, the New Birth, Regeneration; but which is at all times a necessary stage in the perfecting of the saints of God. Pardon and purity are the conditions alike of the prophet's work and of the completeness of his own spiritual life.

(8) **Also I heard the voice of the Lord.** —The work of cleansing has made the prophet one of the heavenly brotherhood. He is as an angel called to an angel's work. (Comp. Judges ii. 1, v. 23; Mal. iii. 1.) He had before seen the glory of Jehovah, and had been overwhelmed with terror. Now he hears His voice (John x. 4), and it rouses him to self-consecration and activity.

Whom shall I send, and who will go for us? —The union of the singular and plural in the same sentence is significant. The latter does not admit of being explained as a *pluralis majestatis*, for the great kings of Assyria, and Babylon, and Persia always spoke of themselves in the singular. (*Records of the Past, passim*), and the "plural of majesty" was an invention of the servility of the Byzantine court. A partial explanation is found in the fact that here, as elsewhere (1 Kings xxii. 19; Job i. 6, ii. 1; and perhaps Gen. i. 26, xi. 7), Jehovah is represented as a king in council. Christian thought has, however, scarcely erred in believing that the words were as a dim foreshadowing of the truth, afterwards to be revealed, of a plurality within the Unity. (See Note on verse 3.) Ps. cx. 1, which Isaiah may have known, suggested at least a duality. The question reveals to the prophet that there is a work to be done for Jehovah, that He needs an instrument for that work. It is implied that no angel out of the whole host, no man out of the whole nation, offers to undertake it. (Comp. chap. lxiii. 3, 5.) The prophet, with the ardour for work which follows on the sense of pardon, volunteers for it before he knows what it is. He reaches in one moment the supreme height of the faith which went forth, not knowing whither it went (Heb. xi. 8).

(9) **Go, and tell this people, Hear ye indeed, but understand not.** — No harder task, it may be, was ever given to man. Ardent dreams of reformation and revival, the nation renewing its strength like the eagle, were scattered to the winds; and he had to face the prospect of a fruitless labour, of feeling that he did but increase the evil against which he strove. It was the very opposite mission of that to which St. Paul was sent, to "open men's eyes, and turn them from darkness to light" (Acts xxvi. 18). It is significant that the words that followed were quoted both by the Christ (Matt. xiii. 14, 15; Mark iv. 12), by St. John (John xii. 40), and by St. Paul (Acts xxviii. 26, 27), as finding their fulfilment in their own work and the analogous circumstances of their own time. History was repeating itself. To Isaiah, as with greater clearness to St. Paul (Rom. ix.—xi.), there was given the support of the thought that the failure which he saw was not total, that even then a "remnant should be saved;" that though his people had "stumbled," they had not "fallen" irretrievably; that the ideal Israel should one day be realised. The words point at once to the guilt of "this people"—we note the touch of scorn ("*populus iste*") in the manner in which they are mentioned (chaps. viii. 11, xxviii. 11, 14; Matt. ix. 3, xxvi. 61)—and to its punishment. All was outward with them. Words did not enter into their minds ("heart," *i.e.*, "understanding," rather than "feeling"). Events that were "signs of the times," calls to repentance or to action, were taken as things of course. For such a state, after a certain stage, there is but one treatment. It must run its course and "dree its weird," partly as a righteous retribution, partly as the only remedial process possible.

(10) **Make the heart of this people fat.**—The thought is the same as that of the "hardening" of Pharaoh's heart (Exod. viii. 19, ix. 34, &c.) and that of Sihon (Deut. ii. 30). It implies the reckless headstrong will which defies restraint and warnings. So the poets of Greece, in their thoughts as to the Divine government of the world, recognised the truth that there is a judicial blindness and, as it were, insanity of will that comes as the consequence of sinful deeds (Æsch. *Agam.* 370—386). The mediæval adage, "*Quem Deus vult perdere prius dementat*," expresses one aspect of the same law; but the *vult perdere* is excluded by the clearer revelation of the Divine purpose (Ezek. xviii. 23; 1 Tim. ii. 4; 2 Peter ii. 9), as "not willing that any should perish."

Shut their eyes.—Literally, as in chap. xxix. 10, *daub*, or *besmear*. Possibly the phrase refers to the barbarous practice, not unknown in the East, of thus closing the eyes as a punishment. Burder (*Oriental Customs*, i. 98) mentions a son of the Great Mogul who was thus punished by his father. For the

The Remnant as the Holy Seed. ISAIAH, VII. *The Siege of Jerusalem.*

(11) Then said I, Lord, how long? And he answered, Until the cities be wasted without inhabitant, and the houses without man, and the land be ¹utterly desolate, (12) and the LORD have removed men far away, and *there be* a great forsaking in the midst of the land. (13) But yet in it *shall be* a tenth, ² and *it* shall return, and shall be eaten: as a teil tree, and as an oak, whose ³ substance *is* in them, when they cast *their leaves*: so the holy seed *shall be* the substance thereof.

CHAPTER VII.—(1) And it came to pass in the days of ᵃAhaz the son of Jotham, the son of Uzziah, king of Judah, *that* Rezin the king of Syria, and Pekah the son of Remaliah, king of Israel, went up toward Jerusalem to war against it, but could not prevail against it. (2) And it was told the house of David, saying, Syria ⁴ is confederate with Ephraim. And his heart was moved, and the heart of his people, as the trees of the wood are moved with the wind.

B.C. cir. 742.

1 Heb., *desolate with desolation.*
2 Or, *when it is returned, and hath been broused.*
3 Or, *stock, or, stem.*
a 2 Kings 16. 5.
4 Heb., *resteth on Ephraim.*

---

ethical fact, as well as for the phrase, we may (with Cheyne) compare Shakespeare—

"For when we in our viciousness grow hard,
Oh, misery on't, the wise gods seal our eyes."

(11) **Lord, how long?**—The prophet asks the question which is ever on the lips of those who are brought face to face with the problems of the world, with the great mystery of evil, sin permitted to work out fresh evil as its punishment, and yet remaining evil. How long shall all this last? So a later prophet, towards the close of the seventy years of exile, cried once again, "How long?" (Dan. viii. 13). So the cry, "How long, O Lord, dost thou not judge?" came from the souls beneath the altar (Rev. vi. 10).

Until the cities be wasted without inhabitant.—The words answer the immediate question of the prophet within its horizon. They suggest an answer to all analogous questions. Stroke after stroke must come, judgment after judgment, till the sin has been adequately punished; but the darkness of the prospect, terrible as it is, does not exclude the glimmer of an eternal hope for the far-off future.

(12) **And the Lord have removed men far away.**—The words point to the policy of deportation adopted by the Assyrian kings. From the first hour of Isaiah's call the thought of an exile and a return from exile was the key-note of his teaching, and of that thought thus given in germ, his whole after-work was but a development, the horizon of his vision expanding and taking in the form of another empire than the Assyrian as the instrument of punishment.

And there be a great forsaking.—Better, *great shall be the deserted space.* (Comp. chaps. v. 9, vii. 22, 23.) The words may have connected themselves in Isaiah's thoughts with what he had heard before from the lips of Micah (Jer. xxvi. 18; Mic. iii. 12).

(13) **But yet in it shall be a tenth . . .**—Better, *And though there should be a tenth in it, yet this shall be again devoured* (*with fire*). What the prophet is led to expect is a series of successive chastisements sifting the people, till the remnant of the chosen ones alone is left. (Comp. the same thought under a different imagery in Ezek. v. 12: Zech. xiii. 8, 9.) The "tenth" is taken, as in Lev. xxvii. 30, for an ideally consecrated portion.

As a teil tree.—Better, *terebinth*; and for "when they cast their leaves" read, *when they are cut down.* The "teil tree" of the Authorised Version is probably meant for the "lime" (*tilier, tilleul*). The thought of this verse is that embodied in the name of his son *Shear-jashub* (see Note on chap. vii. 3), and constantly reappears (chaps. i. 27, iv. 2, 3, x. 20, xxix. 17, xxx. 15, &c.). The tree might be stripped of its leaves, and its branches lopped off, and nothing but the stump left; but from that seemingly dead and decayed stock, pruned by the chastisements of God (John xv. 2), a young shoot should spring, holy, as consecrated to Jehovah, and carry on the continuity of the nation's life. The same thought is dominant in St. Paul's hope for his people. At first the "remnant," and then "all Israel," should be saved (Rom. xi. 5, 26). In chaps. x. 33—xi. 1 the same image is specially applied to the house of David, and becomes, therefore, essentially Messianic.

VII.

(1) **It came to pass in the days of Ahaz.**—The whole reign of Jotham comes between chaps. vi. and vii. On Isaiah's life during that period, see *Introduction.* The work of the prophet now carries him into the main current of history, as recorded in 2 Kings xv., xvi.; 2 Chron. xxviii., and in Assyrian inscriptions. The facts to be borne in mind are—(1) that the kingdom of Israel under Menahem had already become tributary to Assyria (2 Kings xv. 19, 20); (2) that the object of the alliance between Pekah, a bold and ambitious usurper, and Rezin, was to organise a resistance against Assyria, such as that in which Uzziah had taken part (Schrader, *Keil-Inschriften*, pp. 395—421, quoted by Cheyne), that first Jotham (2 Kings xv. 37), and then Ahaz, apparently refused to join the confederacy, and that the object of the attack of the allied kings was either to force Ahaz to join, or else to depose him, bring the dynasty of David to a close, and set a follower of their own, probably a Syrian, on the throne of Judah.

But could not prevail against it.—The words obviously refer to a special stage in the campaign. The king of Syria seems to have been the leading spirit of the confederacy. 2 Chron. xxviii. 5—15 represents Judah as having sustained a great and almost overwhelming defeat. Jerusalem, however, though besieged (2 Kings xvi. 5) was not absolutely taken (2 Kings xvi. 5); 2 Kings xvi. 6 records the capture of the port of Elath, on the Gulf of Akaba, by Rezin.

(2) **Syria is confederate with Ephraim.**—Literally, *rests upon* . . . Ephraim stands, of course, as often elsewhere, for the northern kingdom of Israel as a whole.

His heart was moved.—There was a general panic. King and people alike asked, How could they resist? Would it not be better to join the confederacy, and take their chance with it in attacking the king of Assyria? The image of the trees is generic, but suggests something like the quivering of the aspen leaves.

The Prophet and the King.   ISAIAH, VII.   *Faith the Condition of Stability.*

(3) Then said the LORD unto Isaiah, Go forth now to meet Ahaz, thou, and [1] Shear-jashub thy son, at the end of the [a] conduit of the upper pool in the [2] highway of the fuller's field; (4) and say unto him, Take heed, and be quiet; fear not, [3] neither be fainthearted for the two tails of these smoking firebrands, for the fierce anger of Rezin with Syria, and of the son of Remaliah. (5) Because Syria, Ephraim, and the son of Remaliah, have taken evil counsel against thee, saying, (6) Let us go up against Judah, and [4] vex it, and let us make a breach therein for us, and set a king in the midst of it, *even* the son of Tabeal: (7) thus saith the Lord GOD, It shall not stand, neither shall it come to pass. (8) For the head of Syria *is* Damascus, and the head of Damascus *is* Rezin; and within threescore and five years shall Ephraim be broken, [5] that it be not a people. (9) And the head of Ephraim *is* Samaria, and the head of Samaria *is* Remaliah's son. [6] If ye will not believe, surely ye shall not be established.

---

[1] That is, *the remnant shall return.*
[a] 2 Kings 18. 17.
[2] Or, *causeway.*
[3] Heb., *let not thy heart be tender.*
[4] Or, *waken.*
[5] Heb., *from a people.*
[6] Or, *Do ye not believe? It is because ye are not stable.*

---

(3) **Go forth now to meet Ahaz . . .**—At this crisis the prophet, already recognised as such, and gathering his disciples round him (chap. viii. 16), is told to deliver a message to the king. He finds him halting between two opinions. He is making a show of resistance, but in reality he is not depending either on the protection of Jehovah, or the courage of his people, but on a plan of his own. Why should he not continue to pay tribute to Assyria, as Uzziah and Menahem (2 Kings xv. 19) had done, and write to Tiglath-pileser to attack the territories of the invading kings, as he actually did at a later stage in the war (2 Kings xv. 29)?

Thou and Shear-jashub thy son.—Assuming chap. vi. to give the first revelation of the idea of the "remnant," it would follow that the birth of the son whose name (*Remnant returns*—the return being both literal and spiritual—*i.e.*, "is converted"), embodied a prophecy, must have followed on that revelation, and he was probably, therefore, at the time a stripling of sixteen or eighteen. It may be noted that Isaiah had in the history of Hosea i., ii. the example of a prophet who, as his children were born, gave them names which were terribly or hopefully significant. Each child was, as it were, a sign and portent (chap. viii. 18). The fact that the mother of his children was herself a prophetess (chap. viii. 3), sharing his hopes and fears, gives a yet deeper interest to the fact.

At the end of the conduit . . .—The king was apparently superintending the defensive operations of the siege, probably cutting off the supply of water outside the walls, as Hezekiah afterwards did (2 Chron. xxxii. 3, 4). The "upper pool" has been identified with the Upper Gihon pool (*Birket-el-Mamilla*) or the "dragon's well" of Neh. ii. 13. A lower pool meets us in chap. xxii. 9. The "fuller's field" was near En-rogelim (chap. xxxvi. 2; 2 Sam. xvii. 17).

(4) **Take heed, and be quiet . . .**—The prophet meets the fears of the king by words of comfort. The right temper for such a time was one of calm courage, waiting on the Lord (chap. xxx. 15).

Neither be fainthearted.—Literally, *let not thine heart be soft.*

For the two tails of these smoking firebrands.—The two powers that Ahaz dreaded were, in the prophet's eyes, but as *the stumps of two smoking torches.* Their flame was nearly out. It would soon be extinguished.

The son of Remaliah.—There is a touch of scorn in the omission of the king's name. So men spoke scornfully of Saul as "the son of Kish" (1 Sam. x. 11), and Saul himself of David as "the son of Jesse" (1 Sam. xx. 30). It pointed out the fact that Pekah was after all but an upstart adventurer, who had made his way to the throne by rebellion and murder.

(6) **Let us make a breach therein for us . . .**—The words imply an assault on the line of fortresses that defended Judah (2 Chron. xxvi. 9, 10, xxxii. 1). If they were won the issue of the war would be practically decided. Jerusalem itself does not appear to have been actually besieged.

The son of Tabeal.—The mode of description, as in the last verse, indicates that the man was of low origin. The name "good is God" is Aramaic, and points to his being an officer in Rezin's army. It meets us again in Ezra iv. 7, among the Aramæan adversaries of Israel, and appears in the term *Tibil* in Assyrian inscriptions, which give us his actual name as Asbariah (Schrader, *Keil Inschrift.*, p. 118). Tubaal appears in an inscription of Sennacherib as appointed by him as governor of Zidon (*Records of the Past*, i. 35). Dr. Kay, connecting the name with Tab-rimmon ("Rimmon is good"), conjectures that the substitution of El ("God") for the name of the Syrian deity may indicate that he was the representative of the family of Naaman, and, like him, a proselyte to the faith of Israel.

(8) **The head of Syria is Damascus . . .**—The prediction of the failure of the alliance is emphasised. Each city, Damascus and Samaria, should continue to be what it was, the head of a comparatively weak kingdom, and should not be aggrandised by the conquest of Judah and Jerusalem. There is an implied comparison of the two hostile cities and their kings with Jerusalem and its supreme King, Jehovah. Bolder critics, like Ewald, assume that a clause expressing that contrast has been displaced by that which now follows, and which they reject as a later interpolation.

Within threescore and five years shall Ephraim be broken.—Assuming the genuineness of the clause, we have in it the first direct chronological prediction in the prophet's utterances. Others follow in chaps. xvi. 14, xvii. 1, xxi. 6, xxiii. 1. Reckoning from B.C. 736 as the probable date of the prophecy, the sixty-five years bring us to B.C. 671. At that date Assyrian inscriptions show that Assurbanipal, the "Asnapper" of Ezra iv. 2—10, co-regent with his father Esarhaddon, had carried off the last remnant of the people of Samaria, and peopled it with an alien race (Smith's *Assurbanipal*, p. 363). This completed the work which had been begun by Salmaneser and Sargon (2 Kings xvii. 6). Ephraim then was no more a people.

(9) **If ye will not believe . . .**—The prophet reads the thoughts that were working in the king's mind. He had no faith in these predictions terminating at

The Sign Offered and Refused. ISAIAH, VII. *The Sign of Immanuel.*

(10) ¹ Moreover the LORD spake again unto Ahaz, saying, (11) Ask thee a sign of the LORD thy God; ² ask it either in the depth, or in the height above. (12) But Ahaz said, I will not ask, neither will I tempt the LORD. (13) And he said, Hear ye now, O house of David; *Is it* a small thing for you to weary men, but will ye weary my God also? (14) Therefore the Lord himself shall give you a sign; *a* Behold, a virgin shall conceive, and bear a son, and ³ shall call

1 Heb., *And the LORD added to speak.*
2 Or, *make thy petition deep.*
a Matt. 1. 23; Luke 1. 31.
3 Or, *thou, O Virgin, shalt call.*

a date which he was not likely to live to witness. By look, or possibly by words, he showed his incredulity, and Isaiah offers to meet it, in the consciousness of a Divine power that will not fail him. From Heaven to Hades, Ahaz may take his choice. The method of giving a sign by predicting something in the near future as a pledge for predictions that belong to a more remote time is specially characteristic of Isaiah. (Comp. chaps. xxxvii. 30, xxxviii. 7.) There is something significant in "the Lord thy God." Ahaz, idolater as he was, had not formally abandoned the worship of Jehovah. The tone of authority in which Isaiah speaks may be either that belonging to his consciousness of his mission, or may imply some previous relation to the young king as a counsellor and teacher. (See *Introduction.*)

(12) **I will not ask . . .**—The king speaks as in the very accents of faith. He will not put Jehovah to any such test. Not, perhaps, without a sneer, he quotes almost the very formula of the Law: "Thou shalt not tempt the Lord thy God" (Exod. xvii. 2; Deut. vi. 16). Was the prophet going to forget his own teaching, and become a tempter to that sin? That which lay beneath this show of humble trust was simply self-will and utter unfaith. He had already made up his mind to the Assyrian alliance, against which he knew Isaiah was certain to protest. The fact that the words that follow are spoken to the whole house of David, may, perhaps, imply that the older members of the royal family were encouraging the king in his Assyrian projects, and had, perhaps, suggested his hypocritical answer.

(13) **Is it a small thing for you to weary men . .**—The thought that men may try the long-suffering of God till He is "weary to bear them," is specially characteristic of Isaiah (chap. i. 14). We mark the changed note of "*my* God," as compared with "the Lord *thy* God" in verse 11. Ahaz has involved himself in a sentence of rejection. In the first part of the question Isaiah becomes the mouthpiece of a wide-spread hopeless discontent. Men also were 'weary' of this idolatrous and corrupt misgovernment (chap. viii. 6).

(14) **Behold, a virgin shall conceive, and bear a son . . .**—Better, *behold, the young woman*, or perhaps the *bride, shall conceive.* The first noun has the definite article in the Hebrew, and the word, though commonly used of the unmarried, strictly speaking denotes rather one who has arrived at marriageable age. "Bride," in the old English and German sense of the word as applied to one who is about to become a wife, or is still a young wife, will, perhaps, best express its relation to the two Hebrew words which respectively and distinctively are used for "virgin" and for "wife." In Ps. lxviii. 26, the Authorised Version gives "damsels." The mysterious prophecy which was thus delivered to Ahaz has been very differently interpreted.

(1) We may deal with it as though the Gospel of St. Matthew had never been written, as though the facts which it records had no place in the history of mankind. From this point of view we get what seems at first a comparatively simple exposition. The prophet offers a sign to the faithless king, and the sign is this: he points to some young bride in either sense of that word, and says that she shall conceive and bear a son. The fulfilment of that prediction in a matter which lay outside the range of human knowledge was to be the sign for Ahaz and his court, and she should give that son a name which would rebuke the faithlessness of the king. Immanuel, "God with us," would be a *nomen et omen*, witnessing, not of an incarnate Deity, but of His living and abiding presence. Who was the mother of the child on this theory we have no *data* for deciding. As the two other children of the prophet bore, like Hosea's (chaps. vii. 3; viii. 3), mysterious and prophetic names, the most probable conjecture seems to be that it was Isaiah's own wife, still young, and, as it were, still a bride, or possibly a second wife whom he had married, or was about to marry, after the death of his first. Other guesses have pointed to one of the women of the harem of Ahaz who may have been with him when Isaiah spoke. The hypothesis of some critics that such a one became the mother of Hezekiah, and that he was the Immanuel of the prophet's thoughts, breaks down under the test of dates. Hezekiah, at the time the prophecy was uttered, was a boy of at least nine years of age (2 Kings xvi. 2, xviii. 2). Of this child so born Isaiah predicts that he shall grow up in a time of suffering and privation (verse 15), and that before he has attained to manhood the confederacy of Rezin and Remaliah shall come to a disastrous end. So far all is at least coherent. Immanuel, as a person, stands on the same level as Shear-jashub, representing a great idea to which Isaiah again appeals in chap. viii. 8, 10, but not identified with the Christ, or even with any expectations of the Christ. On the other hand, there are phenomena in Isaiah's prophetic work at large which this explanation does not adequately include. The land of Israel at least appears to be described as in some peculiar sense the land of Immanuel (chap. viii. 10). Isaiah is clearly expecting, even in the first volume that bears his name, not to speak of chaps. xl.—lxvi., the arrival, at some undefined point in the future, of one whose nature, work and character, shall be represented by the marvellous series of names of chap. ix. 6, in whom the spirit of Jehovah, the fear of Jehovah, shall dwell in their fulness—who shall be of the stem of Jesse, and whose reign shall be as the realised ideal of a golden age (chap. xi. 1—10). That expectation connects itself with a like prophecy, associated as this is with the childbirth of a travailing woman, in Micah v. 3—5. In what relation, we ask, did Immanuel stand to these confessedly Messianic predictions?

(2) The other interpretation sets out from an entirely different starting-point. The words of Matt. i. 23 are taken as, once for all, deciding the entire meaning of the Immanuel prophecy. The prophet is supposed to have passed into a state of ecstasy in which he sees clearly, and with a full consciousness of its meaning, the history of the incarnation and the marvel of the travail-pangs of the Virgin mother. The vision of the future Christ thus presented to his mind, colours all his after-thoughts, and forms the basis of his whole work.

The Growth of the Immanuel Child. ISAIAH, VII. *The Downfall of Syria and Ephraim.*

his name Immanuel. ⁽¹⁵⁾ Butter and honey shall he eat, that he may know to refuse the evil, and choose the good. ⁽¹⁶⁾ For before the child shall know to refuse the evil, and choose the good, the land that thou abhorrest shall be forsaken of both her kings.

The article emphasises the definiteness of his visions. He sees "*the* virgin mother" of the far-off future. And the prophet learns to connect the vision with the history of his own time. The growth of that Christ-child in the far-off future serves as a measure of time for the events that were passing, or about to pass, within the horizon of his earthly vision. Before the end of an interval not longer than that which separates youth from manhood, the Syro-Ephraiminitic confederacy should be broken up. So far, here also, we have a coherent and consistent view. It is attended, however, by some serious difficulties. A "sign," in the language of Hebrew prophets, is that which proves to the person to whom it is offered that there is a supernatural power working with him who gives it. If a prediction, it is one which will speedily be tested by a personal experience, the very offer of which implies in the prophet the certainty of its fulfilment. He stakes, as it were, his reputation as a prophet on the issue. (Comp. chaps. xxxvii. 30, xxxviii. 7; Exod. iv. 8—14; 1 Sam. xii. 16.) But how could the prediction of a birth in the far-off distance, divided by several centuries from Isaiah's time, be a sign to Ahaz or his people? And what would be the meaning, we may ask again, of the words "butter and honey shall he eat," as applied to the Christ-child? Do not the words "Before the child shall know to refuse the evil . . ." point, not to a child seen as afar in vision, but to one who was to be born and grow up among the men of that generation? Should we not have expected, if the words had implied a clear revelation of the mystery of the virgin-birth, that Isaiah himself would have dwelt upon it elsewhere, that later prophets would have named it as one of the notes of the Messiah, that it would have become a tradition of the Jewish schools of interpretation? As a matter of fact, no such allusion is found in Isaiah, nor in the prophets that follow him (see Note on Jer. xxxi. 22, for the only supposed, one cannot say even "apparent," exception); the Jewish interpreters never include this among their notes of the Christ. It is indeed, as has been said in the New Testament portion of this *Commentary*, one of the strongest arguments for the historical, non-mythical character of the series of events in Matt. i., Luke i. and ii., that they were contrary to prevailing expectation. (See Note on Matt. i. 23.)

A truer way of interpretation than either of those that have been thus set forth, is, it is believed, open to us. We may remember (1) as regards St. Matthew's interpretation of Isaiah's prophecy, that two other predictions cited, as by the Evangelist himself, in the history of the Nativity, in Matt. i. and ii. are, as it were, detached from their position, in which they had a distinct historical meaning, and a new meaning given to them (see Notes on Matt. ii. 15, 18), and that this holds good of other prophecies cited by him elsewhere (see Notes on Matt. xxi. 5, xxvii. 9). It was not, as some have thought, that facts were invented or imagined that prophecies might appear to be fulfilled, but that the facts being given, prophecies were shown to have a meaning which was fulfilled in them, though that meaning may not have been present to the prophet's own mind. In this case the use of the word for "virgin" in the LXX. version may have determined St. Matthew's interpretation of the words. Here, in the history which had come to him attested by evidence which satisfied him, he found One who, in the truest and highest sense, was the "Immanuel" of Isaiah's prophecy. We must not forget (2) the limits within which the prophets lived and moved, as they are stated in 1 Pet. i. 10. They "enquired and searched diligently" as to the time and manner of the fulfilment of their hopes; but their normal state (the exceptions being only enough to prove the rule) is one of enquiry and not of definite assurance. They had before them the ideal of a righteous king, a righteous sufferer, of victory over enemies and sin and death, but the "times and the seasons" were hidden from them, as they were afterwards from the apostles, and they thought of that ideal king as near, about to burst in upon the stage that was filled with the forms of Assyria, Syria, Ephraim, Judah, as the apostles appear to have thought afterwards that the advent of the Lord would come upon the stage of the world's history that was filled with the forms of Emperors and rebellious Jews and perverse heretics and false prophets (1 Thess. iv. 15; 1 Cor. xv. 51; 2 Thess. ii. 3, 4; 1 Pet. iv. 7; 1 Tim. iv. 1—3; 1 John ii. 18). And neither prophets nor apostles, though left to the limitations of an imperfect knowledge, were altogether wrong. Prophecy has, in Bacon's words, its "springing and germinant accomplishments." The natural birth of the child Immanuel was, to the prophet and his generation, a pledge and earnest of the abiding presence of God with His people. The overthrow of Assyria, and Babylon, and Jerusalem were alike forerunners of the great day of the Lord in which the ultimate and true Immanuel, the name at last fulfilled to the uttermost, shall be at once the Deliverer and the Judge.

⁽¹⁵⁾ **Butter and honey shall he eat, that he may know . . .**—Better, *till he know*, or, *when he shall know* . . . .—By a strange inversion of the familiar associations of the phrase (Exod. iii. 17; Deut. xxxi. 20), probably, as the prophet spoke them, not without a certain touch of the irony of paradox, the words describe a time, not of plenty, but of scarcity. (Comp. verse 22.) Fields and vineyards should be left uncultivated (chap. v. 9), and instead of bread and meat, and wine and oil, the people, flying from their cities and taking refuge in caves and mountains, should be left to the food of a nomadic tribe, such, *e.g.*, as the Kenites (Judg. v. 25; 1 Sam. xiv. 26; Matt. iii. 4). The "butter" of the Bible here, as in Judg. v. 25, is the clotted milk which has always been a delicacy with Arabs.

⁽¹⁶⁾ **For before the child shall know . . .**—The words imply the age of approaching manhood, and predict the downfall of Pekah and Rezin, as the longer period of verse 8 predicted the entire downfall and annihilation of one of the two kingdoms which they represented. The words "good and evil" are better taken of moral choice (Gen. iii. 5; Deut. i. 39) rather than (with some critics, who appeal to 2 Sam. xix. 35) of the child's discernment of food as pleasant or the reverse. (See Gen. ii. 9; 1 Kings iii. 9.)

The land that thou abhorrest.—The words imply the "horror" of fear as well as of dislike. The prediction was fulfilled in the siege of Samaria by Salmaneser, and its capture by Sargon (1 Kings

The King of Assyria. ISAIAH, VII. *The Desolation of Judah.*

(17) The LORD shall bring upon thee, and upon thy people, and upon thy father's house, days that have not come, from the day that Ephraim departed from Judah; *even* the king of Assyria. (18) And it shall come to pass in that day, *that* the LORD shall hiss for the fly that *is* in the uttermost part of the rivers of Egypt, and for the bee that *is* in the land of Assyria. (19) And they shall come, and shall rest all of them in the desolate valleys, and in the holes of the rocks, and upon all thorns, and upon all ¹bushes. (20) In the same day shall the Lord shave with a ᵃrazor that is hired, *namely*, by them beyond the river, by the king of Assyria, the head, and the hair of the feet: and it shall also consume the beard. (21) And it shall come to pass in that day, *that* a man shall nourish a young cow, and two sheep; (22) and it shall come to pass, for the abundance of milk *that* they shall give he shall eat butter: for butter and honey shall every one eat that is left ²in the land. (23) And it shall come to pass in that day, *that* every place shall be, where there were a thousand vines at a thousand silverlings, it shall *even* be for briers and

¹ Or, *commendable trees.*

ᵃ 2 Kings 19. 35.

² Heb., *in the midst of the land.*

---

xvi. 9, xvii. 6), a fulfilment all the more remarkable in that it was preceded by what seemed an almost decisive victory over Judah (2 Chron. xxviii. 5—15), of which the prophet makes no mention.

(17) **The Lord shall bring upon thee . . .**—The prophet's language shows that he reads the secret thoughts of the king's heart. He was bent on calling in the help of the king of Assyria. Isaiah warns him (reserving the name of the king, with all the emphasis of suddenness, for the close of his sentence) that by so doing he is bringing on himself a more formidable invasion than that of Syria and Ephraim, worse than any that had been known since the separation of the two kingdoms (we note the use of the event as a chronological era), than that of Shishak under Rehoboam (2 Chron. xii. 2), or Zerah (2 Chron. xiv. 9), or of Baasha under Asa (2 Chron. xvi. 1), or of the Moabites and Ammonites under Jehoshaphat (2 Chron. xx. 1), or of the Philistines and Arabians under Jehoram (2 Chron. xxi. 16). So in 2 Chron. xxviii. 19, 20, we read that "the Lord brought Judah low and made it naked," that "Tilgath-pilneser, king of Assyria, came unto Ahaz and distressed him," and this was but the precursor of the great invasions under Sargon and Sennacherib.

(18) **The Lord shall hiss for the fly . . .**—See for the phrase the Note on chap. v. 26. The legions of Egypt are represented by the flies that swarmed on the banks of the Nile (Exod. viii. 24, and possibly Isa. xviii. 1), those of Assyria by the bees of their forests and their hills (Deut. i. 44; Ps. cxviii. 12). The mention of Egypt indicates that some of the king's counsellors were then, as afterwards (chaps. xviii. 2, xxxi. 1), planning an Egyptian alliance, as others were relying on that with Assyria. The prophet tells them that each is fraught with danger. No help and much evil would come from such plans. Consistent in his policy from first to last, the one counsel he gives is that men should practise righteousness, and wait upon the Lord.

The uttermost part of the rivers of Egypt.—The phrase points to the whole extent of the Delta of the Nile, probably to the whole Egyptian course of the Nile itself. Historically the prophecy found its fulfilment in the invasion of Pharaoh Necho in the reign of Josiah (2 Kings xxiii. 29), or, nearer Isaiah's time, in the movements of Tirhakah's arms (2 Kings xix. 9).

(19) **The desolate valleys . . .**—The Hebrew adjective has rather the meaning of *precipitous* or *steeply walled*, and the noun that of *torrent valley*, like the Arabic *wady*. The whole verse is a graphic description of the characteristic features of the scenery of Judah.

(20) **Shall the Lord shave with a razor that is hired.**—Better, "with *the* razor." The words find a parallel in the "made him naked" of 2 Chron. xxviii. 19. The term "hired" applies to the tribute which Ahaz was about to pay to Tilgath-pilneser. He thought that he was securing an ally: he was but hiring a razor (there is, perhaps, the implied thought that the razor is in other hands than his) that should sweep away all the signs of strength, and leave him an open shame and scorn to all who looked on him. (2 Sam. x. 4). From head to foot, not sparing even the beard, to maltreat which was the last extreme of Oriental outrage, he and his kingdom should be laid bare and naked to his enemies. Possibly there may be an allusive reference (Kay) to Lev. xiv. 9. The nation, leprous in its guilt (chap. i. 6), needs the treatment which was prescribed for the leper.

(21, 22) **A man shall nourish a young cow, and two sheep . . .**—Better, *two ewes.* Not only should cultivation cease, but the flocks and herds that had before been counted by hundreds or thousands should be counted now by units, two ewes and a heifer for a man's whole stock, and yet (we note the prophet's irony once more in the use of the word "abundance") even that should be enough for a population reduced in proportion. There should be "milk and honey" for the scattered remnant. They should have that, and nothing but that, to eat, *ad nauseam usque.* The words are grouped together with a grim irony as reminding men of the proverbial words of praise which spoke of Canaan as "a land of milk and honey" (Exod. iii. 17).

(23) **Where there were a thousand vines at a thousand silverlings.**—The words seem to contain an allusive reference to Song of Sol. viii. 11, and are therefore worth noting as bearing on the date of that book. There, however, the sum represents the annual produce of the vineyard, here the rent of the vines at a shekel each, a high rent apparently, and indicating a choice quality of vine. The costly vineyards of the hills of Judah should be left to run wild without a keeper (chap. v. 10), and thorns and briers would rapidly cover it. "Silverling" was an old English word for any silver coin, and appears in Tyndale's version of Acts xix. 19, and Coverdale's of Judg. ix. 4, xvi. 5; here it stands for "shekel." The modern rent is said to be a piastre (2¼d.) for each vine; the shekel was worth 2s. 3d. (Kay).

The Desolation of Judah. ISAIAH, VIII. *Birth of Speed-plunder, Haste-spoil.*

thorns. ⁽²⁴⁾ With arrows and with bows shall *men* come thither;¹ because all the land shall become briers and thorns. ⁽²⁵⁾ And *on* all hills that shall be digged with the mattock, there shall not come thither the fear of briers and thorns: but it shall be for the sending forth of oxen, and for the treading of lesser cattle.

¹ Heb., *in making speed to the spoil he hasteneth the prey, or, make speed, &c.*

B.C. cir. 742.

² Heb., *approached unto.*

CHAPTER VIII.—⁽¹⁾ Moreover the LORD said unto me, Take thee a great roll, and write in it with a man's pen concerning ¹ Maher-shalal-hash-baz. ⁽²⁾ And I took unto me faithful witnesses to record, Uriah the priest, and Zechariah the son of Jeberechiah. ⁽³⁾ And I ² went unto the prophetess; and she conceived, and bare a son. Then said

⁽²⁴⁾ **With arrows and with bows shall men come thither . . .**—The words admit of two or three distinct interpretations: (1) the invaders shall march through the desolate vineyards shooting down any whom they found, or (2) the people shall carry bows as a protection against the invaders, or (3) the thickets of thorns and briars shall become coverts for the wolves and jackals, the hyena and the bear, and men shall need bows and arrows for their protection against the beasts of prey. Of these (3) has most in its favour.

⁽²⁵⁾ **And on all hills that shall be digged . . .** —Better, "*that are digged,*" or *that used to be digged with the hoe.* The picture of devastation is completed. On the hill-sides, every inch of which was once brought under careful vine culture, "*Thou wilt not enter for fear of thorns and briars,*" i.e., thou wilt not venture on the task of tilling the soil in face of such disarrangements. What would be the use of hoeing such a tangled mass of brushwood? At the best it must be left for such pasturage as oxen and sheep might find there as they browsed, and they by their trampling should but increase the mischief. The rendering of the Authorised version conveys the thought that where there was the careful culture thus described, there should be an exception to the general desolation. Below this, if we accept it, there may be a spiritual meaning like that of Jer. iv. 3 (Kay).

VIII.

⁽¹⁾ **Moreover the Lord said unto me . . .**— The prophecy that follows was clearly separated by an interval of some kind, probably about a year, from that in chap. vii. In the meantime much that had happened seemed to cast discredit on the prophet's words. The child that was the type of the greater Immanuel had been born, but there were no signs as yet of the downfall of the northern kingdom. The attack of Rezin and Pekah, though Jerusalem had not been taken, had inflicted an almost irreparable blow on the kingdom of Judah. Multitudes had been carried captive to Damascus (2 Chron. xxviii. 5). Many thousands, but for the intercession of the prophet Oded, would have eaten the bread of exile and slavery. The Edomites were harassing the south-eastern frontier (2 Chron. xxviii. 15—17). The commerce of the Red Sea was cut off by Rezin's capture of Elath (2 Kings xvi. 6). To the weak and faithless Ahaz and his counsellors, it might well seem that the prospect was darker than ever, that there was no hope but in the protection of Assyria. If such was the state of things when the word of the Lord came to Isaiah, was he to recant and confess that he had erred? Was he to shrink back into silence and obscurity? Far otherwise than that. He was to repeat all that he had said, more definitely, more demonstratively than ever.

Take thee a great roll . . .—Better, *a large tablet.* The noun is the same as that used for "mirrors" or "glasses" in chap. iii. 23. The writings of the prophet were commonly written on papyrus and placed in the hands of his disciples to be read aloud. For private and less permanent messages men used small wooden tablets smeared with wax, on which they wrote with an iron stylus. (Comp. Job xix. 24; Isa. xxx. 8.) Here the tablet was to be large, and the writing was not to be with the sharp point of the artist or learned scribe, but with a "man's pen," i.e., such as the common workmen used for sign-boards, that might fix the gaze of the careless passer-by (Hab. ii. 2), and on that tablet, as though it were the heading of a proclamation or dedication, he was to write TO MAHER-SHALAL-HASH-BAZ. That mysterious name, which we may render "*Speed-plunder, haste-spoil,*" was, for at least nine months, to be the enigma of Jerusalem.

⁽²⁾ **And I took unto me faithful witnesses.**— That the prophet's challenge to his gainsayers might be made more emphatic, the setting-up of the tablet is to be formally attested. And the witnesses whom the prophet calls were probably men of high position, among those who had been foremost in advising the alliance with Assyria. Of Uriah or Urijah, the priest, we know that he complied with the king's desire to introduce an altar after the pattern which he had seen at Damascus (2 Kings xvi. 10, 11). Of Zechariah we know nothing; but the name was a priestly one (2 Chron. xxiv. 20), and it has been conjectured, from his association with Isaiah, that he may have been the writer of a section of the book that bears the name of a later Zechariah (Zech. ix.—xii.), which bears traces of being of a much earlier date than the rest of the book. The combination of "Zachariah, son of Jeberechiah" reminds us of Zacharias, the son of Barachias, and points to a priestly family. (See Note on Matt. xxiii. 35.) In 2 Chron. xxix. 13 the name appears as belonging to the Asaph section of the Levites. A more probable view is that he was identical with the father of the queen then reigning, and was therefore the grandfather of Hezekiah (2 Chron. xxix. 1). Probably, looking to the prophet's habit of tracing auguries in names, the two witnesses may have been partly chosen for the significance of those which they bore, Uriah, *i.e.,* "Jah is my light," Zechariah, *i.e.,* "Jah will remember," each of which comes in with a special appropriateness.

⁽³⁾ **I . . . the prophetess . . .**—The word may have been given by courtesy to a prophet's wife as such. Elsewhere, however, as in the case of Deborah (Judg. iv. 4) and Huldah (2 Chron. xxxiv. 22), it implies prophetic gifts. Possibly, therefore, we may think of the prophet and his wife as having been drawn together by united thoughts and counsels, in contrast with the celibate life of Jeremiah (Jer. xvi. 2), the miseries of Hosea's marriage (Hosea i., ii.), and the sudden bereavement of Ezekiel (Ezek. xxiv.

the LORD to me, Call his name Maher-shalal-hash-baz. (4) For before the child shall have knowledge to cry, My father, and my mother, ¹ the riches of Damascus and the spoil of Samaria shall be taken away before the king of Assyria.

(5) The LORD spake also unto me again, saying, (6) Forasmuch as this people refuseth the waters of Shiloah that go softly, and rejoice in Rezin and Remaliah's son; (7) now therefore, behold, the Lord bringeth up upon them the waters of the river, strong and many, *even* the king of Assyria, and all his glory: and he shall come up over all his channels, and go over all his banks: (8) and he shall pass through Judah; he shall overflow and go over, he shall reach *even* to the neck; and ² the stretching out of his wings shall fill the breadth of thy land, O Immanuel.

(9) Associate yourselves, O ye people, ³ and ye shall be broken in pieces; and give ear, all ye of far countries: gird yourselves, and ye shall be broken in pieces; gird yourselves, and ye shall be broken in pieces. (10) Take counsel together, and it shall come to nought; speak the word, and it shall not stand: for God *is* with us.

(11) For the LORD spake thus to me ⁴ with a strong hand, and instructed me

---

1 Or, *he that is before the king of Assyria shall take away the riches, &c.*

2 Heb., *the fulness of the breadth of thy land shall be the stretchings out of his wings.*

3 Or, *yet.*

4 Heb., *in strength of hand.*

16—18). We may, perhaps, trace, on this view, the wife's hand in the toilet inventory of chap. iii. 16—24.

(4) **For before the child shall have knowledge to cry . . .**—Here then was another sign like that of chap. vii. 14—16. The two witnesses of verse 2 were probably summoned to the circumcision and naming of the child, and the mysterious name at which all Jerusalem had gazed with wonder was given to the new-born infant. The prediction is even more definite than before. Before the first cries of childhood (Heb. *Abi, Ami*) should be uttered, *i.e.*, within a year of its birth, the spoils of the two capitals of the kings of the confederate armies should be carried to the king of Assyria. The conclusion of the period thus defined would coincide more or less closely with the longer period assigned at an earlier date (chap. vii. 16). Historically the trans-Jordanic region and Damascus fell before Tiglath-pilneser; Samaria, besieged by Salmaneser, before his successor Sargon (2 Kings xv. 29, xvi. 9, xvii. 6).

(6) **Forasmuch as this people refuseth the waters of Shiloah . . .**—Grammatically, the words "this people" might seem to refer to Judah, and suggest the thought that the tyranny of Ahaz had made him so unpopular that his subjects welcomed the invaders. On this view Ahaz sought the alliance with Tiglath-pilneser as against his own subjects no less than against Syria or Ephraim. He was as a Ferdinand of Naples falling back on Austria to protect him against Garibaldi and Victor Emmanuel. What line was the prophet to take? Was he to take the side of the king, or that of his rebellious subjects who were ready to sacrifice their independence? As it is, he sides with neither, and has a warning for each. Each is running blindly into destruction. The prophet could hardly have blamed the people of Syria and Israel for following their own kings; but it was for him a strange and monstrous thing that Judah should follow their example. We must remember, too, that in spite of the weakness and wickedness of Ahaz, the prophet's hopes rested on the house of David (chap. xi. 1), and that Hezekiah was already old enough to justify that hope. The "waters of Shiloah that go softly," issuing from the slope between Moriah and Zion, "fast by the oracles of God" (Ps. xlvi. 4; John ix. 7), presenting so striking a contrast to the great rivers, Nile, Euphrates, Hiddekel (Tigris), on which stood the capitals of great empires, or even to the Abana and Pharpar of Syria, and the Jordan of Ephraim, were a natural symbol of the ideal polity and religion of Judah.

(Comp. Ezek. xlvii. 1—5.) In acting as they did the people were practically apostatising as much as "that king Ahaz" of 2 Chron. xxviii. 22.

(7) **The waters of the river . . .**—"The river" is, as elsewhere (Josh. xxiv. 2, 14), the Euphrates; here used (1) as the symbol of the Assyrian monarchy, as Shiloah had been of that of Judah, and (2) of the Assyrian armies that were to pour down like that river in the time of its inundations. The "channels" and "banks" describe the intended course of that army as invading Syria and Israel; but it was to overflow those banks and sweep over Judah. In the former case, the kingdoms were to be utterly submerged as by the violence of the current. In Judah, it was to reach only "to the neck," *i.e.*, was not to work out so utter a destruction. Jeremiah (xlvii. 2) reproduces the image.

(8) **The stretching out of his wings.**—The metaphor within a metaphor is quite after the manner of Isaiah. The armies of Assyria are like a river in flood; the outspread waters on either side of the main stream are like the expanded wings of a great bird sweeping down on its prey.

Shall fill the breadth of thy land, O Immanuel.—The prophet has not forgotten, however, the *nomen et omen* of the earthly child, now growing towards the time when he would be able to "choose the good and refuse the evil." The land over which the flood sweeps belongs to Him who is, in very deed, "God with us." In Ps. xlvi. 1—4 we have the prophecy turned into a hymn, or, less probably, the hymn which was the germ of the prophecy. The parallelism, in any case, is so clear as to make it certain that the two were contemporary, and refer to the same events. The same may be said, perhaps, of all the psalms of the sons of Korah. The hope of the psalmist fastens on the thought, "the Lord of hosts is *with us*" (Ps. xlvi. 7, 11).

(9) **Associate yourselves, O ye people . . .**—Better, *O ye peoples.* The words are not limited to the confederacy of Syria and Ephraim, but are, as it were, a challenge to all the peoples of the earth, far and near. No plan against the Divine kingdom, of which the earthly kingdom of the house of David was, for the time, the representative, shall prosper. The prophet falls back once more on the abiding promise of the name Immanuel ("with us is God").

(11) **For the Lord spake thus to me.**—We enter on a new section, separated, probably, by a short interval of time, but dealing with the same subject. In the "strong hand" we have an anthropomorphic phrase,

that I should not walk in the way of this people, saying, (12) Say ye not, A confederacy, to all *them to* whom this people shall say, A confederacy; neither fear ye their fear, nor be afraid. (13) Sanctify the LORD of hosts himself; and *let* him *be* your fear, and *let* him *be* your dread. (14) And he shall be for a sanctuary; but for *a* stone of stumbling and for a rock of offence to both the houses of Israel, for a gin and for a snare to the inhabitants of Jerusalem. (15) And many among them shall *b* stumble, and fall, and be broken, and be snared, and be taken.

(16) Bind up the testimony, seal the law among my disciples. (17) And I will wait upon the LORD, that hideth

a ch. 28. 16; Luke 2. 34; Rom. 9. 33; 1 Pet. 2. 8.

b Matt. 21. 44; Luke 20. 18.

---

implying a specially high degree of the intensity of inspiration (1 Kings xviii. 46; 2 Kings iii. 15; Ezek. i. 3, iii. 14, 22, viii. 1, xxxvii. 1). Something had occurred which brought the prophet into a state like that of St. Paul in Acts xvii. 16, xviii. 5. Indignation and zeal were roused to their highest point, and were able to resist all human pressure from without. The result was a lesson which was to be specially impressed on the disciples who gathered round the prophet.

(12) **Say ye not, A confederacy . . .**—The words have been very differently interpreted. (1) The confederacy has been thought to be that between Syria or Ephraim, which had at first filled the people with terror, and then had seemed so powerful that men had been willing to join it (chaps. vii. 2, viii. 6). (2) Translating the word as *conspiracy* as in 2 Kings xvii. 4— it was the word used by Athaliah when she cried, "Treason, treason!" (2 Chron. xxiii. 13)—interpreters have seen in it the cry of the Assyrian alliance party against the prophet and his followers, whom they accused of conspiracy against their country, such as was afterwards imputed to Jeremiah (Jer. xxxvii. 14). (3) Others, following a conjectural amendment of the text, have read, "Ye shall not call everything a holy thing which this people calleth a holy thing," and find in the words a protest against the idolatrous reverence for that which has no real holiness, analogous to the warning against soothsayers or diviners in verse 19; or possibly an allusion to such an object of worship as the brazen serpent, which Hezekiah had destroyed by Isaiah's advice (2 Kings xviii. 4). Of these, (2) seems the most in harmony with the sequence of facts and thoughts.

(13) **Sanctify the Lord of hosts himself . . .**—The words contain an implicit appeal to the revelation of the Divine Name in chap. vi. 3. Had the prophet's disciples entered into the meaning of that "Holy, holy, holy, is the Lord of hosts?" Had they learnt to sanctify Jehovah Sabaoth, to recognise the power of that infinite holiness?

(14) **And he shall be for a sanctuary . . .**—Literally, *he shall become a hallowed thing*, with the implied thought as in Ezek. xi. 16, that the sanctuary is also an asylum (1 Kings i. 50, ii. 28). In that sanctuary, in the presence of Jehovah, there was a refuge from all terror, the answer to all misgivings (Ps. lxxiii. 17).

But for a stone of stumbling and for a rock of offence . . .—The words have become so familiar to us through their Christian application (Matt. xxi. 44; Rom. ix. 33; 1 Pet. ii. 8) that we find it hard to measure their force and meaning as they came from Isaiah's lips. Are the contrasted clauses connected by any common link of imagery? To enter into fellowship with Jehovah, is to enter into the sanctuary. He who stands on the stone which forms the threshold of that sanctuary, has gained an asylum. But to do that requires the clear vision of faith. He who walks blindly (chap. vi. 10; John xi. 10), without faith, may stumble on that very stone of the threshold, and what was safety and life for others, might for him bring pain and shame. He might be there sorely bruised (Matt. xxi. 44) like the wild animals taken in a trap (synonyms are heaped one upon another to increase the force of the imagery), till a helper came to release him. So, Isaiah says, was Jehovah "to both the houses of Israel" (the phrase is peculiar, and implies a hope of the restored unity of the nation's life) in their self-chosen blindness. So St. Peter says, even the head corner-stone is to those who "stumble at the word, being disobedient" a "stone of stumbling and a rock of offence" (1 Pet. ii. 8). It lies in the nature of the case that the fall is not necessarily final and irretrievable. Men may be bruised, but not "ground to powder;" may "stumble" so that they may rise again (Matt. xxi. 44; Luke ii. 34; Rom. xi. 11).

(15) **And many among them shall stumble, and fall . . .**—The accumulation of words more or less synonymous has obviously, as before, the emphasis of iteration. Possibly for the prophet and his disciples, each word had a distinct ethical significance, which we can only partially recover. Looking to the figure implied in verse 14, they seem to describe the several stages of the capture of the animal for whom the trap has been laid. It first stumbles, then falls into the pit, and breaks its limbs, then is fastened in the trap, and is powerless to escape.

(16) **Bind up the testimony . . .**—The intensity of feeling in which the prophetic utterance of verses 11—15 had its birth, is followed by a corresponding solemnity at its close. The words which had been so full of meaning for the prophet himself are to be impressed on the disciples of Jehovah (for it is He who speaks), *i.e.*, on those who looked to Isaiah as their guide and counsellor. They are to be written on a parchment roll, as men wrote the sacred Book of the Law; the roll is to be sealed up, partly as a security against its being tampered with, till the time came for its disclosure (Dan. xii. 4), partly as an attestation, like the seal of a king's letter (1 Kings xxi. 8; Esth. iii. 12), that it was authentic. The two terms "testimony" (Deut. viii. 19; Pss. l. 7, cxix. 2) and "law" are here taken in their wider sense as applicable to any revelation of the mind of God. The "law of the Lord" of Pss. xix. 7, cxix. 1 was wider and higher than the Pentateuchal code.

(17) **And I will wait upon the Lord, that hideth his face . . .**—The words come in somewhat abruptly, but not to the extent that justifies the assumption of some critics that a verse has been lost. The prophet enforces precept by example. He has learnt to conquer the feverish desire to know the future, which led men to trust in soothsayers and diviners, and from which even his own disciples were

Isaiah and his Children as Signs. ISAIAH, VIII. *Familiar Spirits, or the Living God.*

his face from the house of Jacob, and I will look for him. ⁽¹⁸⁾ ^aBehold, I and the children whom the LORD hath given me *are* for signs and for wonders in Israel from the LORD of hosts, which dwelleth in mount Zion.

⁽¹⁹⁾ And when they shall say unto you, Seek unto them that have familiar spirits, and unto wizards that peep, and that mutter: should not a people seek unto their God? for the living to the dead? ⁽²⁰⁾ ^bTo the law and to the testimony: if they speak not according to this word, *it is because there is* ¹no light in them. ⁽²¹⁾ And they shall pass through it, hardly bestead and hungry: and it shall come to pass, that when they shall be hungry, they shall fret

a Heb. 2. 13.

b Luke 16. 29.

¹ Heb., *no morning.*

---

not altogether exempt. He is content to "wait," even though Jehovah "hide His face," though predictions seem to fail (see Note on verse 1), and all seems dark and hopeless. There is, perhaps, a contrast between the fact that Jehovah hides His face from the house of Jacob, that all is dark for the nation's life as such, while yet the prophet, in his own individuality, can "look for Him" with the eye of faith.

⁽¹⁸⁾ **Behold, I and the children whom the Lord hath given me . . .**—In the mystic significance of his own name (Isaiah—*Salvation of Jehovah*) and of the names of his sons: *Remnant shall return,* and *Speed-plunder, Haste-spoil,* possibly also in that of Immanuel, the prophet finds a sufficient revelation of the future. Each was a *nomen et omen* for those who had ears to hear. Could the disciples of Isaiah complain that they had no light thrown upon the future, when, so to say, they had those embodied prophecies? The children disappear from the scene, and we know nothing of their after-history, but all their life long, even with or without a special prophetic work, they must have been, by virtue of their names, witnesses to a later generation, of what Isaiah had predicted. In Isaiah's own life, as including symbolic acts as well as prophetic words (chap. xx. 2), we have a further development of the thought that he was "a sign and a wonder." (Comp. Ezek. xii. 11.) The citation of the words, "I and the children whom thou hast given me," in Heb. ii. 13, is noticeable here chiefly as showing how little the writer of that Epistle cared in this and other quotations for the original meaning of the words as determined by the context. It was enough for him that the Christ, like the prophet, did not stand alone, but claimed a fellowship with the children whom the Father had given him (John xvii. 6, 12), as being alike servants and children of God, called to do His will.

⁽¹⁹⁾ **And when they shall say unto you . . .**—This then was the temptation to which the disciples of Isaiah were exposed, and to which they were all but yielding. Why should not they do as others did, and consult the soothsayers, who were in such great demand (chap. ii. 6), as to the anxious secrets of the coming years. The words point to some of the many forms of such soothsaying (Deut. xviii. 10). The "familiar spirit" (the English term being a happy paraphrase rather than a translation), is closely connected, as in the case of the witch of Endor (1 Sam. xxviii. 1—20), with the idea of necromancy, *i.e.,* with the claim to have a demon or spirit of divination (Acts xvi. 16), on the part of the wizards (comp. Hom. *Il.,* xxiii. 10; Virg. *Æn.,* vi. 492) that "peep" (old English for "pipe," "chirp," "whisper") "and mutter." This peculiar intonation, thrilling each nerve with a sense of expectant awe, seems to have been characteristic of the soothsayers of Isaiah's time (chap. xxix. 4).

Should not a people seek unto their God? . . .—That, the prophet says, is the only true pathway to such knowledge as is good for man. The latter part of the question is abruptly elliptical: *Are men to seek on behalf of the living to the dead?* What ground, he seems to ask, have we for thinking that the spirits of the dead can be recalled to earth, or, if that were possible, that they know more than the living do? May it not even be that they know less? The prophet views the state of the departed as Hezekiah views it (chap. xxxviii. 18), as one, not of annihilation, but of dormant or weakened powers.

⁽²⁰⁾ **To the law and to the testimony.**—The words are only remotely and by analogy an exhortation to the study of Scripture in general, or even to that of the Law of Moses in particular. "The law and the testimony" are obviously here, as in verse 16, the "word of Jehovah," spoken to the prophet himself, the revelation which had come to him with such an intensity of power.

If they speak not according to this word . . .—The personal pronoun refers to the people of verse 19 who were hunting after soothsayers. The second clause should be rendered, *for them there is no light of morning.* The light here is that of hope rather than of knowledge. No morning dawn should shine on those who haunted the caves and darkened rooms of the diviners, the *séances* of the spiritualists of Jerusalem. The verse admits, however, of a different construction. As the Hebrew idiom, "If they shall . . ." stands, as in Ps. xcv. 11; Heb. iv. 3, 5, for the strongest form of negative prediction, so "if they shall not . . ." may stand here for the strongest form of positive. So taken the verse would read, *Surely they will speak according to this word* (*i.e.,* will have recourse to the true Revelation) *when there is no morning-dawn for them,* when they look above and around, and see nothing but darkness.

⁽²¹⁾ **And they shall pass through it . . .**—*i.e.,* through the land over which hangs the sunless gloom. The abruptness with which the verse opens, the absence of any noun to which the pronoun "it" may refer, has led some critics (Cheyne) to transpose the two verses. So arranged, the thought of the people for whom there is no dawning passes naturally into the picture of their groping in that thick darkness, and then the misery of that midnight wandering is aggravated by the horrors of starvation. The words may point to the horrors of a literal famine (chap. ii. 11); but as the darkness is clearly figurative, so probably is the hunger—not a famine of bread, but of hearing the word of the Lord. The Authorised version rightly translates the indefinite singular by the plural.

When they shall be hungry, they shall fret themselves.—The faithful who waited for the Lord might bear even that darkness and that hunger, as soldiers bear their night-march fasting before the battle. Not so with the panic-stricken and superstitious crowd. With them despair would show itself in curses. (Comp.

Trouble and Darkness. ISAIAH, IX. *Light and Joy.*

themselves, and curse their king and their God, and look upward. (22) And they shall look unto the earth; and behold trouble and darkness, dimness of anguish; and *they shall be* driven to darkness.

CHAPTER IX.—(1) Nevertheless the dimness *shall* not *be* such as *was* in her vexation, when at the first he lightly afflicted the land of Zebulun and the land of Naphtali, and afterward did more grievously afflict *her by* the way of the sea, beyond Jordan, in Galilee ¹of the nations.

(2) ᵃ The people that walked in darkness have seen a great light: they that dwell in the land of the shadow of death, upon them hath the light shined. (3) Thou hast multiplied the nation, *and* ²not increased the joy: they joy before thee according to the joy in harvest,

1 Or, *populous.*

a Matt. 4. 16; Eph. 5. 14.

2 Or, *to him.*

Rev. xvi. 11, 21.) They would curse at once the king who had led them to destruction, and the God whom they had neglected. Possibly the words may mean, "the king who is also their God," as in Amos v. 26 (Heb.) and Zeph. i. 5; but the analogy of 1 Kings xxi. 13 is in favour of the more literal meaning. The "upward" look is, we must remember, that of despair and defiance, not of hope. Upwards, downwards, behind, before, there is nothing for them but the darkness in which they are driven, or drifting onward. All seems utterly hopeless. Like Dante, they find themselves in a land "where silent is the sun."

IX.

(1) **Nevertheless the dimness . . .**—It is obvious, even in the English version, that the chapters are wrongly divided, and that what follows forms part of the same prophetic utterance as chap. viii. That version is, however, so obscure as to be almost unintelligible, and requires an entire remodelling:—*Surely there is no gloom to her that was afflicted. In the former time he brought shame on the land of Zebulun and the land of Naphtali; but in the latter he bringeth honour on the way by the sea, beyond Jordan, the circuit of the Gentiles.*

The prophet had seen in the closing verses of chap. viii. the extreme point of misery. That picture, as it were, dissolves, and another takes its place. She that was afflicted, the whole land of Israel, should have no more affliction. The future should be in striking contrast with the past. The lands of Zebulun and Naphtali, the region afterwards known as the Upper and Lower Galilee, had been laid waste and spoiled by Tiglath-pilneser (2 Kings xv. 29). That same region, described by the prophet in different terms (the former representing the tribal divisions, the latter the geographical) is hereafter to be the scene of a glory greater than Israel had ever known before.

The way of the sea . . .—The context shows that the "sea" is that which appears in Bible history under the names of the sea of Chinnereth (Num. xxxiv. 11; Deut. iii. 17), the Sea of Galilee, the Sea of Tiberias (John vi. 1), Gennesaret (Mark vi. 53). The high road thence to Damascus was known as *Via Maris* in the time of the Crusaders (Renan, quoted by Cheyne).

Beyond Jordan.—This, the Peræa of later geography, included the regions of Gilead and Bashan, the old kingdoms of Moab and Ammon, the tribes of Reuben, Gad, and half the tribe of Manasseh. These also had suffered from the ravages of the Assyrian armies under Pul (1 Chron. v. 26).

Galilee of the nations.—The word Galilee, derived from the same root as Gilgal (Josh. v. 9), means strictly "a circle," or "circuit." It was applied to the border-lands of the Phœnician frontier of the northern kingdom, inhabited by a mixed population, and therefore known as "Galilee of the Gentiles" (Matt. iv. 15, 16) what in mediæval German would have been called the *Heidenmark.*

(2) **The people that walked in darkness . . .** —The words throw us back upon chap. viii. 21, 22. The prophet sees in his vision a light shining on the forlorn and weary wanderers. They had been wandering in the "valley of the shadow of death" (the phrase comes from Ps. xxiii. 4; Job iii. 5), almost as in the gloom of Sheol itself. Now there breaks in the dawn of a glorious day. Historically the return of some of the inhabitants of that region to their allegiance to Jehovah and the house of David (2 Chron. xxx. 11, 13) may have been the starting point of the prophet's hopes. The words have to the Christian student a special interest, as having been quoted by St. Matthew (Matt. iv. 15, 16) in connection with our Lord's ministry in Galilee, perhaps with His being "of Nazareth," which was in the tribe of Zebulun. We cannot positively say that such a fulfilment as that was in the prophet's thoughts. The context shows in that he was thinking of Assyrian invasions, and the defeat of Assyrian armies, of a nation growing strong in numbers and prosperity. In this, as in other cases, the Evangelist adapts the words of prophecy to a further meaning than that which apparently was in the mind of the writer, and interprets them by his own experience. When he compared the state of Galilee, yet more, perhaps, that of his own soul, before and after the Son of man had appeared as the light of the world, Isaiah's words seemed the only adequate expression of the change.

(3) **Thou hast multiplied the nation, and not increased the joy. . .**—Better, following the marginal reading of the Hebrew: *Thou hast increased its joy.* The picture is one of unmingled brightness; the return as of a golden age, the population growing to an extent never attained before (comp. chap. xxvi. 15; Jer. xxxi. 27; Ezek. xxxvi. 11), and scarcely admits of the dark shadow introduced by the reading of the text, unless, with some critics (Kay), we see in the words a contrast between the outward prosperity of the days of Solomon and Uzziah, in which there was no permanent joy, and the abundancy of joyfulness under the ideal king.

They joy before thee according to the joy in harvest. . .—The words "before thee" are significant. The gladness of the people is that of worshippers at a sacrificial feast (chap. xxv. 6; Deut. xii. 7, 12, 18), who find the secret spring of blessing in their consciousness of the presence of Jehovah. So the New Testament writers speak of "rejoicing in the Lord" (Phil. iii. 1), of "joy in the Holy Ghost" (Rom. xiv. 17). This "joy of harvest" represents the peaceful side of that gladness, thought of as the gift of God (Acts xiv. 17). But it

The Yoke of the Oppressor Broken. ISAIAH, IX. *The Coming of the Prince of Peace.*

and as *men* rejoice when they divide the spoil. (4) ¹ For thou hast broken the yoke of his burden, and the staff of his shoulder, the rod of his oppressor, as in the day of ᵃMidian. (5) ² For every battle of the warrior *is* with confused noise, and garments rolled in blood;

1 Or, *When thou brakest.*
a Judg. 7. 22; ch. 10. 26.
2 Or, *When the whole battle of the warrior was,* &c.
3 Or, *and it was,* &c.
4 Heb., *meat.*
b John 3. 16.

³ but *this* shall be with burning *and* ⁴fuel of fire. (6) For unto us a child is born, unto us a ᵇson is given: and the government shall be upon his shoulder: and his name shall be called Wonderful, Counsellor, The mighty God, The everlasting Father, The Prince of Peace.

---

had another aspect. It was the rejoicing after a conflict, historically with foes like the Assyrians, spiritually with all powers hostile to the true kingdom of God (Matt. xii. 29). The joy of the conquerors on the battle-field, like that of harvest, had become proverbial (Ps. cxix. 162).

(4) **For thou hast broken the yoke of his burden** . . .—The text comes in the Hebrew with all the emphasis of position. *The yoke of his burden . . . thou hast broken.* The phrase suggests a bondage like that of Egypt, where the "task-masters" (the same word as that here rendered "oppressors") drove the people to their labours with their rods.

As in the day of Midian.—The historical allusion was probably suggested by the division of spoil that had been in the prophet's thoughts. Of all victories in the history of Israel, that of Gideon over the Midianites had been most conspicuous for this feature (Judges viii. 24—27). In Ps. lxxxiii. 9—11 (which the mention of Assur shows to have been nearly contemporary with Isaiah) we find a reference to the same battle. Men remembered "the day of Midian" centuries after its date, as we remember Poitiers and Agincourt.

(5) **For every battle of the warrior** . . .—Here again the whole verse requires re-translating: "*Every boot of the warrior that tramps noisily, and the cloak rolled in blood, are* (i.e., shall be) *for burning,* (as) *fuel for fire.* The picture of the conquerors collecting the spoil is continued from verse 3. The victory is decisive, and the reign of peace begins, and the weapons of war, the garments red with blood (chap. lxiii. 1—3), the heavy boot that makes the earth ring with the warrior's tread, these shall all be burnt up. Like pictures of a time of peace are found in Zech. ix. 10; Ezek. xxxix, 9; Ps. xlvi. 9, lxxvi. 3.

(6) **For unto us a child is born.**—The picture of a kingdom of peace could not be complete without the manifestation of a king. In the description of that king Isaiah is led to use words which cannot find a complete fulfilment in any child of man. The loftiness of thought, rising here as to its highest point, is obviously connected with the words which told that Jehovah had spoken to the prophet "with a strong hand." His condition was one more ecstatic and therefore more apocalyptic than before, and there flashes on him, as it were, the thought that the future deliverer of Israel must bear a name that should be above every name that men had before honoured. And yet here also there was a law of continuity, and the form of the prediction was developed from the materials supplied by earlier prophets. In Ps. cx. he had found the thought of the king-priest after the order of Melchizedek, whom Jehovah addressed as Adonai. In Ps. ii., though it did not foretell an actual incarnation, the anointed King was addressed by Jehovah as His Son. The throne of that righteous king was as a throne of God (Ps. xlv. 6). Nor had the prophet's personal experience been less fruitfully suggestive. He had given his own children mysterious names. That of the earthly Immanuel,

as the prophet brooded over it, might well lead on to the thought of One who should, in a yet higher sense than as being the pledge of Divine protection, be as "God with us." Even the earthly surroundings of the prophet's life may not have been without their share of suggestiveness. The kings of Egypt and Assyria with whom his nation had been brought into contact delighted in long lists of epithetic names (*e.g.,* "the great king, the king unrivalled, the protector of the just, the noble warrior." Inscription of Sennacherib, in *Records of the Past,* i. p. 25), describing their greatness and their glory. It was natural that the prophet should see in the king of whom he thought as the future conqueror of all the world-powers that were founded on might and not on right, One who should bear a name formed, it might be, after that fashion, but full of a greater majesty and glory.

His name shall be called Wonderful.—It is noticeable that that which follows is given not as many names, but one. Consisting as it does of eight words, of which the last six obviously fall into three couplets, it is probable that the first two should also be taken together, and that we have four elements of the compound name: (1) *Wonderful-Counsellor,* (2) *God-the-Mighty-One,* (3) *Father of Eternity,* (4) *Prince of Peace.* Each element of the Name has its special significance. (1) The first embodies the thought of the wisdom of the future Messiah. Men should not simply praise it as they praise their fellows, but should adore and wonder at it as they wonder at the wisdom of God (Judges xiii. 18, where the Hebrew for the "secret" of the Authorised version is the same as that for "wonderful;" Exod. xv. 11; Pss. lxxvii. 11, lxxviii. 11; Isa. xxviii. 29, xxix. 14). The name contains the germ afterwards developed in the picture of the wisdom of the true king in chap. xi. 2—4. The LXX. renders the Hebrew as "the angel of great counsel," and in the Vatican text the description ends there. (2) It is significant that the word for "God" is not Elohim, which may be used in a lower sense for those who are representatives of God, as in Exod. vii. 1, xxii. 28, 1 Sam. xxviii. 13, but *El,* which is never used by Isaiah, or any other Old Testament writer, in any lower sense than that of absolute Deity, and which, we may note, had been specially brought before the prophet's thoughts in the name Immanuel. The name appears again as applied directly to Jehovah in chap. x. 21; Deut. x. 17; Jer. xxxii. 18; Neh. ix. 32; Ps. xxiv. 8; and the adjective in chap. xlii. 13. (3) In " Father of Eternity," (LXX. Alex. and Vulg., " Father of the age to come ") we have a name which seems at first to clash with the formalised developments of Christian theology, which teach us, lest we should "confound the persons," not to deal with the names of the Father and the Son as interchangeable. Those developments, however, were obviously not within Isaiah's ken, and he uses the name of "Father" because none other expressed so well the true idea of loving and protecting government (Job xxix. 16, Isa. xxii. 21). And if the kingdom was to be "for ever and ever," then in some very real

The Kingdom of Righteousness. ISAIAH, IX *The Pride of Ephraim.*

⁽⁷⁾ Of the increase of *his* government and peace *^athere shall be* no end, upon the throne of David, and upon his kingdom, to order it, and to establish it with judgment and with justice from henceforth even for ever. The ^bzeal of the LORD of hosts will perform this.

⁽⁸⁾ The Lord sent a word into Jacob, and it hath lighted upon Israel. ⁽⁹⁾ And all the people shall know, *even* Ephraim and the inhabitant of Samaria, that say in the pride and stoutness of heart, ⁽¹⁰⁾ The bricks are fallen down, but we will build with hewn stones: the sycomores are cut down, but we will change *them into* cedars. ⁽¹¹⁾ Therefore the LORD shall set up the adversaries of Rezin against him, and ¹join his enemies together; ⁽¹²⁾ the Syrians before, and the Philistines behind; and they shall devour Israel ²with open mouth.

^cFor all this his anger is not turned away, but his hand *is* stretched out still.

⁽¹³⁾ For the people turneth not unto him that smiteth them, neither do they

a Luke 1. 32, 33.

b 2 Kings 19. 31; ch. 37. 32.

1 Heb., *mingle.*

2 Heb., *with whole mouth.*

c ch. 5. 25, & 10. 4.

---

sense he would be, in that attribute of Fatherly government, a sharer in the eternity of Jehovah. Another rendering of the name, adopted by some critics, "Father (*i.e.*, Giver) of booty," has little to recommend it, and is entirely out of harmony with the majesty of the context. (4) "Prince of Peace." The prophet clings, as all prophets before him had done, to the thought that peace, and not war, belonged to the ideal Kingdom of the Messiah. That hope had been embodied by David in the name of Absalom ("father of peace") and Solomon. It had been uttered in the prayer of Ps. lxxii. 3, and by Isaiah's contemporary, Micah (v. 5). Earth-powers, like Assyria and Egypt, might rest in war and conquest as an end, but the true king, though warfare might be needed to subdue his foes (Ps. xlv. 5), was to be a "Prince of Peace" (Zech. ix. 9, 10). It must be noted as remarkable, looking to the grandeur of the prophecy, and its apparently direct testimony to the true nature of the Christ, that it is nowhere cited in the New Testament as fulfilled in Him; and this, though verse 1 is, as we have seen, quoted by St. Matthew and verse 7, finds at least an allusive reference in Luke i. 32, 33.

(7) **Of the increase . . .**—Better, "*For the increase of the government, and for peace with no end . . .*" The "throne of David," though in harmony with the whole body of prophetic tradition as to the Messiah, may be noted as the first appearance of that tradition in Isaiah.

Henceforth even for ever.—The words admit, as in the parallels of Pss. xxi. 4, lxi. 6, 7; 2 Sam. vii. 12—16, of being interpreted of the perpetuity of the dynasty of which the anointed king is to be the founder; but the "Everlasting Father" of the context, and the parallels of Pss. xlv. 6, cx. 4, are in favour of its referring to a personal immortality of sovereignty.

The zeal of the Lord of hosts will perform . . .—As in Greek so in Hebrew, we have the same root-word and root-idea for "zeal" and "jealousy," and here, perhaps, the latter thought is dominant. It is because Jehovah loves the daughter of Zion with an absorbing love that He purposes such great things for her future, and that what He purposes will be assuredly performed. (Comp. Ezek. v. 13.)

(8) **The Lord sent a word into Jacob . . .** —For "hath lighted" read *it lighteth.* A new section, though still closely connected with the historical occasion of chap. vii., begins. The vision of the glory of the far-off king comes to an end, and the prophet returns to the more immediate surroundings of his time. The "word" which Jehovah sends is the prophetic message that follows. It is a question whether the terms "Jacob" and "Israel" stand in the parallelism of identity or contrast, but the use of the former term in chap. ii. 3, 5, 6, makes the former use more probable. In this case both names stand practically for the kingdom of Judah as the true representative of Israel, the apostate kingdom of the Ten Tribes being no longer worthy of the name, and therefore described here, as in chap. vii. 5, 8, 17, simply as Ephraim. The occasion of the prophecy is given in verse 9. Pekah, the king of Ephraim, was still confident in his strength, and in spite of his partial failure, and the defeat of his ally (2 Kings xvi. 9), derided the prophet's prediction.

(10) **The bricks are fallen down . . .**—Sundried bricks and the cheap timber of the sycamore (1 Kings x. 27) were the common materials used for the dwellings of the poor, hewn stones and cedar for the palaces of the rich. Whatever injury Samaria had sustained (the words are too proverbially figurative to make literal interpretation probable), through the intervention of Tiglath-pileser, was, its rulers thought, but as the prelude to a great and more lasting victory even than that of 2 Chron. xxviii. 6.

(11) **Therefore the Lord shall set up the adversaries . . .**—The Hebrew tenses are in the past (*has set up*), but probably as representing the prophet's visions of an accomplished future. The "adversaries" of the text can hardly be any other than the Assyrians; yet the context that follows clearly points to an attack on Ephraim in which the armies of Rezin were to be conspicuous. The natural explanation is that Syria, after the conquest by the Assyrian king (2 Kings xvi. 9), was compelled to take part in a campaign against Samaria. The reading of the text may be retained with this explanation, and the sentence paraphrased thus, "Jehovah will stir up the adversaries of Rezin (the Assyrians who have conquered Syria) against him (Ephraim and the inhabitant of Samaria), and shall join his enemies against him, and those enemies shall include the very nations on whose support he had counted, the Syrians and the Philistines" (Ps. lxxxiii. 7, 8). The latter people were, it is true, enemies to Judah (2 Chron. xxviii. 18), but their hostilities extended to the northern kingdom also.

(12) **For all this his anger is not turned away . . .**—The formula which in chap. v. 25 had been applied to Judah is here and in verses 17, 21 used of Israel at large, and specially of Ephraim. It embodied the law which governed God's dealing with both.

(13) **For the people turneth not . . .**—What follows was the word that was meant for all Israel.

446

The Branch and Rush Cut off.   ISAIAH, X.   *The Land Darkened.*

seek the LORD of hosts. ⁽¹⁴⁾ Therefore the LORD will cut off from Israel head and tail, branch and rush, in one day. ⁽¹⁵⁾ The ancient and honourable, he *is* the head; and the prophet that teacheth lies, he *is* the tail. ⁽¹⁶⁾ For ¹the leaders of this people cause *them* to err; and ²*they that are* led of them *are* ³destroyed. ⁽¹⁷⁾ Therefore the Lord shall have no joy in their young men, neither shall have mercy on their fatherless and widows: for every one *is* an hypocrite and an evildoer, and every mouth speaketh ⁴folly.

For all this his anger is not turned away, but his hand *is* stretched out still.

⁽¹⁸⁾ For wickedness burneth as the fire: it shall devour the briers and thorns, and shall kindle in the thickets of the forest, and they shall mount up *like* the lifting up of smoke. ⁽¹⁹⁾ Through the wrath of the LORD of hosts is the land darkened, and the people shall be as the ⁵fuel of the fire: no man shall spare his brother. ⁽²⁰⁾ And he shall ⁶snatch on the right hand, and be hungry; and he shall eat on the left hand, and they shall not be satisfied: they shall eat every man the flesh of his own arm: ⁽²¹⁾ Manasseh, Ephraim; and Ephraim, Manasseh: *and* they together *shall be* against Judah.

For all this his anger is not turned away, but his hand *is* stretched out still.

CHAPTER X.—⁽¹⁾ Woe unto them that decree unrighteous decrees, and ⁷that write grievousness *which* they have

---

Marginal notes:
1 Or, *they that call them blessed.*
2 Or, *they that are called blessed of them.*
3 Heb., *swallowed up.*
4 Or, *villainy.*
B.C. cir. 738.
5 Heb., *meat.*
6 Heb., *cut.*
7 Or, *to the writers that write grievousness.*

They had not "turned" to the Lord, there were no proofs of that conversion which true prophets and preachers have at all times sought after.

⁽¹⁴⁾ **Head and tail, branch and rush . . .**—The "branch" is strictly that of the palm-tree, which in its stately height answered to the nobles of the land, while the "rush," the emblem of a real or affected lowliness (chap. lviii. 5) represented the "mean man" of chap. ii. 9. The same proverbial formula meets us in chap. xix. 15.

⁽¹⁵⁾ **The ancient and honourable . . .**—Comp. chap. iii. 2, 3, for the meaning of the words. These, the prophet seems to say, were the true leaders of the people. The ideal work of the prophet was, indeed, that of a teacher who was to lead even them, but *corruptio optimi pessima;* and to Isaiah, as to Jeremiah, there was no class so contemptible and base as that of spiritual guides whose policy was that of a time-serving selfishness. The verse is rejected by some critics as a marginal note that has found its way into the text; but the prophet may well have given his own interpretation of this formula. (Comp. chap. xxviii. 7, xxix. 10; Jer. xiv. 14, xxiii. 9—40.)

⁽¹⁷⁾ **Therefore the Lord shall have no joy. . .**—The Hebrew tenses are in the past, *The Lord had no joy.* The severity of the coming judgment is represented as not sparing even the flower of the nation's youth, the widows and orphans who were the special objects of compassion both to God and man. The corruption of the time was universal, and the prophet's formula, "For all this his anger is not turned away . . ." tolls again like the knell of doom.

Folly.—Better, *blasphemy* or *villainy.*

⁽¹⁸⁾ **It shall devour the briers and thorns . . .**—The words are obviously figurative for men who were base and vile, as in 2 Sam. xxiii. 6; but the figure may have been suggested by chap. vii. 23, 24. The outward desolation, with its rank growth of underwood, was to the prophet's eye a type of the moral condition of his people. And for such a people sin becomes the punishment of sin, and burns like a fire in a forest thicket, leaving the land clear for fresh culture and a better growth. (Comp. chap. xxxiii. 11, 12; Jas. iii. 5; Heb. vi. 8.)

⁽¹⁹, ²⁰⁾ **Through the wrath of the Lord of hosts is the land darkened . . .**—The vision of darkness and famine which had come before the prophet's eyes in chap. viii. 21 appears once again, and here, as there, it is a question whether the words are to be understood literally or figuratively. The definiteness of the language of verse 20 suggests the thoughts of the horrors of a famine like that of Samaria (2 Kings vi. 28, 29), or of Deut. xxviii. 53—57; Zech. xi. 9. But even that scene of horror might be only typical of a state of chaos and confusion pervading the whole order of society, fierce passions, jealousies, rivalries working out the destruction of the nation's life; such as Thucydides (iii. 82—84) has painted as the result of the Peloponnesian war. The mention of Ephraim and Manasseh as conspicuous in the self-destructive work confirms the figurative interpretation. They were devouring "the flesh of their own arm" when they allowed their old tribal jealousies (Judg. viii. 1, xii. 1—4; 2 Sam. xix. 43) to break up the unity of the nation.

And they together shall be against Judah.—This formed the climax of the whole. The only power of union that showed itself in the northern kingdom was to perpetuate the great schism in which it had its origin. The idea that Israel as such was a nation was forgotten. Ephraim and Manasseh could join in a common expedition against Judah when they could join in nothing else. Of this the alliance of Pekah with Rezin was the most striking instance (2 Chron. xxviii. 6—15). Traces of internal division are found in the conspiracy of the Gileadites of the trans-Jordanic district of Manasseh, against Pekah's predecessor in Samaria (2 Kings xv. 25).

X.

⁽¹⁾ **Woe unto them that decree unrighteous decrees . . .**—The division of the chapters is again misleading. Verses 1—4 continue the discourse of chap. ix., and end with the final knell, "For all this . . ." With verse 5 a new section begins, and is carried on to chap. xii. 6, which deals, for the first time in the collection of Isaiah's writings, exclusively with Assyria, and is followed in its turn by utterances that deal with Babylon and other nations. The formula

prescribed; (2) to turn aside the needy from judgment, and to take away the right from the poor of my people, that widows may be their prey, and *that* they may rob the fatherless! (3) And what will ye do in the day of visitation, and in the desolation *which* shall come from far? to whom will ye flee for help? and where will ye leave your glory? (4) Without me they shall bow down under the prisoners, and they shall fall under the slain.

a For all this his anger is not turned away, but his hand *is* stretched out still.

(5) ¹O ²Assyrian, the rod of mine anger, ³and the staff in their hand is mine indignation. (6) I will send him against an hypocritical nation, and against the people of my wrath will I give him a charge, to take the spoil, and to take the prey, and ⁴to tread them down like the mire of the streets.

(7) Howbeit he meaneth not so, neither doth his heart think so; but *it is* in his heart to destroy and cut off nations not

a ch. 5. 25, & 9. 12.

1 Or, *Woe to the Assyrian.*

2 Heb., *Asshur.*

3 Or, *though.*

4 Heb., *to lay them a treading.*

---

with which the section opens reminds us of that of chap. v. 8, 11, 18, 22, and suggests the thought that the prophet is speaking not only or chiefly of the northern kingdom, as in chap. ix. 21, but of Israel as including Judah. The evils the prophet denounces are, it will be noted, identical with those in chaps. i. 23, v. 23. For the second clause of the verse, read, "*and the scribes who register oppression.*" All the formalities of justice were observed punctiliously. The decision of the unjust judge was duly given and recorded, but the outcome of it all was that the poor, the widow, and the fatherless got no redress. The words for "prey" and "rob" are those used in the mysterious name of chap. viii. 1. They occur again in verse 6. It would seem as if the prophet sought in this way to impress the thought of the great law of divine retribution. Men were reaping as they had sown.

(3) **And what will ye do in the day of visitation . . . ?**—The question was not without a certain touch of irony. Had those corrupt judges asked themselves what they would do when the Supreme Judge should call them to account? Had they an ally who could protect them against Jehovah? Or had they found a hiding-place for the treasures which they had made their "glory"? Had they made a covenant with Hades and with death? (chap. xxviii. 18).

(4) **Without me they shall bow down . . .**—The Hebrew text is obscure, but these words were probably intended as the answer to the taunting question that had preceded them. Dropping the direct address, and passing to the third person, the prophet seems to say as with a kind of ominous "aside," "No, there is no ally, no hiding-place but this, *except they bow down among the captives or fall among the slain.*" Exile or death, that was their only alternative. When that sentence has been uttered, the doom-bell, as we have called it, "For all this . . ." tolls once more. If we adopt the Authorised version we have the same fact asserted, with the suggested thought that there was a refuge to be found in God.

(5) **O Assyrian.**—The words open, as has been said above, a perfectly distinct section. Assyria had been named in connection with the Syro-Ephraim alliance against Judah (chap. vii. 17—20, viii. 7, 8); but this is the first prophetic utterance of which it is the direct subject. Anticipating the phraseology of chap. xiii. 1, we might call it the "burden of Assyria." In the judgment of the best Assyrian scholars, some years had passed since the date of the alliance and invasion. Tiglath-pileser had taken Damascus and reduced Samaria to submission. Pekah and Ahaz had met at Damascus to do homage to their common suzerain. In B.C. 727 Salmaneser succeeded to the throne of Assyria, and began the conquest of Samaria and the deportation of the Ten Tribes in B.C. 722 (2 Kings xvii. 3—6). On his death, in B.C. 721, the throne was seized by Sargon, who had been his Tartan, or commander-in-chief (chap. xx. 1). The achievements of this king are recorded at length in an inscription discovered by M. Botta at Khorsabad (*Records of the Past*, vii. 28. Lenormant's *Manual*, i. p. 392). In it he says:—"I besieged, took, and occupied the city of Samaria, and carried into captivity 27,280 of its inhabitants. I changed the form of government of the country, and placed over it lieutenants of my own." In another inscription discovered at Kouyunyik, but unfortunately incomplete, Sargon speaks of himself as "the conqueror of the far-off land of Judah" (Layard, *Inscriptions*, xxxiii. 8). It was probably to this king, exulting in his triumphs and threatening an attack on Judah, and not (as was commonly thought prior to the discovery of the inscription) to his son Sennacherib, who succeeded him B.C. 704, that the prophet now addressed himself. The first words proclaim that the great king was but an instrument working out the Divine intent, the "rod," and the "staff," the "axe" and the "saw" (verse 15). So in chap. vii. 20, the earlier king of Assyria is as "the razor that is hired." So Nebuchadnezzar in Jer. li. 20 is the "battle-axe" or "hammer" of Jehovah. (Comp. chap. xxxvii. 26.)

(6) **I will send him against an hypocritical nation.**—Better, *impious*. The verb admits of the various renderings, "I will send," "I did send," and "I am wont to send." The last seems to give the best meaning—not a mere fact in history, nor an isolated prediction, but a law of the Divine government.

To take the spoil.—The series of words, though general in meaning, contains probably a special reference to the recent destruction of Samaria, walls pulled down, houses and palaces turned into heaps of rubbish, the soldiers trampling on flower and fruit gardens, this was what the Assyrian army left behind it. Judah had probably suffered in the same way in the hands of Sargon.

(7) **Howbeit he meaneth not so.**—The thoughts which Isaiah puts into the mouth of the Assyrian are exactly in accord with the supreme egotism of the Sargon inscription, "I conquered," "I besieged," "I burnt," "I killed," "I destroyed"; this is the ever-recurring burden, mingled here and there with the boast that he is the champion of the great deities of Assyria, of Ishtar and of Nebo.

The Boasts of the Assyrian King.   ISAIAH, X.   *The Punishment of Pride.*

a few. (8) ^a"For he saith, Are not my princes altogether kings? (9) *Is* not Calno as Carchemish? *is* not Hamath as Arpad? *is* not Samaria as Damascus? (10) As my hand hath found the kingdoms of the idols, and whose graven images did excel them of Jerusalem and of Samaria; (11) shall I not, as I have done unto Samaria and her idols, so do to Jerusalem and her idols?

(12) Wherefore it shall come to pass, *that* when the Lord hath performed his whole work ^bupon Mount Zion and on Jerusalem, I will ¹punish the fruit ²of

a 2 Kings 18. 24, 33, & 19. 10, &c.
b 2 Kings 19. 31.
¹ Heb., *visit upon.*
² Heb., *of the greatness of the heart.*

---

(8) **Are not my princes altogether kings?**—So Tiglath-pileser names the twenty-three kings (Ahaz and Pekah among them) who came to do homage and pay tribute at Damascus (*Records of the Past*, v. 5—26).

(9) **Is not Calno as Carchemish?**—The six names obviously pointed to more recent conquests in which Sargon and his predecessors had exulted. One after another they had fallen. Could Judah hope to escape? (1) Calno, the Calneh of Gen. x. 10, Amos vi. 2. That prophet had held up its fate in vain as a warning to Samaria. It has been identified by Kay with Ctesiphon on the east bank of the Tigris, by Lenormant (*Manual*, i. 80) with Ur of the Chaldees and with the ruins known now as the *Mugheir*, by Rawlinson (*Five Great Monarchies*, i. 20) with *Nipur*. The Assyrian form, Kil-Anu, means the "house" or "temple" of Anu, an Assyrian deity). Sennacherib (Lenormant i. 398), speaks of having reconquered it after a Chaldean revolt, and sold its inhabitants as slaves. The LXX. version, which instead of naming Carchemish, gives "Calanè, where the tower was built," seems to imply a tradition identifying that city with the Tower of Babel of Gen. xi. 4. (2) Carchemish. Few cities of the ancient world occupied a more prominent position than this. Its name has been explained as meaning the Tower of Chemosh, and so bears witness to the widespread *cultus* of the deity whom we meet with in Biblical history as the "abomination of the Moabites" (1 Kings xi. 7). It has been commonly identified with the Circesium of Greek historians, but the inscriptions found by Mr. George Smith at *Tarabolos* (the Hierapolis of the Greeks) on the banks of the Euphrates, at its junction with the *Kyabur*, prove that this is the true representative of the great commercial city of the old Hittite kings (*Times*, Aug. 23, 1876). Its importance is shown by the frequent occurrence of the name, in its Egyptian form of Karakumusha, in the record of Egyptian kings. Thothmes I. (circa B.C. 1600) conquered it, and, as a result of his campaign, strengthened the forces of Egypt with the chariots and horses for which it was afterwards conspicuous (Lenormant, *Manual*, i. p. 229). Thothmes III. built a fortress there to guard the passage of the Euphrates (*ibid.* i. p. 232), the ruins of which, with Egyptian inscriptions and works of Egyptian manufacture, have recently been found there (*ibid.* i. p. 263). It revolted against Ramses II. (the Sesostris of the Greeks), with the Hittites and Phœnicians, and other nations, but was subdued by him in the expedition in which the victorious issue is recorded on the monument on the *Nahr-el-Kelb* near *Beyrût*. Shalmaneser IV. (contemporary with Ahab) records that he demolished and burnt it (*ibid.* i. p. 380). Tiglath-pileser II., the king to whom Ahaz paid tribute, received tribute from its king in B.C. 742 (*ibid.* i. p. 389). The last two victories are probably referred to in the boast now before us. At a later period it was conspicuous for the great defeat of Pharaoh-Necho's army by Nebuchadnezzar (see notes on Jer. xlvi. 2). Its commercial importance is indicated by the fact that the "*mana* (Heb., *manah*) of Carchemish" appears in numerous cuneiform inscriptions as the standard weight of the time, just as that of Troyes, in the commerce of the Middle Ages, is shown by the survival of the name in the "Troy weight" of our arithmetic books (*Records of the Past*, vii. 114).

Is not Hamath as Arpad?—(1) Hamath on the Orontes, the capital of an Aramæan kingdom, was prominent in the history of the East. Under its kings Toi and Joram it paid tribute to David (2 Sam. viii. 9, 10). It fell under the power of Jeroboam II. of Israel (2 Kings xiv. 25). In conjunction with Damascus it revolted against Shalmaneser IV., and was subdued by him (Lenormant's *Manual*, i. p. 380). Its king was first among the tributary princes under Tiglath-pileser II. after having joined with Pekah and Rezin in their revolt (*ibid.* i. p. 389). Lastly, to come to the date of the present prophecy, it again revolted, in conjunction, as before, with Damascus and Samaria, and was again subdued by Sargon (*ibid.* i. p. 393). (2) Of the early history of Arpad we know less, but it appears as having sustained a three years' siege from the forces of Tiglath-pileser II. It joined Hamath in its revolt against Sargon, and was again, as this verse implies, subdued by him. It is always united in the Old Testament with Hamath (chaps. xxxvi. 19; xxxvii. 13). Under the name of *Erfad* it is still traceable about nine miles from Aleppo (Lenormant, i. pp. 389, 393).

Is not Samaria as Damascus?—These cities, which under Rezin and Remaliah had, as we have seen (chap. vii.) revolted against Tiglath-pileser, and the latter of which had sought to strengthen itself by an alliance with the Egyptian king So, or Sabaco (2 Kings xvii. 4), of the Ethiopian dynasty, against Shalmaneser IV., close for the present the list of Sargon's conquests.

(10) **As my hand hath found the kingdoms of the idols.**—The word "idols" seems hardly appropriate as a word of scorn in the mouth of an idolatrous king; but Isaiah probably puts into his lips the words which he himself would have used. It is, however, quite in character with the Assyrian inscriptions that Sargon should ascribe his victories to Asshur as the Supreme God, before whose sovereignty all local deities were compelled to bow. To the Assyrian king the name of Jehovah would represent a deity whose power was to be measured by the greatness of the nation that worshipped Him, and inferior, therefore, to the gods of Carchemish or Hamath. The worship of Baal, Moloch, and other deities, in both Israel and Judah, had of course tended to strengthen this estimate. (Comp. Rabshakeh's language in chap. xxxvi. 18, 19.)

(11) **Shall I not, as I have done . . .**—The verse gives the occasion of Isaiah's utterance. Sargon was threatening Jerusalem, probably in the early years of Hezekiah's reign. The inscriptions show, as chap. xx. 1 also does, that he made war against Philistia and besieged Ashdod (*Records of the Past*, vii. 40).

(12) **Wherefore it shall come to pass . . .**—Better, *And it shall come to pass . . .* The boast of the proud king is interrupted by the reassertion of the

the stout heart of the king of Assyria, and the glory of his high looks. (13) For he saith, By the strength of my hand I have done *it*, and by my wisdom; for I am prudent: and I have removed the bounds of the people, and have robbed their treasures, and I have put down the inhabitants ¹like a valiant *man*: (14) and my hand hath found as a nest the riches of the people: and as one gathereth eggs *that are* left, have I gathered all the earth; and there was none that moved the wing, or opened the mouth, or peeped. (15) Shall the ax boast itself against him that heweth therewith? *or* shall the saw magnify itself against him that shaketh it? ²as if the rod should shake itself against them that lift it up, *or* as if the staff should lift up ¹itself, *as if it were* no wood. (16) Therefore shall the Lord, the Lord of hosts, send among his fat ones leanness; and under his glory he shall kindle a burning like the burning of a fire. (17) And the light of Israel shall be for a fire, and his Holy One for a flame: and it shall burn and devour his thorns and his briers in one day; (18) and shall consume the glory of his forest, and of his fruitful field, ⁴both soul and body: and they shall be as when a standardbearer fainteth. (19) And the rest of the trees of his forest shall be ⁵few, that a child may write them.

---

1 Or, *like many people.*

2 Or, *as if a rod should shake them that lift it up.*

3 Or, *that which is not wood.*

4 Heb., *from the soul and even to the flesh.*

5 Heb., *number.*

---

fact that he is but an instrument in the hand of Jehovah, and that when his work was done he too will be punished for his pride. The "fruit" of the "stout heart" includes all the words and acts in which his arrogance had shown itself.

(13) **For he saith, By the strength of my hand . . .**—Another reproduction of the style of the royal inscriptions of Assyria. (Comp. chap. xxxvii. 10—13.)

I have removed the bounds of the people. —The practice has, of course, more or less characterised the conquerors of all ages in their attempts to merge independent nationalities into one great empire; but it was pursued more systematically by Assyria than by most others. To be "a remover of boundaries and landmarks" was the title in which an Assyrian king most exulted. (Comp. inscription of Rimmon-nirari, in Smith's *Assyrian Discoveries*, pp. 243, 244. *Records of the Past*, xi. 3).

I have put down the inhabitants like a valiant man.—Better, *I have put down those that sat firmly.* The Hebrew word for "valiant man" means primarily a "bull," and then figuratively, as in chap. xxxiv. 7; Ps. xxii. 12, a "mighty one." The fact that the bull appears so frequently in Assyrian monuments as a symbol of sovereignty, makes it probable that the word is used in that symbolic sense here. In Ps. lxxviii. 25, the "mighty ones" to whom it is applied are those of the host of heaven, the angels of God.

(14) **My hand hath found as a nest.**—The inscription of Sargon presents an almost verbal parallelism (*Records of the Past*, vii. 28). In other documents the king looks on himself as a colossal fowler, and the kingdoms are but as birds'-nests for him to spoil, and the nests are left empty.

There was none that . . . peeped—*i.e.*, chirped. See Note on chap. viii. 19. Not a fledgling was left in the nests which the royal fowler had despoiled.

(15) **Shall the ax boast itself . . . ?**—The words spoken by the prophet as the mouthpiece of Jehovah remind us of the way in which Christian writers of the fifth century spoke of Attila as "the scourge of God." There was comfort in that thought for the nations that were scourged. The man's lust for power might be limitless, but there was the limit of the compassion and longsuffering of God.

As if the rod should shake itself against them that lift it up.—Better, *As if the rod should shake them.* The plural is used either as generalising the comparison, or more probably as suggesting the thought that Elohim (God) is the true wielder of the rod. (Comp. verse 5.)

As if the staff should lift up itself, as if it were no wood.—The multiplied italics show that the translators found the clause difficult. Better and more simply, *As if the staff should lift that which is not wood, i.e.,* the living arm that holds it. Was it for the king of Assyria to assume that he could alter and determine the purposes of Jehovah? Did the man wield the rod, or the rod the man?

(16) **Therefore shall the Lord . . . send among his fat ones leanness.**—The overthrow of the Assyrian is painted in the two-fold imagery of famine and of fire. (Chap. xvii. 4; comp. Pharaoh's vision in Gen. xli. 18—24.) The "fat ones" are the warriors of the Assyrian army. The fire that burns the glory of the king is explained in the next verse as the wrath of Jehovah.

(17) **And the light of Israel shall be for a fire.** —The Divine glory, which is as a consuming fire (chap. xxvii. 4) to the enemies of Israel, is to Israel itself as the very light of life. The "briars and thorns" (we note the recurrence of the combination of chap. ix. 18) are the host of the Assyrian army (comp. 2 Sam. xxiii. 6; Ezek. ii. 6), as "the glory of his forest" in the next verse are the captains and princes. The emphatic "in one day" points to some great catastrophe, such as that which afterwards destroyed the army of Sennacherib.

(18) **Both soul and body.**—Literally, *from the soul even to the flesh.* The metaphor is for a moment dropped, and the reality is unveiled.

As when a standardbearer fainteth.—The Authorised version represents the extremity of misery and exhaustion. The "standard-bearer" was chosen for his heroic strength and stature. When he "fainted" and gave way, what hope was there that others would survive? A more correct rendering, however, gives *As a sick man pineth away.*

(19) **And the rest of the trees of his forest shall be few.**—To number the host of an army, to count killed and wounded after a battle, was commonly the work of the royal scribe, who appears so often as

The Return of the Remnant. ISAIAH, X. *The Slaughter of Midian repeated.*

(20) And it shall come to pass in that day, *that* the remnant of Israel, and such as are escaped of the house of Jacob, shall no more again stay upon him that smote them; but shall stay upon the LORD, the Holy One of Israel, in truth. (21) The remnant shall return, *even* the remnant of Jacob, unto the mighty God. (22) *a*For though thy people Israel be as the sand of the sea, yet a remnant [1]of them shall return: [2]the consumption decreed shall overflow [2]with righteousness. (23) *c*For the Lord GOD of hosts shall make a consumption, even determined, in the midst of all the land.

(24) Therefore thus saith the Lord GOD of hosts, O my people that dwellest in Zion, be not afraid of the Assyrian: he shall smite thee with a rod, [3]and shall lift up his staff against thee, after the manner of *d*Egypt. (25) For yet a very little while, and the indignation shall cease, and mine anger in their destruction. (26) And the LORD of hosts shall stir up a scourge for him according to the slaughter of *e*Midian at the rock of Oreb: and *as* his rod *was* upon the sea, so shall he lift it up after the manner of Egypt. (27) And it shall come to pass in that day, *that* his burden [4]shall be taken away from off thy shoulder, and his yoke from off thy neck, and the yoke shall be destroyed because of the anointing.

(28) He is come to Aiath, he is passed

a Rom. 9. 27.
[1] Heb., *in, or, amongst.*
b ch. 28. 22.
[2] Or, *in.*
c ch. 28. 22.
[3] Or, *but he shall lift up his staff for thee.*
d Ex. 14.
e Judg. 7. 25; ch. 9. 4.
[4] Heb., *shall remove.*

---

in that employment in Assyrian sculptures. Here the survivors (the "remnant" as before) were to be so few (literally, *a number*) that even the boy who could hardly count but on his fingers would be skilled enough to number them.

(20) **The remnant of Israel . . .**—For the remnant of Assyria there is as yet no word of hope. (See, however, chap. xix. 23.) For that of Israel, the prophet, falling back on the thought embodied in the name Shear-jashub (see Note on chap. vii. 3), predicts a brighter future.

Shall no more again stay upon him that smote them.—The smiter is the king of Assyria, whose protection Ahaz and his counsellors had courted instead of trusting in the Holy One of Israel. Their experience of the failure of that false policy should lead them to see that faith in God was, after all, the truest wisdom.

(21) **The remnant shall return . . .**—The very form of the words (*Shear-jashub*) shows that the prophet had the "Immanuel" promise in his thoughts, just as "the mighty God" (the same word as in chap. ix. 6) must have reminded men of the Child who was to bear that name in the age to come. (Comp. Hezekiah's proclamation in 2 Chron. xxx. 6.)

(22) **Though thy people Israel be as the sand of the sea.**—The word "remnant" has, however, its aspect of severity as well as of promise. Men are not to expect that they, the hypocrites and evildoers, shall escape their punishment. The promise of restoration is for the remnant only. (Comp. St. Paul's application of the text in Rom. ix. 27, 28).

The consumption decreed shall overflow with righteousness.—Literally, *a finished* (or *final*) *work, decisive, overflowing with righteousness.* A like phrase meets us again in chap. xxviii. 22; Dan. ix. 27. The "finished work" is that of God's judgment, and it "overflows with righteousness" at once punitive and corrective.

(24) **O my people . . . be not afraid of the Assyrian.**—The practical conclusion of all that has been said is, that the people should not give way to panic as they had done in the days of Ahaz (chap. vii. 2), but should abide the march of Sargon, or his successor, with the tranquillity of faith. They were not to faint beneath the blows of the "rod" and "staff," even though it were to reproduce the tyranny of Egypt. In that very phrase, "after the manner of Egypt," there was a ground of hope, for the cruelty of Pharaoh was followed by the Exodus. As the later Jewish proverb had it, "When the tale of bricks is doubled, then Moses is born."

(25) **The indignation shall cease . . .**—The "indignation" is the wrath of Jehovah poured out upon His people. That wrath is to cease, and His anger *shall be for* the destruction of their enemies.

(26) **According to the slaughter of Midian.**—The historical associations of chap. ix. 4 are still in the prophet's mind. In the history of Judges (vii. 25), Oreb and Zeeb are the names at once of the Midianite chiefs and of the places where they were slain.

As his rod was upon the sea.—The italics spoil the sense. Better, *His rod upon the sea . . . He shall lift it up after the manner of Egypt.* The ambiguous formula which had been taken as primarily of evil boding in verse 24, is repeated as an augury of good. There was another rod prominent in that Egyptian history besides that of the oppressor, and that rod had been wielded by the deliverer.

(27) **The yoke shall be destroyed because of the anointing . . .**—The English, as it stands, is scarcely intelligible, but suggests the idea that the "anointing" was that which marked out the kings and priests of Judah as a consecrated people, and the remembrance of which would lead Jehovah to liberate them from bondage. Most commentators, however, render "by reason of the fat," the implied figure being that of a bullock which grows so fat that the yoke will no longer go round his neck, as the symbol of a people waxing strong and asserting its freedom. Comp. "Jeshurun waxed fat and kicked" (Deut. xxxii. 15).

(28) **He is come to Aiath . . .**—There is an obvious break between this and the preceding verse, and a new section begins, connected with the former by unity of subject, both referring to Sargon's invasion of Judah. That such an invasion took place at or about the time of that king's attack on Ashdod (chap. xx. 1) the inscriptions leave no doubt. The Koujunyik cylinder names the king of Judah as having joined with the king of Ashdod; and in another, Sargon speaks of himself as "the subduer of the lands of Judah".

to Migron; at Michmash he hath laid up his carriages: ⁽²⁹⁾ they are gone over the passage: they have taken up their lodging at Geba; Ramah is afraid; Gibeah of Saul is fled. ⁽³⁰⁾ ¹Lift up thy voice, O daughter of Gallim: cause it to be heard unto Laish, O poor Anathoth. ⁽³¹⁾ Madmenah is removed; the inhabitants of Gebim gather themselves to flee. ⁽³²⁾ As yet shall he remain at Nob that day: he shall shake his hand *against* the mount of the daughter of Zion, the hill of Jerusalem.

⁽³³⁾ Behold, the Lord, the LORD of hosts, shall lop the bough with terror: and the high ones of stature *shall be* hewn down, and the haughty shall be humbled. ⁽³⁴⁾ And he shall cut down the thickets of the forest with iron, and Lebanon shall fall ²by a mighty one.

CHAPTER XI.—⁽¹⁾ And there shall come forth a rod out of the stem of

1 Heb., *Cry shrill with thy voice.*

2 Or, *mightily.*

(Layard, *Inscriptions*, xxxiii. 8). There is nothing in the passage itself to determine whether verses 28—32 are predictive or historical, or when they were first uttered. Assuming that the Messianic prophecy of chap xi. is in close connection with them, it seems most probable that now, as in the earlier attack of Pekah and Rezin (chap. vii.), as in the later invasion of Sennacherib (chap. xxxvii.), the bright vision of the future came to sustain the people when they were at their lowest point of depression. This would obviously be when Sargon's armies were actually encamped round the city, when they had reached the last halting-place of the itinerary which Isaiah traces out. We may infer accordingly that the Assyrian armies were then at or near Nob, and that the prophet, supplied, either by human agency or supernaturally, with a knowledge of the movements of the Assyrian armies, describes their progress to a terrified and expectant people, and fixes the final goal. That progress we now have to trace. (1) Aiath is probably identical with the Ai of Josh. vii. 2, the Aija of Neh. xi. 31, in the tribe of Benjamin, not far from Bethel. (2) Migron. The route taken was not the usual one, but passed over three valleys, probably with a view to surprise Jerusalem by an unexpected attack. The modern name, *Bure Magrun*, survives, a short distance from Bethel. (3) Michmash. Now *Muchmas*, on the east side of the Migron valley. Here the carriages, *i.e.*, the *baggage* (Acts xxi. 15; 1 Sam. xvii. 22), the *impedimenta*, of the Assyrian army was left behind that the host might advance with greater rapidity to immediate action. (4) Geba, in the tribe of Benjamin (1 Chron. vi. 60). Here, after defiling through the "passages," probably the gorge of *Wady Suweinit* memorable for Jonathan's adventure (1 Sam. xiv. 4, 5), the army halted and encamped. (5) The panic spread rapidly to Ramah, memorable as the chief residence of Samuel (1 Sam. vii. 17). (6) The inhabitants of Gibeah, still retaining in its name its old association with the hero-king of Israel (1 Sam. xi. 4), left their town deserted and undefended. (7) Gallim, not now identifiable, but mentioned in 1 Sam. xxv. 44. (8) Laish, not the northern city of that name (Judges xviii. 29), but near Jerusalem. Read, *Listen, O Laish*, as if to the tramp of the armies as they passed. (9) Anathoth; about four miles north of Jerusalem, the birth-place of Jeremiah (Jer. i. 1). There is a special pathos in the prophet's accents, *ăniyah Anathôth*. A various reading adopted by many critics gives, *Answer, O Anathoth*. (10) Madmenah, or Madmen, appears in Jer. xlviii. 2, as a Moabite city. The name ("dung-hill") was, however, not an uncommon one. It is named (Josh. xv. 31) as one of the south-eastern cities of Judah. (11) The people of Gebim ("water-pits;" locality not identified) *gather their goods for flight.*

(12) At last the army reaches Nob, memorable as having been one of the resting-places of the Tabernacle in the time of Saul (1 Sam. xxi. 1). The site has not been identified with certainty, but it was obviously a position that commanded Jerusalem, between it and Anathoth, probably not far from the hill *Scopos* ("watch-tower") where Titus and his troops encamped during the siege of Jerusalem. The prophet's narrative leaves the invader there shaking his hand, as with defiant menace, against the holy city. For "that day," read *this very day*, fixing, as it were, the very hour at which Isaiah spoke.

⁽³³⁾ **Behold, . . . the Lord of hosts . . .**—The sudden change of tone indicates another pressure of the "strong hand" of Jehovah (chap. viii. 11), another burst of intensest inspiration. So far shalt thou go, the prophet says to Sargon, as he said afterwards to Sennacherib (chap. xxxvii. 28—32), and no farther. In the "boughs" that are to be lopped, and the "thickets of the forest" that are to be cut down, we have the same imagery as in verses 17—19. The constant boasts of the Assyrian kings that they cut down the forests of the nations they conquered, gave a special fitness to this emblem of the work of the Divine Nemesis. High as the cedars of Lebanon might rise in their majesty, the "Mighty One" of Israel (better, *Glorious One*; comp. verse 18, chap. xxxiii. 21; Ps. xciii. 4) would lay them low.

XI

There shall come forth a rod out of the stem of Jesse . . .—We enter on another great Messianic prophecy developing that of chap. ix. 6, 7. More specifically than before the true King is named as springing from the house of David, and His reign is painted as the return of a golden age, almost as one of the "new heavens and the new earth wherein dwelleth righteousness" (2 Pet. iii. 13). The figure with which the section opens is carried on from the close of chap. x. The cedar of Lebanon, the symbol of the Assyrian power, was to be cut down, and being of the pine genus, which sends forth no suckers, its fall was irretrievable. But the oak, the symbol of Israel, and of the monarchy of the house of David (chap. vi. 13), had a life remaining in it after it had been cut down, and the rod or sucker that was to spring from its roots should flourish once again in greater glory than before. (Comp. Ezek. xvii. 22.) In the Branch (Heb. *netzer*) we have the word which suggested St. Matthew's generalisation of the prophecies of this type in the words, "He shall be called a Nazarene" (see Note on Matt. ii. 23), and which corresponds, in idea though not in words, to the great prophecies which speak of the Messiah as the Branch (Heb. *Zemach*) in Jer. xxiii. 5, and Zech. iii. 8, and in

The Branch out of the Root of Jesse. ISAIAH, XI. *The restored Paradise.*

ᵃJesse, and a Branch shall grow out of his roots: ⁽²⁾ and the spirit of the LORD shall rest upon him, the spirit of wisdom and understanding, the spirit of counsel and might, the spirit of knowledge and of the fear of the LORD; ⁽³⁾ And shall make him of ¹quick understanding in the fear of the LORD: and he shall not judge after the sight of his eyes, neither reprove after the hearing of his ears: ⁽⁴⁾ but with righteousness shall he judge the poor, and ²reprove with equity for the meek of the earth: and he shall ᵇ smite the earth with the rod of his mouth, and with the breath of his lips shall he slay the wicked. ⁽⁵⁾ And righteousness shall be the girdle of his loins, and faithfulness the girdle of his reins. ⁽⁶⁾ ᶜ The wolf also shall dwell with the lamb, and the leopard shall lie down with the kid; and the calf and the young lion and the fatling together; and a little child shall lead them. ⁽⁷⁾ And the cow and the bear shall feed; their young ones shall lie down together: and the lion shall eat

a Acts 13. 23.

1 Heb., *scent, or, smell.*

B.C. cir. 713.

2 Or, *argue.*

b Job 4. 9; 2 Thes. 2. 8.

c ch. 65. 25.

---

which Isaiah himself had led the way in chap. iv. 2. In identifying the future King with a representative of the house of David, Isaiah was following in the track of Micah v. 2. It is obvious here, as in chap. ix. 6, 7, that he is not speaking of Hezekiah as the actual sovereign of Judah, or of any prince then within the horizon of his earthly vision, though we may legitimately think of the virtues of that king as having been welcomed by him as a pledge and earnest of the ideal future.

⁽²⁾ **And the spirit of the Lord shall rest upon him . . .**—The words throw us at once back upon the memories of the past, and forwards upon the hopes of the future. It was the "spirit of the Lord" that had made men true heroes and judges in the days of old (Judg. xi. 29, xiii. 25). It was in the "spirit of the Lord" descending on Jesus of Nazareth and abiding on Him (John. i. 33) that men were taught to see the token that He was the Christ of God. And in this case the spirit was to give more than the heroic daring which had characterised Jephthah and Samson. The future King was to be as a David and Solomon in one, pre-eminent, chiefly, as the Prince of Peace (chap. ix. 7), in the wisdom and counsel which had been the glory of the latter. "Wisdom," in its highest form, as implying the comprehension of the secret things of God; "understanding," as the sagacity which discerned the right thing to do and the right word to say (Heb. v. 14) in all human relationships; these formed the first link in the chain of supernatural gifts. With these there was to be the "spirit of counsel and might," the clear purpose and strength which fits a king for the right exercise of sovereignty; and lastly, as at once the crown and source of all, the "spirit of knowledge and of the fear of the Lord," the reverence and faith which is "the beginning of all wisdom" (Prov. i. 7). The copious use of the vocabulary of the Book of Proverbs is interesting as showing the part which that book played in the prophet's education. (See *Introduction.*)

⁽³⁾ **And shall make him of quick understanding . . .**—Better, *he shall draw his breath in the fear of the Lord.* It shall be, as it were, the very air in which he lives and breathes. Some commentators, however, interpret *he shall find a sweet savour.* The Hebrew word rendered "understanding" means primarily, as the margin shows, "scent" or "smell," either as the organ or the object of perception.

He shall not judge after the sight of his eyes . . .—Earthly kings are apt to judge "according to the appearance" (John vii. 24), and the reports of interested or corrupt advisers, but the true King shall "know what is in man" (John ii. 25), and judge righteous judgment.

⁽⁴⁾ **With righteousness shall he judge the poor . . .**—The picture which Isaiah had drawn of the corrupt judges of his time gives point to the contrast (chaps. i. 23, ii. 14, 15, x. 1, 2). The poor whom they trampled on should be the special objects of the care of the true King (Matt. xi. 5).

He shall smite the earth. . .—The "earth" stands here, if we accept the reading, for the rulers who are for the time supreme in it. A slight alteration of the Hebrew gives *shall smite the tyrant,* which forms a better parallelism with the "ungodly" of the next clause. The phrase "the *sceptre* of his mouth" is significant. The word which the Messiah-King speaks shall be as the sceptre which is the symbol of authority. So in Rev. i. 16, "a sharp two-edged sword" comes forth from the mouth of the Christ of St. John's vision. The latter clause, "with the breath of his lips shall he slay . . .," has a parallel in Hos. vi. 5.

⁽⁵⁾ **Righteousness shall be the girdle of his loins . . .**—The image of clothing as the symbol of habit or character was already familiar (Ps. cix. 18, 19). The repetition of "girdle" has needlessly offended some fastidious critics, but the emphasis of iteration is quite after Isaiah's manner (chaps. xv. 8, xvi. 7, xvii. 12, 13). It perhaps implies an upper and a lower girdle as the symbol of complete equipment. In the "loins girt about with truth" of Eph. vi. 14, we may probably trace an allusive reference. The armour of the followers of Christ was to be like that of Christ Himself.

⁽⁶⁾ **The wolf also shall dwell with the lamb . . .**—It is significant of the prophet's sympathy with the animal world that he thinks of that also as sharing in the blessings of redemption. Rapine and cruelty even there were to him signs of an imperfect order, or the consequences of a fall, even as to St. Paul they witnessed of a "bondage of corruption" (Rom. viii. 21). The very instincts of the brute creation should be changed in "the age to come," and "the lion should eat straw like the ox." Men have discussed the question whether and when the words shall receive a literal fulfilment, and the answer to that question lies behind the veil. It may be that what we call the laws of animal nature in these respects are tending to a final goal, of which the evolution that has tamed the dog, the bull, the horse, is as it were a pledge and earnest (Soph., *Antig.,* 342—351). It may be, however, that each form of brute cruelty was to the prophet's mind the symbol of a human evil, and the imagery admits, therefore, of an allegorical rather than a literal interpretation. The

The Golden Age to come. ISAIAH, XI. *The Remnant returning from Exile.*

straw like the ox. ⁽⁸⁾ And the sucking child shall play on the hole of the asp, and the weaned child shall put his hand on the ¹cockatrice' den. ⁽⁹⁾ They shall not hurt nor destroy in all my holy mountain: for the earth shall be full of the knowledge of the LORD, as the waters cover the sea.

⁽¹⁰⁾ And in that day there shall be a root of Jesse, which shall stand for an ensign of the people; to it shall the ᵃGentiles seek: and his rest shall be ²glorious.

⁽¹¹⁾ And it shall come to pass in that day, *that* the Lord shall set his hand again the second time to recover the remnant of his people, which shall be left, from Assyria, and from Egypt, and from Pathros, and from Cush, and from Elam, and from Shinar, and from Hamath, and from the islands of the sea. ⁽¹²⁾ And he shall set up an ensign for the nations, and shall assemble the outcasts of Israel, and gather together the dispersed of Judah from the four

¹ Or, *adder's.*

ᵃ Rom. 15. 12.

² Heb., *glory.*

---

classical student will remember the striking parallelism of the fourth Eclogue of Virgil, which, in its turn, may have been a far-off echo of Isaiah's thoughts, floating in the air or embodied in apocryphal Sibylline Oracles among the Jews of Alexandria and Rome.

⁽⁸⁾ **And the sucking child shall play on the hole of the asp . . .**—The description culminates in the transformation of the brute forms which were most identified with evil. As it is, the sight of a child near the hole of the asp (the *cobra*) or cockatrice (better, perhaps, *basilisk*, the great viper), would make its mother scream with terror. There was still "enmity between the seed of the woman and the seed of the serpent" (Gen. iii. 15), but in the far-off reign of the Christ even that enmity should disappear, and the very symbols of evil, subtle, malignant, venomous, should be reconciled to humanity. Some critics translate the last clause, "*shall stretch out his hand to the eye-ball of the basilisk,*" as if alluding to the power of fascination commonly assigned to it.

⁽⁹⁾ **They shall not hurt nor destroy . . .**—The pronoun may possibly refer to the evil beasts, the lion, the bear, the leopard, of the previous verses. The prophet, on this view, sees in his vision, as it were, a restored Eden, a paradise life, in which the fiercest brutes have lost their fierceness. The words admit, however, of being taken as a generalised statement: "None shall hurt nor destroy . . ." The "holy mountain" is none other than the "mountain of the Lord's house" of chap. ii. 2 in its future apocalyptic glory (Ezek. xl. 2; Zech. xiv. 10), but may, perhaps, include the whole of the hill-country of Israel, as in chap. lvii. 13; Ps. lxxviii. 54; Exod. xv. 17.

The earth shall be full of the knowledge of the Lord.—If, as some have thought, the "earth" here should be the *land* (*i.e.,* as in chaps. ix. 19, x. 23, the land of Judah), that region is represented as the paradise centre of a restored world, to which, as in chap. ii. 2, all nations turn for light and blessing. Probably, however, the words may be taken in their wider significance. This was for the prophet the crown and consummation of the work of redemption. More than all removal of physical evil, he thought of a victory over moral and spiritual darkness. As it is, in the existing order of the world, few fear God; still fewer know Him as He should be known. But in that new earth "the knowledge of Jehovah" shall flow far and wide. Even as the waters of the Mediterranean (the sea which must have suggested the prophet's comparison) washed the shores of the far-off isles of the Gentiles, the coasts of Chittim (Num. xxiv. 24), as well as those of Israel, so should the knowledge of the truth of God expand beyond the limits of the people of Israel. Hence the transition was natural to the prophecies which speak at once of the restoration of Israel and the in-gathering of the heathen. It should be remembered that in Hos. iii. 5; Joel ii. 28, iii. 17, prophecies like in kind had preceded Isaiah's utterance. In Hab. ii. 14 it is all but verbally reproduced.

⁽¹⁰⁾ **In that day there shall be a root of Jesse . . .**—The "root," as in chap. liii. 2; Deut. xxix. 18, is the same as the "rod" and "branch" growing from the root in verse 1. The new shoot of the fallen tree of Jesse is to grow up like a stately palm, seen afar off upon the heights of the "holy mountain," a signal round which the distant nations might rally as their centre. So the name of "the root of David" is applied to the glorified Christ in Rev. v. 5, xxii. 16. The word for "seek" implies, as in chap. viii. 19, xix. 3, lv. 6, the special seeking for wisdom and illumination.

His rest shall be glorious.—Better, *his resting-place shall be glory;* *i.e.,* he shall abide evermore in the eternal glory which is the dwelling-place of Jehovah.

⁽¹¹⁾ **The Lord shall set his hand again the second time . . .**—The "first" time, implied in the "second," was obviously that of the Exodus. Then, as from a state of extremest misery, they had entered on their life as a nation, and what had been in the past should be reproduced yet more wonderfully in the future. The list of countries that follows rests in part on the fact of a dispersion already begun, as in 2 Kings xv. 29, xvii. 6, and Isa. xliii. 5, 6, partly on the prophet's prevision of the coming years. The great kingdoms by which Judah was surrounded are all enumerated :—(1) Assyria; (2) Egypt, *i.e.,* Lower Egypt; (3) Pathros, probably the region of Upper Egypt, of which Thebes was the capital (the name has been interpreted as "Southland," or as connected with the worship of the goddess Athor; (4) Cush, *i.e.,* Ethiopia, higher up the valley of the Nile, governed at this time by a warlike and powerful dynasty (see chap. xxxvii. 9) ; (5) Elam, often translated Persia, but probably used, with a wider range, for the region east of the lower course of the Tigris and Euphrates; (6) Shinar, as in Gen. xi. 1, the plain south of the junction of those rivers; (7) Hamath, the nearest of the hostile kingdoms (see Note on chap. x. 9); and, lastly, the "island" or *coast regions* of the Mediterranean Sea. In Zeph. iii. 10 we have traces of an Ethiopian captivity; in Ezra ii. 7, of exiles in Elam.

⁽¹²⁾ **And he shall set up an ensign . . .**—The thought of verse 10 re-appears. The "signal" is, as before, "the root of Jesse," and the exiles gather round it. In the Hebrew the "outcasts" are men, and the "dispersed" are women, the prophet thus implying that in the case of both Israel and Judah both sexes should alike be sharers in the blessings of restoration.

Judah and Ephraim reconciled. ISAIAH, XII. *The Return from Assyria.*

¹ corners of the earth. (13) The envy also of Ephraim shall depart, and the adversaries of Judah shall be cut off: Ephraim shall not envy Judah, and Judah shall not vex Ephraim. (14) But they shall fly upon the shoulders of the Philistines toward the west; they shall spoil ² them of the east together: ³ they shall lay their hand upon Edom and Moab; ⁴ and the children of Ammon shall obey them. (15) And the LORD shall utterly destroy the tongue of the Egyptian sea; and with his mighty wind shall he shake his hand over the river, and shall smite it in the seven streams, and make *men* go over ⁵ dryshod. (16) And there shall be an highway for the remnant of his people, which shall be left, from Assyria; *a* like as it was to Israel in the day that he came up out of the land of Egypt.

CHAPTER XII.—(1) And in that day thou shalt say, O LORD, I will praise thee: though thou wast angry with me, thine anger is turned away, and thou

1 Heb., *wings.*
2 Heb., *the children of the east.*
3 Heb., *Edom and Moab shall be the laying on of their hand.*
4 Heb., *the children of Ammon their obedience.*
5 Heb., *in shoes.*
a Ex. 14. 29.

(13) **The envy also of Ephraim shall depart . . .**—The prophet's vision of the future would not have been complete if national unity had not been included in it. He looked back on the history of the past, and saw almost from the first the deep line of cleavage between north and south, Israel and Judah. Century by century the chasm had grown deeper and wider; sub-sections of antagonism had increased its bitterness (chap. ix. 21); but in the times of the Christ the sense of unity should be stronger than the old hostilities. The prophet's hope connects itself with Hezekiah's efforts after a restored unity (2 Chron. xxx. 1—12). The "envy" of Ephraim" is, as the parallelism shows, that of which Ephraim was the object. By a subtle turn of thought, however, the latter half of the verse represents Ephraim as not *feeling* envy or ill-will against Judah, *i.e.*, he is neither object nor subject, and Judah, free from its own adversaries, is no longer an adversary to Ephraim.

(14) **They shall fly upon the shoulders of the Philistines . . .**—The English version is ambiguous, and half suggests the thought that the Philistines should bear the returning Israelites as on their shoulders; so the LXX. gives, "And they shall speed their wings in the ships of the aliens." What is meant, however, is that the returning exiles shall *swoop down*, as a bird of prey after its flight, "upon the *shoulder* of the Philistines," that name being applied (as in Ezek. xxv. 9; Josh. xv. 10) to the shape of the seaward-sloping country occupied by that people. From this victorious onset in the West, they are to pass on to "the children of the East," the generic name for the nomadic tribes that are found associated with the Midianites and Amalekites (Judges vi. 3, 33, vii. 12), and in chap. ii. 6, with the Philistines themselves, and then to complete their triumph by avenging themselves on their old enemies of Edom, and Moab, and Ammon. The whole verse is singularly characteristic of what has been already spoken of as the limitation of prophetic knowledge. The seer has had revealed to him the glory of the Messianic kingdom as a restored Eden, full of the knowledge of Jehovah, the Gentiles seeking light and salvation from it. Suddenly he blends this with anticipations that belong to the feelings and complications of his own time. He sees Philistines, Moabites, Ammonites, in that far future. They will be then, as they were in his own times, the persistent foes of Israel (comp. Zeph. ii. 7—9), but will be, at last, subdued.

(15) **The tongue . . .**—Better, as in Josh. xv. 2, 5, xviii. 19, the "bay" or "gulf." The "Egyptian sea" is the Gulf of Suez, and the prophet pictures to himself another marvel like the passage of the Red Sea in Exod. xiv. 22. The "river," on the other hand, is the word commonly used for the Euphrates (Gen. xxxi. 21; Josh. xxiv. 2), and that meaning is assigned to it here by most commentators, who refer to chap. xliv. 27 as a parallel. In chap. xix. 5, however, it is found, as here, in parallelism with the "sea" of Egypt, and as it there refers to the Nile, that meaning may well be accepted here. The prophet describes, in language which almost excludes the thought of a merely literal fulfilment, a renewal of wonders transcending those of the Exodus, and it was natural that his description should bear the local colouring of the region. He contemplates a return from Egypt as much as from Assyria (verse 11). On this view the words that follow, "will smite it in the seven streams," refer naturally enough to the seven mouths that enclose and intersect the Delta of the Nile. On the other view, the words may be interpreted as meaning literally, "I will smite it [Euphrates] into seven streams," and figuratively, "I will reduce the power of Assyria [or Babylon, as an Assyrian city] to insignificance."

(16) **And there shall be an highway for the remnant . . .**—The "highway" is, as in chap. xix. 23, xlix. 11, and elsewhere, the raised embanked road, made by Eastern kings for the march of their armies. Such a road the prophet sees in his vision (here as in chap. xl. 3), stretching across the great plains of Mesopotamia for the return of Israel. It was to be for that "second time" of restoration what the passage of the Red Sea had been for the "first time" of the Exodus, for the exiles in Assyria what another passage of the Egyptian sea was to be for those in Egypt.

XII.

(1) **In that day thou shalt say . . .**—The prophet becomes the psalmist of that new Exodus, and the hymn that follows is based upon the type of that in Exod. xv., though with less of local and historical colouring. He has been taught that confession must be blended with thanksgiving—that those only can rightly estimate the comfort which God gives who have first felt His wrath. The fact that the prophet appears as a psalmist was a natural result of the training of the schools of the prophets, as described in 1 Sam. xix. 20, possibly also of his familiarity with the Temple service as a priest or Levite. The group of psalms ascribed to the sons of Korah presents so many parallelisms to the writings of Isaiah, and so obviously belongs to the same period, that we may reasonably think of him as having been associated with that goodly company. (See *Introduction*.)

comfortedst me. (2) Behold, God *is* my salvation; I will trust, and not be afraid: for the LORD JEHOVAH *is* my ᵃ strength and *my* song; he also is become my salvation. (3) Therefore with joy shall ye draw water out of the wells of salvation.

(4) And in that day shall ye say, ᵇ Praise the LORD, ¹ call upon his name, declare his doings among the people,

ᵃ Ex. 15. 2; Ps. 118. 14.

ᵇ 1 Chron. 16. 8; Ps. 105. 1.

¹ Or, *proclaim his name.*

² Heb., *inhabitress.*

make mention that his name is exalted. (5) Sing unto the LORD; for he hath done excellent things: this *is* known in all the earth. (6) Cry out and shout, thou ² inhabitant of Zion: for great *is* the Holy One of Israel in the midst of thee.

CHAPTER XIII.—(1) The burden of Babylon, which Isaiah the son of Amoz did see.

---

(2) **Behold, God is my salvation . . .**—The words admit of the rendering, *Behold the God of my salvation.* In either construction "salvation" is taken, as in the New Testament (John iv. 22; 1 Pet. i. 9, 10), as meaning more than mere deliverance from danger, and including the highest spiritual blessings.

The Lord Jehovah . . .—The Hebrew here and in chap. xxvi. 4 presents the exceptional combination of the two Divine Names (*Yah Yahveh*). (See Ps. lxviii. 4.) With this exception the second clause of the verse is a verbal reproduction of Exod. xv. 2.

(3) **Therefore with joy shall ye draw water . . .**—Literally, *And with joy.* The words may be either part of the hymn, or addressed to those who are to join in it. The latter seems most in harmony with the context. In the later ritual of the Feast of Tabernacles, the priests went in solemn procession to the Pool of Siloam, filled a golden vase with water, carried it to the Temple, and poured it out on the western side of the altar of burnt offering, while the people chanted the great Hallel (Hymn of Praise) of Pss. cxiii.—cxviii. (See Note on John vii. 37.) If we may assume that this represented the ritual of the monarchy, we may reasonably infer that the words of Isaiah pointed to it. The Talmud expressly connects the act with the symbolism of Isaiah's words (*Jer. Succa*, v. 1), and the prophet's reference to the "waters of Shiloah" in chap. viii. 6, confirms the inference.

(4) **Declare his doings among the people.**—Literally, *among the peoples.* The prophet quotes from the hymn which had been sung when the Ark was placed in Zion (1 Chron. xvi. 8), and in part from Ps. cv. 1.

(5) **For he hath done excellent things.**—Here, again, the Hebrew indicates an echo from Exod. xv. 1: "He hath triumphed gloriously."

(6) **Thou inhabitant of Zion.**—The Hebrew is feminine. The inhabitant is the *daughter* of Zion, the restored Church, that has Zion for her dwelling-place.

Great is the Holy One of Israel . . .—The hymn ends with the Divine Name which is characteristic of Isaiah. The presence of the Holy One was to be a joy and blessing to the remnant who were worthy of their calling. With this hymn the whole of what has been called the Immanuel volume of Isaiah's prophecies comes to its close.

XIII.

(1) **The burden of Babylon . . .**—The title "burden," which is repeated in chaps. xv. 1, xvii. 1, xix. 1, xxi. 1, xxii. 1, xxiii. 1, indicates that we have in this division a collection of prophetic utterances, bearing upon the future of the surrounding nations, among which Babylon was naturally pre-eminent. The authenticity of the first of these oracles has been questioned, partly on the ground of differences of style, partly because it seems to anticipate the future destruction of Babylon with a distinctness which implies a prophecy after the event. The first of these objections rests, as will be seen from the numerous coincidences between these and other portions of Isaiah, on no sufficient evidence. The second implies a view of prophecy which excludes the element of a divinely given foreknowledge; and that view the present writer does not accept.

Accepting the two chapters as Isaiah's, we have to ask how Babylon came at the time within the prophet's historical horizon, and what were at the time its political relations with Assyria. (1) It is obvious that the negotiations which Ahaz had opened with Tiglath-pileser, the passage to and fro of armies and ambassadors, the journeys of prophets like Jonah and Nahum, the commerce of which we have traces even in the days of Joshua (Josh. vii. 21), must have made Babylon, as well as Nineveh, familiar to the leading men of Judah. As a matter of fact, it was probably more familiar. Babylon was the older, more famous, more splendid city Nineveh (if we accept the conclusions of one school of historians) had been overpowered and destroyed by the Medes under Arbaces, and the Babylonians under Belesis (B.C. 739), the Pul of Bible history, under whom Assyria was a dependency of Babylon (Lenormant, *Anc. Hist.*, p. 38). In Tiglath-pileser the Assyrians found a ruler who restored their supremacy. The Chaldæans, however, revolted under Merôdach-baladan, and Sargon records with triumph how he had conquered him and spoiled his palace. As the result of that victory, he took the title of king of Babylon. Merôdach-baladan, however, renewed his resistance early in the reign of Sennacherib, and though again defeated, we find him courting the alliance of Hezekiah either before or after the destruction of that king's army (chap. xxxix.). We can scarcely doubt that the thought of a Babylonian, as of an Egyptian, alliance had presented itself to the minds of the statesmen of Judah as a means of staying the progress of Assyrian conquests. The chapters now before us, however, do not seem written with reference to such an alliance, and in chap. xiv. 25 Babylon seems contemplated chiefly as the representative of the power of Assyria. It seems probable, accordingly, that the king of Babylon in chap. xiv. 4 is to be identified with Sargon, the Assyrian king, who took the title of "Vicar of the Gods in Babylon" (*Records of the Past*, vol. xi. 17).

The word "burden," prefixed to this and the following prophecies, is a literal translation of the Hebrew. It seems to have acquired a half-technical sense as announcing the doom which a nation or a man was called to bear, and so to have acquired the meaning of an "oracle," or "prophecy." This meaning, which is first prominent in Isaiah (in Prov. xxx. 1, xxxi. 1 it is used of an ethical or didactic utterance thought of as inspired), was afterwards given to it in the speeches of the false prophets (Lam. ii. 14); and in Jer. xxiii. 33

Mustering of the Hosts of Battle. ISAIAH, XIII *The Day of Jehovah.*

(2) Lift ye up a banner upon the high mountain, exalt the voice unto them, shake the hand, that they may go into the gates of the nobles. (3) I have commanded my sanctified ones, I have also called my mighty ones for mine anger, *even* them that rejoice in my highness. (4) The noise of a multitude in the mountains, ¹ like as of a great people; a tumultuous noise of the kingdoms of nations gathered together: the LORD of hosts mustereth the host of the battle. (5) They come from a far country, from the end of heaven, *even* the LORD, and the weapons of his indignation, to destroy the whole land.

(6) Howl ye; for the day of the LORD is at hand; it shall come as a destruction from the Almighty. (7) Therefore shall all hands ²be faint, and every man's heart shall melt: (8) and they shall be afraid: pangs and sorrows shall take hold of them; they shall be in pain as a woman that travaileth: they shall ³be amazed ⁴one at another; their faces *shall be as* ⁵flames. (9) Behold, the day of the LORD cometh, cruel both with wrath and fierce anger, to lay the land desolate: and he shall destroy the sinners thereof out of it. (10) For the stars of heaven and the constellations thereof shall not give their light: the sun shall be ᵃdarkened in his going forth, and the moon shall not cause her

1 Heb., *the likeness of.*
2 Or, *fall down.*
3 Heb., *wonder.*
4 Heb., *every man at his neighbour.*
5 Heb., *faces of the flames.*
a Ezek. 32. 7; Joel 2. 31, & 3. 15; Matt. 24. 29; Mark 13. 24; Luke 21. 25.

—40 we have a striking play upon the primary and derived meaning of the word. (See Note on Jer. xxiii. 33.) It continued in use, however, in spite of Jeremiah's protest, and appears in Zech. ix. 1, xii. 1; Mal. i. 1. *Oracle* is perhaps the best English equivalent. We note as characteristic (see chaps. i. 1, ii. 1), that the "burden" is described as that which Isaiah *saw*.

(2) **Lift ye up a banner upon the high mountain . . .**—Strictly speaking, *a bare mountain*, where there were no trees to hide the standard round which the forces that the prophet sees were to rally. The word and thought are the same as in chap. v. 26; but there the summons lies for the invaders of Israel, here for its avengers. The voice that summons is, as the next verse shows, that of Jehovah. The "shaking the hand" is, as in chap. x. 32, the act of the generals pointing with emphatic gesture to the city that is to be destroyed.

The gates of the nobles.—The word is used to heighten the contrast between the greatness of the city to be destroyed, with its gates that had witnessed for centuries the entrance of kings and princes, and the wild roughness of the barbarian destroyers.

(3) **I have commanded my sanctified ones . . .**—The word is applied even to the fierce tribes of the future destroyers, as being appointed, or *consecrated*, by Jehovah for that special work. The thought and the words (there translated "prepare") appear in Jer. vi. 4, xxii. 7, li. 27. So in the later prophecies Cyrus appears as "the anointed" of the Lord (chap. xlv. 1).

Even them that rejoice in my highness.—In Zeph. iii. 11 the same phrase occurs in a bad sense. Here, apparently, it denotes the proud consciousness of the invaders that they are doing God's work.

(4) **The noise of a multitude . . .**—The prophet hears, as it were, the tramp of the armies gathering on the mountains north of Babylonia (possibly the Zagros range, or the plateau of Iran, or the mountains of Armenia; but the prophet's geography was probably vague) before they descend to the plain, and march against the haughty city. (Comp. Jer. li. 27.)

(5) **They come from a far country . . .**—The same phrase is used of Cyrus in chap. xlvi. 11, and in chap. xxxix. 3 of Babylon itself in relation to Jerusalem. The "end of heaven" represents the thoughts of Isaiah's time, the earth as an extended plain, and the skies rising like a great vault above. The phrase represents (Deut. iv. 32; Ps. xix. 6), as it were, the *ultima Thule* of discovery. For the "whole land," the Hebrew noun hovers, as often elsewhere, between the meanings of "earth," or "country." The LXX. favours the former meaning.

(6) **Howl ye; for the day of the Lord is at hand.**—The verse is an almost verbal reproduction of Joel i. 15. On the "day of Jehovah," see Note on chap. ii. 12.

As a destruction from the Almighty.—The Hebrew *shodmish-Shaddai* comes with the emphasis of assonance, possibly coupled with that of etymology, the Hebrew *Shaddai* being derived by many scholars from the verb *Shadad* = to destroy. On this assumption, "*destruction from the destroyer*" would be a fair equivalent. The name, occurring frequently in the earlier books of the Old Testament (twenty-three times in Job and eight in the Pentateuch), was characteristic of the pre-Mosaic creed of Israel (Exod. vi. 3), and occurs but seldom in the prophets: here, and in Joel i. 15; Ezek. i. 24, x. 5.

(7) **Shall all hands be faint.**—Better, *be slack*, hanging down in the helpless despondency of the terror which the next clause paints (Heb. xii. 12).

(7) **They shall be in pain as a woman that travaileth.**—The image of powerless agony occurs both in earlier and later prophets (Hosea xiii. 3; Micah v. 9; Jer. vi. 24, *et al.*). Perhaps the most striking parallelism is found in Ps. xlviii. 6, probably, like the other psalms of the sons of Korah, contemporary with Isaiah.

Their faces shall be as flames.—The comparison seems at first to describe those who cause terror rather than those that feel it. What is described is, however, the moment of horror, when the dejected pallor of ordinary fear flashes into a new intensity, and the eyeballs glare, and the face glows as with a terrible brightness.

(10) **The constellations thereof.**—The noun in the singular (*kesil*, foolhardy, or impious) is translated as Orion in Job ix. 9; Amos v. 8. It is significant, as pointing to some widely-diffused legend, that the Persian name for the constellation is *Nimrod* and the Arabian *Giant*. In Greek mythology Orion is a giant hunter, conspicuous for acts of outrage against the gods, and finally slain by Zeus. It is obvious that the words in their first application had a figurative, and not a literal, fulfilment. Such imagery has been at all times

The Heavens and the Earth shaken. ISAIAH, XIII. *The Medes stirred up against Babylon.*

light to shine. (11) And I will punish the world for *their* evil, and the wicked for their iniquity; and I will cause the arrogancy of the proud to cease, and will lay low the haughtiness of the terrible. (12) I will make a man more precious than fine gold; even a man than the golden wedge of Ophir. (13) Therefore I will shake the heavens, and the earth shall remove out of her place, in the wrath of the Lord of hosts, and in the day of his fierce anger. (14) And it shall be as the chased roe, and as a sheep that no man taketh up: they shall every man turn to his own people, and flee every one into his own land. (15) Every one that is found shall be thrust through; and every one that is joined *unto them* shall fall by the sword. (16) Their children also shall be *a* dashed to pieces before their eyes; their houses shall be spoiled, and their wives ravished.

(17) Behold, I will stir up the Medes against them, which shall not regard silver; and *as for* gold, they shall not delight in it. (18) *Their* bows also shall dash the young men to pieces; and they shall have no pity on the fruit of the womb; their eye shall not spare children. (19) And Babylon, the glory of kingdoms, the beauty of the Chaldees'

a Ps. 137. 9.

the natural symbolism of a time of terror (Joel ii. 31, iii. 15; Matt. xxiv. 29; Mark xiii. 24; Luke xxi. 25).

(12) **I will make a man more precious.**—Both the words for man (*ĕnosh* and *ădam*) express, as in Ps. viii. 2, the frailty of man's nature. The words may point to the utter destruction, in which but few men should be left. The "gold of Ophir" (the gold coast near the mouth of the Indus) was proverbial for its preciousness (Job xxii. 24; xxviii. 16; 1 Chron. xxix. 4; 1 Kings ix. 28; xxii. 48).

(13) **Therefore I will shake.**—The description of the great day of the Lord meets us in like terms in Haggai ii. 6, Heb. xii. 26, carried in both instances beyond the overthrow of Babylon or any particular kingdom to that of every world-power that resists the righteousness of God.

(14) **And it shall be as the chased roe.**—Better, *as with a chased roe . . . . as with sheep* . . . The roe and the sheep represent the "mixed multitude" (Æsch., *Pers.* 52) of all nations who had been carried into Babylon, and who would naturally take to flight, some, though without a leader, returning to their own lands on the approach of the invader.

(15) **Every one that is joined unto them.**—Better, *every one that is caught*. The first clause of the verse refers to those that are in the city at the time of its capture, the second to those who are taken as they endeavour to escape.

(16) **Their children also shall be dashed.**—Better, *their sucklings*. The words of the prediction seem to have been in the minds of the exiles in Babylon when they uttered their dread beatitude on those who were to be the ministers of a righteous vengeance (Ps. cxxxvii. 9). Outrages such as these were then, as they have been ever since, the inevitable accompaniments of the capture of a besieged city.

(17) **Behold, I will stir up the Medes.**—The Hebrew form *Madai* meets us in Gen. x. 2, among the descendants of Japheth. Modern researches show them to have been a mixed people, Aryan conquerors having mingled with an earlier Turanian race, and differing in this respect from the Persians, who were pure Iranians, both in race and creed. The early Assyrian inscriptions, from Rimmon Nirari III. onward (Cheyne), name them, as also does Sargon (*Records of the Past*, xi. 18), among the enemies whom the kings subdued. Their name had been recently brought before the prophet's notice by Salmaneser's deportation of the Ten Tribes to the cities of the Medes (2 Kings xvii. 6).

In naming the Medes, and not the Persians, as the conquerors of Babylon, Isaiah was probably influenced by the greater prominence of the former, just as the Greeks spoke of them, and used such terms as "Medism" when they came in contact with the Medo-Persian monarchy under Darius and Xerxes. So Æschylus (*Pers.* 760) makes "the Median" the first ruler of the Persians. It is noticeable that they were destined to be the destroyers both of Nineveh and Babylon: of the first under Cyaxares, in alliance with Nabopolassar, and of the second under Cyrus the Persian, and, we may add, the Mede Darius of Dan. v. 31. If we accept the history of a yet earlier attack on Nineveh by Arbaces the Mede and Belesis of Babylon, we can sufficiently account for the prominence which Isaiah, looking at Babylon as the representative of Assyrian rather than Chaldæan power, gives to them as its destroyers. (See Lenormant, *Anc. Hist.*, i., p. 337.)

Which shall not regard silver.—The Medes are represented as a people too fierce to care for the gold and silver in which Babylon exulted. They would take no ransom to stay their work of vengeance. So Xenophon, in his *Cyropædia* (v. 3), represents Cyrus as acknowledging their unbought, unpaid service.

(18) **Their bows also shall dash the young men to pieces.**—These, as in chap. xxii. 6, Jer. l. 9—14, were the characteristic weapons of the Medo-Persian armies.

(19) **And Babylon, the glory of kingdoms.**—The words paint the impression which the great city, even in Isaiah's time, made upon all who saw it. So Nebuchadnezzar, though his work was mainly that of a restorer, exulted in his pride in the greatness of the city of which he claimed to be the builder (Dan. iv. 30). So Herodotus (i. 178) describes it as the most famous and the strongest of all the cities of Assyria, adorned beyond any other city on which his eyes had ever looked. (Compare the descriptive notices in Jer. li. 41, and the constantly recurring epithet of "gold-abounding Babylon" in the *Persians* of Æschylus.)

As when God overthrew Sodom and Gomorrah.—The phrase had clearly become proverbial, as in chap. i. 9; Jer. l. 40; Deut. xxix. 23, carrying the picture of desolation to its highest point. The present state of the site of Babylon corresponds literally to the prediction. It is "a naked and hideous waste" (Layard, *Nineveh and Babylon*, p. 484). The work was, however, accomplished by slow degrees, and was not, like the destruction of Nineveh, the result of a single

excellency, shall be [1] as when God overthrew *a* Sodom and Gomorrah. [20] It shall never be inhabited, neither shall it be dwelt in from generation to generation: neither shall the Arabian pitch tent there; neither shall the shepherds make their fold there. [21] But [2] wild beasts of the desert shall lie there; and their houses shall be full of [3] doleful creatures; and [4] [5] owls shall dwell there, and satyrs shall dance there. [22] And [6] the wild beasts of the islands shall cry in their [7] desolate houses, and dragons in *their* pleasant palaces: and her time *is* near to come, and her days shall not be prolonged.

CHAPTER XIV.—[1] For the LORD will have mercy on Jacob, and will yet choose Israel, and set them in their own land: and the strangers shall be joined with them, and they shall cleave to the house of Jacob. [2] And the people shall take them, and bring them

[1] Heb., *as the overthrowing.*
a. Gen. 19. 24; Jer. 50. 40.
B.C. cir. 712.
[2] Heb., *Ziim.*
[3] Heb., *Ochim.*
[4] Or, *ostriches.*
[5] Heb., *daughters of the owl.*
[6] Heb., *Iim.*
[7] Or, *palaces.*

---

overthrow. Darius dismantled its walls, Xerxes pulled down the Temple of Belus. Alexander contemplated its restoration, but his designs were frustrated by his early death. Susa and Ecbatana, Seleucia and Antioch, Ctesiphon and Bagdad, became successively the centres of commerce and of government. By the time of Strabo (B.C. 20) the work was accomplished, and "the vast city" had become a "vast desolation" (Strabo, xvi. 15). At no time within the range of Old Testament literature did such a consummation come within the range of the forecast which judges of the future by an induction from the past.

[20] **Neither shall the Arabian pitch tent there . . .**—The word "Arabian" is used in its widest extent, as including all the nomadic tribes of the Bedouin type east and north of Palestine as far as Babylon (2 Chron. xxi. 16; Strabo, xvi., p. 743). Here, again, we note a literal fulfilment. The Bedouins themselves, partly because the place is desolate, partly from a superstitious horror, shrink from encamping on the site of the ancient temples and palaces, and they are left to lions and other beasts of prey. On the other hand, Joseph Wolff, the missionary, describes a strange weird scene, pilgrims of the Yezidis, or devil-worshippers, dancing and howling like dervishes amid the ruins of Babylon.

[21] **Wild beasts of the desert . . .**—The Hebrew term, which in Ps. lxxii. 9, and perhaps in Isaiah xxiii. 13, is used of men, has been rendered by "wild cats," but is probably generic, the *feræ naturæ* that haunt such desolate regions. The "doleful creatures" (literally *groaners*) are probably "horned owls;" while the word rendered "owls" (literally, *daughters of screaming*) may be taken as *ostriches* (Job xxxix. 13—18). In the "satyrs" (literally, *hairy* or *shaggy ones*) we may find either "goats" (as in Lev. iv. 24, xvi. 9), or, as the English version suggests, a mythical form of grotesque animal life (the "demons" or "devils" of Lev. xvii. 7; 2 Chron. xi. 15, a goat-shaped form, like that of the Greek Pan), or more probably (with Tristram), the species of baboon (*Macacus Arabicus*) still found in Babylonia.

[22] **Wild beasts of the islands . . .**—The Authorised version rests on a false etymology of the words, which strictly mean "wailers," and in its form *ey* probably represents the cry of a wild beast, such as the *jackal*, with which it is commonly identified (see chap. xxxiv. 14; Jer. l. 39), or, possibly, the hyæna. Perhaps, however, as the word "jackal" is wanting in the next clause, it would be best to keep "wailers."

In their desolate houses.—Literally, as the text stands, *among their widows*; but the word closely resembles that for "castles" or "fortresses" in chaps. xxxii. 14, xxxiv. 13. The Authorised version is either an attempt to combine the two meanings, or to take the word "widow" figuratively, as in chap. xlvii. 8, for a house bereaved of its owner.

Dragons in their pleasant palaces.—Better, *jackals* (chap. xxxiv. 13; Jer. li. 37, and elsewhere) *in their palaces of pleasure.*

Her time.—The appointed day of visitation (Jer. xlvi. 21, l. 27).

The whole passage finds a singular parallel in an inscription of Assurbanipal's recording his devastation of the fields of Elam: "Wild asses, serpents, beasts of the desert and *galhus* (bull-shaped demons), safely I caused to lie down in them" (*Records of the Past*, i., p. 80). Isaiah may have known of such boasts, and if so, his words may have pointed to the working of a law of retribution like that invoked by the Babylonian exiles in Ps. cxxxvii. 8. The doom that Babylon had inflicted on others was to come upon herself. The language of modern travellers illustrates the fulfilment of the prediction. "Owls start from the scanty thickets, and the foul jackal stalks among the furrows" (Layard, *Nineveh and Babylon*, p. 484, quoted by Kay).

XIV.

[1] **For the Lord will have mercy on Jacob . . .**—The words imply a prevision of the return of the Israelites from exile, and therefore of the exile itself. The downfall of Babylon was certain, because without it the mercy of the Lord to Israel could not be manifested. The whole section is an anticipation of the great argument of chaps. xl.—lxvi., and the question of its authorship stands or falls on the same grounds.

The strangers shall be joined with them . . .—The thought is one specially characteristic of the later prophecies of Isaiah (chaps. xliv. 5, lv. 5, lvi. 3—6), but is prominent in the earlier also (chap. ii. 2). In later Hebrew the same words came to be applied to the proselytes who are conspicuous in the apostolic age (Acts ii. 10, vi. 5), and in them, as before in the adhesion and support of the Persian kings and satraps, and as afterwards in the admission of the Gentiles into the kingdom of the Christ, we may trace successive fulfilments of the prophet's words.

[2] **The people shall take them . . .**—Literally, *the peoples.* In Ezra i. 1—4, vi. 7, 8, we have what answered, in a measure, to the picture thus drawn; but here, as elsewhere, the words paint an ideal to which there has been as yet no historical reality fully corresponding. No period of later Jewish history has beheld the people ruling over a conquered race; and if we claim a real fulfilment of the last clause of the verse, it is only in the sense in which the Latin poet said that *Græcia capta ferum victorem cepit* (Horat. *Ep.* II. i. 156). The

Rest from Bondage. ISAIAH, XIV. *The King of Babylon in Hades.*

to their place: and the house of Israel shall possess them in the land of the LORD for servants and handmaids: and they shall take them captives, ¹ whose captives they were; and they shall rule over their oppressors.

⁽³⁾ And it shall come to pass in the day that the LORD shall give thee rest from thy sorrow, and from thy fear, and from the hard bondage wherein thou wast made to serve, ⁽⁴⁾ that thou shalt take up this ² proverb against the king of Babylon, and say,

How hath the oppressor ceased! the ³ golden city ceased! ⁽⁵⁾ The LORD hath broken the staff of the wicked, *and* the sceptre of the rulers. ⁽⁶⁾ He who smote the people in wrath with ⁴ a continual stroke, he that ruled the nations in anger, is persecuted, *and* none hindereth. ⁽⁷⁾ The whole earth is at rest, *and* is quiet: they break forth into singing. ⁽⁸⁾ Yea, the fir trees rejoice at thee, *and* the cedars of Lebanon, *saying*, Since thou art laid down, no feller is come up against us.

⁽⁹⁾ ⁵ Hell from beneath is moved for thee to meet *thee* at thy coming: it stirreth up the dead for thee, *even* all the ⁶ ⁷ chief ones of the earth; it hath

1 Heb., *that had taken them captives.*
2 Or, *taunting speech.*
3 Or, *exactress of gold.*
4 Heb., *a stroke without removing.*
5 Or, *The grave.*
6 Heb., *leaders.*
7 Or, *great goats.*

---

triumph of Israel has, so far, been found in that of its leading ideas, and in the victory of the faith of Christ. In chap. lvi. 3 the proselyte appears as admitted on terms of equality, here on those of subjugation.

⁽³⁾ **It shall come to pass . . .**—The condition of the exiles in Babylon is painted in nearly the same terms as in Hab. ii. 13. A monarch bent on building towers and walls and palaces, who had carried off all the skilled labour of Jerusalem, was likely enough to vex their souls with "fear" and "hard bondage." So Assurbanipal boasts that he made his Arabian prisoners carry heavy burdens and build brick-work (*Records of the Past,* i. 104).

⁽⁴⁾ **That thou shalt take up this proverb against the king of Babylon.**—The prophet appears once more (comp. chaps. v. 1, xii. 1) in his character as a psalmist. In the *mashal* or *taunting-song* that follows, the generic meaning of "proverb" is specialised (as in Micah ii. 4; Hab. ii. 6; Deut. xxviii. 37, 1 Kings ix. 7, and elsewhere) for a derisive utterance in poetic or figurative speech. The LXX., singularly enough, renders the word here by "lamentation."

How hath the oppressor ceased.—If we take "the golden city" of the English version as the correct rendering, it finds a parallel in the epithet of "gold-abounding" applied to Babylon by Æschylus (*Pers.* 53). The word so translated is, however, not found elsewhere, and the general consensus of recent critics, following in the wake of the Targum and the LXX., is in favour of the rendering, *the task-master,* or *the place of torture.* The Vulgate, *how has the tribute ceased,* expresses substantially the same thought. The marginal reading, *exactress of gold,* seems like an attempt to combine two different etymologies.

⁽⁵⁾ **The Lord hath broken the staff of the wicked . . .**—The "staff" and the "sceptre" are alike symbols of power, the former being that on which a man supports himself, the other that which he wields in his arm to smite those who oppose him.

⁽⁶⁾ **He who smote . . .**—Better, *which smote,* the whole verse being of the nature of a relative clause, with the "sceptre" for antecedent.

A continual stroke.—Literally, *a stroke without ceasing.*

Is persecuted, and none hindereth.—Better, completing the parallelism, *with a trampling that is not stayed.*

⁽⁷⁾ **They break forth into singing . . .**—The phrase is noticeable as characteristic of Isaiah (chaps. xliv. 23, xlix. 13, lii. 9, liv. 1, lv. 12), and is not found elsewhere. The emancipated nations are represented as exulting in the unfamiliar peace that follows on the downfall of their oppressor.

⁽⁸⁾ **Yea, the fir trees rejoice at thee.**—The tree has been identified (Carruthers, in *Bible Educator,* iv., 359) with the Aleppo pine (*Pinus halepensis*), which grows abundantly on the Lebanon range above the zone of the evergreen oaks. The LXX. often translates it by "cypress," the Vulgate and Authorised version commonly by "fir tree." Its wood was largely used in house and ship-building, but was less precious than the cedar (1 Kings v. 10, vi. 15, 34; Isa. xli. 19; Ezek. xxvii. 5).

No feller is come up against us.—The literal and figurative senses melt into each other, the former perhaps being the more prominent. It was the boast of Assurbanipal and other Assyrian kings that wherever they conquered they cut down forests and left the land bare. (Comp. chap. xxxvii. 24: *Records of the Past,* i. 86.) As the fir tree, the cedar, and the oak were the natural symbols of kingly rule (Jer. xxii. 7; Ezek. xvii. 3, xxxi. 3), this devastation represented the triumph of the Chaldæan king over other princes. On his downfall, the trees on the mountain, the kings and chieftains in their palaces, would alike rejoice.

⁽⁹⁾ **Hell from beneath is moved for thee . . .**—"Hell," or *Sheol,* is, as elsewhere, the shadow-world, the region of the dead. Into that world the king of Babylon descends. The "dead" and the Rephaim are there, the *giant-spectres,* now faint and feeble (Deut. ii. 11, iii. 11), of departed forms of greatness. The verb ("it stirreth up"), which is masculine, while the noun is feminine, seems to personify Sheol, as Hades is personified in Rev. xx. 14. The "chief ones" are, literally, *the he-goats,* or "bell-wethers" of the flock (chap. xxxiv. 6; Zech. x. 3), of which Hades is the shepherd (Ps. xlix. 14). Even in Sheol the kings of the earth retain their former majesty, and sit on thrones apart from the vulgar dead. In Ezek. xxxii. 17—32 we have a reproduction of the same imagery, and the kings appear, each with his "weapons of war." The whole passage finds a striking parallel in the Assyrian legend of the Descent of Ishtar (*Records of the Past,* i. p. 144), where Hades is described.

"The abode of darkness and famine.
 * * * * *
Night is not seen—in darkness they dwell.
Ghosts, like birds, flutter their wings there.
On the door and gate-posts the dust lies undisturbed.
 * * * * *
To be the ruler of a palace shall be thy rank;
A throne of state shall be thy seat."

The Fall of the Morning Star. ISAIAH, XIV. *His Boasting in Vain.*

raised up from their thrones all the kings of the nations. (10) All they shall speak and say unto thee, Art thou also become weak as we? art thou become like unto us? (11) Thy pomp is brought down to the grave, *and* the noise of thy viols: the worm is spread under thee, and the worms cover thee. (12) How art thou fallen from heaven, ¹ O Lucifer, son of the morning! *how* art thou cut down to the ground, which didst weaken the nations!

(13) For thou hast said in thine heart, I will ascend into heaven, I will exalt my throne above the stars of God: I will sit also upon the mount of the congregation, in the sides of the north: (14) I will ascend above the heights of the clouds; I will be like the most High. (15) Yet thou shalt be brought down to hell, to the sides of the pit.

(16) They that see thee shall narrowly look upon thee, *and* consider thee, saying, *Is* this the man that made the earth to tremble, that did shake kingdoms; (17) *that* made the world as a wilderness, and destroyed the cities thereof; *that* ² opened not the house of his prisoners?

1 Or, *O day star.*

2 Or, *did not let his prisoners loose homeward.*

---

(10) **Art thou also become weak as we?**—The question implies, of course, an affirmative answer. The king of Babylon, the report of whose coming had roused awe and wonder, is found to be as weak as any of the other Rephaim, the *eidôla*, or shadowy forms, of Homer (*Il.*, xxiii., 72). With these words the vision of the spectral world ends, and the next verse takes up the taunting song of the liberated Israelites, the language of which is, however, influenced by the imagery of the vision.

(11) **Thy pomp is brought down to the grave.** Literally, *to Sheol*, as in verse 9. The "pomp" is the same as the "beauty" of chap. xiii. 19.

The noise of thy viols.—Perhaps *harps*, or *cymbals*, representing one of the prominent features of Babylonian culture (Dan. iii. 5). The singers see, as it were, all this kingly state mouldering in the grave, *maggots* and worms (the two words are different in the Hebrew) taking the place of the costly shawls and carpets on which the great king had been wont to rest.

(12) **How art thou fallen from heaven, O Lucifer, son of the morning!**—The word for Lucifer is, literally, *the shining one*, the planet Venus, the morning star, the *son of the dawn*, as the symbol of the Babylonian power, which was so closely identified with astrolatry. "Lucifer" etymologically gives the same meaning, and is used by Latin poets (Tibull. i., 10, 62) for Venus, as an equivalent for the *phôsphoros* of the Greeks. The use of the word, however, in mediæval Latin as a name of Satan, whose fall was supposed to be shadowed forth in this and the following verse, makes its selection here singularly unfortunate. Few English readers realise the fact that it is the king of Babylon, and not the devil, who is addressed as Lucifer. While this has been the history of the Latin word, its Greek and English equivalents have risen to a higher place, and the "morning star" has become a name of the Christ (Rev. xxii. 16).

(13) **I will ascend into heaven.**—The boast of the Chaldæan king is represented as nothing less than an apotheosis, which they themselves claimed. So Shalmaneser describes himself as "a sun-god" (*Records of the Past*, iii. 83), Assurbanipal as "lord of all kings" (*ib.*, iii. 78). In contrast with the *Sheol* into which the Chaldæan king had sunk, the prophet paints the heaven to which he sought to rise. He, the brightest star, would raise his throne above all the stars of God.

I will sit also upon the mount of the congregation . . .—The words have often been interpreted of Jerusalem or the Temple, as the "mountain of assembly" (as the tabernacle was "the tent of the congregation," or "of meeting"), and "the sides (better, *recesses*) of the north" have been connected, like the same phrase in Ps. xlviii. 2, with the portion of the Temple which the king of Babylon is supposed to threaten. Most modern scholars are, however, agreed that this interpretation is untenable. What is brought before us is the heaven, the "mountain of assembly," where the great gods in whom the king of Babylon believed sat in council. So Assyrian hymns speak of "the feasts of the silver mountains, the heavenly courts" (as the Greeks spoke of Olympus), where the gods dwell eternally (*Records of the Past*, iii. 133). And this ideal mountain was for them, like the Meru of Indian legend, in the farthest north. So in the legendary geography of Greece, the Hyperborei, or "people beyond the north wind," were a holy and blessed race, the chosen servants of Apollo (Herod., ii. 32—36). In Ezek. xxviii. 14 the prophet recognises an ideal "mountain of God" of like nature, and the vision of the future glory of a transfigured Zion, in chap ii. 1—3, implies, as we have seen, an idea of the same kind. Possibly the same thought appears in Ezekiel's vision, "out of the north" (chap. i. 4).

(14) **I will be like the most High.**—The Chaldæan king is rightly represented as using a Divine name (*Eliôn*), which was not essentially Israelite, but common to the Phœnicians and other kindred nations. (See Gen. xiv. 18; Dan. iv. 24; Luke viii. 28; Acts xvi. 17.) The Persians carried their adulation still further, and applied the title "god" to their kings (Æsch. *Pers.* 623), as the Syrians afterwards did in the case of Antiochus Theos. The Assyrian and Babylonian inscriptions, for the most part, fall short of this, and describe the king as the "servant," or "priest," of Assur, or Bel, or Nebo, "the viceroy, or vicar, of the gods."

(15) **Yet thou shalt be brought . . .**—We note in the use of the same words ("the sides, or *recesses*," of the pit), as in the previous verse, the contrast of an indignant sarcasm. Yes, the prophet seems to say, the proud king has found his way to those "recesses;" but they are not in heaven, but in Hades.

(16) **They that see thee . . .**—The context shows that the picture before the prophet's eye is no longer the shadow-world of Hades, but the field of battle. Men look at the corpse of the mighty conqueror as it lies dishonoured, bloody, and unburied.

(17) **That opened not the house of his prisoners.**—Better, as in the margin, *he loosed not his prisoners to their homes*. This was, we may note, a

The Corpse of the great King. ISAIAH, XIV. *The Besom of Destruction.*

(18) All the kings of the nations, *even* all of them, lie in glory, every one in his own house. (19) But thou art cast out of thy grave like an abominable branch, *and as* the raiment of those that are slain, thrust through with a sword, that go down to the stones of the pit; as a carcase trodden under feet. (20) Thou shalt not be joined with them in burial, because thou hast destroyed thy land, *and* slain thy people: *a* the seed of evil-doers shall never be renowned.

(21) Prepare slaughter for his children *b* for the iniquity of their fathers; that they do not rise, nor possess the land, nor fill the face of the world with cities. (22) For I will rise up against them, saith the LORD of hosts, and cut off from Babylon the name, and remnant, and son, and nephew, saith the LORD. (23) I will also make it a possession for the bittern, and pools of water: and I will sweep it with the besom of destruction, saith the LORD of hosts.

a Job 18. 19; Ps. 21. 10 & 37. 28 & 109. 13.

b Ex. 20. 5; Matt. 23. 35.

---

characteristic feature of the cruelty of the Assyrian kings. So Sennacherib and Assurbanipal boast of having carried off captive kings in "chains of iron" (*Records of the Past*, i. pp. 43, 62, 72), and kept them chained like dogs in the court of their palace (*ib.*, pp. 93, 97). So Jehoiachin was kept in prison for thirty-seven years (Jer. lii. 31).

(18) **All the kings of the nations . . .**—The "house" in which the monarchs lie is, of course, their sepulchre. Such sepulchres, as in the case of the pyramid graves of the Egyptian kings, the "eternal home" as they themselves called it (comp. Eccles. xii. 5), were often almost literally the "house," or palace, of the dead.

(19) **Like an abominable branch.**—The noun is the same as in chaps. xi. 1, lx. 21. The idea seems to be that of a scion or shoot which is mildewed and blasted, and which men fling away as loathsome.

As the raiment of those that are slain . . .—The image reminds us of the "garments rolled in blood" of chap. ix. 5, gathered after the battle, and "cast forth" to be burnt. In such raiment, not in stately robes nor kingly grave-clothes, would the great ruler be found. To lie thus unburied, "a prey to dogs and vultures" (Homer, *Iliad*, i. 4), was, as with the Homeric heroes, the shame of all shames.

That go down to the stones of the pit.—By some critics these words are joined with the following verse: *Those that go down . . . with them thou shalt not be joined in burial*, *i.e.*, shalt have no proper sepulchre. As the passage stands, "the stones of the pit" represent the burial-place into which the carcases of the slain were indiscriminately thrown.

(20) **Thou shalt not be joined with them in burial . . .**—The curse of the dishonoured death is connected with its cause. The conqueror had inflicted that shame even on his own people, and was punished in like kind himself. Comp. Jeremiah's prediction as to Jehoiakim (Jer. xxii. 19), and parallel instances in 2 Chron. xxi. 20, xxiv. 25; Ezek. xxix. 5.

The seed of evildoers shall never be renowned.—Literally, *shall not be named for ever*. Here we have a parallel in the sentence on Coniah (Jer. xxii. 30). In the inscription of Eshmunazzar, king of Sidon (quoted by Cheyne), we have both elements of the imprecation: "Let him (the man who violates the sacredness of the king's tomb) not have a couch with the shade, and let him not be buried in the grave, and let him not have son or seed in his stead." In the inscriptions of Tiglath-pileser (*Records of the Past*, v. 26) and Merôdach-baladan III. (*ib.*, ix. 36) we find like curses. Historically, as the *Behistun* inscription shows, the dynasty of Nabopolassar disappeared from history, and Darius boasts of having subdued an impostor, a second Nebuchadnezzar, who claimed to represent it (*Records of the Past*, i. 114).

(21) **Prepare slaughter for his children.**—Literally, as in Jer. li. 40, *a slaughter house*. The command may be addressed to the Medes of chap. xiii. 17, or to any minister of the Divine vengeance. In the judgment of God, as seen in history, that judgment falls necessarily on the last members of an evil and cruel dynasty. In this sense the sins of the fathers are visited on the children, while, in the eternal judgment which lies behind the veil, each single soul stands, as in Ezek. xviii. 4, on its own personal responsibility, and may win pardon for itself. Penitent or impenitent (and the latter seems here implied), the children of the evil-doers should cease to be conquerors and rulers.

Nor fill the face of the world with cities.—The words describe the boast of the great monarchs, who, like Nimrod, built cities to perpetuate their fame. (Comp. Gen. x. 10—12; Dan. iv. 30.) The Babylonian and Assyrian kings record their destructive and constructive work with equal exultation (*Records of the Past*, v., pp. 80, 119, 123). Various readings have been suggested, giving *ruined heaps*, or *terrible ones*, or *enemies*, or *conflicts*; but there seems no need for any change.

(22) **Son, and nephew . . .**—The latter word, as throughout the Bible, is used in its true sense as "grandson," or "descendant." (Comp. 1 Tim. v. 4.) Every word that could express descent is brought together to express the utter extirpation of the Babylonian dynasty. The Hebrew adds the emphasis of alliteration, as in our "bag and baggage," and other like phrases.

(23) **I will also make it a possession for the bittern . . .**—Naturalists are not agreed as to the meaning of the noun. In the LXX. and Vulgate it appears as "hedgehog," or "porcupine," and the "tortoise," "beaver," "otter," and "owl" have all been suggested by scholars. Its conjunction with "pelican" in chap. xxxiv. 11 and Zeph. ii. 14, and with "pools of water" here, is in favour of some kind of water-fowl. The "hedgehog" frequents dry places, and not marshes, and does not roost, as in Zeph. ii. 14, on the capitals of ruined columns. On the whole, therefore, "bittern" (*Botaurus stellaris*) may as well stand.

Pools of water.—These were the natural result of the breaking up of the canals, sluices, reservoirs, which had kept the overflow of the Euphrates within bounds (Diod. Sic., ii. 7).

I will sweep it with the besom of destruction . . .—The phrase has its parallel in the "sieve of vanity," in chap. xxx. 28. (Comp. chap. xxxiv. 11.) The force of the image must not be lost sight of.

The Purpose of the Lord of Hosts. ISAIAH, XIV. *The Burden of the Philistines.*

(24) The LORD of hosts hath sworn, saying, Surely as I have thought, so shall it come to pass; and as I have purposed, *so* shall it stand: (25) that I will break the Assyrian in my land, and upon my mountains tread him under foot: then shall his yoke depart from off them, and his burden depart from off their shoulders. (26) This *is* the purpose that is purposed upon the whole earth: and this *is* the hand that is stretched out upon all the nations. (27) For the LORD of hosts hath *a* purposed, and who shall disannul *it?* and his hand *is* stretched out, and who shall turn it back?

(28) In the year that king Ahaz died was this burden.

(29) Rejoice not thou, whole Palestina, because the rod of him that smote thee is broken: for out of the serpent's root shall come forth a [1] cockatrice, and his fruit *shall be* a fiery flying serpent. (30) And the firstborn of the poor shall feed, and the needy shall lie down in safety: and I will kill thy root with famine, and he shall slay thy remnant. (31) Howl, O gate; cry, O city; thou,

a 2 Chron. 20. 6; Job 9. 19; Prov. 21. 30; Dan. 4. 32.

[1] Or, *adder.*

Babylon is to be swept away as men sweep away some foul rubbish from their house. The world is cleaner for its destruction. The solemn doom closes the "burden" of Babylon.

(24) **The Lord of hosts hath sworn . . .**—The long "oracle" of Babylon is followed by a fragmentary prophecy against Assyria (verses 24—27), possibly misplaced, possibly, as opening with a solemn asseveration, like that of the preceding verse, added by way of proof, that the word of the Lord of Hosts would be fulfilled on Babylon, as it had been on Assyria, with which, indeed, Babylon was closely connected—almost, perhaps, identified—in his thoughts.

(25) **That I will break the Assyrian in my land . . .**—The words found their fulfilment in the destruction of Sennacherib's army. The "mountains" are the hills round Jerusalem on which the army of the Assyrians was encamped. They were sacred, as the phrase, "*my* mountains," shows, to Jehovah (comp. chaps. xlix. 11, lxv. 9; Zech. xiv. 5), and He, therefore, would put forth His power to rescue them from the proud invader.

(26) **This is the hand that is stretched out . . .**—The words point, as it were, to the idea of a universal history. The fall of the Assyrian power and of Babylon does not stand alone, but forms part of a scheme embracing all nations and all ages (chap. ix. 12).

(27) **His hand is stretched out.**—Literally, and more emphatically, *His is the outstretched hand.*

(28) **In the year that king Ahaz died was this burden.**—The prophecies against Babylon and Assyria are naturally followed by a series of like predictions, dealing with other nations which played their part in the great drama of the time. The date of that which comes next in order is obviously specified, either by Isaiah himself or by the compiler of his prophecies, that it might be seen that it was not a prophecy after the event. The death-year of Ahaz was B.C. 727. It was natural that the prophet's thoughts should be much exercised then, as in the year of Uzziah's death (chap. vi. 1), on the uncertainties of the coming future, and the "burden" was the answer to his searchings of heart. It was probably delivered *before* the king's death. (See Note on chap. vi. 1.)

(29) **Rejoice not thou, whole Palestina.**—Better, *Rejoice not thou, Philistia, all of thee; i.e.,* give not thyself wholly to rejoicing. Here, as in Exod. xv. 14, "Palestina" is used, not in the wider meaning with which we are familiar, but specifically as the country of the Philistines. The historical circumstances connected with the "oracle" before us are found in 2 Chron. xxviii. 18. The Philistines had invaded the low country (*Shephēlah*), and the district known as the *Negeb,* or "south" of Judah, in the reign of Ahaz. He had called in the help of Tiglath-pileser, the Assyrian king, to assist him as against Rezin and Pekah (chap. vii.), so probably against these new invaders. Sargon (who succeeded Tiglath-pileser, B.C. 723) invaded Ashdod in B.C. 710 (chap. xx. 1; *Records of the Past,* vii. 40). Sennacherib records a like attack on Ashkelon and (according to Rawlinson's interpretation) Ekron (*Records of the Past,* vii. 61). With these data we are able to enter on the interpretation of Isaiah's prediction.

Because the rod of him that smote thee is broken.—The "rod," as in chap. x. 24, is the power of Tiglath-pileser. The Philistines were exulting in his death, or in that of Ahaz as his ally, as though their peril was past. They are told that their exultation was premature.

Out of the serpent's root.—The three forms of serpent life (we need not be careful about their identification from the zoologist's point of view) may represent the three Assyrian kings named above, from whose invasions the Philistines were to suffer. Each form was more terrible than the preceding. The fiery flying serpent (chap. xxx. 6; Num. xxi. 6), which represented Sennacherib, was the most formidable of the three. So in chap. xxvii. 1, the "piercing serpent," the "crooked serpent," and the "dragon" are symbols of the Assyrian power. Some critics, however, led chiefly by the first words of the next verse, find in the three serpents—(1) Ahaz, (2) Hezekiah, (3) the ideal king of chap. xi. 1—9.

(30) **And the firstborn of the poor shall feed.**—As the "children of the needy" in Ps. lxxii. 4 are simply the poor as a class, so the "firstborn" are those who, as it were, inherit the double portion, not of riches, but of poverty. (Comp. "the firstborn of death" in Job xviii. 13.) The people spoken of are those of Judah, which in the days of Ahaz had been "brought very low" (2 Chron. xxviii. 19). For these the prophet foretells a time of plenty; not so for Philistia. Either through the sieges of their towns or the devastation of their fields, they would be reduced to the last extremities of famine. With them there should be no "remnant" to return.

(31) **Howl, O gate . . .**—The "gate," as elsewhere, is the symbol of the city's strength. The "city" stands probably for Ashdod, as the most conspicuous of the Philistine cities.

From the north.—Here of the Assyrian invaders, as in Jer. i. 14, x. 22, xlvi. 20 of the Chaldean. The

The Lord hath founded Zion. ISAIAH, XV. *The Burden of Moab.*

whole Palestina, *art* dissolved: for there shall come from the north a smoke, and ¹none *shall be* alone in his ²appointed times. ⁽³²⁾ What shall *one* then answer the messengers of the nation? That ᵃthe LORD hath founded Zion, and the poor of his people shall ³trust in it.

1 Or, *he shall* not *be alone.*
2 Or, *assemblies.*
a Ps. 87. 1, 5, & 102. 16.
3 Or, *betake themselves unto it.*
4 Or, *cut off.*

CHAPTER XV.—⁽¹⁾ The burden of Moab.

Because in the night Ar of Moab is laid waste, *and* ⁴brought to silence; because in the night Kir of Moab is laid waste, *and* brought to silence; ⁽²⁾ he is gone up to Bajith, and to Dibon, the

---

"smoke" may be either that of the cities which the Assyrians burnt, or, more probably, the torch-signals, or beacons, which they used in their night marches or encampments (Jer. vi. 1, l. 2). (See Note on chap. iv. 5.)

None shall be alone in his appointed times.—Better, *there is no straggler at the appointed places:* *i.e.,* all the troops shall meet at the rendezvous which was indicated by the column of fiery smoke as a signal.

⁽³²⁾ **What shall one then answer . . . ?**—The words obviously imply that the prophet either had received, or expected to receive, a message of inquiry from the Philistines, and that this is his answer. It seems not improbable, indeed, that the series of prophecies that follow were delivered in answer to such inquiries. The fame of the prophet had spread beyond the confines of Israel, and men of different nations came to Jerusalem to consult him. So Jeremiah's oracles are delivered to the ambassadors who came to propose an alliance against Nebuchadnezzar in the time of Zedekiah (Jer. xxvii. 3). Commonly, however, the words are referred to the embassies of congratulation, which came with plans of new alliances after the destruction of Sennacherib's army (2 Chron. xxxii. 23).

That the Lord hath founded Zion.—This is the answer to all such inquiries. Zion stands firm and safe in the protection of Jehovah. The "poor" (obviously those of verse 30) shall trust (better, *shall find refuge*) in it. (Comp. chap. xxviii. 16.) They need no foreign alliances, no arm of flesh.

XV.

⁽¹⁾ **The burden of Moab.**—The oracle which fills the next two chapters deals with the coming history of Moab. The comparative obscurity of that history, the names of towns and villages which it is difficult to identify, present a striking contrast to the evolution of the great world-drama which is brought before us in the "burden" of Babylon. What light can be thrown on that obscurity must be gathered from what we can learn of the contemporary history of Moab and its relation to Israel. This we know partly from the record of 2 Kings iii., partly from the inscription of the Moabite stone found at Diban, in 1860, by Mr. Klein, and translated by Dr. Ginsburg in *Records of the Past,* xi. 163. Combining the information from these two sources, we find that Omri and Ahab had subdued Moab when that nation was governed by Chemosh-Gad of Dibon, and had compelled him to pay a sheep tribute reckoned by hundreds of thousands. When Jehoram succeeded Ahab, Mesha, the son of Chemosh-Gad, revolted, and the Moabite inscription records the successful issue of the campaign. Jehoram entered into an alliance with Jehoshaphat and the king of Edom. The Moabites were defeated. Their trees were cut down, their wells stopped, and their land made barren. The king of Moab in his despair offered up his son as a sacrifice to Chemosh in the sight of both armies. With that sacrifice apparently the tide of victory turned. Mesha, in his inscription, records how he took Nebo from Israel and slew seven thousand men, and built or restored fortified towns, and offered the vessels of Jehovah, taken probably from the sanctuaries of the "high places" of Nebo. Exulting in the memory of this victory, Moab became "exceeding proud" (chap. xvi. 6), and in a psalm, probably contemporary with Isaiah (see the mention of Assur, or Assyria, in Ps. lxxxiii. 8), they are named as among the enemies of Judah, joined with the Philistines and Assyrians. It is probable enough that, having been kept in check by the prosperous rule of Uzziah, they took advantage of the weakness of Ahaz to renew hostilities, and were looking, half with dread, half with hope, to the Assyrian power. It may be noted here that the following cities named in these chapters—Dibon, Medeba, Nebo, Horonaim—occur also in the Moabite stone, which thus renders a striking testimony to their antiquity, and, so far, to their authenticity. (Comp. Jer. xlviii., which is, to a large extent, a reproduction of Isaiah's language.)

Ar of Moab is laid waste.—This was apparently the older capital (Num. xxi. 28; Deut. ii. 9), sometimes known as Rabbath Moab. In Jerome's time it was known as Areopolis, the Greeks catching, probably, at the resemblance between the name Ar and that of their god, Ares. Probably Ar was a Moabite form of the Hebrew *Ir,* a city. One of the names survives in the modern *Rabba;* but the ruins are comparatively insignificant. The prophet begins with words of threatening. Both that city and Kir (here again the word means "city," and if we identify it, as most experts do, with *Kerek,* the castle on a hill, which rises to 1,000 feet above the Dead Sea, it must have been the strongest of the Moabite fortresses) were to be attacked at night, when resistance was most hopeless. So Mesha boasts (*Records of the Past,* xi. 66) that he had taken Nebo by a night attack. We note the emphasis of iteration in the words "laid waste and brought to silence." The latter clause would be more accurately rendered *cut off,* or *destroyed.*

⁽²⁾ **He is gone up to Bajith . . .**—The noun is better taken not as a proper name, but as "the house" or "temple" of the Moabite god. In this and in the "high places" (*Bamôth*) we may probably recognise the Bamoth-baal (high places of Baal) which appears in Josh. xiii. 17, side by side with Dibon, and the Beth-Bamoth of the Moabite stone (*Records of the Past,* xi. 167). That stone was, it may be noted, found at *Dibân,* which stands on two hills, and represents the ancient city of that name. What the prophet sees as following on the destruction of Ar and Kir is the terror which leads men to join in solemn processional prayers to the temples of their gods.

Nebo.—Not the mountain that bore that name as such (Deut. xxxiv. 1), but a city named after the same deity. Mesha boasts of having taken it, and slain seven thousand men (*Records of the Past,* xi. 166). Medeba is named by him (*ib.*) as having been taken by Omri, and held by the Israelites for forty years.

On all their heads shall be baldness . . .—This, originally, perhaps, sacrificial in its character,

The Wailing of Moab. ISAIAH, XV. *Destruction and Desolation.*

high places, to weep: Moab shall howl over Nebo, and over Medeba: *a* on all their heads *shall be* baldness, *and* every beard cut off. (3) In their streets they shall gird themselves with sackcloth: on the tops of their houses, and in their streets, every one shall howl, ¹weeping abundantly. (4) And Heshbon shall cry, and Elealeh: their voice shall be heard *even* unto Jahaz: therefore the armed soldiers of Moab shall cry out; his life shall be grievous unto him. (5) My heart shall cry out for Moab; ²his fugitives *shall flee* unto Zoar, an *b*heifer of three years old: for by the mounting up of Luhith with weeping shall they go it up; for in the way of Horonaim they shall raise up a cry of ³destruction. (6) For the waters of Nimrim shall be ⁴desolate: for the hay is withered away, the grass faileth, there is no green thing. (7) Therefore the abundance they have gotten, and that which they have laid up, shall they carry away to the ⁵brook of the willows. (8) For the cry is gone round about the borders of Moab; the howling thereof unto Eglaim, and the howling thereof unto Beerelim. (9) For the waters of Dimon shall be full of blood: for I will bring

a Jer. 48. 37, 38; Ezek. 7. 18.

1 Heb., *descending into weeping:* or, *coming down with weeping.*

B.C. clr. 726.

2 Or, *to the borders thereof, even to Zoar, as an heifer.*

b Jer. 48. 5, 34.

3 Heb., *breaking.*

4 Heb., *desolations.*

5 Or, *valley of the Arabians.*

---

became at a very early period a symbol of intensest sorrow among Eastern nations. It was forbidden to Israel, probably as identified with the worship of other deities than Jehovah (Lev. ix. 27, xxi. 5; Deut. xiv. 1; Job i. 20; Micah i. 16; Amos viii. 10).

(3) **In their streets . . .**—The picture of lamentation is continued. The flat roofs of Eastern houses were a natural resort for such wailings (chap. xxii. 1). The "broad places," the *bazaars* or *market-places*, were also, like the *agora* of Greek cities, a natural place of concourse. The prophet represents them as filled with the sound of wailing.

(4) **And Heshbon shall cry, and Elealeh . . .**—Of the places thus named (1) Heshbon (now *Hesban*) was twenty miles east of the Jordan, on a line from the northern extremity of the Dead Sea. It is first mentioned as in the power of Sihon king of the Amorites (Num. xxi. 26). On his overthrow it was assigned to the tribe of Reuben (Num. xxxii. 37), and became a city of the Levites (Josh. xxi. 39). It had probably fallen into the hands of the Moabites, to whom it had originally belonged (Num. xxi. 26). Its ruins exhibit architecture of various periods, Jewish, Roman, and Saracenic; (2) Elealeh, obviously near Heshbon, had shared its fate (Num. xxxii. 3, 37). The ancient name still attaches to its ruins in the form *El-A'al*; (3) Jahaz was the scene of the battle between Sihon and the Israelites (Num. xxi. 23; Deut. ii. 32; Judg. xi. 20), and was also within the region assigned to Reuben (Josh. xiii. 10) north of the Arnon. The language of Isaiah implies that it was at some distance from the other two cities. Their cry was to be heard even there. In the Moabite inscription it appears as annexed to Dibon (*Records of the Past*, xi. 167). Eusebius (*Onomast.*) names it as between Medeba and *Debus*, the latter name being probably identical with Dibon. The panic is intensified by the fact that even the "armed soldiers" of Moab are powerless to help, and can only join in the ineffectual wailing.

(5) **My heart shall cry out for Moab . . .**—The prophet, though a stranger to Moab, and belonging to a hostile people, is touched with pity at the sight—the fugitives fleeing before the army coming from the north to Zoar, at the extreme south of the Dead Sea (see Note on Gen. xix. 22), in the wild scare as of a frightened heifer as yet untamed by the yoke (Jer. xxxi. 18, xlviii. 34, l. 11). The English "fugitives" answers to the marginal reading of the Hebrew, the text of which (followed by the Vulg.) gives, "his bars reach unto Zoar:" but it is not easy to connect this with the context.

By the mounting up of Luhith . . .—No city has been identified as bearing this name. Probably "the *ascent of Luhith*" (the name may indicate a staircase of boards) was the well-known approach (Jer. xlviii. 5) to a Moabite sanctuary. Eusebius (*Onomast.*) speaks of it as between Zoar and Areopolis (Rabbath Moab). Horonaim (here and in Jer. xlviii. 3, 5, 34) is as little known as its companion. The name, which in Hebrew means "two caverns," is, perhaps, descriptive of the nature of the sanctuary. The point of the description is that the fugitives when they reach Horonaim, are met with the cry of destruction, "All is over."

(6) **The waters of Nimrim . . .**—These also appear in Jer. xlviii. 34. They were probably a reservoir from which the fields were irrigated so as to be conspicuous for their verdure. Eusebius (*Onomast.*) places it north of Zoar. The name appears to survive in the *Wady en Nemeirah* on the south-eastern shore of the Dead Sea (De Saulcy, *Voyage*, i. 284; Tristram, *Land of Israel*, 340). Beth-Nimrah appears as the name of a town in Num. xxxii. 36). The desolation predicted was probably thought of as caused by the stoppage of the wells, one of the common acts of an invading army (2 Kings iii. 25).

(7) **Therefore the abundance . . .**—The picture of the flight is completed. The fugitives carry with them all that they can collect together of their household goods, and bear them in their flight.

To the brook of the willows.—This, which has been variously translated as (1) "the torrent of the poplars," or (2) "the Arabians," or (3) "of the wilderness," was probably the *Wady el Achsar*, where a stream falls into the Dead Sea, between the territory of Moab and Edom, the brook Zered of Num. xxi. 12, Deut. ii. 13. It is obviously named here as being the point where the fugitives pass the boundary of their own lands. With less probability it has been taken as a poetical equivalent for the Euphrates (Ps. cxxxvii. 2).

(8) **The cry is gone round about . . .**—The extent of the lamentation is emphasised by naming its farthest points. It reaches (1) Eglaim ("two pools"), probably the same as the En-Eglaim of Ezek. xlvii. 10, as near the Dead Sea. Eusebius (*Onomast.*) names it as eight miles south of Areopolis or Rabbath Moab. Josephus mentions a town Agalla as near Zoar (*Ant.* xii. 1, 4); (2) Beer-Elim ("the well of the terebinths"), perhaps the same as the "well" on the borders of Moab of Num. xxi. 16.

(8) **The waters of Dimon.**—Probably the same as Dibon, the name being slightly altered (*m* and *b*, as

¹more upon Dimon, lions upon him that escapeth of Moab, and upon the remnant of the land.

CHAPTER XVI. — ⁽¹⁾ Send ye the lamb to the ruler of the land from ²³ Sela to the wilderness, unto the mount of the daughter of Zion. ⁽²⁾ For it shall be, *that*, as a wandering bird ⁴cast out of the nest, *so* the daughters of Moab shall be at the fords of Arnon. ⁽³⁾ ⁵Take counsel, execute judgment; make thy shadow as the night in the midst of the noonday; hide the outcasts; bewray not him that wandereth. ⁽⁴⁾ Let mine outcasts dwell with thee, Moab; be thou a covert to them from the face of the spoiler: for the ⁶extortioner is at an end, the spoiler ceaseth, ⁷the oppressors are consumed out of the land. ⁽⁵⁾ And in mercy ᵃshall the throne be ⁸established: and he shall sit upon it in truth in the tabernacle of David, judging, and seeking judgment, and hasting righteousness.

⁽⁶⁾ We have heard of the ᵇpride of Moab; *he is* very proud: *even* of his haughtiness, and his pride, and his wrath: *but* his lies *shall* not *be* so. ⁽⁷⁾ Therefore shall Moab ᶜhowl for Moab, every one shall howl: for the foundations of Kir-hareseth shall ye ⁹mourn;

---

1 Heb., *additions.*
2 Or, *Petra.*
3 Heb., *A rock.*
4 Or, *a nest forsaken.*
5 Heb., *Bring.*
6 Heb., *wringer.*
7 Heb., *the treaders down.*
a Dan. 7. 14, 27; Mic. 4. 7; Luke 1. 33.
8 Or, *prepared.*
b Jer. 48. 29.
c Jer. 48. 20.
9 Or, *mutter.*

---

labial letters, are closely connected in all languages) so as to resemble the Hebrew word for "blood" (*dam*), or *dum* ("silent"). Men should call the stream no more by the name of Dimon, but by that of *the blood*, or *the silent river*. (See Note on chap. xxi. 11.)

I will bring more . . .—*i.e.*, sorrow upon sorrow. The "lions" are either literally such, as in 2 Kings xvii. 25, prowling through the streets of the deserted city (see Notes on chap. xiii. 21), or symbols of Assyrian or other invaders (Jer. iv. 7, v. 6).

XVI.

⁽¹⁾ **Send ye the lamb to the ruler of the land.** —In the days of Ahab, Mesha, the then king of Moab, had paid a tribute of sheep and lambs to the king of Israel (2 Kings iii. 4). On his revolt (as recorded in the *Moabite Inscription*) that tribute had ceased. The prophet now calls on the Moabites to renew it, not to the northern kingdom, which was on the point of extinction, but to the king of Judah as the true "ruler of the land." The name Sela ("a rock") may refer either to the city so-called (better known by its Greek name of Petra), 2 Kings xiv. 7, or to the rock-district of Edom and the confines of Moab generally. In either case the special direction implies that the presence of the invaders described in chap. xv. would make it impossible to send the tribute across the fords of the Jordan, and that it must accordingly be sent by the southern route, which passed through Sela and the desert country to the south of the Dead Sea (Cheyne). Possibly the words are a summons to Edom, which had attacked Judah in the reign of Ahaz (2 Chron. xxviii. 17), to join in a like submission.

⁽²⁾ **As a wandering bird cast out of the nest.** —Better as in the margin, *a forsaken nest*. The "daughters of Moab" either literally, the women driven from their homes, or figuratively (as in verse 1) the whole population of its towns and villages, are represented as fluttering in terror, like birds whose nests are spoiled (comp. chap. x. 14), like the fledglings in the nest, on the fords of Arnon, uncertain whether to return to their old homes or to cross into a strange land. The imagery reminds us of Ps. xi. 1, Prov. xxvii. 8, so also of Æsch. *Agam.* 49—52.

⁽³⁾ **Make thy shadow as the night . . .**—The whole verse is addressed, as the context shows, not by the prophet to Moab, but by Moab to the rulers of Judah. The fugitives call on those rulers to plead for them and act as umpires, to be to them "as the shadow of a great rock in a weary land" (chap. xxxii. 2), black as night whilst the hot sun glares all around. Some critics, however, hold that the prophet still speaks to the Moabites and calls on them to protect the fugitives from Judah as they had done of old (Ruth i. 2; 1 Sam. xxii. 3), and so to secure a return of like protection (Kay).

⁽⁴⁾ **Let mine outcasts dwell with thee . . .** Better, *let the outcasts of Moab dwell with thee*. Judah, as being herself in safety, is once more appealed to to show mercy to the Moabite fugitives. The "oppressors" are, literally, *they that trample under foot*.

⁽⁵⁾ **And in mercy shall the throne . . .**— Better, less definitely, *in mercy shall a throne be established, and one shall sit upon it in truth*. The prophet has in mind the ideal king of chaps. ix. 4—7, xi. 1—5 (of whom Hezekiah was a partial type and representative), whom he expected after the downfall of the Assyrian oppressor. For the "tabernacle of David," comp. Amos ix. 11.

⁽⁶⁾ **We have heard of the pride of Moab . . .** —The hopes of the prophet are clouded by the remembrance of the characteristic sin of Moab. Of this the *Moabite Inscription* gives sufficient evidence. (See Notes on chap. xv.) Isaiah's language finds an echo in Jer. xlviii. 29.

But his lies shall not be so.—Better, "*his lies, or boasts, are of no worth*," are "not so" as they seem to be.

⁽⁷⁾ **Therefore shall Moab howl for Moab.**— Either the whole nation wailing for its downfall, or the survivors wailing for the fallen.

The foundations of Kir-hareseth.—The name has been commonly explained as the "brick fortress," (*city of pottery*). Others, with a different derivation, make it "city of the sun." Others, again (E. H. Palmer, in the *Athenæum* of August 19, 1871), connect it with *háreith*, the modern Moabite name for the hillocks on which the rock fortresses were built. The word for *foundations* occurs in Hos. iii. 1, for *raisin-cakes* ("flagons of wine" in the Authorised version (comp. 2 Sam. vi. 19, Song Sol. ii. 5), and has been supposed to refer to this as the main product of Kir-hareseth, the traffic in which she lost through the destruction of the vineyards, mentioned in the next verse. *Ruins* would, in any case, be better than "foundations."

surely *they are* stricken. (8) For the fields of Heshbon languish, *and* the vine of Sibmah: the lords of the heathen have broken down the principal plants thereof, they are come *even* unto Jazer, they wandered *through* the wilderness: her branches are ¹stretched out, they are gone over the sea.

(9) Therefore I will bewail with the weeping of Jazer the vine of Sibmah: I will water thee with my tears, O Heshbon, and Elealeh: for ²the shouting for thy summer fruits and for thy harvest is fallen. (10) And ªgladness is taken away, and joy out of the plentiful field; and in the vineyards there shall be no singing, neither shall there be shouting: the treaders shall tread out no wine in *their* presses; I have made *their* vintage shouting to cease. (11) Wherefore my bowels shall sound like an harp for Moab, and mine inward parts for Kirharesh. (12) And it shall come to pass, when it is seen that Moab is weary on the high place, that he shall come to his sanctuary to pray; but he shall not prevail.

(13) This *is* the word that the LORD hath spoken concerning Moab since that time. (14) But now the LORD hath spoken, saying, Within three years, as the years of an hireling, and the glory

1 Or, *plucked up.*

2 Or, *the alarm is fallen upon, &c.*

a Jer. 48. 33.

---

(8) **The fields of Heshbon languish . . .**—For Heshbon see Note on chap. xv. 4. Sibmah appears as assigned to the tribe of Reuben, in Num. xxxii. 38, Josh. xiii. 19, and in Jer. xlviii. 32 as famous for its vines. Jerome (*Comm. in Esai.* v.) speaks of it as about half a Roman mile from Heshbon, and as one of the strongest fortresses of Moab. It has not been identified by recent travellers. The names of the chief Moabite cities are brought together by Milton with a singular rhythmical majesty in *Par. Lost*, i., 406—411.

The lords of the heathen . . .—The words admit of this rendering; but another version, equally admissible grammatically, is preferred by most recent critics. *Its branches smote down the lords of the nations,* i.e., the wine of Sibmah was so strong that it "overcame" the princes who drank of it (chap. xxviii. 1; Jer. xxiii. 9). In the word for "lords" (*baalim*), we have a parallel to the "lords of the high places of Arnon," in Num. xxi. 28.

They are come even unto Jazer.—The pronoun may be referred either to the "branches of the vine," or to the "lords of the heathen," as destroyers. Adopting the former construction, we find in the words a description of the extent of the culture of the Sibmah vine. Northward it spread to Jazer on the Gilead frontier (Num. xxxii. 1, 3; 1 Chron. xxvi. 31), rebuilt by the Gadites (Num. xxxii. 35), eastward to the wilderness, westward it crossed the Dead Sea, and re-appeared in the vine-clad slopes of Engedi (Song of Sol. i. 14). In Jer. xlviii. 32, we have "the sea of Jazer." See Note there.

(9) **Therefore I will bewail with the weeping of Jazer . . .**—The prophet, in his sympathy with the sufferings of Moab (see chap. xv. 5), declares that he will weep with tears as genuine as those of Jazer itself over the desolation of its vineyards.

The shouting for thy summer fruits . . .—Better, as in the margin, *on thy summer-fruits, and on thy harvest a shout is fallen,* i.e., not the song of the vintage gatherers and the reapers, but the cry of the enemy as they trample on the fields and vineyards. The force of the contrast is emphasised, as in Jer. xlviii. 33 ("a cheer which is no cheer," Cheyne), by the use of the same word (*hedad*) as that which in the next verse is employed for the song of those that tread the grapes. (Comp. Jer. xxv. 30.) Possibly the word for "harvest" is used generically as including the vintage.

(10) **Out of the plentiful field.**—Literally, *out of the Carmel,* one of Isaiah's favourite words, as in chaps. x. 18, xxix. 17. The word for "shouting" is the *hedad* of the previous verse. In the words, "I have made . . ." Jehovah speaks as declaring that the work of desolation, though wrought by human hands, is yet His. The prophet, while he weeps in true human pity, is taught not to forget that the desolation is a righteous punishment.

(11) **My bowels shall sound like an harp . . .**—The context leaves it uncertain whether the speaker is the prophet as in verse 9, or Jehovah as in verse 10. The former seems, perhaps, the most natural. On the other hand, the very phrase is used of the compassion of Jehovah in chap. lxiii. 15. The "bowels," as in modern language the "heart," were looked on as the seat of the emotions, and as such they vibrate, like the chords of the harp or lyre (*kinnûr*) used at funerals, with the thrills of pity.

(12) **When it is seen . . .**—Better thus: When Moab *appeareth* (*sc.,* as a worshipper), *when he wearies himself on the high place* (the scene of Chemosh-worship), *though he enter into the sanctuary to pray, yet shall he not prevail.* The prophet draws a picture of the unavailing litanies which Moab, like the priests of Baal in 1 Kings xviii. 26, shall offer to his gods.

(13) **Since that time.**—The phrase is used of an indefinite past, like our "of yore," or "of old time." It is variously translated by "hitherto" (2 Sam. xv. 34), "from the beginning" (chap. xlviii. 3, 5, 7). It seems to imply that thus far Isaiah had been in part reproducing the "burden" of an older prophet, or of one given to him to deliver at an earlier date.

(14) **But now the Lord hath spoken . . .**—The point of contrast seems to lie in the vaguer character of what had gone before, and the specific defined prediction that follows. "Within three years," measured with the exactness of the hired labourer, who will not give more than he has contracted for, and of the employer, who will not take less. The same phrase meets us in chap. xxi. 16.

The glory of Moab shall be contemned.—We may infer from the fact that the prophecy was recorded when the writings of Isaiah were collected, whether by himself or another, that men looked on it as an instance of his prevision. History is, indeed, silent as to the manner of its fulfilment. It was probable, however, that the armies of Salmaneser or Sargon swept, as those of Pul and Tiglath-pileser had done

of Moab shall be contemned, with all that great multitude; and the remnant *shall be* very small *and* ¹feeble.

CHAPTER XVII.—⁽¹⁾ The burden of Damascus.

Behold, Damascus is taken away from *being* a city, and it shall be a ruinous heap. ⁽²⁾ The cities of Aroer *are* forsaken: they shall be for flocks, which shall lie down, and none shall make *them* afraid. ⁽³⁾ The fortress also shall cease from Ephraim, and the kingdom from Damascus, and the remnant of Syria: they shall be as the glory of the children of Israel, saith the LORD of hosts.

⁽⁴⁾ And in that day it shall come to pass, *that* the glory of Jacob shall be made thin, and the fatness of his flesh shall wax lean. ⁽⁵⁾ And it shall be as when the harvestman gathereth the corn, and reapeth the ears with his arm; and it shall be as he that gathereth ears in the valley of Rephaim. ⁽⁶⁾ Yet gleaning grapes shall be left in it, as the shaking of an olive tree, two *or* three berries in the top of the uppermost bough, four *or* five in the outmost fruitful branches thereof, saith the LORD God of Israel.

⁽⁷⁾ At that day shall a man look to his Maker, and his eyes shall have respect to the Holy One of Israel. ⁽⁸⁾ And he shall not look to the altars, the work of his hands, neither shall respect *that* which his fingers have made, either the groves, or the ²images.

1 Or, *not many.*

2 Or, *sun images.*

(1 Chron. v. 26), over the region east of the Jordan, and so invaded Moab. (See Note on chap. xvii. 1.) We note that here also there was to be a "remnant," but not like that of Israel, the germ of a renewed strength.

XVII.

⁽¹⁾ **The burden of Damascus.**—Syria, it will be remembered, had been "confederate with Ephraim," *i.e.*, with the kingdom of Israel, against Judah in the reign of Ahaz, and the prophet had then foretold its overthrow by Assyria (chap. vii. 1—16). In 2 Kings xvi. 9, 2 Chron. xxviii. 29, we have a partial fulfilment of that prediction. Writing probably early in the reign of Hezekiah, Isaiah now looks forward to a further fulfilment in the future.

Damascus is taken away from being a city . . .—The words emphasise the result of the Assyrian invasion. The city of ancient days (Gen. xv. 2) should lose glory and be no more worthy of the name; struck out, as it were, from the list of the great cities of the world.

⁽²⁾ **The cities of Aroer are forsaken.**—The LXX. and other versions seem to have followed a different text, and give, "The cities are forsaken for ever." Taking Aroer as the right reading, we note that there were two cities of the name, one in the tribe of Reuben (Deut. ii. 36, iii. 12), afterwards in the possession of Moab (Jer. xlviii. 19), and the other in that of Gad, near Rabbah of Ammon (Num. xxxii. 34; Josh. xiii. 25; 2 Sam. xxiv. 5). The present passage seems to imply a closer connection with Damascus, and therefore a more northern position than that of either of these cities. The latter of the two just named may, however, have been in alliance with Damascus, and so have shared its fate during the Assyrian invasion. Possibly it may have been chosen for special mention on account of the significance of its name ("laid bare") as ominous of utter ruin. The picture of the "flocks" wandering through the streets of the city reminds us of that of Babylon in chap. xiii. 21.

⁽³⁾ **The fortress also shall cease from Ephraim.**—The alliance of the two kingdoms is still prominent in Isaiah's thoughts. Both shall fall, he predicts, together; and, with a stern, grave irony, he paints the downfall of "the remnant of Syria." It shall be "as the glory of the children of Israel," *i.e.*, shall be fleeting and transient as that had been proved to be. There is, perhaps, a special reference to Hosea ix. 11, "Ephraim, their glory shall fly away like a bird."

⁽⁴⁾ **The glory of Jacob shall be made thin.**—The word is the same as that rendered "impoverished" in Judges vi. 8. "Jacob" stands as commonly in the prophets, like Israel, for the northern kingdom, and the words point, therefore, to the downfall, or, adopting the prophet's figurative language, the *emaciation*, of that kingdom.

⁽⁵⁾ **And it shall be as when the harvestman gathereth the corn.**—The work of devastation is described under another image. The conqueror shall plunder the cities of Israel as the reaper cuts off the ears of corn. With his usual Dantesque vividness the prophet localises the imagery. The valley of Rephaim, or, as in Josh. xv. 8, xviii. 16, "of the giants," lay to the south-west of Jerusalem in the direction of Bethlehem. It was famous for its fertility, and was often on that account attacked by the Philistines, who came to carry off its crops (2 Sam. xxiii. 13). The prophet had looked on the reaper's work and had seen in it a parable of that of the Assyrian invader.

⁽⁶⁾ **Yet gleaning grapes shall be left in it.**—The idea of the "remnant" is still in the prophet's thoughts, even in the case of the northern kingdom. First the vineyard, then the olive-yard, supplies a similitude. The "shaking" followed on the "beating" of Deut. xxiv. 20 (comp. chap. xxiv. 13), but even after that a few berries might be seen on the topmost bough.

⁽⁷⁾ **At that day shall a man look to his Maker.**—The words are words of warning hardly less than of promise. There is to be a return to the true faith of Israel, but that return will be brought about by a bitter experience of the results of idolatry. The eyes of men will turn in that hour of their calamity to the Holy One of Israel.

⁽⁸⁾ **The groves or the images.**—Literally, *the Asherah or the sun-images.* The former were conical, tree-like pillars which symbolised the worship of a Canaanite goddess, the giver of good fortune. (See Notes on 2 Kings xxi. 7; 2 Chron. xxxiv. 3—7.)

Scant Harvest of the pleasant Plants. ISAIAH, XVIII. *Trouble at Eveningtide.*

(9) In that day shall his strong cities be as a forsaken bough, and an uppermost branch, which they left because of the children of Israel: and there shall be desolation. (10) Because thou hast forgotten the God of thy salvation, and hast not been mindful of the rock of thy strength, therefore shalt thou plant pleasant plants, and shalt set it with strange slips:

(11) In the day shalt thou make thy plant to grow, and in the morning shalt thou make thy seed to flourish: but the harvest *shall be* a ¹heap in the day of grief and of desperate sorrow.

(12) Woe to the ²multitude of many people, *which* make a noise like the noise of the seas; and to the rushing of nations, *that* make a rushing like the rushing of ³mighty waters! (13) The nations shall rush like the rushing of many waters: but *God* shall rebuke them, and they shall flee far off, and shall be chased as the chaff of the mountains before the wind, and like ⁴a rolling thing before the whirlwind. (14) And behold at eveningtide trouble; *and* before the morning he *is* not. This *is* the portion of them that spoil us, and the lot of them that rob us.

CHAPTER XVIII.—(1) Woe to the

---

1 Or, *removed in the day of inheritance, and there shall be deadly sorrow.*

2 Or, *noise.*

3 Or, *many.*

4 Or, *thistledown.*

---

(9) **In that day shall his strong cities be as a forsaken bough.**—Better, *his fortified cities shall be like a forsaken tract of forest and hill-top.* These were naturally the usual sites of fortresses (2 Chron. xxvii. 4), and the gist of the prediction is that they shall be left uninhabited and in ruins. The LXX., it may be noticed, either followed a different reading or else give a curious paraphrase, "thy cities shall be forsaken, like as the Amorites and Hivites forsook them before the face of the children of Israel." The whole verse reminds us of the "great forsaking" of chap. vi. 12.

(10) **Hast not been mindful of the rock of thy strength.**—Jehovah, as the true defence, the fortress rock of His people (Deut. xxxii. 4), is contrasted with the rock-fortresses in which the people had put their trust. They had forsaken the One, and therefore, by a just retribution, the others should be forsaken.

Therefore shalt thou plant pleasant plants. —Better, *thou didst plant.* The word for "pleasant" is found here only as a common noun. The singular appears as a proper name in Gen. xlvi. 21, Num. xxvi. 40, and in the more familiar instance of *Naaman the Syrian* (2 Kings v. 1). It would appear that the prophet chose the peculiar term to indicate the foreign, in this case the Syrian, character of the worship to which he refers as the "plant" which Israel had adopted. Mr. Cheyne, following an ingenious suggestion of Lagarde's, connects it (1) with the Arabic *Nahr No'man,* the name of the river Belus near Acre, and (2) with the Arabic name (*Shakaiku-'n-nomân*) for the red anemone. The former was near the head-quarters of the worship of Thammuz, the Phœnician Adonis, and the flower was sacred to him, and so it is inferred that the prophet refers to "the gardens of Adonis," fair but perishable (Plato, *Phædr.* p. 276 B), in which Israel had delighted (Ezek. viii. 14). The addition of "strange slips," literally, *vine-slips of a strange one* —i.e., of a strange god (comp. Jer. ii. 21)—confirms at least the general drift of this interpretation.

(11) **In the day shalt thou make.**—Better, *thou makest,* or, *thou fencest, thy plant.* The alliance between Syria and Ephraim is compared in the rapidity of its growth with the "gardens of Adonis." All the "harvest heaps" from such a planting would end, not in the wonted joy of harvest (chap. ix. 3), but in "grief and *incurable* pain." There is no sufficient evidence for the marginal reading of the Authorised version.

(12) **Woe to the multitude of many people.**— The three verses 12—14 stand as an isolated fragment, probably placed here as beginning like chap. xviii. 1. They may have been connected with the progress of Sennacherib's army. In the "rushing of mighty waters" to describe the march of an army we have a parallel to chap. viii. 7, 8.

(13) **But God shall rebuke them.**—Better, *He shall rebuke.* The insertion of the word "God" weakens the force of the sublime indefiniteness of the Hebrew.

Like a rolling thing.—The Hebrew word is the same as the "wheel" of Ps. lxxxiii. 13, and probably refers, like the "chaff of the mountains," to the *whirling dust-clouds* driven from an elevated threshing-floor before the wind (Ps. i. 4; xxxv. 5). There is no sufficient authority for the "thistle-down" of the margin.

(14) **And behold at eveningtide trouble.**—The words, though spoken in general terms, received a special fulfilment in the destruction of Sennacherib's army (chap. xxxvii. 36). Possibly the parallelism they present to verse 11 may have led to the insertion of the oracle in this place.

XVIII.

(1) **Woe to the land shadowing with wings.**— A new kingdom, hitherto unnamed by Isaiah, comes now within his horizon. The movements of Tirhakah, king of Cush or Ethiopia, from the upper valley of the Nile, subduing Egypt, and prepared to enter into conflict with the great Assyrian king (chap. xxxvii. 9), had apparently excited the hopes of such of Hezekiah's counsellors as put their trust in an arm of flesh. To these Isaiah now turns with words of warning. The words "shadowing with wings" have been very variously interpreted as implying (1) the image of a mighty eagle stretching out its imperial wings (Ezek. xvii. 1—8); (2) the *urœus* or disk with outspread wings which appears in Egyptian paintings as the symbol of Ethiopian sovereignty; (3) the rendering *resounding* being adopted instead of "shadowing," the swarms of the *tse-tse* fly that have been the terror of all travellers in Abyssinia. Of these (2) has most to commend it, and receives confirmation from the inscription of Piankhi-Mer-Amon, translated by Canon Cook in *Records of the Past* (ii. p. 89), in which that king, an Ethiopian, who had conquered Egypt, appears with the *urœus* on his head, and

The Messengers to Ethiopia.   ISAIAH, XIX.   *The Gift to the Lord of Hosts in Zion.*

land shadowing with wings, which *is* beyond the rivers of Ethiopia: (2) that sendeth ambassadors by the sea, even in vessels of bulrushes upon the waters, *saying,* Go, ye swift messengers, to a nation ¹scattered and peeled, to a people terrible from their beginning hitherto; ²³a nation meted out and trodden down, ⁴whose land the rivers have spoiled! (3) all ye inhabitants of the world, and dwellers on the earth, see ye, when he lifteth up an ensign on the mountains; and when he bloweth a trumpet, hear ye.

(4) For so the LORD said unto me, I will take my rest, and I will ⁵consider in my dwelling place like a clear heat ⁶upon herbs, *and* like a cloud of dew in the heat of harvest. (5) For afore the harvest, when the bud is perfect, and the sour grape is ripening in the flower, he shall both cut off the sprigs with pruning hooks, and take away *and* cut down the branches. (6) They shall be left together unto the fowls of the mountains, and to the beasts of the earth: and the fowls shall summer upon them, and all the beasts of the earth shall winter upon them.

(7) In that time shall the present be brought unto the LORD of hosts of a people ⁷scattered and peeled, and from a people terrible from their beginning hitherto; a nation meted out and trodden under foot, whose land the rivers have spoiled, to the place of the name of the LORD of hosts, the mount Zion.

CHAPTER XIX.—(1) The burden of Egypt.

Behold, the LORD rideth upon a swift cloud, and shall come into Egypt: and the idols of Egypt shall be moved at his presence, and the heart of Egypt shall

---

Marginal notes:
1 Or, *outspread and polished.*
2 Or, *a nation that meteth out, and treadeth down.*
3 Heb., *a nation of line, line, and treading under foot.*
4 Or, *whose land the rivers despise.*
B.C. cir. 714.
5 Or, *regard my set dwelling.*
6 Or, *after rain.*
7 Or, *outspread and polished, &c.*

---

the chiefs of the north and south cry out to him, "Grant us to be under thy shadow." (Comp. chap. xxx. 2, 3.) The phrase, "beyond the river," points, as in Zeph. iii. 10, to the region of the White and the Blue Nile, south of Meroe or *Sennar,* and not far from the Lake Nyanza of modern explorers.

(2) **That sendeth ambassadors . . .**—The words point to the embassies which the Ethiopian king had sent, in the papyrus boats used for the navigation of the Upper Nile, down that river to Hezekiah and other princes, inviting them to join the alliance against Assyria.

Go, ye swift messengers . . .—The interpolated "saying" being omitted, the words that follow are as the prophet's address to the messengers, as he sends them back to their own people. Instead of "scattered and peeled," we are to read *tall and polished,* as describing the *physique* which had probably impressed itself on Isaiah's mind. (Comp. the Sabeans as "men of stature" in chap. xlv. 14.) They were terrible then, as they had ever been (*i.e.,* imperious and mighty), a nation *that treadeth down* its foes. Instead of "meted out and trodden down," they are a nation of *command, command* (or, perhaps, "strength, strength"). The rivers are literally the affluents of the Nile that *intersect* and fertilise (not "spoil") the hills and valleys of Nubia. Some commentators, however, though with less probability, accept the Authorised version, and refer the words to Israel, as "scattered and plundered," with its land "spoiled" by the "rivers" of invading armies (chap. viii. 7).

(3) **When he lifteth up an ensign . . .**—Both clauses are better taken as indefinite, *when an ensign is set up . . . when a trumpet is sounded.* The prophet calls on all nations (Ethiopia being specially included) to watch for the signal that shall be given, distinct as the beacon-fire on the hill, or the alarm of the trumpet, to proclaim the downfall of Assyria.

(4, 5) **I will take my rest . . .**—The words that follow paint with marvellous vividness the calmness and deliberation of the workings of Divine judgments.

God is at once unhasting and unresting. He dwells in His resting-place (*i.e.,* palace or throne), and watches the ripening of the fruit which He is about to gather. *While there is a clear heat in sunshine, while there is a dew-cloud in harvest-heat,* through all phenomenal changes, He waits still. Then, *before the harvest, when the blossom is over, and the fruit becomes the full-ripe grape,* He comes as the Lord of the vineyard, and cuts off the branches with His pruning-hooks. (Comp. the striking parallels of Æsch. *Suppl.* 90—98, and Shakespeare, *Henry VIII.,* iii. 2.)

(6) **They shall be left together unto the fowls of the mountains . . .**—The figure and the reality are strangely blended. The grapes of that vintage cut off by those pruning-hooks are none other than the carcases of the host of the Assyrians left unburied, to be devoured by the dogs and vultures.

(7) **In that time shall the present be brought . . .**—Not "of the people," but *a people,* as being themselves the present. The prophet foresees, as one result of the defeat of the Assyrian armies, that the nation, which he again describes instead of naming, will offer themselves to the service of Jehovah. So taken the words have an interesting parallel in Ps. lxviii. 31, "Ethiopia stretches out her hands unto God," or in the mention of Ethiopia in Ps. lxxxvii. 3, as among the nations whose children are to be enrolled among the citizens of Zion. Messengers who may have justified Isaiah's words were probably found among the envoys mentioned in 2 Chron. xxxii. 23. Here, again, the words have been referred as before, to Israel.

XIX.

(1) **The burden of Egypt.**—In its political bearings, as Egypt and Ethiopia were at this time under the same ruler, Tirhakah, as they had been before under Piankhi-Mer-Amon, this prophecy presents nearly the same features as the preceding. Its chief characteristic is that it presents the condition of the conquered nation as distinct from that of the conqueror. The opening

The Burden of Egypt. ISAIAH, XIX. *The Failure of the Waters of the Nile.*

melt in the midst of it. (2) And I will ¹set the Egyptians against the Egyptians: and they shall fight every one against his brother, and every one against his neighbour; city against city, *and* kingdom against kingdom. (3) And the spirit of Egypt ²shall fail in the midst thereof; and I will ³destroy the counsel thereof: and they shall seek to the idols, and to the charmers, and to them that have familiar spirits, and to the wizards. (4) And the Egyptians will I ⁴give over into the hand of a cruel lord; and a fierce king shall rule over them, saith the Lord, the LORD of hosts. (5) And the waters shall fail from the sea, and the river shall be wasted and dried up. (6) And they shall turn the rivers far away; *and* the brooks of defence shall be emptied and dried up: the reeds and flags shall wither. . (7) The paper reeds by the brooks, by the mouth of the brooks, and every thing sown by the brooks, shall wither, be driven away, ⁵and be no more. (8) The fishers also shall mourn, and all they that cast angle into the brooks shall lament, and they that spread nets upon the waters shall languish. (9) Moreover they that work in fine flax, and they that weave ⁶networks, shall be confounded. (10) And they shall be broken in the ⁷purposes thereof, all that make sluices *and* ponds ⁸for fish.

(11) Surely the princes of Zoan *are* fools, the counsel of the wise counsellors of Pharaoh is become brutish: how say ye unto Pharaoh, I *am* the son of the

1 Heb., *mingle.*
2 Heb., *shall be emptied.*
3 Heb., *swallow up.*
4 Or, *shut up.*
5 Heb., *and shall not oe.*
6 Or, *white works.*
7 Heb., *foundations.*
8 Heb., *of living things.*

---

words declare that the long-delayed judgment is at last coming, swift as a cloud driven by the storm-wind, upon the idols of Egypt. Men shall feel that the presence of the Mighty One is among them.

(2) **I will set the Egyptians against the Egyptians** . . .—The discord predicted was probably the natural consequence of the overthrow of the Ethiopian power by Sargon, the Assyrian king, in B.C. 720. Under Piankhi each *nome*, or district, had been governed by a chief, owning the suzerainty of the Ethiopian king, and these, when the restraint was removed, would naturally assert their independence. So Herodotus (ii. 147) relates that on the overthrow of Sabaco, the last of the Ethiopian dynasty, the unity of Egypt was broken up into a dodecarchy.

(3) **The charmers, and to them that have familiar spirits** . . .—The old reputation of Egypt for magic arts (Exod. vii. 22, viii. 7) seems to have continued. The "charmers" or *mutterers* were probably distinguished, like "those that peep" in chap. viii. 19, by some peculiar form of ventriloquism. A time of panic, when the counsels of ordinary statesmen failed, was sure there, as at Athens in its times of peril, to be fruitful in oracles and divinations.

(4) **Into the hand of a cruel lord.**—The later history of Egypt presents so many pictures of oppressive government, that it is hard to say to which of them the picture thus drawn bears most resemblance. Sargon, or Esarhaddon, or Psammetichus, who became king of Egypt on the breaking up of the dodecarchy, or Nebuchadnezzar, or Cambyses, has, each in his turn, been identified as presenting the features of the "cruel lord."

(5) **The waters shall fail from the sea.**—The "sea," like the river, is, of course, the Nile (Homer calls it *Oceanus*), or, possibly, indicates specially the Pelusiac branch of the river. So the White and Blue Niles are respectively the White and Blue Seas (*Bahr*). The words that follow seem to describe partly the result of the failure of the annual rising of the Nile, partly of the neglect of the appliances of irrigation caused by the anarchy implied in verse 2 (Herod. ii. 137).

(6) **And they shall turn the rivers far away.**—Better, *the river shall stagnate*; *i.e.*, in consequence of the Nile's inundation failing.

The brooks of defence.—The latter noun (Heb., *matzor*) is better treated as a proper name, the singular of the dual form Mitsraim, commonly used for Egypt. Here it would seem to be used for Lower Egypt, the region of Zoan and Memphis, as distinct from Upper Egypt or the Thebaid. The same form occurs in chap. xxxvii. 25; 2 Kings xix. 24; Micah vii. 12. Its primary meaning is that of a fortified land. The "flags" are strictly the papyrus of the Nile; the "brooks" are the canals or Nile-branches of the Delta.

(7) **The paper reeds by the brooks.**—Better, *the meadows by the Nile*. And so in the other clauses, the Hebrew word for "brooks" being used specifically for that river. For "shall wither and be driven away," read, *shall dry up and vanish*. The valley of the Nile is to become as parched and barren as the desert on either side of it.

(8) **The fishers also shall mourn.**—With the failure of the river, one at least of the industries of Egypt failed also. Fish had at all times formed part of the diet of the working-classes of Egypt (Herod. ii. 93; Num. xi. 5), and the pictures of Egyptian life continually represent the two modes of fishing, with the "angle" or hook, and with the net.

(9) **Moreover they that work in fine flax.**—Another class also would find its occupation gone. The "fine flax" was used especially for the dress of the priests (Herod. ii. 81), and for the mummy clothes of the dead (1 Kings x. 28; Ezek. xxvii. 7).

They that weave networks. — Better, *white cloths*, the cotton or byssus fabrics for which Egypt was famous.

(10) **And they shall be broken in the purposes thereof.**—Better, *the pillars thereof* (*i.e.*, the props and columns of the state) *shall be broken in pieces, and all those who work for wages* (*i.e.*, the great masses of the people) *shall be troubled in mind*. The word translated "purposes," occurs in the sense here given in Ps. xi. 3, and is there translated "foundations." (Compare the like figure in Ezek. xxx. 4; Gal. ii. 9.)

(11) **Surely the princes of Zoan are fools.**—Zoan, the great city of the Delta, was known to the Greeks as Tanis, founded, as stated in Num. xiii. 22, seven years after Hebron. Here the great Rameses II.

The Wisdom of Egypt   ISAIAH, XIX.   *turned to Folly.*

wise, the son of ancient kings? ⁽¹²⁾ Where are they? where are thy wise men? and let them tell thee now, and let them know what the LORD of hosts hath purposed upon Egypt. ⁽¹³⁾ The princes of Zoan are become fools, the princes of Noph are deceived; they have also seduced Egypt, *even* ¹²*they that are* the stay of the tribes thereof. ⁽¹⁴⁾ The LORD hath mingled ³a perverse spirit in the midst thereof: and they have caused Egypt to err in every work thereof, as a drunken *man* staggereth in his vomit. ⁽¹⁵⁾ Neither shall there be *any* work for Egypt, which the head or tail, branch or rush, may do.

¹ Or, *governors.*

² Heb., *corners.*

³ Heb., *a spirit of perversities.*

⁴ Heb., *the lip.*

⁵ Or, *of Heres,* or *of the sun.*

⁽¹⁶⁾ In that day shall Egypt be like unto women: and it shall be afraid and fear because of the shaking of the hand of the LORD of hosts, which he shaketh over it. ⁽¹⁷⁾ And the land of Judah shall be a terror unto Egypt, every one that maketh mention thereof shall be afraid in himself, because of the counsel of the LORD of hosts, which he hath determined against it.

⁽¹⁸⁾ In that day shall five cities in the land of Egypt speak ⁴the language of Canaan, and swear to the LORD of hosts; one shall be called, The city ⁵of destruction.

⁽¹⁹⁾ In that day shall there be an altar

---

fixed his capital, and the city thus acquired the name of Pi-Rameses.

How say ye unto Pharaoh . . . ?—The princes of Zoan, probably priest-princes and priest-magicians (Exod. vii. 11), boasting at once of their wisdom and their ancestry, are represented as speaking to the Pharaoh of the time (probably, as in chap. xviii., of Ethiopian origin) in something like a tone of superiority. They claim to be the only counsellors; and the prophet challenges their claim. Can they disclose, as he can, the future that impends over their country?

⁽¹³⁾ **The princes of Noph.**—Probably, as in the LXX., Noph is the same as Memphis. The name has been derived (1) from *Ma-m-pthah* ("the house of Pthah," an Egyptian deity of the Hephæstos, or Vulcan type); or (2), and more correctly, from *Men-nepher* ("place of the good"). This also was, as in Hosea ix. 6 (where we have the form Moph), one of the chief royal cities of Lower Egypt, and the seat of the Ethiopian dynasty then ruling.

Even they that are the stay of the tribes thereof.—Better, *the corner-stone of the castes.* The word is the same as the "corner" of Zech. x. 4, the "chief" of Judges xx. 2; 1 Sam. xiv. 38, and describes the position of superiority among the Egyptian castes claimed by the priest-rulers of Zoan and Noph.

⁽¹⁴⁾ **The Lord hath mingled a perverse spirit.**—Better, *hath poured a spirit of giddiness.* As in 1 Kings xxii. 22; 1 Sam. xvi. 14, the infatuation of the Egyptian rulers is thought of as a judicial blindness. Prostrate or vacillating amid the wrecks of frustrated hopes and plans, they are as the drunkard staggering in his foulness. (Comp. chap. xxix. 9.)

⁽¹⁵⁾ **The head or tail, branch or rush.**—For this figurative description of all classes of the people, see Note on chap. ix. 14.

⁽¹⁶⁾ **In that day shall Egypt be like unto women.**—This image of panic, terror, and weakness has been natural in the poetry of all countries (comp. Homer, "Achæan women, not Achæan men"), and appears in its strongest form in Jer. xlviii. 41. In such a state, even the land of Judah, once so despised, shall become a source of terror.

⁽¹⁸⁾ **In that day shall five cities in the land of Egypt speak the language of Canaan.**—The prophecy is, it will be noticed, parallel to that affecting Ethiopia in chap. xviii. 7, and at least expresses the yearnings of the prophet's heart after the conversion of Egypt to the worship of Jehovah. Like the previous prediction, it connects itself with Ps. lxxxvii., as recording the admission of proselytes as from other countries, so also from Rahab (*i.e.*, Egypt). The "five cities" stand either as a certain number for an uncertain (chap. xxx. 17, xvii. 6; Lev. xxvi. 8; 1 Cor. xiv. 19), or possibly as the actual number of the chief or royal cities of Egypt. The "language of Canaan" is Hebrew, and the prediction is that this will become the speech of the worshippers of Jehovah in the Egyptian cities. There is to be one universal speech for the universal Church of the true Israel.

And swear to the Lord of hosts.—The oath, as in the parallel phrase of chap. xlv. 23, is one of allegiance, and implies, therefore, something like a covenant of obedience.

The city of destruction.—There is probably something like a play on the name of the Egyptian city On, the Greek Heliopolis, the City of the Sun (Heb., *Ir-ha-kheres*), and the word which the prophet actually uses (*Ir-ha-cheres*), the "city of destruction." The paronomasia, like in character to Ezekiel's transformation of On into Aven, "nothingness," or "vanity" (Ezek. xxx. 17), or Hosea's of Beth-el ("house of God") into Bethaven ("house of nothingness") (Hos. iv. 15), was intended to indicate the future demolition of the sun-idols, and is so interpreted in the Targum on this passage, "Bethshemesh (*i.e.*, Heliopolis), whose future fate shall be destruction." The word for destruction is cognate with the verb used of Gideon's breaking down the image of Baal, in Judges vi. 25; and in Jeremiah's prophecy (xliii. 13), "He shall break the pillars in the house of the sun," we may probably trace an allusive reference to Isaiah's language. Other meanings, such as "city of rescue," "city of protection," "city of restoration," have been suggested, but on inadequate grounds. The Vulg. gives *civitas solis.* The LXX. rendering, "city *asedek,*" apparently following a different reading of the Hebrew, and giving the meaning, "city of righteousness," was probably connected historically with the erection of a Jewish temple at Leontopolis by Onias IV., in the time of Ptolemy Philomêtor, which for some two centuries shared with the Temple at Jerusalem the homage of Egyptian Jews. Onias and his followers pointed to Isaiah's words as giving a sanction to what their brethren in Palestine looked on as a rival and sacrilegious worship.

⁽¹⁹⁾ **In that day shall there be an altar to the Lord . . .**—The words naturally tended to bring about their own fulfilment, as related in the preceding

to the LORD in the midst of the land of Egypt, and a pillar at the border thereof to the LORD. (20) And it shall be for a sign and for a witness unto the LORD of hosts in the land of Egypt: for they shall cry unto the LORD because of the oppressors, and he shall send them a saviour, and a great one, and he shall deliver them. (21) And the LORD shall be known to Egypt, and the Egyptians shall know the LORD in that day, and shall do sacrifice and oblation; yea, they shall vow a vow unto the LORD, and perform *it*. (22) And the LORD shall smite Egypt: he shall smite and heal *it*: and they shall return *even* to the LORD, and he shall be intreated of them, and shall heal them.

(23) In that day shall there be a highway out of Egypt to Assyria, and the Assyrian shall come into Egypt, and the Egyptian into Assyria, and the Egyptians shall serve with the Assyrians.

(24) In that day shall Israel be the third with Egypt and with Assyria, *even* a blessing in the midst of the land:

---

note. From the prophet's own stand-point, however, the altar was probably thought of, not as the centre of a rival worship, but, like that erected by the trans-Jordanic tribes in the time of Joshua, as an altar of "witness" (Josh. xxii. 27), and the words that follow supply a distinct confirmation of this view. Substantially the prophet saw in the distant future a time in which the connection between Judah and Egypt should be one influencing the latter for good, and not the former for evil. The admission of Egyptian and Ethiopian proselytes, already referred to, was as the first fruits of such an influence. It may not be without interest to note some of its later workings. (1) In the time of Manasseh, who gave to his son Amon a name singularly Egyptian in its sound, a body of Jewish settlers were invited by Psammetichus to station themselves on the frontiers of Upper Egypt ("Pseudo-Aristeas," in Hudson's *Josephus*). (2) Under Ptolemy I. large numbers of Jewish emigrants fixed themselves at Alexandria, with full toleration of their faith and worship. (3) Under Ptolemy Philadelphus the intercourse between the Palestinians and Egyptians led to the translation of the Old Testament Scriptures known as the LXX., and this was followed by the growth of a Hellenistic or a Græco-Jewish literature, of which we have the remains in the Apocrypha and in Philo. (4) There was the erection of the Leontopolis Temple, already spoken of, and this was followed by that of numerous synagogues, perhaps also of monasteries for communities of Jewish ascetics of the Essene type, such as that which Philo describes under the name of the *Therapœutæ* (Euseb. *H.E.* ii. 17).

A pillar at the border thereof . . .—The pillar was the familiar obelisk of the Egyptians, commonly associated with the worship of the sun. The point of Isaiah's prediction was that the symbol should be rescued from its idolatrous uses, and stand on the borderland of Egypt and of Judah, as a witness that Jehovah, the Lord of hosts, was worshipped in both countries.

(20) **For they shall cry unto the Lord because of the oppressors** . . .—The words are almost as an anticipation of the great truth proclaimed in John iv. 21. The prayers of the worshippers in spirit and in truth, whether Jews or proselytes, in Egypt should find as immediate an access to the ear of Jehovah as if they had been offered in the Temple at Jerusalem. If the people suffered under the oppression of a Pharaoh, or a Cambyses, or a Ptolemy, and prayed for deliverance, He would as certainly send them a saviour who should free them from the yoke as He had sent saviours to Israel of old in the persons of the judges (Judg. iii. 9, 15, iv. 4). It is open to us to see a yet higher fulfilment in the fact that the message of the Gospel brought peace and joy to those who were weary and heavy laden in Egypt, as well as in Galilee; to those who were looking for redemption in Alexandria not less than to those who were looking for it in Jerusalem.

(21) **The Egyptians shall know the Lord** . . . —Here also we note what we may venture to call the catholicity of Isaiah's mind. The highest of all blessings, the knowledge of God as He is (John xvii. 3), was not to be the exclusive inheritance of Israel, but was to be shared even by the nation whom she had reason to regard as her hereditary enemy.

Sacrifice and oblation.—The two words describe respectively the slain victims and the meat, or rather, *meal*, offerings of the Law. Did the prophet, we ask, think of such sacrifices as literally offered in Egypt, or did he look beyond the symbol to the thing symbolised? The builders of the temple at Leontopolis took the former view. Those who have entered into the mind and spirit of Isaiah will be inclined, perhaps, to take the latter. A literal fulfilment has been found in the fact that Ptolemy Euergetes (B.C. 244) came to Jerusalem to offer sacrifices in the Temple.

(22) **And the Lord shall smite Egypt** . . . —The tone of the preceding verses seems at first at variance with the stern prophecies of disaster with which the chapter opened. The prophet, however, is no eater of his words. What he has learnt is to look beyond the chastisement, and to see that it is as true of Egypt as of Israel, that "whom the Lord loveth He chasteneth." The sword of Jehovah smote but to heal, and the healing could not come without the smiting. Through it they would be led to pray, and prayer was the condition of all spiritual recovery.

(23) **In that day shall there be a highway out of Egypt to Assyria.**—The prophet's horizon at once brightens and expands. Palestine was in his time the battle-field of the two great empires. The armies of one of the great powers crossed it both before and after, as in the case of Shishak, Zerah, Tirhakah, Necho, Sargon, Sennacherib, Nebuchadnezzar, on their march against the other. The prophet looks forward to a time when the long-standing discord should cease (Assyria, or the power which succeeded her, gaining for a time the suzerainty), and both should be joined with Israel, as in "a three-fold cord, not easily broken." Like other bright ideals of the future, it yet waits for its complete fulfilment. The nearest historical approximation to it is, perhaps, found in the Persian monarchy, including, as it did, the territory of Assyria, of Israel, and of Egypt, and acknowledging,

(25) whom the LORD of hosts shall bless, saying, Blessed be Egypt my people, and Assyria the work of my hands, and Israel mine inheritance.

CHAPTER XX.—(1) In the year that Tartan came unto Ashdod, (when Sargon the king of Assyria sent him,) and fought against Ashdod, and took it; (2) at the same time spake the LORD [1]by Isaiah the son of Amoz, saying, Go and loose the sackcloth from off thy loins, and put off thy shoe from thy foot. And he did so, walking naked and barefoot. (3) And the LORD said, Like as my servant Isaiah hath walked naked and barefoot three years for a sign and wonder upon Egypt and upon Ethiopia: (4) so shall the king of Assyria lead away [2]the Egyptians prisoners, and the Ethiopians captives, young and old, naked and barefoot, even with their buttocks uncovered, to the [3]shame of Egypt. (5) And they shall be afraid and ashamed of Ethiopia their expectation, and of Egypt their glory. (6) And the inhabitant of this [4]isle shall say in that day, Behold, such is our

[1] Heb., by the hand of Isaiah.
[2] Heb., the captivity of Egypt.
[3] Heb., nakedness.
[4] Or, country.

---

through the proclamations of Cyrus, Jehovah as the God of heaven (Ezra i. 2). May we connect this prediction with Isaiah's distinctly defined anticipation of the part which Persia was to play in the drama of the world's history as an iconoclastic and monotheistic power, and so with the dominant idea of chaps. xl—lxvi.?

(25) **Whom the Lord of hosts shall bless . . .**—In this tripartite holy alliance Israel is to retain the spiritual supremacy. Egypt, once alien, becomes the people of the Lord. (Comp. Hosea i. 9, 10.) Assyria is recognised as the instrument which He has made to do His work (comp. chaps. x. 15, xxxvii. 26); but Israel has the proud pre-eminence of being His "inheritance."

XX.

(1) **In the year that Tartan came unto Ashdod.**—Better, *the Tartan*. The word was an official title borne by the generalissimo of the Assyrian armies, who was next in authority to the king. He may, or may not, have been the same with the officer of the same rank who appears in 2 Kings xviii. 17 as sent by Sennacherib to Jerusalem.

When Sargon the king of Assyria sent him.—Much light has been thrown by the Assyrian inscriptions on the events connected with this king. Prior to that discovery, there was no trace of his name to be found elsewhere than in this passage, and his very existence had been called in question. As it is, he comes before us as one of the greatest of Assyrian monarchs. He succeeded Shalmaneser VI., the conqueror of Israel, in B.C. 721, at first as guardian and co-regent of his son Samdan-Malik, and afterwards in his own name. His reign lasted till B.C. 704, when he was succeeded by Sennacherib. Long inscriptions, giving the annals of his reign, were found by M. Botta at Khorsabad, and have been interpreted by M. Oppert (*Records of the Past*, vii. 21, ix. 1, xi. 17, 27, 33) and others.

And fought against Ashdod.—The occasion of the campaign is related by Sargon in the annals just mentioned as happening in his eleventh year. Azuri, the king of Ashdod, refused to pay tribute, and revolted. Sargon deposed him, and placed his brother Akhismit, on the throne. The people, in their turn, rose against Akhismit, and chose Yaman as their king. Sargon then marched against the city, took it, and carried off its gods and its treasures as booty (*Records of the Past*, vii. 40). These events naturally excited the minds of Hezekiah and his counsellors, and led them to look to an alliance with Egypt as their best protection.

(2) **Go and loose the sackcloth from off thy loins.**—Against these schemes Isaiah was prompted to prophesy in act as well as words. Month by month, for three whole years, he was seen in the streets of Jerusalem as one who was already as a prisoner of war, ready to be led into an ignominious exile. The "sackcloth" was the "rough garment" which, like Elijah (2 Kings i. 8) and John the Baptist, the prophets habitually wore (Zech. xiii. 4), and the "nakedness" was confined to the laying aside this outer robe, and appearing in the short tunic worn near the body (1 Sam. xix. 24; 2 Sam. vi. 14—20; John xxi. 7). Like instances of prophetic symbolism are the horns of Zedekiah in 1 Kings xxii. 11, the yokes worn by Jeremiah (Jer. xxvii. 2), Ezekiel's lying on his side (Ezek. iv. 4), and the girdle with which Agabus bound himself (Acts xxi. 11).

(3) **For a sign and wonder upon Egypt and upon Ethiopia.**—Apparently Isaiah prophesied in act, but in silence, and did not unfold the meaning of the symbol till the three years came to an end. There are no adequate grounds for limiting his dramatic action to a single day or three days. Egypt and Ethiopia are, as in chaps. xviii., xix., closely connected, both countries being under a king of Ethiopian origin, Sabaco.

(4) **So shall the king of Assyria lead away the Egyptians . . .**—The prediction did not receive its fulfilment in the reign either of Sargon or Sennacherib, but Esarhaddon subdued the whole of Egypt, carried off its treasures, and appointed satraps over its provinces (Budge's *Esarhaddon*, pp. 111—129). The prophet paints the brutality with which prisoners were treated on a march in vivid colours. What would men say of their boasted policy of an Egypto-Cushite alliance when they saw that as its disastrous issue? It may be noted that Rabshakeh's scornful phrase, "This bruised reed," seems to imply that Assyria had ceased to fear the power of Egypt; and Nahum (Nah. iii. 8) speaks of No (*i.e.*, No-Amun or Thebes) as having, when he wrote, been conquered, and his people carried into captivity.

(6) **The inhabitant of this isle . . .**—Better, as elsewhere, *coast-land*. Here it probably refers to the whole coast of Philistia, which had been foremost in the revolt, and Phœnicia, Tyre also having joined in it (*Annals of Sargon* in Lenormant's *Anc. Hist.*, i. 396). Cyprus, the conquest of which Sargon records (*Records of the Past*, vii. 51), may also be included. The whole sea-board population would find out too late that they could not resist Assyria even with the help of Egypt and Ethiopia.

The Burden of the Desert of the Sea.   ISAIAH, XXI.   *The Vision of the Watchman.*

expectation, whither we flee for help to be delivered from the king of Assyria: and how shall we escape?

CHAPTER XXI.—⁽¹⁾ The burden of the desert of the sea.

As whirlwinds in the south pass through; *so* it cometh from the desert, from a terrible land. ⁽²⁾ A ¹ grievous vision is declared unto me; the treacherous dealer dealeth treacherously, and the spoiler spoileth. Go up, O Elam: besiege, O Media; all the sighing thereof have I made to cease. ⁽³⁾ Therefore are my loins filled with pain: pangs have taken hold upon me, as the pangs of a woman that travaileth: I was bowed down at the hearing *of it;* I was dismayed at the seeing *of it.* ⁽⁴⁾ ² My heart panted, fearfulness affrighted me: the night of my pleasure hath he ³ turned into fear unto me.

⁽⁵⁾ Prepare the table, watch in the watchtower, eat, drink: arise, ye princes, *and* anoint the shield. ⁽⁶⁾ For thus hath the Lord said unto me, Go, set a watchman, let him declare what he seeth. ⁽⁷⁾ And he saw a chariot *with a*

B.C. cir. 714.

1 Heb., *hard.*

2 Or, *My mind wandered.*

3 Heb., *put.*

XXI.

⁽¹⁾ **The burden of the desert of the sea . . .**—The title of the prophecy is obviously taken from the catch-word of "the desert" that follows. The "sea" has been explained (1) as the Euphrates, just as in chaps. xviii. 2, xix. 5, it appears as used of the Nile (Cheyne). (2) As pointing to the surging flood of the mingled myriads of its population. (3) Xenophon's description of the whole plain of the Euphrates, intersected by marshes and lakes, as looking like a sea affords, perhaps, a better explanation.

As whirlwinds in the south . . .—The "South" (or *Negeb*) is here, as elsewhere, the special name of the country lying south of Judah. The tempests of the region seem to have been proverbial (Zech. ix. 14; Jer. iv. 11, xiii. 24; Hos. xiii. 15).

So it cometh.—The absence of a subject to the verb gives the opening words a terrible vagueness. Something is coming "from the wilderness, a terrible land," beyond it. The "wilderness" in this case is clearly the Arabian desert, through part of which the Euphrates flows. The context determines the "terrible land" as that of Elam and Media.

⁽²⁾ **A grievous vision . . .**—The verse contains, as it were, the three tableaux that came in succession before the prophet's gaze: (1) The treacherous dealer, the Assyro-Chaldæan power, spoiling and oppressing, breaking treaties, and, as its kings boasted (Hab. ii. 5; *Records of the Past*, vii. 42, 44), "removing landmarks." (2) The summons to Elam and Media to put an end to this tyranny. (3) The oppressed peoples ceasing to sigh, and rejoicing in their liberation.

Elam appears here as combined with Media, which is named in chap. xiii. 17 as the only destroyer of Babylon, and this has been urged as evidence of a later date. As a matter of fact, however, Sargon at this very time was carrying on a fierce war against Elam (*Records of the Past*, vii. 41—49) as well as against Media (*ibid*, p. 37). In Ezek. xxxii. 24, Elam is numbered among the extinct nations, but the name, at all events, re-appears as applied to the Persians, though they were of a distinct race. It was, even as a mere forecast, perfectly natural that the two should be associated together as the future destroyers of the Nineveh and Babel empires, which to the prophet's eye were identical in character and policy. The advance described as "from the wilderness" implies a march of part at least of the Medo-Persian army down the Choaspes and into the lowland of Chuzistan, bordering on the great Arabian desert.

⁽³⁾ **Therefore are my loins filled with pain . . .** —Comp. Nah. ii. 10; Ezek. xxi. 6; and for the image of the "woman in travail," chap. xiii. 8; Jer. xxx. 6. The vision of destruction is so terrible that it overpowers all feeling of exultation, and oppresses the prophet like a horrible nightmare.

⁽⁴⁾ **The night of my pleasure . . .**—The words point to the prophet's longing for the darkness of night, either as a time of rest from his labour, or, more probably, for contemplation and prayer (Ps. cxix. 148), and to the invasion of that rest by the vision of terror. The suggestion that the prophet speaks as identifying himself with the Babylonians, and refers to the capture of their city during a night of revelry (Dan. v. 1, 30; Herod., i. 121; Xenoph. *Cyrop.*, vii. 23), is hardly tenable.

⁽⁵⁾ **Prepare the table, watch in the watchtower.**—The words (historical infinitive) are better taken as indicative: *They prepare . . . they watch.* The last clause has been variously rendered, *they spread the coverlet; i.e.,* for the couches of the revellers (Amos vi. 4); and *they take a horoscope* (Ewald). Here, with hardly a shadow of a doubt, there is a reference to the temper of reckless revel such as was the immediate forerunner of the capture of Babylon. The prophet had, perhaps, an analogue of such blind security before his eyes at the very time he wrote (chap. xxii. 13), which led him to anticipate a like state of things in Babylon.

Anoint the shield . . .—The summons is one which in the prophet's vision breaks in on the songs and music of the revel. The shields thought of were those covered with leather, which was oiled, partly to protect it from wet, partly to make the stroke of the sword glide off from it. The call implies that even this precaution had been neglected by the revellers.

⁽⁶⁾ **Go, set a watchman . . .**—The prophet is, as it were, placed in vision on a lofty watch-tower, and reports what meets his gaze, or that of the watchman with whom he identifies himself (Ezek. xxxiii. 7). (Comp. the striking parallel of Hab. ii. 1, 2.)

⁽⁷⁾ **A chariot with a couple of horsemen.**— Better, *a troop, a couple.* Both asses and camels were employed in the Persian army (Herod., i. 80, iv. 129). They probably indicate, the former an Arab, the latter a Carmanian contingent. Both are named (11,173 asses, 5,230 camels) among the spoil taken by Sennacherib on the defeat of Merôdach-baladan (Bellino Tablet in *Records of the Past*, i. 26).

He hearkened diligently with much heed. —Literally, *he listened sharply, listened sharply,* with

The Fall of Babylon. ISAIAH, XXI. *The Burden of Dumah and Arabia.*

couple of horsemen, a chariot of asses, and a chariot of camels; and he hearkened diligently with much heed: ⁽⁸⁾ and ¹he cried, A lion: My lord, I stand continually upon the ᵃwatchtower in the daytime, and I am set in my ward ²whole nights: ⁽⁹⁾ and, behold, here cometh a chariot of men, *with* a couple of horsemen. And he answered and said, ᵇBabylon is fallen, is fallen; and all the graven images of her gods he hath broken unto the ground.

⁽¹⁰⁾ O my threshing, and the ³corn of my floor: that which I have heard of the LORD of hosts, the God of Israel, have I declared unto you.

⁽¹¹⁾ The burden of Dumah.

He calleth to me out of Seir, Watchman, what of the night? Watchman, what of the night? ⁽¹²⁾ The watchman said, The morning cometh, and also the night: if ye will enquire, enquire ye: return, come.

⁽¹³⁾ The burden upon Arabia.

In the forest in Arabia shall ye lodge, O ye travelling companies of Dedanim. ⁽¹⁴⁾ The inhabitants of the land of Tema ⁴brought water to him that was thirsty,

¹ Or, *cried as a lion.*
ᵃ Hab. 2. 1.
² Or, *every night.*
ᵇ Jer. 51. 8; Rev. 14. 8 & 18. 2.
³ Heb., *son.*
⁴ Or, *bring ye.*

---

the iteration of intensity. What had met the watchman's eye in his vision had passed by in silence, and had left him in doubt as to its meaning. Was it the symbol of a Babylonian army marching out against rebels, or of a rebel army on the way to attack Babylon? He listened, but no voice came out of the darkness to interpret the vision for him.

⁽⁸⁾ **And he cried, A lion.**—Better, *As a lion.* The cry seems to be the low murmur of the eager, almost angry, impatience by which the prophet or the ideal watchman was stirred.

⁽⁹⁾ **And, behold, here cometh . . .**—Better, *Behold, there came . . .* The words narrate a second vision, not the watchman's narrative of the first. He sees now, as it were, a part of the cavalcade which he had beheld before, and now it is no longer silent, but reports what has been accomplished. "Babylon is fallen, is fallen!" The words are applied to the destruction of the mystical Babylon in Rev. xiv. 8, xviii. 2. Stress is laid on the destruction of the idols of Babylon by the iconoclastic Persians.

⁽¹⁰⁾ **O my threshing, and the corn of my floor.**—Literally, *and child of my threshing-floor.* . . . The words are abrupt, and we have to read the thoughts that lie below them. The "child of the threshing-floor" is none other than Israel, thought of as the corn which is under God's chastisements, Assyrian and Chaldæan invasions, Babylonian exile, and the like, severing the wheat from the chaff (Mic. iv. 12, 13; Jer. li. 33; Matt. iii. 3). The prophet looks on those chastisements with yearning pity, but he cannot "go beyond the word of the Lord" (Num. xxiv. 13), and this is all that he has to tell his people. The oppressor shall in the end be overthrown, but that which lies between the present and that far-off future is, as yet, concealed from him.

⁽¹¹⁾ **The burden of Dumah.**—Several places of the name are mentioned in the Old Testament (Gen. xxv. 14; Josh. xv. 52), but these are not in the direction of Seir. Probably here, as in verse 1 and chap. xxii. 1, we have a mystical prophetic name, Edom being altered to Dumah, *i.e.,* "silence," as in Pss. xciv. 17, cxv. 17, the silence of the grave. In this case, as in the preceding, there is first the oppressive silence of expectancy, and then of desolation.

He calleth . . . out of Seir . . .—The subject is indefinite: *one calleth.* The watchman hears the silence of the night broken by a voice from Seir. It is probable that the prophet had actually been consulted by the Edomites, and that this is his answer to their enquiries. The cry is, "Watchman, what *part* of the night?" In the weary night of calamity the sufferer desires to know what hour it is, how much of the darkness still remains to be lived through. The answer is mysterious and ill-boding. There is a "morning" coming, a time of light and hope, but the day which is so opened closes too quickly in the blackness of night (Amos v. 18). The words sum up the whole future of Edom, subject as it was to one conqueror after another, rising now and then, as under Herod and the Romans, and then sinking to its present desolation.

⁽¹²⁾ **If ye will enquire . . .**—The words pre-suppose a craving to know the meaning of the mysterious oracle just given. The prophet declines to answer. If they like to ask, they may, and return and go back after a bootless journey. Some interpreters, however, have seen in the "return" a call to repentance like that conveyed by the same word in Jer. iii. 22, but hardly on sufficient grounds. We should, in that case, have expected "return to Jehovah."

⁽¹³⁾ **The burden upon Arabia.**—Better, *of the evening land.* Here, again, the prophet alters the form of the word (*Arab* into *Ereb*) so as to convey a mystic meaning. The land of which he is about to speak is a land of shadow and of gloom. Evening is falling on it. It is a question whether the second Arabia is to retain its geographical form or to be translated "evening," as before. In any case, of course, Arabia is the country spoken of. The "Dedanites" appear in Jer. xlix. 8; Ezek. xxv. 13, and seem from Ezek. xxvii. 15 to have been dwelling in the neighbourhood of the Edomites (Jer. xlix. 8) as a commercial people trading with Tyre in ebony and ivory. The point of the oracle against them is that they shall be compelled by the presence of the Assyrian armies to leave the main lines of their traffic, probably, as before, on their way westward to Tyre, and to take bye-paths, pitching their tents not near towns and villages, but in the low brushwood of the wilderness.

⁽¹⁴⁾ **The inhabitants of . . . Tema . . .**—Another element of suffering comes into the picture. The Dedanites, driven out of their usual route into the desert, find their provisions fail them, and the men of Tema, fearing to invite them to their tents, lest they too should be smitten by the invader, are compelled to take out bread and water stealthily. The name of Tema (now *Taima*), is found on the pilgrim route from Damascus to Mecca, and again on that between Palmyra and Petra, on the east of the Haurân mountains.

They prevented with their bread—*i.e.,* they went out to welcome him (the fugitive), without waiting

they prevented with their bread him that fled. ⁽¹⁵⁾ For they fled ¹ ²from the swords, from the drawn sword, and from the bent bow, and from the grievousness of war. ⁽¹⁶⁾ For thus hath the Lord said unto me, Within a year, according to the years of an hireling, and all the glory of Kedar shall fail: ⁽¹⁷⁾ and the residue of the number of ³archers, the mighty men of the children of Kedar, shall be diminished: for the LORD God of Israel hath spoken *it*.

CHAPTER XXII.—⁽¹⁾ The burden of the valley of vision.
What aileth thee now, that thou art wholly gone up to the housetops?

⁽²⁾ Thou that art full of stirs, a tumultuous city, a joyous city: thy slain *men are* not slain with the sword, nor dead in battle. ⁽³⁾ All thy rulers are fled together, they are bound ⁴by the archers: all that are found in thee are bound together, *which* have fled from far. ⁽⁴⁾ Therefore said I, ᵃ Look away from me; ⁵I will weep bitterly, labour not to comfort me, because of the spoiling of the daughter of my people. ⁽⁵⁾ For *it is* a day of trouble, and of treading down, and of perplexity by the Lord GOD of hosts in the valley of vision, breaking down the walls, and of crying to the mountains. ⁽⁶⁾ And Elam bare the quiver with chariots of men *and*

1 Or, *for fear.*
2 Heb., *from the face.*
3 Heb., *bows.*
4 Heb., *of the bow.*
a Jer. 4. 19, & 9. 1.
5 Heb., *I will be bitter in weeping.*

---

till he came as a suppliant. Their very hospitality, in strange contrast with Arab usage, had to be practised in secret.

⁽¹⁵⁾ **For they fled from the swords.**—The fourfold repetition of the somewhat full form of the Hebrew preposition (literally, *from the face of*) seems as if intended to emphasise the several stages of retreat.

⁽¹⁶⁾ **According to the years of an hireling** . . . The prophet uses, as in chap. xvi. 14, the formula which expressed the most precise measurement, and so gives a test as to his forecast of the future.

And all the glory of Kedar shall fail.—Kedar is used, as in Ps. cxx. 5, Song of Sol. i. 5, generically for the nomadic tribes of Arabia, including Dedan.

⁽¹⁷⁾ **And the residue** . . .—The Hebrew word is the same as the characteristic "remnant" of Isaiah's earlier prophecies. The words point primarily to the subjugation of Arabia by Sargon and Sennacherib, who narrate their victories over the Arabian tribes (*Records of the Past*, vii. 34). In Jer. xlix. 28, 29 we have an echo of the prediction, which, in that case, pointed to their conquest by Nebuchadnezzar.

XXII.

⁽¹⁾ **The burden of the valley of vision.**—The "valley of vision" is Jerusalem, lying as it did (Jer. xxi. 13) in a valley, as compared with the hills round about it (Ps. cxxv. 2). If we think of the prophet's dwelling as being in the lower city, in the valley of Tyropœon, the epithet becomes still more appropriate. That valley would be to him in very deed a "valley of vision," where he saw things present and to come. Possibly the name became more characteristic from the impulse given to the prophetic dreams of all who claimed to be seers. The prophet looks out, and sees the people in a state of excitement, caused probably by the near approach of the Assyrian armies. They are "on the house-tops," the flat roofs of which were a customary place of concourse (Judges xvi. 27; Neh. viii. 16), keeping their revels, as those do who meet the approach of danger with a reckless despair (verse 13). By some commentators (Birks, Kay), the "valley of vision" has been identified with Samaria.

⁽²⁾ **A joyous city** . . .—It would seem from chap. xxxii. 13 as if this was the characteristic on which Jerusalem, like Athens afterwards (Thucyd. ii. 40), specially prided itself.

Thy slain men are not slain with the sword . . .—The words imply something like a reproach of cowardice. Those who had perished had not died fighting bravely in battle, but by the pestilence which then, as at all times, was prevalent in the crowded streets of a besieged city.

⁽³⁾ **They are bound by the archers.**—Better, *fettered without the bow.* The taunting charge of cowardice is carried farther. The rulers had ventured on a sortie, and had been captured without a struggle, not even drawing their bows in their defence.

⁽⁴⁾ **Therefore said I, Look away from me.**—The tone is that of one who wishes to be alone in his sorrow. It is too deep for visits of consolation. He "refuses to be comforted." Isaiah bewails the destruction of "the daughter of his people" in much the same strain as that of Jeremiah over a later catastrophe (Lam. iii. 48).

⁽⁵⁾ **For it is a day of trouble.**—The earlier clauses paint the mental emotions of the coming day of judgment. In the latter we hear the actual crash of the battering-rams across the walls. The cry of the panic-stricken people shall rise to the surrounding mountains, possibly as to the hills from whence they expected help, either as true worshippers looking to Mount Zion (Ps. cxxi. 1), or to the high places which were so long the objects of their worship, and which led their enemies to say that their gods were "gods of the hills, and not of the valleys" (1 Kings xx. 23).

⁽⁶⁾ **Elam . . . Kir** . . .—The two nations are named as the chief elements of the Assyrian army then invading Judæa. Elam, previously named as the destroyer of Babylon (chap. xxi. 2), was at this time, as the inscriptions of Sargon show, subject to Assyria (*Records of the Past*, vii. 29). As in later history (Herod. i. 73, iii. 21; Jer. xlix. 35), it was conspicuous chiefly for its archers. "Kir," named in 2 Kings xvi. 11 as the region to which Tiglath-pileser carried off the people of Damascus, has been identified with the region near the river Kyros, the modern Georgia. There are, however, both linguistic and historical grounds against this identification, and we must be content to look on it as an otherwise unknown region of Mesopotamia. To "uncover the shield" was to draw it out of its leather case (comp. "*Scutis tegumenta detrahere*"; Cæs. *Bell. Gall.* ii. 21), and so to be prepared for battle.

Jerusalem preparing for a Siege. ISAIAH, XXII. *The reckless Revelry of its Defenders.*

horsemen, and Kir ¹uncovered the shield. ⁽⁷⁾ And it shall come to pass, that ²thy choicest valleys shall be full of chariots, and the horsemen shall set themselves in array ³at the gate. ⁽⁸⁾ And he discovered the covering of Judah, and thou didst look in that day to the armour of the house of the forest. ⁽⁹⁾ Ye have seen also the breaches of the city of David, that they are many: and ye gathered together the waters of the lower pool. ⁽¹⁰⁾ And ye have numbered the houses of Jerusalem, and the houses have ye broken down to fortify the wall. ⁽¹¹⁾ Ye made also a ditch between the two walls for the water of the old pool: but ye have not looked unto the maker thereof, neither had respect unto him that fashioned it long ago. ⁽¹²⁾ And in that day did the Lord GOD of hosts call to weeping, and to mourning, and to baldness, and to girding with sackcloth: ⁽¹³⁾ and behold joy and gladness, slaying oxen, and killing sheep, eating flesh, and drinking wine: ᵃ let us eat and drink; for to morrow we shall die. ⁽¹⁴⁾ And it was revealed in mine ears by the LORD of hosts, Surely this iniquity shall not be purged from you till ye die, saith the Lord GOD of hosts.

⁽¹⁵⁾ Thus saith the Lord GOD of hosts, Go, get thee unto this treasurer, *even* unto Shebna, which *is* over the house,

---

1 Heb., made naked.
2 Heb., the choice of thy valleys.
3 Or, towards.
a ch. 56. 12; Wisd. 2. 6; 1 Cor. 15. 32.

⁽⁷⁾ **That thy choicest valleys ...**—These were the valleys of Gibeon, Rephaim, Hinnom, and Jehoshaphat, which encircled Jerusalem on the west and south. They are painted as filled with the chariots and cavalry of the Assyrian army, ready to make their attack on the very gate of the city, the "great gate" named in Sennacherib's inscription (*Records of the Past*, i. 39).

⁽⁸⁾ **And he discovered the covering of Judah**—*i.e.*, Jehovah removed the veil which till then had hidden the approaching danger from the eyes of the inhabitants, and laid bare their weakness to those of the invaders. The verbs which in the English version are in the past tense are really in a kind of prophetic present, painting the future as if actually passing before the prophet's gaze.

The armour of the house of the forest.—More fully (as in 1 Kings vii. 2, x. 17), "the house of the forest of Lebanon," which appears to have been used as an arsenal, and to which the people now turn as their chief resource.

⁽⁹⁾ **Ye have seen also the breaches ...**—The prophet paints the hasty preparations for defence. So in 2 Chron. xxxii. 5: "Hezekiah built up all the wall that was broken, and raised it up to the towers," and added an outer line of defence. The "city of David" is, of course, the fortress of Zion.

The waters of the lower pool.—This was the Lower Gihon, now the *Birket-es-Sultan*. The operation is described more fully in 2 Chron. xxxii. 3, 4. Its object was to stop the outflow of the streams, and gather them into a reservoir, partly, of course, for the supply of the inhabitants during the siege, but still more that the Assyrian armies might find little or no water in the immediate neighbourhood of the city. Sargon, in his inscriptions, describes like preparations at Ashdod (Smith, *Assyr. Discov.*, p. 291).

⁽¹⁰⁾ **Ye have numbered the houses of Jerusalem.**—The preparations for defence are continued. The houses were numbered that some might be pulled down and others left, as strategical plans might determine. (Comp. 2 Chron. xxxii. 5.) So in what was probably a contemporary psalm we have, "Walk about Zion ... tell the towers thereof ... mark ye well her bulwarks" (Ps. xlviii. 12). So in the later siege of Jerusalem houses were thrown down by (or, more accurately, *on account of*) the mounds that were employed by the besiegers (Jer. xxxiii. 4).

⁽¹¹⁾ **Ye made also a ditch between the two walls.**—Better, *a pond* or *pool*, to form a reservoir for the supply of the city. This was probably identical with the "pool of Hezekiah," known also as the *Birket-el-Batrak* ("pool of the patriarchs"), between two walls, that to the north of Zion, and that which runs to the north-east round the Acra. During the rainy season this is supplied by the small conduit which runs from the upper pool along the surface of the ground, and then under the wall near the Joppa gate (Robinson, *Researches*, i., 437—439). The "old pool" was probably the pool of Siloam (John ix. 7), or the king's pool (Neh. ii. 14).

Ye have not looked unto the maker thereof.—These material defences, the prophet affirms, will avail but little if they forget Him who was the true "builder and maker" of the city, and who alone can secure its safety.

⁽¹²⁾ **To weeping, and to mourning, and to baldness ...**—National danger, Isaiah adds, should call to a national repentance in its outward manifestations, like the fast described in Joel ii. "Baldness," produced by the tearing of the hair in extreme grief, took its place naturally, with weeping and sackcloth, in those manifestations.

⁽¹³⁾ **And behold joy and gladness ...**—As things were, however, the danger, imminent as it was, led, as in the plague at Athens in the time of Pericles, and that of Florence in the time of Boccaccio, not to repentance, but to recklessness and sensuality. The cry of the baser form of epicureanism in all ages (1 Cor. xv. 32) was uttered, or acted on, and the prophet echoes the spoken words, or gives utterance to the unspoken thought, in tones of burning indignation.

⁽¹⁴⁾ **It was revealed in mine ears ...**—The special form indicates that the warning was "borne in," ringing, as it were, on the inward ears of the prophet, as an oracle of God. That sensual recklessness could have but one end in all countries and ages, and that end was death. No formal religion, no chastisement, even, would avail to purge an iniquity like that in the absence of a true repentance.

⁽¹⁵⁾ **Go, get thee unto this treasurer, even unto Shebna.**—The section that follows opens a chapter in the internal politics of the reign of Hezekiah. The word for "treasurer" (literally, *companion*) implies a position like that of a vizier, identical, probably,

and say, (16) What hast thou here? and whom hast thou here, that thou hast hewed thee out a sepulchre here, ¹ *as* he that heweth him out a sepulchre on high, *and* that graveth an habitation for himself in a rock? (17) Behold, ² the LORD will carry thee away with ³ a mighty captivity, and will surely cover thee. (18) He will surely violently turn and toss thee *like* a ball into a ⁴ large country: there shalt thou die, and there the chariots of thy glory *shall be* the shame of thy lord's house. (19) And I will drive thee from thy station, and from thy state shall he pull thee down. (20) And it shall come to pass in that day, that I will call my servant Eliakim the son of Hilkiah: (21) and I will clothe him with thy robe, and strengthen him with thy girdle, and I will commit thy government into his hand: and he shall be a father to the inhabitants of Jerusalem, and to the house of Judah. (22) And the key of the house of David will I lay upon his shoulder; so he shall ᵃ open, and none shall shut; and he

1 Or, *O he.*
2 Or, *the LORD who covered thee with an excellent covering, and clothed thee gorgeously, shall surely, &c.,* ver. 18.
3 Heb., *the captivity of a man.*
4 Heb., *large of spaces.*
ᵃ Job 12. 14; Rev. 3. 7.

---

with that of the "king's friend" of Gen. xxvi. 26; 2 Sam. xv. 37; 1 Kings iv. 5. In addition to this office Shebna had the position of being "over the house," an office, like that of a Lord Chamberlain, of such importance that it was sometimes held by a king's son (2 Chron. xxvi. 21). It gave him supreme control over the treasury of the king and the internal affairs of his kingdom, and made him almost like a *maire du palais* under the Merovingian kings. It is obvious that his influence was exercised to thwart the prophet's counsels; and the probable sequence of thought connecting the two sections is that he was prominent as the representative of the false security and luxury which the prophet had condemned; probably also of the party which rested their hope on an alliance with Egypt. What follows seems to show that he was a *novus homo*, with no ancestral dignities in his house, possibly even a foreigner (the name is Aramæan in form), pushing himself forward with an obtrusive ambition. We note the touch of scorn in "*this* Shebna."

(16) **What hast thou here?** . . .—The prophet's indignation is roused by Shebna's last act of arrogance. He had no "sepulchre of his fathers" to deck with fresh stateliness, and, like the kings and great ones of the earth (the kings of Sidon, the Pharaohs of Egypt, the kings of Assyria), had built one for himself, hollowed out of the wells (probably on one of the hills of Jerusalem), to be his own everlasting "habitation," his *domus æterna*. So in Eccles. xii. 5, the grave is the "long home" of man. Rock-hewn sepulchres of this type are found on the slopes of all the hills in the neighbourhood of the holy city.

(17) **The Lord will carry thee away with a mighty captivity.**—Better, *will hurl thee with the hurling of a mighty man*—i.e., strongly and effectually. The words have, however, been rendered (Cheyne), "will hurl, will hurl thee, O mighty man." The marginal rendering rests on no sufficient grounds.

Will surely cover thee.—Better, *Will surely grasp thee,* so that thou shalt not escape.

(18) **Like a ball into a large country.**—The picture is that of a ball flung violently on a smooth, even plain where it bounds on and on with nothing to stay its progress. The "large country" is, probably, the plain of Mesopotamia, where Shebna is to end his days in exile.

There the chariots of thy glory shall be the shame of thy lord's house.—Better, *Thither shall go the chariots of thy glory, the shame of thy lord's house.* The words point to another form of Shebna's ostentatious pride. Not content with riding on an ass or mule, as even judges and counsellors rode (Judges v. 10, x. 4, xii. 14; 2 Sam. xvii. 23), he had appeared in public in stately chariots, such as were used by kings (Song Sol. i. 9, iii. 9). These were to accompany him in his exile, but it would be as the spoil of the conqueror. There are no records of the fulfilment of the prediction, and the judgment may have been averted by repentance; but when we next meet with Shebna (chap. xxxvi. 22) he is in the inferior position of a scribe, and Eliakim occupies his place as being "over the household."

(19) **I will drive thee . . . shall he pull thee down.**—The change of person has led some interpreters to refer the latter clause to Hezekiah. Such changes, however, are common enough in Hebrew prophetic speech (*e.g.*, chap. x. 12, xlii. 13, 14), and Jehovah is the subject of both clauses.

(20) **Eliakim the son of Hilkiah.**—Nothing is known of Eliakim's previous history, but the epithet, "my servant," bears witness to his faith and goodness; and we may well believe him to have been in heart, if not openly, one of Isaiah's disciples. He was apparently, at the time, in some subordinate office.

(21) **I will clothe him with thy robe . . .**—The words point to an actual transfer of the robe and girdle which were Shebna's insignia of office. There was to be, in this case, a literal investiture.

He shall be a father . . .—The words were, perhaps, an official title given to the king's vizier or chamberlain. (Comp. 2 Kings v. 13.) Here, however, the words indicate that the idea of the title should be fulfilled, and that the government of Eliakim should be, in the truest sense, paternal.

(22) **And the key of the house of David will I lay upon his shoulder . . .**—The key of the king's treasure-chambers and of the gates of the palace was the natural symbol of the chamberlain's or vizier's office, and, as in chap. ix. 6, it was solemnly laid upon the shoulder of the new official, perhaps as representing the burden of the responsibilities of the duties of his office. In the "keys of the kingdom of heaven," in Matt. xvi. 19, and again in Rev. iii. 7, as also in the custom of admitting a Rabbi to his office by giving him a key, we have a reproduction of the same emblem.

So he shall open, and none shall shut . . .—The words paint vividly the supremacy of the office to which Eliakim was to be called. He alone was to decide who was to be admitted into the king's chamber, and for whom the king's treasury was to be opened. In Rev. iii. 7, the symbolism is reproduced in its higher application to the King of kings.

The Downfall of Eliakim. ISAIAH, XXIII. *The Burden of Tyre.*

shall shut, and none shall open. ⁽²³⁾ And I will fasten him *as* a nail in a sure place; and he shall be for a glorious throne to his father's house. ⁽²⁴⁾ And they shall hang upon him all the glory of his father's house, the offspring and the issue, all vessels of small quantity, from the vessels of cups, even to all the ¹vessels of flagons. ⁽²⁵⁾ In that day, saith the LORD of hosts, shall the nail that is fastened in the sure place be removed, and be cut down, and fall; and the burden that *was* upon it shall be cut off: for the LORD hath spoken *it*.

CHAPTER XXIII.—⁽¹⁾ The burden of Tyre.

Howl, ye ships of Tarshish; for it is laid waste, so that there is no house, no entering in: from the land of Chittim it

B.C. cir. 712.

¹ Or, *instruments of viols.*

⁽²³⁾ **I will fasten him as a nail in a sure place** . . .—The word for "nail" is used both for the peg that fastens a tent to the ground, as in the "stakes" of chaps. xxxiii. 20, liv. 2; Judges iv. 21, or, as in Ezek. xv. 3, for a nail driven into the wall. Here the context shows that the latter meaning is preferable. It was, as the sequel shows, a symbol of the support upon which others can depend. (Comp. the "nail in his holy place" of Ezra ix. 8.)

He shall be for a glorious throne . . .—Another symbol of sovereignty follows. The form, *throne of glory*, is found in its highest application in 1 Sam. ii. 8, and Jer. xiv. 21, xvii. 12. Such a throne, kingly in its state, is to be the pride of the hitherto obscure house of Eliakim.

⁽²⁴⁾ **And they shall hang upon him all the glory of his father's house** . . .—The metaphor of the nail is resumed. Not without a touch of irony, as the sequel shows, the prophet paints the extent to which those who belong to Eliakim will hang upon his support. There will be the "glory" or the "weight" (the Hebrew word has both meanings) of his next-of-kin. Besides these there will be the remoter *off-shoots* and *side-shoots* of his family. But the number will increase, and upon that single nail, or peg, would hang the "vessels of small quantity," cups such as were used by the priests for the blood of the victims in sacrificing (Exod. xxiv. 6), or for wine in common use (Song Sol. vii. 2), flagons, or earthen pitchers, as in chap. xxx. 14; Lam. iv. 2, *i.e.*, the whole crowd of the retainers of a great official. The prophet obviously paints the picture as a warning. There was the danger even for Eliakim, upright and religious as he was, as there has been for others like him, of giving way to nepotism, and the fault would not remain unpunished.

⁽²⁵⁾ **Shall the nail that is fastened in a sure place be removed** . . .—There is, the prophet says, a judgment for the misuse of power portrayed in the previous verse. The "nail" that seems so firmly fixed should be removed, *i.e.*, Eliakim should cease to hold his high office, and with his fall should come that of all his kindred and dependents. Here, as in the case of Shebna, we have no record of the fulfilment of the prediction, but it is a natural inference, from its remaining in the collected prophecies of Isaiah, either that it was fulfilled, or that it did its work as a warning, and that the penalty was averted by a timely reformation.

XXIII.

⁽¹⁾ **The burden of Tyre** . . .—The chapter calls us to enquire into the political relations of Tyre at the time of Isaiah. These we learn, partly from Scripture itself, partly from Assyrian inscriptions. In the days of David and Solomon there had been an intimate alliance between Israel and Hiram, King of Tyre. Ps. xlv. 12 indicates at least the interchange of kingly gifts, if not the acknowledgment of sovereignty by payment of tribute. Ps. lxxxiii. 7, which we have some reason to connect with the reign of Uzziah, shows that this alliance had passed into hostility. The position of Tyre naturally threw it into more intimate relations with the northern kingdom; "its country was nourished by the king's country" then as in the days of Herod Agrippa (Acts xii. 20), and there seems reason to believe that the son of Tabeal, whom Pekah and Rezin intended to place upon the throne of Judah, was the son of a Tyrian ruler. (See Note on chap. vii. 6.) It was, at this time, the most flourishing of the Phœnician cities, and had succeeded to the older fame of Zidon. The action of Ahaz in inviting the help of Tiglath-pileser against Israel and the Syrians had tended to make Tyre also an object of attack by the Assyrian armies. The prophecy now before us would seem to have been connected with that attack, and foretells the issue of the conflict on which Tyre had rashly entered. Upon that issue light is thrown by the inscriptions of the Assyrian kings. Sargon records that he "plundered the district of Samaria and the whole house of Omri," and "reigned from Yatnan (Cyprus), which is in the midst of the sea of the setting sun . . . from the great Phœnicia and Syria . . . . to all the cities of remote Media" (*Records of the Past*, vii. 27). Sennacherib boasts of a victory over the land of the Hatti (*i.e.*, Hittites); "fear overwhelmed Luti, the king of Zidon," and "he fled to Yatnan, which is in the midst of the sea," and the Assyrian "placed Tubalu" (the Tabeal of Isaiah) on the throne of the kingdom (*Records of the Past*, vii. 61). In anticipation of these events, the prophet utters his note of warning to the great merchant city. It seems more natural to connect it with those events, which came within the horizon of his vision, than to refer it, as some interpreters have done, to the later siege of Tyre by Nebuchadnezzar. The mention of the Chaldeans as having been subdued by the Assyrians, which fits in with Sargon's and Sennacherib's victories over Merôdach-baladan (*Records of the Past*, vii. 45, 59), who endeavoured to establish an independent kingdom in Babylon (see Note on chap. xxxix. 1), and is, of course, entirely inapplicable to the time of Nebuchadnezzar, seems, indeed, to be decisive as to this question.

Howl, ye ships of Tarshish . . .—See Note on chap. ii. 16. The prophet sees, as in vision, the argosies of Tyre speeding on their way homeward across the Mediterranean from Tarshish (Spain), and bids them raise their lamentation over the coming fate of their city. They will hear that their city has been taken, that there is no access to its harbours. At Chittim (Cyprus, or, probably, Citium, the chief Phœnician colony of the island), the tidings which burst upon them were as a revelation, confirming the vague rumours they had heard before.

Tyre as the Mart of Nations. ISAIAH, XXIII. *City whose Merchants are Princes.*

is revealed to them. (2) Be ¹still, ye inhabitants of the isle; thou whom the merchants of Zidon, that pass over the sea, have replenished. (3) And by great waters the seed of Sihor, the harvest of the river, *is* her revenue; and she is a mart of nations. (4) Be thou ashamed, O Zidon: for the sea hath spoken, *even* the strength of the sea, saying, I travail not, nor bring forth children, neither do I nourish up young men, *nor* bring up virgins. (5) As at the report concerning Egypt, so shall they be sorely pained at the report of Tyre.

(6) Pass ye over to Tarshish; howl, ye inhabitants of the isle. (7) *Is* this your joyous *city*, whose antiquity *is* of ancient days? her own feet shall carry her ²afar off to sojourn. (8) Who hath taken this counsel against Tyre, the crowning *city*, whose merchants *are* princes, whose traffickers *are* the honourable of the earth? (9) The LORD of hosts hath purposed it, ³to stain the pride of all glory, *and* to bring into contempt all the honourable of the earth.

(10) Pass through thy land as a river, O daughter of Tarshish: *there is* no more ⁴strength. (11) He stretched out his hand over the sea, he shook the kingdoms: the LORD hath given a commandment ⁵against ⁶the merchant *city*, to

1 Heb., *silent.*
2 Heb., *from afar off.*
3 Heb., *to pollute.*
4 Heb., *girdle.*
5 Or, *concerning a merchant-man.*
6 Heb., *Canaan.*

---

(2) **Inhabitants of the isle . . .**—Better, *coast.* The word was specially appropriate to the narrow seaboard strip of land occupied by the Phœnicians—Zidon, the older city, the "great Zidon" of Josh. xi. 8, xix. 28, appearing as the representative of Phœnicia generally. It was her commerce that had filled Tyre and the other daughter cities. The "dumbness" to which the prophet calls the people is that of stupefied terror.

(3) **By great waters the seed of Sihor . . .**—Sihor ("the dark river") is as in Jer. ii. 18, a Hebrew name for the Nile. The corn-trade with Egypt (Ezek. xxvii. 7, adds the linen-trade) was naturally a chief branch of Tyrian commerce. Practically, indeed, as the Egyptians had no timber to build ships, and, for the most part, hated the sea, their navy consisted of Phœnicians. Tyre practically reaped the harvest that sprang from the inundation of the Nile. For "mart," read *gain.* The "great waters" are those of the great sea, *i.e.,* of the Mediterranean.

(4) **Be thou ashamed, O Zidon . . .**—Zidon is addressed as the mother-city of Tyre. The "strength" (or *fortress*) of the sea is the rock-island on which the new Tyre was built. She sits as a widow bereaved of her children, with no power to renew the population which once crowded her streets. (Comp. Lam. i. 1.)

(5) **As at the report concerning Egypt . . .**—Better, *When the report cometh to Egypt* . . . The news of the capture of Tyre would cause dismay in Egypt, partly because the export trade of their corn depended upon it, partly because it had served as a kind of outpost against the Assyrians, who, under Sargon (*Records of the Past,* vii. 34) and Sennacherib (2 Kings xviii. 21, xix. 8), were pressing on against the Ethiopian dynasty then dominant in Egypt.

(6) **Pass ye over to Tarshish . . .**—The words have the ring of a keen irony. The Tyrians are told to go to Tarshish, the extreme point of their commerce; not, as before, to bring back their wealth, but to seek safety there as exiles. No nearer asylum would give them safety. So, in the siege of Tyre by Alexander the Great, the Tyrians sent their old men, women, and children to Carthage (Diod. Sic. xvii. 41). So Layard (*Nineveh,* plate 71) represents enemies of the Assyrians taking refuge in ships (Cheyne). The "isle" or "coast" is, as before, Tyre, and its neighbourhoods.

(7) **Is this your joyous city . . . ?**—Tyre was, as has been said, of later origin than Zidon, but was the oldest of the daughter cities. Josephus (*Ant.* viii. 3. 1) fixes the date of its foundation at 240 years before Solomon.

Her own feet shall carry her.—The English version (tenable grammatically) points to the wanderings of exile. Another rendering, *her feet are wont to carry her* . . . is also legitimate, and fits in better with the context, which paints the past glory of Tyre in contrast with her coming calamities. So taken, the words point to her numerous colonies, of which Carthage was the chief.

(8) **The crowning city.**—The participle is strictly transitive in its force. Tyre was the distributor of crowns to the Phœnician colonies. The Vulg., however, gives "crowned."

Whose merchants are princes.—It is a fact worth noting in the history of language that the word for "merchants" here, and in Hos. xii. 7; Prov. xxxi. 24, is the same as that for Canaanite. The traffickers of the earth were pre-eminently of that race.

(9) **The Lord of hosts hath purposed . . .**—This is the prophet's answer. The kings of Assyria were but instruments in the hand of Jehovah Sabaoth, working out what He had planned.

To stain the pride . . .—The primary meaning of the verb is to pollute or desecrate, possibly in reference to the destruction of the temples of Tyre, such *e.g.* as that of Melkarth, which was reported to be one of the most ancient in the world.

(10) **Pass through thy land as a river . . .**—The word for "river" is that used in verse 3 with special reference to the Nile. Here the inundation of the Nile gives special force to the comparison. The daughter of Tarshish (*i.e.,* Tarshish itself) is to spread and overflow in independent action. The colonies of Tyre are no longer subject to her, paying tribute or custom duties as she might ordain. There is no "strength," no "*girdle*" now to restrain them, no limit such as Tyre had imposed on their commerce or colonisation. It is significant that Cyprus revolted about this time, and that the Phœnician colonies took part in attacking the mother city under Sennacherib (Jos. *Ant.* ix. 14. 2).

(11) **He shook the kingdoms.**—The picture of the great convulsion of the time includes more than Tyre and its subject states. Egypt, Ethiopia, Babylon, Syria, Israel, Judah, were all affected, shaken as to their very foundations, by the rapid progress of the restored Assyrian empire under Tiglath-pileser and his successors.

The Howling of the Ships of Tarshish. ISAIAH, XXIII. *Tyre Singing as an Harlot.*

destroy the ¹strong holds thereof. ⁽¹²⁾ And he said, Thou shalt no more rejoice, O thou oppressed virgin, daughter of Zidon: arise, pass over to Chittim; there also shalt thou have no rest. ⁽¹³⁾ Behold the land of the Chaldeans; this people was not, *till* the Assyrian founded it for them that dwell in the wilderness: they set up the towers thereof, they raised up the palaces thereof; *and* he brought it to ruin. ⁽¹⁴⁾ Howl, ye ships of Tarshish: for your strength is laid waste.

⁽¹⁵⁾ And it shall come to pass in that day, that Tyre shall be forgotten seventy years, according to the days of one king: after the end of seventy years ²shall Tyre sing as an harlot. ⁽¹⁶⁾ Take an harp, go about the city, thou harlot that hast been forgotten; make sweet melody, sing many songs, that thou mayest be remembered. ⁽¹⁷⁾ And it shall come to pass after the end of seventy years, that the LORD will visit Tyre, and she shall turn to her hire, and shall commit fornication with all the kingdoms of the world upon the face of the earth. ⁽¹⁸⁾ And her merchandise and her hire shall be holiness to the LORD: it shall not be treasured nor laid up; for her

1 Or, *strengths.*

2 Heb., *it shall be unto Tyre as the song of an harlot.*

Against the merchant city.—Literally, *Canaan* (the word "city" being an interpolation), taken here as equivalent to Phœnicia. So in Josh. v. 1, the LXX. translates "Canaanites" by " Phœnicia."

⁽¹²⁾ **Thou oppressed virgin.**—Strictly speaking, the noun and adjective are incompatible, the latter conveying the sense of "defiled," or "deflowered." Till now Tyre had known no defeat. Her fortress was a virgin citadel. Now the barbarian conqueror was to rob her of that virginity.

Pass over to Chittim.—With a keen irony the prophet gives a counsel which he declares will be of no avail. They may flee to Chittim (Cyprus); but the power of the Assyrians would reach them even there. Once and again the inscriptions of the Assyrian kings record how they subdued and took tribute from "Yatnan," the "island in the sea of the setting sun," which can be none other than Cyprus (*e.g.*, Sargon in *Records of the Past*, vii. 26).

⁽¹³⁾ **Behold, the land of the Chaldeans.**—Heb., *land of Kasdim.* The prophet points to the destruction of one power that had resisted Assyria as an example of what Tyre might expect. The Assyrian inscriptions record the conquests referred to. Sargon relates his victory over the "perverse and rebellious Chaldæans," who had rebelled under Merôdach-baladan (*Records of the Past*, vii. 41, 45). Towns were pillaged, 80,570 men carried away captive from a single city. Sennacherib (*ibid.*, p. 59) boasts of having plundered Babylon itself, and all the "strong cities and castles of the land of the Chaldæans"; and again, of having crushed another revolt under Suzab the Babylonian (*ibid.*, i. 47—49). The words that follow on this survey are better rendered: *This people is no more: Asshur appointeth it for the desert beasts. They set up their towers, they destroy its palaces.* The "towers" are those of the Assyrian besiegers attacking Babylon; the palaces, those of the attacked. The words have, however, often been interpreted as pointing to the origin and migration of the Chaldæans, as having had scarcely any national existence till Assyria had brought them into the plains of the Euphrates. The English version seems based upon this interpretation of the passage. It is obvious, however, that such a fragment of ethnological history does not cohere well with the context, and gives a less satisfactory meaning. It is doubtful, too, whether the supposed history itself rests on any adequate evidence.

⁽¹⁴⁾ **Howl, ye ships of Tarshish: for your strength is laid waste.**—The prophecy of woe ends as it began in verse 1. The "strength" is the *fortress* of Tyre.

⁽¹⁵⁾ **Tyre shall be forgotten seventy years.** —If we take the number literally, the seventy years may coincide with those of the captivity of Judah, during which, under the Chaldæan supremacy, Tyre was reduced to a state of comparative insignificance. It seems better, however, with Cheyne, to take it as a symbolic number for a long period of indefinite duration, and so, bringing it into closer connection with the context, to reckon the period from its conquest by the Assyrians.

According to the days of one king.—We look in vain for any ruler of Assyria or Babylon whose reign was of this length, and the words probably mean, *as the days fixed by a king*—*i.e.*, by a despotic and absolute decree. Possibly, however, the "one king" may stand for one dynasty.

Shall Tyre sing as an harlot.—Literally, *there shall be to Tyre as the song of the harlot*, possibly referring to some well-known lyric of this type. The commercial city, welcoming foreigners of all nations as her lovers for the sake of gain, is compared to the prostitute who sells herself for money. (Comp. Rev. xvii. 2.)

⁽¹⁶⁾ **Take an harp, go about the city . . .**—In a tone half of irony and half of pity, the prophet tells the "harlot that had been forgotten" to return to her old arts of song (the singing women of the East were commonly of this class), and to go about once more with song and lyre, recalling her old lovers (*i.e.*, her old allies) to the memory of their past love.

⁽¹⁷⁾ **She shall turn to her hire.**—The words indicate, in the strong imagery of verse 15, the revival of the commercial prosperity of Tyre under the rule of the Persian kings. To that commerce there was to be no limit. The ships of all nations were once more to crowd her harbours.

⁽¹⁸⁾ **Her merchandise and her hire shall be holiness to the Lord.**—The words seem to reverse the rule of Deut. xxiii. 18, which, probably not without a reference to practices like those connected with the worship of Mylitta (Herod., i. 99), forbade gifts that were so gained from being offered in the Sanctuary. Here, it seems to be implied, the imagery was not to be carried to what might have seemed its logical conclusion. The harlot city, penitent and converted, might be allowed, strange as it might seem, to bring the gains of her harlotry into the temple of the Lord. Interpreted religiously, the prophet sees the admission of proselytes to the worship of Israel in the future, as he had seen it

The Land utterly Spoiled. ISAIAH, XXIV. *The Mourning of the new Wine.*

merchandise shall be for them that dwell before the LORD, to eat sufficiently, and for [1] durable clothing.

CHAPTER XXIV.—(1) Behold, the LORD maketh the earth empty, and maketh it waste, and [2] turneth it upside down, and scattereth abroad the inhabitants thereof. (2) And it shall be, as with the people, so with the [3] *a* priest; as with the servant, so with his master; as with the maid, so with her mistress; as with the buyer, so with the seller; as with the lender, so with the borrower; as with the taker of usury, so with the giver of usury to him. (3) The land shall be utterly emptied, and utterly spoiled: for the LORD hath spoken this word.

(4) The earth mourneth *and* fadeth away, the world languisheth *and* fadeth away, [4] the haughty people of the earth do languish. (5) The earth also is defiled under the inhabitants thereof; because they have transgressed the laws, changed the ordinance, broken the everlasting covenant. (6) Therefore hath the curse devoured the earth, and they that dwell therein are desolate: therefore the inhabitants of the earth are burned, and few men left. (7) The new wine mourneth, the vine languisheth, all the merryhearted do sigh. (8) The mirth *b* of tabrets ceaseth, the noise of them that rejoice endeth, the joy of the harp ceaseth. (9) They shall not drink wine with a song; strong drink shall be bitter to them that drink it. (10) The city of confusion is broken down: every house is shut up, that no man may come

1 Heb., *old.*
2 Heb., *perverteth the face thereof.*
3 Or, *prince.*
a Hos. 4. 9.
4 Heb., *the height of the people.*
b Jer. 7. 34 & 16. 9 & 25. 10; Ezek. 26. 13; Hos. 2. 11.

---

probably in the days of Hezekiah (Ps. lxxxvii. 4). Interpreted politically, the words point to a return to the old alliance between Judah and Tyre in the days of David and Solomon (1 Kings v. 1—12), and to the gifts which that alliance involved (Ps. xlv. 12).

For them that dwell before the Lord . . .—These were probably, in the prophet's thoughts, the citizens of Jerusalem, who were to find in Tyre their chief resource both for food and raiment. Traces of this commerce after the return of the Jews from the captivity are found in Neh. xiii. 16, "men of Tyre" bringing "fish and all manner of ware" to the gates of Jerusalem. Of the more direct service we find evidence in the fact that Tyrians and Zidonians contributed to the erection of the second Temple, as they had done to that of the first (Ezra iii. 7).

XXIV.

(1) **Behold, the Lord maketh the earth empty . . .**—The chapters from xxiv. to xxvii., inclusive, are to be taken as a continuous prophecy of the overthrow of the great world-powers which were arrayed against Jehovah and His people. Of these Assyria was then the most prominent within the horizon of the prophet's view; but Moab appears in chap. xxv. 10, and the language, with that exception, seems deliberately generalised, as if to paint the general discomfiture in every age (and, above all, in the great age of the future Deliverer) of the enemies of Jehovah and His people. The Hebrew word for "earth" admits (as elsewhere) of the rendering "land"; but here the wider meaning seems to predominate, as in its union with the "world," in verse 4.

(2) **It shall be, as with the people . . .**—In the apparently general classification there is, perhaps, in the last two clauses a trace of the prophet's indignation at the growing tendency of the people to the luxury which led to debt, and to the avarice which traded on the debtor's necessities. Israel, it would seem, was already on the way to become a nation of money lenders.

(4) **The haughty people of the earth.**—Literally, *the heights,* or, to use an English term with a like history, "the *highnesses* of the people."

(5) **The earth also is defiled.**—The verb is used of blood-guiltiness in Num. xxxv. 33, of impurity in Jer. iii. 1, 2, 9. It includes, therefore, all the sins that, in modern phrase, desecrate humanity. Taking the word in its wider range, each form of evil was a transgression of the "everlasting covenant" of Gen. ix. 16.

(6) **Therefore hath the curse . . .**—The definite article may be either generic, *the* curse which always follows on evil-doing, or, more specifically, *the* curse of the Book of the Covenant, as in Lev. xxvi.; Deut. xxviii. The curse is personified as a beast of prey or a consuming fire, ready to devour. (Comp. Gen. iv. 7, 11.)

They that dwell therein are desolate.—Better, *bear their punishment,* or *are dealt with as guilty.*

Are burned.—The word determines, perhaps, the sense of the word "devour" in the previous clause. The curse, the symbol of the wrath of Jehovah, is the consuming fire that burns.

(7) **The new wine mourneth.**—Each feature takes its part in the picture of a land from which all sources of joy are taken away. The vine is *scorched* with the fire of the curse, there is no wine in the winepress, the song of the grape-gatherers (proverbially the type of the "merry-hearted") is hushed in silence.

(8) **The mirth of tabrets . . .**—The words point to the processions of women with timbrels (tambourines) and sacred harps or lyres, like those of Exod. xv. 20; Judg. xi. 34; 1 Sam. xviii. 6, as was customary in seasons of victory. (Comp. the striking parallel of 1 Macc. iii. 45.)

(9) **They shall not drink wine with a song . . .**—Literally, *in their song they drink no wine; i.e.,* the music of the feasts (Amos vi. 5) should cease, and if they sang at all it should be a chant of lamentation (Amos viii. 10). The very appetite for "strong drink" (probably the palm-wine of the East) should pass away, and it would be bitter as the wine of gall (Deut. xxxii. 33).

(10) **The city of confusion.**—Better, *the city of chaos,* the *tohu* of Gen. i. 2, "without form and void." The world should be cast back out of its *cosmos* into

All Joy darkened. ISAIAH, XXIV. *Fear, the Pit, and the Snare.*

in. ⁽¹¹⁾ There *is* a crying for wine in the streets; all joy is darkened, the mirth of the land is gone. ⁽¹²⁾ In the city is left desolation, and the gate is smitten with destruction. ⁽¹³⁾ When thus it shall be in the midst of the land among the people, *there shall be as the shaking of an olive tree, and as the gleaning grapes when the vintage is done.* ⁽¹⁴⁾ They shall lift up their voice, they shall sing for the majesty of the LORD, they shall cry aloud from the sea. ⁽¹⁵⁾ Wherefore glorify ye the LORD in the ¹fires, *even* the name of the LORD God of Israel in the isles of the sea. ⁽¹⁶⁾ From the ²uttermost part of the earth have we heard songs, *even* glory to the righteous. But I said, ³My leanness, my leanness, woe unto me! the treacherous dealers have dealt treacherously; yea, the treacherous dealers have dealt very treacherously. ⁽¹⁷⁾ *ᵃ Fear, and the pit, and the snare, are* upon thee, O inhabitant of the earth. ⁽¹⁸⁾ And it shall come to pass, *that* he who fleeth from the noise of the fear shall fall into the pit; and he that cometh up out of the midst of the pit shall be taken in the snare: for the windows from on high are open, and the foundations of the earth do shake. ⁽¹⁹⁾ The earth is utterly broken down, the earth is clean dissolved, the

1 Or, *valleys.*
2 Heb., *wing.*
3 Heb., *Leanness to me,* or, *My secret to me.*
a Jer. 48. 43, 44.

---

its primeval chaos. The word is a favourite one with Isaiah (chap. xxxiv. 11, lix. 4, and nine other passages).

Every house is shut up—*i.e.,* to complete the picture, not because its gates are barred, but because its own ruins block up the entrance.

⁽¹¹⁾ **There is a crying for wine in the streets.**—Literally, *because of wine in the fields.* The Hebrew noun for the latter word hovers between the meaning of an open place within and one without a city. The context seems in favour of the latter sense. Men weep in the fields because there is no vintage.

All joy is darkened.—The English verb exactly expresses the force of the Hebrew, which is used, as in Judg. xix. 9, of the gloom of sunset. (Comp. Micah iii. 6.) The light of joy had passed into the blackness of darkness.

⁽¹²⁾ **In the city is left desolation.**—Better, *of the city.* Nothing should be left but its crumbling ruins. The "gate," usually, in an Eastern town, the pride of the city, and the chief place of concourse, had been battered till it lay in ruins.

⁽¹³⁾ **There shall be as the shaking of an olive tree . . .**—The prophet's characteristic thought of the "remnant" that should escape is presented under familiar imagery, that of the few olives on the olive tree, and the gleaning of the grapes when the vintage is over. (Comp. chap. xvii. 5, 6; Judg. viii. 2.)

⁽¹⁴⁾ **They shall cry aloud from the sea . . .**—The utterers of the praise are obviously the remnant of the saved, whether of the "Jews of the dispersion," or of the Gentiles. To them there appears in the midst of the desolation, the vision of the glory of the Lord, and far off, from *the* sea (the Mediterranean, as the great sea of the ancient world) they raise their song of praise.

⁽¹⁵⁾ **Wherefore glorify ye the Lord in the fires.**—The last word, which is identical in form with the Urim of the high priest's breastplate, has been very differently interpreted:—(1) Taking it in the sense of "light," it has been taken as meaning the east, as contrasted with the "isles of the sea" as a synonym for the west, and so standing parallel to the familiar phrase "from the rising of the sun to the going down of the same" (Mal. i. 11; Isa. lix. 19), and, we may add, to the like formula in Assyrian inscriptions, *e.g.,* that of Esarhaddon (*Records of the Past,* iii. 111). So Homer, "the dawn and the sun" (*Il.,* xii. 239) as a phrase for the East; and our Orient and East have substantially the same significance. (2) It has been rendered simply "regions," or "countries" (Cheyne). (3) It has been interpreted of the "fiery trial" of tribulation, or of the "light" of Divine truth. Of these, (1) has the merit of being more in harmony with the primary meaning of the word, and giving a more vivid antithesis. The "isles of the sea" we have met in chap. xi. 11.

⁽¹⁶⁾ **From the uttermost part of the earth . . .**—The words "glory to the righteous" sound at first like a doxology addressed to Jehovah as essentially the Righteous One. Two facts militate, however, against this view. The word translated "glory" is not that commonly used in doxologies, but rather "honour" or "praise," such as is applied to men (chaps. iv. 2, xxiii. 9, xxviii. 1, 4, 5; 2 Sam. i. 19). (2) The term "the Righteous One" is never used absolutely as a name of God. On these grounds, therefore, it seems better to render "honour to the righteous" (comp. Rom. ii. 7), to the true Israel of God as a righteous people. The "uttermost part" is, literally, *the wing* or *skirt* of the earth.

But I said, My leanness, my leanness . . .—The prophet is recalled from the ideal to the actual, from the glory of the future to the shame and misery of the present. "Leanness," as in Pss. xxii. 17, cix. 24, was the natural symbol of extremest sorrow. In the "treacherous dealers," literally, *robbers,* or *barbarians,* we may find primarily the Assyrian invaders, who were making the country desolate, or the unjust rulers of Judah, who oppressed the people.

⁽¹⁷⁾ **Fear, and the pit, and the snare . . .**—The words paint the rapid succession of inevitable calamities, in imagery drawn from the several forms of the hunter's work. There is first the terror of the startled beast; then the pit dug that he might fall into it; then the snare, if he struggled out of the pit, out of which there was no escape (chap. viii. 15). The passage is noticeable as having been reproduced by Jeremiah in his prophecy against Moab (chap. xlviii. 43, 44).

⁽¹⁸⁾ **The windows from on high are open . . .**—The phrase reminds us of the narrative of the Flood in Gen vii. 11, viii. 2. There was a second judgment on the defiled and corrupted land like that of the deluge. The next clause and the following verses were probably reminiscences of the earthquake in Uzziah's reign, and of the panic which it caused (chap. ii. 19; Amos i. 1; Zech. xiv. 5).

⁽¹⁹⁾ **The earth is utterly broken . . .**—We note the characteristic form of Hebrew emphasis in the threefold iteration of "the earth." (Comp. chap. vi. 3; Jer. xxii. 29.) There the form (more visibly in the

The Punishment of the High Ones. ISAIAH, XXV. *The Lord reigning in Mount Zion.*

earth is moved exceedingly. ⁽²⁰⁾ The earth shall reel to and fro like a drunkard, and shall be removed like a cottage; and the transgression thereof shall be heavy upon it; and it shall fall, and not rise again.

⁽²¹⁾ And it shall come to pass in that day, *that* the LORD shall ¹punish the host of the high ones *that are* on high, and the kings of the earth upon the earth. ⁽²²⁾ And they shall be gathered together, ²*as* prisoners are gathered in the ³pit, and shall be shut up in the prison, and after many days shall they be ⁴visited. ⁽²³⁾ Then the ᵃmoon shall be confounded, and the sun ashamed, when the LORD of hosts shall reign in mount Zion, and in Jerusalem, and ⁵before his ancients gloriously.

CHAPTER XXV.—⁽¹⁾ O LORD, thou *art* my God; I will exalt thee, I will praise thy name; for thou hast done wonderful *things*; *thy* counsels of old *are* faithfulness *and* truth. ⁽²⁾ For thou hast made of a city an heap; of a defenced city a ruin: a palace of strangers to be no city; it shall never be built.

---

1 Heb., *visit upon.*
B.C. cir. 712.
2 Heb., *with the gathering of prisoners.*
3 Or, *dungeon.*
4 Or, *found wanting.*
ᵃ ch. 13. 10; Ezek. 32. 7; Joel 2. 31 & 3. 15.
5 Or, there shall be *glory before his ancients.*

Hebrew than in the English) is a climax representing the three stages of an earthquake: the first cleavage of the ground; the wide open gaping; the final shattering convulsion. The rhythm of the whole passage is almost an echo of the crashes.

⁽²⁰⁾ **The earth shall reel to and fro . . .**—The point of the first comparison is obvious. (Comp. the like illustration of a ship tossed by the waves in Ps. cvii. 27.) The second becomes clearer if we render *hammock* instead of cottage, a hanging mat, suspended from a tree, in which the keeper of the vineyard slept, moving with every breath of wind; the very type of instability. In the words that follow the prophet traces the destruction to its source. The physical catastrophe is not the result of merely physical causes. The earth totters under the weight of its iniquity, and falls (we must remember the Hebrew idea of the world as resting upon pillars, 1 Sam. ii. 8), never to rise again. In its vision of the last things the picture finds a parallel, though under different imagery, in 2 Peter iii. 10-13.

⁽²¹⁾ **The Lord shall punish the host of the high ones that are on high . . .**—The prophet's utterance becomes more and more apocalyptic. He sees more than the condemnation of the kings of earth. Jehovah visits also the "principalities and powers in heavenly places" (Eph. iii. 10) or "on high" (Eph. vi. 12). Perhaps identifying these spiritual evil powers with the gods whom the nations worshipped, and these again with the stars in the firmament, Isaiah foresees a time when their long-protracted rebellion shall come to an end, and all authority and power be put down under the might of Jehovah (1 Cor. xv. 25). The antithetical parallelism of the two clauses is decisive against the interpretation which sees in the "high ones on high" *only* the representatives of earthly kingdoms, though we may admit that from the prophet's stand-point each rebel nation is thought of as swayed by a rebel spirit. (Comp. Dan. x. 20; Ecclus. xvii. 14; and the LXX. of Deut. xxxii. 8: "He set the bounds of the nations according to the number of the angels of God.") The same thought is found in a Rabbinic proverb, "God never destroys a nation without having first of all destroyed its prince" (Delitzsch, but without a reference).

⁽²²⁾ **As prisoners are gathered in the pit . . .**—The imagery is drawn from the deep underground dungeons of Eastern prisons (Jer. xxxviii. 6), which are here the symbol of the abyss of Hades, in which the rebel powers of earth and heaven await the final judgment (2 Peter ii. 4; Jude verse 6).

After many days shall they be visited.—The verb is the same as that translated "punish" in the previous verse, but does not in itself involve the idea of punishing, and in some of its forms is used of visiting in mercy. Interpreters have, according to their previous bias, assigned this or that meaning to it. Probably the prophet used it in a neutral sense, drawing his imagery from the custom of Eastern kings, who, after leaving their enemies in prison for an appointed time, came to inspect them, and to award punishment or pardon according to their deserts. In such a company there might be "prisoners of hope" (Zech. ix. 12), waiting with eager expectation for the coming of the king. The passage is interesting in the history of Christian doctrine, as having furnished to Origen and his followers an argument in favour of the ultimate restitution of all created spirits.

⁽²³⁾ **The moon shall be confounded . . .**—The thought implied is that the most glorious forms of created light will become dim, the moon red as with the blush of shame, the sun turning pale, before the glory of Jehovah's presence.

The Lord of hosts shall reign . . .—Better, *hath become king*, the phrase being that used as in 2 Sam. v. 4; 1 Kings xv. 1, for a king's accession to his throne.

And before his ancients gloriously.—Better, *and before his elders shall he glory*. The "elders" are, like the seventy of Exod. xxiv. 9, like the twenty-four of Rev. iv. 4, the chosen ones of the new Jerusalem, to whom it shall be given, as the counsellors of the great King, to see His glory, that glory resting on them as in old time it rested upon Moses.

XXV.

⁽¹⁾ **O Lord, thou art my God.**—The burst of praise follows, like St. Paul's in Rom. xi. 33—36, upon the contemplation of the glory of the heavenly city.

Thy counsels of old are faithfulness and truth.—It is better to omit the words in italics, and to treat the words as standing in the objective case, in apposition with "wonderful things." The "counsels of old" are the eternal purposes of God made known to His prophets. The absence of a conjunction in the Hebrew, emphasises the enumeration.

⁽²⁾ **Thou hast made of a city an heap.**—The city spoken of as "the palace of strangers" was, probably in the prophet's thought, that which he identified with the oppressors and destroyers of his people—*i.e.*, Nineveh or Babylon; but that city was also for him the representation of the world-power which in every

(3) Therefore shall the strong people glorify thee, the city of the terrible nations shall fear thee. (4) For thou hast been a strength to the poor, a strength to the needy in his distress, a refuge from the storm, a shadow from the heat, when the blast of the terrible ones *is* as a storm *against* the wall. (5) Thou shalt bring down the noise of strangers, as the heat in a dry place; *even* the heat with the shadow of a cloud: the branch of the terrible ones shall be brought low.

(6) And in this mountain shall the LORD of hosts make unto all people a feast of fat things, a feast of wines on the lees, of fat things full of marrow, of wines on the lees well refined. (7) And he will ¹destroy in this mountain the face of the covering ²cast over all people, and the vail that is spread over all nations. (8) He will ᵃswallow up death in victory; and the Lord GOD will ᵇwipe away tears from off all faces; and the rebuke of his people shall he take away from off all the earth: for the LORD hath spoken *it*.

(9) And it shall be said in that day, Lo, this *is* our God; we have waited for him, and he will save us: this *is* the LORD; we have waited for him, we will be glad and rejoice in his salvation. (10) For in this mountain shall the hand of the LORD rest, and Moab shall be ³trodden down under him, even as straw is ⁴trodden down for the dunghill.

¹ Heb., *swallow up.*
² Heb., *covered.*
ᵃ 1 Cor. 15
ᵇ Rev. 7. 17 & 21. 4.
³ Or, *threshed.*
⁴ Or, *threshed in Madmenah.*

---

age opposes itself to the righteousness of God's kingdom. The Babylon of Isaiah becomes the type of the mystical Babylon of the Apocalypse. The words as they stand expand the thought of chap. xxiv. 10. (Comp. chap. xxvii. 10.)

(3) **Therefore shall the strong people** . . . — Better, "*a fierce people* and a city," the Hebrew having no article before either noun. The words paint the effect of the downfall of the imperial oppressor on the outlying fiercer nations, who were thus taught to recognise the righteous judgments of the God of Israel. (Comp. Rev. xi. 13, xv. 4.)

(4) **Thou hast been a strength** . . . —Literally, *a fortress.* The fierceness of the oppressor is represented by the intolerable heat, and the fierce tornado of an eastern storm, dashing against the wall, threatening it with destruction. From that storm the faithful servants of the Lord should find shelter as in the castle of the great King.

(5) **Thou shalt bring down the noise of strangers** . . . —The thought of verse 4 is reproduced with a variation of imagery, the scorching "heat" in a "dry" (or *parched*) "land." This is deprived of its power to harm, by the presence of Jehovah, as the welcome shadow of a cloud hides the sun's intolerable blaze. (Comp. chap. xxxii. 2.) It is noticeable that the LXX. in both passages gives "Sion" for "dry place" (Heb. *tsayôn*), perhaps following a various reading, perhaps interpreting.

The branch of the terrible ones . . . —Better, *the song.* The Hebrew noun is a rare one, but is found in this sense in Song Sol. ii. 12. The triumph song of the dread oppressors is thought of as blighting the world like a spell of evil; but this also is to be brought low, and hushed in silence.

(6) **And in this mountain shall the Lord** . . . —The mountain is, as in chap. ii. 1, the hill of Zion, the true representative type of the city of God. True to what we may call the catholicity of his character, Isaiah looks forward to a time when the outlying heathen nations shall no longer be excluded from fellowship with Israel, but shall share in its sacrificial feasts even as at the banquet of the great King. In the Hebrew, as even in the English, the rhythm flows on like a strain of music appropriate to such a feast. The "wines on the lees" are those that have been allowed to ripen and clarify in the cask, and so, like the "fat things full of marrow," represent the crowning luxuries of an Eastern banquet.

(7) **The face of the covering cast over all people** . . .—To cover the face was, in the East, a sign of mourning for the dead (2 Sam. xix. 4); and to destroy that covering is to overcome death, of which it is thus the symbol. With this there probably mingled another, though kindred, thought. The man whose face is thus covered cannot see the light, and the "covering" represents the veil (2 Cor. iii. 15) which hinders men from knowing God. The final victory of God includes a triumph over ignorance and sorrow, as well as over sin and death.

(8) **He will swallow up** . . . —The verb is the same as the "destroy" of verse 7. The words are an echo of the earlier promise of Hosea xiii. 14. They are, in their turn, re-echoed in the triumph-anthem of St. Paul in 1 Cor. xv. 54. The clause, "the Lord God shall wipe away tears," is in like manner reproduced in Rev. vii. 17, xxi. 4.

The rebuke of his people . . . —The taunt to which they were exposed in the time of their affliction, when the heathen took up their proverb of reproach and asked, "Where is now their God?" (Ps. lxxix. 10).

(9) **It shall be said in that day.**—The speakers are obviously the company of the redeemed, the citizens of the new Jerusalem. The litanies of supplication are changed into anthems of praise for the great salvation that has been wrought for them.

(10) **Moab shall be trodden down** . . . — There seems at first something like a descent from the great apocalypse of a triumph over death and sin and sorrow, to a name associated with the local victories or defeats of a remote period in the history of Israel. The inscription of the Moabite stone, in connection with chap. xv., helps to explain the nature of the allusion. Moab had been prominent among the enemies of Israel; the claims of Chemosh, the god of Moab, had been set up against those of Jehovah, the God of Israel (*Records of the Past*, xi. 166), and so the name had become representative of His enemies. There was a mystical Moab, as there was afterwards a mystical Babylon, and in Rabbinic writings a mystical Edom (*i.e.*, Rome). The proud nation was to lie wallowing in the mire of shame, trampled on by its conquerors, as the straw on the

The Gates opened for the Righteous.   ISAIAH, XXVI.   *Everlasting Strength in Jehovah.*

(11) And he shall spread forth his hands in the midst of them, as he that swimmeth spreadeth forth *his hands* to swim: and he shall bring down their pride together with the spoils of their hands. (12) And the fortress of the high fort of thy walls shall he bring down, lay low, *and* bring to the ground, *even* to the dust.

CHAPTER XXVI.—(1) In that day shall this song be sung in the land of Judah; We have a strong city; salvation will God appoint *for* walls and bulwarks. (2) Open ye the gates, that the righteous nation which keepeth the ¹truth may enter in. (3) Thou wilt keep *him* in ²perfect peace, *whose* ³mind *is* stayed *on thee*: because he trusteth in thee. (4) Trust ye in the Lord for ever: for in the Lord JEHOVAH *is* ⁴everlasting strength: (5) for he bringeth down them that dwell on high; the lofty city, he layeth it low; he layeth it low, *even* to the ground; he bringeth it *even* to the dust. (6) The foot shall tread it down, *even* the feet of the poor, *and* the steps of the needy.

(7) The way of the just *is* uprightness: thou, most upright, dost weigh the path of the just. (8) Yea, in the way of thy judgments, O Lord, have we waited for thee; the desire of *our* soul *is* to thy name, and to the remembrance of thee. (9) With my soul have I desired thee in

¹ Heb., *truths.*
² Heb., *peace, peace.*
³ Or, *thought,* or, *imagination.*
⁴ Heb., *the rock of ages.*

---

threshing-floor is trampled by the oxen till it looks like a heap of dung. In the Hebrew word for "dunghill" (*madmēnah*) we may probably trace a reference to the Moabite city of that name (Jer. xlviii. 2), in which Isaiah sees an unconscious prophecy of the future condition of the whole nation.

(11) **As he that swimmeth spreadeth forth his hands to swim.**—The structure of the sentence leaves it uncertain whether the comparison applies (1) to Jehovah spreading forth His hands with the swimmer's strength to repress the pride of Moab, or (2) to the outstretched hands upon the Cross, or (3) to Moab vainly struggling in the deep waters of calamity. Each view has the support of commentators. The last seems beyond question most in harmony with the context. Ineffective struggles for preservation naturally suggest the parallel, "like some strong swimmer in his agony" (Ps. lxix. 1, 2, 14). In the second clause there is, of course, no reason for doubt. It is Jehovah who "brings down the pride" of the guilty nation.

(12) **And the fortress of the high fort of thy walls . . .**—Primarily the words, as interpreted by verse 10, point to Kir-Moab (chap. xv. 1) as the stronghold of the nation. Beyond this they predict a like destruction of every stronghold, every rock-built fortress (2 Cor. x. 5) of the great world-power of which Moab was for the time the symbol.

XXVI.

(1) **In that day shall this song be sung . . .**—The prophet appears once more, as in chaps. v. 1, xii. 4, in the character of a psalmist, and what he writes is destined for nothing less than the worship of the new city of the heavenly kingdom.

Salvation will God appoint for walls.—Better, *salvation He appoints*. The walls of the heavenly city are not of stone or brick, but are themselves as a living force, saving and protecting. The same characteristic thought appears in chap. lx. 18.

(2) **Open ye the gates . . .**—The cry comes as from the heralds of the king of the heavenly city, proclaiming that the gates are open to those who are worthy to enter into it, *i.e.*, to the righteous people who alone may dwell in the city of God (Ps. xv. 1, 2, xxiv. 3, 4, cxviii. 19, 20; Rev. xxi. 27.)

The truth.—Literally, *truths*; all the many forms of truthfulness in heart and life.

(3) **Thou wilt keep him in perfect peace.**—The italics show that the English version is made up with several interpolated words. More literally, and more impressively, we read, *Thou establishest a purpose firm; peace, peace, for in Thee is his trust.* Completeness is expressed, as elsewhere, in the form of iteration. No adjectives can add to the fulness of the meaning of the noun.

(4) **For in the Lord Jehovah.**—The Hebrew presents, as in chap. xii. 2, the exceptional combination of the two names Jah (Ps. lxviii. 4) and Jehovah. In the Hebrew for "everlasting strength," we have, literally, the *Rock of Ages* of the well-known hymn. We have the same name of Rock applied to express the unchangeableness of God, as in Deut. xxxii. 4.

(5) **The lofty city, he layeth it low . . .**—The "city" is probably the great imperial "city of confusion" that had exalted itself against God and his people. To that city, Moab, in all its pride, was but as a tributary.

(6) **Even the feet of the poor . . .**—The downfall of the haughty city is emphasised by the fact that the instruments of its destruction are to be the very people it had oppressed. The "saints of God" are in this sense to judge the world.

(7) **The way of the just is uprightness.**—The English version seems somewhat tautologous. Better, *is straight*, or *is even*—*i.e.*, leads on without interruption to its appointed end. So, in the second clause, instead of "thou shalt weigh the path," which conveys a not very intelligible thought, we render, *makest smooth the path*. Probably, too, the word translated, "most upright," as if it were a vocative, should be taken adverbially. The verse is, as it were, an echo of Prov. iv. 26, v. 6, 21.

(8) **To thy name, and to the remembrance of thee . . .**—The "name" of God is, as always, that which reveals His character and will. Those who have waited for Him in the path of His judgments long for a fuller manifestation of that character. Comp. the prayer, "Father, glorify thy Name," in John xii. 28. In the next verse the prophet identifies himself in spirit with the longing expectation of the time that precedes the final manifestation.

(9) **With my soul have I desired thee in the night . . .**—Soul and spirit are joined together to express the fulness of personality. The "night" is the

the night; yea, with my spirit within me will I seek thee early: for when thy judgments *are* in the earth, the inhabitants of the world will learn righteousness. (10) Let favour be shewed to the wicked, *yet* will he not learn righteousness: in the land of uprightness will he deal unjustly, and will not behold the majesty of the LORD. (11) LORD, *when* thy hand is lifted up, they will not see: *but* they shall see, and be ashamed for *their* envy ¹at the people; yea, the fire of thine enemies shall devour them.

(12) LORD, thou wilt ordain peace for us: for thou also hast wrought all our works ²in us. (13) O LORD our God, *other* lords beside thee have had dominion over us: *but* by thee only will we make mention of thy name. (14) They are dead, they shall not live; *they are* deceased, they shall not rise: therefore hast thou visited and destroyed them, and made all their memory to perish. (15) Thou hast increased the nation, O LORD, thou hast increased the nation: thou art glorified: thou hadst removed *it* far *unto* all the ends of the earth. (16) LORD, in trouble have they visited thee, they poured out a ³prayer *when* thy chastening *was* upon them. (17) Like as a woman with child, *that* draweth near the time of her delivery, is in pain, *and* crieth out in her pangs; so have we been in thy sight, O LORD. (18) We have been with child, we have been in pain, we have as it were brought forth

¹ Or, *towards thy people.*
² Or, *for us.*
³ Heb., *secret speech.*

---

time of sorrow and expectation, in which the saints of God shall "watch for the morning" of the great day of judgment and deliverance. They welcomed the "judgments" as the discipline, by which those who had failed to learn before would at last, it might be, learn and acknowledge the righteousness of God.

(10) **Let favour be shewed to the wicked . . .**—The thought of verse 9 is presented under another aspect. The judgments of God manifested against evil are the only discipline by which the doers of evil can be taught; without them, under a system of mere tolerance and favour, they remain as they are. In the very "land of uprightness" (Ps. cxliii. 10) they will still work unrighteousness. "The mind is its own place," and can make a hell of heaven itself. The eyes that see "the majesty of the Lord" are those of the pure in heart (Matt. v. 8).

(11) **They will not see . . .**—Better, *they did not see*, or, *they see not*, so as to bring out the contrast with the clause that follows. When the "arm of Jehovah," the symbol of His power, was simply lifted up for the protection of His people, the evildoers closed their eyes and would not see it. A time will come when judgments shall fall on them, and so they shall be made to see.

Shall be ashamed for their envy at the people.—Better, *they shall see (and be ashamed) the jealousy (of God) for the people.* They shall understand something of God's watchful and zealous care for those whom He loves. It shall be seen that it is as a consuming "fire" (Ps. lxxix. 5) that shall devour His adversaries.

(12) **Thou also hast wrought all our work in us . . .**—Better, *for us*. The "work" is the great work of salvation and deliverance.

(13) **Other lords beside thee have had dominion over us . . .**—The "other lords" are the conquerors and oppressors by whom Israel had been enslaved; possibly also, the false gods with whom those conquerors identified themselves.

By thee only will we make mention of thy name.—Better, *Through Thee alone we celebrate Thy Name.* The power to praise God with hymns of thanksgiving (Ps. xlv. 17) had been restored to Israel, not by man's strength, but through His interposition on behalf of His people.

(14) **They are dead . . .**—We get a more vivid rendering by omitting the words in italics, *Dead, they live not; shadows* (*Rephaim*, as in Ps. lxxxviii. 10), *they rise not.* Those of whom the prophet speaks are the rulers of the great world-empires, who, as in chap. xiv. 9; Ezek. xxxii. 21, have passed into the gloomy world of Hades, out of which there was, for them at least, no escape. Their very names should perish from the memories of men. The LXX., adopting another etymology of the word *Rephaim*, gives the singular rendering, "Physicians shall not raise them up to life."

(15) **Thou hast increased the nation . . .**—The nation is, if we follow this rendering, Israel, whose prosperity the prophet contrasts with the downfall of its oppressors (comp. chap. ix. 3). The LXX., however, gives, "Add thou evils to all the glorious ones," as if referring to the "chastening" of exile in the next verse, and the use of the word "nation" (*i.e.*, heathen) instead of "people," is, perhaps, in favour of this rendering. "Nation," however, is used for Israel in chap. ix. 3, which is partly parallel to this passage.

Thou hadst removed it far unto all the ends of the earth.—Better, *Thou hast moved far off the borders of the land.* The English Version seems to speak of the exile and dispersion of the people. What is really meant is, probably, that Jehovah will restore it to its old remoter boundaries, as in the days of David and Solomon. This belongs, of course, to the ideal, and not the historical, restoration.

(16) **Lord, in trouble have they visited thee.**—Better, *have they missed Thee* (as in 1 Sam. xx. 6, xxv. 15), or *sought after Thee*, or, *remembered Thee.*

They poured out a prayer . . .—The word for "prayer" is a peculiar one, commonly used, as in chaps. iii. 3, viii. 19, for the whispered incantations of the heathen. Here it appears to mean the low-toned prayers, pitched as in a minor key, of the afflicted. In chap. xxix. 4 we have the same thought more fully developed.

(17) **Like as a woman with child.**—This, as in Matt. xxiv. 8, John xvi. 21, comes as the most natural image of longing, painful expectation, followed by great joy.

(18) **We have as it were brought forth wind.**—Left to themselves, the longing expectations of Israel had been frustrated. It was, "as it were" (the words imply the prophet's consciousness of the boldness of the

wind; we have not wrought any deliverance in the earth; neither have the inhabitants of the world fallen. ⁽¹⁹⁾ Thy dead men shall live, *together with* my dead body shall they arise. Awake and sing, ye that dwell in dust: for thy dew *is as* the dew of herbs, and the earth shall cast out the dead.

⁽²⁰⁾ Come, my people, enter thou into thy chambers, and shut thy doors about thee: hide thyself as it were for a little moment, until the indignation be overpast. ⁽²¹⁾ For, behold, the LORD ^acometh out of his place to punish the inhabitants of the earth for their iniquity: the earth also shall disclose her ¹blood, and shall no more cover her slain.

CHAPTER XXVII.—⁽¹⁾ In that day the LORD with his sore and great and strong sword shall punish leviathan the ²piercing serpent, even leviathan that crooked serpent; and he shall slay the dragon that *is* in the sea.

⁽²⁾ In that day sing ye unto her, A vineyard of red wine. ⁽³⁾ I the LORD do keep it; I will water it every moment: lest *any* hurt it, I will keep it night and day. ⁽⁴⁾ Fury *is* not in me: who would set the briers *and* thorns against me in

a Mic. 1. 3.

1 Heb., *bloods.*

2 Or, *crossing like a bar.*

---

figure), like a false pregnancy, a disease with no birth as its outcome.

Neither have the inhabitants of the world fallen.—Better, *Neither were the inhabitants of the world brought to birth,* the verb to "fall" being used, as in Wisd. vii. 3; Hom., *Il.,* xix. 10, of the delivery of a woman with child. The words continue the picture of the fruitlessness of mere human strivings and expectations. The LXX., "They that are in the tombs shall rise," connects itself with John v. 28, 29. (Comp. the like imagery in chap. xxxvii. 3.) The "creation" was "subject unto vanity," as in Rom. viii. 20—22.

⁽¹⁹⁾ **Thy dead men shall live.**—Better, *Thy dead shall live; my corpses shall rise.* The words, though they imply a belief more or less distinct in a resurrection, are primarily like the vision of dry bones in Ezekiel xxxvii. 1—14, and like St. Paul's "life from the dead" in Rom. xi. 15 (comp. also Hosea vi. 2), used of national and spiritual resurrection.

For thy dew is as the dew of herbs.—The rendering is a tenable one, and expresses the thought that as the dew that falls upon the parched and withered plant quickens it to a fresh life, so should the dew of Jehovah's grace (comp. 2 Sam. xxiii. 4) revive the dying energies of His people. Most interpreters, however, render the words *the dew of lights* (plural expressing completeness), the dew which is born of the womb of the morning (Ps. cx. 3). This, coming as it does from the "Father of Lights" (so the LXX., "The dew that is from Thee shall be healing for them"), shall have power to make the earth cast forth even the shadowy forms of the dead. The verb for "cast forth" is another form of that used in verse 18 of childbirth, and is, in this interpretation, used in the same sense.

⁽²⁰⁾ **Come, my people, enter thou into thy chambers.**—The vision of the judgments and the glory of the future leads the prophet to his work as a preacher of repentance in the present. His people also need the preparation of silent and solitary prayer (Matt. vi. 6; Pss. xxvii. 5, xxxi. 21). As men seek the innermost recesses of their homes while the thunderstorm sweeps over the city, so should they seek God in that solitude till the great tempest of His indignation has passed by.

⁽²¹⁾ **The earth also shall disclose her blood.**—Literally, *her bloods* (plural of intensity). The prophet has in his thoughts the reckless destruction of life which characterised the great world-powers of Assyria and Babylon. As in the case of Abel's blood that cried from the ground (Gen. iv. 16), so here the earth first brings to light the blood of those that have been slain, and then the forms of the murdered ones themselves.

XXVII.

⁽¹⁾ **Leviathan the piercing serpent.**—Rather, *fleet,* or *fugitive.* The verse paints in vivid symbolic language the judgment of Jehovah on the great world-powers that had shed the blood of His people. The "sword of the Lord" (primarily, perhaps, representing the lightning-flash) is turned in its threefold character as sore, and swift, and strong, against three great empires. These are represented, as in Ezek. xvii. 3, xxix. 3 Dan. vii. 3—7, by monstrous forms of animal life. The "dragon" is as in chap. li. 19; Ps. lxxiv. 13, 14; Ezek. xxix. 3; xxxii. 2, the standing emblem of Egypt: the other two, so generically like, that the "leviathan" ("crocodile" in Job xli. 1, but here, probably, generically for a monster of the serpent type) serves as a common type for both, while each has its distinctive epithet, may refer respectively to Assyria and Babylon, the epithets indicating (1) the rapid rush of the Tigris and the tortuous windings of the Euphrates; and (2) the policy characteristic of each empire, of which the rivers were looked upon as symbols, one rapidly aggressive, the other advancing as by a sinuous deceit. By some commentators, however, Egypt is represented in all three clauses; while others (Cheyne) see in them the symbols not of earthly empire, but of rebel powers of evil and darkness, quoting Job xxvi. 12, 13 in support of his view.

⁽²⁾ **In that day sing ye . . .**—The prophet appears once again, as in chap. xxvi. 1, as the hymn-writer of the future day of the triumph of the redeemed. He had chanted a dirge over the vineyard that was unfruitful, and therefore given over to desolation. He now changes the wailing into a poem. The word translated "red wine" (comp. Deut. xxxii. 14) signifies "fiery," or "foaming." The LXX. seems to have followed a different text, giving (with the alteration of a single letter) the meaning, "a *pleasant* vineyard."

⁽³⁾ **I the Lord do keep it.**—The words imply a distinct reversal of the sentence passed in chap. v. 1—7. Instead of abandonment, there is constant care. Instead of the clouds being commanded to give no rain, the vineyard is watered whenever it requires watering. Instead of being wasted by the wild boar or by spoilers, Jehovah tends it both by day and night.

⁽⁴⁾ **Fury is not in me.**—Better, *There is no wrath in me. Who will set briars and thorns before me? With war will I go forth against them; I will burn*

Israel shall Blossom and Bud. ISAIAH, XXVII. *The Iniquity of Jacob Purged.*

battle? I would ¹go through them, I would burn them together. ⁽⁵⁾ Or let him take hold of my strength, *that* he may make peace with me; *and* he shall make peace with me.

⁽⁶⁾ He shall cause them that come of Jacob to take root: Israel shall blossom and bud, and fill the face of the world with fruit. ⁽⁷⁾ Hath he smitten him, ²as he smote those that smote him? or is he slain according to the slaughter of them that are slain by him? ⁽⁸⁾ In measure, ³when it shooteth forth, thou wilt debate with it: ⁴he stayeth his rough wind in the day of the east wind. ⁽⁹⁾ By this therefore shall the iniquity of Jacob be purged; and this *is* all the fruit to take away his sin; when he maketh all the stones of the altar as chalkstones that are beaten in sunder, the groves and ⁵images shall not stand up. ⁽¹⁰⁾Yet the defenced city *shall be* desolate, *and* the habitation forsaken, and left like a wilderness: there shall the calf feed, and there shall he lie down, and consume the branches there-

B.C. cir. 712.

1 Or, *march against.*

2 Heb., *according to the stroke of those.*

3 Or, *when thou sendest it forth.*

4 Or, *when he removeth it.*

5 Or, *sun images.*

---

them up together. The reversal of the sentence is continued. Wrath against this vineyard has passed away from Jehovah. Should briars and thorns (symbols of the enemies of His people, as in chaps. ix. 18, x. 17; 2 Sam. xxiii. 6, 7; Ezek. ii. 6) spring up, he will do battle against them, and consume them utterly.

⁽⁵⁾ **Or let him take hold of my strength.**—Or, *Let him lay hold on my fortress: let him make peace with Me.* The thought implied is that even the enemies of Jehovah, if repentant, may find in Him "their castle and deliverer." To them, too, there is the gracious invitation to make peace.

⁽⁶⁾ **He shall cause them that come of Jacob . . .**—Better, *In the days that come Jacob shall strike root.* The figure of Israel as the vine of Jehovah's vineyard is carried to its close. The true Israel of God shall go through its normal stages of growth, and its restoration shall be as "the riches of the Gentiles" (Rom. xi. 12; Hosea xiv. 6). With this picture of blessedness the psalm of the Church of the future comes to an end.

⁽⁷⁾ **Hath he smitten him . . .**—The pronouns are left in the English Version somewhat obscure, but the use of capitals makes the meaning plain: "Hath *He* (Jehovah) smitten him (Israel) as *He* smote those that smote him; or is he slain according to the slaughter of those that are slain by Him?" A slight alteration in the last clause in the text gives, *according to the slaughter of his slayers.* In any case the thought is that Jehovah had chastised the guilt with a leniency altogether exceptional. They had not been punished as others had been. The words admit, however, of another meaning, which is preferred by some critics, viz., that Jehovah doth not smite Israel with the smiting like that with which his (Israel's) smiters smote him—*i.e.*, had not punished, as the oppressors had punished, ruthlessly and in hate, but had in His wrath remembered mercy.

⁽⁸⁾ **In measure . . .**—Literally, with the force of iteration, *with measure and measure.* The verse continues the thought of the preceding. The word for "measure" is strictly definite: the *seah,* or third part of an *ephah* (comp. chap. v. 10), and therefore used as proverbial for its smallness; to express the extreme moderation of God's chastisements.

When it shooteth forth, thou wilt debate with it.—Better, *When thou didst put her away, thou didst plead with her.* The prophet falls back upon the thought of Hosea i.—iii., that Israel was the adulterous wife to whom Jehovah had given, as it were, a bill of divorcement, but against whom He did not carry the pleadings to the furthest point that the rigour of the law allowed. Comp. for this meaning chap. l. 1; Deut. xxiv. 1; Mal. ii. 16.

He stayeth his rough wind . . .—The words have become familiar, as expressing the loving-kindness which will not heap chastisement on chastisement, lest a man should be swallowed up of overmuch sorrow, which keeps the "rough wind" from completing the devastation already wrought by the scorching "east wind." That rendering, however, can scarcely be maintained. The word translated "stay" is found elsewhere in Prov. xxv. 4, 5, and there has the sense of "separating," or "sifting." And this is its sense here also, the thought expressed asserting, though in another form than the traditional rendering, the compassion of Jehovah, in that He *sifts with his rough wind in the day of east wind;* though punishment come on punishment, it is reformatory, and not simply penal, to *sift,* and not to destroy. A rendering accepted by some critics gives, *He sigheth with His rough wind,* as though with a sorrowing pity mingled with the chastisement.

⁽⁹⁾ **By this therefore shall the iniquity of Jacob be purged.**—The pronoun may refer either to the chastisement of the previous verse as the instrument of purification (preferably), or to the destruction of idols which follows as the result and proof of that purification, the end contemplated by Jehovah in His chastisements.

This is all the fruit to take away his sin. —Better, *of taking away his sin.* The words repeat the thought of the previous clause. The fruit of repentance and forgiveness will be found in rooting out all vestiges of idol-worship. The LXX., "when I shall take away their sins," is quoted by St. Paul in Rom. xi. 27.

The groves and images.—Literally, as elsewhere, the *Asherahs,* or *the sun-images,* the two leading features of the *cultus* which Israel had borrowed from the Phœnicians. In the action of Josiah (2 Chron. xxxiv. 3, 4) we may, with little doubt, trace a conscious endeavour to fulfil the condition which Isaiah had thus proclaimed. He sought to "purge" Judah and Jerusalem from the "groves and the carved (sun) images, and molten images."

⁽¹⁰⁾ **The defenced city shall be desolate . . .** —The key to this prediction is found in chap. xxv. 2, where the same words occur. The "defenced city" is that of the strangers, who are the enemies of God's people, and its destruction is contrasted with the restoration of the purified Jerusalem of the preceding verse. To see in the "defenced city" which is to be laid low Jerusalem itself is at variance with the natural sequence of thought. The picture of desolation—calves

Gathering of the Children of Israel. ISAIAH, XXVIII. *The Drunkards of Ephraim.*

of. ⁽¹¹⁾ When the boughs thereof are withered, they shall be broken off : the women come, *and* set them on fire : for it *is* a people of no understanding : therefore he that made them will not have mercy on them, and he that formed them will shew them no favour.

⁽¹²⁾ And it shall come to pass in that day, *that* the LORD shall beat off from the channel of the river unto the stream of Egypt, and ye shall be gathered one by one, O ye children of Israel. ⁽¹³⁾ And it shall come to pass in that day, *that* the great trumpet shall be blown, and they shall come which were ready to perish in the land of Assyria, and the outcasts in the land of Egypt, and shall worship the LORD in the holy mount at Jerusalem.

CHAPTER XXVIII.—⁽¹⁾ Woe to the crown of pride, to the drunkards of Ephraim, whose glorious beauty *is* a fading flower, which *are* on the head of the fat valleys of them that are [1]overcome with wine ! ⁽²⁾ Behold, the Lord hath a mighty and strong one, *which* as a tempest of hail *and* a destroying storm, as a flood of mighty waters overflowing, shall cast down to the earth with the hand. ⁽³⁾ The crown of pride, the drunkards of Ephraim, shall be trodden [2]under feet : ⁽⁴⁾ and the glorious beauty, which *is* on the head of the fat

1 Heb., *broken.*
2 Heb., *with feet.*

---

feeding in what had been the busy streets of a populous city—is analogous to that of the "wild beasts of the desert," roaring among the ruins of Babylon, in chap. xiii. 21, 22.

⁽¹¹⁾ **When the boughs thereof are withered . . .**—The picture of the wasted city receives another touch. Shrubs cover its open spaces (perhaps the prophet thinks of the gardens and parks within the walls of a city like Babylon), and women come, without fear of trespassing, to gather them for firewood.

For it is a people of no understanding.—The words are generic enough, and may be applied, like similar words in chap. i. 3; Jer. viii. 7; Deut. xxxii. 28, to Israel as apostate, or to the world-power, which was the enemy of Israel. In this case, as we have seen, the context turns the scale in favour of the latter reference. So taken, the words are suggestive, as witnessing to the prophet's belief that the God of Israel was also the Maker and the Former of the nations of the heathen world.

⁽¹²⁾ **The Lord shall beat off . . .**—The English Version conveys scarcely any meaning. The verb used is that which we find in chap. xxviii. 27 for the "beating out" of seeds from their husks, as a form of threshing. In Deut. xxiv. 20 it is used of the beating down of the olive crop. So understood, the words imply a promise, like that of chap. xvii. 6, but on a far wider scale. Instead of the gleaning of a few olives from the topmost boughs, there should be a full and abundant gathering, and yet each single olive, "one by one," should receive an undivided care. Judah and Israel should once more be peopled as in the days of old, and the ideal boundaries of their territory should be restored.

The channel, or *flood of the river*, is the Euphrates.

The stream of Egypt.—As in Gen. xv. 18, 1 Kings viii. 65, not the Nile, but the river which divides Palestine from Egypt, known by the Greeks as Rhinocolura, and now the *Wady-el-'Arish*.

⁽¹³⁾ **The great trumpet shall be blown . . .**—The symbolism had a probable origin in the silver trumpets which were used in the journeys of the Israelites " for the calling of the assembly and for the journeying of the camps " (Num. x. 1—10), and which were solemnly blown in the year of Jubilee on the eve of the Day of Atonement (Lev. xxv. 9). It re-appears in the Apocalyptic eschatology of Matt. xxiv. 31; 1 Cor. xv. 52; 1 Thess. iv. 16, standing there, as here, for any great event that heralds the fulfilment of a Divine purpose. That purpose, in this instance, is the proclamation of the Year of Redemption, the restoration of the dispersed of Israel from the countries of their exile, of which, as in chaps. xi. 11, xix. 23, Assyria and Egypt are the two chief representatives. (Comp. Zeph. iii. 10.)

XXVIII.

⁽¹⁾ **Woe to the crown of pride . . .**—Better, *the proud crown of the drunkards of Ephraim.* The chapter is remarkable, as showing that the prophet's work was not limited to Judah and Jerusalem, but extended to the northern kingdom. The warning was clearly uttered before the capture of Samaria by Salmaneser, or, more probably, by Sargon, and paints in vivid colours—reminding us in part of Amos vi. 4—6, not without a side glance at the like vices in Jerusalem (chap. xxii. 13)—the license into which the capital of the northern kingdom had fallen. With a bold personification the words paint (1) the banquet with its revellers, crowned, as in the later days of Rome, with wreaths of flowers ; and (2) Samaria itself as such a wreath, once beautiful, now fading, crowning the "head" of the "fat," or luxuriant, valley (literally, *valley of oils*, or, *fat things*) in which the revellers held their feasts. Cheyne notes that the inscription of Salmaneser records that the tribute of Jehu consisted of bowls, cups, and goblets of gold, as illustrating the luxury of the palace of Samaria (*Records of the Past*, v. 41). The LXX. strangely renders the last clause, "drunk without wine," as if from a reminiscence of chap. xxix. 9, and gives the " hirelings of Ephraim " instead of " drunkards."

⁽²⁾ **The Lord hath a mighty and strong one . . .**—The Hebrew may be either neuter, as in the LXX. and Targum, or masculine, as in the Authorised Version. In either case it refers to the King of Assyria as the instrument of Jehovah's vengeance, the similitudes employed to describe his action reproducing those of chaps. viii. 7, 8, xxv. 4. Here the picture is that of the "destroying storm," the *pestilent* or *blasting* tempest withering, and the flood sweeping away, the beautiful "garland" of Samaria.

⁽⁴⁾ **And the glorious beauty . . .**—Better, *And the fading flower of his glorious beauty . . . shall be*

491

valley, shall be a fading flower, *and* as the hasty fruit before the summer; which *when* he that looketh upon it seeth, while it is yet in his hand he ¹ eateth it up.

⁽⁵⁾ In that day shall the LORD of hosts be for a crown of glory, and for a diadem of beauty, unto the residue of his people, ⁽⁶⁾ and for a spirit of judgment to him that sitteth in judgment, and for strength to them that turn the battle to the gate.

⁽⁷⁾ But they also have erred through wine, and through strong drink are out of the way; the priest and the prophet have erred through strong drink, they are swallowed up of wine, they are out of the way through strong drink; they err in vision, they stumble *in* judgment. ⁽⁸⁾ For all tables are full of vomit *and* filthiness, *so that there is* no place *clean*.

⁽⁹⁾ Whom shall he teach knowledge? and whom shall he make to understand ²doctrine? *them that are* weaned from the milk, *and* drawn from the breasts. ⁽¹⁰⁾ For precept ³*must be* upon precept, precept upon precept; line upon line, line upon line; here a little, *and* there a little: ⁽¹¹⁾ for with ⁴ᵃstammering lips and another tongue ⁵will he speak to this people. ⁽¹²⁾ To whom he said, This *is* the rest *wherewith* ye may cause the weary to rest; and this *is* the refreshing: yet they would not hear. ⁽¹³⁾ But the word of the LORD was unto them precept upon precept, precept upon precept; line upon line, line upon line; here a little, *and* there a little; that they might go, and fall backward, and be broken, and snared, and taken.

Marginal notes:
1 Heb., *swalloweth*.
2 Heb., *the hearing?*
3 Or, *hath been*.
4 ¹Heb., *stammerings of lips*.
a 1 Cor. 14. 21.
5 Or, *he hath spoken*.

---

as the early fig before the fruit-gathering. The "early fig," as a special delicacy (Hos. ix. 10; Micah vii. 1), becomes a type of the beauty and pride of Samaria, doomed to inevitable destruction. (Comp. Nahum iii. 12.) Such a fig the passer-by seizes, and eagerly devours. So, the prophet says, with a Dante-like homeliness of comparison, should the Assyrian king treat Samaria.

⁽⁵⁾ **In that day shall the Lord of hosts be for a crown of glory.**—The words are obviously used in direct contrast with the "crown of pride" in verses 1—3. The true glory of the people for "the remnant that should be left" of Israel, as well as Judah, should be found in the presence of Jehovah, whom they would then acknowledge. In the gathering of some of the Ten Tribes at Hezekiah's passover (2 Chron. xxx. 11) there had already been an earnest of such a restored union.

⁽⁶⁾ **And for a spirit of judgment . . .**—The words remind us of the list of spiritual gifts in chap. xi. 2. The injustice of corrupt judges was the crying evil of both Samaria and Jerusalem, and their place was to be taken by those who should be just and faithful. And brave warriors, able to drive back the enemy to the gate of the city from which they had issued forth (2 Sam. xi. 23)—or, perhaps, to defeat them *at the gate* of that which they attacked—should be the companions of the upright judges.

⁽⁷⁾ **But they also have erred through . . .**—Better, *yet these also reel . . .* Isaiah acts on the method of Nathan when he said, "Thou art the man." He has painted the drunkards of Ephraim; now he turns and paints in yet darker colours the drunkards of Judah. Priests were seen reeling to their services, prophets reeling in the very act of their counterfeit inspiration. The threefold iteration of the word for "reel" emphasises the scandals of the scene. The sins of the sons of Eli, those of which Micah (chap. ii. 11) had spoken, were reproduced in all their enormity. The most loathsome features of their drunkenness are printed in verse 8 with a boldness which is almost photographic. The prohibition of wine during the time when the priests were on duty (Lev. x. 1—9) adds to the guilt thus represented.

⁽⁹⁾ **Whom shall he teach knowledge?**—The two verses that follow reproduce the language of the drunkards as they talk scornfully of the prophet. "To whom does he come with what he calls his 'knowledge' and his 'doctrine?' (better, *message*, as in verse 19). Does he think that they are boys just weaned, who are to be taught the first elements of the religion of the infant school?" Then in their mockery they describe (verse 10) his teaching, with what was to them its wearisome iteration, "Always precept upon precept, line upon line . . ."—petty rebukes and puerile harping upon the same note, *semper eandem canens cantilenam*. We can scarcely doubt that Isaiah was indignantly reproducing, as St. Paul does in 2 Cor. x. 10, xi. 16, 17; the very words, almost the drunken accents, in which the priests and false prophets had spoken of him.

⁽¹¹⁾ **With stammering lips and another tongue . . .**—The "stammering lips" are those of the Assyrian conquerors, whose speech would seem to the men of Judah as a barbarous *patois*. They, with their short sharp commands, would be the next utterers of Jehovah's will to the people who would not listen to the prophet's teaching. The description of the "stammering tongue" re-appears in chap. xxxiii. 19. (Comp. Deut. xxviii. 49.) In 1 Cor. xiv. 21, the words are applied to the gift of "tongues," which, in its ecstatic utterances, was unintelligible to those who heard it, and was therefore, as the speech of the barbarian conquerors was in Isaiah's thoughts, the antithesis of true prophetic teaching.

⁽¹²⁾ **To whom he said, This is the rest . . .**—The prophet vindicates himself against the charge of being a repeater of wearisome messages of rebuke. Rather had he pointed the way to a time of repentance, and therefore of rest and refreshment. But to this also they closed their ears. They had but one formula of derision, whatever might be the subject of the prophet's teaching; and the prophet, with all the scorn of irony, repeats that formula in the words that follow.

⁽¹³⁾ **That they might go, and fall backward . . .**—The words are an echo of those in chap. viii. 14, 15. The preaching which might have led to "rest and

The Precious Corner-stone in Zion. ISAIAH, XXVIII. *Covenant with Death Disannulled.*

(14) Wherefore hear the word of the LORD, ye scornful men, that rule this people which *is* in Jerusalem. (15) Because ye have said, We have made a covenant with death, and with hell are we at agreement; when the overflowing scourge shall pass through, it shall not come unto us: for we have made lies our refuge, and under falsehood have we hid ourselves: (16) therefore thus saith the Lord GOD, Behold, I lay in Zion for a foundation *ᵃ*a stone, a tried stone, a precious corner *stone*, a sure foundation: he that believeth shall not make haste. (17) Judgment also will I lay to the line, and righteousness to the plummet: and the hail shall sweep away the refuge of lies, and the waters shall overflow the hiding place. (18) And your covenant with death shall be disannulled, and your agreement with hell shall not stand; when the overflowing scourge shall pass through, then ye shall be ¹trodden down by it. (19) From the time that it goeth forth it shall take you; for morning by morning shall it pass over, by day and by night: and it shall be a vexation only ²to understand the report. (20) For the bed is shorter than that *a man* can stretch himself *on it*: and the covering narrower than that he can wrap himself *in it*. (21) For the LORD shall rise up as *in* mount *ᵇ*Perazim, he shall be wroth as *in* the valley of *ᶜ*Gibeon, that he may do his work, his strange work; and bring to pass his

ᵃ Ps. 118. 22; Matt. 21. 42; Acts 4. 11; Rom. 9, 33 & 10. 11; 1 Pet. 2. 6, 7, 8.

¹ Heb., *a treading down to it.*

² Or, *when he shall make* you *to understand doctrine.*

ᵇ 2 Sam. 5. 20; 1 Chr. 14. 11.

ᶜ Josh. 10. 10. 12; 2 Sam. 5. 25; 1 Chr. 14. 16.

---

refreshing " would become to those who scorned it a " stumbling stone " on which they would fall, a " net " in which they, who boasted of their freedom, would be entangled.

(14) **Ye scornful men, that rule this people . . .**—The last words emphasise the fact that the men who derided the prophet in their worldly wisdom were found among Hezekiah's chief princes and counsellors, the partizans now of an Assyrian, now of an Egyptian alliance—anything rather than the policy of righteousness and repentance.

(15) **We have made a covenant with death . . .**—The phrase was a proverbial one. (Comp. Job v. 23; Hos. ii. 18.) Cheyne quotes Lucan, ix. 394, *Pax illis cum morte data est* (They have made peace with death"). "Hell" is the Hebrew Sheol (Hades), the region of the dead. The two are joined together, as in Hos. xiii. 14; Rev. xx. 13, 14.

When the overflowing scourge . . .—The words probably implied a sneer at the imagery which the prophet had used, painting the Assyrian invasion first as a flood (chap. viii. 7, 8), and then as a scourge (chap. x. 24). (Comp. verse 2.) The scorners think that their " lies " will give them a refuge from the danger under either form.

(16) **Behold, I lay in Zion for a foundation . . .**—We have first to deal with the imagery, then with the interpretation. The former connects itself with the importance which attached, in ancient as in modern architecture, to the foundation stone of a building (1 Kings v. 17). So in Zion the foundation stone was laid, as witnessed in the Arabic name of the Mosque of Omar (*Kubhet-es-Sakhra*), (*i.e.*, " dome of the rock "), on the solid rock. In the stone which was made " the head of the corner " (Ps. cxviii. 22) we have a like thought. From the prophet's stand-point this was identical with the manifestation of Jehovah's righteousness in and through the Temple in its higher spiritual aspect. Christian interpreters have rightly found the true fulfilment of the words in the person of the Christ (Eph. ii. 20; 1 Peter ii. 6, 7). The " corner stone," the *lapis angularis* of the Vulg. is that upon which two walls at right angles to each other rest and are bonded together. The " tried stone " (literally, *stone of proof*) may be one (1) which stands every test, or (2) one which tries those who come in contact with it, becoming an asylum, or a " stone of stumbling," according to their character. (Comp. Luke ii. 34, 35; xx. 18.)

He that believeth shall not make haste.—The LXX. and some other versions give " shall not be ashamed," which is a paraphrase rather than a translation. The English Version, following the Vulgate, represents the meaning of the Hebrew, haste and hurry being regarded in their contrast to the calm temper of a steadfast faith. (Comp. chap. v. 19.)

(17) **Judgment also will I lay to the line . .**—Rather, *I make judgment for a line, and righteousness for a plummet.* The architectural imagery is continued. The " elect corner stone " shall come up to the standard of perfection, laid four-square (Rev. xxi. 16), and, therefore, should be the true place of refuge; while the boast of the scorners, which the prophet repeats in the words that follow, should prove a false one. They would see their place of refuge swept away by the great waters. (Comp. Matt. vii. 26, 27.) Their treaty with death and Hades should be treated as null and void. They should be trampled under foot by the invading armies.

(19) **From the time that it goeth forth it shall take you.**—The words that follow remind us of Deut. xxviii. 66, 67. Day by day would come the dread rumours of the Assyrian march. Then the " report " would no longer be unintelligible. Instead of the " line upon line, precept upon precept," there would be " mourning upon mourning," " day and night," each with its sad burden of alarming tidings. To understand those tidings would be a vexation and a terror. The word for " report " is the same as the " doctrine " of verse 9, and stands, in each case, for the derided " *message* " of the prophet.

(20) **For the bed is shorter . . .**—The image represents vividly a policy that ended in failure. Hezekiah's counsellors had " made their bed," and would have to lie on it, in their Egyptian alliance, but it would not meet their wants. Bed and blankets would be all too scanty, and leave them in a restless disquietude.

(21) **The Lord shall rise up as in mount Perazim . . .**—The point of the reference to David's victories at Baal Perazim (2 Sam. v. 20; 1 Chron. xiv. 11), and at Gibeon (1 Chron. xiv. 16) is that then Jehovah had interposed on behalf of His people against

The Parable of the Ploughman. ISAIAH, XXVIII. *Wisdom of the Sower and the Reaper.*

act, his strange act. (22) Now therefore be ye not mockers, lest your bands be made strong: for I have heard from the Lord God of hosts a consumption, even determined upon the whole earth.

(23) Give ye ear, and hear my voice; hearken, and hear my speech. (24) Doth the ploughman plow all day to sow? doth he open and break the clods of his ground? (25) When he hath made plain the face thereof, doth he not cast abroad the fitches, and scatter the cummin, and cast in ¹the principal wheat and the appointed barley and the ²rie in their ³place? (26) ⁴For his God doth instruct him to discretion, *and* doth teach him. (27) For the fitches are not threshed with a threshing instrument, neither is a cart wheel turned about upon the cummin; but the fitches are beaten out with a staff, and the cummin with a rod. (28) Bread *corn* is bruised; because he will not ever be threshing it, nor break *it with* the wheel of his cart, nor bruise it *with* his horsemen. (29) This also cometh forth from the Lord of hosts,

1 Or, *the wheat in the principal place, and barley in the appointed place.*
2 Or, *spelt.*
3 Heb., *border?*
4 Or, *And he bindeth it in such sort as his God doth teach him.*

their enemies. The "new and strange" work—the very paradox of prophecy—was that He would now rise up to overthrow His own people.

(22) **Now therefore be ye not mockers . . .**—The rulers are warned that the scorn in which they indulge so freely will only make the fetters which already gall them tighter and heavier. In the words that follow the prophet reproduces his own language in chap. x. 23 (where see Notes), probably because they had been singled out as a special subject for derision.

(23) **Give ye ear . . .**—The words remind us of the style of the "wisdom" books of the Old Testament (Prov. ii. 1, iv. 1, v. 1; Ps. xxxiv. 11) in which Isaiah had been trained. Isaiah is about to set before those who have ears to hear a parable which he does not interpret, and which will, therefore, task all their energies. The idea that lies at the root of the parable is like that of Matt. xvi. 2—4, that men fail to apply in discerning the signs of the times the wisdom which they practise or recognise in the common phenomena of nature and the tillage of the soil. As that tillage presents widely varied processes, differing with each kind of grain, so the sowing and the threshing of God's spiritual husbandry presents a like diversity of operations. What that diversity indicates in detail the prophet proceeds to show with what may again be called a Dante-like minuteness.

(24) **Doth the plowman plow all day . . . ?**—Better, *every day*. Ploughing represents naturally, as in Jer. iv. 3, the preparatory discipline by which the spiritual soil is rendered fit for the sower's work. It is a means, and not an end, and is, therefore, in its very nature but for a season. To a nation passing through this stage, Assyrian invaders scoring their long furrows visibly on the surface of the land, the parable gave the hope that this was preparing the way for the seed-time of a better harvest.

(25) **Doth he not cast abroad the fitches . . . ?**—Modern English would give *vetches*. Each verb is carefully chosen to describe the special process that belonged to each kind of seed. We have, as it were, an excerpt from the "Georgics" of Palestine. Identification in such cases is not always easy; but I follow Mr. Carruthers (*Bible Educator*, i. 38) in reading "fennel seed" for the "fitches" of the English version. This, proverbially among the smallest of seeds, so as to be a type of the microscopic unseen, was scattered broadcast; "cummin," also proverbial for its smallness, was sown by a like process, with some technical variation, indicated by the use of the Hebrew words. Wheat and barley were "dropped in" more deliberately by the hand of the sower, and then (instead of "the rie in their place"), "*vetches for the borders thereof*," these being used in the East as a kind of herbaceous hedge round the field of corn. The point of the enumeration is that the wise tiller of the soil is discriminating in his methods, and deals with each seed according to its nature. So is it, the prophet suggests through the parable which he does not interpret, with the great Husbandman, whose field is the world, and for whom the nations are as seed. For "cast in the principal wheat . . ." read *set the wheat in lines and the barley in the appointed place*.

(26) **For his God doth instruct him to discretion . . .**—Better, as in the margin, with a slight variation, *He treateth each as is fitting, his God instructing him*. The prophet looks on the skill of the tiller of the soil, which seemed the outcome of a long experience, as nothing less than a gift of God. The legends of the Gentiles embraced that thought in the myths of Osiris and Oannes, of Dionysius and Triptolemos; Isaiah states the fact without the mythos.

(27) **For the fitches are not threshed . . .**—Better, *fennel seed*, as before. The eye of the prophet passes from the beginning to the end of the husbandman's work. He finds there also the varying methods of a like discrimination. A man would be thought mad who threshed his fennel seed and cummin with the same instrument that he uses for his barley and his wheat. It is enough to beat or tap them with the "rod," or "staff," which was, in fact, used in each case. Interpreting this parable, we may see in the fennel and the cummin the little ones of the earth, with whom God deals more gently than with the strong. "Tribulation," as the etymology of the word (*tribulum*, a threshing instrument) tells us, is a threshing process. The lesson of the parable is that it comes to nations and individuals in season and in measure. The main idea is familiar enough in the language of the prophets (Micah iv. 13; Hab. iii. 12). The novelty of Isaiah's treatment of it consists in his bringing in the minute details, and drawing this lesson from them.

(28) **Bread corn is bruised.**—Better, as a question, *Is bread corn crushed to pieces?* As the poor and meek of the earth were as the fennel and the cummin, so Israel, in its national greatness, was as the "bread corn" of the wheat and barley. For this a severer chastisement, a more thorough threshing, was needed; but the end of threshing is the preservation, not the destruction, of the true grain. It is for a time, not for ever. It separates the worthless from the precious. The wheels stop when they have done their work.

(29) **This also cometh forth from the Lord of hosts.**—The force of the climax lies in the use of the

The Distress of the City of David. ISAIAH, XXIX. *Dream of the Hungry and the Thirsty.*

which is wonderful in counsel, *and* excellent in working.

CHAPTER XXIX.—⁽¹⁾ Woe ¹ to Ariel, to Ariel, ² the city *where* David dwelt! add ye year to year; let them ³ kill sacrifices. ⁽²⁾ Yet I will distress Ariel, and there shall be heaviness and sorrow: and it shall be unto me as Ariel. ⁽³⁾ And I will camp against thee round about, and will lay siege against thee with a mount, and I will raise forts against thee. ⁽⁴⁾ And thou shalt be brought down, *and* shalt speak out of the ground, and thy speech shall be low out of the dust, and thy voice shall be, as of one that hath a familiar spirit, out of the ground, and thy speech shall ⁴ whisper out of the dust.

⁽⁵⁾ Moreover the multitude of thy strangers shall be like small dust, and the multitude of the terrible ones *shall be* as chaff that passeth away: yea, it shall be at an instant suddenly. ⁽⁶⁾ Thou shalt be visited of the LORD of hosts with thunder, and with earthquake, and great noise, with storm and tempest, and the flame of devouring fire. ⁽⁷⁾ And the multitude of all the nations that fight against Ariel, even all that fight against her and her munition, and that distress her, shall be as a dream of a night vision. ⁽⁸⁾ It shall even be as when an hungry *man* dreameth, and, behold, he eateth; but he awaketh, and his soul is empty: or as when a thirsty man dreameth, and, behold, he drinketh; but he awaketh, and, behold, *he is* faint, and his soul hath appetite: so shall the multitude of all the nations be, that fight against mount Zion.

⁽⁹⁾ Stay yourselves, and wonder; ⁵ cry

B.C. cir. 725.

1 Or, O *Ariel, that is, the lion of God.*

2 Or, *of the city.*

3 Heb., *cut off the heads.*

4 Heb., *peep, or, chirp.*

5 Or, *take your pleasure, and riot.*

---

highest of the Divine names instead of "God" (Elohim), as in verse 26. The wisdom of the husbandman was His gift in the highest aspect of the being that had been revealed to men, and that gift was in itself a parable of the method of His own government.

XXIX.

⁽¹⁾ **Woe to Ariel, to Ariel.**—The name belongs to the same group of poetic synonyms as Rahab (Pss. lxxxvii. 4, lxxxix. 10) and the Valley of Vision (Ps. xxii. 1). It may have been coined by Isaiah himself. It may have been part of the secret language of the prophetic schools, as Sheshach stood for Babel (Jer. xxv. 26), Rahab for Egypt (chap. li. 9), and in the language of later Rabbis, Edom, and in that of the Apocalypse, Babel, for Rome (Rev. xvii. 5). Modern language has, it will be remembered, like names of praise and scorn for England and France, though these (John Bull, the British Lion, Crapaud, and the Gallic Cock) scarcely rise to the level of poetry. "Ariel" has been variously interpreted as "the lion of God," or "the hearth of God." The first meaning has in its favour the use of the same word for men of special heroism in 2 Sam. xxiii. 20 ("lion-like men," as in the margin, "lions of God"), and perhaps in Isa. xxxiii. 7 (see Note). The "lion" was, it may be noted, the traditional symbol of Judah (Rev. v. 5). In the words that follow, "the city where David dwelt," the prophet interprets the mystic name for the benefit of his readers. The verb for "dwelt" conveys the sense of "encamping." David had dwelt securely in the rock-fortress of Zion.

Add ye year to year.—The word implies the solemn keeping of the New Year festival. The people might keep that festival and offer many sacrifices, but this would not avail to ward off the tribulation which they deserved, and at which the prophet had hinted in the last verse of the preceding chapter.

⁽²⁾ **And it shall be unto me as Ariel.**—Better, *But she* (the city) *shall be unto me as Ariel.* That name would not falsify itself. In the midst of all her "heaviness and sorrow," Jerusalem should still be as "the lion of God," or, taking the other meaning, as the "altar-hearth" of God. (Comp. Ezek. xliii. 15.)

⁽³⁾ **I will encamp against thee . . .**—The words describe the strategy of an Eastern siege, as we see it in the Assyrian sculptures—the mound raised against the walls of the city, the battering-ram placed upon the mound, and brought to bear upon the walls. (See Jer. xxxiii. 4; Ezek. iv. 2.)

⁽⁴⁾ **Shalt speak out of the ground.**—The words paint the panic of the besieged, the words pointing probably to Sennacherib's invasion. They spoke in whispers, like the voice of the spectres which men heard in the secret chambers of the soothsayers. The war-cry of the brave was changed into the feeble tones of those that "peep and mutter." (See Note on chap. viii. 19.)

⁽⁵⁾ **Moreover the multitude . . .**—Better, *But.* The words interpret those of chap. xxx. 28. The tribulation should be great, but it should last but for a while. As in chap. xxv. 5, the "strangers"—*i.e.,* the "enemies," and the "terrible ones"—should be brought low. A sudden catastrophe, pointing, probably, to the destruction of Sennacherib's army, should bring them low. They, too, should pass under the "threshing instrument" of God's judgments, and be as chaff before the wind.

⁽⁶⁾ **Thou shalt be visited . . .**—Better, *She* (*i.e.,* Jerusalem). The words may be figurative, but they may also be literal. Some terrific storm, acting as an "angel of the Lord" (chap. xxxvii. 36; Ps. civ. 4), should burst at once upon Jerusalem and the hosts that were encamped against her, bringing to her safety, but to them destruction. As in the next verse, the "multitude of all nations" of the great host of Assyria should be as "a dream, a vision of the night."

⁽⁷⁾ **Against her and her munition.**—The word is a rare one, but probably stands here for the new fortifications by which Uzziah and Hezekiah had defended Jerusalem.

⁽⁸⁾ **It shall even be as when an hungry man . . . eateth.**—The foes of Jerusalem were greedy of their prey, eager to devour; they thought it was already theirs. The rude awakening found them still empty. The lion of Judah was not to be devoured even by the strong bull of Assyria.

⁽⁹⁾ **Stay yourselves . . .**—Better, *Astonish yourselves.* We can perhaps best understand the words by

ye out, and cry: they are drunken, but not with wine; they stagger, but not with strong drink. ⁽¹⁰⁾ For the LORD hath poured out upon you the spirit of deep sleep, and hath closed your eyes: the prophets and your ¹ rulers, the seers hath he covered. ⁽¹¹⁾ And the vision of all is become unto you as the words of a ² book that is sealed, which *men* deliver to one that is learned, saying, Read this, I pray thee: and he saith, I cannot; for it *is* sealed: ⁽¹²⁾ and the book is delivered to him that is not learned, saying, Read this, I pray thee: and he saith, I am not learned.

⁽¹³⁾ Wherefore the Lord said, ᵃ Forasmuch as this people draw near *me* with their mouth, and with their lips do honour me, but have removed their heart far from me, and their fear toward me is taught by the precept of men: ⁽¹⁴⁾ Therefore, behold, ³ I will proceed to do a marvellous work among this people, *even* a marvellous work and a wonder: ᵇ for the wisdom of their wise *men* shall perish, and the understanding of their prudent *men* shall be hid.

⁽¹⁵⁾ Woe unto them that seek deep to hide their counsel from the LORD, and their works are in the dark, and they say, ᶜ Who seeth us? and who knoweth us? ⁽¹⁶⁾ Surely your turning of things upside down shall be esteemed as the potter's clay: for shall the ᵈ work say of him that made it, He made me not? or shall the thing framed say of him that framed it, He had no understanding? ⁽¹⁷⁾ *Is* it not yet a very little while, and Lebanon shall be turned into a fruitful field, and the fruitful field shall

---

1 Heb., *heads*.
2 Or, *letter*.
a Matt. 15. 8; Mark 7. 6.
3 Heb., *I will add*.
b Jer. 49. 7; Obad. 8; 1 Cor. 1. 19.
c Ecclus. 23. 18.
d ch. 45. 9.

---

picturing to ourselves the prophet as preaching or reciting the previous prediction to his disciples and to the people. They are staggered, startled, incredulous, and he bursts into words of vehement reproof. The form of the verb implies that their astonished unbelief was self-caused. The change from the second person to the third implies that the prophet paused for a moment in his address to describe their state as an observer. Outwardly, they were as men too drunk to understand, but their drunkenness was not that of the "wine" or the "strong drink" of the fermented palm-juice, in which, as in chap. xxviii. 7, the prophet implies that they habitually indulged. Now their drunkenness was of another type.

⁽¹⁰⁾ **The Lord hath poured out upon you . . .**—The prophet sees in the stupor and panic of the chief of the people what we call a judicial blindness, the retribution of those who had wilfully closed their eyes against the light. (Comp. Rom. xi. 8.)

Your rulers.—Literally, *your heads*, the word being in apposition with the *seers*. The word is emphasised with a keen irony, precisely because they did *not* see. They were as those who sleep, and are "covered," their mantle wrapped round their head, as when men settle themselves to sleep.

⁽¹¹⁾ **The vision of all . . .**—Better, *the whole vision*, *i.e.*, the entire substance of Isaiah's teaching. The words perhaps imply that this had been committed to writing, but that to the unbelievers they were as "the roll of a sealed book." The same imagery meets us in Rev. v. 2. The wise of this world treated its dark sayings as seals, which forbade their making any attempt to study it. The poorer unlearned class could plead a more genuine and less guilty ignorance, but the effect was the same with both.

⁽¹³⁾ **Wherefore the Lord said . . .**—We pass from the effect to the cause. The blind stupor was the outcome of a long hypocrisy. Lip-homage and an estranged heart had been the notes of the religious life of Israel, and they could bear no other fruit.

Their fear toward me . . .—The words point to what we may call an anticipated Pharisaism. Side by side with the great commandments of the Law and with the incisive teaching of the prophets there was growing up even then a traditional system of ethics and religion, based upon wrong principles, ending in a dishonest casuistry and a formal devotion. Commentaries even then were darkening counsel by words without knowledge, as they did in the Mishna and the Gemara of the later days of Judaism (Matt. xv. 3; Mark vii. 6).

⁽¹⁴⁾ **I will proceed to do a marvellous work . . .**—The sure doom of hypocrisy would come upon the hypocrites: not loving the light, they would lose the light they had, and be left to their self-chosen blindness. Here, again, history was to repeat itself, and the words of Isaiah were to be fulfilled in an age and in a manner that lay beyond the horizon of his thoughts.

⁽¹⁵⁾ **Woe unto them . . .**—The words sound like an echo of chap. v. 8, 11, 18, and show that Isaiah had not lost the power of adding to that catalogue of woes. The sins of which he speaks here may have been either the dark sensualities which lay beneath the surface of religion, or, more probably, their clandestine intrigues with this or that foreign power—Egypt, Ethiopia, Babylon—against the Assyrian invader, instead of trusting in the Lord of hosts.

⁽¹⁶⁾ **Surely your turning of things upside down.**—The words are better taken as exclamatory, *O your perversity!* Isaiah was indignant at that habit of always taking things at their wrong end, and looking on them from the wrong side.

Shall be esteemed as the potter's clay . . .—Better, *Shall the potter be counted as the clay?* The Authorised version is scarcely intelligible. Taken as a question, the words bring out the character of the perversity, the upside-downness, of which the prophet speaks. The men whom he condemns were inverting the relations of the Creator and the creature, the potter and the clay, acting practically as atheists, denying that there was a Divine order of which they formed a part.

⁽¹⁷⁾ **Is it not yet a very little while . . .?**—The image of the potter does not suggest to Isaiah the thought of an arbitrary sovereignty, but of a love which will in the long run fulfil itself. He paints as not far off the restoration at once of the face of nature and of the life of man. Lebanon, that had been stripped of its cedars by the Assyrian invader (chap.

The Joy of the Meek and Poor.   ISAIAH, XXX.   *The Woe of the Rebellious Children.*

be esteemed as a forest? ⁽¹⁸⁾ And in that day shall the deaf hear the words of the book, and the eyes of the blind shall see out of obscurity, and out of darkness. ⁽¹⁹⁾ The meek also ¹ shall increase *their* joy in the LORD, and the poor among men shall rejoice in the Holy One of Israel. ⁽²⁰⁾ For the terrible one is brought to nought, and the scorner is consumed, and all that watch for iniquity are cut off: ⁽²¹⁾ that make a man an offender for a word, and lay a snare for him that reproveth in the gate, and turn aside the just for a thing of nought. ⁽²²⁾ Therefore thus saith the LORD, who redeemed Abraham, concerning the house of Jacob, Jacob shall not now be ashamed, neither shall his face now wax pale. ⁽²³⁾ But when he seeth his children, the work of mine hands, in the midst of him, they shall sanctify my name, and sanctify the Holy One of Jacob, and shall fear the God of Israel. ⁽²⁴⁾ They also that erred in spirit ² shall come to understanding, and they that murmured shall learn doctrine.

CHAPTER XXX.—⁽¹⁾ Woe to the rebellious children, saith the LORD, that take counsel, but not of me; and that cover with a covering, but not of my spirit, that they may add sin to sin: ⁽²⁾ that walk to go down into Egypt, and

1 Heb., *shall add.*

2 Heb., *shall know understanding.*

---

x. 34), so as to be as the wilderness of chap. xxxii. 15, should regain its glory, and once more be as Carmel, or "the fruitful field," while the fields that had rejoiced in the rich growth of herbage and shrubs should attain the greatness of the forests of Lebanon as they had been. (See chap. xxxii. 15, where "the wilderness" answers to the "Lebanon" of this verse.) The thought and the language would seem to have been among Isaiah's favourite utterances.

⁽¹⁸⁾ **In that day shall the deaf hear the words of the book.**—The open vision of the future is contrasted with the self-chosen ignorance of verse 11. The "book" (the Hebrew has, however, no definite article) is, perhaps, the prophet's own message, or the book of the law of the Lord, which will then be understood in all its spiritual fulness. The doom of the "closed eyes" of chap. vi. 10 shall then be in force no more.

⁽¹⁹⁾ **The meek also shall increase their joy in the Lord.**—A new element enters into the ideal restoration of the future. Men had been weary of the name of the Holy One of Israel (chap. xxx. 11). In that better time it should be the source of joy and peace for the poor and the lowly, on whom Isaiah looked with all the yearnings of a prophet's sympathy.

⁽²⁰⁾ **The terrible one.**—The word stands, as in verse 5, for the Assyrian invader; the "scorner," for the prophet's enemies who derided his message, and sought, "watching for iniquity," to find an accusation against him.

⁽²¹⁾ **That make a man an offender for a word** . . .—The words indicate that Isaiah had been accused, as Jeremiah was afterwards (Jer. xxxvii. 13), of being unpatriotic, because he had rebuked the sins of Israel and its rulers. Another interpretation gives, "that make men sinners in word," *i.e.*, suborn false witnesses against him. The former seems preferable, but the general drift of the passage is the same. The "snare" was laid for the "righteous man," precisely because he "reproved in the gate:" *i.e.*, preached in the open air in the places of public concourse, even in the presence of the rulers and judges as they sat there.

Turn aside the just.—The phrase is used in Exod. xxiii. 6; Amos v. 12; Mal. iii. 5, for the deliberate perversion of justice.

A thing of nought.—The Hebrew word is once more the *tohu* ("without form") of Gen. i. 1. The accusations brought against the prophet were, as we say, incoherent, absolutely *chaotic* in their falsehood.

⁽²²⁾ **Thus saith the Lord, who redeemed Abraham.**—The words gain in vividness if we think of them as referring to the Jewish tradition that Abraham had been accused by his kinsmen before Nimrod for not worshipping the host of heaven. That history was for the prophet the assurance that Jehovah would not abandon him to his accusers.

Jacob shall not now be ashamed . . .—The patriarch appears, as Rachel does in Jer. xxxi. 15, as if watching over the fortunes of his descendants with varying emotions. Those emotions had been of shame and terror; now there was the dawning of a brighter day.

⁽²³⁾ **The work of mine hands.**—Possibly the direct object of the verb "seeth," the word "his children" being an interpretative insertion, to explain the change from the singular to the plural. The joy of the patriarch as he watched his people centred in the fact that they repented, and once more worshipped God as the Holy and the Dread, entering at last into that true fear of the Lord which is the beginning of wisdom (Prov. i. 7; Job xxviii. 28).

⁽²⁴⁾ **They that murmured shall learn doctrine.** —Better, *instruction*. The word is prominent in the sapiential books of Israel, and is therefore adapted to describe the process of growth and education that followed on conversion. The word, too, "murmured" is noticeable, as occurring only in Deut. i. 27; Ps. cvi. 25, of which its use here may be an echo.

XXX.

⁽¹⁾ **Woe to the rebellious children . . .**—The interjection perhaps expresses sorrow rather than indignation, *Alas, for . . !* as in chap. i. 4. The prophet hears that the intrigues of the palace have at last issued in favour of an alliance with Egypt, and that an embassy has been already sent.

That cover with a covering.—Better, *that weave a web*. The word was fitly chosen then, as now, to describe the subtle intricacies of a double-dealing diplomacy. Some, however, render "form a molten image," not as referring to actual idolatry, but to the trust in human plans which the prophet condemns.

⁽²⁾ **To strengthen themselves in the strength of Pharaoh.**—Literally, *the fortress of Pharaoh*, used

have not asked at my mouth; to strengthen themselves in the strength of Pharaoh, and to trust in the shadow of Egypt! ⁽³⁾ Thererore shall the strength of Pharaoh be your shame, and the trust in the shadow of Egypt *your* confusion. ⁽⁴⁾ For his princes were at Zoan, and his ambassadors came to Hanes. ⁽⁵⁾ They were all ashamed of a people *that* could not profit them, nor be an help nor profit, but a shame, and also a reproach.

⁽⁶⁾ The burden of the beasts of the south: into the land of trouble and anguish, from whence *come* the young and old lion, the viper and fiery flying serpent, they will carry their riches upon the shoulders of young asses, and their treasures upon the bunches of camels, to a people *that* shall not profit *them*. ⁽⁷⁾ For the Egyptians shall help in vain, and to no purpose: therefore have I cried ¹ concerning this, Their strength *is* to sit still.

⁽⁸⁾ Now go, write it before them in a table, and note it in a book, that it may be for ² the time to come for ever and ever: ⁽⁹⁾ that this *is* a rebellious people, lying children, children *that* will not hear the law of the LORD: ⁽¹⁰⁾ which say to the seers, See not; and to the prophets, Prophesy not unto us right things, speak unto us smooth things, prophesy deceits: ⁽¹¹⁾ get you out of the way, turn aside out of the path, cause the Holy One of Israel to cease from before us.

⁽¹²⁾ Wherefore thus saith the Holy One of Israel, Because ye despise this word, and trust in ³ oppression and perverseness, and stay thereon: ⁽¹³⁾ therefore

1 Or, *to her.*

2 Heb., *the latter day.*

B.C. cir. 718.

3 Or, *fraud.*

---

as the symbol of his kingdom. This, then, was the course into which even Hezekiah had been led or driven, and it had been done without consulting Isaiah as the recognised prophet of Jehovah. For the "shadow of Egypt" see Note on chap. xviii. 1.

⁽⁴⁾ **His princes were at Zoan . . .**—Better, *are*, in the vivid use of the historic present of prophecy. Zoan, the Tanis of the Greeks, was one of the oldest of Egyptian cities. Hanes, identified with the Greek *Heracleopolis*, as lying in the delta of the Nile, would be among the first Egyptian cities which the embassy would reach.

⁽⁵⁾ **They were all ashamed . . .**—Better, *are*: historic present, as before. The prophet paints the dreary disappointment of the embassy. They found Egypt at once weak and false, without the will or power to help them. So Rabshakeh compares that power to a "broken reed," which does but pierce the hand of him who leans on it. So Sargon (Smith, *Assyrian Canon*, p. 133, quoted by Cheyne), describing the resistance of his foes, says that they "carried presents, seeking his alliance, to Pharaoh, king of Egypt, a monarch who could not help them."

⁽⁶⁾ **The burden of the beasts of the south.**—It has been conjectured that this, which reads like the heading of a new section, was first placed in the margin by a transcriber, as suggested by the mention of the lions, the vipers, the camels, and the asses, and then found its way into the text (Cheyne). There seems no reason, however, why the prophet should not have prefixed it as with the sarcasm of an indignant irony. "You ask for an oracle," he seems to say, "and you shall have one; but its very heading will imply condemnation and derision;" and then he continues his picture of the journey of the embassy. They pass through the *Negeb*, the south country, arid and waste, haunted only by lions, and vipers, and fiery (*i.e.*, venomous) serpents, and they had their asses and camels with them, laden with the treasures with which they hoped to purchase the Egyptian alliance.

⁽⁷⁾ **Concerning this.** — Better, *it*, or *her* — *i.e.*, Egypt.

Their strength is to sit still.—The Authorised version fairly gives the meaning: "Their boasted strength will be found absolute inaction," but the words, as Isaiah wrote or spoke them, had a more epigrammatic point—"Rahab, they are sitting still." He uses the poetical name for Egypt which we find in chap li. 9; Job xxvi. 12; Pss. lxxxvii. 4, lxxxix. 10, and which conveyed the idea of haughty and inflated arrogance. "Rahab sitting still" was one of those *mots* which stamp themselves upon a nation's memory, just as in modern times the Bourbons have been characterised as "learning nothing, forgetting nothing," or Bismarck's policy as one of "blood and iron." It was, so to speak, almost a political caricature.

⁽⁸⁾ **Now go, write it before them in a table.**—We have before seen this in one of Isaiah's methods for giving special emphasis to his teaching (chap. viii. 1). The word, we may believe, passed into the act in the presence of his astonished hearers. In some way or other he feels sure that what he is about to utter goes beyond the immediate occasion, and has a lesson for all time which the world would not willingly let die. Others, following the Vulg., take the verb as an imperative: "*They are boasters; cease from them.*" (*Superbia tantum est; quiesce.*)

⁽⁹⁾ **That this is a rebellious people.**—The words that follow were those which were thus written on the tablet. The people did not know the law of the Lord, the eternal law of right, themselves. They wished the seers, like Isaiah, to be as blind as themselves, and would fain have made the prophets tune their voice according to the time.

⁽¹¹⁾ **Cause the Holy One of Israel to cease from before us.**—It would seem as if the iterated utterance of this Divine name by Isaiah caused a bitterness of irritation which was not roused by the more familiar "Lord," or even by "Jehovah." It made men feel that they stood face to face with an infinite holiness, and this they could not bear.

⁽¹²⁾ **Because ye despise this word**—*i.e.*, the message which Isaiah had delivered against the alliance with Egypt. We note how the prophet enforces it, as coming from that very Holy One of Israel of whom they were tired of hearing.

⁽¹³⁾ **As a breach ready to fall.**—The ill-built, half-decayed houses of Jerusalem may have furnished

this iniquity shall be to you as a breach ready to fall, swelling out in a high wall, whose breaking cometh suddenly at an instant. (14) And he shall break it as the breaking of ¹the potters' vessel that is broken in pieces; he shall not spare: so that there shall not be found in the bursting of it a sherd to take fire from the hearth, or to take water *withal* out of the pit.

(15) For thus saith the Lord God, the Holy One of Israel; In returning and rest shall ye be saved; in quietness and in confidence shall be your strength: and ye would not. (16) But ye said, No; for we will flee upon horses; therefore shall ye flee: and, We will ride upon the swift; therefore shall they that pursue you be swift. (17) One thousand *shall flee* at the rebuke of one; at the rebuke of five shall ye flee: till ye be left as ²a beacon upon the top of a mountain, and as an ensign on an hill.

(18) And therefore will the Lord wait, that he may be gracious unto you, and therefore will he be exalted, that he may have mercy upon you: for the Lord *is* a God of judgment: *a* blessed *are* all they that wait for him. (19) For the people shall dwell in Zion at Jerusalem: thou shalt weep no more: he will be very gracious unto thee at the voice of thy cry; when he shall hear it, he will answer thee. (20) And *though* the Lord give you the bread of adversity, and the water of ³affliction, yet shall not thy teachers be removed into a corner any more, but thine eyes shall see thy teachers: (21) and thine ears shall hear a word behind thee, saying, This *is* the way, walk ye in it, when ye turn to the right hand, and when ye turn to the left. (22) Ye shall defile also the

1 Heb., *the bottle of potters*.

2 Or, *a tree bereft of branches*, or, *boughs*: or, *a mast*.

a Pss. 2. 12 & 34. 8; Prov. 16. 20; Jer. 17. 7.

3 Or, *oppression*.

---

the outward imagery of the parable. First comes the threatening bulge, then the crack, and then the crash. That was to be the outcome of the plans they were building up on the unsound foundation of corrupt intrigue. In Ezek. xiii. 10 we have the additional feature of the "untempered mortar" with which such a wall is built.

(14) **As the breaking of the potters' vessel** . . . Ps. ii. 9 had given currency to the figure. In Jer. xviii. 4, xix. 10, it passes into a parable of action. The schemes of the intriguers were to be not crushed only but pulverised.

(15) **In returning and rest** . . .—The words describe a process of conversion, but the nature of that conversion is determined by the context. In this case it was the turning from the trust in man, with all its restless excitement, to a trust in God, full of calmness and of peace.

(16) **We will flee upon horses.**—These were expected as the Egyptian contingent of the forces of Judah. With them and the prestige attaching to their fame, the generals and statesmen reckoned on being able to resist Assyria. Isaiah, with his keen insight into the present temper of Egypt, tells them that the only use of the horses will be for a more rapid retreat, not for the charge of battle.

(17) **One thousand shall flee at the rebuke of one.**—The hyperbole is natural and common enough (Deut. xxxii. 30; Josh. xxiii. 10; Lev. xxvi. 8); but the fact that the inscription of King Piankhi Mer. Amon., translated in *Records of the Past*, ii. 84, gives it in the self-same words ("many shall turn their backs on a few; and one shall rout a thousand") as his boast of the strength of Egypt, may have given a special touch of sarcasm to Isaiah's words.

As a beacon upon the top of a mountain.— Literally, *as a pine*. As with a poet's eye, the prophet paints two of the most striking emblems of solitariness: the tall pine standing by itself on the mountain height, the flag-staff seen alone far off against the sky. (Comp. the lowlier imagery of chap. i. 8.)

(18) **And therefore . . .**—The words seem to embody the thought that "man's extremity is God's opportunity." Precisely because of this isolated misery Jehovah was "waiting," *i.e.*, longing, with an eager expectation, to come to the rescue.

And therefore will he be exalted.—A very slight alteration gives a meaning more in harmony with the context, *will wait in stillness* (Cheyne). If we adhere to the existing text, we must take the meaning *will withdraw himself on high*, will seem to wait, that He may at last interpose effectually.

A God of judgment.—Better, *of righteousness*.

All they that wait for him.—This waiting is, as in the first clause, that of wistful longing.

(19) **Shall dwell in Zion at Jerusalem.**—The two words are, of course, practically synonymous; but the prophet dwells with a patriot's affection on both the names which were dear to him. The words admit of being taken as a vocative, "Yea, O people that dwellest."

(20) **The bread of adversity.**—Better, *bread in small quantity, and water in scant measure*. The words seem to imply an allusion to the scant rations of a siege such as Jerusalem was to endure from the Assyrian armies. For this there should be the compensation that the true "teachers" of the people, Isaiah and his fellow-workers, should at least be recognised— no longer thrust into a corner, as they had been in the days of Ahaz. The clearer vision of the truth was to be the outcome of the sharp teaching of chastisement. A various reading gives "*thy teacher*," *i.e.*, Jehovah Himself; but the plural seems more in harmony with the context. In the mission of chap. xxxvii. 2 we have a virtual fulfilment of the prediction.

(21) **Thine ears shall hear a word behind thee.** —The voice of the human teacher on whom the people looked as they listened would find an echo in that inner voice telling them which was the true way, when they were tempted to turn to the right hand or the left.

(22) **Ye shall defile also . . .**—The first effect of the turning of the people was to be the putting away

covering of ¹thy graven images of silver, and the ornament of thy molten images of gold: thou shalt ²cast them away as a menstruous cloth; thou shalt say unto it, Get thee hence. ⁽²³⁾ Then shall he give the rain of thy seed, that thou shalt sow the ground withal; and bread of the increase of the earth, and it shall be fat and plenteous: in that day shall thy cattle feed in large pastures. ⁽²⁴⁾ The oxen likewise and the young asses that ear the ground shall eat ³ ⁴ clean provender, which hath been winnowed with the shovel and with the fan. ⁽²⁵⁾ And there shall be upon every high mountain, and upon every ⁵ high hill, rivers *and* streams of waters in the day of the great slaughter, when the towers fall. ⁽²⁶⁾ Moreover the light of the moon shall be as the light of the sun, and the light of the sun shall be sevenfold, as the light of seven days, in the day that the LORD bindeth up the breach of his people, and healeth the stroke of their wound. ⁽²⁷⁾ Behold, the name of the LORD cometh from far, burning *with* his anger, ⁶ and the burden *thereof is* ⁷ heavy: his lips are full of indignation, and his tongue as a devouring fire: ⁽²⁸⁾ And his breath, as an overflowing stream, shall reach to the midst of the neck, to sift the nations with the sieve of vanity: and *there shall be* a bridle in the jaws of the people, causing *them* to err. ⁽²⁹⁾ Ye shall have a song, as in the night *when* a holy solemnity is kept; and gladness of heart, as when one goeth with a pipe to come into the

1 Heb., *the graven images of thy silver.*
2 Heb., *scatter.*
3 Or, *savoury.*
4 Heb., *leavened.*
5 Heb., *lifted up.*
6 Or, *and the grievousness of flame.*
7 Heb., *heaviness.*

of what had been their besetting sin. The "graven" image possibly refers to the "carved" wooden figure which was afterwards overlaid with silver and gold. (Comp. chap. xl. 19.) These, which had been worshipped, were now to be cast aside, like that which was the very type of loathsomeness.

⁽²³⁾ **Then shall he give the rain . . .**—Following in the steps of Joel (ii. 21—26), the prophet draws a picture of the outward plenty that should follow on the renewal of the nation's inner life.

⁽²⁴⁾ **The oxen likewise and the young asses . . .**—It is, perhaps, hardly necessary to remind the reader that the verb "ear" means "plough."

Clean provender.—Literally, *salted*. The epithet describes what in modern phrase would be the favourite "mash" of the highest class of cattle-feeding, corn mixed with salt or alkaline herbs; and this was to be made, not, as commonly, of inferior barley and chopped straw, but of the finest winnowed grain. That this should be given not to oxen and horses only, but to the lowlier asses, made up the *ne plus ultra* of plenty.

⁽²⁵⁾ **There shall be upon every high mountain . . .**—The picture of a golden age is continued. The mountains and hills, often so dry and barren, should flow down with rivers of waters, and irrigate the valleys. And this should coincide with the day of a "great slaughter," perhaps of the enemies of Israel, perhaps also of the people themselves (judgment coming before the blessing), and of the fall of the "towers" in which they had put their trust. (Comp. chap. xl. 4.) As before, man's extremity was to be God's opportunity. Possibly, however, the "towers" are those of the besiegers of the city.

⁽²⁶⁾ **The light of the moon shall be . . .**—The vision of the future expands, ascending from the new earth to the new heaven. With the passionate joy in light which sees in it, in proportion to its intensity, the symbol of the Divine glory, Isaiah beholds a world in which sun and moon shall shine with a brightness that would now be intolerable, but which shall then be an element of delight.

In the day that the Lord bindeth up.—The day of blessing follows on the day of judgment. Even that had, for God's true servants, been the beginning of blessings, but this was but the earnest of a more glorious future. Isaiah reasons as St. Paul does. If one is the "reconciling of the world," what shall the other be but "life from the dead"? (Rom. xi. 15). (Comp. also Deut. xxxii. 39.)

⁽²⁷⁾ **Behold, the name of the Lord cometh from far . . .**—The use of "the Name of Jehovah" for Jehovah Himself is noticeable as an anticipation of the later use of the *memra* (sc., "word") in the Targumim (or paraphrases) of the sacred writings, and of the *logos* of St. John, a distinct, though not defined, conception of a duality in the Divine essence. In other respects the vision of the Theophany has its parallels in Judg. v. 4, 5; Exod. xxiv. 17.

And the burden thereof is heavy.—Better, *in thick uplifting of smoke.*

⁽²⁸⁾ **His breath, as an overflowing stream.**—Water supplies its symbolism, as well as fire. The wrath of the judge sweeps onward like an autumn torrent, threatening to engulf all that stand in its way.

To sift the nations with the sieve of vanity.—Better, *the winnowing fan of nothingness*. Sifting is, as elsewhere, the symbol of judgment (so Osiris appears in Egyptian monuments armed with a flail, as the judge of the dead; Cheyne), and the "fan" in this case is one which threatens to annihilate the guilty.

A bridle in the jaws of the people.—The words find a parallel in chap. xxxvii. 29. The enemies of Jehovah should find themselves under a constraining power, leading them on against their will to their own destruction. *Quem Deus vult perdere, prius dementat.*

⁽²⁹⁾ **Ye shall have a song . . .**—The "holy solemnity," or feast, was probably the Feast of Tabernacles, the feast of in-gathering, of all the festivals of the Jewish year the most abounding in its joy. In later times, and probably, therefore, in earlier, it had a night-ritual of special solemnity, the court of the Temple being illuminated with a great candelabrum. It was known as being pre-eminently "*the* feast" (1 Kings viii. 2, 65, xii. 32; Ezek. xlv. 25; 2 Chron. vii. 8, 9). The second clause of the verse completes the picture, by introducing the day-ritual of the procession of pilgrims from the country, bringing their firstfruits and playing on their flutes. (Comp. 1 Sam. x. 5.)

mountain of the LORD, to the ¹mighty One of Israel. ⁽³⁰⁾ And the LORD shall cause ² his glorious voice to be heard, and shall shew the lighting down of his arm, with the indignation of *his* anger, and *with* the flame of a devouring fire, *with* scattering, and tempest, and hailstones. ⁽³¹⁾ For through the voice of the LORD shall the Assyrian be beaten down, *which* smote with a rod. ⁽³²⁾ And ³ *in* every place where the grounded staff shall pass, which the LORD shall ⁴ lay upon him, *it* shall be with tabrets and harps: and in battles of shaking will he fight ⁵ with it. ⁽³³⁾ For Tophet *is* ordained ⁶ of old; yea, for the king it is prepared; he hath made *it* deep *and* large: the pile thereof *is* fire and much

1 Heb., *rock.*
2 Heb., *the glory of his voice.*
3 Heb., *every passing of the rod founded.*
4 Heb., *cause to rest upon him.*
5 Or, *against them.*
6 Heb., *from yesterday.*
7 Heb., *remove.*

wood; the breath of the LORD, like a stream of brimstone, doth kindle it.

CHAPTER XXXI.—⁽¹⁾ Woe to them that go down to Egypt for help; and stay on horses, and trust in chariots, because *they are* many; and in horsemen, because they are very strong; but they look not unto the Holy One of Israel, neither seek the LORD! ⁽²⁾ Yet he also *is* wise, and will bring evil, and will not ⁷ call back his words: but will arise against the house of the evildoers, and against the help of them that work iniquity. ⁽³⁾ Now the Egyptians *are* men, and not God; and their horses flesh, and not spirit. When the LORD shall stretch out his hand, both he that helpeth shall

---

The mighty One of Israel.—Literally, *the Rock of Israel*, as a name of Jehovah (chap. xvii. 10; Deut. xxxii. 4, *et al.*).

⁽³⁰⁾ **And the Lord shall cause his glorious voice . . .**—The peace and joy at home are contrasted with the judgments that fall on the enemies of Israel. They are exposed to the full thunderstorm of the wrath of Jehovah. "Hailstones and coals of fire" were the natural symbols of His anger.

⁽³¹⁾ **Shall the Assyrian be beaten down, which smote with a rod.**—Better, *and He* (Jehovah) *shall smite with the rod.* Asshur appears as the foremost and most dreaded enemy of Judah. The prediction points to the destruction of the armies of Sennacherib.

⁽³²⁾ **And in every place where the grounded staff . . .**—It is not clear what meaning the English was intended to convey. Better, *Wherever shall pass the destined rod* (literally, *the rod of foundation) which the Lord causes to fall upon him.*

It shall be with tabrets and harps . . .—*i.e.*, at every stroke of God's judgments upon Asshur Israel should raise its song of triumph with the timbrels and harps (or, perhaps, *lutes*), which were used by the people in their exultation after victory. So after Jephthah's and David's victories we have like processions (Judges xi. 34; 1 Sam. xviii. 6). Israel was to sing, as it were, its *Te Deum* over the fall of Assyria. So the long walls that connected Athens and the Piræus were pulled down by the Spartans to the sound of music.

In battles of shaking will he fight with it.—Literally, *battles of swinging*, as marking the action of the warrior, who swings his sword rapidly to and fro, smiting his enemies at every stroke. The Hebrew pronoun for "it" is feminine, and has been referred by some critics to Jerusalem.

⁽³³⁾ **Tophet is ordained of old.**—Literally, *the Tophet*, or *place of burning*, with perhaps the secondary sense of "a place of loathing." Tophet was the name given to the Valley of Hinnom, outside Jerusalem, where, within the memory of living men, Ahaz had made his son to pass through the fire to Moloch (2 Kings xvi. 3), and where like sacrifices had taken place up to the time of Hezekiah's accession. "The king" is, of course, the king of Assyria; but the Hebrew, "for the *melek*," suggests a sarcastic reference to the god there worshipped, as if it were "for Moloch." There was to be a great sacrifice of the *Melek* to the *Moloch*, who was as a mighty king (the name of the Ammonite god being a dialectic form of the Hebrew *Melek*) exulting in his victims. (Comp. for the idea chap. xxxi. 9.)

The pile thereof is fire and much wood.—The word seems partly literal, and partly figurative. The king of Assyria, though he did not die at Jerusalem, is represented as burnt with stately ceremonial in Tophet. Probably, as a matter of fact, it was the burial place of the corpses that were lying round the city after the pestilence had destroyed the Assyrian army, and they were literally burnt there. For such a Moloch funeral, making the valley of Hinnom then, as it afterwards became, a fit type of Gehenna, a trench deep and wide and a mighty pyre were needed. Comp. Jer. xix. 12, where like words are spoken of Jerusalem.

XXXI.

⁽¹⁾ **Woe to them that go down . . .**—The Egyptian alliance was, of course, the absorbing topic of the time, and Isaiah returns to it yet again. As in chap. xxx. 16, the princes of Judah were attracted by the prospect of strengthening themselves in their weakest point, and reinforcing the cavalry of Judah, which could hardly be mentioned by an Assyrian ambassador without a smile (chap. xxxvi. 9), with an Egyptian contingent. Isaiah once more condemns this as trusting in an "arm of flesh" instead of in the "Holy One of Israel."

⁽²⁾ **Yet he also is wise.**—The words have a ring of sarcasm in them. Isaiah admits ironically that the counsellors of Hezekiah were wise in their generation. He reminds them that there might be some little wisdom in Jehovah, and in the prophet by whom He spake.

And will not call back his words.—Such words, *e.g.*, as those of the preceding chapter (verses 12, 13, 16, 17).

⁽³⁾ **The Egyptians are men . . .**—We hear again the key-note of Isaiah's teaching. The true strength of a nation lay in its spiritual, not in its material, greatness: in seeking the Holy One of Israel by practising holiness. Without that condition the alliance with Egypt would be fatal both to those that sought for help and those who gave it.

The Lord defending Jerusalem. ISAIAH, XXXII. *The King reigning in Righteousness.*

fall, and he that is holpen shall fall down, and they all shall fail together.

⁽⁴⁾ For thus hath the LORD spoken unto me, Like as the lion and the young lion roaring on his prey, when a multitude of shepherds is called forth against him, *he* will not be afraid of their voice, nor abase himself for the ¹ noise of them: so shall the LORD of hosts come down to fight for mount Zion, and for the hill thereof. ⁽⁵⁾ As birds flying, so will the LORD of hosts defend Jerusalem; defending also he will deliver *it; and* passing over he will preserve *it*.

⁽⁶⁾ Turn ye unto *him from* whom the children of Israel have deeply revolted. ⁽⁷⁾ For in that day every man shall ᵃcast away his idols of silver, and ² his idols of gold, which your own hands have made unto you *for* a sin. ⁽⁸⁾ Then shall the Assyrian fall with the sword, not of a mighty man; and the sword, not of a mean man, shall devour him: but he shall flee ³ from the sword, and his young men shall be ⁴ ⁵ discomfited. ⁽⁹⁾ And ⁶he shall pass over to ⁷his strong hold for fear, and his princes shall be afraid of the ensign, saith the LORD, whose fire *is* in Zion, and his furnace in Jerusalem.

CHAPTER XXXII.—⁽¹⁾ Behold, a king shall reign in righteousness, and princes shall rule in judgment. ⁽²⁾ And a man shall be as an hiding place from the wind, and a covert from the tempest; as rivers of water in a dry place, as the

---

1 Or, *multitude.*
a ch. 2. 20.
2 Heb., *the idols of his gold.*
3 Or, *for fear of the sword.*
4 Or, *tributary.*
5 Heb., *for melting,* or, *tribute.*
6 Heb., *his rock shall pass away for fear.*
7 Or, *his strength.*

⁽⁴⁾ Like as the lion . . .—The similitude is noteworthy, as for its fulness and vividness, so also for the fact that the lion is made the symbol, not of destruction, but protection. As the king of beasts stands haughtily defiant over the prey which he has made his own against the shepherds who seek to rob him of it, so will Jehovah, in His character as the Lord of hosts, refuse to surrender Jerusalem, His peculiar possession, to the armies of the Assyrians. (Comp. Homer, *Il.*, xviii. 161.)

To fight for Mount Zion.—The preposition has been differently rendered as *for*, *on*, *against*. The lion in the last case is claiming the sheep as his own prey, and will not suffer interference from without. Jehovah, using the Assyrian armies as His instruments, will fight against Jerusalem, and will not allow the Egyptian allies to interfere with His chastisements. (Comp. chap. xxix. 7, 8.) The second clause simply marks Jerusalem as the scene of the conflict, but agrees in substance with the first. Looking to the verse that follows, the idea of protection seems more natural than that of hostility. The thought of supreme ownership, however, includes both; Jerusalem belonged to Jehovah to protect or to chastise.

⁽⁵⁾ As birds flying . . .—The picture that follows (Æschylean, as the former was Homeric; see Æsch. *Agam.* 49—54, though there the point is the wailing of the parent birds over the plundered nest) is, at least, not doubtful in its meaning, whether it be meant as a counterpart or antithesis to that which precedes it. The eagles hovering over their nest, and scaring off man or beast that attacked their nestlings, supplied the most vivid image possible of protection. (Comp. the image, like, but not the same, in Deut. xxxii. 11.)

Passing over.—The word is the same as that used in connection with the Passover festival, and may perhaps imply a reference to it.

⁽⁶⁾ Turn ye unto him.—Then, as ever, this was the sum and substance of the prophet's teaching, conversion; with that, all was hope; without it, all was fear. (Comp. 2 Chron. xxx. 6.)

⁽⁷⁾ In that day every man shall cast away . . .—The act is the same as that of chap. ii. 20, but with a marked difference of motive: there it springs from the terror of despair, here from the repentance which is the ground of hope.

⁽⁸⁾ Not of a mighty man . . .—The Hebrew has no adjectives, but the nouns are those which are commonly opposed to each other in this way, as in chap. ii. 9, like the Latin *vir* and *homo*. The thought expressed is, of course, that the whole work would be of God, and not of man. The "sword" was that of the Divine judgment (Deut. xxxii. 41), perhaps, as in 1 Chron. xxi. 16, of the destroying angel of the pestilence.

⁽⁹⁾ He shall pass over to his strong hold for fear.—Most recent critics translate, *His rock will pass away for terror*, the "rock" (not the same word, however, as that elsewhere, *e.g.*, Deut. xxxii. 31, used for God) being the symbol of Assyria's strength. The laws of parallelism point to our taking the noun as the subject of the sentence, corresponding to "princes" in the next clause, and so exclude the Authorised version.

Whose fire is in Zion.—Fire, as the symbol of the Divine glory, giving light and warmth to the faithful, and burning up the evil. (Comp. chap. x. 16, 17.)

XXXII.

⁽¹⁾ **Behold, a king shall reign . . .**—More accurately, *the king*. Verses 1—8 form a separate section, standing in the same relation to the foregoing chapter that the picture of the ideal king in chap. xi. does to the anti-Assyrian prophecy of chap. x. "The king" is accordingly the true Anointed one of the future, not, of course, without a reference to the character of Hezekiah as the partial and present embodiment of the idea. The addition of "princes" worthy of their king emphasises this reference. The words are as an echo of Prov. viii. 15, 16.

⁽²⁾ **A man shall be . . .**—The word is that used in chap. xxxi. 8 for "mighty man," in chap. ii. 9 for "great man," and probably retains that meaning here. The nobles of Judah, who had been tyrannous and oppressive (chap. i. 23), should become a true aristocracy, beneficent and protecting. Of both the "king" and the "man" it is true that they find their fulfilment in the true servant of the Lord, who is also the ideal king.

As rivers of water . . .—The words paint the picture of the two great blessings of an Eastern landscape: the streams that turn the desert into an oasis, the "rock" throwing its dark shadow as a shelter from

shadow of a ¹great rock in a weary land. ⁽³⁾ And the eyes of them that see shall not be dim, and the ears of them that hear shall hearken. ⁽⁴⁾ The heart also of the ²rash shall understand knowledge, and the tongue of the stammerers shall be ready to speak ³plainly. ⁽⁵⁾ The vile person shall be no more called liberal, nor the churl said *to be* bountiful. ⁽⁶⁾ For the vile person will speak villany, and his heart will work iniquity, to practise hypocrisy, and to utter error against the LORD, to make empty the soul of the hungry, and he will cause the drink of the thirsty to fail. ⁽⁷⁾ The instruments also of the churl *are* evil: he deviseth wicked devices to destroy the poor with lying words, even ⁴when the needy speaketh right. ⁽⁸⁾ But the liberal deviseth liberal things; and by liberal things shall he ⁵stand.

⁽⁹⁾ Rise up, ye women that are at ease; hear my voice, ye careless daughters; give ear unto my speech. ⁽¹⁰⁾ ⁶Many days and years shall ye be troubled, ye careless women: for the vintage shall fail, the gathering shall not come. ⁽¹¹⁾ Tremble, ye women that are at ease; be troubled, ye careless ones: strip you, and make you bare, and gird *sackcloth* upon *your* loins. ⁽¹²⁾ They shall lament for the teats, for ⁷the pleasant fields, for the fruitful vine. ⁽¹³⁾ Upon the land of my people shall come up thorns *and* briers; ⁸yea, upon all the houses of joy *in* the joyous city: ⁽¹⁴⁾ because the palaces shall be forsaken; the multitude

B.C. cir. 713.

1 Heb., *heavy.*
2 Heb., *hasty.*
3 Or, *elegantly.*
4 Or, *when he speaketh against the poor in judgment.*
5 Or, *be established.*
6 Heb., *Days above a year.*
7 Heb., *the fields of desire.*
8 Or, *burning upon,* &c.

---

the noontide heat. The word for "rock" is the same as that used for Assyria in chap. xxxi. 9, and is obviously chosen to emphasise the contrast.

⁽³⁾ **The eyes of them that see** . . .—Another reversal, like that of chap. xxix. 18, of the sentence of judicial blindness with which Isaiah's work as a prophet had begun (chap. vi. 10).

⁽⁴⁾ **The heart also of the rash** . . .—"Heart," as in Prov. iv. 23 and elsewhere, for the intellect rather than the emotions. The "rash" are those that are "hurried," precipitate, reckless; the "stammerers," those who have no power to speak clearly of the things of God, who hesitate and are undecided.

⁽⁵⁾ **The vile person shall be no more called liberal.**—Better, *noble*, the καλοκἀγαθος of the Greeks, the *ingenuus* of the Latin. So for "bountiful," read *gentle*. Here, again, we have a picture, the exact contrast of that which met us at the beginning of Isaiah's work, when men "called good evil, and evil good" (chap. v. 20).

⁽⁶⁾ **The vile person will speak villany.**—Another echo, like that of chap. xxviii. 23—29, of the teaching of the Book of Proverbs. In that better day men would learn to see men as they are, and not as they pretend to be. "By their fruits ye shall know them" was to be one of the blessings of the reign of the true king (Matt. vii. 20).

To utter error against the Lord.—The "error" is either that of "heresy," or of hollow profession, or of open scoffing. In either case it finds its practical outcome, like the hypocrisy of the Pharisees (Matt. xxiii. 14), in violence and wrong towards the poor and weak.

⁽⁷⁾ **To destroy the poor with lying words** . . .—The words, though perfectly generic in their form, are probably not without an implied reference to those who had thus acted towards Isaiah himself, making even him an "offender for a word" (chap. xxix. 21).

⁽⁸⁾ **The liberal deviseth liberal things** . . .—Better, as before, *noble*.

⁽⁹⁾ **Rise up, ye women that are at ease** . . .—The beginning of a new section, probably a distinct sermon, or, as it were, pamphlet, against the evils of which the prophet had spoken in chap. ii. 16—26, and which continued, it would seem, unabated, in spite of Hezekiah's reformation. It probably finds a place here as painting the *harem* influence, which then, as in the policy of modern Eastern monarchies, Constantinople and elsewhere, lay behind the counsels of the king and his ministers. The whole tone is that of invective against the women of the pseudo-aristocracy that had been covertly attacked in the preceding verses.

Give ear unto my speech . . .—Another echo of the teaching of the Proverbs (Prov. ii. 1, iii. 1, iv. 1, vi. 1, 20.

⁽¹⁰⁾ **Many days and years** . . .—Literally, *days to the year*, a phrase after the pattern of "add ye year to year" in chap. xxix. 1, but implying, not the long continuance of the trouble, but its quick arrival, as in "a year and a day."

The vintage shall fail . . .—The words are commonly taken as predicting a literal failure of the vine-crop, and therefore of the supply of wine for the banquets of the rich. A truer insight into the language of a poet-prophet would lead to our seeing in it a symbol of the failure of all forms of earthly joy.

⁽¹¹⁾ **Tremble, ye women that are at ease** . . .—The words find at once a parallel and a contrast in those spoken to the daughters of Jerusalem in Luke (chap. xxiii. 28—30). The call to repentance includes their stripping themselves of their costly finery, and putting on the "sackcloth" (the word is implied, though not expressed in the Hebrew), which was the outward symbol of repentance (Jonah iii. 5—8). The words, it may be noted, are masculine, the call not being limited to the women.

⁽¹²⁾ **They shall lament for the teats** . . .—Better, *shall smite upon the breasts*. The Hebrew nouns for "teats" and "fields," *Shádaim* and *Sadè*, have an assonance which may be represented by the Latin *ubera* and *ubertas*. In the renewed, unabated luxury of the women of Jerusalem Isaiah sees the precursor of another time of desolation like that which he had foretold before in the reign of Ahaz (chap. vii. 24). "Thorns and briers" are again to take the place of the fair gardens in the outskirts of Jerusalem during the invasion of Sennacherib, as they had once before in that of Rezin and Pekah. The "houses of joy" are manifestly what we should call the stately villas of the rich.

⁽¹⁴⁾ **The palaces shall be forsaken.**—With a bold pencil and rapid strokes the picture of desolation is

of the city shall be left; the ¹forts and towers shall be for dens for ever, a joy of wild asses, a pasture of flocks; (15) until the spirit be poured upon us from on high, and ᵃthe wilderness be a fruitful field, and the fruitful field be counted for a forest. (16) Then judgment shall dwell in the wilderness, and righteousness remain in the fruitful field. (17) And the work of righteousness shall be peace; and the effect of righteousness quietness and assurance for ever. (18) And my people shall dwell in a peaceable habitation, and in sure dwellings, and in quiet resting places; (19) when it shall hail, coming down on the forest; ²and the city shall be low in a low place.

(20) Blessed *are* ye that sow beside all waters, that send forth *thither* the feet of the ox and the ass.

CHAPTER XXXIII.—(1) Woe to thee that spoilest, and thou *wast* not spoiled; and dealest treacherously, and they dealt not treacherously with thee! when thou shalt cease to spoil, thou shalt be spoiled; *and* when thou shalt make an end to deal treacherously, they shall deal treacherously with thee. (2) O LORD, be gracious unto us; we have waited for thee: be thou their arm every morning, our salvation also in the time of trouble. (3) At the noise of the tumult the people fled; at the lifting up of thyself the nations were scattered.

1 Or, *clifts and watchtowers.*

ᵃ ch. 29. 17.

2 Or, *and the city shall be utterly abased.*

---

sketched in outline. The forts are those of Ophel (so in Heb.), the fortified south-eastern slope of the Temple mountain; the towers, probably such as "the tower of the flock," mentioned in conjunction with Ophel in Mic. iv. 8. These would serve as dens for the wild asses, which commonly roved in the open country.

(15) **Until the spirit be poured upon us from on high . . .**—There was, then, a fixed limit of the desolation then described. Isaiah dwelt, as Joel (chap. ii. 28) had dwelt before him, on the outpouring of the Spirit which should sweep away the frivolities of a profligate luxury and lead to a nobler life. The effect of that outpouring is described in symbolic language which had been used before (see Note on chap. xxix. 17), the "wilderness" taking the place of Lebanon.

(16) **Then judgment shall dwell . . .**—Outward blessings, themselves symbols of something beyond themselves, are followed by spiritual. Over the whole country, from the one extreme of cultivation to the other, the judgment and righteousness which had been so lacking should now find a home, and bring their blessed fruits of peace, and confidence, and calm. The whole picture is that of a smiling land, a God-fearing and contented people, all in striking contrast with the panic and unrest with which the people had been but too familiar.

(19) **When it shall hail, coming down on the forest.**—Better, *But it shall hail.* A time of sharp judgment, "hailstones and coals of fire," is to precede that of blessedness and peace. Of such a judgment "hail" was the natural symbol. (Comp. chap. xxx. 30; Ezek. xiii. 13.) The "forest" stands in the symbolism of prophecy for the rulers and princes of any kingdom, as in chap. x. 34 for those of Assyria, and here probably of Judah. Not a few commentators refer the words here also to Assyria, but the city that follows is clearly Jerusalem, and the interpretation given above harmonises accordingly better with the context. Of that city Isaiah says that it shall be "brought down to a low estate," its pride humbled even to the ground, in order that it may afterwards be exalted.

(20) **Blessed are ye that sow beside all waters.** —The picture of a golden age of agriculture receives its final touch. The whole land should be irrigated by calmly flowing streams, and men should cast their seed broadcast, and the oxen and the asses should draw the plough over a rich and fertile land. The whole land should be under tillage, instead of being left to supply (as in chap. vii. 21, 22) a poor and meagre pasturage, or to bring forth nothing but the "thorns and briars" of verse 13. It is obvious that here also a spiritual meaning underlies the literal.

XXXIII.

(1) **Woe to thee that spoilest . . .**—No chapter in the prophet's writings presents so little traceable connection. A thought is expressed in one, or it may be two, verses, and then another follows without anything to link it on. This may be, perhaps, explained either by the strong emotion which filled the prophet's mind as he looked on the coming perils of his country, or, as I think, more probably, on the assumption that we have a series of rough notes, memoranda for a long discourse, which was afterwards delivered in a more continuous form. They would, perhaps, be more intelligible if they were printed separately, as we print Pascal's *Pensées*, the verse arrangement giving a fictitious semblance of continuity. The opening words are addressed to Sennacherib when he entered on his second campaign against Judah, as it seemed to Isaiah, without the slightest provocation. Hezekiah had submitted, and had paid an enormous indemnity for the costs of the war (2 Kings xviii. 13—16) at the close of the first campaign, and had, in the meantime, taken no aggressive action. The invasion was one of undisguised spoliation and rapacity. (For "treacherously," read *rapaciously*.) Upon such aggressiveness there was sure to come a righteous retribution, and in that thought the prophet finds comfort.

(2) **O Lord, be gracious . . .**—Faith transforms itself into prayer. The prophet will still "wait" upon God. In the change of person, "*their* arm," "*our* salvation," we hear the very words of the prayer as it was spoken, the first referring to the soldiers who were to fight the battles of their country, the second to the non-combatants who were assembled with Isaiah in supplication.

(3) **At the noise of the tumult . . .**—The "people" are the mingled nations of the Assyrian armies; the "tumult" is that of the rush and crash, as of a mighty tempest, when Jehovah should at last uplift Himself for the deliverance of His chosen ones.

(4) And your spoil shall be gathered *like* the gathering of the caterpiller: as the running to and fro of locusts shall he run upon them. (5) The LORD is exalted; for he dwelleth on high: he hath filled Zion with judgment and righteousness. (6) And wisdom and knowledge shall be the stability of thy times, *and* strength of ¹salvation: the fear of the LORD *is* his treasure.
(7) Behold, their ²valiant ones shall cry without: the ambassadors of peace shall weep bitterly. (8) The highways lie waste, the wayfaring man ceaseth: he hath broken the covenant, he hath despised the cities, he regardeth no man. (9) The earth mourneth *and* languisheth: Lebanon is ashamed *and* ³hewn down: Sharon is like a wilderness; and Bashan and Carmel shake off *their fruits*.
(10) Now will I rise, saith the LORD; now will I be exalted; now will I lift up myself. (11) Ye shall conceive chaff, ye shall bring forth stubble: your breath, *as* fire, shall devour you. (12) And the people shall be *as* the burnings of lime: *as* thorns cut up shall they be burned in the fire. (13) Hear, ye *that are* far off, what I have done; and, ye *that are* near, acknowledge my might.
(14) The sinners in Zion are afraid; fearfulness hath surprised the hypocrites. Who among us shall dwell with the devouring fire? who among us shall dwell with everlasting burnings? (15) He that ᵃwalketh ⁴righteously, and speaketh ⁵uprightly; he that despiseth the gain of ⁶oppressions, that shaketh his hands from holding of bribes, that stoppeth his ears from hearing of ⁷blood, and shutteth his eyes from seeing evil; (16) he shall dwell on ⁸high: his place of defence *shall be* the munitions of rocks: bread shall be given him; his waters shall be sure.

---

1 Heb., *salvations.*
2 Or, *messengers.*
3 Or, *withered away.*
a Ps. 15. 2 & 24. 4.
4 Heb., *in righteousnesses.*
5 Heb., *uprightnesses.*
6 Or, *deceits.*
7 Heb., *bloods.*
8 Heb., *heights,* or, *high places.*

---

(4) **Your spoil . . .**—The words are addressed to the invader. He who came to spoil should find himself spoiled. As caterpillars and locusts devour the green herbage, so should he (or they, the indefinite pronoun standing for the people of Jerusalem) strip his camp of all its treasures.

(5) **The Lord is exalted . . .**—The vision of the seer takes in the ideal city of God, Jehovah dwelling on high in His holy Temple, the city at last filled with "judgment and righteousness."

(6) **Wisdom and knowledge . . .**—The words are used in the higher sense, as in Prov. i. 1—4, in contrast with the craft and devices of men, just as the "fear of the Lord" is the true treasure, in contrast with the silver and gold in which Hezekiah had been led to place his trust.

(7) **Behold, their valiant ones.**—Literally, *their lions of God.* Heb., *Arielam,* probably with a reference to the "Ariel" of chap. xxix. 1, the lion-like heroes of the lion-like city. (Comp. 2 Sam. xxiii. 20; 1 Chron. xi. 22.) The whole passage paints the panic caused by the approach of Sennacherib.

The ambassadors of peace.—The envoys sent by Hezekiah to Sennacherib at Lachish. They "weep bitterly" at the hard conditions imposed on them, which may be either those of 2 Kings xviii. 14, or some yet harder terms, demanding the surrender of the city.

(8) **The highways lie waste . . .**—Another feature in the picture of terror. No traveller dared to show himself in the main road. (Comp. Judg. v. 6.)

He hath broken.—Sennacherib is denounced as having broken the treaty of 2 Kings xviii. 14. Hezekiah had complied with his conditions, and yet there was no suspension of hostilities.

(9) **The earth mourneth . . .**—Lebanon, with its cedars, *the* Sharon (as we say, *the* Campagna), Bashan, with its oaks (chap. ii. 13), Carmel, with its copse-wood, are the types of beauty and fertility, now languishing and decaying. Possibly the embassy referred to was sent in the autumn, so that the prophet saw in the natural features of that season the symbols of failure and decay.

(10) **Now will I rise . . .**—We note the emphatic iteration of the adverb of time. Man's necessity was, as ever, to be God's opportunity. He had been, as it were, waiting for this crisis, and would at once arise in His might.

(11) **Ye shall conceive chaff . . .**—Primarily the words are addressed to the Assyrian invaders, but not without a side glance at all who had been weaving their own webs of policy instead of trusting in Jehovah. Scheme and result, conception and parturition, would be alike worthless.

Your breath, as fire . . .—"Breath," the hot panting of rage; this, instead of working the destruction of Judah, should prove suicidal.

(12) **And the people shall be . . .**—The two images of destruction are singularly vivid. The lime-kiln and the oven which was fed with thorns were alike in this. The outcome of their work was seen in a residuum of ashes.

(13) **Hear, ye that are far off . . .**—The fate of Assyria is proclaimed as a warning to other nations, and to Israel itself. For the "sinners in Zion" also there is the furnace of fire of the wrath of God. "Who," they ask, "can dwell with that consuming fire, those everlasting (*æonian?*) burnings," which are one aspect of the righteousness of God?

(15, 16) **He that walketh righteously . . .**—The answer to the question shows that the words point not to endless punishments, but to the infinite holiness of God. The man who is true and just in all his dealings can dwell in closest fellowship with that holiness which is to others as a consuming fire. To him it is a protection and defence, a "rock fortress," in which he can dwell securely, where he will find all that he needs for the sustenance of soul and body, the bread and the water of life. The picture of the righteous man is in part an echo, probably a conscious echo, of Pss. xv. and xxiv.

Jerusalem as a quiet Habitation. ISAIAH, XXXIV. *A Place of broad Rivers.*

(17) Thine eyes shall see the king in his beauty: they shall behold ¹the land that is very far off. (18) Thine heart shall meditate terror. ᵃWhere *is* the scribe? where *is* the ²receiver? where *is* he that counted the towers? (19) Thou shalt not see a fierce people, a people of a deeper speech than thou canst perceive; of a ³stammering tongue, *that* thou canst not understand. (20) Look upon Zion, the city of our solemnities: thine eyes shall see Jerusalem a quiet habitation, a tabernacle *that* shall not be taken down; not one of the stakes thereof shall ever be removed, neither shall any of the cords thereof be broken. (21) But there the glorious LORD *will be* unto us a place ³of broad rivers *and* streams; wherein shall go no galley with oars, neither shall gallant ship pass thereby. (22) For the LORD *is* our judge, the LORD *is* our ⁵lawgiver, the LORD *is* our king; he will save us. (23) ⁶ Thy tacklings are loosed; they could not well strengthen their mast, they could not spread the sail: then is the prey of a great spoil divided; the lame take the prey. (24) And the inhabitant shall not say, I am sick: the people that dwell therein *shall be* forgiven *their* iniquity.

CHAPTER XXXIV.—(1) Come near,

1 Heb., *the land of far distances.*
a 1 Cor. 1. 20.
2 Heb., *weigher?*
3 Or, *ridiculous.*
4 Heb., *broad of spaces, or, hands.*
5 Heb., *statute-maker.*
6 Or, *They have forsaken thy tacklings.*

---

(17) **Thine eyes shall see the king in his beauty** . . .—Torn from their context, the words have been not unfitly used to describe the beatific vision of the saints of God in the far-off land of heaven. So the Targum gives "Thine eyes shall see the Shekinah of the King of Ages." Their primary meaning is, however, obviously historical. The "king" is Hezekiah, who shall be seen no longer in sackcloth and ashes, and with downcast eyes (chap. xxxvii. 1), but in all the "beauty" of triumph and of majesty, of a youth and health renewed like the eagle; and the "land that is very far off" is the whole land of Israel, all prosperous and peaceful, as contrasted with the narrow range of view which the people had had during the siege, pent up within the walls of Jerusalem. (Comp. Gen. xiii. 14, 15.) Comp. as to form, chaps. xxix. 18, xxx. 20.

(18) **Thine heart shall meditate terror**—*i.e.,* shall recall the memory of the past evil days, as a dream that had passed away, leaving behind it the thankful joy which rises out of such recollections.

Where is the scribe?—Then, in those times of panic, each Assyrian official was an object of dread. There was the "scribe," who fixed the amount of tribute to be paid by each village or landowner; the "receiver" (literally, *weigher*), who weighed the gold and silver as it was brought in for payment; the "counter of towers," who formed his plans for the operation of the "siege." In Ps. xlviii. 13 the same phrase is used of those who defend the city.

(19) **Thou shalt not see a fierce people** . . .—Better, *The fierce people thou shalt not see* . . . The words answer the question just asked. The whole Assyrian army, with their barbarous, unintelligible speech (chap. xxviii. 11), shall have passed away.

(20) **Look upon Zion** . . .—The words sound like an echo of Pss. xlvi. and xlviii., which were probably written by the sons of Korah on the destruction of Sennacherib's army. Men had seen Zion desecrated by Ahaz, besieged by Sennacherib; now they should see it once again as it had been at the beginning of Hezekiah's reign, emphatically a "city of solemnities," *a tent that shall not be removed*, the latter words probably referring to Sennacherib's threat of deportation (chap. xxxvi. 17).

(21) **A place of broad rivers and streams** . . . —Better, *rivers and canals*. The bold imagery has its starting-point in what the prophet had heard of the great cities of the Tigris and Euphrates. What those rivers were to Nineveh and Babylon, that the presence of Jehovah would be to Jerusalem, that could boast only of the softly going waters of Shiloah (chap. viii. 6). Here, again, we have an echo of Ps. xlvi.: "There is a river, the streams whereof shall make glad the city of God." The words help us to understand the symbolism of Ezekiel's vision of the "river that could not be passed over," flowing out of the Temple (Ezek. xlvii. 1 —5). And the spiritual river of the Divine Presence would have this advantage over those of which the great cities boasted, that no hostile fleet, no pirate ships, could use it for their attacks. So in Ps. xlviii. 7 the "ships of Tarshish" are probably to be taken 'figuratively rather than literally' for the Assyrian forces.

(22) **The Lord is our judge** . . .—The verb is better omitted, and the threefold iteration of the name of Jehovah, in each case with a special characteristic, taken as the subject of the final verb: "The Lord, our judge, the Lord, our lawgiver . . . He will save us."

(23) **Thy tacklings are loosed** . . .—The words have been taken as applicable either to Assyria, as one of the "ships of Tarshish" that had been wrecked, or to Zion, as a vessel that had been driven by the wind and tossed, but had escaped shipwreck. On the whole, the first view seems most in harmony with the context. The terms have been taken by some critics for the cords, poles, and canvas of a tent, but the rendering of the Authorised version seems preferable.

The lame take the prey.—The wrecked Assyrian ship is represented as being plundered by those whom it came to plunder. "The lame" were commonly excluded, as incapable of active service, from sharing in the spoils. Here they also were to have their portion.

(24) **The inhabitant shall not say, I am sick** . . .—The words seem to have had their starting-point in the pestilence which attacked the Assyrian army, and which had probably been felt, during the siege, in Jerusalem itself. The prophet, seeing in such a pestilence the punishment of iniquity, couples together the two blessings of health and pardon. Healthy, because holy, was his report as to the restored Jerusalem. (Comp. Matt. ix. 2.)

XXXIV.

(1) **Come near, ye nations, to hear** . . .— The two chapters that follow have a distinct character of their own. They form, as it were, the closing epilogue of the first great collection of Isaiah's prophecies, the historical section that follows (chaps. xxxvi. — xxxix.) serving as a link between them and the great second

The Enemies of Israel destroyed. ISAIAH, XXXIV. *The Day of the Lord's Vengeance.*

ye nations, to hear; and hearken, ye people: let the earth hear, and ¹all that is therein; the world, and all things that come forth of it. ⁽²⁾ For the indignation of the LORD *is* upon all nations, and *his* fury upon all their armies: he hath utterly destroyed them, he hath delivered them to the slaughter. ⁽³⁾ Their slain also shall be cast out, and their stink shall come up out of their carcases, and the mountains shall be melted with their blood. ⁽⁴⁾ And all the host of heaven shall be dissolved, and the heavens shall be ᵃrolled together as a scroll: and all their host shall fall down, as the leaf falleth off from the vine, and as a ᵇfalling *fig* from the fig tree.

⁽⁵⁾ For my sword shall be bathed in heaven: behold, it shall come down upon Idumea, and upon the people of my curse, to judgment. ⁽⁶⁾ The sword of the LORD is filled with blood, it is made fat with fatness, *and* with the blood of lambs and goats, with the fat of the kidneys of rams: for the LORD hath a sacrifice in Bozrah, and a great slaughter in the land of Idumea. ⁽⁷⁾ And the ²unicorns shall come down with them, and the bullocks with the bulls; and their land shall be ³soaked with blood, and their dust made fat with fatness. ⁽⁸⁾ For *it is* the day of the LORD's ᶜvengeance, *and* the year of recompences for the controversy of Zion.

⁽⁹⁾ And the streams thereof shall be turned into pitch, and the dust thereof into brimstone, and the land thereof shall become burning pitch. ⁽¹⁰⁾ It shall not be quenched night nor day; ᵈthe

---

B.C. cir. 713.

1 Heb., *the fulness thereof.*

a Rev. 6. 14.

b Rev. 6. 13.

2 Or, *rhinocerots.*

3 Or, *drunken.*

c ch. 63. 4.

d Rev. 18. 18 & 19. 3.

---

volume, which comes as an independent whole. Here, accordingly, we have to deal with what belongs to a transition period, probably the closing years of the reign of Hezekiah. The Egyptian alliance and the attack of Sennacherib are now in the back-ground, and the prophet's vision takes a wider range. In the destruction of the Assyrian army he sees the pledge and earnest of the fate of all who fight against God, and as a representative instance of such enemies, fixes upon Edom, then, as ever, foremost among the enemies of Judah. They had invaded that kingdom in the days of Ahaz (2 Chron. xxviii. 17). The inscriptions of Sennacherib (Lenormant, *Anc. Hist.*, i. 399) show that they submitted to him. They probably played a part in his invasion of Judah, in his attack on Jerusalem, analogous to that which drew down the bitter curse of the Babylonian exiles (Ps. cxxxvii. 7). The chapters are further noticeable as having served as a model both to Zephaniah throughout his prophecy, and to Jer. xxv., xlvi. 3—12, l., li., parallelisms with which will meet us as we go on.

The prophecy opens, as was natural, with a wider appeal. The lesson which Isaiah has to teach is one for all time and for all nations: "They that take the sword shall perish by the sword." There rises before his eyes once more the vision of a day of great slaughter, such as the world had never known before, the putrid carcases of the slain covering the earth, as they had covered Tophet, the Valley of Hinnom, after the pestilence had done its work on Sennacherib's army. (Comp. as an instance of like hyperbole, the vision of the destruction of Gog and Magog, in Ezek. xxxix. 11—16.)

⁽⁴⁾ **And all the host of heaven shall be dissolved . . .**—No prophetic picture of a "day of the Lord" was complete without this symbolism (see chap. xiii. 10, 11), probably written about this period. Like the psalmist (Ps. cii. 26), Isaiah contrasts the transitoriness of sun, moon, and stars, with the eternity of Jehovah. The Greek poets sing that the "life of the generations of men is as the life of the leaves of the trees" (Homer, *Il.* vi. 146). To Isaiah's sublime thoughts there came the vision of a time when even the host of heaven would fall as "a leaf from the vine, and as a fig from the fig-tree."

⁽⁵⁾ **My sword shall be bathed in heaven . . .**—Literally, *hath drunk to the full.* The words find an echo in Deut. xxxii. 41, 42, and Jer. xlvi. 10. There, however, the sword is soaked, or made drunk with blood. Here it is "bathed *in heaven*," and this seems to require a different meaning. We read in Greek poets, of the "dippings" by which steel was tempered. May not the "bathing" of Isaiah have a like significance?

It shall come down upon Idumea . . .—Better, *for Edom*, . . . here and in the next verse. No reason can be assigned for this exceptional introduction of the Greek form.

⁽⁶⁾ **The Lord hath a sacrifice in Bozrah . . .**—Two cities of this name appear in history; one in the Haurân, more or less conspicuous in ecclesiastical history, and the other, of which Isaiah now speaks, in Edom. It was a strongly fortified city, and is named again and again. (Comp. chap. lxiii. 1; Amos i. 12; Jer. xlix. 13, 22.) The image both of the sword and the sacrifice appears in Jer. xlvi. 10.

⁽⁷⁾ **And the unicorns shall come down with them . . .**—Better, *the aurochs*, or *wild bulls* . . . The Hebrew, *rem*, which meets us in Deut. xxxiii. 17; Ps. xxii. 21, has been identified with the buffalo, the antelope (*Antilope leucoryx*), and by Mr. Houghton, a naturalist as well as a scholar, on the strength of Assyrian inscriptions, pointing to the land of the Khatti (Hittites) and the foot of the Lebanon as its *habitat*, and of bas-reliefs representing it, with the *Bos primigenius* of zoologists (*Bible Educator*, ii. 24—29). Here, the fierce wild beasts stand for the chiefs of the Edomites. (Comp. Ps. xxii. 12, 21.) The verb, "shall come down," as in Jer. xlviii. 15, l. 27, li. 40, implies going down to the shambles, or slaughtering house.

⁽⁸⁾ **The year of recompences for the controversy of Zion . . .**—The long-delayed day of retribution should come at last. This would be the outcome from the hand of Jehovah for the persistent hostility of the Edomites to the city which He had chosen.

⁽⁹, ¹⁰⁾ **The streams thereof shall be turned into pitch . . .**—The imagery of the punishment which is to fall on Edom is suggested partly by the scenery of the Dead Sea, partly by the volcanic character

The Line of Confusion.   ISAIAH, XXXV.   *Gathering of Owls and Vultures.*

smoke thereof shall go up for ever: from generation to generation it shall lie waste; none shall pass through it for ever and ever. (11) ᵃBut the ¹cormorant and the bittern shall possess it; the owl also and the raven shall dwell in it: and he shall stretch out upon it the line of confusion, and the stones of emptiness. (12) They shall call the nobles thereof to the kingdom, but none *shall be* there, and all her princes shall be nothing. (13) And thorns shall come up in her palaces, nettles and brambles in the fortresses thereof: and it shall be an habitation of dragons, *and* a court for ²³owls. (14) ⁴The wild beasts of the desert shall also meet with ⁵the wild beasts of the island, and the satyr shall cry to his fellow; the ⁶screech owl also shall rest there, and find for herself a place of rest. (15) There shall the great owl make her nest, and lay, and hatch, and gather under her shadow: there shall the vultures also be gathered, every one with her mate.

(16) Seek ye out of the book of the LORD, and read: no one of these shall fail, none shall want her mate: for my mouth it hath commanded, and his spirit it hath gathered them. (17) And he hath cast the lot for them, and his hand hath divided it unto them by line: they shall possess it for ever, from generation to generation shall they dwell therein.

CHAPTER XXXV.—(1) The wilderness and the solitary place shall be glad

a Zeph. 2. 14; Rev. 18. 2.
1 Or, *pelican.*
2 Or, *ostriches.*
3 Heb., *daughters of the owl.*
4 Heb., *Ziim.*
5 Heb., *Ijim.*
6 Or, *night-monster.*

---

of Edom itself, with its extinct craters and streams of lava. (Comp. Jer. xlix. 18.) The prophet sees the destruction, as continuing not merely in its results, but in its process, the smoke of the burning craters rising up perpetually, and making the land uninhabitable.

(11) **But the cormorant and the bittern shall possess it . . .**—The picture of a wild, desolate region, haunted by birds and beasts that shun the abode of men, is a favourite one with Isaiah (comp. chaps. xiii. 20—22, xiv. 23), and is reproduced by Zephaniah (Zeph. ii. 14). Naturalists agree in translating, *The pelicans and hedgehogs; the owl, and the raven.*

The line of confusion, and the stones of emptiness . . .—The "line" and the "stones" are those of the builder's plumb-line, used, as in 2 Kings xxi. 13; Amos vii. 7—9; Lam. ii. 8, for the work, not of building up, but for the destroying as with a scientific completeness. "Confusion" and "emptiness," are the *tohu v'bohu*, "without form and void" of the primeval chaos (Gen. i. 1).

(12) **They shall call the nobles thereof . . .**—The monarchy of Edom seems to have been elective, its rulers being known, not as kings, but by the title which the English version renders by "dukes" (Gen. xxxvi. 15—43). It will be noticed that no chief in the list of dukes is the son of his predecessor. Isaiah foretells as part of the utter collapse of Edom that there shall be neither electors nor any to elect.

(13) **An habitation of dragons, and a court for owls . . .**—The wild creatures named are identified, as elsewhere, with "jackals" ("wild dogs," Delitzsch) and "ostriches."

(14) **The wild beasts of the desert . . .**—Better, *wild cats* or *hyenas shall meet wolves.* The nouns that follow belong, apparently, to the region of mythical zoology. The English "satyr" expresses fairly enough the idea of a "demon-brute" haunting the waste places of the palaces of Edom, while the "screech-owl" is the *Lilith,* the she-vampire, who appears in the legends of the Talmud as having been Adam's first wife, who left him and was turned into a demon. With the later Jews, *Lilith,* as sucking the blood of children, was the bugbear of the nursery. *Night-vampire* would, perhaps, be the best rendering.

(15) **The great owl . . .**—Better, *the arrow-snake.*

(16) **Seek ye out of the book of the Lord . . .** —The phrase is an exceptional one. Isaiah applies that title either to this particular section, or to the volume of his collected writings. When the time of the fulfilment comes, men are invited to compare what they shall then find with the picture which Isaiah had drawn. Keith and others have brought together from the descriptions of modern travellers, illustrations of the condition of Edom as it is well summed up by Delitzsch *in loc.* "It swarms with snakes, and the desolate heights and barren table-lands are only inherited by wild crows and eagles, and great flocks of birds." It has to be remembered, however, that the decay was very gradual. The ruins of Petra and other Idumæan cities are of Roman origin, and indicate a period of culture and prosperity stretching far into the history of the Empire.

His spirit.—In the sense of the creative Breath of the Almighty working in Nature (Ps. civ. 30).

(17) **He hath cast the lot for them . . .**—*i.e.,* hath allotted, or assigned it as by a formal deed of transfer, to the savage beasts who are to be its future possessors. The thought is the same as that of Acts xvii. 26. God is represented as the Supreme Ruler assigning to each nation its place in the world's history, its seasons of prosperity and judgment.

XXXV.

(1) **The wilderness and the solitary place shall be glad for them . . .**—The desolation of the chief enemy of Israel is contrasted with the renewed beauty of Israel's own inheritance. The two last words are better omitted. The three nouns express varying degrees of the absence of culture, the wild pasture-land, the bare moor, the sandy steppe.

Shall . . . blossom as the rose.—Better, *as the narcissus,* but the primrose and the crocus (*Colchicum autumnale*) have also been suggested. The words paint the beauty of the chosen land flourishing once more as "the garden of Jehovah" (Gen xiii. 10), and therefore a fit type of that which is in a yet higher sense the "Paradise of God" (Rev. ii. 7).

The Blind seeing and the Deaf hearing. ISAIAH, XXXV. *Songs and Everlasting Joy.*

for them; and the desert shall rejoice, and blossom as the rose. (2) It shall blossom abundantly, and rejoice even with joy and singing: the glory of Lebanon shall be given unto it, the excellency of Carmel and Sharon, they shall see the glory of the LORD, *and* the excellency of our God.

(3) *a* Strengthen ye the weak hands, and confirm the feeble knees. (4) Say to them *that are* of a ¹fearful heart, Be strong, fear not: behold, your God will come *with* vengeance, *even* God *with* a recompence; he will come and save you. (5) Then the *b* eyes of the blind shall be opened, and *c* the ears of the deaf shall be unstopped. (6) Then shall the *d* lame *man* leap as an hart, and the *e* tongue of the dumb sing: for in the wilderness shall *f* waters break out, and streams in the desert. (7) And the parched ground shall become a pool, and the thirsty land springs of water: in the habitation of dragons, where each lay, *shall be* ²grass with reeds and rushes. (8) And an highway shall be there, and a way, and it shall be called The way of holiness; the unclean shall not pass over it; ³but it *shall be* for those: the wayfaring men, though fools, shall not err *therein*. (9) No lion shall be there, nor *any* ravenous beast shall go up thereon, it shall not be found there; but the redeemed shall walk there: (10) and the *g* ransomed of the LORD shall return, and come to Zion with songs and everlasting joy upon their heads: they shall obtain joy and

a Heb. 12. 12.
1 Heb., *hasty*.
b Matt. 9. 27 & 11. 5 & 12. 22 & 20. 30 & 21. 14; John 9. 6, 7.
c Matt. 11. 5; Mark 7. 32.
d Matt. 11. 5 & 15. 30 & 21. 14; John 5. 8, 9; Acts 3. 2 & 8. 7 & 14. 8.
e Matt. 9. 32 & 12. 22 & 15. 30.
f John 7. 38, 39.
2 Or, *a court for reeds*, &c.
3 Or, *for he shall be with them*.
g ch. 51. 11.

---

(2) **The glory of Lebanon . . .**—The three types of cultivated beauty are contrasted with the former three of desolation. See Note on chap. xxxiii. 9. And over this fair land of transcendent beauty, there will shine not the common light of day, but the glory of Jehovah. (Comp. chap. xxx. 26; Rev. xxi. 23.)

(3) **Strengthen ye the weak hands . . .**—Here the words are obviously, as they are quoted in Heb. xii. 12, figurative and not literal, and so far suggest a like interpretation for what follows.

(4) **Be strong, fear not: . . .**—The words are, of course, wide and general enough, but looking to the probable date of this section, we may perhaps connect them with the tone of Hezekiah's speech in 2 Chron. xxxii. 7. Both king and prophet had the same words of comfort for the feeble and faint-hearted, and the ground of comfort is that the government of God is essentially a righteous government, punishing the oppressor, and saving the oppressed. (Comp. Josh. i. 6, 7.)

(5, 6) **Then the eyes of the blind shall . . .**—The words are obviously to be interpreted, like those that precede them, and chap. xxix. 18, of spiritual infirmities. If they seem to find a literal fulfilment in the miracles of the Christ, it is, as it were, *ex abundante*, and as a pledge and earnest of something beyond themselves.

(7) **The parched ground . . .**—The Hebrew word is essentially what we know as the *mirage*, or *fata morgana*, the silvery sheen which looks like a sparkling lake, and turns out to be barren sand. Instead of that delusive show, there shall be in the renewed earth the *lake* itself.

In the habitation of dragons . . .—Better, as elsewhere, *jackals*, which had their lair in the sandy desert.

Shall be grass with reeds and rushes.—Better, *grass shall grow as* (or *unto*) *reeds and rushes*, the well-watered soil giving even to common herbage an intensified fertility.

(8) **An highway shall be there.**—The raised causeway, as distinct from the common paths. (See Judg. v. 6.) We are still in the region of parables, but the thought has a special interest as a transition, at the close of the first volume of Isaiah's writings, to the opening of the second. The use of the road has been referred, by some interpreters, to the return of the exiles from Babylon. Rather is it the road by which the pilgrims of all nations shall journey to the mountain of the Lord's house (chap. ii. 1).

The way of holiness . . .—The name of the road confirms the interpretation just given. There was to be a true *Via Sacra* to the earthly temple, as the type of that eternal Temple, not made with hands, which also was in the prophet's thoughts. Along that road there would be no barbarous invaders polluting the ground they trod, no Jews ceremonially or spiritually unclean. The picture of the heavenly Jerusalem (Rev. xxi. 27) into which "there entereth nothing that defileth," presents a like feature. *It shall be for them*, i.e. . . *It is appointed for those, for whosoever walketh therein* (the Hebrew verb is in the singular). Then, in strict order, comes the final clause: *Even the simple ones shall not lose their way.* A curious parallel is found in Eccles. x. 15, where "he knoweth not how to go to the city," is one of the notes of the man who is void of understanding.

(9) **No lion shall be there . . .**—We have to remember that the lion had not ceased to haunt the valley of the Jordan, as it had done in the days of Samson (Judg. xiv. 5), and David (1 Sam. xvii. 3, 4; 2 Sam. xxiii. 20). The recent depopulation of the northern kingdom had probably laid the country more open to their attack (2 Kings xvii. 25), and thus gave a special force to the prophet's description. For "any ravenous beast," read *the most* ravenous.

The redeemed . . . ** (10) **. . . the ransomed.—The Hebrew words express simply the idea of release and freedom, without implying, as the English words do, a payment as its condition.

(10) **With songs and everlasting joy . . .**—The first volume of Isaiah's prophecy closes fitly with this transcendent picture, carrying the thoughts of men beyond any possible earthly fulfilment. The outward imagery probably had its starting-point in the processions of the pilgrims who came up to the Temple singing psalms, like those known as the "songs of degrees" at their successive halting-places (Pss. cxx.—cxxxiv.).

Sorrow and sighing shall flee away.—The words have a special interest as being the closing utterance of Isaiah's political activity, written, therefore,

gladness, and sorrow and sighing shall flee away.

CHAPTER XXXVI.— (1) Now *it came to pass in the fourteenth year of king Hezekiah, *that* Sennacherib king of Assyria came up against all the defenced cities of Judah, and took them. (2) And the king of Assyria sent Rabshakeh from Lachish to Jerusalem unto king Hezekiah with a great army. And he stood by the conduit of the upper pool in the highway of the fuller's field.
(3) Then came forth unto him Eliakim, Hilkiah's son, which was over the house, and Shebna the ¹scribe, and Joah, Asaph's son, the recorder. (4) And Rabshakeh said unto them, Say ye now to Hezekiah, Thus saith the great king, the king of Assyria, What confidence *is* this wherein thou trustest? (5) I say, *sayest thou*, (but *they are but* ²vain words) ³*I have* counsel and strength for war: now on whom dost thou trust, that thou rebellest against me? (6) Lo, thou trustest in the *b*staff of this broken reed, on Egypt; whereon if a man lean, it will go into his hand, and pierce it: so *is* Pharaoh king of Egypt to all that trust in him.

a 2 Kin. 18. 13; 2 Chron. 32. 1.
¹ Or, *secretary*.
² Heb., *a word of lips*.
³ Or, *but counsel and strength are for the war*.
b Ezek. 29. 6, 7.

---

probably, in his old age, and in the midst of much trouble, whether he wrote at the close of Hezekiah's reign, or the beginning of Manasseh's, which must have been sufficiently dark and gloomy. (See 2 Chron. xxxii. 26, xxxiii. 1—10.) The hopes of the prophet were, however, inextinguishable, and they formed a natural starting-point for the words: "Comforty ye, comfort ye, my people," with which the second collection opens, the intermediate chapters being obviously of the nature of an historical appendix. They find their echo in Rev. vii. 17, "God shall wipe away all tears from their eyes."

XXXVI.

(1) **It came to pass in the fourteenth year of king Hezekiah . . .**—In the judgment of nearly all Assyriologists (Sir Henry Rawlinson, Sayce, Hinckes, Lenormant, Schrader, Cheyne), we have to rectify the chronology. The inscriptions of Sennacherib fix the date of his campaign against Hezekiah in the third year of his reign (B.C. 700), and that coincides not with the fourteenth, but with the twenty-seventh year of the king of Judah. The error, on this assumption, arose from the editor of Isaiah's prophecies taking for granted that the illness of Hezekiah followed on the destruction of Sennacherib's army, or, at least, on his attack, and then reckoning back the fifteen years for which his life was prolonged from the date of his death. Most of the scholars named above have come to the conclusion that the illness preceded Sennacherib's campaign by ten or eleven years, and this, of course, involves throwing back the embassy from Babylon (chap. xxxix.) to about the same period. Lenormant (*Manual of Ancient History*, i. 181) keeping to the Biblical sequence, real or apparent, of the events, meets the difficulty by assuming that Hezekiah reigned for forty-one instead of twenty-nine years, and that Manasseh was associated with him in titular sovereignty even from his birth, and the fifty years of his reign reckoned from that epoch.

Sennacherib king of Assyria.—According to the Assyrian inscriptions, the king succeeded Sargon, who was assassinated in his palace, B.C. 704, and after subduing the province of Babylon which had rebelled under Merôdach-baladan, turned his course southward against Hezekiah with four or five distinct complaints— (1) that the king had refused tribute (2 Kings xviii. 14); (2) that he had opened negotiations with Babylon and Egypt (2 Kings xviii. 24) with a view to an alliance against Assyria; (3) that he had helped the Philistines of Ekron to rise against their king who supported Assyria, and had kept that king as a prisoner in Jerusalem (*Records of the Past*, i. 36—39).

(2) **The king of Assyria sent Rabshakeh.**—The word is a title (*the* Rabshakeh) probably the chief officer or cup-bearer. In 2 Kings xviii.; 2 Chron. xxxii., we have the previous history of the war. Hezekiah, on hearing Sennacherib's reproach, began to strengthen the fortifications of Jerusalem, called his officers and troops together, and made an appeal to their faith and courage. In chap. xxii. we have the prophet's view of those preparations. Probably by Isaiah's advice, who put no confidence in this boastful and blustering courage, Hezekiah sent to Sennacherib, who was then besieging Lachish, to sue for peace, acknowledging that he had offended. A penalty of three hundred talents of silver and thirty talents of gold was imposed and paid, Hezekiah being reduced to empty his own treasury and that of the Temple, and even to strip the Temple doors and pillars of the plates of gold with which they were overlaid. Peace, however, was not to be had even at that price. Encouraged, perhaps, by this prompt submission, and tearing up the treaty (the breach of covenant of which Isaiah complains in chap. xxxv. 1), Sennacherib sent his officers, the Tartan, the Rabsaris, and the Rabshakeh (the names are all official titles) to demand an unconditional surrender.

He stood by the conduit of the upper pool.—The spot was the same as that at which Isaiah had addressed Ahaz thirty or more years before (chap. vii. 3). It was probably chosen by the Rabshakeh as commanding one end of the aqueduct which supplied the city with water, and thus enabling him to threaten that he would cut off the supply (verse 12).

(3) **Eliakim.**—It is significant that Eliakim now fills the office which, a short time before, had been filled by Shebna, while the latter is reduced to the inferior position of a scribe (chap. xxii. 15—25). The change is clearly traceable to Isaiah's influence. The "scribe" was the secretary who formulated despatches and degrees; the "recorder," probably the registrar of the official annals.

(5, 6) **I have counsel and strength for war . . .** —Reports of Hezekiah's speech, probably also of his negotiations with Egypt, had reached the ears of the Assyrian king. So Sennacherib, in his inscriptions, speaks of "the king of Egypt as a monarch who could not save those who trusted in him" (Smith, *Assyrian Canon*). The Pharaoh in this case was Shabatoka, or Sabaco II., the father of the Tir-hakah of chap. xxxvii.

The Rabshakeh's Oration.   ISAIAH, XXXVI.   *A Royal Proclamation.*

(7) But if thou say to me, we trust in the LORD our God: *is it* not he, whose high places and whose altars Hezekiah hath taken away, and said to Judah and to Jerusalem, Ye shall worship before this altar? (8) Now therefore give ¹pledges, I pray thee, to my master the king of Assyria, and I will give thee two thousand horses, if thou be able on thy part to set riders upon them. (9) How then wilt thou turn away the face of one captain of the least of my master's servants, and put thy trust on Egypt for chariots and for horsemen? (10) And am I now come up without the LORD against this land to destroy it? the LORD said unto me, Go up against this land, and destroy it.

(11) Then said Eliakim and Shebna and Joah unto Rabshakeh, Speak, I pray thee, unto thy servants in the Syrian language; for we understand *it:* and speak not to us in the Jews' language, in the ears of the people that *are* on the wall. (12) But Rabshakeh said, Hath my master sent me to thy master and to thee to speak these words? *hath he* not *sent me* to the men that sit upon the wall, that they may eat their own dung, and drink their own piss with you?

(13) Then Rabshakeh stood, and cried with a loud voice in the Jews' language, and said, Hear ye the words of the great king, the king of Assyria. (14) Thus saith the king, Let not Hezekiah deceive you: for he shall not be able to deliver you. (15) Neither let Hezekiah make you trust in the LORD, saying, The LORD will surely deliver us: this city shall not be delivered into the hand of the king of Assyria. (16) Hearken not to Hezekiah: for thus saith the king of Assyria, ²³Make *an agreement* with me *by* a present, and come out to me: and eat ye every one of his vine, and every one of his fig tree, and drink ye every one the waters of his own cistern; (17) until I come and take you away to a

Marginal notes:
1 Or, *hostages.*
B.C. 710.
2 Or, *seek my favour by a present.*
3 Heb., *Make with me a blessing.*

9, one of the Ethiopian dynasty that reigned in Egypt from B.C. 725—665.

(7) **Is it not he, whose high places . . .**—This was this impression left on the mind of the Rabshakeh by what he heard of Hezekiah's reformation. From the Assyrian stand-point a god was honoured in proportion as his sanctuaries were multiplied, but wherever he went, the Rabshakeh had found "high places" where Jehovah had been worshipped, which Hezekiah had desecrated. How could one who had so acted hope for the protection of his God?

(8) **Now, therefore, give pledges.**—Better, *make a wager.* This would seem to be a taunt interpolated by the Rabshakeh in the midst of his official message. There was something absurd in the idea of Judah coming out as strong in its cavalry. Had they two thousand men who could manage their horses if they had them?

(10) **Am I now come up without the Lord . . .**—The words may be simply an empty boast. Possibly, however, Isaiah's teaching that it was Jehovah who brought the King of Assyria into Judah, and used him as an instrument (chap. vii. 17, 18), had become known, or Sennacherib may have dreamt, or have said that he had dreamt, that the God of Judah, irritated with the destruction of the high places, had given him this mission. He assumes the character of a defender of the faith. The inscriptions of Sennacherib are, it may be noted, conspicuous for like assertions. He delights, apparently, to claim a Divine sanction for the wars in which he is engaged (*Records of the Past,* i. 25, ix. 23).

(11) **Speak, I pray thee, unto thy servants . . .**—The king's officers, knowing the "little faith" of their people, are not, perhaps, without misgivings of their own. Might not the townsmen, listening eagerly on the wall, recognise in Rabshakeh's words an echo of Isaiah's, and lose courage, as feeling that they were fighting against the God who was chastising them? The Syrian or Aramaic was a common ground for the ambassadors on both sides, as being the language of commerce and diplomacy. Rabshakeh, it would seem, could speak three languages, Assyrian, Syrian, and Hebrew; Hezekiah's ministers the two latter; the "people on the wall" only the last.

In the Jews' language.—It is uncertain whether this means simply Hebrew, which Isaiah elsewhere calls the language of Canaan (chap. xix. 18), or a special dialect of Judah. The Moabite stone, on the one hand, shows that Hebrew was the common speech of Palestine and the border countries. On the other hand, dialects spring up quickly. Nehemiah xiii. 24 is the only other passage (the parallels of 2 Kings xviii. 26 and 2 Chron. xxxii. 18 excepted) in which the term meets us in the narrower sense, and that is after the exile.

(12) **Hath he not sent me to the men that sit upon the wall . . . ?**—The words, which in their brutal coarseness have hardly a parallel in history, till we come to Bismarck's telling the Parisians that they may "stew in their own gravy," imply that the Assyrians were in a position to cut off the supplies both of food and water.

(15, 16) **Neither let Hezekiah make you trust in the Lord . . .**—Rabshakeh had apparently heard from spies or deserters of Hezekiah's speech to his people (2 Chron. xxxii. 7, 8). In contrast with what he derides as trust in a God who was against those who trusted Him, he offers tangible material advantages. They have only to leave the besieged city, and to go to the Assyrian camp, and they will be allowed provisionally to occupy their own houses and till their own fields, and, instead of dying of thirst, shall have each man the waters of his own cistern; and then, not without a latent sarcasm, worse than the *væ victis* which is the normal utterance of conquerors, he offers the doom of exile as if it were a change for the better, and not the worse, as though the conquered had no love of country as such, no reverence for the sepulchres of their fathers, no yearning for the Temple of their

land like your own land, a land of corn and wine, a land of bread and vineyards. (18) *Beware* lest Hezekiah persuade you, saying, The LORD will deliver us. Hath any of the gods of the nations delivered his land out of the hand of the king of Assyria? (19) Where *are* the gods of Hamath and Arphad? where *are* the gods of Sepharvaim? and have they delivered Samaria out of my hand? (20) Who *are they* among all the gods of these lands, that have delivered their land out of my hand, that the LORD should deliver Jerusalem out of my hand?

(21) But they held their peace, and answered him not a word: for the king's commandment was, saying, Answer him not.

(22) Then came Eliakim, the son of Hilkiah, that *was* over the household, and Shebna the scribe, and Joah, the son of Asaph, the recorder, to Hezekiah with *their* clothes rent, and told him the words of Rabshakeh.

CHAPTER XXXVII.—(1) And *it came to pass, when king Hezekiah heard *it*, that he rent his clothes, and covered himself with sackcloth, and went into the house of the LORD.

(2) And he sent Eliakim, who *was* over the household, and Shebna the scribe, and the elders of the priests covered with sackcloth, unto Isaiah the prophet the son of Amoz. (3) And they said unto him, Thus saith Hezekiah, This day *is* a day of trouble, and of rebuke, and of ¹blasphemy: for the children are come to the birth, and *there is* not strength to bring forth. (4) It may be the LORD thy God will hear the words of Rabshakeh, whom the king of Assyria his master hath sent to reproach the living God, and will reprove the words which the LORD thy God hath heard: wherefore lift up *thy* prayer for the remnant that is ²left.

(5) So the servants of king Hezekiah came to Isaiah. (6) And Isaiah said unto them, Thus shall ye say unto your master, Thus saith the LORD, Be not afraid of the words that thou hast heard, wherewith the servants of the king of

a 2 Kin. 19.1, &c.

¹ Or, *provocation*.

² Heb., *found*.

God. The taunt and the promise may, perhaps, be connected with Sennacherib's boast that he had improved the water-supply of the cities of his empire (*Records of the Past*, i. 32, ix. 23, 26, 28).

(18) **Hath any of the gods of the nations . . .**—The Rabshakeh speaks in the natural language of polytheism. The Jehovah of Israel was one of gods many and lords many, a simple national deity; but Asshur and Ishtar, the gods of Assyria, were supreme above them all (*Records of the Past*, i. 25, 33).

(19) **Hamath and Arphad . . .**—See Note on chap. x. 9. Looking to the practice of the Assyrians, the question would have had for its answer, not the echoing "Where?" which it suggests to modern ears, but "They are to be seen in the Temples of Assyria, as trophies of its victories."

Sepharvaim.—The southernmost city of Mesopotamia, on the left bank of the Euphrates, probably the same as the "sun-city" Sippara, in which Xisuthros, the Noah of Chaldæan mythology, was said to have concealed the sacred books before the great flood (*Records of the Past*, vii. 143).

(21) **But they held their peace . . .**—Hezekiah seems to have commanded silence, as if distrustful either of the wisdom of the ambassadors or of the effect which any chance words might have upon the garrison and people of Jerusalem. As it was, the only words they had spoken (verse 11) had made matters infinitely worse.

(22) **With their clothes rent.**—The act was the natural expression of their horror at the blasphemy of Rabshakeh's words. (Comp. Matt. xxvi. 65; Acts xiv. 14.) They would not reply to that blasphemy, and trusted to the effect of this silent protest on the minds of the people who had heard it.

XXXVII.

(1) **Covered himself with sackcloth.**—The king was probably accompanied by his ministers, all in the penitential sackcloth of mourners (Joel i. 8—13; Jonah iii. 5, 6).

(2) **Unto Isaiah the prophet.**—At last, then, the people did "see their teacher" (chap. xxx. 20). In that supreme hour of calamity the prophet, who had been despised and derided, was their one resource. What could he do to extricate them from the evil net which was closing round them, and to vindicate the honour of his God?

(3) **The children are come to the birth.**—The bold language of the text stands where we should use an adjective of which we half forget the meaning. Things had come to such a pass that all plans and counsels were literally *abortive*. (Comp. chap. xxvi. 17, 18, and Hosea xiii. 13 for a like simile.)

(4) **Lift up thy prayer for the remnant . . .**—Isaiah's characteristic words (chaps. i. 9, x. 21) had impressed itself on the king's mind. Now that town after town of Judah had fallen into Sennacherib's hands (forty-six, according to his inscriptions—*Records of the Past*, i. 38), those who were gathered within the walls of Jerusalem were as a mere remnant of the people.

(5) **So the servants . . .**—Literally, *And . . .* The Authorised Version suggests that there was only one coming of the messengers. Possibly, however, the words imply a withdrawal between the delivery of their message and their coming a second time to receive his answer.

(6) **The servants of the king of Assyria.**—Not the usual word for "servants," which might include

Assyria have blasphemed me. (7) Behold, I will ¹send a blast upon him, and he shall hear a rumour, and return to his own land; and I will cause him to fall by the sword in his own land.

(8) So Rabshakeh returned, and found the king of Assyria warring against Libnah: for he had heard that he was departed from Lachish. (9) And he heard say concerning Tirhakah king of Ethiopia, He is come forth to make war with thee. And when he heard *it*, he sent messengers to Hezekiah, saying, (10) Thus shall ye speak to Hezekiah king of Judah, saying, Let not thy God, in whom thou trustest, deceive thee, saying, Jerusalem shall not be given into the hand of the king of Assyria.

¹ Or, *put a spirit into him.*

(11) Behold, thou hast heard what the kings of Assyria have done to all lands by destroying them utterly; and shalt thou be delivered? (12) Have the gods of the nations delivered them which my fathers have destroyed, *as* Gozan, and Haran, and Rezeph, and the children of Eden which *were* in Telassar? (13) Where *is* the king of Hamath, and the king of Arphad, and the king of the city of Sepharvaim, Hena, and Ivah?

(14) And Hezekiah received the letter from the hand of the messengers, and read it: and Hezekiah went up unto the house of the LORD, and spread it before the LORD. (15) And Hezekiah prayed unto the LORD, saying, (16) O LORD of hosts, God of Israel, that dwell-

---

high officers of state, but a less honourable one (*na'arê*), like *puer* in Latin, or *garçon* in French. He speaks of Rabshakeh (probably the king's cup-bearer) as though he were only, after all, a *valet*.

(7) **I will send a blast upon him.**—Better, *I will put a spirit in him.* The Authorised Version suggests the idea of some physical calamity, like that which actually destroyed the Assyrian army. Here, however, the "spirit," stands for the impulse, strong and mighty, which overpowers previous resolves. (Comp. chap. xxx. 28.)

He shall hear a rumour.—The words admit of being explained either as a prediction rising out of a purely supernatural foresight, or as resting on some secret intelligence which Israel had received as to the movements of Tirhakah.

(8) **Warring against Libnah . . . Lachish.**—Both names occur in Josh. xv. 39, 42, as belonging to Judah. The step would seem to indicate a strategic movement, intended to check the march of Tirhakah's army; but in our ignorance of the topography, we can settle nothing further. By some writers Libnah has been identified with Pelusium, or some other town in the Delta of the Nile. The narrative seems, perhaps, to suggest something more than a transfer of the attack from one small fortress in Judah to another; but that is all that can be said.

(9) **Tirhakah.**—The third of the twenty-fifth, or Ethiopian dynasty of kings. So, or Sabaco, with whom Hoshea, the last king of Israel, allied himself, being the first (2 Kings xvii. 4). He is described in Assurbanipal's inscriptions (*Records of the Past*, i. 60) as king of Mizr and Cush—*i.e.*, Egypt and Ethiopia. The policy of Hezekiah's counsellors had led them to court his alliance, as in chaps. xxx., xxxi. Now, however, the Egyptian army was at least mobilised. "Rahab" was no longer "sitting still" (chap. xxx. 7).

When he heard it.—The message is in substance a repetition of its predecessors, more defiant, perhaps, as if in answer to the threatened attack of Tirhakah's armies, which Sennacherib could scarcely fail to connect with Hezekiah's confident hope of deliverance.

(12) **Gozan . . .**—The induction drawn from the enumeration of conquered nations is continued. Strictly speaking, Sargon, the father of Sennacherib, was the founder of a new dynasty; but the "fathers" are, as commonly in the formulæ of Eastern kings, the predecessors of the reigning king. The position of Gozan is defined by 2 Kings xvii. 6 as being on the Habor, or *Khabûr*, which flows into the Tigris from the east, above Mosul. Haran is probably identical with Abraham's resting-place (Gen. xi. 31), and the Charran of Josephus and St. Stephen's speech (Acts. vii. 4). "Rezeph" is identified with the Rheseper of Ptolemy (chap. v. 13, 6) below Thapsacus, between the Euphrates and Tadmor (= Palmyra). Telassar is probably an altered form of Tel-Assur (the hill of Assur), and was probably a new name given to a conquered city, after the manner in which Shalmaneser records that he gave names to cities that he had taken belonging to Akhuni, the son of Adini (*Records of the Past*, iii. 87, v. 30). In the patronymic we may trace *the sons of Eden* of this verse. In Amos i. 5 we have a Beth-Eden named as connected with Damascus; and in Ezek. xxvii. 23 an "Eden" connected with Haran and Asshur, as carrying on traffic with Tyre. The latter is probably identical with that named by Sennacherib.

(13) **Where is the king of Hamath . . .**—The question which had been asked in chap. xxxvi. 19 as to the gods of the cities named is now asked of their kings, and the implied answer is that they are in the dungeons of Nineveh.

Hena, and Ivah.—The sites have not been identified, but Anah is found as the name of a city on the Euphrates, and Ivah may be the same as the Ava of 2 Kings xvii. 24.

(14) **Hezekiah received the letter.**—The Hebrew noun is plural, as though the document consisted of more than one sheet.

And spread it before the Lord.—The act was one of mute appeal to the Supreme Arbiter. The *corpus delicti* was, as it were, laid before the judge, and then the appellant offered up his prayer. Mr. Cheyne quotes a striking parallel from the "Annals of Assurbanipal" (*Records of the Past*, vii. 67), who, on receiving a defiant message from the King of Elam, went into the Temple of Ishtar, and, reminding the goddess of all he had done for her, besought her aid, and received an oracle from her as a vision of the night.

(16) **That dwellest between the cherubims.**—A like phrase in Ps. xviii. 10 refers, apparently, to the dark thunder-clouds of heaven. Here, probably, the

| The Assyrian Army destroyed. | ISAIAH, XXXVIII. | The Death of Sennacherib. |

Assyrians a hundred and fourscore and five thousand: and when they arose early in the morning, behold, they were all dead corpses. ⁽³⁷⁾ So Sennacherib king of Assyria departed, and went and returned, and dwelt at Nineveh. ⁽³⁸⁾ And it came to pass, as he was worshipping in the house of Nisroch his god, that Adrammelech and Sharezer his sons smote him with the sword; and they

¹ Heb., *Ararat.*

B.C. 713.

a 2 Kin. 19. 1; 2 Chron. 32, 34.

² Heb., *Give charge concerning thy house.*

escaped into the land of ¹Armenia: and Esar-haddon his son reigned in his stead:

CHAPTER XXXVIII.—⁽¹⁾ In *a*those days was Hezekiah sick unto death. And Isaiah the prophet the son of Amoz came unto him, and said unto him, Thus saith the LORD, ²Set thine house in order: for thou shalt die, and not

presented by the account which Herodotus gives (chap. ii. 141), on the authority of the Egyptian priests, of the destruction of Sennacherib's army when he invaded Egypt, then under the rule of Sethon, a priest of Ptha or Hephæstos. The priest-king prayed to his gods, and the Assyrian army, then encamped before Pelusium, were attacked by myriads of field-mice, who gnawed the straps of quivers, bows, and shields, and so made all their weapons useless, and led to their taking flight. Therefore, the historian adds, there stood a statue of Sethon in the Temple of Hephæstos at Memphis, with a mouse in one hand and with the inscription, "Whosoever looks at me let him fear the gods." Some writers (*e.g.*, Ewald and Canon Rawlinson) have been led by this to the conclusion that the pestilence fell on Sennacherib's army at Pelusium, and not at Jerusalem. It may be questioned, however, whether, even admitting that the narrative in its present form may be later than the exile, the probabilities are not in favour of the Biblical record, compiled as it was by writers who had documents and inherited traditions, rather than of the travellers' tales which the vergers of Egyptian temples told to the good Herodotus.

In the camp of the Assyrians.—Josephus (*Bell. Jud.*, v. 7, 2) names a site in the outskirts of Jerusalem which in his time still bore this name. The narrative of Isaiah leaves room for a considerable interval between his prophecy and the dread work of the destroyer (2 Kings xix. 35). "In that night" does not necessarily imply immediate sequence, the demonstrative adjective being used, like the Latin *iste*, or *ille*, for "that memorable night."

⁽³⁷⁾ **So Sennacherib . . .**—We have to remember that the Assyrian king had been engaged in the siege of Libnah, probably also in an Egyptian expedition, which from some cause or other was unsuccessful. The course of events was probably this: that in Egypt he heard of the ravages of the pestilence, returned to find his army too weak to fight, and then, abandoning all further action in the south, withdrew to Nineveh.

Departed, and went and returned.—We are reminded by the three synonyms of the proverbial "*abiit, evasit, erupit*" of Cicero, *in Catil.* ii. (Del.).

⁽³⁸⁾ **And it came to pass.**—The Assyrian inscriptions fill up the gap of twenty years between the events which appear here, as if in immediate sequence, with five campaigns in the north and east of the Assyrian Empire, chiefly against the Babylonians, who revolted again under the son of Merodach-baladan.

Nisroch.—Some experts (Oppert and Schrader) have found the name in the Khorsabad inscriptions, in a prayer of Sargon to Nisroch as the patron of marriage, but the identification is disputed by others, as G. Smith, Sayce, and Cheyne. The etymology of the name, as meaning the "eagle" deity, is also one of the open questions of Assyrian research.

Adrammelech and Sharezer.—The former name appears in that of a deity of Sepharvaim in 2 Kings xvii. 31—its probable meaning being "the king of glory," that of Sharezer, "the ruler preserves," or, in a variant form, Sanatzu, "Sin (the moon-god) preserves." The Assyrian records, so far as they are yet interpreted, make no mention of the murder, but an inscription of Esar-haddon's, mutilated at the beginning, begins with an account of his victory over rebel princes, and the narrative of his campaign speaks of snowy mountains, which at least suggest Armenia (Heb. Ararat), (*Records of the Past*, iii., 101). Armenian traditions make the two parricides the founders of royal houses, the Sasserunians and Aizerunians. From the latter, in which the name of Sennacherib was common, sprang the Byzantine Emperor, Leo the Armenian. Esar-haddon is further memorable as having peopled Samaria with the mixed population of Babylonians, Cutheans, and others (2 Kings xvii. 24; Ezra iv. 10), from whom the later Samaritans were descended—as having taken Zidon and deported its inhabitants (*Records of the Past*, iv., p. 111)—as having left inscriptions at *Nahr-el-kelb*, near Beyrout, in which he describes himself as "King of Egypt, Thebes, and Ethiopia," as having probably been the "king of Assyria" who carried Manasseh bound in fetters to Babylon. The will of Sennacherib (*Records of the Past*, i. 136), giving him his chief treasures, and re-naming him with a new title of sovereignty (Assur-Ebil-Muni-pal, *i.e.*, "Assur is lord, the establisher of the son"), seems to imply that he was a younger son, whom the fondness of Sennacherib had exalted above his elder brothers, who accordingly revenged themselves by the murder of their father.

XXXVIII.

⁽¹⁾ **In those days.**—On any supposition, the narrative of Hezekiah's illness throws us back to a time fifteen years before his death, and therefore to an earlier date than the destruction of the Assyrian army, which it here follows. So in verse 6, the deliverance of the city is spoken of as still future. Assuming the rectified chronology given above, we are carried to a time ten or eleven years before the invasion, which was probably in part caused by the ambitious schemes indicated in chap. xxxix. It follows from either view that we have no ground for assuming, as some commentators have done, (1) that the illness was an attack of the plague that destroyed the Assyrian army, or (2) that the treasures which Hezekiah showed to the Babylonian ambassadors were in part the spoil of that army.

Set thine house in order.—Literally, *Give orders to thy house*, euphemistic for "make thy will." The words are a striking illustration, like Jonah's announcement that Nineveh should be destroyed in three days (Jonah iii. 4), of the conditional character

Hezekiah's Sickness. ISAIAH, XXXVIII. *The Sign on the Sun-dial of Ahaz.*

live. (2) Then Hezekiah turned his face toward the wall, and prayed unto the LORD, (3) and said, Remember now, O LORD, I beseech thee, how I have walked before thee in truth and with a perfect heart, and have done *that which is* good in thy sight. And Hezekiah wept ¹sore. (4) Then came the word of the LORD to Isaiah, saying, (5) Go, and say to Hezekiah, Thus saith the LORD, the God of David thy father, I have heard thy prayer, I have seen thy tears: behold, I will add unto thy days fifteen years. (6) And I will deliver thee and this city out of the hand of the king of Assyria: and I will defend this city.

(7) And this *shall be* a sign unto thee from the LORD, that the LORD will do this thing that he hath spoken; (8) behold, I will bring again the shadow of the degrees, which is gone down in the ²sun dial of Ahaz, ten degrees backward. So the sun returned ten degrees, by which degrees it was gone down.

(9) The writing of Hezekiah king of Judah, when he had been sick, and was recovered of his sickness:

(10) I said in the cutting off of my days, I shall go to the gates of the grave: I am deprived of the residue of my years. (11) I said, I shall not see the LORD, *even* the LORD, in the land of the

¹ Heb., *with great weeping.*
² Heb., *degrees by,* or, *with the sun.*

---

of prophecy. It would seem as if Isaiah had been consulted half as prophet and half as physician as to the nature of the disease. It seemed to him fatal; it was necessary to prepare for death. The words may possibly imply a certain sense of disappointment at the result of Hezekiah's reign. In the midst of the king's magnificence and prosperity there was that in the inner house of the soul, as well as in that of the outer life, which required ordering.

(2) **Turned his face toward the wall . . .**—The royal couch was in the corner, as the Eastern place of honour, the face turned to it, as seeking privacy and avoiding the gaze of men. (Comp. Ahab in 1 Kings xxi. 4.)

(3) **Remember now, O Lord.**—Devout as the prayer is, there is a tone of self-satisfaction in it which contrasts with David's prayer (Ps. li. 1—3). He rests on what he has done in the way of religious reformation, and practically asks what he has done that he should be cut off by an untimely death. The tears may probably have been less egotistic than the words, and, therefore, were more prevailing.

(5) **Fifteen years.**—The words fix the date of the illness, taking the received chronology, as B.C. 713. The next verse shows that there was danger at the time to be apprehended from Assyria, but does not necessarily refer to Sennacherib's invasion. Sargon's attack (chap. xx. 1) may have caused a general alarm.

(7) **This shall be a sign unto thee . . .**—The offer reminds us of that made to Ahaz; but it was received in a far different spirit. In 2 Kings xx. 8—11 the story is more fully told. Hezekiah asks for a sign, and is offered his choice. Shall the shadow go forward or backward? With something of a child-like simplicity he chooses the latter, as the more difficult of the two. The sun-dial of Ahaz, probably, like his altar (2 Kings xvi. 10), copied from Syrian or Assyrian art [the mention of a sun-clock is ascribed by Herodotus (ii. 109) to the Chaldæans], would seem to have been of the form of an obelisk standing on *steps* (the literal meaning of the Hebrew word for dial), and casting its shadow so as to indicate the time, each step representing an hour or half-hour. The nature of the phenomenon seems as curiously limited as that of the darkness of the crucifixion. There was no prolongation of the day in the rest of Palestine or Jerusalem, for the backward movement was limited to the step-dial. At Babylon no such phenomenon had been observed, and one ostensible purpose of Merôdach-baladan's embassy was to investigate its nature (2 Chron. xxxii. 31). An inquiry into the causation of a miracle is almost a contradiction in terms, but the most probable explanation of the fact recorded is that it was the effect of a supernatural, but exceedingly circumscribed, refraction. A prolonged after-glow following on the sunset; and reviving for a time the brightness of the day, might produce an effect such as is described to one who gazed upon the step-dial.

(9) **The writing of Hezekiah . . .**—Verses 21 and 22 would seem to have their right place before the elegiac psalm that follows. The culture which the psalm implies is what might have been expected from one whom Isaiah had trained, who had restored and organised the worship of the Temple (2 Chron. xxix. 25—30), who spoke to Levites and soldiers as a preacher (2 Chron. xxx. 22, xxxii. 6), "speaking comfortably" (literally, *to their heart*), and who had directed the compilation of a fresh set of the proverbs ascribed to Solomon (Prov. xxv. 1). It will be seen, as we go through the hymn, that it presents echoes of the Book of Job as well as of the earlier Psalms.

(10) **I said in the cutting off of my days . . .**—The words have been very differently interpreted —(1) "in the *quietness*," and so in the even tenor of a healthy life. As a fact, however, the complaint did not, and could not, come in the "quiet" of his life, but after it had passed away; (2) "in *the dividing point*," *scil.*, the "half-way house of life." Hezekiah was thirty-nine, but the word might rightly be used of the years between thirty-five and forty, which were the moieties of the seventy and eighty years of the psalmist (Ps. xc. 10). We are reminded of Dante's "*Nel mezzo del cammin di nostra vita*" (*Inf.* i. 1).

The gates of the grave.—The image is what we should call Dantesque. Sheol, the Hades of the Hebrews, is, as in the Assyrian representations of the unseen world, and as in the *Inferno* of Dante (iii. 11, vii. 2, x. 22), a great city, and, therefore, it has its gates, which again become, as with other cities, the symbol of its power. So we have "gates of death" in Job xxxviii. 17; Pss. ix. 18, cvii. 18.

The residue . . .—The words assume a normal duration, say of seventy years, on which the sufferer, who had, as he thought, done nothing to deserve punishment, might have legitimately counted.

(11) **I shall not see the Lord . . .**—The words are eminently characteristic of the cheerless dimness of the Hebrew's thoughts of death. To St. Paul and those who share his faith death is to " depart, and to be

Hezekiah's Psalm   ISAIAH, XXXVIII.   *of Thanksgiving.*

living: I shall behold man no more with the inhabitants of the world. (12) Mine age is departed, and is removed from me as a shepherd's tent: I have cut off like a weaver my life: he will cut me off ¹with pining sickness: from day *even* to night wilt thou make an end of me. (13) I reckoned till morning, *that*, as a lion, so will he break all my bones: from day *even* to night wilt thou make an end of me. (14) Like a crane *or* a swallow, so did I chatter: I did mourn as a dove: mine eyes fail *with looking* upward: O LORD, I am oppressed; ²undertake for me. (15) What shall I say? he hath both spoken unto me, and himself hath done *it*: I shall go softly all my years in the bitterness of my soul. (16) O Lord, by these *things men* live, and in all these *things is* the life of my spirit: so wilt thou recover me, and make me to live. (17) Behold, ³for peace I had great bitterness: but ⁴thou hast in love to my soul *delivered it* from the pit of corruption: for thou hast cast all my sins behind thy back. (18) For the grave cannot praise

¹ Or, *from the thrum.*
² Or, *ease me.*
³ Or, *on my peace came great bitterness.*
⁴ Heb., *thou hast loved my soul from the pit.*

---

with Christ" (Phil. i. 23), to be "ever with the Lord" (1 Thess. iv. 17). To Hezekiah, it would seem, the outward worship of the Temple, or possibly, the consciousness of God's presence in the full activity of brain and heart, was a joy which he could not bear to lose. The spiritual perceptions of the life after death would be spectral and shadowy, like the dead themselves. (Comp. the Greek idea of Hades in Homer (*Od.* xi. 12—19). It may be noted that the Hebrew for "the Lord" is the shorter, possibly the poetical, form "Jah" (as in Ps. lxviii. 4). The LXX paraphrases "I shall not see the salvation of God."

(12) **Mine age is departed** . . .—Better, *my home*, or *habitation* . . . as in Ps. xlix. 19, and thus fitting in better with the similitude that follows. The "home" is, of course, the body, as the dwelling-place of the spirit. (Comp. Ps. lii. 5, "hurl thee away tentless," Heb., and Job xxi. 28, "Is not their tent-cord torn away?" Heb.) The "shepherd's tent" is the type of a transitory home (2 Cor. v. 1—4).

I have cut off like a weaver my life . . . —The words express the feeling of one who had been weaving the web of his life with varied plans and counsels (comp. chap. xxx. 1), and now had to roll it up, as finished before its time, because Jehovah had taken up the "abhorred shears" to cut it *from the thrum*, which takes the place of "with pining sickness." There is, perhaps, a tone of reverence in the impersonal form of the statement. The sufferer will not name Jehovah as the author of his trouble.

From day even to night.—The words speak of the rapidity rather than of the prolongation of suffering. The sick man expects that death will come before the morrow's dawn.

(13) **I reckoned till morning** . . .—Better, *I quieted myself*, as in Ps. cxxxi. 2. He threw himself into the calm submission of the weaned child; yet when the morning came there was a fresh access of suffering. Life had been prolonged, contrary to his expectations; but it was only for renewed agony. Surely that would end his sufferings.

(14) **Like a crane** . . .—The three birds—strictly, the "swift," the "crane," the "dove"—each with its special note of lamentation, represent, as it were, the cries of pain and the low suppressed wail of the sufferer. The three appear again together in Jer. viii. 7.

Undertake for me—*i.e.*, as in Gen. xliii. 9, xliv. 32; Job xvii. 3, *Be surety for me*. The idea is that of Death, who, yet in another sense, is but the minister of Jehovah, as being the creditor pressing for immediate payment. The words involve (as Cheyne points out) something like an appeal to the judge, who is also the accuser, to be bail for the accused.

(15) **What shall I say?**—With the same force as in 2 Sam. vii. 20; Heb. xi. 32. Words fail to express the wonder and the gratitude of the sufferer who has thus been rescued for the fulfilment which followed so immediately on the promise.

I shall go softly . . .—Better, *That I should walk at ease upon* (*i.e.*, *because of*, or, as others take it, *in spite of*) *the trouble of my soul*. The verb is used in Ps. xlii. 4 of a festal procession to the Temple, but here refers simply to the journey of life, and implies that it is to be carried on to the end as with calm and considerate steps. The Authorised Version suggests wrongly the thought of a life-long bitterness.

(16) **By these things** . . .—*i.e.*, by the word of God and the performance which fulfils it. For "in all these things," read *wholly through them*. The words remind us of Deut. viii. 3, "Man doth not live by bread alone . . ."

(17) **For peace I had great bitterness** . . .— The words in the Authorised Version read like a retrospect of the change from health to suffering. Really, they express the very opposite. *It was for my peace* (*i.e.*, *for my salvation*, in the fullest sense of the word) *that it was bitter, was bitter unto me* (emphasis of iteration). All things were now seen as "working together for good."

Thou hast in love to my soul . . .—The italics show that the verbs "delivered it" are not in the present Hebrew text. A slight change, such as might be made to correct an error of transcription, would give that meaning, but as it stands, we have the singularly suggestive phrase, *Thou hast loved me out of the pit of corruption*. The very love of Jehovah is thought of as *ipso facto* a deliverance.

Thou hast cast all my sins . . .—As in our Lord's miracles, the bodily healing was the pledge and earnest of the spiritual. "Arise and walk" guaranteed, "Thy sins be forgiven thee" (Matt. ix. 2—5). (For the symbols of that forgiveness, comp. Micah vii. 19.)

(18) **For the grave** . . .—*i.e.*, *Sheol*, or *Hades*. We return to the king's thoughts of the dim shadow-world, *Death and Sheol* (joined together, as in chap. xxviii. 15; Ps. vi. 5). In that region of dimness there are no psalms of thanksgiving, no loud hallelujahs. The thought of spiritual energies developed and intensified after death is essentially one which belongs to the "illuminated" immortality (2 Tim. i. 10), of Christian thought. (Comp. Pss. vi. 5, xxx. 9, lxxxviii. 11, 12, cxv. 17; Eccl. ix. 4, 5, 10).

The Plaister laid upon the Boil. ISAIAH, XXXIX. *The Ambassadors from Babylon.*

thee, death can *not* celebrate thee: they that go down into the pit cannot hope for thy truth. ⁽¹⁹⁾ The living, the living, he shall praise thee, as I *do* this day: the father to the children shall make known thy truth. ⁽²⁰⁾ The LORD *was ready* to save me: therefore we will sing my songs to the stringed instruments all the days of our life in the house of the LORD.

⁽²¹⁾ For Isaiah had said, Let them take a lump of figs, and lay *it* for a plaister upon the boil, and he shall recover. ⁽²²⁾ Hezekiah also had said, What *is* the sign that I shall go up to the house of the LORD?

CHAPTER XXXIX.—⁽¹⁾ At *a* that time Merodach-baladan, the son of Baladan, king of Babylon, sent letters and a present to Hezekiah: for he had heard that he had been sick, and was recovered. ⁽²⁾ And Hezekiah was glad of them, and shewed them the house of his ¹precious things, the silver, and the gold, and the spices, and the precious ointment, and all the house of his ^{2 3}armour, and all that was found in his treasures: there was nothing in his house, nor in all his dominion, that Hezekiah shewed them not.

⁽³⁾ Then came Isaiah the prophet unto king Hezekiah, and said unto him, What said these men? and from whence came they unto thee? And Hezekiah said, They are come from a far country

a 2 Kin. 20. 12, &c.

1 Or, *spicery.*

2 Or, *jewels.*

B.C. 712.

3 Heb., *vessels,* or, *instruments.*

B.C. cir. 712.

⁽¹⁹⁾ **The father to the children . . .**—The words are perfectly general, but they receive a special significance from the fact that Hezekiah's son and successor, Manasseh, who was only twelve years old at his father's death (2 Kings xxi. 1), was not born till two or three years afterwards. At the time of his illness the king may still have been childless, and the thought that there was no son to take his place may have added bitterness to his grief. "Thy truth," has here the sense of "faithfulness" rather than of the truth about God which is the object of belief.

⁽²⁰⁾ **Was ready.**—Better, as fitting in with the praise and hope of the close of the prayer, *is ready.*

We will sing.—The king identifies himself with the great congregation, perhaps even yet more closely with the Levite minstrels of the Temple whom he had done so much to train and re-organise.

⁽²¹⁾ **For Isaiah had said . . .**—The direction implies some medical training on the part of Isaiah (see Note on chap. i. 6, and *Introduction*), such as entered naturally into the education of the prophet-priests. They were to Israel, especially in the case of leprosy and other kindred diseases, what the priests of Asclepios were to Greece. The Divine promise guaranteed success to the use of natural remedies, but did not dispense with them, and they, like the spittle laid on the eyes of the blind in the Gospel miracles (Mark vii. 33, John ix. 6), were also a help to the faith on which the miracle depended. Both this and the following verse seem, as has been said, to have been notes to verse 8, supplied from the narrative of 2 Kings xx., and placed at the end of the chapter instead of at the foot of the page, as in modern MSS. or print. The word for "boil" appears in connection with leprosy in Exod. ix. 9, Lev. xiii. 18, but is used generically for any kind of abscess, carbuncle, and the like. (Comp. Job ii. 7.)

XXXIX.

⁽¹⁾ **Merodach-baladan.**—The name is conspicuous in the Assyrian inscriptions of Sargon (*Records of the Past,* ix. 13), as having rebelled against him and set up an independent monarchy. He is described in them as *son of Yakin,* but this is, probably, a dynastic appellative, just as Jehu is described in the Assyrian records (*Records of the Past,* v. 41) as "the son of Khumri" (*i.e.,* Omri). The mission had two ostensible objects: (1) congratulation on Hezekiah's recovery; (2) to inquire and report as to the phenomenon of the sun-dial (2 Chron. xxxii. 31). Really, we may believe the object of Merôdach-baladan was to open negotiations for an alliance with Judah. The "present," interpreted after the manner of the East, would seem almost like an acknowledgment of Hezekiah's *hegemony,* or even *suzerainty,* in such a confederacy.

⁽²⁾ **Shewed them the house of his precious things.**—This fixes the date of the embassy at a time prior to the payment to Sennacherib (2 Kings xviii. 15, 16), unless we were to assume that the treasury had been replenished by the gifts that followed on the destruction of Sennacherib's army; but this, as we have seen, is at variance with both the received and the rectified chronology. The display was obviously something more than the ostentation of a Crœsus showing his treasures to Solon (Herod. i. 3). It was practically a display of the resources of the kingdom, intended to impress the Babylonian ambassadors with a sense of his importance as an ally.

The spices, and the precious ointment . . .—The mention of these articles as part of the king's treasures is characteristic of the commerce and civilisation of the time. "Spices"—probably myrrh, gum-benzoin, cinnamon—had from a very early period been among the gifts offered to princes (Gen. xliii. 11; 1 Kings x. 10). The "ointment," or perfumed oil, finds its parallel in the costly unguent of the Gospel history (Matt. xxvi. 7; John xii. 3). Esar-haddon's account of the magnificence of his palace (*Records of the Past,* iii., 122) supplies a contemporary instance of like ostentation.

⁽³⁾ **Then came Isaiah . . . .**—The words that follow, like those in chap. vii. 3, are spoken with the authority at once of age and of a Divine mission, perhaps also of a master speaking to one who had been his pupil. No sooner does the arrival of the embassy from Babylon reach his ear than he goes straight to the king to ask him what it all meant. The king's answer seems to plead that they came "from a far country" as an excuse. Could he refuse to admit those who had taken so long a journey in his honour? Could intercourse with a land so distant bring any moral or political danger? It was not like the alliance with Egypt, to which Isaiah was so strenuously opposed.

unto me, *even* from Babylon. ⁽⁴⁾ Then said he, What have they seen in thine house? And Hezekiah answered, All that *is* in mine house have they seen: there is nothing among my treasures that I have not shewed them.

⁽⁵⁾ Then said Isaiah to Hezekiah, Hear the word of the LORD of hosts: ⁽⁶⁾ Behold, the days come, that all that *is* in thine house, and *that* which thy fathers have laid up in store until this day, shall be carried to Babylon: nothing shall be left, saith the LORD. ⁽⁷⁾ And of thy sons that shall issue from thee, which thou shalt beget, shall they take away; and they shall be eunuchs in the palace of the king of Babylon.

⁽⁸⁾ Then said Hezekiah to Isaiah, Good *is* the word of the LORD which thou hast spoken. He said moreover, For there shall be peace and truth in my days.

CHAPTER XL.—⁽¹⁾ Comfort ye, comfort ye my people, saith your God. ⁽²⁾ Speak ye ¹comfortably to Jerusalem, and cry unto her, that her ²warfare is accomplished, that her iniquity is pardoned: for she hath received of the LORD'S hand double for all her sins.

---

1 Heb., *to the heart.*

2 Or, *appointed time.*

---

(4) What have they seen in thine house?—The question was pressed home. Had the king contented himself with such hospitality as would have satisfied the demands of the code of Eastern ethics? or had he, as the prophet rightly suspected, done more than that, in his vain-glorious hope of figuring among the "great powers" of the East? On the minds of the ambassadors, we may well believe the impression left was like that made on Blucher as he passed through London: that it would be "a grand city to plunder."

(6, 7) Behold, the days come . . .—The words, it may be noted, received a two-fold fulfilment, under widely different conditions. Hezekiah's son Manasseh, at the time when Isaiah spoke unborn, was carried as a prisoner to Babylon by Esar-haddon, king of Assyria (2 Chron. xxxiii. 11). The last lineal heir of the house of David, Jehoiachin, died there after long years of imprisonment (2 Kings xxv. 27). Daniel and his three companions were "of the king's seed and of the princes," and were, probably, themselves reduced to that state, placed under the care of "the master of the eunuchs" (Dan. i. 3). The actual treasures which Hezekiah showed were probably handed over to Sennacherib (2 Kings xviii. 15, 16); but looking to the fact that that king records his capture of Babylon, after defeating Merodach-baladan, and established his son Esar-haddon there (Lenormant, *Ancient History,* i., p. 400), it is probable enough that the treasures may have been taken thither, and displayed, as if in irony, to the king and the counsellors, who had hoped to profit by them. Sennacherib indeed boasts that he had carried off not only the king's treasures, and his musicians to Nineveh, but his daughters also (*Records of the Past,* vii. 63).

(8) Good is the word of the Lord . . .—The words have the appearance of a pious resignation, but we feel that they are less true and noble than those of David on a like occasion: "I have sinned and done wickedly; but these sheep, what have they done? Let thy hand, I pray thee, be against me, and against my father's house" (2 Sam. xxiv. 17). Hezekiah's thanksgiving reminds us a little too much of "*Après moi le déluge.*"

Peace and truth.—The latter word is used in the sense of "stability" (so Ps. liv. 5). The two words are used in the same way in Jer. xiv. 13, where we find "assured peace" in the text of the Authorised Version, and "peace of truth" in the margin.

XL.

⁽¹⁾ Comfort ye . . .—I start with the assumption that the great prophetic poem that follows is the work of Isaiah himself, referring to the *Introduction* for the discussion of all questions connected with its authorship and arrangement. It has a link, as has been noticed, with the earlier collection of his writings in chap. xxxv. 9, 10. The prophet's mind is obviously projected at the outset into the future, which it had been given him to see, when the time of punishment and discipline was to be succeeded, having done its work, by blessedness and peace. The key-note is struck in the opening words. The phrase "my people" is a distinct echo of Hos. ii. 1. *Lo Ammi* (*i.e.* "not my people,") has been brought back to his true position as *Ammi* (*i.e.* "my people").

Saith your God.—Noticeable as a formula which is at once peculiar to Isaiah and common to both his volumes (chaps. i. 11, 18, xxxiii. 10, xli. 21, lxvi. 9).

⁽²⁾ Speak ye comfortably . . .—Literally, *Speak ye to the heart.* The command is addressed to the prophets whom Isaiah contemplates as working towards the close of the exile, and carrying on his work. In Haggai i. 13, ii. 9, iii. 19—23, and Zechariah i. 13, ii. 5—10, ix. 9—12, we may rightly trace the influence of the words as working out their own fulfilment.

That her warfare is accomplished.—The time of war, with all its suffering, becomes the symbol of sufferings apart from actual war. The exile was one long campaign with enemies who were worse than the Babylonian conquerors. In Job vii. 1, xiv. 14, the word is applied (rendered by "appointed time") to the battle of life from its beginning to its end. This, too, may be noted as one of the many parallelisms between Isaiah and Job.

That her iniquity is pardoned.—Strictly, as in Lev. xxvi. 41, 43, *is paid off,* or *accepted.* The word implies not exemption from punishment, but the fact that the punishment had been accepted, and had done its work.

She hath received of the Lord's hand . . .—Primarily, the thought is that Jerusalem has suffered a more than sufficient penalty. (Comp. Exod. xxii. 9; Rev. xviii. 6.) This seems more in harmony with the context than the view which takes the meaning that Jerusalem shall receive a double measure of grace and favour. In the long run, however, the one meaning does not exclude the other. It is the mercy of Jehovah which reckons the punishment sufficient, because it has been

The Cry of the Herald of Jehovah.   ISAIAH, XL.   *The Message of Good Tidings.*

(3) *a*The voice of him that crieth in the wi'derness, Prepare ye the way of the LORD, make straight in the desert a highway for our God. (4) Every valley shall be exalted, and every mountain and hill shall be made low: and the crooked shall be made ¹straight, and the rough places ²plain: (5) and the glory of the LORD shall be revealed, and all flesh shall see *it* together: for the mouth of the LORD hath spoken *it*.

(6) The voice said, Cry. And he said, What shall I cry? *b*All flesh *is* grass, and all the goodliness thereof *is as* the flower of the field: (7) the grass withereth, the flower fadeth; because the spirit of the LORD bloweth upon it: surely the people *is* grass. (8) The grass withereth, the flower fadeth: but the *c*word of our God shall stand for ever.

(9) ³O Zion, that bringest good tidings, get thee up into the high mountain; ⁴O Jerusalem, that bringest good tidings, lift up thy voice with strength; lift *it* up, be not afraid; say unto the cities of Judah, Behold your God!

a Matt. 3. ; Mark 1. 3; Luk 3. 4; John 1. 23.
¹ Or, *a straight place.*
² Or, *a plain place.*
b Job 14. 2; Ps. 102. 11 & 103. 15; James 1. 10; 1 Pet. 1. 24.
c John 12. 34; 1 Pet. 1. 25.
³ Or, *O thou that tellest good tidings to Zion.*
⁴ Or, *O thou that tellest good tidings to Jerusalem.*

"accepted" (Lev. xxvi. 41), and has done its work. (Comp. Jer. xvi. 18.)

(3) **The voice of him that crieth . . .**—The laws of Hebrew parallelism require a different punctuation: *A voice of one crying, In the wilderness, prepare ye . . .* The passage is memorable as having been deliberately taken by the Baptist as defining his own mission (John i. 23). As here the herald is not named, so he was content to efface himself—to be a *voice* or nothing. The image is drawn from the march of Eastern kings, who often boast, as in the Assyrian inscriptions of Sennacherib and Assurbanipal (*Records of the Past*, i. 95, vii. 64), of the roads they have made in trackless deserts. The wilderness is that which lay between the Euphrates and Judah, the journey of the exiles through it reminding the prophet of the older wanderings in the wilderness of Sin (Ps. lxviii. 7; Judg. v. 4). The words are an echo of the earlier thought of chap. xxxv. 8. We are left to conjecture to whom the command is addressed: tribes of the desert, angelic ministers, kings and rulers—the very vagueness giving a grand universality. So, again, we are not told whether the "way of Jehovah" is that on which He comes to meet His people, or on which He goes before and guides them. The analogy of the marches of the Exodus makes the latter view the more probable.

(4) **Every valley shall be exalted.**—The figure is drawn from the titanic engineeering operations of the kingly road-makers of the East, but the parable is hardly veiled. The meek exalted, the proud brought low, wrong ways set right, rough natures smoothed: that is the true preparation for the coming of the Lord, and therefore the true work of every follower of the Baptist in preparing the way. (Comp. Matt. iii. 5—7; Luke iii. 3—9.)

(5) **The glory of the Lord shall be revealed.**—Did the prophet think of a vision of a glory-cloud, like the Shechinah which he had seen in the Temple? or had he risen to the thought of the glory of character and will, of holiness and love? (John i. 14.)

All flesh.—The revelation is not for Israel only, but for mankind. So in Luke iii. 6, the words are quoted from the LXX., "all flesh shall see the salvation of God." The phrase meets us here for the first time, and occurs again in chaps. xlix. 26, lxvi. 16, 23, 24, marking, so to speak, the growing catholicity of the prophet's thoughts. (See Note on chap. xxxviii. 11.)

(6) **The voice said, Cry.**— Literally, *A voice saith, Cry.* The questioner ("and *one* said") is probably the prophet himself, asking what he is to proclaim. The truth which he is to enforce thus solemnly is the ever-recurring contrast between the transitoriness of man and the eternity of God and of His word, taking that term in its highest and widest sense. Two points of interest may be noted: (1) that this is another parallelism with Job (xiv. 2); (2) the naturalness of the thought in one who, like Isaiah, was looking back, as Moses looked (Ps. xc. 5, 6) in extreme old age upon the generations whom he had survived, and forward to the fall of mighty monarchies one after another. The marginal references show how dominant the thought is in the mind of Isaiah. Isaiah himself had uttered it in chap. ii. 22.

(7) **The spirit of the Lord bloweth upon it.**—Better, *the breath,* or *the wind* of Jehovah, as we are still in the region of the parable, and the agency is destructive, and not quickening. A "wind of Jehovah" would be a mighty storm-blast, tearing up the grass and hurling it to destruction. The image of the fading flower reminds us of the well-known Homeric simile, "As are the generations of leaves, so are those of men." (Comp. Ps. ciii. 15, 16.)

The word of our God . . .—Primarily the prophetic word revealing the will of God, but including all manifestations of His being (Ps. cxix. 41, 65, 89; John i. 1)

(9) **O Zion, that bringest good tidings.**—A new section begins. In some versions (LXX. and Targum) and by some interpreters "Zion" is taken as in the objective case, *O thou that bringest glad tidings to Zion;* but as the participle, "thou that bringest," is in the feminine, and a female evangeliser other than Jerusalem has not appeared on the scene, the Authorised Version is preferable. In that rendering the ideal Zion, seeing or hearing of the return of the exiles, becomes the bearer of the good news to the other cities of Judah. It is not without emotion that we note the first occurrence of the word which, passing through the Greek of the LXX. and the New Testament (ευαγγελίζεσθαι), has had so fruitful a history, as embodying the message of the Gospel—good-spell, glad tidings—to mankind. The primary meaning of the Hebrew word is *to make smooth,* or bright, and so "to gladden." (Comp. the connection of this English word with the German *glatten.*)

The high mountain.—There is no article in the Hebrew, but the word is probably connected with the ideal exaltation of the holy city, as in chap. ii. 1.

Behold your God!—The words have, in one sense, only an ideal fulfilment; but the prophet contemplates the return of the exiles and the restoration of the Temple worship, as involving the renewed presence of Jehovah in the sanctuary which He had apparently abandoned. He would come back with His people, and abide with them.

The Shepherd Feeding his Flock. ISAIAH, XL. *The Greatness and Wisdom of God.*

(10) Behold, the Lord GOD will come ¹with strong *hand*, and his arm shall rule for him: behold, ᵃhis reward *is* with him, and ²his work before him. (11) He shall ᵇfeed his flock like a shepherd: he shall gather the lambs with his arm, and carry *them* in his bosom, *and* shall gently lead those ³that are with young. (12) Who hath measured the waters in the hollow of his hand, and meted out heaven with the span, and comprehended the dust of the earth in ⁴a measure, and weighed the mountains in scales, and the hills in a balance? (13) ᶜWho hath directed the Spirit of the LORD, or *being* ⁵his counsellor hath taught him? (14) With whom took he counsel, and *who* ⁶instructed him, and taught him in the path of judgment and taught him knowledge, and shewed to him the way of ⁷understanding? (15) Behold, the nations *are* as a drop of a bucket, and are counted as the small dust of the balance: behold, he taketh up the isles as a very little thing. (16) And Lebanon *is* not sufficient to burn, nor the beasts thereof sufficient for a burnt offering. (17) All nations before him *are* as ᵈnothing; and they are counted to him less than nothing, and vanity. (18) To whom then will ye ᵉliken God? or what likeness will ye compare unto him? (19) The workman melteth a graven image, and the goldsmith spreadeth it

---

1 Or, *against the strong.*
a ch. 62, 11.
2 Or, *recompence for his work.*
b Ezek. 34. 23; John 10. 11.
3 Or, *that give suck.*
4 Heb., *a tierce.*
e Wis. 9. 13; Rom. 11. 34; 1 Cor. 2. 16.
5 Heb., *man of his counsel.*
6 Heb., *made him understand.*
7 Heb., *understandings?*
d Dan. 4. 35.
e Acts 17. 29.

---

(10) **The Lord God.**—*Adonai Jehovah*; each word commonly translated Lord. The combination is characteristic both of 1 and 2 Isaiah (chaps. iii. 15, xxviii. 16, xxx. 15).

With strong hand.—Literally, *with*, or *in strength of hand*, as the essence of His being. The "arm" of the Lord is a favourite phrase of Isaiah (chaps. li. 5, 9, lii. 10) for His power.

His reward is with him . . .—The noun "work" has also the sense of *recompense* for the faithful worker (Lev. xix. 13; Deut. xxiv. 15, and is rightly taken in that sense here and in chap. lxi. 11).

(11) **He shall feed his flock** . . .—Ps. xxiii. is the great embodiment of the thought in the Old Testament, as John x. is in the New, but the thought itself is everywhere (Pss. lxxvii. 20, lxxx. 1; Jer. xiii. 17, xxxi. 10, l. 19; Ezek. xxxiv. 11—16; Matt. ix. 36, xviii. 12; Luke xv. 4, &c.). The tender care of the shepherd for the ewes and lambs finds a parallel in Jacob's pleas (Gen. xxxiii. 13).

(12) **Who hath measured** . . .?—Another section opens, expanding the thought of the eternal majesty of Jehovah, as contrasted with the vanity of the idols, or "no-gods," of the heathen. The whole passage in form and thought supplies once more a parallelism with Job xxxviii. 4, 25, 37. The whole image is divinely anthropomorphic. The Creator is the great Work-master (Wisd. xiii. 1) of the universe, ordering all things, like a human artificer, by number and weight and measure. The mountains of the earth are as dust in the scales of the Infinite.

(13) **Who hath directed the Spirit of the Lord?**—The term, which had been used in a lower sense in verse 7, is here clothed as with a Divine personality, answering, as it were, to the wisdom of Prov. viii. 22—30, with which the whole passage has a striking resemblance. Eastern cosmogonies might represent Bel or Ormuzd, as calling inferior deities into counsel (Cheyne). The prophet finds no other counsellor than One who is essentially one with the Eternal.

(14) **Counsel . . . judgment.**—The cluster of words belonging to the sapiential vocabulary of the Book of Proverbs is to be noted as parallel with chaps. xi. 23, xxxiii. 15.

(15) **The nations are as a drop** . . .—"Nations" and "isles" bring us into the region of human history, as distinct from that of the material world. "Isles" as elsewhere, stands vaguely for *far-off lands*, or *sea-coasts*. The word is that of one who looks on the Mediterranean, and thinks of the unexplored regions that lie in it and around. It is one of Isaiah's favourite words in this aspect of its meaning.

A drop of a bucket.—Better, *on a bucket*. Such a drop adds nothing to the weight which the bearer feels; as little do the nations and the isles to the burden which Jehovah bears. The "small dust in the balance" presents another illustration of the same idea.

(16) **Lebanon is not sufficient.**—The thought is the same as that of Ps. l. 10—12. Lebanon is chosen as the type of the forests that supply the wood for burnt-offerings, in which Judah was comparatively poor. In Nehemiah's organisation of the Temple ritual the task of supplying wood for this purpose was assigned by lot to priests or Levites (Neh. x. 34).

(17) **Less than nothing.**—Literally, *as things of nought.*

Vanity.—Once more the *tohu*, or chaos, of Gen. i. 2—one of Isaiah's favourite phrases (chaps. xxiv. 10, xxix. 21, xxxiv. 11).

(18) **To whom then will ye liken God** . . .— The thought of the infinity of God leads, as in St. Paul's reasoning (Acts xvii. 24—29), to the great primary argument against the folly of idolatry. It is characteristic, partly of the two men individually, partly of the systems under which they lived, that while the tone of Isaiah is sarcastic and declamatory, that of St Paul is pitying, and as with indulgent allowance for the "times of ignorance." We must remember, of course, that the Apostle speaks to those who had known nothing better than the worship of their fathers, the prophet to those who were tempted to fall into the worship of the heathen from a purer faith.

(19) **The workman melteth** . . .—The reign of Ahaz, not to speak of that of Manasseh, must have supplied the prophet with his picture of the idol factory not less fully than if he had lived in Babylon or Nineveh.

Spreadeth it over with gold.—The image of lead was covered over, as in the well-known story of Phidias's "Zeus," with plates of gold. The "silver chains" fastened it to the wall.

over with gold, and casteth silver chains. (20) He that ¹*is* so impoverished that he hath no oblation chooseth a tree *that* will not rot; he seeketh unto him a cunning workman to prepare a graven image, *that* shall not be moved. (21) Have ye not known? have ye not heard? hath it not been told you from the beginning? have ye not understood from the foundations of the earth? (22) ²*It is* he that sitteth upon the circle of the earth, and the inhabitants thereof *are* as grasshoppers; that ᵃstretcheth out the heavens as a curtain, and spreadeth them out as a tent to dwell in: (23) that bringeth the ᵇprinces to nothing; he maketh the judges of the earth as vanity. (24) Yea, they shall not be planted; yea, they shall not be sown: yea, their stock shall not take root in the earth: and he shall also blow upon them, and they shall wither, and the whirlwind shall take them away as stubble.

(25) To whom then will ye liken me, or shall I be equal? saith the Holy One. (26) Lift up your eyes on high, and behold who hath created these *things*, that bringeth out their host by number: he calleth them all by names by the greatness of his might, for that *he is* strong in power; not one faileth. (27) Why sayest thou, O Jacob, and speakest, O Israel, My way is hid from the LORD, and my judgment is passed over from my God? (28) Hast thou not known? hast thou not heard, *that* the everlasting God, the LORD, the Creator of the ends of the earth, fainteth not, neither is weary? ᶜ*there is* no searching of his understanding. (29) He giveth power to the faint; and to *them that have* no might he increaseth strength. (30) Even the youths shall faint and be weary, and the young men shall utterly fall: (31) but they that wait upon the LORD shall ³renew *their* strength; they shall mount up with wings as eagles;

Marginal notes:
1 Heb., *is poor of oblation.*
2 Or, *Him that sitteth, &c.*
a Ps. 104. 2.
b Job 12. 21; Ps. 107. 40.
c Ps. 147. 5.
3 Heb. *change.*

---

(20) **He that is so impoverished . . .**—The transition is abrupt, but the intention apparently is to represent idolatry at its opposite extremes of the elaborate art in which kings and princes delighted, and the rude rough image, hardly more than a *fetiche*, the *inutile lignum* of Horace, "which cannot be moved," standing on its own wide base, so as not to fall.

(21) **Have ye not known? . . .**—Strictly speaking, the first two verbs are potential futures: *Can ye not know? . . .* We note that the prophet appeals to the primary intuitions of mankind, or, at least, to a primitive revelation, rather than to the commandments of the Decalogue. (Comp. Rom. i. 20; Ps. xix. 4.)

(22) **The circle of the earth**—*i.e.*, the vault of heaven over-arching the earth (Job xxii. 14; Prov. viii. 27).

As grasshoppers.—The word indicates some insect of the locust tribe. The comparison may have been suggested by Num. xiii. 33.

That stretcheth out the heavens.—A favourite phrase of 2 Isaiah (chaps. xlii. 5, xliv. 24, *et al.*), taken probably from Ps. civ. 2.

As a curtain . . . as a tent.—The words indicate a clearer perception of space than the older Hebrew word for the "firmament" of Gen. i. 7. The visible heavens are thought of as a thin, filmy veil of gauze, the curtains of the tent of God.

(23) **That bringeth the princes to nothing.**—The words imply, like those of chap. xiv. 9, the prophetic strain of experience. The past is full of the records of kingdoms that are no more; so also shall the future be; *mortalia facta peribunt.* In "vanity" we have the familiar *tohu* once more.

(24) **They shall not be planted . . .**—Better, *Hardly are they planted, hardly are they sown.* Such are empires before the eternity of Jehovah: so soon withered that we cannot say that they were ever really planted (Ps. cxxix. 6).

(26) **Who hath created . . .**—The verb may be noted as a characteristic of 2 Isaiah, in which it occurs twenty times.

That bringeth out their host . . .—The words expand the idea implied in Jehovah-Sabaoth (comp. Ps. cxlvii. 4). He marshals all that innumerable host of stars, as a supreme general who knows by sight and name every soldier in a vast army, or as a shepherd who knows his flock (John x. 3).

(27) **Why sayest thou, O Jacob.**—The eternity and infinity of God is presented not only as rebuking the folly of the idolater, but as the ground of comfort to His people. His is no transient favour, no capricious will. (Comp. Rom. xi. 29—36.)

(28) **Hast thou not known? . . .**—The questions are parallel to those of verse 21, but are addressed to the Israel of God, rather than, as those were, to mankind.

The Creator of the ends of the earth.—The word emphasises the thought that the whole earth, from the Euphrates to the "islands" of the sea, is subject to the power of the Eternal.

Fainteth not, neither is weary? . . .—Had Isaiah learnt to feel that even his own phrase as to men "wearying God" (chap. vii. 13) was too boldly anthropomorphic, and might, therefore, be misleading?

No searching of his understanding.—The words come, like so many others like it, from Job (chaps. v. 9, ix. 10), and must have been in St. Paul's mind as he wrote Rom. xi. 33.

(29) **He giveth power to the faint . . .**—*i.e.*, to them pre-eminently—their very consciousness of weakness being the condition of their receiving strength. (Comp. Matt. v. 6; Luke i. 52, 53, vi. 21.)

(30) **Even the youths . . .**—The second word implies a nearer approach to manhood than the first, the age when vigour is at its highest point.

(31) **They that wait upon the Lord.**—The waiting implies, of course, the expectant attitude of faith.

they shall run, and not be weary; *and* they shall walk, and not faint

CHAPTER XLI.—(1) Keep silence before me, O islands; and let the people renew *their* strength: let them come near; then let them speak: let us come near together to judgment.

(2) Who raised up ¹the righteous *man* from the east, called him to his foot, gave the nations before him, and made *him* rule over kings? he gave *them* as the dust to his sword, *and* as driven stubble to his bow. (3) He pursued them, *and* passed ²safely; *even* by the way *that* he had not gone with his feet.

1 Heb., *righteousness.*
2 Heb., *in peace.*
a ch. 43. 10 & 44. 6 & 48. 12; Rev. 1. 17 & 22. 13.
3 Heb., *Be strong.*
4 Or, *founder.*
5 Or, *the smiting.*
6 Or, *saying of the soder, It is good.*

(4) Who hath wrought and done *it*, calling the generations from the beginning? I the LORD, the ᵃfirst, and with the last; I *am* he.

(5) The isles saw *it*, and feared; the ends of the earth were afraid, drew near, and came. (6) They helped every one his neighbour; and *every one* said to his brother, ³Be of good courage. (7) So the carpenter encouraged the ⁴goldsmith, *and* he that smootheth *with* the hammer ⁵him that smote the anvil, ⁶saying, It *is* ready for the sodering: and he fastened it with nails, *that* it should not be moved.

(8) But thou, Israel, *art* my servant,

Shall mount up with wings.—Better, *shall lift up their wings,* or, *shall put forth wings' feathers,* the last, like Ps. ciii. 5, implying the belief that the eagle renewed its plumage in extreme old age. For the faithful there is no failure, and faith knows no weariness.

XLI.

(1) **O islands.**—See Note on chap. xl. 15.

Let the people renew their strength . . .—The same phrase as in chap. xl. 31, but here, perhaps, with a touch of irony. The heathen are challenged to the great controversy, and will need all their "strength" and "strong reasons" if they accept the challenge. In what follows we have to think of the prophet as having, like Balaam, a vision of what shall come to pass in the "latter days" (Num. xxiv. 20), and seeing not only the forms of the old empires on their way to Hades, as in chap. xiv. 9—12, but the appearance on the scene of the new conqueror.

(2) **Who raised up . . .**—More accurately, *Who hath raised up from the East the man whom Righteousness calls* (or, *whom He calls in righteousness*) *to tread in His steps.* (Comp. chap. xlv. 2.) The man so raised up to rule over the "islands" and the "peoples" is none other than Koresh (Cyrus), the future restorer of Israel. The thought of Cyrus as working out the righteousness of God is dominant in these chapters (chaps. xlii. 6, xlv. 13). In the rapidity of his conquest, the prophet bids men see the proof that he is doing God's work. So Jeremiah speaks of Nebuchadnezzar as the servant of Jehovah (Jer. xxvii. 6). One may notice, if only to reject, the exposition of the Targum, followed by some commentators, which refers the verse to the call of Abraham and the victory of Gen. xiv.

He gave them.—Better, *He giveth them*, the future seen as present. The LXX. and some modern critics follow a reading which gives, *he maketh them as dust, their sword as stubble.*

(3) **He pursued . . .**—Tenses in the present, as before.

By the way that he had not gone—*i.e.*, by a new untrodden path. So Tiglath-Pileser and other Assyrian kings continually boast that they had led their armies by paths that none had traversed before them. (*Records of the Past*, i. 15, v. 16.)

(4) **I the Lord . . .**—The words are the utterance of the great thought of eternity which is the essence of the creed of Israel (comp. Exod. iii. 14; Pss. xc. 2, cii. 26), and appear in the Alpha and Omega of Rev. i. 11, iv. 8. The identical formula, "I am He" meets us in chaps. xliii. 10, 13, xlvi. 4, xlviii. 12. It is probably used as an assertion of an eternal being in the "I AM" of John viii. 58.

(5) **The isles saw it, and feared . . .**—The words paint the terror caused by the rapid conquests of Cyrus, but the terror led, as the following verses show, to something very different from the acknowledgment of the Eternal. As the sailors in the ship of Tarshish called each man on his God (Jonah i. 5), so each nation turned to its oracles and its shrines. The gods had to be propitiated by new statues, and a fresh impetus was given to the manufacture of idols, probably for the purpose of being carried forth to battle as a protection. (Comp. 1 Sam. iv. 5—7; Herod. i. 26.)

(6) **Be of good courage.**—Literally, *Be strong:* *i.e.*, work vigorously.

(7) **So the carpenter.**—The process is described even more vividly than in chap. xl. 19. For "the carpenter," read *the caster*, the idol being a metal one. The image of lead or copper is then covered with gold plates, which are laid on the anvil, and are smoothed with the hammer; the soldering is approved by the artist, and then (supreme touch of irony) the guardian deity is fixed with nails, that it may not totter and fall.

(8) **But thou, Israel, art my servant . . .**—The verse is important as the first introduction of the servant of the Lord who is so conspicuous throughout the rest of the book. The idea embodied in the term is that of a calling and election, manifested now in Israel according to the flesh, now in the true Israel of God, realising its ideal, now, as in the innermost of the three concentric circles, in a person who gathers up that ideal in all its intensity into himself. The three phrases find their parallel in St. Paul's language as to (1) the seed of Abraham according to the flesh; (2) the true seed who are heirs of the faith of Abraham; (3) *the* seed, which is none other than the Christ Himself (Rom. ix. 7; Gal. iii. 7, 16). Here we have the national aspect, Israel as he is in the idea of God. So in the later language of Christian thought we have (1) the visible Church falling short of the ideal; (2) the spiritual Church approximating to the ideal; (3) Christ Himself, as identified with His people.

The seed of Abraham my friend.—The word for "friend" implies loving as well as being loved. Of

Jacob whom I have *a* chosen, the seed of Abraham my *b* friend. (9) *Thou* whom I have taken from the ends of the earth, and called thee from the chief men thereof, and said unto thee, Thou *art* my servant; I have chosen thee, and not cast thee away. (10) Fear thou not; for I *am* with thee: be not dismayed; for I *am* thy God: I will strengthen thee; yea, I will help thee; yea, I will uphold thee with the right hand of my righteousness. (11) Behold, all they that were incensed against thee shall be *c* ashamed and confounded: they shall be as nothing; and ¹they that strive with thee shall perish. (12) Thou shalt seek them, and shalt not find them, *even* ²them that contended with thee: ³they that war against thee shall be as nothing, and as a thing of nought. (13) For I the LORD thy God will hold thy right hand, saying unto thee, Fear not; I will help thee. (14) Fear not, thou worm Jacob, *and* ye ⁴men of Israel; I will help thee, saith the LORD, and thy redeemer, the Holy One of Israel. (15) Behold, I will make thee a new sharp threshing instrument having ⁵teeth: thou shalt thresh the mountains, and beat *them* small, and shalt make the hills as chaff. (16) Thou shalt fan them, and the wind shall carry them away, and the whirlwind shall scatter them: and thou shalt rejoice in the LORD, *and* shalt glory in the Holy One of Israel.

(17) *When* the poor and needy seek water, and *there is* none, *and* their tongue faileth for thirst, I the LORD will hear them, *I* the God of Israel will not forsake them. (18) I will open *d* rivers in high places, and fountains in the midst of the valleys: I will make the *e* wilderness a pool of water, and the dry land springs of water. (19) I will plant in the wilderness the cedar, the shittah

a Deut. 7. 6 & 10. 15 & 14. 2; Ps. 135. 4; ch. 43. 1 & 44. 1.
b 2 Chr. 20. 7; Jam. 2. 23.
c Ex. 23. 22; ch. 60. 12; Zech. 12. 3.
1 Heb., *the men of thy strife.*
2 Heb., *the men of thy contention.*
3 Heb., *the men of thy war.*
4 Or, *few men.*
5 Heb., *mouths.*
d ch. 35. 7 & 44. 3.
e Ps. 107. 35.

---

all the names of Abraham, it has had the widest currency (comp. 2 Chron. xx. 7; Jas. ii. 23). For the Arabs of the present time Abraham is still *Khalil Allah—*the friend of God, or simply, *el Khalil, the* friend.

(9) **From the ends of the earth.**—Ur of the Chaldees, as belonging to the Euphrates region, is on the extreme verge of the prophet's horizon.

From the chief men thereof.—Better, *from the far-off regions thereof.*

I have chosen . . .—Isaiah becomes the preacher of the Divine election, and finds in it, as St. Paul found, the ground of an inextinguishable hope for the nation of which he was a member. As in St. Peter's teaching, it remained for them to "make their calling and election sure" (2 Pet. i. 10), though God, in the unchangeableness of His nature, had chosen them before the foundation of the world.

(10) **Fear thou not . . .**—The thought of the election of God gives a sense of security to His chosen.

I will strengthen thee.—The verb unites with this meaning (as in chap. xxxv. 3; Ps. lxxxix. 21) the idea of attaching to one's self, or choosing, as in chap. xliv. 14.

(11, 12) **Behold . . .**—The choice of the Servant has, as its complement, the indignation of Jehovah against those who attack him, and this thought is emphasised by a four-fold iteration. "They that strive with thee, &c.," represents the Hebrew idiom, *the men of thy conflict,* which stands emphatically at the end of each clause.

(14) **Fear not, thou worm Jacob.**—The servant of Jehovah is reminded that he has no strength of his own, but is "as a worm, and no man" (Ps. xxii. 6). He had not been chosen because he was a great and mighty nation, for Israel was "the fewest of all people" (Deut. vii. 7). As if to emphasise this, the prophet in addressing Israel passes from the masculine to the feminine, resuming the former in the second clause of verse 15, where he speaks of its God-given strength.

Thy redeemer . . .—*i.e.,* the *Goel* of Lev. xxv. 48, 49, the next of kin, who was the protector, the deliverer, of his brethren (Lev. xxv. 43—49). Looking to the numerous traces of the influence of the Book of Job in 2 Isaiah, it seems not improbable that we have in these words an echo of the hope, "I know that my Redeemer liveth" (Job xix. 25).

(15) **A new sharp threshing instrument.**—The instrument described is a kind of revolving sledge armed with two-edged blades, still used in Syria, and, as elsewhere (Mic. iv. 13), is the symbol of a crushing victory. The next verse continues the image, as in Jer. xv. 7, li. 2.

(17) **When the poor and needy . . .**—The promise may perhaps take as its starting-point the succour given to the return of the exiles, but it rises rapidly into the region of a higher poetry, in which earthly things are the parables of heavenly, and does not call for a literal fulfilment any more than "wines of the lees," of chap. xxv. 6.

(18) **I will open rivers.**—The words have all the emphasis of varied iteration. Every shape of the physical contour of the country, bare hills, arid steppes, and the like, is to be transformed into a new beauty by water in the form adapted to each: streamlets, rivers, lakes, and springs. (Comp. chap. xxxv. 7.)

(19) **I will plant in the wilderness.**—A picture as of the Paradise of God (chap. li. 3), with its groves of stately trees, completes the vision of the future. The two groups of four and three, making up the symbolic seven, may probably have a mystic meaning. The "shittah" is the *acacia,* the "oil tree" the *wild olive,* as distinguished from the cultivated (Rom. xi. 17), the "fir tree" is probably the *cypress,* the "pine" stands for the *plane,* always—as in the opening of Plato's *Phædrus,* and the story of Xerxes in Herod. vii. 31,—the glory of Eastern scenery and the "box-tree" is perhaps the *larch,* or a variety of cedar. The "myrtle" does not appear elsewhere in the Old Testament till after the exile (Neh. viii. 15; Zech. i. 8,

tree, and the myrtle, and the oil tree; I will set in the desert the fir tree, *and* the pine and the box tree together: ⁽²⁰⁾ that they may see, and know, and consider, and understand together, that the hand of the LORD hath done this, and the Holy One of Israel hath created it.

⁽²¹⁾ ¹Produce your cause, saith the LORD; bring forth your strong *reasons*, saith the King of Jacob. ⁽²²⁾ Let them bring *them* forth, and shew us what shall happen: let them shew the former things, what they *be*, that we may ²consider them, and know the latter end of them; or declare us things for to come. ⁽²³⁾ Shew the things that are to come hereafter, that we may know that ye *are* gods: yea, do good, or do evil, that we may be dismayed, and behold *it* together. ⁽²⁴⁾ Behold, ye *are* ³of nothing, and your work ⁴of nought: an abomination *is he that* chooseth you.

⁽²⁵⁾ I have raised up *one* from the north, and he shall come: from the rising of the sun shall he call upon my name: and he shall come upon princes as *upon* mortar, and as the potter treadeth clay. ⁽²⁶⁾ Who hath declared from the beginning, that we may know? and beforetime, that we may say, *He is* righteous? yea, *there is* none that sheweth, yea, *there is* none that declareth, yea, *there is* none that heareth your words. ⁽²⁷⁾ The first *shall say* to Zion, Behold, behold them: and I will give to Jerusalem one that bringeth good tidings. ⁽²⁸⁾ For I beheld, and *there was* no man; even among them, and *there was* no counsellor, that, when

---

1 Heb., *Cause to come near.*

2 Heb., *set our heart upon them.*

3 Or., *worse than nothing.*

4 Or., *worse than of a viper.*

10, 11), but then it appears as if indigenous. It supplies the proper name Hadassah (Esther) in Esth. ii. 7.

⁽²⁰⁾ **That they may see.**—The outward blessings, yet more the realities of which they are the symbols, are given to lead men to acknowledge Him who alone would be the giver.

⁽²¹⁾ **Produce your cause.**—The scene of verse 1 is reproduced. The worshippers of idols, as the prophet sees them in his vision hurrying hither and thither to consult their oracles, are challenged, on the ground not only of the great things God hath done, but of His knowledge of those things. The history of Herodotus supplies some striking illustrations. Crœsus and the Cumœans, and the Phocœans, and the Athenians are all sending to Delphi, or consulting their seers, as to this startling apparition of a new conqueror.

Your strong reasons.—Literally, *bulwarks*, or *strongholds*. So we speak of *impregnable* proofs.

⁽²²⁾ **The former things.**—Not, as the Authorised Version suggests, the things of the remote past, but those that lie at the head, or beginning of things to come—the near future. Can the false gods predict them as the pledge and earnest of predictions that go further? Can they see a single year before them? We note that the challenge exactly corresponds to Isaiah's own method of giving "signs" that his words are not idly spoken (chaps. vii. 10—14, xxxviii. 7, 8). The other meaning is maintained, however, by some critics as more in harmony with chap. xliii. 18. The things "for to come" lie, as it were, in the middle future, the "hereafter" of verse 23, in the more remote. All are alike hidden from the gods of the heathen oracles.

⁽²³⁾ **Do good, or do evil.**—The challenge reminds us of Elijah's on Mount Carmel (1 Kings xviii. 27). Can the heathen point to any good or evil fortune which, as having been predicted by this or that deity, might reasonably be thought of as his work? It lies in the nature of the case that every heathen looked to his gods as having sent blessings, or the reverse, but it was only Jehovah who could give the proof supplied by prediction.

⁽²⁴⁾ **Behold, ye are of nothing.**—This is the summing up of the prophet, speaking as in the Judge's name. The idol was "nothing in the world" (1 Cor. viii. 4). The demonic view of the gods of the heathen does not appear, as in St. Paul's argument (1 Cor. x. 20), side by side with that of their nothingness.

⁽²⁵⁾ **I have raised up one from the north.**—The north points to Media, the east to Persia, both of them under the rule of the great Deliverer.

Shall he call upon my name.—The word admits equally of the idea of "invoking" or "proclaiming." It may almost be said, indeed, that the one implies the other. The words find a fulfilment in the proclamations of Cyrus cited in 2 Chron. xxxvi. 22, 23; Ezra i. 2—4.

He shall come upon princes.—The Hebrew noun *Sagan* is a transitional form of a Persian (Delitzsch) or Assyrian (Cheyne) title for a viceroy or satrap.

As the potter treadeth clay.—Commonly the image describes the immediate action of Jehovah. (Jer. xviii. 6, xix. 10). Here it is used for the supreme dominance of His instrument.

⁽²⁶⁾ **Who hath declared . . .**—The words paint once more the startling suddenness of the conquests of the Persian king. He was to come as a comet or a meteor. None of all the oracles in Assyria or Babylon, or in the far coasts to which the Phœnicians sent their ships of Tarshish, had anticipated this.

⁽²⁷⁾ **The first shall say to Zion.**—The italics show the difficulty and abruptness of the originals. A preferable rendering is, (1) *I was the first that said to Zion, &c.* No oracle or soothsayer anticipated that message of deliverance (Ewald, Del.); or (2) *a forerunner shall say . . .* The words "Behold them" point to the returning exiles. The second clause fits in better with (2), and explains it. Jehovah sends a herald of good news (not Cyrus himself, but a messenger reporting his victories, or possibly Isaiah himself, as a more distant herald) to Jerusalem, to say that the exiles are returning.

⁽²⁸⁾ **For I beheld, and there was no man** —*i.e.*, no one who had foretold the future. Jehovah, speaking through the prophet, looks round in vain for that.

I asked of them, could ¹answer a word. ⁽²⁹⁾ Behold, they *are* all vanity; their works *are* nothing: their molten images *are* wind and confusion.

CHAPTER XLII.— ⁽¹⁾ Behold ᵃmy servant, whom I uphold; mine elect, *in whom* my soul ᵇdelighteth; I have put my spirit upon him: he shall bring forth judgment to the Gentiles. ⁽²⁾ He shall not cry, nor lift up, nor cause his voice to be heard in the street. ⁽³⁾ A bruised reed shall he not break, and the ²smoking flax shall he not ³quench: he shall bring forth judgment unto truth. ⁽⁴⁾ He shall not fail nor be ⁴discouraged, till he have set judgment in the earth: and the isles shall wait for his law. ⁽⁵⁾ Thus saith God the LORD, he that created the heavens, and stretched them out; he that spread forth the earth, and that which cometh out of it; he that giveth breath unto the people upon it, and spirit to them that walk therein: ⁽⁶⁾ I the LORD have called thee in righteousness, and will hold thine hand, and will keep thee, and give thee for a covenant of the people, for ᶜa light of

---

1 Heb., *return.*
a Matt. 12. 18.
b Matt. 3. 17 & 17. 5; Eph. 1. 6.
2 Or, *dimly burning.*
3 Heb., *quench it.*
4 Heb., *broken.*
c ch. 49. 6; Luke 2. 32; Acts 13. 47.

---

(29) They are all . . . their works . . .—The first pronoun refers to the idols themselves, the second to the idolaters who make them. In "confusion" we have the familiar *tohu.*

XLII.

(1) Behold my servant . . .—Here the words point not, as before, to the visible, or even the ideal Israel, but to One who is the centre of both, with attributes which are reproduced in His people in the measure of their fulfilment of the ideal. "Elect" is another of the words with which Isaiah has fashioned the theology of Christendom. It meets us there four times (xlv. 4, lxv. 9, 22), and is echoed and interpreted in the voice from heaven of Matt. iii. 17. That voice fixed on the human consciousness of the Son of Man that He was "*the* servant of the Lord," and throughout His life we trace an ever expanding and conscious reproduction of the chief features of Isaiah's picture. Disciples like St. Matthew learnt to recognise that likeness even in what might seem to us subordinate details (Matt. xii. 17—21).

I have put my spirit . . .—An echo from chap. xi. 2, heard once more in chap. lxi. 1. The promise we note as fulfilled in closest connection with the utterance of the previous words in Matt. iii. 16; Luke iii. 22; John i. 32, 33.

He shall bring forth judgment to . . .—The ministry of "*the* servant," as extending to the Gentiles, is prominent in 2 Isaiah (xlix. 6, 7, lii. 15). It expands the thought of chap. ii. 1—4. There the Temple is the centre from which the knowledge and the "judgment" (used here in the sense of *law,* or *ordinance*) flow; here it is from the personal teaching of "*the* servant."

(2) He shall not cry . . .—Isaiah's ideal of a teacher, but partly realised in himself, is that of one exempt from the violence of strong feelings, calm in the sereneness of authority, strong in his far-reaching and pitying sympathy. False prophets might rave as in orgiastic frenzy. We are reminded of Solon affecting the inspiration of a soothsayer in order to attract attention to his converts. Even true prophets might be stirred to vehement and incisive speech, but it should not be so with him. No point of resemblance between the archetype and the portrait seems to have impressed men so deeply as this (Matt. vii. 29, xii. 17—21). The "street" describes the open space of an Eastern city, in which, as in the Greek *agora,* men harangued the people, while "the gate of the city" was reserved for the more formal administration of justice. (Ruth iv. 1; Prov. xxxi. 23.)

(3) A bruised reed shall he not break . . .—Physical, moral, spiritual weakness are all brought under the same similitude. In another context the image has met us in chap. xxxvi. 6. The simple negative "he shall not break" implies, as in the rhetoric of all times, the opposite extreme, the tender care that props and supports. The humanity of the servant of the Lord was to embody what had been already predicated of the Divine will (Ps. li. 17). The *dimly burning flax,* the wick of a lamp nearly out, He will foster and cherish and feed the spiritual life, all but extinguished, with oil till it burns brightly again. In Matt. xxv. 1—13 we have to deal with lamps that are going out, and these not even He could light again unless the bearers of the lamps "bought oil" for themselves.

Judgment unto truth—*i.e.,* according to the perfect standard of truth, with something of the sense of St. John's "true" in the sense of representing the ideal (John i. 9, xv. 1).

(4) He shall not fail nor be discouraged . . .—Both verbs in the Hebrew point back to those of the previous verse, *He shall not burn dimly nor be crushed,* as if to teach that in helping others to strength and light, the servants of the Lord, after the pattern of *the* Servant, gain light and strength for themselves.

The isles shall wait for his law.—The relation of "the servant" to the far off Gentile world is still dominant in the prophet's mind. The LXX. Version, given in Matt. xii. 21, "In His name shall the Gentiles hope," is a paraphrase rather than a translation. The words describe the "earnest expectation," the unconscious longing of the heathen for One who shall be a true teacher (Rom. viii. 22).

(5) He that created.—The accumulation of Divine attributes, as enhancing the solemnity of a revelation, has an earlier parallel in Amos v. 8; a later one in Zech. xii. 1.

(6) Have called thee in righteousness . . .—The words apply to the personal servant. His call was in accordance with the absolute righteousness of God, manifesting itself in love.

A covenant of the people.—The context limits the "people" to Israel. The "servant of the Lord" is to be in Himself not only the mediator of the covenant, but *the* covenant, the meeting-point between God and man, just as He is the the "peace" as well as the peacemaker (Mic. v. 5; Eph. ii. 14). The words may well have furnished a starting-point for the "new covenant" of Jer. xxxi. 31, and the whole series of thoughts that have grown out of it.

A light of the Gentiles.—Re-echoed in Luke ii. 32.

the Gentiles ; ⁽⁷⁾ to open the blind eyes, to ^abring out the prisoners from the prison, *and* them that sit in ^bdarkness out of the prison house. ⁽⁸⁾ I *am* the LORD: that *is* my name: and my ^cglory will I not give to another, neither my praise to graven images.

⁽⁹⁾ Behold, the former things are come to pass, and new things do I declare : before they spring forth I tell you of them. ⁽¹⁰⁾ Sing unto the LORD a new song, *and* his praise from the end of the earth, ye that go down to the sea, and ¹all that is therein; the isles, and the inhabitants thereof. ⁽¹¹⁾ Let the wilderness and the cities thereof lift up *their voice*, the villages *that* Kedar doth inhabit : let the inhabitants of the rock sing, let them shout from the top of the mountains. ⁽¹²⁾ Let them give glory unto the LORD, and declare his praise in the islands.

⁽¹³⁾ The LORD shall go forth as a mighty man, he shall stir up jealousy like a man of war : he shall cry, yea, roar ; he shall ²prevail against his enemies. ⁽¹⁴⁾ I have long time holden my peace ; I have been still, *and* refrained myself : now will I cry like a travailing woman ; I will destroy and ³devour at once. ⁽¹⁵⁾ I will make waste mountains and hills, and dry up all their herbs ; and I will make the rivers islands, and I will dry up the pools. ⁽¹⁶⁾ And I will bring the blind by a way *that* they knew not ; I will lead them in paths *that* they have not known : I will make darkness light before them, and crooked things ⁴straight. These things will I do unto them, and not forsake them. ⁽¹⁷⁾ They shall be ^dturned back, they shall be greatly ashamed, that trust in graven images, that say to the molten images, Ye *are* our gods.

⁽¹⁸⁾ Hear, ye deaf ; and look, ye blind,

---

a ch. 61. 1 ; Luke 4. 18 ; Heb. 2. 14, 15.

b ch. 9. 2.

c ch. 48. 11.

1 Heb., *the fulness thereof.*

2 Or, *behave himself mightily.*

3 Heb., *swallow, or, sup up.*

4 Heb., *into straightness.*

d Ps. 97. 7 ; ch. 1. 29, & 44. 11, & 45. 16.

⁽⁷⁾ **To open the blind eyes.**—The prophet must have felt the contrast between this and his own mission (chap. vi. 10). The words all point to spiritual blessings. (Comp. St. Paul's call in Acts xxvi. 18.) The "prison" is that of the selfishness and sin which hinder men from being truly free. In the "prisoners of hope" of Zech. ix. 11, and the "spirits in prison" of 1 Pet. iii. 18, we have different aspects of the same thought.

^(8, 9) **I am the Lord . . . .**—The prophet grasps the full meaning of the name revealed in Exod. iii. 15. It follows from that meaning that God cannot look with indifference on the transfer to the "graven image" of the worship due to Him. With his vision of Cyrus still present to his thoughts, the prophet again presses the unique point of prediction as distinguishing the religion of Israel from that of the heathen. The "former things" refer probably not to the remote past, but to Isaiah's earlier prophecies, say the whole Assyrian cycle, on which he now looks back from his new stand-point ; or even, as in chap. xli. 22, to the near future of the conquests of Cyrus as compared with that which was to usher in the restoration of Israel.

⁽¹⁰⁾ **Sing unto the Lord a new song.**—The words are familiar in the Psalms (xxxiii. 3, xl. 3, xcviii. 1) and are probably quoted from them. The only touch of definite localisation is found in the mention of Kedar. (See Note on chap. xxi. 16.) Starting from this, the other terms gain a more defined significance. The proclamation seems to be addressed to the nations of the Eastern, not the Western world, as if to the ships that sailed from Elath or Ezion-geber down the Elanitic Gulf. The rock, or Sela (see chap. xvi. 1), is the Petra of Roman Idumæa ; the ships are those that trade to Ophir or the land of Sinim. The cities and the nomad tribes are all invited to join in the hymn of praise, and it is to be echoed in the far-off "islands," or *coasts*, of the Indian Ocean.

⁽¹³⁾ **The Lord shall go forth . . .**—The boldly anthropomorphic image prepares the way for the yet more awful picture of chap. lxiii. 1, which belongs outwardly to the same region. As if roused from slumber, Jehovah stirs up His jealous indignation against the idols, which had seemed to sleep, and rushes to the battle as with the war-cry of a mighty one.

⁽¹⁴⁾ **I have long time holden my peace . . .**—The change of person indicates that Jehovah is the speaker. "Long time," literally, *for an age,* or *an eternity.* What is actually meant is the period of the exile, during which, till the advent of the deliverer, there had been no interposition on behalf of Israel. To the exiles this had seemed endless in its weariness. Now there were the travail-pangs of a new birth for the nation. (Comp. Matt. xxiv. 8.) Was it strange that there should be the convulsions and catastrophes which are as the thunder-roaring of the voice of Jehovah?

I will destroy and devour.—Better, *I pant and gasp.* The verbs express strong emotion, the cries of the travailing woman rather than destructive acts.

⁽¹⁵⁾ **I will make waste mountains . . .**—The whole description is symbolic, and points to the subjugation of the heathen nations, the "rivers" and "pools" probably representing the kingdoms of the Tigris and Euphrates (chap. viii. 7). All this seems a purely destructive work, but through it all mercy and truth are working, and a way is being opened for the return of Israel, in painting which, as elsewhere, the literal melts into the spiritual, as in a dissolving view. (See Note on chap. xl. 4.) "These things" include the whole work of judgment and of mercy.

⁽¹⁷⁾ **They shall be greatly ashamed . . .**—Manifestly the winding up of a section. The foretold victories of Cyrus shall bring shame and confusion on the worshippers of the idols which he, the representative of a purer faith, should overthrow.

⁽¹⁸⁾ **Hear, ye deaf . . .**—The words form the beginning of a new section. The prophet feels or sees that the great argument has not carried conviction as it ought to have done. The people to whom Jehovah speaks through him are still spiritually blind and deaf, and that people is ideally the servant of the Lord (ch. xli. 8), in whom the pattern of the personal servant ought to have been reproduced. (Comp. John ix. 39—41.)

that ye may see. (19) Who *is* blind, but my servant? or deaf, as my messenger *that* I sent? who *is* blind as *he that is* perfect, and blind as the LORD's servant? (20) Seeing many things, *a* but thou observest not; opening the ears, but he heareth not. (21) The LORD is well pleased for his righteousness' sake; he will magnify the law, and make ¹*it* honourable. (22) But this *is* a people robbed and spoiled; ²*they are* all of them snared in holes, and they are hid in prison houses: they are for a prey, and none delivereth; for ³a spoil, and none saith, Restore.

(23) Who among you will give ear to this? *who* will hearken and hear ⁴for the time to come? (24) Who gave Jacob for a spoil, and Israel to the robbers? did not the LORD, he against whom we have sinned? for they would not walk

a Rom. 2. 21.

1 Or, him.

2 Or, *in snaring all the young men of them.*

3 Heb., *a treading.*

4 Heb., *for the after time?*

in his ways, neither were they obedient unto his law. (25) Therefore he hath poured upon him the fury of his anger, and the strength of battle: and it hath set him on fire round about, yet he knew not; and it burned him, yet he laid *it* not to heart.

CHAPTER XLIII.—(1) But now thus saith the LORD that created thee, O Jacob, and he that formed thee, O Israel, Fear not: for I have redeemed thee, I have called *thee* by thy name; thou *art* mine. (2) When thou passest through the waters, I *will be* with thee; and through the rivers, they shall not overflow thee: when thou walkest through the fire, thou shalt not be burned; neither shall the flame kindle upon thee. (3) For I *am* the LORD thy God, the Holy One of Israel, thy Saviour:

---

(19) **Deaf, as my messenger . . .**—The work of the messenger of God had been the ideal of Isaiah, as it was of *the* servant in whom the ideal was realised (Rom. x. 15; verse 1). But how could a blind and deaf messenger, like the actual Israel, do his work effectually? (Ps. cxxiii. 2).

As he that is perfect.—Strictly speaking, *the devoted*, or *surrendered one*. The Hebrew *meshullam* is interesting, as connected with the modern *Moslem* and *Islam*, the man *resigned* to the will of God. The frequent use of this, or a cognate form, as a proper name after the exile (1 Chron. ix. 21; Ezra viii. 6, x. 15; Neh. iii. 4) may (on either assumption as to the date of 2 Isaiah) be connected with it by some link of causation. Other meanings given to it have been "perfect" as in the Authorised Version, "confident," "recompensed," "meritorious."

(20) **Seeing many things . . .**—With a clear vision into the future, the prophet sees that the future Israel will be as far from the ideal as his contemporaries had been. In the actual work of *the* Servant we find the fulfilment of his vision. Scribes and Pharisees are as those who "learn nothing and forget nothing," on whom all the lessons of experience are cast away, reproducing the state from which Isaiah started (chap. vi. 10; Matt. xiii. 14; Mark iv. 12; Luke viii. 10; John xii. 40; Acts xxviii. 26). The transfer of the words to the sufferings of the Christ, who bore them as though He neither heard nor saw, is scarcely tenable.

(21) **The Lord is well pleased . . .**—The tenses require a change: *The Lord was well pleased . . He made His law great and glorious.* This had been His purpose, and He had not failed in it. He had done all that it was possible to do. (Comp. chap. v. 4; Rom. ix. 4.)

(22) **But this is a people robbed and spoiled . . .**—It is hard to say whether the prophet contemplates the state of the exiles in Babylon, or sees far off yet another exile, consequent on a second and more fatal falling off from the true ideal.

None delivereth . . . none saith, Restore.—The tone of despondency seems to come in strangely after the glorious promise of deliverance. On the whole, therefore, the second view seems the more probable; and, so taken, the verse finds its best commentary in Rom. ix.—xi., which is permeated through and through with the prophecies of 2 Isaiah. The "holes" are, primarily, rock-caves, used, not as places of refuge (chap. ii. 19), but as dungeons.

(24) **Who gave Jacob for a spoil . . . ?**—The sufferers, whether in the nearer or more distant exile, are reminded that they have brought their sufferings upon themselves, and that it is Jehovah who sends them in the wrath which, as aiming at their restoration, is but another aspect of His love.

(25) **The fury of his anger.**—Better, *the burning heat of His wrath, and the violence of war.* Historically, the words seem to find a better fulfilment in the "wars and rumours of wars" (Matt. xxiv. 6) than in the long equable continuance of the exile.

XLIII.

(1) **But now . . .**—The outpouring of love that follows is contrasted with the wrath of the preceding verse.

The Lord that created thee.—The title implies something more than "the Maker of heaven and earth." Jehovah has created Israel as specially answering, as other created things did, to an archetype in His own purpose. To "call by name" is everywhere, but pre-eminently in the East, the mark of an individualising tenderness (John x. 3), almost of a predestinating love that makes the name a witness of its purpose.

(2) **When thou passest through the waters . . .**—The two contrasted forms of elemental perils are used, as elsewhere, proverbially for all forms of danger (Ps. lxvi. 12).

(3) **I gave Egypt for thy ransom . . .**—Speaking after the manner of men, the prophet paints Jehovah as surrendering Egypt and other kingdoms to the arms of Cyrus, as if they were a price paid to him for liberating the Jews of Babylon. Ethiopia (Heb., *Cúsh*) may be taken of either the Asiatic or African people that bore that name—Seba as Meroe, between the Blue and White Nile, the modern *Dár Sennár*. His-

I gave Egypt *for* thy ransom, Ethiopia and Seba for thee. (4) Since thou wast precious in my sight, thou hast been honourable, and I have loved thee: therefore will I give men for thee, and people for thy ¹life. (5) ᵃFear not: for I *am* with thee: I will bring thy seed from the east, and gather thee from the west; (6) I will say to the north, Give up; and to the south, Keep not back: bring my sons from far, and my daughters from the ends of the earth. (7) *Even* every one that is called by my name: for I have created him for my glory, I have formed him; yea, I have made him.

(8) Bring forth the blind people that have eyes, and the deaf that have ears. (9) Let all the nations be gathered together, and let the people be assembled: ᵇwho among them can declare this, and shew us former things? let them bring forth their witnesses, that they may be justified: or let them hear, and say, It *is* truth. (10) Ye *are* my witnesses, saith the LORD, and my servant whom I have chosen: that ye may know and believe me, and understand that I *am* he: ᶜbefore me there was ²no God formed, neither shall there be after me. (11) I, even I, ᵈ*am* the LORD; and beside me *there is* no saviour. (12) I have declared, and have saved, and I have shewed, when *there was* no strange *god* among you: therefore ye *are* my witnesses, saith the LORD, that I *am* God. (13) Yea, before the day *was* I *am* he; and *there is* none that can deliver out of my hand: I will work, and who shall ³ᵉlet it? (14) Thus saith the LORD, your redeemer, the Holy One of Israel; For your sake I have sent to Babylon, and have brought down all their ⁴nobles, and the Chaldeans, whose cry *is* in the ships. (15) I *am* the LORD, your Holy One, the creator of Israel, your King. (16) Thus saith the LORD, which ᶠmaketh

1 Or, *person.*
a ch. 44. 2; Jer. 30. 10 & 46. 27.
b ch. 41. 21.
c ch. 41. 4 & 44. 8.
2 Or, *nothing formed of God.*
d ch. 45. 21; Hos. 13. 4.
3 Heb., *turn it back?*
e Job 9. 12; ch. 14. 27.
4 Heb., *bars.*
f Ex. 14. 16, 22.

---

torically, the words find a fulfilment in the conquest of Egypt by Cambyses, who carried into effect his father's plans. For the thought of the "ransom" comp. Prov. xi. 8, xxi. 18, and the next verse. As a man would sacrifice any number of slaves to ransom a son, so was it in Jehovah's dealings with His people.

(5) **From the east** . . .—Even from Isaiah's stand-point, the dispersion of Israel might well be contemplated in all this wide extent. The Ten Tribes were already carried off to the cities of the Medes (2 Kings xvii. 6). The Babylonian exile had its beginning under Esar-haddon (2 Chron. xxxiii. 11); others may have been found before the time of Zephaniah (Zeph. iii. 10) beyond the rivers of Ethiopia. Even in the time of Joel the slave-trade of the Phœnicians had carried the sons of Judah and Jerusalem to the western isles of Javan, or Ionia (Joel iii. 6).

(6) **Bring my sons** . . .—The words imply an escort of honour, given by the heathen nations to the returning exiles.

(7) **Every one that is called by my name** —*i.e.*, who is marked as belonging to the people that is chosen as the Lord's servant.

(8) **Bring forth the blind people** . . .—The command comes abruptly, as from a Divine voice, and is, as it were, a reversed echo of chap. xlii. 18—20. There Israel saw but did not observe, had eyes and yet was blind. Here the blind and deaf—*i.e.*, the heathen, or the Israel that had fallen into heathenism—are spoken of as having capacities for sight and hearing which will one day be developed.

(9) **Who among them** . . .—The challenge of chap. xli. 22, 23 is repeated. Who among their gods has foretold the "former things"? has predicted events that were then in the future, and have now come to pass?

(10) **Ye are my witnesses** . . .—These are collectively addressed as the servant of Jehovah. Their calling and election had not been cancelled, and they might yet fulfil it. They, in that restoration from exile which Isaiah had foretold, should be a living proof of the foresight granted to the prophets, and, therefore, of the foreknowledge of Him who alone could say, "I am He," to whom past, present, and future were as one; and He, the Eternal, proclaims Himself as being also the only Saviour.

(12) **When there was no strange god among you.**—Better, *and there was* . . . It was no heathen oracle or soothsayer that had foretold the restoration. Israel as a people, through its whole future history, was to be a living witness of the oneness and eternity of its God, and the eternity implies (verse 13) omnipotence.

(13) **Who shall let it?**—Literally, *who shall turn it back?* One of the numerous echoes from Job (chaps. ix. 12, xi. 10).

(14) **I have sent to Babylon.**—For the first time in 2 Isaiah, the place of exile is named. For "have brought down all their nobles" read, *I will bring them all down as fugitives.* The marginal "bars" represents a various reading, *defences,* in the sense of *defenders.*

The Chaldeans, whose cry is in the ships. —Better, *into the ships of their shouting* — *i.e.*, the ships which used to echo with the exulting joy of sailors. The word for "shouting" is purposely chosen to suggest the thought that there will be a shout of another kind, even the wailing cry of despair. The commerce of Babylon, and its position on the Euphrates, made it, as it were, the Venice of the earlier East (Herod., i. 194). The prophet sees the inhabitants of Babylon fleeing in their ships from the presence of their conqueror.

(16) **Which maketh a way in the sea** . . .— A distinct echo of Exod. xiv. 16 and Ps. lxxvii. 19. The return from Babylon is to be as a second Exodus from another house of bondage. In the one, as in the other, the "horse and his rider" are to be thrown into the sea.

Rivers in the Desert. ISAIAH, XLIII. *Transgressions Blotted Out.*

a way in the sea, and a ᵃpath in the mighty waters; ⁽¹⁷⁾ which bringeth forth the chariot and horse, the army and the power; they shall lie down together, they shall not rise: they are extinct, they are quenched as tow. ⁽¹⁸⁾ Remember ye not the former things, neither consider the things of old. ⁽¹⁹⁾ Behold, I will do a ᵇnew thing; now it shall spring forth; shall ye not know it? I will even make a way in the wilderness, *and* rivers in the desert. ⁽²⁰⁾ The beast of the field shall honour me, the dragons and the ¹²owls: because I give waters in the wilderness, *and* rivers in the desert, to give drink to my people, my chosen. ⁽²¹⁾ ᶜThis people have I formed for myself; they shall shew forth my praise.

⁽²²⁾ But thou hast not called upon me, O Jacob; but thou hast been weary of me, O Israel. ⁽²³⁾ Thou hast not brought me the ³small cattle of thy burnt offerings; neither hast thou honoured me with thy sacrifices. I have not caused thee to serve with an offering, nor wearied thee with incense. ⁽²⁴⁾ Thou hast bought me no sweet cane with money, neither hast thou ⁴filled me with the fat of thy sacrifices: but thou hast made me to serve with thy sins, thou hast wearied me with thine iniquities. ⁽²⁵⁾ I, *even* I, am he that ᵈblotteth out thy transgressions for mine own sake, and will not remember thy sins. ⁽²⁶⁾ Put me in remembrance: let us plead together: declare thou, that thou mayest be justified. ⁽²⁷⁾ Thy first father hath sinned, and thy ⁵teachers have transgressed against me. ⁽²⁸⁾ Therefore I have profaned the ⁶princes of the sanctuary, and have given Jacob to the curse, and Israel to reproaches.

---

a Josh. 3. 13, 16.
b 2 Cor. 5. 17; Rev. 21. 5.
1 Or, *ostriches.*
2 Heb., *daughters of the owl.*
c Luke 1. 74, 75.
3 Heb., *lambs,* or, *kids.*
4 Heb., *made me drunk,* or, *abundantly moistened.*
d Ezek. 36. 22, &c.
5 Heb., *interpreters.*
6 Or, *holy princes.*

⁽¹⁷⁾ **Quenched as tow**—*i.e.*, as the wick of a lamp going out. (See Note on chap. xlii. 3.)

⁽¹⁸, ¹⁹⁾ **Remember ye not . . .**—All the wonders of the great historic past of Israel were to be as nothing compared with the new manifestation of the power of Jehovah, which Isaiah sees as already dawning in the future.

Shall ye not know it?—Better, *Will ye not give heed to it?*

I will even make a way in the wilderness . . .—The literal and the spiritual senses melt into each other. The very beasts of the field shall lose their ferocity in the presence of the saints of God. For "dragons and owls," read *jackals and ostriches.*

⁽²²⁾ **But thou hast not called upon me.**—The startling abruptness of the complaint has led many critics to question the genuineness of these verses (22—24). Their insertion, however, by a later writer would be at least as hard to understand as their having come from the hand of the same writer as the glowing picture that precedes them. May we not find the solution of the problem in the fact that Isaiah's experience taught him that there would be in the future, as in the past, a dark as well as a bright side to the picture? that the mercies shown to the exiles would not be according to their merits, but to God's great goodness? The worship of the restored exiles would be as that of the people had been in his own time, meagre and unthankful. Visions of failure alternate with the glowing hope that the ideal will be realised, and this alternation constitutes the great problem of the book, as it does of all like apocalyptic intimations.

But thou hast been weary.—Better, *so that thou shouldest be weary.* Others render it, *Much less hast thou toiled for me.* Sacrifices elsewhere than in the Temple were forbidden by the Law, and the prophet does not so much blame the people for not offering these as for not compensating for their absence by the true worship of which they were the symbols.

⁽²³⁾ **I have not caused thee to serve . . .**—The words practically imply the suspension of sacrifices during the exile. Jehovah had not imposed that bond-service on them—had not wearied them with demanding incense when they were far away from the Temple to whose ritual it belonged.

⁽²⁴⁾ **No sweet cane . . .**—Probably some species of *Amomum* for the anointing oil (Exod. xxx. 23). It is distinguished from the incense, and is not one of the ingredients (Exod. xxx. 34).

Thou hast made me to serve.—The verbs of verse 23 are repeated with the emphasis of scorn, the thought being analogous to that of chap. i. 14. The people had made this hypocritical worship as a service which their God had to endure, till He was altogether weary of it.

⁽²⁵⁾ **I, even I . . .**—As in chap. i. 2, 18, the analogy with which may be noted as evidence of identity of authorship, the incisive words that prove the guilt of Israel are followed by the fullest offer of pardon on repentance. And this he does "for His own sake," to manifest the everlasting righteousness which is also the everlasting love. The "blotting out" finds an echo in Col. ii. 14.

⁽²⁶⁾ **Put me in remembrance . . .**—The object of the verb has been differently supplied: (1) "Remind me, if thou canst, *of thy merits;* plead in thine own defence for an acquittal;" and (2) "Remind me *of my promise to thee,* of that electing grace which called thee to be my servant." The former seems to fit in best with what follows.

⁽²⁷⁾ **Thy first father hath sinned . . .**—The words have been interpreted: (1) of Adam; (2) of Abraham; (3) of Jacob; (4) of the ancestors of Israel collectively; (5) of this or that high priest individually. (3) fits in best. (See verse 28.)

Thy teachers.—Literally, *thy interpreters* (Job xxxiii. 23), or *thy mediators.* The term is used in 2 Chron. xxxii. 31 of the "ambassadors" of the king of Babylon, and stands here for the priests and the prophets, who ought officially to have been the expounders of the Divine will.

⁽²⁸⁾ **I have profaned the princes of the sanctuary.**—Better, *holy princes.* The title is given to the chief priests in 1 Chron. xxiv. 5. In the exile their priestly functions were in abeyance. They were practically desecrated.

The Outpouring of the Spirit. ISAIAH, XLIV. *The Shame of the Makers of Idols.*

CHAPTER XLIV.—⁽¹⁾ Yet now hear,^a O Jacob my servant; and Israel, whom I have chosen: ⁽²⁾ thus saith the LORD that made thee, and formed thee from the womb, *which* will help thee; Fear not, O Jacob, my servant; and thou, Jesurun, whom I have chosen. ⁽³⁾ For I will ^bpour water upon him that is thirsty, and floods upon the dry ground: I will pour my spirit upon thy seed, and my blessing upon thine offspring: ⁽⁴⁾ and they shall spring up *as* among the grass, as willows by the water courses. ⁽⁵⁾ One shall say, I *am* the LORD'S; and another shall call *himself* by the name of Jacob; and another shall subscribe *with* his hand unto the LORD, and surname *himself* by the name of Israel.

⁽⁶⁾ Thus saith the LORD the King of Israel, and his redeemer the LORD of hosts; ^cI *am* the first, and I *am* the last; and beside me *there is* no God. ⁽⁷⁾ And who, as I, shall call, and shall declare it, and set it in order for me, since I appointed the ancient people? and the things that are coming, and shall come, let them shew unto them. ⁽⁸⁾ Fear ye not, neither be afraid: have not I told thee from that time, and have declared *it*? ye *are* even my witnesses. Is there a God beside me? yea, ^d*there is* no ¹God; I know not *any*.

⁽⁹⁾ They that make a graven image *are* all of them vanity; and their ²delectable things shall not profit; and they *are* their own witnesses; ^ethey see not, nor know; that they may be ashamed. ⁽¹⁰⁾ Who hath formed a god, or molten a graven image *that* is profitable for nothing? ⁽¹¹⁾ Behold, all his fellows shall be ^fashamed: and the workmen, they *are* of men: let them all be gathered together, let them stand up; *yet* they shall fear, *and* they shall be ashamed together.

⁽¹²⁾ ^gThe smith ³with the tongs both worketh in the coals, and fashioneth it with hammers, and worketh it with the

a ch. 41. 8 & 43. 1; Jer. 30. 10 & 46. 27.
b ch. 35. 7; Joel 2. 28; John 7. 38; Acts 2. 18.
c ch. 41. 4 & 48. 12; Rev. 1. 8, 17 & 22. 13.
d Deut. 4. 35, 39 & 32. 39; 1 Sam. 2. 2; ch. 45. 5.
¹ Heb., *rock*.
² Heb., *desirable*.
e Ps. 115. 4, &c.
f Ps. 97. 7; ch. 1. 29, & 42. 17, & 45. 16.
g Jer. 10. 3; Wis. 13. 11.
³ Or, *with an axe*.

The curse.—The *cherem*, or *ban*, answering to the *anathema*. The state described answers to that of Hos. iii. 4.

XLIV.

⁽¹⁾ **Yet now hear . . .**—The thoughts of Israel are turned from their own sins to the unchanging love of God, and that is the ground of their hope.

⁽²⁾ **Thou, Jesurun . . .**—The ideal name of Israel as "the upright one;" so the Book of Jasher is the book of the "upright," of the heroes of Israel. (See Note on Deut. xxxii. 15.) The name is substituted for the Israel of the preceding verse, as pointing to the purpose of God in their election.

⁽³⁾ **I will pour water . . .**—The latter words of the verse interpret the former. It is not the union of material or spiritual blessings, but first the symbol, and then the reality. The "thirst" is that of Ps. xlii. 1; John iv. 13, 14. In the promise of the Spirit we have an echo of Joel ii. 28.

⁽⁴⁾ **As willows.**—The same word as in Ps. cxxxvii. 2 and chap. xv. 7. Botanists identify it with a species of *Viburnum*, which grows on the banks of streams, rather than with the "weeping" or other species of *Salix*.

⁽⁵⁾ **One shall say, I am the Lord's.**—The words paint, like Ps. lxxxvii. 4, 5, the eagerness of heathen proselytes to attach themselves to Israel. The forms of adhesion rise in emphasis: (1) the convert declares himself to belong to Jehovah; (2) he calls upon the name of Jacob; (3) he writes upon his hand, To Jehovah!—brands himself, as it were, as His servant (comp. Ezek. ix. 4), as showing that the prohibition of idolatrous marks (Lev. xix. 28) did not exclude this; and see also Rev. vii. 3, ix. 4; (4) he takes the name of Israel in addition to his own as a title of honour.

⁽⁶⁾ **Thus saith the Lord . . .**—A new section opens, repeating the argument of chaps. xli., xliii. against idolatry.

⁽⁷⁾ **Since I appointed the ancient people . . .**—Literally, *the people of the age*, or *of eternity*. The phrase is used of the dead in Ezek. xxvi. 20. Here it has been referred either to the antediluvian fathers of mankind (Job xxii. 15) or to the patriarchs of Israel, or, more fitly, to Israel, as having before it a far-off future as well as a far-off past, and, therefore, *an everlasting people*. The same phrase is used for the "perpetual covenant" of Exod. xxxi. 16. (Comp. Exod. xl. 15; 2 Sam. vii. 13, 16.)

⁽⁸⁾ **Yea, there is no God . . .**—Literally, *no Rock*. That word, as expressing eternal strength, being used, as in Deut. xxxii. 4; 2 Sam. xxii. 3, xxiii. 3, as a Divine name.

⁽⁹⁾ **Are all of them vanity . . .**—Once more Isaiah's favourite *tohu*—the symbol of the primeval chaos.

Their delectable things . . .—The generic term used for works of art (chap. ii. 16), specially for what men delight to worship. (Comp. chap. lxiv. 11; Lam. i. 10.)

They are their own witnesses . . .—Better, *their witnesses* (*i.e.*, the worshippers who sing their praises) *see not and know not*.

⁽¹¹⁾ **Behold, all his fellows . . .**—The noun has a half-technical sense, as describing a member of a religious guild or fraternity, such as were attached to heathen temples. In this sense "Ephraim was *joined* to idols" (Hos. iv. 17). In Hos. vi. 9, the noun is used for the "company" of priests.

Let them stand up.—The words gain in vividness when we remember that the challenge is addressed to the guild of idol-makers. They are but men; how can they make a god?

⁽¹²⁾ **The smith with the tongs.**—We begin with the metal idol. Better, *The smith uses a chisel*. The work involves stooping over the charcoal furnace. The maker of the god is exhausted with his toil, and requires food and drink to sustain him.

strength of his arms: yea, he is hungry, and his strength faileth: he drinketh no water, and is faint. (13) The carpenter stretcheth out *his* rule; he marketh it out with a line; he fitteth it with planes, and he marketh it out with the compass, and maketh it after the figure of a man, according to the beauty of a man; that it may remain in the house. (14) He heweth him down cedars, and taketh the cypress and the oak, which he ¹strengtheneth for himself among the trees of the forest: he planteth an ash, and the rain doth nourish it. (15) Then shall it be for a man to burn: for he will take thereof, and warm himself; yea, he kindleth *it*, and baketh bread; yea, he maketh a god, and worshippeth *it*; he maketh it a graven image, and falleth down thereto. (16) He burneth part thereof in the fire; with part thereof he eateth flesh; he roasteth roast, and is satisfied: yea, he warmeth *himself*, and saith, Aha, I am warm, I have seen the fire: (17) and the residue thereof he maketh a god, *even* his graven image: he falleth down unto it, and worshippeth *it*, and prayeth unto it, and saith, Deliver me; for thou *art* my god.

(18) They have not known nor understood: for he hath ²shut their eyes, that they cannot see; *and* their hearts, that they cannot understand. (19) And none ³considereth in his heart, neither *is there* knowledge nor understanding to say, I have burned part of it in the fire; yea, also I have baked bread upon the coals thereof; I have roasted flesh, and eaten *it*: and shall I make the residue thereof an abomination? shall I fall down to ⁴the stock of a tree? (20) He feedeth on ashes: a deceived heart hath turned him aside, that he cannot deliver his soul, nor say, *Is there* not a lie in my right hand?

(21) Remember these, O Jacob and Israel, for thou *art* my servant: I have formed thee; thou *art* my servant: O Israel, thou shalt not be forgotten of me. (22) I have blotted out, as a thick cloud, thy transgressions, and, as a cloud, thy sins: return unto me; for I have redeemed thee. (23) Sing, O ye heavens; for the LORD hath done *it*: shout, ye lower parts of the earth: break forth into singing, ye mountains, O forest, and every tree therein: for the LORD hath redeemed Jacob, and glorified himself in Israel.

1 Or, *taketh courage*.
2 Heb., *daubed*.
3 Heb., *setteth to his heart*.
4 Heb., *that which comes of a tree?*

---

(13) **The carpenter.**—The wooden idol comes next. First there is the rough measurement with the "rule;" then the artificer draws the outline of the figure in red chalk. "Plane" and "compasses" come in to make the form more definite. The human figure is complete; then there is the artist's final touch to add the element of beauty; and so it is ready for the "house," or *temple*.

(14) **He heweth him down cedars.**—The manufacture is traced further back, possibly by way of protest against the belief current in all nations that some archaic image had fallen from heaven (Acts xix. 35). The "cypress" is probably the *Quercus ilex*, and the "ash" a *fig tree;* but the identification of trees in the language of a remote time and language is always somewhat uncertain.

Which he strengtheneth for himself.—Better, *fixeth his choice among*. The eye travels, it will be noted, backward from the workshop.

(15—17) **Then shall it be. . . .**—The point on which the prophet dwells with indignant iteration is that it is a mere chance which half of the shapeless log is to be worshipped as a god, and which to be used for cooking the workmen's dinner. Diagoras of Melos, the reputed atheist disciple of Democritus, is said to have thrown a wooden Hercules on his hearth, bidding the herogod do a thirteenth labour, and boil his turnips (Del.).

(18) **He hath shut their eyes.**—Better, *their eyes are smeared over*. The state described is the judicial blindness of Rom. i. 20—25. It will be remembered that blindness thus inflicted was one of the tortures of Eastern cruelty.

(20) **He feedeth on ashes.**—The verb passes readily through the meanings "feeding," "pasturing," "following after," and the last is commonly accepted. The first, however, has the merit of greater vividness. (Comp. Hosea xii. 1.) The "ashes" of the smith's furnace become the symbols of the vanity of his work (Eccles. vii. 6), and yet he has not even the germ of truth which lies in the questions of the sceptic.

(21) **Remember these.**—Better, *these things*—i.e., the whole argument against idolatry. In contrast with the blind worshippers of idols, Israel is addressed in its ideal character as the "servant of Jehovah" with all the emphasis of iteration.

Thou shalt not be forgotten of me.—The LXX., Vulg., and some other versions take the verb as middle, *thou shalt not forget*, but the evidence for the passive sense preponderates, to say nothing of its greater fitness in connection with the next verse, and its bearing upon complaints like those of chaps. xl. 27, xlix. 14.

(22) **I have blotted out, as a thick cloud.**—Better, *mist*. The Authorised Version half suggests the idea that it is the cloud that hides the sins from view. What is meant is that the sins of Israel are put away, as the sun and wind drive away the mists and fogs (Job xxx. 15); and that this is, in idea at least, if not in time, prior to the conversion as that which makes it possible.

(23) **The Lord hath done it.**—The pronoun supplied in the Authorised Version refers to the redemption of verse 22; but the word may be taken absolutely in the sense *hath done mightily*.

The Promise of Deliverance.   ISAIAH, XLV.   *Cyrus as the Anointed One.*

(24) Thus saith the LORD, thy redeemer, and he that formed thee from the womb, I *am* the LORD that maketh all *things;* that stretcheth forth the heavens alone; that spreadeth abroad the earth by myself; (25) that frustrateth the tokens of the liars, and maketh diviners mad; that turneth wise *men* backward, and maketh their knowledge foolish; (26) that confirmeth the word of his servant, and performeth the counsel of his messengers; that saith to Jerusalem, Thou shalt be inhabited; and to the cities of Judah, Ye shall be built, and I will raise up the ¹decayed places thereof: (27) that saith to the deep, Be dry, and I will dry up thy rivers : (28) that saith of Cyrus, He *is* my shepherd, and shall perform all my pleasure : even saying to Jerusalem, *ᵃ*Thou shalt be built; and to the temple, Thy foundation shall be laid.

CHAPTER XLV.—(1) Thus saith the LORD to his anointed, to Cyrus, whose right hand I ²have holden, to subdue nations before him; and I will loose the loins of kings, to open before him the

1 Heb., *wastes.*

a 2 Chron. 36. 22; Ezra. 1. 1; ch. 45. 13.

2 Or, *strengthened.*

Ye lower parts of the earth.—These, as in Ephes. iv. 9, are equivalent to Sheol, or Hades. Even they, commonly thought of as echoing no song of praise (Pss. vi. 5, lxxxviii. 12; Isa. xxxviii. 18), are invited to join in the great doxology.

(24) **Thus saith the Lord.**—A new section begins, which is carried on to the end of chap. xlv. The contrast between the foreknowledge of Jehovah and the no-knowledge of the worshippers of idols culminates in the proclamation, in verse 28, of the name of the deliverer and his restoration of the Temple.

That spreadeth abroad the earth by myself.—The Hebrew written text gives the more emphatic reading: *that spreadeth forth the earth; who was with me?* (Comp. chaps. xl. 13, lxiii. 3; and Job ix. 8.)

(25) **That frustrateth the tokens of the liars.**—Better, *of the praters*—i.e., the false prophets of Babylon. It is implied that they, after the manner of the false seers of Judah (Jer. xxiii. 16, 17), predicted for the kings of Babylon a time of prosperity and peace.

(26) **That confirmeth the word of his servant.**—The parallelism of "servant" in the singular with "messengers" in the plural suggests the thought that the prophet is not speaking of himself, but of Israel, as the ideal "servant of the Lord," the prophetic nation represented by the individual "messengers" or prophets. Comp. as to the word chap. xlii. 19; Mal. iii. 1, and that prophet's own name ("my messenger").

(27) **That saith to the deep**—i.e., to the Euphrates. The words find a literal fulfilment in the strategical operation by which Cyrus turned the river from its usual bed into the Sepharvaim channel, and thus enabled his soldiers to cross on foot (Herod. i. 191). Symbolically the words may mean simply the destruction of the power of Babylon, of which its river was the emblem. (Comp. Rev. xvi. 12.)

(28) **That saith of Cyrus.**—The Hebrew form is *Koresh,* answering to the *Kur'us* of the inscription of the king's tomb in the Murghab valley. The prediction of the name of the future deliverer has its only parallel in that of Josiah (1 Kings xiii. 2). Such a phenomenon admits of three possible explanations:—(1) That it is a prophecy after the event—i.e., that the whole of Isaiah, or this part of it, was written at the close of the exile. (2) That the name was revealed to the prophet in a way altogether supernatural. (3) That the name came within the horizon of the prophet's vision from his natural stand-point, the supernatural element being found in the facts which he is led to connect with it. Of these, (3) seems to commend itself as most analogous with the methods of prophetic teaching. The main facts in the case are these—(1) Events had made Isaiah acquainted with the name of the Medes, and with a people bearing the name (Elam), afterwards given by the Jews to the Persians of the Greeks (xi. 1, xiii. 7, xxi. 2; 2 Kings xvii. 6, xviii. 11). (2) *Koresh* or *Kyros* was the name of a river in that region, and the conqueror is said to have changed his previous name (Agradates) for it (Strab. xv. 3, 6). (3) The name has been said to mean "the sun" (Plutarch, Ctesias), and this, though not accepted by many modern scholars as philologically accurate, at least indicates that the Greeks assigned that meaning to it. It would be a natural name for one who, as a worshipper of Ormuzd, saw in the sun the supreme symbol of the God of heaven. (4) The grandfather of the great Cyrus is said to have borne the same name (Herod. i. 111). (5) The facts point to the conclusion that the name *Kur'us,* if not a titular epithet, like the Pharaoh of Egypt, may yet have had the prestige of antiquity and dignity, historical or mythical. (6) Is it altogether impossible that the prophecy, circulating among the Babylonian exiles, helped to bring about its own fulfilment, and that Agradates may have been led to take the name of *Kur'us* because he found his work described in connection with it (Josh. *Ant.,* xii. 1. 2)?

My shepherd.—As guiding the flock of Jehovah, each to their own pasture.

Thou shalt be built.—Both verbs are better taken as imperatives, *Let her be built; Let thy foundations be laid.*

XLV.

(1) **To his anointed . . .**—The name is none other than the Messiah, the Christ, with which we are familiar, here and here only applied to a heathen king. It has to be remembered that the words had not yet received the special application given to it in Dan. ix. 26, and had been used of the theocratic kings, of Saul (1 Sam. xxvi. 9, 11, 16), of the house of David (2 Sam. xxii. 51, xxiii. 1), and of the patriarch Abraham (Ps. cv. 15). What is meant, therefore, is that Cyrus, the future deliverer, would be as truly a king "by the grace of God" as David had been, not only, like Nebuchadnezzar, "a servant of Jehovah" (Jer. xxvii. 6, xliii. 10), but "fulfilling all his pleasure," whom He *grasps* by the right hand and guides.

I will loose the loins.—Literally, *I will ungird,* either as a general symbol of weakening, or specifically for disarming, the sword being suspended from the girdle. The "two-leaved gates" are those of

two leaved gates; and the gates shall not be shut; ⁽²⁾ I will go before thee, and make the crooked places straight: I will break in pieces the gates of brass, and cut in sunder the bars of iron: ⁽³⁾ and I will give thee the treasures of darkness, and hidden riches of secret places, that thou mayest know that I, the LORD, which call *thee* by thy name, *am* the God of Israel. ⁽⁴⁾ For Jacob my servant's sake, and Israel mine elect, I have even called thee by thy name: I have surnamed thee, though thou hast not known me. ⁽⁵⁾ I *am* the LORD, and *there is* none else, *there is* no God beside me: I girded thee, though thou hast not known me: ⁽⁶⁾ that they may know from the rising of the sun, and from the west, that *there is* none beside me. I *am* the LORD, and *there is* none else. ⁽⁷⁾ I form the light, and create darkness: I make peace, and create evil: I the LORD do all these *things*.

⁽⁸⁾ Drop down, ye heavens, from above, and let the skies pour down righteousness: let the earth open, and let them bring forth salvation, and let righteousness spring up together; I the LORD have created it.

⁽⁹⁾ Woe unto him that striveth with his Maker! *Let* the potsherd *strive* with the potsherds of the earth. ^bShall the clay say to him that fashioneth it, What makest thou? or thy work, He hath no hands? ⁽¹⁰⁾ Woe unto him that saith unto *his* father, What begettest thou? or to the woman, What hast thou brought forth?

⁽¹¹⁾ Thus saith the LORD, the Holy One of Israel, and his Maker, Ask me of things to come concerning my sons, and concerning the work of my hands

a Deut. 4. 35, 39 & 32. 39; ch. 44. 8.

b Jer. 18. 6; Rom. 9. 20.

---

kingly palaces; the "gates," those of cities, which will have to open to him. The words here, and in the next verse, may have been used with a special reference to the "hundred brazen gates" of Babylon (Herod. i. 179).

⁽²⁾ **Make the crooked places straight.**—Better, *make the dwelling-places smooth—i.e.,* remove all obstacles (comp. xl. 4, xlii. 16).

⁽³⁾ **The treasures of darkness . . .**—The heaped-up wealth of "gold-abounding" Babylon. The capture of Sardis, with all the riches of Crœsus, must have been almost as fruitful in plunder. (Herod. i. 84). The conqueror was to see in his victories the token of the protection of Jehovah, and so accept his vocation as the redeemer of His people.

⁽⁴⁾ **For Jacob my servant . . .**—The words "servant" and "elect" show that the prophet speaks of the ideal Israel, the true *Ecclesia*, rather than of the nation as such outwardly, though this also, as including the other, shared in the outward blessings of the election. Essentially, the words declare that the world's history is ordered with a view to the true *Ecclesia*.

Called thee by thy name.—Either as predicting the actual name of Koresh, or as giving the titles of "Messiah" and "shepherd." The surname clearly refers to these.

Though thou hast not known me.—Better, *when thou didst not know me,* either as referring to a time prior to the recognition by Cyrus of Jehovah as the God of heaven (Ezra i. 1, 2), or, possibly, prior to his birth (comp. chap. xlix. 1; Jer. i. 5).

⁽⁵⁾ **There is no God beside me.**—Commonly, the formula is used in antithesis to polytheism. Possibly we may think of it here as in contrast with the dualism of Persia, or, if that be assigned to a later date, of Babylonia.

I girded thee.—The opposite of the "loosing," or "ungirding," of verse 1, and so implying the idea of giving strength.

⁽⁷⁾ **I make peace, and create evil . . .**—The words have no bearing on the insoluble problem of what we call the origin of evil. "Evil," as opposed to "peace" or prosperity, is suffering, but not sin; normally, in the Divine counsels, at once the consequence and corrective of moral evil (comp. chap. xlvii. 11, lvii. 1.)

⁽⁸⁾ **Let the skies pour down righteousness . . .**—The vision is that of a new heaven and a new earth, in which righteousness is at once as the rain that falls from the one, and as the product of the other.

⁽⁹⁾ **Woe unto him that striveth . . .**—The sequence of thought is not at first apparent. Were those who strove, the heathen nations who resisted Cyrus, or Israelites who desired some other deliverer, say a prince of the house of David? The latter seems more probable. In either case men were guilty of the folly of criticising the Almighty.

Let the potsherd strive . . .—The sentence, as the italics show, is abrupt, but is better taken without inserting the verbs, and in apposition with the pronoun —*Woe unto him . . . a potsherd among the potsherds;* a frail mortal like all his fellows.

Shall the clay say . . .—The potsherd suggests the potter, not without an allusive reference to the history of man's creation in Gen. ii. 7. As in Jer. xviii. 1—10; Rom. ix. 20, 21, the thought pressed is that of absolute sovereignty, the belief in the wisdom and equity of that sovereignty being kept in the background, as a reserve force. The two clauses represent different aspects of presumption—the first questions, the other arrogantly condemns. The potter's vessel says that the potter "has no hands," is without creative power or skill.

⁽¹⁰⁾ **Woe unto him . . .**—The implied argument is that men accept the accident of birth without questioning father or mother as to that which lay beyond the control of either. Should they not *a fortiori* accept what God orders for nations and individual men?

⁽¹¹⁾ **Ask me of things to come . . .**—As it stands, the verse calls men to consult the Holy One of Israel, and not the oracles of the heathen, about the future, to leave His works to His own control, and this falls in with chap. xliv. 25, 26. A slight alteration of the text gives a meaning much more coherent with the immediate context: *Will ye question me concerning things*

command ye me. (12) I have made the earth, and created man upon it: I, *even* my hands, have stretched out the heavens, and all their host have I commanded. (13) I have raised him up in righteousness, and I will ¹direct all his ways: he shall ᵃbuild my city, and he shall let go my captives, not for price nor reward, saith the LORD of hosts.

(14) Thus saith the LORD, The labour of Egypt, and merchandise of Ethiopia and of the Sabeans, men of stature, shall come over unto thee, and they shall be thine: they shall come after thee; in chains they shall come over, and they shall fall down unto thee, they shall make supplication unto thee, *saying,* Surely God *is* in thee; and *there is* none else, *there is* no God.

(15) Verily thou *art* a God that hidest thyself, O God of Israel, the Saviour.

(16) They shall be ashamed, and also confounded, all of them: they shall go to confusion together *that are* ᵇmakers of idols. (17) *But* Israel shall be saved in the LORD with an everlasting salvation: ye shall not be ashamed nor confounded world without end.

(18) For thus saith the LORD that created the heavens; God himself that formed the earth and made it; he hath established it, he created it not in vain, he formed it to be inhabited: I *am* the LORD; and *there is* none else. (19) I have not spoken in ᶜsecret, in a dark place of the earth: I said not unto the seed of Jacob, Seek ye me in vain: I the LORD speak righteousness, I declare things that are right. (20) Assemble yourselves and come; draw near together, ye *that are* escaped of the nations: they have no knowledge that set up the wood of their graven image, and pray unto a god *that* cannot save. (21) Tell ye, and bring *them* near; yea, let them take counsel together: who hath declared this from ancient time? *who* hath told it from that time? *have* not I the LORD? and *there is* no God else beside me; a just God and a Saviour; *there is* none beside me. (22) Look unto me, and be ye saved, all the ends of the earth: for I *am* God,

¹ Or, *make straight.*

a 2 Chron. 36. 22; Ezra 1. 1; ch. 44. 28.

b ch. 44. 11.

c Deut. 30. 11.

---

to come, concerning my sons . . . *will ye command me!* This was what they were practically doing when they murmured against the providence of God.

(12) **I have made . . .**—The Creator is also the Ruler, supreme in history as in nature.

(13) **I have raised him up in righteousness . . .**—This was the answer to the murmurers. It would be seen by the results, the city rebuilt, the exiles restored to their home, that the conquests of Cyrus had been ordered by the loving righteousness of Jehovah; and he would do this, not through the greed and ambition of other conquerors, but because the spirit of the Lord stirred him (2 Chron. xxxvi. 22).

(14) **Thus saith the Lord . . .**—A new section opens. In chap. xliii. 3, Egypt, Ethiopia, Seba, had been given to Cyrus, as a reward, or ransom, for the deliverance of Israel. Here the prophet goes a step farther, and contemplates them as coming, in the spirit of a voluntary surrender, as proselytes to the faith of Israel, in self-imposed bondage, offering to Israel, as one with God, the "supplication" which, elsewhere, is offered to Jehovah. The promise reminds us of Pss. lxviii. 31, lxxii. 10, and yet more of chaps. xix. 23, lx. 5—7. A partial fulfilment may have been found in the command given by Cyrus, that these and other nations should assist in the work of rebuilding the Temple (Ezra i. 4). Egypt and Ethiopia send the products of their labour. The Sabæans (*sc.* the people of Meroe), strong, but not wealthy, come freely to offer their own labour.

(15) **Verily thou art a God that hidest thyself . . .**—The words have been variously taken: (1) as continuing the wondering homage of the heathen; (2) as spoken by the prophet as he surveys the unsearchable ways of God. (Comp. Rom. xi. 33.) Through the long years of exile He had seemed to hide Himself, to be negligent of His people (chaps. viii. 17, liv. 8; Ps. lv. 1) or unable to help them. Now it would be seen that He had all along been as the Strong one (*El*) working for their deliverance.

(17) **World without end.**—Literally, *for the ages,* or *æons on æons* in Ps. lxxvii. 5.

(18) **He hath established it . . .**—*i.e.,* prepared it (see Deut. xxxii. 6; Gen. xlii. 16) for human habitation. It was not a *tohu* or chaos (Gen. i. 2; Isa. xxiv. 10), but the scene of human action. We note the grandeur of the prophet's thoughts of creation.

(19) **I have not spoken in secret.**—The words are in marked contrast to the thought expressed in verse 15. God had been all along revealing Himself, not like the oracles of the heathen, in the gloom of caves and darkened shrines (chaps. viii. 19, lxv. 4, xxix. 4), but in the broad daylight of history and in the law written on men's hearts. He had bidden men seek Him not in chaos, but in a world of order, and to recognise His utterances by their righteousness.

(20) **Ye that are escaped of the nations.**—Primarily, the words point to the survivors of the conquests of Cyrus, who are contemplated as acknowledging the God of Israel. Ultimately the words find their fulfilment in the conversion of the heathen to the true anointed of Jehovah, of whom Cyrus was a type. They will bear witness from their experience to the vanity of idols. They will learn that it does not avail to set up (or *carry*) their idols in religious processions (Jer. x. 5; Amos v. 26; 1 Sam. iv. 4).

(21) **Tell ye, and bring them near.**—Yet another challenge to the idols and their worshippers.

A just God and a Saviour.—Stress is laid on the union of the two attributes which in human actions are often thought incompatible. (Comp. Ps. lxxxv. 10.) In virtue of that union the invitation of verse 22 is

Jehovah's Care for ISAIAH, XLVI. *the Remnant of Israel.*

and *there is* none else. (23) I have sworn by myself, the word is gone out of my mouth *in* righteousness, and shall not return, That unto me every *a*knee shall bow, every tongue shall swear. (24) [1]Surely, shall *one* say, in the LORD have I [2]righteousness and strength: *even* to him shall *men* come; and all that are incensed against him shall be ashamed. (25) In the LORD shall all the seed of Israel be justified, and shall glory.

CHAPTER XLVI.—(1) Bel boweth down, Nebo stoopeth, their idols were upon the beasts, and upon the cattle: your carriages *were* heavy loaden; they are a burden to the weary *beast*. (2) They stoop, they bow down together; they could not deliver the burden, but [3]themselves are gone into captivity.

(3) Hearken unto me, O house of Jacob, and all the remnant of the house of Israel, which are borne *by me* from the belly, which are carried from the womb: (4) and *even* to *your* old age I *am* he; and *even* to hoar hairs will I carry *you*: I have made, and I will bear; even I will carry, and will deliver *you*.

(5) *b*To whom will ye liken me, and make *me* equal, and compare me, that we may be like? (6) They lavish gold out of the bag, and weigh silver in the balance, *and* hire a goldsmith; and he maketh it a god: they fall down, yea, they worship. (7) They bear him upon the shoulder, they carry him, and set him in his place, and he standeth; from his place shall he not remove: yea, *one* shall cry unto him, yet can he not answer, nor save him out of his trouble. (8) Remember this, and shew yourselves men: bring *it* again to mind, O ye transgressors.

a Rom. 14. 11; Phil. 2. 10.

[1] Or, *Surely he shall say of me, In the* LORD *is all righteousness and strength.*

[2] Heb., *righteousnesses.*

[3] Heb., *their soul.*

b ch. 40. 18, 25.

---

addressed to all the ends of the world. The offer of salvation is universal.

(23) **I have sworn by myself.**—The highest conceivable form of asseveration (Gen. xxii. 16; Jer. xxii. 5; Heb. vi. 13).

Unto me every knee shall bow.—The faith of Israel becomes the religion of mankind, though, from the prophet's standpoint, Israel does not lose its distinctive nationality. We note the application of the words to the Christ in Phil. ii. 10; Rom. xiv. 11.

(24) **Surely, shall one say.**—The prophet hears that confession as uttered in the far-off time.

(25) **In the Lord.**—We note the germ of the New Testament thought of the mystic union of man with God, in the phrases "in the Lord," "in the Holy Spirit," "in Christ," which embody that thought. Jehovah is the sphere, or region, in which men "live and move and have their being." The seed of Israel, as interpreted by verse 23, includes all who have joined themselves to the true Israel of God.

XLVI.

(1) **Bel boweth down, Nebo stoopeth.**—Bel or Belus ("Lord"), is perhaps identical with Marduk or Merôdach, but see Note on Jer. l. 2. Nabu ("the Revealer") was a kind of Assyrian Hermes. Isaiah sees the idols carried off as spoil, at the command of Cyrus, a heavy burden for the beasts that drag them. An inscription recently deciphered by Sir H. Rawlinson (*Journal of Asiatic Society*, Jan. 1880, quoted by Cheyne) presents the conduct of the conqueror under a somewhat different aspect. In that inscription he describes himself as a worshipper of Bel and Nebo, and prays to them for length of days. The king would seem from this to have been as wide in his syncretic liberalism as Alexander the Great was afterwards. How are we to reconcile the two? May we say that the prophet idealises the policy and character of the king, or that the monotheistic element which appears in his treatment of the Jews (2 Chron. xxxvi. 22, 23; Ezra i. 1, 2) was, after all, dominant in his action, in spite of episodes like that indicated in the inscription. It is possible that the recognition of the Babylonian deities may have followed on the submission of the people, and been preceded by some rougher treatment. Anyhow the contrast makes it probable that the prophecy was not written after the inscription.

Your carriages.—Here, as elsewhere (1 Sam. xvii. 22; Acts xxi. 15) in the sense of things carried; *i.e.*, in this case, the images of the gods, which used to be carried in solemn procession, but are now represented as packed into a load for transport. So Herod. (i. 183) states that Xerxes carried off from Babylon the golden image of Zeus (*sc.* Bel), the grandson thus fulfilling the prediction which his grandfather apparently had left unfulfilled.

(2) **They could not deliver the burden.**—The deities are, for the moment, distinguished from their images. They are powerless to rescue them. So far as they have a soul or being at all, that very being is carried away captive.

(3) **Hearken unto me.**—The prophet's choice of words is singularly emphatic. The false gods are borne away as a burden. The true God bears, *i.e.*, supports, His people. He is able to bear that burden. Every "I" is emphasised in the Hebrew.

(4) **Even to your old age.**—The care of a mother ceases, in the natural course of things, before a man grows old, but the fatherly, we might almost say the *mother-like*, maternal care of Jehovah for His chosen ones endures even to the end of life.

(5) **To whom will ye liken me?**—The argument against idolatry is renewed in nearly its old form (chap. xl. 18—25, xliv. 9—17). The fate of Bel and Nebo is urged against those who thought that they might worship Jehovah as those deities had been worshipped. Such had been the sin of the calves at Bethel and at Dan. Like it had been the act of Israel when it had carried the ark into battle against the Philistines (1 Sam. iv. 5).

(8) **Shew yourselves men.**—As elsewhere, the prophet's challenge is couched in the language of

(9) Remember the former things of old: for I *am* God, and *there is* none else; *I am* God, and *there is* none like me, (10) declaring the end from the beginning, and from ancient times *the things* that are not *yet* done, saying, *a* My counsel shall stand, and I will do all my pleasure: (11) calling a ravenous bird from the east, ¹ the man that executeth my counsel from a far country: yea, I have spoken *it*, I will also bring it to pass; I have purposed *it*, I will also do it.

(12) Hearken unto me, ye stouthearted, that *are* far from righteousness: (13) I bring near my righteousness; it shall not be far off, and my salvation shall not tarry: and I will place salvation in Zion for Israel my glory.

CHAPTER XLVII.—(1) Come down, and sit in the dust, O virgin daughter of Babylon, sit on the ground: *there is* no throne, O daughter of the Chaldeans: for thou shalt no more be called tender and delicate. (2) Take the millstones, and grind meal: uncover thy locks, make bare the leg, uncover the thigh, pass over the rivers. (3) Thy nakedness shall be uncovered, yea, thy shame shall be seen: I will take vengeance, and I will not meet *thee as* a man. (4) *As for* our redeemer, the LORD of hosts *is* his name, the Holy One of Israel. (5) Sit thou silent, and get thee into darkness, O daughter of the Chaldeans: for thou shalt no more be called, The lady of kingdoms.

(6) I was wroth with my people, I have polluted mine inheritance, and given them into thine hand: thou didst shew them no mercy; upon the ancient hast thou very heavily laid thy yoke. (7) And thou saidst, I shall be *b* a lady for ever: so that thou didst not lay these *things* to thy heart, neither didst remember the latter end of it. (8) Therefore hear now this, *thou that art* given to pleasures, that dwellest carelessly, that sayest in thine heart, I *am*, and none else beside

a Ps. 33. 11; Pro. 19. 21 & 21. 30; Heb. 6. 17.

1 Heb., *the man of my counsel.*

b Rev. 18. 7.

---

irony. The worshippers of idols should at least have the courage of their convictions. A conjectural emendation gives the opposite meaning, *Be ye deeply ashamed.*

(9) **I am God.**—The first predicate is *El*, the mighty and strong one, the second *Elohim*, the one true object of worship. The verse that follows asserts what in modern language would be called the omniscience and the omnipotence of God.

(11) **Calling a ravenous bird.**—Cyrus is thus described as Nebuchadnezzar is in Jer. xlix. 22; Ezek. xvii. 3. The image derives a special significance from the fact that the standard borne by Cyrus and his successors was a golden eagle (Xen.; *Cyrop.* vii. 1. 4; *Anab.* i. 10, 12). (Comp. also Matt. xxiv. 28; Luke xvii. 37.) The "sun-rising" is, of course, Persia; the "far country" probably represents Media.

I have spoken.—The word of Jehovah passes, unlike that of the false gods, into a certain and immediate act.

(12) **Ye stouthearted.**—The word, like analogous terms in Ezek. ii. 4, iii. 7, implies at once obduracy and ignorance. Such as these are self-excluded at once from the "righteousness" and the "salvation" of Jehovah, which ultimately imply, and coincide with each other. Their unfaithfulness, however, does not hinder the faithfulness of God. He brings near His salvation to all who are ready to receive it. (Comp. chap. lvi. 1.)

XLVII.

(1) **Come down . . .**—*The virgin daughter of Babylon, i.e.,* Babylon itself, personified as till now unconquered, is called to leave her throne and sit in the dust as a menial slave. The epithets "tender" (better, perhaps, *wanton*) and "delicate" point to the luxury which had been identified with Babylon, and which was now to cease.

(2) **Take the millstones.**—Always the most servile form of female labour (Exod. xi. 5; Job xxxi. 10; Matt. xxiv. 41).

Uncover thy locks.—The picture of suffering is heightened by the fact that the female slave has to wade unveiled, and bare-legged, all sense of shame outraged, to the scene of her labours. The picture is, of course, to be taken symbolically, not literally.

(3) **I will not meet thee as a man.**—The words in italics show that the phrase is difficult. Omitting them we get *I shall not meet a man, i.e.,* there will be none to oppose me, or *I will not spare a man.*

(4) **As for our redeemer . . .**—The verse comes in somewhat abruptly, but may be viewed (unless we suppose it to have been originally a marginal addition, which has found its way into the text) as Israel's song of praise, as it looks on the overthrow of Babylon. As such it finds a parallel in the overthrow of the mystical Babylon in Rev. xviii. 20.

(5) **Sit thou silent.** — Another contrast between the stir of the rejoicing city and the stillness of its later desolation. "The lady" (we might almost say, *the empress*) "of kingdoms" was reduced to the loneliness of widowhood.

(6) **I was wroth with my people . . .**—The sin of Babylon was that she had gone beyond her commission as the chastiser of Israel, casting off all reverence for age, and making even the *old men* do the hard tasks of bond-slaves (Lam. iv. 16, v. 12). (Comp. Zech. i. 15.)

(7) **Thou saidst . . .**—The boastful confidence of Babylon in her own perpetuity blinded her, as it had long blinded other nations, to "these things," *scil.* the Divine law that pride and cruelty bring their own Nemesis.

(8) **I am, and none else beside me . . .**—The boasts of Babylon are purposely embodied by the

me; I shall not sit *as* a widow, neither shall I know the loss of children: ⁽⁹⁾ but these two *ᵃthings* shall come to thee in a moment in one day, the loss of children, and widowhood: they shall come upon thee in their perfection for the multitude of thy sorceries, *and* for the great abundance of thine enchantments. ⁽¹⁰⁾ For thou hast trusted in thy wickedness: thou hast said, None seeth me. Thy wisdom and thy knowledge, it hath ¹perverted thee; and thou hast said in thine heart, I *am*, and none else beside me. ⁽¹¹⁾ Therefore shall evil come upon thee; thou shalt not know ²from whence it riseth: and mischief shall fall upon thee; thou shalt not be able to ³put it off: and desolation shall come upon thee suddenly, *which* thou shalt not know.

⁽¹²⁾ Stand now with thine enchantments, and with the multitude of thy sorceries, wherein thou hast laboured from thy youth; if so be thou shalt be able to profit, if so be thou mayest prevail. ⁽¹³⁾ Thou art wearied in the multitude of thy counsels. Let now the ⁴astrologers, the stargazers, ⁵the monthly prognosticators, stand up, and save thee from *these things* that shall come upon thee. ⁽¹⁴⁾ Behold, they shall be as stubble; the fire shall burn them; they shall not deliver ⁶themselves from the power of the flame: *there shall* not *be* a coal to warm at, *nor* fire to sit before it. ⁽¹⁵⁾ Thus shall they be unto thee with whom thou hast laboured, *even* thy merchants, from thy youth: they shall wander every one to his quarter; none shall save thee.

CHAPTER XLVIII.— ⁽¹⁾ Hear ye this, O house of Jacob, which are called by the name of Israel, and are come forth out of the waters of Judah, which swear by the name of the LORD, and make mention of the God of Israel, *but* not in truth, nor in righteousness. ⁽²⁾ For they call themselves of the holy city, and stay themselves upon the God of Israel; The LORD of hosts *is* his name.

⁽³⁾ I have declared the former things from the beginning; and they went forth out of my mouth, and I shewed them; I did *them* suddenly, and they came to pass. ⁽⁴⁾ Because I knew that

a ch. 51. 19.

1 Or, *caused thee to turn away.*

2 Heb., *the morning thereof.*

3 Heb., *expiate.*

4 Heb., *viewers of the heavens.*

5 Heb., *that give knowledge concerning the months.*

6 Heb., *their souls.*

---

prophet in p_£¹⁷ₐₛ that recall Jehovah's assertion of His own eternity. She practically deified herself. So a like boast is put into the mouth of Nineveh in Zeph. ii. 15, and was repeated almost verbally by the poets of Rome: *Terrarum dea gentiumque Roma, cui par est nihil, et nihil secundum* (Martial).

⁽⁹⁾ **In their perfection.**—Better, *in their completeness.* She should taste the full bitterness of widowhood and bereavement.

For the multitude of thy sorceries.—Better, *in spite of* . . .

⁽¹⁰⁾ **For thou hast trusted in thy wickedness** . . .—Babylon, like other nations that have followed in her steps, took for its law that Might was Right, practically denied the existence of a Ruler who saw and judged, and boasted of its wisdom. The context implies that the special form of wisdom spoken of was that of astrology and magic.

⁽¹¹⁾ **Thou shalt not be able to put it off** . . .—The words have been variously rendered: (1) *of which thou shalt know no dawn,* i.e., after the night of calamity; and (2) *which thou shalt not be able to charm away.* Stress is laid on the destruction being at once unforeseen and irretrievable.

⁽¹²⁾ **If so be thou shalt be able** . . .—The words come with a subtle tone of irony. *Persevere in thy enchantments . . . perchance thou wilt be able to profit, perchance thou wilt strike terror.*

⁽¹³⁾ **Let now the astrologers** . . .—The three words describe two aspects of the same art—(1) the *dividers of the heavens,* assigning stellar influences to the signs of the Zodiac; (2) the "star-gazers," further defined as *those who make known things to come at the new moon.* The Assyrian and Chaldæan observers compiled an almanack, in which the days of the month were noted as severally lucky or unlucky for the incidents of war or of home-life, as the case might be.

⁽¹⁴⁾ **There shall not be a coal to warm at.**—Better, *it shall not be* . . . The destroying flame shall be altogether other than the fire on the hearth, at which a man can sit and warm himself.

⁽¹⁵⁾ **Thy merchants, from thy youth** . . .—The commerce of Babylon is specially prominent in all descriptions. (Comp. Herod. i. 194—196; Ezek. xvii. 4.) The time was coming when those who had thronged her markets would desert her and leave her to her desolation.

XLVIII.

⁽¹⁾ **Are come forth out of the waters of Judah.**—The words limit the wider terms of Jacob and Israel to the Judæan exiles. For the phrase, comp. "ye that are of the fountains of Israel" (Ps. lxviii. 26). The ideal attributes of Israel, "swearing by the name of Jehovah . . ." are pressed in contrast with their actual state of hypocrisy and unrighteousness.

⁽²⁾ **They call themselves of the holy city** . . .—The words of praise are spoken, as the preceding words show, with a touch of irony. Those who so boasted were not true citizens of Zion (Ps. xv. 1; Matt. iii. 9). They did not enter into all that was implied in their confession of Jehovah Sabaoth.

⁽³⁾ **I have declared** . . .—Once more, for the seventh time, the prophet presses the fact of the Divine foreknowledge, not, as before, against the "no-faith" of the heathen, but against the "little faith" of Judah.

⁽⁴⁾ **Because I knew that thou art obstinate** . . .—The point is that Jehovah foresees not only the

The Argument from Prophecy.   ISAIAH, XLVIII.   *Cyrus, the Beloved of Jehovah.*

thou art ¹ obstinate, and thy neck *is* an iron sinew, and thy brow brass; ⁽⁵⁾ I have even from the beginning declared *it* to thee; before it came to pass I shewed *it* thee: lest thou shouldest say, Mine idol hath done them, and my graven image, and my molten image, hath commanded them. ⁽⁶⁾ Thou hast heard, see all this; and will not ye declare *it?* I have shewed thee new things from this time, even hidden things, and thou didst not know them. ⁽⁷⁾ They are created now, and not from the beginning; even before the day when thou heardest them not; lest thou shouldest say, Behold, I knew them. ⁽⁸⁾ Yea, thou heardest not; yea, thou knewest not; yea, from that time *that* thine ear was not opened: for I knew that thou wouldest deal very treacherously, and wast called a transgressor from the womb. ⁽⁹⁾ For my name's sake will I defer mine anger, and for my praise will I refrain for thee, that I cut thee not off. ⁽¹⁰⁾ Behold, I have refined thee, but not ²with silver; I have chosen thee in the furnace of affliction. ⁽¹¹⁾ For mine own sake, *even* for mine own sake, will I do *it*: for how should *my name* be polluted? and ᵃI will not give my glory unto another.

⁽¹²⁾ Hearken unto me, O Jacob and Israel, my called; I *am* he; I *am* the ᵇfirst, I also *am* the last. ⁽¹³⁾ Mine hand also hath laid the foundation of the earth, and ³my right hand hath spanned the heavens: *when* I call unto them, they stand up together. ⁽¹⁴⁾ All ye, assemble yourselves, and hear; which among them hath declared these *things?* The LORD hath loved him: he will do his pleasure on Babylon, and his arm *shall be on* the Chaldeans. ⁽¹⁵⁾ I, *even* I, have spoken; yea, I have called him: I have brought him, and he shall make his way prosperous.

⁽¹⁶⁾ Come ye near unto me, hear ye this; I have not spoken in secret from

---

1 Heb., *hard.*

2 Or, *for silver.*

a ch. 42. 8.

b ch. 41. 4 & 44. 6; Rev. 1. 17 & 22. 13.

3 Or, *the palm of my right hand hath spread out.*

---

conquests of Cyrus, but the obduracy of His own people. In Egypt (Jer. xliv.) and in Babylon, as of old, they were still a stiff-necked people, inclined (verse 5), to ascribe their deliverance to another god, and to worship that god in the form of a graven image.

⁽⁶⁾ **Thou hast heard . . .**—The appeal is to the conscience of the exiles. They had heard the prediction. They are bidden to consider it all. Should not they declare the impression it had made on them?

I have shewed thee.—Better, *I shew thee,* as a present incipient act.

New things.—The "new things" are those that lie in a more distant future than the conquests of Cyrus, which are referred to as "former things."

⁽⁷⁾ **They are created now . . .**—The verb is an unusual one, as applied to the events of history. What is meant is that the things which had been from the beginning in the mind of God are now, for the first time, manifested, through the prophet, as about to pass into act. What these are the prophet develops in the following chapters, as including the spiritual redemption and restoration of Israel. They were kept in store, as it were, to make men wonder (Rom. xvi. 25, 26).

Even before the day when . . .—Better, *and before to-day thou heardest them not. . . .* The reason given for what we might almost call this method of reserve and reticence, was that the people had been till now unprepared to receive the truth, and in their state it would but have increased their condemnation (John xvi. 12; Mark iv. 33).

⁽⁹⁾ **For my name's sake . . .**—The thought is two-fold, in answer to the implied question why Jehovah had not punished so guilty a people: (1) after the manner of men, that had He destroyed His chosen people, the nations of the world would have thought Him changeable and capricious; (2) taking "name" as the symbol of character, that He might assert His own everlasting righteousness and love, as willing to save rather than destroy.

⁽¹⁰⁾ **I have refined thee, but not with silver . . .**—The meaning is obscure, and perhaps depends on some unknown process in ancient metallurgy. Commonly the refining of silver is taken as a parable of God's dealings with His people (chap. i. 25; Ezek. xxii. 18—22; Mal. iii. 3). Here the thought seems to be that the discipline had been less fierce than that of the refiner's fire. Silver was "purified seven times in the fire" (Ps. xii. 6); but that would have brought about the destruction of Israel, and He sought to spare them.

I have chosen thee.—Better, *I have tested thee.*

⁽¹¹⁾ **Will I do it . . .**—The neuter pronoun includes the whole work of redemption.

For how should my name be polluted?—The italics show that "my name" is not in the Hebrew, but the context requires its insertion as from verse 9, or that of "my glory" from the clause that follows. The "pollution" or desecration of the name of Jehovah would follow, it is implied, on the non-completion of His redeeming work.

⁽¹²⁾ **Hearken unto me, O Jacob.**—The prophet is drawing near to the end of the first great section of his book, and his conclusion takes the form of a condensed epitome of the great argument of chaps. xl.—xlvii., asserting the oneness, the eternity, the omnipotence, the omniscience of Jehovah.

⁽¹⁴⁾ **All ye, assemble yourselves.**—The challenge is addressed as before (chap. xliii. 9) to the worshippers of idols.

The Lord hath loved him.—Better, *He whom the Lord loveth will do his pleasure.* The context leaves it uncertain whether the "pleasure" and the "arm" are those of Cyrus or Jehovah. The latter seems to give a preferable meaning. There is, perhaps, an allusive reference to the idea implied in the name of the great king of Israel (David, "beloved," or "darling"). Cyrus was to be even as a second David, beloved of the Lord.

⁽¹⁶⁾ **Come ye near unto me.**—Here the address would seem to be made to Israel. At first Jehovah

| *The Departure from Babylon.* | ISAIAH, XLIX. | *The polished Staff.* |

the beginning; from the time that it was, there *am* I: and now the Lord God, and his Spirit, hath sent me. ⁽¹⁷⁾ Thus saith the Lord, thy Redeemer, the Holy One of Israel; I *am* the Lord thy God which teacheth thee to profit, which leadeth thee by the way *that* thou shouldest go. ⁽¹⁸⁾ O that thou hadst hearkened to my commandments! then had thy peace been as a river, and thy righteousness as the waves of the sea: ⁽¹⁹⁾ thy seed also had been as the sand, and the offspring of thy bowels like the gravel thereof; his name should not have been cut off nor destroyed from before me. ⁽²⁰⁾ Go ye forth of Babylon, flee ye from the Chaldeans, with a voice of singing declare ye, tell this, utter it *even* to the end of the earth; say ye, The Lord ^a hath redeemed his servant Jacob. ⁽²¹⁾ And they thirsted not *when* he led them through the deserts: he ^b caused the waters to flow out of the rock for them: he clave the rock also, and the waters gushed out.

⁽²²⁾ ^c *There is* no peace, saith the Lord, unto the wicked.

CHAPTER XLIX.—⁽¹⁾ Listen, O isles, unto me; and hearken, ye people, from far; The Lord hath called me from the womb; from the bowels of my mother hath he made mention of my name. ⁽²⁾ And he hath made my mouth like a sharp sword; in the shadow of his hand hath he hid me, and made me a polished shaft; in his quiver hath he hid me; ⁽³⁾ and said unto me, Thou *art* my servant, O Israel, in whom I will be

a Exod. 19. 4, 6.

b Exod. 17. 6; Num. 20. 11.

c ch. 57. 21.

---

appears as the speaker, and as using much the same language as before. At the close the prophet appears abruptly, as speaking in his own person. Perhaps, indeed, the prophet is the speaker throughout. A paraphrase will perhaps help to explain the sequence of thought. "I have not from the beginning of my prophetic work spoken in dark, ambiguous speeches like the oracles of the heathen. From the time that the great work began to unfold itself I was present, contemplating it. Now the time of revelation has come. *The Lord God hath sent me* (this is the Hebrew order); *and His Spirit.* This gives, it is believed, an adequate explanation. By some interpreters the closing words are referred to the mysterious "Servant of the Lord," and by others the Spirit is made the object and not the subject of the word "sent."

⁽¹⁷⁾ **The Lord thy God which teacheth thee to profit.**—The words applied to the natural human, perhaps we may add, to the specially national, desire, to make a good investment. The question what was profitable? was one to which men returned very different answers. It was the work of the true Redeemer to lead men to the one true imperishable gain (comp. Matt. xvi. 26), to lead them in the one right way (John xiv. 4—6).

⁽¹⁸⁾ **Then had thy peace been as a river.**—Literally, "as *the* river," *i.e.*, the Euphrates, which for the Babylonian exiles was a natural standard of comparison. "Righteousness," as elsewhere, includes the idea of the blessedness which is its recompense. United with "peace" it implies every element of prosperity.

⁽¹⁹⁾ **Like the gravel thereof.**—Literally, *as the bowels thereof, i.e.*, as that within the bowels of the sand, the living creatures that swarm in countless myriads in the sea. The two verses utter the sigh which has come from the heart of all true teachers as they contemplate the actual state of men and compare it with what might have been. (Comp. Deut. xxxii. 29, 30; Luke xix. 42.)

⁽²⁰⁾ **Go ye forth of Babylon . . .**—The sorrow and sighing are past, and the prophet speaks to the remnant that shall return. They are to act without fear on the promises of God, on the decree of Cyrus, and to start at once on their homeward journey, and as they go, to proclaim what great things God hath done for them.

⁽²¹⁾ **He caused the waters to flow . . .**—A dead prosaic literalism makes men wonder that there is no record of such wonders on the return from Babylon. A truer insight recognises that the "water out of the rock" is, as ever, the symbol of spiritual refreshment (chaps. xli. 17—19, xliii. 19, 20; John iv. 10).

⁽²²⁾ **There is no peace.**—The warning was needed even for the liberated exiles. There was an implied condition as to all God's gifts. Even the highest blessings, freedom and home, were no real blessings to those who were unworthy of them.

XLIX.

⁽¹⁾ **Listen, O isles . . .**—The argument against idolatry has been brought to its close, and a new section opens, and with it there is a new speaker, the mysterious "Servant of the Lord," (chap. xlii. 1), at once identified with Israel (verse 3), in fulfilling its ideal, and yet distinguished from it, as its Restorer and Redeemer. "Isles" as before stand vaguely for "far-off countries." The invitation is addressed to the heathen far and wide.

The Lord hath called me from the womb. —The words indicate a predestined vocation. (Comp. Jer. i. 5; Luke i. 15, 41; Gal. i. 15.) Admitting the thought of a Divine order working in human history, the idea of such a vocation follows in inevitable sequence.

⁽²⁾ **He hath made my mouth like a sharp sword.**—The words indicate at once the spiritual nature of the "Servant's" victories. It is his speech that wounds and heals, his words that go like winged arrows to their mark. The description finds an echo in Heb. iv. 12; Rev. i. 16, xix. 15; Eph. vi. 17. The "shaft" is "polished," as piercing without impediment. It is "hid in the quiver," reserved, in the drama of the world's history, and in each crisis of the Servant's life, till the "hour was come," the appointed "fulness of time" (John ii. 4, vii. 6; Gal. iv. 4).

⁽³⁾ **Thou art my servant, O Israel.**—Not that the "Servant" is merely the nation, but that he fulfils

The Servant of Jehovah as a   ISAIAH, XLIX.   *Light to the Gentiles*

glorified. (4) Then I said, I have laboured in vain, I have spent my strength for nought, and in vain: *yet* surely my judgment *is* with the LORD, and ¹my work with my God. (5) And now, saith the LORD that formed me from the womb *to be* his servant, to bring Jacob again to him, ²Though Israel be not gathered, yet shall I be glorious in the eyes of the LORD, and my God shall be my strength. (6) And he said, ³It is a light thing that thou shouldest be my servant to raise up the tribes of Jacob, and to restore the ⁴preserved of Israel: I will also give thee for a ᵃlight to the Gentiles, that thou mayest be my salvation unto the end of the earth.

(7) Thus saith the LORD, the Redeemer of Israel, *and* his Holy One, ⁵to him whom man despiseth, to him whom the nation abhorreth, to a servant of rulers, Kings shall see and arise, princes also shall worship, because of the LORD that is faithful, *and* the Holy One of Israel, and he shall choose thee.

(8) Thus saith the LORD, ᵇIn an acceptable time have I heard thee, and in a day of salvation have I helped thee: and I will preserve thee, and give thee for a covenant of the people, to ⁶establish the earth, to cause to inherit the desolate heritages; (9) that thou mayest say ᶜto the prisoners, Go forth; to them that *are* in darkness, Shew yourselves. They shall feed in the ways, and their pastures *shall be* in all high places. (10) They shall not ᵈhunger nor thirst; neither shall the heat nor sun smite them: for he that hath mercy on them shall lead them, even by the springs of water shall he guide them. (11) And I will make all my mountains a way, and my highways shall be exalted. (12) Behold, these shall come from far: and, lo, these from the north and from the west; and these from the land of Sinim.

1 Or, *my reward.*
2 Or, *That Israel may be gathered to him, and I may, &c.*
3 Or, *Art thou lighter than that thou shouldest &c.*
4 Or, *desolations.*
ᵃ ch. 42. 6.
5 Or, *to him that is despised in soul.*
ᵇ 2 Cor. 6. 2.
6 Or, *raise up.*
ᶜ ch. 42. 7.
ᵈ Rev. 7. 16.

---

its ideal. "Israel" had begun with being an individual name. It should be so once more in the person of Him who would be truly "a prince with God."

In whom I will be glorified.—Better, *in whom I will glorify myself.* The words find a conscious echo in John xiii. 31, 32, xvii. 1–5.

(4) **Then I said.**—The accents of disappointment sound strangely on coming from the lips of the true Servant; but the prophet had learnt by his own experience that this formed part of the discipline of every true servant of God, in proportion to the thoroughness of his service, and therefore it was not strange to him that *the* ideal Servant should also taste that bitterness. We find in the prophet of Anathoth a partial illustration of the law (Jer. xx. 14). We find its highest fulfilment in the cries of Gethsemane and Golgotha, The sense of failure is surmounted only, as here, by looking to another judgment than man's, and another *reward* (better than "work"). (Comp. 1 Cor. iv. 3.)

(5) **Though Israel be not gathered.**—Better, *and that Israel be gathered to him.* The negative, as in chap. ix. 3, comes from an error of transcription; for "yet" read *and*. The Servant falls back upon the greatness of the work committed to him, that of restoring Israel, and is certain that sooner or later it will be accomplished. Comp. the argument of Rom. ix.–xi.

(6) **And he said.**—The words are repeated from "saith the Lord" of the preceding verse, where they had been followed by a long parenthesis. The Servant becomes conscious of a higher mission. All national barriers are broken down. He is to be the bearer of a message of peace to the whole race of mankind, and has "other sheep not of this fold" (John x. 16).

(7) **To him whom man despiseth.**—Literally, *to one despised of soul*, where "soul" may either stand for "men" as in the Authorised version, or imply that the contempt enters into the soul of the sufferer. (Comp. Ps. cv. 18.) The point of the words lies in the fact that the doer of the great work is to be despised by the world's judgment or by his own people, by proud rulers (comp. 1 Cor. i. 27); and yet he, and no other, will accomplish it.

(8) **In an acceptable time.**—Literally, *in the season of good pleasure.* The message is borne in on the soul of the servant as the secret of confidence and strength. It will be his work to be the link in a new covenant with the people, an idea afterwards developed by Jeremiah (xxxi. 31), and reaching its fulfilment in Matt. xxvi. 28; Luke xxii. 20.

To cause to inherit the desolate heritages.—The prophet may have thought of a literal fulfilment such as was probably in part accomplished by Zerubbabel. We, seeing the prediction in the light of its fulfilment, look to the spiritual inheritance.

(9) **That thou mayest say to the prisoners . . .**—Comp. chap. xlii. 6, 7. Here, perhaps, the thought of the deliverance of Israel is more exclusively prominent; but the words have obviously a yet wider and higher application.

(10) **Neither shall the heat . . .**—The word is the same as the "parched ground" of chap. xxxv. 7, and stands, as there, for the mirage of the scorching desert.

(11) **My mountains . . . my highways . . .**—The pronoun asserts the universal lordship of Jehovah. The whole earth is His.

(12) **From the west.**—Literally, *from the sea*, which commonly has this meaning. In Ps. cvii. 3, however, it clearly stands for the south, and is probably used in that sense here. In this case "from far" stands for the south, probably for the distant Ethiopia, where Jewish exiles had already found their way (Zeph. iii. 10).

From the land of Sinim.—The region thus named is clearly the *ultima Thule* of the prophet's horizon, and this excludes the "Sinites" of Canaan (Gen. x. 17), and the Sin (Pelusium) of Egypt. Modern scholars are almost unanimous in making it refer to the Chinese. Phœnician or Babylonian commerce may have made

The pitying Love of Jehovah. ISAIAH, XLIX. *Kings the nursing Fathers of Israel.*

(13) Sing, O heavens; and be joyful, O earth; and break forth into singing, O mountains: for the LORD hath comforted his people, and will have mercy upon his afflicted.

(14) But Zion said, The LORD hath forsaken me, and my Lord hath forgotten me. (15) Can a woman forget her sucking child, [1] that she should not have compassion on the son of her womb? yea, they may forget, yet will I not forget thee. (16) Behold, I have graven thee upon the palms of *my* hands; thy walls *are* continually before me. (17) Thy children shall make haste; thy destroyers and they that made thee waste shall go forth of thee. (18) *a* Lift up thine eyes round about, and behold: all these gather themselves together, *and* come to thee. *As* I live, saith the LORD, thou shalt surely clothe thee with them all, as with an ornament, and bind them *on thee*, as a bride *doeth*. (19) For thy waste and thy desolate places, and the land of thy destruction, shall even now be too narrow by reason of the inhabitants, and they that swallowed thee up shall be far away. (20) The children which thou shalt have, after thou hast lost the other, shall say again in thine ears, The place *is* too strait for me: give place to me that I may dwell. (21) Then shalt thou say in thine heart, Who hath begotten me these, seeing I have lost my children, and am desolate, a captive, and removing to and fro? and who hath brought up these? Behold, I was left alone; these, where *had* they been?

(22) Thus saith the Lord GOD, Behold, I will lift up mine hand to the Gentiles, and set up my standard to the people: and they shall bring thy sons in *their* [2] arms, and thy daughters shall be carried upon *their* shoulders. (23) And kings shall be thy [3] nursing fathers, and their [4] queens thy nursing mothers: they shall bow down to thee with *their* face toward the earth, and *b* lick up the dust of thy feet; and thou shalt know

[1] Heb., *from having compassion.*
a ch. 60. 4.
[2] Heb., *bosom.*
[3] Heb., *nourishers.*
[4] Heb., *princesses.*
b Ps. 72. 9.

---

that people known, at least by name, to the prophet. Recent Chinese researches have brought to light traditions that in B.C. 2353 (and again in B.C. 1110) a people came from a strange western land, bringing with them a tortoise, on the shell of which was a history of the world, in strange characters "like tadpoles." It is inferred that this was a cuneiform inscription, and the theory has been recently maintained that this was the origin of the present Chinese mode of writing. (See Cheyne's "Excursus," ii. p. 20, and an elaborate article on "China and Assyria" in the *Quarterly Review* for October, 1882.) Porcelain with Chinese characters has been found, it may be added, in the ruins of the Egyptian Thebes (Wilkinson, *Ancient Egyptians*, 1st ser., iii. 106—109). All recent discoveries tend to the conclusion that the commerce of the great ancient monarchies was wider than scholars of the sixteenth century imagined. The actual immigration of Jews into China is believed to have taken place about B.C. 200 (Delitzsch *in loc*).

(13) **Sing, O heavens.**—As in chap. xliv. 23, all nature is invited to join in the chorus of praise for the deliverance of Israel.

(14) **But Zion said . . .**—In the midst of all that Jehovah was doing for his people they were still showing their little faith, and thinking of themselves as forsaken. They shared the misgivings which were felt even by *the* Servant, but they did not rise out of them as quickly as He did into the full assurance of faith.

(15) **Can a woman forget . . . ?**—The love of Jehovah for His chosen ones is more than that of a father, more tender and unchangeable even than the maternal love which exists often in the most depraved. Even that may perish, but not so His pitying affection.

(16) **Behold, I have graven thee . . .**—The words point to the almost universal practice of tattooing. A man thus "engraved" the name of his god, or the outlines of his home, or the face of her he loved, upon his hands or arms. So, by a boldly anthropomorphic figure, Jehovah had "graven" Jerusalem on His hands. He could not open them, *i.e.*, could not act, without being reminded of her. The "walls" may be either those of the earthly city lying in ruins, or those of the heavenly Jerusalem.

(17) **Thy children shall make haste.**—A various reading adopted by the LXX., Targum, and Vulg., gives *thy builders*. They rush to their work of restoration; the destroyers and ravagers go forth.

(18) **Lift up thine eyes.**—The daughter of Zion is called on to gaze on the returning exiles. They shall be her gems and her girdle as the bride of her new espousals. A distant parallel is found in the story of the mother of the Gracchi pointing to her children as more precious jewels than those of her wealthy rival.

(19) **Shall even now be too narrow.**—Literally, with a vivid abruptness, *thou shalt be* . . . The over population of the future is contrasted with the depopulation of the past (chaps. iii. 6, iv. 1).

(20) **The children which thou shalt have . . .** —Better, *the children of thy bereavement* (*i.e.*, born when Zion thought herself bereaved) *shall yet say* . . .

(21) **Who hath begotten me these . . . ?**—Better, *who hath borne* . . . ? The widowed daughter of Zion cannot believe that these crowding children are her own, and asks, Who then is their mother? She, the widowed one, the prisoner, dragged hither and thither, could not claim them.

(22) **The Gentiles . . . the people . . .**—Both words are used of the heathen. They are summoned by the uplifted signal of Jehovah to do their work as nursing fathers, carrying the children *in their bosom*. (Num. xi. 12).

(23) **Kings shall be thy nursing fathers . . .**— As a rule kings gave their children to be brought up by their nobles (2 Kings x. 5). Zion should have

that I *am* the LORD; for they shall not be ashamed that wait for me. (24) Shall the prey be taken from the mighty, or ˡthe lawful captive delivered? (25) But thus saith the LORD, Even the ²captives of the mighty shall be taken away, and the prey of the terrible shall be delivered: for I will contend with him that contendeth with thee, and I will save thy children. (26) And I will feed them that oppress thee with their own flesh; and they shall be drunken with their own ᵃ blood, as with ³sweet wine: and all flesh shall know that I the LORD *am* thy Saviour and thy Redeemer, the mighty One of Jacob.

CHAPTER L.—(1) Thus saith the LORD, Where *is* the bill of your mother's divorcement, whom I have put away? or which of my creditors *is it* to whom I have sold you? Behold, for your iniquities have ye sold yourselves, and for your transgressions is your mother put away. (2) Wherefore, when I came, *was there* no man? when I called, *was there* none to answer? ᵇIs my hand shortened at all, that it cannot redeem? or have I no power to deliver? behold, at my rebuke I ᶜdry up the sea, I make the ᵈrivers a wilderness: their fish stinketh, because *there is* no water, and dieth for thirst. (3) I clothe the heavens with blackness, and I make sackcloth their covering.

(4) The Lord GOD hath given me the tongue of the learned, that I should know how to speak a word in season to *him that is* ᵉweary: he wakeneth morning by morning, he wakeneth mine ear to hear as the learned. (5) The Lord GOD hath opened mine ear, and I was not ᶠrebellious, neither turned away back. (6) ᵍI gave my back to the smiters, and my cheeks to them that plucked off the hair: I hid not my face from shame

1 Heb., *the captivity of the just.*

2 Heb., *captivity.*

a Rev. 14. 20 & 16. 6.

3 Or, *new wine.*

b Nu. 11. 23; ch. 59. 1.

c Ex. 14. 21.

d Josh. 3. 16.

e Matt. 11. 28.

f John 14. 31; Phil. 2. 8; Heb. 10. 5, &c.

g Matt. 26. 67 & 27. 26.

---

kings themselves and their queens to rear her children. They shall bow down to her, the true Israel, the true *Ecclesia*, as the dwelling-place of Jehovah.

(24) **Shall the prey be taken . . . ?**—The question is asked by Zion in her little faith. The next phrase, "lawful captive," literally "captive of righteousness," may mean, (1) as in the Authorised version, a captive whom the conqueror had a right to take, or (2) one who was righteous and yet had been given into captivity. Neither meaning is quite satisfactory. A conjectural emendation gives *the captives of the terrible one*, which fits in with the parallelism of the next verse.

(25) **I will contend . . .**—The pronoun is specially emphatic. The question of verse 24 is answered in the affirmative, because Jehovah is the deliverer.

(26) **I will feed them that oppress thee . . .**—The words are, of course, symbolical of the utter collapse, the self-destructive struggles of the enemies of Zion, *i.e.*, of the company, or *Ecclesia*, of the redeemed.

The mighty One of Jacob.—Same word, and that a rare one, as in chap. i. 24.

L.

(1) **Where is the bill . . . ?**—The thought seems suggested by chap. xlix. 14, but expands in a different direction. Both questions imply a negative answer. Jehovah had not formally repudiated the wife (Judah) whom he had chosen (Deut. xxiv. 1) as he had done her sister Israel (Jer. iii. 8; Hos. ii. 2). He had no creditors among the nations who could claim her children. On the law of debt which supplies the image, comp. Exod. xxi. 7; 2 Kings iv. 1; Neh. v. 5. The divorce, the sale, were her acts and not His.

(2) **Wherefore, when I came . . . ?**—The "coming" of Jehovah must be taken in all its width of meaning. He came in the deliverance from Babylon, in a promise of still greater blessings, in the fullest sense, in and through His Servant, and yet none came to help in the work, or even to receive the message. (Comp. chap. lxiii. 3.) Not that He needed human helpers. In words that remind us, in their sequence, of the phenomena of the plagues of Egypt, the prophet piles up the mighty works of which He is capable. The words are echoed in Rev. vi. 12, viii. 9, 12.

(4) **The Lord God . . .**—A new section begins in the form of an abruptly introduced soliloquy. As in chap. xlix. 4, the speaker is the Servant of Jehovah, not Isaiah, though we may legitimately trace in what follows some echoes of the prophet's own experience. The union of the two names Adonai Jahveh (or Jehovah) indicates, as elsewhere, a special solemnity.

The tongue of the learned.—Better, *of a disciple*, or, well-trained scholar.

That I should know how to speak.—Better, *that I should know how to sustain* (or, *refresh*) *the weary with a word*.

He wakeneth.—The daily teaching of the morning communion with God is contrasted by implication with the dreams and night visions of a less perfect inspiration. An illustration, perhaps a conscious fulfilment, may be found in Mark i. 35; Luke iv. 42.

To hear as the learned.—Read *disciples*, as before. The true Servant is also as a scholar, studious of the Master's will, as are other scholars.

(5, 6) **The Lord God.**—*Jehovah Adonai*, as before. The Servant continues his soliloquy. What has come to him in the morning communings with God is, as in the next verse, that he too is to bear reproach and shame, as other disciples had done before him. The writer of Ps. xxii. 7, the much-enduring Job (Job xxx 10), the prophet Jeremiah (Jer. xx. 7), were but foreshadowings of the sufferings that should fall on him. And all this the true Servant-Scholar accepts willingly, because it is his Father's will. Here again we cannot fail to trace the influence of Isaiah's words in all our Lord's utterances as to His passion. (Comp. Matt. xvi. 21; Mark x. 34; Luke xviii. 32.)

and spitting. ⁽⁷⁾ For the Lord God will help me; therefore shall I not be confounded: therefore have I set my face like a flint, and I know that I shall not be ashamed. ⁽⁸⁾ ᵃ*He is* near that justifieth me; who will contend with me? let us stand together: who *is* ¹mine adversary? let him come near to me. ⁽⁹⁾ Behold, the Lord God will help me; who *is* he *that* shall condemn me? lo, they all shall wax old as a garment; the moth shall eat them up.

⁽¹⁰⁾ Who *is* among you that feareth the Lord, that obeyeth the voice of his servant, that walketh *in* darkness, and hath no light? let him trust in the name of the Lord, and stay upon his God. ⁽¹¹⁾ Behold, all ye that kindle a fire, that compass *yourselves* about with sparks: walk in the light of your fire, and in the sparks *that* ye have kindled. ᵇThis shall ye have of mine hand; ye shall lie down in sorrow.

a Rom. 8. 32, 33.

¹ Heb., *the master of my cause?*

b John 9. 39.

CHAPTER LI.—⁽¹⁾ Hearken to me, ye that follow after righteousness, ye that seek the Lord: look unto the rock *whence* ye are hewn, and to the hole of the pit *whence* ye are digged. ⁽²⁾ Look unto Abraham your father, and unto Sarah *that* bare you: for I called him alone, and blessed him, and increased him. ⁽³⁾ For the Lord shall comfort Zion: he will comfort all her waste places; and he will make her wilderness like Eden, and her desert like the garden of the Lord; joy and gladness shall be found therein, thanksgiving, and the voice of melody.

⁽⁴⁾ Hearken unto me, my people; and give ear unto me O my nation: for a law shall proceed from me, and I will make my judgment to rest for a light of the people. ⁽⁵⁾ My righteousness *is* near; my salvation is gone forth, and mine arms shall judge the people; the isles shall wait upon me, and on mine arm shall they trust. ⁽⁶⁾ Lift up your

---

⁽⁷⁾ **The Lord God will help me.**—That one stay gives to the suffering Servant an indomitable strength. (Comp. for the phrase Jer. i. 18; Ezek. iii. 9.)

⁽⁸⁾ **He is near that justifieth**—*i.e.*, declares innocent and righteous. Appealing from the unrighteous judges of the earth, the Servant commits himself to Him who judges righteously (Luke xxiii. 46). With that Judge to declare his innocence, what does he care for the accuser? (Comp. Rom. viii. 33, 34.)

Who is mine adversary?—Literally, *the master of a law-suit, i.e.*, the prosecutor.

⁽⁹⁾ **They all shall wax old as a garment.**—An echo of Job xiii. 28; Ps. cii. 26; reproduced in chap. li. 6.

⁽¹⁰⁾ **That obeyeth the voice of his servant.**—The question may be asked of *any* servant of Jehovah, such as was Isaiah himself, but receives its highest application in *the* Servant who has appeared as speaking in the preceding verses.

That walketh in darkness.—The words grow at once out of the prophet's own experience and that of the ideal Servant. All true servants know what it is to feel as if the light for which they looked had for a time failed them, to utter a prayer like that of Ajax, "Give light, and let us die" (Hom. *Il.* xvii. 647). *The* Servant felt it when he uttered the cry, "My God, my God, why hast thou forsaken me?" (Matt. xxvii. 46). For such an one there were the words of counsel, "Trust, in spite of the darkness." So the cry of the forsaken Servant was followed by the word "Father, into thy hands I commend my spirit." (Luke xxiii. 46).

⁽¹¹⁾ **All ye that kindle a fire.**—The words obviously point to any human substitute for the Divine light, and thus include the two meanings which commentators have given them: (1) Man's fiery wrath, that worketh not the righteousness of God; and (2) man's attempt to rest in earthly comforts or enjoyments instead of in the light and joy that comes from God.

That compass yourselves about with sparks. —The words are rendered by many commentators, *gird yourselves with burning darts,* or *firebrands, i.e.,* with calumnies and execrations as your weapons of warfare. (Comp. Ephes. vi. 16.)

Ye shall lie down in sorrow.—The words point to a death of anguish, perhaps to the torment that follows death (comp. Luke xvi. 24), as the outcome of the substitution of the earthly for the heavenly light.

LI.

⁽¹⁾ **Look unto the rock.**—The implied argument is, that the wonder involved in the origin of Israel is as a ground of faith in its restoration and perpetuity. The rock is, of course, Abraham, the pit, Sarah.

⁽²⁾ **I called him alone.**—Literally, *as one.* If so great a nation had sprung from one man (Heb. xi. 12), so would God out of the faithful remnant once more create a people. (Comp. Ezek. xxxiii. 24, where the exiles are represented as boastfully inverting the argument: "Abraham was one, and we are many; therefore we shall prosper, the chances are in our favour.")

⁽³⁾ **He will make her wilderness like Eden.** —Interesting as showing Isaiah's acquaintance with Gen. i.—iii. (Comp. Ezek. xxxi. 9, 16, xxxvi. 35; Joel ii. 3.) "Paradise" has already entered into the idea of future restoration (Rev. ii. 7).

⁽⁴⁾ **A law shall proceed.**—"Law" and "judgment" include all forms of divine revelation, and specially the "glad tidings" which are the groundwork of the highest law. (Comp. Luke i. 77; Rom. i. 17.)

⁽⁵⁾ **Mine arms shall judge the people.**—Literally, *the peoples,* including Israel and the heathen. The work of judgment thus, as ever, comes first; after it the *isles* (*i.e.,* far-off countries), as representing the heathen, shall be converted, and trust the very Arm that smote them.

⁽⁶⁾ **Shall die in like manner**—*i.e.*, shall vanish into nothingness. Many commentators, however, render, *shall die like gnats;* shall live their little day and pass away; thus supplying a third similitude, in

eyes to the heavens, and look upon the earth beneath: for *a* the heavens shall vanish away like smoke, and the earth shall wax old like a garment, and they that dwell therein shall die in like manner: but my salvation shall be for ever, and my righteousness shall not be abolished.

(7) Hearken unto me, ye that know righteousness, the people *b* in whose heart *is* my law; *c* fear ye not the reproach of men, neither be ye afraid of their revilings. (8) For the moth shall eat them up like a garment, and the worm shall eat them like wool: but my righteousness shall be for ever, and my salvation from generation to generation.

(9) Awake, awake, put on strength, O arm of the LORD; awake, as in the ancient days, in the generations of old. Art thou not it that hath cut Rahab, *and* wounded the *d* dragon? (10) *Art* thou not it which hath *e* dried the sea, the waters of the great deep; that hath made the depths of the sea a way for the ransomed to pass over? (11) Therefore *f* the redeemed of the LORD shall return, and come with singing unto Zion; and everlasting joy *shall be* upon their head: they shall obtain gladness and joy; *and* sorrow and mourning shall flee away.

(12) I, *even* I, am he that comforteth you: who *art* thou, that thou shouldest be afraid *g* of a man *that* shall die, and of the son of man *which* shall be made *h as* grass; (13) and forgettest the LORD thy maker, that hath stretched forth the heavens, and laid the foundations of the earth; and hast feared continually every day because of the fury of the oppressor, as if he ¹were ready to destroy? and where *is* the fury of the oppressor? (14) The captive exile hasteneth that he may be loosed, and that he should not die in the pit, nor that his bread should fail. (15) But I *am* the LORD thy God, that *i* divided the sea, whose waves roared: The LORD of hosts *is* his name. (16) And I have put my words *k* in thy mouth, and I have covered thee in the shadow of mine hand, that I may plant the heavens, and lay the foundations of the earth, and say unto Zion, Thou *art* my people.

a Ps. 102. 26; Matt. 24. 35.
b Ps. 37. 31.
c Matt. 10. 28.
d Ps. 74. 13, 14; Ezek. 29. 3.
e Ex. 14. 21.
f ch. 35. 10.
g Ps. 118. 6.
h ch. 40. 6; 1 Pet. 1. 24.
¹ Or, *made himself ready.*
i Jer. 31. 35.
k ch. 49. 2, 3.

---

addition to the "smoke" and the "garment." We are reminded once again of Ps. cii. 26; and we may add, Matt. xxiv. 35; 2 Peter iii. 10.

(7) **Ye that know righteousness.**—Jehovah, through His Servant, speaks to the Israel within Israel, the Church within the Church. They need support against the scorn and reproach of men, and are to find it in the thought that the revilers perish and that Jehovah is eternal.

(8) **The moth . . . the worm.**—The two words in Hebrew have the force of an emphatic assonance—*ash* and *sāsh*.

(9) **Awake, awake.**—Who is the speaker that thus bursts into this grand apostrophe? (1) The redeemed and ideal Israel, or (2) the Servant of the Lord, or (3) the prophet, or (4) Jehovah, as in self-communing, after the manner of men, like that of Deborah in Judges v. 12. On the whole the first seems the preferable view; but the loftiness of poetry, perhaps, transcends all such distinctions. The appeal is, in any case, to the great deeds of God in the past, as the pledge and earnest of yet greater in the future. "Rahab," as in chap. xxx. 7, Ps. lxxxix. 10, is Egypt; and the "dragon," like "leviathan" in Ps. lxxiv. 13, stands for Pharaoh. (Comp. Ezek. xxix. 3.) Cheyne quotes from Bunsen's "Egypt," vol. vi., an invocation to the god Ra, from the Egyptian Book of the Dead, "Hail, thou who hast cut in pieces the scorner and strangled the Apophis (*sc.* the evil serpent)," as a striking parallel.

(11) **Therefore the redeemed.**—Noteworthy as being either a quotation by Isaiah from himself (chap. xxxv. 10), or by the unknown writer of Isaiah from the earlier prophet. The assumption that it is an interpolation by a copyist rests on no adequate ground.

(12) **I, even I.**—The iterated pronoun emphasises the true grounds of confidence. If God be with us, what matter is it who may be against us? The enemies are mortal and weak; the Protector is the Eternal and the Strong.

(13) **As if he were ready.**—Better, *as he makes him ready to destroy.* The Authorised version unduly minimises the amount of danger. In the case contemplated by the prophet, the oppressor was the Babylonian monarchy, which he sees as already belonging to the past; but the words have, of course, a far wider application.

(14) **The captive exile.**—Literally, *he that is bowed down, i.e.,* bound in fetters. The "pit," as in the case of Jeremiah (Jer. xxxviii. 6), is the underground dungeon, in which the prisoner was too often left to starve.

(15) **But I am . . .**—Better, *Seeing that I am.* The fact which follows is not contrasted with that which precedes, but given as its ground. The might of Jehovah is seen in the storm-waves of the sea. It is seen not less in the fall and rise of empires.

(16) **And I have put my words in thy mouth . . .**—Some interpreters assume, that while verse 12 was spoken to the Jewish exiles, this, which reminds us of chap. xlix. 2, is addressed to *the* Servant of the Lord. Of these, some (Cheyne), struck by the apparent abruptness, assume it to be misplaced. There seems no adequate reason for adopting either hypothesis. The words were spoken to Israel, contemplated as in its ideal, as were the others to the actual Israel. It remains true, as ever, that that ideal is fulfilled only in *the* Servant.

That I may plant.—Noteworthy as the first intimation of the new heaven and the new earth, implying

The Dregs of the Cup of Trembling. ISAIAH, LII. *The Holy City in its Beauty.*

(17) "Awake, awake, stand up, O Jerusalem, which hast drunk at the hand of the LORD the cup of his fury; thou hast drunken the dregs of the cup of trembling, *and* wrung *them* out. (18) *There is* none to guide her among all the sons *whom* she hath brought forth; neither *is there any* that taketh her by the hand of all the sons *that* she hath brought up. (19) *b*These two *things* ¹are come unto thee; who shall be sorry for thee? desolation, and ²destruction, and the famine, and the sword: by whom shall I comfort thee? (20) Thy sons have fainted, they lie at the head of all the streets, as a wild bull in a net: they are full of the fury of the LORD, the rebuke of thy God. (21) Therefore hear now this, thou afflicted, and drunken, but not with wine: (22) thus saith thy Lord the LORD, and thy God *that* pleadeth the cause of his people, Behold, I have taken out of thine hand the cup of trembling, *even* the dregs of the cup of my fury; thou shalt no more drink it again: (23) but I will put it into the hand of them that afflict thee; which have said to thy soul, Bow down, that we may go over: and thou hast laid thy body as the ground, and as the street, to them that went over.

CHAPTER LII.—(1) Awake, *c*awake; put on thy strength, O Zion; put on thy beautiful garments, O Jerusalem, the holy city: for henceforth there shall no more come into thee the uncircumcised and the unclean. (2) Shake thyself from the dust; arise, *and* sit down, O Jerusalem: loose thyself from the bands of thy neck, O captive daughter of Zion.

(3) For thus saith the LORD, Ye have sold yourselves for nought; and ye shall be redeemed without money. (4) For thus saith the Lord GOD, My people went down aforetime into *d*Egypt to sojourn there; and the Assyrian oppressed

a ch. 52. 1.
b ch. 47. 9.
1 Heb., *happened.*
2 Heb., *breaking.*
c ch. 51. 17.
d Gen. 46. 6.

---

a restitution of all things, of which we find the expression in chaps. lxv. 17, lxvi. 22.

(17) **Awake . . .**—The words present a strange parallelism to verse 9. There they were addressed to the arm of Jehovah, and were the prelude of a glorious promise. Here they are spoken to Jerusalem as a drunken and desperate castaway, and introduce a painfully vivid picture of her desolation. They seem, indeed, prefixed to that picture to make it bearable. They are a call to Zion to wake out of that drunken sleep, and therefore show that her ruin is not irretrievable.

The dregs of the cup.—Literally, *the goblet cup,* but with the sense, as in the Authorised version, of the cup being drained.

(19) **These two things . . .**—The two things are amplified into four: (1) the two effects, and (2) the two causes.

Who shall be sorry for thee?—Better, Be sorry *with* thee, or *who shall console thee?* Even Jehovah is represented as failing, or seeming to fail, in finding a comforter for such affliction.

(20) **As a wild bull . . .**—Better, *as an antelope.* The picture explains that of verse 17. The sons cannot help the mother, for they, too, have drunk of the same cup of fury, and lie like corpses in the open places of the city. (Comp. Lam. ii. 12.)

(21) **Drunken, but not with wine . . .**—Same phrase as in chap. xxix. 9.

(22) **Thy Lord the Lord . . .**—Note the emphatic combination of *Adonai* (or rather, in this solitary instance, of the plural *Adonim* used like Elohim) with Jehovah. Man's necessity is once more God's opportunity. He will plead for His people when none else will plead. The cup of trembling shall be taken from the hand of the forlorn castaway, and given to her enemies. (Comp. Jer. xxv. 15.)

(23) **Thou hast laid thy body . . .**—The image is startlingly bold; but our word "prostration," as applied to the condition of a people, embodies precisely the same thought. (Comp. Ps. cxxix. 3.) The previous words paint the last humiliation of Eastern conquest (Josh. x. 24).

LII.

(1) **Awake, awake . . .**—The repetition of the burden of chap. li. 9, 17, indicates, by a subtle touch of art, the continuity of thought. The call is addressed as before to Zion, as a castaway. It summons her to the highest glory. She is to put on the *garments of beauty,* which belong to her as the priestly queen of cities. (Comp. Exod. xxviii. 2.) The alien and the impure shall no longer ride victorious through her streets, as in chap. li. 23. (Comp. Ezek. xliv. 9, and the picture of the heavenly Jerusalem in Rev. xxi. 2.)

(2) **Sit down . . .**—As Jerusalem has risen from the dust, the "sitting" here implies a throne, and so stands in contrast with that of Babylon in chap. xlvii. 1.

(3) **Ye have sold yourselves . . .**—Literally, *ye were sold.* The people had complained that Jehovah had "sold them" into the hands of their enemies (Ps. xliv. 12). "Not so," is the answer. "There was no real sale, only a temporary transfer, and therefore Jehovah can redeem you at His own pleasure. A comparison with chap. xliii. 3, shows how spiritual truths may present aspects that require the most opposite illustrations.

(4) **My people went down . . .**—Stress is laid on the unprovoked character of the oppression in the case both of Egypt and the Assyrian invaders Sargon and Sennacherib. It is possible that Assyria may be used in its wider sense as including Babylon. If so, the fact tends to the conclusion that the book was written at a time when the kings of Assyria included Babylon in their titles. Probably, however, the prophet refers to the deliverance from the army of Sennacherib as a pledge of the deliverance from Babylon.

them without cause. (5) Now therefore, what have I here, saith the LORD, that my people is taken away for nought? they that rule over them make them to howl, saith the LORD; and my name continually every day is ᵃblasphemed. (6) Therefore my people shall know my name: therefore *they shall know* in that day that I *am* he that doth speak: behold, *it is* I.

(7) ᵇHow beautiful upon the mountains are the feet of him that bringeth good tidings, that publisheth peace; that bringeth good tidings of good, that publisheth salvation; that saith unto Zion, Thy God reigneth! (8) Thy watchmen shall lift up the voice; with the voice together shall they sing: for they shall see eye to eye, when the LORD shall bring again Zion. (9) Break forth into joy, sing together, ye waste places of Jerusalem: for the LORD hath comforted his people, he hath redeemed Jerusalem. (10) The LORD hath made bare his holy arm in the eyes of all the nations; and ᶜall the ends of the earth shall see the salvation of our God.

(11) ᵈDepart ye, depart ye, go ye out from thence, touch no unclean *thing*; go ye out of the midst of her; be ye clean, that bear the vessels of the LORD. (12) For ye shall not go out with haste, nor go by flight: for the LORD will go before you; and the God of Israel *will* ¹*be* your rereward.

(13) Behold, my servant shall ²deal

---

a Ezek. 36. 20, 23; Rom. 2. 24.

b Nah. 1. 15; Rom. 10. 15.

c Ps. 98. 3; Luke 3. 6.

d 2 Cor. 6. 17; Rev. 18. 4.

¹ Heb., *gather you up.*

² Or, *prosper.*

---

(5) **What have I here . . . ?**—*i.e.*, What have I to do? As in Gen. xi. 4, Jehovah is represented as deliberating after the manner of men. Again the people have been gratuitously, wantonly attacked; and their groans mingle with the taunting blasphemies of their conquerors. Has not the time come for Him to vindicate His outraged Majesty?

(7) **How beautiful . . .**—The image is reproduced, with variations, from chap. xl. 9. There Zion herself was the herald proclaiming the glad tidings; here the heralds are seen coming to Zion, to tell her that her God is verily reigning, and their feet are beautiful on the mountains like those of an antelope (Song of Sol. ii. 8, 9; Nah. i. 15).

(8) **Thy watchmen . . .**—The sentinels see the heralds from their watch-towers (chap. xxi. 6; Hab. ii. 1), and sing out for joy, as they see, not only afar off, but "eye to eye," the presence of the God who has *become the King.*

(9) **Ye waste places of Jerusalem . . .**—The history of the return of the exiles in Ezra i., iii., seems a somewhat poor and prosaic fulfilment of the glorious vision; but it lies in the nature of the case, that the words of the prophet, contemplating the distant future, idealise that return, and connect it unconsciously, it may be, with another city than the earthly Jerusalem.

(10) **The Lord hath made bare . . .**—The warrior preparing for action throws off his mantle, tucks up the sleeve of his tunic, and leaves his outstretched arm free.

(11) **Depart ye . . .**—The command is addressed to the exiles in Babylon. They are not to plunder or carry off spoil that would render them unclean. They are to bring only "the vessels of Jehovah," *i.e.*, the gold and silver which had been taken from His temple, and which Cyrus restored by them (Ezra i. 7). In this case the bearers are the Levites. Commonly, however, the phrase is used of "armour-bearers," and this meaning is given to it by many commentators, as pointing to the whole body of the people as filling that function for the great king (1 Kings xiv. 27, 28).

(12) **Ye shall not go out with haste . . .**—The words contrast the exodus from Babylon with that from Egypt (Exod. xii. 39; Deut. xvi. 3). In the essential point, however, of Divine protection, the resemblance would be greater than the contrast. Jehovah would still be once more both the vanguard and the rear-guard of the great procession.

(13) **Behold, my servant . . .**—There is absolutely no connection between verses 12 and 13, absolutely no break between the close of chap. lii. and the opening of chap. liii. The whole must be treated as an entirely distinct section (all the more striking, from its contrast to the triumphant tone of what precedes it), and finds its only adequate explanation in the thought of a new revelation made to the prophet's mind. That may have had, like other revelations, a starting-point in the prophet's own experience. He had seen partially good kings, like Uzziah and Jotham; one who almost realised his ideal of what a king should be, in Hezekiah. None of these had redeemed or regenerated the people. So far as that work had been done at all, it had been through prophets who spake the word of the Lord and were mocked and persecuted because they spake it. Something like a law was dawning upon his mind, and that law was the power of a vicarious suffering, the might of martyrdom in life and death. Did it not follow from this that that ideal must be wrought out on a yet wider scale in the great work of restoration to which he was looking forward? The Servant of the Lord, in all the concentric developments of the thought which the word implied, the nation, the prophetic kernel of the nation, the individual Servant identifying himself with both, must himself also be made perfect through suffering and conquer through apparent failure. Granting that such a law exists, it will be no wonder that we should find examples of its working both before and after the great fulfilment, in Isaiah himself, in Jeremiah, in the exiles of the captivity, in the heroes of the Maccabean struggle, in the saints and martyrs of the Church of Christ. It remains true that the Christ alone fulfils the idea of the perfect sufferer, as He alone fulfils that of the perfect King. Measuring Isaiah from a purely human stand-point, and by the standard of other poets, this manifold symbolism of "the Servant," will hardly seem strange to the student of literature who remembers the many aspects presented by the Beatrice of Dante, the St. George and Gloriana of Spenser, the Piers Plowman of Langland.

Shall deal prudently.—The words imply, as in Josh. i. 8; Jer. x. 21, the idea of prospering. The same

The Man of Sorrows, despised   ISAIAH, LIII.   *and rejected of Men*

prudently, he shall be exalted and extolled, and be very high. (14) As many were astonied at thee; his *a* visage was so marred more than any man, and his form more than the sons of men: (15) so shall he sprinkle many nations; the kings shall shut their mouths at him: for *that* *b* which had not been told them shall they see; and *that* which they had not heard shall they consider.

a ch. 53. 3.
b Rom. 15. 21.
c John 12. 38; Rom. 10. 16.
1 Or, *doctrine.*
2 Heb., *hearing.*
d ch. 52. 14; Mark 9. 12.

CHAPTER LIII.—(1) Who *c* hath believed our ¹²report? and to whom is the arm of the LORD revealed? (2) For he shall grow up before him as a tender plant, and as a root out of a dry ground: he hath no form nor comeliness; and when we shall see him, *there is* no beauty that we should desire him. (3) *d* He is despised and rejected of men; a man of sorrows, and acquainted with grief: and

---

verb is used of the "righteous branch" in Jer. xxiii. 5, and is there so translated.

Shall be exalted.—It is noteworthy that the phrase impressed itself, through the LXX., on the mind of the Christ in reference to His crucifixion (John iii, 14, viii. 28, xii. 32), on that of the Apostles in reference to His ascension (Acts ii. 33; Phil. ii. 9). (Comp. chaps. vi. 1, lvii. 15; Ps. lxxxix. 27.)

(14) **As many were astonied . . .**—The words point to the correspondence of the supreme exaltation following on the supreme humiliation.

His visage was so marred . . .—The words conflict strangely with the type of pure and holy beauty with which Christian art has made us familiar as its ideal of the Son of Man. It has to be noted, however, that the earlier forms of that art, prior to the time of Constantine, and, in some cases, later, represented the Christ as worn, emaciated, with hardly any touch of earthly comeliness, and that it is at least possible that the beauty may have been of expression rather than of feature or complexion, and that men have said of Him, as of St. Paul, that his "bodily presence was weak" (2 Cor. x. 10).

(15) **So shall he sprinkle many nations . . .**—The words have been very differently rendered by, *He shall cause to spring up,* i.e., *shall startle, He shall scatter, He shall fling away,* or, *Many nations shall marvel at him.* On the whole, however, admitting the difficulty of the passage, the Authorised version seems preferable. The "sprinkling" is that of the priest who cleanses the leper (Lev. iv. 6, 17), and this was to be done by Him who was Himself counted as a leper "smitten of God" (chap. liii. 4). We may probably trace an echo of the words in the "sprinkling clean water" of Ezek. xxxvi. 25, in the "blood of sprinkling," of Heb. x. 22, xii. 24. Here it comes as an explanation of the paradox that *the* Servant of Jehovah was to bring in "many nations" into the holy city, and yet that the "uncircumcised and unclean" were not to enter it (verse 1).

The kings shall shut their mouths . . .—The reverence, as in chap. xlix. 7, Job xxix. 9, xl. 4, is that of silent wonder at the change which has passed over the suffering Servant. Wisd. v. 1—5 presents an interesting parallel, the reference there being to the person of the ideal righteous sufferer. In that case, as in this, there was, so to speak, a transfiguration "beyond all that men looked for."

LIII.

(1) **Who hath believed our report? . . .**—The question has been variously interpreted as coming from the lips of the prophet or of Israel. The former view commends itself most, and the unusual plural is explained by his mentally associating with himself the other prophets, probably his own disciples, who were delivering the same message. The implied answer to the question may be either "None," or, "Not all." St. Paul (Rom. x. 16) adopts the latter.

(2) **For he shall grow up . . .**—The Hebrew tenses are in the perfect, the future being contemplated as already accomplished. The words present at once a parallel and a contrast to those of chap. xi. 1. There the picture was that of a strong vigorous shoot coming out of the root of the house of David. Here the sapling is weak and frail, struggling out of the dry ground. For "before Him" (*i.e.,* Jehovah) some critics have read "before us," as agreeing better with the second clause; while others have referred the pronoun "him" to the Jewish people. Taking the received text and interpretation, the thought expressed is that Jehovah was watching this humble and lowly growth, as a mother watches over her weakest and most sickly child.

He hath no form nor comeliness.—See Note on chap. lii. 14. The thought which has been constantly true of the followers of the Christ, was to be true of the Christ Himself.

"Hid are the saints of God,
Uncertified by high angelic sign;
Nor raiment soft, nor empire's golden rod,
Marks them divine."
                J. H. NEWMAN (*Lyra Apostolica.*)

(3) **He is despised and rejected.**—Better, for the last word, *forsaken.* This had been the crowning sorrow of the righteous sufferer of the Old Testament (Job xvii. 15, xix. 14). It was to complete the trial of the perfect sufferer of the New (Matt. xxvi. 56).

A man of sorrows . . .—The words "sorrow" and "grief" in the Heb. imply the thought of bodily pain or disease. (Comp. Exod. iii. 7; Lam. i. 12, 18.) Men have sometimes raised the rather idle question whether the body of our Lord was subject to disease, and have decided on *à priori* grounds that it was not. The prophet's words point to the true view, that this was an essential condition of His fellowship with humanity. If we do not read of any actual disease in the Gospel, we at least have evidence of an organisation every nerve of which thrilled with its sensitiveness to pain, and was quickly exhausted (Luke viii. 46; John iv. 6; Mark iv. 36). The intensity of His sympathy made Him feel the pain of others as His own (Matt. viii. 17), the "blood and water" from the pierced heart, the physical results of the agony in Gethsemane (Luke xxii. 44; John xix. 34), indicate a nature subject to the conditions of our humanity.

We hid as it were . . .—Literally, *As the hiding of the face from us,* or, *on our part.* The words start from the picture of the leper covering his face from men, or their covering their own faces, that they might not look upon him (Lev. xiii. 45). In Lam. iv. 15, we have a like figurative application. (Comp. also Job xix. 13—19, xxx. 10.)

¹² we hid as it were *our* faces from him; he was despised, and we esteemed him not.

⁽⁴⁾ Surely ᵃhe hath borne our griefs, and carried our sorrows: yet we did esteem him stricken, smitten of God, and afflicted. ⁽⁵⁾ But he was ³ᵇ wounded for our transgressions, *he was* bruised for our iniquities: the chastisement of our peace *was* upon him; and with his ᶜ⁴stripes we are healed. ⁽⁶⁾ All we like sheep have gone astray; we have turned every one to his own way; and the LORD ⁵hath laid on him the iniquity of us all.

⁽⁷⁾ He was oppressed, and he was afflicted, yet ᵈhe opened not his mouth: he is brought as a ᵉlamb to the slaughter, and as a sheep before her shearers is dumb, so he openeth not his mouth. ⁽⁸⁾ ⁶He was taken from prison and from judgment: and who shall declare his generation? for he was cut off out of the land of the living: for the transgression of my people ⁷was he stricken. ⁽⁹⁾ And he made his grave with the

1 Or, *he hid as it were his face from us.*
2 Heb., *as a hiding of faces from him, or, from us.*
a Matt. 8. 17.
3 Or, *tormented.*
b Rom. 4. 25; 1 Cor. 15. 3.
c 1 Pet. 2. 24.
4 Heb., *bruise.*
5 Heb., *hath made the iniquity of us all to meet on him.*
d Matt. 26. 63 & 27. 12; Mark 14. 61 & 15. 5.
e Acts 8. 32.
6 Or, *He was taken away by distress and judgment: but, &c.*
7 Heb., *was the stroke upon him.*

⁽⁴⁾ **Surely he hath borne our griefs . . .**—The words are spoken as by those who had before despised the Servant of Jehovah, and have learnt the secret of His humiliation. "Grief" and "sorrow," as before, imply "disease" and "pain," and St. Matthew's application of the text (Matt. viii. 17) is therefore quite legitimate. The words "stricken, smitten of God," are used elsewhere specially of leprosy and other terrible sicknesses (Gen. xii. 17; Lev. xiii. 3, 9; Num. xiv. 12; 1 Sam. vi. 9; 2 Kings xv. 5). So the Vulg. gives *leprosus*. The word for "borne," like the Greek in John i. 29, implies both the "taking upon himself," and the "taking away from others," *i.e.*, the true idea of vicarious and mediatorial atonement.

⁽⁵⁾ **He was wounded . . .**—*Bruised*. Both words refer to the death which crowned the sufferings of the Servant. That also was vicarious.

The chastisement of our peace—*i.e.*, the punishment which leads to peace, that word including, as elsewhere, every form of blessing. (Comp. the "reproof of life" in Prov. xv. 31.) In Heb. ii. 10, v. 8, 9, we have the thought which is the complement of this, that the chastisement was also an essential condition of the perfection of the sufferer.

With his stripes we are healed.—The words stretch wide and deep. Perhaps the most touching application is St. Peter's use of them as a thought of comfort for the slaves who were scourged as He, their Lord, had been (1 Peter ii. 24).

⁽⁶⁾ **All we like sheep have gone astray . . .**—The confession of repentant Israel (Ps. cxix. 176), of repentant humanity (1 Peter ii. 25), was also the thought present to the mind of the Servant, as in Matt. ix. 36; John x. 11.

Hath laid on him.—Better, as in the margin, *hath made to light on him.* The words express the fact, but do not explain the mystery of the substitutive satisfaction. The two sides of that mystery are stated in the form of a seeming paradox. God does not punish the righteous *with* the wicked (Gen. xviii. 25). He accepts the suffering of the righteous *for* the wicked (Mark x. 45).

⁽⁷⁾ **He was afflicted . . .**—More accurately, *He let himself be afflicted*, as implying the voluntary acceptance of the suffering.

Opened not his mouth.—The silence of absolute acquiescence, as in Pss. xxxviii. 14, xxxix. 9.

As a lamb to the slaughter.—It is suggestive, as bearing both on the question of authorship, and that of partial fulfilment, that Jeremiah (chap. xi. 19) appropriates the description to himself. In our Lord's silence before the Sanhedrin and Pilate it is allowable to trace a conscious fulfilment of Isaiah's words (Matt. xxvi. 62, xxvii. 14). (Comp. 1 Peter ii. 23.)

⁽⁸⁾ **He was taken from prison . . .**—The Hebrew preposition admits of this rendering, which is adopted by many commentators, as describing the oppression and iniquitous trial which had preceded the death of the servant. It admits equally of the sense, *through oppression and through judgment*; and, on the whole, this gives a preferable sense. The whole procedure was tainted with iniquity.

Who shall declare his generation?—The words are, perhaps, the most difficult of the whole section, and have been very differently explained: (1) "Who shall declare his life, the mystery of his birth, his eternal being?" (2) "Who shall count his spiritual offspring?" as in Ps. xxii. 30. (3) "As to his generation (*i.e.*, his contemporaries, as in Jer. ii. 31), who will consider rightly?" (4) "Who shall set forth his generation in all the intensity of their guilt?"—to say nothing of other renderings, which render the noun as "his dwelling," *i.e.*, the grave, or his "course of life," or his "fate." Of these (3) seems most in harmony with the context, the words that follow pointing to the fact which ought to have been considered, and was not, that though the Servant of Jehovah was smitten, it was not for his own sins, but theirs.

⁽⁹⁾ **And he made his grave . . .**—Literally, *one* (or, *they) assigned him a grave . . .* The words are often interpreted as fulfilled in our Lord's crucifixion between the two robbers and his burial in the tomb of Joseph of Arimathea. It has to be noted, however, (1) that this requires an inversion of the clauses; (2) that it introduces a feature scarcely in harmony with the general drift of the description; (3) that the laws of parallelism require us to take the "rich" of one clause as corresponding to the "wicked" of the other, *i.e.*, as in the sense of the wrongfully rich, the oppressors, as in Pss. xlix. 6, 16, lxxiii. 3—5. Men assigned to the Servant, not the burial of a saint, with reverence and honour (such, *e.g.*, as that of Stephen, Acts viii. 2), but that of an unjust oppressor, for whom no man lamented, saying, "Ah lord! Ah my brother! Ah his glory!" (Jer. xxii. 18), and this *although* (not "because") he had done no violence to deserve it. (Comp. Job xvi. 17.) The rendering "because" has been adopted as giving a reason for the honourable burial which, it has been assumed, the words imply. It may be questioned, however, when we remember Isaiah's words as to Shebna (chap. xxii. 16), whether he would have looked on such a burial as that recorded in the Gospels, clandestine, and with no public lamentation, as an adequate recognition of the holiness of the victim. The point of the last two

wicked, and with the rich in his ¹death; because he had done no violence, neither was any ᵃdeceit in his mouth. ⁽¹⁰⁾ Yet it pleased the LORD to bruise him; he hath put *him* to grief: ²when thou shalt make his soul an offering for sin, he shall see *his* seed, he shall prolong *his* days, and the pleasure of the LORD shall prosper in his hand. ⁽¹¹⁾ He shall see of the travail of his soul, *and* shall be satisfied: by his knowledge shall my righteous servant justify many; for he shall bear their iniquities. ⁽¹²⁾ Therefore will I divide him *a portion* with the great, and he shall divide the spoil with the strong; because he hath poured out his soul unto death: and he was ᵇnumbered with the transgressors; and he bare the sin of many, and ᶜmade intercession for the transgressors.

CHAPTER LIV.—⁽¹⁾ ᵈSing, O barren, thou *that* didst not bear; break forth into singing, and cry aloud, thou *that* didst not travail with child: for more *are* the children of the desolate than the children of the married wife, saith the LORD. ⁽²⁾ Enlarge the place of thy tent, and let them stretch forth the curtains of thine habitations: spare not, lengthen thy cords, and strengthen thy stakes; ⁽³⁾ for thou shalt break forth on the

Margin references: ¹ Heb. *deaths.* ᵃ 1 Pet. 2. 22; 1 John 3. 5. ² Or, *when his soul shall make an offering.* ᵇ Mark 15. 28; Luke 22. 37. ᶜ Luke 23. 34. ᵈ Gal. 4. 27.

---

clauses is that they declare emphatically the absolute rectitude of the sufferer in act, his absolute veracity in speech.

⁽¹⁰⁾ **Yet it pleased the Lord . . .**—The sufferings of the Servant are referred not to chance or fate, or even the wickedness of his persecutors, but to the absolute "good-pleasure" of the Father, manifesting itself in its fullest measure in the hour of apparent failure. (Comp. Ps. xxii. 15.)

When thou shalt make . . .—Better, *if his soul shall make a trespass offering, he will see his seed; he will prolong his days . . .* The sacrificial character of the death of the Servant is distinctly defined. It is a "trespass offering" (Lev. vi. 6, 17, xiv. 12), an expiation for the sins of the people. The words declare that such a sacrifice was the condition of spiritual parentage (Ps. xxii. 30), of the immortality of influence, of eternal life with God, of accomplishing the work which the Father had given him to do (John xvii. 4). The "trespass offering" was, it must be remembered, distinct from the "sin offering," though both belonged to the same sacrificial group (Lev. v. 15, vii. 1—7), the distinctive element in the former being that the man who confessed his guilt, voluntary or involuntary, paid his shekels, according to the judgment of the priest, and offered a ram, the blood of which was sprinkled upon the altar. It involved, that is, the idea not of an atonement only, but of a satisfaction, according to the nature of the sin.

⁽¹¹⁾ **He shall see of the travail . . .**—Better, *On account of the travail of his soul, he shall see, and be refreshed.* We may find the truest explanation in the words, "To-day thou shalt be with me in paradise" (Luke xxiii. 43). The refreshment *after* travail, *because* of the travail, was already present to the sufferer's consciousness.

By his knowledge . . .—The phrase admits of two meanings, objective and subjective : (1) by their knowledge of Him; or (2) by His own knowledge; and each expresses a truth. Men are saved by knowing Christ. To know Him and the Father is eternal life (John xvii. 3). On the other hand, the Christ Himself makes His knowledge of the Father the ground of His power to impart that knowledge to men, and so to justify and save them (John xvii. 25). Without that knowledge He could not have led them to know God as He knew. If we dare not say that the prophet distinctly contemplated both meanings, we may rejoice that he was guided to use a phrase which includes both. Chap. xi. 2 and Mal. ii. 7 are in favour of (2).

For he shall bear.—The conjunction is not necessarily more than *and.* The importance of the renewal of the assurance given in verse 4 lies in its declaring the perpetuity of the atoning work. The sacrifice of the Servant is "for ever" (Heb. x. 12). He "ever liveth to make intercession for us" (Heb. vii. 25). He taketh away the sin of the world, through the æons of all duration (John i. 29).

⁽¹²⁾ **Therefore will I divide . . .**—The "great" and the "powerful" are words which describe the kings and rulers of mankind. The Servant, once despised and forsaken, takes his place with them, though not in the same manner, or by the same means. We may have echoes of the words in our Lord's language as to the "spoiling of the strong man" (Matt. xii. 29) as to the contrast between the greatness of His Kingdom and that of the rulers and great ones of the world (Matt. xx. 25; Mark x. 42; Luke xxii. 25). The LXX., Vulg., Luther, and some modern scholars render, *I will give him the multitude as a prey,* the spoil "of the mighty ones."

Because he hath poured out . . .—The absolutely voluntary character of the sacrifice is again emphasised. The next clause is better taken as *he let himself be numbered.* So it was that he bore (and took away) *the sin of many,* and gained the power for availing intercession, both in the hour of death (Luke xxiii. 34) and in the eternal triumph (Heb. vii. 25). The ideal Servant, contemned, condemned, failing, is seen, at last, to be identical with the ideal King.

LIV.

⁽¹⁾ **Sing, O barren . . .**—The words seem to carry on the jubilant strain of chaps. li., lii. 1—12, leaving the section lii. 13—liii. 12, as a mysterious episode, inserted, it may be, by the prophet to show how it was that the restoration of Israel and the victory of righteousness had become possible. We note, as bearing on Isaiah's studies, the parallelism with 1 Sam. ii. 5. The "children of the desolate" are primarily the returning exiles, ultimately all the citizens of the heavenly Jerusalem.

⁽²⁾ **Enlarge the place of thy tent.**—Interesting parallels are found in chap. xxxiii. 20; Jer. x. 20.

⁽³⁾ **On the right hand and on the left.**—Comp. Gen. xxviii. 14. Strictly speaking, the words indicate specially the north and the south, in relation to one who

right hand and on the left; and thy seed shall inherit the Gentiles, and make the desolate cities to be inhabited. (4) Fear not; for thou shalt not be ashamed: neither be thou confounded; for thou shalt not be put to shame: for thou shalt forget the shame of thy youth, and shalt not remember the reproach of thy widowhood any more. (5) For thy maker *is* thine husband; the ^aLord of hosts *is* his name; and thy Redeemer the Holy One of Israel; The God of the whole earth shall he be called. (6) For the Lord hath called thee as a woman forsaken and grieved in spirit, and a wife of youth, when thou wast refused, saith thy God. (7) For a small moment have I forsaken thee; but with great mercies will I gather thee. (8) In a little wrath I hid my face from thee for a moment; but with everlasting kindness will I have mercy on thee, saith the Lord thy Redeemer.

(9) For this *is as* the waters of ^bNoah unto me: for *as* I have sworn that the waters of Noah should no more go over the earth; so have I sworn that I would not be wroth with thee, nor rebuke thee. (10) For the mountains shall depart, and the hills be removed; but my kindness shall not depart from thee, neither shall the covenant of my peace be removed, saith the Lord that hath mercy on thee.

(11) O thou afflicted, tossed with tempest, *and* not comforted, behold, I will lay thy stones with ^cfair colours, and lay thy foundations with sapphires. (12) And I will make thy windows of agates, and thy gates of carbuncles, and all thy borders of pleasant stones. (13) And all thy children *shall be* ^dtaught of the Lord; and great *shall be* the peace of thy children. (14) In righteous-

a Luke i. 33.

b Gen. 9. 11.

c 1 Chron. 29. 2.

d John 6. 45.

---

stands looking towards the East. Here, of course, they mean "on every side." The words that follow have, like others, a lower or material and a higher or spiritual meaning.

(4) **Thou shalt forget.**—The "shame of thy youth," was the Egyptian bondage, from which Jehovah chose Israel to be His bride (Jer. iii. 1—11; Ezek. xvi. 1—14). The "reproach of widowhood" was the captivity in Babylon.

(5) **The Lord of Hosts . . . the Holy One of Israel.**—We note the combination of the two names so prominent in 1 Isaiah. The "Redeemer" in this context suggests the idea of the next of kin (such, *e.g.*, as Boaz was to Ruth), taking on himself the kinsman's duty of protection (Ruth iv. 4—6).

(6) **For the Lord hath called thee.**—The words find their explanation, perhaps their starting-point, in the history of Hosea and Gomer (Hos. i.—iii.). The husband has punished the faithless wife by what seemed a divorce, but his heart yearns after her, and he takes her back again.

When thou wast refused.—Some critics render *Can she be rejected . . . ?* with the implied answer. "No, that is impossible," but the Authorised version is tenable, and gives an adequate meaning.

(7) **For a small moment.**—Historically the words point to the seventy years of exile, as being but a transient interruption of the manifestation of the everlasting mercies. Spiritually they have wider and manifold fulfilments in the history of individuals, of the Church, of mankind.

(8) **In a little wrath.**—The Hebrew has the rhetorical emphasis of rhyme, *běshetsheph, quetseph,* literally, *in a gush or burst, of wrath,* which, however terrible at the time, endured but for a moment.

(9) **This is as the waters of Noah.**—Interesting (1) as showing the writer's knowledge of the book of Genesis (see chap. li. 2); (2) as one of the few references to the Deluge, outside that book, in the Old Testament. Strictly speaking, Gen. ix. 11 speaks of a "covenant," not an "oath," but it would be idle to find a difficulty in the use of words which, as referring to a Divine act, are almost or altogether interchangeable. It is obvious that the words have found their fulfilment not in any earthly city but in the heavenly Jerusalem.

(10) **For the mountains shall depart.**—Better, *"may depart."* The same bold hyperbole is found in Ps. xlvi. 3; Jer. xxxi. 36; Matt. xxiv. 35.

The covenant of my peace.—The phrase is taken from Num. xxv. 12, and re-appears in Ezek. xxxiv. 25. xxxvii. 26. "Peace," as elsewhere in the Old Testament, includes well-nigh all that is wrapped up in the "salvation" of the New.

(11) **I will lay thy stones with fair colours.**—The first germ of the idealising symbolism of the new Jerusalem. The language of Tobit xiii. 16, 17, shows the impression which it made on the Jews of the captivity. It takes its highest form, excluding all thoughts of a literal fulfilment, in Rev. xxi. 19—21. The Hebrew word for "fair colours" indicates the *kohl,* the black powder of antimony, or manganese, used by women in the East on eyelids and eyebrows, so as to enhance the brilliancy of the eyes. (2 Kings ix. 30, 1 Chron. xxix. 2, Jer. iv. 30.) Here, apparently, it is used in the same way as the setting of the sapphires and other gems. For "windows" read *pinnacles.*

Sapphires . . .—As with the choice of the twelve gems for the High Priest's breast-plate, it is probable that each stone, over and above its visible beauty, had a symbolical significance. Sapphire, *e.g.*, represented the azure of the firmament, as the "sapphire throne" of the Eternal (Exod. xxiv. 10, Ezek. i. 26, x. 1), and the *rubies* (not "agates") and carbuncles may, in like manner, have answered to the fiery glow of the Divine love and the Divine wrath.

(13) **All thy children shall be taught of the Lord . . .**—More accurately, *shall be the disciples of Jehovah;* quoted by our Lord as fulfilled in His disciples (John vi. 45).

(14) **Thou shalt be far from oppression . . .**—On the assumption of Isaiah's authorship the words stand out in contrast with his own experience of the

The Heritage of Jehovah's Servants. ISAIAH, LV. *The Sure Mercies of David.*

ness shalt thou be established: thou shalt be far from oppression; for thou shalt not fear: and from terror; for it shall not come near thee. (15) Behold, they shall surely gather together, *but not by me*: whosoever shall gather together against thee shall fall for thy sake. (16) Behold, I have created the smith that bloweth the coals in the fire, and that bringeth forth an instrument for his work; and I have created the waster to destroy. (17) No weapon that is formed against thee shall prosper; and every tongue *that* shall rise against thee in judgment thou shalt condemn. This *is* the heritage of the servants of the LORD, and their righteousness *is* of me, saith the LORD.

CHAPTER LV.—(1) Ho, *a* every one that thirsteth, come ye to the waters, and he that hath no money; come ye, buy, and eat; yea, come, buy wine and milk without money and without price. (2) Wherefore do ye ¹spend money for *that which is* not bread? and your labour for *that which* satisfieth not? hearken diligently unto me, and eat ye *that which is* good, and let your soul delight itself in fatness. (3) Incline your ear, and come unto me: hear, and your soul shall live; and I will make an everlasting covenant with you, *even* the *b*sure mercies of David. (4) Behold, I have given him *for* a witness to the people, a leader and commander to the people. (5) Behold, thou shalt call a nation *that* thou knowest not, and nations *that* knew not thee shall run unto thee because of the LORD thy God, and for the Holy One of Israel; for he hath glorified thee.

(6) Seek ye the LORD while he may be found, call ye upon him while he is

a John 7. 37.

1 Heb., *weigh.*

b Acts 13. 34.

"oppression" of Ahaz, of the "fear" and "terror" caused by Sargon and Sennacherib.

(15) **But not by me . . .**—Another contrast with Isaiah's experience. The power of Sargon and Sennacherib rested on the fact that they were instruments in God's hands (chap. x. 15, xxxvii. 26). Against the new Jerusalem no command would be given such as had been given to them.

(16) **Behold, I have created the smith . . .**—The words assert the same thought. The "axe," the "hammer," the "sword," of the great ravagers of the earth are formed by the great Work-Master, and He would fashion no such weapon against the new Jerusalem.

(17) **Every tongue that shall rise . . .**—The thought implied is that war comes as the punishment of guilt, and that it is preceded by the "cry" of accusation. Many such cries had risen up against the old Jerusalem (chap. v. 7). There should be none such heard against the new.

This is the heritage.—The solemn asseveration indicates the close of a distinct section.

LV.

(1) **Ho, every one that thirsteth . . .**—The whole context shows that the water, the wine, the milk are all symbols of spiritual blessings as distinctly as they are, *e.g.*, in John iv. 10; Matt. xxvi. 29; 1 Pet. ii. 2. The word "buy" *is* elsewhere confined to the purchase of corn, and would not rightly have been used of wine and milk. The invitation is addressed, as in a tone of pity, to the bereaved and afflicted one of chap. liv. 6, 7.

Without money and without price.—Literally, *For not-money and not-price.* The prophet had used the word "buy," but he feels that that word may be misinterpreted. No silver or gold can buy the blessing which He offers. Something, indeed, is required, and therefore the word "buy" is still the right word; but the "price" is simply the self-surrender that accepts the blessing. Comp. Prov. iii. 14, 15; Matt xiii., 45, 46.

(2) **Wherefore do ye spend money . . .**—Here again the "bread" is that which sustains the true life of the soul. "Labour" stands for the "earnings of labour." Israel had given her money for that which was "not-bread," she is called to accept the true bread for that which is "not-money," *scil.*, as the next verse shows, for the simple "hearing of faith." "Fatness," as in chap. xxv. 6, and the "fatted calf" of Luke xv. 23, represents the exuberance of spiritual joy.

(3) **Your soul shall live . . .**—Better, *revive.* The idea is that of waking to a new life.

I will make an everlasting covenant . . . —The words find their explanation in the "new covenant" of Jer. xxxi. 31, Luke xxii. 20, but those which follow show that it is thought of as the expansion and completion of that which had been made with David (2 Sam. vii. 12—17; Ps. lxxxix. 34, 35), as the representative of the true King, whom Isaiah now contemplates as identical with the "servant of the Lord." For "sure mercies" read *the unfailing loving-kindnesses,* which were " of David," as given to him and to his seed by Jehovah.

(4) **I have given him . . .**—Better, *I gave,* the words referring primarily to the historic David (Comp. Ps. lxxviii. 70, 71), though realised fully only in Him who was the "faithful and true witness" (John xviii. 37; Rev. i. 5, iii. 14), the "captain" or "leader" of our salvation (Heb. ii. 10).

(5) **Thou shalt call a nation.**—The calling of the Gentiles and the consequent expansion of the true idea of Israel is again dominant. The words sound like an echo from Ps. xviii. 43.

Because of the Lord thy God . . .—The words are repeated, as expressing a thought on which the prophet loved to dwell, in chap. lx. 9.

(6) **While he may be found . . .**—The appeal shows that the promised blessings are not unconditional. There may come a time (as in Matt. xxv. 11) when "too late" will be written on all efforts to gain the inheritance which has been forfeited by neglect (2 Cor. vi. 2).

The Parable of the Rain and Snow. ISAIAH, LVI. *Instead of the Brier the Myrtle Tree.*

near: (7) let the wicked forsake his way, and ¹the unrighteous man his thoughts: and let him return unto the LORD, and he will have mercy upon him; and to our God, for ²he will abundantly pardon. (8) For my thoughts *are* not your thoughts, neither *are* your ways my ways, saith the LORD. (9) For *as* the heavens are higher than the earth, so are my ways higher than your ways, and my thoughts than your thoughts. (10) For as the rain cometh down, and the snow from heaven, and returneth not thither, but watereth the earth, and maketh it bring forth and bud, that it may give seed to the sower, and bread to the eater: (11) so shall my word be that goeth forth out of my mouth: it shall not return unto me void, but it shall accomplish that which I please, and it shall prosper *in the thing* whereto I sent it. (12) For ye shall go out with joy, and be led forth with peace: the mountains and the hills shall *a* break forth before you into singing, and all the trees of the field shall clap *their* hands. (13) Instead of the thorn shall come up the fir tree, and instead of the brier shall come up the myrtle tree: and it shall be to the LORD for a name, for an everlasting sign *that* shall not be cut off.

CHAPTER LVI.—(1) Thus saith the LORD, Keep ye ³judgment, and do justice: for my salvation *is* near to come, and my righteousness to be revealed. (2) Blessed *is* the man *that* doeth this, and the son of man *that* layeth hold on it; that keepeth the sabbath from polluting it, and keepeth his hand from doing any evil. (3) Neither let the son of the stranger, that hath joined himself to the LORD, speak, saying, The LORD hath utterly separated me from his people: neither

1 Heb., *the man of iniquity.*

2 Heb., *he will multiply to pardon.*

a ch. 35. 1.

3 Or, *equity.*

---

(8) **My thoughts are not your thoughts . . .**—The assertion refers to both the promise and the warning. Men think that the gifts of God can be purchased with money (Acts viii. 20). They think that the market in which they are sold is always open, and that they can have them when and how they please (Matt. xxv. 9—13).

(10) **For as the rain cometh down . . .**—The verse includes well-nigh every element of the parables of agriculture. The "rain" and the "dew" are the gracious influences that prepare the heart; the "seed" is the Divine word, the "sower" is the Servant of the Lord, *i.e.*, the Son of Man (Matt. xiii. 37); the "bread" the fruits of holiness that in their turn sustain the life of others.

(11) **So shall my word be . . .**—The point of the comparison is that the predominance of fertility in the natural world, in spite of partial or apparent failures, is the pledge of a like triumph, in the long run, of the purposes of God for man's good over man's resistance. It does not exclude the partial, or even total, failure of many; it asserts that the saved are more than the lost. Comp. chap. liii. 11.

(12) **The mountains and the hills . . .**—Cheyne aptly compares—

"Ipsi lætitia voces ad sidera jactant
Intonsi montes." VIRG., *Æclog.*
(The very hills, no more despoiled of trees,
Shall to the stars break forth in minstrelsies.)

The waving of the branches of the trees is, in the poet's thoughts, what the clapping of hands is with men, a sign of jubilant exultation (Ps. xcvi. 12).

LVI.

(1) **Thus saith the Lord.**—Verses 1—8 form a distinct section, and obviously had an historical starting-point. It has been said (Cheyne, following many other critics) that "the writer of this section presupposes the circumstances of a period long subsequent to the reign of Hezekiah." It will be seen in the following notes that I cannot altogether accept that statement, and find circumstances in the closing years of Isaiah's life which may well have given occasion to his teaching here. It obviously does not stand in any close connection with the preceding chapter.

Keep ye judgment—*i.e.*, the righteousness of the law. The general exhortation is specialised in the next verse.

(2) **That keepeth the sabbath from polluting it . . .**—It lies in the nature of the case that a devout king like Hezekiah would be an observer of the Sabbath. It is almost certain that the counsellors of the young Manasseh (probably the Shebna party), abandoning the religion of Israel in other things, would also disregard this. I take the prophet's teaching accordingly as directed against that evil. He utters his beatitude for those who are faithful to the *régime* of Hezekiah's reign, even though their alien birth or their condition as eunuchs seemed to exclude them from the polity of Israel (Deut. xxiii. 1—8).

(3) **Neither let the son of the stranger . . .**—Two classes of persons were likely to suffer specially from Manasseh's policy—(1) the heathen proselytes, who, as in Ps. lxxxvii., had been admitted as citizens of Zion under Hezekiah's special protection; and (2) in the highest degree, those of that body who had been taken, as Ebed-Melech afterwards was (Jer. xxxviii. 7), into the king's household as eunuchs. The courtiers of Manasseh would taunt them as aliens and in the second case would press the letter of Deut. xxiii. 2. The principle of Isaiah's teaching was, of course, applicable to the Israelites who, like Daniel and his friends, had been mutilated against their will by heathen conquerors (Dan. i. 3), and most commentators refer the words to such cases. It is scarcely probable, however, that the household of Hezekiah would have been supplied with home-born eunuchs, and, on the hypothesis which I have adopted, I find in the eunuchs a sub-section of the proselytes. The words put into the mouths of the complainers are

The Blessings of the Strangers.   ISAIAH, LVI.   *Dumb Dogs that cannot Bark.*

let the eunuch say, Behold, I *am* a dry tree. ⁽⁴⁾ For thus saith the LORD unto the eunuchs that keep my sabbaths, and choose *the things* that please me, and take hold of my covenant; ⁽⁵⁾ even unto them will I give in mine house and within my walls a place and a name better than of sons and of daughters: I will give them an everlasting name, that shall not be cut off. ⁽⁶⁾ Also the sons of the stranger, that join themselves to the LORD, to serve him, and to love the name of the LORD, to be his servants, every one that keepeth the sabbath from polluting it, and taketh hold of my covenant; ⁽⁷⁾ even them will I *ᵃ* bring to my holy mountain, and make them joyful in my house of prayer: their burnt offerings and their sacrifices *shall be* accepted upon mine altar; for *ᵇ*mine house shall be called an house of prayer for all people.

⁽⁸⁾ The Lord GOD which gathereth the outcasts of Israel saith, Yet will I gather *others* to him, ¹beside those that are gathered unto him.

⁽⁹⁾ All ye beasts of the field, come to devour, *yea,* all ye beasts in the forest. ⁽¹⁰⁾ His watchmen *are* blind: they are all ignorant, they *are* all dumb dogs, they cannot bark; ² sleeping, lying down, loving to slumber. ⁽¹¹⁾ Yea, *they are* ³ greedy dogs *which* ⁴ can never have enough, and they *are* shepherds *that* cannot understand: they all look to their own way, every one for his gain, from his quarter. ⁽¹²⁾ Come ye, *say they,* I will fetch wine, and we will fill ourselves with strong drink; and to morrow shall be as this day, *and* much more abundant.

ᵃ ch. 2. 2.

ᵇ Matt. 21. 13; Mark 11. 17; Luke 19. 46.

¹ Heb., *to his gathered.*

² Or, *dreaming,* or, *talking in their sleep.*

³ Heb., *strong of appetite.*

⁴ Heb., *know not to be satisfied.*

---

the natural utterances of men treated as they had been.

⁽⁵⁾ **Even unto them will I give . . .**—The words may refer simply to the spiritual blessedness of the faithful (Rev. ii. 17, iii. 5), but the customs of Eastern temples and of the later synagogues suggest that they may refer primarily to the memorial tablets which were put up in such places in commemoration of distinguished benefactors. For "place" read *memorial.* We note, of course, the special adaptation of the words "better than of sons and daughters" to the case which the prophet has in view; but it has to be remembered also that the whole promise substitutes the principle of catholicity for the rubrics of exclusiveness which we find in Deut. xxiii. 1.

⁽⁶⁾ **Also the sons of the stranger . . .**—Proselytes also were to share in the blessings of the wider covenant. The words "to serve him" have been referred to some menial offices like that of the Nethinim, "hewers of wood and drawers of water" (Josh ix. 27; Ezra viii. 20). The usage of the word, however, limits it to honourable functions. The germ of Isaiah's thought appears in Solomon's dedication prayer (1 Kings viii. 41—43). It receives its highest development (in its entire separation from the building with which there and here it is associated), in John iv. 23. Comp. a further emancipation from the bondage of the law in chap. lxvi. 21.

⁽⁷⁾ **Even them will I bring . . .** The words foreshadow the breaking down of the "middle wall of partition" (Eph. ii. 14). Every privilege of the Israelite worshipper is to belong also to the proselyte. It is perhaps assumed that the proselyte is circumcised. The development of truth is in such cases gradual, and it was left for St. Paul to complete the work of Isaiah (Rom. ii. 26—29; Gal. vi. 15).

⁽⁸⁾ **The Lord God . . . saith.**—The phrase is the normal one for introducing an oracle of special importance. This, so to speak, was to be one of the "faithful sayings" of Isaiah. We can hardly fail to find in John x. 16 a deliberate reproduction of Isaiah's thought. The first clause refers clearly to the gathering of the heathen as following on that of the "outcasts" of Israel.

⁽⁹⁾ **All ye beasts of the field . . .**—The sudden change of tone indicates that we enter on an entirely new section, which extends to the close of chap. lvii. The contents of that section fit in with the assumption of its having been written early in the reign of Manasseh, better than with that of a date after the exile. The opening words summon the enemies of Israel to do their work of punishment, and this is followed naturally by a denunciation of the sins which had made it necessary. For the form of the summons, comp. Ezek. xxxiv. 8; Jer. xii. 9.

⁽¹⁰⁾ **His watchmen are blind.**—These are the guides of the people, and specially the self-styled prophets, who are "blind" to the signs of the times, who are "dumb," and give no warning to the people of the real dangers that threaten them, who prophesy for the rewards of divination (Num. xxii. 7; 1 Sam. ix. 7; Neh. vi. 12), who are conspicuous for their luxury and intemperance. Given the men who are described in chap. v. 22, xxviii. 7, 8, xxx. 10, and the circumstances of Manasseh's reign, no other result could be expected.

Sleeping.—The prophet, with a scornful irony, substitutes *hozim* ("dreamers") for *khozim* ("seers"). The "lying down" contrasts their indolent and easy life with the vigil and the fast of a true prophet.

⁽¹¹⁾ **Shepherds that cannot understand . . .**—Better, *and such are shepherds; they cannot understand.* There is no confusion or change of metaphors. What is implied is that the prophets who are not fit to be watch-dogs of the flock, assume the office of its shepherds.

From his quarter—*i.e.,* in modern phrase, from his own sphere of influence.

⁽¹²⁾ **Come ye, say they . . .**—The words in italics are necessary to complete the sense; but their absence from the Hebrew is noticeable, and noteworthy as an example of the prophet's bold use of a dramatic form. He represents the false prophet as giving a feast to his friends, and promising a yet more splendid banquet on the morrow. Here again we note continuity of character (chap. xxii. 13). Comp. Luke xii. 19, which reads almost like an echo of this passage. (Comp. the dramatic form of chap. xxviii. 9, 10.)

The Righteous taken away   ISAIAH, LVII.   *from the Evil to Come.*

CHAPTER LVII.—⁽¹⁾ The righteous perisheth, and no man layeth it to heart: and ¹ᵃ merciful men *are* taken away, none considering that the righteous is taken away ² from the evil *to come.* ⁽²⁾ He shall ³enter into peace: they shall rest in their beds, *each one* walking ⁴ *in* his uprightness.

⁽³⁾ But draw near hither, ye sons of the sorceress, the seed of the adulterer and the whore. ⁽⁴⁾ Against whom do ye sport yourselves? against whom make ye a wide mouth, *and* draw out the tongue? *are* ye not children of transgression, a seed of falsehood. ⁽⁵⁾ Enflaming yourselves ⁵with idols ᵇ under every green tree, slaying the children in the valleys under the clifts of the rocks? ⁽⁶⁾ Among the smooth *stones* of the stream *is* thy portion; they, they *are* thy lot: even to them hast thou poured a drink offering, thou hast offered a meat offering. Should I receive comfort in these? ⁽⁷⁾ Upon a lofty and high mountain hast thou set thy bed: even thither wentest thou up to offer sacrifice. ⁽⁸⁾ Behind the doors also and the posts hast thou set up thy remembrance: for thou hast discovered *thyself to another* than me, and art gone up; thou hast enlarged thy bed, and ⁶made thee *a* covenant with them; thou lovedst their

Marginal notes: 1 Heb., *men of kindness, or, godliness.* / a Ps. 12. 1; Mic. 7. 2. / 2 Or, *from that which is evil.* / 3 Or, *go in peace.* / 4 Or, *before him.* / 5 Or, *among the oaks.* / b 2 Kings 16. 4. / 6 Or, *hewed it for thyself larger than their's.*

LVII.

⁽¹⁾ **The righteous perisheth . . .**—The words seem written as if in the anticipation or in the actual presence of Manasseh's persecution of the true prophets. Even before that persecution burst out in its full violence, the "righteous" survivors of Hezekiah's *régime* may well have vexed their souls even to death with the evils that were around them. The prophet finds comfort in the thought that their death was a deliverance from yet worse evils. The singular number points to the few conspicuous sufferers.

⁽²⁾ **He shall enter into peace . . .**—Noticeable as presenting the brighter side of the dim thoughts of Israel as to the life behind the veil, and so far contrasted with Hezekiah's shrinking fear. (Comp. Job iii. 17.) For the righteous there was peace in death as in life. For the wicked there was peace in neither (verse 21).

They shall rest in their beds.—The "bed" is obviously the grave, the thought following naturally on that of death being as the sleep "after life's fitful fever." (Ezek. xxxii. 25.)

Each one walking in his uprightness.—Better, *every one who has walked straight before him—has taken,* i.e., the straight path of duty (chap. xxx. 21.)

⁽³⁾ **Ye sons of the sorceress.**—The words may be purely figurative, as meaning those who practise sorcery, but it is also possible that they may have reference to the female soothsayers, such as are described in Ezek. xiii. 17–23.

The adulterer.—Here again the epithet may have had both a figurative and a literal application. (Comp. Matt. xii. 39, xvi. 4; James iv. 4.)

⁽⁴⁾ **Against whom do ye sport yourselves?**—The question, as in chap. xxxvii. 23, is one of indignant scorn, the implied answer being that the mockers were deriding the servants of Jehovah. (Comp. Wisd. ii.), and, in so doing, mocking Jehovah himself. The "wide mouth," and the "drawn-out tongue," are the natural symbols of derision.

⁽⁵⁾ **Enflaming yourselves.**—The best illustration of the phrase is found in the real or supposed derivation of "fanatic" as meaning one who is *circa fana calefactus*. No word could better describe the orgiastic excitement of heathen rites. For "with idols" read *among the terebinths*, which were prominent, with other trees, in the groves dedicated to idol-worship (Hos. iv. 13; Ezek. vi. 13).

Under every green tree is almost a stereotyped formula in this connection (Deut. xii. 2; 1 Kings xiv. 23; Jer. ii. 20), the tree itself becoming a direct object of the *cultus*.

Slaying the children in the valleys. . . .—This had been done by Ahaz (2 Chron. xxviii. 3). It was perfectly natural that it should be done by Manasseh. There is not the slightest trace of the revival of the practice among the exiles in Babylon or after their return. The scenery described—the torrent-stream, the clefts of the rock—belongs distinctively to Palestine.

⁽⁶⁾ **Among the smooth stones . . .**—The worship of stones was almost as widely diffused as that of trees and serpents. In Gen. xxviii. 18 we have, at least, an analogous practice, which might easily become identical. Among the Phœnicians such stones were known as *Bœtulia* (probably a Grecised form of Bethel), and were connected with the worship of the reproductive powers of nature. As the true portion of Israel was emphatically Jehovah (Jer. x. 16; Ps. xvi. 5) there is an indignant irony in the word thus used. The idolaters had chosen a *fetish* instead of the Eternal One. In *thy portion,* we have the feminine singular, designating Israel as the faithless wife.

Should I receive comfort in these?—i.e., better, *Should I be quiet in spite of all this?* (Comp. Jer. v. 7.)

⁽⁷⁾ **Set thy bed . . .**—Idolatry being as adultery, the "bed" follows naturally as representing the locality of the idol-worship. Comp. Ezek. xvi. 31, xxiii. 17.

⁽⁸⁾ **Hast thou set up thy remembrance . . .**—The noun has been commonly referred to the *Mesusah,* or memorial text, "Jehovah is our God; Jehovah is one," which was to be written on the door-posts of each house (Deut. vi. 9, xi. 20); and the prophet is supposed to point to the fact that this had been written *behind* the door, as showing that Israel had been ashamed to confess her creed. The explanation seems tenable, but it is possible that "remembrance" may stand for some idolatrous symbol or inscription which had been substituted for the true confession.

Thou hast discovered thyself.—The figure of the unfaithful wife is carried into its details almost with Ezekiel's boldness.

Made thee a covenant with them . . .—The noun, as the italics show, is implied in the verb. The faithless wife forsook the covenant of her youth with her husband, and made a fresh compact with the adulterers.

556

bed ¹where thou sawest *it*. ⁽⁹⁾ And ²thou wentest to the king with ointment, and didst increase thy perfumes, and didst send thy messengers far off, and didst debase *thyself even* unto hell. ⁽¹⁰⁾ Thou art wearied in the greatness of thy way; *yet* saidst thou not, There is no hope: thou hast found the ³life of thine hand; therefore thou wast not grieved.

⁽¹¹⁾ And of whom hast thou been afraid or feared, that thou hast lied, and hast not remembered me, nor laid *it* to thy heart? have not I held my peace even of old, and thou fearest me not? ⁽¹²⁾ I will declare thy righteousness, and thy works; for they shall not profit thee. ⁽¹³⁾ When thou criest, let thy companies deliver thee; but the wind shall carry them all away; vanity shall take *them*: but he that putteth his trust in me shall possess the land, and shall inherit my holy mountain; ⁽¹⁴⁾ and shall say, ᵃCast ye up, cast ye up, prepare the way, take up the stumbling-block out of the way of my people.

⁽¹⁵⁾ For thus saith the high and lofty One that inhabiteth eternity, whose name *is* Holy; I dwell in the high and holy *place*, with him also *that is* of a contrite and humble spirit, to revive the spirit of the humble, and to revive the heart of the contrite ones. ⁽¹⁶⁾ For I will not contend for ever, neither will I be always wroth: for the spirit should fail before me, and the souls which I

1 Or, *thou providedst room.*
2 Or, *thou respectedst the king.*
3 Or, *living.*
a ch. 40. 3 & 62. 10.

Where thou sawest it.—*And thou sawest the place*, the words being used euphemistically for the obscene image of a Chemosh-like idol.

⁽⁹⁾ **Thou wentest to the king . . .**—The alteration of a single letter would give *to Molech*; and this may be the meaning even of the text as it stands. Looking to the Manasseh-surroundings of the passage, however, it is more natural to refer the words to the king, the great king of Assyria, whose religion Judah had basely and shamefully adopted. The sin of Ahaz (2 Kings xvi. 11) had been reproduced by his grandson. The description that follows is that of a harlot adorning herself for her evil calling, and finds its best illustration in Prov. vii. 14—17. Looking to the previous traces of Isaiah's study of that book (chap. xi. 1—4, &c.) we may, perhaps, find in it a deliberate reproduction of that passage. The "ointment" and "perfumes" are symbols of the treasures which were lavished to secure the Assyrian alliance. The words help us to understand Isaiah's indignation at what must have seemed to him the initial step of a like policy on the part of Hezekiah (chap. xxxix. 3—7). The words which point to the "far-off" land, to which the messengers were sent, seem almost like an echo from that king's apology.

Even unto hell—*i.e.*, Hades or Sheol, the world of the dead—as the symbol of an abysmal depth of degradation.

⁽¹⁰⁾ **Thou art wearied in the greatness of thy way . . .**—Better, *with the length of thy journey*—*i.e.*, with the long embassies to Assyria, and to Babylon, as for the time the residence of its kings. For "there is no hope," read, *there is no result*, or *profit*. Judah would not acknowledge that the negotiations were fruitless.

Thou hast found the life of thine hand . . .—The words are a literal rendering, and convey the meaning, *Thou didst renew the strength of thine hand*—*i.e.*, Judah found a fancied increase of power in the alliance she was seeking, and therefore did not repent of her ignominious diplomacy.

⁽¹¹⁾ **And of whom hast thou been afraid . . . ?**—The question implies that Judah had been led by the fear of man to forsake the fear of Jehovah, and this had led her to what was, in the fullest sense of the word, the false step of an alliance with Assyria, which was an acted lie.

Have I not held my peace . . . ?—The words suggest, half-pityingly, the cause of the people's little faith. From "of old," *i.e.*, during the period that preceded the captivity, or perhaps in the dark time of Manasseh, Jehovah had been silent, and His long-suffering had been mistaken for apathy, and therefore the people had not feared Him.

⁽¹²⁾ **I will declare thy righteousness . . .**—Accepting the Hebrew text, we must look on the word as used ironically, the righteousness which is no righteousness. Comp. chap. lxiv. 6. A slight alteration, adopted by many critics, gives "*my righteousness.*"

⁽¹³⁾ **Let thy companies . . .**—The word is used contemptuously of the crowd of gods introduced by the confluent idolatry of Manasseh. (Comp. 2 Chron. xxxiii. 3—7.) The prophet taunts the worshipper with their impotence, "Let them save thee, if they can," but that taunt is followed by a declaration that true help and strength will be given to all who trust in Jehovah.

⁽¹⁴⁾ **And shall say . . .**—Better, *And one said*. The prophet hears, as it were, a voice behind him, bringing an oracle from Heaven, which renews the cry of the herald in chap. xl. 3. The verb, *cast up*, points to the construction of the "highway" of a spiritual return, from which all impediments are removed.

⁽¹⁵⁾ **For thus saith the high and lofty . . .**—The central truth for the comfort of God's people is that the infinitely Great One cares even for the infinitely little. The truth of the greatness of lowliness manifested in the life of Christ was but the reflection of the permanent law of the Divine government. The "high and holy place" is, of course, the heavenly temple, the "light inaccessible." The verse, as a whole, combines the truths of 2 Chron. vi. 18, and Ps. li. 17.

⁽¹⁶⁾ **I will not contend for ever . . .**—The words come as a message of comfort to the penitent who is still bearing the chastisement of his sins. The time during which God "contends" with him as an accuser and a judge has its limits. Were it not so, the souls which he had made would be utterly consumed, and His purpose in creation would be frustrated. The words seem like an echo of Gen. vi. 3, viii. 21. (Comp. Ps. ciii. 9, 10).

The Healing of the Transgressor. ISAIAH, LVIII. *The Counterfeit and the True Fast.*

have made. (17) For the iniquity of his covetousness was I wroth, and smote him: I hid me, and was wroth, and he went on ¹frowardly in the way of his heart. (18) I have seen his ways, and will heal him: I will lead him also, and restore comforts unto him and to his mourners. (19) I create the fruit of the lips; Peace, peace to *him that is* far off, and to *him that is* near, saith the LORD; and I will heal him. (20) But the wicked *are* like the troubled sea, when it cannot rest, whose waters cast up mire and dirt. (21) ᵃ*There is* no peace, saith my God, to the wicked.

CHAPTER LVIII.—(1) Cry ²aloud,

1 Heb., *turning away.*

a ch. 48. 22.

2 Heb., *with the throat.*

3 Or, *things wherewith ye grieve others.*

4 Heb. *griefs.*

5 Or, *ye fast not as this day.*

B.C. cir. 698.

spare not, lift up thy voice like a trumpet, and shew my people their transgression, and the house of Jacob their sins. (2) Yet they seek me daily, and delight to know my ways, as a nation that did righteousness, and forsook not the ordinance of their God: they ask of me the ordinances of justice; they take delight in approaching to God.
(3) Wherefore have we fasted, *say they*, and thou seest not? *wherefore* have we afflicted our soul, and thou takest no knowledge? Behold, in the day of your fast ye find pleasure, and exact all your ³⁴labours. (4) Behold, ye fast for strife and debate, and to smite with the fist of wickedness: ⁵ye shall not fast as

---

(17) **For the iniquity of his covetousness . . .** —Literally, *of his gain.* This was the root-evil, out of which all others sprang (Jer. vi. 13; Ezek. xxxiii. 31; 1 Tim. vi. 10), and for this, therefore, a sharp chastisement was needed that men might learn what their true wealth consisted in. The last clause may either state the guilt which caused the wrath, or paint the obduracy which went on doing evil in spite of it.

(18) **I have seen his ways . . .** —The words have been interpreted: (1) of the evil ways described in the previous verse; (2) of the way of repentance into which Israel had been led by chastisement. (1) seems most in harmony with the context. The paths had been rough and thorny, but Jehovah presents Himself as the Healer to those who had been wounded by them, and leads them into a better way. The "mourners" are those who have been touched as with the "godly sorrow" of 2 Cor. vii. 10, 11.

(19) **The fruit of the lips . . .** —The words point primarily to the praise and thanksgiving of the pardoned penitent (comp. Hos. xiv. 2; Heb. xiii. 15), but include also all true utterances of the wise of heart (Prov. x. 31). All these alike have their origin in the creative fiat of Jehovah, which proclaims "peace" (*i.e.*, salvation) to all, whether near or far, Jews in Jerusalem, or Jews in exile, or (as in Eph. ii. 17) the Gentiles whose distance was that of spiritual remoteness. The message of healing is for all.

(20) **The wicked are like the troubled sea . . .** —The promise of healing is, however, not unconditional. The acceptance of peace requires calmness; but for the wicked, whose thoughts are restlessly seething with evil ripening into act, this true peace is, in the nature of the case, impossible. We note the recurrence of the watchword of chap. xlviii. 22, as indicating the close of another section of the prophecy. The MSS. and versions present a curious variation in verse 21: some "saith Jehovah," some "God," some "the Lord God." It would almost seem as if transcribers and translators had shrunk from the prophet's boldness in claiming God as in some special sense his God. It has a parallel, however, in chap. vii. 13, and may be noted, accordingly, as one of the characteristic touches common to the two parts of Isaiah. The "Sea" of which Isaiah speaks may possibly have been the Dead Sea, casting up its salt bituminous deposits.

LVIII.

(1) **Cry aloud . . .** —Literally, *with the throat, i.e.,* with no faint whisper as from stammering lips, but with full strength of voice. The work of the preacher of repentance is not to be done slightly or by speaking smooth things (comp. Ezek. xiii. 10—15). The "trumpet" of the next clause emphasises the thought yet further.

(2) **Yet they seek me daily . . .** —The "seeking" is that of those who come, like the elders in Ezek. xx. 1, to "enquire" of Jehovah, and looking for an oracle from Him. The words point to the incongruous union, possible in the reign of Manasseh, but hardly possible after the exile, of this formal recognition of Jehovah with an apostate life. Every phrase rings in the tone of an incisive irony, describing each element of a true devotion which the people did *not* possess.

(3) **Wherefore have we fasted . . .** —The words remind us of those of a much later prophet (Mal. iii. 14), but the complaints of the unconscious hypocrites who are amazed that their service is not accepted as sincere are in every age the same. Only one fast, that of the Day of Atonement, was prescribed by the Law. In practice, however, they were often held in times of calamity (comp. chap. xxxii. 12; Joel i. 13; 2 Chron. xx. 3), and we may legitimately think of them as having been more or less frequent under Hezekiah (chap. xxxvii. 1, 2). Now, as though that had been a meritorious work, the people ask what good had come of it? After the exile fasts were instituted, commemorative of the siege of Jerusalem, its capture, its destruction, and the murder of Gedaliah (Zech. vii. 3, viii. 19), and those who maintain the later date of the book naturally suppose that these are the fasts referred to.

In the day of your fast ye find pleasure . . . —Better, *ye carry on your business.* Fasts were not governed, like the Sabbath, by a fixed law, and the people consequently lost sight of the true end of fasting—prayer, meditation, penitence.

Exact all your labours.—The words are rendered by some critics more vividly, though with the same meaning, *ye oppress all your labourers.* (Comp. Jas. v. 4.)

(4) **Behold, ye fast for strife and debate.**—The words possibly point to the psychological fact that

The Fast of the Hypocrite. ISAIAH, LVIII. *The Fast of the Godly.*

ye do this day, to make your voice to be heard on high. ⁽⁵⁾ Is it ^a such a fast that I have chosen? ^{b 1}a day for a man to afflict his soul? *is it* to bow down his head as a bulrush, and to spread sackcloth and ashes *under him?* wilt thou call this a fast, and an acceptable day to the LORD? ⁽⁶⁾ *Is* not this the fast that I have chosen? to loose the bands of wickedness, to undo ²the heavy burdens, and to let the ³oppressed go free, and that ye break every yoke? ⁽⁷⁾ *Is it* not ^cto deal thy bread to the hungry, and that thou bring the poor that are ⁴cast out to thy house? when thou seest the naked, that thou cover him; and that thou hide not thyself from thine own flesh? ⁽⁸⁾ Then shall thy light break forth as the morning, and thine health shall spring forth speedily: and thy righteousness shall go before thee; the glory of the LORD ⁵shall be thy rereward. ⁽⁹⁾ Then shalt thou call, and the LORD shall answer; thou shalt cry, and he shall say, Here I *am*. If thou take away from the midst of thee the yoke, the putting forth of the finger, and speaking vanity; ⁽¹⁰⁾ and *if* thou draw out thy soul to the hungry, and satisfy the afflicted soul; then shall thy light rise in obscurity, and thy darkness *be* as the noon day: ⁽¹¹⁾ and the LORD shall guide thee continually, and satisfy thy soul in ⁶drought, and make fat thy bones: and thou shalt be like a watered garden, and like a spring of water, whose waters ⁷fail not. ⁽¹²⁾ And *they that shall be* of thee ^dshall build the old waste places: thou shalt raise up the foundations of

a Zech. 7. 5.
b Lev. 16. 29.
1 Or, *to afflict his soul for a day?*
2 Heb., *the bundles of the yoke.*
3 Heb., *broken.*
c Ezek. 18. 7.
4 Or, *afflicted.*
5 Heb., *shall gather thee up.*
6 Heb., *droughts.*
7 Heb., *lie, or, deceive.*
d ch. 61. 4.

---

an unspiritual fasting irritates the nerves and embitters the temper. Extremes meet, and the disputes of fasting controversialists are often as fierce as those of drunken disputants. (Comp. the conspiracy of Acts xxiii. 21.)

⁽⁵⁾ **A day for a man to afflict his soul.**—The phrase comes from Lev. xvi. 29, and describes the soul-sorrow which was the true ideal of fasting. In contrast with this we have the picture, reminding us of Matt. vi. 16, of the mechanical prostrations, which are as the waving of a bulrush in the breeze. The image suggests a new aspect of our Lord's statement, that the Baptist was not as "a reed shaken by the wind" (Matt. xi. 7), *scil.*, that his fasting was not outward and ceremonial, like that of the Pharisees.

⁽⁶⁾ **To loose the bands of wickedness.**—The words do not exclude abstinence from food as an act of discipline and victory over self-indulgence, but declare its insufficiency by itself. So in the practice of the ancient Church fasting and almsgiving were closely connected, as indeed they are in Matt. vi. 1, 16. The history of the emancipation of the slaves and of their subsequent return to bondage presents a curious illustration of the prophet's words (Jer. xxxiv. 8—22). The truth which he proclaimed was recognised in the hour of danger and forgotten in that of safety. Comp. Joel ii. 13.

To undo the heavy burdens.—Literally, *the thongs of the yoke,* the leather straps which fastened the yoke on the head of the oxen as they ploughed. Again we trace an echo of the thought and almost of the phraseology in our Lord's teaching (Matt. xi. 29, 30, xxiii. 4). The Pharisees who fasted laid heavy burdens on men's shoulders. He, who was thought not to fast, relieved them of their two-fold yoke of evil selfishness and ceremonial formalism.

⁽⁷⁾ **To deal thy bread.**—Literally, *to break bread,* as in the familiar phrase of the New Testament (Matt. xxvi. 26; Acts xx. 11, xxvii. 34). The bread of the Jews seems to have been made always in the thin oval cakes, which were naturally broken rather than cut.

The poor that are cast out.—The words include all forms of homelessness—tenants evicted by their landlords, debtors by their creditors, slaves fleeing from their masters' cruelty, the persecuted for righteousness' sake, perhaps even political refugees. Note the parallelism with Matt. xxv. 35, 36.

From thine own flesh.—Usage, as in Gen. xxix. 14; Neh. v. 5, leads us to refer the words primarily to suffering Israelites, but those who have learnt that "God hath made of one blood all the nations of the earth" (Acts xvii. 26) will extend its range to every form of suffering humanity.

⁽⁸⁾ **Then shall thy light . . .**—The dawning of a new day, as in 2 Sam. xxiii. 4; the growth as of new and healthy flesh after long illness; "righteousness," *i.e.,* the sentence of acquittal in the eyes of all the world, as leading the van of a triumphant march, the "glory of Jehovah" following in the rear as a protection; all these images are heaped together to paint the fulness of blessing that follows on that true renunciation of the old evil selfishness of which fasting is but a symbol and a part.

⁽⁹⁾ **Then shalt thou call.**—The words point to the secret of the prayer which is answered in contrast to the formal worship that found no acceptance (verses 2, 4).

The putting forth of the finger.—The gesture (Cheyne compares the "*infamis digitus*" of Persius ii. 33) has in well-nigh all nations been a natural symbol of scorn. It is in action what the words "Raca" and "Thou fool" are in the language of Matt. v. 22.

⁽¹⁰⁾ **Draw out thy soul.**—The words have been interpreted as meaning (1) giving up sensuous desires for the sake of others; (2) ministering of thy substance; (3) extending thy sympathy. On the whole, (3) seems preferable.

Then shall thy light rise.—We note the recurrence of the imagery of chap. ix. 2.

⁽¹¹⁾ **In drought.**—Literally, *droughts,* either with the force of intensity or as meaning "dry places."

And make fat.—Better, *shall strengthen,* or *make supple.*

Like a watered garden.—Comp. Ps. i. 3, Isa. xliv. 3, 4, Jer. xxxi. 12, in the last of which we have the self-same phrase.

⁽¹²⁾ **Shall build the old waste places.**—The prophet contemplates primarily the restoration of the

many generations; and thou shalt be called, The repairer of the breach, The restorer of paths to dwell in. ⁽¹³⁾ If thou turn away thy foot from the sabbath, *from* doing thy pleasure on my holy day; and call the sabbath a delight, the holy of the LORD, honourable; and shalt honour him, not doing thine own ways, nor finding thine own pleasure, nor speaking *thine own* words: ⁽¹⁴⁾ Then shalt thou delight thyself in the LORD; and I will cause thee to ^aride upon the high places of the earth, and feed thee with the heritage of Jacob thy father: for the mouth of the LORD hath spoken *it*.

CHAPTER LIX.—⁽¹⁾ Behold, the LORD's hand is not ^bshortened, that it cannot save; neither his ear heavy, that it cannot hear: ⁽²⁾ but your iniquities have separated between you and your God, and your sins ¹have hid *his* face from you, that he will not hear. ⁽³⁾ For ^cyour hands are defiled with blood, and your fingers with iniquity; your lips have spoken lies, your tongue hath muttered perverseness. ⁽⁴⁾ None calleth for justice, nor *any* pleadeth for truth: they trust in vanity, and speak lies; ^dthey conceive mischief, and bring forth iniquity. ⁽⁵⁾ They hatch ²cockatrice' eggs, and weave the spider's web: he that eateth of their eggs dieth, and ³that which is crushed breaketh out into a viper. ⁽⁶⁾ ^eTheir webs shall not become garments, neither shall they cover themselves with their works: their works *are* works of iniquity, and the act of violence *is* in their hands. ⁽⁷⁾ ^fTheir feet run to evil, and they make haste to shed innocent blood: their thoughts *are* thoughts of iniquity; wasting and ⁴destruction *are* in their paths. ⁽⁸⁾ The way of peace they know not; and *there is* no ⁵judgment in their goings: they have made them crooked paths: whosoever goeth therein shall not know peace.

⁽⁹⁾ Therefore is judgment far from us, neither doth justice overtake us: we wait for light, but behold obscurity; for

---

a Deut. 32. 13.

b Num. 11. 23; ch. 50. 2.

¹ Or, *have made him hide.*

c ch. 1. 15.

d Job 15. 35; Ps. 7. 14.

² Or, *adders'*.

³ Or, *that which is sprinkled is as if there brake out a viper.*

e Job. 8. 14, 15.

f Prov. 1. 16; Rom. 3. 15.

⁴ Heb., *breaking.*

⁵ Or, *right.*

---

public and private buildings of Jerusalem, but the words have obviously a wider spiritual application.

The foundations of many generations—*i.e.*, those that had been lying in ruins, with no superstructure, for even a longer period than the seventy years of exile.

Thou shalt be called . . .—This was to be the special work, and was to constitute the enduring fame, of the new Israel.

Paths to dwell in—*i.e.*, the streets of the city shall be once more flanked with houses on either side, and not merely roads from one point to another.

⁽¹³⁾ **If thou turn away thy foot.**—The teaching of chap. lvi. 4—7, as to the Sabbath is resumed. The form of the phrase implies the idea that the Sabbath is as holy ground, on which no profane foot must tread (Exod. iii. 5).

Thy pleasure.—Better, *thy business.*

Nor speaking thine own words.—Literally, *speak words*, as in Hos. x. 4, for idle unprofitable talk (Prov. x. 19, Eccles. v. 3).

⁽¹⁴⁾ **I will cause thee to ride upon the high places of the earth.**—Better, *of the land:* i.e., of Canaan, the idea being that of a victorious march to occupy all commanding positions, and thus connecting itself with the full enjoyment of the heritage of Israel in the next clause.

LIX.

⁽¹⁾ **Behold, the Lord's hand . . .**—The declaration is an implied answer to the complaint, like that of chap. lviii. 3, that the glorious promises had not as yet been fulfilled. The murmurers are told that the hindrance is on their side.

⁽²⁾ **Have separated**—*i.e.*, have become, as it were, a "middle wall of partition" excluding them from the Divine presence.

His face.—Better, *the face.* The Hebrew has neither article nor possessive pronoun, the substantive being treated almost as a proper name.

⁽³⁾ **Your hands are defiled with blood.**—The accusation of the "grand indictment" of chap. i. 15 is reproduced *verbatim.*

⁽⁴⁾ **None calleth for justice.**—Better, *none preferreth his suit with truthfulness.* The words point chiefly to the guilt of unrighteous prosecutions, but may include that of false witness also.

They trust in vanity.—Literally, *in chaos*—the characteristic *tohu* of both parts of Isaiah (chaps. xxiv. 10, xxix. 21, xl. 17, 23).

⁽⁵⁾ **They hatch cockatrice' eggs.** — Better, *basilisk's*, as in chap. xiv. 29. The schemes of the evil-doers are displayed in their power for evil and their impotence for good. To "eat of the eggs," which are assumed to be poisonous, is to fall in with their schemes, and so be ruined: to "crush" them is to oppose and so to rouse a more venomous opposition. Men break the egg, and the living viper darts forth to attack them.

⁽⁶⁾ **Their webs shall not become garments.**—See the same figure in chap. xxx. 1. The point of the comparison lies chiefly in the uselessness of the spider's webs, but the second clause emphasises also the fact that the only purpose which the webs serve is one of mischief. They may catch flies, they cannot clothe men.

⁽⁷⁾ **Their feet run to evil.**—Note the parallelisms, entirely after the manner of Isaiah, with Prov. i. 16, xvi. 17. So the four words "paths," "goings," "ways," and "paths" (another word in the Hebrew) are all from the same book.

⁽⁹⁾ **Therefore is judgment.**—The pleading of the prophet is followed by the confession which he makes on their behalf. They admit that the delay in

The Groping of the Blind.   ISAIAH, LIX.   *The Armour of Righteousness.*

brightness, *but* we walk in darkness. ⁽¹⁰⁾ We grope for the wall like the blind, and we grope as if *we had* no eyes: we stumble at noon day as in the night; *we are* in desolate places as dead *men.* ⁽¹¹⁾ We roar all like bears, and mourn sore like doves: we look for judgment, but *there is* none; for salvation, *but* it is far off from us. ⁽¹²⁾ For our transgressions are multiplied before thee, and our sins testify against us: for our transgressions *are* with us; and *as for* our iniquities, we know them; ⁽¹³⁾ in transgressing and lying against the LORD, and departing away from our God, speaking oppression and revolt, conceiving and uttering from the heart words of falsehood. ⁽¹⁴⁾ And judgment is turned away backward, and justice standeth afar off: for truth is fallen in the street, and equity cannot enter. ⁽¹⁵⁾ Yea, truth faileth; and he *that* departeth from evil ¹maketh himself a prey:

And the LORD saw *it,* and ²it displeased him that *there was* no judgment. ⁽¹⁶⁾ And he saw that *there was* no man, and wondered that *there was* no intercessor: *ᵃ* therefore his arm brought salvation unto him; and his righteousness, it sustained him. ⁽¹⁷⁾ *ᵇ* For he put on righteousness as a breastplate, and an helmet of salvation upon his head; and he put on the garments of vengeance *for* clothing, and was clad with zeal as a cloke. ⁽¹⁸⁾ *ᶜ* According to *their* ³deeds, accordingly he will repay, fury to his adversaries, recompence to his enemies; to the islands he will repay recompence. ⁽¹⁹⁾ So shall they fear the name of the LORD from the west, and his glory from the rising of the sun. When the enemy

Marginal notes:
¹ Or, *is accounted mad.*
² Heb., *it was evil in his eyes.*
ᵃ ch. 63. 5.
ᵇ Eph. 6. 17; 1 Thess. 5. 8.
ᶜ ch. 63. 6.
³ Heb., *recompences.*

---

the manifestation of God's judgment against their enemies, and of His righteousness (*i.e.,* bounty) towards themselves, has been caused by their own sins.

We wait for light.—The cry of the expectant Israelites is, *mutatis mutandis,* like that of the "How long?" of Zech. i. 12; Rev. vi. 10. On the assumption that the words come ideally from the Babylonian exiles, the first of these passages presents an interesting coincidence.

⁽¹⁰⁾ **We grope for the wall . . .**—The words present a striking parallelism with Deut. xxviii. 29, and may have been reproduced from, or in, it.

We are in desolate places . . .—Many critics render, (1) *among those full of life,* or (2) *in luxuriant fields,* of which (1) is preferable, as giving an antithesis like that of the other clauses. So taken, we have a parallelism with Ps. lxxiii. 5—8.

⁽¹¹⁾ **We roar all like bears . . .**—The comparison is not found elsewhere in Scripture, but Horace (*Epp.* xvi. 51) gives "*circumgemit ursus ovile.*" For the dove, comp. chap. xxxviii. 14; Ezek. vii. 16.

⁽¹²⁾ **For our transgressions . . .**—The parallelism with the confessions of Daniel (chap. ix. 5—15) and Ezra (chap. ix. 6—15) is singularly striking, but is as explicable on the hypothesis that they reproduced that of 2 Isaiah as on the assumption that this also was written at the close of the exile. It would, of course, be as true in the time of Manasseh as at any subsequent period. The self accusations of the people are now, as they ought to be, as full and severe as the prophet's original indictment had been.

⁽¹³⁾ **In transgressing . . .**—The clauses point respectively (1) to false and hypocritical worship; (2) to open apostacy; (3) to sins against man, and these subdivided into (*a*) sins against truth, and (*b*) sins against justice.

⁽¹⁴⁾ **Truth is fallen in the street**—*i.e.,* the broad open place, or *agora,* of the city. The words point naturally to Jerusalem. If they refer to Babylon, we must assume, unless we deal with the language as altogether figurative, that the exiles had a quarter of their own, in which they had an *agora* for business and judicial proceedings.

⁽¹⁵⁾ **Truth faileth**—*i.e.,* is banished, and becomes as a missing and lost thing. The man who departs from evil is but the victim of the evil-doers. Other renderings are (1) *is outlawed,* and (2) *is counted mad,* but the Authorised Version is quite tenable. The words remind us of the terrible picture of Greek demoralisation in Thuc. iii.

And the Lord saw it . . .—The verse at first suggests the thought that what Jehovah saw were the sins thus described. The sequence of thought, however, tends to the conclusion that the words are properly the beginning of a new section, and that the supplied pronoun refers to the repentance and confession of the people. It displeased Him—literally, *was evil in His eyes*—that the penitents were still subject to oppression, that they found no leader and deliverer, and therefore He came, as it were, alone and unaided, to the rescue. (Comp. Joel ii. 17—19.)

⁽¹⁶⁾ **He saw that there was no man . . .**—If the words mean no "righteous man," we have a parallel in Jer. v. 1, and the "intercessor" points to action like that of Aaron (Num. xvi. 48) or Phinehas (Num. xxv. 7). On the interpretation here adopted, "no man" is equivalent to "no champion."

⁽¹⁷⁾ **He put on righteousness . . .**—The close parallelism with chap. xi. points, as far as it goes, to identity of authorship; and that with Eph. vi. 14—17 suggests a new significance for St. Paul's "whole armour of God."

The garments of vengeance . . .—As parts of a warrior's dress the "garments" are the short tunic, or tabard, which hung over the breast-plate; the "cloke" the scarlet mantle (the *chlamys* of the Roman soldier), its colour probably making it a fit symbol of the zeal of Jehovah.

⁽¹⁸⁾ **To his adversaries . . .**—The judgment is generally against all, in Israel or outside it, who come under this description. The word "islands" is used, as elsewhere, for far-off lands. The words point to every such judgment, from that of Cyrus to the great final day.

⁽¹⁹⁾ **When the enemy shall come in . . .**—The noun admits of the senses "adversary," "adversity,"

shall come in ª like a flood, the Spirit of the LORD shall ¹lift up a standard against him. (20) And ᵇthe Redeemer shall come to Zion, and unto them that turn from transgression in Jacob, saith the LORD.

(21) As for me, this *is* my covenant with them, saith the LORD; My spirit that *is* upon thee, and my words which I have put in thy mouth, shall not depart out of thy mouth, nor out of the mouth of thy seed, nor out of the mouth of thy seed's seed, saith the LORD, from henceforth and for ever.

CHAPTER LX.—(1) Arise, ²shine; for thy light is come, and the glory of the LORD is risen upon thee. (2) For, behold, the darkness shall cover the earth, and gross darkness the people: but the LORD shall arise upon thee, and his glory shall be seen upon thee. (3) And the ᶜGentiles shall come to thy light, and kings to the brightness of thy rising. (4) ᵈLift up thine eyes round about, and see: all they gather themselves together, they come to thee: thy sons shall come from far, and thy daughters shall be nursed at thy side. (5) Then thou shalt see, and flow together, and thine heart shall fear, and be enlarged; because the ³abundance of the sea shall be converted unto thee, the ⁴forces of the Gentiles shall come unto thee. (6) The multitude of camels shall cover thee, the dromedaries of Midian and Ephah; all they from Sheba shall come: they shall bring ᵉgold and incense; and they shall shew forth the praises of the LORD. (7) All the flocks of Kedar shall be gathered together unto thee, the rams of Nebaioth shall minister unto thee: they shall come up with acceptance on mine altar, and I will glorify the house of my glory.

(8) Who *are* these *that* fly as a cloud, and as the doves to their windows? (9) Surely the isles shall wait for me,

a Rev. 12. 15.
¹ Or, *put him to flight.*
b Rom. 11. 26.
² Or, *be enlightened? for thy light cometh.*
c Rev. 21. 24.
d ch. 49. 18.
³ Or, *noise of the sea shall be turned toward thee.*
⁴ Or, *wealth.*
e ch. 61. 6.

"hemmed in," "rushing," and the verse has accordingly been very differently rendered. (1) *He (Jehovah) shall come like a rushing stream which the breath of Jehovah (i.e.,* a strong and mighty wind) *driveth.* (2) *Adversity shall come like a stream.* The verse is difficult, but the Authorised Version is, at least, as tenable as any other rendering, and finds parallelisms in Jer. xlvi. 7, 8 for the image of a flood, and in Ps. lx. 4 for that of the banner. (Comp. also chap. xi. 10.)

(20) **And the Redeemer shall come. . .**—The picture of the Theophany is continued—Jehovah comes as a Redeemer (Goel, as in chaps. xli. 14, xliii. 1, Job xix. 25) to the true Zion, to those who have turned from their transgression. The verse is noticeable as being quoted, with variations, by St. Paul in Rom. xi. 26.

(21) **As for me, this is my covenant . . .**—The words are, as to their form, an echo of Gen. xvii. 4; as to their meaning, the germ of Jer. xxxi. 31; Heb. viii. 10, x. 16. The new covenant is to involve the gift of the Spirit, that writes the law of God inwardly in the heart, as distinct from the Law, which is thought of as outside the conscience, doing its work as an accuser and a judge.

LX.

(1) **Arise, shine . . .**—The description of the redeemed Zion—*i.e.,* the new Jerusalem—seen in the prophet's vision as under the forms of the old. She has been prostrate, as in the darkness of Sheol (as in chaps. li. 23, lvii. 9). The word comes that bids her rise to a new life, radiant with the glory of the Lord. In Eph. v. 14 we have, perhaps, an echo, though not a quotation, of the prophet's words.

(2) **The darkness shall cover the earth . . .**—The darkness which had shrouded Zion still spreads its veil over the heathen nations of the world, but they also are to share in the light which is to stream forth from the new Jerusalem. (Comp. Mal. iv. 2; Ps. lxxxiv. 11.)

(4) **Lift up thine eyes . . .**—Repeated from chap. xlix. 18.

Thy daughters shall be nursed at thy side . . .—As in chap. lxvi. 12, the words point to the Eastern custom of carrying young children on the hip of their mother, with their arms clasped round her waist.

(5) **Then thou shalt see.**—A various reading adopted by many commentators gives *thou shalt fear.*

Thine heart shall fear . . .—Literally, *shall throb,* as with an awe-stricken joy at the marvellous prosperity, but that throb of awe is followed by the *expansion* of ecstatic joy.

The abundance of the sea—*i.e.,* the riches of the Western isles, with which the new Jerusalem was to be filled, as Tyre and Zidon had been of old. (Ezek. xxvii. 1—25).

(6) **The multitude of camels . . .**—The verse paints the commerce of the East, as verse 5 had described that of the West. For the camels and riches of Midian, see Judg. vi. 5, viii. 26. "Ephah" appears in Gen. xxv. 4 among the sons of Midian. "Sheba" keeps up its traditional fame for gold and incense (Ps. lxxii. 10; Strabo xvi. 4, 19).

(7) **Kedar.**—The nomad tribes (chap. xxi. 17) come as well as the trading ones. Nebaioth, mentioned with Kedar, in Gen. xxv. 13, among the descendants of Ishmael, expanded in the centuries preceding the Christian era, into the kingdom of the Nabathœan Arabs, spreading from the Ælanitic Gulf to the Haurân. The two names together include what were known to the Roman geographers as Arabia Felix and Arabia Petræa. The primary thought is that the Temple of the new Jerusalem will be supplied with its sacrifices from the inexhaustible flocks of these regions.

(8) **Who are these . . .**—The vision of the prophet brings before him the cloud-like sails of the ships that are bringing back the exiles over the Mediterranean and the Red Seas, hastening to their home like doves to their dove-cote. (Comp. Hos. xi. 11.)

(9) **The isles . . .**—*i.e.,* as in chap. xlix. 1, the far-off maritime regions of the West.

and the ships of Tarshish first, *a* to bring thy sons from far, their silver and their gold with them, unto the name of the LORD thy God, and to the Holy One of Israel, because he hath glorified thee. (10) And the sons of strangers shall build up thy walls, and their kings shall minister unto thee: for in my wrath I smote thee, but in my favour have I had mercy on thee. (11) Therefore thy gates *b* shall be open continually; they shall not be shut day nor night; that *men* may bring unto thee the ¹forces of the Gentiles, and *that* their kings *may be* brought. (12) For the nation and kingdom that will not serve thee shall perish; yea, *those* nations shall be utterly wasted. (13) The glory of Lebanon shall come unto thee, the fir tree, the pine tree, and the box together, to beautify the place of my sanctuary; and I will make the place of my feet glorious. (14) The sons also of them that afflicted thee shall come bending unto thee; and all they that despised thee shall *c* bow themselves down at the soles of thy feet; and they shall call thee, The city of the LORD, The Zion of the Holy One of Israel.

(15) Whereas thou hast been forsaken and hated, so that no man went through *thee*, I will make thee an eternal excellency, a joy of many generations. (16) Thou shalt also suck the milk of the Gentiles, and shalt suck the breast of kings: and thou shalt know that I the LORD *am* thy Saviour and thy Redeemer, the mighty One of Jacob. (17) For brass I will bring gold, and for iron I will bring silver, and for wood brass, and for stones iron: I will also make thy officers peace, and thine exactors righteousness. (18) Violence shall no more be heard in thy land, wasting nor destruction within thy borders; but thou shalt call thy walls Salvation, and thy gates Praise.

a Gal. 4. 26.

b Rev. 21. 25.

¹ Or, *wealth.*

c Rev. 3. 9.

Ships of Tarshish.—These are, as in chap. ii. 16, the first-class trading ships, whether trading with that country (Spain) or in the Indian Ocean. (Comp. 1 Kings x. 22, xxii. 48.) The mention of silver and gold may, therefore, point to Ophir as well as Spain.

The Holy One of Israel.—We note once more the recurrence of the characteristic Name.

(10) **The sons of strangers shall build . . .**—Either as willing proselytes or as being brought into subjection. (Comp. Zech. vi. 15.) To build the temples or palaces of conquerors was, as in the case of the Egyptian and Babylonian bondage, the almost inevitable lot of the conquered.

(11) **Thy gates shall be open continually.**—The words imply (1) a state of peace in which there would be no danger of attack; and (2) the constant stream of caravans of pilgrims, with their offerings, entering by night as well as day. It is interesting to note St. John's transfer of the thought to the heavenly Jerusalem (Rev. xxi. 25, 26).

The forces of the Gentiles.—Better, *the riches,* or *the possessions.*

That their kings may be brought . . .—The verb, as in chap. xx. 4, 1 Sam. xxx. 2, implies that they are brought as captives, acknowledging, with or against their will, the sovereignty of Zion.

(13) **The glory of Lebanon . . .**—The prophet sees in the new Jerusalem a revival of the glories of the days of Solomon. The cedars of Lebanon, and other trees of the forest, are to furnish timber for its buildings, or even to be planted in the courts of the Temple, or in its open places and streets (Pss. lii. 8, xcii. 12, 13; Isa. xxxv. 2).

The box is probably, as in chap. xli. 19, a species of cedar.

The place of my feet is clearly parallel with the "sanctuary" of the previous clause. So the word "footstool" is used of the Temple in Pss. xcix. 5, cxxxii. 7.

(14) **The sons also of them that afflicted thee . . .**—The explanation commonly given is that the "sons" are named because the persecutors themselves are thought of as no more. It seems better, however, to see in the words an expression of the law of inherited retribution, which entered so largely into the Hebrew's thought of the moral government of the world. That law will show itself in the prostrate homage with which the descendants of the old oppressors will recognise that the restored city is indeed the Zion of the Holy One of Israel.

(15) **Whereas thou hast been forsaken . . .**—The figure of the daughter of Zion, who had been as a forsaken and slighted wife (comp. chap. lxii. 4), mingles with the literal picture of a city in ruins, abandoned and unvisited.

(16) **Thou shalt also suck the milk of the Gentiles . . .**—The metaphor is bold, but the prophet had already presented it in a less startling form in chap. xlix. 23. What is meant in either case is that the new Jerusalem shall be supported by the offerings of the Gentiles.

(17) **For brass I will bring gold . . .**—The material wealth of the days of Solomon (1 Kings x. 21—27) furnishes another element in the picture of the ideal city, but with this striking difference: that there the "officers" and "exactors" of the king had been instruments of oppression (1 Kings xii. 4), while now they were to be the very embodiment of righteousness, and, in the widest sense, of "peace," and, therefore, of prosperity.

(18) **Violence shall no more . . .**—Following the thought of the previous verse, we see in the words a picture of freedom from internal misgovernment rather than from external invasion.

Thou shalt call thy walls Salvation . . .—The idea, almost the very phrase, has met us before in chap. xxvi. 1. They probably found a starting-point in the Eastern practice of giving to the walls of a city names that implied a consecration. Thus the walls of Babylon were named Imgur Bel and Nimetti Belkit (*Records of the Past,* v. 124, 125).

Jehovah the Everlasting Light of Zion. ISAIAH, LXI. *The Acceptable Year of the Lord.*

(19) *a*The sun shall be no more thy light by day; neither for brightness shall the moon give light unto thee: but the LORD shall be unto thee an everlasting light, and thy God thy glory. (20) Thy sun shall no more go down; neither shall thy moon withdraw itself: for the LORD shall be thine everlasting light, and the days of thy mourning shall be ended. (21) Thy people also *shall be* all righteous: they shall inherit the land for ever, the branch of my planting, the work of my hands, that I may be glorified. (22) A little one shall become a thousand, and a small one a strong nation: I the LORD will hasten it in his time.

CHAPTER LXI.—(1) The *b*Spirit of the Lord GOD *is* upon me; because the LORD hath anointed me to preach good tidings unto the meek; he hath sent me to bind up the brokenhearted, to proclaim liberty to the captives, and the opening of the prison to *them that are* bound; (2) to proclaim the acceptable year of the LORD, and the day of vengeance of our God; to comfort all that mourn; (3) to appoint unto them that mourn in Zion, to give unto them beauty for ashes, the oil of joy for mourning, the garment of praise for the spirit of heaviness; that they might be called trees of righteousness, the planting of the LORD, that he might be glorified.

(4) And they shall *c*build the old wastes, they shall raise up the former

a Rev. 21. 23 & 22. 5.

b Luke 4. 18.

c ch. 58. 12.

---

(19) **The sun shall be no more . . .**—The ideal picture becomes bolder and more transcendent. Sun and moon may still shine, but, as in Rev. xxi. 23 (obviously derived from this), they shall not be needed in the radiance of the greater glory of the presence of Jehovah. Here on earth the sun sets and the moon wanes, but in that Divine glory there is no waning and no setting. "Mourning" will belong to the past (comp. Rev. xxi. 4), everlasting joy to the future.

(21) **Thy people also shall be all righteous . . .**—The city is to realise the as yet unfulfilled ideal of Pss. xv. and xxiv. Evil will be blotted out, and, therefore, there will be no forfeiture of the inheritance. In the "branch" we have the words which had been prominent in chap. xi. 1, and which is now extended from the ideal representative of the nation to the whole body of the people.

(22) **A little one shall become a thousand.**—The noun is probably to be taken not in its merely numerical value, but, as in Judges vi. 15, 1 Sam. xxiii. 23, Micah v. 2, for a clan or sub-division of a tribe.

LXI.

(1) **The Spirit of the Lord God is upon me . . .**—We have obviously a new poem in the form of a soliloquy, and we ask, "Who is the speaker?" The Jewish Targum and many modern critics hear only the voice of Isaiah. Guided by chaps. xli. 1, l. 4—9, we recognise here, as there, the utterance of the ideal Servant of Jehovah. That view, it needs scarcely be said, is the one suggested to all Christian minds by our Lord's application of the passage to His own work in Luke iv. 16—22. The opening words repeat what had been said by Jehovah of the Servant in chap. xlii. 1. The "anointing," as it stands, might be that of king (1 Sam. ix. 16, x. 1), or priest (Exod. xxix. 2; Lev. vii. 36), or prophet (1 Kings xix. 16). As interpreted by its fulfilment, it may be held to include all three.

To preach good tidings . . .—Comp. Note on chap. xl. 9. To this passage, more than any other, even than chap. xl. 9, we may trace the use of the word "gospel" ("evangel," "good tidings") in our Lord's teaching and that of the Apostles. Claiming the promise as fulfilled in Himself, He became the great evangelist, and all who followed Him were called to the same office.

To bind up the broken-hearted . . .—The primary thought is that of a healing bandage applied to the heart's wounds. (Comp. i. 6). The Servant of Jehovah is the great physician as well as the evangelist.

To proclaim liberty.—Phrase and thought are taken from the law of the Year of Jubilee (Lev. xxv. 10; Ezek. xlvi. 17; Jer. xxxiv. 8).

The opening of the prison.—The LXX., adopted in Luke iv. 18, gives "recovery of sight to the blind;" and as the verb is never used for the opening of a room or door, and is used in chaps. xxxv. 5, xlii. 7, for the opening of the eyes, that is probably its meaning here.

(2) **To proclaim the acceptable year . . .**—The Year of Jubilee is still, perhaps, in the prophet's thoughts; but the chief point of the promise is the contrast between the "year" of favour and the single "day" of vengeance, reminding us of the like contrast in Exod. xx. 5, 6.

(3) **To appoint unto them that mourn . . .**—The verb (literally, *to set*) has no object either in the Hebrew or English, and it would seem as if the prophet corrected himself in the act of writing or dictating, and substituted for a word which would have applied only to the *coronet* one which was better fitted for the whole context.

Beauty for ashes.—Literally, a *diadem*, or *coronet*, which is to take the place of the ashes that had been sprinkled on the head of the mourners or penitents (2 Sam. i. 2, xiii. 19; Josh. vii. 6). The assonance of the two Hebrew words, *épher, paer*, deserves notice.

Oil of joy.—Same phrase as in Ps. xlv. 7.

The spirit of heaviness . . .—The second noun is that used for the "smoking" or "dimly burning" flax in chap. xlii. 3, and in its figurative sense in chap. xlii. 4; Ezek. xxi. 7.

That they might be called trees of righteousness . . .—Strictly, *terebinths*, or *oaks*, as the symbols of perennial verdure—the "righteousness" being thought of as the gift of the Spirit of Jehovah, and, therefore, life-giving and enduring—and in their beauty and strength manifesting His glory.

(4) **They shall build the old wastes . . .**—Literally *the waste places of olden time*: *i.e.*, not merely

desolations, and they shall repair the waste cities, the desolations of many generations. ⁽⁵⁾ And strangers shall stand and feed your flocks, and the sons of the alien *shall be* your plowmen and your vinedressers. ⁽⁶⁾ But ye shall be named the Priests of the LORD: *men shall call you the Ministers of our God:* ^aye shall eat the riches of the Gentiles, and in their glory shall ye boast yourselves.

⁽⁷⁾ For your shame *ye shall have* double; and *for* confusion they shall rejoice in their portion: therefore in their land they shall possess the double: everlasting joy shall be unto them. ⁽⁸⁾ For I the LORD love judgment, I hate robbery for burnt offering; and I will direct their work in truth, and I will make an everlasting covenant with them. ⁽⁹⁾ And their seed shall be known among the Gentiles, and their offspring among the people: all that see them shall acknowledge them, that they *are* the seed *which* the LORD hath blessed.

⁽¹⁰⁾ I will greatly rejoice in the LORD, my soul shall be joyful in my God; for he hath clothed me with the garments of salvation, he hath covered me with the robe of righteousness, as a bridegroom ¹decketh *himself* with ornaments, and as a bride adorneth *herself* with her jewels. ⁽¹¹⁾ For as the earth bringeth forth her bud, and as the garden causeth the things that are sown in it to spring forth; so the Lord GOD will cause righteousness and praise to spring forth before all the nations.

CHAPTER LXII.—⁽¹⁾ For Zion's sake will I not hold my peace, and for Jerusalem's sake I will not rest, until the

a ch. 60. 6.

¹ Heb., *decketh as a priest.*

---

the cities that had fallen into ruins during the exile, but those that had been lying waste for generations. The words are parallel with those of chap. lviii. 12. By some commentators *strangers* is supplied from verse 5 as the implied subject, as in chap. lx. 10. Here, however, it would seem as if the prophet looked on the rebuilding as being Israel's own work, while service of another kind was assigned to the aliens.

⁽⁵⁾ **Strangers shall stand** . . .—*i.e.*, like servants waiting for their master's orders. The implied thought of the whole passage is, as in the next verse, that all Israel is raised to the dignity of a priestly caste, leaving the rough work of the world to be done by foreigners, who stood on a lower level. (Comp. Ecclus. xxxviii. 31—34.)

⁽⁶⁾ **But ye shall be named the Priests of the Lord** . . .—This had been the original ideal of the nation's life (Exod. xix. 6), forfeited for a time through the sins of the people (Exod. xxviii. 1), to be fulfilled at last in the citizens of the new Jerusalem. (Comp. 1 Pet. ii. 9.) The thought implies, it may be noted, that as Israel has succeeded to the position of the sons of Aaron, so mankind at large is to occupy the position of Israel, as chosen and redeemed. Even the heathen Gentiles shall speak of the new Israel as "Ministers of our God."

Ye shall eat the riches of the Gentiles . . .—St. Paul seems to see a partial fulfilment of the promise in the collection made among the Gentiles for the Church at Jerusalem (Rom. xv. 27). On the other hand, the phrase that the conversion of the Jews shall be the riches of the Gentiles (Rom. xi. 12), affords an illustration of the varying aspects of prophetic imagery.

⁽⁷⁾ **For your shame ye shall have double** . . .—*i.e.*, double compensation for the suffering of years (comp. Zech. ix. 12), the general idea passing in the next clause into a double inheritance of territory. See Note on chap. xl. 2.

⁽⁸⁾ **I hate robbery for burnt offering.**—The Authorised Version follows the Vulg. and Luther, but the words, commonly applied as condemning the formal sacrifices of the wicked, do not fit in with the context, and it is better to take the rendering of the LXX. and the Targum, *I hate robbery with violence*, as referring to the spoliation which Israel had suffered at the hands of the Chaldæans.

I will direct their work in truth.—Better—the word for "work" standing, as in Lev. xix. 13, Ezek. xxix. 20, for its reward—*I will appoint their recompense in faithfulness.*

⁽⁹⁾ **Their seed shall be known**—*i.e.*, as in Prov. xxxi. 23, shall be "renowned," or "honourably recognised," even by the heathen, as the people whom Jehovah hath blessed. (Comp. chap. lxv. 23.)

⁽¹⁰⁾ **I will greatly rejoice** . . .—The speaker is again, as in verse 1, the ideal Servant of Jehovah, who identifies himself with the people and slaves. The Targum, it may be noted, makes Jerusalem the speaker.

The garments of salvation . . .—The imagery is the same as that of chap. lix. 17 and verse 3, its entirely spiritual significance being, perhaps, still more strongly accentuated.

As a bridegroom decketh himself with ornaments.—Literally, *wears a turban* (or *mitre*), *as a priest.* It would appear from Song Sol. iii. 11 that bridegrooms wore a special head-dress on the day of their espousal, and this is here compared to the priestly "bonnet," or "mitre" (Exod. xxviii. 4, xxxix. 28; Ezek. xliv. 18). On the special occasion which may have suggested the image, see Note on chap. lxii. 4.

⁽¹¹⁾ **As the earth bringeth forth her bud** . . .—The passage is memorable as at least suggesting the leading thought of the parable of the sower, and the appropriation of that title to Himself by the Son of Man (Matt. xiii. 3—23, 37; Mark iv. 26—29).

LXII.

⁽¹⁾ **For Zion's sake** . . .—Opinions again differ as to the speaker. Is he the prophet, or the Servant of Jehovah, or Jehovah Himself? On the whole, the second view seems to be most in harmony with what follows. The true Servant will carry on what in the language of later theology may be called his mediatorial intercessory work, that there may be no delay in the fulfilment of the glorious promises that have just been uttered.

righteousness thereof go forth as brightness, and the salvation thereof as a lamp *that* burneth. ⁽²⁾ And the Gentiles shall see thy righteousness, and all kings thy glory: and thou shalt be called by a new name, which the mouth of the LORD shall name. ⁽³⁾ Thou shalt also be a crown of glory in the hand of the LORD, and a royal diadem in the hand of thy God. ⁽⁴⁾ ᵃThou shalt no more be termed Forsaken; neither shall thy land any more be termed Desolate: but thou shalt be called ¹Hephzi-bah, and thy land ²Beulah: for the LORD delighteth in thee, and thy land shall be married. ⁽⁵⁾ For *as* a young man marrieth a virgin, *so* shall thy sons marry thee: and ³*as* the bridegroom rejoiceth over the bride, *so* shall thy God rejoice over thee. ⁽⁶⁾ I have set watchmen upon thy walls, O Jerusalem, *which* shall never hold their peace day nor night: ⁽⁷⁾ ye that make mention of the LORD, keep not silence, ⁽⁷⁾ and give him no ⁵rest, till he establish, and till he make Jerusalem a praise in the earth. ⁽⁸⁾ The LORD hath sworn by his right hand, and by the arm of his strength, ⁶Surely I will no more give thy corn *to be* meat for thine enemies; and the sons of the stranger shall not drink thy wine, for the which thou hast laboured: ⁽⁹⁾ but they that have gathered it shall eat it, and praise the LORD; and they that have brought it together shall drink it in the courts of my holiness.

⁽¹⁰⁾ Go through, go through the gates; ᵇprepare ye the way of the people; cast up, cast up the highway; gather out the stones; lift up a standard for the people. ⁽¹¹⁾ Behold, the LORD hath pro-

a Hos. 1. 10; 1 Pet. 2. 10.
¹ That is, *My delight is in her.*
² That is, *Married.*
³ Heb., *with the joy of the bridegroom.*
⁴ Or, *ye that are the Lord's remembrancers.*
⁵ Heb., *silence.*
⁶ Heb., *If I give,* &c.
b ch. 40. 3 & 57. 14.

As brightness.—Better, *as the brightness of morning*, the word being thus used in chap. lx. 3, Prov. iv. 18.

As a lamp . . .—Better, *as a burning torch*.

⁽²⁾ **Thou shalt be called by a new name . . .**—So in Jer. xxxiii. 16, the name of the restored city is to be "Jehovah our Righteousness." The root-thought is that the altered state is to be embodied, as in the case of Abraham and Israel, in a new name. Here, however, the effect of the promise is heightened, as in Rev. ii. 17, iii. 12, by the absence of the new name, as something which is to transcend all experience.

⁽³⁾ **A crown of glory . . .**—The "crown" as distinctively kingly; the "diadem" implies a "tiara," like the mitre of the High Priest (Exod. xxviii. 4; Zech. iii. 5). The two "hands" are expressed by different words in the Hebrew, the second having the sense of the open *palm* of the hand. The "new crown," *i.e.*, the new glory accruing to Jehovah from the restoration of Jerusalem, is not worn on the head (thought of, we may believe, as already crowned from eternity), but held forth in the hand for the gaze of the adoring nations.

⁽⁴⁾ **Thou shalt no more be termed Forsaken . . .**—The change of name is here partially indicated, and probably finds its starting-point in the marriage of Hezekiah with Hephzi-bah (2 Kings xxi. 1), which, on the assumption of Isaiah's authorship of these chapters, would be fresh in the prophet's memory. It would be entirely after his manner to see in the bride's name, as in those of his own sons, an omen of the future. The fact that the Hebrew word for Forsaken (*Azubah*) had been borne by a previous queen, the mother of Jehoshaphat (1 Kings xxii. 42), confirms the view here taken. "Hephzi-bah" means "my delight is in her;" and "Beulah," "married."

⁽⁵⁾ **So shall thy sons marry thee . . .**—The image of the bride is presented under another aspect. The people of a country are, in their collective unity, as the bridegroom, and the country is as the bride. They are bound, as the husband is to the wife, to cherish and protect it, to be ready to live and die for it.

⁽⁶⁾ **I have set watchmen upon thy walls . . .**—The "watchmen" have been differently interpreted as (1) angelic guardians and (2) prophets. Zech. i. 12, and Dan. x. 16—21 may be alleged in favour of (1), but on the whole, (2) seems preferable. The prophets of the return from exile, Zechariah, Haggai, Malachi, may be thought of as representative examples of such "watchmen," as also are the prophets of the Christian Church, which takes partly, at least, the position of the new Jerusalem.

Ye that make mention . . .—Better, *ye that are the remembrancers*. They are to remind Jehovah of His promises day and night, that He may hasten their fulfilment, never resting till the future Jerusalem is in very deed "a praise in the earth." (Comp. Zech. i. 12.)

⁽⁸⁾ **The Lord hath sworn . . .**—The principle of the Epistle to the Hebrews (Heb. vi. 13) is recognised here. Jehovah can swear by nothing less than that which is the symbol of His own greatness, identified with Himself.

I will no more give thy corn . . .—The words throw us back upon the early history of Israel, subject at any time to the desolating attacks of Midianites (Judges vi. 4, 11), Assyrians (Isa. xvi. 9), and Philistines (2 Chron. xxviii. 18). The new blessing stands in special contrast with the curse of Deut. xxviii. 33, 51.

⁽⁹⁾ **In the courts of my holiness.**—Better, *of my sanctuary*. The harvest and the vintage festivals are to be kept, as of old, without interruption, the master of the house, with his family and the Levites and the poor (Deut. xiv. 22—27), eating of the first-fruits "before the Lord."

⁽¹⁰⁾ **Go through . . .**—Here, probably, we have the cry of the prophet himself (but, possibly, also that of the Servant of Jehovah) addressed to the heralds, who are to go forth and summon the exiles to return to the restored city. On the special phrases, see Notes on chaps. xl. 3, lvii. 14.

Lift up a standard for the people.—Literally, *peoples*, the plural indicating that the prophet thinks of the Gentile nations as escorting Israel. It follows from this that the command itself is addressed, like the previous clauses, to the returning exiles.

⁽¹¹⁾ **The Lord hath proclaimed . . .**—A partial fulfilment of the words is found in the decree of Cyrus

Zion as a City not Forsaken. **ISAIAH, LXIII.** *The Conqueror with Dyed Garments.*

claimed unto the end of the world, ^aSay ye to the daughter of Zion, Behold, thy salvation cometh; behold, his ^breward *is* with him, and his ¹work before him. ⁽¹²⁾ And they shall call them, The holy people, The redeemed of the LORD: and thou shalt be called, Sought out, A city not forsaken.

CHAPTER LXIII.—⁽¹⁾ Who *is* this that cometh from Edom, with dyed garments from Bozrah? this *that is* ²glorious in his apparel, travelling in the greatness of his strength?

I that speak in righteousness, mighty to save.

⁽²⁾ Wherefore *art thou* red in thine apparel, and thy garments like him that treadeth in the winefat?

⁽³⁾ I have trodden the winepress alone; and of the people *there was* none with me: for I will tread them in mine anger, and trample them in my fury; and their blood shall be sprinkled upon my garments, and I will stain all my raiment. ⁽⁴⁾ For the ^dday of vengeance *is* in mine heart, and the year of my redeemed is come. ⁽⁵⁾ And I looked, and *there was* none to help; and I wondered that *there was* none to uphold: therefore mine own ^earm brought salvation unto me; and my fury, it upheld me. ⁽⁶⁾ And I will tread down the people in mine anger, and make them drunk in my

a Zech. v. 9; Matt. 21. 5; John 12. 15.
b ch. 40. 10.
1 Or, *recompence.*
2 Heb., *decked.*
c Rev. 19. 13.
d ch. 34. 8.
e ch. 59. 16.

(Ezra i. 1, 2); but they have also a wider range, and take in all the events by which history becomes as the voice of God, proclaiming His will.

The end of the world has been restricted by some commentators to the western regions of the Mediterranean, but without sufficient reason.

Behold, his reward is with him.—Repeated from chap. xl. 10, where see Notes.

⁽¹²⁾ **The redeemed of the Lord.**—Literally, *ransomed*, as in chaps. xxxv. 10, li. 10.

Sought out . . .—*i.e.*, a city which men would seek after to honour, and promote its welfare. (Comp. the opposite, "Zion, which no man seeketh after," in Jer. xxx. 17.)

A city not forsaken.—With special reference to the name "Azubah" in verse 4. (Comp. the change of names in Hosea ii. 1.)

LXIII.

⁽¹⁾ **Who is this that cometh from Edom?** . . .—There is no apparent connection between verses 1—6 and what precedes and follows. They must be dealt with, accordingly, as a separate section, though not, as some critics have suggested, by a different writer. To understand its relation to the prophet's mind, we must remember the part which Edom had taken during the history of which Isaiah was cognisant, perhaps also that which he foresaw they would take in the period that was to follow. That part had been one of persistent hostility. They had been allied with the Tyrians against Judah, and had been guilty of ruthless atrocities (Amos i. 9—11). They had carried off Jewish prisoners as slaves (Obad. 10, 11). They had been allies of the Assyrian invaders (Ps. lxxxiii. 6), and had smitten Judah in the days of Ahaz (2 Chron. xxviii. 17). If we think of the prophet as seeing in spirit the working of the old enmity at a later period, we may extend the induction to their exultation at the capture of Jerusalem (Ps. cxxxvii. 7; Lam. iv. 21). The memory of these things sank deep into the nation, and the first words of the last of the prophets echo the old hatred (Mal. i. 2—4). In the later days of Judaism, when Rabbis uttered their curses against their oppressors, Edom was substituted for Rome, as St. John substitutes Babylon (Rev. xviii. 2). Isaiah, possibly starting from the memory of some recent outrages in the reign of Hezekiah, and taking Edom as the representative of all the nearer hereditary enemies of Israel, passes into an ecstacy of jubilation, and sees the conquering king returning from his work of vengeance. The form is that of a warrior coming from the Idumæan Bozrah (as distinct from that in the Haurân, Jer. xlviii. 24) in *bright-red* garments. And the colour (as in Rev. xix. 13) is not that of the scarlet dress worn by soldiers (Nahum ii. 3), but that of blood just shed.

Travelling.—The Hebrew verb (*bending*, or *tossing* the head) indicates the movement and gestures of a conqueror exulting in his victory.

I that speak . . .—The hero-avenger, the righteous king who represents Jehovah, hears the wondering question, and makes answer for himself. "Righteousness" and "salvation," which he claims as his attributes, show that he is none other than the ideal Servant of the Lord of Hosts, sharing His attributes.

⁽²⁾ **Wherefore art thou red . . . ?**—The wondering question shows that the colour is not that of the warrior's usual dress. The Hebrew word for "red" (*ādom*) connects itself with Edom (comp. Gen. xxv. 30), as *batsir* ("vintage") probably with Bozrah.

⁽³⁾ **I have trodden the winepress alone . . .**—The "winepress" is here, as elsewhere (Joel iii. 13; Lam. i. 15; Rev. xiv. 18—20), the received symbol of the carnage of battle. What the hero-conqueror asserts is that the battle was fought by him single-handed. He had no human allies, but God was with him. A slight change in the vowel-points, adopted by some interpreters, turns the verbs into futures: "*I will* tread . . . *will* trample, . . .*"* as in the second clause of the Authorised Version. It is better, perhaps to take the latter verb also as in the past. The work of slaughter is clearly thought of as accomplished before the warrior is seen.

⁽⁴⁾ **The day of vengeance is.**—Better, in both clauses, *was*, as pointing to the motive of the action, of which the blood-stained garments were the result.

The year of my redeemed . . .—Better, *the year of my redemption*, scil., the work of redeeming my people.

⁽⁵⁾ **I looked . . .**—As in chap. l. 2, the absolute isolation of the avenger and redeemer is emphasised again and again. Nothing but his own indomitable and righteous zeal against evil had sustained him.

⁽⁶⁾ **I will tread down . . .**—Better, *I trod*; and so throughout the verse.

The Angel of God's Presence ISAIAH, LXIII. *Saving His People.*

fury, and I will bring down their strength to the earth. ⁽⁷⁾ I will mention the lovingkindnesses of the LORD, *and* the praises of the LORD, according to all that the LORD hath bestowed on us, and the great goodness toward the house of Israel, which he hath bestowed on them according to his mercies, and according to the multitude of his lovingkindnesses. ⁽⁸⁾ For he said, Surely they *are* my people, children *that* will not lie: so he was their Saviour. ⁽⁹⁾ In all their affliction he was afflicted, and the angel of his presence saved them: ᵃin his love and in his pity he redeemed them; and he bare them, and carried them all the days of old. ⁽¹⁰⁾ But they ᵇrebelled, and vexed his holy Spirit: therefore he was turned to be their enemy, *and* he fought against them. ⁽¹¹⁾ Then he remembered the days of old, Moses, *and* his people, *saying*, Where *is* he that ᶜbrought them up out of the sea with the ¹shepherd of his flock? where *is* he that put his holy Spirit within him? ⁽¹²⁾ That led *them* by the right hand of Moses with his glorious arm, ᵈdividing the water before them, to make himself an everlasting name? ⁽¹³⁾ That led them through the deep, as an horse in the wilderness, *that*

a Deut. 7. 7, 8.

b Ex. 15. 24; Num. 14. 11; Ps. 78. 56 & 95. 9.

c Ex. 14. 30.

¹ Or, *shepherds,* as Ps. 77. 20.

d Ex. 14. 21; Josh. 3. 16.

Make them drunk, implies a change of imagery from that of the battle to that of the cup of wrath, as in chap. li. 17, Ps. lxxv. 8, Jer. xxv. 15. The section which thus closes has often been applied (as, *e.g.,* in the Prayer-Book Epistle for the Monday before Easter) to the passion of our Lord. In that agony and death it has been said He was alone, and none was with Him. He trod the wine press of the wrath of God. It is obvious, however, that this, though we may legitimately apply some of Isaiah's phrases to it, is not an interpretation of this passage, which paints a victory, and not a passion. The true analogue in the New Testament is that of the victory of the triumphant Christ in Rev. xix. 11—13; but it may be conceded that, from one point of view, the agony and the cross were themselves a conflict with the powers of evil (John xii. 31, 32; Col. ii. 15), and that as He came out of that conflict as a conqueror, the words in which Isaiah paints the victor over Edom may, though in a much remoter analogy, be applicable to Him in that conflict also.

⁽⁷⁾ **I will mention . . .**—The words begin an entirely new section, of the nature of a psalm of thanksgiving for redemption (verse 16). Possibly, in the arrangement of the book it was thought that such a psalm followed rightly on the great dramatic dialogue which represented the victory of the Redeemer. The psalm begins, according to the implied rule of Ps. l. 23, with praise, and passes afterward to narrative and supplication.

⁽⁸⁾ **For he said . . .**—The words throw us back to the starting-point of God's covenant with His people, based, so to speak, on the assumption that they would not fail utterly in the fulfilment of their promises. (Comp. Exod. xix. 3—6.)

⁽⁹⁾ **In all their affliction . . .**—Literally, *there was affliction to Him.* So taken, the words speak of a compassion like that of Judges x. 16. The Hebrew text gives, *In all their affliction there was no affliction:* i.e., it was as nothing compared with the salvation which came from Jehovah. The Authorised Version follows the *Kĕri,* or marginal reading of the Hebrew. It may be inferred, from the strange rendering of both clauses in the LXX. ("neither a messenger, nor an angel, but He himself saved them"), that the variation in the text existed at an early date, and was a source of perplexity, and therefore of conjectural emendation.

The angel of his presence . . .—Literally, *the angel of His face.* As in Exod. xxiii. 20—23, xxxii. 34, xxxiii. 2, so here, Jehovah is thought of as working out His purpose of deliverance for Israel through the mediation of an angel, who is thus described either as revealing the highest attributes of God, of which the "face" is the anthropomorphic symbol, or as standing ever in the immediate presence of the King of kings, ready for any mission.

He bare them . . .—The same image of fatherly care meets us in chap. xlvi. 3, Exod. xix. 4, Deut. i. 31, xxxii. 11.

⁽¹⁰⁾ **Vexed his holy Spirit . . .**—Literally, *his Spirit of holiness.* So St. Paul speaks of Christians as "grieving the Holy Spirit." Here, and in Ps. li. 11, as in the 'Angel of the Presence," we may note a foreshadowing of the truth of the trinal personality of the unity of the Godhead, which was afterwards to be revealed. That which "vexed" the Holy Spirit was, in the nature of the case, the unholiness of the people, and this involved a change in the manifestation of the Divine Love, which was now compelled to show itself as wrath.

⁽¹¹⁾ **Then he remembered . . .**—The readings vary, and the construction is difficult. Probably, the best rendering is, *His people remembered the ancient days of Moses.* In any case, it is Israel that remembers, and by that act repents. (Comp. the tone and thoughts of Pss. lxxvii., lxxviii., cv., cvi.)

With the shepherd . . .—Many MSS., as in the margin, give the plural, "shepherds," probably as including Aaron and Miriam as among the leaders and deliverers of the people. (Comp. Ps. lxxvii. 20; Mic. vi. 4.)

Within him.—Not Moses only, but Israel collectively. Note the many instances of the gift of the Spirit, to Bezaleel (Exod. xxxv. 31), to the Seventy Elders (Num. xi. 25), to Joshua (Deut. xxxiv. 9). (Comp. Neh. ix. 20.)

⁽¹²⁾ **With his glorious arm.**—Literally, *with the arm of His glory,* or *majesty.* This, the arm of the Unseen Guide, is thought of as accompanying the leader of Israel, ready to grasp his hand and support him in time of need.

Dividing the water.—The words may include the passage of the Jordan, but refer primarily to that of the Red Sea. (Comp. Pss. lxxvii. 16, cvi. 9.)

⁽¹³,¹⁴⁾ **That led them . . .**—Each comparison is singularly appropriate. Israel passes through the sea as a horse through the wide grassy plain (not the sandy desert, as "wilderness" suggests). Then, when its wanderings are over, it passes into Canaan, as a herd

they should not stumble? ⁽¹⁴⁾ As a beast goeth down into the valley, the Spirit of the LORD caused him to rest: so didst thou lead thy people, to make thyself a glorious name.

⁽¹⁵⁾ ^a Look down from heaven, and behold from the habitation of thy holiness and of thy glory: where *is* thy zeal and thy strength, ¹the sounding of thy bowels and of thy mercies toward me? are they restrained? ⁽¹⁶⁾ Doubtless thou *art* our father, though Abraham be ignorant of us, and Israel acknowledge us not: thou, O LORD, *art* our father, ²our redeemer; thy name *is* from everlasting.

⁽¹⁷⁾ O LORD, why hast thou made us to err from thy ways, *and* hardened our heart from thy fear? Return for thy servants' sake, the tribes of thine inheritance. ⁽¹⁸⁾ The people of thy holiness have possessed *it* but a little while: our adversaries have trodden down thy sanctuary. ⁽¹⁹⁾ We are *thine*: thou never barest rule over them; ³they were not called by thy name.

CHAPTER LXIV.—⁽¹⁾ Oh that thou wouldest rend the heavens, that thou wouldest come down, that the mountains might flow down at thy presence, ⁽²⁾ as *when* ⁴the melting fire burneth, the fire causeth the waters to boil, to make thy name known to thine adversaries, *that* the nations may tremble at thy presence! ⁽³⁾ When thou didst terrible things *which* we looked not for, thou camest down, the mountains flowed down at thy presence.

⁽⁴⁾ For since the beginning of the

---

a Deut. 26. 15.

¹ Or, *the multitude.*

² Or, *our redeemer from everlasting is thy name.*

³ Or, *thy name was not called upon them.*

⁴ Heb., *the fire of meltings.*

---

of cattle descends from the hills into the rich pasturage of the valleys, that guidance also coming from the Spirit of Jehovah.

⁽¹⁵⁾ **Look down from heaven . . .**—The form of the prayer reminds us of 2 Chron. vi. 21. Perhaps there is a latent remonstrance, as though Jehovah, like an Eastern king, had withdrawn to the recesses of His palace, and had ceased to manifest His care and pity for His people, as He had done of old.

The sounding of thy bowels.—See Note on chap. xvi. 11. The words jar upon modern ears, but were to the Hebrew what "the sighs of thy heart" would be to us.

⁽¹⁶⁾ **Doubtless thou art our father, though Abraham . . .**—Better, *For Abraham is ignorant of us.* The passage is striking as being an anticipation of the New Testament thought, that the Fatherhood of God rests on something else than hereditary descent, and extends not to a single nation only, but to all mankind. Abraham might disclaim his degenerate descendants, but Jehovah would still recognise them. Implicitly, at least, the words contain the truth that "God is able of these stones to raise up children unto Abraham" (Matt. iii. 9). He is still their Redeemer. The words may possibly imply the thought that, as in the case of Jeremiah (2 Macc. xv. 13, 14), and Rachel (Jer. xxxi. 15), Abraham was thought of as watching over his posterity, and interceding for them. So, eventually, Abraham appears in the popular belief of Israel, as welcoming his children in the unseen world (Luke xvi. 22).

⁽¹⁷⁾ **Why hast thou made us to err . . .**—The prophet identifies himself with his people, and speaks as in their name. Have their sins led God to abandon them, and to harden their hearts as He hardened Pharaoh's? (Comp. Rom. ix. 17—22.) Are they given over as to a reprobate mind? Against that thought he finds refuge, where only men can find it, in prayer, and in pleading God's promise and the "election of grace," to which He at least remains faithful, though men are faithless. Conscious that they have no power without Him to return to Him, they can ask Him to return to them.

⁽¹⁸⁾ **The people of thy holiness . . .**—Better, *For a little while have they possessed thy sanctuary,* or, with a various reading, *thy holy mountain.* The plea is addressed to Jehovah, on the ground of His promise that the inheritance was to be an everlasting one. Compared with that promise, the period of possession, from Joshua and David to the fall of the monarchy, was but as a "little while." (Comp. Ps. xc. 4.) The seeming failure of the promise was aggravated by the fact that the enemies of Israel had trodden down the sanctuary.

⁽¹⁹⁾ **We are thine . . .**—*Thine,* as the italics show, is not in the Hebrew, and its insertion distorts the meaning. Better, *We are become as those over whom Thou hast never ruled, upon whom Thy name hath never been called* (Cheyne). What the prophet presents as a plea is not the contrast between Israel and the heathen, but the fact that Israel has been left to sink to the level of the heathen who had not known God. Would not that thought move Jehovah, as it were, to remember this covenant?

LXIV.

⁽¹⁾ **Oh that thou wouldest rend . . .**—The division of chapters hinders the English reader from seeing that this is really a continuation of the prayer of chap. lxiii. 15—19. The prophet asks that Jehovah may not only "look down" from heaven, but may rend, as it were, the dark clouds that hide the light of His countenance from His people, and that the mountains might *tremble* at His presence. (Comp. Ps. lxviii. 8; Exod. xix. 18.)

⁽²⁾ **As when the melting fire burneth . . .** —Better, *as when fire kindleth brushwood, as when fire causeth the water to boil.* The two-fold action of material fire is used, as elsewhere, as a symbol of the "consuming fire" (Heb. xii. 29) of the wrath of Jehovah.

⁽³⁾ **When thou didst terrible things . . .**— The latter clause, "thou camest down . . ." is supposed by some critics to be an accidental repetition from verse 1. By others it is taken as an intentional repetition, emphasising the previous assertion, after the manner of Hebrew poetry. The latter view seems to have most in its favour.

⁽⁴⁾ **Neither hath the eye seen, O God, beside thee . . .**—The best commentators are in favour

world *men* have not heard, nor perceived by the ear, neither hath the eye ¹seen, O God, beside thee, *what* he hath prepared for him that waiteth for him. ⁽⁵⁾ Thou meetest him that rejoiceth and worketh righteousness, *those that* remember thee in thy ways: behold, thou art wroth; for we have sinned: in those is continuance, and we shall be saved. ⁽⁶⁾ But we are all as an unclean *thing*, and all our righteousnesses *are* as filthy rags; and we all do ᵇfade as a leaf; and our iniquities, like the wind, have taken us away. ⁽⁷⁾ And *there is* none that calleth upon thy name, that stirreth up himself to take hold of thee: for thou hast hid thy face from us, and hast ²consumed us, because of our iniquities.

⁽⁸⁾ But now, O Lord, thou *art* our father; we *are* the clay, and thou our potter; and we all *are* the work of thy hand. ⁽⁹⁾ Be not ᶜwroth very sore, O Lord, neither remember iniquity for ever: behold, see, we beseech thee, we *are* all thy people. ⁽¹⁰⁾ Thy holy cities are a wilderness, Zion is a wilderness, Jerusalem a desolation. ⁽¹¹⁾ Our holy and our beautiful house, where our fathers praised thee, is burned up with fire: and all our pleasant things are laid waste. ⁽¹²⁾ Wilt thou refrain thyself for these *things*, O Lord? wilt thou hold thy peace, and afflict us very sore?

CHAPTER LXV.—⁽¹⁾ I ᵈam sought of *them that* asked not *for me;* I am found of *them that* sought me not: I

a Ps. 31. 19; 1 Cor. 2. 9.
¹ Or, *seen a God beside thee, which doeth so for him, &c.*
b Ps. 90. 5, 6.
² Heb., *melted.*
c Ps. 79. 8.
d Rom. 9. 24, 25, 26 & 10. 20; Eph. 2. 12.

---

of rendering, *Neither hath the eye seen a God beside Thee, who will work for him that waiteth for Him.* The sense is not that God alone knows what He hath prepared, but that no man knows (sight and hearing being used as including all forms of spiritual apprehension) any god who does such great things as He does. St. Paul, in 1 Cor. ii. 9, applies the words freely, after his manner, to the eternal blessings which God prepares for His people. Clement of Rome (1 Cor. xxxiv.), it may be noted, makes a like application of the words, giving "those who wait for Him" (as in Isaiah), instead of "those who love Him."

⁽⁵⁾ **Thou meetest him . . .**—The "meeting" is obviously one of favour. That was the law of God's dealings with men. He met, in this sense, those who at once rejoiced in righteousness and practised it. But with Israel it was not so. Their sins had brought them under His anger, not under His favour.

In those is continuance . . — The clause is difficult, and has been variously interpreted—(1) "*In these* (the ways of God) *there is permanence* (literally, eternity), *that we may be saved;*" and (2) "*In these* (the ways of evil) *have we been a long time, and shall we be saved!*" The latter seems preferable. So taken, the clause carries on the confession of the people's sinfulness.

⁽⁶⁾ **We are all as an unclean thing . . .**—Better, *as he who is unclean, scil.*, like the leper of Lev. xiii. 45.

Filthy rags point to that which to the Israelite was the other extremest form of ceremonial uncleanness, as in Ezek. xxxvi. 17.

Have taken us away—*scil.*, afar off from the light and favour of Jehovah.

⁽⁷⁾ **Hast consumed us, because of our iniquities.**—Better, *hast delivered us into the hand (scil., the power) of our iniquities.* The previous clause had pointed to the people's forgetfulness of God—what we should call their indifference—as the root-evil. This states that that sin led, in the righteous judgment of God, to open iniquities. The thought is parallel to that of Rom. i. 21—24.

⁽⁸⁾ **We are the clay, and thou our potter . . .**—Commonly, partly, perhaps, from St. Paul's application of the image in Rom. ix. 20, 21, and Isaiah's own use of it in chap. xxix. 16, we associate the idea of the potter with that of simple arbitrary sovereignty. Here, however (as in Jer. xviii. 6), another aspect is presented to us, and the power of the Great Potter is made the ground of prayer. The "clay" entreats Him to fashion it according to His will, and has faith in His readiness, as well as His power, to comply with that prayer. The thought of the "potter" becomes, in this aspect of it, one with that of the Fatherhood of God.

⁽¹⁰⁾ **Thy holy cities . . .**—There is no other instance of the plural, and this probably led the LXX. and Vulg. to substitute the singular. It probably rests on the thought that the whole land was holy (Zech. ii. 12), and that this attribute extended, therefore, to all its cities, especially to those which were connected with historical memories. Possibly, however, Zion and Jerusalem—the former identified with the Temple, the latter with the people of Jehovah—are thought of as two distinct cities, locally united. The "wilderness" is, as elsewhere, rather open pasture-land than a sandy desert.

⁽¹¹⁾ **Our holy and our beautiful house . . .**—The destruction of the Temple, which, on the assumption of Isaiah's authorship, the prophet sees in vision, with all its historic memories, comes as the climax of suffering, and, therefore, of the appeal to the compassion of Jehovah.

All our pleasant things . . .—Probably, as in 2 Chron. xxxvi. 19, the precincts, porticoes, and other "goodly buildings" of the Temple.

⁽¹²⁾ **Wilt thou refrain . . . ?**—The final appeal to the fatherly compassion of Jehovah reminds us of the scene when Joseph could not "refrain" (Gen. xlv. 1), and natural tenderness would find a vent. Could the God of Israel look on the scene of desolation, and not be moved to pity?

LXV.

⁽¹⁾ **I am sought of them . . .**—Is this the answer to the previous prayer? Most commentators say "Yes;" but there is, at least, an apparent absence of continuous sequence. A more probable view is that it was written after an interval more or less considerable, and that the prophet utters what had been revealed to him as explaining why the plaintive appeal of chap.

said, Behold me, behold me, unto a nation *that* was not called by my name. (2) I have spread out my hands all the day unto a rebellious people, which walketh in a way *that was* not good, after their own thoughts; (3) a people that provoketh me to anger continually to my face; that sacrificeth in gardens, and burneth incense ¹upon altars of brick; (4) which remain among the graves, and lodge in the monuments, which eat swine's flesh, and ²broth of abominable *things is in* their vessels; (5) which say, Stand by thyself, come not near to me; for I am holier than thou. These *are* a smoke in my ³nose, a fire that burneth all the day. (6) Behold, *it is* written before me: I will not

<small>1 Heb., *upon bricks*.
2 Or, *pieces*.
3 Or, *anger*.</small>

---

lxiv. 12 did not meet at once with the answer that might have been looked for.

A further question meets us, which has received different answers. Do the opening words speak, as St. Paul implies they do, of the calling of the Gentiles, contrasting their faith with the unbelief of Israel (Rom. x. 20)? Taking the text as it stands, the most natural interpretation (there being no reference afterwards to the Gentiles) seems to be that Jehovah speaks to the same people in verses 1 and 2, and that both alike speak of indifference and hardness. On this view the words may be translated, *I was ready to answer those who did not enquire, was nigh at hand to be discovered by those who did not seek.* . . . Such words were a true description of the state of Israel, as they have been of Christian Churches since, and are in close agreement with what follows. On this view St. Paul's free use of the LXX. rendering must be looked on as analogous to the like application of Hosea i. 10, ii. 1, by him (Rom. ix. 25, 26) and by St. Peter (1 Peter ii. 10), though in these instances it is beyond question that the words primarily referred to the Jews, and not to the Gentiles.

A nation that was not called by my name.—Better, with the LXX., as in chaps. xliii. 22, lxiv. 7, *that has not called on my name.* The meaning, on either rendering, is that Israel has sunk to the level of the heathen.

(2) **I have spread out my hands** . . .—Here, of course, the words were meant for Israel, as St. Paul applies them. It may not be without interest to note the fact that the words stand over the portal of the Church of Santa Maria, which stands at the entrance of the Ghetto at Rome. Of how many churches at Rome and elsewhere might it not be said, "Thou art the man," "The beam is in thine own eye"?

(3) **That sacrificeth in gardens.**—It is not without significance, as bearing on the date of the chapter, that the practice was common in Judah under Ahaz. (Comp. chaps. i. 29, lvii. 5; Ezek. xx. 28.)

Burneth incense upon altars of brick.—Literally, *on the bricks*, and possibly, therefore, on the roofs of houses, as was common in the idolatrous practices of Judah (2 Kings xxiii. 12; Jer. xix. 13). By some interpreters the words are referred, though with less probability, to the brick altars which the exiles are supposed to have used at Babylon, and were forbidden by the Law (Exod. xx. 24, 25).

(4) **Which remain among the graves.**—Probably the rock graves of Palestine, which, although they were ceremonially unclean, were not unfrequently used as dwellings (Matt. viii. 28; Mark v. 3). The charge may be one merely of neglecting the precepts of the Law, but possibly also may imply that the graves were frequented, as in chaps. viii. 19, xxix. 4, for necromantic purposes.

Lodge in the monuments . . .—Here, again, the words probably point to practices more or less idolatrous, and common among the heathen of the time. Jerome (*in loc.*) notes the fact that men went to sleep in the crypts of the Temple of Æsculapius, in the hope of gaining visions of the future, and translates *in delubris idolorum.*

Which eat swine's flesh.—The flesh of swine was apparently forbidden, not on sanitary grounds only or chiefly, but because that animal was sacrificed in the festivals of Thammuz (Ezek. viii. 14), or Adonis. (Comp. chap. lxvi. 17.) It may be noted, as against the view that the verse points to the practices of the Babylonian exiles, that no reference to swine has been found in any cuneiform inscriptions. In Egypt, as in Palestine, it was looked upon as unclean (Herod. ii. 47, 48). On the worship of Thammuz, see an article by the Rev. A. H. Sayce, in the *Contemporary Review* for September, 1883.

Broth of abominable things.—The words indicate, as before, a sacrificial feast of unclean meats, and therefore connected with a violation of the Mosaic law, possibly with some form of heathen mysteries or divination from the viscera of slaughtered animals. The word occurs here and in chap. lxvi. 3, once in Deuteronomy (chap. xxix. 17), and frequently in Leviticus (chaps. xi. 11, 13; xviii. 26, 30).

(5) **Which say, Stand by thyself** . .—The picture, in its main outlines, reminds us of the proud exclusiveness of the later Pharisees, and the root-evil is, of course, identical. Here, however, the ground of the exclusiveness is not the consciousness of the peculiar privileges of Israel, but rests on what was an actual apostasy. Those of whom Isaiah speaks boasted of their initiation into heathen mysteries (Baal, Thammuz, or the like) as giving them a kind of consecrated character, and separating them from the *profanum vulgus* of the Israelites, who were faithful to the God of their fathers.

I am holier than thou.—Literally, *I am holy to thee: i.e.,* one whom thou mayest not approach. (Comp. Lev. xxi. 8.) By some commentators the verb is taken as transitive, *I make thee holy: i.e.,* have power to impart holiness; but this is less satisfactory, both grammatically and as to meaning.

These are a smoke in my nose . . .—The point of the clause is that the punishment is represented as not future. The self-exalting idolaters are already as those who are being consumed in the fire of the Divine wrath, and their smoke is "a savour of death" in the nostrils of Jehovah.

(6) **It is written before me** . . .—The thought is that of the great register, the book of God's remembrance, in which men's deeds, good and evil, are ever being recorded. (Comp. Jer. xvii. 1; Ps. lvi. 8; Dan. xii. 1; Mal. iii. 16.)

But will recompense . . .—Literally, *without recompensing,* or, *except I recompense.* Men took the long-suffering of God as if it indicated forgetfulness

keep silence, but will recompense, even recompense into their bosom, (7) your iniquities, and the iniquities of your fathers together, saith the LORD, which have burned incense upon the mountains, and blasphemed me upon the hills: therefore will I measure their former work into their bosom.

(8) Thus saith the LORD, As the new wine is found in the cluster, and *one* saith, Destroy it not; for a blessing *is* in it: so will I do for my servants' sakes, that I may not destroy them all. (9) And I will bring forth a seed out of Jacob, and out of Judah an inheritor of my mountains: and mine elect shall inherit it, and my servants shall dwell there. (10) And Sharon shall be a fold of flocks, and the valley of Achor a place for the herds to lie down in, for my people that have sought me.

(11) But ye *are* they that forsake the LORD, that forget my holy mountain, that prepare a table for that ¹troop, and that furnish the drink offering unto that ²number. (12) Therefore will I number you to the sword, and ye shall all bow down to the slaughter: *a*because when I called, ye did not answer; when I spake, ye did not hear; but did evil before mine eyes, and did choose *that* wherein I delighted not. (13) Therefore thus saith the Lord GOD, Behold, my servants shall eat, but ye shall be hungry: behold, my servants shall drink, but ye shall be thirsty: behold, my servants shall rejoice, but ye shall be ashamed: (14) behold, my servants

1 Or, *Gad*.
2 Or, *Meni*.
a Prov. 1. 24, &c.; ch. 66. 4; Jer. 7. 13.

(Rom. ii. 4; 2 Pet. iii. 9). They are told that He will at last requite the impenitent "into their very bosom," their inmost self, for all the evil they have done.

(7) **Which have burned incense upon the mountains . . .**—The old inveterate sin of the worship of high places (comp. chap. lvii. 7; Hos. iv. 13; Ezek. vi. 13; 2 Kings xv. 4, 35). The worship paid there to other gods, or nominally to Jehovah in a way which He had forbidden, was practically a "blasphemy" or "reproach" against Him.

Their former work.—Better, *I will measure their work first into their bosoms*. That was, as it were, the primary duty of the Supreme Ruler.

(8) **As the new wine . . .**—Literally, *the must*, or *unfermented juice of the grape*. The transition from the denunciations of the preceding verse is abrupt, and suggests the thought of an interval of time and absence of direct continuity. Possibly, however, a link may be found in the "first" of the amended translation, which prepares the way for something that is to follow. God chastens, but does not destroy.

Destroy it not . . .—The thought is that as even one fruitful cluster of grapes will lead the vine-dresser to spare an otherwise fruitless vine in the hope of a fuller blessing in the future, so Jehovah will spare a sinful nation for the twenty or the ten righteous (Gen. xviii. 23—33). The words "destroy it not" are those which stand at the head of Pss. lvii.—lix., as indicating the tune to which they were to be sung; and it is a natural inference that it may have been a popular vintage song, and therefore doubly apt for the prophet's purpose. May we compare our own song of "Woodman, spare that tree?" applied, as it has been, to the trees of ancient institutions.

(9) **I will bring forth a seed out of Jacob . . .**—Jacob (*i.e.*, Israel) and Judah are used to represent respectively the remnants of the two kingdoms that had been carried into captivity.

My mountains.—One of Isaiah's characteristic phrases (comp. chaps. xiv. 25, xxix. 11; Ezek. vi. 2, 3). Not Zion only, but every hill in Canaan was a sharer in a derived sanctity.

(10) **Sharon.**—As elsewhere, the name appears in the Hebrew with the article—*the* Sharon, the rich plain stretching along the coast from Joppa to the foot of Carmel. The LXX., Josephus, and Strabo render it by *the plain*, or *the woodland*. (Comp. chaps. xxxiii. 9, xxxv. 2.)

The valley of Achor.—The name, traditionally connected with the sin of Achan (Josh. vii. 24—26), belonged to a valley running into the plain of Jericho, and is here taken as the Eastern limit of the region bounded by the Sharon on the west. The whole district was to be as a "garden of the Lord" for the restored remnant. (Comp. the striking parallelism of Hos. ii. 15.)

(11) **That forget my holy mountain . . .**—The words imply, like verses 3—5, the abandonment of the worship of the Temple for a heathen ritual, but those that follow point, it will be seen, to Canaanite rather than Babylonian idolatry, and, so far, are in favour of the earlier date of the chapter. The same phrase occurs, however, as connected with the exiles in Ps. cxxxvii. 5.

That prepare a table for that troop.—Hebrew, "for *the Gad*," probably the planet Jupiter, worshipped as the "greater fortune," the giver of good luck. The LXX. renders "for the demon" or "Genius." The name of Baal-Gad (Josh. xi. 17, xii. 17) indicates the early prevalence of the worship in Syria. Phœnician inscriptions have been found with the names Gad-Ashtoreth and Gad-Moloch. The "table" points to the *lectisternium* (or "feast"), which was a prominent feature in Assyrian and other forms of polytheism.

Unto that number.—Here, again, we have in the Heb. *Mĕni* the proper name of a Syrian deity, probably of the planet Venus as the "lesser fortune." Some scholars have found a name *Manu* in Babylonian inscriptions; and Manât, one of the three deities invoked by the Arabs in the time of Mahomet, is probably connected with it (Cheyne). See Sayce, as in Note on verse 4.

(13) **My servants shall eat . . .**—The form of the punishment is apparently determined by that of the sin. That had been the orgy of an idol's feast; the penalty would be hunger and thirst, while joy and gladness would be the portion of those who had abstained from it. The words present a striking parallelism to Luke vi. 20—26.

The New Heavens ISAIAH, LXV. *and the New Earth.*

shall sing for joy of heart, but ye shall cry for sorrow of heart, and shall howl for ¹vexation of spirit. (15) And ye shall leave your name for a curse unto my chosen: for the Lord God shall slay thee, and call his servants by another name: (16) that he who blesseth himself in the earth shall bless himself in the God of truth; and he that sweareth in the earth shall swear by the God of truth; because the former troubles are forgotten, and because they are hid from mine eyes.

(17) For, behold, I create ᵃnew heavens and a new earth: and the former shall not be remembered, nor ²come into mind. (18) But be ye glad and rejoice for ever *in that* which I create: for, behold, I create Jerusalem a rejoicing, and her people a joy. (19) And I will rejoice in Jerusalem, and joy in my people: and the ᵇvoice of weeping shall be no more heard in her, nor the voice of crying. (20) There shall be no more thence an infant of days, nor an old man that hath not filled his days: for the child shall die an hundred years old; but the sinner *being* an hundred years old shall be accursed. (21) And they shall build houses, and inhabit *them*; and they shall plant vineyards, and eat the fruit of them. (22) They shall not build, and another inhabit; they shall not plant, and another eat: for as the days of a tree *are* the days of my people, and mine elect ³shall long enjoy the work of their hands. (23) They shall not labour in vain, nor bring forth for trouble; for they *are* the seed of the blessed of the Lord, and their offspring with them. (24) And it shall come to pass, that ᶜbefore they call, I will answer; and while they are yet speaking, I will hear. (25) The ᵈwolf and the lamb shall feed together, and the lion shall eat straw like the bullock: and

1 Heb., *breaking*.
a ch. 66. 22; 2 Pet. 3. 13; Rev. 21. 1.
2 Heb., *come upon the heart*.
b Rev. 21. 4.
3 Heb., *shall make them continue long*, or, *shall wear out*.
c Ps. 32. 5.
d ch. 11. 6, 7.

---

(15) **Ye shall leave your name for a curse** . . . —The phrase has parallels in Num. v. 21; Zech. viii. 13; Jer. xxix. 22, the thought in each case being that the person named is under so heavy a penalty from the wrath of Jehovah that he becomes a representative instance of what that wrath can accomplish, and because the old name, say of Jacob or of Judah, has been thus identified with evil. He will call His chosen ones, the true Israel, as by another name, which shall be for blessing, and not for cursing. (Comp. lxii. 2, Rev. ii. 17, iii. 12.)

(16) **Shall bless himself in the God of truth** . . . —Literally, *the God of the Amen*. In Rev. iii. 14 we have an echo of the Hebrew; in John xvii. 3 we have as distinct an echo of the LXX. rendering, τὸν Θεὸν τὸν ἀληθινόν. The words seem to imply that the prophet had entered into the inner meaning of what was to most men only a liturgical formula.

Because the former troubles . . . —The addition of the clause emphasises the thought that it is the truth or faithfulness of God, who keepeth His promise for ever, that will lead men to use that new Name as a formula of benediction.

(17) **Behold, I create new heavens** . . . —The thought reappears in many forms in the New Testament—verbally in 2 Pet. iii. 13; Rev. xxi. 1, substantially in the "restitution of all things" (Acts iii. 21), in the "manifestation of the sons of God" (Rom. viii. 19). The "former things," the sin and sorrow of the past, shall then fade away from the memory of God's people, absorbed in the abounding and everlasting joy.

(18) **I create Jerusalem** . . . —From the prophet's stand-point, as elsewhere, both in 1 and 2 Isaiah, the earthly city, transformed and transfigured, occupies the central place in the new creation. In the New Testament we note the transfer of the promise to the unseen eternal city, the Jerusalem which is above (Gal. iv. 26; Rev. xxi. 10).

(20) **There shall be no more thence** . . . —The prophet sees in the restored city not so much an eternal and a deathless life as the return of the traditional longevity of the prediluvian and patriarchal age (Gen. v., xi.). Life will not be prematurely cut off, as it had been, by pestilence and war. (Comp. Zech. viii. 4.) He who dies at the age of a hundred will be thought of as dying young; even the sinner, dying before his time as the penalty of his guilt, shall live out the measure of a century. The noticeable fact is that sin is thought of as not altogether extinct—as still appearing, though under altered conditions, even in the restored Jerusalem.

(21) **They shall build houses** . . . —The proverbial type of national security and peace, as the opposite was of national misfortune (Lev. xxvi. 16; Deut. xxviii. 30).

(22) **As the days of a tree** . . . —We may think of the cedars of Lebanon or the oaks of Bashan as furnishing the prophet with the ideal standard of longevity. Commonly, as by Homer and other poets, the lives of men have been compared to that of the leaves of deciduous trees; here they are compared to the life of the tree itself. The prophet is still speaking, not of national, but of individual life.

(23) **Their offspring with them** . . . —The picture presented is that of a patriarchal family, including many generations, fathers no longer outliving their children and mourning for their death, as Jacob did (Gen. xxxvii. 35, xlii. 38), and as men had often done in the times of war, famine, and pestilence, through which Isaiah had lived.

(24) **Before they call** . . . —In man's experience of men, often, as things are now, in his relations with God, there is an interval between prayer and the answer. In the new Jerusalem the two would be simultaneous, or the answer would anticipate the prayer.

(25) **The wolf and the lamb** . . . —The words point to what have been called the discords in the harmony of Nature, the pain and death involved, of necessity, in the relation of one whole class of animals

dust *shall be* the serpent's meat. They shall not hurt nor destroy in all my holy mountain, saith the LORD.

CHAPTER LXVI.—⁽¹⁾ Thus saith the LORD, ᵃ"The heaven *is* my throne, and the earth *is* my footstool: where *is* the house that ye build unto me? and where *is* the place of my rest? ⁽²⁾ For all those *things* hath mine hand made, and all those *things* have been, saith the LORD: but to this *man* will I look, *even* to *him that is* poor and of a contrite spirit, and trembleth at my word.

⁽³⁾ He that killeth an ox *is as if* he slew a man; he that sacrificeth a ¹lamb, *as if* he cut off a dog's neck; he that offereth an oblation, *as if he offered* swine's blood; he that ²burneth incense, *as if* he blessed an idol. Yea, they have chosen their own ways, and their soul delighteth in their abominations. ⁽⁴⁾ I also will choose their ³delusions, and will bring their fears upon them; ᵇbecause when I called, none did answer; when I spake, they did not hear: but they did evil before mine eyes, and chose *that* in which I delighted not.

⁽⁵⁾ Hear the word of the LORD, ye that tremble at his word; Your brethren that hated you, that cast you out for my name's sake, said, ᶜLet the LORD be glorified: but he shall appear to your joy, and they shall be ashamed. ⁽⁶⁾ A voice of noise from the city, a voice from the temple, a voice of the LORD that rendereth recompence to his ene-

ᵃ 1 Kin. 8. 27; 2 Chr. 6. 18; Acts 7. 49 & 17. 24.

¹ Or, *kid.*

² Heb., *maketh a memorial of.*

³ Or, *devices.*

ᵇ Prov. 1. 24; ch. 65. 12; Jer. 7. 13.

ᶜ ch. 5. 19.

---

to another. In St. Paul's language, the "whole creation groaneth and travaileth together" (Rom. viii. 22). In the new heaven and the new earth of the prophet's vision there would be no such discords. The flesh-eating beasts should change their nature; even the serpent, named, probably, with special reference to Gen. iii., as the starting-point of the discords, shall find food in the dust in which he crawls, and shall be no longer a destroyer. The condition of the ideal Paradise should be restored. The picture finds a parallel, perhaps a *replica*, in Virgil, *Ecl.* iv. Do the poet and the prophet stand on the same footing? or may we look for a literal fulfilment of the words of the one, though not of the other? The answer must be given in words that are "wary and few." We dare not, on the one hand, fix times and seasons, or press the *letter* of prophetic visions as demanding a fulfilment. On the other, the permanence of Israel as a people suggests the possibility of a restored Jerusalem, and modern theories of evolution point to the gradual elimination of the fiercer animals as part of the conquests of humanity.

LXVI.

⁽¹⁾ **The heaven is my throne . . .**—We are left to conjecture the historical starting-point of this utterance of a Divine truth. Was the prophet condemning in advance the restoration of the temple on the return from Babylon, or, as some critics have supposed, the intention of some of the exiles to build a temple in the land of their captivity, as others did afterwards at Leontopolis in Egypt? Was he anticipating the vision of the Apocalypse, that in the new Jerusalem there was to be "no temple" (Rev. xxi. 22)? Neither of these views is satisfactory, chaps. lvi. 7, lx. 7, and the writings of Ezekiel, Haggai, Zechariah, all pre-supposing the existence of a new temple. It seems better to see in the words the utterance, in its strongest form, of the truth that God dwelleth not in temples made with hands, that utterance being compatible, as in the case of Solomon himself (2 Chron. vi. 18), of our Lord (John ii. 16, 17, iv. 21—23), of St. Stephen, who quoted this passage (Acts vii. 48—50), with the profoundest reverence for the visible sanctuary. Cheyne quotes a striking parallel from an Egyptian hymn to the Nile of the fourteenth century B.C., in which we find the writer saying of God, "His abode is not known . . . there is no building that can contain Him." (*Records of the Past*, iv. 109.)

⁽²⁾ **All those things . . .**—The sequence of thought runs thus:—God, the Maker of the universe, can need nothing that belongs to it. The most stately temple is to Him as the infinitely little. What He does delight in is something which is generically different, the spiritual life which answers to His own, the "contrite heart," which is the true correlative of His own holiness. He who offers that is a true worshipper, with or without the ritual of worship; in its absence, all worship is an abomination to the Eternal. Here 1 and 2 Isaiah are essentially one in teaching. (Comp. chaps. i. 11—18, lvii. 15.)

⁽³⁾ **He that killeth an ox . . .**—The truth of the previous verse is emphasised by iteration, each clause presenting a distinct illustration of it. Chapter lxv. 3—11 had pointed to tendencies, not yet extinct, which led to open apostasy. Now the prophet declares that there may be as real an apostasy beneath an orthodox creed and an irreproachable ritual. Each act of the hypocrite's worship is as an idolatrous abomination.

⁽⁴⁾ **I also will choose their delusions . . .**—The Hebrew noun conveys the thought of the turnings and windings of fortune—what has been called the irony of history. These are the instruments with which God, as it were, mocks and has in derision those who mock Him by their hypocrisy. Their choice did not delight Him; what He chooses will be far other than delightful for them. (Comp. Ps. ii. 4; Prov. i. 24—26.)

⁽⁵⁾ **Hear the word of the Lord . . .**—The prophet turns from the hypocrites to the persecuted remnant. The self-righteous, self-exalting Pharisee (comp. chap. lxv. 5) repudiates, and, as it were, excommunicates, the true worshippers, and taunts them with their devotion to a God who does not help them. In words which find an echo in Matt. xxvii. 42, they said, "Let Jehovah glorify Himself, that we may look on your joy." The prophet adds the doom that shall fall upon the mockers: "They, and not those whom they deride, shall be put to shame."

⁽⁶⁾ **A voice of noise . . .**—The form reminds us of chap. xiii. 4. The words represent dramatically the wonder with which men will behold the great judgments of God, proceeding, as with the thunders of

mies. (7) Before she travailed, she brought forth; before her pain came, she was delivered of a man child. (8) Who hath heard such a thing? who hath seen such things? Shall the earth be made to bring forth in one day? *or* shall a nation be born at once? for as soon as Zion travailed, she brought forth her children. (9) Shall I bring to the birth, and not ¹cause to bring forth? saith the Lord: shall I cause to bring forth, and shut *the womb*? saith thy God.

(10) Rejoice ye with Jerusalem, and be glad with her, all ye that love her: rejoice for joy with her, all ye that mourn for her: (11) that ye may suck, and be satisfied with the breasts of her consolations; that ye may milk out, and be delighted with the ²abundance of her glory. (12) For thus saith the Lord, Behold, I will extend peace to her like a river, and the glory of the Gentiles like a flowing stream: then shall ye suck, ye shall be *ᵃ*borne upon *her* sides, and be dandled upon *her* knees. (13) As one whom his mother comforteth, so will I comfort you; and ye shall be comforted in Jerusalem. (14) And when ye see *this*, your heart shall rejoice, and your bones shall flourish like an herb: and the hand of the Lord shall be known toward his servants, and *his* indignation toward his enemies.

(15) For, behold, the Lord will come with fire, and with his chariots like a whirlwind, to render his anger with fury, and his rebuke with flames of fire. (16) For by fire and by his sword will the Lord plead with all flesh: and the slain of the Lord shall be many. (17) They that sanctify themselves, and purify themselves in the gardens ³behind one

¹ Or, *beget.*
² Or, *brightness.*
ᵃ ch. 49. 22 & 60. 4.
³ Or, *one after another.*

Sinai (Amos i. 2; Joel iii. 16), from the city and the temple, that seemed to have been given over to destruction.

(7) **Before she travailed** . . .—The mother, as the next verse shows, is Zion; the man-child, born at last without the travail-pangs of sorrow, is the new Israel, the true Israel of God. The same figure has met us in chaps. xlix. 17—21, liv. 1, and is implied in Matt. xxiv. 8. Its antithesis is found in chap. xxxvii. 3.

(8) **Shall the earth be made** . . .—Better, *Shall a land be made to travail.* The usually slow processes of national development are contrasted with the supernatural rapidity of the birth and growth of the new Israel.

(9) **Shall I bring to the birth** . . .—The implied thought is that God will not leave His work of national restoration unfinished. There shall not be that frustration of hopes when they seem just on the point of being fulfilled which the history of the world so often records. (Comp. chap. xxxvii. 3.)

(10) **Rejoice ye with Jerusalem** . . .—The holy city is still thought of as a mother rejoicing in her new-born child; friends and neighbours (*i.e.*, the nations friendly to Israel) who had shown pity for her sufferings are now invited to participate in her joy.

(11) **That ye may suck** . . .—The figure takes a new and bolder form. The friends who visit the rejoicing mother are invited to take their place with the new-born child, and to share his nurture. The underlying thought is, of course, that the heathen nations who had been friendly to Zion were to become converts, and be incorporated with her citizens.

(12) **Ye shall be borne upon her sides.**—Better, *upon the side,* or *upon the knee, or hip.* (See Note on chap. lx. 4.) The outward figure is now presented as in an inverted form, to express a new spiritual fact. The children of Zion will find a maternal tenderness and care at the hands of the heathen nations, who are to be as their "nursing mothers." (Comp. lx. 16.)

(13) **One whom his mother comforteth** . .—The image of maternal love, with which the prophet's mind is full, is presented in yet another aspect. The love which Zion gives, the love which her children receive from the nations, are both but shadows of the infinite tenderness of Jehovah. In this instance the object of the mother's love that comforts is not the child at the breast, but the full-grown man, returning, like the prodigal, to his home after long years of exile. The words are characteristic at once of the special tie which unites the son to the mother, almost more than to the father, in most Eastern nations, and, perhaps also, of the prophet's personal memories of his own mother's love.

(14) **Your bones shall flourish** . . .—"Heart" and "bones" stand respectively as symbols of the inner and outer life. The "bones," the branches, so to speak, of the body, which had been dry and sere, should revive as with the sap of a new life, and be as the succulent herbage. His "hand," *i.e.*, His manifested power, will show itself in love to His people, in indignation to their enemies.

(15) **With his chariots** . . .—*i.e.*, the storm-clouds sweeping on their way, while the lightnings and the winds do their work. (Comp. Pss. xviii. 10, lxviii. 33.)

(16) **Will the Lord plead** . . .—Better, *will the Lord hold judgment.* The thoughts of the seer pass on to the retributive side of the Divine righteousness. Fire and sword have been used by the enemies of God against His people, and shall, in turn, be the instruments of His vengeance. The "sword" may, however, be the symbol of the Divine judgment, apart from any reference to its human instrument (Deut. xxxii. 41; Rev. i. 16).

(17) **They that sanctify themselves** . . .—Better, *they that consecrate themselves* . . . As in chap. lxv. 3, 4, the prophet has in his thoughts the apostates, who gloried in mingling heathen rites with the worship of Jehovah. Such a blending of incompatible elements was, as we have seen, eminently characteristic of the reign of Manasseh. We have no trace of anything corresponding to it among the Babylonian exiles, either before or after their return. The "consecration" and "purification" are the initiatory rites of heathen mysteries, connected probably with the worship of Baal or Ashtoreth, or, as the

Vengeance on the Wicked.   ISAIAH, LXVI.   *Reward for the Righteous.*

tree in the midst, eating swine's flesh, and the abomination, and the mouse, shall be consumed together, saith the LORD. ⁽¹⁸⁾ For I *know* their works and their thoughts: it shall come, that I will gather all nations and tongues; and they shall come, and see my glory. ⁽¹⁹⁾ And I will set a sign among them, and I will send those that escape of them unto the nations, *to* Tarshish, Pul, and Lud, that draw the bow, *to* Tubal, and Javan, *to* the isles afar off, that have not heard my fame, neither have seen my glory; and they shall declare my glory among the Gentiles. ⁽²⁰⁾ And they shall bring all your brethren *for* an offering unto the LORD out of all nations upon horses, and in chariots, and in ¹ litters, and upon mules, and upon swift beasts, to my holy mountain Jerusalem, saith the LORD, as the children of Israel bring an offering in a clean vessel into the house of the LORD. ⁽²¹⁾ And I will also take of them for *a*priests *and* for Levites, saith the LORD.

¹ Or, *coaches.*

a Ex. 19. 6; ch. 61. 6; 1 Pet. 2. 9; Rev. 1. 6.

---

context, with its reference to gardens and swine's flesh, renders probable, with that of Thammuz. (See Note on chap. lxiv. 4.)

Behind one tree in the midst.—The noun "tree" is a conjectural explanation. The Hebrew text gives the "one" in the masculine, and is explained as referring either (1) to the Hierophant, who led the worshippers; or (2), as with a contemptuous reluctance to utter the name of the false deity, to Thammuz. The Hebrew margin gives "one" in the feminine, and this may have been meant for the *Asherah*, the "grove," or Phallic symbol of idolatrous worship. If we adopt the masculine, and refer it to Thammuz, the word may connect itself with the lamentations of the Syrian maidens over Thammuz (Adonis) as over an only son. (Comp. Milton, *Paradise Lost*, i.)

The abomination.—The word stands in Lev. vii. 21, xi. 11, for various kinds of unclean beasts, among which the mouse, or jerboa, still eaten by the Arabs, was conspicuous (Lev. xi. 29). It is probable that all these, as well as the swine's flesh, were used in the idol-feasts. In any case the apostate worshippers would seem to have exulted in throwing off the restraints of the Mosaic law.

⁽¹⁸⁾ **For I know their works . . .**—The Hebrew has no verb, either—as in the *Quos ego . . .* of Virgil, *Æn.*,i. 139—for the sake of emphasis, or through an accidental omission in transcription. *I know* is supplied by many versions and commentators; *I will punish* or *I have seen* by others. The thought, in any case, is that the eye of Jehovah sees the evil things that are done in the secret places, caves or groves, in which the heathen rites were celebrated.

All nations and tongues . . .—The phrase, though not incompatible with Isaiah's authorship, is specially characteristic of the prophets of the Exile (Dan. iii. 4, 7, 29, iv. 1; Zech. viii. 23).

They shall come, and see my glory.—The "glory" in the prophet's thoughts is that of Jehovah manifested in His righteous judgments on open enemies and concealed apostates.

⁽¹⁹⁾ **I will set a sign among them . . .**—The "sign" may be one of supernatural terror in the work of judgment, or, as the context makes more probable, of supernatural deliverance. The thought of a "remnant" to be saved is still characteristically dominant, and that "remnant" is to act as heralds of Jehovah to the far-distant nations who had not been sharers in any open antagonism to Israel, and who were, therefore, not involved in the great judgment. Of these the prophet names Tarshish, either definitely for Spain, or vaguely for the far west.

Pul is not found elsewhere as the name of a nation, and stands probably for "Phut," as in the LXX., found in common with "Lud" in Ezek. xxvii. 10, xxx. 5, and standing for an African people (Phint, or Phet) on the east coast of Northern Africa.

Lud, joined with "Pul" here, in Ezek. xxvii. 10 with Phut, and with Ethiopia and Libya in Ezek. xxxvii. 5, stands, in the judgment of most scholars, not for the Lydians of Asia Minor, but for an African nation, the Ludim of Gen. x. 13 and Jer. xlvi. 9, where they are named, as here, as famous for their skill as archers. On the other hand, Mr. Sayce (Cheyne, ii. 287) identifies "Pul" with the Apuli of Italy and "Lud," with the Lydian soldiers, by whose help Psammitichus made himself independent of Assyria.

Tubal (comp. Ezek. xxvii. 13, xxxviii. 2, 3, xxxix. 1) points to the shores of the Black Sea and tribes of Scythian extraction.

Javan (Ionia), Gen. x. 2, is here used widely for any Greek settlements, and points probably to those on the Black Sea, which, together with Tubal and Meshech, carried on an active slave-trade with Tyre (Ezek. xxvii. 3). It completes the list of nations named as representing the far-off lands that had not before heard of the God of Israel, but were now to know Him through the preaching of the remnant.

⁽²⁰⁾ **They shall bring all your brethren . . .**—The offering is the *minchah*, the bloodless meat-offering of the Levitical law (Lev. ii. 1, 2). The underlying thought is that the returning exiles would be the most acceptable offering that could be brought to Jehovah. The same idea appears in Zeph. iii. 10, and a similar one, transferred, however, to the Gentile converts, in Rom. xv. 16.

Upon horses, and in chariots . . .—The list of the modes of transport, as in Zech. xiv. 15, points to the various habits of the many nations who are to be sharers in the work.

As the children of Israel . . .—The "clean offering" is, as before, the *minchah*. The heathen, or, perhaps, even the chariots and litters on which they brought the exiles, are as the "clean vessels" in which the *minchah* was brought to the Temple.

⁽²¹⁾ **I will also take of them for priests . . .**—We are left to determine whether the promise is that even Gentile converts should be enrolled among the priests and Levites of the new Jerusalem, or that Israelites of the non-priestly tribes should be so enrolled. Was the prophet breaking down in thought the middle wall of partition, or clinging to its maintenance? Chap. lxi. 6 seems in favour of the latter view, and we are probably right in looking on this thought, that

The Undying Worm ISAIAH, LXVI. *and the Unquenched Fire.*

(22) For as the *ª new heavens and the new earth, which I will make, shall remain before me, saith the LORD, so shall your seed and your name remain. (23) And it shall come to pass, *that* ¹from one new moon to another, and from one sabbath to another, shall all flesh come to worship before me, saith the LORD. (24) And they shall go forth, and look upon the carcases of the men that have transgressed against me: for their *ᵇ worm shall not die, neither shall their fire be quenched; and they shall be an abhorring unto all flesh.

ª ch. 65. 17; 2 Pet. 3. 13; Rev. 21. 1.

¹ Heb., *from new moon to his new moon, and from sabbath to his sabbath.*

ᵇ Mark 9. 44.

---

of all Israel being eligible for the priesthood, as that which was in the prophet's mind. Like other such thoughts, however, it was capable of expansion, so as to include the whole Israel of God, who were by faith the children of Abraham. (Comp. 1 Pet. ii. 5, 9, with Exod. xix. 6.)

(22) **As the new heavens and the new earth . . .**—The transformation of chap. lxv. 17 is pre-supposed, but that future kingdom of God shall perpetuate the historical continuity of that which has preceded it. Israel (the prophet's range of vision seems limited to the outward Israel, while St. Paul extends it to the spiritual) shall still exist. The ideal represented by that name will have an indestructible vitality.

(23) **From one new moon to another . . .**— Under the Mosaic law Israelites were bound, at least in theory, to attend the temple at the three great feasts. In the new Jerusalem, as the prophet thought of it, the pilgrimages would be both more frequent and more universal. Every sabbath and new moon would witness not Israel only, but "all flesh," thronging into the courts of the temple. It lies in the nature of the case that the words never have received, and never can receive, a literal fulfilment. The true realisation is found in the new Jerusalem of Rev. xxi. 22—27, of the perpetual sabbatism of Heb. iv. 9, and even that glorious vision is but the symbol of spiritual realities.

(24) **And they shall go forth . . .**—As at the close of chaps. xlviii., lvii., each ending a great section of the volume, so here, the vision of restoration and blessedness is balanced by that of the righteous condemnation of the wicked. The outward imagery is suggested, as in Joel iii. 12; Zech. xiv. 12, by that of the great battle of the Lord (verses 15, 16). Those who are slain in that battle are thought of as filling the valleys round about Jerusalem, especially the valley of Jehoshaphat ("Jehovah judges"), devoured by worms, or given to the flames. Taken strictly, therefore, the words do not speak of the punishment of the souls of men after death, but of the defeat and destruction upon earth of the enemies of Jehovah. The words that tell us that "the worm shall not die" and that "the fire shall not be quenched" point, however, to something more than this, to be read between the lines. And so those words became the starting-point of the thoughts of later Judaism as to Gehenna (Ecclus. vii. 17; Judith xvi. 17; and the Targum on this passage), of the words in which our Lord Himself gave utterance to what, at least, seemed to express those thoughts (Mark ix. 44—48), of the dominant eschatology of Christendom. Even so taken, however, with this wider range, it is still a question whether the words are to be taken literally or figuratively (though this, perhaps, is hardly a question), whether the bodies, which represent souls, are thought of as not destroyed, but only tormented, or as consumed to nothing, by the fire and by the worm, whether those two agents represent sufferings of sense or spirit. The one aspect of the future life which they tend to exclude is that which presents the idea of a suffering that may be purifying. That idea is not without apparent support in other passages of Scripture (*e.g.*, Rom. v. 17—21, xi. 32; 1 Pet. iii. 19, iv. 6); but we cannot say that it entered into the prophet's thoughts here. What he emphasises is the eternal antagonism between the righteousness of God and man's unrighteousness, and this involves the punishment of the latter as long as it exists. In any case there is a strange solemnity in this being the last word of the prophet's book of revelation, even as there is a like awfulness in the picture of the final judgment, which appears in Matt. xxv. 46, at all but the close of our Lord's public teaching. Cheyne quotes a singular rubric of the Jewish ritual, that when this chapter, or Eccles. xii., or Mal. iii., was read in the synagogue, the last verse but one should be repeated after the last, so that mercy might appear as in the end triumphant after and over judgment.

www.ingramcontent.com/pod-product-compliance
Lightning Source LLC
Chambersburg PA
CBHW080529300426
44111CB00017B/2653